1 MONTH OF
FREE
READING

at
www.ForgottenBooks.com

By purchasing this book you are eligible for one month membership to ForgottenBooks.com, giving you unlimited access to our entire collection of over 1,000,000 titles via our web site and mobile apps.

To claim your free month visit:
www.forgottenbooks.com/free1213384

ISBN 978-0-332-09983-5
PIBN 11213384

This book is a reproduction of an important historical work. Forgotten Books uses
state-of-the-art technology to digitally reconstruct the work, preserving the original format
whilst repairing imperfections present in the aged copy. In rare cases, an imperfection in
the original, such as a blemish or missing page, may be replicated in our edition. We do,
however, repair the vast majority of imperfections successfully; any imperfections that
remain are intentionally left to preserve the state of such historical works.

PUBLICATIONS

OF THE

ODERN LANGUAGE ASSOCIATIO

OF

AMERICA

EDITED BY

WILLIAM GUILD HOWARD

SECRETARY OF THE ASSOCIATION

VOL. XXX

NEW SERIES, VOL. XXIII

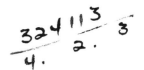

PUBLISHT QUARTERLY BY THE ASSOCIATION
PRINTED BY J. H. FURST COMPANY
BALTIMORE
1915

CONTENTS

PUBLICATIONS

OF THE

Modern Language Association of America

1915

| VOL. XXX, 1 | NEW SERIES, VOL. XXIII, 1 |

I.—GUILLAUME DE MACHAUT AND *THE BOOK OF THE DUCHESS*

Chaucer's *Book of the Duchess* opens, as is generally agreed, with five lines rather closely translated from Froissart's *Paradys d'Amours.*[1] Froissart, however, was himself imitating a passage from Guillaume de Machaut's *Fontaine Amoureuse,*[2] and Chaucer, who knew both works, utilized the *Fontaine,* along with Ovid, for the tale of Ceyx and Alcyone, which occupies most of his Proem.[3] Yet, in the midst of this story, he darted back to the *Paradys* for a moment to pick up the strange name *Eclympasteyr,*[4] and, near the end of the Proem, the influence of Froissart is

---

[1] Cf. also B. *Duch.,* 14-15, with *Par.,* 7-9; B. *Duch.,* 23, with *Par.,* 7; B. *Duch.,* 45 with *Par.,* 13.

[2] See *Englische Studien,* XXVI, pp. 321-2, 335-6.

[3] Vv. 62-217. The happy thought of making the tale reveal to the speaker the existence of gods of sleep hitherto unsuspected (231-7) is Chaucer's own. Froissart has no occasion to use the story of Ceyx and Alcyone in the *Paradys,* but he seems to take more than a hint from it in the curious story of Architeles and Orphane in *Le Joli Buisson de Jonece* (2102-2209), where it is easy to see the influence of the *Fontaine Amoureuse.*

[4] B. *Duch.,* 167; *Par.,* 28.

again visible in a few details.[5]   One of these is amusing.
Froissart prayed not only to Morpheus, but to Juno and
Oleus:

> Car tant priai a Morpheus,
> A Juno et a Oleus—(15-16).

Who Oleus may be, is a puzzle equal to that of Eclympasteyr's origin.   The latter deity Chaucer accepted with a
certain zest, but he shied at Oleus:

> I wolde yive thilke Morpheus,
> Or his goddesse, dame Juno,
> *Or som wight elles, I ne roughte who*—(242-4).

Let us return, however, to the opening paragraph of the
Proem (1-43).

Vv. 16-21 have a noteworthy resemblance to the beginning of Machaut's first *Complainte*.

> And wel ye wite, *agaynes kynde*
> *It were to liven in this wyse;*
> For *nature wolde nat suffyse*
> To noon erthely creature
> *Not longe tyme to endure*
> Withoute sleep, and been in sorwe.[6]

> Amours, tu m'as tant esté dure,
> Et si m'a tant duré et qure
> *La durté que pour toy endure,*
>   *Que d'endurer*
> Sui si mis a desconfiture
> Que de garir est aventure;

---

[5] Cf. *B. Duch.*, 222-3, with *Par.*, 19-22; B. *Duch.*, 242-5, with *Par.*,
15-18; B. *Duch.*, 272-5, with *Par.*, 14, 31.

[6] Cf. B. *Duch.*, 466-9:

> For, by my trouthe,
> It was gret wonder that nature
> Mighte suffren any creature
> To have swich sorwe and be not deed.

Here the Dreamer is speaking of the Knight in Black, who is composing a "compleynt" (464).

> *Et croy que c'est contre nature*
> *D'einsi durer.*[1]

Vv. 23-29, 42, are much like vv. 109-112, 126-128, of *Le Jugement dou Roy de Navarre,* a poem which Chaucer knew.[8]

And thus melancolye	Et pour ce que merencolie	109
And drede I have for to dye,		
Defaute of sleep, and hevinesse		
Hath sleyn my spirit of quiknesse 26	Esteint toute pensée lie,	
That I have lost al lustihede—		
Swiche fantasies been in myn hede—		
So I not what is best to do. 29	Et aussi que je bien veoie	
	Que mettre conseil n'i pooie,	112
. . . . . .	. . . . .	
	N'i a il conseil si soutil	126
That wil not be, moot nede	Comme de tout laissier ester,	
be left. 42	Puis qu'on ne le puet contrester.	128

---

[1] Chichmaref, I, p. 241. This same *Complainte* (13-16) shows also the metaphor of the *amie* as a physician (see p. 4, below):

> Ne je ne m'en sçay où clamer,
> Puis que ma dame reclamer
> Ne me vuet ne ma joie amer
> N'estre mon mire.

[8] See *Mod. Philol.*, VII, pp. 471-3, where some connection is suggested between the *Navarre* and the *Prologue* to the *Legend of Good Women.* It may here be noted that the figure of Winter's sword occurs in both poems.

> Forgeten hadde the erthe his pore estat
> Of winter, that him naked made and mat,
> And *with his swerd of cold* so sore greved (B, 125-7).

> Car ce qu' estre soloit tout vert
> Estoit mué en autre teint,
> Car bise l'avoit tout desteint

A long passage of the *Navarre* (309-487), far above Machaut's usual level, describes the pestilence of 1349. It is not surprising, therefore, that Chaucer remembered this poem when he was composing the *Book of the Duchess* in the plague season of 1369.[9]

The Dreamer's long sickness and his remark that there is but one physician who can cure him (30-40), have been shown by Professor Sypherd to be commonplaces.[10]   Since it is certain, however, that Chaucer made extensive use of Machaut's *Remede de* Fortune in the *Book of the Duch-ess,*[11] and almost equally certain that he translated or adapted the same author's *Dit dou Lyon,* the following comparisons may well be significant:

Ther is phisicien[12] but oon	39	Qu'en monde n'a homme ne fame
That may me hele—but that		Qui medecine
is doon:		Y sceüst, se ce n'est ma dame.
		(*R. F.,* 1467-9.)
Passe we over until eft;		Mais laissier vueil ceste matiere,
That wil not be, moot nede		
be left;		
Our firste matere is good to		Et revenir a la premiere.
kepe.	43	(*Lyon,* 67-68.)

The trite transitional turn in *B. Duch.,* 41, 43, and *Dit dou Lyon,* 67-68, would not be worth noting, were it not that the verses that immediately precede it in the *Lyon* involve the metaphor that we are considering:

> Qui mainte fleur a decopée
> Par la froidure de s'espée (32-36).

Chaucer (as Skeat notes) is imitating the *Roman de la Rose* (56-57) both here and in B. *Duch.,* 410-12, but the sword does not occur in the *Roman.*

[9] See also, p. 14, below.
[10] *Modern Language Notes,* XX, pp. 241-3.
[11] See pp. 10 ff., below.
[12] Cf. also *R. F.,* 1574-7, 1591-1607; first *Complainte,* 13-16 (see p. 3, n. 7, above).

Einsi est il, si Dieus me gart,
De ma dame et de son regart:
Car je sui de tous maus gardez
Quant je suis de li regardez,
Ne doubtance n'ay de morir.
Helas! et je ne puis garir,
Eins suis en paour de ma vie,[13]
Quant ses dous regars signefie
Ma mort: c'est quant elle le tourne
Ailleurs, dont trop griefment m'atourne.
Mais laissier vueil ceste matiere,
Et revenir a la premiere. (57-68.)

The relations, already mentioned, between Chaucer'
story of Ceyx and Alcyone and its two source Fon
taine Amoureuse and Book XI of Ovid's *Metamorphoses,*
are familiar to scholars,[14] and need not detain us. We
will pass, therefore, from the Proem to the Dream itself.
Here the indebtedness of the *Book of the Duchess* to
Machaut's *Jugement dou Roy de Behaingne* is a proved
fact.[15] Some further parallels to that poem will be cited
in the present paper, not in confirmation,—which is needless,—but merely to illustrate Chaucer's craftsmanship.

For convenience we may divide the Dream roughly into
seven parts:—(1) The Hunt, (291-386); (2) The Walk
Through the Forest, (387-442); (3) The Encounter With
the Knight in Black (443-617); (4) The Knight's Tirade
Against Fortune (618-709); (5) The Conversation (710-
58); (6) The Story of the Knight in Black (759-1297);
(7) Conclusion (1298-1334).

I. *The Hunt* (291-386).—Here nothing of any account
has ever been cited by way of parallel. V. 291 ("Me

---

[13] Cf. B. *Duch.,* 24: "drede I have for to dye."
[14] Add to ten Brink's remarks (*Chaucer, Studien,* pp. 7-12) the
note by Professor Shannon in *Mod. Philol.,* XI, p. 227.
[15] *Mod. Philol.,* VII, pp. 465-71.

thoughte thus—that it was May ") might, *de rigueur,* be construed as a translation of v. 45 of the *Roman de la Rose* ("Avis m'iere qu'il estoit mais") [16] but the thing is a commonplace, recurring, in substance, in both the *Paradys* (45) and the *Behaingne* (9). The emperor Octavian (368) is mentioned in *Behaingne* (421), but he is a stock figure in romantic poetry. Sandras's references for 354 ff., 375 ff., come to nothing, and are not valued, even by Sandras himself.[17] Vv. 339-43 have been compared with *R. R.,* 123-4, but are rather closer to *Behaingne,* 13-14:

> And eek the welken was so fair,
> Blew, bright, clere was the air,
> And ful atempre, for soth, it was,
> For nother cold nor hoot it nas
> Ne in al the welken was a cloude.

> Et li jours fu attemprez par mesure,
> Biaus,[18] clers, luisans, nès et purs, sans froidure.

II. *The Walk Through the Forest* (387-442).—In this *passus* occur several pieces of description, long ago recognized as borrowed from the *Roman de la Rose.*[19] Vv. 398-399 suggest *Behaingne,* 43-44:

Doun by a floury grene wente	Par une estroite voie Pleinne d'erbette.
Ful thikke of gras ful softe and swete.	

---

[16] Kaluza's reading.

[17] *Étude,* pp. 91-92, 296-7; ten Brink, *Chaucer, Studien,* p. 12; Furnivall, *Trial-Forewords,* 1871, pp. 50-51; Skeat, n. on v. 376.

[18] Did Chauser read *blaus?*

[19] Cf. B. *Duch.,* 402-3, with *R. R.* 8448-50 Méon (9160-62 Michel); B. *Duch.,* 405-9, with *R. R.,* 8464-7 (9176-9); B. *Duch.,* 410-13, with *R. R.,* 56-57 (57-58); B. *Duch.,* 414-18, with *R. R.,* 49-55 (50-56); B. *Duch.,* 419-33, with *R. R.,* 1372-89 (1373-90); B. *Duch.,* 434-42, with *R. R.,* 12992-9 (13730-7).

But this is a mere trifle. Far more significant is the charming picture of the lost puppy that had tried in vain to follow the hounds (388-397).

The mourning lady in *Behaingne* is accompanied by a *chiennet,* which does not know Guillaume, but barks at him and sets its futile teeth in the skirt of his mantle (46, 1204-15). Whoever will take the trouble to compare these verses with *Le Dit dou Lyon,* 325-49, will cheerfully agree that Chaucer was writing under the spell of both passages, and will at the same time admit the originality of the English poet.

Ther cam by me	388	*Lors vint vers moy,* tout belement	325
A whelp that fauned me as I stood,		Li lions, *aussi humblement*	
That hadde yfolwed, and coude no good.	390	*Com se fust un petit chiennet.*	
It com and *creep to me as lowe*		Et quant ce vi, je dis, " Bien est,"	
Right as it hadde me yknowe,		Si li mis ma main sua la teste.	
Hild doun his heed and *ioyned his eres*		Mais plus doucement qu'autre beste	
And leyde al smothe doun his heres.	394	Le souffri et *joint les oreilles.*	331

III. *The Encounter With the Knight in Black* (443-617).—Chaucer has his eye on the *Behaingne* throughout, as is abundantly evident from quotations made in a previous paper.[20] A few other comparisons are worth making.

The Black Knight's lay of complaint (475-86) may

[20] *Mod. Philol.,* VII, pp. 465-6. The following parallels are cited: —*B. Duch.,* 502-4, *Beh.,* 56, 58, 60-62; *B. Duch.,* 519-21 (*read* 519-25)', *Beh.,* 70-74; *B. Duch.,* 547-50 (*read* 54), 560-4, *Beh.,* 88-97; *B. Duch.,* 583-4, *Beh.,* 196-8; *B. Duch.,* 599-616, *Beh.,* 177-87.

have been inspired either by *Behaingne*, 193-200, or by
the first eight lines of Machaut's third *Motet*.

> I have of sorwe so greet woon
> That ioye gete I never noon,
>   Now that I see my lady bright,
>   Which I have loved with al my might,
> Is fro me deed and is agoon.
>
> Allas, deth! what ayleth the,
>   That thou noldest have taken me
>   Whan that thou toke my lady swete,
> That was so fayr, so fresh, so fre,
> So good, that men may wel yse
>   Of al goodnesse she hadde no mete?   (475-86.)

> N'a mon las cuer jamais bien ne vendra,
> N'a nul confort n'a joie n'ateindra,
> Jusques atant que la mort me prendra,
>   Qui a grant tort
> Par devers moy, quant elle ne s'amort
> A moy mordre de son dolereus mort,
> Quant elle m'a dou tout tollu et mort
>   Mon dous ami.   (*Behaingne*, 193-200.)

> Hé! Mors, com tu es haïe
> De moy, quant tu as ravie
> Ma joie, ma druerie,
>   Mon solas,
> Par qui je sui einsi mas
> Et mis de si haut si bas,
> Et ne me pouiés pas
>   Assaillir.   (*Motet* iii, 1-8.) [21]

Note that after her lament in *Behaingne* the lady faints
(208 ff.), as the Black Knight comes near doing in Chaucer (487 ff.).[22]

---

[21] Chichmaref, II, p. 487. For an assured instance of borrowing
from the eighth Motet, see pp. 10-11, below.

[22] Chaucer dwells upon the physiology of the matter in a fashion
that shows his interest in medical science, so learnedly and convincingly illustrated in a recent paper by Professor Lowes (*Mod.
Philol.*, XI, pp. 491-546).

Vv. 526-55 are not continuously taken from *Behaingne,* but show occasional resemblances:

		Li chevaliers, sans faire plus de plait,	75
"Yis, thamendes is light to make,"	526	Dist doucement:	
Quod he, "for ther lyth noon ther-to;		"Dame, il n'affiert ci nul pardonnement,	
Ther is no-thing missayd nor do."	528	Car il n'y a meffait ne mautalent."	78
. . . .			
And I saw that, and gan me aqueynte	532	Et cils prist a traire	85
With him.	533	Plus près de li,	
. . . .			
Anoon-right I gan fynde a tale	536		
To him, to loke wher I mighte ought			
Have more knowing of his thought.	538	pour sa pensée attraire.	86
. . . .			
"And telleth me of your sorwes smerte."	555	Mais je vous pri que vostre pensement	79
		Me vueilliez dire.	80

V. 600 of the *Book of the Duchess* ("And al my laughter to weping") translates *Remede de Fortune,* 1198 ("En grief plour est mué mon ris").

IV. *The Black Knight's Tirade Against Fortune* (618-709).—The indebtedness of the *Book of the Duchess* to Guillaume de Machaut's *Remede de Fortune* was strongly asserted by Sandras, more than fifty years ago, in his tantalizing *Étude sur G. Chaucer,* but with scanty quotations that by no means prove his case, even if one makes generous allowance for characteristic hyperbole.[23] The

---

[23] Pp. 90, 290-4. Sandras quotes the following verses from the *Remede:* 1189-92 (P. 290); 1162, 1137-8, 931-3 (p. 291); 217-24

obligation, it now appears, is really considerable. It involves (to say nothing of scattered borrowings) a substantial portion of the Black Knight's tirade against Fortune, of his autobiography, and of his description of the Lady Blanche.

In the tirade against Fortune (618-709), Chaucer has utilized at least four of Machaut's poems—the *Remede de Fortune,* the *Jugement dou Roy de Behaingne,* the eighth *Motet,*[24] and the *Lay de Confort.* The allegory of the Game of Chess, which he takes, as is well known, from the *Roman de la Rose,* also appears in the *Remede.* The whole tirade affords so instructive an example of Chaucer's artistic method in his so-called French Period, that I reproduce most of it, with the appropriate comparisons.[25]

For fals Fortune hath pleyd
     a game   618
Atte ches with me—allas the
     whyle!

                La desloyal renoïe, parjure,
The trayteresse fals and ful   Fausse, traître, perverse.[26]
     of gyle,   620   (*M.,* 16-17.)
That al behoteth, and no-   Elle promet largement,
     thing halt;

                Et en son pis couvertement
                Traïson noe. (*R. F.,* 1054-6.) [27]

(p. 293); 52-56, 26-30 (p. 294). The passage which he credits to the *Remede* on p. 292 is from *Le Jugement dou Roy de Behaingne* (178-83); that which he credits to the *Remede* at the top of p. 294 is from *Le Dit dou Lyon* (215-220, 224).

[24] Chichmaref, II, pp. 497-8.

[25] *M.* means the eighth *Motet; R. F., Remede de Fortune;* B., *Le Jugement dou Roy de Behaingne.*

[26] This line is literally translated in B. *Duch.,* vs. 813: "The false trayteresse perverse."

[27] Cf. *R. F.,* 1117-19:

     Promettre assez puet des ses biens,
     Mais tu yes trop fols, se tu tiens
     Qu'il en y ait nul qui soit tiens.

Cf. *R. F.,* 998: "Riens ne tient qu'elle ait en couvent."

She goth upright, and yet she
    halt;

That baggeth foule, and
    loketh faire,
The dispitouse debonaire,   624
That scorneth many a crea-
    ture!
An ydole of fals portraiture

Is she, for she wol sone
    wryen;
She is the monstres heed
    ywryen,   628
As filth over ystrawed with
    floures.
Her moste worship and her
    flour is
To lyen, for that is her nat-
    ure,
Withoute feyth, lawe, or
    mesure,   632
She is fals,
    and ever laughing
With oon eye, and that other
    weping.
That is broght up, she set al
    doun.
I lykne her to the scor-
    pioun,   636
That is a fals flatering
    beste,
For with his hed he maketh
    feste,
But al amid his flateringe
With his tayle he wol stinge   640
And envenyme, and so wol
    she.
She is thenvyous·charite,

Un piet a droit, l'autre clopie,
La droite torte.
        (R. F., 1167-8.)

Une ydole est de fausse pour-
    traiture. (M., 9.)[28]

C'est fiens couvers de riche cou-
    verture,
Qui dehors luist et dedens est
    ordure. (M., 7-8.)

Sans foy, sans loy, sans droit,
    et sans mesure. (M. 6.)
Elle est non seüre. (M., 5.)
D'un oueil rit,
    de l'autre larmie.
        (R. F., 1162.)
Le sormonté au bas retourne.
        (R. F., 918.)
Oint et puis point de si mortel
    pointure. (M., 18.)
Cf. the next Motet (No. 9):

Tua cum garrulitas

Nos affatur dulcius,
Retro pungit sevius,
Ut veneno scorpius. (45-48.)[29]

C'est l'envieuse charité.
        (R. F., 1138.)

---

[28] In R. F., 1001-1112, Fortune is elaborately compared with the image (estature) that Nebuchadnezzar saw in his dream.
[29] Cf. Skeat's note.

That is ay fals, and semeth
   wel
So turneth she her false
   whel   644

                                        Et n'est estable,

Aboute, for it is no-thing
   stable,   Eins est toudis changant et
Now by the fyre, now at   variable,
   table.   Puis ci, puis la, or au feu, a la
Ful many oon hath she   table. (*B.*, 1072-4)
   yblent.   Les yeux esbloe
                              Et aveugle de mainte gent.
                                          (*R.* F., 1052-3.)
She is pley of enchaunte-   C'est droitement li gieus d'en-
   ment   648   chantement,
That semeth oon and is nat   Que ce qu'on cuide avoir cer-
   so.   teinnement,
The false theef! What hath   On ne l'a mie.
   she do,   (*B.*, 1078-80.) [20]
Trowest thou? By our
   Lord, I wol the seye.
Atte ches with me she gan
   to pleye;   652
With her false draughtes
   divers
She stal on me and took my
   fers;   Car la fierche avoit esté prise
And whan I saw my fers   Au gieu de la premiere assise.
   aweye,   (*R. R.*, 6734-5.)
Alas! I couthe no lenger
   pleye,   656
But seyde, " Farwel, swete,
   ywis,
And farwel al that ever ther
   is! "
Therwith Fortune seyde   " Eschec et mat! " li ala dire,[21]
   " Chek here,

---

[20] Cf. *Motet* VIII, 12-13:

      Car c'est tous vens, ne riens qu'elle figure
      Ne puet estre fors de fausse figure.

[21] Cf. *R. F.*, 1190-1:

      De ses gieus telement s'esbat
      Qu'en veinquant dit: " Eschac et mat! "

And mat!" in mid point of
the chekkere,
With a poun erraunt, alas! 661
Ful craftier to pleye she was
Than Athalus, that made the
game
First of the ches: so was his
name.   664
But God wolde I hadde ones
or twyes
Ykoud and knowe the ieu-
pardyes
That coude the Grek Pitha-
gores?
I shulde have pleyd the bet
at ches,   668
And kept my fers the bet
therby.
And thogh wherto? For
trewely
I holde that wish nat worth
a stree;
It hadde be never the bet for
me;   672
For Fortune can so many a
wyle,
Ther be but fewe can her
begyle.
And eek she is the las to
blame:
My-self I wolde have do the
same.   676

Desus son destrier auferrant,
Du trait d'un paonnet errant,

Ou milieu de son eschiquier.
            (R. R., 6675-8).
Car ainsinc le dist Athalus,

Qui des eschez controva l'us.
            (R. R., 6714-15.)

·   ·

Fortune a plus de mil engiens

Pour penre et decevoir les siens. ✓
            (R. F. 1113-14.)

The curiously learned remark of the Black Knight
(693-6) that all the planets and all the elements "give
him a gift of weeping" in solitude, is literally translated
from Machaut's *Lay de Confort*:

> Ther nis planete in firmament,
> Ne in air ne in erthe noon element,
> That they ne yive me a yift echoon
> Of weping, whan I am aloon.

> Qu'en terre n'a element,
> Ne planette en firmament,
> Qui de pleur don
> Ne me face. (10-13.)[32]

V. *The Conversation* (710-58).—In the conversation
that follows the Tirade against Fortune, Chaucer is known
to have had recourse to the *Roman de la Rose*[33] and the
Jugement dou Roy de Behaingne.[34] The three examples
of Medea (726-7), Phyllis (728-731), and Dido (731-4),
all occur in a famous passage of the Old Woman's discourse
in the *Roman*,[35] and in Medea and Phyllis there are coin-
cidences in phraseology that are manifestly not accidental.
But Machaut knew the *Rose* as well as Chaucer did, and
it is instructive to observe that in the *Remede* he, like
Jean de Meun[36] and Chaucer, brings in Socrates as a
model of constancy or fortitude,[37] and that, in still another
poem which Chaucer knew and utilized,[38] *Le Jugement
dou Roy de Navarre,* he mentions Medea's murder of her
children in terms very like Chaucer's[39] and dwells upon
the suicide of Dido. The Dido passage, indeed, is so much
closer than Jean de Meun's to Chaucer's verses that one
cannot hesitate in recognizing it, rather than Jean's, as

[32] Chichmaref, II, p. 415. The only other passage in *Le Lay de
Confort* that Chaucer seems to have imitated anywhere is 164-6,
which much resemble B. *Duch.*, 844-5 (see p. 18, below). We may
note that the speaker in this poem of Machaut's is a lady addressing
her absent lover, (see 96, 187 ff., 255).

[33] See Skeat's notes.

[34] *Mod. Phil.*, VII, p. 466 (B. *Duch.*, 746, 749-52; *Beh.*, 251, 253-6).
Cf. also B. *Duch.*, 724, with *Beh.*, 234; B. *Duch.*, 753, with the oath
in *Beh.*, 114-121, 251-2; B. *Duch.*, 755-7, with *Beh.*, 257-8.

[35] Méon, II, pp. 431-6 (see Skeat's n. on 726). The order in *R. R.*
is *Dido, Phyllis, [Œnone,] Medea.*

[36] *R. R.*, 5868-91.

[37] *R. F.*, 118-22; cf. *Confort d'Ami*, Tarbé, p. 94.

[38] *Mod. Phil.*, VII, pp. 471-3; see also pp. 3-4 above.

[39] 2793-7.

Chaucer's immediate model.   In both Machaut and Chaucer the emphasis is on Dido's " rage " and " folly ": not
so in the *Rose,* which uses neither word, but insists rather
on the compassion that one must feel in contemplating
her fate.

> *Another rage*
> *Hadde Dido, quene eek of Cartage,*
> That slow herself, for Eneas
> Was *fals.* Which a fool she was!   (731-4.)

2095

> *Dydo, roïne de Cartage,*
> *Ot si grant dueil et si grant rage*
> Pour l'amour qu'elle ot a Enée,
> Qui li avoit sa foy donnée
> Qu'a mouillier l'aroit et a femme;
> Et *li faus* l'appeloit sa dame.   2100

>   .   .   .   .

> Quant failli li ot dou couvent   2107
> Qu'eü li avoit en couvent,   2108

>   .   .   .   .

> La desesperée, *la fole,*   2111
> Qu'amours honnist, qu'amours *afole,*
> L'espée d'Eneas trouva
> Et en son corps si l'esprouva.   2114

>   .   .   .   .

> Dont elle morut a dolour   2117
> Pour amer, et *par sa folour.*   2118

In Chaucer, the example of Dido is immediately followed by a brief mention of Echo:

> And Ecquo dyed for Narcisus
> Nolde nat love her (735-6).

Here again one naturally refers to the *Roman de la Rose,*
which tells the story of Echo and Narcissus.[40]   But it is
worth noting that the same tale is summarized by Machaut
in his seventh *Motet,* with which Chaucer, who borrows
from the *eighth,*[41] must have been familiar:

[40] Méon, I, pp. 58-61.   In the application "rage" is mentioned,
(1590).

[41] See pp. 10-11, above.

Narcisus

. · . . . . . .

... onques entendre le depri
Ne deingna d'Echo, qui pour li
Reçut mort amere et obscure.[42]

VI. *The Story of the Knight in Black* (759-1297).—
After the conversation which we have just been studying,
the Knight in Black tells the story of his youthful love
(759 ff.). His autobiography begins, as I have shown in
a previous essay,[43] with a number of extracts from *Le
Jugement dou Roy de Behaingne,* which, artistically rearranged, account for vv. 759-776 of the English poem.
With v. 777 Chaucer turns to the *Remede de Fortune,*
which he excerpts freely in vv. 777-804.

That I did thus, and niste why:	777	Pour ç'a li mes cuers s'encli-noit,	61
I trowe it cam me kyndely.		Et Nature li aprenoit,	
		Ce m'est vis.	63
Paraunter I was therto able		Car le droit estat d'innocence	26
As a whyt wal or a table;	780	Ressamble proprement la table	
For it is redy to cacche and take		Blanche, polie, qui est able	
Al that men wil therin make,		A recevoir, sans nul con-traire,	
Wher-so men wol portreye or peynte,		Ce qu'on y veut peindre et pourtraire.	30
Be the werkes never so queynte.	784		
		Einsi est il certainnement	35
And thilke tyme I ferde so		De vray humein entendement,	
I was able to have lerned tho		Qui est ables a recevoir	
		Tout ce qu'on vuet et con-cevoir	
And to have coud as wel or bettre,		Puet tout ç'a quoy on le vuet mettre,	

---

[42] *Motet* vii, 38, 42-44 (Chichmaref, II, p. 496).
[43] *Mod. Phil.,* VII, pp. 467-8 (*Beh.,* 261-3, 125-33, 264-73).

Paraunter, other art or
   lettre,   788
But, for love cam first in
   my thought,
Therfore I forgat it nought.
I 'chees love to my firste
   craft,
Therfore it is with me laft; 792
For-why I took it of so yong
   age
That malyce hadde my cor-
   age
Nat that tyme turned to no-
   thing
Through to mochel knowlech-
   ing.   796
For that tyme

   youthe, my maistresse,
Governed me in ydelnesse,
For it was in my firste
   youthe,
And tho ful litel good I
   couthe,   800
For al my werkes were flit-
   ting,
And al my thoghtes varying;
Al were to me yliche good
That I knew tho; but thus it
   stood.   804

Armes, amours, autre art
   ou lettre.   40

Et l'entreprengne en juene
   aäge,   23
Eins qu'en malice son corage

Mue

   par trop grant congnois-
   sance.   25
Por ce l'ay dit que, quant
   j'estoie   45
De l'estat qu' innocence
   avoie,
Que juenesse me gouvernoit
Et en oiseuse me tenoit,   48
[With *B. D.*, 799, cf. *R. F.*, 46,
   above.]

Mes ouevres estoient volages,

Varians estoit mes corages,
Tout m'estoit un,
      quanque vëoie.   51

Then Chaucer returns to *Le Jugement dou Roi de Behaingne,* to which he is indebted for a large part of vv. 805-832.[44] With v. 833 he once more utilizes the *Remede.*

She hadde so stedfast coun-
   tenaunce   833
So noble port and meynten-
   aunce.

Et sa maniere asseürée, . .   197

Son biau port, son gentil
   maintieng.   199

---

[44] *Mod. Phil.*, VII, p. 468 (*Beh.*, 281-90).

And Love, that hadde herd my bone	Et quant Amours vit qu'en ce point	71
Hadde espyed me thus sone, 836	Estoie, elle n'atendi point.	72
That she ful sone, in my thoght,	Eins l'avoit	95
As helpe me God, so was ycaught	entrepris.	95
So sodenly that I ne took	Qu'einc congié ne conseil n'en pris	96
No maner counseyl but at her look 840	Fors a mon cuer et a ses yeus,	97
And at myn herte, for-why her eyen	Qui en riant m'ont en mains lieus	98
So gladly, I trowe, myn herte seyen	Prié que par amour l'amasse.	99
	. . . .	
That purely tho myn owne thoght	Et mes cuers voloit que je fusse	102
Seyde it wer bet serve her for noght 844	Tous siens.	103
Than with another to be wel.		
And it was soth, for, every-del,		
I wil anoon-right telle thee why.		

The only lines in *B. Duch.*, 833-47, that are not present in the *Remede* (except for such as are merely transitional) are 844-5:

> Seyde it were bet to serve her for nought
> Than with another to be wel.

These strongly resemble three lines in Machaut's *Lay de Confort,* a poem from which (as we have already found) four other verses of the *Book of the Duchess* are literally translated.[45]

> Miex vaut assez s'acointence
> Que puissence
> D'autre avoir (164-6).[46]

---

[45] See p. 13, above. V. 836 is reminiscent of *R. R.*, 1690 (Skeat).
[46] Chichmaref, II, p. 420.

With v. 848 Chaucer reverts to the *Behaingne,* which continues to be his main source through v. 1041, though he handles the material with his accustomed freedom and felicity. Vv. 848-1041 are also indebted, in places, to the *Remede.*

Duchess	Behaingne	Remede
848-58	297-303	
859-74	312, 316, 318, 321-30	
883-7	331-5	
895-903	292-6	
904-5	356-8	
906		1629-30
907-11	397-403	
912-13	411-14	
918	580-1	
919-26		217-224
927-32		234, 225-30
933-6		234-6
937		238
939-47	361-3	
948-51		54-56
952-60	364-83	
966-74		167-74
985-7 [47]		123-4
1035-40 [48]	148-53, 156-8	

Vv. 1042-51 are a conversation. With v. 1052 the Knight in Black resumes his discourse, and from v. 1056 through v. 1182 we have a remarkable series of parallels to the *Remede de Fortune.* Machaut, in a truly mediæval outburst,[49] protests that he should not have been good

[47] In the interval between this group of verses and the next in the column falls the famous passage (1024-33) about sending lovers to Wallachia, Prussia, etc., to the Dry Sea and the Carrenar—the general resemblance of which to *Le Dit dou Lyon,* 1368 ff., is noted by Skeat.

[48] Vv. 1037-39 are compared by Sandras (p. 294) with *Dit dou Lyon,* 215-17, 220, 224 (lines which he credits to the *Remede*).

[49] 107 ff. .The fashion is well-recognized and examples are countless. There is a pretty instance in Machaut's 38th *Balade Notée* (Chichmaref, II, pp. 560-1).

enough for his lady if he had been as wise as Solomon, as valorous as Alexander or Hector, as honored as Godfrey of Bouillon, as fair as Absalom, as patient as Job, as constant as Judith and Socrates, as humble as Esther, and as loyal as Abraham. This protestation the Black Knight imitates in 1054-74 ; but Chaucer shows good taste in avoiding Machaut's mixture of sacred and profane worthies.[50] There is a shorter passage of a similar character in *Behaingne,* 421-5.[51] Continuing the narrative of his love, v. 1089, the Black Knight goes back to the early part of the *Remede* for materials.

But wherfor that I telle thee 1088	
Whan I first my lady sey?	Quant tel fais voloie entre-dame vi, 89
	Sa grant biauté mon cuer ravi,
	Et quant de s'amour fui espris,
I was right yong, soth to sey,	Juenes estoie et desapris,
And ful gret need I hadde to lerne;	S'avoie bien mestier d'apren-dre,
Whan my herte wolde yerne 1092	Quant tel fais voloie entre-prendre. 94
To love it was a gret em-pryse.	
But as my wit coude best suffyse	
	Et quant Amour m'ot a ce mis 135

---

[50] *Per contra,* he inserts a little bit of learning about the death of Hector and Antilochus (1066-71). It is certainly malapropos, but is of some value as a landmark in Chaucer's literary travels, for it doubtless comes from the *Roman de Troie,* 21799-22256 (Joly): cf. *Publ. Mod. Lang. Assoc.,* XXIV, pp. 345-7. The substitution of Alcibiades for Absalom was prompted by a reminiscence of the *Roman de la Rose,* 8980-4 (see Skeat).

[51] Here Octavian is mentioned (421); cf. *B. Duch.,* 368 (see p. 6, above).

After my yonge childly wit,

Without drede, I besette it 1096

[With *R. F.*, vv. 139-40, cf.

B. Duch., vv. 1285-6.]

To love her in my beste
   wyse,
To do her worship and
   servyse

That I tho coude, by my
   trouthe,
Withoute feyning outher
   slouthe; 1100
For wonder fayn I wolde
   her se.

So mochel it amended me

That, whan I saw her first
   a-morwe
I was warished of al my
   sorwe 1104
Of al day after, til it were
   eve;
Me thoghte no-thing mighte
   me greve,
Were my sorwes never so
   smerte. 1107

Que pris fui et loiaus amis,
Elle congnut bien ma jue-
   nesse,
Mon innocence, ma sim-
   plesse;
Et pour ce qu'estoie en en-
   fance,
Me prist elle en sa gouver-
   nance;
Si me moustra la droite voie,
Comment ma dame amer de-
   voie,
Servir, oubeïr, honnourer,

Humblement croire et aou-
   rer. 144

Selonc mon juene entende-
   ment 64
La vëoie moult volentiers. 65

Et son trés dous plaisant
   regart 295
Attraioit mon cuer de sa
   part
Tout aussi, par son dous at-
   trait,
Com l'aïmant le fer attrait.
Et ce tenoit mon cuer en
   joie,
Car quant ce dous regart
   vëoie,
En moy prenoit son repaire

Riens qui fust a joie contraire. 302

With the next four lines compare *Dit dou Lyon,* 207-212:

	Car la très douce imprecion 207
	Don son ymagination
And yit she sit so in myn herte　1108	Est en mon cuer si fort em-preinte
That, by my trouthe, I nolde noght,	Que encor y est et yert em-preinte,
For al this world, out of my thoght .	Ne jamais ne s'en partira
Leve my lady,—no, trewly!　1111	Jusques a tant qu'il par-tira.　　212 [53]

Vv. 1115-1125, in which the Knight in Black declares that he will never repent of loving, and that if he should, he should be the worst of traitors, look like a development of vv. 1140-7 of the *Behaingne,*—a passage which also shows some resemblance to vv. 1109-1111.

The Knight goes on with his story at v. 1146, after some conversation with the Dreamer, and parallels to the *Remede* continue.

On her was al my love leyd;　1146	Et je la servi longuement　357
	De cuer si amoureusement
	Qu' a nulle autre rien n'en-tendoie
	Fors a s'amour ou je ten-doie.　　360
And yet she niste it never a del	Mais de tout ce riens ne savoit,
Noght longe tyme, leve it wel,	Ne comment elle pris m'avoit;
For be right siker, I durste noght	Car pour riens ne li des-couvrisse
For al this world telle her my thoght　1150 [*]	L'amour de mon cuer, ne deïsse.　　364
. . . .	. . . .
But for to kepe me fro ydelnesse,　1155	Et pour ce que n'estoie mie 401

---

[*] Cf. also *R. F.*, 131-4:—

> Si que siens sans riens retenir
> Sui, que qu'il m'en doie avenir.
> Et seray, tant com je vivray.
> Ne jamais autre n'ameray.

[53] Vv. 1152-4 are from *R. R.*, 2005-6 (Skeat).

Trewly I did my besinesse		Toudis en un point, m'es-
To make songes, as I best		tudie
coude.	1157	Mis en faire chansons et lais. 403
. . . .		. . . .
And lo! this was alder-		Fist je ce dit qu'on claimme
firste,	1173	lay. 430
I not wher it were the		
werste.	1174	

Here follows a short song (1175-1180) in the *Book of the Duchess,* a long lay. (431-680) in the *Remede.*

Now have I told thee, soth		·Einsi me fist ma dame faire 681
to saye,	1181	
My firste song.		Ce lay qu' oÿ m'avez retraire. 682

Then the poet passes over to the *Jugement,* which he utilizes, with an occasional touch from the *Remede,* until the Knight's story is finished.

DUCHESS	BEHAINGNE	REMEDE
1183-91	453-6	
1192	466	
1195-8	461-2	1671-83
1203-18	467-76	
1216		696
1219	504-5	
1226-30	656-8	
1236-8	509-12	
1239-44	541-8	
1250-1		·751-2
1258-67	592-8	
1270	641 (cf. 670)	
1271	610	
1273		4074-5
1275-8	622-4	
1285-6		139-40
1289-95	166-76	

Some of these parallels are quite unmistakable; others are vague, and would have no significance if we did not positively know that Chaucer drew extensively on both the *Behaingne* and the *Remede.* One passage in the list de-

serves particular notice, for it shows the Chaucerian
reaction in full force.

Machaut's Knight, in *Behaingne,* gives an elaborate
form of rejection that was used by his lady:

> Si que, biau sire, alez devers Amours,
> Si li faites vos plains et vos clamours;
> Car en li gist vos mors et vos secours,
>   Nom pas en moy;
> Et pas ne sui cause de vostre anoy,
> Ce m'est avis, si que souffrir m'en doy.
> Plus ne vous say que dire, en bonne foy:
>   *Adieu* vous di.   (541-8.)

Contrast the Knight in Black:

> To telle shortly as it is,
> Trewly her answere, it was this—
> I can not now wel counterfete
> Her wordes, but this was the grete
> Of her answere: she sayde *Nay,*
> Al-outerly.   (1239-44.)

VII. *Conclusion* (1298-1334).—The conclusion of the
Book of the Duchess is Chaucer's own, but at the very end
there is, as was to be expected, a reminiscence of Froissart's
Paradys d'Amours.[54]

We have studied Chaucer's lovely and pathetic elegy,
with some particularity, in comparison with its sources,—
not, one may trust, for the sake of accumulating parallel
passages, but rather for the sake of getting a better insight
into his methods as an artist.   Whatever the result, one
thing emerges triumphantly from our investigation,—the
essential originality of Chaucer's genius.

                                   G. L. KITTREDGE.

[54] Cf. B. *Duch.*, 1324-5, with *Par.*, 1685-92; *B. Duch.*, 1350, with
Par., 1693-5; B. *Duch.*, 1334, with *Par.*, 1722-3.

II.—THE *POEMA BIBLICUM* OF ONULPHUS

The attention of students of mediæval drama has often been arrested by a short dramatic text from a Vienna manuscript published by DuMéril among the examples of the liturgical Epiphany play in his *Origines Latines du Théâtre Moderne.*[1]   Among the mediæval Latin plays of Epiphany this slight specimen is unique in its rhetorical form, in the names of the *dramatis personæ,* and in the absence of liturgical elements.   The play is composed of thirteen leonine hexameters, which provide thirty-one speeches, each of the last ten hexameters being divided among three speakers.   The first three lines, in the nature of an invitatory, are assigned to *Stella* as a speaking character, and the Magi appear under the names of *Aureolus, Thureolus,* and *Myrreolus.*   The play bears no marks from the liturgy.   Although the introductory rubric *Ad adorandum Filium Dei per Stellam invitantur Eoy* might serve well enough for launching a liturgical play, there is no concluding rubric to indicate a liturgical association, and the text itself contains no formulæ reminiscent of the liturgy.

Before receiving this text, then, into the history of liturgical drama, we should do well to scrutinize its credentials.   DuMéril's text is an excerpt from the eighteenth-century catalogue compiled by Denis,[2] and is re-

[1] E. DuMéril, *Les Origines Latines du Théâtre Moderne,* Paris, 1849, pp. 151-152.

[2] M. Denis, *Codices Manuscripti theologici bibliothecae palatinae vindobonensis latini aliarumque occidentis linguarum,* Vol. I, Part iii, Vienna, 1795, col. 3054-3056.   Denis numbers the manuscript 841. DuMéril's No. 941 is apparently a misprint.

25

presented as showing an independent and complete "my-stère" upon the subject of the Magi.[3] Succeeding writers have added nothing to the data transmitted by DuMéril. Köppen[4] and Meyer[5] give this play no consideration. Chambers,[6] Anz,[7] and Creizenach[8] appear to derive their information exclusively from DuMéril.

In a search for further knowledge, therefore, we must first revert to DuMéril's immediate source, the catalogue of Denis. In this generous compilation we are surprised to discover that the text presented by DuMéril as an inde-pendent "mystère" is, in reality, only part of a larger poem in the form of a cycle of small dramatic pieces, to which Denis gives the collective title *Poema biblicum de generis humani Reparatione*. In view of the substantial accuracy of Denis's description of the cycle, we may well quote it *in extenso:* [9]

Fol. 30. absque inscriptione incipit *Poema* biblicum de generis

---

[3] DuMéril speaks of the text as follows: " Il y avait aussi dans un MS. du xive siècle, de la Bibliothèque de Vienne, No 941 [misprint for No 841], un mystère sur ce sujet, dont il ne resterait plus que l'ar-gument, selon Denis, *Codices manuscripti theologici*, t. I, col. 3049; mais nous croirions volontiers que la pièce est complète." This state-ment misrepresents Denis, who in his remark (col. 3054), " Verum hujus Scenae non nisi Argumentum superest," refers not to the play before us, but to the dialogue " Inter Magos et Herodem," which in the manuscript follows immediately upon our play, and of which the manuscript preserves only part of the *argumentum*, as may be seen in my complete text printed below.

[4] W. Köppen, *Beiträge zur Geschichte der deutschen Weihnachts-spiele*, Marburg, 1892.

[5] W. Meyer, *Fragmenta Burana*, Berlin, 1901, pp. 38-48.

[6] E. K. Chambers, *The Mediœval Stage*, Vol. II, Oxford, 1903, p. 51.

[7] H. Anz, *Die lateinischen Magierspiele*, Leipzig, 1905, pp. 9-49.

[8] W. Creizenach, *Geschichte des neueren Dramas*, Vol. I, Halle, 1911, p. 56.

[9] Denis, col. 3054-3056.

humani Repar̦atione autore *Onulpho* quodam, ut patet e sequenti
Prǫœmio:

> Adlardo patri uirtutibus inuigilanti
> Annuit Onulphus pietatis amabile munus.
> Sim licet exilis populi seu portio vilis
> Rebus in extremis multo minor atque coeuis
> Fascibus illatis humeros nostros oneratis,
> Quas vix tangendas fragili datis ecce ferendas,
> Atque panegyricum de paupere fonte rogatis
> Quod ḃic scribatur Christi ut natale loquatur.
> Hic cogor mixtum cum dramate carmen inire,
> Quod sub personis alternat opus Salomonis etc.

Ad modum itaque *Cantici Cantic.* διαλόγιχως scribere decernit, idque
praestat sequentibu₃ Scenis: 1°. inter Serpentem et Evam. 2°. inter Deum Patrem et Filium. 3°. inter Prophetas et Terrigenas.
4°. inter Prophetas, Deum Patrem et Filium. 5°. inter Mariam et
Gabrielem. 6°. inter Misericordiam et Veritatem. 7°. inter Coeli-
genas et Terrigenas, cui subjicitur Poetae Epilogus. 8°. inter Stellam et Magos, cui praemissum est metricum proœmium. 9°. inter
Magos et Herodem. Verum hujus Scenae non nisi Argumentum superest, deperditis omnibus, quae non exiguo fortasse numero seque-
bantur. Scenis singulis praefigitur Argumentum rhythmicum, ita
Scenae 1.

> Gloriam primi parentis euacuauit suggestio dyri serpentis.
> Et dum deitatis ius expectatur auarum.
> Inuidia dyaboli introiuit mors in orhem terrarum.

Scenam ult. speciminis loco exscribam: Argumentum. . . .

After the word *Argumentum* follows the text printed by
DuMéril.[10] At the conclusion of this extract, Denis com-
pletes his description of the fragment as follows:

Nihil Noster aeuo suo de tribus *Regibus*, qui, si *Onulphus* Monachus
est, qui in vitam *Popṛonis* Abb. *Stabulensis* autore *Everhelmo* apud
Bollandum T. II. Jan. ad'diem 25. p. 638. praefatur, ad medium Sec.
XI, et Coenobium *Blandiniense* prope *Gandavum* pertinet. Certiora
dicent fortasse, apud quos integrum *Onulphi* Poema fuerit, de quo nil
Leyserus, nec, quod sciam, alii.

---

[10] DuMéril, pp. 151-152.

The information communicated by Denis may best be interpreted through the *Poema biblicum* itself, of which I offer a text based upon the manuscript: [11]

<POEMA BIBLICUM DE GENERIS HUMANI REPARATIONE>

Adlardo patri   uirtutibus inuigilanti
Annuit Onulphus   pietatis amabile munus.

Prohemium.

   Sim licet exilis   populi seu portio uilis
   Rebus in extremis   multo minor atque coeuis,
5 Fascibus illatis   humeros nostros oneratis,[12]
   Quas uix tangendas   fragili datis ecce ferendas,
   Atque panegyricum de paupere fonte rogatis
   Quod sic scribatur   Xpisti ut natale loquatur.
   Hinc cogor mixtum cum dramate [13] carmen inire,

---

[11] In preparing this text I have had the great advantage of consultations with Professor Grant Showerman and Professor E. K. Rand, to whom I am deeply grateful for generous assistance. To Professor Rand I owe numerous editorial suggestions, a few of which I have been able to acknowledge specifically below. Professor Rand, however, should not be held responsible for any errors that I may have committed in my use of his suggestions.

The manuscript is described by Denis, col. 3049-3058, and in *Tabulae codicum manu scriptorum in Bibliotheca Palatina Vindobonensi Asservatorum*, Vol. I, Vienna, 1864, p. 185. The press-mark of the manuscript given by Denis as 841, is now " 1054· [Theol. 452]." Cod. 1054 is a miscellany of 40 folios, containing some ten separate entries written in hands of the twelfth and fourteenth centuries. The entry with which we are concerned is written in double columns in a hand of the fourteenth century, and occupies the lower two-thirds of folio 30 recto and all of folio 30 verso. In my text, asterisks mark the beginning and end of the part printed, from Denis, by DuMéril.

[12] In the manuscript this word is preceded by a false stroke.

[13] Ms. diamate.

10 Quod sub personis   alternat opus Salomonis,
    Necdum deprendi   quamuis hoc scema canendi
    Quod personarum   facit alternatio clarum
    Datque decus rebus,   grandeuo iunctus ephebus
    Par persona pari   cum deposcit sociari
15 Persone interdum comite persona repugnat,
    Astute prauus   satagit cum fallere Dauus,[14]
    Iratusque Chremes tumido delitigat ore,[15]
    Id genus et plura   comitis potius placitura
    Que fidei sane doctrina studet reprobare.
20 Sed qui preclare   uis personas uariare
    Has dum componis   morem gerito Salomonis,
    Nam satyram quod olet,   mens Xpisto dedita nolet.
       Virgo parit Xpistum,   res tanta diem sacrat
                           istum,
    Cuius natalem persona pudica loquatur.
25 Omnis ab hoc festo   uates gentilis abesto,
    Pindarus, Alceus,   mendose pulcher Homerus.
    Nec maculent fucis   presentis gaudia lucis,
    Sed prestent de te,   Deus, argumenta prophete,
    Ac patriarcharum   concurrunt dicta tuorum.
30 Secla quoque ex Ade   ueteris pereuntia clade
    Deplorent flendo,   miserendo, compatiendo,
    Per lacrimas quorum,   Ihesu, miserere reorum,
    Et per Mariam   pie cum uacuaueris Euam,
    Antydoto [16] leni   gustum compesce ueneni.

Argumentum primum:

Gloriam primi parentis
Euacuauit suggestio dyri serpentis;

---

[14] Ms. clauus.

[15] Horace, Ars Poetica, line 94.

[16] The manuscript appears to have antydotū, altered to antydoto.

Et du*m* deitatis ius expectatu*r* auarum,
Inuidia dya*boli* introiuit mors i*n* orbe*m* te*rr*arum.

Serpens: <fol. 30^r, col. 2>

35   Qui te plantaui*t*   lignu*m* uitale negauit,
    Q*uo*d si gustares,   · bona uel mala tanta negares.
    Vim q*uoque* magnoru*m*   posses equare deor*um*.

Eua:
    Legem dictauit,   qui uos a*n*im*ando* creauit,
    Ut n*on* gustetu*r*   medius q*ui* fructu*s* ha*b*etur,
40   Ne c*um* gustatur,   qu*o* [17] uiuimu*s* hoc pe′ri-
                      matu*r*.

Se*r*pens:
    Saluat saluificu*m*,   nouit nocuisse nociuu*m*.
    Nec ualet e*ss*e malu*m*   uirtutis ma*nder*e malu*m*.

Eua:
    Parce*n*du*m* statui, q*uia* rem u*irtus* comitatur.
    Nec fruar absq*ue* uiro   re q*uam* fru*i*tura re-
       q*ui*ro;
45   *Et* cibus iste p*ro*bus   stabi*t* i*n* co*m*mune duobu*s*
    Du*m* liquet h*oc* tali bo*na* uel mala p*o*sse notari.

Argume*n*tum:

Hoc inobedientie reatu i*m*mortalitate*m* homo exuit,
Morte*m*que i*n* omn*e*s ia*m* posteros transmisit,
Cui*us* lapsum De*us* Pa*t*er miseratus ab alto
P*ro* reparatio*ne* ipsius t*r*actat c*um* Deo Filio.

De*us* Pa*t*er:
    Nate, mee uires   *et* mag*n*ificentia diues,
    Cernis co*n*fundi   q*uia* crimine clymata mu*n*di.
    Hu*n*c repa*r*es mecu*m*   q*ui* corrui*t*; arbitro*r*
                    equu*m*.

[17] Ms. q*uo*d.

Deus Filius:

50 Res manet ad cunctas   tecum mihi iuncta uo-
                                                luntas.
     Per me decerne   quecumque gerenda superne,
     Quidquid et est infra   uel quidquid respicit
                                                extra.

Deus Pater:

     Testantes de te   patriarche necne prophete
     Hii premittantur,   mundoque futura loquantur,
55 Post quorum aduentum   mitteris secla redemp-
                                                tum.

Deus Filius:

     Pneumate de nostro   uatum perflabitur ordo,
     Peccati morbis   per quos si non caret orbis,
     Perfectam faciam, te disponente, salutem.

Argumentum:

     Patriarche cum prophetis ad terrigenas mittuntur,
     Sed ab hiis non recipiuntur.

Prophete:

     Misit rex celi nos uulnera uestra mederi,
60 Res etenim uestra   prorsus perit intus et extra;
     Absque salute ulla   cordis languetque medulla.

Terrigene:

     Languida mens egri   satis indiget ipsa mederi.
     Quos sanos scitis   frustra curare uenitis,
     Nam non languemus   sana qui mente uigemus.

Prophete:

     Per mali morsum   postquam ruit Eua retror-
                                                sum,
     Ira necis dire   passim porrexerat [18] ire.

[18] Ms. perrexerat.

Mortifere pestis   pressi sic cladibus estis.

Terrigene ad prophetas Domini: <fol. 30^v, col. 1>

Vulnus id obduxit satis inueterata cycatrix;

Quidquid et est hominum   post dampna manet

recidiuum,

70   Nullaque splendet ita   uelud hec clarissima uita.

Argumentum:

Prophete Deo quem nullum latet secretum audita renunciant atque redimendo homini consilium instauratur Domini.

Prophete:

Rebus in humanis   sic preualet error inanis,

Ut bona praua putent   ueluti mala recta refu-

tent,

Et preter mundum   nil credant esse secundum.

Deus Pater ad prophetas:

Dure ceruicis   datur hec si plebs inimicis

75   Inpie perdetur;   sed nunc ne tota necetur,

Iram suspendi,   quia sit tempus miserendi.

Deus Filius:

Si, Pater, intendis   pietatis rebus agendis,

Est opis id graue me queque gerenda patrare.

Deus Pater:

In terris tibi mater erit noua, Virgo Maria,

80   Illa quod ut sciscat,   Gabrielis dogmata discat.

Deus Filius:

Pareo preceptis,   et tu, Pater, annue ceptis,

Maiestate [19] pari   quia constat nos sociari.

[19] Ms. maiestati.

Argumentum:

Gabriel archangelus ad uirginem Mariam destinatur,
Natiuitas quia Xpisti per eum nunciatur.

Gabriel archangelus:
    O Maria, uale!   templum Domini speciale!
    Pulchra maris stella,   sed et intemerata puella!
85   Innuba mater eris,   sed mater uirgo manebis.

Maria:
    Qualiter absque uiro   ualeam generare requiro;
    Nec dubitans quero,   quod posse geri pie spero
    Huius iura rei,   sed sum studiosa doceri.

Gabriel archangelus:
    Inbuet internum   pectus tibi pneuma supernum;
90   Sicque Dei ueri   gaudebis prole repleri.
    Post partum prolis   nec habebis dampna pudoris.

Maria:
    Annuat ancille   mihi rerum conditor ille,
    Huius iura rei   ualeam quo sancta mereri,
    Atque status mentis   formetur rebus agendis.

Argumentum:

Xpisto nato, Misericordia et Veritas obuiauerunt sibi;
Iusticia et Pax osculate sunt.

Misericordia:
95   Per Xpistum natum   uideo mundum gratula-
                                tum,
    Et quia perpendi   uenisse diem miserendi
    Omni pro mundo [20]   pietatis amore redundo.

[20] The manuscript may read promendo.

3

Veritas:

    Hec presens etas   meruit‾ res cernere letas,
    Verbum namque Dei   nunc stillabant quia celi.
100   Vera fides crescat,   fallacia cuncta facescat.

Iusticia:

    Qui bona formauit   me Iusticiam uocitauit.
    Iussit et ipse sequi   nati uestigia Xpisti,
    Ut mala pellantur,   fraus, ira, dolus sopiantur.

Pax:

    Sim comes ut tecum   prorsus res postulat equum,
105   Et quoniam Xpisti   gressus comitata fuisti,
    Mecum coniura   componere federa pura.

Argumentum:

Natiuitatem Xpisti cum hec leta prosequuntur,
Inter celigenas et terrigenas uerba de pace oriuntur.

Celigene:

    Actenus immitem   tenuerunt secula litem.
    Sed cum uirgo parit   uerbum quod cuncta cre-
                                         auit,
    Pax quoque uera redit,   lis inueterata recedit.

Terrigene:

110   Maiestate Dei   coguntur cuncta moueri
    Nam cum uirgo parit,   cum pax litem superarit,
    Re licet insueta   procedunt tempora leta.

Celigene:

    Res cum mira datur   nullus uestrum moueatur.
    Hic puer a uobis   Bethlem cernetur in oris
115 .   Cui cunas tantum   presepia dant animantum.

Terrigene: <fol. 30ᵛ, col. 2>

    Morte quidem uicta   deitas iuge sit benedicta;
    Sed pia dona Dei   properabimus ecce tueri,
    Ut regem regum   per nos sciat orbis in euum.

POETA SUB APOSTROPHA FACIT EPYLOGUM.

    Hiis sum personis Xpistum tibi, Domne, locutus,
120 Pallentes hederas,   nenias [21] spernens et Hyberas,
    Quas qui stultus amat   Xpisto precando re-
                                 clamat,
    Sed quia nil triste,   Pater alme, dies habent iste,
    Iam nunc mente pari   nos conuenit exhilarari,
    Peccatisque mori,   uirtutibus atque renasci.
125 Sed quia tempus abit,   finiri sermo rogabit,
    Sit licet egregium numquam te, Xpiste, tacere,
    Qui cum Patre Deo   uiuis sine temporis euo
    Iure coeterno   cum pneumate necne superno.

PERSONE DE EPYPHANIA DOMINI.

PROHEMIUM.

    Prodiit ex stella   lux hec radiante nouella,
130 Xpistum monstrando,   gentiles atque uocando.
    ᵛHec neque nunc orbi   recoletur laude minori,
    Quam que [22] nascentem   iam uiderat omnipoten-
                                    tem,
    Rex unus quamuis sibi consignarit utramuis.
    Illa dedit Xpistum,   hec gentes traxit ad ipsum.
135 Plebi Iudee   celestia tunc patuere;

---

[21] Since Professor Rand has called my attention to Ovid, Fasti, vi, 519, Appulerat ripae vaccas Œtæus Hyberas, I can suggest the emendation uaccas.

[22] Ms. quamque.

  Stella *sed* absentes   trax*it* *nunc* *preuia* *gentes,*
  Et c*um* de longe   *populus* *conuenit* uterq*ue*
  Diu*er*sus dudu*m*   *paries* respondet i*n* unu*m.*
  Vocib*us* hinc eque   parib*us* uene*r*entur utreq*ue,*
140 Sed cu*m* personis   alternatim speciosis
  Dele*ct*at [23] rursum   ` scribendi [24] tend*ere* cursum,
  Voce s*ub* alterna   resonet q*uo* [25] laus hodierna
  Ex re d*iu*ina   cui sunt mysteria trina:
  R*e*gu*m* dona triu*m*   baptisma † uonīs † aq*ua* ui-
    nu*m;* [26]
145 Que tria cu*m* dant*ur*   *uirtutem* in nos op*er*antur;
  Na*m* per s*anct*or*um*   tria mystica dona magorum
  P*r*imicias gentis   pietas uocat om*n*ipot*en*tis;
  N*ost*ra mala exti*n*guit   cum se baptismate ti*n*git,
  Resq*ue* p*ar*at letas   laticu*m* signa*n*do metretas.
150 Sicq*ue* dies unus   cum dat t*r*iplicabile munu*s,*
  Multiplicata salus   n*ost*ros *concurrit* i*n* usus.

      Argum*entum:*

*Ad adorandu*m* Filium Dei p*er* Stella*m* inuita*ntur*
  Eoy.
[1] Stella, Aureolus, Thureolus, Myrreolus.[1]

Stella:

  Nato ferte Dei   redolencia thura, Sabei,
  Et iunctis Arabis   exotica plebs p*r*operabis,
  Auru*m* c*um* myrra   tellus sudabis eoa.

---

[23] Professor Rand suggests the conjectural emendation Me liceat.
[24] Ms. scribende corrected to scribendi.
[25] Ms. q*ua.*
[26] My difficulty in this line may be due to a scribal error.
*** Reprinted from Denis by DuMéril.
[1-1] Omitted by DuMéril. Before the word *Stella* Denis interpolates
the word *Interlocutores.*

Aureolus:

155   Quid parat hec stella?

Thureolus:
Stupeo.

Myrreolus:
Lux ista nouella!

Aureolus:
Hec nimis ignescit.

Thureolus:
Sol cedit.

Myrreolus:
Luna facescit.

Aureolus:
O quam candescit.

Thureolus:
Frix [27] pallet.

Mirreolus:
Taurus [28] ebescit.

Aureolus:
O quam feruescit.

Thureolus:
Iouis horret.

Myrreolus:
Mars tenebrescit.

Aureolus:
Iamque magis crescit.

Thureolus:
Leo pallet.

Myrreolus:
Virgo tabescit.

[27] I. e., Phryx.
[28] Ms. Laurus.

Aureolus:

160   Hec regem regum monstrat.

               Thureolus:
                 Dominumque.

                      Myrreolus:
                        Hominemque.

    Aureolus:
      Hinc inquiratur.

               Thureolus:
                 Veneretur.

                      Myrreolus:
                        Nonne colatur?

    Aureolus:
      Aurum sumamus.

               Thureolus:
                 Seu thus.

                      Myrreolus:
                        Myrramque feramus.

    Aureolus:
      Aurum sit regi.

               Thureolus:
                 Domino thus.

                      Myrreolus:
                        Myrra hominique.

    Aureolus:
      Stellam sectemur.

               Thureolus:
                 Precedit nos.

                      Mirreolus:
                        Comitemur.*

Argumentum

Apud Herodem regem Iudeorum natum regem regum inuestigat sollicitudo magorum. Magi . . .[29]

The content of the cycle of dialogues may be indicated schematically as follows:

Procemium.

(1) Argumentum.
    Dialogus: Serpens et Eva.
(2) Argumentum.
    Dialogus: Deus Pater et Deus Filius.
(3) Argumentum.
    Dialogus: Prophetæ et Terrigenæ.
(4) Argumentum.
    Dialogus: Prophetæ, Deus Pater, et Deus
       Filius.
(5) Argumentum.
    Dialogus: Gabriel et Maria.
(6) Argumentum.
    Dialogus: Misericordia, Veritas, Justitia, et
       Pax.
(7) Argumentum.
    Dialogus: Cœligenæ et Terrigenæ.
  Epilogus.

Procemium.

(8) Argumentum.
    Dialogus: Stella, Aureolus, Thureolus, et
       Myrreolus.
(9) Argumentum. [Magi apud Herodem.]

---

[29] Thus the fragment ends at the bottom of the second column of fol. 30v. At the top of fol. 31r another hand begins a separate work under the rubric: Incipit prologus super commento Apocalipsis.

The fragment preserves, then, eight dialogues, and part of the *argumentum* preceding a ninth dialogue. The first seven dialogues by themselves seem to constitute a complete and separate play, for the series is introduced by a *prooemium* and is concluded by an *epilogus*. The second *prooemium* was probably followed by a considerable number of dialogues on subjects from the New Testament, and the complete text may well have extended to considerable length. The succession of subjects in the fragment is not precisely paralleled in any Latin or vernacular play known to me.[30]

As to the authorship of the cycle we have only the evidence of the text itself. It appears that for the sake of a certain Adlardus Pater a poet named Onulphus composed a dramatic poem upon a Christian subject in the manner of the *Canticum Canticorum Salomonis*. The identity of the author is not easy to determine. To the literary history of the middle ages are known two personages bearing the name Onulphus:

(1) Onulphus Blandiniensis was a Benedictine monk at Blandigny (Blandinium, Blandinberg,), near Ghent. He collaborated with Abbot Everhelmus († 1069) in writing the life of Saint Poppo, abbot of Stavelot (1020-1048). Thus Onulphus Blandiniensis had associations with two Belgian monasteries.[31]

(2) Onulphus Spirensis is known to us only as the author of the *Colores Rhetorici*, a fragment preserved in a twelfth-century manuscript, to which is attached the following colophon: *Finiunt rethorici colores ab Onulfo*

---

[30] As to the formation of Old Testament cycles see Hardin Craig, *The Origin of the Old Testament Plays*, in *Modern Philology*, Vol. X, pp. 473-487.

[31] See A. Potthast, *Bibliotheca Historica Medii Aevi*, Vol. II, Berlin, 1896, p. 1532; U. Chevalier, *Répertoire des Sources Historiques du Moyen Age: Bio-Bibliographie*, Vol. II, Paris, 1907, col. 3420.

Spirensi magistro beatae memoriae editi. Wattenbach assigns the writing of the *Colores Rhetorici* to the middle of the eleventh century.[32]

From the information at my disposal I should feel no certainty in identifying the Onulphus of our dramatic fragment with either of the writers mentioned above. One is tempted to identify Adlardus Pater of the dedication with Adalardus I († 1033/4) or Adalardus II († 1082), each an abbot of St. Trond, Belgium,[33] and hence to assign the fragment itself to the Belgian Onulphus Blandiniensis. On the other hand, certain literary aspects of the fragment are suggestive of the *Colores Rhetorici.* The knowledge of Horace and Terence shown by the author of the *Poema Biblicum,* and his mention of Pindar, Alcæus, and Homer, recall the classical learning displayed by Onulphus Spirensis in the *Colores Rhetorici.*

Whoever the author of the fragment may have been, the dramatic cycle before us hardly lies in the main channel of mediæval dramatic development, for it betrays no connection with either the liturgical or the vernacular cycles. Since, moreover, it bears no evidence of scenic production, it may be regarded as an isolated academic exercise of a pious rhetorician of classical attainments, and as such it brings to mind the more imposing dramatic achievement of Hrotsvitha of Gandersheim.

KARL YOUNG.

[32] Concerning Onulphus Spirensis I have no information beyond that given by W. Wattenbach, *Magister Onulf von Speier,* in *Sitzungsberichte der königlich Preussischen Akademie der Wissenschaften zu Berlin,* 1894, Part I, pp. 361-386, and by M. Manitius, *Zu Onulfs von Speier Rhetorici Colores,* in *Neues Archiv der Gesellschaft für ältere deutsche Geschichtskunde,* Vol. xx (1894), pp. 441-443. These references are used by Chevalier (*Répertoire,* Vol. II, col. 3420), who, however, assigns Onulphus to the twelfth century.

[33] Chevalier, Vol. I, col. 27.

III.—THE *ENUEG* AND *PLAZER* IN MEDIÆVAL FRENCH AND ITALIAN

About three years ago an article was published by the present writer [1] defining the essential features of the *enueg* and the *plazer* and showing the rise of this type of poetry in Provençal and its subsequent spread to Catalan, French, Italian, and Portuguese. The *enueg* was found to be a rimed composition on the subject of vexations and annoyances, while the *plazer* took pleasures as its theme. Except for this difference, the important characteristics of both are the same: (A) the enumeration of a series of vexations or pleasures, usually without continuity; (B) the repetition of a word or phrase which indicates the attitude of the poet, such as 'it vexes me' or 'it pleases me.' Since that time the investigations have been continued, especially in French and Italian.

Thanks to a suggestion of Prof. Jeanroy, my attention was turned to collections of Old French proverbs. Many of these aphorisms consist of a list of three or more incongruous subjects for which displeasure is expressed, at times merely by the statement that they are useless or will not succeed, as

> Feux sans creux, gasteau sans mische,
> Et bourse sans argent
> Ne vallent pas gramment [2]—

or

> Soleil qui luisarne au matin,
> Femme qui parle latin,

---

[1] R. T. Hill, "The Enueg," *Pub. Mod. Lang. Assoc.*, xxvii (1912), pp. 265-296.

[2] Le Roux de Lincy, *Le Livre des Proverbes Français*, Paris, 1859, I, p. 69.

> Et enfant nourri de vin,
> Ne viennent jamais à bonne fin.[3]

Others mention things to be loved, as

> Vin, or et ami vieux
> Sont en prix en tous lieux.[4]

Most of these proverbs contain only three or four lines in rime. The *ennuis* are usually quite incongruous. There are a few [5] which are somewhat longer, but these do not show any attempt at arrangement. There is an absence of any repeated word and of any personal expression of dislike.

Another quite similar type is the entreaty for deliverance from troubles. This form is distinguished by the phrase *Dieu me garde, Dieu nous garde,* or in one case *Libera nos, Domine,*[6] and the repetition of *de* at the beginning of each line. Most of these are anonymous and in general they do not differ much from the class described in the preceding paragraph. Sometimes the same line is found in several, as *De boucons de Lombards* and *D'et caetera de notaires, De qui pro quo d'apoticaires.*[7] The four-line strophe of the *Comédie des Proverbes* [8] is found in almost identical form.[9]

> De plusieurs choses Dieu nous garde:
> De toute femme qui se farde,
> D'un serviteur qui se regarde,
> Et de bœuf salé sans moutarde.

The verbal similarity, the disjointed structure, and the fact that the order of the lines varies in the different pieces

---

[3] *O. c.,* I, p. 131.

[4] *O. c.,* II, p. 221. Others are I, p. 221, II, pp. 137, 172, 191, 206, 216, 221, 278, etc.

[5] *O. c.,* II, pp. 270, 375, 471.   [8] Hill, *o. c.,* p. 294 n.

[6] *O. c.,* II, p. 284.   [9] Le Roux, *o. c.,* II, pp. 283, 284.

[7] I, p. 382, II, pp. 142, 283.

indicate that the longer forms (one has 37 vv.) are in
reality merely a series of proverbs loosely joined together.[10]   There is not any verbal resemblance between
this class and the first.

The annoyances refer to a large variety of things, one
of the most common subjects being women.   Occasionally
an entire piece is given up to the enumeration of the unpleasant qualities of the frail sex.   Such for instance is
the *Contredictz de Songecreux* by P. Gringoire, of which
a fragment is printed by Le Roux de Lincy, Vol. I,
p. lvii:

> Femme est l'ennemy de l'amy;
> Femme est péché inévitable;
> Femme est familier ennemy.
> Femme déçoyt plus que le diable, etc.

A fondness for long enumerations in metrical compositions is seen in Guillaume Alexis: *Le Contrablason de
Faulses Amours*,[11] whole strophes of which consist entirely of names of different classes of evil doers, and in a ballad [12] on the coming of Antichrist, where each line, introduced by *puisque,* states a reason for the coming.   In the
first case the *ennuis* are various classes of people, whereas
in the second they are abuses of society.   A tedious list of
faults and sins is the *Vergier d'honneur* [13] by André de la
Vigne, in which *chascun* is frequently repeated.   A simi-

---

[10] Prof. Jeanroy in a review (*Romania*, XLII, p. 318) of my former
article, points out two short pieces of this kind in a MS. at Clermont-
Ferrand, besides a long ballad by Deschamps.   He also adds to my
list in Provençal one strophe by Gaucelm Faidit and a poem by
Guillem Peire de Toulouse.   The latter had already been mentioned
by me, p. 275, where I attributed it to Guillem Peire de Casals.
According to Appel (*Revue des Lang. Rom.* XXXIX, p. 183) the
authorship is uncertain.

[11] *Soc. d. Anc. Textes*, Vol. I, p. 310.

[12] Montaiglon: *Anc. Poés. Fr.*, v, p. 319.

[13] *Ibid.*, x, p. 152.

lar use of this pronoun is seen in the *Ditz de Chascun*,[14] in which 'each one' tells his ambition and its failure. The use of *chascun* is common in proverbs, of which both of these compositions seem to be developments.

But the *enueg* is not confined to anonymous aphorisms nor to long disconnected lists, for one well-known author of the 14th century, Eustache Deschamps, has a striking fondness for enumerations of pains and pleasures. Some of these are merely lists, as in a piece attributed to Deschamps [15] where each line of three strophes begins by *on voit* which introduces some pessimism. One ballad mentions the successful men in each profession, each line beginning with *bon*,[16] while in another the poet bids farewell to all his pleasures with frequent repetition of *adieux*.[17] Deschamps was not content with a list of incongruities thrown together pell-mell, but consecrated entire poems to special subjects, such as the causes of diseases and the proper remedies. No less than six [18] of his poems deal with this subject and all are of the same general form with enumerations.

> Vivre d'eaues de terre marcageuse,
> Estre au gros air quant li brouillas est fors,
> Trop main lever, vie luxurieuse,
> Sanz mouvement soy courcier est la mors.

There is a delightfully personal note about these compositions in the way in which the poet urges the avoidance of unsanitary places, swamps, and public baths, and especially contaminated water. The use of salt meat

---

[14] *Ibid.*, x, p. 156.

[15] Deschamps, *Œuvres complètes, Soc. d. Anc. Textes*, Vol. x, p. xxviii.

[16] *O. c.*, VII, p. 71.   [17] *O. c.*, v, p. 51.

[18] *O. c.*, VI, p. 100; VII, pp. 38, 40; VIII, pp. 139, 145, 339.

is also mentioned several times as being very disagreeable, whereas the advocacy of short repasts seems not
inappropriate at the present time. One ballad,[19] with
its list of remedies, seems to be an answer to the list
of diseases in the poem directly preceding. Bread one day
old, and good wine with a little game, appear to form the
ideal diet, from which all heavy meats, strong spices, fish,
and fruit are to be excluded. He is also an advocate of
light suppers and early rising.

Several of these poems refer to the life in Bohemia, to
which country the poet was sent by the Duc d'Orléans [20]
in 1397, charged with a special mission to King Wences-
las. This visit was not entirely pleasant, if one may judge
from these poems and his ballad *Contre la Bohème* [21]
where the author does not limit his complaints to food, but
criticises the manner of serving (*Vint gens mangier en
deux plateaux*), the poor beds, the bitter beer, etc. The
alliterative line at the beginning, *Poulx, puces, puour et
pourceaulx,* which is repeated several times, shows a few
of the discomforts which he probably experienced. The
poem immediately following in the edition serves as a
pendant. The poet, thinking of his own country, describes what he considers an ideal repast.

> Bon poisson d'eaue et de mer,
> Bon vins et chars a son voloir,
> L'en doit bien le pais amer.

In most of the poems described above there is lack of any
repeated word except that in one case *de* is so used; but
the general character of lists of disagreeable or attractive
subjects renders them worthy of consideration in any study
of this kind.

---

[19] *O. c.,* VII, p. 40.   [21] *O. c.,* VII, p. 90.
[20] XI, pp. 80 ff.

A virelay [22] is the only perfect *enueg* in the voluminous works of Deschamps. The commencement of this poem

> Tout ne me plaist pas ce que j'oy,
> Tout me desplaist ce que je voy.

recalls the negative *plazer* of Guillem Peire de Casals, or de Toulouse as Prof. Jeanroy prefers to call him. Nearly every line begins with *tout* and there is a complete lack of continuity, for it is merely a series of pessimistic aphorisms varied by the occasional repetition of *tout ne me plaist pas*. So in every particular it illustrates the typical *enueg*, or *desplaisir* which would perhaps be a better name for these compositions in the Northern French.

One other group of Deschamps's poems remains to be considered. These are the six poems devoted to imprecations, in which he conjures up all sorts of evils against his enemies. In three [23] of these ballads he names various diseases which are to be sent on the victim of the curse. Nearly every line begins with *de*.

> Du mal saint Fremin d'Amiens,
> Du saint Fiacre et du saint Quentin,
> De la rage qui prent les chiens,
> Du mau saint Leu, de l'esvertin,
> Du saint Josse et saint Matelin,
> Et de tous maulx, soir et matin,
> Soit maistre Mahieu confondu.

In another [24] he sends wounds from all sorts of weapons,

> De males dagues de Bourdeaulx,
> Et d'espées de Cleremont,
> De dondaines et de cousteaulx
> D'acier qui a Milan se font, etc.

---

[22] *O. c.*, VI, p. 178.
[23] *O. c.*, IV, pp. 315, 321; VII, p. 33.
[24] *O. c.*, VII, p. 34.

or again,[25] it is a question of vermin as well as maladies. In one the first strophe is limited to curses against the different parts of the body, the second is filled with a series of vile epithets, and in the final one various forms of death are to fall upon the victim of the curse.

We have seen how fond Deschamps is of lists of *ennuis,* how he frequently devotes an entire poem to a single class of troubles, such as maladies, how at times he uses them in imprecations against his enemies or in prayers for deliverance, and how in at least one piece he conforms to the regular *noie* type. However, it is not so much in the form as in the personal nature revealed in the discomforts that he shows his relationship to the Monk of Montaudon and to Girard Pateg. This is a feature which must not be lost sight of in treating the subject, for the *genre* is essentially popular in tone and the material is largely taken from the personal experiences of the poet, or his own observations of society. For this reason these compositions serve as a guide to the habits and customs of the later Middle Ages. It has also been pointed out that the germs of the *enueg* and *plazer* are at times found in the rhymed proverbs and that the latter are occasionally expanded into long series which contain at times the same expressions as the shorter forms. However, with the exception of Deschamps, this style of writing seems to have met with little favor with the French authors of this period. Nor is this surprising if one considers the vogue of allegorical compositions due to the popularity of the *Roman de la Rose.*

It is however in Italy that this form of poetry has been most cultivated ever since its first appearance in the *noie* of Girard Pateg. This has been shown in the article

---

[25] *O. c.,* IV, p. 315.

already referred to, but no mention has yet been made of the existence of a number of maledictions of the same general type as those written by Deschamps. Perhaps the best known is Dante's sonnet *Io maledico il dì ch'io vidi in prima* [26] in which the poet curses the day he met his love, his own verses, etc. *Maledico* is repeated several times, but the subject matter is more or less homogeneous. A longer poem by Antonio da Beccari (1315-circ. 1363) or Antonio da Ferrara [27] is given up entirely to curses. Antonio heaps maledictions upon the universe and all that it contains and everything that has contributed to his own existence. He does not spare his father nor his mother nor the day of his birth. He curses the very beginning of his life, the water and the salt used at his baptism, then passing to his youth he decries his labors, his intelligence, his sufferings, in short his whole life and even death which does not come to end his pains.

> Maledetta la 'ntenza—e quel sudore
> Che per mio studio spese,
> Maledetta la 'mpresa intelligenza,
> Che fa centuplicar il mio dolore:
> Maledetto 'l paese,
> Dove io la 'mpresi ché mi tien pensando
> Più tristo assai che Ecuba furiando.
>
> . . . .
>
> Maledetti i servigi reverenti,
> Maledetto 'l servire
> Ch' io feci ad altri o con borsa o con bocca,

[26] Ed. Fraticelli, *Opere minori*, I, p. 139; son. 32. Ed. Moore, son. 33.

[27] Carducci: *Antica lirica italiana*, Firenze, 1907, p. 98. Volpi *Rime di Trecentisti Minori*, Firenze, 1907, p. 47. Cf. Volpi: *Il Trecento* in *Storia Lett. D'Italia*, pp. 165 ff. for a discussion of the author and this poem. Volpi cites a *canzone* by Fazio degli Uberti *Lasso che quando* and the third chapter of the Book of Job as works of a similar style, but I fail to find sufficient resemblance in either to class them among the productions of this *genre*.

> Maledetto 'l tacere e'l sofferire
> De' miei dolor cocenti,
> Maledetta la morte che no scocca
> L'ultimo stral di sua possente rocca.[28]

The repetition and the lack of continuity as well as the general tone make this a masterpiece of *disperate*. Volpi calls it the oldest example of this type.

Besides these two entire poems there are several groups of verses beginning with *maledetto*, such as the *Crudeltà* [29] of Verini (16th century) where the subject is love and the lines *Io maledico l'ora e'l punto e'l dì,* etc.,[30] resemble Dante's sonnet mentioned above. Cino da Pistoia in his sonnet *Io maledico il dì, ch'io veddi primo* [31] treats the same theme in a similar manner. The sonnet by Guittone d'Arezzo, *Deo, che mal aggia mia fede, mi' amore* [32] belongs also to this class, although the introductory word is not the same.

Older than any of the examples mentioned is the Latin poem by Arrigo da Settimello called *De Diversitate Fortunae et Philosophiae Consolatione* [33] written about 1200. Two of the four *libri* treat the misfortunes which the author has experienced through the loss of his property. Lists of troubles are numerous and there is considerable repetition at the beginning of lines.

> Nunc nimis est altum, nimium nunc decidit, unquam
>   Pulvinar medium nescit habere modum.
> Nunc caput inclino, nunc elevo, parte sinistra
>   Nunc ruo, nunc dextra, nunc cado, nuncque levor;

---

[28] Volpi: *Rime di trecentisti*, pp. 48 f.

[29] D'Ancona, *Poesia Pop. It.*, 2nd ed., Livorno, 1906, p. 464.

[30] Carducci: *Cantilene e Ballate*, p. 268. D'Ancona: *o. c.*, p. 510.

[31] Ed. Fiodo, Lanciano, 1913, p. 142.

[32] Guittone d'Arezzo, *Rime* ed. Pellegrini, Bologna, 1901; Vol. I, No. LIV, p. 82.

[33] Pub. by Manni, Firenze, 1730. There is an Italian translation called *Arrighetto*, with introduction by Tiraboschi, pub. at Prato, 1841.

Nunc hac, nunc illac, nunc sursum, nunc rotor infra,
Et modo volvo caput qua mihi parte pedes.[34]

Vade per Hispanos, et nigros vade per Indos,
Vade per insidias, vade per omne nemus;
Vade per hostiles cuneos, turmasque latronum,
Dummodo sis verus, tutus egenus eris.[35]

In one instance, after reciting the many woes that afflict him the poet breaks out into maledictions which are strikingly similar to those found in the Italian.

Sit maledicta dies, in qua concepit, et in qua
Me mater peperit, sit maledicta dies.
Sit maledicta dies, qua suxi pectus, et in qua
In cunis vagii, sit maledicta dies.
Sit maledicta dies. Vita de ventre sepulcro
Me transmutasset. o Deus, illa dies.[36]

This is important not only because of its similarity to some of the Italian maledictions in both form and subject, but also because it antedates the forms in Romance literatures. There is no reason however to believe that the Italian verses of this type are due to the influence of Arrigo; [37] they seem rather to reflect a tendency of the age which manifests itself in different authors who wrote independently of one another, drawing on their personal experiences for the material, while using a form which may have been imitated.

All these poems possess the essential qualities of the

[34] O. c., p. 10.

[35] O. c., p. 28. For other cases of repetition and lists of ennuis cf. pp. 11, 18, 29.

[36] O. c., pp. 12, 13. One should note the lists of curses with repetition of maledictus in Deut. 27, 15-26; 28, 16-19, and the series of lamentations introduced by vae Isaiah, 5, 18-22, Mat. 23, 13-16, Luke 6, 24-26. For corresponding lists of blessings, cf. the Beatitudes, Mat. 5, 3-11, Luke 6, 20-22.

[37] This poem has been mentioned by Volpi: Il Trecento, p. 268, who also points out the similarity of the curses of Job in Chap. III.

enueg, of which they form a special subdivision. It is not then surprising to find a corresponding group which attaches itself to the *plazer*. These poems repeat *benedico* or *benedetto* in the same way as the others employed *maledico,* etc. Such is Petrarch's sonnet *Benedetto sia 'l giorno e 'l mese e l'anno,* in which the poet praises the time and place where he first met his love, the arrows that made the wound. In a sonnet by Antonio da Ferrara (*Io benedico il dì che dio ti cinse*)[38] there is frequent repetition of *benedetti*. The poet addresses his love who has just died and blesses her eternal happiness, while praying that he may join her. It is quite natural that Antonio should write both kinds of these poems, for he is merely following the example of his illustrious prototype, the Monk of Montaudon who added a *plazer* to his three *enueg*. This habit of writing benedictions as well as maledictions is seen also in Verini's *Ardore,*[39] where several verses begin with *sia benedette*. This appears to be a form of popular poetry, if one may judge from the lines

> Benedetto quel Dio che t'ha creato,
> E quella madre che t'ha partorito.
> E il padre tuo che t'ha ingenerato;
> Benedetto il compar che t'ha assistito!
> Il sacerdote che t'ha battezzato,
> E alla luce di Dio t'ha istituito!
> Benedette parole, e quella mano,
> E poi quell' acqua che ti fe cristiano! [40]

Three versions, two in Sicilian and one in Venetian, show that it was widespread. From Venice too comes a short group of verses [41] where the eyes are the subject of the

---

[38] Carducci, *Antica lir. it., ed. cit.,* col. 333.

[39] D'Ancona, *o. c.,* pp. 462, 510.

[40] D'Ancona, *o. c.,* pp. 238 f. and 553 f. Tigri, *Canti pop. toscani,* Firenze, 1860, p. 69.

[41] D'Ancona, *o. c.,* p. 299.

blessing. Another popular refrain which is found appended to several songs is

> Sia benedetto e benedetta sia
> La casa del mio Amore e po' la mia.[42]

Somewhat more elaborate is the one beginning, *io benedico la mano al maestro*,[43] in which blessing is asked for the hand of the builder who made the house where the lady lives and for the hand that carved the window through which he first saw her. Sometimes the prayer is put in the mouth of the girl who addresses a youth setting out to war, and asks blessings for the mother that bore him and the father that trained him in arms;[44] in another case it is dedicated to the Creator, who made the land and sea and guides the ships that sail.[45] In the last example the repetition consists merely of *fece,* which is the first word in several lines.

Besides the anonymous popular refrains, several stanzas of a similar type are found in the works of well known writers, as the third strophe of Boiardo's *Ancor dentro dal cor vago mi sona*,[46] in which *beato* is repeated several times. The poet is addressing his lady and asks blessings for her heart, her eyes and ' the loving key that opens and unlocks the gentle soul.' The same form is applied to a similar theme by Panfilo Sasso (circ. 1455-1527) of Modena, author of sonnets and *strambotti,* in the sonnet, *Sia benedetta la notte che'l giorno.*[47] The subject is the pangs of love, ' the sweet and bitter poison,' ' the quiver and the arrow,' etc. Lorenzo Moschi used the same form in the sonnet

---

[42] Tigri, pp. 114, 122. D'Ancona, pp. 463, 510.
[43] Cf. Tigri, p. 121, where three forms of this ballad are quoted.
[44] Tigri, p. 126.   [46] Carducci, *o. c.,* p. 214.
[45] *Ibid.,* p. 130.   [47] Carducci, *o. c.,* p. 434.

Benedetta sia l'ora e la stagione
E l'anno e'l mese e'l dì ch'i' fu' legato,
Da si dolze catena incatenato
I' fui da 'more in eterna prigione.
Benedetta la pena e l'affrizione
Che nel cor porto e quant' i' ho sospirato,
E tutte quelle cose che m'ha dato
A farmi innamorar vera cagione, etc.[48]

Benedetta continues throughout the rest of the poem, wheras in a sonnet by Andrea Baiardi [49] it is found only in the latter part; the poet blesses not only the house of his lady, but the town and the entire region where she lives.

It has been shown that enumerations marked by the repetition of *benedetto* or a similar word occur in sonnets and in popular refrains, but that this is not confined to short poems is shown by the *canzone* of Franco Sacchetti, whose title to fame is due to his large number of lyrics as well as his *Novelle*. In *Sia benedetto in cielo e in terra l'ora* [50] a regular and sustained repetition of *benedetto* occurs throughout the five strophes and the *envoi*. The theme is the usual type of the ballads, but instead of the simple language of the popular song, Sacchetti has introduced numerous mythological references and used a highly artificial style. The 'happy day' has given place

---

[48] Volpi, *o. c.*, pp. 233 f. Cf. the recent article by Oliver M. Johnston, *Pub. Mod. Lang. Assoc.*, XXIX, p. 542 n. where this sonnet is mentioned. Several pages are devoted to the *enueg* and the *noie*, but no new material of importance is added. There is a slight error, p. 537, n. 1, where the initial phrase of the poem by Christine de Pisan should be *seulete suy*, not *je congnois*. The latter phrase is repeated in a poem by Villon (Bartsch-Wiese, *Chrest. de l'anc. fr.* no. 93, d., François Villon, *Œuvres, les Classiques Fr. du Moyen-Age*, pp. 80, 81.) For other cases of repetition in Villon cf. the latter edition pp. 58, 79, 80, 81, 82.

[49] Carducci, *o. c.*, p. 464.

[50] Carducci, *o. c.*, p. 155.

to ' the coming of the rays of Phaethon,' ' the *notricante latte*' has supplanted the ' mother,' while the beauty of the suitor is such that neither Narcissus nor Absalom could rival it, and the lady far surpasses Leda's daughter. The elements of the popular form are still discernible in blessing the time and place of the first meeting of the lovers, the land where she lives, etc.

It has thus been seen that: (A) Verses with a repetition of *benedetto, maledetto* or similar words were frequent in popular poetry in Italy; (B) Occasionally well-known poets have used these forms either in parts of poems or in entire compositions, often confining themselves to a similar theme and always adhering to the same form. Now let us see if verses of this type conform to the general definition of *enueg* and *plazer*. It has been shown [51] that the *enueg* is distinguished (A) by enumerations in epigrammatic style of a series of vexations and (B) by the repetition of a word or phrase which indicates the attitude of the poet. The *plazer* is of the same type except that *pleasures* take the place of *vexations*. From the preceding description it is evident that the curses or maledictions, with their lists of objectionable persons or things and marked by frequent use of the ' curse,' clearly belong to the *enueg,* whereas the *benedetti* are but a special form of the *plazer*. It may be rather surprising that in the examples which have been cited the latter should outnumber the former in Italian, when one recalls the preponderance of the *enueg*. This may be due entirely to chance, but it should not be forgotten that the regular *plazers* were apparently more popular in Italian than in the other Romance Languages, as the complete ring by Chiaro Davanzati [52] would seem to indicate.

[51] *Publ. Mod. Lang. Assoc.,* XXVII, p. 266.
[52] Cf. Hill, *o. c.,* pp. 284-285.

Besides the special class of *noie* there are several poems which enumerate a series of disagreeable things. One of these is the sonnet *Lingua ria, pensier fello, e oprar maligno*,[53] by Annibal Caro (1507-1566). It consists in part of contrasts, as *lodar aperto chiuso mal dir, gran vanti e picciol merto*, etc. All the evil qualities are supposed to belong to the person to whom the poem is addressed. There is a total absence of repeated words.

Francesco da Barberino in his *Documenti d'Amore* [54] refers at times to things that displease him. These are introduced by *noia, dispiacemi, dispiacevol, folle*, etc.,[55] but these words are not repeated and the passages where they are found form but short parts of long poems. Hence there is no real reason to consider these as *noie*, for they serve only to indicate that sometimes Barberino has this

---

[53] *Parnaso Italiano*, Venezia, 1787, Vol. XXVII, p. 188.

[54] *I Documenti d'Amore di* Francesco da Barberino, ed. F. Egidi, Roma, 1902, I, pp. 127, 225, 264, 266, 304.

[55] The use of different words or phrases to indicate the attitude of the poet is seen to better advantage in a *plazer* by Guittone d'Arezzo, *Tanto sovente dett' aggio altra fiata* (ed. Valeriani, Vol. I, No. x, p. 56). Five of the six strophes have each a special repeated word which is not found in the others, while nearly all of them are included in the final strophe. Thus the first uses *aggrada*, the second *bello m'è*, the third *piace*, the fourth *diletto* and the fifth *sa mi bel*. These phrases are repeated at irregular intervals and serve to introduce different classes of people whom the poet desires to praise. In subject matter as well as in form each strophe possesses unity; the first deals with peace, the second humility, and the others have as their subjects honesty, women, and ecclesiastics. The poem ends with an outburst of religious fervor in the later manner of Guittone. This careful arrangement in subject matter recalls the *noie* of Pucci, whereas the use of a special repeated word for each strophe suggests a possible prototype for Bindo Bonichi's *canzone, Guai a chi*, etc. (Cf. *Pub. Mod. Lang. Assoc.*, XXVIII, p. 286-7). When my first article on the *enueg* was written, I had not been able to examine this poem of Guittone and so was unable to put this note where it might have been more appropriate.

tendency. One of the best instances is [56] the part which treats of different kinds of ingratitude, where *ingrato* is used four times, each time to introduce a special variety of that sin. Another passage [57] refers particularly to table etiquette and reminds one a little of a part of Pucci's *noie*.[58]

> Folle chi prima leva
> da se il taglier, ancor gli altri mangiando;
> e chi non netto stando
> fa de la mensa panier di rilievo
> e colui etc.

Another group of precepts on the same subject is found in an anonymous didactic poem of the thirteenth century, published by Bartsch.[59] In this case however there is a complete lack of repetition, and the do's and don't's are intermingled.

Another special type of enumerations of annoyances is the list of beasts hostile to mankind in a sonnet by Annibal Caro.[60] After a long series of serpents, chimæras and wild animals, fearing lest something may have been omitted the author concludes ' *e quanto aborre e quanto ha 'l mondo a schivo.*' There are also lists of pleasant things, a sort of lyric Utopia, in the sonnet attributed to Lapo Gianni, *Amor, eo chero mia donna in domino.*[61] Guido

[56] *O. c.*, I, i, p. 225.

[57] *O. c.*, I, i, p. 127.

[58] Pub. by Ildefonso di San Luigi in Vol. VI of the *Delizie degli eruditi toscani*, pp. 275-285; reprinted without change in *Raccolta di rime antiche toscane*, Palermo, 1817, Vol. III, 311-320 and by F. Ferri, *La poesia pop. in Antonio Pucci*, Bologna, 1909, pp. 235-242. Pub. from the Oxford Ms. by Prof. K. McKenzie, *Kittredge Anniversary Papers*, Boston, 1913, pp. 175-183. Prof. McKenzie has also published the version found in the *Codice Kirkupiano, Studii publ. in onore di F. Torraca*, Napoli, 1912.

[59] *Rivista d. Fil. Rom.*, II, pp. 45-48.

[60] *Parnaso It.*, Venezia, 1787, Vol. XXVII, p. 190.

[61] E. Rivalta: *Liriche del " Dolce Stil Nuovo,"* p. 133.

Cavalcanti in the beautiful sonnet *Beltà di donna e di piagente core* [62] enumerates many attractions such as 'the songs of birds,' 'the quiet of the dawn,' 'the calm of the falling snow,' all of which are less beautiful than his lady. In a sonnet by Francesco Ismera,[63] a contemporary of Lapo Gianni, it is a question of the pleasures afforded by hunting and music. The '*canti d' augelli*' and '*veder fioccar la neve senza venti*' suggest Cavalcanti's sonnet. None of the enumerated poems belong to the *noie*, but they are interesting in so far as they illustrate a class of compositions of which the *noie* are but a special form.

Besides the *benedetti*, another type of the *plazer* is marked by the frequent use of *vorrei*, as the few lines quoted by D'Ancona [64] from the *Nova Fenice* of Olimpo, where the poet in his despair wishes 'every lamb to be changed into a lion,' 'every light to become obscured,' and 'summer to be turned into winter.' Other instances of *vorrei*, etc., in popular verse are two stanzas [65] where the poet expresses his desire to fly over the mill in which love is to grind him. Both of these are combined with the *benedetto* refrain already discussed. In another *vorrei* [66] the wish is that the window might be opened and the lady appear there.

[62] P. Ercole, *G. Cavalcanti e le sue rime*, Livorno, 1885, pp. 269 f.

[63] G. Navone, *Le Rime di Folgore da San Gimignano e di Cene da la Chitarra*, Bologna, 1880; p. cxv.

[64] *Poesia Pop.*, p. 467; cf. pp. 186, 187.

[65] Tigri, *o. c.*, pp. 114, 122.

[66] Tigri, *o. c.*, p. 338. Prof. Zenatti in a short study of the *Noie* of Patecchio or Pateg (*Atti d. R. Accad. lucchese*, xxix) calls attention, pp. 9 ff., to certain forms which resemble the *noie*, mentioning Bonichi's sonnet already discussed by me, the poem by Lapo Gianni and the *vorrei*. Most of the latter, especially the famous one by Dante, *Guido, i' vorrei que tu e Lapo ed io*, do not, I think, belong to the *noie* type, since they usually lack all its essential characteris-

This feature of enumerations of pleasures is extensively developed in the poems of Folgore da San Gimignano.[67] It is seen to best advantage in the ring of sonnets on the twelve months and in another group on the different days of the week. The former treat of the pleasures more or less appropriate to each month, but it is not the ordinary forms of enjoyment that interest the poet, but rather the extravagant forms of ámusement, in which the gilded youth of the time indulged. These sonnets are addressed to a *brigata nobile e cortese* which was probably one of the *brigate spendereccie* [68] formed at Siena in the second half of the thirteenth century, and to which Dante alludes in *Inf., xxix, 130.* In the case of several months the pleasures are more or less confined to a single type; the sonnet for February emphasizes hunting, that for March fishing, May tournaments, July banquets, August riding in the mountains, etc.

> Di Marzo si vi do una pischiera
> D'anguille, trote, lamprede e salmoni,
> Di dentali, delfini e storioni,
> D'ogni altro pesce in tutta la rivera;
> Con pescatori e navicelle a schiera
> E barche saettíe e galeoni,
> Le qual ve porteno tutte stasoni
> A qual porto vi piace a la primera, etc.[69]

There is not the same appropriateness in subject matter in the sonnets for the different days of the week, most of them being concerned with hunting. Even the enumeration in those for *lunidie* and *giovedi* is not well carried out. This characteristic is not confined to these

tics. Zenatti's suggestions and explanations regarding the poems ascribed to Patecchio deserve consideration.

[67] G. Navone, *o. c.*   [69] *O. c.,* p. 9.
[68] *O. c.,* pp. LXXIX f.

two *corone,* but may be seen equally well in sonnets XXIII and XXVII.[70]

Of equal if not of greater importance in connection with the *noie* is a group of sonnets by Cene de la Chitarra d'Arezzo, in which he presents the discomforts peculiar to the different months. These poems appear to be replies or parodies to the *corona* of Folgore, as Navone has pointed out.[71] However, it is the general idea of extravagant pleasures for each month that is parodied rather than the details of the individual sonnets.

> Di marzo vi riposo en tal manera
> en pugla piana tra molti lagoni,
> en esse gran mignatte e ranagloni,
> poi da mangiar abiate sorbe e pera,
> oleo di noce veglo mane e sera
> per far calde gli arance e gran cidroni,
> barchette assai con remi e con timoni,
> ma non possiate uscir de tal rivera, etc.[72]

> Di decembre vi pongo en un pantano
> con fango, ghiaccio et ancor panni pochi,
> per vostro cibo fermo fave e mochi,
> per oste abiate un troio maremmano;
> un cuocho brutto secho tristo e vano
> ve dia colli guascotti e quigli pochi,
> e qual tra voi a lumi dadi o rochi
> tenuto sia come tra savii un vano; [73]

There is a realistic appropriateness shown in the choice of the *ennuis* which indicates a careful observation of

---

[70] D'Ancona (*Archivio per la tradiz. pop.,* II, p. 257) mentions the sonnets by Folgore and calls attention to the fact that they do not refer to ordinary pastimes appropriate to the different months, but indicate the distractions of a select society fond of lavishness and artificiality. For popular poems on the pleasures of the months, cf. Gianini: *Canti pop. della Montagna Lucchese,* pp. 233-239. The idea is the same but the treatment is more popular.

[71] *O. c.,* p. lxxxv.   [72] *O. c.,* p. 65.   [73] *O. c.,* p. 83.

.social conditions of the time. In this way they recall Antonio Pucci, who did not confine his lists of discomforts to his *noie,* but refers in one instance to the same *brigate* mentioned in the sonnets of Folgore.

> E poi il dì di calen di gennaio
> vanno in camicia con allegra fronte
> curando poco scirocco o rovaio
> E dove avean gli tordi e la pernice
> la vitella e i capponi lessi e arrosto
> hanno per cambio il porro e la radice.[74]

Although Cene mentions many vexations, still the word *noia* is nowhere found. However, popular poems with the phrase existed, as is shown by the refrain *a noia gli verran*[75] which is used three times to introduce a new annoyance.[76]

In many of the compositions of the *genre* one of the subjects most frequently treated is woman. This is seen particularly well in a sonnet assigned by D'Ancona[77] to Buto Giovanni. Nearly every verse begins with *femina* introducing a series of bitter sarcasms against women.

> Femina è d'ogni mal convento
> Femina è dell' uom vergogna e danno,
> Femina mal pensa tutto l'anno,
> Femina d'ogni ben è struggimento.

Another important instance of this sort of repetition is one canto of *Il Manganello,* a curious poem written probably in the fifteenth century.[78] This work is divided into

---

[74] A. Pucci, *La proprietà di Mercato Vecchio.* F. Ferri, *o. c.,* pp. 234-5.

[75] Tigri, *o. c.,* p. 157.

[76] In many of the poems of Guittone d'Arezzo the word *noia* occurs often riming with *gioia.*

[77] *Saggi di Lett. Pop.,* p. 381. The same sonnet with slight changes is printed among the poems of Burchiello, Londra, 1751, p. 199.

[78] There are three editions, two of which bear no date but appear

13 *capitoli,* throughout which the unknown author devotes
himself to a most virulent satire on women. There is
little connection between the chapters except that all deal
with the evil conduct of women, many examples being
cited from mythology, antiquity, and the Middle Ages.
At the beginning of the poem the author adduces the
authority of Juvenal and Boccaccio, but except for choice
of subject he does not appear to have been influenced by
these writers. There are only two chapters which bear a
direct resemblance to the *noie.* In the first (*cap.* 11)
each *terzina* begins with *la femina è,* just as in the sonnet
ascribed to Buto Giovanni. There is a complete lack of
continuity:

> La femina è cagion d'ogni heresia,
>   Incendio, guerra, sangue e dura morte,
>   Stupro, adulterio, furto e robbaria,
> La femina è del diavolo consorte,
>   Apparecchiata sempre nel mal fare,
>   Con la malitia e con l'animo forte.

Of course this is not a perfect *enueg,* but it acts as a fitting
introduction to the following *capitolo* (No. 12), of which
each *terzina* is introduced by *anoia a me* and is an independent unit, the only connection being the general theme
of the entire poem. It begins as follows:

> Anoia a me la femina, Signori,
>   A dirvi'l ver come si dice al prete,

to have been printed in the sixteenth century. The third is a reprint
issued by a society cf bibliophiles at Paris, 1860, and limited to 100
copies. It is the last that I have consulted. D'Ancona (*La Poesia
Pop.*, p. 16, n.) mentions this poem as belonging to the fifteenth
century. There exists also a *Riprehensione contro Il Manganello* by
Antonio Cornazzano, who died about 1500. Cf. Melzi, *Dizionario di
Anon. e Pseud.*, II, p. 154; Affò, *Mem. degli Scrittori e Lett. parmi-
giana*, III, pp. 29-57 and Cristoforo Poggiali: *Mem. per la Storia lett.
di Piacenza*, Piacenza, 1789, pp. 64-130. Because of the literary interest and the rarity of *Il Manganello*, it is my intention to publish an
edition of the entire poem in the near future.

Perch'ella è piena di tutti i dolori.
Anoia a me perch'ella pute e fete
 Più che non fa lo stronzo d'una gatta;
 E voi che le toccate, il sentirete.
 . . . .
Anoia a me la femina barbuta;
 Ma quando tu la senti a te venire,
 Da lunghi con tre sassi la saluta.
Anoia a me verderla imbizzarire
 Con le vicine per una gallina
 C'ha fatto l'ovo, e non glie'l voglion dire.

This twelfth *capitolo,* consisting of 33 *terzine,* both on account of its length and subject matter constitutes an important example of the *noie.* At first sight it seems to resemble Pucci's poem, but careful comparison shows that it differs markedly from that well-known composition both in the choice of subject and the disconnected manner of treatment. Not only does *Il Manganello* offer a perfect case of the *noie,* but in *cap.* 11 it presents some of the characteristics, such as repetition and lack of continuity, whereas in other passages it contains lists of *ennuis* (*cap.* 13) referring to the same general subject. This shows that often the *enueg* is not so much an independent *genre,* but that rather it is a special form of the satire.

The aim of this article has been to supplement the work already done on this subject by bringing up other examples in French and Italian and showing how some of the individual characteristics of the *genre* appear in rhymed proverbs, popular ballads, and enumerative poems. In this way certain well defined classes can be made, such as the *benedetti* and the *maledetti,* both of which are comparatively common in both popular and artistic poetry. While few perfect specimens of the *noie* or the *plazer* are added to those already studied, still the various manifestations of the tendencies are of importance in order to gain a comprehensive view of the whole matter.

RAYMOND THOMPSON HILL.

IV.—THE "CHARACTER" IN RESTORATION COMEDY

Every reader of the Restoration comedy of manners cannot fail to be impressed with the frequent occurrence of the character-sketch. Often this is of a typical personage having no part in the action, as when in Wycherley's *Plain Dealer,* Novel and Olivia together in dialogue form describe Lady Autumn, her daughter, and a fop, none of whom appears in the play. Again, one notices a marked use of the dramatic convention of making one actor describe another who is about to enter. A typical instance occurs in the scene just mentioned [1] when Novel describes in the form of a " character," Lord Plausible, and is interrupted by that gentleman's entrance.

These " characters," which we find so often in Restoration comedies, though new in the English drama, appealed to a taste sedulously cultivated in English literature for more than a generation.

The English character-sketch, or " character " as it came universally to be called in the seventeenth century, was a short account usually in prose, of the properties, qualities, or peculiarities that serve to individualize a type. Sir Thomas Overbury, himself one of the best-known of the " character " writers, defined it thus: " To square out a character by our English level, it is a picture (real or personal) quaintly drawn in various colors, all of them heightened by one shadowing. It is a quick and soft touch of many strings, all shutting up in one musical close; it is wit's descant on any plain song."

The immediate source of the English " character " was

---

[1] Act II, sc. I.

64

Theophrastus's *Ethical Characters,* translated into Latin by Casaubon, and published in 1592.   The influence of Theophrastus upon all the " character " writers of the early part of the seventeenth century, upon the men who set the fashion for those who were to follow, is clearly apparent.[2]   To the strength of this influence is due, no doubt, the fact that in a general way the " character " remained even to the time of the Restoration, in a remarkable degree unchanged.   Yet, in spite of its general adherence to a tradition, the " character " did slowly, with the progress of the century, acquire greater freedom of form, thereby approaching constantly nearer to that later stage of its development in the hands of Addison and Steele, when, through the periodical essay, it merged into the novel and became a part of it.

Among the changes that accompanied the growing emancipation of the " character " from the Theophrastian tradition, one notices that, while it always remained properly speaking a description of a type, rather than of an individual, it, nevertheless, showed an incorrigible tendency to lose its generic quality and to become biographical.   This tendency is exemplified as early as 1642 in Thomas Fuller's *Holy and Profane States.*   Of the seventy-nine " characters " that this book contains, only four are genuine types of ethical character, and some are biographical. The " Character of a Good King," for example, is a disguised, but by no means unidealized portrait of Charles I. Moreover, the portrait is frequently used to exemplify the " character."   Twenty-seven of them are followed by short

---

[1] Some account of the influence of Theophrastus upon the early writers of " characters," and of the development of " character " writing in England, may be found in my articles in *The Publications of the Modern Language Association of America,* vol. XVIII, July, 1903, and vol. XIX, March, 1904.

5

biographies of noted men and women who embodied, or were thought by Fuller to embody, the quality typified by the "character." In the latter part of the century, when the "character" had become completely nationalized, the biographical portraits multiplied. They became a favorite form of campaign "literature," the various leaders of the Whig and Tory parties being lampooned alternately. Moreover the poetical satires of the period teemed with them. Such, to mention the most notable example, was Dryden's portrait of the Duke of Buckingham in "Zimri," which Dryden, not unreasonably, considered the best part of *Absalom and Achitophel*.[3]

From the beginning, English dramatists had recognized the kinship between the character-sketch (character in repose) and the drama (character in action). To Ben Jonson has been attributed the first step toward a popularization of the "character."[4] More than once Jonson proves his familiarity with Theophrastus by adapting to dramatic uses certain passages from the Greek author. In *Volpone*,[5] for example, Jonson repeatedly paraphrases Theophrastus.[6] It is not mainly by direct adaptations, however, that Jonson shows most clearly the influence of Theophrastus. He was much too original a worker to content himself with mere borrowing. Hence we find him amusing himself by writing "characters" of his own, quite in the Theophrastian manner. To the list of *dramatis personœ* of two of his plays, *Everyman Out of His Humour* and *The New Inn,* he affixed short "characters of the persons," which, because each of "the persons" is

---

[3] Ll. 544-568.

[4] Professor Schelling in *English Literature in the Lifetime of Shakespeare*, p. 332.

[5] Act IV, sc. I and Act III, sc. I.

[6] Some account of Jonson's indebtedness is furnished by my article in *Modern Language Notes* for Nov. 1901, vol. XVI, pp. 385 ff.

the embodiment of some " humour," are, except for their brevity, exactly like the " ethical characters " of Theophrastus.   There is indeed considerable plausibility in the suggestion [7] that Jonson's whole notion of character portrayed by a ruling trait or " humour " may have come from the Greek character-sketch.   Such a hint is rendered more probable by the facts concerning the origin of Morose in *The Silent Woman.*   The play is simply a dramatic expansion of a rhetorical declamation, written in the form of a dramatic character-sketch, by Libanius, the Greek sophist of Antioch.[8]   This material Jonson utilized exactly as Goldsmith in the character of Croaker in *The Good-Natured Man* later utilized Doctor Johnson's " character " of " Suspirius, the human Screech-owl." [9]   The Δύσκολος of Libanius, like Doctor Johnson's Suspirius, is a " humourist," and as such appealed to the analytical and expository nature of Jonson's mind—a mind more interested in the type than in the individual, and more in the exhibition than in the development of character. Whether or not we accept the suggestion that Jonson may have owed his theory of " humours " to the Greek character-sketch, we may at least assert without fear of contradiction that he was the first to recognize the kinship, afterward more generally acknowledged,[10] between the " char-

[7] Professor Schelling in *English Literature in the Lifetime of Shakespeare,* p. 332.

[8] The title is " A Morose Man who has Married a Talkative Wife denounces Himself."   Vol. IV, Reiske's edition of the Works of Libanius.

[9] Contained in *The Rambler* for Oct. 9th, 1750.

[10] La Bruyère, in his " Discours sur Théophraste," the first chapter of his *Caractères,* was the first formally in writing to recognize this kinship.   " Les savants, faisant attention à la diversité des mœurs qui y sont traitées et à la manière naïve dont tous les caractères y sont exprimés, et la comparant d'ailleurs evec celle du poëte Ménandre, disciple de Théophraste, et qui servit ensuite de modèle à Té-

acter " and the drama. The former portrays character
in its statical relations. The latter, by means of the
counterplay of action upon action, makes the characters
reveal themselves. The one shows character fixed, sta-
tuesque, separate from all that could lend it human interest. The other shows character in vital relations.

Now Ben Jonson, it will be remembered, exerted a
powerful influence upon the Restoration comedy of manners. It was his satirically heightened pictures of contemporary life, composed with classical restraint and polish,
that reappeared after the Restoration in the work of such
men as John Wilson,[11] and in no small degree affected,
also, the dramatic methods of Davenant, Dryden, Etherege, and Vanbrugh.

Though Jonson's influence unquestionably encouraged
an interest in character portrayal, and though by 1660 the
writing of " characters " had become a prevalent literary
fashion, the dramatic character-sketch of Restoration comedy cannot be explained thereby. The " character," as
we find it in Restoration plays, differs in a marked degree
from the " character " as it had been written hitherto
in England, resembling much more, in the extent of its
departure from the Theophrastian tradition, the French
portrait as written by La Bruyère, and afterwards imitated
by Addison.[12]

rence, qu' on a dans nos jours si heureusement imité, ne peuvent
s'empêcher de reconnaître dans ce petit ouvrage la première source
de tout le comique; je dis de celui qui est épuré des pointes, des ob-
scénités, des équivoques, qui est pris dans la nature, qui fait rire
les sages et les vertueux " (p. 5, edition of 1750).

[11] Wilson's first play, *The Cheats*, written 1662, enjoyed a remarkable popularity. Scarcely less popular was *The Projectors*, 1664.
Both these plays followed the Jonsonian tradition, and revived the
comedy of humours.

[12] Upon the influence of La Bruyère on Addison, see my article in
the *Publications of the Modern Language Association*, vol. XIX, Dec.
1904.

Though the development of an interest in character-writing had been almost exactly contemporary in France and England, it had in the former country taken a slightly different direction. Hall's *Characters of Virtues and Vices* had been translated into French in 1619, and had been followed by many imitations. Among the most famous of these was Le Moine's *Peintures Morales* (1643), and, more famous still, La Bruyère's *Les Caractères ou Les Mœurs de ce Siècle* (1688). Yet the French "character" was, even in the work of those who aimed to follow the fashion set by Hall, somewhat different from the English, being more akin to the biographical portrait as written in England by Clarendon, the historian. Indeed the French often called the "character" a *portrait*. It consists in a description of the physiognomy, complexion, figure, appearance, and mannerisms of an individual, designated under a classical pesudonym.

The art of portraiture was cultivated in the *salons* that flourished during the first half of the seventeenth century in France. Of these *salons,* the most famous was the Hôtel de Rambouillet. From 1620 to 1650, this was the rendezvous of the wits of both sexes. Among those who gathered about the Marquise de Rambouillet, and who, like her, had revolted from the rudeness of the court of Louis XIII, were such men as Balzac, the letter writer, Voiture, the poet, Ménage, the scholar. There were also women of refined taste, such as Madame de Longueville, who is said to have inspired the *Maximes* of La Rochefoucauld, Madame de Sablé, and, later, Mademoiselle de Scudéry, Madame de Lafayette, and Madame de Sévigné. The chief aim of this brilliant coterie was to purify the language by the avoidance alike of pedantry and of vulgarity, and so to improve it by a process of refining and polishing as to render it a better instrument of social intercourse. They appear themselves to have reduced conversation to something of a fine art.[13]   One of their favorite exercises of wit was the composition, in both oral and written form, of *portraits*.   One of the most characteristic figures among the frequenters of the Hôtel de Rambouillet was the Abbé d'Aubignac (François Hédelin, 1604-1676), author of *Les Portraits égarés* (1660), a book that clearly shows to what length the fashion of writing these personal character-sketches was carried.   The book contains five *portraits,* and is dedicated to a certain Laodamie, whose *portrait* the author gives to the length of thirty-seven pages.   This he claims to have painted in a dream, but at the lady's own request, Cupid standing by and furnishing the materials.

In such a school, and among such associates was trained Mademoiselle de Scudéry, the most distinguished authoress of the *romans de longue haleine*,[14] the heroic-gallant romance invented by Gomberville (1600-1674) and perfected by La Calprenède (1610-1663).   Their most prominent characteristic is that of describing contemporary society under the thin disguise of ancient history.   Thus in the *Cyrus* Mademoiselle de Scudéry borrows her plot from the *Cyropædia* of Xenophon (with suggestions from Herodotus) but the personages are her friends and contemporaries.[15]

---

[13] See Brander Matthews, *Molière,* pp. 70 ff.

[14] The *Cyrus* contained 12,946 pages, not including prefaces, dedications, and appeared (1649-1653) in ten volumes.   Besides the thirty-two volumes containing her four romances, she published (1665) *Les Femmes illustres,* and (1680-1692) ten volumes of *Conversations.*

[15] These have been identified by V. Cousin, with the help of a key discovered in the Library of the Arsenal at Paris.   A similar " key," though somewhat less complete, has been found for the *Clélie.* See *La Societé Française au XVII Siècle,* 2 vols., Paris, 1886.

The origin of Mademoiselle de Scudéry's interest in character-drawing seems to have been in a sense accidental. In her *Mémoires*,[16] she tells us:

> Dès que je sus la cour à Paris (automne de 1657) j'y envoyai un gentilhomme pour lui faire mes excuses de ne m'y être pas rendue aussitôt, mais que mes affaires m'obligeoient de demeurer encore à Champigny, Madame la princesse de Tarente et mademoiselle de la Tremoille y vinrent deux ou trois fois, et y furent longtemps à chacune. Elles me montrèrent leurs portraits qu'elles avoient fait faire en Hollande. Je n'en avois jamais vu; je trouvai cette manière d'écrire fort galante, et je fis le mien, Mademoiselle de la Tremoille m'envoya le sien de Thouars.

These portraits she continued to collect from her friends, with much the same avidity that people a generation ago collected autographs, till a little later (1659) Segrais, her secretary, published them.[17]

The custom of writing portraits, carried to an extreme by Mademoiselle de Scudéry, did not escape the strictures of the satirists. Charles Sorel (1599-1674) in his attack upon the fantastic pastoral [18] satirized the passion for *portraits* under the form of an imaginary journey: [19]

> On nous disoit encore que la passion des portraits avoit si bien gagné le cœur des personnes de ce sexe dans toute l'Europe, et principalement dans la France, qu'il en venoit tous les jours plusieurs dans l'île de Portraiture pour s'y instruire, sans que les périls du voyage et le regret de quitter leur patrie les pussent toucher.[20]

[16] Ed. Cheruel, II, p. 181.

[17] The fashion seems to have spread like an epidemic. V. Cousin says: Les portraits se multiplièrent à Paris et dans les provinces; ils descendèrent du grand monde dans la bourgeoisie; il y en eut d'excellentes, il y en eut de médiocres et aussi de détestables, jusqu' à ce qu'en 1688 La Bruyère renouvela et éleva le genre, et, sous le nom de Caractères, au lieu de quelques individus peignit son siècle et l'humanité (*Madame de Sablé*, p. 77).

[18] The *Histoire comique de Francion* is frankly picaresque, and the *Berger extravagant* is a direct parody of the pastoral romance.

[19] *La Description de l'Ile de Portraiture et la Ville de Portraits*, in *Voyages Imaginaires*. Amsterdam, 1788, vol. XXVI.

[20] Page 364.

Sorel ridicules especially the custom of autobiographic portraits such as Mademoiselle de Scudéry had made of herself in *Artamène ou le Grand Cyrus* under the name of " Sapho." [21]

Il y en avoit aussi qui, pour faire leur portrait, prenoient des masques des plus fins, et de ceux qui imitoient mieux le naturel, ou bien elles se fardoient de sorte que c'étoit elles-mêmes, et si ce n'étoit plus elles-mêmes. A les voir, on les eût prises pour des poupées de cire, ou pour ces figures d'horloges qui sont de bois ou d'ivoire, dont les yeux ont du mouvement par le moyen des ressorts, sans que leur front et leurs joues fassent aucun pli; comme elles leur étoient pareilles, cela donnait assez à connoître qu' elles étoient contrefaites.

Molière also satirized the preciosity in style and the artificial *galanterie* in love making of the romances. In *Les Précieuses ridicules,* the description by Madelon [22] is no exaggeration of what romance was to Mademoiselle de Scudéry:

Il faut qu'un amant, pour être agréable, sache débiter les beaux sentiments, pousser le doux, le tendre et le passionné, et que sa recherche soit dans les formes. Premièrement, il doit voir au temple, ou à la promenade, ou dans quelque cérémonie publique, la personne dont il devient amoureux; ou bien être conduit fatalement chez elle par un parent ou un ami, et sortir de là tout rêveur et mélancolique. Il cache un temps sa passion à l'objet aimé, et cependant lui rend plusieurs visites, où l'on ne manque jamais de mettre sur le tapis une question galante qui exerce les esprits de l'assemblée. Le jour de la déclaration arrive, qui doit se faire ordinairement dans une allée de quelque jardin, tandis que la compagnie s'est un peu éloignée: et cette déclaration est suivie d'un prompt courroux, qui parait à notre rougeur et qui, pour un temps, bannit l'amant de notre présence. Ensuite il trouve moyen de nous apaiser, de nous accoutumer insensiblement au discours de sa passion, et de tirer de nous cet aveu qui fait tant de peine. Après cela viennent les aventures, les rivaux qui se jettent à la traverse d'une inclination établie, les persécutions des pères, les jalousies conçues sur les fausses apparences, les plaintes, les désespoirs, et tout ce qui s'en suit. Voilà comment les choses se traitent dans les belles manières; et ce sont des règles dont, en bonne galanterie, on ne saurait se dispenser.

[21] Vol. x, pp. 554 ff.   [22] Scene IV.

The *précieuse* fad of making *portraits* provokes Molière's most caustic ridicule.   In the tenth scene Madelon tells Mascarille that she is madly fond of *portraits,* and that in her opinion nothing is more elegant.   " Portraits," Mascarille answers, " are difficult, and require a deep insight into character."   The insight requisite he claims to possess, for he modestly confesses having written "two hundred songs, as many sonnets, four hundred epigrams, and more than a thousand madrigals, without reckoning enigmas and *portraits.*"

The satire of Sorel and of Molière discouraged the art of portraiture as a social diversion, without diminishing its influence, already developed, upon literature.[23]   Indeed Molière himself, while he laughed at the *précieuse* fondness for *portraits,* shows clearly by his own *penchant* for the dramatic " character " that the art of literary portraiture, developed as a social amusement among the bluestockings he ridiculed, had no inconsiderable influence upon his own dramatic methods.   It seems impossible otherwise to explain his predilection for the portrait-character.   It is found in all his plays; and one, *Les Fâcheux,* is hardly more than a collection of them—a kind of rogues' gallery, or, more accurately, a bores' gallery.   Nearly the whole of the first scene is made up of a " character " of the blustering gallant at a play, who disturbs the audience and interrupts the actors.   This is the prelude to the successive appearance of ten other bores, who are simply " characters '" dramatized—that is, presented in action.   More individualized, and, therefore, more analogous to the methods of the *précieuses,* is the portrait that Covielle and Cléonte together compose of Lucille in *Le Bourgeois Gentilhomme* (Act III, sc. ix.).   It is easily

[23] It is evident in the work of the memoir-writers, especially Saint Simon, and, of course, in La Bruyère.

recognizable as a picture of Molière's wife, Armande Béjart. Molière continually employs the "character" as a means of introducing players about to come upon the stage. Two notable instances occur in *La Critique de L'École des Femmes*. In the second scene, Élise gives us a portrait of Climène before the latter appears, and, similarly, in the sixth scene Dorante performs the same service for the Marchioness Araminte, the *précieuse*.[24] In *L'Impromptu de Versailles* Molière ingeniously contrives that he himself, as one of the actors, shall introduce each of the others. This he does by giving a brief portrait of the person each is to impersonate. So, we have the courtier, the poet, the *précieuse*, etc.

Now the strongest extra-English influence upon Restoration comedy was Molière. The Restoration dramatists seem to have regarded him much as the Elizabethans regarded such books as Painter's *Palace of Pleasure*. They looked upon his plays as a kind of public store house of plots, incidents, and characters, to be drawn upon at will, and without acknowledgment. They simply took from Molière whatever incidents, situations, and characters struck their fancy.[25] So prevalent did the fashion of plundering Molière become that it furnished a frequent theme to the satirists of the age. So Caryll says in his Epilogue to his adaptation of *L'École des Femmes* (1669-70)

> Faith, be good natur'd to this hungry crew,
> Who, what they filch abroad, bring home to you.

[24] Cf. *Le Bourgeois Gentilhomme*, Act I, sc. i, in which the music master and the dancing master prepare us for the entrance of Jourdain by giving us his "character."

[25] See Besing, *Molière's Einfluss auf das englische Lustspiel bis 1700*, Inaugural-Dissertation, Leipzig, 1913, and Miles, *The Influence of Molière upon Restoration Comedy*, Columbia Univ. Press, 1910.

But still exclude those Men from all Relief,
Who steal themselves, yet boldly cry, Stop Thief;
Like talking Judges, these without Remorse
Condemn all petty Thefts, and practice worse;
As if they Robb'd by Patent, and alone
Had right to call each Foreign Play their own.
  What we have brought before you, was not meant
For a new Play, but a new President;
For we with Modesty our Theft avow,
(There is some Conscience us'd in stealing too)
And openly declare, that if our Cheer
Does hit your Pallate, you must thank Molliere.

In 1681 Thomas Durfey ironically asks, in a song that is a part of his play *Sir Barnaby Whig*,

Molière is quite rifled, then how shall I write?[26]

Samuel Butler probably had dramatic pilferers in mind when he wrote in his *Satyr upon Plagiary Privateers*,[27]

The World's as full of curious Wit
Which those, that father, never writ,
As 'tis of Bastards, which the Sot
And Cuckold owns, that ne'er begot;
Yet pass as well, as if the one
And th' other By-blow were their own.
For why should he that's impotent
To judge and fancy, and invent,
For that Impediment be stopt
To own, and challenge, and adopt,
At least th' expos'd, and fatherless
Poor Orphans of the Pen, and Press,
Whose Parents are obscure, or dead,
Or in far Countries born and bred?

The satire was fully justified by the facts. The borrowing from Molière began very early in the Restoration period. The first to practice it was Davenant in *The*

---

[26] Both quotations are cited by Miles, p. 81.
[27] Butler's *Remains*, Thyer's ed., Vol. I, pp. 168 ff.

Playhouse to Let (1663). Here he inserted into the play a garbled version of *Sganarelle ou le Cocu Imaginaire.* The precedent established by Davenant of transferring practically an entire play from Molière was followed by Medbourne in *Tartuffe, or the French Puritan* (1670), by Shadwell in *The Miser* (1671),[28] by Otway in his *Cheats of Scapin* (1677),[29] by Dryden in his *Amphitryon, or the two Sosias* (1690),[30] and by Vanbrugh in *The Mistake* (1705).[31] More often, instead of taking the whole play, the English playwrights contented themselves with transferring one or two scenes; as when Sedley made *The Mulberry Garden* open with a scene almost identical with the opening scene of *L'École des Femmes,* and as Congreve used the third scene of the fourth act of *Don Juan* as the opening of his *Love for Love* (1695). The most potent and pervasive influence of Molière is evident, not so much in the wholesale thefts of such men as Dryden and Otway, as in the lesser pilferings of men like Etherege, Wycherley, and Congreve, who owe comparatively little to Molière's plots, but who imitated his sprightly dialogue, and adapted his characters and situations to their own uses.[32]

Both classes of borrowers, however,—those whose plagiarisms were so great as to entitle them to be called literary embezzlers, and those whose thefts were more of the nature of literary shoplifting—were alike attracted by Molière's use of the *portraits.* These the Restoration

---

[28] The play is practically a paraphrase of *L'Avare.*

[29] This is a translation, with some omissions, of *Les Fourberies de Scapin.*

[30] The play is an adaptation, with some changes from the original, of Molière's *Amphitryon.*

[31] The play is scarcely more than a translation of *Le Dépit Amoureux.*

[32] Miles enumerates sixty-four plays that owe more or less to Molière.

dramatists simply appropriated. Shadwell who, by the way, laid his borrowing from the French to laziness,[33] and confessed that he was "ashamed on't,"[34] borrowed the plot of *The Sullen Lovers* mainly from *Le Misanthrope,* but adapted six scenes and six characters from *Les Fâcheux.* These six characters are the "bores" of both plays, and the scenes Shadwell adapted, in which they appear, are the scenes that contain the *portraits.* In the opening scene, for example, Stanford (Eraste) gives satiric characterizations of the three "bores" he has met that day, all of whom later appear in the action. This is quite similar to the opening of *Les Fâcheux,* except that Eraste describes only one bore, who does not afterwards appear. Wycherley, though in general far more independent and original in his use of the material he borrowed from Molière, nevertheless illustrates the attraction that the French *portrait* exerted upon the minds of the English playwrights. His *Plain Dealer* is an adaptation from *Le Misanthrope* and *La Critique de l'Ecole des Femmes.* Of the four scenes that Wycherley adapts from the former, one is the famous "portrait scene."[35] In this scene, the six characters that Wycherley borrowed from Molière[36] all appear; and Olivia, composes satiric portraits of her ac-

[33] " 'Tis not barrenness of wit or invention, that makes us borrow from the French but laziness; and this was the occasion of my making use of *l'Avare.* This play was wrote in less than a moneth" (Preface to *The Miser*).

Beljame says the smallness of the audiences, since the majority of the people retained the Puritan prejudice against the theatre, made necessary a larger repertoire than playwrights could supply without borrowing (*Le Public et les Hommes de Lettres en Angleterre au XVIII Siècle,* pp. 50 ff.).

[34] The Preface to *The Sullen Lovers.*

[35] *Le Misanthrope,* Act II, sc. IV.

[36] Wycherley took nearly half his *Dramatis Personæ* from Molière. There are thirteen named characters in *The Plain Dealer.*

quaintances, exactly as Célimène in *Le Misanthrope* had done, except that one,[37] at least, of the latter's has been identified as that of an individual, whereas Olivia's spiteful caricatures were, so far as is known, not personal. That they have every appearance of being portraits, Wycherley, nevertheless, fully recognizes; for he makes Eliza say of them:

So, cousin, I find one may have a collection of all one's acquaintances as well at your house as at Mr. Lely's. Only the difference is, there we find 'em much handsomer than they are, and like; here much uglier, and like; and you are the first of the profession of picture-drawing I ever knew without flattery.

Olivia answers:

I draw after the life; do nobody wrong, cousin.

The inevitable conclusion to which we are led is that the peculiar form of " character " found in Restoration comedy is in origin not English, but French. Though Ben Jonson's influence predisposed the Restoration dramatists to the " character," he did not supply the models for it. These were furnished by Molière. Molière's art was in turn influenced by that of the *précieuses,* who, after serving an apprenticeship in the social portraiture of the *salon,* had introduced the *portrait* into fiction.

EDWARD CHAUNCEY BALDWIN.

---

[37] Timante represents the Comte de Saint-Gilles according to Brossette (in notes on *Boileau,* quoted in *Œuvres de Molière,* Tome V, p. 481).

V.—THOMAS WARTON AND THE HISTORICAL METHOD IN LITERARY CRITICISM

Thomas Warton's *Observations on the 'Fairy Queen'
of Spenser* [1] has hardly yet received due recognition as
the first important piece of modern historical criticism in
the field of English literature. By the variety of its
new tenets and the definitiveness of its revolt against pseudo-classical criticism by rule, it marks the beginning of a
new school. Out of the turmoil of the quarrel between
the 'ancients' and the 'moderns' the pseudo-classical
compromise had emerged. The 'moderns,' by admitting
and apologizing for a degree of barbarity and uncouthness in even their greatest poets, had established their
right to a secure and reputable place in the assembly of
immortals, although on the very questionable ground of
conformity with the ancients and by submitting to be
judged by rules which had not determined their development. It was thus by comparisons with the ancients that
Dryden found Spenser's verse harmonious but his design
imperfect; [2] it was by applying the classical rules for epic
poetry that Addison praised *Paradise Lost*, [3] and that
Steele wished an 'Encomium of *Spencer* also.' [4]

Impossible as was the task of reconciling literature
partly romantic and modern with classical and ancient
standards, the critics of a rationalistic age did not hesitate
to attempt it: common sense was the pseudo-classical handmaiden that justified the rules, methodized nature, stand-

---

[1] London, 1754. Second edition, corrected and enlarged, 2 vols.,
1762. References in this article are to the third edition, 1807.

[2] *Essay on Satire.*

[3] *Spectator*, January to May, 1712.

[4] *Spectator*, No. 540.

ardized critical taste, and restrained the ' Enthusiastick Spirit ' and the *je ne sais quoi* of the school of taste. The task was a hard one, and the pseudo-classical position dangerous and ultimately untenable. A more extended study of literary history—innocuously begun by Rymer—[5] and an enlightened freedom from prejudice would show at the same time the inadequacy of the rules and the possibility of arriving at sounder critical standards.

These are the two principal gifts that Thomas Warton had with which he revolutionized criticism: intelligent independence to throw off the bondage of the rules, and broad knowledge to supply material for juster criteria. When he said, ' It is absurd to think of judging either Ariosto or Spenser by precepts which they did not attend to,' [6] he not merely asserted their right to be judged by Gothic or romantic, as opposed to pseudo-classical, standards, but he sounded the death-knell of criticism by rule, and the bugle-note of the modern school. When, in the same critical work, and even more impressively in two later ones,[7] he brought to bear upon the subject in hand a rich store of ideas and illustrations drawn from many literatures—Latin, Greek, Italian, French, and English in its obscure as well as its more familiar eras—he rendered an even more important service on the side of constructive criticism.

Warton's *Observations* is connected not only with the history of critical theory in the eighteenth century, but also with what is called the Spenserian revival. It was partly the culmination of one of several related movements tending toward the restoration of the older English

[5] *A Short View of Tragedy*, 1693. See Chapter v.
[6] *Observations*, I, p. 21.
[7] *History of English Poetry*, 1774, 1778, 1781. Milton's *Poems upon Several Occasions*, 1785.

classics. While Chaucer was slowly winning a small circle
of appreciators; Shakespeare, from ignorantly apologetic
admiration and garbled staging, through serious study and
intelligent comprehension, was coming into his own; and
Milton was attaining a vogue that left its mark on the
new poetry; the Spenserian revival was simultaneously
preparing to exert an even greater influence. Although
Spenser was never without a select circle of readers, that
circle was small and coldly critical during the pseudo-
classical period when his principal charm was that which
his moral afforded readers who held that the purpose of
poetry was to instruct. Most readers assented to Jonson's
dictum that Spenser ' writ no language ' without attending to the caveat that followed, ' Yet I would have him
read for his matter.' The difficulties of his language, the
tiresomeness of his stanza,[8] the unclassical imperfection of
his design, and the extravagance of the adventures too often
obscured even the beauty of his moral. Therefore it was
after a pretty general neglect of his poetry that the eighteenth century saw a species of Spenserian imitation arise
which showed to what low ebb the study of Spenser had
sunk. The first of these imitators either ignorantly fancied that any arrangement of from six to ten iambic
pentameter lines capped with an Alexandrine, with distinctly Popeian cadence and a sprinkling of ' I ween,' ' I
weet ' and ' whilom ' by way of antiquated diction, could
pass for Spenserian verse,[9] or followed the letter of the

[8] Hughes, *Remarks on the ' Fairy Queen '* prefixed to Ed. *Spenser's Works*, 2nd. ed., 1750, I, p. lxvii.

[9] Prior: *Ode to the Queen, written in Imitation of Spenser's Style*, 1706, Preface. Whitehead: *Vision of Solomon*, 1730, and two *Odes to the Hon. Charles Townsend*. Boyse: *The Olive: an Heroic Ode*, etc., in the stanza of Spenser (ababcdcdee), 1736-7. *Vision of Patience: an Allegorical Poem*, 1741; *Psalm XLII: In Imitation of the Style of Spenser* (ababcc, no Alexandrine), 1736-7. Blacklock: *Hymn to*

6

stanza closely enough, but failed to take their model seriously, and misapplied it to vulgar burlesque, social and political satire, and mere moralizing.[10] Their ignorance of the poet whom they professed to imitate is marked. Often they knew him only through Prior's imitations: usually their attempts at antiquated diction betray them.[11] Occasionally, as in the case of Shenstone, a study of Spenser followed imitation of him, and led to a new attitude, changes in the imitation, and finally, apparently, to an admiration that he neither understood nor cared to admit.[12]

Divine Love, and *Philantheus* (ababcc), 1746. T. Warton, Sr.: *Philander* (ababcc), 1748. Lloyd: *Progress of Envy* (ababcdedd), 1751. Smith: *Thales* (ababccc), 1751. See W. L. Phelps: *Beginnings of the English Romantic Movement*, Boston, 1902. Ch. on Spenserian Revival, and Appendix I, for a more complete list.

[10] Pope: *The Alley*, date unknown, an exercise in versification, and ill-natured burlesque. Croxall: *Two Original Cantos of the Fairy Queen*, 1713 and 1714. Akenside: *The Virtuoso*, 1737, mild satire. G. West: *Abuse of Travelling*, 1739, satire. Cambridge: *Archimage*, 1742-50, a clever parody. Shenstone: *The Schoolmistress*, 1742, satirical. Pitt: *The Jordan*, 1747, vulgar burlesque. Ridley: *Psyche*, 1747, moral allegory. Mendez: *The Seasons*, 1751, *Squire of Dames*, 1748-58. Thomson: *Castle of Indolence*, 1748. See also Phelps, as above.

[11] Such slips as 'nor ceasen he from study' and 'he would oft ypine' in Akenside's *Virtuoso*, and even Thomson's note: 'The letter *y* is frequently placed in the beginning of a word by Spenser to lengthen it a syllable; and *en* at the end of a word for the same reason' (Glossary to the *Castle of Indolence*).

[12] I cannot agree with Professor Phelps that, 'as people persisted in admiring "The School-Mistress" for its own sake, he finally consented to agree with them, and in later editions omitted the commentary explaining that the whole thing was done in jest' (*The Beginning of the English Romantic Movement*, p. 66). On the contrary, it seems pretty clear that although Shenstone had probably not come to any very profound appreciation for the older poet, his admiration for him became more and more serious, but that he lacked the courage of his convictions, and conformed outwardly with a public opinion wholly ignorant of Spenser. Two later letters of Shenstone's indicate pretty clearly that it was he, and not 'the

Of course by far the best of the Spenserian imitators was James Thomson, whose work was the first to rise above the merely imitative and to have an independent value as creative poetry. Although his 'Advertisement' and a few burlesque touches throughout the poem are evidence of the influence of the *Schoolmistress* and of the prevailing attitude toward Spenser, Thomson went further than mere external imitation, and reproduced something of the melody and atmosphere of the *Fairy Queen.* Thus poetical enthusiasm began the Spenserian revival; it remained for a great critical enthusiasm to vindicate the source of this inspiration and to establish it on the firm basis of scholarly study and intelligent appreciation.

The first attempt at anything like an extended criticism of the *Fairy Queen* was in the two essays, *On Allegorical Poetry* and *Remarks on the 'Fairy Queen,'* which profaced John Hughes's edition of Spenser's works in 1715, the first eighteenth-century edition.[13] Steele, in the 540th

people,' whose taste for Spenser had developed. In November, 1745, he wrote to Graves (to whom he had written of his early contempt) that he had ' read Spenser once again and added full as much more to my *School-mistress* in regard to *number of lines; something* in point of *matter* (or *manner* rather) *which* does not displease me. I would be glad if Mr. ———— were, upon your request, to give his opinion of particulars, etc.' Evidently the judgment was unfavorable, for he wrote the next year, ' I thank you for your perusal of that trivial poem. If I were going to print it, I should give way to your remarks *implicitly,* and would not *dare* to do otherwise. But so long as I keep it in manuscript, you will pardon my silly prejudices, if I chuse to read and shew it with the addition of most of my new stanzas. I own, I have a fondness for several, imagining them to be *more* in Spenser's way, yet more independent on the antique phrase, than any part of the poem; and, on that account, I cannot yet prevail on myself to banish *them* entirely; but were I to print, I should (with *some* reluctance) give way to your sentiments' (Shenstone's Works, 1777, III, pp. 105-6).

[13] And the first attempt at an annotated edition. *Spenser's Works, to which is prefix'd .... an Essay on Allegorical Poetry* by Mr.

Spectator, three years before had desired an 'Encomium of *Spencer,*' ' that charming author,' like Addison's Milton papers, but nothing further than his own meagre hints was forthcoming. And Hughes's attitude, like that of the imitators, was wholly apologetic.

Hughes seems almost to have caught a glimpse of the promised land when he refused to examine the *Fairy Queen* by the classical rules for epic poetry, saying: 'As it is plain the Author never design'd it by those Rules, I think it ought rather to be consider'd as a Poem of a particular kind, describing in a Series of Allegorical Adventures or Episodes the most noted Virtues and Vices: to compare it therefore with the Models of Antiquity wou'd be like drawing a Parallel between the *Roman* and the *Gothick* Architecture.' [14] At first sight one is inclined to think this very near to Warton's revolutionary dicta, but the bungling way in which he spoiled the effect of so striking a statement by preparing in advance a set of pseudo-classical and misfit standards to apply as he exposed the unsuitability of the old, merely by the substitution of allegory for epic, shows that he was a true pseudo-classicist after all. He could not, nor would, throw off his allegiance to the ancients. If the *Fairy Queen* could not be considered as an epic, it could be judged as an allegory, the rules of which, though not described by the ancients, were easily determinable. And in attempting to set forth the rules for allegorical poetry, he tried to conform to the spirit of the classical critics as he understood it, and to illustrate his subject by examples from classical poets. Nevertheless he felt some reluctance in introducing a sub-

---

Hughes, 6 vols., London, 1715. Second edition, 1750. There is a second preface, *Remarks on the 'Fairy Queen.'* References are to the second edition.

[14] *Remarks on the 'Fairy Queen,'* I, p. xliii.

ject which was 'something out of the way, and not expressly treated upon by those who have laid down Rules
for the Art of Poetry.' [15]   Hughes's ideas of what should
constitute successful allegory were therefore embodied in
his *Essay on Allegorical Poetry*, by the uncertain light
of which the critic hoped 'not only to discover many Beauties in the *Fairy Queen*, but likewise to excuse some of its
Irregularities.' [16]

Hughes did not, however, yield to the spell of 'magic
Spenser's wildly-warbled song.'   While he admitted that
his fable gave 'the greatest Scope to that Range of Fancy
which was so remarkably his Talent,' [17] and that his plan,
though not well chosen, was at least well executed and
adapted to his talent, he apologized for and excused both
fable and plan on the score of the Italian models which he
followed, and the remnants of the 'old Gothic Chivalry'
which yet survived.   The only praise he could give the
poem was wholly pseudo-classical,—for the moral and
didactic bent which the poet had contrived to give the
allegory,[18] and for some fine passages where the author
rises above himself and imitates the ancients.[19]   In spite
of his statement that the *Fairy Queen* was not to be
examined by the strict rules of epic poetry, he could not
free himself from that bondage, and the most of his essay
is taken up with a discussion of the poem in the light of
the rules.   Moreover Hughes was but ill-equipped for his
task; he failed even to realize that a great field of literary
history must be thoroughly explored before the task of
elucidating Spenser could be intelligently undertaken, and
that genuine enthusiasm for the poet could alone arouse
much interest in him.   These are the reasons why nearly

---

[15] *Essay on Allegorical Poetry*, I, p. xxi.
[16] *Remarks on the 'Fairy Queen*,' I, p. xlii.
[17] I, p. xliv.   [18] I, p. xl.   [19] I, p. l.

forty years elapsed before the edition was reprinted, and
why it failed to give a tremendous impetus to the Spenserian revival. Yet, notwithstanding its defects, it is extremely significant that Hughes should have undertaken
at all the editing of so neglected a poet.[20]   It is a straw
that points the direction of the wind.

The next attempt at Spenserian criticism was a small
volume of *Remarks on Spenser's Poems and on Milton's
'Paradise Regained,'* published anonymously in 1734, and
soon recognized as the work of Dr. Jortin, a classical
scholar of some repute.   This is practically valueless as a
piece of criticism.   But Jortin was at least partly conscious of his failure and of a reason for it, though he was
more anxious to have the exact text determined by a ' col-
lation of editions, and by comparing the author with himself' than to furnish an interpretive criticism; and he
acknowledged himself unwilling to bestow the necessary
time and application for the work,[21]—a gratifying acknowledgment of the fact that no valuable work could
be done in this field without special preparation for it.

And when Thomas Warton was able to bring this special
preparation for the first time to the study of the *Fairy
Queen,* he produced a revolution in criticism.   Freed from
the tyranny of the rules by the perception of their limitations, he substituted untried avenues of approach and

[20] The neglect of Spenser is best shown by the few editions of either
the *Fairy Queen* or the complete works which had appeared since
the first three books of the former were published in 1590. *Faerie
Queene,* 1st ed., 4to., 1590-6; 2nd, 1596; 3rd, fol., 1609; Birch ed.,
3 vols., 4to., 1751. *Poetical Works,* 1st fol. ed., 1611; 2nd, 1617-18;
3rd, 1679. Hughes, 1st ed., 1715, 2nd, 1750.

[21] Jortin's conclusion quoted in Nichols's *Literary Anecdotes,* II, p.
53. H. E. Cory says nothing of Jortin's Remarks in his monograph,
The Critics of Edmund Spenser, Univ. of California *Pub. in Mod.
Phil.,* II, 2, pp. 81-182.

juster standards of criticism, and revealed beauties which
could never have been discovered with the old restrictions.
That he should be without trace of pseudo-classicism is
something we cannot expect; but that his general critical
method and principles are ultimately irreconcilable with
even the most generous interpretation of that term, is a
conclusion one cannot escape after a careful study of the
Observations on the 'Fairy Queen.'

Briefly, the causes of Warton's superiority over all previous critics of Spenser, the reasons why he became through
this piece of critical writing the founder of a new kind of
criticism, are four. First, he recognized the inadequacy
of the classical rules, as interpreted by Boileau and other
modern commentators, as standards for judging modern
literature, and declared his independence of them and his
intention of following new methods based upon the belief
that the author's purpose is at least as important a subject for critical study as the critic's theories, and that pure
imagination is as important a factor in creative literature
as reason. Second, he introduced the modern historical
method of criticism by recognizing that no work of art
could be independently judged, isolated from the conditions under which it was produced, without reference to
the influences which determined its character; and without considering its relation to other literatures. In taking
so broad a view of his subject, Warton was, of course,
recognizing the necessity for a comparative study of literature. In the third place, and as a consequence of this independence and this greater breadth of view, Warton understood more fully than his contemporaries the true relation between classical and modern literature, understood
that the English writers of the boasted Augustan age, in
renouncing their heritage from the middle ages, had deprived themselves of the qualities which alone could have

redeemed their desiccated pseudo-classicism. And last, Warton made a place in criticism for the reader's spontaneous delight and enthusiasm.

Few critics of the 18th century recognized any difference between their own rules and practice and those of the ancients, or saw the need for modern standards for judging modern poems. Just here comes the important and irreparable break between Warton and his contemporaries. While Hughes and the rest attempted to justify Spenser by pointing out conformities to the rules [22] where they existed or might be fancied, and condemned his practice when they failed to find any, Warton was at some pains to show that Hughes failed and that such critics must fail because their critical method was wrong.[23] He pointed out that the *Fairy Queen* cannot be judged by rule, that 'the plan and conduct' of Spenser's poem 'is highly exceptionable,' ' is confused and irregular,' and has ' no general unity '; [24] it fails completely when examined by the rules. To Warton this clearly showed the existence of another standard of criticism—not the Aristotelian, but the poet's: Spenser had not tried to write like Homer, but like Ariosto; his standard was romantic, not classical; and he was to be judged by what he tried to do.

Warton's declaration of independence of pseudo-classical criticism was a conscious revolt; yet it was one to which he made some effort to win the assent of his contemporaries

---

[22] Dryden had done the same thing in the *Dedication to the Translation of Juvenal* by pointing out how the ' character of Prince Arthur shines throughout the whole poem,' and Warton took issue squarely with him on the point and denied any such unity. See *Observations*, I, pp. 10-11. Addison used the same method in his papers on *Paradise Lost*. Beni was probably the originator of this sort of misapplied criticism in his comparison of Tasso with Homer and Virgil (I, p. 3).

[23] I, pp. 11 ff.   [24] I, p. 17.

by conceding that Spenser's frequent extravagances [25] did violate the rules approved by an age that took pride in its critical taste. His desire to engage their interest, however, neither succeeded in that purpose nor persuaded him that those rules were properly applied to poems written in ignorance of them. There is no uncertainty, no compromise with pseudo-classical criticism in the flat defiance, ' it is absurd to think of judging either Ariosto or Spenser by precepts which they did not attend to.' [26]

Having thus condemned the accepted standards as inadequate for a just criticism of the *Fairy Queen,* Warton's next purpose was to find those by which it could be properly judged: not the rules of which the poet was ignorant, but the literature with which he was familiar. He recognized quite clearly a distinction between a classical and a romantic poet, and accounted for it by a difference of circumstances. Warton's even then extensive knowledge of the neglected periods of earlier English literature gave him a power that most of his contemporaries lacked, and enabled him to see that Spenser's peculiarities were those of his age, that the ' knights and damsels, the tournaments and enchantments of Spenser ' were not oddities but the familiar and admired features of romance, a prevailing literary form of the age, and that ' the fashions of the time ' determined Spenser's purpose of becoming a ' *romantic* poet.' [27]

Warton determined, therefore, not only to judge but to praise Spenser as a romantic [28] poet. He found that as the characteristic appeal of pseudo-classical poetry was to the intellect, to the reason, romantic poetry addressed

[25] I, p. 18.   [26] I, p. 21.   [27] II, p. 72.
[28] Warton used the word *romantic* as a derivative of ' romance,' implying the characteristics of the mediæval romances, and I have used the word frequently in this paper with that meaning.

itself to the feelings, to the imagination. Its excellence, therefore, consisted not in design and proportion, but in interest and variety of detail. The poet's business was 'to engage the fancy, and to interest the attention by bold and striking images, in the formation, and disposition of which, little labour or art was applied. The various and the marvellous were the chief sources of delight.' [29] Hence Spenser had ransacked 'reality and romance,' 'truth and fiction' to adorn his 'fairy structure,' and Warton revelled in the result, in its very formlessness and richness, which he thought preferable, in a romantic poem, to exactness. 'Exactness in his poem,' he said, 'would have been like the cornice which a painter introduced in the grotto of Calypso. Spenser's beauties are like the flowers of Paradise.' [30]

When beauties thus transcend nature, delight goes beyond reason. Warton did not shrink from the logical result of giving rein to imagination; he was willing to recognize the romantic quest for beauties beyond the reach of art, to sacrifice reason and 'nature methodiz'd' in an exaltation of a higher quality which rewarded the reader with a higher kind of enjoyment. 'If the *Fairy Queen*,' he said, 'be destitute of that arrangement and œconomy which epic severity requires, yet we scarcely regret the loss of these, while their place is so amply supplied by something which more powerfully attracts us: something which engages the affections, the feelings of the heart, rather than the cold approbation of the head. If there be any poem whose graces please, because they are situated beyond the reach of art, and where the force and faculties of creative imagination [31] delight, because they are unas-

---

[29] I, p. 22.   [30] I, p. 23.

[31] Without the same precision in nomenclature but with equal clearness of idea Warton distinguished between creative and imita-

sisted and unrestrained by those of deliberate judgment, it is this. In reading Spenser, if the critic is not satisfied, yet the reader is transported.' [32]

When Warton thus made a place for transport in a critical discourse, he had parted company with his contemporaries and opened the way for the whole romantic exaltation of feeling. He had turned from Dr. Johnson, who condemned ' all power of fancy over reason ' as a ' degree of insanity,' [33] and faced toward Blake, who exalted the imagination and called ' reason . . . the only evil.' [34] Every propriety of Queen Anne criticism had now been violated. Not satisfied with condemning all previous Spenserian criticism as all but nonsense, Warton dared to place the uncritical reader's delight above the critic's deliberate disapproval, and then to commend that enthusiasm and the beauties that aroused it. In repudiating the pseudo-classical rules, Warton enunciated two revolutionary dicta : there are other critical standards than those of Boileau and the ancients (save the mark!) ; there

---

tive power in exactly the same way that Coleridge differentiated imagination and fancy. He did not compose exact philosophical definitions of the two qualities, but in a careful contrast between the poetic faculties of Spenser and Ariosto, he made the same distinction. Spenser's power, imagination, he described as creative, vital; 'it endeavours to body forth the unsubstantial, to represent by visible and external symbols the ideal and abstracted (II, p. 77). Ariosto's faculty, fancy, he called imitative, lacking in inventive power (I, p. 308; II, p. 78). Although Warton at times applied the term imagination loosely to both, there was no confusion of ideas; when he used both terms it was with the difference in meaning just described. In speaking of the effect of the marvels of romance upon the poetic faculty he said they ' rouse and invigorate all the powers of imagination' and 'store the fancy with . . . images' (II, p. 323).

[32] I, p. 24.
[33] *Rasselas*, Ch. XLIV.
[34] Crabbe Robinson's *Diary*. Ed. Sadler, Boston, 1870, II, p. 43.

are other poetical beauties than those of Pope and ' nature
methodiz'd.'

Revolutionary as he was in his enjoyment of Spenser's
fable, Warton had not at the time he wrote the Observations freed himself from the pseudo-classical theories of
versification [35] and he agreed with his predecessors in his
discussion of this subject. Although he did not feel the
romanticist's enthusiasm for Spenser's versification, he
was nevertheless sufficiently the poet to appreciate and to
enjoy his success with it. 'It is indeed surprising,' he
said, ' that Spenser should execute a poem of uncommon
length, with so much spirit and ease, laden as he was with
so many shackles, and embarrassed with so complicated
a *bondage* of *riming*. . . . His sense and sound are equally
flowing and uninterrupted.' [36] Similarly, with respect to
language, we neither expect nor find enthusiasm. Warton
thought Jonson ' perhaps unreasonable,' [37] and found the
origin of his language in the language of his age, as he
found the origin of his design in its romances. Long acquaintance enabled him to read the *Fairy Queen* with
ease; he denied that Spenser's language was either so
affected or so obsolete as it was generally supposed, and
asserted that ' For many stanzas together we may frequently read him with as much facility as we can the same
number of lines in Shakespeare.' [38] In his approval and

[35] Somewhat later he took a not insignificant part in the romantic
movement in poetry.

[36] I, pp. 168-170.

[37] In his opinion that ' Spenser, in affecting the ancients, writ no
language ' (I, p. 184).

[38] I, p. 185. This parallel does not greatly help the case in an age
when Atterbury could write to Pope that he found ' the hardest part
of Chaucer . . . more intelligible ' than some parts of Shakespeare
and that ' not merely through the faults of the edition, but the
obscurity of the writer ' (Pope's *Works*, Elwin-Courthope ed., IX,
p. 26).

appreciation of Spenser's moral purpose Warton was, of course, nearer to his pseudo-classical predecessors than to his romantic followers; however, without relinquishing that prime virtue of the old school, the solidity that comes from well-established principles, he attained to new virtues, greater catholicity of taste and flexibility of judgment.

In seeking in the literature of and before the sixteenth century and in the manners and customs of the ' spacious times of Great Elizabeth ' for the explanation of Spenser's poem—so far as explanation of genius is possible—Warton was, as has been said, laying the foundations of modern historical criticism. Some slight progress had been made in this direction before, but without important results. Warton was by no means original in recognizing Spenser's debt to the Italian romances which were so popular in his day, and to Ariosto in particular. And many critics agreed that he was ' led by the prevailing notions of his age to write an irregular and romantic poem.' They, however, regarded his age as one of barbarity and ignorance of the rules, and its literature as unworthy of study and destitute of intrinsic value. No critic before Warton had realized the importance of supplementing an absolute with an historical criticism, of reconstructing, so far as possible, a poet's environment and the conditions under which he worked, in order to judge his poetry. ' In reading the works of a poet who lived in a remote age,' he said, ' it is necessary that we should look back upon the customs and manners which prevailed in that age. We should endeavour to place ourselves in the writer's situation and circumstances. Hence we shall become better enabled to discover how his turn of thinking, and manner of composing, were influenced by familiar appearances and established objects, which are utterly different from those with which we are at present surrounded.' [39]   And, realizing that the neglect of these details was fatal to good criticism, that the 'commentator,'[40] whose critical enquiries are employed on Spenser, Jonson, and the rest of our elder poets, will in vain give specimens of his classical erudition, unless, at the same time, he brings to his work a mind intimately acquainted with those books, which though now forgotten, were yet in common use and high repute about the time in which his authors respectively wrote, and which they consequently must have read,' [41] he resolutely reformed his own practice.

Warton not only perceived the necessity of the historical method of studying the older poets, but he had acquired what very few of his contemporaries had attained, sufficient knowledge of the earlier English literature to undertake such a study of Spenser.   He embarked upon the study of the *Fairy Queen,* its sources and literary background, with a fund of knowledge which, however much later scholars, who have taken up large holdings in the territory charted by that pioneer, may unjustly scorn its superficiality or inexactness, was for that time quite exceptional, and which could not fail to illuminate the poem to the point of transfiguration.   Every reader of Spenser had accepted his statement that he took Ariosto as his model,

---

[39] II, p. 71.

[40] Warton ably and sharply met Pope's attack on Theobald for including in his edition of Shakespeare a sample of his sources, of " '——All such reading as never was read,' " and concluded 'If Shakespeare is worth reading, he is worth explaining, and the researches used for so valuable and elegant a purpose, merit the thanks of genius and candour, not the satire of prejudice and ignorance' (II, p. 319). In similar vein he rebuked such of his own critics as found his quotations from the romances 'trifling and uninteresting': 'such readers can have no taste for Spenser' (I, p. 91).

[41] II, pp. 317-18.

but no one before Warton had remarked another model, one closer in respect of matter, which the poet no doubt thought too obvious to mention, the old romances of chivalry. Warton observed that where Spenser's plan is least like Ariosto's, it most resembles the romances; that, although he 'formed his Faerie Queene upon the fanciful plan of Ariosto,' he formed the particular adventures of his knight upon the romances. 'Spenser's first book is,' he said, 'a regular and precise imitation of such a series of action as we frequently find in books of chivalry.' [42]

In proof of Spenser's indebtedness to the romances Warton cited the prevalence of romances of chivalry in his day, and pointed out particular borrowings from this popular poetry. In the first place he insisted again and again not only that the 'encounters of chivalry' which appeared so extraordinary to modern eyes were familiar to readers in Spenser's day,[43] but that the practices of chivalry were even continued to some extent.[44] Warton's close acquaintance with the literature of the sixteenth century and before showed him that the matter of the romances was common property and had permeated other works than those of mediæval poets. He discovered that the story of Arthur, from which Spenser borrowed most,

---

[42] I, p. 26.

[43] And even later to the time of Milton. Warton found Milton's mind deeply tinctured with romance reading and his imagination and poetry affected thereby (I, pp. 257 and 350). Even Dryden wanted to write an epic about Arthur or the Black Prince but on the model of Virgil and Spenser, not Spenser and the romances (*Essay on Satire*).

[44] I, p. 27 and II, pp. 71-72. Warton cited Holinshed's Chronicles (Stowe's contin.) where is an account of a tourney for the entertainment of Queen Elizabeth, in which Fulk Grevill and Sir Philip Sidney, among others, entered the lists (Holin., *Chron.*, ed. 1808, IV, pp. 435 ff.).

was so generally known and so great a favourite that incidents from it were made the basis for entertainment of
Elizabeth at Kenilworth,[45] and that Arthur and his
knights were alluded to by writers so various as Caxton,
Ascham, Sidney, Puttenham, Bacon, and Jonson; [46] that
even Ariosto [47] himself borrowed from the story of Arthur.
At the same time his first-hand knowledge of the romances
enabled him to point out among those which most directly
influenced the *Fairy Queen,* Malory's *Morte Arthur,* the
largest contributor, of course, from which such details as
the story of Sir Tristram, King Ryence and the mantle
of beards, the holy Grail, and the Blatant Beast were
drawn; [48] *Bevis of Southampton,* which furnished the incident of the well of marvellous healing power; [49] the ballad of the Boy and the Mantle, from the French romance,
Le Court Mantel, which suggested Spenser's conceit of
Florimel's girdle.[50] Warton also carefully discussed Spenser's fairy mythology, which supplanted the classical mythology as his romantic adventures replaced those of anti-

---

[45] Warton quotes Laneham's 'Letter wherein part of the Entertainment untoo the Queen's Majesty at Killinworth Castl in Warwick-
sheer in this Soomer's progress, 1575, is signified,' and Gascoigne's
'Pleasures of Kenilworth Castle,' *Works,* 1576.
[46] I, pp. 50-74.   [48] I, pp. 27-57.
[47] I, pp. 53-57.   [49] I, pp. 69-71.
[50] I, p. 76. Warton says an 'ingenious correspondent communicated' to him this 'old ballad or metrical romance.' Part of *Le
Court Mantel* he found in Sainte Pelaye's *Mémoires sur l'ancienne
Chevalerie,* 1760. Other details, which could not be traced to particular romances, Warton attributed to 'a mind strongly tinctured
with romantic ideas.' One of these, the custom of knights swearing
on their swords, Upton had explained as derived from the custom of
the Huns and Goths, related by Jornandes and Ammianus Marcelli-
nus, but Warton pointed out that it was much more probably derived from the more familiar romances (II, p. 65). A Bodleian MS.
containing Sir Degore and other romances is quoted from and
described (II, pp. 5-9).

quity, ascribing its origin to romance and folk-lore of Celtic and ultimately Oriental origin.[51]

As in the case of mediæval romance, Warton was the first critic to consider in any detail Spenser's indebtedness to Chaucer. Antiquarians and a few poets had been mildly interested in Chaucer, but his importance for the study of the origins of English poetry had been ignored in the prevalent delusion that the classics were the ultimate sources of poetry. Dryden, to be sure, had remarked that Spenser imitated Chaucer's language,[52] and subsequent readers, including Warton, concurred. But it still remained for Warton to point out that Spenser was also indebted to Chaucer for ideas, and to show the extent and nature of his debt by collecting 'specimens of Spenser's imitations from Chaucer, both of language and sentiment.'[53] Without, of course, attempting to exhaust the subject, Warton collected enough parallel passages to prove that Spenser was not only an 'attentive reader and professed admirer,' but also an imitator of Chaucer. For example, he pointed out that the list of trees in the wood of error was more like Chaucer's in the *Assembly of Fowls* than similar passages in classical poets mentioned by Jortin;[54] that he had borrowed the magic mirror which Mer-

---

[51] I, pp. 77-89. Warton often used the terms Celtic and Norse very loosely without recognizing the difference. Like Huet and Mallet and other students of romance he was misled by the absurd and fanciful ethnologies in vogue in the 17th and 18th centuries. For his theory of romance see his dissertation *On the Origin of Romantic Fiction in Europe* prefixed to the first volume of his *History of English Poetry*, 1774. In spite of the absurdity of his theory as a whole, many details are surprisingly correct and illuminating.

[52] *Essay on Satire.* Dryden frequently referred to Chaucer as Spenser's master, meaning in the matter of language. See also *Dedication of the Pastorals* and *Preface to the Fables.*

[53] Section V, *Of Spenser's Imitations from Chaucer.*

[54] In his *Remarks on Spenser's Poems.* See *Observations* I, p. 190.

7

lin gave Ryence from the *Squire's Tale*,[55] and from the
Romance of the Rose, the conceit of Cupid dressed in flowers.[56] By a careful comparison with Chaucer's language,
Warton was able to explain some doubtful passages as well
as to show Spenser's draughts from ' the well of English
undefiled.'

One can scarcely overestimate the importance of Warton's evident first-hand knowledge of Chaucer in an age
when he was principally known only through Dryden's
and Pope's garbled modernizations, or Milton's reference
to him who

> . . . . . . left half-told
> The story of Cambuscan bold.

Warton was not satisfied that Chaucer should be studied
merely to illustrate Spenser; he recognized his intrinsic
value as well, and suffered his enthusiasm for Chaucer to
interrupt the thread of his criticism of Spenser, while he
lauded and recommended to his neglectful age the charms
of the older poet.[57] To be sure Warton's reasons for admiring Chaucer were somewhat too romantic to convince
an age that preferred regular beauties; his ' romantic
arguments ', ' wildness of painting ', ' simplicity and
antiquity of expression ', though ' pleasing to the imagination ' and calculated to ' transport us into some fairy.
region ' were certainly not the qualities to attract Upton

---

[55] I, p. 205. Warton showed many instances of Spenser's interest
in Cambuscan, including his continuation of part of the story. See
also pp. 210 ff.

[56] I, p. 221.

[57] Warton found opportunity to express more fully his enthusiasm
for Chaucer in a detailed study comparable to this of Spenser, in his
History of English Poetry twenty years later. This contributed quite
as much to the restoration of Chaucer as did Tyrwhitt's accurate
elucidation of textual difficulties.

or Hughes or Dr. Johnson. Unlike the pseudo-classical admirers of Chaucer, Warton held that to read modern imitations was not to know Chaucer; that to provide such substitutes was to contribute rather to the neglect than to the popularity of the original. With characteristic soundness of scholarship Warton condemned the prevalence of translations because they encouraged 'indolence and illiteracy', displaced the originals and thus gradually vitiated public taste.[58]

The study of Spenser's age yielded the third element which Warton introduced into Spenserian criticism—the influence of the mediæval moralities and allegorical masques. Warton's study of Spenser's allegory is of quite another sort than Hughes's essay. Instead of trying to concoct a set of *a priori* rules for a kind of epic which should find its justification in its moral, Warton, as usual, was concerned with forms of allegory as they actually existed and were familiar to his poet, and with the history of allegorical poetry in England. Without denying the important influence of Ariosto, he pointed out that his predecessors had erred in thinking the *Orlando Furioso* a sufficient model; he saw that the characters of Spenser's allegory much more resembled the 'emblematical personages, visibly decorated with their proper attributes, and actually endued with speech, motion, and life'[59] with which Spenser was familiar upon the stage, than the less symbolical

---

[58] I, pp. 269-71. Warton extended this criticism to translations of classical authors as well. Of course the greatest of the classicists, Dryden and Johnson, realized the limitations of translation, that it was only a makeshift. See Preface to translation of Ovid's epistle, to *Sylvae* and to the *Fables*, and Boswell's *Johnson*, Hill Ed., III, p. 36. But the popularity of Dryden's translations, and the large number of translations and imitations that appeared during his and succeeding generations, justified Warton's criticism.

[59] II, p. 78.

characters of Ariosto. Warton could support his position by quoting references in the *Fairy Queen* to masques and dumb shows,[60] and by tracing somewhat the progress of allegory in English poetry before Spenser.[61] It is characteristic that he should not have been satisfied to observe that allegory was popular in Spenser's age, but that he should wish to explain it by a ' retrospect of English poetry from the age of Spenser.' [62] Superficial and hasty as this survey is, it must have confirmed Warton's opinion that a thorough exploration of early English poetry was needed, and so anticipated his *magnum opus*. And we can find little fault with its conclusions, even when he says that this poetry ' principally consisted in visions and allegories ' when he could add as a matter of information, ' there are, indeed, the writings of some English poets now remaining, who wrote before Gower or Chaucer.'

In rejecting the conclusions of pseudo-classical criticism, in regarding Spenser as the heir of the middle ages, Warton did not by any means overlook the influence of the renaissance, of the classical revival, upon his poetry. His study of the classical sources from which Spenser embellished his plan [63] is as careful and as suggestive as his study of the mediæval sources; it is only not so strikingly new. His attack on Scaliger, who subordinated a comparative method to the demonstration of *a priori* conclusions, shows that he was a sounder classicist than that

[60] II, pp. 78-81. ' Spenser expressly denominates his most exquisite groupe of allegorical figures, the *Maske of Cupid*. Thus, without recurring to conjecture, his own words evidently demonstrate that he sometimes had representations of this sort in his eye.'

[61] II, pp. 93-103. Beginning with Adam Davy and the author of *Piers Plowman*. Like Spence, Warton recognized in Sackville's *Induction* the nearest approach to Spenser, and a probable source of influence upon him.

[62] II, p. 92.   [63] I, pp. 92-156.

pseudo-classical leader.   Scaliger, he said, more than once 'betrayed his ignorance of the nature of ancient poetry'; [64] he 'had no notion of simple and genuine beauty; nor had ever considered the manners and customs which prevailed in early times.' [65]   Warton was a true classicist in his admiration for Homer and Aristotle, and in his recognition of them as the 'genuine and uncorrupted sources of ancient poetry and ancient criticism'; [66] but, as has been said, he did not make the mistake of supposing them the sources of modern poetry and criticism as well.

Warton shows in this essay an extraordinarily clear recognition of the relation between classical, mediæval and modern literatures, and a corresponding adaptation of criticism to it.   By a wide application of the historical method, he saw that English poetry was the joint product of two principal strains, the ancient or classical, and the mediæval or romantic; and that the poet or critic who neglected either disclaimed half his birthright.   The poetry of Spenser's age, Warton perceived, drew from both sources.   Although the study of the ancient models was renewed, the 'romantic manner of poetical composition introduced and established by the Provencial bards' was not superseded by a 'newer and more legitimate taste of writing.' [67]   And Warton as a critic accepted—as Scaliger would not—the results of his historical study; he admired and desired the characteristic merits of classical poetry, 'justness of thought and design,' 'decorum,' 'uniformity,' [68] he 'so far conformed to the reigning maxims of modern criticism, as . . . to recommend classical propriety'; [69] but he wished them completed and adorned with the peculiar imaginative beauties of the 'dark ages,' those

[64] I, p. 147.   [66] I, p. 1.   [68] I, p. 2.
[65] I, p. 133.   [67] I, p. 2.   [69] II, pp. 324-5.

fictions which ' rouse and invigorate all the powers of
imagination [and] store the fancy with those sublime and
charming images, which true poetry best delights to display.' [70]

The inevitable result of recognizing the relation between
the classical and romantic sources of literature was contempt for pseudo-classicism, for those poets and critics who
rejected the beauties of romance for the less natural per-
fections approved by the classical and French theorists,
who aped the ancients without knowing them and despised
their own romantic ancestry.   The greatest English poets,
Warton perceived, were those who combined both elements
in their poetry; those who rejected either fell short of the
highest rank.   And therefore he perceived the loss to English poetry when, after the decline of romance and allegory,
' a poetry succeeded, in which imagination gave way to
correctness, sublimity of description to delicacy of sentiment, and majestic imagery to conceit and epigram.'   Warton's brief summary of this poetry points out its weakness.
' Poets began now to be more attentive to words, than to
things and objects.   The nicer beauties of happy expression were preferred to the daring strokes of great conception.   Satire, that bane of the sublime, was imported
from France.   The muses were debauched at court; and
polite life, and familiar manners, became their only themes.
The simple dignity of Milton [71] was either entirely neglected, or mistaken for bombast and insipidity, by the
refined readers of a dissolute age, whose taste and morals
were equally vitiated.' [72]

The culminating—perhaps the crowning—glory of War-

---

[70] II, pp. 322-3.

[71] There is a digression on Milton in the *Observations* (I, pp. 335-
353) the prelude to his edition of Milton, 1785 and 1791.

[72] II, pp. 106-8.

ton's first piece of critical writing is his keen delight in the task. Addison had praised and popularized criti-cism,[73] but with reservations; and most people—even until recent times (if indeed the idea has now wholly disappeared from the earth)—would agree with Warton that the 'business of criticism is commonly laborious and dry.' Yet he affirms that his work 'has proved a most agreeable task'; that it has 'more frequently amused than fatigued [his] attention,' and that 'much of the pleasure that Spenser experienced in composing the Fairy Queen, must, in some measure, be shared by his commentator; and the critic, on this occasion, may speak in the words, and with the rapture, of the poet.'

> The wayes through which my weary steppes I guyde
> In this *delightfull land of faerie*,
> Are so exceeding spacious and wyde,
> And sprinkled with such sweet varietie
> Of all that pleasant is to ear or eye,
> That I nigh ravisht with rare thoughts delight,
> My *tedious travel* do forgett thereby:
> And when I gin to feele decay of might,
> It strength to me supplies, and cheares my dulled spright.

Warton's real classicism and his endeavours to carry his contemporaries with him by emphasizing wherever possible his accord with them, blinded them for a time to the strongly revolutionary import of the *Observations on the 'Fairy Queen,'* and the book was well received by pseudo-classical scholars. Its scholarly merits and the impulse it gave to the study of literature were generously praised by Dr. Johnson.[74] This is however scarcely a fair test;

---

[73] In his critical essays in the *Spectator.*

[74] July 16, 1754. 'I now pay you a very honest acknowledgement, for the advancement of the literature of our native country. You have shewn to all, who shall hereafter attempt the study of our ancient authours, the way to success; by directing them to the peru-

for the 'watch-dog of classicism,' although an indifferent
scholar when compared with Warton, had an almost om-
nivorous thirst for knowledge, and although he despised
research for its own sake, his nearest sympathy with the
romantic movement was when its researches tended to
increase the sum of human knowledge. Warburton was
delighted with the *Observations,* and told Warton so.[75]
Walpole complimented the author upon it, though he had
no fondness for Spenser.[76] The reviewer for the *Monthly
Review* [77] showed little critical perception. Although he
discussed the book section by section, he discovered nothing extraordinary in it, nothing but the usual influence of
Ariosto, defects of the language, parallel passage and
learned citation; and he reached the height of inadequacy
when he thus commended Warton's learning: ' Upon the
whole, Mr. *Warton* seems to have studied this author with
much attention, and has obliged us with no bad prelude
for the edition, of which he advises us.[78] His acquaint-

sal of the books which those authours had read. Of this method,
Hughes and men much greater than Hughes, seem never to have
thought. The reason why the authours, which are yet read, of the
sixteenth century, are so little understood, is, that they are read
alone; and no help is borrowed from those who lived with them,
or before them ' (Boswell's *Johnson,* Hill Ed., I, p. 270).

[75] Warburton's *Letters,* No. CLVII, Nov. 30, 1762. *Works,* XIII,
p. 338.

[76] Walpole to Warton, October 30, 1767. Walpole's *Letters,* Toyn-
bee Ed., VII, p. 144.

[77] August, 1754, XI, pp. 112-124.

[78] Probably Upton's Edition of the *Fairy Queen,* which is frequently
referred to in the second edition of the *Observations.* There is ample
evidence in Johnson's letters and Warton's comments upon them, as
well as his own manuscript notes in his copy of Spenser's Works
that he intended a companion work of remarks on the best of Spenser's works, but this made so little progress that it cannot have been
generally known. See Boswell's *Johnson,* I, p. 276, and Warton's
copy of Spenser's works, ed. 1617. This quarto volume, which I have
examined in the British Museum, contains copious notes which sub-

ance with our earliest writers must have qualified him with such a relish of the *Anglo-Saxon* dialect, as few poets, since *Prior,* seem to have imbibed.' A scurrilous anonymous pamphlet, *The Observer Observ'd, or Remarks on a certain curious Tract, intitl'd, 'Observations of the Faiere Queen of Spencer,' by Thomas Warton, A. M.,* etc., which appeared two years after the *Observations,* deserved the harsh treatment it received at the hands of the reviewers.[79] The immediate results on the side of Spenserian criticism were not striking. Two editions of the *Fairy Queen,* by John Upton and Ralph Church, appeared in 1758. Of these, the first was accused at once of borrowing without acknowledgment from Warton's *Observations;*[80] the second is described as having notes little enlightening;[81] both editors were still measuring Spenser by the ancients.[82]

From this time the Spenserian movement was wholly poetical. Warton's essay put a new seal of critical approval upon the *Fairy Queen* and Spenser's position as the poet's poet was established with the new school. He was no longer regarded judicially as an admirable poet who unfortunately chose inferior models for verse and fable with which to present his moral; he was enthusiastically adopted as an inexhaustible source of poetic inspiration, of imagination, of charming imagery, of rich colour, of elusive mystery, of melodious verse.

---

sequently formed the basis for the *Observations.* The notes continue partly through the shorter poems as well as the *Fairy Queen.* Some of them were evidently made for the second edition, for they contain references to Upton's edition.

[79] *Mon. Rev.,* July, 1756, xv, p. 90. *Crit. Rev.,* May, 1756, I, p. 374.

[80] *An impartial Estimate of the Rev. Mr. Upton's notes on the 'Fairy Queen,'* reviewed in *Crit. Rev.,* VIII, pp. 82 ff.

[81] *Crit. Rev.,* VII, p. 106.

[82] H. E. Cory: *The Critics of Edmund Spenser,* Univ. of California *Pub. in Mod. Phil.* II, 2, pp. 81-182, pp. 149-50.

Although Warton's pseudo-classical contemporaries did not perceive the full significance of his study of Spenser, his general program began to be accepted and followed; and his encouragement of the study of mediæval institutions and literature gave a great impetus to the new romantic movement. His followers were, however, often credited with the originality of their master, and their work was apt to arouse stronger protest from the pseudo-classicists.[83] When Hurd's very romantic *Letters on Chivalry and Romance* appeared, they were credited with having influenced Warton to greater tolerance of romance and chivalry.[84] This unjust conclusion was de-

---

[83] While even Dr. Johnson had only praise for the *Observations*, Joseph Warton's *Essay on Pope*, on the whole a less revolutionary piece of criticism, touched a more sensitive point. He found the essay instructive, and recommended it as a 'just specimen of literary moderation' (Johnson's *Works*, Ed. 1825, v, p. 670). But as an attack on the reputation of the favourite Augustan poet, its drift was evident, and pernicious. This heresy was for him an explanation of Warton's delay in continuing it. 'I suppose he finds himself a little disappointed in not having been able to persuade the world to be of his opinion as to Pope' (Boswell's *Life*, Hill Ed., I, p. 448).

[84] *Crit. Rev.*, XVI, p. 220. It is perfectly evident, however, that the debt does not lie on that side. Hurd's *Letters* and the second edition of the *Observations* appeared in the same year, which would almost conclusively preclude any borrowings from the first for the second. But Warton's first edition, eight years before, had enough of chivalry and romance to kindle a mind in sympathy. Hurd was a less thorough student of the old romances themselves than Warton was. He seems to have known them through Sainte Palaye's *Mémoires sur l'Ancienne Chevalerie* (1750-81); for he said 'Not that I shall make a merit with you in having perused these barbarous volumes myself. . . . Thanks to the curios'ty of certain painful collectors, this knowledge may be obtained at a cheaper rate. And I think it sufficient to refer you to a learned and very elaborate memoir of a *French* writer' (*Letters on Chivalry and Romance*. Letter IV, Hurd's *Works*, ed. 1811, IV, p. 260). Warton also new this French work (Ste. Pelaye's at least) and quoted from it, *Observations*, I, p. 76, and frequently in his *History of English Poetry*.

rived no doubt from the tone of greater confidence that
Hurd was able to assume. Following both the Wartons,
Hurd sharpened the distinction between the prevailing
pseudo-classical school of poetry and what he called the
Gothic; insisted upon the independence of its standards;
and even maintained the superiority of its subjects.[85] In
all this however he made no real departure from Warton,
the difference being one of emphasis; Hurd gave an important impetus to the movement his master had begun.
But with all his modernity, his admiration for the growing
school of imaginative poets, he lacked Warton's faith in his
school; he had no forward view, but looked back on the
past with regret, and toward the future without hope.[86]

On the side of pure literary criticism Warton's first and
most important follower was his elder brother, Joseph,
whose *Essay on Pope* was a further application of his
critical theories to the reigning favourite. This very
remarkable book was the first extensive and serious attack
upon Pope's supremacy as a poet, and it is credited with
two very important contributions to the romantic movement: the overthrow of Pope and his school; and the substitution of new models, Spenser, Shakespeare, Milton,

---

[85] ' May there not be something in the *Gothic* Romances peculiarly
suited to the views of a genius, and to the ends of poetry?' (Hurd,
IV, p. 239). 'Under this idea than of a *Gothic*, not classical poem,
the *Fairy Queen* is to be read and criticized' (IV, p. 292). 'So far as
the heroic and *Gothic* manners are the same, the pictures of each
. . . must be equally entertaining. But I go further, and maintain
that the circumstances, in which they differ, are clearly to the advantage of the *Gothic* designers . . . could Homer have seen . . . the
manners of the feudal ages, I make no doubt but he would certainly
have preferred the latter,' because of '*the improved gallantry of the
Gothic Knights* and the *superior solemnity of their superstitions*'
(IV, p. 280).

[86] Hurd's *Letters*, IV, p. 350.

and the modern school; [87] it contained the first explicit statement of the new poetic theories.[88]

Warton's *Observations on the 'Fairy Queen'* thus wrought so great and so salutary a change in literary criticism that it is practically impossible to exaggerate its importance. Here first the historical method was appreciated and extensively employed. Here first the pseudo-classicism of the age of Pope was exposed. Here first is maintained a nice and difficult balance between classical and romantic criticism: without underestimating the influence of classical literature upon the development of English poetry, Warton first insisted that due attention be paid the

---

[87] Joseph Warton placed Spenser, Shakespeare, Milton, ' our only three sublime and pathetic poets ' in the first class, at the head of English poets. The object of the essay was to determine Pope's place in the list. ' I revere the memory of POPE,' he said, ' I respect and honour his abilities; but I do not think him at the head of his profession. In other words, in that species of poetry wherein POPE excelled, he is superior to all mankind: and I only say, that this species of poetry is not the most excellent one of the art ' (*Dedication* i-ii). ' The sublime and pathetic are the two chief nerves of all genuine poetry. What is there transcendently sublime or pathetic in POPE?' (*Ded.* vi). After a careful examination of all Pope's works Joseph Warton assigned him the highest place in the second class, below Milton and above Dryden. He was given a place above other modern English poets because of the ' excellencies of his works *in general,* and *taken all together;* for there are *parts* and *passages* in other modern authors, in Young and in Thomson, for instance, equal to any of POPE, and he has written nothing in a strain so truly sublime, as the B*ard* of *Gray*' (II, p. 405). References are to the fifth edition, 2 vols., 1806.

[88] The first volume of Joseph Warton's *Essay on Pope* appeared in 1756, two years after the *Observations.* Though its iconoclasm was more apparent, the latter essay made little advance in the way of new theory upon the earlier one, and there is rather more of hedging in the discussion of Pope than in that of Spenser. The greater variety of revolutionary dicta enunciated by the younger brother, and his greater activity in promulgating them, lead us to regard him as the more original thinker of the two.

neglected literature of the Middle Ages, which with quite independent but equally legitimate traditions contributed richly not only to the poetry of Spenser but to all great poetry since. His strength lies in the solidity and the inclusiveness of his critical principles. Without being carried away by romantic enthusiasm to disregard the classics, he saw and accounted for a difference between modern and ancient poetry and adapted his criticism to poetry as he found it instead of trying to conform poetry to rules which were foreign to it. This new criticism exposed the fatal weakness in the prevailing pseudo-classical poetry and criticism; it showed the folly of judging either single poems or national literature as independent and detached, and the necessity of considering them in relation to the national life and literature to which they belong. Thus Warton's freedom from prejudice and preconceived standards, his interest in the human being who writes poetry, and the influences both social and literary which surround him, his—for that day—extraordinary knowledge of all those conditions, enabled him to become the founder of a new school of criticism.

CLARISSA RINAKER.

That Thomas Middleton was the author of the London Lord Mayor's Show for 1623 has long been known; that he was not the sole author no one has suspected. His pamphlet describing the occasion is entitled *The Triumphs of Integrity;* it was printed by Dyce,[1] and from him by Bullen;[2] Dyce does not tell where the pamphlet which he reprints may be found; and I have not been able to discover it in the libraries of the British Museum, the Guildhall, the Society of Antiquaries, or the Bodleian.

There is, however, in the British Museum a pamphlet by Anthony Munday—who wrote several of these triumphs —which seems to indicate that he had a hand in planning the festivities with which Lumley was inaugurated. The title-page reads: The Trivmphs of the Golden Fleece. Performed at the cost and charges of the Auncient and Honourable *Societie* of the *Drapers:* for the enstaulment of their Worthy Brother, Mr. *Martin Lvmley* in the Maioraltie of London. On Wednesday . . . the nine and twentieth day of October 1623. Written by A. Mundy, citizen and Draper of London. London . . . 1623.[3]

---

[1] In his edition of Middleton's Works, v, pp. 305 f.

[2] In his edition of Middleton, VII, pp. 381 f. The title is recorded by Greg, *A List of Masques, Pageants, &c.* (1902) p. 18. For mention of this show, see Fairholt, *Lord Mayor's Pageants* (1843), pt. I, p. 49. Bullen says he has not seen the original of this very rare pamphlet; nor had J. Nichols (writing in the *Gent. Mag.* for August, 1824, p. 117) seen any copy.

[3] Aside from a page and three lines of dedication (addressed to the Drapers and signed " your poore louing Brother, A. Mundy "), this pamphlet consists of four pages of description. I find no suggestion of a pageant—in the strict sense of the word—beyond the *Argo.* Of course the companies in their barges accompanied the Mayor to Westminster, as the custom was.

Munday describes the show on the Thames, when the Lord Mayor made his customary trip by water to take his oath at Westminster. This show included a barge, designed like the *Argo,* with Medea " attended with the faire Queene Irene her daughter, and accompanied with the famous Princes *Jason, Hercules, Telamon, Orpheus, Castor* and P*ollux* all armed with fayre guilt Armours; and bearing Triumphall Lances wreathed about with guilded Laurell. . . . Sixe Tributarie Indian Kings, holding their seuerall dominions of *Medea,* and liuing in vassalage to her: are commaunded by her to rowe the Argoe, all of them. . . . Antickely attired in rich habiliments.

" The Seruice being performed vpon the Water, the like is done on the Land, all the rest of the day following · always attending his honors seruice and for adding the more splendor to the Triumphs Solemnite.

" Whatsoeuer credit or commendation (if any at all) may attend on the Artefull performance of this poore deuise: it belongeth to the Arts-Maisters *Richard Simpson,* and *Nicholas Sotherne,* and freely I giue it to them.

" A. M."

The water-show as described in Middleton's pamphlet does not correspond with that described by Munday; my first impulse, in my attempt to settle the question of the authorship of this show, was to suppose that Munday wrote a plan for the festivities on the water, which had not proved acceptable to the Drapers. In 1617—when the show was written by Middleton—both Dekker and Munday were unsuccessful competitors; we find, in the Grocers' records, the following items:

" Payde and given in benevolence to Anthony Monday, gent[n], for his paynes in drawing a project for this busynesse which was offered to the Comyttee, £5.

" Payde and given to Mr Deckar for the like, £4." [1]

Reference to the records of the Drapers' Company, however, showed that such an assumption would not be justified. The Wardens' Accounts for 1621-2,—the mayoralty of Sir Edward Barkham,—show that Munday assisted Middleton in his show for 1621. We find in these accounts:

Item paid to Mr Thomas Middleton, Garrett Christmas and
Anthony Munday by agreement for makinge and settinge out
of the Pageants and shewes, viz. the one in forme or likenes
of a Mountaine one other of a fountaine with a triple Crowne ⎱cxvli
a third called the tower of Vertue or the brazen tower and the
fourth a chariott drawne with twoe pellited lyons and for all
charges incident to these shewes

Item given and allowed for scarfes, viz. to Mr Middleton⎱ iijli iiijs
and Mr Christmas to each of them xxijs and to Bell xx s⎰

These preparations were for *The Svnne in Aries,* Middleton's show for 1621.[2] In the same accounts for 1622-3, we read:

Sir Martyn Lumley, lord mayor.
Item paid to Mr. Thomas Middleton and Garret Christmas by
agreement for making and setting out of the pageants and shewes
viz. the one in forme or likenes of a mountayne one other a ⎱clli
charriott drawne with twoe Pellited Leyons a Third chaistall
Temple and the fourth a royall canopy of state and for all
chardges incident to those shewes

Item paid Anthony Munday for an argot   xxxvli

---

[1] Reprinted in Heath, *Some Account of the Worshipful Company of Grocers* (2d ed., 1854), p. 413.

[2] This pamphlet, which is in the British Museum, has been reprinted by Dyce, v, pp. 293 f.; Bullen, vii, pp. 335 f.; in *Prog. James,* iv, pp. 724 f. Cf. Greg, p. 17; J. G. Nichols, *London Pageants* (1831), p. 103; J. Nichols, in *Gent. Mag.* for August, 1824, p. 116, and Fairholt, pt. i, p. 48. Cf. Bullen, vii, pp. 341, 346, and 348, for descriptions of the pageants here enumerated. Garrett Christmas was the engineer who had charge of the scenic effects of more than one Lord Mayor's Show planned by Middleton.

Item to Mr Monday & his partener for the like [*i. e.*, "in liewe of his scarfe"] xl^s [1]

The "argot" of the above item is evidently the "Argoe" of the pamphlet in which Munday describes his show. The appropriateness of the *Argo* and the story of the Golden Fleece to the Drapers is too obvious to need comment; suffice it to say that Munday had used it before.[2] It is possible that the similarities which we find in so many of these civic triumphs are due to the fact that certain properties owned by the companies had to be used when one of their number was elected mayor; such a limitation must have hampered the poet, whose genius must have strained more than once at the bonds fastened by Economy.

Middleton's reference to the water-show of 1623 is

---

[1] The "partener" is Mr. Richard Simpson, or Mr. Nicholas Sotherne. This looks as if the poet chosen to write the Show could select the engineer who was to realize his "projects." If there were an honor in having a "scarf" it is comforting to know that Monday received its equivalent in 1623, though it was denied him in 1621.

[2] As early as 1522, when Charles V came to London, the Drapers exhibited "a pagiaunt of the story of Jason and medea wyth the dragon and ij bollys (*bulls*) beryng the goldyn flese, by cause the emperowr is lorde and gever of the tewson (*Toison d'Or*) and hedde & maker of all the knyghtys off the tewson, lyke as the kyng of englonde is of the ordyr of the knyghtys off the garter" Corp. Christi (Cantab.) MS. 298; cf. also on this entry, Stow, *Annals*, p. 516; Hall, pp. 637 f.; Grafton, ii, pp. 322 f. My own *English Pageantry—an Historical Outline*, which is in preparation, will contain a detailed account of this "royal-entry."

In 1615 Munday wrote the show for the inauguration of Sir John Jolles, Draper, as Lord Mayor. (The pamphlet is in the British Museum, Guildhall, and Bodleian; it is reprinted in John Nichols, *Progresses, &c. of James I*, III, pp. 107 f.). In this show a goodly Argo, with Jason, Medea, and the Argonauts appeared on the Thames; the companions of Jason were "seated about him in their several degrees, attired in fair gilt armors." Jason also appeared in the 1621 show; he sat in the "Chariot of Honour." See Bullen, *op. cit.*, VII, pp. 339 f.

8

brief:[1] "After his lordship's return from Westminster, having received some service upon the water by a proper and significant masterpiece of triumph called the Imperial Canopy, being the ancient arms of the Company, an invention neither old nor enforced, the same glorious and apt property, accompanied with four other triumphal pegmes,[2] are, in their convenient stages, planted to honour his lordship's progress through the city." These four are the Mount Royal; a Chariot,—with various famous mayors of London, to whom an allegorical significance has been given, —" drawn by two pelleted lions, being the proper supporters of the Company's arms ";[3] the Crystal Sanctuary; and the " thrice-royal Canopy of State, being the honoured arms of this fraternity, the three Imperial Crowns cast into the form and bigness of a triumphal pageant, with cloud and sunbeams, those beams by enginous art, made often to mount and spread like a golden and glorious canopy over the deified persons that are placed under it, which are eight in number, figuring the eight Beatitudes;[4] to improve which conceit, *Beati pacifici,* being the king's word or motto, is set in fair great letters near the uppermost of the three crowns."[5] The speech, delivered from this pageant, contained no reference to Jason, Medea, or the *Argo.*[6]

---

[1] Bullen's ed., VII, pp. 385 f.

[2] "Movable stage-erections (Gr. πῆγμα, Lat. *pegma*) "—Bullen. The word was a common synonym for *pageant* in the XVII century.

[3] Bullen's *Middleton*, VII, p. 389.

[4] These were personified, and sat in a pageant at Sopers-Lane end, when Queen Elizabeth passed through London before her coronation in January, 1558-9. For an account of this " royal entry," see the pamphlet printed by Richard Tottill, and reprinted in John Nichols, *Progresses, &c., of Queen Elizabeth,* I, pp. 38 f.; and in Edward Arber, *An English Garner,* IV, pp. 217 f.

[5] Bullen, *op. cit.,* VII, pp. 393 f. This may be the " fountaine with a triple Crowne " of the 1621 records, remodelled.

[6] Bullen, VII, pp. 394 f.

It is, of course, possible that, after Middleton's pamphlet had been printed, the *Argo* was substituted for the Canopy which he had intended to put on the river; the fact that this ship had appeared in 1615,—and perhaps in 1621,— would make such a substitution easy.[1] Thirty-five pounds, however, was a big sum to pay for getting the ship ready.

The extracts from the Drapers' records serve to clear up the relation between the two descriptive pamphlets for the Lord Mayor's Show of 1623. It is quite clear that Munday was not—as were he and Dekker in 1617—unsuccessful in his attempts to get his plans for the show accepted. As in 1621, he collaborated with Middleton; the nature of the collaboration is, however, clearer in 1623—for Munday planned the festivities on the water, and Middleton confined himself to those on land. If the latter had intended to show an Imperial Canopy on the Thames, his plans were evidently changed; for it is clear that the *Argo* appeared on the river when the show took place.[2]

ROBERT WITHINGTON.

---

[1] Cf. Middleton's *The Sun in Aries* (the show for 1621—Bullen's ed. VII, pp. 335 f.). The water-show is dismissed with a word— the mayor "received some service upon the water" (p. 339). The first character to greet him on land was Jason, who with Hercules, Alexander, Cæsar, and others, awaited his "most wished arrival," in St. Paul's Churchyard.

[2] Fairholt, *op. cit.*, p. 50, echoes Middleton's descriptive pamphlet, and makes no mention of the *Argo*.

VII.—THE POSITION OF GROUP C IN THE *CANTERBURY TALES*

It has for a long time been generally agreed among Chaucerian scholars that the most serious defect of the Chaucer Society's arrangement of the *Canterbury Tales* is its placing of the *Physician's Tale,* Pardoner's prolog, and *Pardoner's Tale,* which constitute what is generally known as Group C, between the *Nun's Priest's Tale* and the Wife of Bath's prolog. This arrangement has absolutely no MS. authority, for no MS. is known to exist in which Group C either precedes Group D or follows Group B. Nor does Group C contain any references to time or place which make the Chaucer Society's arrangement a probable one. Indeed, the arrangement was adopted for no better reason than to make the tales of the third day not less than those of the second,[1] a reason which we can only characterise as a trivial one.

But altho the *Physician's Tale* and the *Pardoner's Tale* contain, as Furnivall said, " no internal evidence as to their proper place in the work ",[2] the MS. evidence is decisive in indicating at least which tales they shall precede, for the sequence CB[2] (*Pardoner's Tale* followed by *Shipman's Tale* and the rest of Group B) is almost invariable in the MSS. Of the MSS. with regard to which information is accessible, thirty-three contain the tales in this sequence.[3] In addition to these, three MSS. which do not

---

[1] Furnivall, *Temporary Preface*, p. 42; cf. *ibid.*, pp. 24 ff.

[2] *Ibid.*, p. 25.

[3] These MSS. (indicated by means of Miss Hammond's abbreviations, *Chaucer*, pp. 163 ff.) are these: Adds. 5140; Adds. 35286; Egerton 2726; Harley 1758; Harley 7333; Harley 7334; Lansd. 851; Royal 17; Royal 18; Sloane 1685; Sloane 1686; Barlow; Bodl. 414; Bodl.

show the sequence CB^2 contain clear evidence of their derivation from mss. which did have this sequence.[4]   Five other mss. which do not exhibit the sequence CB^2, but which are so confused in their arrangement as not even to preserve the internal integrity of Groups C and B^2,[5] must be entirely disregarded, for it is clear that a ms. of this character is useless as an authority with regard to the order in which these groups shall be arranged.   In opposition to the thirty-three mss. which exhibit the sequence CB^2 we have the testimony of one ms., Arch. Selden B 14, in which the tales are arranged in the order A E^1 D E^2 F^1 B^1 B^2 G C F^2 H I.[6]   Now it is entirely possible that a single ms. might preserve the correct sequence of the *Canterbury Tales* and that all the other mss. might be incorrect in arrangement, for the single ms. might be de-

686; Laud 600; Laud 739; Rawl. poet. 149; Ch. Ch.; Corpus; New; Dd.; Gg.; Ii.; Del.; Dev.; Ellesmere; Hengwrt; Egerton 2863; Egerton 2864; Hodson-Ashb.; Hodson; Lichfield; Paris. The data concerning nearly all of these mss. are given by Miss Hammond, pp. 173 ff., for the most part from her own collations. The order of the tales in Hengwrt is not given by her but must be ascertained from Furnivall's Trial-Tables, *Six-Text Print*, Part I.

[4] Tho the Hatton ms. places E^1 between C and B^2, and the Petworth ms. places the first part of B^2 (Shipman and Prioress) before B^1 with the rest of B^2 after C, the presence in both of the spurious Pardoner-Shipman link shows that the present arrangement is not original but the result of displacement; for the data see Hammond, pp. 184, 200. Ms. Mm divides B^2 into three fragments, one of them following C, but the presence of the spurious Pardoner-Shipman link and the numbers attached to the tales show that the original arrangement was CB^2; for the data see Hammond, pp. 192, 188.

[5] These mss. are Rawl. poet. 223, Trinity 49, Trinity 3, Trinity 15, Northumberland; for the data see Hammond, pp. 186, 189, 193, 199.

[6] Hammond, p. 187. B^1 and B^2 are connected by means of the Man of Law's end-link, which is here converted into a Shipman's prolog. That the Selden ms. is not a trustworthy authority as to arrangement is the opinion of Hammond (*Chaucer*, p. 187), and it was also that of Skeat (*Modern Language Review*, v, pp. 430 ff.).

rived from a superior textual tradition altogether independent of that of the other MSS.   But we cannot accept
the authority of the Selden MS. against that of the other
MSS. unless we assume for it such an origin as I have indicated.   Have we any evidence for making this assumption?
If the Selden MS. is derived from a superior and independent textual tradition, its arrangement ought at least to be
better on the whole than that of the other MSS.   We actually find, however, that the Selden MS. is in no respect
better in its arrangement than others, but that in certain
important particulars it is demonstrably wrong where
other MSS. are right.   It shares with all the other MSS.
the defect of placing the reference to Rochester (B 3116)
after the reference to Sittingbourne (D 847).   It is unquestionably wrong (a) in placing the *Clerk's Tale* (with
its reference to the Wife of Bath in E 1170) before the
Wife of Bath's prolog and tale;[7] (b) in splitting Group
F by placing some 7000 lines of text between the *Squire's
Tale* and the *Franklin's Tale*.   In view of these facts it is
impossible for us to concede any authority whatever to the
Selden MS. when its testimony is opposed to that of all the
other MSS.   Its testimony against the order CB² is therefore of no weight.

Since there is nothing in the text itself that would lead
an editor or scribe to introduce the order CB² if he did
not find it in his original, only one explanation will account satisfactorily for the fact that our MSS. of the *Canterbury Tales,* with all their varieties of arrangement, so
consistently preserve CB² as a solid block of text,—namely, that this part of the *Canterbury Tales* was a solid

---

[7] The separation of the *Merchant's Tale* from the *Clerk's Tale* must
be the result of accidental displacement, for the linking of the two
is complete in the text of the Selden MS., even tho the interposition
of Group D breaks the continuity of Group E.

block of text in those MSS. of Chaucer himself from which our MSS. are derived.[8] In this respect at least, however defective may be their arrangement in other respects, the MSS. must be right, and no arrangement of the tales can be considered a good one which disregards the testimony of the MSS. by breaking up the order CB².

But what position should CB² occupy in relation to other portions of the text? It cannot be placed between Group A and B¹, for this sequence is attested by such an overwhelming weight of MS. evidence that we are obliged to accept it as that of Chaucer's own MSS.[9] Nor can we place CB² between the *Manciple's Tale* and the Parson's prolog, for as to the correctness of the sequence

---

[8] For the alternative hypothesis, that all existing MSS. are derived from a single MS. which was not Chaucer's own and in which the tales were arranged in an order for which he was not responsible, we have not a particle of evidence, and the hypothesis is improbable in itself.

[9] The order AB¹ is found in the following 35 MSS.: Adds. 5140; Adds. 35286; Egerton 2726; Harley 1758; Harley 7333; Harley 7334; Harley 7335; Lansd. 851; Royal 17; Royal 18; Sloane 1685; Sloane 1686; Barlow; Bodl. 414; Bodl. 686; Laud 739; Rawl. poet. 141; Rawl. poet. 149; Rawl. poet. 223; Corpus; New; Dd.; Gg.; Ii.; Trinity 3; Trinity 15; Dev.; Ellesmere; Egerton 2863; Hodson-Ashb.; Hodson; Egerton 2864; Lichfield; Northumberland; Paris. For the data concerning their arrangement see Hammond, pp. 173 ff. It is clear from the state of the links that this was also the order back of MSS. Hatton and Petworth (see Hammond, pp. 184 and 200, and note 4 above); the numbers attached to the tales in MS. Mm show that this MS. also was derived from one having the order AB¹ (see Hammond, p. 192). Mss. Laud 600, Ch. Ch., Del., Hengwrt, and Holkham do not have the order AB¹, but place B¹ elsewhere, always in some position which cannot possibly be correct and not the same in any two MSS. See Hammond, pp. 185, 188, 195, 196, 198. Ms. Trinity 49 places B¹ in still a different position, between the *Pardoner's Tale* and a fragment of B² (see Hammond, p. 189), but the state of its links has never been ascertained and it is therefore not possible to say what may have been the arrangement of the MS. from which it was derived. MS. Selden and its arrangement have already been discussed.

HI there can be no question at all; not only is it that of virtually all the MSS., but the two so-called groups are inseparably linked together by the opening line of the Parson's prolog:

> By that the maunciple hadde his tale al ended.[10]

Finally, it is impossible to break up DEF by placing CB^2 between D and E or between E and F, for from the evidence of the text itself as well as from the evidence of the MSS. it is certain that the arrangement DEF represents Chaucer's maturest accomplishment with regard to this part of the text.[11] We have therefore to choose one of three positions for CB^2: (1) between B^1 and D;[12]

---

[10] Of the MSS. which contain both groups, all but five have them in the order HI. These MSS., Adds. 35286, Rawl. poet 223, Ch. Ch., Trinity 3, Hengwrt, have different arrangements, of which all must be wrong and none is found in more than one MS. For the data see Hammond, pp. 173, 186, 188, 193, and the Trial-Tables.

[11] For the internal evidence see Kittredge's article, *Chaucer's Discussion of Marriage, Modern Philology*, IX, pp. 435 ff. The MS. evidence is too complex to be stated here. In general it may be said that all the MSS. which have all of D E F either (1) present the groups as a solid block of text, arranged in the order in which I have named them; or (2) present all of the material of these groups as a solid block of Text, but with various misarrangements of the members of which the groups are composed; or (3) present as a solid block of text the great bulk of the material, but with various mismanagements of the members of the groups and with one member separated altogether from its fellows by the interposition of other sections of text. Of (1) an example is the Ellesmere MS., of (2) an example is Harley 7333, and of (3) an example is the Hatton MS. Two MSS. Ch. Ch. and Hengwrt, break up D E F to a greater extent than MSS. of the third class; for the arrangement of these see Hammond, p. 188 and the Trial-Tables. In MSS. Adds. 35286, Harley 7335, and Laud 600 the arrangement of the text resembles that of the MSS. of the first class but is not identical with it; see Hammond, pp. 173, 179, 185.

[12] To place D E F between G and H would be against the clear evidence of the MSS., for (except in MS. Selden) the only group which ever breaks the sequence G H is CB^2.

(2) between F and G; (3) between G and H. The MSS. furnish no decisive evidence to guide us in choosing between these three positions, for they are divided between the arrangements CB^2G and CB^2H.[13] The question of the best position for CB^2, however, is not exactly of the same nature as the question of the best position for Group C alone.   Group C, as we observed, contains no internal evidence to show what ought to be its position in relation to the rest of the tales.   We have only the evidence of the MSS., and that evidence is so unanimous that we cannot hesitate to accept it as conclusive.   But the testimony of the MSS. is not conclusive with regard to the position of CB^2; moreover, when CB^2 is accepted as a solid block of text we have as a guide internal evidence which is not available as long as we fail to recognise that CB^2 is virtually a single group.   Now if we take into account this internal evidence, there can be no doubt as to which is the best position for CB^2.   If we place it between F and G, the Summoner's reference in D 847 to Sittingbourne, which is 41 miles from London, will precede the Host's reference in B 3116 to Rochester, which is only 30 miles from London.   If we place CB^2 between G and H, the reference to Rochester will occur between Chaucer's reference in G 556 to Boughton, which is 50 miles from London, and his reference in H 2 to Bob-up-and-down, which is between Boughton and Canterbury.[14]   If, however, we place CB^2 between B^1 and D, the references to Deptford,[15] Rochester, Sittingbourne, Boughton, and Bob-up-and-down occur

[13] For the data see Hammond, pp. 173 ff. and the Trial-Tables.

[14] The exact location of Bob-up-and-down has never been satisfactorily determined, but since Group G certainly precedes Group HI Bob-up-and-down must have been farther along the road to Canterbury than Boughton.

[15] A 3906.

in the text in the same order as that in which the places succeed each other along the road. These references are not so numerous that it would have been difficult for Chaucer to keep track of them, and it seems reasonable to assume that he intended them to occur in the right order. The inference is therefore a justifiable one that Chaucer referred to Rochester in the Monk's prolog and to Sittingbourne in the Wife of Bath's prolog because he intended that the Monk should precede the Wife of Bath.

If we accept this internal evidence as supplementary to the external evidence of the MSS., we must conclude that the best arrangement of the *Canterbury Tales* is A B¹ C B² D E F G H I.[16] Tho it is not known to exist in

---

[16] That is, assuming that we are justified in arranging the *Canterbury Tales* at all. Skeat in his later years was of the opinion that we are not, but that the sole duty of the editor with regard to the arrangement of the tales is to ascertain precisely the order in which Chaucer left them and print them in that order (*The Eight-Text Edition of the Canterbury Tales*, pp. 35 f.). He accordingly recommended to future editors the course of printing the tales in what is virtually the order of MS. Harley 7334 (*Modern Language Review*, v, p. 434). Scholars who do not share Skeat's belief that Harley 7334 "gives the best and latest authoritative arrangement of the tales" (*The Eight-Text Edition of the Canterbury Tales*, p. 35), might, if they wished to follow this principle, print the tales in the order in which they occur in some other MS. The principle, tho a perfectly defensible one on abstract grounds, would be difficult to apply in practice and its application could scarcely give any very valuable result. A better principle seems to me to be that which Tatlock states when he says that "if we can devise an arrangement without serious inconsistencies, we are justified in preferring it to a self-contradictory one, and in accepting it as coming near Chaucer's intention, even tho the one be the arrangement of no MS., and the other that of many" (*The Harleian Manuscript 7334 and Revision of the Canterbury Tales*, p. 26). The suggestion that B² should be followed by C is not a new one, for Skeat (*The Eight-Text Edition of the Canterbury Tales*, p. 30) says, "If we are to regard evidence at all, there is no other place for it." Compare also his recommendation in the *Modern Language Review* which is

any MS., it expresses better than any other Chaucer's intentions, so far at least as his intentions were ever expressed in literary form.

SAMUEL MOORE.

cited above. Tatlock says likewise (*The Harleian Manuscript and Revision of the Canterbury Tales,* p. 27) that MS. Harley 7334 in putting C before B² " could not easily be proved wrong." It is interesting to note in this connection that Lawrence (*Modern Philology,* XI, p. 257) argues in favor of the sequence Nun's Priest-Wife of Bath, tho on grounds altogether independent of those set forth in the present paper.

PUBLICATIONS

OF THE

Modern Language Association of America

1915

VOL. XXX, 2   NEW SERIES, VOL. XXIII, 2

VIII.—THE VOGUE OF *GUY OF WARWICK* FROM THE CLOSE OF THE MIDDLE AGES TO THE ROMANTIC REVIVAL

Among the questions which still await investigation in the literary history of sixteenth and seventeenth century England, not the least important is that of the survival of the vernacular writings of the Middle Ages. No one can have studied the records of publishing activities during the Tudor and Stuart periods without becoming aware that a considerable number of the romances, tales, poems, chronicles, lives of saints of the fourteenth and fifteenth centuries still continued to circulate, and to find, though probably in ever smaller numbers, appreciative readers. Nor can anyone who has noted this persistence of medieval literature beyond the Middle Ages fail to draw from it inferences not a little damaging to our current conceptions of sixteenth and seventeenth century taste. As yet, however, no historian of literature has dealt with the problem in a systematic or detailed way—no one has tried to set clearly before us precisely which works, out of the total body of medieval writings, remained in vogue, how

125

long the popularity of each of them lasted, how far they
were modified in form or content to suit the taste of successive generations, by what sort of " public " they were read,
and of what nature was the influence which they exercised
upon the newer writers. Some day perhaps we shall have
such a history of the survival of medieval literature in
early modern England. In the meantime, as a preliminary treatment of a single phase of the subject, the present study of *Guy of Warwick* may not be without its
interest. It proposes to trace from the days of the early
printers to the close of the eighteenth century the fortunes
of but one—though perhaps the most typical one—of the
many romances whose popularity survived the Middle
Ages.[1]

I

In the little library of English books collected by John
Paston, probably during the reign of Edward IV, were
two romances dealing with Guy of Warwick—" Guy Earl
of Warwyk " and " Guy and Colbronde." [2] Paston was

[1] The later history of the legend of Guy of Warwick has received
comparatively little attention from scholars. Zupitza (" Zur Literaturgeschichte des Guy von Warwick," in *Sitzungsberichte der phil.-
hist. Classe der kais. Akademie*, Bd. 74, Vienna, 1873, pp. 623-668)
discusses a few of the more important texts, but without exhausting
the subject. Some details are also to be found in *Bishop Percy's
Folio Manuscript*, II (1867), pp. 511, 514, 515, 517; in *The Dictionary of National Biography*, art. " Guy of Warwick "; and in A. C. L.
Brown, " The Source of a Guy of Warwick Chap-Book " (*The Journal
of Germanic Philology*, III, 1900, pp. 14-23). A bibliography of the
prose versions of the story is given by Arundell Esdaile, *A List of
English Tales and Prose Romances printed before 1740* (1912), pp.
233-234.

[2] *The Inventory off Englysshe Boks off John Paston*, in *The Paston
Letters*, ed. Gairdner, III (1910), p. 300. On the date see Gairdner's
note, *ibid*.

in many respects a typical member of the English reading public of the time; and the favor which he thus displayed toward the story of Guy was characteristic of the attitude of readers generally in the latter years of the fifteenth century. No legend, it would seem, of all those then in circulation was more widely familiar than that which told how the son of the steward of Warwick, in order to win the hand of Phelis, the daughter of his Earl, had twice gone to seek honor and adventures on the Continent; how, finally successful in his ambition and married to his lady, he had left her almost immediately after and had set out for the Holy Land in the guise of a palmer, to expiate in the service of God the wrongs he had done in the service of Phelis; and how, learning on his return that England was in the power of the Danes and the King besieged in Winchester, he had slain the Danish champion Colbrond, and then, still unknown to Phelis, had retired to spend his last days in a hermit's cave near Warwick. Of the romance itself there were in existence at least four translations of the French original, one in a twelve line stanza, the other three in couplets.[3] One episode of the story, moreover—the conflict between Guy and Colbrond—was recounted as sober history in several of the leading chronicles,[4] and Lydgate had recently versified it, from the

[3] Zupitza, *The Romance of Guy of Warwick, E. E. T. S.*, E. S., xxvi (1876), pp. v-vii. The poem entitled *Guy & Colebrande* in Bishop Percy's folio manuscript (ed. Hales and Furnivall, ii, 1867, pp. 527-549) may not improbably be of this period. See, on its relations to other versions of the story, Kölbing, in *Germania*, xxxiv (1889), pp. 191-194, and Weyrauch, *Die mittelenglischen fassungen der sage von Guy of Warwick* (1901), pp. 61-65.

[4] Girardus Cornubiensis, *De Gestis Regum Westsaxonum* (cited in *Liber Monasterii de Hyda*, ed. Edwards, Rolls Series, 1866, pp. 118-123); Knighton, *Chronicon de Eventibus Angliae*, b. 1366 (quoted in *Bishop Percy's Folio Manuscript*, ii, pp. 512-513); Rudborne, *Historia Major Wintoniensis*, c. 1454 (*ibid.*, p. 514); Hardyng,

Latin of Girardus Cornubiensis, in a poem written at the request of the Countess of Shrewsbury, who claimed descent from the hero.[5]   Such, indeed, was the popularity of the tale in the late fifteenth century that the owners of the early presses, who almost without exception were content to follow without changing the taste of their public, hastened to print it among the first of the old English romances.

Editions of *Guy* began to appear shortly before 1500. One of them, perhaps the first, issued from the shop of Richard Pynson, who with Wynkyn de Worde shared the bulk of the general English book-trade after the death of Caxton.[6]   The version of Guy's adventures which this edition contained was one already long familiar to the public.   Though abridged in places and slightly modernized in language, it was in all essential respects identical with a version in short couplets composed as early as the fourteenth century, which narrated in considerable detail the whole story of Guy and of Raynburn his son as it

Chronicle, c. 1465 (ed. Ellis, 1812, pp. 210-211) ; Rous, notes on the Earls of Warwick, b. 1491 (*Bishop Percy's Folio Manuscript*, II, pp. 515-516).

[6] " Her nowe begynnyth an abstracte owte the cronycles in latyn made by Gyrade Cornubyence the worthy the cronyculer of Westsexse & translatid into Englishe be lydegate Daun Iohan at the request of Margret Countasse of Shrowesbury lady Talbot ffournyvale & lysle of the lyffe of that moste worthy knyght Guy of Warrewyk of whos blode she is lenyally descendid " (Shirley's rubric, *Harvard MS.*, printed by F. N. Robinson in *Harvard Studies and Notes*, v, 1896, p. 197).   The facts set forth in this rubric serve to fix the date of composition of Lydgate's poem between 1442 and 1468 (Ward, *Catalogue of Romances*, I, 1883, pp. 494-495).   Of the six known manuscripts of the work, two only have been printed: Bodl. MS., Laud 683, by Zupitza, *Zur Literaturgeschichte des Guy von Warwick*, pp. 649-665, and Harvard MS., by Robinson, *l. c.*, pp. 197-220 (with variants from Leyden MS.).

[6] See the list of his publications in *Hand-lists of Early English Printers* (Bibliographical Society, 1896).

had been conceived by the old French poet.[7] For the
greater part of the sixteenth century this remained for
English readers the favorite, if not the only easily accessible, form of the legend. It was several times reprinted:
by Wynkyn de Worde perhaps not long after 1500;[8] by
William Copland, the leading publisher of romances in
the next generation, between 1562 and 1569;[9] and by

[7] Of Pynson's edition, a fragment consisting of sig. L. i and two
following leaves (not " preceding," as they are catalogued) is in the
British Museum (IA. 55533). One page is reproduced in Duff, *Early
English Printing* (1896), Plate xxv, 1. The fragment has no date,
but from the type in which it is printed may be placed between
about 1496 and 1500. Cf. Duff, *l. c.*, pp. 19, 39. Changes in spelling
apart, the text is identical with that of the edition printed by
William Copland (see below, p. 129, note 9) ; the three leaves of the
fragment corresponding to sigs. U. [4], l. 25—X. j. l. 24; Y. ii,
l. 25—Y. iii, l. 24; Y. iii, l. 25—Y [4], l. 24 of the later impression.
The source must therefore have been the same. Now, as Zupitza has
shown (*Zur Literaturgeschichte*, pp. 635-640), Copland's version is
a modernization of a version closely resembling that in B. M.,
Addit. ms. 14408, dating from the fourteenth century. Cf. Ward,
Catalogue of Romances, I, pp. 490-491.

[8] The only sample of this edition which has survived is a fragment
of one leaf preserved among the Douce fragments in the Bodleian
(e 14). It belongs to the portion of the romance describing the
conflict between Guy and Colbrond, a circumstance which has led E.
Gordon Duff, in the Bibliographical Society's *Hand-lists*, Part I
(1895), "Wynkyn de Worde," Part I, p. 3, to catalogue it under
the misleading title of " Guy and Colbrond." It is, strictly speaking, not a fragment of a real edition at all, but merely an " off-
print." This becomes clear on comparison with Copland's edition,
which has, except for a few changes in spelling, exactly the same
text. Thus the recto of the fragment, as bound, corresponds to sig.
Ii. iij. of Copland's reprint; the verso, to sig. Ii. ii.; so that between
the recto and the verso of the leaf a full page of thirty lines of
text is wanting. The value of the fragment as evidence that a
real edition was printed is not, of course, destroyed by this circumstance. The printer is identified as De Worde by the character of
the type. See the manuscript note in the Bodleian copy.

[9] An imperfect copy of this edition, wanting everything before
sig. F. i., is in the British Museum (C. 21. c. 68). It is a black

John Cawood, the royal printer, probably about the same
date.[10]   All these editions—and there were in all likelihood others besides—were rudely printed in black letter;
and at least one of them—Copland's—was furnished with
rough woodcut illustrations of incidents in the story.[11]
Like the editions of all the other metrical romances issued
by the early printers, they were purely commercial ven-
tures, intended to sell cheaply and to reach a general
audience.[12]

letter quarto, poorly printed, and containing a number of woodcuts.
The colophon reads: "Here endeth the Booke of themoste victoryous
Prynce, Guy of Warwick. Imprynted at London in Lothbury, ouer
agaynst Margarits Church by wylliam Copland." The address furnishes an approximate date for the edition; for it is known that
Copland printed here between 1562 and his death in 1568 or 1569.
See Duff, *A Century of the English Book Trade* (1905), p. 33.
Henry Morley's unsupported statement (*Early Prose Romances*,
1889, p. 27) that "the earliest edition [of *Guy*] in English prose
was printed by William Copland" has caused a good deal of confusion. See in particular W. P. Reeves, "The So-Called Prose Version of Guy of Warwick" (*Modern Language Notes*, XI, 1896, cols.
404-408); Alexis F. Lange, *The Gentle Craft. By Thomas Deloney*
(1903), pp. x, xxxiv-xxxv (Dr. Lange is so far deceived by Morley's
words as to quote passages from a chapbook account of Guy first
published in 1706 as the probable source of an episode in Deloney's
Gentle Craft, 1597-1598!); W. L. Cross, *The Development of the
English Novel* (1906), p. 4. No such edition, however, has ever been
shown to exist.

[10] Ames-Herbert, *Typographical Antiquities*, II, p. 798. Cawood
printed from 1546 to 1572 (Duff, *l. c.*, p. 23).

[11] There are four of these in the British Museum copy. Some of
them did duty also in contemporary and later editions of other
works. Cf. Jusserand, *The English Novel in the time of Shakespeare*, Eng. tr. (1899), p. 67 (who reproduces the cut of Guy and
Phelis in the garden), and *Beuis of Hampton* (B. M., C. 57.e.7),
sig. E.

[12] In a list of books which Richard Pynson agreed to furnish to
John Russhe, an itinerant merchant, sometime before 1498, single
copies of "bevys off hampton" (a romance resembling *Guy of
Warwick* in type and format) were valued at 10d; this was one of

And, indeed, there were probably few Englishmen during the first seventy or more years of the century, among those who read at all, who did not read in them the story of the old Saxon hero. Among literary men the romance was known to Skelton,[13] Udall,[14] Puttenham,[15] Drayton,[16] Shakepeare,[17] and doubtless many others. With the mass of readers it remained a sort of popular classic, familiar to them from boyhood,[18] a pleasant tale to beguile the long winter evenings in the country.[19]

The causes of this survival of interest in the romance of *Guy of Warwick* were at least three in number. In the first place, notwithstanding the many social and intellectual changes which characterized the first half of the century, the English people were still, even as late as the

the cheapest books in the lot, which included besides, " bocas off the falle of prynces " (2s), " canterbery Talys" (5s), and " Isoppys fabullys" (3s. 4d). See *The Library*, N. S., x (1909), pp. 126-128.

[13] See Warton, *Observations on the Fairy Queen of Spenser* (ed. 1807), II, pp. 9-12.

[14] *Ralph Roister Doister*, Actus I, Scæna II, ed. C. G. Child (1912), p. 65.

[15] *The Arte of English Poesie* (ed. Smith, *Elizabethan Critical Essays*, II, 1904, pp. 43-44).

[16] *Poly-olbion*, Cantos XII and XIII (Spenser Society reprint, II, 1890, pp. 198-202, 220-221).

[17] Anders, *Shakespeare's Books* (1904), p. 160.

[18] See, for example, Robert Ashley's account of his early reading in his autobiography, B. M., Sloane MS. 2131, fol. 18 (printed by the present writer in *Modern Philology*, XI, 1913, p. 271). Ashley was born in 1565.

[19] . . . in winter nights [in the country] we vse certaine Christmas games very propper, & of much agilitie; wee want not also pleasant mad headed knaues, yt bee properly learned, and will reade in diuerse pleasant bookes and good Authors: As Sir Guy of Warwicke, ye foure Sonnes of Amon, the Ship of Fooles, the Budget of Demaundes, the Hundreth merry Tales, the Booke of Ryddles, and many other excellent writers both witty and pleasaunt " (*The English Courtier and the Cŭtrey-gentleman*, 1579, in Hazlitt, *Inedited Tracts*, 1868, p. 56).

accession of Elizabeth, more than half medieval in their literary tastes. The movement of the Renaissance, which after two generations of silent growth had come into a temporary prominence in the early years of Henry VIII, was as yet confined almost exclusively to the limited environment of the Universities and the Court. Moreover, the reforms which its leaders had in view were not literary at all in the strict sense of the word, but moral and religious.[20] It was but natural, then, that the general public of Englishmen should remain attached to the intellectual habits and interests of the Middle Ages; all the more perhaps as the selection of their reading was to a large extent in the hands of persons in no way sympathetic with the ideals of humanists, English or Continental. The early English printers, unlike many of their contemporaries in France and Italy, were men of but limited culture, and that culture was thoroughly medieval in character. Thus the writers and works which appear to have been most in the thoughts of Caxton were Saint Bernard, the *Golden Legend,* Boethius, Chaucer, Lydgate, and the French prose romances of chivalry. In short, not only did there continue to be an extensive public interested in the literature of the Middle Ages, but the printers whose policy it was to satisfy the demands of this public were themselves conservatives in matters of taste. The result was that a considerable proportion of the books which issued from the early presses of Westminster and London were books which had been written in the thirteenth, fourteenth, or fifteenth centuries.

Among these the romances naturally occupied a promi-

---

[20] On the general character of the early English Renaissance see A. Feuillerat, *John Lyly* (1910), pp. 45-49, and G. L. Hamilton, in *Modern Language Notes,* xx (1905), pp. 57-58.

nent place.[21]   For no other class of medieval writings, indeed, was the demand so strong as for the old stories of knightly adventure and courtly love.   In supplying this demand the printers drew from two sources: the English metrical romances, the work mainly of the fourteenth and early fifteenth centuries, and the newer prose romances of fifteenth-century France.   The movement of importation began first: between 1474 and 1491, Caxton brought out English editions of no fewer than eight romances of the type then popular across the Channel—*The Recuyell of the Historyes of Troye* (printed abroad, but with English readers quite definitely in view),[22] *The History of Jason, Le Morte Darthur* (the only one not translated by Caxton himself), *Charles the Great, Paris and Vienne, Blanchardine and Eglantine, The Four Sons of Aymon,* and *Eneydos.*   Wynkyn de Worde carried on and extended this work of his " Master."   Not only did he reprint the more important of Caxton's romances, but, in consequence either of his own interest or of his desire to please his patrons and public, he put forth a number of new translations.   Among them were *Helias, Knight of the Swan, Robert the Devil, Ponthus and Sidone, The Seven Wise Masters,* and, probably, *Huon of Bordeaux* and *Valentine and Orson.*   With later publishers interest in the medieval French tales took the form rather of new editions of romances translated in the preceding generation than of fresh versions or adaptations.   Of these publishers

[21] The present paragraph and the pages which follow on the survival of the medieval romances in the sixteenth century are a summary of material gathered for my doctorate thesis at the University of Pennsylvania in 1911. The full results of my study I hope to publish shortly.

[22] See Caxton's statement in the Prologue of Book I, ed. Sommer, I (1894), p. 4.

the most important was William Copland, whose activity
fell between about 1546 and 1569.   He appears to have
confined his efforts almost entirely to reprinting the romances issued by his predecessors; and his editions of
Le Morte Darthur, The Four Sons of Aymon, and *The
Recuyell of the Historyes of Troye* did good service in
making the old French stories accessible to the public of
early Elizabethan England.   But while the printers were
thus helping to bring into the language a large number
of medieval prose romances hitherto little known in England, they were not neglecting the older English metrical
versions.   From the shop of Wynkyn de Worde romances
of the type of *Bevis of Hampton, Generides, Ipomydon,
Richard Cœur de Lion, Sir Degore, Sir Eglamour, Sir
Triamour,* and *The Squire of Low Degree*—all old favor-
ites with story-loving Englishmen—issued perhaps more
frequently than did the newer importations from France.
And, like the French romances, their popularity lasted
well into the days of Queen Elizabeth: between the forties
and the seventies of the century they were nearly all reprinted by William Copland.   Now, while Englishmen
were buying and reading the stories of Arthur and Charlemagne, Robert the Devil, Sir Bevis, Sir Degore, and
numerous worthies more, it was not to be expected that
they should forget the equally celebrated story of Sir Guy.
As one of the most typical of medieval heroes, he was
bound to share the vogue of his fellow knights.

But with many readers the romance owed its popularity
to still other circumstances than the general survival of
interest in the fiction of the Middle Ages.   For one thing,
Guy was not merely a good knight, the conqueror of treacherous Dukes, Saracens, wild boars, dragons, and giants:
he was also a national hero.   The popular chroniclers of
the time—Fabyan, Grafton, Holinshed, Stow—told how

in the reign of King Athelstan he had fought to free his country from a foreign invader.[23] His combat with Colbrond, as they narrated it, was not romance at all, but a fully accredited part of that glorious past of which all Englishmen were coming to be so proud. Local patriotism, too, doubtless played a part in keeping the romance alive. The people of the Midland county in which the story was localized had not forgotten that Guy had been one of the most celebrated of their Earls.[24] His sword and armor were preserved in Warwick Castle in the charge of a custodian appointed by royal patent;[25] and nearby,

[23] Fabyan, *The New Chronicles of England and France*, 1516, and many later editions (repr. Henry Ellis, 1811), pp. 183-185 (Fabyan's account is admittedly based upon Lydgate's poem, one stanza of which is quoted); Grafton, *A Chronicle at Large*, 1569 (repr. 1809), I, pp. 118-119 (Grafton's narrative is taken word for word from Fabyan); Holinshed, *The Historie of England*, 1577, Book VI, ch. xx (repr. 1807), I, p. 688; Stow, *A Summarie of the Chronicles of England . . . vnto this present yeare of Christ 1575* (London, Richard Tottle and Henry Binneman, n. d.), pp. 75-76.

[24] On August 12, 1572, in an oration before Elizabeth, the recorder of Warwick made the following reference to Guy: " But to returne to the auncient estate of this towne of Warwik, wee reade in olde writings and autenticall cronycles the same to have bene a citie or wallid towne in the tyme of the Brytayns, callid then Carwar; and afterwards, in the tyme of the Saxons, that name was chaungid into 'Warwik. We reade also of noble earles of the same, namely of one Guido or Guye, who being baron of Wallingford, became earle of Warwik by mariage of the ladie Felixe, the sole doughter and heyre of that house in the tyme of king Athelston, who rayned over this lande about the yere of our Lorde God 933." " The Black Book of Warwick," in Nichols's *Bibliotheca Topographica Britannica*, No. XVII (1783), pp. 17-18.

[25] William Hoggeson, yeoman of the buttery of the Archbishop of Canterbury, was appointed, on 20 June 1509, "keeper of Guy of Warwick's sword in Warwick Castle," in place of William Lowman (Brewer, *Letters and Papers*, I, No. 202). In May 1531 John Thoroughgood was associated with Hoggeson in the keepership (*Ibid.*, v, No. 278/19). On 14 March 1542, after Thoroughgood's death, the

at Guyscliffe, a chapel and a statue erected early in the fifteenth century [26] marked the spot where, as tradition told, Guy had withdrawn after his victory over the Danish champion at Winchester. The existence of these relics, visited as they were by travelers from other sections of the country,[27] must have attracted numerous readers to the romance.

Not all readers, however, were equally friendly. As the century grew older, the surviving medieval romances became the object of increasingly severe attacks from several different groups of writers: humanists and educational reformers, Puritanical moralists, and students and men of letters imbued with the literary culture of the Renaissance.[28] Much of this criticism was directed specifically against *Guy of Warwick*. What was perhaps the earliest attack came from the world of the humanists: it occurred in a translation of one of the works of the Spanish scholar Juan Luis Vives. In 1523 Vives published a treatise in Latin on the education of women, entitled *De Institutione feminae christianae,* in which he gave particular consideration to the question of what women should read.

office passed to Edward Cresswell, to be held during his life (Rymer, *Foedera*, 2nd ed., XIV, London, 1728, p. 745).

[26] Ward, *Catalogue of Romances*, I, p. 482; *Bishop Percy's Folio Manuscript*, II, p. 515.

[27] Leland, *Itinerary*, c. 1535-1543 (ed. Lucy Toulmin Smith, II, 1908, pp. 45-46); Johannes Caius, *De Rariorum Animalium . . . Historia*, 1570 (in *The Works of John Caius, M.D.*, Cambridge, 1912, p. 42); Camden, *Britannia*, 1586 (tr. Edmund Gibson, London, 1695, cols. 502, 506).

[28] For examples of these three kinds of criticism of the romances see, besides the passages cited in the text, Ascham, *The Scholemaster*, 1570, *English Works*, ed. Wright (1904), pp. 230-231; Gosson, *Playes Confuted in fiue Actions*, 1582, ed. Hazlitt, *The English Drama and Stage* (1869), pp. 188-189; Jonson, *An Execration upon Vulcan*, c. 1619-1629, *Works*, ed. Gifford-Cunningham, III (1872), p. 320.

Under no conditions, he maintained, should they be allowed to soil their minds with such pestiferous books as "in Spain, Amadis, Esplandian, Florisanda, Tirante, Tristan, . . . Celestina; in France, Lancelot of the Lake, Paris and Vienna, Ponthus and Sidonia, . . . Melusine; in Flanders, Floris and Blanchefleur, Leonella, . . . Pyramus and Thisbe." [29] Although he evidently wrote with a view to English as well as Continental readers—he dedicated his treatise to Queen Catherine—he omitted to give any English examples. During the same year in which *De Institutione* first appeared, Vives came to Oxford.[30] His fame, already great among scholars, soon spread to the Court; [31] he won the favor of the King and Queen, who gave him the office of Latin tutor to the Princess Mary; [32] and, as a result no doubt of his personal success, his writings came more and more into demand with the educated English public. None seems to have been more popular than *De Institutione*. Sometime before 1535, a certain Richard Hyrde undertook a translation of this work, which was published about 1540.[33] Into the passage

[29] " Hoc ergo curare leges & magistratus congruit. Tum et de pestiferis libris, cuiusmodi sunt in Hispania Amadisus, Splandianus, Florisandus, Tirantus, Tristranus: quarum ineptiarum nullus est finis, quotidie prodeunt nouae: Cœlestina laena, nequitiarum parens, carcer amorum. In Gallia Lancilotus a lacu, Paris et Vienna, Ponthus & Sydonia, Petrus Prouincialis & Maguelona, Melusina, domina inexorabilis: in hac Belgica Florius, & Albus flos, Leonella, & Cana morus, Curias & Floretta, Pyramus & Thisbe. . . ." *Opera* (Basle, 1555), II, p. 658. The preface of *De Institutione* bears the date " Brvgis, nonis Aprilis. 1523 " (*ibid.*, II, p. 650).

[30] On Vives's stay in England see Foster Watson, *Vives on Education* (1913), pp. lxxiii-lxxxii.

[31] See the documents analysed in *Letters and Papers*, III, Nos. 838, 2052; IV, No. 941.

[32] *Ibid.*, IV, No. 4990.

[33] *A very frutefull and pleasant boke called the Instructiõ of a Christen womã*. . . . London, Thomas Berthelet, n. d. (B. M., G.

condemning the reading of romances, Hyrde introduced one significant change: to the list of forbidden stories given by Vives he added the names of several romances especially popular in England: "Parthenope, Genarides, Hippomadon, William and Melyour, Libius and Arthur, Guye, Beuis, and many other."[34] Hyrde's translation enjoyed not a little fame during the remainder of the sixteenth century; it was reprinted in 1541, again in 1557, and finally in 1592.[35] Thus Vives's authority as a guide in education, which long remained high among the more serious sort of readers,[36] continued to tell against *Guy of Warwick.*

From about 1570 onwards condemnations of the romance for its immorality became more numerous. In 1572 appeared a little book entitled *A bryefe and necessary Catechisme or instruction, very needfull to be knowne of al Housholders.* The author was Edward Dering, a learned clergyman of decided Puritanical leanings.[37] In his preface addressed " To the Christian Reader " Dering included *Guy of Warwick* among books of " childish fol-

---

11884). The translation seems to have been completed before the death of Sir Thomas More in 1535. See Watson, *l. c.*, p. lxxvi.

[34] " And this [the singing of ribald songs] the lawes ought to take hede of; and of those vngracious bokes, suche as be in my countre in Spayn Amadise, Florisande, Triante, Tristane, and Celestina ye baude mother of noughtynes. In France Lancilot du Lake, Paris and Vienna, Ponthus and Sidonia, & Melucyne. In Flanders, Flori and Whit flowre, Leonel and Canamour, Curias and Floret, Pyramus and Thysbe. In Englande, Parthenope, Genarides, Hippomadon, William and Melyour, Libius and Arthur, Guye, Beuis, and many other . . . what delyte can be in those thynges. . . . (*The Instructiõ of a Christen womã,* sig. E. iiij—F).

[35] Bonilla y San Martin, *Luis Vives y la Filosofia del Renacimiento* (Madrid, 1903), pp. 766-767.

[36] Watson, *l. c.,* pp. xxx-xiii.

[37] Mullinger in *D. N. B.,* art. " Dering."

lye," the " spiritual enchauntmentes " of the generations
which preceded the Reformation.[38]   His words must have
been read by many during the later years of the century,
for the *Bryefe and necessary Catechisme* was reprinted several times, reaching a fourth edition in 1606.[39]   In the
meantime other critics of *Guy* had come forward.   In
1598, in a passage admittedly inspired by François de la
Noue's recent condemnation of *Amadis de Gaule,*[40] Francis Meres drew up a catalogue of twenty-four romances
which in his estimation were " hurtfull to youth ": *Guy*
stood second in the list.[41]   Five years later, in a pamphlet called *Vertues Common-wealth,* Henry Crosse was even
more outspoken in his disapproval.   " If," he declared,
speaking of the popular literature of the time, " if a view
be had of these editions, the Court of *Venus,* the Pallace
of Pleasure, *Guy* of *Warwick, Libbius* and *Arthur, Beuis*
of *Hampton,* the wise men of *Goatam, Scoggins* Ieasts,
Fortunatus, and those new delights that haue succceded
these, and are now extant, too tedious to recken vp: what
may we thinke? but that the floudgates of all impietie are
drawne vp, to bring a vniuersall deluge ouer all holy and
godly conuersation: for there can be no greater meanes to
affright the mind from honestie, then these pedling bookes,
which haue filled such great volumes, and blotted so much
paper, theyr sweete songs and wanton tales do rauish and
set on fire the young vntempered affections, to practice that

[38] Dering's preface is printed in *Shakespeare-Jahrbuch,* XL (1904),
pp. 228-229.   It is dated 22 April 1572.

[39] See *Catalogue of Books in the Library of the British Museum
. . . to the year 1640,* I (1884), pp. 458, 470.

[40] In *Discours Politiques et Militaires,* 1587; translated into English by E. A., 1587.   The passage to which Meres refers is on pages
87-95 of the English edition.

[41] *Palladis Tamia,* Wits Treasury, ed. Smith, *Elizabethan Critical
Essays,* II, pp. 308-309.

whereof they doo intreate." [42] Not long after this came
an equally severe criticism from a somewhat different
quarter. The author of *Lingua,* a play written primarily
for an academic audience, but long a favorite with the
general reading public, put into the mouth of Mendacio, a
page, this characteristic boast: " For the ' Mirror of
Knighthood,' ' Bevis of Southampton,' ' Palmerin of England,' ' Amadis of Gaul,' ' Huon of Bordeaux,' ' Sir Guy
of Warwick,' . . . and a thousand such exquisite monu-
ments as these, no doubt but they breathe in my breath up
and down." And Appetitus, another character, was made
to answer: " Downwards, I'll swear, for there's stinking
lies in them." [43]

Not all of the criticism of the romances, however, was
directed against their supposed immorality. Much of it,
particularly that which concerned the older metrical romances, was purely literary in character. To many of the
critics and men of letters of the later sixteenth century,
who had no ethical prepossessions against imaginative literature, the verse, the language, the sentiments of the old
stories seemed crude and antiquated in the extreme, quite
incapable of giving pleasure to readers accustomed to the
new literature of Renaissance Italy or Elizabethan England. What Thomas Nashe wrote of *Bevis of Hampton*
no doubt represented the judgment of many of the younger

---

[42] See the reprint by Grosart (1878), pp. 102-103.

[43] Dodsley's *Old English Plays,* ed. Hazlitt, IX (1874), pp. 365-
366. *Lingua* was first printed in 1607; three other editions appeared before 1632 (Greg, *A List of English Plays,* 1900, p. 134). For
other contemporary expressions of skepticism regarding the truth
of the story of Guy, see Camden, *Britannia,* 1586 (tr. Gibson, 1695),
col. 507; Robert Ashley's autobiography (*Modern Philology,* XI, p.
271); and John Lane, *The corrected historie of Sir Guy, Earle of
Warwick,* 1621, Prologue to the Reader (In *Bishop Percy's Folio
Manuscript,* II, p. 524).

wits at the close of the century;[44] and few of them but must have included *Guy of Warwick*—a romance of precisely the same type as *Bevis*—in the condemnation. "Who is it," Nashe wrote in *The Anatomie of Absurditie* (1589) " that reading Beuis of Hampton, can forbeare laughing, if he marke what scambling shyft he makes to ende his verses a like?   I will propound three or foure payre by the way for the Readers recreation.

> *The Porter said, by my snout,*
> *It was Sir Beuis that I let out.*

or this,

> *He smote his sonne on the breast,*
> *That he neuer after spoke with Clark nor Priest.*

or this,

> *This almes by my crowne,*
> *Giues she for Beuis of South-hamptoune.*

or this,

> *Some lost a nose, some a lip,*
> *And the King of Scots hath a ship.*

But I let these passe as worne out absurdities." [45]

When Nashe wrote these words, nearly a century had elapsed since the metrical romance of *Guy of Warwick* had first been printed by Pynson and Wynkyn de Worde. Its life was now fast drawing to a close. Copies of the early Elizabethan editions, it is true, doubtless remained in circulation, and found readers, though probably in no great numbers; [46] but there was no longer a demand for new impressions; and after about 1575 the metrical version apparently ceased to be reprinted. For this disap-

[44] Cf. Melbancke, *Philotimus* (1583), sig. L2: " This followes as well as that in Beuis of Hampton: Some lost a nose, and some their lip, and the King of Scots hath a ship."

[45] *The Works of Thomas Nashe*, ed. McKerrow, I, (1904), p. 26. Cf. *ibid.*, IV (1908), p. 26.

[46] See below, pp. 151, 153, 158-160, 164-165.

2

pearance of a poem which during so many generations
had been a special favorite with English readers, the attacks of the moralists and critics from Vives on were no
doubt in part responsible.   But only in part: a still more
potent factor was probably the growing strangeness of the
language in which the romance was written, a language
still, in spite of successive " modernizations," predomi-
nantly medieval in character.   It is significant that while,
with the single exception of *Bevis of Hampton,* all of the
other surviving metrical romances disappeared from circulation at about the same time as *Guy,* many of the more
recently translated prose romances, such as *Arthur, Huon
of Bordeaux, Valentine and Orson,* and the like, some of
which had been as severely handled by the critics and
moralists as *Guy,* continued to be reprinted.[47]

Whatever were the causes, however, they did not include
any very general or lasting decline of interest in the legend
of which the old poem treated.   The English reading
public still continued to think of Guy of Warwick as a
national hero only a little below King Arthur in renown;
and when, between 1592 and 1640, a number of writers
composed new versions of the story more in harmony with
the prevailing taste, it gave to nearly all of them a hearty
welcome.

II

These new versions were in no sense isolated phenomena
in the literary life of the time.   They were, in fact, but
one manifestation of a general revival of interest in chivalrous romance and the legends of the Middle Ages which
characterized the later years of the sixteenth century.

While individuals like Nashe were denouncing the

[47] See below, p. 145.

" worne out impressions of the feyned no where acts, of Arthur of the rounde table, Arthur of litle Brittaine, sir Tristram, Hewon of Burdeaux, the Squire of low degree, the foure sons of Amon," [1] not a few of the leaders of later Elizabethan culture retained a measure of sympathetic regard for the old stories. Thus, in the very year in which Nashe's condemnation appeared, Puttenham, avowedly addressing an audience of courtiers, criticised those who " reproue and disgrace euery *Romance* or short historicall ditty for that they be not written in long meeters or verses *Alexandrins,* according to the nature and stile of large histories." In doing this, he added, " they should do wrong, for they be sundry formes of poems, and not all one." [2] Sidney, classicist as he was, was familiar with romances of the type of *Amadis de Gaule, Valentine and Orson,* and *King Arthur;* [3] and at one time seems to have planned to transform the *Arcadia* into a collection of Arthurian legends. [4] So thoroughly modern a poet as William Drummond of Hawthornden, an admirer of the literature of Renaissance France, was in his youth a diligent reader of medieval romances; between 1606 and 1609 he devoured seven out of the twenty-four volumes of *Amadis de Gaule* in French, and dipped into the English translation of *The Mirror of Knighthood.* [5] Ben Jonson, hostile on the whole, was yet not unreservedly so: in 1619 he could

[1] *The Anatomie of Absurditie* (1589), in *Works,* ed. McKerrow, I, p. 11.

[2] *The Arte of English Poesie,* in Smith, *Elizabethan Critical Essays,* II, p. 44. Cf. *ibid.,* p. 166.

[3] *An Apologie for Poetrie,* in Smith, *l. c.,* I, pp. 173, 188, 198. See also Brunhuber, *Sir Philip Sidneys Arcadia und ihre Nachläufer* (1903), pp. 13-19.

[4] *Ben Jonson's Conversations with William Drummond of Hawthornden,* ed. D. Laing, Shakespeare Society (1842), p. 10.

[5] *Archæologica Scotica,* IV, i (1831), pp. 73-74.

assure Drummond that for " a Heroik poeme . . . ther
was no such ground as King Arthur's fiction." [6] But the
writer who took perhaps the deepest interest of all the
literary men of his time in the old romances was Spenser.
He had read *Le Morte Darthur* and *Huon of Bordeaux*
among the prose versions, and probably *Bevis of Hampton*
and *The Squire of Low Degree* among the metrical; and
he did not disdain to draw from them hints not only for
the details but for the general conception and plan of *The
Faerie Queene*.[7] Plainly, the medieval romances—or at
least some of them—had admirers as well as critics among
the cultivated classes of late Elizabethan England.

The critics, however, were probably in the majority.
And at any rate it was not among the cultivated classes but
among the great public of imperfectly educated or old-
fashioned readers that interest in the old stories had its
true center. No one recognized this better than the realistic playwrights, in whose pictures of London merchants
and their apprentices and of country gentlemen a love for
the knightly romances of the Middle Ages was an oft-re-
curring trait. " He is eene wel inough serv'd, Sin," declared Gertrude, a goldsmith's daughter in *Eastward Hoe*
(1605), of her husband, " that so soone as ever he had got
my hand to the sale of my inheritance, run away from me

[6] *Conversations with Drummond*, p. 10.
[7] See on Spenser's knowledge and use of the medieval romances
Warton, *Observations on the Fairy Queen of Spenser* (ed. 1807),
I, pp. 27-75, II, pp. 144-145, 205; J. B. Fletcher, " Huon of Burdeux
and the Fairie Queene " (in *The Journal of Germanic Philology*, II,
1898, pp. 203-212); J. R. Macarthur, " The Influence of Huon of
Burdeux upon the Fairie Queene " (*ibid.*, IV, 1902, pp. 215-238);
Marie Walther, *Malorys Einfluss auf Spensers Faerie Queene*
(1898); Howard Maynadier, *The Arthur of the English Poets*,
(1907), pp. 257-277; Edgar A. Hall, " Spenser and Two Old French
Grail Romances " (in *P. M. L. A.*, XXVIII, 1913, pp. 539-554).

. . . Would the knight o' the sunne, or Palmerin of England, have used their ladies so, Syn? or Sir Lancelot, or Sir Tristram? . . . The knighthood now a daies are nothing like the knighthood of old time. They rid a horseback; 'ours goe a foote. They were attended by their squires; ours by their lacquaies. They went buckled in their armor; ours muffled in their cloaks. . . They were stil prest to engage their honour; ours stil ready to paune their cloaths. They would gallop on at sight of a monster; ours run away at sight of a serjeant. They would helpe poore ladies; ours make poore ladies." [8]

To supply this growing demand of the middle-class public for chivalric fiction the booksellers found it necessary to bring out new editions of the old stories. After the death of Copland, his practice of publishing medieval romances was continued by a number of younger printers and booksellers, of whom the most prominent were Thomas Purfoot, Cuthbert Burby, and Thomas Creede. With the exception of *Bevis of Hampton,* they neglected the older metrical romances. But from early in Queen Elizabeth's reign to the days of the Civil War they kept the market supplied with editions of many of the prose romances first brought into the language by Caxton and Wynkyn de Worde: *Arthur of Little Britain, The Four Sons of Aymon, Apollonius of Tyre, Blanchardine and Eglantine, Gesta Romanorum, The Histories of Troy, Huon of Bordeaux, Le Morte Darthur, Paris and Vienna, The Seven Wise Masters,* and *Valentine and Orson.* [9] They revived

[8] Ed. Schelling (Belles Lettres Series, 1903), pp. 112-113. Cf. also the texts cited by Koeppel, " Reflexe der Ritter-Romane im Drama " (in his *Ben Jonson's Wirkung auf zeitgenössische Dramatiker,* 1906, pp. 195-222).

[9] See Esdaile, *A List of English Tales and* Prose *Romances printed before 1740* (1912), under the titles of the romances named in the text.

in all fully half of the medieval prose romances which had been in circulation before the accession of Elizabeth. Nor did they always content themselves with merely reprinting the earlier impressions. In some cases,[10] they made attempts to modernize the language of the old editions; in others,[11] they substituted entirely new versions for the somewhat antiquated translations of the late fifteenth or early sixteenth century.

But the activity of the Elizabethan and Jacobean publishers of romances was not confined to the revival of stories already in circulation. They were likewise instrumental in introducing to the public a considerable body of narratives of knightly adventure not hitherto known in England. The most important of these consisted of romances belonging to the late medieval cycles of Amadis and Palmerin, which, although immensely popular in Spain and in France, had remained up to the last quarter of the sixteenth century closed books for all but a few Englishmen.[12] Thereafter, thanks in the main to the initiative of the booksellers, translations came out in rapid succession. In 1567-68 appeared *The treasurie of Amadis of Fraunce;* in 1578, the first part of *The Mirror of Knighthood;* sometime after 1581, *Palmerin of England;* in 1583, *Gerileon of England;* in 1588, *Palladine of England* and *Palmerin d'Oliva;* in 1589, *Palmendos;* in 1595, *Primaleon of Greece* and *Amadis of Gaule;* in 1598,

---

[10] E. g., *The Auncient Historie, of the destruction of Troy* (1596), *Huon of Bordeaux* (1601), and *The Seven Wise Masters* (1633).

[11] E. g., *Appollonius of Tyre* (c. 1594), *Blanchardine and Eglantine* (1595), and *Paris and Vienna* (1621).

[12] The British Museum possesses the manuscript (Lansdowne 766) of a translation of the first chapter and a half of *Amadis*, made in 1571 by Charles Stewart (afterwards Earl of Lennox), at the request of his mother. Cf. Ward, *Catalogue of Romances*, I, pp. 787-788.

Bellianis of Greece.[13]   For the most part the translations
were made from the French; in only a single case,[14]
indeed, did the translators who did the work for the booksellers go to the original Spanish. The vogue of the new
romances was enormous. Most in demand perhaps during
the nineties of the sixteenth century, they continued to be
reprinted and read far into the seventeenth. Wherever
they penetrated they helped greatly to strengthen the
taste for chivalric fiction.

In the meantime, there had begun to appear, in forms
dictated by the literary fashions of the day, fresh versions
of some of the medieval stories. Probably the most popular, if not the largest, group of these versions was composed of ballads. Among the common people of Elizabethan England, the old taste for this form of literature,
so far from dying out with the advent of grammar-schools
and the printing press, flourished even more vigorously.
At " Christmasse diners & brideales, and in tauernes &
alehouses, and such other places of base resort," [15] the
ballad-man with his repertory of songs—heroic, comic, or
sentimental—was an important and welcome personage.
Scores of ballads, moreover, issued yearly from the presses
of London during the early part of the reign, and the production increased as time went on.[16] In their search for
themes that would please their public, the ballad writers
turned naturally to the old romances; with the result that
there were ballads on King Arthur,[17] on Sir Lancelot of

---

[13] For a complete bibliography of these translations, see Esdaile,
l. c., under the various titles.

[14] *The Mirror of Knighthood.*

[15] Puttenham, *The Arte of English Poesie*, in Smith, *Elizabethan
Critical Essays*, II, p. 87.

[16] F. E. Bryant, *A History of English Balladry and Other Studies*
(1913), pp. 141-145, 163-172.

[17] A ballad entitled " a pleasaunte history of an adventurus

the Lake,[18] on Sir Eglamour,[19] and doubtless on other medieval heroes besides. Again, many of the new versions of the old stories took the form of plays.[20] Thus, between 1593 and 1603, Philip Henslowe bought, or drew revenue from, six pieces founded upon old romances—*Huon of Bordeaux*,[21] *Uther Pendragon*,[22] *The Life of King Arthur*,[23] *Valentine and Orson*,[24] *Tristram of Lyons*,[25] and *The Four Sons of Aymon*.[26] The last play was still being performed in 1624.[27] Finally, there appeared a number of treatments of particular legends in narrative prose or verse. Such were Lodge's pamphlet account of the life of Robert the Devil,[28] and " the Birth, Life and

knyghte of kynges Arthurs Couurte " was licensed to Richard Jones between July 1565 and July 1566 (*Stationers' Registers*, I, p. 297).

[18] Deloney, " The Noble Acts of Arthur of the round Table " (in *The Garland of Good Will*, ed. F. D. Mann, *The Works of Thomas Deloney*, 1912, pp. 323-326). Cf. R. Sievers, *Thomas Deloney* (1904), pp. 96-98.

[19] *Courage Crowned with Conquest; or, A brief Relation, how . . . Sir Eglamore bravely fought with . . . a Dragon.* The British Museum has an edition of 1672 (C. 40. m. 10/18); but the ballad itself is much older. It was quoted in 1615 in Rowlands's *The Melancholie Knight* (*The Complete Works of Samuel Rowlands*, II, 1880, pp. 33-34).

[20] See on this general subject, Schelling, *Elizabethan Drama* (1908), I, pp. 198-205; and Creizenach, *Geschichte des neueren Dramas*, IV, i (1909), pp. 228-230.

[21] *Henslowe's Diary*, ed. W. W. Greg (1904), Part I, p. 16.

[22] *Ibid.*, pp. 52-53.

[23] *Ibid.*, pp. 86, 87.

[24] *Ibid.*, p. 90.

[25] *Ibid.*, p. 112.

[26] *Ibid.*, pp. 173, 176. Cf. Part II (1908), p. 227.

[27] *Ibid.*, Part II, p. 227.

[28] *The Famous, true and historicall life of Robert second Duke of Normandy, surnamed for his monstrous birth and behauiour, Robin the Diuell . . .* 1591 (reprinted in *The Complete Works of Thomas Lodge*, Hunterian Club, II, 1883).

Death of honourable Arthur King of Brittaine " in Robert Chester's *Loves Martyr*.[29]

Thus, in spite of much unfriendly criticism from individual writers, a large and apparently a growing public in the late sixteenth and early seventeenth centuries continued to find enjoyment in the fiction of the Middle Ages. It was doubtless this general taste for medieval romances, quite as much as the more special interest which Englishmen took in the story out of patriotic sentiment, that called forth the new versions of the legend of Guy of Warwick.[30]

The first of these versions to appear was an anonymous stall-ballad entitled *A plesante songe of the valiant actes*

[29] First published in 1601; reprinted by Grosart, 1878. See pp. 34-37. On the sources of Chester's poem, cf. *Journal of English and Germanic Philology*, XIV (1915), pp. 75-88.

[30] In addition to the independent versions described in the text, there were at least two others which formed part of longer works. One was in Puttenham's lost *Romance or historical ditty . . . of the Isle of great Britaine* (before 1589). Such at least seems to me to be the correct interpretation of the following passage in *The Arte of English Poesie* (Smith, *Elizabethan Critical Essays*, II, pp. 43-44): " And we our selues who compiled this treatise haue written for pleasure a litle brief *Romance* or historicall ditty in the English tong, of the Isle of great *Britaine*, in short and long meetres, and by breaches or diuisions to be more commodiously song to the harpe in places of assembly, where the company shalbe desirous to heare of old aduentures & valiaunces of noble knights in times past, as are those of king *Arthur* and his knights of the round table, Sir *Beuys* of *Southampton*, *Guy* of *Warwicke*, and others like." The other was in Drayton's *Poly-olbion* (1613), Canto XII of which contained an account of the fight with Colbrond, and Canto XIII, a summary of the leading incidents in the whole legend. See the Spenser Society reprint, Part II, pp. 198-202, 220-221. The sources of Drayton's versions cannot be determined with exactness; but he seems to have known, besides the Middle English romance, Lydgate's poem (probably in the prose rendering of Fabyan or Grafton) and the ballad of 1592.

*of Guy of Warwicke, to the tune of ' Was ever man soe
tost in love.'* It was licensed for publication on January
5, 1592, to Richard Jones, a printer who during his long
career made a specialty of ballads.[31]   Innumerable editions were printed during the seventeenth and eighteenth
centuries, most of them on broadsides illustrated with
rude woodcuts of scenes from the story.[32] Hawked about
the streets or countryside by ballad-men,[33] they found a
ready audience, and helped to perpetuate the memory of
Guy among classes of people who for the most part were
inaccessible to literature of a more formal sort.[34]

   The ballad narrated in a very summary way the whole
story of Guy's career. Guy himself was the speaker, and

[31] *Stationers' Registers*, II, p. 601. On Jones see McKerrow, *A
Dictionary of Printers and Booksellers . . . 1557-1640* (1910), p. 159.

[32] No bibliography of these editions exists, and probably the
greater part of them have disappeared. The British Museum has a
few, chiefly of the late seventeenth and early eighteenth centuries.
See especially B. M., C. 40. m. 10/19, and Rox. III., 50, 51, and 708.
All these have the same woodcut below the title—Guy on horseback
in full armor, carrying a boar's head on his lance, and followed by
a lion. This design is identical with that on the title-page of the
1632 edition of Rowlands's *The Famous History of Guy Earle of
Warwicke* (B. M., G. 11467). For other broadside editions of the
ballad, see *Stat. Reg.*, IV, pp. 131-132; Hazlitt, *Collections and Notes*,
p. 194; *The Bagford Ballads*, I, p. lxiii; *Harvard Catalogue of Chap-
books*, No. 881. In addition to the numerous independent editions,
the ballad was regularly printed in the eighteenth century as a sort
of appendix to the prose chapbook *The Noble and Renowned History
of Guy Earl of Warwick* (1706). Cf. below, p. 184. It also appeared
in Percy's *Reliques* (1765).

[33] See *The London Chanticleers* (1637), in Hazlitt's *Dodsley*, XII
(1875), p. 330. ·

[34] Evidences of the vogue of the ballad in the early seventeenth
century may be found in *The Knight of the Burning Pestle*, 1607-08
(*The Works of Beaumont and Fletcher*, ed. Waller, VI, 1908, p.
193); *The Little French Lawyer*, 1619 (*ibid.*, III, 1906, p. 398);
Cal. of State Papers, Dom., Addenda, 1580-1625, p. 679; *Bishop
Percy's Folio Manuscript*, II, pp. 201-202.

his first words gave the reader the secret of his subsequent
adventures and wanderings:

> Was ever Knight for Lady's sake,
>   so tost in love, as I, Sir *Guy;*
> For Phillis fair, that Lady bright,
>   as ever Man beheld with eye;
> She gave me leave my self to try,
>   the valiant Knight with shield and spear,
> E're that her love she would grant me,
>   which made me venture far and near.[35]

Then he proceeded to tell of his exploits in Normandy and
Germany, his victories over the Saracens at Constantinople, his rescue of a lion from the jaws of a dragon, his
marriage to Phillis and his desertion of her forty days
later, his adventures as a pilgrim in the Holy Land, his
return to England, his battle with Colbrond, his retirement to a cave near Warwick, and finally his death.

All this material the writer of the ballad found ready to
his hand in the printed editions of the old metrical
romance. He was not, however, content to stop with a
mere summary of the longer poem. After making Guy
relate his successful conflict with the Danish champion,
and his slaying of a boar in Windsor Forest, he put into
his mouth the following stanza, describing an event not
mentioned in the old romance, nor indeed in any of the
earlier literary versions of the story:

> On Dunsmore-heath I also slew
>   a monstrous wild and cruel beast,
> Call'd the dun-cow of Dunsmore-heath,
>   which many People had opprest;
> Some of her bones in Warwick yet
>   still for a monument doth lie,
> Which unto every Looker's view,
>   as wondrous strange they may espy.

[35] My quotations from the ballad are from an edition in the British Museum (C. 40. m. 10/19), dated by the compilers of the Catalogue about 1670.

This incident the ballad-maker in all likelihood borrowed directly from popular oral tradition. A legend of how the great Earl had delivered the countryside from the ravages of a terrible Dun Cow seems to have been current among the people of Warwickshire at least a hundred years before the ballad was published.[36] Throughout the sixteenth century, though apparently never written down, the legend survived. Thus when Johannes Caius, the naturalist, visited Warwick not long after 1550, he was shown in the chapel at Guyscliffe an enormous bone, nine inches in diameter in the smallest part and six feet and a half long, which many of the common people declared to be the very rib of the famous beast.[37] However unconnected with Guy the story may have been in its origin, by the latter half of the sixteenth century it would seem to have become an integral part of the Guy tradition. In introducing it into his verse, the author of the ballad of 1592 no doubt helped greatly to spread its fame beyond the narrow limits of a locality and to give it currency among the reading public at large.

About sixteen years after the first publication of the *Plesante Songe,* appeared a somewhat more extended account of the story of Guy of Warwick. Its author, Samuel Rowlands, was one of the numerous writers of miscellaneous pamphlets in prose or verse whose active pens kept the presses busy during the early years of the seventeenth century.[38] He had already published a number of popular tracts, when sometime before 1608 he con-

---

[36] See the evidence set forth by Professor A. C. L. Brown in *The Journal of Germanic Philology,* III, p. 21.

[37] *De Rariorum Animalium . . . Historia* (1570) in *The Works of John Caius, M. D.,* p. 42.

[38] On Rowlands see Gosse's memoir in *The Complete Works of Samuel Rowlands,* Hunterian Club, I (1880), pp. 3-24.

ceived the idea, or had it suggested to him by some book-
seller, of versifying the legend of Sir Guy. The result
was a short poem in twelve cantos, entitled *The Famous
History of Guy Earle of Warwick*.[39] It was written—so
the prefatory matter in the printed edition declared—to
revive the fame of a "dustconsumed Champion," whose
"deeds of old, writ with an ancient Pen," had now out-
worn the memory of the public.[40]

Not ambitious of pleasing the critical, Rowlands was
content, in writing *The Famous History,* to rely for his
material on the most easily accessible sources. The substance and order of his narrative and perhaps most of his
details he took from the metrical romance. In only one
passage, indeed, does he seem to have made use of any

[39] Reprinted *ibid.,* III. Neither the date nor the publisher of the
first edition can be established with certainty. The known facts are
these: (1) On 23 June 1608, a book called "the famous history of
Guy Erle of Warwick" was entered at Stationers' Hall to William
Ferbrand (*Stat. Reg.* III, p. 382). That this was Rowlands's poem
there can be little doubt. No trace, however, of any edition by
Ferbrand has survived. (2) The British Museum (C. 39. c. 21) has
a copy of *The Famous History* bearing the imprint "Printed at
London by *Elizabeth All-de.* 1607." This was long regarded as a
copy of the first edition, and as such was reproduced by the editors
of *The Complete Works.* More critical examination showed, however, that the title-page, the lower half of the next two leaves, and
the last leaf were in reality manuscript facsimiles, while the text
itself belonged to some edition of the late seventeenth century
(*Complete Works,* I, p. 44). Furthermore, as Elizabeth Allde did not
begin to publish until 1628 (McKerrow, *Dictionary of Printers and
Booksellers,* p. 6), there is no ground for the assumption that the
person who supplied the missing leaves may have copied from an
edition of 1607 subsequently lost. We are therefore thrown back
on the entry in the Registers for 1608 as our only source of information regarding the date of appearance of Rowlands's poem. (3) The
earliest edition of which a copy is known dates from 1632 (B. M.,
G. 11467). It was printed for Elizabeth Allde.

[40] Hunterian Club reprint, pp. 2, 3.

other literary authority. In his account of Guy's conflict
with Colbrond,[41] he described the battle as taking place
in Hide Mead, a meadow near Winchéster—

> *Amen*, quoth *Guy*, and with great courage goes
> Forth *Winchester's* North gate unto *Hide-Mead*
> Where that same Monster of a man he found,
> Treading at every step two yards of ground.

For this detail he must have gone to some other version of
the story than the romance, which left the scene of the
combat unnamed.   This other version may have been
Lydgate's poem of the fifteenth century, or, more probably, some sixteenth century prose chronicle.[42]   Yet, for
all his reliance on a single source, Rowlands did not produce a mere slavish compilation.   On the contrary, he
took not a few liberties with the material which he found
in the old romance.   Not only did he omit several episodes here and there,[43] but he made more or less signifi-

---

[41] Canto XII.

[42] The possibility that Rowlands had among his sources Lydgate's
Guy was suggested by Professor Brown (*The Journal of Germanic
Philology*, III, p. 19, note 4).   It must be remembered, however, that
Lydgate's poem had never been printed, and was, therefore, if not
entirely unknown in the sixteenth century (see Ward, *Catalogue of
Romances*, I, p. 496), at least not very easily accessible.   Lydgate,
moreover, was not, as Professor Brown seems to imply, the *only*
authority for the location of the fight with Colbrond in Hide-Mead.
The fact was also attested by a rather long line of chroniclers, from
Girardus Cornubiensis (Lydgate's source), probably in the fourteenth century (*ibid.*, I, p. 480), through Thomas Rudborne in
the fifteenth (*Bishop Percy's Folio Manuscript*, II, p. 514), to
Fabyan (*The New Chronicles of England*, 1516; ed. Ellis, 1811, p.
184), Grafton (*A Chronicle at Large*, 1569; repr. 1809, p. 118), and
Stow (*A Summarie of the Chronicles of England . . . vnto . . .
1575*, p. 76), in the sixteenth.   The last three of these chronicles
at least were still well known when Rowlands wrote.   That it was
from one of them rather than from Lydgate that he learned of Hide-
Mead seems to me highly probable.

[43] As, for example, the narrative of Guy's relations with the

cant alterations in others, and added one or two new ones of his own. Of the alterations, perhaps the most important occurred in the passage narrating the fight with Colbrond. In the romance, King Athelstone, directed by an angel, sought out Guy among the pilgrims at Winchester gate and urged upon him the great task of defending England against the Danes. Guy at first hesitated:

> Redest thou me to fight quod guy whereto
> Seest thou not me readily,
> Unneathes for feeblenesse alyue am I.

In the end, however, he consented to become the English champion.[44] In treating this episode in *The Famous History*, Rowlands directly reversed the situation, making Guy petition Athelstone for the privilege of the combat:

> At length great *Guy* no longer could refrain,
> Seeing all strain court'sies to express their love:
> But comes unto the King, and says, Dread Lord!
> This combate to thy unknown Knight afford.
> Although in simple habit I am hid,
> Yielding no shew of that I undertake,
> I ne're attempted ought but what I did;
> An end of *Colbrond*, on my soul, I'le make.
> Palmer (quoth *Athelstone*) I like thy sprite.
> God send thee thither, and He aid thee right.
> His Powerful Hand lend vigour to thy blows,
> And grant thy foot upon thy Foe may tread.[45]

daughter of the Emperor of Constantinople and of the intrigues of Morgadour, the steward (Copland's edition, sigs. O. ijᵛ—S. ij, *passim*); the incident of King Valentine (*ibid.*, sig. Bb. iij); and the story of the birth and early life of Raynburne (*ibid.*, sigs. Dd. i, Ff. iiᵛ—Ff. [4]ᵛ, Kk. i—end).

[44] Copland's edition, sig. Hh. [4]ᵛ.

[45] Hunterian Club reprint, pp. 76-77. Changes were also made in the circumstances of Guy's rescue of the lion (Canto VII, and cf. Copland's edition, sig. R. ijᵛ); in the whole course of the Terry-Osile-Duke Otton episode (Cantos VII and VIII; cf. Copland, sigs. S. iijᵛ—Aa. iijᵛ); in the incident of Amarant, the giant (Canto x;

The principal additions which Rowlands made to the legend were two—a vision which transformed Phelice's indifference to Guy into love,[46] and a dialogue between Guy and a skull during his wanderings in the East.[47] Though he alluded once to the tradition of the Dun Cow, he made no attempt to narrate it in detail.[48] Such were the chief modifications which Rowlands introduced into the substance of the old story. On the side of form, he substituted for the medieval style of the romance a style full of the fashionable classical imagery and reference. The whole he wrote in a six-line stanza, riming *ababcc,* his favorite measure during most of his career.[49]

The Famous History became, and long remained, widely popular. More than any other of the new versions,

---

cf. Copland, sigs. Dd. iij—Ff. ij^v). These changes, unlike the one noted in the text, seem to have been made merely in the interest of brevity and simplicity. For another change, which appeared in some of the later editions of *The Famous History,* Rowlands cannot be held responsible. Following his source, the Middle English romance as printed in the sixteenth century, he gave to Guy's chief opponent in the fight outside Constantinople (Canto VI) the name of "Coldran." It so appears in the edition of 1632 (sig. G3). But in all of the impressions of the later seventeenth century and in at least four of the prose chapbooks founded on Rowlands's poem, the warrior in question is called "Colbrond" or "Colbron"; with the result that, as Professor Brown notes (*l. c.*, p. 19, note 1), "we have . . . the strange phenomenon of Colbrond's being killed *twice,* once, as here, in the East, and later in England."

[46] Canto II; Hunterian Club reprint, pp. 13-16.

[47] Canto XI; pp. 66-67.

[48] The passage occurs in Athelstone's speech to Guy after the slaying of Colbrond (Canto XII; p. 80).

[49] He used it, for example, in the following pieces: *The Betraying of Christ* (1598), *Tis Merrie when Gossips meete* (1602), *Aue Caesar. God saue the King* (1603), *Looke to it: For, Ile Stabbe ye* (1604), *Hell's Broke Loose* (1605), *A Terrible Battell betweene . . . Time, and Death* (n. d.). In some of the later editions of *The Famous History* the stanza divisions are disregarded; they appear, however, in the edition of 1632.

it succeeded to the place formerly occupied by the metrical romance in the affections of the English public. Reprinted at frequent intervals in cheap, illustrated editions, it continued in active circulation to the end of the seventeenth century.[50] The ballad alone, of all contemporary versions, enjoyed a longer life.

To at least one reader in the early seventeenth century, however, Rowlands's poem, on account of its brevity, seemed to do Guy an injustice. Among the acquaintances of the elder John Milton was a gentleman named John Lane, a somewhat old-fashioned person, who spent a great deal of his time in writing and rewriting long poems, most of which for some reason he never printed.[51] Although apparently self-educated, he seems to have been a man of some reading; in particular, he took a deep interest in the English literature of the Middle Ages. Thus one of his unpublished poems was a continuation of Chaucer's *Squire's Tale,* written first in 1616, and revised in 1630.[52] He was likewise a declared admirer, though probably no great student, of Lydgate;[53] and sometime before 1617, possibly as a result of his knowledge that Lydgate had written a poem on the subject, he read a number of the

---

[50] Hazlitt (*Handbook*, p. 523) records editions in 1632, 1635, 1649, 1654, 1667, 1679, 1682, 1699, and c. 1700. These represent probably by no means all of the impressions actually printed. See Arber, *Term Catalogues*, III, p. 114, and Turnbull, *The Romance of Sir Guy of Warwick*, Abbotsford Club (1840), p. xxv. Four copies of "Guy of Warwick" (Rowlands's?) were in the stock of John Foster, a York stationer, in 1616 (Davies, *A Memoir of the York Press*, 1868, pp. 362, 366).

[51] On Lane see Furnivall, *John Lane's Continuation of Chaucer's 'Squire's Tale,'* Chaucer Society (1888-1890).

[52] Ed. Furnivall, *ibid.*

[53] See the Prologue to the Reader in his poem on Guy (printed in *Bishop Percy's Folio Manuscript*, II), *passim*, and Zupitza, *Zur Literaturgeschichte*, pp. 646-647.

3

existing versions of the legend of Guy of Warwick, both
in print and in manuscript. Among them were the metrical romance, some of the older chronicles,[54] and perhaps
Lydgate's poem.[55] All of these versions, however, were
survivals from a more or less distant past; some of them,
being in manuscript, were inaccessible to the general public; all were in a language too nearly obsolete to be read
with ease or pleasure by Englishmen of the early seventeenth century.[56] And latterly, as it seemed to Lane, Guy
had been neglected, particularly by the English chroniclers.[57] It is true that a little tract had recently appeared,
in which the legend had been " renewed in verse ";, but
this version, which could have been none other than Rowlands's, omitted, " for brevitie sake," much of the original
history as told by the ancient English poets.[58] Clearly—

[54] Prologue, *l. c.*, II, p. 523.

[55] " Now, for my own part (vnder correction) I endevour to call a
general muster of all our noblest Guions whole historie, in the same
kind also, as beinge most proper for it, and him; but without dero-
gatinge from the desert of our ancient English poets first plott:
the *which* . . . was written allmost three hundred yeeres gonn, by
Don Lidgate. . . ." (*Ibid.*, pp. 522-523). In spite of this apparently plain statement, it seems to me likely that Lane had in view
here, not Lydgate's actual poem, which treated only an episode in
Guy's career, but the metrical romance, with which, as it contained
the "whole historie," it would be more natural for him to compare
his own work. This hypothesis harmonizes with the considerations
set forth below, page 159.

[56] " And him (Guy) have they sunge in deed into the fabrick of
sownd poetrie, although in terms obsolete . . ." *Ibid.*, p. 522.

[57] *Ibid.*, p. 523.

[58] *Ibid.*, p. 522. The following passage may perhaps contain an
allusion to Rowlands's altered version of the fight with Colbrond (cf.
above, p. 155): ". . . som of oures . . . woold faine decline the
credite of all ye ancient*es*, concerninge the conditions of Guyes fight-
inge the Duello for this kingdom, when hee slewe Colbrond the Affri-
can giant challenginge for the Danes: as yf Sir Guy, beinge then a
man retired to obscuritie, and besides overtaken of old age; shoold, or

Lane seems to have concluded—it would be a service to the memory of the old English hero to retell in modern verse the complete story of his career. To this task he therefore set himself after finishing his continuation of *The Squire's Tale*. For his material he boasted later that he had ransacked "ancient historiens, poetes, heraltes recordes, publick monumentes, and tradicion." [59] However true this may be, his chief reliance was on the old metrical romance; even for his account of Guy's exploit at Winchester, this, rather than Lydgate's poem, which he professed to be completing, was his principal source. [60]

woold runn at a masterie so daungerous for glorie, which hee contemned: and not vppon the necessitie of that occasion, but this presumptuous kind of novitious writinge, maie rest assured, that onlie one of yonder ancientes livinge neerer the time of the famous Guy by some hundreds of yeeres will carrie more credite! then one thowsand such news, offringe so forwardly, which must needes bee ignorantlie, sith not havinge seene anie of the manuscriptes before mentioned " (*Ibid.*, p. 523).

[59] *Ibid.*, p. 525. Cf. the sonnet by John Milton the elder, prefixed to the manuscript of Lane's completed poem:

> . . . .
> Heralds' records and each sound antiquary
> For Guy's true being, life, death, eke hast sought,
> To satisfy those which *praevaricari;*
> Manuscript, chronicle, if might be bought;
> Coventry's, Winton's, Warwick's monuments,
> Trophies, traditions delivered of Guy,
> With care, cost, pain, as sweetly thou presents,
> To exemplify the flower of chivalry:
> From cradle to the saddle and the bier,
> For Christian imitation, all are here.

(Masson, *The Life of John Milton*, I, 1881, pp. 57-58).

[60] Cf. Zupitza, *Zur Literaturgeschichte*, p. 646: " Ich selbst hatte, wie ich aufrichtig gestehen muss, nicht Zeit und Lust, mich durch die gesammten 26 Cantos auf mehr denn einem halben Tausend Spalten von über 30 Zeilen durchzuwinden. Ich begnügte mich mit einer Lectüre derjenigen Stellen, an denen sich eine Benützung von Lydgate's Gedicht, wenn sie vorhanden wäre, zeigen müsste: indessen

He followed it closely, keeping almost everywhere the same order of incidents, and even of details, through all the adventures of Guy and Raynburne. However, though he added little or nothing in the way of substance to what he found in this source,[61] he succeeded in greatly amplifying the narrative. When he finished his work, sometime before the middle of the year 1617,[62] he had written upwards of twelve thousand lines, about four thousand more than in the romance as printed in the preceding century.[63] He called his poem *The corrected historie of Sir Gwy, Earle of Warwick, surnamed the Heremite;* and added on the title-page a note to the effect that the story begun by Lydgate was " now dilligentlie exquired from all Antiquitie by John Lane." The work was divided into twenty-six cantos; it began with a Prologue and ended with an Epilogue, both spoken by Lydgate.

The general public, for whom Lane evidently designed his compilation, never received it. Like his continuation of *The Squire's Tale, The corrected historie of Sir Gwy,* though licensed to be printed, remained in manuscript: perhaps he could find no publisher willing to undertake the risk; perhaps he was not altogether satisfied with his work. In 1621, four years after he secured his license, he subjected it to a thorough revision, increasing its length to over seventeen thousand lines.[64] In this form it

.ich konnte nicht die geringste Spur einer solchen entdecken." In my own examination of the poem I failed to note any matter not to be found in the romance as printed by Copland.

[61] Thus, though he spoke of his indebtedness to " tradicion," he quite ignored the tradition of the Dun Cow.

[62] It was licensed for publication on July 13 of that year (Ward, *Catalogue of Romances,* I, p. 497).

[63] *Ibid.,* p. 497. The exact number was 12,180.

[64] 17,450 (*ibid.,* p. 497). The manuscript in this revised form is in the British Museum (Harl. MS. 5243). The only portions that

remained, read no doubt by the author's own circle of friends, but unknown to the public at large. Although, on this account, its influence on either the content or the vogue of the Guy legend could have amounted to very little, it was nevertheless significant of the continued interest in the story.

In 1636 still another attempt was made to retell the old legend in modern English verse. In June of that year a license was issued to a stationer named Richard Oulton for the publication of a poem entitled *The famous and worthy History of Guy Earle of Warwick.*[65] It was the work of John Carpenter, an obscure popular writer, who had already turned out earlier in the year a pamphlet called *A Merry fortune Booke wherein all Trades and professions may read their owne good and bad fortunes,* and a book called *Ovids remedie of Loue.*[66]

In the meantime, the story of Guy had found its way to the stage. In October 1618, the Earl of Derby's company was giving performances at Islington of a play called *The Life and Death of Guy of Warwick.*[67] On January 15, 1620, this play was licensed to be published as the work of John Day and Thomas Dekker.[68] Twelve years later it was apparently still being played in the country.[69]

have been printed are the long prose preface and the sonnet by Milton. The manuscript is described by Ward, *l. c.,* I, pp. 497-499.

[65] *Stationers' Registers,* IV, p. 366. No copies of this edition are known.

[66] *Ibid.,* IV, pp. 356, 364.

[67] John Taylor, *The Pennyles Pilgrimage* (in *The Workes of John Taylor,* 1630. Spenser Society reprint, p. 150). For the date, cf. *ibid.,* p. 132.

[68] *Stationers' Registers,* III, p. 662. The stationer to whom the license was granted was John Trundle. On December 13, 1620, he assigned his rights in the play to Thomas Langley (*ibid.,* IV, p. 44).

[69] The fact is alluded to in Thomas Nabbes's *Covent Garden,* 1632

Its success may have been a factor in calling forth another dramatization of the legend, which appeared on the boards a few years before the closing of the theatres. This was *The Tragical History, Admirable Atchievments and various events of Guy Earl of Warwick. A Tragedy,* which was authorized to be printed on April 6, 1639.[70] The piece belonged to the repertory of the King's players, by whom it was acted " very Frequently with great Applause " in the days before the Civil War.[71] On the title-page of the printed edition it was ascribed to one B. J.[72] Its five acts, each of which began with a Prologue spoken by " Time," told the story of Guy's career from his marriage to his death, in rude

(*The Works of Thomas Nabbes*, ed. Bullen, 1887, I, pp. 8-9). It was perhaps this production that suggested to Jonson some of the details of his description of popular plays in *The Magnetic Lady* (1632): " So if a child could be born in a play, and grow up to a man, in the first scene, before he went off the stage: and then after to come forth a squire, and be made a knight: and that knight to travel between the acts, and do wonders in the Holy Land or elsewhere; kill Paynims, wild boars, dun cows, and other monsters; beget him a reputation, and marry an emperor's daughter for his mistress: convert her father's country; and at last come back home lame, and all-to-be-laden with miracles." Act I, sc. i (*The Works of Ben Jonson*, ed. Gifford-Cunningham, II, 1872, p. 402).

[70] Two copies of a quarto edition of this play " printed for Thomas Vere and William Gilbertson without Newgate, 1661 " are among the Dyce books at South Kensington. Both are imperfect. There is also a copy in the British Museum (643. c. 18). The leaf preceding the title-page contains what must have been the original imprimatur: " Imprimatur. April. 6. 1639. Math. Clay." No copy of this first edition, however, seems to have survived. I am indebted to Mr. G. H. Palmer, of the Victoria and Albert Museum, for information regarding the copies at Kensington, and to Professor W. Bang, of Louvain, for the loan of a transcript of the play made for an edition, now shortly forthcoming, in *Materialien zur Kunde*.

[71] Title-page of the edition of 1661.

[72] In the Epilogue the author is described as a young man: " he's but young that writes of this Old Time " (l. 1597).

blank verse interspersed with patches of rime and prose. The plot ran as follows: While the wedding guests were still gathered in the house of Rohon, the old Earl of Warwick, Guy announced his determination to leave Phillis and go on a pilgrimage to Jerusalem. In spite of her entreaties to him to stay for the sake of her unborn child, he clad himself as a palmer and set out, accompanied only by a clown named Sparrow. On his way, after meeting with a hermit, he came to "the stately Tower of *Donather*," the scene, as he recalled, of one of the exploits of Huon of Bordeaux. From the spells of the enchanter who inhabited the place he was delivered by Oberon, who gave him, for the sake of Huon, a magical wand which enabled him to destroy the tower. Arrived in Palestine, he helped to drive back the Saracens from Jerusalem, and captured and converted the Sultan Shamurath. Finally, after a number of years, he returned to England, and, still in disguise, did battle with Colbron for the control of the kingdom. Then, having revealed his identity only to King Athelstone, he retired to a cave in a wood near Warwick, where he lived as a hermit, depending for his food on the charity of his unsuspecting wife, until an angel appeared to warn him of his approaching end. Just before he died he summoned Phillis to him by means of a ring she had given him before he left England. She hastened to the cave, accompanied by Rainborn, who had spent many years in a futile search for his father; but when she arrived the old warrior was dead. To console her, King Athelstone, who presently appeared, promised that

> the shield-bone of the bore of *Callidon*,
> shall be hang'd up at *Coventries* great Gate;
> the Ribs or the Dun Cow of *Dunsmore* Heath,
> in *Warwick* Castle for a monument;

and on his Cave where he hath left his life,
a stately Hermitage I will erect,
in honour of Sir *Guy* of *Warwicks* Name.[73]

Into the making of this "dolent history," as the Epilogue described it, went elements from three different sources. The inclusion among the youthful exploits of Guy of the destruction of the Dun Cow was probably suggested by the ballad of 1592. The encounter with Oberon and the adventure of the tower of Donather came from one of the most popular of the surviving medieval romances, *Huon of Bordeaux*.[74] The remainder of the

[73] *The Tragical History*, ll. 1574-1580. There are several other allusions to the episode of the Dun Cow. See ll. 23-26, 71-72, 292-294, 328-329.

[74] Ed. Sidney Lee, *E. E. T. S.*, *E. S.*, XL, pp. 60-109. The hero of this story, sent by Charlemagne on a dangerous mission to the Admiral of Babylon, happened to encounter on his way an aged hermit, who warned him against taking the shortest road to his destination lest he should fall under the power of Oberon, the dwarf king of fairy-land. Huon's curiosity, however, was aroused by the hermit's description of Oberon, and he made light of the prophecy of danger. Accordingly, he continued his journey by the shorter path, and presently caught a glimpse of the fairy king riding by with his bow and magic horn. Several other encounters followed, until finally Huon, though he had been expressly commanded by the hermit not to speak to Oberon, could contain himself no longer, and saluted him kindly. Thereupon Oberon gave him as a reward his ivory horn, one blast of which would suffice to summon the dwarf to his side with a hundred thousand men. Huon then proceeded upon his way, and after a number of adventures came to the tower of Dunother, the abode of the giant Angolafer. Against the advice of Oberon and the entreaties of his own companions, he entered the tower, and fought and overcame the giant. In Act II of *The Tragical History* this narrative is clearly alluded to. After the departure of the hermit, Guy beholds the tower of Donather. "This," he says to Sparrow,

"This is the stately Tower of *Donather*,
wher *Huon* of *Burdeaux* a couragious Knight
slew *Angolofar* in a single Fight:
375 go *Sparrow*, seek find me an entrance in."

play, with the exception of the scenes at Jerusalem, was based upon the common source of nearly all the contemporary versions of the legend, the metrical romance.[75]

III

With the middle of the seventeenth century began a new period in the fortunes of *Guy of Warwick,* a period marked not only by the appearance of a second group of new versions, but also by the completion of a change—begun far back in the preceding century—in the character of the public which read the old story. For at least seventy-five years after the introduction of printing, the popularity of the surviving medieval romances was probably quite as great among the upper classes as among the lower. The patrons for whom Caxton brought out his editions were without exception gen-

And again, after delivering Guy from the spells of the enchanter, Oberon tells him:

> "I am the Fairy King that keeps these Groves,
> 455 for *Huon* ot *Burdeaux* sake, thy Warlike friend,
>   the dear loved Minion of the Fairy King,
>   will I make *Guy* of *Warwicks* name be fear'd;
>   for conquest of the Tower of *Donather.*"

On the vogue of Lord Berners's translation of *Huon* in the sixteenth and early seventeenth centuries, see Lee, *l. c.,* XL, pp. xxxviii-lvii; L. p. 791.

[75] The number of details which could have come from the romance and from no other extant version is considerable. They include, in Act I, Guy's charge to Phillis respecting the upbringing of her child (cf. Copland's edition, sig. Dd. j); in Act IV, King Athelstone's vision, his interview with Guy at Winchester gate, and Guy's prayer before the battle (Copland, sigs. Hh. [4]v, I i. j); in Act V, Guy's interview with Phillis and the visit of the angel (Copland, sig. I i. iijv); and, throughout the play, the story of Rainborn (simplified somewhat from the account given in the romance).

tlemen or nobles;[1] *Le Morte Darthur,* for example, he dedicated expressly to "alle noble prynces lordes and ladyes gentlymen or gentylwymmen."[2] Wynkyn de Worde likewise published romances at the instance of members of the aristocracy;[3] and in the early sixteenth century, Lord Berners, a nobleman high in the favor of Henry VIII, and a man of no mean culture, himself turned into English *Huon of Bordeaux* and *Arthur of Little Britain.*[4] That the old stories should thus continue to find favor with the fashionable classes was owing in large part no doubt to the paucity of other narrative literature. Until the early years of the reign of Elizabeth, medieval romances comprised the bulk of the fiction accessible to the English public. Here and there, it is true, as early as the forties, individuals were becoming familiar with the *novelle* of Renaissance Italy;[5] but it was only after the sixties, when the importation of the new romances began in earnest, that the relative position of the medieval tales underwent a change. Thereafter, though they did not cease to be reprinted and read, they no longer attracted so many readers from the cultivated public; on the contrary, neglected or criticised by men of

[1] Cf. *Charles the Grete,* 1485 (*E. E. T. S., E. S.,* XXXVI), pp. 2-3; *Blanchardyn and Eglantine,* c. 1489 (*ibid.,* LVIII), p. 1; *The Four Sons of Aymon,* c. 1489 (*ibid.,* XLIV), p. 4; *Eneydos,* c. 1490 (*ibid.,* LVII), p. 3.

[2] Ed. Sommer, I (1889), p. 4.

[3] See, for example, the "Prologue of the Translatour," in his edition of *Helyas, Knight of the Swan* (Thoms, *Early English Prose Romances,* III, pp. 15-16).

[4] On Berners see Lee, *Huon of Burdeux* (*E. E. T. S., E. S.,* XL), pp. xl-xlvi.

[5] See Friedrich Brie, "Die erste Übersetzung einer italienischen Novelle ins Englische," in *Archiv für das Studium der neueren Sprachen und Literaturen,* CXXIV (1910), pp. 46-57.

letters,[6] they came more and more to be the special property of the uneducated and the old-fashioned. This evolution, which was well under way before the close of the
sixteenth century, had by the middle of the seventeenth
practically run its course. Henceforth, for over a hundred years, the admirers of the old stories—of *Guy of
Warwick* no less than the others—were to be found almost
exclusively among the plebeian and uncultivated classes.[7]

In spite of this narrowing of its audience, however, the
popularity which *Guy of Warwick* had enjoyed during
the first half of the seventeenth century continued
unabated. The old Middle English metrical version, it
is true, had probably long ago disappeared from general
circulation; many years had elapsed since the last edition
had been printed; and by 1650 both its language and its
style had become hopelessly old-fashioned. But the case
was different with at least three of the versions written
during the previous half-century. *The Tragical History
of Guy Earl of Warwick* survived the closing of the
theatres, and was re-issued in 1661;[8] reprints of Rowlands's *Famous History* appeared in 1649, 1654, 1667,
and at short intervals during the remainder of the cen-

---

[6] See above, pp. 136-141.

[7] The facts upon which this generalization rests are of three sorts:
(1) the lack of any evidence of a general interest in the medieval
romances on the part of seventeenth-century men of letters; (2) the
monopoly of the surviving stories by the lower class of booksellers,
including many who made a specialty of publishing for the country
chapmen; and (3) the existence in the plays and other literary
works of the time of numerous passages in which a taste for the
chivalric romances is treated as especially characteristic of old
women, servants, country squires, the sons and daughters of citizens, and children. I hope to treat the question in detail in a forthcoming study of the survival of the romances after 1500.

[8] Above, p. 162, note 70.

tury; [9] while editions of the *Plesante Song of the Valiant
Deeds of Chivalry Atchiev'd by that Noble Knight, Sir
Guy of Warwick* were so numerous as to excite the wonder
of contemporaries.   Thus Pepys, wishing to record his
impression of the number of ballads written on the Duke
of Albemarle, thought it sufficient to say, " There are so
many, that hereafter he will sound like Guy of Warwicke." [10]   A significant indication of the popular favor
in which the old legend was still held was the inclusion,
in a manuscript collection of ballads and romances written shortly before 1650, of no less than three distinct
poems on Guy—the ballad, a portion of Rowlands's
Famous History, and a poem, doubtless of much greater
antiquity than either of these, on the battle with Colbrond.[11]

Meanwhile, Guy's fame as a local hero had in no wise
diminished.   Visitors to Warwick were still shown his
relics in the castle and in the chapel at Guyscliff.   " Wednesday morning," wrote Nehemiah Wharton, an officer

[9] Above, pp. 157, note 50.

[10] *Diary,* 6 March 1667. *The Plesante Song* was not the only ballad
on Guy known in the seventeenth century. " May all the ballads
be call'd in and dye," wrote Richard Corbet in *Iter Boreale* (b.
1635), " Which sing the warrs of *Colebrand* and Sir *Guy* " (quoted
in *Roxburghe Ballads,* VI, 1889, p. 732). Among the Roxburghe
Ballads in the British Museum (III, 218, 219), is a fragment entitled " THF [*sic*] HEROICK HISTORY OF GVY, Earle of Warwick. *WRITTEN BY HUMPHREY CROVCH. LONDON.* Printed
for *Jane Bell* at the East end of Christ-Church. 1655." This fragment is apparently a proof of portions of the ballad taken off on
a waste copy of the ballad of *Mock-Beggers Hall.* It is reprinted in
Roxburghe Ballads, VI, p. 737.

[11] This was the manuscript which afterwards belonged to Percy.
See the edition by Hales and Furnivall, II, pp. 136-143, 201-202, 527-
549; and, on the date, I, pp. xii-xiii. The copyist seems to have been
a North of England man, perhaps from Lancashire or Cheshire.

in the Parliamentary Army, in a letter dated September 26, 1642, "we marched toward Warwick, leaving Kenilworth Castle upon the right; and after we had marched six miles our forces met again and quartered before Warwick until 40 pieces of ordnance passed by; in which time I viewed the antiquities about one mile on this side Warwick, as S^r. Guy's cave, his chapel, his picture, and his stables all hewed out of the main rock, as also his garden and two springing wells."[12] In 1654 John Evelyn, while on a visit to Warwick, was shown in the castle "Sir Guy's great two-handed sword, staff, horse-arms, pot, and other relics of that famous knight-errant." He also examined the cave and chapel at Guyscliff; and, on proceeding to Coventry, saw at the gate the bone of a wild boar, said to have been killed by Sir Guy, which he suspected, however, to be only the chine of a whale.[13] In 1656 William Dugdale, the antiquary, in writing his history of Warwickshire, thought it proper to devote several pages to an account of that most famous of Guy's exploits, the victory at Winchester.[14]

But the most significant manifestation of the interest which the public of the later seventeenth century took in the story of Guy was the reception it accorded to a number of new versions of the legend. Between 1640 and 1706 as many as six fresh accounts of the old warrior's adventures issued from the presses of London. They were

[12] *Cal. of State Papers, Dom.*, 1641-43, p. 392.

[13] *Diary*, 3 August 1654. See also Celia Fiennes's account of her visit to Warwick between 1689 and 1694 (quoted in Dobson's edition of *The Diary of John Evelyn*, II, 1906, p. 86 n.).

[14] *The Antiquities of Warwickshire illustrated* . . . (1656), 299a-301a. His sources he enumerated as follows: "Hist. MS. Tho. Rudburn in bibl. C. C. C. Cantab. p. 35. Hist. MS. Gerardi Cornub. in bibl. Coll. S. M. Magd. Oxon. f. 227. a. Chron. MS. H. Knighton, f. 6b."

rudely and cheaply printed pamphlets, ranging in size
from twenty-four pages to a hundred and fifty, provided
with crude woodcuts, and intended primarily for the con-
sumption of the humble customers of the popular booksellers and the country chapmen.[15]   In substance, at least
five of them were based directly or indirectly upon Rowlands's *Famous History of Guy Earle of Warwick*.   In
form, they differed not only from Rowlands's work but
from all earlier accounts of the story in being written not
in verse but in prose.

The first of the new versions was the work of Martin
Parker, an active writer of popular fiction and ballads
in the middle years of the century.[16]   It bore the title *The
true story of Guy Earle of Warwick,* and was entered at
Stationers' Hall on November 24, 1640, by Richard
Oulton, the publisher of Carpenter's *Famous and Worthy
History.*[17]

Whatever may have been the success of this version,
it was not, however, until the last twenty years of the seventeenth century that prose accounts of Guy began to appear

[15] See, for example, the advertisement of W. Thackeray (1685), in
which *Guy of Warwick* is included among "Small Books, Ballads
and Histories" ready to be furnished to "any Chapman . . . at
Reasonable Rates" (*The Bagford Ballads*, ed. Ebsworth, I, 1878,
pp. liv, lv).

[16] On Parker, see Seccombe in *D. N. B.*

[17] Stat. Reg. MS.: "24 Novembris 1640 Master Oulton Entred for
his copies under the hands of Master Stansby and Master Man
Warden a book called The true story of Guy Earle of Warwick in
prose by Martyn Parker vjd." Cf. Hazlitt, *Handbook*, p. 439. As
Oulton had but recently (April 22, 1640; see *Stat. Reg.*, IV, p. 507)
acquired the copyright of Rowlands's *Famous History* from his
mother-in-law, Elizabeth Allde, it is not an unreasonable conjecture
that this was the source of Parker's narrative. I owe thanks to the
Clerk of Stationers' Hall for a transcript of the original entry,
which occurs in a portion of the Registers not printed by Arber.
No copy of Parker's work is known.

with any frequency. About 1680 there was printed for
four London booksellers, all of them well-known dealers
in popular literature, a small black-letter book of twenty-
four pages entitled *The Famous History of Guy Earl of
Warwick*. The author was advertised on the title-page
as one Samuel Smithson;[18] and his work consisted simply
of abridging in prose the old poem of the same title by
Samuel Rowlands. Throughout the thirteen chapters,
into which he divided his narrative, he preserved the same
order of incidents, neither adding nor omitting anything
of consequence, spelled the names of the characters in the
same way, and even retained, here and there, bits of the
original wording. His fidelity to his source appeared
most clearly in the chapter recounting Guy's victory over
Colbrond. Rowlands had written:

> King *Athelstone* was forced to retire
> To *Winchester*. Which when the *Danes* once knew,
> Towards the City all their strength they drew,
> Which was too strong for spear and Shield to win.
>
> . . . .
>
> Beholding now how they repulsed were,
> That *Winchester* by no means could be won:
> They do conclude to summon parley there,
> And with a Challenge have all quarrels done;
> An *English* man to combat with a *Dane*,
> And that King lose, that had his Champion slain.
> Wherewith a huge great Giant doth appear,
> Demanding where the Foxes all were crept;
> Saying, if one dare come and meet me here,
> That hath true valour for his Countrey kept,

[18] " The Famous HISTORY OF *GUY* Earl of *WARWICK*. By *Samuel Smithson. Licensed and Entered according to Order. London,
Printed for F. Coles, T. Vere, J. Wright,* and *J. Clarke.*" 8°. The
only copy I have seen is in the Bodleian (Wood, 254/2); it bears a
note in Anthony à Wood's hand, "Bought at Oxon. 1687." The
date of this edition, which was apparently the first, could hardly
have been later than 1681, as Coles died in that year (Plomer, *A
Dictionary of Printers and Booksellers,* 1907, p. 49).

Let him come forth, his manhood to disclose,
Or else the *English* are but cowards foes.

.   .   .   .

Is *English* Courage now become so rare,
That none will fight, because they fear to dye?
That I pronounce you all faint-hearted fools,
Afraid to look on manly martial tools?
What slanders I have heard in foreign lands,
Of these poor men for deeds which they have done?
Most false they are belied of their hands;
But he says true, who says their feet can run;
They have a Proverb to instruct them in,
That 'tis good sleeping in a sound whole skin.
Thus did he vaunt in terms of proud disdain,
And threw his Gauntlet down; sa'ing, There's my glove:
At length great *Guy* no longer could refrain,
Seeing all strain court'sies to express their love:
But comes unto the King, and says, Dread Lord!
This combate to thy unknown Knight afford.

Athelstone accepts his offer, whereupon Guy

with great courage goes
Forth *Winchester's* North gate unto *Hide-Mead*
Where that same Monster of a man he found,
Treading at every step two yards of ground.
Art thou the man (quoth *Colbrond*) art thou he
On whom the King will venture *England's* Crown?
Can he not find a fitter match for me,
Than this poor Rascal in a thred-bare Gown?
Where's all his Knights and worthy Champions now?
I do disdain so base a Slave as thou.
Giant, said *Guy*, Manhood should never rail,
To breathe the air with blast of idle wind;
A Soldier's weapon best can tell his tale,
Thy destiny upon my Sword I find;
'Twill let thee blood, while thou hast drops to bleed,
And spell thy death for all the *Danes* to read.
Thus I begin   .   .   .[19]

This passage Smithson abridged as follows:

[19] Hunterian Club reprint, pp. 75-77.

The Danes having Intelligence of King Athelstone's being at Winchester, they drew all their Forces thither: and seeing there was no
Means to win the City, the bloody Danes sent in a Summons to King
Athelstone, desiring that an Englishman might combat with a Dane,
and that Side to lose all that had their Champion killed.

Upon this, mighty Colbron singles himself from the Danes, and
entered into Hide-mead, near Winchester, breathing out venemous
Words, calling the English cowardly Dogs, and that he would make
their Carcases meat for Crows and Ravens. Is now, said Colbron,
all your English Courage become so timerous that you dare not fight?
What mighty boasting hath there been in foreign Nations of these
English Cowards, as if they had done deeds of Wonder, who now like
Foxes hide their Heads saying, It is good to sleep in a whole Skin.

Guy hearing the proud Disdain of Colbron could no longer forbear,
but presently goes to King Athelstone, and begs the Combat upon his
Knee, at the King's Hand; the King liking well the Courage of the
Pilgrim (so Guy was habited) he bid him go on and Prosper, so he
walked forth of the North Gate unto Hide-mead, where Colbron, the
Danes Champion, was treading every Step two Yards of Ground.

When Colbron espied Guy in his Palmer's weed, the Giant disdain'd
him with much Ire and Scorn, saying, Art thou the best Champion
that England can afford for the Honour of a King, Crown and
Country?

Giant, quoth Guy, your Words are tedious, and it is uncivil for
profest Champions to rail, filling the Air with idle Words; I have a
Sword that shall be my Orator, and make deep Impression in thy
Blood. No longer stood they to parley, but with great Vigour and
Courage they fought manfully. . . .[20]

Smithson's *Famous History* long remained one of the
favorite versions of the story with the chapmen and their
customers. It was reprinted for another group of booksellers in 1686 [21] and continued to be issued, both in

---

[20] I quote from a Newcastle reprint of about 1785 (B. M., 11621.
c. 8/8, pp. 22-23), which gives the text substantially unaltered from
the first edition. Other examples of Smithson's fidelity to the
phrasing of his source may be found in Guy's speech to Phillis on
his return from the continent (*ibid.*, p. 11; cf. Rowlands, p. 24), in
the account of his fight with the pagan warriors (pp. 13-14; Rowlands, pp. 37-39), and in his soliloquy on the skull (pp. 19-20;
Rowlands, pp. 66-68).

[21] Esdaile, *A List of English Tales and Prose Romances printed*

London and elsewhere, until at least the end of the eighteenth century.[22]   Sometime before 1750 the abridgment was itself abridged, and the shorter version seems to have become no less popular than the longer.[23]

In the meantime, rival publishers had come forward with other chapbook accounts of Guy's career.   The first of these, a much more complete and circumstantial relation than Smithson's, appeared in 1681, under the title *The Renowned History, or the Life and Death of Guy Earl of Warwick.*[24]   The compiler, John Shurley (or

before 1740, p. 233. The publishers were J. Clark, W. Thackeray, and T. Passinger. An edition of *Guy of Warwick* was advertised among " Small Merry Books " in Thackeray's list of 1685 (*Bagford Ballads*, I, p. lv).

[22] The British Museum has a copy of a Newcastle edition of about 1785 (11621. c. 8/8). This has the same title and virtually the same text as the Bodleian copy of c. 1680; but the name of the author does not occur.

[23] There seem, indeed, to have been two abridgments: one represented by a Newcastle edition of c. 1800 (B.M., 1078. i. 19/7), in which a few paragraphs only are omitted; the other represented by a London edition of c. 1750 (B.M., 1079. i. 14/3; the date is that of the British Museum Catalogue, and must not be taken too seriously). Of this version, which is considerably shortened from the original, the Museum has a Derby reprint of 1796 (12331. aaaa. 56/1), a Nottingham reprint of the same date (12331. aaaa. 56/7), and a London reprint of about the end of the century (12804. de. 53/2). The title in all cases is *The History of Guy, Earl of Warwick.* For the text see Ashton, *Chap-books of the Eighteenth Century* (1882), pp. 140-153.

[24] " The Renowned HISTORY, or the LIFE and DEATH of GUY Earl of WARWICK, Containing His Noble EXPLOITS and VICTORIES. *LONDON.* Printed by *H. Brugis* for P. *Brooksby* at the *Golden Ball* near the *Hospital-Gate* in *west-Smithfield.* MDCLXXXI." 4o. B. L. There is a copy in the British Museum (12403. aa. 35). It contains 78 unnumbered pages, with sixteen large cuts. The text is divided into sixteen chapters with headings. This edition was advertised in Hilary Term, 1680/81, among new books (*Term Catalogues*, I, p. 428).

Shirley), was a professional writer of popular fiction during the last quarter of the century, the author, in addition to *Guy*, of *The History of Reynard the Fox, in heroic verse; The Honour of Chivalry; The Famous History of Aurelius;* and abridgments of *Amadis of Gaul* and of the story of King Arthur.[25]   His version of Guy of Warwick was probably his first venture, and, it would seem, one of his most ambitious. He aimed to give a more complete account of the legend than any of his predecessors. " Courteous Reader," he announced in his prefatory epistle, " I have here undertaken to give you a full and satisfactory Account of the *Life* and *Death* of the far-Famed and Most Renowned *English* Champion *GUY* Earl of *Warwick,* according to what can be Collected out of the best Historians, both Antient and Modern. No work in this Nature ever yet appearing to the World with more then half a Face, or an imperfect Relation, the which has rather sullied the Heroick Actions of so brave a man, then caused them to shine in their Native brightness." [26]   He appears, indeed, to have derived his materials from various sources. For the general framework of the narrative, and for the details of most of the incidents, he went no farther than *The Famous History of Guy Earle of Warwick* by Samuel Rowlands.[27]   But he added several matters not

---

[25] Cf. *D. N. B.*, art. " Shirley, John," and Esdaile, *l. c.*, p. 306.

[26] " Epistle to the Reader."

[27] Of the modifications made by Rowlands in the story as told in the romance (see pp. 154-156, above), all but one—the dialogue with the skull—reappear in Shurley. The character of the latter's borrowing, which was material rather than verbal, and involved considerable amplification, may be seen in the following passage from the narrative of the fight with Colbrond, (chapter xv):
" . . . the King being much perplexed turned to his Nobles, demanding if any of them would adventure on the Noble Enterprize: Remember said he how great Goliah fell by David's hand; and

included in Rowlands's poem: an account of the early
history of Britain and of Guy's descent from Cassibilain,
a British chieftain who fought against the Romans; [28] a
story of how Guy, after landing in Normandy, "fought
with three Champions, killing two of them, and wounded
the third, taking from them a Lady wrongfully condemned
to dy by the young Duke of Bilois, who had Ravisht her,"
and of how he later defeated and captured the Duke who
pursued him by the sea; [29] a narrative of his conquest of
the Dun Cow; [30] and finally a description of his fight with
three pirate ships while on his way to Constantinople. [31]
Of these additions the first two and the fourth may well
have been the invention of Shurley himself; it is not

shall this Pagan outbrave us thus, for shame my Lords let it not
be known . . . So said the King but all around stood mute,
looking on each other who should first Reply, which Guy (who had
stood all that while undiscovered) observing, with anger groaned,
and coming to the King most humbly besought his Majesty to confer
on him the Honour of the Combate, to which the King (not dreaming
who it was, for all supposed Guy then dead, by reason he had not
been heard of in so long a time) made answer, Alas poor Pilgrim,
for so thou seemest to be, thou art not able to contend with one
so mighty, I had a Champion once, whom Death has now snatch'd
from me, on whose head I would have ventured my Life and Crown,
Oh . . . Renowned Guy, for ever lost, thou wouldst not have
seen thy Soveraign thus affronted and abused, with that he turn'd
and wept, whose Royal Tears grieved Guy for to behold, still with
supplications, pressing him that he would give consent: Saying, Dread
Lord, though I'm now unknown to you, yet trust my Courage for
this once, and by Heaven, I vow before the Sun descends beneath the
Western deep, he that has braved you now shall pay his Life for
the affront, at which Heroick speech the King stood amazed, and
wondered at the greatness of his saying, I have accepted thee, thou
shalt be the man on whom I'l venture England . . . Go thou
worthy man and Heaven direct thy hand to quell thy Foe; at which
Guy returning humble thanks departed." Compare with this the
extract from Rowlands cited on page 155, above.

[28] Chapter I.   [30] Chapter VII.
[29] Chapters IV, V.   [31] Chapter IX.

likely that he found them in any earlier versions of the story of Guy. With the tale of the Dun Cow the case was different. As a result partly of the continued influence of local tradition, partly of that of the ballad of 1592, this particular adventure had become extremely well known. In 1593 Gabriel Harvey alluded to " the furious dun Cowe of Dunsmore heath " as the " terriblest foman of Sir Guy." [32] In 1612 an anonymous writer of ballads gave the exploit a prominent place among Guy's claims to honor in a piece called *Saint George's Commendation to all Souldiers:*

> The noble Earl of Warwick, that we call'd Sir *Guy,*
> The Infidels and Pagans stoutly did defie;
> He slew the Giant *Brandimore,* and after was the death
> Of that most ghastly Dun Cowe, the divell of *Dunsmore* Heath.[33]

In 1613 Drayton mentioned the story, apparently on the authority of *The Plesante Song,* in *Poly-olbion.*[34] In 1639 the author of *The Tragical History* included it among the adventures which Guy undertook to win the hand of Phillis.[35] And in 1663, in the first part of

---

[32] *Pierces Supererogation,* in Works, ed. Grosart, II (1884), p. 223.
[33] *Roxburghe Ballads,* VI, p. 781.
[34] Canto XIII, Spenser Society reprint, Part II, p. 221.
[35] The passage occurs in the scene in which Guy, just married to Phillis, hints at his intention of leaving her. Rohon, his father-in-law, speaks:

> Live then in peace, my fair high-hearted Sonne
> since all men muse to think what thou hast done,
> the *Calledonian* savage Bore is dead,
> and by thy hand the wild Cow slaughtered,
> that Kept such Revels upon *Dunsmore* Heath;
> and many adventures hath thou past beside
> to make my Daughter *Phillis* thy fair Bride.

Quarto of 1661, ll. 68-74. For other allusions to the Dun Cow in the play see above, p. 164, note 73.

Hudibras, Butler employed it to give point to his description of Talgol, the butcher:

> Right many a Widow his keen blade,
> And many a Fatherless, had made.
> He many a *Bore* and huge *Dun Cow*
> Did like another *Guy* o'erthrow.
> But *Guy* with him in fight compar'd,
> Had like the *Bore* or *Dun Cow* far'd.[36]

Without betraying his ideal of completeness, Shurley could scarcely have omitted some mention of the famous Dun Cow. He wrote, in fact, probably the most detailed account of the legend that had yet appeared.

Dismissed for the second time by Phillis, Guy was waiting in the harbor for a favorable wind, when he learned that a " monstrous Beast, formed by Majick skill into the likeness of a Cow, or rather a Cow of vast bulk possessed by some tempestuous spirit " was terrifying the neighboring country, destroying the cattle and putting their keepers to flight. According to rumor, the beast was " so strong and swift in motion, that it was thought no humane force could have destroy'd it; the monstrous description of her as followeth, is affirmed by Authors of great integrity and worth, that she was four yards in height, six in length, and had a head proportionable, armed with two sharp hornes growing direct, with Eyes all red and fiery, which seemed to dart Lightning from afar, she being of a Dun colour, from whence she was named the Dun .Cow and the place not many miles distant from Warwick, where she haunted; from that Monster took the name of Dunsmore Heath, which name it keeps unto this day." Although the King had offered Knighthood and various other rewards to anyone who would slay the Dun Cow, no one

[36] Ed. A. R. Waller (1905), p. 36.

had as yet dared to risk his life in the attempt. Guy, however, glad of the opportunity for a little excitement before he sailed, immediately seized battle-ax and bow and arrow, and set out for Dunsmore Heath. "He no sooner came within bow shot of the place but the Monster espyed him, and putting out her head through the thicket, with dreadful eyes glared on him, and began to roar horribly, at which Guy who was one of the expertest Archers England then had, bent his Bow of Steel, and drawing an Arrow to the head let fly, the which as swift as Lightning, striking on the Monster's hide rebounded as from a wall of Adamant, not making the least impression." Then the Dun Cow charged, and not minding the blows Guy rained on her with his battle-ax, dinted his "high proofed Armour" with her terrible horns. Wheeling his horse, Guy met her again, and this time directed his blows behind her ear, "the only place she was sensible of being wounded in," till she finally fell to the ground. After that it was an easy matter to dispose of her; he simply "hewed upon her so long that through her impenitrable skin he battered her skull, till with a horrid groan she there expired." When the result of the fight became known, Guy was summoned by the King to York, and the order of knighthood, with many other rich gifts, conferred upon him. As for the Dun Cow, one of her ribs was ordered to be hung up in Warwick Castle as a trophy of the victory.[37]

Shurley's chapbook enjoyed a vogue which, though not so long-lived as that of Smithson's *Famous History*, was nevertheless considerable while it lasted. Not only was it frequently reprinted during the twenty-five years following its appearance,[38] but it also furnished mate-

---

[37] *The Renowned History* (1681), sig. D.
[38] Esdaile, *l. c.*, p. 233.

rial to the compilers of at. least three new versions of the story.

One of these was a simple abridgment. Inspired perhaps by the success of Smithson's *Guy,* an obscure bookseller named Charles Bates, who after 1695 issued several editions of Shurley,[39] put forth a new and greatly abbreviated account of the legend under the title, *The History of the Famous Exploits of Guy Earl of Warwick.*[40] It was a poorly printed black-letter tract, with a text taken directly, though with much condensation and not a little verbal change, from *The Renowned History.*[41] It was reissued at least once, sometime after 1728.[42]

[39] *Ibid.,* p. 233 and *Harvard Catalogue of Chapbooks,* No. 484.

[40] "The HISTORY of the FAMOUS EXPLOITS of Guy Earl of Warwick. His Encountring and Overcoming of Monstrous Gyants and Champions, and his killing the Dun Cow of *Dunsmore-heath,* with many other Gallant Atchievements performed by him in his life, and the manner of his death. Printed for *Charles Bates,* at the *Sun* and *Bible* in *Pye-Corner.*" 4°. B. M. (12450. f. 8).

[41] The episode of Guy's service with the Duke of Lovain (Shurley, Chap. VII) was omitted altogether, and the narrative throughout greatly condensed. The following extracts will serve to illustrate the relation of the two texts:

SHURLEY, CHAP. VII.

. . . the terrour of her [the Dun Cow's] fierceness had spread it self in such a dreadful shape, that none durst undertake the enterprize, but each one wishing for Guy whom all supposed by this time in France; glad of this opportunity, he leaves the ship, and having changed his Armour to avoid being known, he takes a strong battle Ax his Bow and Quiver with him, and so incognito riding to the place where this Monster used to lodge, which

The History of the Famous Exploits, Chap. V.

. . . *Guy,* who was by all thought to be far beyond sea, privately arming himself with a strong Battle-Ax, and his Bow and Quiver, made his way towards the Place where this Monster was, and approaching near the Den, he beheld upon the Heath, the sad Objects of Desolation, the Carcasses of Men and Beasts she had destroyed: *Guy* no whit daunted at that, pursued on his way, till such time she

Meanwhile, probably not long after 1690, there issued from the shop of G. Conyers, an active publisher of popular literature, two small volumes each bearing the title *The Famous History of Guy Earl of Warwick. Written by Samuel Rowland.* One of these volumes contained a reprint of Rowlands's poem; [43] the other, a new rendering

was among a great thicket of trees that grew upon the Plain, near to a Poole or standing water finding as he had passed along all the Shepherds Cottages deserted and the Carcasses of men and beasts ly scattered round about; he no sooner came within bow shot of the place but the Monster espyed him, and putting out her head through the thicket, with dreadful eyes glared on him, and began to roar horribly, at which Guy who was one of the expertest Archers England then had, bent his Bow of Steel, and drawing an Arrow to the head let fly, the which as swift as Lightning, striking on the Monster's hide rebounded as from a wall of Adamant, not making the least impression. . . .

espyed *Guy*, staring with her dreadful Eyes upon him, and roaring most hediously, he bent his Bow of Steel, and let fly an Arrow, which rebounded from her Hide, as if it had been shot against a Brazen Wall. . . .

[42] "The HISTORY of the FAMOUS EXPLOITS of Guy Earl of Warwick. . . . Printed for *Sarah Bates*, at the *Sun* and *Bible* in *Guilt-spurr-street*." B.M. (12403 d. 1). The succession of Sarah Bates to the business formerly belonging to Charles Bates took place between 1728 and 1735. See Esdaile, *l. c.*, pp. 318-319.

[43] B.M. (G. 18792/1). The imprint gives Conyers's place of business as "the Gold-Ring in Little Britain." He began to publish at this address in Michaelmas Term, 1690 (*Term Catalogues*, II, p. 333). A peculiar feature of this edition of Rowlands was the interpolation, at the end of the canto describing Guy's marriage (pp. 52-54), of an account of the Dun Cow, versified apparently from the narrative in Shurley.

of the story in prose.[44] In preparing this prose version,
the compiler relied chiefly on what he found in *The
Famous History* in verse. But, while he retained here
and there bits of the original phrasing,[45] he made no
attempt to preserve the arrangement or proportions of his
source. Thus, in Rowlands, Guy's first adventure after
leaving England was a tournament for the hand of the
daughter of the Emperor of Almain; [46] this the maker of
the chapbook postponed until after the knight's return
from Constantinople.[47] Again, Guy's rescue of a lion
who was fighting for his life with a dragon, an episode
which in Rowlands had occurred on the return journey
from the East,[48] the writer of the *Famous History* in prose
introduced long before the expedition against the Sultan
had been planned.[49] Nor did his changes stop with these

[44] "The FAMOUS HISTORY of *GUY* of W*arwick*. Written by
Samuel Rowland. LONDON, Printed for *G. Conyers,* at the *Golden-
Ring* in *Little-Britain.*" 8°, 30 pp. B.M. (G. 18792/2). The text
is divided into two chapters of very unequal length (pp. 3-5, 5-30).

[45] As, for example, in his account of Guy's victory over the Sultan
(P. 12): "With that at each other they ran, their Launces broke,
and each forsook his Horse, and betook them to their Swords: *Guy*
struck such forcible blows, that he cut through the *Souldain's* Armour, and by loss of Blood the *Souldain* fell to ground, casting
handfuls of his Blood at *Guy.*" Rowlands had described the event
as follows (Hunterian Club reprint, p. 39):

> With that at *Guy* he ran with all his force,
> Their Launces brake, and each forsook his Horse.
> Then by the Sword the Victor must prevail,
> Which manly force makes deadly wounds withal,
> Cutting through Armour, mangling shirts of Mail,
> That at the last down did the *Souldan* fall,
> Sending blasphemous curses to the skye,
> And casting handfulls of his blood at *Guy.*

In general, however, the chapbook departed rather widely from the
style of the original.

[46] Canto III.   [47] Pp. 12-15.   [48] Canto VII.   [49] Pp. 8-9.

shifts in the order of the story. He added accounts of. Guy's parentage,[50] of his slaughter of the Dun Cow,[51] and of his encounter with a giant named Rumbo, who after being overcome in a fight agreed to become Guy's man, and, though his native cowardice now and then got the better of him, yet proved a faithful servant until his death in a sortie against the Germans.[52] The first two of these additions plainly came from Shurley's *Renowned History,* although in rewriting them the compiler of the new chapbook ascribed to Guy's father a Latin name which Shurley had given to Guy himself,[53] and shifted the episode of the Dun Cow to a position among Guy's youthful exploits in the opening chapter.[54] The incident of Rumbo may

---

[50] P. 3. [51] Pp. 3-5. [52] Pp. 7-10.

[53] "Guyraldus Cacibylanius."

[54] The narrative begins as follows: " One of his Atchievements was, the destroying of a monstrous Dun-Cow upon *Dunsmore-heath,* that destroy'd both Man and Beast: She is said by some to be six Yards in length, and about four in breadth; her Head was proportionable, and her Horns large and sharp, her Eyes was fiery and sparkling, her Colour, as I said before, Dun; and in short, she was so strong and swift in Motion, that no Humane Force could prevail against her; for she destroy'd Man and Beast, and put all her keepers to flight.

" The King hearing of this monstrous Beast, and the great slaughters that was made by her, offer'd Knighthood and a great Reward to any that would undertake to destroy her; whereupon *Guy,* after many others had attempted in vain, privately goes and engages this Curst-Cow, with a strong Battle-Ax, and his Bow and Quiver. The Plain the Cow used to lodge in, was a great Thicket of Trees near a Pool of Water, and above it laid the Carcases of Men and Beasts. . . .

" Being at last come within Bow-shot, the cow espy'd him, who began to make a horrid roaring, but *Guy* quickly bent his Bow, and let an Arrow fly, which could not penetrate nor make the least Impression." A comparison of this passage with the accounts in Shurley, in *The Famous Exploits,* and in *The Noble and Renowned History* (see above, pp. 178 ff. and p. 180, note 41, and below p. 187, note 69) leaves little doubt that the direct source was Shurley.

perhaps have grown out of a reminiscence of the story of
the giant Ascapart in the romance of *Bevis of Hampton.*[55]

Neither *The History of the Famous Exploits* nor Conyers's *Famous History* in prose appears to have caught the
fancy of the chapbook-reading public as did the productions of Smithson and Shurley. A much greater success attended *The Noble and Renowned History of Guy Earl of
Warwick,* which was published in 1706 as the work of
" G. L." [56] Of all the prose treatments of the legend this
was destined to achieve perhaps the greatest popularity.
It reached a seventh edition in 1733,[57] and after that was
reprinted at frequent intervals, in London and in various
provincial towns, during more than a hundred years:[58]
to the publisher of an edition of 1821 it seemed that

[55] Cf. *The Romance of Sir Beues of Hampton,* ed. Kölbing, *E. E.
T. S., E. S.,* XLIV (1885), ll. 2506-2802.

[56] " The Noble and Renowned HISTORY OF *GUY* Earl of *Warwick:*
CONTAINING A Full and True Account of his many Famous and
Valiant Actions, Remarkable and Brave Exploits, and Noble and
Renowned Victories. Also his Courtship to fair *Phaelice,* Earl *Ro-
band's* Daughter and Heiress, and the many Difficulties and Hazards
he went thorow, to obtain her Love. Extracted from Authentick
Records; and the whole Illustrated with Cuts suitable to the History.
LONDON: Printed by W. O. for *E.* B[rewster] and sold by *A.
Bettesworth,* at the Sign of the Red Lion on *London-bridge.* 1706."
12°. Pp. 157. B. M. (12450. b. 16). The work is divided into
fourteen chapters. It was dedicated by G. L. to "his Honour'd and
Worthy Friend, Mr. Zachariah Hayward, Citizen of London." For a
modern reprint see Morley, *Early Prose Romances,* Carisbrooke
Library (1889), pp. 331-408. Edward Brewster, the publisher, also
issued editions of Rowlands's *Famous History.* See *Term Catalogues,*
III, p. 114 and Hazlitt, *Handbook,* p. 523.

[57] Esdaile, *l. c.,* p. 234.

[58] A. C. L. Brown, in *The Journal of Germanic Philology,* III, p. 14.
The British Museum owns copies of the " twelfth edition," published
about 1785 (12403. aaaa. 12, and 12410. aaa. 18), and of an edition
of 1821, printed by C. Whittingham of Chiswick for booksellers in
Warwick, Coventry, London, and Edinburgh (12410. aaa. 9).

"almost innumerable editions" had been given to the public.[59]

The composition of *The Noble and Renowned History* could have cost its author but little pains. For the main divisions of his narrative and at least two-thirds of his text, he followed Rowlands, and followed him, too, in a singularly slavish way. Unlike Smithson and Shurley, he did not even attempt a paraphrase, but contented himself with turning the verse of his original into prose by the easy method of dropping the rimes, changing here and there the order of a sentence, or adding an occasional phrase of transition.[60] Thus, in the fourth canto of *The Famous History* Rowlands had made Guy on his return from the continent address Phaelice in these words:

> Fair Foe (quoth *Guy*), I come to challenge thee,
> For there's no man that I can meet will fight;
> I have been where a Crew of Cowards be,
> Not one that dares maintain a Ladies right:
> Good proper fellows of their tongues, and tall,
> That let me win a Princess from them all.
> *Phaelice*, this sword hath won an *Emp'rors* Daughter,
> As sweet a Wench as lives in *Europe's* space:
> At price of blows, and bloody wounds I bought her,
> Well worth my bargain; but thy better face
> Hath made me leave her to some others Lot;
> For, I protest by Heaven, I love her not.
> This stately Steed, this Faulcon and these Hounds,
> I took, as in full payment of the rest:

[59] "Advertisement" in *The Noble and Renowned History of Guy Earl of Warwick*, 1821 (B. M., 12410. aaa. 9). Percy alluded to it in 1765 as "the common story book" (*Reliques*, ed. Wheatley, 1886, III, p. 114); and Ellis in 1805 declared that it was to be found "at almost every stall in the metropolis" (*Specimens of Early English Metrical Romances*, II, p. 3).

[60] The first writer to note the character of G. L.'s indebtedness to Rowlands seems to have been Thomas Percy (*Reliques*, ed. cit., III, p. 114). Professor Brown has treated the question with fullness in *The Journal of Germanic Philology*, III, pp. 14-21.

> For I will keep my love within the bounds
> That do inclose the compass of my breast:
> My constancy to thee is all my care,
> Leaving all other Women as they are.
> But Sweet-heart, tell me, shall I have thee now,
> Wilt thou consent the Priest shall do his part?
> Art thou resolved still to keep thy Vow?
> Is none but I half with thee in thy heart?
> Canst thou forsake the world, change Maiden-life,
> And help thy faithful Lover to a Wife? [61]

In *The Noble and Renowned History* this speech appeared transformed as follows:

" Fair foe," said he, " I come to challenge thee; for there is no man that I can meet will fight me. I have been where a crew of cowards are, but none that dare maintain the right of ladies; good, proper, and well spoken men, indeed, but let me win a Princess from them all. Phaelice, this sword hath won an Emperor's daughter, as sweet a wench as any lives in all Europe. I bought her at the price of blood and wounds; well worth my bargain: but thy better face hath made me leave her to some other's lot; for I protest, by Heaven, I could not love her. This stately steed, this falcon, and these hounds I took, as in full payment of the rest; for I have always kept my love to thee enclosed within the centre of my heart. My constancy to thee I have still preserved, leaving all other women as they are. But say, my Phaelice, shall I now obtain thee? wilt thou consent that Hymen tie our hands? art thou resolved to keep still to thy vow, that none but I shall ever have thy heart? canst thou forsake the world, change thy condition, and now become thy true and faithful lover's wife." [62]

By this simple process of writing Rowlands's verse as prose, G. L. composed the greater part of *The Noble and Renowned History*.[63] Rowlands, however, was not his only source. Every now and then he turned aside from *The Famous History* to pilfer a sentence, a paragraph, a

[61] Hunterian Club reprint, pp. 24-25.
[62] Morley's reprint, pp. 349-350.
[63] For further parallels see the article, previously cited, of Professor Brown.

chapter from his more recent predecessor, Shurley. From Shurley he took, besides shorter or less important passages, the details of Guy's parentage and early life,[64] the story of the rescue of Dorinda from death at the stake,[65] the accounts' of the killing of the Dun Cow,[66] and of the sea-fight with the three Saracen pirates,[67] and portions of the narrative of the combat with Colbrond.[68] The verbal changes which he made in these passages in fitting them into his work, although numerous, were not sufficient to destroy their original character.[69] In short, as regards both style and content, *The Noble and Renowned History* was little more than a composite of the two earlier versions of Rowlands and Shurley.

IV

The eighteenth century was for *Guy of Warwick* a period of both revival and decline.

The revival centered in that little group of critics and antiquaries who during the third quarter of the century pioneered in England the study of the older literature of northern Europe. These men, of whom the most prominent were Thomas Warton, Richard Hurd, Thomas Percy, and Thomas Gray, found in the medieval romances a fruitful subject of inquiry and speculation. Some of them knew, perhaps from their childhood, the few late versions

[64] G. L., *The Noble and Renowned History*, Morley's reprint, pp. 331-332; cf. Shurley, *The Renowned History*, 1681, A2 and verso.
[65] G. L., 340-345; Shurley, B2v-C.
[66] G. L., 352-354; Shurley, D and verso.
[67] G. L., 360-362; Shurley, E-E3.
[68] G. L. 399-400; Shurley, I2v-I3.
[69] Compare, for example, G. L.'s narrative of the Dun Cow episode (Morley's reprint, pp. 352-353) with the corresponding passage from Shurley, quoted above, pp. 178-179, and p. 180, note 41.

still in circulation. But for the most part they disregarded these, and went back, at first to the editions of the sixteenth century, and later, as their interest grew, to the medieval manuscripts themselves. The results of their studies they gave to the public at intervals after 1750. Warton began the movement with his *Observations on the Fairy Queen of Spenser,* published in 1754 and reissued, in a revised and enlarged form, in 1762; Hurd followed in the latter year with his *Letters on Chivalry and Romance;* in 1765 came Percy's essay " On the Ancient Metrical Romances," included along with much other material on the medieval stories in his *Reliques;* in 1774 Warton devoted to the subject a large part of the first volume of his *History of English Poetry.* These writers approached the old stories in the spirit partly of the antiquary and partly of the lover of romantic poetry. Romances, wrote Warton in 1762, " preserve many curious historical facts, and throw considerable light on the nature of the feudal system. They are the pictures of ancient usages and customs; and represent the manners, genius, and character of our ancestors. Above all, such are their Terrible Graces of magic and enchantment, so magnificently marvellous are their fictions and failings, that they contribute in a wonderful degree, to rouse and invigorate all the powers of imagination: to store the fancy with those sublime and alarming images, which true poetry best delights to display." [1]

---

[1] *Observations on the Fairy Queen* (1807), II, p. 323; the passage appeared first in the second edition. The full story of this phase of the medieval revival of the eighteenth century remains to be told. Professors Beers and Phelps in their works on the English Romantic Movement give to it but the merest passing notice; while Professor Ker in his chapter on " The Literary Influence of the Middle Ages " in *The Cambridge History of English Literature* (vol. x, 1913, pp. 245-273) leaves it out of account altogether.

The first person to deal from the new point of view with *Guy of Warwick* was Thomas Percy. His knowledge of the romance was derived from a considerable variety of sources. In the folio manuscript given him early in life by Humphrey Pitt he possessed texts of the ballad, of an old poem entitled *Guy and Colebrande,* and of a portion of Rowlands's *Famous History;*[2] and he knew, perhaps from boyhood, the prose chapbook of G. L.[3] He was not, however, content to stop here. In 1764 he addressed a letter to Dr. Ducarel, a prominent antiquary, requesting aid in securing copies of certain old poems and romances: among the pieces which he declared would be "particularly acceptable" was the metrical romance of *Sir Guy.*[4] Whether or not as the result of this letter, he eventually gained access to a copy of Copland's quarto edition ("preserved among Mr. Garrick's collection of old plays"[5]), and learned of the existence of manuscripts of *Guy* at Cambridge and Edinburgh.[6] On the basis of this knowledge he devoted several pages in his *Reliques of Ancient English Poetry* (1765) to an exposition of facts about the legend. Of the texts known to him he printed three: the ballad of Guy and Phelis,[7] a fragment of Rowlands's poem recounting Guy's fight with Amarant,[8] and a short passage from Copland's edition of the metrical romance.[9] To these specimens he added various bits of information concerning the accessible manuscripts of the poem, its popularity in England and on the Continent.

---

[2] *Bishop Percy's Folio Manuscript,* II, pp. 136-143, 201-202, 527-549.

[3] *Reliques,* ed. Wheatley, III, p. 114.

[4] Percy to Dr. Ducarel, quoted in Nichols, *Literary Anecdotes of the Eighteenth Century,* III (1812), p. 753.

[5] *Reliques,* ed. cit., III, p. 107.   [7] *Ibid.,* III, pp. 109-113.

[6] *Ibid.,* III, pp. 364-365.   [8] *Ibid.,* III, pp. 115-121.

[9] *Ibid.,* III, p. 108.

5

its historical foundation, and the relations of the different versions.[10] Altogether he contributed something, if not a great deal, to current knowledge of the story.

Two years after the first publication of the *Reliques,* another, and somewhat more critical, scholar addressed himself to the study of *Guy of Warwick.* On May 7, 1767, Samuel Pegge, a well-known student of English antiquities, read before the Society of Antiquaries a brief memoir on the legend.[11] In it he dealt exclusively with one problem—the historical basis of the story of Guy's duel with Colbrand. That this episode was in the main, if not entirely, founded on fact, had been the almost universal opinion of the Middle Ages and the sixteenth century.[12] Moreover, in spite of occasional expressions of skepticism,[13] belief in its truth had remained alive during the succeeding hundred and fifty years. Thus, in 1656 William Dugdale wrote in his *Antiquities of Warwickshire:* " The story . . . however it may be thought fictitious by some, forasmuch as there be those that make a question whether there was ever really such a man; or, if so, whether all be not a dream which is reported of him, in regard that the monks have sounded out his praises so hyperbolically; yet those that are more considerate will neither doubt the one nor the other, inasmuch as it hath been so usual with our antient historians, for the encouragement of after-ages unto bold attempts, to set forth the exploits of worthy men with the highest encomiums imaginable; and therefore should we for that cause be so conceited as to explode it ? All the history of

[10] *Ibid.,* II, pp. 182-183; III, pp. 107-108, 114, 364-365.
[11] Printed in Nichols's *Bibliotheca Topographica Britannica,* No. XVII (1783), pp. 29-39.
[12] Above, pp. 127, 134.
[13] Above, p. 140, note 43.

those times might as well be villified." [14] Dugdale's opinion was shared, in the next century, by Thomas Hearne and Percy. In 1733 Hearne printed a text of Girardus Cornubiensis's version of the story without the slightest suggestion that he doubted the truth of the narrative; [15] and in 1765, in the *Reliques*, Percy cited Dugdale's conclusions with evident approval.[16] Pegge rejected the theory *in toto*. With no more texts at his disposal than any of his predecessors—he seems, indeed, to have known only the accounts in the medieval chronicles [17]—he reached the conclusion, which he supported with numerous arguments, that while "there might be such a person as Guy in the Saxon times, and a soldier of eminence," still the supposition "that he was earl of Warwick, and fought a duel with Colbrond for the crown of England," was improbable in the extreme.[18] The whole story he set down as the invention of some writer of romance in the period after the Norman Conquest.[19]

Pegge's "Memoir" remained unpublished until 1783, when it was issued, along with several other pieces, in the seventeenth number of Nichols's *Bibliotheca Topographica Britannica*. It seems to have attracted but little attention.

In the meantime a third investigator had added his quota to the knowledge of the romance possessed by the scholarly public. In the first volume of Thomas Warton's *History of English Poetry*, published in 1774, por-

---

[14] Quoted by Pegge, *l. c.;* p. 31.

[15] *Ibid.*, p. 30, note.

[16] *Reliques*, ed. cit., III, p. 108.

[17] He cites Girardus Cornubiensis, Knighton, Hardyng, and Rous. See his "Memoir," *passim*. He appears to have known the metrical romance only through Percy. *Ibid.*, p. 32.

[18] *Ibid.*, p. 29.   [19] *Ibid.*, p. 38.

tions of sections III and v were devoted to *Guy of War-wick*.[20] Unlike Percy and Pegge, who had treated the story largely by itself, apart from the extensive body of medieval narrative literature to which it belonged, Warton aimed to present the poem in its historical perspective, first as a popular French romance, second as one of the numerous metrical tales which flourished in England from the end of the thirteenth century. In doing so he brought together nearly all of the facts about *Guy* which Percy had scattered through the *Reliques,* and added some new ones from his own research. Among these additions were a few new items in the list of French manuscripts, one or two fresh details in the history of the story's vogue, and several pages of quotations from the romance as printed by Copland.

Thus there was taking place in the second half of the eighteenth century something like a revival of interest in the older forms of *Guy of Warwick*. As a part of the general current of medieval influence characteristic of the time, this revival was not without its importance. Study of *Guy* was but one of the many paths by which Englishmen were coming to a clearer and more sympathetic knowledge of the life and literature of the Middle Ages. Judged, however, by its effect on the popular vogue of the story in the later eighteenth century, the revival had no significance whatever. If *Guy* continued to appeal to the general reading public, the reason was to be found in the persistence of a long-established tradition, not in any influence exerted by the writings of Percy or Warton or Pegge.

But, in truth, this long-established tradition was itself breaking up; and the later eighteenth century, which saw

---

[20] Pp. 144-145 and 170-175 of the edition of 1840.

the beginning of scholarly interest in the legend, saw also the end, or nearly the end, of popular interest. It is true that editions of the ballad and of the chapbooks of Smithson and G. L. continued to be printed and sold.[21] But these survivors constituted only a small part of the literature about Guy which had come into existence since the end of the sixteenth century; and after 1706 no fresh accounts of the legend seem to have been written. The audience, moreover, which read the current versions was becoming more and more restricted in its composition. Throughout the eighteenth century *Guy of Warwick* seems to have found its readers almost exclusively among children. It was as a child's story, indeed, that it was most frequently mentioned in the literature of the time. Thus, in 1709, in a paper in *The Tatler*, Steele included it along with other romances among the favorite classics of a boy under eight. " We were pleasing our selves," he wrote, " with this fantastical Preferment of the young Lady, when on a sudden we were alarmed with the Noise of a Drum, and immediately entered my little Godson to give me a Point of War. . . I found upon Conversation with him, . . . that the Child had excellent Parts, and was a great Master of all the Learning on t'other Side Eight Years old . . . I found he had very much turned his Studies for about a Twelvemonth past, into the Lives and Adventures of Don *Bellianis* of *Greece, Guy* of *Warwick,* the *Seven Champions,* and other Historians of that Age. . . . He would tell you the Mismanagements of *John Hickathrift,* find Fault with the passionate Temper in *Bevis* of *Southampton,* and loved St. *George* for being the Champion of *England*." [22] So also, in 1765, Percy spoke of *Guy* as a

[21] See above, pp. 150, note 32, 173-174, 184.
[22] *The Tatler*, No. 95, November 17, 1709.

book "once admired by all readers of wit and taste," but
"now very properly resigned to children." [23]   And some
sixty years later, in a conversation reported by Hazlitt,
James Northcote made much the same observation. " You
are to consider," he said, " that there must be books for all
tastes and ages. You may despise it, but the world do
not.   There are books for children till the time they are
six years of age, such as Jack-the-Giant-killer, the Seven
Champions of Christendom, Guy of Warwick, and
others." [24]   To such uses had come a story once read and
admired by all Englishmen!

RONALD S. CRANE.

[23] *Reliques*, ed. cit., III, p. 107.
[24] Hazlitt, *Conversations of James Northcote, Esq., R.A.*, in *The Collected Works of William Hazlitt*, ed. Waller and Glover, VI (1903), pp. 412-413.

IX.—THE ORIGINAL OF *THE NON-JUROR*

Colley Cibber declared that for *The Non-juror,* the most important of his dramas, he employed Molière's *Tartuffe* as the basis.[1] His declaration has been accepted by later writers. Genest says, "it is taken from Moliere's Tartuffe."[2] Ward repeats, "Crowne may have helped to suggest to Cibber the composition of *The Non-Juror* (1717), which however more closely follows *Tartuffe.*"[3] Van Laun declares: "Cibber has been accused of having stolen the plot, characters, incidents, and most part of the language from Medbourne; but this is untrue. What he has taken from him is the servant Charles (Laurence), who also betrays his master."[4] The ever-present German dissertation solemnly copies the statement: a certain Wilhelm Schneider concludes: "Medbournes 'Tartuffe' kann, zumal er zunächst Übersetzung ist, nach van Launs Artikel nur für wenige Anregungen herangezogen werden."[5] Joseph Knight in his article on Cibber in the *Dictionary of National Biography* remarks: "A

[1] *An Apology for the Life of Colley Cibber,* ed. Lowe, London, 1889, II, p. 186.

[2] *Some Account of the English Stage from the Restoration in 1660 to 1830,* Bath, 1832, II, p. 615.

[3] *A History of English Dramatic Literature to the Death of Queen Anne,* London, 1899, III, p. 405, note 4.

[4] *Dramatic Works of Molière Rendered into English,* Edinburgh, 1876, IV, p. 122. His fourth article on "Les Plagiaires de Molière en Angleterre" in *le Moliériste,* ler mai 1881, pp. 60-1, holds slightly different language: "En 1717, le 6 Décembre, Colley Cibber fit représenter une comédie: *The Nonjuror* qui est en partie imitée de la pièce de Crowne, en partie de celle de Medbourne, et surtout basée sur celle de Molière. . . . Cibber, comme Medbourne, a donné aussi au domestique de l'hypocrite un des rôles principaux."

[5] *Das Verhältnis von Colley Cibbers Lustspiel "The Non-Juror" zu Molières "Tartuffe,"* Halle, 1903, p. 53.

strong Hanoverian, as was natural from his origin, Cibber saw his way to adapting the ' Tartuffe ' of Molière to English politics. ' Tartuffe ' became accordingly in the ' Non-juror ' an English catholic priest." Americans have joined the chorus. A Western man asserts: "*The Non-Juror* is based directly on Molière's *Tartuffe*. . . . Cibber was no doubt familiar with Medbourne's play, but he used Molière as a basis, and owed practically nothing to any play other than the *Tartuffe* of Molière." [6] More recently Professor Nettleton speaks of "*The Non-Juror* (1717), an adaptation of Molière's *Tartuffe* to English setting," and quotes with approval the words of Cibber.[7]

Now, in spite of this cloud of witnesses, a critical examination leads one to conclude that Cibber actually employed, not the original French play, but Medbourne's English translation made only a few months after Molière's triumphal production in February, 1669. The actor Matthew Medbourne presented at Drury Lane sometime after May, 1670, a piece called *Tartuffe, or the French Puritan,*[8] which the title-page informed the public was "Written in French by Moliere; and rendered into English with much Addition and Advantage." The dedication added: " How successful it has prov'd in the Action, the advantages made by the Actors, and the satisfaction

[6] Croissant, *Studies in the Work of Colley Cibber* (Bulletin of The University of Kansas, Humanistic Studies, i, No. 1), Lawrence, 1912, pp. 23-24.

[7] *English Drama of the Restoration and Eighteenth Century*, Macmillan, New York, 1914, p. 151.

[8] *Tartuffe: or the French Puritan. A Comedy, Lately Acted at the Theatre Royal. Written in French by Moliere; and rendered into English with much Addition and Advantage, By M. Medbourne, Servant to His Royal Highness.* London: Printed by H. L. and R. B. for James Magnus at the Posthouse in Russel-street near the Piazza in Covent Garden. M.DC.LXX.

received by so many Audiences, have sufficiently pro-claim'd." The book is a translation into the blankest of miserable blank verse, in an ignorantly literal manner, scene by scene, the only changes being the addition and advantage modestly confided to the reader by the title-page. This consists of eighty-five lines added to i, v; of fourteen lines added to ii, iv, and all of the fifth scene; of scenes viii and ix added to the third act; of a new scene ii in act iv and an added scene viii; and of numerous alterations and additions to bring act v into conformity with these various changes. The features of this adaptation will become clear from the analysis of the new material presently.

The only other known edition of the play is that of 1707;[9] in which the text, page by page, is reproduced with more profuse capitalization than in the first (1670) edi-tion, and with the front matter reset in a different style. The second publisher, having within the decade moved his shop from the Dolphin and Crowne in St. Paul's Churchyard to King George's Head over against St. Clement's Church in the Strand, inserted the following advertisement in *The Daily Courant* for Friday, December 27, 1717: " This Day is Published, Tartuffe; or, The French Puritan. Written in French by Moliere, and render'd into English with Improvements by the late Mr. Medbourne; in which Play may be seen the Plot, Charac-ters, Incidents, and most part of the Language of The Nonjuror." The Advertisement was repeated on Satur-

---

[9] *Tartuffe: or, the French Puritan. A Comedy, Acted at the Theatre-Royal. Written in French by Moliere, and Render'd into English, with much Addition and Advantage, By M. Medbourne, Servant to His Royal Highness.* London: Printed for Richard Well-ington, Bookseller, at the Dolphin and Crowne in St. Paul's Church-yard. 1707.

day, December 28, on Wednesday, January 1, and on Monday, January 6, to take advantage of the swelling flood of interest raised by Cibber's sensationally successful play. As indicated above, Genest does not take very seriously this charge of plagiarism by Cibber's enemies, for he implies that Cibber used Medbourne merely for a suggestion: "Charles is borrowed from Medbourne's Tartuffe, but is altered greatly for the better." [10] Nevertheless, an examination of plot, characters, and language in *The Non-juror* will show that Cibber need never have seen the original and that in all likelihood he worked with Medbourne's translation before him.

It is obvious that whichever text Cibber used, he would introduce great changes. His purpose was to ride to a firm success on the crest of the wave of hostility to the Nonjurors which had been mounting for more than a year before the production of his play. He would therefore be obliged to make his plot and characters include the main centers of this hostility. How he accomplished this purpose I have shown in another paper. But an examination of more technical matters indicates that other considerations had some weight in determining what alterations he should introduce into his management of the action.

Molière, to make clear the hypocritical character of his villain, deferred his entrance for two whole acts. Because he wished to offer up incense to the king, he launched no intrigue against Tartuffe, but saved Orgon at the very end by the intervention of the royal hand. Both Medbourne and Cibber are more regular in the structure of their plays. The chief character is in each case introduced in the first act. Medbourne at the end of act I has him call from the wings for his servant. Then *"Enter* Tartuffe,

[10] *Op. cit.,* II, p. 615.

*and passes over the stage in a demure posture With books
as going to Church.*"[11]   He briefly remarks, " Come,
Laurence, you neglect your Prayers too much." [12]   Cibber
also has him enter with his servant, whom he commands
to " bid the Butler ring to Prayers." [13]   But Cibber introduces a conversation to reveal his treasonable Jacobitish
ambitions.[14]   He gives him a second entry to make clear
his insolent authority in the family.[15]

In the second act of both Medbourne and Cibber it is
hinted that the servant of the villain is much better than
his station.   Laurence declares to Dorina, with whom he
is in love, " Though *I* am *Tartuff's* Man, and receive
wages of him, His Agreement with my friends was otherwise." [16]   Charles gives Maria, with whom he is in love,
a much more circumstantial account of his past life.[17]
Laurence hints that Tartuffe does not intend to marry
the daughter, but seeks the estate and the wife of his
patron.[18]   Charles reveals much more circumstantially
how the estate is to be transferred to the villain,[19] who has
previously explained what his interest in the daughter is.[20]

In the fourth act Laurence hands over to Dorina the
deed and cabinet by which Tartuffe hopes to secure complete control of Orgon's estate.[21]   In Cibber's second act

[11] Medbourne: *Tartuffe,* I, v, p. 13.
[12] *Ibid.*
[13] Cibber: *The Non-Juror. A Comedy. As it is Acted at the
Theatre-Royal, By His Majesty's Servants.* London: Printed for
B. Lintot, at the Cross-Keys in Fleetstreet. MDCCXVIII. P. 12.
[14] *Op. cit.,* pp. 12-14.
[15] *Op. cit.,* pp. 14-15.
[16] Medbourne: *Tartuffe,* II, v, p. 26.
[17] Cibber: *The Non-Juror,* pp. 30-32.
[18] Medbourne: *Tartuffe,* II, v, p. 27.
[19] Cibber: *The Non-Juror,* p. 32.
[20] *Op. cit.,* p. 28.
[21] Medbourne: *Tartuffe,* IV, viii, p. 51.

Charles shows to Maria a "Writing" which has been approved by the villain and is to be executed that evening.[22] Again Cibber is more detailed and plausible. The quick-witted Maria at once repairs to a lawyer, who makes important alterations in a duplicate to replace the original among the villain's papers.

In the first act Dorina boasts concerning her deed,

> And when it come to th' issue 'twill appear,
> *I* have been active in another sphere.[23]

In the fourth act Maria says of the writing she has secretly altered, "when you have done all you can, I am resolv'd to reserve some Merit against him to my self." [24] At the climax of the final scene Dorina brings in "Laurence *with a Cabinet and Writings.* Dorina *with the Assignment,*"[25] which restores everything to Orgon. At the climax of the final scene in *The Non-juror* Maria explains the substitution of the second deed for the original and the part which Charles had in the outwitting of Wolf.[26]

These correspondences indicate that Cibber acted on the suggestions afforded by Melbourne in planning the structure of his play, since his method of outwitting the villain follows so closely the plan introduced by the first adaptor.

A more important part of Cibber's plan evidently came from the same source. He was not content with the intrigue of Maria against Dr. Wolf. His political satire required in addition that the villain be a traitor, and that this traitor be unmasked before the audience. For this

[22] Cibber: *The Non-Juror*, p. 32.
[23] Medbourne: *Tartuffe*, v, i, p. 52.
[24] Cibber: *The Non-Juror*, p. 56.
[25] Medbourne: *Tartuffe*, v, scen. ult., p. 62.
[26] Cibber: *The Non-Juror*, p. 75.

purpose he created the Colonel, a character totally different from Damis in Molière's play. The evidence suggests that this thread of action was spun from some scenes which Medbourne inserted. In the second scene of the fourth act (original with Medbourne), Laurence gives these directions:

> · You must procure a meeting 'twixt *Elmira*
> And my Master, to which by some means you
> Must make *Orgon* privy, that his own ears may
> Witness to him what from the mouth of truth
> He'd not believe. This must be done, though
> For a time it breed a strange confusion, then let *Cleanthes*
> *Damis*, and *Valere* inform the King and Council
> Before hand of *Orgons* former services; lay before
> Them his fidelity.[27]

Dorina performs her part in five inserted lines at the beginning of the next scene.[28] In the first scene of act v (also original) Cleanthes reports that he has accomplished all that Laurence directed.[29] In the fifth scene (likewise original) he decides he will

> give an Information 'gainst this Villain
> That he may be secur'd.[30]

In the next scene Valere reports:

> The Work is done, the Villain is secur'd,
> ` And does not know it yet, but thinks he's Victor.
> We have the Deed and Cabinet; by these means
> The traitors malice ceases, and all's safe—
> But we must fright *Orgon*. You shall, *Cleanthes*,
> Go to the Messenger, in whose Custody.
> *Tartuffe* remains at present, and bring with him
> His prisoner, as if he came to put
> Him in possession.[31]

---

[27] Medbourne: *Tartuffe*, IV, ii, p. 43.
[28] *Op. cit.*, IV, iii, pp. 43-44.
[29] *Op. cit.*, v, i, p. 52.
[30] *Op. cit.*, v, v, p. 57.
[31] *Op. cit.*, v, vi, p. 58.

Near the end of the play Valere interrupts Cleanthes's account of their activities with the exclamation:

> Let me tell that; *Cleanthes*, 'twas your *Genius*
> Brought it to this perfection. He, Sir, perceiving
> How strongly you had noos'd your self by Law,
> Accuses *Tartuffe* of prodigious crimes:
> Crimes that entrencht on Royal Majesty,
> Which he confirm'd by noble Witnesses.[32]

It will be noted that these additions and alterations by Medbourne change the villain from a mere *fourbe renommé* to a traitor to his king, and afford a second intrigue for his overthrow.

Cibber had to make the villain of his piece a traitor in order to carry out his satire against Jacobites and Nonjurors. But the suggestion for the change and indeed for his whole adaptation may well have come from Medbourne. Along with making the villain a traitor, he would adopt the manner of unmasking his treason. Cleanthes was made over into the Colonel for the obvious reason that the *raisonneur* was much more tedious than the arch-conspirator and loyal young military man.

As in the case of the deed, Cibber is more specific than Medbourne. In the first act the Colonel declares, " I am now upon the scent of a Secret, that I hope shortly will prove him a Rogue to the whole Nation." [33]   He later tells of Dr. Wolf's having been in Flanders under suspicious circumstances,[34] and at the very close of the act refers to him as the " Traytor." [35]   Laurence's suggestion of a second meeting between Tartuffe and Elmira, as a more plausible explanation of such an act by an English wife, was transferred to the Colonel, who, as prime mover

[32] *Op. cit.*, v, scen. ult., pp. 63-62 [64].   [34] *Op. cit.*, p. 14.
[33] Cibber: *The Non-Juror*, p. 9.   [35] *Op. cit.*, p. 16.

against Dr. Wolf, in the second act suggests the first meeting also, because " it's the only way in the World to
expose him." [36]   In the fourth act Cibber very much
bettered the instruction offered by Medbourne in the sixth
scene of the fifth act.   The Colonel reports that he has
" Substantial Affidavits! that will puzzle him to Answer;
I have planted a Messenger at the next Door, who has a
Warrant in his Pocket, when I give the Word, to take
him." [37]   When his sister asks him for an immediate arrest, he explains just as Cleanthes does in Medbourne,
" No; our seizing him now for Treason, I am afraid won't
convince my Father of his Villany." [38]   His plan, like
Laurence's, is to secure a second interview between the
Doctor and Lady Woodvil.   Surely Cibber's is a much less
childish arrangement than Medbourne's, who has Tartuffe
under arrest during a good part of the fifth act, yet one obviously suggested by it.   A further divergence from Molière toward Medbourne is that, instead of keeping the
outcome a secret till the end, Cibber prepares us for the
dénouement.   The " Crimes that entrencht on Royal Majesty " the Colonel proves more specifically by " noble
Witnesses," who testify that the Doctor was in arms in the
Rebellion of 1715 and that as a priest in popish orders he
had officiated at public mass.[39]

In short, it is clear from this consideration of the elements which Medbourne added to Molière's plot that Cibber is indebted to him for the more regular structure of
The Non-juror, (1) that he drew suggestions for the intrigue against Wolf as a private villain, that for this purpose he took over that villain's servant and enlarged the
part to serve his political satire also, and that he adopted

[36] *Op. cit.,* p. 22.   [38] *Ibid.*
[37] *Op. cit.,* p. 55.   [39] *Op. cit.,* pp. 74-75.

the means of carrying out this intrigue by having the servant secure the villain's papers; (2) that he drew suggestions for the intrigue against Wolf as a public traitor, that for this purpose he used the addition to Cléante's rôle to build up an entirely new conception for the son which fitted in much better with his political satire.

Besides these two newly conceived characters, the servant of the villain and the son of his benefactor, which may be traced to Medbourne's additions, Cibber is evidently indebted to his predecessor for modifications in two other characters. (1) The wife, as in Medbourne, becomes a less prominent, daring, and resourceful character, becomes a more conventional English wife, who undertakes interviews with the villain only because the Colonel tells her it is necessary. (2) The villain not only becomes a traitor instead of a notorious rogue, as I have shown above, but he likewise becomes a much less wary and consummate hypocrite. Medbourne did not regard the servant Laurence's explanations as sufficient to make clear his master's hypocrisy. He added a whole scene of thirty-three lines, the eighth in the third act, to allow Tartuffe to explain his purposes and motives to his servant.[40] This scene, altered to suit his changed plot and characters, Cibber introduces into his second act.[41] Each scene is entirely out of keeping with Molière's conception of Tartuffe. In the fourth act, after Tartuffe has been unmasked, Medbourne added a scene, numbered eight, in which Tartuffe declares his purpose to wreak vengeance on Orgon. This too Cibbey adapts after the corresponding scene, with the necessary changes.

[40] Medbourne: *Tartuffe*, pp. 37-38.
[41] Cibber: *The Non-Juror*, p. 28.

Tart. Laurence, look you to the chamber, and be sure
You're careful of the cabinet stands there.
Orgon himself delivered it to me,
And I will give't the King to ruine him.
If any offer to intrude, be quick,
And pocket up the writings with the seals;
While I immediately find out the Sheriff. [*Exit* Tartuffe.[42]

Doct. [*Apart.*] No. It ends not here. He was not brought to
listen to this proof alone! There's something deeper yet design'd
against me—I must be speedy—suppose I talk with *Charles,* allarm
him with our Common Danger, Point out his Ruine as our only
means of Safety, and like the Panther in the Toil provok'd, turn
short with Vengeance on my Hunters! [43]

In brief, Cibber follows Medbourne, not only in making
the villain a traitor, but in making him a much more
transparent hypocrite than was consistent with Molière's
conception.

To sum up, in his changes in plot and management of
the action, and in his introduction and modification of
characters, Cibber corresponds with Medbourne at the
very points where Medbourne differs from Molière. What
is more remarkable, all of Medbourne's important changes
he embodies in his adaptation. The conclusion to be
drawn is obvious.

If we turn now to the elements which are common to
all three pieces, we shall have a further test of Cibber's
indebtedness. These elements may be grouped into three
classes: (i) scenes that are altered considerably in Cibber;
(ii) scenes that are pretty closely copied; (iii) scattered
reminiscences—echoes, for the most part, of passages that
in the original appear in a different connection.

[42] Medbourne: *Tartuffe,* n. 51.
[43] Cibber: *The Non-Juror,* p. 70.

6

I. Scenes that are Altered Considerably in Cibber

In this class his language is so much his own that he might have worked from either the original or the translation.   The list follows:—

1) The opening of *The Non-juror,* which corresponds to *le Tartuffe,* i, v, ll. 409-426 [44] and to the corresponding lines in Medbourne, i, v. Cibber substitutes the Colonel for Cléante or Cleanthes.

2) *The Non-juror,* ii, p. 20. " Sir *John.* 'Tis very well . . . *Enter* Charles." The independent Maria takes the place of the impertinent Dorine of *le Tartuffe,* ii, ii, ll. 456-494, or of the corresponding lines of Medbourne, ii, ii.

3) *The Non-juror,* iv, pp. 59-60, beginning, " *Enter* Colonel, *unseen* " and extending to the end of the act. The intervention of the Colonel must have been suggested by the similar action of Dorine in the quarrel of the lovers in *le Tartuffe,* ii, iv, ll. 753-788, or in the corresponding lines in Medbourne, ii, iv.

4) *The Non-juror,* v, pp. 64-65. " Sir *John.* What, do you brave me, Madam? . . . *Lady W.* Indeed, my Dear." The passage is altered almost beyond recognition from *le Tartuffe,* iv, iii, ll. 1276-1300, or from the corresponding lines of Medbourne, iv, iii.

II. Scenes that are Pretty Closely Copied

1) A good example of this class is a scene in the third act of *The Non-juror* which corresponds to act iii, scene iii, in *le Tartuffe* and Medbourne's translation. An ex-

---

[44] Line numberings are taken from *Œuvres de Molière,* ed. Despois-Mesnard, iv, Hachette, Paris, 1878.

amination of the three versions reveals correspondences between Medbourne and Cibber in points where Medbourne diverges from Molière which cannot be the result of chance coincidence.

a)

ELMIRE.

C'est pousser bien auant la charité Chrestienne;
Et je vous dois beaucoup, pour toutes ces bontez.

TARTVFFE.

Ie fais bien moins pour vous, que vous ne méritez.[45]

Medbourne translates this passage thus:

Elm. Your charity methinks extends too far;
Tart. I have done much less than you have merited.[46]

Cibber follows him with:

Lady W. Your Charity was too far concern'd for me.
Doct. Ah! don't say so, don't say so—you merit more,
        than mortal Man can do for you.[47]

(*b*)

TARTVFFE.

Il luy serre les bouts des doigts.
Oüy, Madame, sans doute; et ma ferueur est telle. . . .

ELMIRE.

Ouf, vous me serrez trop.

---

[45] *Le Tartvffe, ov l'Impostevr, comedie.* Par I. B. P. de Moliere. Imprimé aux despens de l'Autheur, et se vend a Paris, Chez Iean Rihov, au Palais, vis-à-vis la Porte de l'Eglise de la Sainte Chapelle, à l'Image S. Loüis, M.DC.LXIX. Avec privilege dv Roy. In " Réimpression des éditions originales de Molière. Tartuffe. Edition originale. Réimpression textuelle par les soins de Louis Lacour. Paris, Librairie des Bibliophiles. M DCCC LXXVI." III, iii, pp. 48-49.

[46] Medbourne: *Tartuffe*, III, iii, p. 29.

[47] Cibber: *The Non-Juror*, p. 40.

TARTVFFE.

C'est par excés de zele.
De vous faire autre mal, je n'eus jamais dessein,
Et j'aurois bien plutost. . . .[48]

Medbourne translates the passage thus:

> Tart. . . . . .   [He presses her Hand.
> Elm. Oh Sir! you hurt my hand. [She cries out.
> Tart. 'Tis through excess of zeal.[49]

Cibber follows with:

> Doct. . . . .   [Presses her Hand.
> Lady W. O dear! you hurt my Hand, Sir.
> Doct. Impute it to my Zeal.[50]

(c)

TARTVFFE.

Il duy met la main sur le genoû.

ELMIRE.

Que fait là vostre main?

TARTVFFE.

Ie taste vostre habit, l'étoffe en est moüelleuse.

ELMIRE.

Ah! de grace, laissez, je suis fort chatoüilleuse.[51]

Medbourne translates the passage thus:

> Tart. . . . . .   [Puts his hand upon her knees.
> Elm. What does your Hand do here? [Draws back her Chair,
>   and he approaches his.
> Tart. I feel the softness of your garment, Madam.
> Elm. Pray, Sir, forbear, I'me very ticklish.[52]

---

[48] Molière: Le Tartvffe, p. 49.
[49] Medbourne: Tartuffe, p. 30.
[50] Cibber: The Non-Juror, p. 41.
[51] Molière: Le Tartvffe, pp. 49-50.
[52] Medbourne: Tartuffe, p. 30.

Cibber follows with:

> *Doct.* . . . .   [*Laying his Hand on her Knee.*
> *Lady W.* Your Hand need not be there, Sir.
> *Doct.* Ah! I was admiring the Softness of this Silk, Madam.
> *Lady W.* Ay, but I am ticklish.[53]

(*d*)   When Medbourne expands:

> Mon sein n'enferme pas vn cœur qui soit de pierre.[54]

into:

> Madam, I'm humane, made of flesh and blood,
> My breast does not enclose a heart of stone—[55]

Cibber neglects Molière's form entirely to expand the new idea introduced by Medbourne:

> I find this mortal Cloathing of my Soul is made like other Mens, of sensual Flesh and Blood, and has its Frailties.[56]

(*e*)   Where Medbourne translates:

> Elle surmonta tout, jeusnes, prieres, larmes,[57]

by:

> And conquer'd all my fasting, pray'rs and tears,[58]

Cibber embodies the change in:

> I may resist, call all my Prayers, my Fastings, Tears and Penance to my Aid.[59]

(*f*)   Where Medbourne breaks a long speech of Tartuffe's with an aside from Elmira:

> How little does my husband think of this,[60]

[53] Cibber: *The Non-Juror*, p. 41.   [57] Molière: *Le Tartvffe*, p. 52.
[54] Molière: *Le Tartvffe*, p. 50.   [58] Medbourne: *Tartuffe*, p. 31.
[55] Medbourne: *Tartuffe*, p. 30.   [59] Cibber: *The Non-Juror*, p. 42.
[60] Cibber, *The Non-Juror*, p. 42.   [60] Medbourne: *Tartuffe*, p. 31.

Cibber breaks the corresponding speech at the corresponding point with:

> Hold, Sir, you've said enough to put you in my Power.[61]

In only one place does Cibber approach Molière more closely than he does Medbourne. Where Medbourne translates:

> L'amour qui nous attache aux Beautez éternelles[62]

by:

> That love we fix upon eternal Beauty,[63]

Cibber uses:

> And yet our Knowledge of Eternal Beauties.[64]

2) Another scene in the third act of *The Non-juror* beginning: "Sir *John*. What! mute!" and extending to the end of the act, which corresponds to III, vi, vii, in *le Tartuffe* and in Medbourne's translation.

(*a*) Where Medbourne changes:

> Vous le haïssez tous, et je vois aujourd'huy,
> Femme, Enfans, et Valets, déchaînez contre luy[65]

into:

> You hate him all, and *I'm* convinc'd on't now.
> Wife, Children, Servants, all combine against him,[66]

Cibber follows the changed form:

> I see your Aim; Wife, Children, Servants, all are bent against him.[67]

[61] Cibber: *The Non-Juror*, p. 42.
[62] Molière: *Le Tartvffe*, p. 50.
[63] Medbourne: *Tartuffe*, p. 30.
[64] Cibber: *The Non-Juror*, p. 42.
[65] Molière: *Le Tartvffe*, p. 58.
[66] Medbourne: *Tartuffe*, pp. 35-36.
[67] Cibber: *The Non-Juror*, p. 44.

3) In the fifth act of *The Non-juror,* in preparation for the unmasking, appears a scene corresponding to *le Tartuffe,* iv, iii, iv, or the translation in Medbourne, iv, iii, iv.

(*a*)   At one point Medbourne translates the figure:

> Et donner vn champ libre à ses temeritez [68]

by the prosaic:

> Or yield a freedom to his rash attempts. [69]

Cibber, though elsewhere introducing many figurative expressions, here employs the prosaic one of Medbourne:

> You must not winch nor stir too soon, at any freedom
> you Observe me take with him. [70]

4) In the unmasking scene in the fifth act of *The Non-juror* corresponding to the *scène de la table* and the two following in *le Tartuffe* (iv, v, vi, vii), or the same scenes in Medbourne's translation.   The wording is nowhere close enough to the original to furnish any evidence.

5) In the third act of *The Non-juror* there is a scene between Heartly and Maria in which the general idea of a lovers' quarrel and one passage in particular are taken from *le Tartuffe,* ii, iv, ll. 685-705, or the corresponding lines in Medbourne's translation, ii, iv. Medbourne makes several changes in the dialogue:

VALERE

. Vous n'aurez pas grand'peine à le suiure, je croy.

MARIANNE.

Pas plus qu'à le donner en a souffert vostre ame.

VALERE.

Moy, je vous l'ay donné pour vous plaire, Madame.

---

[68] Molière: *Le Tartvffe,* p. 72.   [70] Cibber: *The Non-Juror,* p. 66.
[69] Medbourne: *Tartuffe,* p. 46.

MARIANNE.

Et moy, je le suiuray, pour vous faire plaisir.[71]

His translation runs:

> *Val.* 'Twill not pain you much to follow it.
> *Mar.* Not quite so much as you have felt to give it.
> *Val.* I gave't a purpose, Madam, for to please you.
> *Mar.* And to please you I shall accept it, Sir.[72]

In all but the first speech Cibber is obviously following Medbourne:

> *Hear.* O! that won't cost you much Trouble, I dare say,
> Madam.
> *Mar.* About as much, I suppose, as it cost you to give
> it me.
> *Hear.* Upon my Word, Madam, I gave it purely to
> oblige you.
> *Mar.* Then to return your Civility, the least I can do
> is to take it.[73]

III. REMINISCENCES FROM VARIOUS PLACES

1) In the first act of *The Non-juror* the Colonel says to Heartly:

> Now she's the only one in the Family, that has Power
> with our precise Doctor, . . . by the way you must
> know, I have some shrewd Suspicions, that this sanc-
> tify'd Rogue is carnally in love with her.[74]

The superlatives here more closely resemble the speech of Dorina to Damis in Medbourne, III, i, than they do the language of Molière:

[71] Molière: *Le Tartvffe*, p. 36.
[72] Medbourne: *Tartuffe*, pp. 21-22.
[73] Cibber: *The Non-Juror*, p. 36.
[74] Cibber: *The Non-Juror*, pp. 11-12.

Your mother is best able to prevail.
She has some Influence upon *Tartuffe*,
If *I* have any skill in Divination;
And he'll accomplish what she shall request,
For I have observ'd him very sweet upon her.[15]

The polished original runs:

Sur l'esprit de Tartuffe, elle a quelque credit:
Il se rend complaisant à tout ce qu'elle dit,
Et pourroit bien auoir douceur de cœur pour elle.[16]

The six remaining reminiscences are embodied in such free paraphrase that they afford no evidence on either side.

In these three classes of borrowing from his source, scenes that are altered considerably, scenes that are pretty closely copied, and scattered reminiscences, Cibber follows so often the phrasing of Medbourne where it differs notably from that of Molière that chance cannot explain the correspondences. Taken in connection with his correspondences with Medbourne in plot and character where Medbourne altered or enlarged upon Molière, these similarities in language drive one to the conclusion that Cibber did not use the French of Molière at all in making his adaptation of the famous drama, but employed the English translation of 1670.

This conclusion should surprise no one. There is no evidence in Cibber's other writings that he was nearly so familiar with French as he was with English. Moreover, there was no advantage in using the original, and a distinct advantage in employing the work of a previous adaptor. The conclusion must lessen the estimate of Cib-

[15] Medbourne: *Tartuffe*, pp. 27-28.
[16] Molière: *Le Tartvffe*, pp. 44-45.

ber's originality in adapting the action of Molière to the demands of an English audience. But it little affects the estimate of his sagacity in introducing the political satire into dialogue and delineation of character. The political satire, it must be remembered, was what caused its sensational and unprecedented run.

DUDLEY H. MILES.

X.—GOETHE'S THEORY OF THE *NOVELLE:*
1785-1827

In attempting to trace the theory of the German *novelle* back to its' beginnings, a century and more ago, the student finds that Goethe's famous epigram of 1827: " Was ist die Novelle anders als eine sich ereignete unerhörte Begebenheit?" [1] is rightly given third place chronologically among the more important contributions to the discussion before Tieck. Goethe's predecessors in this field were the brothers Schlegel, and their contributions were pioneer work in a truly peculiar sense of the word; for at the time they wrote, the German *novelle* was as good as non-existent, and criticism is wont to follow, not precede, literary production. It is true that both had foreign models from which to deduce their theory; in the case of Friedrich Schlegel, Boccaccio [2] furnished the norm, for August Wilhelm, both Boccaccio and Cervantes. [3] But it is also true that, as the foremost critical talents of the Romantic movement, the Schlegels were in search of a new literary form into which might be poured the new literary content of the movement with which they were allied; and so their critical state-

[1] *Gespräch mit Goethe*, 29. Jan. 1827.

[2] The essay has been published four times: 1) A. W. und Fr. Schlegel, *Charakteristiken und Kritiken*, 2 Bde., Königsberg, 1801, II, pp. 360-400. 2) Fr. Schlegel, *Sämtl. Wke.*, Wien, 1825-46, x, pp. 3-36. 3) *Sämtl. Wke.*, 2. Orig.-Ausg., Wien, 1846, VIII, pp. 5-29. 4) J. Minor, *Friedrich Schlegel 1794-1802: seine prosaischen Jugendschriften*, 2 Bde., Wien, 1882, II, pp. 396-414, from which I quote.

[3] A. W. Schlegel, *Vorlesungen über schöne Literatur und Kunst*, nach der Hs. hgb. von J. Minor, 8 Bde., Heilbron, 1884 (*Seufferts Literaturdenkmale*, Bd. XVII, XVIII, XIX).

ments are, in a certain sense, more or less conscious propaganda for Romanticism. It was in their characteristically Romantic flight from an uncongenial present that they rediscovered Boccaccio and Cervantes and realised that these two masters had excelled in a form not native to Germany. In introducing this form in theory into German literature theirs was pioneer criticism of the first order, and it is with no thought of belittling their attainment that attention may be called to the fact that their work was anticipated in a fashion by the greatest figure in literature among their contemporaries.

That is to say, Goethe's epigrammatic definition of 1827 was only his final word on the theory of the *novelle,* and it contains only the briefest possible statement of essentials brought to light in the course of a long investigation which goes back to his *Unterhaltungen deutscher Ausgewanderten* (1795), thus antedating the work of the Schlegels by over half a decade. But since the theoretical statements of the *Unterhaltungen* are of real import only in the light of the later definition, and since the latter depends on the former for its elucidation and interpretation,[4] it is evident that the Schlegels were the first among German critics to attempt a full and formal theory of the *novelle,* and to recognise in it a highly developed form as yet without counterpart in their own literature.

Goethe, like the Schlegels, based his conception on foreign models,—at first, it would seem, almost entirely on Boccaccio and the French *contes moraux.* The striking

---

[4] Paul Joh. Arnold in his article on *Goethes Novellenbegriff* (Literar. Echo. XIV, Sp. 1251-54) has given an excellent interpretation of the definition, but he makes no attempt to trace the growth of the conception chronologically. His elucidation is based on no material earlier than that in the *Wahlverwandtschaften* (1809).

similarity between the frame stories of the *Decamerone*
and the *Unterhaltungen* has frequently been pointed
out,[5] and in this connection it is interesting to note
how little evidence we have to show that Goethe knew the
rich *novella* literature of Italy aside from the *Decamerone*.
It is, of course, unthinkable that a man of Goethe's wide
reading and thorough knowledge of the various foreign
literatures should have neglected this one branch entirely,
and yet one looks in vain through the indices of the best
Goethe biographies and the index volumes of the chief
editions, even of the Weimar edition, for reference to
such names as Bandello, Basile, Masuccio, Sacchetti,
Straparola. The last entry in the *Tages- und Jahreshefte*
for 1811 shows Goethe escaping "mit unschuldigem
Behagen" from the gallant Bandello to the *Vicar of
Wakefield*,[6] but up to 1795 we have no evidence that
he was acquainted with the best products in the domain
of the *novella* outside the *Decamerone*.

Even for Boccaccio the direct evidence is meagre
enough. On the 7th of December, 1765, Goethe forbids
his sister Cornelia to read the *Decamerone*,[7] but on

---

[5] Cf., e. g., R. M. Meyer, *Goethe*, 2. Aufl., Berlin, 1898, pp. 346 f.:
"Der berühmteste Erzählungszyclus solcher Art, Boccaccios Decamerone, hebt damit an, dasz eine Anzahl vornehmer Florentiner
sich vor der in der Stadt herrschenden Pest flüchtet und in fröhlichen
Gesprächen auf dem Lande weilt. Dies gibt den heiteren Erzählungen
einen dunklen historischen Hintergrund, und der Kontrast ruft
uns zu, in schlimmer Zeit sei Heiterkeit die beste Hygiene. Nach-
drücklicher noch tritt die gleiche lehrhafte Absicht bei Goethe hervor.
Wie in 'Hermann und Dorothea' bilden die Wirren, welche die
französische Revolution auf deutschem Boden hervorgerufen, den
Hintergrund: eine Anzahl von Personen, die vertrieben waren, kehren
nach der Heimat zurück und suchen die alte Form des Lebens zu
erneuern."

[6] *Werke, Weimarer Ausg.*, XXXVI, 2, p. 73.

[7] *Wke.*, Abt. IV, Bd. I, p. 28.

the 23d he relents so far as to suggest that their father might make a proper selection for her.[8]   A passing reference to Boccaccio in a review which appeared in the *Frankfurter gelehrte Anzeigen* in 1772 is equally prudish in tone.[9]   Indirect evidence is furnished by the frame story of the *Unterhaltungen,* as we have seen, and we know that in the summer of 1776 Goethe attempted a dramatization of Boccaccio's Falcon *novella.*[10]   And this is the sum total of the evidence.

R. M. Meyer [11] has given us a very happy characterization of the stories of the *Unterhaltungen:* " Die Aufgabe dieser kleinen Reihe von Novellen meist fremden, vorzugsweise romanischen Ursprungs ist es also, in ihrer Gesamtheit die ideale Unterhaltung einer feingebildeten Gesellschaft darzustellen.   Die Klage der Baronesse, dasz jede gesellige Bildung geschwunden sei, ist dem Dichter aus der Seele gesprochen; für ihn gehört auch die Geselligkeit zu den Künsten, oder mindestens zu den Beschäftigungen, die durch schöne Form geadelt werden wollen. . . .   Als Heilmittel gegen diese einreiszende Formlosigkeit bietet Goethe das Beispiel der Besten dar, die mit Selbstbeherrschung und Ernst vorangehen.   Die Erzählungen der Ausgewanderten werden daher gewissermaszen zu 'Musternovellen,' wie Cervantes die seinen benannte."   Aside from the *Märchen,* which obviously falls under another category, there are six stories of varied length and character within the frame story of the *Unterhaltungen,* and two of these are real *novellen* in the

---

[8] *Loc. cit.,* p. 32.

[9] Max Morris, *Der junge Goethe,* 2. Aufl., Leipzig, 1912, VI, p. 227.

[10] Alb. Bielschowski, *Goethe, sein Leben und seine Werke,* 9. Aufl., München, 1905, I, pp. 517 f.   Cf. *Briefe,* 8-12. Aug. 1776, and *Tagebücher,* 10-12. Aug. 1776.

[11] *Op. cit.,* p. 347.

modern sense of the term: the *Prokurator* and *Ferdinand*.
These two are true *novelas exemplares,* both in the moral
implication of the term as Cervantes used it, and also in
the sense that they are models for the *genre*. Goethe lays
due stress on both these aspects in the course of the frame
story. But it must not be inferred that he was writing
directly under the inspiration of Cervantes, for all the
evidence goes to show that he first became acquainted with
the *Novelas exemplares* after the *Unterhaltungen* had
appeared in print.

The composition of the stories for the *Unterhaltungen*
began in October or November, 1794,[12] and they appeared
in the *Horen* [13] between January and October, 1795. On
the 17th of December Goethe wrote to Schiller: " Dagegen
habe ich an den *Novellen* des Cervantes einen wahren
Schatz gefunden, sowohl der Unterhaltung als der Be-
lehrung. Wie sehr freut man sich, wenn man das aner-
kannte Gute auch anerkennen kann, und wie sehr wird
man auf seinem Wege gefördert, wenn man Arbeiten
sieht, die nach eben den Grundsätzen gebildet
sind, nach denen wir nach unserm Masze und
in unserm Kreise selbst verfahren." [14] Here there
is nothing to indicate a previous acquaintance with the
Novelas exemplares; on the contrary, Goethe is apparently rejoicing over a new discovery.[15] In later years

[12] The first reference is in Goethe's letter to Schiller of Oct. 26,
1794, and Schiller's reply of Oct. 28.

[13] Nos. 1, 2, 4, 7, 9, 10.

[14] *Wke.,* Abt. IV, Bd. x, p. 350. The spacing of letters here and in
subsequent quotations from Goethe does not appear in the original.

[15] This is clearly the opinion of Gervinus: " Cervantes griff zu
dieser Gattung [Novelle] und ist das grosze Beispiel darin auch
für Tieck, und Goethe durfte sich fühlen, mit ihm, ohne ihn zu
kennen, hier auf gleichem Wege gewandelt zu sein " (*Gesch. d.
deutschen Lit.,* 5 Aufl., Leipzig, 1874, V, p. 775).

he turned again to the *Novelas exemplares* with undiminished admiration,[16] but evidently it was not Cervantes to whom he owed inspiration in 1795. The inspiration, if any, seems rather to have come from the French *contes moraux,* possibly from Marmontel direct.

In this connection it is interesting to note that two out of the six stories in the *Unterhaltungen* are of Goethe's own invention, while the remaining four are French in source.[17] Among the latter is the *Prokurator* which, though a " moral tale " *par excellence,* seems to have been suggested to the poet by one of the *Cent Nouvelles nouvelles.* Schiller thought its source the *Decamerone* at a time when he knew only the plan of the story in Goethe's mind,[18] and evidently Goethe took no trouble to correct the impression, for even with the finished manuscript in hand Schiller is still of the same opinion.[19] Schiller's mistake would be immaterial except that, as Max Herrmann suggests, it may well have given Goethe the idea of incorporating the different tales in an elaborate frame story.[20]

[16] H. Voss an K. W. F. Solger, 8. Feb. 1805: "Nun liest Goethe die Cervantischen Novellen, die ihm Freude machen." Cf. Biedermann, *Goethes Gespräche*, Gesamtausg., 2. Aufl. Leipzig, 1909, I, p. 384.

[17] Cf. *Wke.*, Hempel'sche Ausg., XVI, pp. 9 ff.

[18] Schiller an Goethe, 28. Oct. 1794: "Da Sie mich auffordern, Ihnen zu sagen, was ich für die ersten Stücke noch von Ihrer Hand wünsche, so erinnere ich Sie an Ihre Idee, die Geschichte des ehrlichen Prokurators aus dem Boccaz zu bearbeiten" (*Schillers Briefe*, krit. Gesamtausg. hgb. von Fritz Jonas, Stuttgart, 1892 ff., IV, p. 49).

[19] Schiller an Goethe, 20. März 1795: "Die Erzählung liest sich mit ungemeinem Interesse; was mich besonders erfreute war die Entwicklung. Ich gestehe, dasz ich diese erwartete, und ich hätte mich nicht zufrieden geben können, wenn Sie hier das Original nicht verlassen hätten. Wenn ich mich nämlich anders recht erinnere, so entscheidet beim Boccaz blosz die zeitig erfolgte Rückkehr des Alten das Glück der Kur" (*loc. cit.*, p. 150).

[20] *Wke.*, Jubiläums-Ausg., XVI, p. xlv: "Alte Geschichten neu

Though reminiscent of Boccaccio in general plan and purpose, this frame story possesses individual features that later find an echo, particularly in Wieland and Tieck. No less than three provinces of the story-teller's domain come up for theoretical discussion: the "moral tale," the fairy tale, and the *erzählung*. This latter Goethe would surely have termed *novelle,* had he been writing even a few years later; for an analysis of this discussion of the *erzählung* in the light of the later definition shows the two conceptions to be essentially one and the same. It should be remembered also that it seems to have occurred to nobody at this time to give any German product the name *novelle,*[21] and that a definition even of the foreign product had not yet been attempted.[22]

When in the course of the frame story the Baroness

erzählt, jede für sich allein den Lesern vorzusetzen, ist offenbar der Wunsch des Horenredakteurs, und erst dessen Irrtum, dasz die für den Anfang in Aussicht genommene Prokuratornovelle aus Boccaccios Dekameron stamme, führt Goethe auf den Gedanken, für diese Erzählungen einen lockeren Rahmen zu zimmern, der sie alle umfaszt und der der Rahmenerzählung Boccaccios deutlich nachgebildet ist."

[21] Bernhard Seuffert, in the article on *Goethes Novelle, Goethe-Jahrbuch,* xix (1898), pp. 133 ff., asserts that the term *novelle* at this time (ca. 1795) "vereinzelt auf Büchertiteln zu erscheinen beginnt." He cites nothing to prove the assertion, and contemporary bibliographies (Sulzer, and Blankenburg's *Zusätze*) fail to mention anything of the sort. His authority is doubtless Goedeke, who lists several titles but does not always make it clear whether the word *novelle* actually appears on the title page or not. I have been able to verify only one case, Grosse's *Des Grafen von Vargas Novellen,* Berlin 1792. In any event the occurence of the word on a title page is very rare before the appearance of Wieland's *Novelle ohne Titel* (1805).

[22] When Wieland in his *Don Sylvio von Rosalva* (1764; p. 18, Anmkg.) refers to the Italian *novella* and the French *nouvelle* as "diese Art von kleinen Romanen" he can hardly be said to have attempted a serious definition.

gives her views on the composition of the *erzählung,* she
is giving expression to the author's own ideal for a terser,
stricter form of prose narrative than existed in contemporary German literature. Just before the beginning of
the *Prokurator*—and it is significant that this is the first
real *novelle* of the series in our modern acceptance of the
term—the Baroness is made to say: "Doch wenn Sie uns
eine Geschichte zur Probe geben wollen, so musz ich
Ihnen sagen, welche Art ich nicht liebe. Jene Erzählungen machen mir keine Freude, bei welchen, nach Weise
der Tausend und Einen Nacht, eine Begebenheit in die
andere eingeschachtelt, ein Interesse durch das andere
verdrängt wird; wo sich der Erzähler genötigt sieht,
die Neugierde, die er auf eine leichtsinnige Weise
erregt hat, durch Unterbrechung zu reizen, und die Aufmerksamkeit, anstatt sie durch eine vernünftige Folge zu
befriedigen, nur durch seltsame und keineswegs lobens-
würdige Kunstgriffe aufzuspannen. Ich tadle das Be-
streben, aus Geschichten, die sich der Einheit des
Gedichts nähern sollen, rhapsodische Rätsel zu
machen, und den Geschmack immer tiefer zu verderben.
Die Gegenstände Ihrer Erzählungen gebe ich Ihnen ganz
frei, aber lassen Sie uns wenigstens an der Form
sehen, dasz wir in guter Gesellschaft sind. Geben
Sie uns zum Anfang eine Geschichte von wenig Personen
und Begebenheiten, die gut erfunden und gedacht ist,
wahr, natürlich und nicht gemein, so viel Handlung als
unentbehrlich und so viel Gesinnung als nötig; die nicht
still steht, sich nicht auf Einem Flecke zu langsam be-
wegt, sich aber auch nicht übereilt; in der die Menschen
erscheinen wie man sie gern mag, nicht vollkommen, aber
gut, nicht auszerordentlich, aber interessant und liebenswürdig. Ihre Geschichte sei unterhaltend, so lange wir

sie hören, befriedigend, wenn sie zu Ende ist, und hinter-
lasse uns einen stillen Reiz nachzudenken." [23]
On the 2nd of December, 1794, Goethe had written
to Schiller: " Ins zweite Stück [der Horen] hoffe ich die
Erzählung [vom Prokurator] zu bringen, überhaupt ge-
denke ich aber wie die Erzählerin in der ' Tausend und
Einen Nacht ' zu verfahren." [24] Of course this may mean
simply that Goethe is planning to enclose the different
tales in a frame story, or it may be merely facetious comment on the rapacity of the editor of the *Horen* for stories,
comparable to that of the Grand Vizier; and yet it would
almost seem from the reference above to the method of
the *Arabian Nights* that Goethe had studied this method
more closely and had discarded it during the three or
four months preceding the completion of the *Prokurator*.[25] Of particular interest in this connection is the
expression " Geschichten, die sich der Einheit des Gedichts nähern sollen," for half a century later we come
upon precisely the same thought in Poe's definition of
the short-story.[26] Goethe's idea that the form of the
story should show us " that we are in good company " is
one which later found amplification at the hands of the
Schlegels, when they point to the high social origin of
the *novelle* as contrasted with the more vulgar origin of
the *schwank* and *fabliau*.[27] Doubtless all three critics go

[23] *Wke.*, XVIII, pp. 158 f.
[24] *Wke.*, Abt. IV, Bd. X, p. 208.
[25] Cf. note 19 above.
[26] *E. g.*, in the essay on *Nathaniel Hawthorne. Works of E. A. Poe*,
ed. by R. H. Stoddard, New York, 1884, VI, pp. 115 f.
[27] Fr. Schlegel speaks of the *novelle* as " so erzählt, wie man sie in
Gesellschaft erzählen würde " (Minor, *op. cit.*, II, p. 412) and A. W.
Schlegel is even more explicit: " Die Erfahrungen des geselligen
Lebens sind eine der beliebtesten und angemessensten Unterhaltungen
in der Gesellschaft; deswegen ist das eigentliche Muster für den

back to Boccaccio direct for this conception, and yet it is
more than possible that A. W. Schlegel at least owes a
certain inspiration to the frame story of the *Unterhaltungen.* Considering the passage as a whole, it would
perhaps be rash to assert that Goethe here has the *novelle*
as a distinct *genre* definitely before his mind; still it is
most significant that the *Prokurator* story, which immediately follows, is the first in the series to meet with the
demands of the later definition in all its implications.

At the close of the story the Baroness comments: " er
[der Prokurator] ist zierlich, vernünftig, unterhaltend
und unterrichtend; so sollen alle diejenigen sein, die uns
von einer Verwirrung abhalten oder davon zurückbringen
wollen. Wirklich verdient die Erzählung vor vielen andern den Titel einer moralischen Erzählung." [28] The
speaker is interested only in the moral content of the
story, not in the form, which had already been duly emphasized, and there follows at this point considerable discussion on the nature of the " moral tale." Finally, however, another person of the frame story gives the conversation a new turn, and what she has to say serves as an
introduction to the *Ferdinand-Novelle:* " Ich leugne nicht,
dasz ich die Geschichten nicht liebe, die unsere Einbildungskraft immer in fremde Länder nötigen. Musz
denn alles in Italien und Sizilien, im Orient geschehen?
Sind denn Neapel, Palermo und Smyrna die einzigen
Orte, wo etwas Interessantes vorgehen kann? Mag man
doch den Schauplatz der Feenmärchen nach Samarcand
und Ormus versetzen, um unsere Einbildungskraft zu
verwirren. Wenn Sie aber unsern Geist, unser Herz

Vortrag der Novelle der gebildete gesellige Erzähler " (*Seufferts
Literaturdenkmale,* XIX, p. 247).

[28] *Wke.,* XVIII, pp. 187 f.

bilden wollen, so geben Sie uns einheimische, geben Sie uns Familiengemälde, und wir werden uns desto eher darin erkennen, und wenn wir uns getroffen fühlen, desto gerührter an unser Herz schlagen." [29]

A distinct echo of this passage is to be found in the prolog to Wieland's *Novelle ohne Titel* (1805): " Bei einer Novelle, sagte [der Erzähler], wird vorausgesetzt, dasz sie sich weder im Dschinnistan der Perser, noch im Arkadien der Gräfin Pembroke, noch im *Pays du Tendre* der Verfasserin der ' Clelia,' noch in einem anderen idealischen oder utopischen Lande, sondern in unserer wirklichen Welt begeben habe, wo alles natürlich und begreiflich zugeht, und die Begebenheiten zwar nicht alltäglich sind, aber sich doch unter denselben Umständen alle Tage allenthalben zutragen könnten." [30] The *Novelle ohne Titel* is the fourth in a series of six stories which, like the six of the *Unterhaltungen,* together with their frame story constitute Wieland's *Hexameron von Rosenhain.* Both the passage just quoted and the general plan of the work show how little Wieland owed directly to Boccaccio, Basile, or the Queen of Navarre. However, the last half of this passage is rather interesting. Even A. W. Schlegel, for all his keen critical mind, was so much the Romanticist, that he doubted whether the *novelle* with its love of realism could find material for literary treatment in the unpoetic present.[31] Years later

---

[29] *Loc. cit.,* pp. 190 f.

[30] *Wke.,* Hempel'sche Ausg., XIII, p. 78.

[31] *Literaturdenkm.,* XIX, p. 245: " . . . . es läszt sich mehr als bezweifeln, ob es in unsern Zeiten, wo das Leben sich in lauter Kleinlichkeiten zerbröckelt, und fast niemand eigentlich das Herz hat, unbekümmert nach seinem Sinne zu leben, möglich sein dürfte, eine solche Masse von Novellen aufzubringen, die in unsern Sitten gegründet und der Denkart des Zeitalters angemessen wären, als die unter den Boccazischen sind, welche einen historischen Grund haben und das damalige Zeitalter schildern."

(1829) Tieck, after he had outgrown his Romantic phase, held the present to be in every way the equal of the past in potential poetic content.[32]   In contrast with the Romanticists, Tieck is intensely modern in his attitude toward the world about him, and it seems a little strange to find a hint of something similar in Wieland so long before what are generally considered the first beginnings of modern realism.

As to the " Familiengemälde," a glance through any one of A. G. Meissner's fourteen volumes of *Skizzen* (1778-96) will show to what depths this type of story had sunk.   In the *Prokurator* Goethe had shown what a master hand could do with the much abused " moral tale," and now in *Ferdinand* he proceeded to do as much for the " Familiengemälde."   Characteristically he has the narrator attack the problem from the psychological side, for here was the weakest element in this type of story: " Auch darin soll Ihnen gewillfahrt werden.   Doch ist es mit den Familiengemälden eine eigene Sache.   Sie sehen einander alle so gleich, und wir haben fast alle Verhältnisse derselben schon gut bearbeitet auf unsern Theatern gesehen. Indessen will ich's wagen und eine Geschichte erzählen, . . . die nur durch eine genaue Darstellung dessen, was in den Gemütern vorging, neu und interessant werden dürfte." [33]   It has always been a prime requisite for the *novelle* that it be " new and interesting " (whence the very name of the species),—if not in content, then at

---

[32] *Schriften*, Berlin, 1828-40, XI, p. lxxxvii: " Aber alle Stände, alle Verhältnisse der neuen Zeit, ihre Bedingungen und Eigentümlichkeiten sind dem klaren dichterischen Auge gewisz nicht minder zur Poesie und edlen Darstellung geeignet, als es dem Cervantes seine Zeit und Umgebung war, und es ist wohl nur Verwöhnung einiger vorzüglichen Kritiker, in der Zeit selbst einen unbedingten Gegensatz vom Poetischen und Unpoetischen anzunehmen."

[33] *Wke.*, XVIII, p. 191.

least in treatment. Goethe appears to lay the emphasis on treatment, though here even the content is " new," being his own invention.

The narrator then begins the story with a brief summary of Ferdinand's inherited traits of character, confining himself absolutely to essentials, and then suddenly interrupts the flow of the narrative with a statement which takes on considerable significance in the light of the later definition: " Ich übergehe mancherlei Szenen, die in seiner Jugend vorfielen, und erzähle nur eine Begebenheit, die seinen ganzen Charakter ins Licht setzt, und in seinem Leben eine entschiedene Epoche machte." [34] It needs no stretch of the imagination to discover here the germ of the final definition. Indeed, the same thought is given better and clearer expression now than later. The entire *novelle* is really nothing more than this single occurrence which is epoch-making in the life of the hero.[35] Goethe seems almost over-anxious to emphasize this " Begebenheit," for just before we learn what it is, the narrator is made to say: " Zu dieser Gemütstimmung traf ein sonderbarer Zufall, der ihm eine reizende Gelegenheit gab, dasjenige zu tun, wozu er nur einen dunklen und unentschiedenen Trieb gefühlt hatte." [36] The occurrence is then related, and 'the remaindei of the narrative is the demonstration of its epoch-making character in the life of the hero. It should be noted that Goethe is careful to make this

[34] *Loe. cit.*, p. 192.

[35] It is possible that Tieck found here the first impulse toward his definition of 1829,—at least it offers a striking parallel: " . . . . die Novelle [sollte] sich dadurch aus allen anderen Aufgaben hervorheben, dasz sie einen groszen oder kleinen Vorfall ins hellste Licht stelle' (*Schriften*, XI, p. lxxxvi).

[36] *Wke.*, XVIII, p. 199.

" strange chance " a really organic element of the story.
It is the same element which Tieck later called the " turning point " in the narrative, and which was the core of his
theory of the *novelle;* [37] and finally Heyse makes of it the
distinctive characteristic of his justly famous " Falcon
Theory." [38]

At the close of the story one of the auditors makes the
comment: " Diese Geschichte gefällt mir, . . . und ob
sie gleich aus dem gemeinen Leben genommen ist, so
kommt sie mir doch nicht alltäglich vor." [39]   Here
the contrast between " aus dem gemeinen Leben " and
" nicht alltäglich " is precisely that of " sich ereignet "
and " unerhört " in the final definition, and the former
furnishes an excellent commentary on the latter. [40]   By
adding the " Begebenheit, die . . . in seinem Leben eine
entschiedene Epoche machte " we have gotten together an
exact equivalent for the final definition, except for the
one word *novelle.*   This, as we have seen, can be supplied,
at least by implication, from the letter of Dec. 17, 1795,
to Schiller; for in comparing his own work with the
novellen of Cervantes there can be no doubt that Goethe
had in mind the *novellen* of the *Unterhaltungen* which

---

[37] " Diese Wendung der Geschichte, dieser Punkt von welchem aus
sie sich unerwartet völlig umkehrt, und doch natürlich, dem Charakter und den Umständen angemessen, die Folge entwickelt, wird sich
der Phantasie des Lesers um so fester einprägen, als die Sache selbst
im Wunderbaren unter andern Umständen wieder alltäglich sein
könnte " (*Schriften,* XI, p. lxxxvi).   And further: " . . . . nur
wird [die Novelle] immer jenen sonderbaren, auffallenden
Wendepunkt haben, die sie von allen anderen Gattungen unter-
scheidet " (*loc. cit.,* p. lxxxvii).

[38] *Deutscher Novellenschatz,* München o. J. (1871-76), I, pp. xix f.

[39] *Wke.,* XVIII, pp. 216 f.

[40] Note the similar juxtaposition in the passages quoted from Wieland and Tieck.   The same thought is expressed or implied in every
serious attempt at a theory of the *novelle.*

had only just appeared in print. Evidently Goethe's informal theory of the *novelle* anticipates the formal state-ment of Friedrich Schlegel in the essay on Boccaccio by six years, and the close of A. W. Schlegel's Berlin Lec-tures by nearly a decade.

In the *Musenalmanach* for May and June, 1796, ap-peared Goethe's *novelle* in verse, *Alexis und Dora,* and here the technic of the *Ferdinand-Novelle* appears again: an entire life and character is depicted in all its essentials in the single epoch-making " Begebenheit." [41] In the year following Goethe began an epic poem, *Die Jagd,* which was, however, soon laid aside and was not taken up again till thirty years later, when it was transformed into prose as the *Novelle,* and gave rise, in discussion with Eckermann, to Goethe's final definition of the species. The material in its epic form was discarded chiefly be-cause of Schiller's objection to the lack of harmony between form and content, and the correspondence of the two poets in April and June, 1797, casts many inter-esting side-lights on the later definition. On the 2nd of April Goethe writes to Schiller: " Mein neuer Stoff hat keinen einzigen retardierenden Moment, es schreitet alles von Anfang bis zu Ende in einer geraden Reihe fort, allein er hat die Eigenschaft, dasz grosze Anstalten ge-macht werden, dasz man viele Kräfte mit Verstand und Klugheit in Bewegung setzt, dasz aber die Entwicklung auf eine Weise geschieht, die den Anstalten ent-

---

[41] K. Heinemann, *Goethe,* 3. Aufl., Leipzig, 1893, pp. 520 f.: " Er verstand es sofort, den springenden Punkt herauszufinden. . . . . Wenn es die Aufgabe des Novellisten ist, in der Darstellung eines einzigen Erlebnisses das ganze Leben und Charakter des Helden zu schildern, so wollte Goethe in dem ' einen Moment das Gehalt eines ganzen Lebens' geben. . . . Alles wird auf diesen einen Augenblick zusammengedrängt, um die Schnelligkeit des Entschlusses und des Liebesgeständnisses auch äuszerlich zu begründen."

gegen ist, und auf einem ganz unerwarteten jedoch natürlichen Wege. Nun fragt sich, ob ein solcher Plan sich auch für einen epischen ausgeben könne.
... Ich habe jetzt keine interessantere Betrachtung, als
über die Eigenschaften der Stoffe, in wie fern sie diese
oder jene Behandlung fordern. Ich habe mich darinnen
so oft in meinem Leben vergriffen, dasz ich endlich einmal
ins Klare kommen möchte, um wenigstens künftig von
diesem Irrtum nicht mehr zu leiden." [42]

Here is an element in the structure of the *novelle* which
had received little emphasis in the *Unterhaltungen,* theoretically at any rate, and which does not reappear in
the final definition, unless it be in the word " unerhört."
But both the Schlegels made much of it under the name
of paradox, and though they nowhere define the term as
clearly as Goethe does without using the term at all, they
evidently mean by it that element in the *novelle* which
brings about a *dénouement* that one is not led to expect
from the beginning of the story. Clearly this conception
of paradox has an intimate connection with Tieck's theory
of the " turning point," and he seems to have gotten the
idea from A. W. Schlegel,[43] not from Goethe. In his
reply Schiller immediately seizes upon this element of
paradox as essentially unepic: " Die Art, wie Sie Ihre
Handlung entwickeln wollen, scheint mir mehr der Ko-
mödie als dem Epos eigen zu sein. Wenigstens werden
Sie viel zu tun haben, ihr das Ueberraschende, Ver-

---

[42] *Wke.,* Abt. IV, Bd. XII, pp. 93 f.

[43] *Literaturdenkm.,* XIX, p. 245: " So viel ist gewisz: die Novelle
bedarf entscheidender Wendepunkte, so dasz die Hauptmassen der
Geschichte deutlich in die Augen fallen, und dies Bedürfnis hat auch
das Drama." For Schlegel the turning points are merely a technical
device, while for Tieck the single turning point is the great characteristic of the *novelle* as a species.

wunderung Erregende zu nehmen, weil dieses nicht
so recht episch ist." [44] To this Goethe replies: " Wird
der Stoff nicht für rein episch erkannt, ob er gleich in
mehr als Einem Sinne bedeutend und interessant ist,
so musz sich dartun lassen, in welcher andern Form er
eigentlich behandelt werden müszte." [45]

Here the discussion is dropped for the time being, but
some two months later Goethe informs Schiller that he
is thinking of recasting the material in strophic form, an
idea to which Schiller agrees: " Zugleich [in der Stro-
phenform] partizipiert es alsdann von gewissen Rechten
des romantischen Gedichts, ohne dasz es eigentlich eines
wäre, es darf sich wo nicht des Wunderbaren, doch
des Seltsamen und Ueberraschenden mehr be-
dienen, und . . . erweckt dann gar kein Befremden
mehr." [46] Goethe's reply on the following day is interesting in furnishing (by implication) what is probably
the first instance of the comparison between the *novelle*
and the ballad, which later became so common: ". . . es
scheint mir jetzt auch ausgemacht, dasz meine Tiger und
Löwen in diese Form gehören, ich fürchte nur fast, dasz
das eigentliche Interessante des Sujets sich zuletzt gar in
eine Ballade auflösen möchte." [47]

In view of the theoretical pronouncements in the *Unterhaltungen* it seems a little strange that Goethe did not
come at once to the conclusion, not reached till thirty years
later, that what he had before him was essentially material for a prose *novelle*. Perhaps the approval show-
ered upon *Alexis und Dora* and *Hermann und Dorothea*,

[44] *Briefe,* v, pp. 181 f. Note the similar connection between the
novelle and the drama in A. W. Schlegel's conception.
[45] *Wke.,* Abt. IV, Bd. XII, p. 100.
[46] *Briefe,* v, pp. 206 f.
[47] *Wke.,* Abt. IV, Bd. XII, p. 170.

after the open disapproval that the *Unterhaltungen* had called forth, made him hesitate to employ any but the popular verse form. At all events he turned from the *novelle* to other forms during the next ten years. We know that in 1805 he turned again to the *Novelas exemplares* and reread them with undiminished enjoyment, and it may well be that his return to the prose *novelle* soon after this time is at least in part due to the revival of his interest in Cervantes.

In 1807, as we learn from his Journal, Goethe was at work on some of the *novellen* which later were to be incorporated in the *Wanderjahre*. Under date of Dec. 9, we find the following entry: " Novellen zu Wilhelm Meisters Wanderjahren." [48] This seems to be Goethe's first specific use of the term for any of his own productions. Again in the *Tages- und Jahreshefte* for the Summer of 1807 we find the poet at work upon stories for the *Wanderjahre,* among them the *Wahlverwandtschaften,* which he at first planned to include with the others.[49] But the story soon outgrew the limits of the original conception and eventually appeared separately with the sub-title " Roman." [50] In the tenth chapter of the second part is the story of *Die wunderlichen Nachbarskinder* with the

---

[48] *Wke.,* Abt. III, Bd. III, p. 305.

[49] *Wke.,* XXXVI, p. 28: " Die . . . . kleinen Erzählungen [Neue Melusine, Mann von 50 Jahren, Pilgernde Törin] beschäftigten mich in heiteren Stunden, und auch die Wahlverwandtschaften sollten in der Art kurz behandelt werden. Allein sie dehnten sich bald aus; der Stoff war allzubedeutend, und zu tief in mir gewurzelt, als dasz ich ihn auf eine so leichte Weise hätte beseitigen können."

[50] It is interesting to note that most later critics, who discuss the matter at all, are inclined to classify the *Wahlverwandtschaften* as a *novelle.* Cf. Th. Mundt, *Kritische Wälder* (1833), pp. 143 f. The same thesis is defended by Spielhagen (*Beiträge zur Theorie und Technik des Romans,* 1883, p. 247 f. and *Neue Beiträge,* 1898, p. 77), but Heyse (*Novellenschatz,* I, p. xviii) takes the opposite view.

sub-title "Novelle," the first of Goethe's stories to come
before the public under this express title. It fulfills all
the requirements of the later definition, and the immediate framework is in places most suggestive, both of
the earlier discussion in the correspondence with Schiller
and the definition given Eckermann.

The narrator of the *novelle* is a man " den eigentlich
auf der Reise nichts mehr interessierte als die sonderbaren Ereignisse, welche durch natürliche und künst-
liche Verhältnisse, durch den Konflikt des Gesetz-
lichen und des Ungebändigten, der Verstandes und
der Vernunft, der Leidenschaft und des Vorurteils her-
vorgebracht werden. . . ." [51]   This is by way of introduction to a story that is paradoxical in the sense that
" die Entwicklung auf eine Weise geschieht, die den
Anstalten ganz entgegen ist und auf einem ganz unerwarteten jedoch natürlichen Wege "—to quote from the
letter of 1797.   Also in the body of the *novelle* itself one
frequently meets with expressions which seem deliberately
to emphasize the idea of paradox, such as " Neigung unter
der Form des Widerstrebens " or " auf eine natürliche
aber doch sonderbare Weise stand er seiner schönen Nach-
barin abermals entgegen."   Again in the frame story, a
few lines below, " bedeutende Bemerkungen " are contrasted with " die trivialsten Aeuszerungen " in such a
way as to furnish an implicit definition for the word
" bedeutend," which Goethe never fails to use in any discussion of the *novelle*.   Then the narrator is asked to
favor the company with " etwas von den vielen ange-
nehmen und bedeutenden Anekdoten und Geschichten " which he had gathered on his travels.   And finally
the story is introduced as follows: " Denn nachdem der

[51] *Wke.*, xx, pp. 321 f.

Begleiter durch manche sonderbare, bedeutende, heitere, rührende, furchtbare Geschichten die Aufmerksamkeit erregt und die Teilnahme aufs höchste gespannt hatte, so dachte er mit einer zwar sonderbaren, aber sanfteren Begebenheit zu schlieszen. . . ."

This is the same conception of the *novelle* that Goethe had held in 1795, with the additional element of paradox, which first appears in the correspondence of 1797; and when in October, 1826, Goethe returned to the material of *Die Jagd* and shaped it to the needs of the prose *Novelle,* the conception had undergone no change whatever. Among the various entries in the Journal two are of special interest: (Oct. 4th) " Erneutes Schema der wunderbaren Jagd," and (Oct. 10th) " Kleines Gedicht zum Abschlusz der projektierten *Novelle.*" [52]   From now on the story is called simply " die Novelle."

After Eckermann had read the completed *novelle* he was considerably puzzled by some of its apparent contradictions, and Goethe offered the following explanation:: " Um für den Gang der Novelle ein Gleichnis zu haben, . . . so denken Sie sich aus der Wurzel hervorschieszend ein grünes Gewächs, das eine Weile aus einem starken Stengel kräftige grüne Blätter nach allen Seiten austreibt und zuletzt mit einer Blume endet.   Die Blume war unerwartet, überraschend, aber sie muszte kommen; ja, das grüne Blätterwerk war nur für sie da und wäre ohne sie nicht der Mühe wert gewesen. . . .   Zu zeigen wie das Unbändige, Unüberwindliche oft besser durch Liebe und Frömmigkeit als durch Gewalt bezwungen werde, war die Aufgabe dieser Novelle. . . .   Dies ist das Ideelle, dies die Blume.   Und das grüne Blätterwerk der durchaus realen Exposition ist nur dieserwegen da. . . .   Schiller war gegen eine Behand-

---

◾ W*ke.*, Abt. III, Bd. X, pp. 252, 255.

lung meines Gegenstandes in Hexametern, wie ich es damals gleich nach Hermann und Dorothea willens war; er riet zu den achtzeiligen Stanzen. Sie sehen aber wohl, dasz ich mit der Prosa am besten gefahren bin. Denn es kam sehr auf genaue Zeichnung der Lokalität an, wobei man doch in solchen Reimen wäre geniert gewesen. Und dann liesz sich auch der anfänglich ganz reale und am Schlusz ganz ideelle Charakter der Novelle in Prosa am besten geben." [53]

The one new element here is the thought that prose is the essential medium for the realistic, an idea that A. W. Schlegel had already developed with considerable fullness in the Berlin Lectures a quarter of a century earlier.[54] That the story drifts away from reality toward the close [55] seems to have presented no obstacle to its being given as a title the name of the whole species, a proceeding which has an earlier parallel in the *Märchen* of the *Unterhaltungen*. As an "exemplary" specimen Goethe might have made a happier choice among his earlier *novellen,* but the choice of the title is important in that it led to the most concise statement, and one of the most famous in German critical literature, on the theory of the *novelle:* "Wissen Sie was, sagte Goethe, wir wollen es die Novelle

[53] Biedermann, *op. cit.,* III, pp. 325 f.

[54] *Litteraturdenkm.,* XIX, pp. 242 ff. It should be remembered that these lectures existed only in manuscript till published by Minor in 1884.

[55] Cf. Heyse, *Novellenschatz,* I, p. viii: "Zu ihrer Zeit waren sie [Tiecks Novellen] eine Tat; ein offener Bruch mit der falschen Kunst, zwei für sich gleichberechtigte Erzählungsgebiete, das Wunderbare und das Natürliche, das Märchen und die Wirklichkeit, zu beiderseitigem Schaden mit einander zu vermengen. Goethes recht ausdrücklich 'Novelle' überschriebene phantastischmystische Erzählung ... schien diesen Miszbrauch zu rechtfertigen, und Tieck hatte ihm, besonders in einigen Erzählungen seines Phantasus, nur allzu sehr gehuldigt."

nennen; denn was ist die Novelle anders als eine sich ereignete unerhörte Begebenheit. Dies ist der eigentliche Begriff, und so vieles, was in Deutschland unter dem Titel Novelle geht, ist gar keine Novelle, sondern blosz Erzählung oder was Sie sonst wollen. In jenem ursprünglichen Sinne einer unerhörten Begebenheit kommt auch die Novelle in den Wahlverwandtschaften vor." [56]

"Was ist die Novelle anders als eine sich ereignete unerhörte Begebenheit." Such is the quintessential result of an investigation which had been conducted intermittently for over thirty years, and which in its beginnings may well lay claim to having given the first definition of a form in which Germany has made perhaps its most valuable and characteristic contribution to literature in the 19th century. Later the discussion was to touch upon many other phases, such as the relation of the *novelle* to the drama and the novel; but the prime essentials could hardly be more happily stated than in the epigrammatic terseness of this single sentence. Extreme brevity has its disadvantages; in this instance the various implications of the definition become clear only after they have been traced to their source. But the advantage of extreme brevity was felt by Heyse when he so formulated his definition of this same species that it might be summed up in the two words: silhouette and falcon. In the mind of any student who has sought a close acquaintance with the *novelle* in its theoretical aspect three definitions will always stand out with peculiar vividness: Goethe's for its "sich ereignete unerhörte Begebenheit," Tieck's for its "Wendepunkt," and Heyse's for its "Silhouette" and "Falken."

McBurney Mitchell.

---

[56] Biedermann, *op. cit.*, III, p. 335.

XI.—CHAUCER AND THE SEVEN DEADLY SINS[1]

In a series of recent articles [2] Professor Frederick Tupper has put forward, with great skill and learning, a view regarding the plan of the *Canterbury Tales* which demands, on account of its originality and its importance, the most respectful and open-minded consideration. As one who was fortunate enough to be present at the inception of the theory, and who welcomed enthusiastically the promise of fresh light which it seemed to hold, I am free, I think, from antecedent prejudice. But as the theory has been developed in article after article I have felt myself compelled to dissent, with steadily strengthening conviction, from Professor Tupper's contention, and it is the purpose of this article to make clear the grounds on which it seems to me that that contention, in spite of its uncommon plausibility, must be rejected. All stu-

---

[1] The *Beiblatt zur Anglia* for October-November, 1914, which contains (pp. 327-32) Koch's review of Tupper's article in the *Publications*, reached me (on account of delays presumably due to the war) on March 2nd, a week after the last sentence of this paper had been written. Professor Koch's conclusions and my own agree in general, and often in detail. I have, however, left this examination precisely as it stood, inasmuch as its angle of approach is somewhat different from Koch's, and its scope considerably wider.

[2] "Chaucer and the Seven Deadly Sins," *Publications of the Modern Language Association of America*, XXIX (March, 1914), pp. 93-128 (hereafter referred to as *Publications*); "Wilful and Impatient Poverty," *Nation*, vol. 99, No. 2558 (July 9, 1914), p. 41 (referred to as *Nation*); "The Pardoner's Tavern," *Journal of English and Germanic Philology*, XIII (Oct., 1914), pp. 553-65 (referred to as *Journal*); "Chaucer's Bed's Head," *Modern Language Notes*, XXX (Jan. 1915), pp. 5-12 (referred to as *Notes*); compare also "Saint Venus and the Canterbury Pilgrims," *Nation*, vol. 97, No. 2520 (Oct. 16, 1913), pp. 354-56.

dents of Chaucer are under a debt to Mr. Tupper, whether
they agree with him or not. A fresh and original conception, maintained with an enthusiasm that vivifies dead
facts, is of all too rare occurrence, and its " Forth, beste,
out of thy stal " is wholesome stimulus. But Mr. Tupper would be the last to wish his vigorous challenge to
gird up our loins and give a reason for the faith that is
in us, to go unanswered. He has already offered hospitality to various objections in his articles,[3] but he and
his critics have not met, apparently, on common ground.
In my own case I wish to accept, without question, his
own choice of field and weapons.

For Mr. Tupper insists with some vehemence that
those who fail to assent to his conclusions thus fail on
account of a lack of " the mediæval perspective," or
because of a " critical astigmatism that either disregards
the text altogether or sees it blurredly through the medium
of modern lenses." [4] In what follows, therefore, I shall
confine myself rigidly to an examination of his argument
*on the basis of those authorities alone which he himself
cites.* And I shall ask regarding these authorities—and
Chaucer as well—only the question which Mr. Tupper
has himself suggested: " What did our mediæval thinker
mean by this ? " [5] And the point of view which I shall
endeavor to maintain throughout is that of the mediæval
reader—the same " every man of the Middle Ages " to

---

[3] See *Publications,* pp. 124 ff.; *Journal,* p. 565.

[4] *Journal,* p. 565; cf. pp. 553-54. One could wish that Mr. Tupper
had left the exemplification of one of his Sins entirely to the
Manciple. "Chydinge and reproche . . . [is] if he repreve him
uncharitably of sinne, as 'thou [Peter Bell of scholarship],' 'thou
[attenuating scholiast!],' and so forth " (*Parson's Tale,* § 42).
Still, like Phoebe, one had rather hear Tupper chide than less racy
writers woo.

[5] *Journal,* p. 554.

whom, in the articles in question, the appeal is constantly made. It is scarcely necessary to say, I think, to those who will read this paper, that I am in the fullest possible accord with the position that mediæval literature must be interpreted in the light of " the conventions, the pre-conceptions, the literary *milieu* " of the mediæval author's times.[6] It is, however, precisely because I regard Mr. Tupper's interpretation, in its postulates and its con-clusions, as inconsistent with mediævál modes of thought that I take issue with it. I am not in the least concerned, for the moment, with its bearing upon Chaucer's art. *A priori,* I could greet Mr. Tupper's Chaucer " as lightly as I were a larke," and as a stranger give him welcome. But the case is not *a priori;* it rests absolutely upon its author's interpretation of the mediæval point of view, upon the way in which he deals with mediæval facts. The merits or demerits of the thesis *per se* are irrelevant, if it is based on a mis-reading of those facts. It is the *foundations* of Mr. Tupper's theory, then, that concern us here.[7] And in examining these foundations my aim is so nearly identical with his, that I cannot find better words for its expression than his own: " This article is an implicit plea not only for the imaginative insight which enables us to enter into the life of another age and to read its poet's words aright, but also for that humbler every-day quality of accurate observation which alone makes it possible for us to read a poet's words at all." [8]

---

[6] See *Journal of English and Germanic Philology*, VIII, pp. 513-69.

[7] I am compelled to emphasize this, for Tupper's skill as an advo-cate is so uncommon, his style so racy and picturesque, and his enthusiasm for his doctrine so contagious, that (*if he is read apart from his authorities*) one feels that Chaucer *should* have done this, even if he *didn't*. It is a necessary, even though an ungrateful task, to view Mr. Tupper's " many-hued theme " in dryer light.

[8] *Journal*, p. 565.

I

The thesis with which we are concerned is that of an
" architectonic use of the *motif* of the Deadly Sins " in
the *Canterbury Tales*.[1] This treatment of the Sins is
" not casual but organic," [2] and it is " as a convenient
and suggestive device of construction " that Chaucer uses
it.[3] The " device of the Sins apparently came to the poet
late," [4] and with the *Parson's Tale* " Chaucer's treatment
of the Sins *motif* is already complete," since " all the
Sins are presented by precept and example." [5]   The
Tales involved are those of the Physician (exemplifying
Lechery), the Pardoner (Avarice and Gluttony), the
Second Nun (Sloth), the Wife of Bath (Pride), the Manciple (Wrath), the Man of Law (Envy), and the Sum-
moner-Friar group (Wrath).   The argument, as applied
to each Tale, rests, (1) on the adequacy of the stories as
exempla of the Sins, as this is established by their use
in Gower or elsewhere, or by their aptness; [6] (2) on the
fact that " each of the stories [is] accompanied by a
preachment against the Sin in question "; [7] (3) on the
further fact that " with delightfully suggestive irony
[Chaucer] oppose[s] practice to precept, rule of life to
dogma, by making several of the story-tellers incarnate
the very Sins that they explicitly condemn "; [8] while
(4) " the crowning argument for Chaucer's deliberate use

---

[1] *Journal*, p. 553; cf. *Publications*, p. 97.
[2] *Publications*, p. 96.
[3] *Ibid.*
[4] *Publications*, p. 117; cf. the whole paragraph.
[5] *Publications*, p. 125, text, and note 56.
[6] *Publications*, pp. 100, 111, 128.
[7] *Ibid.*, pp. 100 ff.; cf. also p. 107.
[8] *Ibid.*, p. 107.

of the Sins *motif* in the Tales under discussion [is] the close connection between these and Chaucer's own detailed discussion of the Sins in his tract on the Deadly Seven which forms so large a part of the Parson's sermon." [9] Such, briefly, are the main outlines of Mr. Tupper's argument.

I have, however, in my statement, greatly simplified the matter at one point. And it is that point which first concerns us. The seven (or eight) Tales just mentioned do not, as Tupper states his case, exemplify outright their respective Sins. The embodiment is *indirect,* through branches, concrete faults, or antitypes. Thus, the *Physician's Tale* represents Lechery, through its antitype Chastity; the *Second Nun's Tale,* Sloth, through its branch, Idleness, the antitype of Undevotion (another branch), and a more general antitype, " bisinesse "; the *Wife of Bath's Tale,* Pride, both directly, and through its branch Inobedience; the *Manciple's Tale,* Wrath, through its branch Chiding; and the *Man of Law's Tale,* Envy, through the fault of " Grucching " against Poverty, and the branches Sorrow at other men's weal, and Detraction. The only Tales which, as Tupper states them, exemplify a Sin *directly* are the Pardoner's (Avarice and Gluttony) and the Friar-Summoner group (Wrath). But in both cases this simplicity is only seeming. For in the *Pardoner's Tale* everything turns (as we shall see) upon the identification of the Sin of which Hazardry and Blasphemy are to be regarded as branches, while in the *Friar's Tale* it is Wrath in its branch of Cursing that is involved. In a word, we have to do with the *branches* of the Sins, as a series of indexes or exponents of the Sins themselves, and Mr. Tupper's uniform assumption is that " every man of

[9] *Ibid.,* p. 114.

the Middle Ages must have recognized at once " the Sin by its exponent.[10] This brings us to the first factor in the theory that gives us pause. For in this assumption lies a very grave difficulty, which the articles in question greatly minimize. Were Mr. Tupper's statements that follow quite in accordance with the facts, this difficulty might not be so serious. But the postulates of his entire argument have to do with the relation of the branches of the Sins to the main categories, and these postulates [11] demand the closest scrutiny. I shall first, then, deal with certain general considerations involved in these preliminary assumptions.

The Vices, we are told, unsystematized at first, " were afterwards adapted to rigid categories, and acquired phases and features which soon became stereotyped." [12] " More formal even than the sequence of the Sins are the traits assigned to each . . . Only voluminous reading in the literature of the Sins will enable one to distinguish readily all the branches and twigs of the deadly tree . . . [But] *generally the limits of variation are so definitely fixed that an exemplum of the Sins, even though its title or tag be lacking, can be referred easily to its appropriate head by the discriminating student of the old formula."* [13] Mr. Tupper grants that there are exceptions. " It is true that the formula of the Sins is not so fixed as to forbid all variations from its categories, *but these varia-*

---

[10] From the various forms in which the categories of the Sins were embodied, " every mediæval reader gleaned as intimate a knowledge of the Sins as of his Paternoster and his Creed, *and hence was able to respond to every reference to these, explicit or implicit!"* (*Publications*, p. 93). The italics are mine. Unless it is otherwise stated, that will uniformly be the case.

[11] *Publications*, pp. 93-96.

[12] *Publications*, p. 93.

[13] *Ibid.*, pp. 94-96.

tions soon become traditional and cause little confusion."[14]
I wish that I could exercise the same unfaltering confidence in the powers of the mediæval mind. But the facts that immediately follow stand seriously in my way.

For it becomes necessary to see just what these supposedly rigid and clear-cut categories really were, and I have the somewhat dismal task of presenting a summary of their intricacies. No *statement* will serve my purpose, for I do not care to set one statement over against another. The Middle Ages must for the moment speak for themselves. I shall use, as I have said, only the sources on which Mr. Tupper himself has drawn, and I shall temper completeness with mercy by omitting many of these.[15] There follow, as compactly as I can put them, the Sins with their branches, subheads, and " speces," as they appear in the *Parson's Tale,* the *Mirour de l'Omme,* the *Confessio Amantis,* the *Ayenbite of Inwit,* and *Jacob's Well.*[16] To promote rapid survey, I shall italicize those branches or twigs which are common to two or more Sins.

PARSON'S TALE.

Pride: *Inobedience,* Vaunting, *Hypocrisy, Despite,* Arrogance, Impudence, Swelling of Heart, Insolence, Elation, *Impatience, Strife,* Contumacy, *Presumption,*

---

[14] *Ibid.*, p. 95.

[15] Among them, the accounts in *Piers Plowman*, the *Pèlerinage, Handlyng Synne*, the *Cursor Mundi*, Frère Lorens, Peraldus, etc. These omissions, it may be remarked, are all in Mr. Tupper's favor. Every additional classification thus analyzed strengthens the case against the assumed rigidity of the categories—as any reader so inclined may easily demonstrate for himself.

[16] Even so, I am omitting in almost every instance numerous " privee speces," some of which are no less ubiquitous than the major branches. I am also omitting, at this point, all but general references. My lists can easily be verified, for they follow in each case the order of treatment. The full references would double the space required.

Irreverence, Pertinacity, *Vain Glory, Jangling*—" and many another twig."

Envy: Sorrow at other men's good, Joy at other men's harm, *Backbiting or Detraction* (five " speces "), *" Grucching " or Murmuration,* arising from *Impatience, Avarice, Pride,* Envy (*Despite*), or *Ire* (resulting in Rancor, *Bitterness, Discord, Scorning, Accusing, Malignity*).

Wrath: *Hate, Discord,* War, *Homicide* (including *Hate, Backbiting, Wicked Counsel, Lechery*), *Hazardry, Anger, Swearing,* Adjuration and *Conjuration,* Divining, *Charms, Lying, Flattery, Cursing, Chiding and Reproach, Scorning, Wicked Counsel, Discord, Double Tongue,* Betrayal of Counsel, *Menace, Idle Words, Jangling, Japing.*

Sloth: Dread to begin good works, *Despair,* Somnolence, Negligence, Idleness, Tarditas, Lachesse, Undevotion, Tristitia.

Avarice: Covetousness, Hard Lordships, Deceit between merchant and merchant, Simony, *Hazardry, False Witness, Theft, Sacrilege.*

Gluttony: Drunkenness, Troubling of Spirit, Devouring of Meat, Distemper, *Forgetfulness.*

Lechery: *Adultery,* Fornication, Deflowering—and the long list of varieties of Adultery.

MIROUR DE L'OMME.[17]

Pride: *Hypocrisy, Vain Glory* [Fool Emprise (1357), *Flattery* (1372)], Overweening [*Presumption* (1526), Vain Curiosity (1611), Derision (1635), Malapertness (1683)], Vaunting, *Inobedience* [*Despite* (2152), Disdain (2257), Danger (2305), " *Grucching* " (2313), *Murmuring* (2323), Rebellion

---

[17] The subheads of each main branch are given in brackets after their respective branches. Since there are no rubrics in the *Mirour* for any but the major subdivisions, I have included in parenthesis, in this case, the line-numbers for the " twigs."

(2325), Contumacy (2326), Perverseness (2403), *Contradiction* (2404), *Blasphemy* (2438)].

Envy: Detraction [Evil Tongue (2679), *Defamation,* (2906), Vituperation (2967), *Reproof* (2989)], Sorrow for others' Joy, Joy for others' Sorrow, Supplantation [*Ambition* (3398), Circumvention (3401), Confusion (3433)], *False-Seeming* [*Double Tongue* (3529), False-Thinking (3651), Dissimulation (3658)].

Wrath: Melancholy [Offense (3952), *Impatience* (3953), Irritation (3975), Provocation (3985)], Contention [*Mocking* (4273), *Slander* (4292), *Defamation* (4292), " Inquietacioun " (4299)], *Hatred* [Malice (4502), *Malignity* (4502), Rancor (4575), Ill-Will (4575)], *Strife* [Mutilation (4706), Fool-Haste (4741)], *Homicide* [*Menace* (4841), Terror (4843), Fright (4843), Murder (4863), *Cruelty* (4983), Vengeance (4993)].

Sloth: Somnolence [Tendresce (5305)], Indolence [Vain Belief (5429), Cowardice (5462), Inconstancy (5462), Desire (5463), Pusillanimity (5463)], Slackness [Sadness (5708), Obstinacy (5732), *Despair* (5761)], Idleness, Negligence (6072).

Avarice: Covetousness [*Accusation* (6315, 6325 ff.), Subtlety (6316, 6373 ff.), Perjury (6318, 6409 ff.), Trickery (6319, 6506 ff.), *Ingratitude* (6320, 6589 ff.), False Occasion (6351), Guile (6380), Plotting (6389), Cunning (6390), *Lying* (6495), Treachery (6506), *Deceit* (6507), Falsity (6408), Fraud (6544), Evil Device (6544), Conspiracy (6566), Confederation (6569), " Champartie " (6571), Circumvention (6578), Brokerage (6579)], Rapine [Robbery (6927), *Theft,* (6929, 7021 ff.), *Sacrilege* (6932, 7141 ff.)], Usury [Subtlety (7309), False Contrivance (7309), Evil Device (7310)], Simony, Niggardliness.

Gluttony: Voracity, Delicacy, Drunkenness, Superfluity, Prodigality [*Extortion* (8438)].

Lechery: Fornication, Rape, *Adultery,* Incest, Wantonness.

CONFESSIO AMANTIS.[18]

Pride: *Hypocrisy, Inobedience* [*Murmur,* Complaint], *Presumption,* Vaunting, *Vain Glory*—antitype, Humility.

Envy: Sorrow for others' Joy, Joy for others' Grief, *Detraction, False Semblant,* Supplantation—antitypes, Charity, Pity.

Wrath: Melancholy, *Cheste, Hate, Contek* [Foolhaste], *Homicide,* War—antitypes, Patience, Mercy.

Sloth: Lachesce, Pusillanimity, *Forgetfulness,* Negligence, Idleness, Somnolence, Tristesce—antitype, Prowess (including Gentilesse).

Avarice: Covetousness, *False Witness, Perjury,* Usury, Parsimony, *Ingratitude,* Ravine, Robbery (including the treatment of Virginity), Stealth, *Sacrilege*—antitype, Liberality.

Gluttony: Drunkenness, Delicacy.

[Lechery]: Incest (not otherwise directly treated).

AYENBITE OF INWYT.[19]

Pride: Untruth [Foulhood or *Ingratitude,* Madness or Folly, *Apostasy* (17-19)], *Despite* [not praising, honoring, or *obeying* aright (19-21)], Arrogance or Overweening [Singularity, *Prodigality, False Strife,* Boasting, *Scorn,* Opposition (21-22)], *Ambition* [*Flattery,* Simulation, *Slander, Deceit, Evil Counsel, Conspiracy, Strife*—" and uele oþre zennes" (22-23)], Idle-bliss or *Vain-Glory* [in goods of nature, of fortune, of grace (23-25)], *Hypocrisy* [+ *Avarice* and Malice (25-26)], Fool-dread, Fool-shame (26).

---

[18] I have given no references in the case of the *Confessio.* They may be easily found in Macaulay's analysis, *Works of John Gower,* II, pp. xxxiii-lxxxix.

[19] Ed. Morris (E. E. T. S.), pp. 16 ff. The numerals in parenthesis are the page-numbers.

Envy: Sorrow in other men's Joy, False-deeming, Wicked Gladness, Worse Sorrow, *Cursing* (27), *Bitterness,* Treachery (28), Sins against the Holy Ghost [*Presumption, Despair,* Hardness of Heart, Contempt of Penance, Striving against Grace, Warring against Truth (28-29)].

Hate (=Wrath): Against one's self [Suicide (29-30)]; against God [*"Grucching," Blasphemy*]; against others [*Chiding, Wrath, Strife,* Desire of Vengeance, *Manslaughter,* War (30)].

Sloth: Slackness, Timidity ("Ar3nesse"), Tenderness, Idleness [*Ribaldry, Lechery*], Heaviness, Wickedness (31), Untruth, Dread, *Forgetfulness* (32), Slackness, Weariness (33), *Unbuxomness, Impatience* (33), *" Grucching,"* Sorrow, Desire of Death, *Despair* (34).

Avarice: Usury [seven varieties (35-37)], *Theft* [four varieties, including *Adultery* and Wicked Judges (37-38)], Robbery [six varieties (38-39)], False Claim (Chalenge) [seven varieties, including *False Witness,* False Judges and Counsellors (39-40)], *Sacrilege* [seven varieties (40-41)], Simony [six varieties (41-42)], Wickedness [*Apostasy, " Grucching," Treason, .Discord,* False Accusation, etc. (43-44)], Chaffer [seven varieties (44-45)], Wicked Crafts, Wicked Games [*Dicing, Lying, Blasphemy* (45-46)].

Lechery: *Adultery* [fourteen kinds (46-50)].

Sin of the Mouth: i) **Gluttony:** Eating before time (50-51) [*Evil Games* (52)], Immoderate Eating and Drinking (52-53), *Hypocrisy* (53), Strong Yearning for Meat (55), *Extravagance* [*Vain Glory* (55)], Undue Anxiety about Eating [three varieties (55-56)]; *Lechery* (56); " Sins of the Tavern " [Gluttony, Lechery, Swearing, Forswearing, *Lying, Slander, Apostasy, Dispute, Cheste, Strife, Manslaughter, Theft* (56-57)]; ii) **Sins of the Tongue:** Idle Words [five sorts, including *Ribaldry, Mocking, Scorn, Manslaughter* (58)], Boasting [five sorts (58-60)], *Flattery* [five boughs (60-61)], *Detraction* [five sorts (61-62)], *Lying* [three sorts, with Guile and *Contek* (62-

63)], *Perjury* and *Swearing* [seven modes of Swearing, including *False Witness* (63-65)], *Cheste* [*Strife, Chiding,* Evil Speaking, *Slander, Reproach, Threatening, Discord* (65-67)], " *Grucching* " ⌊*Murmuring* a) against God, including " *Grucching* " *against Poverty,* b) against man—as a result of *Inobedience, Sloth, Impatience, Envy,* or Felony (67-68)], Opposition (68-69), *Blasphemy* (70).

JACOB'S WELL.[20]

Pride: *Presumption* [Singularity, *Extravagance,* Litigiousness, Avaunting, *Scorn, Anger* (70-71)], *Vain Glory* [three sorts (71)], *Unbuxomness* [*Despite,* Disdain, Defiance (71-72)], Boldness [Unkindness, Wasting Time, *Apostasy*—four kinds (72-73)], *Hypocrisy* [three kinds (73-74)], Disdain (76), Impudence [two kinds (77)], Sturdiness (77).

Envy: False Deeming, Sorrow at others' Good (82), *Slander, Bitterness, Backbiting, Sowing of Discord* (83), Restraining good beginnings, ruining him who would do right, and discrediting a good name (84); Sins against the Holy Ghost [*Presumption, Despair,* Hardness of Heart, Contempt of Penance, Opposition to Grace, Opposition to Truth (85)].

Wrath: *Hate,* Malice (90, 92), Vengeance, Wrath against God [*"Grucching"*], against one's self, against one's household (91) or one's neighbor, Hastiness, *Manslaughter* [*Defamation* (93)], *Impatience* [" *Grucching* "], *Blasphemy* (94), *Sowing of Discord, Scorn* (99).

Sloth: " Slugness " (103-04), Tenderness (104-05), Idleness [*Hazardry, Tavern-revels,* Dancing, etc. (105-106)], Heaviness of Heart, Wickedness of Heart, " Arweness " (106), Delay of Amendment (107), Recklessness or Negligence (108), *Forgetfulness,* Faintheartedness, Lachesce, Slackness (109), *Inobedience, Impatience,* " *Grucching,*" Heaviness, Langour, *Despair* (112).

---

[20] Ed. Brandeis (E. E. T. S.), pp. 68 ff.

Avarice: Idolatry, - *Ambition* (120), Niggardliness (121), *Treason* (122), Usury [twelve kinds (122-24)], Simony (126-27), *Theft* [five kinds (128)], Robbery [six kinds (129)], *Sacrilege* [eight kinds, including *Adultery* (130)], False litigation (130), Wickedness [*Apostasy*, Witchcraft, *Charms* (131), *Conjurations, Manslaughter, Sowing of Discord* (132)], Dishonest Trade [five kinds (133)], Disreputable Crafts [Prostitutes, Jugglers, Sham Cripples, "Lacchedrawers," *Japers,* Heralds-at-arms, Champions, Dishonest Tollers, Hangmen (134)], *Gambling* [nine divisions, including *Blasphemy* and *Inobedience* (135)].

Gluttony: Eating and drinking out of time or out of measure [including *Hypocrisy* (142-43)], Eating greedily, Eating over-dainty meats, Delicacy [*Vain Glory* (144), Distemper, in *Jangling, Boasting, Drunkenness, Tavern-revels, Swearing, Lying, Chiding, Despising, Cursing* (145)]; "Sins of the Tavern" [Gluttony, *Lechery, Forswearing, Slander, Backbiting, Scorn, Chiding, Despite, Apostasy, Theft, Robbery, Strife, Manslaughter* (148)]; Sins of the Tongue [*Idle-talk, Jangling* (148), *Boasting, Flattery* (149), *Backbiting* (150), *Lying* (151), *Forswearing* —seven kinds (152-53), *Chiding and Striving*—seven kinds, including *Disdain, Slander, Reproof, Menace, Discord* (154)], "*Grucching*" [a) against God, including "*Grucching*" against Poverty," b) against man (154-55)], *Frowardness* (155), *Blasphemy* (156).

Lechery: fourteen degrees (160-62).

These, then, are a few of the facts about the "rigid" categories. If we are going to be mediæval, let us *be it, à toute outrance!* [21]

[21] The interweavings of the *antitypes* of the Sins yield little in interest to the overlappings of the Sins themselves, and since Mr. Tupper deals also in antitypes, their inclusion would be highly pertinent. But space is not available. In the *Parson's Tale* the *remedia*

One thing is obvious at a glance. The "definitely fixed limits of variation" among the branches, which Mr. Tupper postulates,[22] simply do not exist. The maze that I have in part reproduced is, both in fact and *ex hypothesi,* what the mediæval reader had. No simplification of the facts is possible, unless we renounce once for all the mediæval point of view. Yet Mr. Tupper sweepingly simplifies. "It is true that the formula of the Sins is not so fixed as to forbid all variations from its categories, *but these variations soon become traditional and cause little confusion."* [23] And he proceeds to illustrate the "limits of variation." "For instance, Swearing or 'Great Oaths' is usually classed under the head of Wrath, and yet in Langland more than once it is transferred to Gluttony both as a fault of the mouth and as a feature of tavern-revel. So, too, Chiding as a Sin of the Tongue, is sometimes found apart, as in the *Ayenbite* and *Mireour du Monde,* from its category of Wrath. Poverty finds a place under both Pride and Envy, and occasionally under Avarice; yet here there are obvious distinctions in the point of view." [24] *That is all.* The list of three variations which Tupper gives is utterly (however unintentionally) misleading, and the impression thus produced is peculiarly unfortunate. For the point involved is one which is absolutely vital to his argument. The relative fixity of the categories—which is the inevitable

follow their respective Sins. See especially Eilers, pp. 567 ff. In the *Mirour de l'Omme* each branch of each Sin has its corresponding antitype. See the long series beginning with l. 10177. The chief antitypes for the *Confessio Amantis* are given above. For the *Ayenbite* see ed. Morris, pp. 130 ff. (summarized in the Introduction, pp. xciv ff.). For *Jacob's Well,* see ed. Brandeis, pp. 238 ff. For one or two concrete instances, see below, pp. 300, n. 74; 327 ff.; 347, n. 21.

[22] *Publications,* p. 96.
[23] *Publications,* p. 95.
[24] *Publications,* pp. 95-96.

implication of his brief enumeration of exceptions, as well- as something which he explicitly asserts—is fundamental to his further assumption of the immediate and accurate convertibility (in the minds of mediæval readers) of branches in terms of head Sins.[25]   Unless the branches *have* these fixed associations, so that they may be intelligibly employed as the constant indexes or exponents of a given Vice, the theory falls to the ground.   The slightest scrutiny of the partial summary given above affords ample evidence that branch after branch [26] moves hither and thither among the categories in a fashion which defies all definite assignment to this Sin or that. Mr. Tupper's list of three traditional variations would be the better for a supplement.   Here is one which, like his, does not even approach completeness, but which is sufficient for our purposes.[27]

Discord appears under Pride,[28] Wrath,[29] Envy,[30] Avarice,[31] and Gluttony (Sins of the Tongue) ; [32] *Scorning,* under Wrath,[33] Envy,[34] Pride,[35] Sloth,[36] and Gluttony

[25] I am not exaggerating Mr. Tupper's position. See *Publications*, p. 93, ll. 8 ff.; p. 96, ll. 5 ff.; *Journal*, p. 555, ¶ 2, ll. 5 ff., etc.

[26] Including seven out of the ten on which Mr. Tupper bases his argument—Inobedience, Chiding, "Grucching" against Poverty, Detraction, Hazardry, Blasphemy, Cursing.

[27] At the risk of the charge of pedantry, I shall give in this article, so far as possible, the reference for every statement of fact that I make. I am challenging assertions, and I wish my own to be susceptible of immediate verification.

[28] *Cursor Mundi*, l. 27604; *Pèlerinage*, l. 14070; Raymund of Pennaforte (Petersen, *Sources of the Parson's Tale*, p. 27).

[29] I, 563 (§ 35), 640 (§ 45) ; *Jacob's Well*, p. 99.

[30] I, 510; *Cursor Mundi*, l. 28174.

[31] *Ayenbite*, p. 43; *Jacob's Well*, p. 132.

[32] *Ayenbite*, pp. 66-67.

[33] I, 635 (§ 43) ; *Jacob's Well*, p. 99.   [34] I, 510.

[35] *Ayenbite*, p. 22; *Jacob's Well*, p. 70; *Handlyng Synne*, p. 109; *Piers Plowman*, C. VII, 22 ff., B. XIII, 277.

[36] *Jacob's Well*, p. 105.

(Sins of the Tongue); [37] *Lying,* under Wrath,[38] Avarice,[39] Pride,[40] Lechery,[41] Sloth,[42] and Gluttony (both independently [43] and as a Sin of the Tongue [44]); *Despite,* under Pride,[45] Envy,[46] Gluttony,[47] and Wrath; [48] *Jangling,* under Pride,[49] Wrath,[50] Gluttony,[51] and Avarice; [52] *Japing,* under Wrath,[53] Avarice,[54] Gluttony,[55] Sloth,[56] and Lechery; [57] *Flattery,* under Wrath,[58] Pride,[59] and Gluttony [60] (Sins of the Tongue); *Charms and Divining,* under Wrath,[61] Avarice,[62] and Sloth; [63] *Prodigality,* under Pride,[64] Gluttony,[65] and the Vice opposite to Avarice; [66] *Despair,* under Sloth,[67] Envy,[68] and Lechery; [69]

---

[37] *Ayenbite,* p. 58.   [38] I, 607 (§ 39).

[39] *Mirour,* ll. 6495 ff.; *Ayenbite,* p. 45; *Pèlerinage,* ll. 18175 ff.; *Cursor Mundi,* l. 27833.

[40] *Piers Plowman,* B. XIII, 288; *Handlyng Synne,* p. 125.

[41] *Cursor Mundi,* l. 27924.

[42] *Jacob's Well,* p. 113.   [43] *Jacob's Well,* p. 145.

[44] *Ayenbite,* pp. 62-63; *Jacob's Well,* p. 151.

[45] I, 390; etc.   [46] I, 505.   [47] *Jacob's Well,* p. 145.

[48] *Pèlerinage,* ll. 15680 ff.; *Jacob's Well,* p. 100.

[49] I, 405; *Ayenbite,* p. 20; *Cursor Mundi,* ll. 27620-22.

[50] I, 648.

[51] *Piers Plowman,* B. II, 94; *Jacob's Well,* pp. 145, 148.

[52] *Mirour,* l. 6286.   [55] *Piers Plowman,* B. II, 94.

[53] I, 650.   [56] *Jacob's Well,* p. 113.

[54] *Jacob's Well,* p. 134.   [57] *Piers Plowman,* B. XIII, 353.

[58] I, 610-15 (§ 40).

[59] *Mirour,* ll. 1369 ff.; *Pèlerinage,* ll. 14644 ff.; *Ayenbite,* p. 23; *Handlyng Synne,* p. 121.

[60] *Ayenbite,* pp. 60-61; *Jacob's Well,* p. 149.

[61] I, 602-605 (§§ 37-38).

[62] *Jacob's Well,* pp. 131-32.   [63] *Cursor Mundi,* l. 28311.

[64] *Ayenbite,* p. 21; *Jacob's Well,* p. 70.

[65] *Mirour,* ll. 8401 ff.; *Ayenbite,* p. 55.

[66] *Confessio,* v, 7644-45.

[67] I, 692 (§ 56); *Pèlerinage,* ll. 13932 ff.; *Handlyng Synne,* p. 170; etc.

[68] *Ayenbite,* p. 29; *Jacob's Well,* p. 85.

[69] Raymund of Pennaforte (Petersen, p. 27); *Mirror of St. Edmund,* p. 24.

Anger, under Wrath,[70] Pride,[71] and Sloth; [72] *Ambition,* under Pride,[73] Avarice,[74] and Envy; [75] *Adultery,* under Lechery [76] and Avarice; [77] *Hypocrisy,* under *Pride,*[78] Gluttony,[79] and Sloth; [80] *Treason,* under Avarice,[81] Envy,[82] and Pride; [83] *Menace,* under Pride,[84] Wrath,[85] and Lechery; [86] *Slander,* under Wrath,[87] Envy,[88] Sloth,[89] and Gluttony[90] (Sins of the Tongue) ; *Malignity,* under Envy,[91] Avarice,[92] and Wrath; [93] *Cursing,* under Wrath,[94] Envy,[95] and Gluttony; [96] *Vain Glory,* under Pride [97] and Gluttony; [98] *Forgetfulness,* under Sloth [99] and Gluttony; [100] *Accusation,* under Envy [101] and Avarice; [102] ; *Apostasy,* under Avarice [103] and Pride; [104] *Homicide,* under

[70] I, 582.   [71] *Jacob's Well,* p. 70.
[72] Gaytryge's Sermon (E. E. T. S., 26), p. 13.
[73] *Ayenbite,* p. 22.   [75] *Mirour,* ll. 3398 ff.
[74] *Jacob's Well,* p. 120.   [76] I, § 75; etc.
[77] *Jacob's Well,* p. 130; *Ayenbite,* p. 37; cf. *Confessio,* v, ll. 6135 ff.
[78] I, 390; *Mirour,* ll. 1057 ff.; *Pèlerinage,* ll. 14588; *Handlyng Synne,* pp. 110 ff.
[79] *Ayenbite,* p. 53; *Jacob's Well,* p. 143.
[80] *Pèlerinage,* ll. 13921 ff.
[81] *Ayenbite,* p. 43; *Jacob's Well,* p. 122; *Cursor Mundi,* l. 27824.
[82] *Pèlerinage,* ll.14982-15232; *Handlyng Synne,* pp. 142-43.
[83] Frère Lorens (Eilers, in " Essays on Chaucer "—Chaucer Soc.— Pt. v, p. 511) ; *Handlyng Synne,* p. 125.
[84] *Handlyng Synne,* p. 126.
[85] *Mirour,* l. 4841.   [86] *Cursor Mundi,* l. 28517.
[87] *Mirour,* l. 4292; *Jacob's Well,* p. 93; Gaytryge, p. 12.
[88] *Jacob's Well,* p. 83; *Mirour,* ll. 2906 ff.
[89] *Jacob's Well,* p. 113.   [94] I, § 41.
[90] *Ayenbite,* p. 66.   [95] *Ayenbite,* p. 27.
[91] I, 510.   [96] *Jacob's Well,* p. 145.
[92] Frère Lorens (Eilers, p. 543). [97] I, 390; etc.
[93] *Mirour,* l. 4502.
[98] *Jacob's Well,* p. 144; *Ayenbite,* p. 55.
[99] *Ayenbite,* p. 32; *Jacob's Well,* p. 109; *Confessio,* iv, 539-886.
[100] I, 825.   [101] I, 510.   [102] *Mirour,* l. 6315.
[103] *Ayenbite,* p. 43; *Jacob's Well,* p. 131.
[104] *Ayenbite,* p. 19; *Jacob's Well,* p. 73.

9

Wrath [105] and Avarice; [106] *Cruelty,* under Wrath [107] and
Pride; [108] *False Semblance,* under Avarice [109] and En-
vy; [110] *Betraying of Counsel,* under Pride [111] and
Wrath; [112] *Mocking,* under Avarice [113] and Wrath; [114]
Extortion, under Avarice [115] and Gluttony; [116] *False Witness,* under Avarice [117] and Envy; [118] *Hate,* under
Wrath [119] and Envy; [120] *Evil Counsel,* under Pride,[121]
W'rath,[122] and Sloth; [123] *Frowardness,* under Pride,[124]
Sloth,[125] and Gluttony [126] (Sins of the Tongue); *Conspiracy,* under Avarice [127] and Envy [128]; *Presumption,*
under Pride [129] and Sloth; [130] *Sacrilege,* under Avarice [131] and Lechery; [132] *Double Tongue,* under Wrath [133]
and Envy; [134] *Ingratitude,* under Pride [135] and Avarice; [136] *Strife,* under Wrath [137] and Pride; [138] *Perjury,*

[105] I, 564; etc.

[106] *Jacob's Well,* p. 132; *Cursor Mundi,* l. 27838.

[107] *Mirour,* ll. 4983 ff.; etc.

[108] *Pèlerinage,* ll. 14192 ff.   [109] *Pèlerinage,* ll. 17879 ff.

[110] *Mirour,* ll. 3469 ff.; *Confessio,* II, 1879 ff.

[111] *Handlyng Synne,* p. 125.   [113] *Handlyng Synne,* p. 196.

[112] I, 645, (§ 47).   [114] *Mirour,* ll. 4273 ff.

[115] I, 750 ff.; *Ayenbite,* pp. 38-39; *Jacob's Well,* p. 129.

[116] *Handlyng Synne,* pp. 218-19; *Mirour,* ll. 8438 ff.

[117] I, 795; *Ayenbite,* pp. 39, 44; *Jacob's Well,* p. 131; *Piers Plowman,* B. XIII, 359; *Confessio,* v, 2863.

[118] *Piers Plowman,* B. v, 89.   [119] I, § 35; etc.

[120] Raymund of Pennaforte (Petersen, p. 27); Gaytryge, p. 12.

[121] Frère Lorens (Eilers, p. 511); *Ayenbite,* p. 23.

[122] I, 566, 637.

[123] *Jacob's Well,* p. 105.   [130] *Cursor Mundi,* ll. 27800, 28358-59.

[124] *Cursor Mundi,* l. 27617.   [131] I, 800; etc.

[125] *Cursor Mundi,* l. 28252.   [132] *Cursor Mundi,* l. 27946.

[126] *Jacob's Well,* p. 155.   [133] I, § 46.

[127] *Mirour,* l. 6566.   [134] *Mirour,* ll. 3529, 3580, 3599, etc.

[128] *Cursor Mundi,* l. 27662.   [135] *Ayenbite,* p. 18.

[129] I, 390; etc.   [136] *Confessio,* v, 4887 (see gloss).

[137] *Mirour,* l. 4633; *Ayenbite,* p. 30.

[138] *Ayenbite,* p. 22.

under Avarice [139] and Gluttony; [140] *Ribaldry,* under Pride,[147] Sloth,[142] and Gluttony.[143]

The branches that definitely link themselves with Mr. Tupper's argument I shall consider later. Here it is sufficient to note that *Inobedience* (Unbuxomness) appears under Pride, Sloth, Avarice, and Gluttony (Sins of the Tongue), and through its antitype Obedience, under Lechery, Wrath, and Envy; *Detraction,* under Pride, Envy, Wrath, and Gluttony (Sins of the Tongue); " *Grucching* " or *Murmuration,* under Envy, Pride, Wrath, Sloth, Avarice, and Gluttony (Sins of the Tongue); *Hazardry,* under Wrath, Avarice, Sloth, and Gluttony; *Blasphemy,* under Wrath, Pride, Avarice, and Gluttony (Sins of the Tongue); *Chiding,* under Wrath, Pride, Envy, Gluttony, and Sins of the Tongue; *Cursing,* under Wrath, Envy, and Gluttony; *Impatience,* under Wrath, Pride, Envy, and Sloth.—Is it true, as Professor Tupper states, that " these variations soon become traditional and cause little confusion " ? *Could* the mediæval reader, even though he were " a discriminating student of the old formula " [144] (which he probably was not), refer any one of a score or two of branches—not to speak of an *exemplum* without its tag—easily to its appropriate head ?

.The truth, of course, is that the categories of the Seven Deadly Sins are neither " rigid," nor " stereotyped," nor " strict." They overlapped and interwove, and the same specific Sin appears now in this group, now in that. That is one salient fact. But there is still another—a mediæval phenomenon of no small significance, which Mr. Tupper has also totally overlooked. For " *summae* and sermons, ' mirrors ' and manuals, hymns, ' moralities,' books

[139] *Confessio,* v, 2866.

[140] *Jacob's Well,* p. 153.

[141] *Handlyng Synne,* p. 126.

[142] *Jacob's Well,* p. 113.

[143] *Piers Plowman,* C. VII, 435.

[144] *Publications,* p. 96.

of *exempla,* rules of nuns and instructions of parish priests, catechisms of lay folk and popular penitentials, such famous allegories as De Guileville's *Pèlerinage"* [145] —not to speak of Dante, and Langland, and Gower, and Spenser—all show a surprising lack of Mr. Tupper's faith in the mediæval reader's powers of divination. One and all, *they employ the most explicit rubrics, titles, headings,* to designate their groups and "place" their branches, so that the wayfaring man, though mediæval, should not err therein.[146] It could not have been otherwise. When Mr. Tupper insists that titles or tags were unnecessary, he is running counter to one of the most striking facts that characterize the mediæval treatment of the Sins—the constant and explicit indication of a given Sin's provenience at the moment among the categories. For a given fault belonged to the Sin where, at the moment, it was *put.* Without explicit indication, the position of scores of faults (and even branches) among the categories was indeterminate. If Mr. Tupper does not feel that, the Middle Ages did, and they consistently guarded against the confusion inherent in the nebulous boundaries between Sin and Sin. Whatever else may be true of the method of dealing with the Sins which Mr. Tupper finds in Chaucer, it is at least unmediæval. And to prove up to the hilt the exemplification in a tale of a given *branch* may be still to leave the question of the *Sin* exemplified an absolutely open one.

Nor is the reason for this state of things far to seek. As Professor Manly has pointed out, "in the Middle

---

[144] *Publications,* p. 93.

[146] Spenser, for example, drew freely on the branches for the traits which he combined in his portraits of the Sins (see these *Publications,* XXIX, pp. 410 ff.)—but each portrait was *named.* Dante's method is also explicit.

Ages the Seven Sins were treated as tempers or tendencies out of which particular misdeeds grow. And, naturally, the same deed, the same sin, may originate in any one of several different tempers or tendencies." [147]   One need go no farther than the *Parson's Tale* for evidence. " And as wel comth Ire of Pryde, as of Envye; for soothly, he that is proude or envious is lightly wrooth." [148]   " In this forseyde develes fourneys there forgen three shrewes: Pryde, that ay bloweth and encreseth the fyr by chydinge and wikked wordes. Thanne stant Envye, and holdeth the hote iren upon the herte of man with a peire of longe tonges of long rancour. And thanne stant the sinne of contumelie or stryf and cheeste, and batereth and forgeth by vileyns reprevinges." [149]   " Envye and Ire maken bitternesse in herte; which bitternesse is moder of Accidie." [150]   " After Glotonye, thanne comth Lecherie; for thise two sinnes been so ny cosins, that ofte tyme they wol not departe." [151]   Nor could a better concrete illustration be given than one which the Parson himself provides. " Grucching or murmuracioun " (I, 497-514) is given as a branch of *Envy.* " Somtyme it springeth of *inpacience* "—and Impatience is the Parson's tenth twig of *Pride.* " Somtyme comth grucching of *avarice* . . . Somtyme comth murmure of *Pryde* ... And somtyme grucching sourdeth of *Envye* ... and [they] grucche, and murmure prively for verray *despyt* ... Som tyme grucching comth of *ire* or prive *hate,* that norisseth *rancour* in herte ... Thanne cometh eek *bitternesse* of herte ... Thanne cometh *discord* . . . Thanne comth *scorninge* ... Thanne comth *accusinge* ... Thanne

---

[147] *Modern Philology,* VII, p. 115. This statement is quoted (*Modern Language Review,* V, p. 19) with assent by R. W. Chambers, whose mediævalism Mr. Tupper accepts.

[148] I, § 32 (*de Ira*).   [150] I, § 53 (*de Accidia*).
[149] I, § 34 (*de Ira*).   [151] I, § 74 (*de Luxuria*).

comth *malignitee* "—and in the section under *Wrath,
hate, discord,* and *scorning* are duly given as branches of
that Sin. The *confusion* of the categories is, to say the
least, as essential a fact as their *rigidity.* The simplification of the complexity inherent in the very conception of
the Sins is not a mediæval, but a modern point of view.

In a word, the premises of Mr. Tupper's argument are
large assumptions. The simplification which he postulates is unwarranted by the facts.[152] It " necessitates "—
if I may quote—" not only a disregard of all evidence
but an insensibility to the trend of mediæval thought." [153]
Yet on that simplification the whole structure rests. I
shall come to that in a moment in detail. Meantime
there is one other general consideration that appears from
even a cursory reading of the summaries that I have given.

The *range* of the categories is practically all-inclusive.
If one is to tell tales at all, one is foredoomed to run into
them. If there is *any* story involving human sin or
frailty (or its opposite—for there are the antitypes) that
could not qualify as an *exemplum* of some branch or other
of the Seven Deadly Sins, such a story would rival " the
sóleyn fenix of Arabyé." Nor is it necessary to go far

---

[152] I have preferred in this discussion to present at first hand the
facts as they lie in Mr. Tupper's own sources, without referring to
the work of others. But anyone who wishes a judgment that carries the weight of absolute authority may turn to the chapter on
" Classification of Sins " in Lea's *History of Auricular Confession
and Indulgences in the Latin Church,* Vol. II, chap. xx, pp. 233-284
(especially pp. 238-44), for statements far stronger than mine
regarding the labyrinth of the Sins. For there was not only the
immeasurable complication of the branches, but the still further
practical impossibility of laying down rules to determine whether
a given fault was even Deadly Sin at all.

[153] *Publications,* p. 105. Mr. Tupper has just been speaking of
Chaucer's close adherence " to *the strict categories of human errors*
recognized by all his contemporaries."

afield for the evidence. The *exemplum*-books are full of
it, but I shall come nearer home. Let us take the stories
that Chaucer told (or meant to tell) in his "Seintes
Legende of Cupyde." What happened to them at the
hands of Gower? Pyramus and Thisbe exemplify *Wrath*,
under its branch of Contek; [154] Dido and Æneas, *Sloth*
(Lachesse); [155] Medea and Jason, *Avarice* (Perjury); [156]
Lucretia (on Mr. Tupper's principle),[157] *Lechery*, under
its antitype of Chastity; [158] Theseus and Ariadne, *Avarice*
(Ingratitude); [159] Philomela and Tereus, *Avarice*
(Ravine); [160] Demophon and Phyllis, *Sloth* (Forgetful-
ness).[161] Of the tales which Chaucer names but does not
tell, Ulysses and Penelope exemplify *Sloth* (Lachesse); [162]
Tristram and Isolde, *Gluttony* ([Love-]Drunken-
ness); [163] Paris and Helen, *Avarice* (Sacrilege); [164]
Canace and Machaire, *Wrath* (Melancholy); [165] Deianira
and Nessus, *Envy* (False-Semblant); [166] and as for
Ceix and Alceone (to round out the Man of Law's list),
they illustrate *Sloth* (Somnolence).[167]   But does even
Mr. Tupper for a moment suppose that these old and
distinguished stories stood for these Sins in the minds of
mediæval readers *apart from Gower's explicit labelling of
them as they entered into the framework of his poem?* [168]
Would the man of the Middle Ages have so "placed"

[154] *Confessio Amantis*, III, 1331 ff.

[155] IV, 77 ff.

[156] V, 3247 ff.

[159] V, 5231 ff.

[157] See below, pp. 306 ff.

[158] VII, 4754 ff.

[160] V, 551 ff. In *Purgatorio*, XVII, 19 ff., Philomela (or Progne)
is an example of *Wrath*.

[161] IV, 731 ff.

[162] IV, 147 ff.

[163] VI, 467 ff.

[164] V, 7195 ff.

[165] III, 143 ff.

[166] II, 2145 ff.

[167] IV, 2927.

[168] It is unnecessary to remark that Chaucer himself did not regard
them as "Sins Tales."

them, without their tag ? [169]   They are simply " impressed soldiers " (as Dr. Mosher has well put it) [170] in Gower's army, and few of the myriads of mediæval tales were
free from liability to such conscription.   The " aptness "
of a story to exemplify a Vice [171] counts for little, for
(once given the all-embracing compass of the Seven
Deadly Sins, their branches, and their antitypes, and the
branches of their antitypes) the story would be far to
seek that was *not* potentially a " Sins Tale."   Nor does
the fact that a story was once so used thereby create for
it a Deadly Sins tradition.   Dido, Medea, Pyramus and
Thisbe, and the rest appear and reappear, after Gower as
before, with no trace of the confessional upon them. [172]
Neither " aptness " nor previous use may be given too
much weight. [173]

These are general considerations.   In the light of them
let us examine the details of Mr. Tupper's argument.

II

I shall consider first the Tales that are not common to
Chaucer and Gower—namely, the *Pardoner's Tale,* the
Friar-Summoner Group, and the *Second Nun's Tale.*

The *Pardoner's Tale,* to which Mr. Tupper has de-

---

[169] I hope I may not be thought so unfair to Mr. Tupper's argument as to imply that the case of the *Legend* stories is parallel *at
all points* with the case, as he states it, for the *Canterbury Tales* in
question.   I am concerned, for the moment, solely with " the *adequacy* of ... stories as *exempla* of the Sins " (*Publications,* p. 100).

[170] *The Exemplum in England* (Columbia University Press, 1911),
p. 126.

[171] *Publications,* p. 111.

[172] See, for example, *Journal of English and Germanic Philology,*
VIII, pp. 546-65.

[173] See below, pp. 304-05.

voted a separate article,[1] is apparently his strongest card among the three. For the Pardoner stands, *ex hypothesi,* for Avarice and Gluttony. He tells a tale which may be—and sometimes is—construed as an *exemplum* against Avarice. He himself is avaricious, and he preaches (as he is the first to tell us) against the very vice which he practices. He also inveighs against Gluttony, and is himself no ascetic. And (as in accordance with the argument he should) he draws upon the *Parson's Tale.* None of this, to be sure (except the heightening of the tavern-setting), is new; the superb irony of prologue, sermon, tale, and epilogue has long been recognised.[2] What *is* new is the contention that "the rascal is *formally illustrating* [*the*] *Deadly Sins*" of Avarice and Gluttony,[3] as his contribution to Chaucer's architectonic use of the Sins *motif.* And it is Avarice and Gluttony alone (it must be noted) for which he stands, for "in his exposition of [these] *two* Sins ... there is little opportunity for any intrusion of other elements."[4] The Pardoner, then, according to the theory, exemplifies two Sins only—Avarice and Gluttony. Let us look for a moment at Mr. Tupper's problem.

The Pardoner starts out with the account of his stock sermon against *Avarice.* Incidentally he mentions, as homiletic motives, Flattery, Hypocrisy, Vain Glory (all branches of *Pride*), and Hate (a branch of *Wrath*).[5]

---

[1] *Journal,* pp. 553-565. Compare *Publications,* pp. 98, 105, 107-08, 115, 124.

[2] See, for example, *The Atlantic Monthly,* LXXII, pp. 829 ff.

[3] *Publications,* p. 115.

[4] *Publications,* p. 124. In the article on "The Pardoner's Tavern" the conception of Gluttony is expanded to "Sins of the Tavern" (*Journal,* p. 559); there is "evidence of the strongest that the Pardoner is exemplifying *only* the vices of the tavern" (*Journal,* p. 558).

[5] C, 409-11.

After a passing glance at his own *lecherous* proclivities,[6] he comes to his " moral tale "—an " ensample " (such as " lewed peple loven "),[7] " which," he distinctly says, *" I am wont to preche,* for to winne " (461). It is one of his own sermons, accordingly, such as he has just described, which he proposes to rehearse. The *exemplum* has its setting in a tavern (463-82),[8] and in the vivid preliminary account of the tavern-revels, *Hazardry* (465, 467), *Gluttony* (468), *Blasphemy* (472-75), and *Lechery* (481-82) all find a place. Having mentioned these Sins, the Pardoner " falls into the well-worn *exempla* track " (for it is his well-worn sermon that he is preaching), and proceeds to take them up in order, and to deal with them in true *exemplum* fashion—first *Lechery* (483-89) and *Homicide* (488-97)[9] as the result of *Drunkenness;* then *Gluttony* in general (498-548), with its subhead *Drunkenness* in particular (549-88). Having finished with Gluttony he comes to *Hazardry* (590-628), especially as it applies to those in high estate (595-628). Hazardry disposed of, he proceeds to *Blasphemy* (629-60)—reverting at the close to the " bicched bones two," whose fruit is " Forswearing, *ire,* falsnesse, *homicyde"* (657). Then follows the *exemplum,* which pays its respects to *Drunkenness* (705), *Blasphemy* (708-09), and *Hazardry* (751), in its course toward its climax, *Homicide,* as the result of *Avarice.* Thereupon we have the peroration:

[6] C, 453.

[7] C, 435-37.

[8] It may well have had this setting in Chaucer's source, as Mr. Tupper (following Miss Petersen, *On the Sources of the Nonne Prestes Tale,* pp. 98-100) hints (*Publications,* p. 98, n. 8). The headings which Miss Petersen quotes, however, do not include " de Gula."

[9] With this paragraph compare particularly the *Summoner's Tale,* D, 2043-78; see below, p. 281.

O cursed sinne, ful of cursednesse!
O traytours *homicyde*, o wikkednesse!
O *glotonye, luxurie*, and *hasardrye!*
Thou *blasphemour* of Crist with vileinye
And *othes grete*, of usage and of *pryde!* [10]

And then the Pardoner ends orderly where he began

Now, goode men, god forgeve yow your trespas,
And ware yow fro *the sinne of avaryce*. [11]

Here is "goddes foyson" of the Seven Deadly Sins! [12]
Avarice, Gluttony, Lechery, Wrath, Pride—five of the
Seven—specifically named; three branches of Pride
(*Flattery, Hypocrisy, Vain Glory*) and two of Wrath
(*Hate, Homicide*) referred to; and *Hazardry* and *Blasphemy* given each its own special and (so far as Chaucer
tells us) independent place. Mr. Tupper's problem is to
reduce all this to *two* sole Sins. For the Pardoner stands
in his scheme for Avarice and Gluttony alone. How does
he solve it?

He does it, in the first place, by dropping the pilot.
The close connection between the Tales concerned and
the Parson's sermon is, as we have seen, "the *crowning
argument* for Chaucer's deliberate use of the Sins *motif*."
And in the present instance it is "*the large plunderings
of the Pardoner* from the Parson's reflections on Avarice
and Gluttony and its auxiliary vices" that "betoken ...
that the rascal is *formally illustrating* those Deadly
Sins." [13]   The argument from the *Parson's Tale*, then,

[10] C, 895-99.
[11] C, 904-05.
[12] I need scarcely say that I have no quarrel with the view that
Chaucer knew the Seven Deadly Sins and made superbly artistic
use of the material that they afforded him. It is from a *schematizing* of them, which stands in sharp conflict with the facts and
with itself, that I dissent.
[13] *Publications*, pp. 114-15.

applies both in general and in particular to the *Pardoner's Tale*. But "the large plunderings of the Pardoner" are not only from Mr. Tupper's two Sins, Avarice and Gluttony; they are even more largely from the Parson's discourse on *Wrath*.[14] That is inconvenient, for even to allow one Tale to represent two Sins is stretching a point; to make it the representative of *three,* by including *Wrath,* would be for the theory a fatal embarrassment of riches. This Mr. Tupper evidently sees. "*It is true,*" he says, "that in the *Parson's Tale,* Hazardry is included under Avarice [he fails to state that it is also included under *Wrath;* see I, 580] ... and Great Oaths under *Wrath; but,*"[15] etc. Again: "*It is interesting* that the Parson, like Peraldus, includes Hazardry under Avarice and Great Oaths under *Wrath.* This arrangement, *however,*"[16] etc. It *is* both true and interesting, and it is also of vital moment to the validity of Mr. Tupper's reasoning. The *Parson's Tale* is the "crowning argument"—till it runs counter to the theory; then, "farewel feldefare"! If Mr. Tupper's thesis is to be accepted, it must be on the basis of his evidence. And it is playing fast and loose with evidence to assert on one page that the Pardoner's borrowings from the Parson show that he is illustrating Avarice and *Gluttony,* and then to announce on another that it is "interesting" that the very points on which most stress is laid belong in the *Parson's Tale* to Avarice and *Wrath.*

And to *Wrath* the Pardoner's "plunderings" undoubtedly belong in large degree. It is under Wrath that the Parson's long discourse on *Blasphemy* is found (I,

[14] See below, pp. 264-67.

[15] *Publications,* p. 105, n. 26.

[16] *Journal,* p. 562. I shall consider the "but" and the "however" below.

587 ff.).   And the greater part of what the Pardoner says of " othes false and grete " [17] is drawn directly from the section " de Ira " of the *Parson's Tale*. [18]   Moreover, Chaucer here (as Professor Tupper does not point out) [19] is in accord with the *Ayenbite*, [20] Raymund of Pennaforte, [21] Frère Lorens, [22] the *Cursor Mundi*, [23] Gaytryge's Sermon, [24] and *Jacob's Well*. [25]   Even Hazardry, in connection with Blasphemy, is brought in the latter directly under Wrath. [26]   Furthermore (and this too Mr. Tupper does not note), the Pardoner's shoulder-bone of a sheep with its use as a charm for curing animals (and even men) comes also from the *Parson's Tale*, under Wrath. [27]   Yet the Pardoner's exposition is " of *the two Sins* of Avarice and Gluttony."   " There is little opportunity," we are told, " for any intrusion of other elements."   But Wrath, unlike " the many-hued theme of Love," [28] is scarcely an intrusion—except upon the necessity of avoiding identification of the Pardoner with too many Sins.   The facts are clear.   Blasphemy in the *Parson's Tale* is a branch of Wrath, and the Pardoner draws his discourse on Blasphemy largely from the *Parson's Tale*.   On Mr. Tupper's

[17] C, 629 ff.   The phrase " as olde bookes trete " is immediately followed by actual quotation from the *Parson's Tale*.

[18] See Herrig's *Archiv*, LXXXVII, pp. 39-41 (and Skeat's notes) for the source of ll. 631-37, 648-50, and 472-75.

[19] He names only Peraldus.

[20] P. 30.

[21] Petersen, p. 27.

[22] Eilers, pp. 525-28.

[23] L. 27736.

[24] P. 12.

[25] Pp. 94-95.

[26] See on p. 100 the *exemplum* of the quarrelsome dicer and his blasphemy.

[27] I, § 37: " But lat us go now to thilke horrible swering of adjuracioun and conjuracioun, as . . . *in a shulder-boon of a sheep*." " Charmes for woundes or maladyes of men, or of bestes " is under belief in " divynailes " (§ 38).   See C, 350-360, 361-71.

[28] *Publications*, p. 124.

own hypothesis, "every man of the Middle Ages must have recognized at once" that along with Avarice and Gluttony the Pardoner represented *Wrath*.[29] Yet Wrath finds no place in the schematizing of the character.

But that is not quite all. With an unconscious irony that Chaucer would have loved, Tupper has treasured up Wrath against the day of Wrath. For he must show that the *Summoner's Tale* draws on the Parson's sermon too. But in this case it is the section "De Ira" on which the Summoner *must* draw, since he exemplifies Wrath. Now the Summoner's borrowings from the Parson, as Mr. Tupper gives them, are these:

> This every lewed viker or person [30]
> Can seye, how *Ire* engendreth *homicyde.*
> *Ire* is, in sooth, executour of *pryde.*[31]

Homicide and Pride, therefore, come under *Wrath,* and the fact that the Summoner in so declaring is drawing on the *Parson's Tale* is one of the arguments[32] advanced by Mr. Tupper to demonstrate that the Summoner stands for Wrath. But when the *Pardoner* asserts in his account of Blasphemy that the fruit of Hazardry is

> Forswering, *ire,* falsenesse, *homicyde;*[33]

---

[29] Tupper has apparently forgotten, when he makes his statement in the *Journal* (p. 562) that "it is interesting that *the Parson, like Peraldus,* includes . . . Great Oaths under Wrath," that he has said in the *Publications* (p. 95): "Swearing or 'Great Oaths' is *usually* classed under the head of Wrath."

[30] *Videlicet,* "Every man of the Midddle Ages."

[31] D, 2008-10. This is the beginning of "the hundred-line homily against Ire" (*Publications,* p. 113), and both Tupper and Skeat refer the lines to I, 564 f., 534: "Of this cursed sinne of *Ire* cometh eek . . . *homicyde* . . . And as wel comth Ire of *Pryde.*"

[32] No. 3, on p. 113 (*Publications*).

[33] C, 657.

when in his final summary he refers to "traytours *homicyde* . . .":

> And othes grete, of usage and of *pryde*—[34]

then we have "an orderly exposition in the true *exemplum* manner of the two Deadly Sins illustrated by his story . . . first, cursed *Avarice,* that leads to homicide; then *Gluttony.*"[35] What is sauce for the Summoner should be sauce (one would think) for the Pardoner. Finally, Mr. Tupper overlooks the fact that his argument from *irony* requires the inclusion of Wrath. No other of the Pilgrims is so angry as the Pardoner:

> This pardoner answerde nat a word;
> *So wrooth he was, no word ne wolde he seye.*[36]

Like Brahma, Wrath might surely say: "They reckon ill who leave me out."

What Mr. Tupper actually does, in order to escape the disastrous saddling of (at least) *three* Sins upon the Pardoner, is no less instructive. Blasphemy may not remain under *Wrath,* where his own insistence on the importance to his argument of the *Parson's Tale* has clearly put it. He is compelled to identify it with another Sin, *Gluttony.* And this brings it at once into close juxtaposition with Hazardry. "The two other accessories of Gluttony[37]—Hazardry and Blasphemy—are always closely associated in mediæval literature."[38] But in the case of Hazardry

---

[34] C, 896, 899.   [35] *Journal,* p. 562.

[36] C, 956-57. He is far more angry than the Summoner, for *he* could speak. See D, 1665 ff.

[37] The third is *Lechery.* The same dire necessities of Mr. Tupper's argument that exclude Wrath forbid also that Lechery should be treated as an independent Sin. It *is* one, of course, in the categories.

[38] *Journal,* p. 560. They are commonly (but not "always") associated *with each other;* they are by no means always, as we shall see, associated with *Gluttony*—which is all that counts.

Mr. Tupper once more runs counter to the *Parson's Tale*.
For the Parson does not include Hazardry under Gluttony. " It is interesting that the Parson, like Peraldus,
includes Hazardry under *Avarice*." [39] And again it is
rather more than " interesting." For the *Pardoner* obviously includes it under Avarice too. In the first place,
he distinguishes it from Gluttony as clearly as words can
make distinctions:

> And *now that I have spoke of glotonye,*
> *Now* wol I yow defenden *hasardrye*.[40]

In the second place, he immediately proceeds, in the very
next lines, *to reproduce part of the Parson's section upon
Avarice:*

> *Hasard* is verray moder of lesinges,
> And of *deceite,* and *cursed forsweringes,*
> Blaspheme of *Crist, manslaughtre,* and *wast* also
> Of *catel and of tyme.*[41]

Now comth *hasardrye* . . . of which comth *deceite, false othes*
. . . *blaspheminge and reneyinge of god* . . . *wast of godes,* mis-
spendinge *of tyme,* and somtyme *manslaughtre.*[42]

What becomes—I can only ask again—of the " crowning
argument "? Either " the Parson's portrayal of the
Vices . . . enters into the framework of the Sins Tales
and makes obvious the ' application ' of each," [43] or it does

[39] *Journal,* p. 562.
[40] C, 589-90. In the Pardoner's sermon Gluttony, Hazardry, and
Blasphemy are *co-ordinate* heads (if clearly marked divisions mean
anything). The last two are not (like Lechery) " annexed un-to
glotonye."
[41] C, 591-94.
[42] I, 793 (*De Auaricia*). See Herrig's *Archiv,* LXXXVII, p. 40. Mr.
Tupper actually quotes this passage from the *Parson's Tale* (*Journal,*
p. 562) as part of his justification of the assignment of Hazardry
to *Gluttony,* without the slightest intimation of the fact that the
Parson is discussing a branch of *Avarice.*
[43] *Publications,* p. 116. On the preceding page Mr. Tupper tells

not. So far as the *Pardoner's Tale* is concerned, Tupper's treatment of his climactic argument, in wresting Blasphemy from Wrath and Hazardry from Avarice, utterly vitiates his own contention.

Let us leave the relation of Hazardry and Blasphemy to the *Parson's Tale,* and consider Hazardry, for the moment, as it appears elsewhere. It is not only the *Parson* (like Peraldus) who includes it under Avarice. It is the tenth bough of Avarice in the *Ayenbite,*[44] where its treatment occupies over half a page, with two *exempla.*[45] It is the tenth bough of Avarice in Frère Lorens.[46] It is one of the ten branches of Avarice in *Jacob's Well,*[47] where it has nine divisions, including Blasphemy. And it is included under Avarice in the *Pèlerinage.*[48] The *Parson's Tale,* Peraldus, the *Ayenbite,* Frère Lorens, and *Jacob's Well,* that is, all class it definitely as one of the subheads of *Avarice,* and the *Pèlerinage* connects it with that Vice. Tupper cites three cases of its occurrence under *Gluttony.* "Both the *Ayenbite,* p. 52, and *Piers Plowman,* B. v, link Gluttony and games of chance." [49] And he compares a mention of "ludi inordinati et prohibiti" from a discussion (apparently) of "Gula" in Bromyard.[50] As for the *Ayenbite,* the case is not quite

us that "the conclusion is irresistible that such a borrowed treatment of each Sin is neither unconscious nor casual, *but deliberately designed.*"

[44] Pp. 45-46.

[45] The *Ayenbite* is one of Mr. Tupper's witnesses for *Gluttony* (*Journal,* p. 561). See below, p. 270.

[46] Eilers, pp. 543, 548.

[47] Pp. 134-35. "þe thredde fote brede wose in coueytise is foly pley; þat is, at þe tabelys & at þe dyse," etc.

[48] Ll. 18426-30.

[49] *Publications,* p. 105, n. 26. This is introduced by the "but" referred to above (p. 264, n. 16). Compare *Journal,* pp. 561-62.

[50] *Ibid.*

10

as Mr. Tupper states it.   For in " The Pardoner's Tavern " he is more explicit: " Hazardry . . . is *one of the
subheads of Gluttony* in the *Ayenbite of Inwit* (p. 52)."
It is not a " subhead " at all—except of *Avarice*. It is
mentioned on p. 52 as one of the " manye kueades " that
men do (" ase playe at ches. oþer ate tables ") under
the first bough of Gluttony, which is " to ete beuore time "
(p. 51).   The " oþer boȝ " comes *after* the bare mention
(in one line, as compared with the full treatment as a
subhead under Avarice) of chess and tables. As for
Piers Plowman, B. v, I am willing to waive the point,
although I find in the passage no mention of what can
fairly be called " games of chance." [51]   The passage from
Bromyard I cannot speak of at first hand. In any case,
the weight of Tupper's own " rigid categories " [52] including his chief witness, the Parson—is against his classification.   His own postulate is that " every mediæval reader
gleaned [from such formulations] as intimate a knowledge of the Sins as of his Paternoster and his Creed, and
hence was able to respond to every reference to these,
explicit or implicit."   If such a reader knew (and the
whole argument rests on the assumption that he did) Peraldus, or the Parson, or Dan Michel, or Deguileville, or
(later) *Jacob's Well,* would he at once recognize Haz-

---

[51] I suppose Mr. Tupper has in mind (he unfortunately gives no
explicit reference) the " chaffare " in ll. 327-43. But on this see
Englische Studien, v, p. 150. " Chaffare " (it may be remarked)
is, as Mr. Chambers rightly points out, the eighth bough of *Avarice*
in the *Ayenbite* (see *Modern Language Review,* v, p. 20). It is
also included under Avarice in *Jacob's Well* (pp. 133-34) and *Piers
Plowman* (B. XIII, 380). And as *Brocage* (with which, as Mr. Chambers notes, it is identical), it appears under Avarice in the *Mirour*
(l. 6579). Compare especially *Mirour,* ll. 6283-85.

[52] In none of his authorities is Hazardry a *branch* of Gluttony,
as in *five* it is of Avarice.

árdry as *Gluttony?* But the point is one that scarcely need be labored further.

We must, however, look at the matter from another (but still mediæval) point of view. Mr. Tupper has called three witnesses—the *Ayenbite, Piers Plowman,* and Bromyard—for Hazardry as associated with Gluttony. For Blasphemy as subordinate to Gluttony he cites *Piers Plowman,*[53] Bromyard,[54] and Barclay.[55] But now we are confronted in still another fashion with the vagaries of those "strict categories of human errors," the strictness of which is the foundation stone of Mr. Tupper's argument. We have seen that Hazardry appears under *Avarice* not only in the *Parson's Tale,* but also in Peraldus, Frère Lorens, the *Ayenbite, Jacob's Well,* and the *Pèlerinage.* But that is not all. It appears under *Sloth* in the *Cursor Mundi,*[56] the *Mirour de l'Omme,*[57] Wyclif,[58] and *Jacob's Well.*[59] And it is included under *Wrath* (as well as under Avarice) not only in the *Parson's Tale* itself,[60] but also in *Jacob's Well.*[61] Blasphemy appears under *Wrath* not only in the *Parson's Tale,* but also in the *Ayenbite,* Raymund of Pennaforte, Frère Lorens, Gaytryge, the *Cursor Mundi,* and *Jacob's Well.*[62] It also appears under *Avarice* in the *Ayenbite,*[63] *Piers Plowman,*[64] the *Mirour,*[65] the *Pèlerinage,*[66] and *Jacob's Well.*[67] And it is included under *Pride* in the *Cursor*

---

[53] *Publications,* p. 105, n. 26; *Journal,* p. 561 ("B, vi, 92" should read "B, ii, 92").

[54] *Ibid.*

[55] *Journal,* p. 561.

[56] L. 28338.

[57] L. 5779.

[58] Ed. Arnold, iii, p. 145.

[59] P. 105, l. 13.

[60] I, 580.

[61] P. 100 (*exemplum*).

[62] See above, p. 265.

[63] P. 45.

[64] B. xiii, 383.

[65] Ll. 6433 ff.

[66] Ll. 18176 ff.

[67] P. 135. It is also included under Sins of the Tongue (Gluttony) on pp. 153, 156.

Mundi [68] and the *Mirour.* [69] Hazardry and Blasphemy,
that is, are classed as branches (in each case) of at least
three Sins besides Gluttony. Moreover, Mr. Tupper's
own illustrations are peculiarly unfortunate.[70] The very
first—that of the unlucky dicer who loses his eye as the
result of his blasphemy—appears in the *Ayenbite* [71] under
Avarice (Wicked Games). The *exemplum* on p. 624 of
Herbert, *Catalogue of Romances,* has the heading: " De
iracundia et blasphemiis et periuriis et *inuidia* superue
gracie "; the others in the list have no headings whatsoever, so far as Herbert indicates. The stanzas immediately preceding the quotation from Barclay's " Of carde
players and dysers " have much to say of *Wrath,* but
nothing of *Gluttony.* [72] Barclay's " Of Blasphemers
and sweres " lays stress on *Envy.* [73] The only one of
the Seven Deadly Sins with which Hazardry and Blasphemy are *not* directly associated in the authorities

---

[68] Ll. 27608-15.   [69] Ll. 2437 ff.

[70] *Journal,* pp. 560-62. He is illustrating the fact that Hazardry
and Blasphemy " are always closely associated in mediæval literature." Their association *with each other* (it must be said again) is
a familiar commonplace—in life as in the categories (see, for instance, *Romanic Review,* II, pp. 116-17). It is only examples of
their association with *Gluttony* that are relevant to Mr. Tupper's
argument.

[71] P. 45.

[72] Exces of watchynge doth players great damage
    And in that space oft Venus doth them blynde . . .
    Also this game troubleth oft theyr mynde
    With *wrath* them makynge vnstable as the wynde . . .
    A *couetous* herte by game is kept in fere
    And styrred to *yre* euer when it can nat wyn . . .
    And so the more that *wrath* doth hym inflame
    The more backwarde and lewdly goeth his game (II, 71).
Mr. Tupper's quotation is from the next stanza but one.

[73] See II, p. 130, stanzas 2-3.

which Mr. Tupper cites is Lechery. And Lechery in the argument is included under Gluttony. Out of these conflicting witnesses Mr. Tupper picks the ones that suit his theory. But what assurance has he that " the mediæval reader " would have hit on the same ones? Or, indeed, how can he tell that that convenient collective, resolved into its constituent individuals, might not have chosen very variously? Is it not possible that some among them might even have been faithful to the Parson? The truth of course is that, *without some tag,* no mortal, however preternaturally mediæval, *could* refer a given branch " easily to its appropriate head." And in the case of the *Pardoner's Tale* it is not " Chaucer, temp. 1390," but that incorrigible modern, Mr. Tupper, who has confined the Pardoner within the pale of just two Sins, by deleting Wrath, and assigning to Hazardry and Blasphemy their place with Gluttony, rather than with Wrath, or Avarice, or Sloth, or Envy, or Pride.

I know that Tupper has taken final refuge in " the develes temple." [74] For his latest position is that the Pardoner's harangues " are directed against those vices which are ever associated with *taverns* in mediæval tradition." [75] And so, " in accounts of the Deadly Seven we find that Gluttony includes ' Sins of the Tavern,' and moreover that *these sins are the very vices enumerated by Chaucer."* [76] It is true that they are, but they are also a

---

[74] See *Journal,* p. 562: " This arrangement, however [i. e., the Parson's interesting slip in his classification of Hazardry and Blasphemy], does not debar the poet, when fashioning the Pardoner, from combining Dicing and Swearing in *the traditional conception of the Glutton as a lord of tavern revels and misrule* rather than as a mere slave of food and drink."

[75] *Journal,* p. 557.

[76] *Journal,* p. 559. Why Mr. Tupper does not say " In *some* accounts," or even " In *three* accounts," I do not know. Among his

good deal more. Mr. Tupper cites the two tavern passages from the *Ayenbite* and *Jacob's Well,* and quotes
them in part. But he does not quote the *list* of the " Sins
of the Tavern " from either. In the *Ayenbite* it is as
follows: " glotounye. lecherie. zuerie. uorzuerie, lyeȝe.
miszigge. reneye god. euele telle. contacky. and to uele
oþre manyeres of zennes. Þer ariseþ þe cheastes. þe
strifs. þe manslaȝþes. Þer me tekþ to stele: and to hongi.
Þe tauerne is a dich to þieues." [77] That includes (besides
Gluttony and Lechery) *Wrath* (in its branches of Contek,
Cheste, Strife, Manslaughter—waiving Forswearing altogether), *Avarice* (as Theft), and *Envy* (as " miszigge ")
—and it does *not* include Hazardry. In *Jacob's Well* the
list is: " glotonye, leccherye, for-sweryng, slaundryng,
bakbyting, to scorne, to chyde, to dyspyse, to reneye god,
to stele, to robbe, to fyȝte, to sle, & manye oþere swiche
synnes. And þus he [the devil] heldyth hem be þe throte
of glotonye in þe scolehous of his tauerne. *he techyth
his dyscyples to mysgouerne here tungys* " [78]—and then
follow immediately, as " Tavern Sins," the ten Sins of
the Tongue: Idle-talk, Boasting, Flattery, Backbiting,
Lying, Forswearing, Chiding and Striving, " Grucching,"
Frowardness, Blasphemy.[79] All the " Deadly Seven "

own authorities " Sins of the Tavern " are given explicit treatment
as such in only the three which he names. And one of these
(*Jacob's Well*) is in all probability a fifteenth-century document
(ed. Brandeis, p. xiii).

[77] Pp. 56-57.

[78] P. 148.

[79] Pp. 148-156. The provenience of the Sins of the Tongue is made
even more explicit at the *close* of the enumeration. " *Out of þis
glotonye* ... springeth out at þe mowth ofte, *in þe feendys scole-
hows of þe tauerne,* a tre, þat is, *euyl tunge* ... þe tre euyll tunge,
þat springeth out of þe wose of glotonye, *hath x. braunches, þat is,
x. spyces,* & iche of þo spyces hath many levis, þat is, many cir-
cumstauncys " (pp. 156-57).

(except perhaps Sloth) are there—once more without *Hazardry*.[80] The "Sins of the Tavern" are on the one hand vastly too inclusive; in one embarrassing particular, on the other hand, they scarcely include enough. Their wide inclusiveness, moreover, is obvious from another fact. The tavern appears in the categories themselves as the *locus* of other Sins than Gluttony. That is the case under *Pride,* in *Piers Plowman;* [81] under *Avarice,* in the *Mirour de l'Omme;* [82] under *Sloth,* in Wyclif [83] and *Jacob's Well;* [84] under Youth, the daughter of *Idleness,* in the *Pèlerinage*.[85] The tavern, in other words, is on precisely the same footing as the Tournament in *Handlyng Synne,* where (under Sloth) Mannyng turns aside, in a famous passage, to demonstrate that tournaments involve *all* the Seven Deadly Sins: "Of tournamentys y preue þerynne, Seuene poyntes of dedly synne." [86] For the "Sins of the Tavern" are far less a formula than a rough sketch of the familiar facts of life. People eat and drink in taverns (that being precisely what they're there for), often to excess. When (as a result) they are drunk, they are apt to grow lecherous. They also amuse

---

[80] Similarly, in the third example (*Ship of Fools,* I, 93) which Mr. Tupper gives (*Journal,* p. 560), Barclay (whose only direct reference to taverns in the whole passage is the line which Tupper quotes) adds to Gluttony and Lechery the following: Discord (P. 93), Murder, Theft (94), Wrath, Cruelty (95), Strife, Chiding, Blasphemy, Hazardry (96). The title of the section is "Of glotons and dronkardes."

[81] C. VII, 50; B. XIII, 304.

[82] Ll. 6285, 6304.

[83] Ed. Arnold, III, p. 145.

[84] P. 105—where the point at issue is the leaving of "þi paryschcherche & þi seruyse" for the tavern, precisely as in the case of *Gluttony* in *Piers Plowman* (B. V, 308-14).

[85] Ll. 11618 ff.

[86] Ll. 4573-74. The passage includes ll. 4571-4606.

themselves there in other ways—playing at dice for one—
and when they play at dice they swear, and frequently
grow angry, and sometimes kill.   That is as much a fact
today as it was " in mediæval tradition "—witness every
morning's paper.   The use of a tavern and its revels as
an apt and integral setting for a character is, *per se,*
absolutely independent of any schematic relation whatsoever to the Seven Deadly Sins.   Or would Mr. Tupper
see a " Sins Character " in Falstaff?   Chaucer has employed the tavern setting in a piece of matchless irony.
But that irony needs no appeal to a categorizing of two
Sins for its support.[87]

Is it not obvious that all this tanglement arises from
a struggle to wrest a magnificent and free creation—a
superb and complex masterpiece of ironical characterization, matched only by that of the Wife of Bath herself—
into conformity with a schematic type?   And an *impossible* schematic type at that, one has to add.   For Chaucer
himself has stated his own theme.   The Pardoner's declaration is explicit and reiterated:

> My theme is alwey oon, and ever was—
> " *Radix malorum est Cupiditas* " . . .

[87] In a racy passage in " The Pardoner's Tavern " Mr. Tupper insists (*Journal*, p. 564) that the pseudo-Chaucerian " Prologue of
the Merry Adventure of the Pardoner with a Tapster at Canterbury "
could not be derived from the Pardoner of the *General Prologue,*
nor from " the hypocritical exponent of *Avarice* known to every
reader," but is, indeed, from " the *gluttonous* Pardoner of his prologue and tale, lickerish, lecherous, blasphemous "—and so on.
This is trichotomy with a vengeance.   Schematizing has now had its
perfect work in the equation: Pardoner = General Prologue (neu-
tral) + exponent of Avarice + exponent of Gluttony.   What the
Tale of Beryn does show is the fact that Chaucer's mediæval contemporaries took his Pardoner not as a schematic figure, but as a
man.

> Therfor my theme is yet, and ever was—
> "*Radix malorum est cupiditas.*"[88]

And the Pardoner and his maker surely knew. The *theme* of the Tale is *Avarice*—and Avàrice is "*radix malorum.*" If most of the other Seven Sins also come in, they have their warrant. Tupper's *two* are either one too many or three or four too few. There is no alternative. To insist that "the Pardoner's summary of sins in the application at' the close of his tale (C, 895-99)[89] . . . is an orderly exposition in the true *exemplum* manner of *the two Deadly Sins* illustrated by his story and by his own practice and assailed in his sermon "[90]—so to insist comes perilously near "high-handed wresting of the evidence into accord with a preconceived verdict."[91]   That summary, as well as the other—"Forswering, ire, falsnesse, homicyde"— can not be brought under Avarice and Gluttony alone even by an appeal to the "Sins of the Tavern." To do so, it is necessary to emulate the Glutton's cooks—to "stampe, and streyne, and grinde" the twigs and branches, "and turnen substaunce in-to accident."[92]

---

[88] C, 333-34, 425-26.   And with the same text the Parson begins *his* sermon on the Vice (I, § 62).

[89] See above, p. 263.

[90] *Journal*, p. 562.

[91] *Publications of the Modern Language Association*, XXV, p. 179. These are Mr. Tupper's own words regarding the members of the Bonn Seminar. I cannot but feel that, without in the least intending it, he has fallen into the same fallacy—against which, he remarks, "argument is impossible."

[92] With Mr. Tupper's statement about the Tale itself I should unreservedly agree, were it not for his "primarily": "Nobody can doubt that the *Pardoner's Tale* is primarily an *exemplum* of Avarice" (*Publications*, p. 98, n. 8). So far as Chaucer is concerned, we have the Pardoner's text to guide us, and that is enough. But one could wish that Mr. Tupper had pointed out the fact that the story is not an *exemplum* of Avarice at all in a large number of its var-

III

In the case of the Pardoner we have had one Tale as
the exemplification of two Sins.   In the Friar-Summoner
group we have one Sin divided between two Tales.   And
precisely as in the *Pardoner's Tale* Mr. Tupper has deleted Wrath in the interest of Gluttony, so in the *Sum-
'moner's Tale* he suppresses Gluttony in the interest of
Wrath.   "That the *Summoner's Tale* is . . . directed
against Wrath is indicated not only by the anger of poor
Thomas and the boar-like frenzy of the friar, *but by the
hundred-line homily against Ire,*[1] which is put into this
same friar's mouth (D, 2005-2090)."[2]   In this same
friar's mouth, however, is also put a *sixty-eight line sermon* (to be precise) *directed against Gluttony* (D, 1873-
1941).   Its purport is unmistakable.   It is a panegyric

iants.   It is not so even in the Buddhist analogue, the 48th
Játaka, which contains the remark about Avarice.   See the " moral
lesson "—the recoil of the plot upon the plotter—with which it
concludes (*Originals and Analogues,* p. 422).   The moral is the same
in the third Arabian version (*ibid.,* p. 430; cf. the moral of the
second, p. 429), and in the analogues from the *Libro di Novelle*
(" cosi paga Domenedio li traditori," p. 133) and the *Morlini No-
vellae* (" Nouella indicat: nec esse de malo cogitandum: nam quod
quis seminat, metit," p. 134).   *Primarily,* the story is an *exemplum*
of " this even-handed justice [which] Commends the ingredients
of our poison'd chalice To our own lips."   Its application to Avarice is *secondary.*   Even the Pardoner does not make this application
explicitly.   It is implicit, however, not only in his text, but also
in ll. 904-05.   Incidentally, Mr. Tupper has incautiously followed
Skeat's summary (*Oxford Chaucer,* III, p. 439) of the version from
Le Ciento Novelle Antike.   In the original Christ does not " warn
his disciples against the fatal effects of *Avarice,*" except by implication.   See the text in *Originals and Analogues,* p. 131.

[1] This touch of rhetorical exaggeration (for the sermon has *eighty-
five* lines) is perhaps not very important, but it happens to have
some bearing upon the point at issue.

[2] *Publications,* p. 113.

on the abstinence of friars as contrasted with the ways of " burel folk," who live " in richesse and despence Of mete and drinke, and in hir foul delyt." [3] Nor does it merely inveigh against Gluttony by implication. It is entirely explicit:

> Fro Paradys first, if I shal nat lye,
> Was man out chaced for his glotonye;
> And chaast was man in Paradys, certeyn.[4]

That is clear enough in its bearing, but happily we have other testimony too. Mr. Tupper has recently shown [5] that " all of the Scriptural *exempla* of fasting put into the mouth of the friar [in the *Summoner's Tale*] are taken directly from one or two chapters in the second book of the [famous tract of Jerome, ' Against Jovinian '] "— although he passes over in absolute silence, in his discussion of the Friar-Summoner group,[6] the presence of these same significant *exempla*. On the three lines just quoted from the *Summoner's Tale,* however, he thus comments in his latest article: " It is significant that this very passage from Jerome *is used by the Pardoner in his attack upon Gluttony* (C, 508 f.). . . . This use of a common source in these two tales of the Sins is suggestive." [7] It *is* significant, and it *is* suggestive, for it proves irrefragably (if proof were needed) that the *friar's* first homily is 'directed against *Gluttony,* and " it seems surprising— if the oversights of Chaucer scholars can any longer awake surprise—that " Mr. Tupper failed to see the implications of his own very sound observation.

---

[3] D, 1874-76. Cf. ll. 1880, 1883, 1898-1900, 1907-08, etc.
[4] D, 1915-17.
[5] *Notes,* pp. 8-9. But see also *Modern Language Notes*, February, 1915, pp. 63-64.
[6] *Publications*, pp. 112-13.
[7] *Notes*, p. 9.

But the friar does not stop with these explicit lines. He is no less unambiguous later:

> Fy on hir pompe and on hir glotonye! . . .
> Me thinketh they ben lyk Jovinian,
> Fat as a whale, and walkinge as a swan;
> Al vinolent as botel in the spence.[8]

He is preaching, then, a sermon against Gluttony.[9] And as in the case of the *Friar's Tale* Chaucer " doubles the story's aptness " by the exquisite irony of the contrast between the homily and the friar's own hypocritical *Delicacie:*

> 'Now dame,' quod he, '*Je vous dy sanz doute,*
> Have I nat of a capon but the livere,
> And of your softe breed nat but a shivere,
> And after that a rosted pigges heed,
> (But that I nolde no beest for me were deed),
> Thanne hadde I with yow hoomly suffisaunce.
> I am a man of litel sustenaunce.
> My spirit hath his fostring in the Bible.' [10]

Indeed, he has *trebled* the aptness. For the Summoner himself, who tells the tale, is both a glutton and a lecher:

[8] D, 1927-31.

[9] Compare also with the friar's repeated emphasis on *abstinence and prayer* (e. g., ll. 1870-73, 1879, 1883-84, 1900, 1905, 1939) the Pardoner's statement (still under *Gluttony*):

> . . . alle the sovereyn actes, dar I seye,
> Of victories in th' olde testament,
> Thurgh verray god that is omnipotent,
> *Were doon in abstinence and in preyere;*
> Loketh the Bible, and ther ye may it lere   (C, 574-78).

The friar's sermon might well be an exposition of that text!

[10] D, 1838-45. This is at least as valid for the argument as Tupper's " boar-like frenzy of the friar," which is also in the Tale itself!

> As hoot he was, and lecherous, as a sparwe . . .
> Wel loved he garleek, oynons, and eek lekes,
> And for to drinken strong wyn, reed as blood.
> Than wolde he speke, and crye as he were wood . . .
> He wolde suffre, for a quart of wyn,
> A good felawe to have his concubyn
> A twelf-month, and excuse him atte fulle.[11]

" With delightfully suggestive irony," then, in the friar's
sermon against Gluttony Chaucer has " opposed practice
to precept, rule of life to dogma, by making [the Sum-
moner] incarnate the very Sin that [he] explicitly condemn[s]." [12]   Even the " homily against *Ire,*" moreover,
includes *Gluttony* too.   For the story of Cambyses (D,
2043-2078) is an *exemplum* against Drunkenness as well
as Wrath.[13]   Indeed (since Tupper has raised the point
of numerical values), if we regard the thirty-five lines of
the Cambyses *exemplum* as common to Gluttony and

---

[11] A, 626, 634-36, 649-51. The implications of his *disease* are
patent to anyone who knows tne significance in mediæval medicine
of the remedies which Chaucer names.

[12] *Publications*, p. 107. The Summoner's Gluttony and Lechery
that are the very essence of the man certainly constitute as valid
evidence (still assuming Mr. Tupper's point of view) as the natural
outbreak of Wrath after the Friar has told his tale.

[13]
> Irous Cambyses was eek *dronkelewe* . . .
> A lord is lost, if he be vicious;
> And *dronkenesse* is eek a foul record
> Of any man, and namely in a lord . . .
> For goddes love, *drink more attemprely;*
> *Wyn maketh man to lesen wrecchedly*
> *His minde, and eek his limes everichon*   (2043-55).

With the last, compare the *Pardoner* on *Gluttony:*

> *A lecherous thing is wyn* and dronkenesse
> Is ful of stryving and of *wrecchednesse* . . .
> *Thou fallest,* as it were a stiked swyn . . .
> For dronkenesse is verray sepulture
> *Of mannes wit*   (C, 549-50, 556, 558-59).

Wrath, we have fifty lines devoted to Wrath alone as
against sixty-eight devoted to Gluttony alone. But we
need not chop logic about numbers. The homily against
Gluttony is of at least equal weight with the homily
against Wrath. Yet Mr. Tupper does not even mention
it. An argument can scarcely be taken very seriously
that deals in this fashion with the facts.

But the *Summoner's Tale* does not stand alone in Tupper's scheme. It forms a Wrath-group with the *Friar's Tale*.
And Tupper gives two "potent reasons" for regarding this
latter Tale as "an *exemplum* of Cursing (Wrath)." [14]
The force of the first I frankly cannot see. How the notorious "strife between friars and *possessioners or beneficed
clergy*" that finds mention in Langland's illustration of
Wrath (B. v, 136-52) furnishes "a wonderfully exact
parallel to the angry quarrel between the Friar and the
Summoner" is beyond my ken. Langland does not describe a quarrel [15] at all, and the Summoner is not a
possessioner. The second reason involves a rather glaring
lapse into the use of the ambiguous middle. "The Friar's
story of the nemesis of hell-pains brought upon a *cursing*
summoner by the heart-felt *curses* of his intended victim
exemplifies most accurately the section on *Cursing* in the
Parson's discussion of Wrath (I, 618 f., § 41)." The two
"cursings" are not the same thing at all. The first
refers (as Tupper himself recognizes [16]) to *the archdea-
con's curse*—that is, excommunication; the second and
third are cursing in the sense of *malediction*. It is not

[14] *Publications*, pp. 112-13.
[15] That does come in, and vividly enough, in the following lines
about the *nuns* (153-65).
[16] *Publications*, p. 113 top. But on p. 115 Mr. Tupper remarks
that Chaucer "draws upon the Parson's discourse on Anger . . . for
the exact motif of the Friar's tale of retribution."

the Summoner's *archidiaconal* curse that has "retorne[d] agayn to him that curseth," and the whole argument is a *non sequitur*. Moreover, Tupper's "poetic justice" of the return upon the offender of "swich cursinge as comth *of irous herte*" precisely reverses the point of the Tale. Can he have remembered Herolt's story of "the grasping [*avarus*] [17] lawyer" at all? The devil and the advocate meet a man leading a pig. The pig is refractory: "Cumque porcus huc illucque diverteretur, *iratus* homo clamavit, 'Diabolus te habeat!'" The devil's reply to the advocate's suggestion is in substance the same as in the *Friar's Tale*. Then a mother says to her crying baby, "Diabolus te habeat!" The advocate again urges the devil to take what has been given him. But the devil replies: "Non mihi illum dedit ex corde: sed talis est consuetudo hominibus loquendi, *cum irascuntur*." It is only when the villagers, who know the advocate all too well, curse him "ex intimo corde" (not in mere sudden anger) that the devil carries off his prize.[18] Cursing from "irous herte" is just what does *not*, in the *Friar's Tale* as in Herolt, come home to roost. Nor is such cursing even deadly sin. Tupper asks us to compare *Handlyng Synne,* 3757 f. Let us do so, and read on four lines:

> Ȝyf a man curse as yn game,
> And yn hys herte wyl hym no shame [19]
> he ne synneþ nat þan dedly,
> For hyt ys seyd al yn rybaudy.

---

[17] See below, p. 285, n. 27.

[18] See the story as printed for the Percy Society, Vol. VIII, pp. 70-71; *Originals and Analogues*, p. 106.

[19] Cf. D, 1567-68: "Heer may ye see, myn owne dere brother, The catl spak oo thing, but he thoghte another."

þis synne ys nat dampnable
But hyt be seyd custummable.[20]

Either Mr. Tupper's understanding of the story or his interpretation of " irous cursing " is wrong. Both cannot be right. His argument for the *Friar's Tale* as " an *exemplum* of the Cursing phase of Wrath " falls to the ground.

It does so, I think, because Tupper has failed to look at Chaucer's story from the mediæval point of view. The situation which underlies the Tale *has* a perfectly definite association with the Seven Deadly Sins in Tupper's own authorities, but it is entirely different from the one he gives.[21]   Let us take first a brief passage from Wyclif:

And þis [i. e., lechery among the poorer classes] is knowen to bischop clerkis, for þei spoylen hom in chapiters, as who wolde spoyle a thef; and *by hor feyned sommenyng* þei drawen hom fro hor laboure, to tyme þat þei have grauntid what silver þei shal paye; and þen *by feyned cursyng* þei maken hom paye þis robbyng. . . . Lord, where slepis þis gode lawe, and when schal hit be wakened? Certis, *not bifore coveytise of þese clerkes be quenchid.*[22]

That is exactly the situation which Chaucer elaborates with such consummate art, and his emphasis, like Wyclif's,[23] is on the Summoner's *Avarice.*[24]   But it is not

---

[20] Ll. 3761-66. So in the *Cursor Mundi* (28563) " wreth þat scort and soden es " is among the " smale sinnes " of which it " es no nede Ilkan for to reken and rede."

[21] Once more, I am assuming Mr. Tupper's premises for the nonce. I do not believe that Chaucer was schematizing at all.

[22] Ed. Arnold III, pp. 166-67.

[23] Compare also *The English Works of Wyclif* (ed. Matthew, E. E. T. S.), p. 35: " Lord, whi schulde curatis pronounsen here breþeren a cursed *for nakid lettris of syche coueitous prelatis* "; p. 75: " Also whanne þei *cursen for here coueitise* "; p. 95: " þes anti-cristis clerkis *cursen men al day for money* "; p. 150: " þei cursen here gostly children *more for loue of worldly catel* þan for brekynge

only Wyclif who so interprets the Summoner's cursing; it is also the " rigid categories " themselves.   Under the fourth bough of Avarice in the *Ayenbite* are included " *þe ualse lettres* [25] uor to greui oþren. and trauayleþ þet uolk myd wrong. *oþer be cristene cort.* oþer be leawede cort." [26] Under the seventh branch of Avarice in *Jacob's Well* occurs the following:

> Offycyallys and denys þat oftyn settyn chapetlys, to gaderyn þat þei may geten, þowȝ þei do wrong, þei recche neuere, *for þei haue more affeccyoun to gadere syluer þan to don correcyoun*, and ȝit þei do noȝt so scharpely reddour to ryche men as to pore, for ryche þey forbere for mede, & pore men þei greue wrongfully, *wyth cursynges* & putting out of cherch to penaunce, to paye vnryȝtfully. þis may be clepyd *raueyn & extorcyoun. Also somnours & bedels, þat dwellyn in offyce vnder hem, spare no conscyens to take what þei may getyn.*[27]

And in the *Mirour de l'Omme* Gower, writing of " les Archedeacnes, Officials et Deans " administers a scathing rebuke to their Avarice.   I may quote but a few lines:

> *Si l'omme lais d'incontinence*
> *Soit accusé,* la violence
> Du nostre dean tost y parra;
> Car devant tous en audience
> *Lors de somonce et de sentence,*
> *S'il n'ait l'argent dont paiera,*
> Sicomme goupil le huera.[28]

---

of goddis hestis "; p. 214: " ȝit worldly clerkis *cursen for dymes and offryngis* "; p. 250: " þes smale curatis schullen haue letteris fro here ordynaries *to summone & to curse pore men for nouȝt but for coueitise* of anticristis clerkis "; etc.

[24] See, for example, D, 1344, 1348-54, 1434-40, 1530-34, 1576-80, 1598-1603, 1613-17.

[25] " He wolde fecche *a feyned mandement* " (D, 1360). Cf. D, 1586, and Wyclif's " feyned sommenyng " above.

[26] P. 39. Cf. p. 43, foot.

[27] P. 129.   Herolt's advocate too is " *immisericors, avarus, faciens graves exactiones in sibi subditos.*"

[28] Ll. 20013-19.   See the whole passage (which is in Gower's sum-

Might not the mediæval reader, who knew his Sins so well, have responded in a different fashion from Mr. Tupper's to the references, explicit and implicit, in Chaucer's *exemplum?*

And he would have had Chaucer's *irony* to guide him too. For *the Friar himself* is avaricious, as his turning of penance into pittance, the implications of his tippet stuffed with knives and pins,[29] his courtesy " ther as profit sholde aryse," his friendship with the rich, his exactions from the poor, all show. And the Avarice of his class is a mediæval commonplace.[30] One has, then, Mr. Tupper's third criterion—the opposition of " practice to precept, rule of life to dogma," exquisitely heightened in this case by the fact that an avaricious limitour tells a tale which turns on the overreaching Avarice of a summoner. And it is to be observed that in Mr. Tupper's interpretation of the Tale this element of " delightfully suggestive irony " is wholly wanting, for Chaucer has not represented the Friar as wrathful.[31] And finally,

mary of contemporary social conditions, not in his account of the Sins), ll. 20089 ff.

[29] " ᵹif þei [the friars] becomen pedderis berynge *knyves*, pursis, *pynnys* and girdlis and spices and sylk and precious pellure and forrouris *for wymmen*, and þerto smale gentil hondis, to gete loue of hem and to haue many grete ᵹiftes for litil good ore nouᵹt; þei *coueiten euyle here neiᵹeboris goodis* " (Wyclif, ed. Matthew, p. 12).

[30] See Jean de Meun *passim;* Wyclif *passim* (especially on " þese coveytouse foolis þat ben *lymytoures,*" ed. Arnold, III, p. 376); *Mirour de l'Omme,* 21217 ff.; etc.

[31] He scowls (D, 1266), and he tells the Summoner at one point that he lies (D, 1761), and that is all. For this is not the friar, of course, of whose " boar-like frenzy " Tupper speaks. Indeed, the irony which the theory demands is a little intricate' in the *Summoner's Tale* (to return to it for a moment). For irony *within the tale* of course does not count in the argument. It is an incongruity between the practice of the teller and the precept of the tale that the theory requires. Now the " homily against Ire "

so far as the *Friar's Tale* is concerned, "the crowning argument" does not apply, for the Friar does not draw upon the *Parson's Tale*.[32] One may cherish some doubt with reference to the Friar-Summoner Tales as a formal exemplification of Wrath.[33]

is put into the mouth *not* of the wrathful Summoner himself, *in propria persona,* but of the representative of the very class against which he is inveighing. It may be that something in my spirit dulleth me, but that seems rather subtle.

[33] Tupper, to be sure, declares that Chaucer "draws upon the Parson's discourse on Anger both for *the exact motif of the Friar's tale of retribution* and for *the angry Summoner's morality against Ire*" (*Publications,* p. 115). This is one of the passages where Mr. Tupper asserts that "the burden of proof certainly rests upon him *who dares claim*" the contrary (cf. *Journal,* p. 558, top). I have already ventured to challenge the relation between "the exact *motif* of the Friar's tale" and the Parson's sermon. As for the *Summoner's Tale* I shall venture farther. The angry Summoner's "hundred line" morality against Ire draws on the discussion of the Sins in the *Parson's Tale* for just three lines, of which Tupper himself notes by implication two (D, 2009-10 = I, 564 f., 534. See above, p. 266. The third line is D, 2075 = I, 617, under Flattery). The flat statement that Chaucer "draws upon the Parson's discourse on Anger . . . for the angry Summoner's morality against Ire" is scarcely calculated to convey to the reader an impression in very close accordance with the facts. Tupper's earlier statement (p. 113) is somewhat less inaccurate: "This sermon is *derived partly* from the *Parson's Tale,* I, 534, 564 f. (Wrath), but *chiefly* from Seneca's *De Ira.*"

[33] It is not without interest that what we really find, by scrupulous application of Mr. Tupper's own methods, is Wrath, Gluttony (*Summoner's Tale*), and Avarice (*Friar's Tale*)—the same triad that emerged from a similar study of the *Pardoner's Tale.* Consistently applied, the theory falls of its own weight—as we shall have further opportunity to see.

IV

There is left, of the stories that are not found in Gower, the legend of St. Cecilia. This particular Tale can not, as we shall see,[1] be regarded as affording evidence for Mr. Tupper's theory, until the theory is established on other grounds. But I prefer to treat it with its group. The arguments in support of the contention that "the Second Nun [illustrates] *Sloth*"[2] are five: (1) the Idleness Prologue;[3] (2) the protest of the "Invocatio ad Mariam" against Sloth in its phase of Undevotion;[4] (3) St. Cecilia's own "bisinesse";[5] (4) the element of irony;[6] (5) the kinship between the Prologue and the *Parson's Tale*.[7] Let us consider them briefly in the reverse order.

The first is the "crowning argument." "The lines in the 'Invocation,'" we are told, "that insist upon the value of works (G, 64-65, 77, 79) are *closely akin to the passage on 'werkes of goodnesse'* in the Parson's discussion of Sloth (I, 690 f.)"[8] The lines of the Invocation are these:

> And, for that feith is deed with-outen werkes,
> So for to werken yif me wit and space (64-65).
> Now help, for to my werk I wol me dresse (77).
> Foryeve me, that I do no diligence (79).[9]

The passage on 'werkes of goodnesse' in the *Parson's Tale* (I, 690 f.) is the section on "*drede to biginne to werke any gode werkes.*" It deals with one of the nine

---

[1] See below, p. 302.   [2] *Publications*, p. 112.

[3] *Publications*, pp. 98, 106.

[4] *Publications*, pp. 106-07; cf. p. 99, n. 10.

[5] *Publications*, pp. 98-99, 106-07, 116, 123.

[6] *Publications*, p. 111.   [7] *Publications*, 107, 115.

[8] *Publications*, p. 107.   [9] See below n. 16.

branches of Accidie—known as *Dilatio* in Peraldus,[10] *Pusillanimites* in *Frère Lorens,*[11] *Pusillanimité* in Gower,[12] *Pusillanimitas* in Raymund of Pennaforte,[13] *Arwenesse* in *Jacob's Well;*[14] etc.—and is followed immediately by Wanhope,[15] with which it *is* closely akin. It has nothing whatever to do with the attitude of mind embodied in the Invocation,[16] and Mr. Tupper's interpretation, of course, assumes the very point at issue. He suggests, however, still another connection. "After a comparison of the Parson's section on Sloth with the Prologue of the *Second Nun's Tale, who can miss the present purport of the Idleness stanzas?*"[17] They *do* both deal with Idleness. But for "*the Parson's* section on Sloth" one might equally well substitute "*Dan Michel's* section"— or any one of half a dozen others. And after stating that there is "a slight verbal connection" (in "conventional epithets") Mr. Tupper himself concludes

[10] Petersen, p. 62.   [11] Eilers, p. 537.
[12] *Mirour,* ll. 5485 ff.   [13] Petersen, p. 27.
[14] Pp. 106-07; cf. *Ayenbite,* p. 32.
[15] *Desperatio* in Peraldus and Raymund of Pennaforte stands in the same position.
[16] Chaucer is calling upon Mary as he calls upon the " cruel Furie " (*T. and C.,* I, 8-11), Clio (II, 8-10), Venus and Calliope (III, 39-49), and the "Herines" (IV, 22-26) in the *Troilus;* the god of sleep (77-80), Cipris and Thought (518-28), and Apollo (109-93) in the *House of Fame;* and the Flower (94-96) in the B-Prologue to the *Legend.* Line 79 above (taken out of its context) looks a little like "Dilatio," but Mr. Tupper has not included the *next* line in his reference:

> *This ilke storie subtilly to endyte,* etc.

The parallel with the Invocation to the third book of the *House of Fame* (for example) is exact:

> [thogh] *that I do no diligence*
> *To shewe craft,* etc. (1099-1100).

[17] *Publications,* p. 115.

that "there is here no proof of direct borrowing" from the Parson.[16] The "crowning argument," therefore, is this time also tenuous indeed.

The argument from *irony* is no less shaky. "Of the Second Nun, who was finally chosen to present the Prologues and Tale against Sloth, *we unfortunately know nothing.*"[19] That should, apparently, settle the matter. But Tupper gallantly throws himself into Chaucer's gap. The Nun was "a member of a notoriously slothful class."[20] As proof, we are referred to one example of the laziness of *nuns*—that of the inmates of the Convent in the *Pèlerinage,* who " ech on ha liberte, at þeir lust, to slepe and wake; and noon other hed ne take forto kepe their observaunce "[21]—and the argument is clinched by the fact that "four of the six illustrations of Sloth in Herolt's *Promptuarium Exemplorum* are lazy *monks* "; that "in *Piers Plowman* Sloth is ... a lazy *priest* "; and that " to the attack upon the Castle of Unity Sloth leads more than a thousand *prelates.*"[22] Apart from the logic, all this is scarcely gentle treatment of the Second Nun, long " deed and nayled in hir cheste," and unable to defend herself. But the theory demands that the association of character and Tale be " ironically apt,' and how should an unknown nun stand in the way? If Chaucer " have nat *seyd* it, leve brother," he *meant* it, none the less. For " *this necessary adjustment* Chaucer relegated to the limbo of many of his undertakings, the morrow."[23] Perhaps! " I nam no divinistre; Of

---

[18] *Publications,* p. 115, n. 45.   [19] *Publications,* p. 111.

[20] *Notes,* p. 11, n. 13; *Publications,* p. 111.

[21] Ll. 23538 ff. The same passage also emphasizes their frowardness and vanity (23599, 23604), their pomp and pride (23611), and their gluttony (23641 ff.).

[22] *Publications,* p. 111, n. 38.   [23] *Notes,* p. 11, n. 13.

[nonnes] finde I nat in this registre." And an irony that confessedly depends on what Chaucer *would* (in Mr. Tupper's judgment) have written, but never *did*, demands an act of faith for its acceptance.

Mr. Tupper's contention rests, then, upon the Tale itself, the Invocation, and the Prologue. So far as the Tale itself is concerned, it is the legend of a *virgin martyr*.[24] And Mr. Tupper leaves (as he must) the story as Chaucer tells it entirely out of the reckoning. It is upon a supposedly traditional view of St. Cecilia herself that his case rests. She is, for him, " that antitype of Sloth ... the ' bee ' of the mediæval homilist, renowned not only for her celibacy but for ' hir lasting bisinesse.' "[25] And he uniformly refers to her as " the traditionally busy Saint Cecilia " ;[26] " the type of busyness, Saint Cecilia ";[27] " a typically busy saint."[28] Do the facts warrant so sweeping a generalization? His evidence proves, on analysis, to be threefold: the testimony of the " Interpretacio "; a sermon of Jacobus de Voragine; and an *exemplum* in the *Flores Exemplorum*.

According to the " Interpretacio,"[29] St. Cecilia stands for (1) " pure chastnesse of virginitee " (virginitatis pudorem); (2) " whytnesse of honestee " (candorem munditiae); (3) " grene of conscience " (virorem con-

---

[24] It is " the lyf of Seint Cecyle," as Chaucer twice designates it himself (G, 554, *Leg.* B, 426 = A, 416). It is the " glorious lyf and passioun " of the " mayde and martir " that he does his " feithful bisinesse " to translate, and it is on her chastity and her martyrdom that the stress is laid (ll. 270-83). Cf. also *Publications of the Modern Language Association*, XXVI, pp. 315-23; XXIX, pp. 129-33. To the examples there given of the symbolic use of roses and lilies for martyrdom and virginity I can now add many others drawn entirely from the Latin hymns.

[25] *Publications*, pp. 98-99.   [26] *Publications*, p. 106; *Notes*, p. 11.

[27] *Publications*, pp. 107, 123.   [28] *Ibid.*, p. 116.

[29] G, 85-119.

scientiae); (4) "ensample ... by good techinge" (exempli informationem); (5) "thoght of holinesse" (jugem contemplationem); (6) "lasting bisinesse" (assiduam operationem); (7) "grete light of sapience" (sapientiae splendorem); (8) "of feith the magnanimitee" (fidei magnanimitatem); (9) "the cleernesse hool of sapience" (sapientiae perspicacitatem); (10) "good werkinge" (operationem sollicitam); (11) "good perseveringe" (perseverantiam); (12) "charitee ful brighte" (caritatem succensam); (13) "sondry werkes, bright of excellence" (virtutum varietatem).[30]   Cecilia's "bisinesse," then, is one out of a list of *ten* [31] qualities. The discarding of the other nine, and the retention of this one alone as Cecilia's "typical" quality stands in need of justification.

That justification the *Sermones Aurei* seem, at first blush, to offer. For in them, we are told, "St. Cecilia is likened to a bee on account of her *five-fold busyness:* her spiritual devotion, humility, contemplation, teaching and exhortation, sagacity." [32]   The testimony of the sermons demands fuller consideration than Professor Tupper accords it, and I shall first give myself the pleasure of stating his case far more strongly than he has stated it himself. For he has overlooked the fact that *in the Tale itself* Cecilia is likened to a bee. It is Urban who is speaking:

> *So, lyk a bisy bee*, with-outen gyle,
> Thee serveth ay thyn owene thral Cecile! [33]

---

[30] For the Latin, see *Originals and Analogues*, p. 192.

[31] I have counted (7) and (9), (6) and (10), each as *one*—although (6) and (10) are really distinct.

[32] *Publications*, p. 99, n. 10.

[33] G, 195-96; cf. 191-99. The bee is not found in the version of the Legend in the Ashmole MS. (*Originals and Analogues*, p. 210), or in the Northern English version (MSS. Harl. 4196) printed by Horst-

Chaucer is here (and in the immediate context) translating the following passage in the *Legenda Aurea:*

> domine Jesu Christe, seminator casti consilii, suscipe seminum
> fructus, quos in Caecilia seminasti, domine Jesu Christe, pastor
> bone, Caecilia famula tua *quasi apis tibi argumentosa deservit;* nam
> sponsum, quem quasi leonem ferocem accepit, ad te quasi agnum
> mansuetissimum destinavit.[34]

And this same passage (as Mr. Tupper also failed to
observe) has found a place in the service of the church.[35]
In the Office for St. Cecilia's day the second lesson of the
first Nocturn closes: " *Quasi apis argumentosa* Domino
deservisti.—Urbanum." The sixth lesson (second Nocturn) closes with the entire passage quoted above from
the Legend.[36] In the Laudes the phrase occurs again:
" Caecilia famula tua, Domine, *quasi apis tibi argumentosa deservit.*" [37] I wish to give these facts their full
weight, and I am doing even more than that by quoting
them as I have done out of their setting. No one can
read the Office impartially without seeing that the references to St. Cecilia as the bee are *incidental.* The Office,
to a far greater degree than the Tale itself, is devoted to
the glorification of Cecilia's *virginity and martyrdom.*
But the Office brings us to the sermons.

For it is precisely that passage from the Legend which
appears in the Office that Jacobus de Voragine elucidates

---

mann (*Altenglische Legenden*, 1881, p. 161), or in Aelfric (ed.
Skeat, E. E. T. S., II, pp. 356 ff.). It is in Caxton (*Originals and
Analogues*, p. 211), but Caxton is following Chaucer.

[34] *Originals and Analogues*, p. 194.

[35] I have not access to the older rituals. I am quoting from the
Breviarium Romanum (Pars Autumnalis) in current use.

[36] With the omission of the second " domine . . . bone."

[37] It is *argumentosa*, not " bisy," which is traditional, it should
be noted. See below, p. 295, n. 43.

in two of his three sermons on St. Cecilia.[38]   At the close
of his second sermon,[39] on the text, " Mulier diligens,
corona est viro suo," he thus comments on the *lectio:*

> Unde dixit Urbanus: Suscipe seminum fructus, quos in Caecilia
> seminasti. Quia erat apis argumentosa, et ille nimis insipidus, id-
> circo ipsum speciali dulcedine dulcoravit. *Brevis in volatilibus est
> apis, et initium dulcoris habet fructus illius.*[40]

The third sermon has for its text the passage from *Ecclesiasticus* (xi, 3) which Jacobus has just quoted.   And he
proceeds:

> Caecilia apis vocata est sicut testatur Urbanus dicens: Caecilia
> . . . deservit [as above]. In istis ergo verbis praedictis a S. Ur-
> bano quinque implicantur, *scilicet quod S. Caecilia fuit apis, et
> brevis apis, et volatilis apis, et mellifica apis, et argumentosa apis.*

This " five-fold busyness," [41] then, is amplified under the
following heads:

> Primo fuit apis in quantum exercitavit se circa dulcedinem devo-
> tionis. Mel quidem generatur a rore, et a flore, miro apis artificio
> aedificata de cera domo, ne mel defluat, sed conservetur. Devotio
> quidem spiritualis habetur a rore S. Spiritus infundente . . . Se-
> cundo fuit apis brevis in quantum se exercitavit circa humilitatem:
> quae consideratur, et quia brevis dicitur, et quia mel ab ipsa gene-
> ratur. Per mel enim humilitas intelligitur. . . Tertio dicitur apis
> volatilis in quantum exercitavit se per contemplationem. Apes
> autem ad olandum per quatuor inducuntur, scilicet per tempus se-
> renum, per abundantiam florum, per dulce vinum, et per sonum. . .
> Quarto dicitur mellificans apis in quantum exercitavit se circa dul-
> cem doctrinam, et exhortationem. . . Quinto dicitur argumentosa
> apis, quae quidem sagacitas attenditur, quantum ad tria, etc.[42]

---

[38] On the entrance of the Legends as *lectiones* into the Office of
the Church, see Horstmann's valuable introduction to his *Altenglische Legenden*, pp. xii ff. On their use in the *homilies*, see pp.
xxiii ff.

[39] *Sermones Aurei* (1760), II, p. 361.   [40] *Ecclesiasticus*, XI, 3.

[41] The phrase is due, I suppose, to the four times repeated " exer-
citavit " below.

[42] I have had to omit, of course, the still more detailed elaboration
of the symbolism.

I have now given, I think, all the pertinent facts. Do they warrant for St. Cecilia the sobriquet of "the traditionally busy saint"?

So far as the *argument* is concerned, I am perfectly willing to waive the point, and save both time and space. The conclusion would not be affected in the least. But the method of interpretation that is involved is more important than the particular point (in this case) at issue. For Mr. Tupper has metamorphosed a subordinate and incidental reference into a typifying formula. The reference is so purely incidental in the Legend and the Tale that Tupper, in his search for evidence, overlooked it altogether.[43] As for the Sermon, the assumption that it gives *traditional* warrant to the view that Cecilia's "*first trait*[44] . . . was the sweetness of spiritual devotion,"[45] leaves out of account once more the "mediæval perspective." It overlooks, that is, the distinction, in the homiletics of the Middle Ages, between what *is* genuinely traditional, and what is purely or largely *ad hoc*. For the allegorizing tendencies of mediæval sermonizing[46] left untried or untortured no remotest possibility of symbolic treatment. This tendency, strong in itself, was heightened by the custom of drawing the texts from the introits, the gospels, and the epistles for the day,[47] or (as in the

[43] Chaucer's translation of "argumentosa" by "bisy" is itself inaccurate, and doubtless represents the "well-worn [convention] track." Given "bee," the chances are large in favor of "busy" as the epithet. Compare E, 2422 (in a very different context!): "for ay *as bisy as bees* Been they [women], us sely men for to deceyve." In Jacobus (who also represents "tradition") the bee is *brevis, volatilis, mellifica,* and *argumentosa*.

[44] On the preceding page it is her "peculiar quality."

[45] *Publications*, p. 107.

[46] See, for example, Crane, *The Exempla of Jacques de Vitry* (Folk Lore Society), pp. lxxx ff.

[47] See Crane, pp. xxxviii, lv, lx, lxiii-iv, lxviii, etc., and the *Sermones Aurei, passim*.

present instance) from the suggestion of the *lectio,* and
by the consequent necessity of finding (in the case of
Sermones de Sanctis) some connecting link between text
and saint.[48]   And in no mediæval preacher is this *penchant* for fine-spun allegorizing stronger than in Jacobus
de Voragine.   St. Paul is compared to a vase; [49] St. Mar-·
garita to a treasure hid in a field; [50] St. Dominic to the
morning star,[51] the full moon,[52] salt,[53] and light; [54] St.
Lawrence to gold [55] and fire; [56] St. Katherine to a field
in which treasure is hid [57]—and so on *ad libitum.*[58]   It

[48] In the *Sermones Aurei* (II, p. 246) St. Hippolytus and his comrades are compared to *sparrows.*   Why?   The text is from Psalm
124: "Anima nostra sicut passer erepta est de laqueo venantium."
And the sermon begins: "Ad honorem sancti Hippolyti et sociorum
ejus *iste versiculus in Missa decantatur.   In Evangelio etiam hodi-
erno in exemplum Sanctorum passeres introducuntur.*"   And so
Jacobus sets himself cheerfully to his exegesis.

[49] II, p. 79: "Primo fuit mirabiliter confictus, quod patet quia de
limo humilitatis profundae, et aqua compunctionis lachrymosae fuit
confictus. . . Secundo istud vas fuit mirabiliter pictum, scilicet colore albo virginalis munditiae"—and so on through six parallels.

[50] II, p. 217: "Thesaurus . . . est autem aurum virginitas, argen-
tum fides, lapides pretiosi opera pietatis," etc.

[51] II, pp. 233-34: "Stella matutina est lucifer qui quidem est calidus, humidus, jucundus, et Solis nuncius.   Sic B. Dominicus fuit
calidus per ferventem zelum . . . fuit humidus per lachramarum
effusionem . . . fuit jucundus, et hoc in mente per conscientiae ser-
enitatem [similarly, in facie, sermone, conversatione]," etc.

[52] P. 234.   I shall not rehearse his "quadruplicem plenitudinem"!

[53] P. 240.

[54] *Ibid.*—with three reasons.

[55] P. 241: "Dicitur aurum in quantum fuit Praelatus.   Et in
quantum fuit Martyr invictus.   Et in quantum fuit Praedicator
gloriosus"—and each of the three is worked out in unimaginable
detail.

[56] P. 243: "Notandum est, quod est quadruplex ignis, scilicet interior sive spiritualis, exterior sive materialis, superior sive caelestis,
et inferior sive infernalis."   I omit the exposition!

[57] P. 368: "Ager iste fuit animus Catherinae, in quo crevit, et
floruit lilium puritatis, rosa charitatis, et viola humilitatis.   In

is in the light of facts like these that Jacobus's account of St. Cecilia's "peculiar virtue" must be read.[59] Nor is this all. For St. Cecilia shares with others her typifying quality. St. Ambrosius is also, by the same token, "the, traditionally busy saint." For he, too, is compared to the bee:

> Assimilatur autem api triplici de causa. Primo, quia sicut ipse dicit in exameron, apis virginitatem custodit . . . Secundo assimilatur api. Apis florem de diversis floribus colligit: In prato quidem caelestis viriditatis sunt diversi flores, etc. . . . Tertio assimilatur api, quia apis alveolum defendit: sic et ipse defendit ecclesiam a tribus persecutoribus [i. e., tyrants, heretics, and demons].[60]

And the Blessed Virgin is "busy" too:

> Apis dicitur Virgo Maria, quia fuit brevis per humilitatem, volatilis per supernorum contemplationem, mellificans per caelestis fructus productionem,[61] etc.

---

isto agro absconditus est thesaurus martyrii . . . et thesaurus divinae sapientiae, et virginalis munditiae, et caelestis gloriae," etc.

[58] The Virgin is compared to Amygdalus, Aquaeductus, Arbor Caelestis, Arca Dei, Arcus caelestis, Aurora, Balsamum, Candela, Cedrus, Caelum, Cinnamomum, Cypressus, Collum, Columba, Crater, Ebur, Elephas, Fons Dei, Gallina, Libanus, Lilium Dei, Luna, Lux, Mare, Myrrha, Nardus, Navis, Nubes, Oliva, Ovis Dei, Palma, Ros, Rosa, Speculum, Stella, Terra, Vellus, Virga, Vitis. See the *tabula* to the *Sermones Aurei de Laudibus Deiparae Virginis*. Each symbol represents the heading of a separate sermon.

[59] I shall quote only the close of the paragraph on her "sweetness of spiritual devotion": "Conservatur autem in vase solido, id est per patientiam, et perseverantiam firmam; alias enim spargitur si per impatientiam frangitur: *Cor fatui quasi vas confractum, et omnem sapientiam non tenebit*." Quite apart from the allegorizing, it is to be observed that (according to the Parson) this is not *Sloth* at all. "Patience, that is another remedye agayns *Ire*" (I, § 50). See below, p. 315.

[60] II, pp. 151-52. He is then compared to a *lion* (after the *Bestiary*), because the lion sleeps with its eyes open, wakens its young, and obliterates its tracks with its tail; then to *honey*, for two reasons. The *text* is Samson's riddle!

[61] *Sermones de Laudibus*, etc., p. 7. The *text* is that of the sermon on St. Cecilia.

In a word, the case stands thus: Mr. Tupper finds in
his documents the fault of Undevotion, one of the chief
phases of Sloth.   For he regards the " Invocatio " as
embodying the *opposite* of Undevotion.   St. Cecilia's
peculiar virtue, then, should also be antipathetic to that.
And so he bases her " sweetness of spiritual devotion "
(which she undoubtedly possessed) *as traditionally her*
" *first trait*," upon a case of *ad hoc* homiletic allegorizing.
St. Cecilia was without question " busy," [62] and she was
endowed with spiritual devotion.   But there is no valid
evidence that these were her two outstanding, *traditional*
qualities.   The other twelve traits [63] which Jean de Vigny
and Jacobus de Voragine enumerate have absolutely equal
claims with the arbitrarily selected two.   Once more, it
is not in this instance so much the fact which counts, as
the principle of interpretation.

The same remark applies to Mr. Tupper's next piece
of evidence.   " In the *Flores Exemplorum* ... Cecilia
exemplifies Fortitude, which, as the Parson tells us (I,
727 f.), is the ' remedy ' against the Sin of Sloth." [64]
Fortitude undoubtedly is, not only in the *Parson's Tale,*
but in other treatments of the Seven Deadly Sins as
well,[65] set over against Sloth.   But Fortitude, even in the
Middle Ages, was not *preëmpted* by the Seven Deadly
Sins.   Mr. Tupper would seemingly have us believe that
the mediæval mind lived and moved and had its being
solely in the Sins; that nothing once associated with them
retained thereafter independent entity.   But the Four

[62] I waive the " argumentosa," and accept Chaucer's " bisinesse "
for " assiduam operationem."

[63] I have counted *contemplation, sagacity* (which appears three
times), and *teaching,* each only once.

[64] *Publications,* p. 98, n. 9.

[65] See below, p. 327.

Cardinal Virtues and the Twelve Moral Virtues survived as such their partial inclusion as antitypes within the categories of the Vices. Thus, in the *Pèlerinage,* Fortitude is the habergeon of the Pilgrim's armor.[66] And Jacobus de Voragine extols the fourfold Fortitude of *another* Virgin martyr, St. Agatha:

> Beata autem Agatha quadruplicem fortitudinem habuit . . . Prima igitur fortitudo fuit, quia sexum fragilem virtute animi superavit . . . Secunda fortitudo fuit, quia contra mundi et tyranni saevitiam pugnavit et vicit [in four contests] . . . Tertio prae dulcedine Dei omnia mundi oblectamenta despexit . . . Quarto in morte per martyrium triumphavit.[67]

Fortitude was, indeed (as we should expect), the peculiar virtue of *all* martyrs, of whom, in the *Ayenbite,* it is again St. Agatha who is the type—"*an suo dede þe martires* . . . huer-of we redeþ of zaynte agase þet mid greate blisse hi yede to torment alsuo ase hi yede to feste oþer to a bredale." [68] The fact that St. Cecilia illustrates Fortitude in an *exemplum* is insufficient warrant for the inference that she was in any special fashion whatsoever regarded as the antitype of Sloth.[69]

The crowning argument does not help us; the irony rests on pure assumption; the Tale itself has quite another emphasis; the tradition of the " busy saint " is at best but incidentally traditional.[70] There is left the testimony

---

[66] Ll. 7553 ff. See especially ll. 7553-69.

[67] II, pp. 90-91.   [68] P. 166 (under " Prouesse ").

[69] Compare the fourteenth-century *exemplum* cited by Herbert (*Catalogue of Romances,* III, p. 632), under the heading " De fortitudine et partibus eius," in which a bishop and his people take refuge from Attila in a church, and suffer martyrdom. Is the bishop to be regarded as an antitype of Sloth?

[70] I have not access at the moment to the vast collections of the *Analecta hymnica.* I know that they are rich in hymns to St. Cecilia. It is possible that Mr. Tupper may find support for his

of the Invocation and the Prologue. "Among the chief phases of [Sloth] is the fault, antipathetic to Cecilia's peculiar virtue,—Undevotion. . . . This Undevotion is definitely represented as neglect of Hymns of our Lord and of our Lady, and of the Daily Service. Now the 'Invocacio ad Mariam' . . . is drawn not only from Dante but from the Hours of the Virgin . . . and is therefore the most effective sort of protest against Sloth in its phase of Undevotion."[71] The Invocation is, indeed, "that antidote to Sloth,"[72] and in it "who can . . . ignore the *formal intent* of the zest of devotion and zeal of good works?"[73] That is (as I make it out), one branch of Sloth is Undevotion, or the neglect of Hymns and Hours. The opposite of Undevotion is Devotion, which does *not* neglect the Hymns and Hours. The "Invocacio" does not neglect them, for it quotes them. Therefore it stands for Devotion, the (*assumed*) opposite of Undevotion,[74] a branch of Sloth, and therefore it is "the most effective sort of protest against Sloth." Just who is to be credited with the freedom from Undevotion —St. Cecilia (its antitype), the Second Nun (its assumed type), or the ironical Chaucer himself—is not

contention there, if it is to be found anywhere. I recall no evidence for it from the hymns. But this point was not in my mind when I read them. At all events, I proffer the reference, which I should use myself, if I could.

[71] *Publications*, pp. 106-07.

[72] *Ibid.*, p. 99, n. 10; cf. *Notes*, p. 11: "its ... Invocation, full of the spiritual devotion that is ever the antidote of this Deadly Sin."

[73] *Publications*, pp. 115-16.

[74] Incidentally it may be remarked that *Devotion*, Cecilia's "peculiar virtue" appears in the *Mirour de l'Omme* as the first branch of Humility, the antitype of Pr*ide*. It is there accompanied by Prayer, and Gower devotes 659 lines to it (ll. 10177-10836). As an antitype of *Sloth* I know it only in *Jacob's Well* (pp. 283-84), where it manifests itself in *weeping*.

quite clear. The point is one which Mr. Tupper, un-troubled by the contagion of his theory, is far too good a scholar to have made.

And in spite of himself he has furnished his own anti-dote. "No one has noted," he tells us in his latest ar-ticle,[75] "that such a prelude to a Miracle of the Virgin or to a Life of a saint *is a literary convention even more common that the 'Idleness' prologue*," and he further points out that "in his large drafts upon the universally familiar Hours, Chaucer was *but following the tradition of the religious lyric*."[76]   And precisely the same thing holds good of the Prologue also.   It *is* an "Idleness" Prologue, but it is also a stock convention.   To the ex-amples pointed out by Professor Carleton Brown [77] Tup-per himself has made two important additions.[78]   I am well aware of the fact that a conventional device may be given a non-conventional turn, but the evidence for such a deflection from common usage must be far stronger than that which Mr. Tupper has thus far presented.   On the face of it, Chaucer is merely doing, in both the Prologue and the Invocation, what had been done again and again —precisely "*the sort of thing*" (as Mr. Tupper himself puts it) "*that every rimer of his time does well*." [79]   The-significance attached to both Prologue and Invocation rests solely, in other words, upon its assumed coincidence with the other elements of the cipher.

---

[75] *Notes*, p. 10.

[76] *Ibid.* He also shows (n. 6) that Barclay as well as Chaucer uses both Idleness Prologue and "an elaborate Invocation to the Virgin richer even than Chaucer's in liturgical phrases."

[77] *Modern Philology*, IX, pp. 1-4.

[78] *Notes*, p. 10, n. 6.

[79] *Notes*, p. 11. Mr. Tupper happens, when he says this, to be arguing for another thesis, which gives his testimony added weight.

For that it is a " Sins cipher " that Mr. Tupper has constructed, there can be, I think, no doubt. One of Cecilia's twelve qualities in the *Legenda Aurea* is " bisinesse " ; one of her five in the *Sermones Aurei* is Devotion; and there is a Fortitude *exemplum*. On the other side are two of the nine branches of Sloth—Idleness and Undevotion—and the *remedium* Fortitude. And as a result of the proper permutations and combinations of these elements, the declaration that the writer is doing his " feithful bisinesse " to avoid the dangers of Idleness becomes an exemplification of the Sin itself; a still more conventional use of Hymns of our Lady in the Invocation to the Virgin becomes " the most effective sort of protest against Sloth " ; and " the glorious lyf and passioun " of the " mayde and martir, seint Cecilie " becomes " the tale of the traditionally busy St. Cecilia "—and therefore " the Second Nun [illustrates] Sloth." If this is a typically mediæval process, where are the parallels ?

And Chaucer himself had none of this in mind when Prologue, Invocation, and Tale came from his pen! Mr. Tupper argues ably, on the ground of " the time-honored function of such a prelude as Chaucer's ' Invocacio ad Mariam' " that the Invocation and the Tale were composed at the same time. That the Prologues and the Tale " were combined at a period prior to the composition of the *Canterbury Tales*," admits (as he grants) no doubt.[80] The whole composition is " *former material converted to the purposes of the motif;* " [81] it is a " treasure-trove of [Chaucer's] portfolio." [82] And the device of the Sins (it will be remembered) came to Chaucer late [83] —" in the latter half of the Canterbury series." So far

---

[80] *Notes*, pp. 10-11.
[81] *Publications*, p. 99, n. 10.
[82] *Notes*, p. 11.
[83] *Publications*, p. 118.

as Chaucer's original purpose is concerned, the intricate significance we are asked to read into the composition is absolutely fortuitous. And in Mr. Tupper's own mature judgment, nothing was added later. The evidence in the case of the *Second Nun's Tale,* even were it ten times as strong as it is, becomes valid, therefore, *only when the validity of the theory as a whole is established.* For on Mr. Tupper's own explicit testimony the association of *this* Tale with the Sins is *ex post facto.* It may therefore be left in its limbo for the present.[84]

[84] Since we are on the subject of Sloth, it is necessary to call attention to a statement of Mr. Tupper's that is not immediately connected with the *Second Nun's Tale.* It is in his general discussion of the categories (*Publications,* p. 95). "From our point of view it is natural to protest against the inclusion of 'the thief on the cross' under Langland's head of Sloth, and yet, as R. W. Chambers points out, that dilatory sinner finds a place *in every formal description of that vice.*" Mr. Chambers does not point this out, and it is not the case. What Chambers says (*Modern Language Review,* V, p. 5) is this: "Now Skeat pointed out long ago that the right place for the penitent thief is under Sloth, *under the sub-heading Wanhope, which always belongs to Accidie.*" (Even that is not quite true, for the *Ayenbite,* p. 29, and *Jacob's Well,* p. 85, put it among the Sins against the Holy Ghost, under *Envy,* and the *Mirror of St. Edmund,* p. 24, places "whanhope of þe blysse of heuene" under *Lechery,* as does also Raymund of Pennaforte; see Petersen, p. 27). That is a very different thing indeed from Mr. Tupper's statement. What Skeat says may be found in his edition of *Piers Plowman,* II, p. 88, where he remarks that "his [the thief's] repentance was the *stock example* of an argument against Wanhope as resulting from Sloth." On p. 97 he refers to the *Parson's Tale, Handlyng Synne,* l. 5171, and the *Ayenbite,* p. 34. In point of fact, the penitent thief does not occur under Wanhope (or even *Sloth*) in the *Cursor Mundi,* Gaytryge's sermon or the *Lay Folks' Catechism, Jacob's Well,* the *Pèlerinage,* the *Confessio Amantis,* the *Mirour de l'Omme*—to name no more. Similarly, Mr. Tupper says (*Publications,* p. 103, n. 22): "*Every mediœval account of Envy records these traits* [its Satanic origin and serpent-like nature]." Many record one, many the other, some both—but the "serpent-like

V

We have now to consider the four Tales—the Physician's, the Man of Law's, the Manciple's, and the Wife of Bath's—the themes of which are common to Chaucer and Gower. And first it may be remarked in general that if Chaucer were to tell *any* tales that Gower told too, they must inevitably be, in Mr. Tupper's theory, " Sins tales." For, the *Confessio Amantis* being what it is, " Sins tales " are the only sort [1] that Gower told. Other considerations aside, every one of Chaucer's Legends except those of Cleopatra, Hypsipyle, and Hypermnestra is as much a " Sins tale " as are the stories of Virginia, Constance, Apollo and the crow, and the Loathly Lady. *In itself,* the coincidence with Gower is wholly without weight.[2] The case for the four tales must rest on other

nature " is wanting, for instance, from the *Parson's Tale* itself. The statement that " the commonplaces [on " gentilesse "] *inevitably* appear in *all* mediæval discourses upon Pride " (*Publications,* p. 100) is another case in point. See below, p. 343, n. 9. The statement (*Journal,* p. 557) that Barclay " devotes *the largest space in his Ship* to the tavern-revelers—drinkers, lechers, dicers, blasphemers," is still another. Even granting Mr. Tupper his own wide latitude in the interpretation of " tavern-revelers," less than a dozen at most, out of the one hundred and fifteen sections of the *Ship of Fools,* may be stretched to come under that head. These are, of course, merely offhand or insufficiently considered statements, but they are none the less somewhat damaging to an argument, when they are used as evidence.

[1] With the exception to be noted below, p. 306.

[2] See above, p.   Did Gower use these stories because they were *per se* " Sins tales," or did they become, *pro tempore,* " Sins tales " because he diverted them to his immediate purpose? The stories of Capaneus (*Confessio,* I, 1977 ff.), Socrates (III, 639 ff.), Daphne (III, 1685 ff.), Phaeton and Icarus (IV, 978 ff.), for example, are all told by Gower as exemplifying Sins. Suppose that Chaucer (who makes use of all these personages) had told their stories as separate

grounds, and it is these grounds that now concern us. We may begin with the *Physician's Tale*. What are its " tags " ?

The first is the " crowning argument." " Only one of the Sins tales—that of the Physician (Gower's *exemplum* of Lechery)—*confesses in its moralities no indebtedness or close resemblance to the Parson's discussion of the corresponding Vice.*" [3]

The second is the element of irony. " No Prologue specifically indicates the Physician's peculiar disqualification for his theme of Lechery, *but* the mediæval reader must have been tickled by the praise of purity from a profession notorious in the fourteenth century for its willingness to increase the passions of lovers [etc.]. . . . *This suggestion of satire in the case of the Doctor is only a plausible conjecture.*" [4] This stand-by also leaves us in the lurch.

Tales, without other indication of his purpose. Would the Middle Ages have interpreted them—" *even though their title or tag were lacking* "—as exemplifying Pride, Wrath (Cheste and Foolhaste) and Sloth respectively, any more than they so interpreted the stories of the *Legend?* Despite Mr. Tupper's words just quoted (*Publications*, p. 96), the application of the story must be made clear. He argues (rather inconsistently with his statement that tags were unnecessary) that the application *is* made clear in the Tales that follow, and that is what we have to see.

[3] *Publications*, p. 116. " *But* "—Mr. Tupper proceeds—" this omission seems the less striking, when we remark the generous use of the section on Lechery in the so-called Marriage Group, particularly in the *Merchant's Tale.*" That is (once more), " if he have not seyd hem, leve brother, In o book, he hath seyd hem in *another*." (The *Merchant's Tale* might have something to say for itself, too. See below, p. 365). Tupper's note on the same page is merely snatching at a straw, as the text makes clear.

[4] *Publications*, pp. 110-11. Tupper, it will be observed, is creating a new category of the *professions*, as exemplifications of the Seven Deadly Sins. " The Gluttony of the Pardoner [is] a traditional trait of that tribe " (*Publications*, p. 117). Nuns exemplify Sloth. Physicians now stand for Lechery. We shall soon see that Lawyers and

We are thrown back, then, exclusively upon the Tale
itself. And the Tale, Mr. Tupper assures us, is " Gower's
exemplum of Lechery." [5]   *But Gower does not include it
under the Seven Deadly Sins at all.* It is in the digression (which occupies all of the seventh book) on Aristotle's philosophy, and it falls under the last of the *Five
Points of Policy*—Truth, Largess, Justice, Pity, and
Chastity.[6] His treatment of Chastity is throughout with
reference to *princes and rulers,*[7] and the *exempla* are
those of Cyrus, Amalech, Solomon, Antonius, Tarquin,
and Appius.[8]   And the moral of the tale of Appius and

Merchants exemplify Envy, as well as Avarice. Five of the Seven
Sins are accounted for. So far as the Physicians are concerned,
Tupper's inferences from the facts he gives are gratuitous. And one
of the facts is wrong. The long passage in the *Confessio Amantis*
(VI, 1292-1358) which he cites (p. 111, n. 37) deals with Sorcery
and Witchcraft (specifically with Geomancy, Hydromancy, Pyro-
mancy, Nigromancy, etc.), and has nothing to do with Physicians.
And anyway, *it is under Gluttony.* See also the gloss opposite ll.
1261 ff.

[5] *Publications,* p. 116. He refers to it elsewhere as "the Physician's version of *Gower's theme of Lechery* in the *Confessio Amantis*" (p. 97; cf. n. 7); as "another Gower story, that of Lechery"
(p. 127); and states again that "in the *Physician's Tale* Chaucer,
like Gower in his version of the theme, . . . is telling a story of
Lechery, and of its antitype, Chastity" (*Notes,* p. 5).

[6] The discussion of Chastity is in ll. 4215-5397; the story of Appius
and Virginia in ll. 5131-5306. Lechery is the only one of the Sins to
which Gower gives no categorical treatment. Each of the other
Vices is specifically named (see Bk. I, ll. 580 ff., and the opening
paragraphs of Books II-VII); Book VIII treats of the Laws of Marriage, and of one branch of Lechery, Incest. It is worth noting that
Gower's specific treatment of *Virginity* is under Robbery, a branch
of *Avarice* (see V, 6338 ff., and especially the heading and gloss to
V, 6359 ff.).

[7] See VII, 4209-14, 4239-56, 4308-12, 4351-60, 4446-58, 4546-73,
5124-30.

[8] The last *exemplum,* that of Tobias, constitutes (as the gloss
makes clear) a transition to the discussion of the Laws of Marriage
in the next book.

Virginia, like that of the others, has specific reference to the Point of Policy:

> And thus thunchaste was chastised,
> *Whereof thei myhte ben avised*
> *That scholden afterward governe,*
> *And be this evidence lerne,*
> *Hou it is good a king eschuie*
> *The lust of vice and vertu suie.*[9]

Precisely similar is its "moral" in Jean de Meun, where it is an *exemplum* of the *inequity of judges:*

> Tex juge fait le larron pendre,
> Qui miex déust estre pendus,
> Se jugemens li fust rendus
> Des rapines et des tors fais
> Qu'il a par son pooir forfais.[10]

Then comes the *exemplum;* and the conclusion of the whole matter, when the tale is told, is this:

> *Briefment juges font trop d'outrages.*[11]

Nor is it different in Hans Sachs: [12]

> Inn der geschicht zu Rom geschehen
> Habt ir als in eym spiegel gsehen,
> *Wie alle ungerechtigkeyt*
> *Kumpt an den tag zu seiner zeyt,*
> Gestraffet ausz götlicher rach . . .
> Auch über das secht ir darbey,
> *Wo herrschaft seins gewalts miszbraucht,*
> *Wie plötzlich sie zu grunde haucht.*
> Wo sie wütet in tyranney . . .
> Desz reich zu grund geht an dem end.
> Dagegen wo gut regiment
> Ist über leut und über land, etc.[13]

---

[9] VII, 5301-06.   [10] Ed. Michel, I, p. 186.

[11] *Ibid.*, p. 189.

[12] Tupper admits Hans Sachs (*Publications*, p. 98, n. 8) as a belated witness, and so may we.

[13] Ed. von Keller, II, pp. 19-20.

What is *Chaucer's* moral?   Here it is:

> Heer men may seen how sinne hath his meryte!
> Beth war, for no man woot whom god wol smyte
> In no degree, ne in which maner wyse
> The worm of conscience may agryse
> Of wikked lyf, though it so privee be,
> That no man woot ther-of but god and he.
> For be he lewed man or elles lered,
> He noot how sone that he shal been afered.
> Therfore I rede yow this conseil take,
> Forsaketh sinne, er sinne yow forsake.[14]

Not a word of Lechery is there.   Mr. Tupper twice refers
to this "moral."   "The ten-line 'application' at the
close of the Tale . . . is the traditional ending of an
'ensample' of *Sin:*[15]

> Heer men may seen how sinne hath his meryte!
> Beth war, for no man woot whom god wol smyte, etc.[16]

So the moral is driven home." [17]   But what moral? Again:
"At the end of another Gower story, that of Lechery,
Chaucer says plainly (C, 277 f.):—[here follow the same
two lines as above].   Evidently," continues Mr. Tupper,
"Chaucer was quite in the dark about himself!"[18]   It
looks a little as if he were.   And Harry Bailly also was
the more deceived:

> 'Harrow!' quod he, 'by nayles and by blood!
> This was a fals cherl *and a fals justyse!*
> As shamful deeth as herte may devyse
> *Come to thise juges and hir advocats!'* [19]

---

[14] C, 277-286. Compare also ll. 267-76 for the real "*leit-motif* of
the Doctor's story" (p. 116, n. 46), as Chaucer tells it.

[15] Italics mine. Mr. Tupper is hard put to it here.

[16] The "etc." is Tupper's. He quotes but the two lines.

[17] *Publications,* p. 104.

[18] *Publications,* p. 127.   [19] C, 288-91.

But our Host had only Jean de Meun and Gower to guide
him—not " Chaucer, temp. 1914." And "his strict confinement within the bounds of fourteenth-century thought"
must be forgiven him.[20] Tupper's remark about another
interpretation of the Appius and Virginia story applies,
I fear, *mutatis mutandis,* to his own: his "unhappy comment upon the moral of the story ignores utterly its traditional function."[21]

[20] *Journal,* p. 553. Still another mediæval reader slipped up
about the purport of the Tale—the scribe of the spurious Prologue
to the *Physician's Tale* in the Lansdowne MS. (*Oxford Chaucer,* III,
p. 435) : "As ye, worschipful Maister of Phisike, Tellith us *somme
tale that is a cronyke*"—and on those terms the Physician complies.
The scribe, who should have recognized the thing without a tag,
somehow missed the point.

[21] *Notes,* p. 7, n. 13. Mr. Tupper lays great stress on "Virginia's
close resemblance to the 'consecrated virgin' ideal of patristic
treatises" (*Publications,* p. 98, n. 7), especially as this ideal is
elaborated in Ambrose's *De Virginibus* (*Publications,* p. 104). This
view is presented in detail in his latest article (*Notes,* pp. 5-7). I
do not feel sure that Mr. Tupper's parallels demonstrate the borrowings from Ambrose, but for the purpose of this argument I am
perfectly willing to grant the point. Virginia *is* a virgin, where-
ever Chaucer got the hints for his description of her. His omni-
vorous reading may well have led him to Ambrose's treatise, but
the fact (if it be such) that he draws from it for Virginia has no
real bearing upon Tupper's case. Is the Prioress unchaste, because
the description of her table manners is taken from the account which
a lecherous old woman gives of women's wiles? Is the first-night
rapture of Troilus holy, because it finds expression in words drawn
from the very Invocation to the Virgin which the Second Nun employs? Every student of Chaucer knows that the implications of his
sources, as carried over to the use he makes of them, must be dealt
with cautiously. It is probably a mere oversight that the example
which Tupper cites from Jacques de Vitry (*Publications,* pp. 103-04)
of "the mediæval moralizer turning him naturally to *father and
mother*" is chosen from a sermon *to boys and young men* (Crane,
p. xlvi).

VI

In the case of the *Man of Law's Tale* Mr. Tupper has laid his stress upon the interpretation of the Prologue, and since his argument hinges almost wholly upon the significance of that puzzling document, it is best to deal with it first. I do not believe that his conclusions would follow, even if all his evidence could stand examination, but I am compelled to subject his arguments to closer scrutiny than I enjoy, because in them statement of fact is frequently vitiated by an admixture of tacit inference.

The Prologue is designated, when it is first referred to, as " a Poverty Prologue "; [1] the next time it has become " the Poverty (or let us say, Envy) Prologue "; [2] in " The Pardoner's Tavern " it is " the Impatient Poverty (Envy) prologue," [3] and the Poverty involved is defined as " more precisely, that Impatient Poverty which is traditionally associated with Envy "; [4] in the *Nation* article it is " a prologue of Impatient Poverty, [which] is . . . a prologue of Envy," [5] or (in the same article) " a prelude of Murmuration." Its stanzas, to be more explicit, illustrate " such a dominant phase of Envy as 'grucching' against one's wretched lot and 'sorwe of other mannes wele' (see *Parson's Tale,* 483, 498)." [6]

" Now Murmuration," Mr. Tupper tells us, " or ' *grucching against poverty,' is one of the chief phases of Envy* in

---

[1] *Publications,* p. 102.   [3] *Ibid.,* p. 118.
[2] *Journal,* p. 565.   [4] *Journal,* p. 555.
[5] P. 41.

[6] *Journal,* p. 555. This properly substitutes Chaucer's " wele " for the misleading " wealth " of *Publications,* p. 103. But the plural " phases " should have been used, as " traits " is properly employed in the earlier article. The two faults mentioned are separate phases of Envy in the categories.

Chaucer's own *Parson's Tale.*" [7]   This is simply not the case.   The identifying " or " is absolutely misleading, for although Murmuration in general is " one of the chief phases of Envy," " grucching against poverty " is *not*. It is one of six particulars under the first of two subheads of Murmuration, and it occupies less than one line out of the one hundred and twenty-nine lines of the section: " After bakbyting cometh grucching or murmuracioun; and somtyme it springeth of inpatience *agayns god,* and somtyme agayns man.   *Agayns god it is,* whan a man gruccheth agayn *the peynes of helle,* or agayns *poverte,* or *los of catel,* or agayn *reyn or tempest;* or elles gruccheth *that shrewes han prosperitee,* or elles *for that goode men han adversitee* " (I, 498-500).   Nor is Murmuration (including " grucching against poverty ") one of the chief phases of Envy *alone* even in the *Parson's Tale.*   The next sentence but one begins: " Somtyme comth grucching of *Avarice* "; the next but one: " Somtyme comth murmure of *Pryde* "; the next: " And somtyme grucching sourdeth of *Envye* "; the next but one: " Som tyme grucching comth of *ire* "—with five subheads.[8]

Moreover, this testimony of the crowning authority is borne out by the " categories."   In the *Confessio Amantis* Murmur and Complaint are branches of *Pride*—" qui super omnes alios *Inobediencie* secreciores vt ministri illi deseruiunt ":

> For thogh fortune make hem wynne,
> *Yit grucchen thei,* and if thei lese,
> Ther is no weie for to chese,
> Wherof thei myhten stonde appesed.
> So ben thei comunely desesed;
> Ther may no *welthe ne poverte*

---

[7] *Nation*, p. 41.   Compare " such a dominant phase of Envy," above.
[8] See also above, p. 257.

> Attempren hem to the decerte
> Of buxomnesse be no wise.[9]

Both " grucching " (*Groucer*) and murmuring are under
Pride (Inobedience) in the *Mirour de l'Omme*.[10]   This
testimony represents Gower, on whose usage the import of
the Tale depends. And Gower includes *neither* under
Envy. Nor is it only Gower who includes them under
Pride. Robert of Brunne does so too—and under precisely the same aspect (that of " grucching against God ")
that is stressed by the Parson and the Man of Law:

> ʒyf þou grucchedest, and seydyst noght,
> But to God haddyst euyl þoght,
> Wete þou wel, *hyt ys grete pryde,*
> *Grucchyng with God,* or for to chyde.[11]

And Frère Lorens, like Gower, associates " murmures "
with *Inobedience* (as well as with Sloth, Impatience, and
Envy),[12] while the *Cursor Mundi* includes " grucching "
under Pride.[13]

Furthermore, in the *Ayenbite*, " grucching " is included
under *Wrath:*

> Vor wreþe and felonye op-bereþ and nimþ zuo oþerhuyl þe herte
> of þe felle uor zome aduersite timlich . . . oþer uor zome misual
> þet his wyl ne is naʒt y-do: þet ha grocheþ aye oure Lhord.[14]

With still greater definiteness it appears under Wrath in
Jacob's Well:

> þe vij. fote of wose in wretthe is blasphemye; þat is, *whanne þou*
> *grucchyst or spekyst aʒens god* in tribulacyoun, in sykenes . . . &
> whanne þou demyst þat god ʒeuyth þe more wo *& lesse wele* þan
> þou were worthy to haue.[15]

---

[9] I, 1348-55.   [10] Ll. 2313 ff., 2323 ff.
[11] *Handlyng Synne*, ll. 3487-90 (under Pride).
[12] Eilers, p. 519.   [13] L. 28100.
[14] P. 30.
[15] P. 94. Cf. the *sixth* foot, " *vnpacyence;* þat is, whan þou grucchyst aʒens resounable chastysing," etc. (See *Parson's Tale*, I, 498:

It is also, in *Jacob's Well,* one of the twenty-two inches of the gravel of misconduct that underlies the ooze of Wrath:

þe secunde inche of mysgouernaunce in þe mowth is *grucching.* As a carte-qweel, dry and vngrecyd, cryeth lowdest of oþere qwelys; So, þou drye & noȝt grecyd wyth grace *grucchyst* lowdest of alle oþere aȝens þi god in ony dyssese & tribulacyoun.[16]

And it is one of the sixteen twigs of Wrath in Frère Lorens.[17]

" Grucching " is the third point of *Sloth* in the *Ayenbite* [18] and in *Jacob's Well,*[19] and " Murmure " is the fifteenth twig of Sloth in Frère Lorens.[20]   " Grucching " is included under *Avarice* in the *Ayenbite,*[21] and also under Sins of the Tongue (*Gluttony*), where it has two boughs:

Vor þe on: is *grouchinge aye god.* and þe oþre aye man regneþ. þis zenne is in uele maneres ase . . . *ine poure: aye þe riche* . . . And wext þe grochinges . . . oþer of *onboȝsamnesse* . . . oþer ine *sleauþe* . . . oþer of *inpacience* . . . oþer of *enuic.* oþer of *felonie* . . . *Grochinge aye god* heþ yet nou ynoȝ mo encheysouns . . . yef me him zent aduersete. *pouerte.* ziknesse. dyere time. rayn. druȝþe . . . he him niymþ anhaste *to grochi aye god.*[22]

Finally, in *Jacob's Well* it is also treated in the chapter "*De gula* et viciis lingue," where (as we have already seen)[23] it grows directly out of " the Devil's tavern ":

þis braunche hath ij. leuys: on is *grucchyng aȝens god,* anoþer is aȝens man. fferst aȝens god, for dyuerse skylles . . . þus þei grucche, ȝif god sende hem . . . *pouerte* . . . or ȝif *god sende a man werdly*

" Somtyme [grucching] springeth of *inpacience*," etc.; Jacob's Well, pp. 91, 100).
    [16] P. 260.   [17] Eilers, p. 525.
    [18] P. 34: " þe þridde is grochynge."
    [19] P. 112: " þe thridde fote is grucchyng."
    [20] Eilers, p. 535.
    [21] P. 43: " þe oþer is þe zenne of grochinge and of traysoun."
    [22] Pp. 67-68.   [23] See above, p. 274.

*good, & take fro an-oþer his good. Þanne þei seyn þat god is noȝt
ryȝtwyse, & blamyn hym for his dede*[24] *. . .* Also þei grucche aȝens
man *. . . as pore men aȝens ryche.*[25]

" Grucching " does not appear under *Envy* at all in the
Confessio, the *Mirour,* the *Ayenbite,* or *Jacob's Well.*   In
the *Parson's Tale,* Peraldus,[26] and Frère Lorens [27] it is
explicitly associated, even in the treatment of Envy itself,
with Avarice,[28] Pride,[29] Sloth,[30] and Wrath.[31]   In Mr.
Tupper's own authorities it is only under Lechery that
" this ' grucching ' or murmuring which characterizes
every mention of [Impatient Poverty]," [32] does not appear.   Yet we are told that *" every man of the Middle
Ages must have recognized at once* the inherent fitness of
prefacing a tale of Envy . . . with stanzas illustrating
such a dominant phase of Envy as ' grucching ' against
one's wretched lot and ' sorwe of other mannes wele.' " [33]
Like Hudibras, presumably, " All this, without a gloss or
comment, He could unriddle in a moment."   The truth
is, the lines are *not* a " Poverty (let us say, *Envy*) Prologue " at all, any more than they are a " Poverty (let us
say, *Pride, Sloth, Gluttony,* or *Wrath*) Prologue."   Mr.
Tupper has overlooked the facts which I have given, and
those facts are fatal to his interpretation of the Prologue.
That is perhaps enough; but he has also failed to observe
another interesting matter.

[24] *" Thou blamest Crist,* and seyst ful bitterly, *He misdeparteth
richesse temporal "* (B, 106-07).

[25] P. 155.   [26] Petersen, pp. 47-48.

[27] Eilers, pp. 518-19.   [28] Parson and Peraldus.

[29] Parson, Peraldus, and (as Inobedience) Frère Lorens.

[30] Frère Lorens.   [31] Parson.

[32] *Nation,* p. 41.

[33] *Journal,* p. 555. " Sorwe of other mannes wele " is, to be sure, a
phase of Envy, but the lines in the Prologue on which Mr. Tupper
relies for this branch (B, 106-12) belong, as we shall see (pp. 316-17
below) in another category.

For one can·readily make, on the basis of the admitted authorities themselves, a far stronger case for a *Wrath* than for an *Envy* Prologue. The phrase which Tupper finally adopts—"Impatient Poverty"—would give at once the clue to any mediæval reader alert for intimations of the Sins, for *Impatient* is itself a definite "tag." "Grucching against God" (under which falls "grucching against poverty") is definitely assigned by the Parson to Impatience as its source: "Somtyme it springeth of *inpatience* agayns god, and somtyme agayns man." [34]   And Impatience is a subdivision of *Wrath* in the *Mirour de l'Omme*,[35] in *Jacob's Well*,[36] and in the *Pèlerinage*.[37] *Patience,* moreover, is the *remedium* for Wrath not only in the *Parson's Tale*,[38] but also in the *Confessio Amantis*,[39] and the *Mirour de l'Omme*.[40]   Furthermore, as we have seen above,[41] "grucching against God" is definitely associated with Wrath, even independently of Impatience, in the *Ayenbite* and *Jacob's Well*. And finally, we have the Man of Law's own testimony. Here is the second stanza, on which Mr. Tupper lays his emphasis:

> Thou *blamest Crist*,[42] and seyst ful *bitterly*,[43]

---

[34] I, 498. Compare "And wext þe grochinges . . . of *inpacience*" (*Ayenbite*, p. 67); "murmur *Impacientie*" (Peraldus; Petersen, p. 48); "et naist cist murmures ... de *inpacience*" (Frère Lorens; Eilers, p. 519); etc.

[35] Ll. 3953 ff.

[36] P. 94. Cf. p. 98, l. 31; p. 100, l. 1.

[37] Ll. 15691-98. Wrath's saw is forged out of iron that "callyd was 'Inpacyence' Wych was dolven out of helle, wher that blake ffendys dwelle."

[38] I, § 50-51.   [39] III, 612-713.

[40] Ll. 13381-14100.   [41] P. 312.

[42] Compare *Tale of Melibeus* under Ire (B, 2317): "'He that is *irous and wrooth*,' as seith Senek, 'ne may nat speke *but he blame thinges*'; and with his *viciouse wordes* he stireth other folk to angre and to ire" (compare Tupper's own characterization [*Publications*,

> He misdeparteth richesse temporal; [44]
> Thy neighebour thou *wytest sinfully.*[45]
> And seyst thou hast to lyte, and he hath al.
> ' Parfay,' seistow, ' sometyme he rekne shal,
> Whan that his tayl shal brennen in the glede,
> For he noght helpeth needfulle in hir nede.' [46]

Indeed, I know but one better characterization of these last lines than Mr. Tupper's " vehement and vindictive," [47] and that is the phrasing of their source. For the testimony of Innocent's chapter [48] is clear: " *Proximum* [mendi-

p. 103] of this stanza as " at once vehement and vindictive "); *Parson's Tale*, under Ire (I, 557): " Outrageous wratthe . . . *spareth neither Crist*, ne his swete mooder. And in his outrageous anger and Ire . . . ful many oon . . . feleth in his herte ful wikkedly, *both of Crist* and of alle hise halwes "; (I, 579): " Yet comen ther of Ire manye mo sinnes . . . as he that arretteth upon god, or *blameth god* "; and see especially above (p. 314) the quotation from *Jacob's* Well, p. 155.

[43] Cf. I, 510: " Som tyme grucching comth of *ire* . . . Thanne comth eek *bitternesse of herte.*"

[44] See the citations from *Jacob's Well*, p. 94 (p. 312 above) and p. 155 (p. 314 above).

[45] See the whole section of the *Parson's Tale* on " Chydinge and *reproche* " under Wrath (I, § 42), especially the portion (I, 623 ff.) which deals with him " that repreveth his neighebor."

[46] B, 106-112.

[47] Cf. *Mirour de l'Omme* (under *Ire*), ll. 3961 ff.: " L'Inpacient envers tres tous Est *fel* et trop contrarious . . . Et en response est *despitous.*"

[48] Tupper does not point out that the chapter in the *De Contemptu Mundi* on which Chaucer here draws (Bk. I, cap. 14: " De miseria pauperis et diuitis ") is *not* from that part of the treatise which deals with the Sins, namely, the *second* book. On the contrary, he definitely brings the passage into association, in his readers' mind, with that discussion of the Sins. The fact that " Innocent's famous tract, . . . which gives so large a space to the Vices, supplied him with Deadly Sins material in the Pardoner's Prologue and Tale " is *not* of value " as an indication of his present purpose " (*Publications*, p. 103)—unless in drawing upon one part of a document Chaucer always meant to carry over into his specific borrowing the implications of every other portion of his source. Cf. also *Publications*, p. 118.

cans] *criminatur* [49] *malignum,*[50] quod non plene subueniat. *Indignatur, murmurat,*[51] *imprecatur."* [52] What (it is pertinent under the theory to ask) was to prevent the mediæval mind from following *this* lead—the lead of the *Parson's Tale,* the *Confessio Amantis,* the *Mirour de l'Omme,* the *Ayenbite,* the *Pèlerinage, Jacob's Well,* Pope Innocent, and the Man of Law? It is a little hard to see.

And Mr. Tupper's own illustrations of the sort of thing that would guide aright every man of the·Middle Ages (and with him us) through the maze towards *Envy* are not felicitously chosen. " According to the author of the ' Romance of the Rose' (ll. 826 ff.),[53] Poverty is the shamefaced spouse of misery, wedding a man to hate, and driving from him all friends and brethren." [54] But this is from a passage that has nothing to do with the Sins, and so far as it may be linked with them at all, the connection with *Wrath* is stronger than with Envy:

> Povreté fait home *despire,*[55]
> Et *haïr.*[56]

---

[49] Compare the Parson's " accusinge " (with reference to "his neighebor "), under " grucching [that] comth of ire or prive hate '· (I, 508).

[50] Cf. " Thanne comth *malignitee* " (*ibid.*).

[51] See above, p. 312.

[52] I. e., " the *Cursing* phase of *Wrath.*"

[53] The reference is wrong, even for Ellis's translation (*Temple Classics,* II, p. 27), from which it is taken. It should be (for Ellis) ll. 8360 ff. The reference for the French is ll. 8712 ff. (ed. Michel, I, p. 265).

[54] *Nation,* p. 41. This is chiefly Ellis. Jean de Meun has nothing about " the shamefaced spouse of misery." The lines so translated (ll. 8712-13; cf. Ellis, II, p. 27) are: " Povreté maint à l'autre chief, Plaine de honte et de meschief." He has nothing about " wedding a man to hate." The lines so translated (ll. 8738-39; cf. Ellis, II, p. 28) are : " Povreté fait home despire, Et haïr et vivre à martire."

[55] *Despite* is incidentally mentioned under Envy in the *Parson's Tale* (I, 505); it is one of the stones of *Wrath* in the *Pèlerinage*

Nor is the next illustration happier. " In Lydgate's translation of De Guileville's " Pilgrimage of Human Life "
(ll. 22716 ff.), Impatient Poverty is an ape-lipped crone
. . . groaning and ' grucching.' It is this ' grucching
or murmuring which characterizes every mention of the
fault." [57]   The treatment of Envy in the *Pèlerinage* [58] is
singularly full and picturesque, but Impatient Poverty is
not there.   Deguileville's account of it comes *after* the
adventures with the Sins, when Grace Dieu has brought
the Pilgrim to the " castle " of the Cistercians, where Lady
Wilful Poverty shows him the crone *Impatient* Poverty.
And the outstanding fact about Impatient Poverty is her
Impatience, not her " grucching."[59]   It is because of her
Impatience that she *is* the " ape-lipped crone ":

> That is thorough my Impacyence,
> And ffor lak of pacyence . . .
> That dothe my lyppes hyghe reyse.[60]

And in the *Pèlerinage* Impatience stands explicitly for
Wrath.[61]   The passage from Hoccleve [62] is not accurately

---

(ll. 15680 ff.) ; it is more commonly a branch of *Pride* (*Parson's
Tale, Mirour, Ayenbite, Jacob's Well*).

[56] *Hate* is a branch (commonly a main one) of Wrath in the *Parson's Tale,* the *Mirour,* the *Confessio,* the *Ayenbite, Jacob's Well,*
Frère Lorens, and Peraldus.   It is a branch of Envy in Raymund
of Pennaforte (Petersen, p. 27).

[57] *Nation,* p. 41.   We have already seen the wide provenience of
" grucching."

[58] Ll. 14763-15500.   [59] See ll. 22741-46.

[60] Ll. 2257-61.

[61] Ll. 15691-98.   There is still another direct association with
Wrath.   Compare the vivid account (ll. 22747-50, 22754-56) of
Impatient Poverty as " the comune ape Affore ffolke to pleye and
Iape " with the Parson's account of the *japeres* (*De Ira,* I, 650),
" the develes apes," at whose " japerie " people laugh as " at the
gaudes of an ape."   The other sin with which Impatient Poverty
associates itself, in this same passage in the *Pèlerinage,* is nót Envy,

quoted. " Whoso gruccheth in poverty, forfeiteth grace "
should read: " And whoso gruchith, forfetith *þat* grace "
—i. e., that grace " that he schuld han, if *þat his pacience*
Wíthstode *þe* grief, and made it resistence " (ll. 1069-71).
And the lines immediately preceding read: " Who-so it
[Pouert] taketh *in pacient suffraunce,* It is ful pleasant
beforn cristes face." That is precisely the Parson's remedy (not to mention Gower's) against *Wrath.*[63] Tupper's
interpolation of " in poverty " (although a fair inference
from the context), coupled with his serious omission of
" that," gives something else than Hoccleve. To " forfeit grace " is a very definite thing—and the line from
the *Regement* says nothing of it. As for the sixteenth-
century Interlude of " Impatient Poverty," [64] I can only
say that two careful readings of the play itself have failed
to disclose to me its bearing on the case. That may well
be my own obtuseness, and I shall content myself here
with observing that, although Mr. Tupper has quoted the
Summoner's words to Impatient Poverty: " Ye be great
slanderer, and full of *envy,*" [65] he has not quoted what
Peace says to him: " Thou art so full of *Wrath* and
Envy " ; [66] and that, although he has quoted one of Peace's
injunctions: " Forsake *Envy* and Misrule," [67] he has left
out another: *" Haunt no taverns* . . . Let not *hassard*

---

but *Sloth:* " I love no maner *besynesse,* But oonly *slouthe* and *ydelnesse* " (ll. 22765-66). Compare the association of Impatience with
Sloth in the *Ayenbite* (p. 33) and *Jacob's Well* (p. 112).

[63] *Regement of Princes* (E. E. T. S.), p. 39 (*Nation,* p. 41). The
passage " in Lydgate's version of Aesop " (for which no reference is
given either) I have not found.

[63] See above, p. 315.

[64] *Nation,* p. 41.

[65] Early English Dramatists (" Lost " Tudor Plays), ed. Farmer,
p. 342.

[66] P. 318.   [67] P. 346.

nor rioter with you be checkmate " [68]—which (as we learn. from " The Pardoner's Tavern ") means *Gluttony*.[69] I am using Mr. Tupper's own evidence alone, and I am willing to leave the conclusion to the impartial scholar.

We may now come to the element of *irony*. The case for the ironical contrast between teller and tale rests upon two assumptions. " The Poverty Prologue . . . shows us clearly that the narrator of this story of Envy *is himself tainted by that Sin*.[70] This evidence is ample for our present purpose. But it is noteworthy that from the point of view of Chaucer's day, there was an ironical fitness in the final assignment of an Envy tale to the Man of Law,[71] *whose profession in the fourteenth century was tainted by Envy* as well as by Avarice." [72] The Man of Law is envious, then, first, because the Prologue shows that he is; second, because he is a member of an envious profession. As regards the first, we may waive, for the moment, the objections to the Prologue as exemplifying

[68] P. 320.

[69] See above, p. 267. It is perfectly easy to show that in the Interlude the tradition which has survived is that of *Impatience*. See, for example, pp. 316, 319, etc.

[70] Compare *Publications*, 118: " Chaucer adheres to the ironical design . . . by making *an envious man* (the anonymous speaker of the Prologue, later identified with the Man of Law merely through the context) furnish in his narrative large evidence against Envy." Compare *Nation*, p. 41: " The cry of *Chaucer's envious man*, ' O riche marchaunts,' " etc.

[71] I shall not dwell on the difficulty (which Mr. Tupper takes lightly) involved in the " final assignment " (see also ·the parenthetical statement in the preceding note above) of " this derelict tale " (Tatlock, *Development and Chronology*, p. 188). As Mr. Tupper himself points out (*Nation*, Oct. 16, 1913, p. 355), " the tale of Constance . . . was inserted here, apparently, *as an afterthought*." It should not be forgotten that the theory has already one " afterthought " to carry, in the *Second Nun's Tale*.

[72] *Publications*, p. 110. Cf. *Nation*, p. 41, fifth paragraph, end.

Envy, and assume that Mr. Tupper's interpretation is so far correct. Even granting that, it ceases at this point to be so. For the *speaker* of the Prologue *is not himself* "*grucching against poverty*" *at all.* He is *addressing* Poverty,[73] and his point of view is that of one who holds the " hateful harm " up to reprobation *because it leads to* "*grucching*." [74] It is *not* the point of view of one who " is himself tainted by that Sin." If the Prologue shows anything whatever about the Man of Law, it shows precisely the reverse of Mr. Tupper's contention.

As for the second point, Mr. Tupper is very hard put to it for his testimony. The association of lawyers with *Avarice* is (as he recognizes) a familiar one.[75] To demonstrate that the profession was regarded as " tainted by *Envy*," he cites the following evidence.[76] (i) Gower's use, to describe the Lawyer (*Vox,* VI, 293), of " the same image of the Basilisk that he employs to picture Envy (*Mirour*, 3748 f.)." There is no reference to the basilisk in *Vox,* VI, 293, nor elsewhere in the chapter, which deals explicitly (see its title, and l. 302) with the *Avarice* of lawyers,

[73] " *Thou* blamest . . . *thou* wytest . . . ' Parfay,' *seistow* "—and so on.
[74] This, of course, is Innocent's attitude too (" O miserabilis mendicantis conditio," etc.).
[75] Not only does it appear in most of the categories (see, for instance, *Ayenbite*, p. 40; *Jacob's Well*, p. 131; *Handlyng Synne*, p. 177; *Mirour*, ll. 6329 ff.; etc.), but it is of constant occurrence elsewhere. See *Sermones Aurei*, II, p. 236: " Quadruplex est lex. Prima est *lex cupiditatis*, quae est *Advocatorum* "; Wyclif, ed. Arnold, III, p. 153: " Bot *men of lawe* and marchauntis . . . synnen more in avarice þen done pore laboreres "; *Roman de la Rose*, l. 5812 (ed. Michel, I, p. 170; cf. Chaucerian Frag.-B, ll. 5721-23), on *advocates* and physicians; etc. Avarice herself becomes an advocate in the *Pèlerinage* (ll. 18244 ff.), and the long section in the *Mirour* (ll. 24817-25176) on the " gens de loy " offers abundant evidence. These are merely representative examples.
[76] *Publications*, p. 110, n. 35.

as do the two preceding sections also. Anyway, the *Parson* uses the basilisk (I, 852) to illustrate the *covetousness* of *Lechery*. (ii) Hoccleve's comparison (*Regement of Princes*, 2815 f.) " of the Law to the *venomous spider,* which catches little flies, and lets big ones go." " Venomous " (which *is* a word that connotes Envy—and the only thing in the passage which does) is Mr. Tupper's own interpolation; it is not in Hoccleve.[77] The reason for this is good; *cobwebs* are not venomous. Tupper has been misled by Furnivall's gloss.[78] The simile of the *spider* is used for *Avarice* in the *Pèlerinage*.[79] (iii) Langland's making Envy instruct friars " to lerne logik and lawe " (C. xxiii, 273). Yes, " and eke *contemplacioun*, And preche men of Plato and prouen hit by Seneca." Did the Clerk of Oxford, " that un-to *logik* badde long y-go," and St. Cecilia, " [quae] fuit ... coelum per jugem *contemplationem* " also exemplify Envy ? Mr. Tupper's logic inexorably requires it. (iv) The testimony of Bromyard of Hereford, which I have not been able to verify. (v) " The sorry part played by ' Civile ' or Civil Law in *Piers Plowman.*" I suppose that this sorry part is the fact that " Civile " is throughout associated with *Simony,* a branch of *Avarice.*[80]

---

[77] P. 102, ll. 2819-21: " Ri3t as lop-webbys, flyes smale and gnattes taken, and suffre grete flyes go, ffor al þis worlde, lawe is now rewlyd so."

[78] For " lop-wehbe " see *Astrolabe*, I, 21, 3: " The Riet of thyn Astrolabie with thy zodiak, shapen in maner of a net or of a *loppe-webbe.*" For " loppe," see I, 19, 3: " crokede strykes lyk to the clawes of a *loppe* "; I, 3, 4: " a wehbe of a *loppe.*"

[79] Ll. 17560 ff.: " And as an yreyne sowketh the flye," etc. It is Avarice herself who is speaking, with reference to her treatment of the poor.

[80] " Symonye and Cyuile " (B, II, 62, 66, 71, 167, 168); " And preide Cyuile to se · and Symonye to rede it " (70); " Bi si3te of sire Symonye · and Cyules leve " (113); " Here-to assenteth Cyuile · ac Symonye ne wolde " (141). See Book II, *passim.*

(vi) This, and many passages in Gower and Wyclif, "prove that the legal profession was then infected by cov- etousness of wealth and *contempt for poverty*—by Avarice intermingled with *Envy.*" No, with P*ride!!* "It is note- worthy that Gower classes *the contempt ... for the poor and humble* under *the Inobedience phase of Pride,* just as Chaucer does here [in the *Wife of Bath's Tale*]." [81] That is Tupper, deplorably divided against himself. (vi) " The advocate is the butt of many *exempla* in such example- books as Jacques de Vitry's and the *Liber Exemplorum.*" True; but one is still to be cited which associates him with *Envy.* I can only say that I have not found it.—In his *Nation* article Mr. Tupper speaks of " Chaucer's final ascription of the prologue of Murmuration ... to the Man of Law as an exponent of Envy [as] vindicated by *the many mediæval illustrations* of the unfavorable conception of *this supposedly envious profession* presented in [his] article on ' Chaucer and the Seven Deadly Sins.' " We have seen " the many mediæval illustrations." And I ac- cept Mr. Tupper's own phrase regarding the " *supposedly* envious profession." For all that has been shown, it is only that and nothing more. The irony, as Mr. Tupper sees it, has no basis whatsoever in the facts.

I do not know whether the next point falls under the head of irony or not. In any case, the theory (in the eyes of which it now begins to seem that all the world's but Sins, and all the men and women merely Vices) is not content with drawing lawyers under the heading *De Invidia,* but must needs hale merchants thither too. " It is no chance coincidence with Chaucer that Envy in the

---

[81] *Publications,* p. 101. " It is *a chief phase of Pride to scorn the poor,*" Tupper goes on (n. 16), and cites Langland's " *poverte to despise* " (B. II, 79) in his support. To make assurance double sure, he *repeats* this slip in the *Nation,* p. 41. See below, p. 324.

Elizabethan interlude makes large mention of *merchants* and men of law. *Both* of these occupations were deemed by men of the Middle Ages to be tainted with a base desire for wealth and a sovereign contempt for the poor." [82]   " A base desire for wealth " is *Avarice:* " a sovereign contempt for the poor " (*teste* Mr. Tupper and the categories) is *Pride.*[83] But of that no fors. As for Envy's " large mention " of merchants in the Interlude, I shall only ask my readers to look up the evidence for themselves.[84] Envy is merely pointing out, in a passage-at-arms with Peace, that both merchants and lawyers are gainers by strife, and (in a similar tilt with Conscience) that both would hang Conscience, could they catch him. But Mr. Tupper cites two more examples " of a score." The first is from Wyclif, in his sermon against Envy (III, p. 133): " And so uneven dealing of goods of this world *engenders much envy* among these worldly men.[85] And so parts of this community [86] and especially merchants *move to this envy* by deceit of their craft." [87] Are merchants therefore envious because their happier state *moves others to Envy?* As for " the rich merchants who but live to gain more wealth," in the *Romance of the Rose,* that is all Ellis [88] except " mer-

---

[82] *Nation*, p. 41.   [83] See above, p. 323.

[84] *Impatient Poverty*, pp. 314-15, 327-28.

[85] I. e., "þo þridde part of þe chirche " (" þo laboreres," " þo puple," " pore men of þo comyne "). The subject of Wyclif's chapter is *the causes of envy* among the laity, as contrasted with priests and knights.

[86] Rather, " commonalty, the commons, the laity."

[87] " Deceite bitwixe marchant and marchant " is under *Avarice* in the *Parson's Tale* (I, 776). Compare the whole section on " Chaffer " (under *Avarice*) in the *Ayenbite* (pp. 44-45); the section on " fals marchaundyse " (under *Avarice*) in *Jacob's Well* (pp. 133-34); *Handlyng Synne*, ll. 5945-50; etc.

[88] *Temple Classics*, I, p. 177. For the text, see ed. Michel, I, p. 166, ll. 5703-07.

chants." It is from a conventional account of the "tribulations of the rich," and even Ellis understood it aright, for his translation goes straight on: "what miseries they are fain To undergo with will to pile Riches on riches; *avarice vile* Hath seized their hearts," etc. The Chaucerian translator (a "man of the Middle Ages") also understood it so, with his "*gredinesse.*"[89] The passage has not the slightest connection with *Envy*. As usual, it is *Avarice* that is involved.[90] In a word, merchants and men of law alike (indubitably classed together in many mediæval documents) were "deemed by men of the Middle Ages to be tainted with" *Avarice*. The addition of *Envy* is unsupported by the facts.

What, in this case, of the "crowning argument?" "Why should we hesitate to regard the Poverty Prologue to the Man of Law's Envy *exemplum*[91] as a studied presentation of the Envious mood,[92] when the Parson himself assures us that the *motif* of these stanzas, 'grucching against poverty' and 'sorwe of other mannes wele' are among the chief traits[93] of this Vice?"[94] This rests entirely on Mr. Tupper's previous contentions, and stands or falls with them. Its upshot is a statement that the Par-

---

[89] B-Fragment, ll. 5590-5600. Compare also *Roman de la Rose*, ed. Michel, I, p. 169 (ll. 5792 ff.), where the connection with Avarice becomes still more explicit, and goes on to include (ll. 5812 ff.) advocates, physicians, and preachers. See the B-Fragment, ll. 5697 ff.

[90] For the *Avarice* of merchants, see above, p. 324, n. 87, and add Wyclif (ed. Arnold), III, p. 153: "þo þridde part of þo Chirche . . . hafs mony partis smytted wiþ avarice, *and specially marchaundis*"; *Vox Clamantis*, Bk. v, chaps. xii-xiv; *Mirour de l'Omme*, ll. 25177-25980; Barclay, II, p. 169 (foot); etc. But the point is too obvious to need illustration.

[91] For this, see below, p. 326.   [92] See above, p. 321.

[93] See above, p. 311.   [94] *Publications*, p. 116.

son's sermon on the Seven Deadly Sins includes a discussion of Envy.

" This is," indeed, " a long preamble of a tale " ! But we may now turn to " the Envy *exemplum*" itself, to wit, the Tale of Constance. In Gower it is used to exemplify Detraction.[95] That is indubitable. But Gower (it is equally indubitable) is merely impressing into the service of his vast schematic plan a tale which has no necessary association whatever with the Sins, but which, on the contrary, has a long and honorable career apart from them.[96] In that development, except for Gower's *ad hoc* employment of the tale, it is the figure of Constance that consistently stands out. And when Mr. Tupper says [97] that " the *Man of Law's Tale,* though *primarily of Envy* (as the little Prologue shows) exalts the loyalty and strength of the stately wife and mother," his theory has led him to a *hysteron proteron.* But since I am scrupulously refraining, in this paper, from all direct consideration of Chaucer's art, in my sole concern with the foundations of a theory, I shall not dwell on what seems to me to have been Chaucer's emphasis.

Instead, since I now know the Sins myself almost as well as my Paternoster and even better than my Creed, I shall offer myself as a fair substitute for the mediæval

[95] It is, of course, Detraction in *love* (see gloss to II, · 587 ff.). Mr. Tupper is mistaken, however, if he supposes that Detraction is a *Merkmal* of Envy alone. It is a " spyce " of *Pride* in *Handlyng Synne* (p. 122); the Parson includes it (as a phase of spiritual homicide) under *Wrath* (I, 565); and in *Jacob's Well* it is classed under *Gluttony*, as a Sin of the Tongue (p. 150; cf. *Ayenbite*, p. 62).

[96] See especially Siefkin, *Das geduldige Weib in der englischen Literatur bis auf Shakspere:* Teil I: Der Konstanzetypus (Rathenow, 1903).

[97] *Publications*, pp. 122-23. Cf. *Nation*, Oct. 16, 1913, p. 355.

adept in the categories. And as such I conceive the Tale of Constance, guided wholly by the manuals that I know, in a fashion very different from Mr. Tupper's interpretation. For to my mediæval prototype the heroine's very name must have betrayed her import. Cecilia was the antitype of Sloth; Virginia the antitype of Lechery; here is a tale in which another noble central figure stands for " *Constaunce,* that is, stablenesse of corage ... in herte by stedefast feith, and in mouth, and in beringe, and in chere and in dede." [98] She is, indeed, own sister to St. Cecilia, for Constance is a branch of that Fortitude which (in the theory) Cecilia represents.[99] Constance is a main division of Prouesce in the *Mirour;* [100] it is the fifth step of Prouesse in the *Ayenbite;* [101] the fifth part of Proesce in Frère Lorens; [102] the fifth part of Fortitudo in the *Summa Virtutum;* [103] in all it is the antitype of *Sloth.* And Chaucer's own interpolation in the Tale (ll. 932-45) is explicit in its emphasis on this high virtue:

> How may this wayke womman han this *strengthe* . . .[104]
> Who yaf Judith *corage* or *hardinesse* . . .[105]
>   . . . I seye, for this entente,

---

[98] *Parson's Tale,* I, 735—under Fortitude, the remedy for *Sloth.*

[99] See above, p. 298. And compare Siefkin (pp. 23, 76), who links the two together.

[100] Ll. 14317 ff.   [101] Pp. 167-68.

[102] Eilers, p. 570.   [103] Petersen, p. 66, n. 1.

[104] A vertu that is called Fortitudo or *Strengthe* " (I, § 60). In the *Ayenbite* (pp. 161 ff.) Prowess is designated as " þe yefþe of *Strengþe.*"

[105] " Constaunce, that is, stableness of *corage* " (I, § 61) ; " Prowesse is huanne *corage* onworþeþ al þet ne is naȝt in his pouer " (*Ayenbite,* p. 164) ; " Ac huanne god yefþ to þe manne þise grace . . . þet me clepeþ þe gost of *strengþe.* he hym yefþ ane newe herte *ane noble herte and hardi . . . Hardyesse* uor to þolie alle þe kueadnesse þet þe wordle may þreapni " (*ibid.,* p. 162) ; " þis ground of *strengthe or hardynesse* " (*Jacob's* Well, p. 288).

> That, right as god spirit of vigour sente
> To hem, and saved hem out of meschance,
> So sent he *might and vigour* to Custance.[106]

Could the mediæval reader go astray ? [107]   Constance, like
Cecilia, is the antitype of Sloth.   And see, now, with what
exquisite aptness the Impatient Poverty Prologue is
adjusted to the Tale.   For Impatience is a *branch* of
Sloth ! [108]   Tale and Prologue fit each other like hand and
glove—a Prologue of " inpacience agayns god " ; [109]   a
Tale of that " pacience. be [which] uirtue þe guode ouer-
comþ alle his uyendes. þane dyeuel. þe wordle. and þet
uless." [110]   Nor has Chaucer left us without other unequivocal indications of his purpose.   Even *Cecilia's* " bisinesse " was not so marked as that of Constance :

> She was *so diligent, with-outen slouthe* ...
> That alle hir loven that loken on hir face.[111]

And as in the Second Nun's Prologue, so in the *Man of
Law's Tale* we have " the most effective sort of protest
against Sloth in its phase of *Undevotion.*"   Only this time
it is not a nameless prologist, but the central figure of the

---

[106] " This vertu [Fortitudo] is *so mighty and so vigorous,* that
it dar withstonde mightily," etc. (I, § 60).   Cf. *Jacob's Well,* p.
289 : " þe ʒyfte of *strengthe,* whiche ʒyfte schal make þe *strong and
myʒty* to dure."

[107] Is not Tupper himself among those who see the light and know it
not ?   Constance " achieves in the end the high reward of her
strength and loyalty " (*Nation,* Oct. 16, 1913, p. 355) ; the Tale
" exalts the loyalty and *strength* of the stately wife and mother "
(*Publications,* p. 123).

[108] " þe oþer poynt [of Sleuþe] is *inpacience* " (*Ayenbite,* p. 33) ;
" þe secunde fote brede [of Accidia] is *vnpacience* " (*Jacob's Well,*
p. 112).   And " inpacience " is the fourteenth twig of Sloth in Frère
Lorens (Eilers, p. 535).

[109] I, 497.

[110] *Ayenbite,* p. 167—under " þe uerþe stape of Prouesse."

[111] B, 530, 532.

Tale herself, who employs " the antidote against Sloth."
For Constance uses Hymns *both* of our Lord and of our
Lady. Her address to the Cross [112] is a cento of reminiscences of the first.[113] The " Invocacio ad Mariam " [114]—
once more on Constance's own lips—is full of phrases
from the second. And we have our Idleness Prologue, too!
Only this time it is no accident. It is the Master of Cere-
monies himself who, *in calling on the speaker,* gives him
his *motif*:

> ' Lordinges, the tyme wasteth night and day,
> And steleth from us, what *prively slepinge,*
> And what *thurgh necligence* in our wakinge,
> As dooth the streem, that turneth never agayn ...
> *Lat us nat moulen thus in ydelnsse.*
> Sir man of lawe,' quod he, ' so have ye blis,
> Tel us a tale anon, as forward is.' [115]

" Who can miss the present purport of the Idleness [lines],
or ignore the formal intent of [Constance's] zest of devotion ? " [116] Even the subtlest sort of *irony* is present too.
For of whom but the Man of Law has Chaucer said:

> No-wher so bisy a man as he ther nas,
> *And yet he semed bisier than he was.*[117]

Nor does the " crowning argument " this time desert us;
the notable correspondence between the " Fortitude stanzas " [118] and the Parson's *remedium* against Sloth is

---

[112] B, 451-462. " O clere, o welful auter, holy croys," etc.

[113] Before Mr. Tupper's article was written I had collected the evidence for this statement, which I may some day print. The hymn
which Skeat quotes (*Oxford Chaucer*, v, p. 155) is only one of several involved.

[114] B, 841-54. " Moder " quod she, " and mayde bright, Marye ...
Thou haven of refut, brighte sterre of day," etc.

[115] B, 20-23, 32-34.   [116] *Publications*, pp. 115-16.

[117] A, 321-22.   [118] B, 932-45 above.

unmistakable. The *Second Nun's Tale* itself is not so unequivocally " tagged." The Host's Idleness Prologue, the Man of Law's Impatience (let us say, Sloth) Prologue, the Fortitude Tale (with Constance's " bisinesse " and her protest against Undevotion), the element of irony, and the crowning argument all unite in one entire and perfect chrysolite.—" Glosinge is a glorious thing, certeyn "] [119]

VII

We need not dwell so long upon the *Manciple's Tale,* the illustration of the Sin of *Chiding.* " Gower tells very briefly (*Confessio,* III, 783-817), the story of Phoebus and Cornis, to illustrate *Chiding or Cheste,* the second of his divisions of Wrath. We shall see that *his moral is exactly the same as Chaucer's,* who *derives his story directly from Ovid."* [1] Tupper's view is here given in a nutshell. Let us examine it.

First, " Cheste " is not necessarily " Chiding " at all. The heading of the section in the Confessio begins: " Ira mouet *litem,* que lingue frena resoluens Laxa per infames currit vbique vias." [2] The gloss begins: " Hic tractat Confessor super secunda specie Ire, *que Lis dicitur."* The story of Socrates is an " exemplum de paciencia in amore *contra lites* habenda." [3] (The tale of Jupiter, Juno, and Tiresias is an " exemplum, quod *de alterius*

---

[119] I shall not take the trouble to shatter this creation of my own. " It is a pratty childe," as Mak's wife says of the *ci-devant* sheep. So are they all—these changelings left of late with Chaucer by the Seven Deadly Sins.

[1] *Publications,* p. 99, n. 12.

[2] III, between lines 416 and 417.

[3] Opposite III, 639 ff. See " *strif* " in l. 650.

lite intromittere cauendum est." [4]   The gloss to the tale of Phoebus and Cornis begins: " Quia *litigantes* ora sua cohibere nequiunt." [5]   *Lis,* of course, is " strife, dispute, quarrel."   Nor is Gower less explicit in his employment of the English word: " To fyhte or for *to make cheste* "; [6] " So is ther noght bot *strif and cheste.*" [7]   And so Macaulay properly defines " Cheste " as " contention (in words)."   Its use in *Piers Plowman* is similar, [8] and Skeat defines it as " strife, quarrelling."   Murray defines it as " strife, contention, quarrelling," and cites Ælfric (where it glosses *Seditio*), and the *Ancren Riwle* (" cheaste oþer *Strif* ").   " Cheaste " in the *Ayenbite* [9] has seven branches: " Strif, chidinge, missigginge, godelinge, atwytinge, þreapninge, vnonynge."   " Cheste ' may *include* Chiding [10] (and a variety of other things), but to *identify* Chiding with Cheste is to deal freely with facts —and also to plunge headlong into difficulties.

For the point of Gower's discussion of Cheste is clear. It is the fact that Cheste *" berth evere his mowth unpinned "*: [11]

> For as a Sive kepeth Ale,
> *Riht so can Cheste kepe a tale.*[12]

That is the point not only of the section in general, but

---

[4] Opposite III, 736 ff. The tale itself begins: " Yit cam ther nevere good of *strif.*"

[5] Opposite III, 783 ff.   [7] v, 541.

[6] *Prologue,* l. 215.   [8] See, for instance, C. I, 103-08.

[9] Pp. 65-67 (Sins of the Tongue). Richard Morris also translates it *Strife,* in both his heading and his gloss (see p. 65).

[10] Wyclif (cited by Murray) translates *James,* IV, 1 (" Unde bella et *lites* in vobis? "): " Wherof bateyles and *cheestes,* or *chidinges,* among ȝou? " The Parson (who does not include it under " Chydinge," I, § 42) is somewhat ambigious: " Thanne stant the sinne of contumelie or stryf and *cheeste* " (I, 555).

[11] III, 424. Compare also the Latin verses at the head of the section.

[12] III, 433-34.

of the tale of Phoebus and Cornis in particular, which is
an "exemplum contra illos qui in amoris causa *alterius
consilium reuelare presumunt.*" [13] It has nothing to do
with Chiding. This Tupper evidently sees. For when
he comes to his "crowning argument," he refers us to
the "Parson's sermon, *in its section upon Wrath* (I,
647 f.)." [14] The part of the section referred to (I, 647 f.)
is the discussion of "*ydel wordes*" (§ 47)[15]—not *chiding*
at all. The discussion of "*Chydinge* and reproche" is
§ 42. Furthermore, Mr. Tupper tells us that "it is interesting to compare the Manciple's lines (H, 343 f.)" on
Jangling "with the Parson's words on the same theme
(I, 648)." [16] The comparison is perfectly apt, but I, 648
is yet *another* subhead of Wrath. "*Chydynge and reproche* . . . scorninge . . . wikked conseil . . . discord
. . . double tongue . . . biwreying of conseil . . . man-
ace . . . ydel wordes . . . *janglinge*" (I, 648)—so the

---

[13] Gloss (III, 783 ff.). See also the introductory lines, quoted below,
p. 334, n. 23.

[14] *Publications,* p. 102.

[15] "Biwreying of conseil" immediately precedes (§ 47).

[16] *Publications,* p. 102, n. 19. It is also interesting to compare the
Manciple's lines on Jangling "with the Parson's words on the same
theme" in *I, 405:* "Janglinge, is when men speken to muche biforn
folk, and clappen as a mille, and taken no kepe what they seye."
But that is P*ride*. (Compare also *Cursor Mundi*, ll. 27620-22;
Pèlerinage, 14414). It is still further interesting to compare what
Gower himself says (*Confessio,* II, 398, 425, 452-54) about *jangling* in
affairs of love (the Manciple's own theme), especially the lover's
conclusion:

> *I telle it noght to ten ne tuelve,*
> Therof I wol me wel avise,
> To speke or *jangle* in eny wise
> That toucheth to my ladi name (II, 524-27).

But that is *Envy*. The interest grows when we compare P*iers
Plowman*, B. II, 93-94: "And alday to drynke. at dyuerse tauernes,
And there to *iangle* and to *iape*." But that is *Gluttony*. See
below, p. 341.

branches run. We are given no evidence for *Chiding* whatsoever. When Mr. Tupper states (in applying the argument from correspondence with the *Parson's Tale*) that the Manciple " concludes his tale of *Chiding* by a *copious use* of the Parson's words *against that fault*," [17] he is running counter to the facts. To argue that a Tale exemplifies one branch of Wrath, because it exemplifies *two other branches,* comes very near what Mr. Tupper himself has called a " perverted endeavor to adapt false premises to a conclusion that admits of large doubt." [18]

But there is the *moral* of the Tale. The moral in Gower is " exactly the same as Chaucer's." The moral which Tupper quotes, however, is *not*, as it happens, *the moral of the story of Phoebus and Cornis.* It follows the *next* tale, that of Jupiter and Laar. The moral of the tale of Phoebus is as follows:

> Be war therfore and sei the beste,
> If thou wolt be thiself in reste,
> Mi goode Sone, as I the rede.[19]

And the story of Jupiter and Laar has its own application too :

> And suche adaies be now felc
> In loves Court, as it is seid,
> *That lete here tunges gon unteid.*[20]

What Tupper quotes is the " application " *of the whole section on Cheste:*

> Mi Sone, be thou non of tho,
> To jangle and telle tales so,
> And namely that thou ne chyde,
> For Cheste can no conseil hide,
> For Wraththe seide nevere wel.[21]

---

[17] *Publications*, p. 116.
[18] *Publications of the Modern Language Association*, XXVI, p. 236.
[19] III, 815-17.   [20] III, 828-30.   [21] III, 831-35.

14

Even apart from the question of the validity of the evidence we are asked to accept, the slip is an unfortunate one. For the reference to *Chiding* harks back to *another* part of the section. Gower, of course, like Dan Michel, makes mention of Chiding *under* Cheste,[22] and the summary includes that. It is not, however, the phase of Cheste which the story of Phoebus and Cornis exemplifies at all. *That* is summed up in " To jangle and telle tales so. . . *For Cheste can no conseil hide.*"[23] Even waiving the implications of the error, however, we are no better off. Let us assume that the lines which Tupper quotes *are* the moral of the tale of Phoebus and the crow. This moral, then, is (according to Tupper) " exactly the same is the fact that the crucial words " chide " or " chiding " the " exactness " of the correspondence between the two[24] is the fact that the crucial words " chide " or " chiding " do not occur in the Manciple's " application " at all, nor do they appear in his Tale from beginning to end. The only point where the two morals do come together is in their insistence on the evils of *jangling* and of *telling tales*—and those are two *other* branches of Wrath. The theme of the Manciple's " morality," both implicitly and explicitly (see ll. 343, 348, 350), is, of course, *jangling.* It begins with the crow (" My sone, thenk on the crowe, a goddes name ") and it ends with the crow (" Kepe wel

---

[22] See III, 472-77, and cf. 443, 492, 534, 552, 565, 575, 580, 591.

[23] See especially the correspondence with the second line of the *introduction* to the tale of Phœbus: " Hold conseil and descoevre it noght, *For Cheste can no conseil hele,* Or be it wo or be it wele: And tak a tale into thi mynde, The which of olde ensample I finde " (II, 778-82)—and the " olde ensample " is the tale of the crow. See also the gloss, quoted above, p. 332. The moral of the next tale (the " tunges unteid ") has been given above.

[24] The one (it may be observed) has *five,* the other *fifty-three* lines.

thy tonge, and thenk up-on the crowe "), and all between is in keeping with that. If Chaucer meant the *Manciple's Tale* to exemplify Chiding, he was singularly careless in affixing his " moral tags to the tale." [25]

And in any case, Chiding, like the other branches, is something of a will-o-the-wisp among the Sins. Mr. Tupper remarks that Langland too deems *Chiding* one of the divisions of *Wrath*.[26] The lines in question are as follows:

> And the erldome of *enuye* · *and wratthe togidres,*
> With the chastelet of *chest* · and chateryng-out-of-resoun.

The identification of Chiding and Cheste [27] we have already seen to be incorrect. And of the two Sins mentioned, it is *Envy,* not Wrath, that claims Chiding proper in *Piers Plowman:*

> Eche a word that he [Enuye] warpe · was of an addres tonge,
> Of *chydynge* and of chalangynge · was his chief lyflode.[28]

Moreover, Chiding is a " spyce " of *Pride* in *Handlyng Synne*.[29] In the same document,[30] and also in *Jacob's Well*,[31] it is included under *Gluttony*. As Mr. Chambers remarks, with reference to the branches of *Wrath:* " If it is objected that we have already had these sins under *Pride,* that is to be ascribed ... *to Mediæval Theology*." [32] And it is just what William James would have called the " blooming welter " of Mediæval Theology that Mr. Tupper refuses to take into account. When we consider the

---

[25] *Publications*, p. 119.   [26] *Publications*, p. 102, n. 20.

[27] In which Mr. Chambers anticipates Tupper. He comments (*Modern Language Review*, v, p. 19) on the lines above: " *Chiding and chattering* rightly come under Wrathe."

[28] B. v, 87-88.

[29] Pp. 121-22, especially ll. 3515-16, 3525-26.

[30] Pp. 221-22, especially ll. 6887 ff.

[31] P. 145, l. 10.   [32] P. 19.

trouble the branches have given in *Piers Plowman,* even
when they are labelled, we may question the mediæval
reader's inerrancy, when, without rubrics or tags, he
enters upon the merry game of " Cherchez le péché."

The conclusion of the whole matter, of course, lies in
the fact which Tupper himself points out: " [Chaucer]
derives his story directly from Ovid." And the key to
Ovid's narrative is succinctly given in two lines:

> *Lingua fuit damno: lingua faciente loquaci,*
> Cui color albus erat, nunc est contrarius albo.[33]

That was quite enough for Chaucer. With Albertano of
Brescia " at his beddes heed," the rest was easy.

We have seen that in the " crowning argument " the
Parson leads us wofully astray among the branches.
What of the element of *irony?* " Amusingly enough, the
chief feature of the Prologue of this teller of a tale against
Chiding is his long revilement of the drunken Cook...
This chiding is reproved by the Host, and the Manciple
makes his *amende.*" [34] I *am* " so incautious as to admit
that [the Manciple] really does chide the Cook " [35]—as
the Host and the Pilgrims " chidde " each other spitously
many times in the give and take of the Pilgrimage! The
Manciple is not even *primus inter pares.* What I wish to
point out is the fact (overlooked by Mr. Tupper) that the
Manciple, according to the rigid categories themselves, did
not thereby exemplify a Deadly Sin, as " every lewed viker
or person " would know. The Parson, who is the last
authority, declares explicitly that " sodeyn Ire or hastif
Ire, withouten avisement and consentinge of resoun " is
different from Ire " that comth of felonye of herte avy-

---

[33] *Met.,* II, 540-41. Compare the emphasis throughout the story:
" loquax " (l. 535), " garrula " (l. 547), and ll. 549-50.

[34] *Publications,* p. 109.   [35] *Journal,* p. 565.

sed and cast biforn." As for the first, " the mening and
the sens of this is, that the resoun of man *ne consente nat*
to thilke sodeyn Ire; *and thanne it is venial.*" [36] The
Manciple says categorically: " That that I spak, *I seyde
it in my bourde.*" [37] Even granting (as I do not) that the
Tale is a tale of Chiding, the Prologue is not a *Sins* Prologue. Moreover, it may be conceded that Harry Bailly
is a fairly good witness. And he suggests (without undue
delicacy) in his " reproof " of the Manciple, that that
worthy's weak spot is his *Avarice:*

> Another day he wol, peraventure,
> Reclayme thee, and bringe thee to lure;
> I mene, he speke wol of smale thinges,
> *As for to pinchen at thy rekeninges,*
> *That were not honeste, if it cam to preef.*[38]

And this is in entire keeping with Chaucer's exposition in
the General Prologue, which reaches its climax in the
closing line:

> And yit this maunciple sette hir aller cappe.[39]

That is good first-hand evidence—if we are Sin-hunting!
In a word, Cheste is not properly Chiding; the parallels
with the *Parson's Tale* are with two other branches; there
is no Chiding in the Tale; Gower's moral (which is not
the right one) and Chaucer's have other things in common,
but *not* Chiding; Chiding is a branch of other Sins besides
Wrath; the Manciple's sort of Chiding is not a mortal Sin
in any case; and the Manciple (so far as he is anything)
is avaricious. Therefore the *Manciple's Tale* exemplifies
" the Chiding phase of Wrath."

Of course it is perfectly obvious that if the *Manciple's
Tale* is to stand for Wrath at all, it should be for Wrath in

[36] I, 540.
[37] H, 81.
[38] H, 71-75.
[39] A, 586.

general. Like the *Summoner's Tale* it has its " homily
against Ire." [40]   The crime itself is committed in Ire
(l. 265), and so comes under Homicide, a branch of Ire in
practically all the categories.[41]   The " rakelnesse " on
which Phœbus dwells (ll. 283, 289) is the " Folhaste " of
the *Confessio*,[42] the ": Fole hastivesse " of the *Mirour*,[43]
etc. The address to the crow as " Traitour ... with tonge
of scorpioun " (l. 271) identifies the crow as a false flatterer,[44] and the P*arson* includes Flattery under Ire (I,
§ 40). Similarly, the crow's *lying* (l. 293) comes under
Wrath (I, § 39). And we have already seen Jangling,
Idle Words, and Betraying of Counsel. The Tale is
an amazingly rich *exemplum* of Wrath pure and simple, on Mr. Tupper's own hypothesis. But he has
already assigned Wrath to *two* Tales (the Summoner's
and the Friar's) and has managed to expel it from
another (the Pardoner's), where it proved embarrassing. It would obviously be overdoing Wrath to bring
it in again, except in some special way. That way (at
the expense of this veritable treasure-trove of Wrath tags)
is through the *Sins of the Tongue*. And this involves
still further inconsistencies, which I shall deal with very
briefly.

" Chaucer's phase of Wrath (Chiding) in the last tale
of the collection might seem to some superfluous after the
elaborate exemplification of Wrath in the Friar-Summoner
quarrel and tales. But as we have seen, *the Sins of the*

---

[40] H, 279-91.

[41] *Parson's Tale*, Peraldus, Raymund of Pennaforte, *Pèlerinage*,
Confessio, Mirour, Ayenbite, Jacob's Well.

[42] III, 1096 ff., 1751 ff., 1861 ff.

[43] Ll. 4741 ff. Compare especially Chaucer's " unavysed " (l. 280)
and Gower's " unavised " (*Confessio*, III, 1098)—adding Spenser's
" unadvized " (F. Q., I, iv, 34, l. 3).

[44] See B, 404-06; E, 2058-59; *Bk. of Duchesse*, ll. 636-41.

Tongue well deserve specific exposition. Compare their place in *Le Mireour du Monde* and the *Ayenbite.*" [45] Here the inclusion of Chiding in the scheme is justified, because it *is* a Sin of the Tongue. Twenty-three pages earlier, however, occurs the following statement: " Significantly enough both Chaucer and Gower deem Chiding one of the divisions of Wrath, *whereas in many mediæval catalogues of the Sins, this fault is classed apart from the Deadly Seven as a Sin of the Tongue.*" [46] That can mean, if I understand English at all, just one thing—namely, that in Chaucer Chiding, as a division of Wrath, is *not* (as in many mediæval catalogues) classed as a Sin of the Tongue.[47] On the one page (where the double treatment of Wrath is justified) the *connection* of Chiding with Sins of the Tongue is stressed; on the other (where the point is the inclusion of Chiding under Wrath) its *disjunction* from Sins of the Tongue is emphasized. But I do not care to dwell on this (at least seeming) discrepancy. It is another matter that concerns us. Mr. Tupper accords to Sins of the Tongue a threefold treatment. First, in many mediæval catalogues of the Sins they are classed *apart* from the Deadly Seven; [48] second, they are included under *Wrath;* [49] third, they are classed with *Gluttony.*[50] As for

---

[45] *Publications*, p. 125, n. 56.

[46] *Publications*, p. 102. On p. 96, " Chiding, as a Sin of the Tongue, is sometimes found *apart ... from its category of Wrath.*"

[47] It *is*, of course, so classed in Chaucer. The Parson concludes his discourse on Ire as follows: " Thise been *the sinnes that comen of the tonge*, that comen of Ire and of othere sinnes mo " (I, 653). The Parson simply happens to include Sins of the Tongue under Wrath.

[48] *Publications*, p. 102 (above).

[49] *Ibid.*, p. 125 (above).

[50] *Ibid.*, p. 125, n. 56: " Compare their place in *Le Mireour du Monde* and the *Ayenbite.*" That place Tupper himself states in " The Pardoner's Tavern ": " Dan Michel, in his *Ayenbite of Inwit* (pp. 56-57), following *Le Mireour du Monde* (pp. 170-171), discusses, *under the*

the first, I do not know the " many mediæval catalogues
of the Sins " in which Chiding (or any other fault) is
classed " *apart from the Deadly Seven* as a Sin of the
Tongue." The Sins of the Tongue are not classed apart
from the Seven in any of the categories on which Tupper
himself relies, nor does he himself so treat them. The contrary is true, as we shall see. The second is the Parson's
classification, which Tupper here accepts. The third (the
usage of the *Ayenbite* and *Jacob's Well*)[51] he follows in
" The Pardoner's Tavern." And this is what happens.

Chiding and Blasphemy are Sins of the Tongue in the
Parson's Tale, under *Wrath;* they are Sins of the Tongue
in the *Ayenbite,*[52] under *Gluttony.* In the *Manciple's Tale*
Chiding deserves specific exposition as a Sin of the Tongue,
and (in accordance with the Parson) it is " Chaucer's
phase of *Wrath.*" In the *Pardoner's Tale* Blasphemy,
another Sin of the Tongue, is withdrawn from Wrath
(where the Parson puts it), and " knitted up " with *Gluttony.* That is, the Sins of the Tongue (which are included
under both Wrath and Gluttony in the categories) are
Wrath, when Mr. Tupper is exemplifying Wrath; they
are Gluttony, when Gluttony is to be exemplified. To put
it another way: the mediæval reader would know, in interpreting the *Manciple's Tale,* that *Chiding,* one Sin of the
Tongue, was *Wrath;* he would also know, in interpreting

---

head of Gluttony, 'the zennes that byeth ydo ine the taverne'"
(*Journal,* p. 559). And in the *Ayenbite,* as Chambers remarks
(*Modern Language Review,* v, p. 20) : "Evil speaking of all kinds goes
with gluttony *as being a sin of the mouth* (*Ayenbite,* p. 50)." The
italics are Chambers's. Tupper's reference is scarcely happy as evidence for the place of Sins of the Tongue under *Wrath.*

[51] Sins of the Tongue are classed with absolute explicitness (as
" Sins of the Tavern ") under Gluttony in *Jacob's Well.* See the
passage quoted above, p. 274. In the *Ayenbite,* Gluttony and Sins of
the Tongue are classed together as Sin of the Mouth (p. 50).

[52] Pp. 65, 69·

the *Pardoner's Tale,* that *Blasphemy,* another Sin of the Tongue, was *Gluttony.* That, however, is not all. The *Manciple's Tale* illustrates *Jangling,* and Mr. Tupper refers Jangling, as we have seen, to Wrath. Here (with its next line added) is the passage from *Piers Plowman* which Tupper quotes [53] in support of his contention that "Great Oaths" denote Gluttony:

> Glotonye he gaf hem eke · and *grete othes* togydere,
> And alday to drynke · at dyuerse tauernes,
> And there *to iangle* and to iape · and iugge here euene cristene.[54]

"Great Oaths" and Jangling stand side by side. The first Tupper refers (in the *Pardoner's Tale*) to Gluttony; the second (in the *Manciple's Tale*) to Wrath. The situation, in other words (to put it plainly), is this. *Blasphemy* in the *Parson's Tale* is under *Wrath;* in *Piers Plowman* it is under *Gluttony.* When Mr. Tupper wishes to prove the Pardoner the embodiment of Gluttony, he abandons the Parson and follows Piers. *Jangling* in the *Parson's Tale* is under *Wrath;* in *Piers Plowman* it is under *Gluttony.* The parallel is exact. When Mr. Tupper wishes to prove the Manciple the embodiment of Wrath, he abandons Piers and holds with the Parson. The tangle in which he has involved himself is hopeless. It could not well be otherwise, on his consistent principle of interpretation—that of selecting out of the mass of conflicting classifications what fits his immediate purpose, and treating the rest as non-existent. I do not believe that Mr. Tupper has realized the inconsistencies into which his initial "fallacy of false assumption"—that of the rigidity of the categories—has betrayed him. But the inconsistencies are there, and they are fatal to his argument.

[53] *Publications,* p. 105, n. 26; *Journal,* p. 561.
[54] B. ii, 92-94.

VIII

" The Wife of Bath," in Mr. Tupper's opinion, " illustrates Pride." [1] More specifically, in the *Wife of Bath's
Tale* Chaucer has " handled Gower's theme of Pride (Inobedience)." [2] The latter statement is true, but it is not all
the truth. Mr. Tupper fails to tell us that the Tale of
Florent in the *Confessio* does not illustrate Inobedience in
general, but " *Murmur and Compleignte* " as a special
phase of it. [3] The section begins as follows :

> Toward this vice of which we trete
> Ther ben yit tweie of thilke estrete,
> Here name is *Murmur and Compleignte:*
> Ther can noman here chiere peinte,
> To sette a glad semblant therinne,
> For thogh fortune make hem wynne,
> *Yit grucchen thei,* and if thei lese,
> Ther is no weie forto chese,
> Wherof thei myhten stonde appesed.
> So ben thei comunly desesed;
> *Ther may no welthe ne poverte*
> Attempren hem to the decerte
> Of buxomnesse be no wise. [4]

Indeed, I know no better characterization of the lines that
precede the Tale of Florent than Mr. Tupper's own phrase
for the Man of Law's Prologue, " a prelude of Murmura-

---

[1] *Publications*, p. 112.   [2] *Publications*, p. 99.

[3] The section has its own heading: " *Murmur* in aduersis ita
concipit ille superbus, Pena quod ex bina sorte perurget eum.
Obuia fortune cum spes in amore resistit,. *Non sine mentali murmure plangit amans.*" (I, before l. 1343). The gloss reads: " H́ic
loquitur *de Murmure et Planctu*, qui super omnes alios Inobediencie
secreciores vt ministri illi deseruiunt." And Macaulay's page-
heading for the section is " [Murmur and Complaint]."

[4] I, 1343-55. Cf. 1363: " Yit wol thei *grucche* be som weie "; l.
1378: " *Of Murmur and Compleignte* of love "; l. 1385: " I *grucche*
anon "; l. 1389: " With *many a Murmur*, god it wot "; etc.

tion; " [5] and (as he tells us) " from the mediæval point of view such a prelude of Murmuration is an apt introduction to a tale of Detraction, its sister phase of *Envy*." [6] The application of Tupper's own principles might lead even a mediæval reader astray just here. That, however, in passing. The Tale of Florent is *not* told to exemplify Envy, but the " murmuring or 'grucching' phase " of Inobedience in love. [7] Mr. Tupper's main arguments for Chaucer's similar use of the Tale are two: [8] (i) the homily of the Loathly Lady is directed against Pride in birth and fortune, and " contempt . . . for the poor and humble "; [9] (ii) the Wife of Bath herself is the embodiment of Pride in general, and of Inobedience in particular. I grant at once that the elements scattered through the categories may be pieced together into this design. A totally differ-

[5] *Nation*, p. 41.

[6] So again: " We must not be surprised to find that to Chaucer and his fellows . . . Murmuration or 'Grucching' against one's own wretched lot belongs as truly to *Envy* as does Detraction of one's neighbors " (*Publications*, p. 95).

[7] With I, 1382-94 (the lover's description of his *silent* " grucching " against his lady) compare ll. 1781-94 of the tale.

[8] *Publications*, pp. 100-101, 108-09.

[9] Which (like Murmuration) Tupper twice interprets (it will be recalled) as *Envy*. When he says that " this excellent sermon is but an expansion of the commonplaces that *inevitably* appear in *all* mediæval discourses upon Pride " (*Publications*, p. 100), he is making a strong overstatement. He himself points out on the very next page (n. 15)—as we shall see below—that this is not the case in the *Confessio Amantis*. Nor is it in the *Pèlerinage;* and others might easily be added. He also greatly exaggerates, when he speaks (p. 115) of " the edifying commonplaces (on Gentilesse) with which, *in much the same language*, the Parson has preached against the first of the Vices " (compare also p. 101, n. 14). The test is perfectly easy to make, line by line. Mr. Tupper has forgotten, apparently, Jean de Meun, Boethius, and Dante (in the *Purgatorio*). The influence of the *Convivio* I have just pointed out. See below, p. 348, n. 23.

ent, yet even more "mediæval" pattern, however, lies ready at our hand. Let us first consider the "homily on Gentilesse."

According to Mr. Tupper, this homily is a preachment against Pride. And Gentilesse undoubtedly appears under Pride in a number of the categories. But the fundamental question (as Mr. Tupper will be the first to grant) is the use that is made of the Gentilesse passage *in the Tale.* And there, I think, the theory has made a slip. For Gentilesse has a perfectly clear and definite association with the categories, which Tupper has completely overlooked— or rather, which he has seen, but failed to recognize—and it is *this* association which Chaucer demonstrably had in mind, if he had any. *"Strangely enough,"* Tupper remarks, " 'Gentilesse' is introduced under *Sloth* by Gower (*Confessio,* IV, 2200 f.)." [10] The only thing strange is the fact that Tupper has been "sadly puzzled by a design so different from [his] twentieth-century conception" of the Sins. For he has forgotten entirely that Fortitude which, on his own assumption, St. Cecilia exemplified [11] —the familiar *Prowess,* which is the antitype of Sloth. For Gentilesse is a phase of *Prowess* in Gower, and it comes at the conclusion of his account of "the corage of hardiesce [which] *Is of knyhthode the prouesce."* [12] The examples of "prouesce" are Lancelot (a knight "of king Arthures hous"), Hercules, Penthesilea, Philemenis, and Æneas. Then comes the conclusion:

[10] *Publications,* p. 101, n. 15.

[11] See above, p. 298.

[12] IV, 2015-16. The discussion of Prowess includes lines 2014-2362. Fortitude, Strength, Force, and Prowess are interchangeable in the categories. Cf. I, § 60: "*Fortitudo* or *Strengthe*"—which in Frère Lorens (Eilers, p. 570) is "Le don de *force,*" or "la vertu de *proesce.*" It is unnecessary to go through the others. See also p. 327 above.

For comunliche in worthi place
The wommen loven worthinesse
Of manhode and of gentilesse,
For the gentils ben most desired.[13]

The lover then asks what Gentilesse is, and the account (which closely parallels the Loathly Lady's in its denial of birth, riches, and contempt of poverty as elements) thereupon follows.[14] Gentilesse, then, precisely as Chaucer interprets it, is one phase of the Prowesse "*that longeth to a knight.*"

What, now, is the situation in the Tale? *The knight is not behaving like a knight.* King Arthur's knight has forgotten knightly Prowess, and with exquisite irony the tables are turned on him. " Is *this* the lawe of king Arthures hous ? " Do his knights not know " *of knyhthode the prouesce,* Which is to love sufficant Aboven al the remenant That unto loves court poursuie " ?[15] *The very situation* was provided for in the books. For " knyhthode of prouesce " made it incumbent upon the *knight* to say what the Lady, " smylinge evermo," found herself compelled to say *for* him. " Hic docetur "—so runs the heading of one chapter in the *De Amore* of Andreas Capellanus—"*qualiter loqui debeat nobilis plebeiae.*"[16] And there the knight courteously meets the very objections—in this case raised by the *woman*— which in the Tale are raised by him.[17] Chaucer is not

[13] IV, 2196-99.

[14] Compare: " aschamed of þi poore freendys, pride of þi riche kyn, or of þi gentyl kyn," in *Jacob's Well* (p. 294). And this is under Shrift (which brings " the ȝyfte of strengthe ") and Shrift is one part of the armor of Strength or Prowesse (p. 292).

[15] IV, 2016-19.

[16] Ed. Trojel, pp. 70 ff. I quote the heading from the Codex Parisinus.

[17] The Knight speaks: " *Sed in plebeia probitas ex solius animi innata virtute optima mentis dispositione procedit, et sic quasi natur-*

túrning aside to preach a little sermon upon Pride; he is developing an exquisitely ironical situation *inherent in the Tale*—a situation whose point depends on the familiar conventions of *Prowesse*. And he makes absolutely clear what he is doing. *It is true Prowesse, which is Gentilesse, that is the Lady's theme:*

> Ful selde up ryseth by his branches smale
> Pro*wesse* of man; for god, of his goodnesse,
> Wol that of him we clayme our *gentilesse.*[18]

She has translated Dante's *probitate* by the very word that *places* Gentilesse precisely where, in the scheme of the Tale, it belongs. Yet *"strangely enough"* Gower classes Gentilesse, as Prowesse, under Sloth.[19]

Nor could better evidence possibly be given for the asso-

---

ale censetur. Tua igitur non possunt exempla procedere, unde merito dicendum credo, *magis in plebeia quam in nobili probitatem esse laudandam* " (p. 72). The woman objects: " Nam quum nobilis sanguine ac generosus inveniaris, patenter ipsi conaris nobilitati detrahere et contra ipsius placitare jura contendis," etc. (p. 73). The knight replies: " Amor enim personam saepe degenerem et deformem tanquam nobilem et formosam repraesentat amanti et facit, eam plus quam omnes alias nobilem atque pulcherrimam deputari . . . *Mirari ergo non debes, si te quamvis ignobilem genere omni tamen decoris fulgore et morum probitate fulgentem tota contendo amare virtute*," etc. (p. 75). The whole chapter is worth reading in the present connection.

[18] D, 1128-30.

[19] It is interesting to observe, too, that the Gentilesse-Prowesse passage is linked in another way with the theme of the Tale. The key to the story, of course, is the question, four times repeated, " What thing is it *that wommen most desyren?* " (D, 905, 1007), or, " What *wommen loven moost* " (D, 985, 921; cf. also D, 925 ff.). In Gower, " *The wommen loven worthinesse* Of manhode and of *gentilesse, For the gentils ben most desired* " (I, 2197-99). The knight in the Wife's Tale had found out *one* thing that women loved; he had not discovered all—and he is taught his lesson. Mr. Tupper insists on " the context of romantic love " (*Journal*, p. 555). The Lady's retort courteous is exquisitely pertinent to that.

ciation of Gentilesse with Prowesse (and so for the aptness of its employment in the Tale) than Mr. Tupper himself affords. For he cites the commandments of the God of Love in the *Roman de la Rose*.[20] " The verbal parallels between the Dame's exhortation to ' gentilesse ' (D, 1109 f.) and the God of Love's command, *Romaunt of the Rose,* 2187 f., have been often noted with never a thought of the bearing of this relation upon the essential purpose of the Wife's Tale." Tupper adds the four words " of obedience in love." [21]   But he has not, I fear, compared the Chaucerian fragment

[20] *Journal*, p. 554.

[21] In this connection Tupper has overlooked, I think, two rather important facts. The first is that " obedience in love " is ("strangely enough," perhaps, but none the less truly) not the antitype of Pride (even of Inobedience) in the *Parson's Tale* (which Tupper has now quite abandoned) at all, nor is it in Frère Lorens (Eilers, p. 568). " Obedience in love " is part of *the remedium against Lechery* in the *Parson's Tale* (§ 80), and it is there considered at great length. Obedience is not necessarily the antitype of Inobedience, any more than Devotion is necessarily the antitype of Undevotion (see above, p. 300, n. 74). Even in Gower (*Mirour*, ll. 12109 ff.), where Obedience *is* one of the five daughters of Humility, it is not treated from Tupper's point of view, but in its *religious* aspects. The same is true of the discussion of " Boȝsamnesse " in the *Ayenbite* (pp. 140-41). Obedience is also in the *Parson's Tale* part of the *remedium* of Wrath (I, 674). In *Jacob's Well* (pp. 268-72) Obedience is the " clene grounde " that appears when the gravel beneath the ooze of Wrath is removed; it is also (p. 254) part of the ground of Friendship underneath the ooze of Envy. I point all this out in the interest of a sympathetic attitude towards the mediæval reader, who was supposed to play his Sins unerringly. The second point is the fact that pride in birth or riches and contempt for the poor (the opposite of Gentilesse) have no immediate connection whatever with *Inobedience*. They belong to a different part of Pride's territory altogether. The homily on Gentilesse is *not* a harangue against the Wife's own (supposedly) particular type of Pride at all. Mr. Tupper adduces no evidence (nor is there any) that she had either pride of birth or riches, or contempt for the poor.

with the French. Line 2099 in Guillaume [22] is:
" N'est pas *proesce* de mesdire." [23] The next line
in the French is: " En Keux le séneschal te mire."
That is line 2206 in the English translation.[24] *And between the two French lines* are inserted in the English by
the translator, as a fit amplification of Guillaume's " *proesce,"* the lines to which Tupper refers (2187-2205),
*which are reminiscences of the Gentilesse passage in the
Wife of Bath's Tale.*[25] That particular man of the Middle Ages who translated the *Roman* understood the Lady's
homily (as she did too!) as a discourse upon *Prowesse,* and
he inserted it as pertinent comment on *proesce* in his rendering of the God of Love's first command.[26] As for the

---

[22] Ed. Michel, I, p. 68.

[23] " Proesce " and " gentillèce " appear together in the long passage
in Jean de Meun (ed. Michel, II, pp. 251-61) on which Chaucer draws
to some extent in the Loathly Lady's discourse. See especially pp.
251, 257, 258. In a paper (*Modern Philology*, May, 1915) which was
in the printer's hands before this article was begun, I have presented
evidence that in the Gentilesse passage in the *Wife of Bath's Tale*
Chaucer is drawing largely on Dante's *Convivio.* And it is worth
noting that in Dante's discussion of *Gentilezza,* too, this same virtue
of Prowesse appears. " Il nobile uomo," in his prime of life (between
adolescence and old age) must manifest five virtues: " Lealtà, Cor-
tesia, Amore, *Fortezza* e Temperanza " (*Convivio,* IV, 26, 143-44).

[24] " Thou mayst ensample take of Keye."

[25] I have had for several years abundant proof of this statement,
which I shall print when I have time to put the evidence together.

[26] Tupper cites (*Journal* p. 554) the God's command against Pr*ide.*
This command, however, has no bearing on the Lady's homily. Tupper has put a *period* after l. 2249 in his quotation of the passage,
where the text has a *comma,* thus changing materially the sense of
the lines. If he had continued, we should have seen what the
God of Love had in mind: " Shun pride—but *dressing well* is not
pride "—

 Cointerie n'est mie orguiex,
 Qui cointes est, il en vaut miex
 Por quoi il soit d'orgoil vuidiés,
 Qu'il ne soit fox n'outrecuidiés (ll. 2147-50).

stanza from the *Troilus*,[27] that is *Prowesse* too. Not only does the previous stanza give the other aspect of it—" worthinesse of manhode " (" And in the feld he pleyde the leoun ")—but the last line of the stanza quoted summarizes not only the stanza itself, but also to perfection the Confessor's statement of the results of Prowesse.

> Dede were his japes and his crueltee,
> His heighe port and his manere estraunge,
> And eche of tho gan for a vertu chaunge.

So Chaucer ; now the Confessor :

> . . . for it [love honeste] *doth aweie*
> *The vice,* and as the bokes sein,
> It makth curteis of the vilein,
> And to the couard hardiesce
> It yifth, *so that verrai prouesse*
> *Is caused upon loves reule*
> To him that can manhode reule.[28]

" So far from being ' irrelevant,' the sermon of the Wife's story is . . . admirably suited to the context of romantic love. *How obvious all this must have been to the mediæ-*

And then he goes on with his " costly thy habit as thy purse can buy." He has *already* dealt (under " vilonnie ") with what Mr. Tupper has in mind.

[27] *T. & C.*, I, 1079-85. Cited in *Journal*, p. 555.

[28] IV, 2298-2304. Tupper does not note, when he says that Troilus " divests himself utterly . . . of the Sin of *Pride* " that " his japes and his crueltee " are not Pride but Wrath, or that in another stanza Chaucer says of Troilus :

> Thus wolde Love, y-heried be his grace,
> That *Pryde, Envye, Ire, and Avarice*
> He gan to flee, *and every other vyce* (III, 1804-06).

But the idea is a commonplace in the *Troilus*—and elsewhere. See, for example, Andreas Capellanus : " Effectus autem amoris hic est, quia verus amator nulla posset *avaritia* offuscari, amor horridum et incultum omni facit formositate pollere, infimos natu etiam morum novit nobilitate ditare, *superbos* quoque solet humilitate beare," etc. (pp. 9-10).

15

val reader! " [29]   Its admirable fitness is indubitable, but
would not the thing most obvious to the mediæval reader
have been the association—in the Tale itself, in Gower,
in Guillaume de Lorris, and in Jean de Meun—of Gentilesse and *Prowesse?* [30]

It may be added incidentally in connection with the
" strangeness " of putting Gentilesse under Sloth (where
it belongs), that the *Ayenbite* (p. 33) and *Jacob's Well*
(p. 112) treat *" Unbuxomness" itself* (in precisely the
sense of the Parson's use of Inobedience) as a subhead of
Sloth.   And in Frère Lorens [31] *Inobedience* is a subhead
of *Accide.*   What, then, was to prevent some mediæval
reader who knew *those* categories from putting together an
Inobedience (let us say, Sloth) Prologue, and a *remedium*
(Prowesse) Tale, precisely as he was to put together an
Idleness (Sloth) Prologue and a *remedium* (Prowesse)
Tale in the case of St. Cecilia?   It would, I think, be
difficult to say.   So much for the " homily."   What of the
Wife herself?

" For god it woot, *I chidde hem spitously.*" [23]   *That*

---

[29] *Journal*, p. 555.

[30] I do not wish the interpretation which I have just given of the
Gentilesse passage to be regarded in quite the same light as my
purely *ad hoc* construction, on the basis of Fortitudo, in the case of
The Tale of Constance (see above, pp. 326 ff.)   That the *general* association of Gentilesse and Prowesse (which seems to have been overlooked until Mr. Tupper's remark drew my attention to it) was
in Chaucer's mind, there can be, I think, little doubt, in view of his
mention of Prowesse in the passage.   But I do not believe for a
moment that Chaucer was thereby exemplifying *Sloth!*   And my
present purpose is chiefly to demonstrate that from the mediæval
point of view (which Tupper has abandoned) Gentilesse as a phase
of *Prowesse* (Sloth) fits the case far better than Gentilesse as an
antitype of *Pride.*

[31] Eilers, p. 535.   " Unbuxomness " also appears under *Avarice* in
Jacob's Well (p. 135).

[23] D, 223.

is the key to the Wife of Bath's place among the Sins, if such a place she has to have. Beside her the Manciple is a farthing-candle to the sun. What the Parson says of *Inobedience* is this:

Inobedient, is he that disobeyeth for despyt to the commandements of god and to hise sovereyns, and to his goostly fader.[33]

What the Parson says of *Chiding* is (among other things) this:

And how that chydinge be a vileyns thing bitwixe alle manere folk, *yet it is certes most uncovenable bitwixe a man and his wyf;* for there is nevere reste. And therfore seith Salomon, '*an hous that is uncovered and droppinge, and a chydinge wyf, been lyke.*'[34] A man that is in a droppinge hous in many places, though he es-chewe the droppinge in o place, it droppeth on him in another place; *so fareth it by a chydinge wyf. But she chyde him in o place, she wol chyde him in another.* And therefore, 'bettre is a morsel of breed with joye than an hous ful of delyces, with chydinge,' seith Salomon. *Seint Paul seith: 'O ye wommen, be ye subgetes to youre housbondes as bihoveth in god; and ye men, loveth youre wyves.'*[35]

That is where the Parson puts the Wife of Bath, and *that* is where he classes *Inobedience* in the sense in which Tup-per is applying it. And even though Tupper himself keeps forgetting his own crowning argument, we may not: " *The Parson's portrayal of the Vices* thus enters into the frame-work of the Sins Tales and makes obvious the 'applica-tion" of each." [36]

[33] I, 392.   [34] Cf. D, 278-80.   [35] I, 630-34.

[36] *Publications,* p. 116. The Inobedient Wife appears under Pride (besides her appearance in the *Mirour,* which Tupper—*Publications,* p. 109—points out) in the *Cursor Mundi,* ll. 28152-55 (" I womman haue vn-buxum bene And tarid myn husband to tene, In many thyng þat i suld don, And noght queþer my lagh vndon ") and *Jacob's Well,* p. 72 ("Also þou wyif, vnbuxom to þin husbonde vnleffully, þou servaunt vnbuxom to þi mayster," etc.). In all these cases the reference is (like " grucching against poverty " under Envy) a single minor detail in a larger treatment.

And, indeed, the Wyf's Prologue is a very antiphonal of chiding " bitwixe a man and his wyf."

> For god it woot, *I chidde hem spitously* (223).
> And if I have a gossib or a freend,
> With-outen gilt, *thou chydest as a feend* (243-44).
> Thow seyst that dropping houses, and eek smoke,
> And *chyding wyves,* maken men to flee
> Out of hir owene hous; a! ben'cite!
> *What eyleth swich an old man for to chyde?* (278-81).
> *Ther wolde I chyde* and do hem no plesaunce (408).
> That made me that *ever I wolde hem chyde* (419).
> ' Bet is,' quod he, ' thyn habitacioun
> Be with a leoun or a foul dragoun,
> *Than with a womman usinge for to chyde.*
> ' Bet is,' quod he, ' hye in the roof abyde
> Than with *an angry wyf* doun in the hous ' (775-79).

And where in the world is there such matchless chiding as that which the Wife rehearses with fresh gusto for the pilgrims' ears, in the consummate tirade [37] with which she parallels the Pardoner's self-revelation? Beside her robust phrases the Parson's " thou holour," " thou dronkelewe harlot " pale their uneffectual fire: " sir olde lechour "; " olde barel ful of lyes "; " sire olde fool "; " olde dotard "; " sir shrewe "; " olde dotard shrewe "; " lorel "; " sir olde kaynard "—" never did I hear such gallant chiding "! Moreover, the other branch which Tupper links with Chiding is there too. Is the Manciple's morality directed against *Jangling?* " Stiborn I was as is a leonesse, And of my tonge *a verray jangleresse* " (637-38). Is Gower's emphasis in his Tale of Cheste upon " *biwreying of conseil* "?

> To hir, and to another worthy wyf,
> And to my nece, which that I loved weel,
> *I wolde han told his conseil every-deel.*
> *And so I dide ful often,* god it woot.[38]

---

[37] D, 235-378.   [38] D, 536-39.

Would not the mediæval reader begin to smell *Wrath* in the wind? And it would be with likelihood to lead him, too. Does the *Friar's Tale* represent "the *Cursing* phase of W'rath"? Beside the Wife of Bath old Mabely is the veriest amateur:

> With wilde thonder-dint and firy levene
> Mote thy welked nekke be to-broke! [39]

Is it "attry angre" that we wish, to give good measure?

> . . . in his owene grece I made him frye
> *For angre*, and for verray jalousye.
> *By god*, in erthe I was his purgatorie— [40]

which reminds the man of the Middle Ages that "*swering*" is wrath too. As for actual *Strife* (Tençon, Contek, what you will):

> I with my fist so took him on the cheke,
> That in our fyr he fil bakward adoun.
> And he up-stirte as dooth a wood leoun,
> And with his fist he smoot me on the heed,
> That in the floor I lay as I were deed. [41]

The mediæval reader must have revelled in the signs of Wrath, "as thikke as motes in the sonne-beem." [42]

But Wrath, of course, does not make up the Wife's sum.

---

[39] D, 276-77.   [40] D, 487-89.   [41] D, 792-96.

[42] That they were so read we know on the testimony of the one unimpeachable, first-hand witness that we have—the Clerk of Oxford. For the Clerk, at the close of his Tale, sets the Wife of Bath over against Griselda. And Griselda is the type of Patience, and Patience (still to keep the point of view demanded by the theory itself) is the antitype, not of Pride, but of *Wrath*. (It is so in the *Parson's Tale*, §§ 50-52, in the *Mirour*, ll. 13381-14100, and in the *Confessio*, III, 612-713; cf. 1-18, 1098, etc.). And the matchless irony of the Clerk's Envoy is directed against the very Chiding to which the Wife herself has given the first place—"the arwes of [hir] crabbed eloquence." If we are to think in terms of the Sins at all, the verdict of the Clerk of Oxford is unequivocally for *Wrath*.

Mr. Tupper has had much to say about Virginity, in connection with his Tale of Lechery. But he passes over in silence (as he passed over the Friar's homily on Gluttony) the Wife's long and explicit depreciation of Virginity (which occupies the first part of her Prologue), her frank distaste for Chastity,[43] and her outspoken avowal of her own "likerousness"[44]—except that he gently refers to her as "the epitome of worldly affection."[45] Nor has he said a word of her *Gluttony,* the "ny cosin" of Lechery:

> And, after wyn, on Venus moste I thinke:
> For al so siker as cold engendreth hayl,
> A likerous mouth moste han a likerous tayl.[46]

Even her "love of fine clothes"[47] meant more than Pride:

> . . . what wiste I when my grace
> Was shapen for to be, or in what place?
> *Therefore* I made my visitaciouns . . .
> And wered upon my gaye scarlet gytes.[48]

In Absolon's expert phrase, "That is a signe of kissing atte leste." To the mediæval mind the Wife of Bath's Prologue was thick inlaid with signs of Lechery and Wrath. And when Mr. Tupper says that her other traits " are *nei-*

---

[43] See, for example, ll. 46, 138, etc.

[44] Ll. 604-26; and *passim.*

[45] *Publications,* p. 108. He *does,* however, recognize her "desclaiming" of Virginity, in connection with his Saint Venus theory (*Nation,* Oct. 16, 1913, p. 355, col. 3). It furthers there; it hinders here.

[46] D, 464-66. See the rest of the passage.

[47] *Publications,* p. 108.

[48] D, 553-55, 559. See 550-62, and cf. 337-61. "Now as of the outrageous array of wommen," says the Parson, " . . . yet notifie they in hir array of atyr *likerousnesse* and pryde" (I, 429). For the same implications, compare the warnings against fine clothes (among them "curchefs crisp and bendes bright") under *Lechery,* in the *Cursor Mundi* (ll. 28018 ff., 28514 ff.), and cf. Deschamps, *Miroir de Mariage,* ch. XLII.

ther so dominant nor conspicuous as that phase of Pride, which she . . . proclaims, with all the frankness of the Pardoner, to be her chief fault—'Unbuxomness' or 'Inobedience' in love "[49] —in saying that, he is substituting an inference for a fact. The Pardoner *does* proclaim frankly that Avarice is his chief fault; the Wife of Bath proclaims with equal frankness that she is " al Venerien," " likerous," " vinolent," " a verray jangleresse," a chider, a betrayer of secrets. *Inobedience* is Mr. Tupper's inference, not her proclamation. I have not the least intention of denying that the Wife of Bath was proud— " unbuxom," if you will; she was, as Mr. Tupper says, a " complex personality." [50] But in order to make her *stand* for " Inobedience in love," Mr. Tupper has to throw overboard the Parson, who puts the chiding and inobedient wife under *Wrath;* overlook entirely the light which Gower, Guillaume de Lorris and his translator, and the Wife herself throw on the place of Gentilesse " in a context of romantic love "—a place which connotes the antitype of *Sloth,* not of Pride; and minimize the most salient features (including *Lechery*) of the Prologue as it stands. And that he *is* imposing his own inferences upon facts, he has himself made clear.

For he has treated Barclay in precisely the same way. But Barclay, unlike Chaucer, uses *labels,* so that we have a check. Among the types preserved in the *Ship of Fools,* Mr. Tupper tells us, is " the *Proud* and Shrewish Wife." [51] He gives no reference, but the line which he quotes [52] identifies the passage. It is the first portrait in the second volume. Its actual title is: " Of the *yre im-*

---

[49] *Publications*, pp. 108-09.
[50] *Publications*, p. 108.   [51] *Journal*, p. 556·
[52] II, 5—second line from foot of page.

moderate, the *wrath* and great *lewdness* of wymen " (in the
Tabula: " Of wymens *malyce & wrath* "). Professor Tupper is absolutely right in his implied parallel with the
Wife of Bath; it is patent throughout the thirty-eight
stanzas. In this case, however, the type *is* tagged, and
the tag is not what Mr. Tupper gives. That again—his
" *Proud* and Shrewish Wife,"—is *his* interpretation of
facts, the *mediæval* interpretation of which we can this
time verify. In the 304 lines of the poem there is just
one mention of Pride (p. 7) : " Hir proude aparayle sholde
make his thryst ful thyn "—which Tupper paraphrases:
" Emptying by her proud apparel her husband's purse."
Tupper's next phrase—" *acknowledging* P*ride as lady and
mistresse* " (which forms the climax of his paraphrase of
Barclay's picture)—is nowhere in the poem. It is interpretation pure and simple, unwarranted by fact. The
lines which *do* follow are:

> As well can some spende as theyr good man can wyn
> And moche faster, but if that coyne do fayle
> She labowryth nat to get it without syn
> But craftely to forge it with hir tayle.

In view of the *title,* it is scarcely necessary to enumerate
the " tags " of Wrath and Lechery of which the poem is
full—chiding, again and again (four times on page 4);
wrath; cruel words; rancor; etc., etc. These Mr. Tupper mentions too,—only to bring in P*ride* as his climax,
exactly as in the case of the Wife of Bath. Yet Barclay's
conclusion is explicit. He puts the " unbuxom " *wife*
precisely where the Parson puts her, namely, under
Wrath. The Envoy begins:

> *Ye wrathfull wymen* by vyce lesynge your name ...
> Let *chastyte* you gyde and *pacience.*
> For to be frowarde, it is a thynge in vayne

Vnto hym to whom ye owe obedyence.
The lawe commaundyth you to do reverence
Vnto your spousys with honour and mekenesse, etc.[53]

The parallel with the Wife of Bath is perfect. Mr. Tupper's interpretation in the one case is at sharp variance with the mediæval point of view. And the evidence I have given points to a similar variance in the other.[54]

The Wife of Bath is a magnificent abstract of the Deadly but Delightful Seven—all their strength and all their sweetness rolled up into one ball! So is Falstaff; so (in her excellent differences) is Cleopatra. And who is there to match them? They are the lust of the flesh, and the lust of the eyes, and the pride of life—and more!—incarnate. But neither the Wife of Bath nor her peers may be cabined within the confines of a Sin. The supreme creations of the poets and the categories of the theologians have a common source—the mingled yarn of *life*. Each comes by its own separate path from that, and each in its own way embodies it. But it is a fatal fallacy to confound cognates with derivatives.

---

[53] P. 10.

[54] Beginning on p. 122 of his *Publications* article, Mr. Tupper proceeds to discuss the blending of the "*Sins motif*" with the "*love motif*," which he had earlier elaborated in the *Nation*, Oct. 16, 1913 (Vol. 97, No. 2520), pp. 354-56. Once more I plead guilty to welcoming at the outset what seemed to be new light, only to find, upon closer investigation, that (to me at least) the light was darkness. In spite of much that is suggestive in the first *Nation* article, its method is open to many of the same objections that lie against the treatment of the "*Sins motif*." But this last theory stands or falls altogether independently of the first, and I do not wish to prolong a discussion that has exceeded bounds already. I shall therefore pass over this part of Mr. Tupper's argument.

IX

The truth of the whole matter is that Mr. Tupper wishes us to play a game in which there are no rules. The deal is nothing—one may pick one's cards. Ace may be high in one hand, low the next. Trumps may or may not take the trick. One does not even have to follow suit. Out of the maze of the categories, with their nebulous dividing lines, their innumerable overlappings and interlacings, one may choose at will, ignore at will, combine at will. By such a method anything whatever may be proved. And that is easy to demonstrate. Now that Tupper has fished the murex up, Nokes may outdare Stokes in azure feats. It is possible to prove, with scrupulous adherence to the principles on which Mr. Tupper's theory is based, that at least three more Tales should be added to his list. And in so doing I shall again confine myself rigidly to his own authorities.

The *Monk's Tale,* in the first place, exemplifies *Pride.* The Parson, in his discourse " De Superbia," has stated the theme of the Tale as clearly as the Monk:

Certes also, who-so prydeth him in the goodes of fortune, he is a ful greet fool; for som-tyme is a man a greet lord by the morwe, that is a caitif and a wrecche er it be night: and somtyme the richesse of a man is cause of his deeth;[1] somtyme the delyces of a man is cause of the grevous maladye thurgh which he dyeth.[2] Certes, the commendacioun of the peple is somtyme ful fals and ful brotel for to triste;[3] this day they preyse, tomorwe they blame.[4]

---

[1] Compare *Croesus* (B, 3917 ff.).

[2] Compare *Antiochus* (B, 3789 ff.).

[3] Compare *Nero* (B, 3717 ff.).

[4] I, 470. Compare also the *Ayenbite* (p. 24) for the wheel of Fortune, and Pride; *Jacob's Well* (p. 78) for comments, under Pride, on the text: " Qui se exaltat, humiliabitur "; and in general compare *Jacob's Well,* p. 237; *Pèlerinage,* ll. 14233-42; *Mirour,* ll. 1274-96, 1828-31, 2596 ff.; etc.

And the "present purport" of the *exempla* is unmistakable. *Lucifer* exemplifies *Pride* in Dante,[5] Pope Innocent,[6] the *Confessio*,[7] the *Mirour*,[8] the *Ayenbite*,[9] the
Pèlerinage,[10] Wyclif,[11] Lydgate,[12] and Barclay; [13] *Adam,*
in the *Pèlerinage*,[14] the *Confessio*,[15] and Barclay; [16]
Nebuchadnezzar, in the *De Contemptu*,[17] the *Pèlerinage*,[18]
the *Confessio*,[19] and the *Mirour*;[20] *Belshazzar,* in Barclay; [21] *Holofernes,* in the *De Contemptu*,[22] Dante,[23] and
Barclay; [24] *Antiochus,* in the *De Contemptu*[25] and Barclay; [26] *Cæsar,* in Lydgate.[27] Nor does the Monk himself
leave us in doubt regarding his " formal intent ":

> This *proude* king (3349); This king of kinges *proud* was and
> elaat (3357); For *proud* he was (3376); And he was *proud* (3402);
> Eek thou . . . art *proud* also (3413); More *proud* was never em-
> perour than he (3662); The hye *pryde* of Nero (3710); The more
> pompous in heigh *presumpcioun* (3745); His hye *pryde* (3767); The
> *proude* wordes that he seyde (3770); Fortune him hadde enhaunced
> so in *pryde* (3773); Wening that god ne mighte his *pryde* abate
> (3780); God daunted al his *pryde* and al his *bost* (3799); Swich
> guerdon as-bilongeth unto *pryde* (3820); Yit was he caught amiddes
> al his *pryde* (3919); Of which he was so *proud* (3931); Cresus, the
> *proude* king (3949).

And the conclusion of the whole matter is no less explicit:

[5] *Purg.*, XII, 25-27.   [9] P. 16.
[6] *De Contemptu Mundi*, II, 31.   [10] Ll. 14030 ff.
[7] I, 3299 ff.   [11] Ed. Matthew, pp. 2, 3, 123.
[8] Ll. 1873 ff.

[12] *Story of Thebes* and *Troy-book* (see *Serpent of Division*, ed.
MacCracken, pp. 5-6).
[13] II, 159, 163-65.   [20] Ll. 1886 ff.
[14] Ll. 14048 ff., 14435 ff.   [21] II, 165.
[15] I, 3303-04.   [22] II, 32.
[16] II, 165.   [23] *Purg.*, XII, 58-60.
[17] II, 32.   [24] II, 162, 165.
[18] Ll. 14220 ff.   [25] II, 32.
[19] I, 2785 ff.   [26] II, 165.
[27] *Serpent of Division*, pp. 50 (l. 3), 65 (l. 28). Cæsar is also an
exemplum, in the *Serpent*, of Fortune's mutability; see p. 65, ll. 21 ff.

> Tragedie is noon other maner thing . . .
> But for that fortune alwey wol assaille
> With unwar strook *the regnes that ben proude.*[25]

The Tale itself, then, is, from Mr. Tupper's point of view, an unsurpassed " morality " on Pride.

The element of *irony,* moreover, could scarcely be more striking. The Monk himself might have been drawn to exemplify the Parson's discourse on Pride. His " ful many a deyntee hors " (A, 168) parallels the " manye delicat horses " against which the Parson inveighs (I, 430) ; his jingling bridle (A, 169-70) repeats the " curious harneys " and the " brydles covered with ... barres and plates of gold and of silver " (I, 433) ; his " sleves pur-filed at the hond With grys, and that the fyneste of a lond " (A, 193-94) recall the " costelewe furringe in hir gounes " (I, 417) ; his love for a fat swan (A, 206) is the Parson's " Pryde of the table " (I, 444).[29] The Monk is guilty of the very Sin against which he tells his Tale.

Nor is there the slightest question regarding the " crown-ing argument." We have seen that the *Parson's Tale* both states the theme of the Monk's *exempla,* and gives the direct suggestion for the irony. I submit that no one of all Professor Tupper's candidates meets the requirements of the theory so perfectly as mine. Yet in this case we know with absolute certainty just what the Monk *did* mean

---

[25] B, 3951-54.

[29] So " grete hors " are mentioned by Wyclif as one " ensaumple " of the pride of prelates (ed. Matthew, p. 30); compare the still fuller and more explicit statements on pp. 60, 92, 121. With the Monk's " grehoundes " (A, 190) compare the delight " yn horsys, haukys, or yn *houndes* " (especially in the case of clerks) in *Hand-lyng Synne* (ll. 3083-86). Tupper has used the General Prologue in his treatment of the Wife of Bath (*Publications,* p. 108), so it is open to us here. But in any case the theory allows for " after-thoughts."

to exemplify—namely, *the fickleness of Fortune.* For we have not only his initial and his closing statements of his purpose, the explicit rehearsal of the point at the close of *exemplum* after *exemplum*,[30] the numerous references to Fortune in the body of the *exempla*,[31] the Knight's entire understanding of the point,[32] the Host's concurrence in the Knight's recognition of the purport of the Tale,[33] but we have also the similar *exemplum* treatment of the same theme in Chaucer's sources, Boccaccio and Jean de Meun, together with the whole mediæval conception of the Monk's specific term, " tragedie." Unless " Chaucer was quite in the dark about himself," the *Monk's Tale* is *not* a " Sins Tale." Yet it bears all the ear-marks that the theory requires.

It is, however, not the only one. The *Nun's Priest's Tale* is also an exemplification of *Pride,* in its branch *Flattery.* One need only recall the Tale to recognize its purport, but this time we have the " tag " as well:

> Allas! ye lordes, *many a fals flatour*
> *Is in your courtes, and many a losengeour,*
> That plesen yow wel more, by my feith,
> Than he that soothfastnesse unto yow seith.
> *Redeth Ecclesiaste of flaterye;*
> *Beth war, ye lordes, of hir trecherye.*[34]

And the close of the Tale " is the traditional ending of an ' ensample ' of Sin "; indeed, " nothing could be more in the true *exemplum* manner ":

[30] Ll. 3325 ff., 3429 ff., 3557 ff., 3587-88, 3647 ff., 3740, 3858-60, 3912-16.

[31] Ll. 3191, 3566, 3591, 3635-36, 3709-10, 3746-47, 3773-74, 3823, 3851-52, 3868, 3876, 3884, 3924, 3927.

[32] Ll. 3957-69.

[33] Ll. 3970-77.

[34] B, 4515-20. This follows the line: " So was he ravisshed with his *flaterye.*"

> Lo, swich it is for to be recchelees,
> And necligent, *and truste on flaterye.*
> But ye that holden this tale a folye,
> As of a fox, or of a cok and hen,
> Taketh the moralitee, good men.
> For seint Paul seith, that al that writen is,
> To our doctryne it is y-write, y-wis.
> Taketh the fruyt, and lat the chaf be stille.[35]

That is, of course, enough, but the Nun's Priest has given us still further help, through hints delightfully obvious to adepts in the Sins. Chanticleer " song *merier than the mermayde in the see.*"[36] Now it is not only " Phisiologus " who discourses on the mermaid's singing. *Flattery's* song, in the Pèlerinage, " ys swettere... *Than off meremaydenys in the se.*"[37] In the *Ayenbite,* flatterers and mis-sayers " byeþ þe tuo nykeren þet we uyndeþ ine bokes of kende of bestes ... þet habbeþ bodyes of wyfman and ... zuetelich zingeþ ... þet byeþ þe blonderes."[38] In *Jacob's Well,* " losengers, in þe book of kynde, are lykenyd to *a mermayden of þe se* ... and sche *syngeth so merye* in þe se " etc.[39] The connotation of the simile is unmistakable.[40] And, indeed, Chanticleer *was* himself a flatterer. As Miss Petersen has pointed out, " he addresses polite and elegant flattery to Pertelote, and enjoys the mockery of the Latin tribute which she cannot understand."[41] There is, accordingly, in the Tale, the delicate irony of the flatterer flattered, just as we have (in Mr.

---

[35] B, 4626-33. The " *exemplum* formula " becomes even more explicit in the closing prayer (ll. 4634-36).

[36] B, 4460. Incidentally, *singing* (*Handlyng Synne,* p. 107), or one's *voice* (*Jacob's Well,* p. 69), is one of the gifts which lead to Pri*de.*

[37] Ll. 14688-93.   [38] P. 61.   [39] P. 150.

[40] And, I imagine, was present in Chaucer's mind—yet without Sin.

[41] *On the Sources of the N. P. T.,* p. 91.

Tupper's opinion) the curser cursed in the *Friar's Tale*.[42]
Moreover, the choice of the *fox* is itself significant. The
fox's tail is the symbol of the flatterer in the *Mirour*,[43]
the *Ayenbite*,[44] and *Jacob's Well*,[45] and in the last two, flatterers are, therefore, "ycleped in writinge: tayles." [46]
And finally, the *exemplum* has pointed a like moral elsewhere. For the fable of the fox and the raven occurs as
an " Exaumple " under Pride in the *Pèlerinage*.[47] And
the moral there is clear. Like the cock, the raven " koude
nat espye Hys [the fox's] tresoun *nor hys fflaterye*," [48] and
Pride asserts that the deceit was wrought "thorgh the
blast off *fflaterye*." [49] We have, then, the testimony of an
analogue. Moreover, Flattery is included under Pride in
the *Mirour*,[50] the *Pèlerinage*,[51] the *Ayenbite*,[52] and *Handlyng Synne*.[53] " It is interesting that the Parson, like
Peraldus, includes [Flattery] under [Wrath]. This arrangement, however," [54] puts the Parson hard to it, as
everybody knows.[55] And this unusual collocation, in the
light of the other authorities, need not trouble us.[56] The
Nun's Priest's Tale is an *exemplum* of Flattery; it is

---

[42] And as in the *Friar's Tale* so here Chaucer " doubles the story's
aptness " by making the *fox's* downfall the punishment of *his* Pride:

> Lo, how fortune turneth sodeinly
> The hope and *pryde* eek of hir enemy!—

and Chantecleer's counter-trick follows.

[43] Ll. 1405-10.   [44] P. 61.   [45] P. 150.

[46] *Ayenbite*, p. 61; cf. *Jacob's Well*, p. 150. In the *Pèlerinage*
Pride's mantel of Hypocrisy is lined with fox-skin (ll. 14590 ff.).

[47] Ll. 14247-89.   [51] Ll. 14645-14762.

[48] Ll. 14275-76.   [52] P. 23.

[49] Ll. 14283-89.   [53] Ll. 3501 ff.

[50] Ll. 1369 ff.   [54] *Journal*, p. 562.

[55] See the last five lines of I, § 40.

[56] Flattery is also among the Sins of the Tongue in the *Ayenbite*
(p. 60) and *Jacob's Well* (p. 149). It is treated under the Points
of Policy in the *Confessio* (VII, 2177-2694).

therefore a " Sins tale "; and its place, in accordance with
the weight of authority, is under Pride.

As for the element of *irony,* " no Prologue specifically
indicates the [Nun's Priest's] peculiar disqualification
for his theme of [Flattery]; but the mediæval reader must
have been tickled by [a sermon against Flattery] from a
profession notorious, in the fourteenth century," [57] for its
use of flattery to attain its ends. The pages of Wyclif
teem with references to the employment of flattery by
ecclesiastics:

> But what man comeþ now to ony fat benefice or prelacie wiþouten
> ʒifte of money or servyce, or *flateryng?* . . . Who getiþ ony fat bene-
> fice of þe Bischop of Rome *wiþouten siche flateryng?* [58] *þei flatren
> lordis* . . . & ʒeuen lordis grete ziftis of gold & iuelis & pardons. [59]
> A symple pater noster of a plouʒman þat his in charite is hetre
> þan a þousand massis of coueitouse prelatis & veyn religious *ful of
> . . . fals flaterynge.* [60]

But we need not rely on Wyclif for the evidence. Every
mediæval reader must have seen the irony at a glance.
For in innumerable versions of the tale " the fox and
various other animals *play the part of priest.*" [61] Indeed,
as Miss Petersen points out, " the ' monking ' of the enemy

---

[57] *Publications,* p. 110.

[58] Ed. Arnold, III, p. 281.

[59] Ed. Matthew, p. 63.

[60] *Ibid.,* p. 274. Cf. pp. 237, 246, etc.; *Mirour,* ll. 21250-21432.
Compare also the Summoner's remark (D, 1294) about the "*flateringe* limitour." As for the Nun's Priest, Professor Lawrence has
pointed out—not, I hasten to add, in even remote connection with
the present theme—that he " is subject to a lady who is his ecclesiastical superior " (*Modern Philology,* XI, p. 254). He was therefore
at least in a position where flattery might " avaunce." And we
know that the Prioress loved " chere of court," and " as forto speke
[of] court real . . . there it [flaterie] is most special " (*Confessio,*
VII, 2209-10). "This suggestion . . . is only a plausible conjecture."

[61] Petersen, p. 43.

is one of the commonest forms of this general theme," [62] and her numerous examples of the fox as priest, from both mediæval tales and mediæval sculpture,[63] offer ample evidence. In the tale itself, in other words, *the arch-flatterer frequently takes the guise of the very class to which the teller of the tale belongs.* The irony is complete. " How obvious all this must have been to the mediæval reader ! "

As for the " crowning argument," the *Nun's Priest's Tale,* like that of the Physician, " confesses in its moralities no indebtedness or close resemblance to the Parson's discussion of the corresponding Vice; but this omission seems the less striking, when we remark the generous use of the section on [Pride] in the [*Monk's Tale*]." [64] The *Nun's Priest's Tale,* accordingly, fulfills all the requirements of an *exemplum* of Pride (Flattery). Moreover, it should be observed that if we accept the order of the Tales to which Mr. Tupper (I believe rightly) subscribes,[65] the Wife of Bath's Prologue and Tale immediately follow the *Nun's Priest's Tale.* We have, therefore, three Pride Tales in succession—the Monk's (Pride in general), the Nun's Priest's (Pride in its phase of Flattery), the Wife of Bath's (Pride as Inobedience)—a treatment worthy of the Vice which is " des autres capiteine." [66]

Finally (since the time would fail me to tell of all), the *Merchant's Tale* is a perfect exemplification of *Lechery*— not this time by way of its antitype, but directly, and with an astonishing inclusiveness. January is one of " thise olde dotardes holours " [67] for whom the staid Parson

---

[62] P. 42.   [63] Pp. 42-45.   [64] *Publications,* p. 116.

[65] *Nation,* Oct. 16, 1913, p. 355; *Publications,* p. 97. See Lawrence, *Modern Philology,* XI, pp. 256-57, for a fuller statement of the evidence.

[66] *Mirour,* l. 1045.

[67] I, 857. Compare the masterly description in the Tale, E, 1842-54.

employs a simile unsurpassed for vividness by any modern master of a realistic pen. We have his habits before his marriage (E, 1248-50); his use of aphrodisiacs (E, 1807 ff.); " avoutrie bitwixe a man and his wyf "; [68] adultery between Damian and May—there are few details in the categories that could not be illustrated from the Tale.[69] Moreover, as regards the " crowning argument," Professor Tatlock has pointed out that " the *Parson's Tale* is quoted in the *Merchant's* more frequently than in any other of Chaucer's works except the *Pardoner's Prologue* and *Tale.*" [70] Even Mr. Tupper, in explaining why *his* Tale of Lechery fails to borrow from the *Parson's Tale* at all, remarks " the generous use of the section on Lechery in the so-called Marriage Group, *particularly in the Merchant's Tale.*" [71] And the argument from irony is at least as good in the case of the *Second Nun's Tale*. For over against one reference to lazy nuns I shall set one reference to lecherous merchants: " þei [false marchauntis] *lyuen in glotonye, dronkenesse & lecherie as hoggis.*" [72] Anyway, on Mr. Tupper's own law of compensation, the meagreness of the argument from irony may be offset by the uncommon richness of the crowning argument.

The *Clerk's Tale* and the *Franklin's Tale* afford, by way of antitypes, a no less fruitful field. Their conformity

---

[68] I, 904, 858; cf. *Jacob's Well*, p. 161; etc. It is unnecessary to rehearse the passages from the Tale.

[69] Mr. Tupper's Tale of Lechery exemplifies (through its *antitype,* and through thwarted *intent* alone) only " that phase of Lechery " which consists in " birev[ing] a mayden of hir maydenhede " (*Publications*, p. 97, n. 7).

[70] *Development and Chronology of Chaucer's Works*, p. 202. See Herrig's *Archiv*, LXXXVII, pp. 35-36, 41-43; *Modern Philology*, VIII, pp. 171-75.

[71] *Publications*, p. 116.   [72] Wyclif, ed. Matthew, p. 186.

at point after point with the requirements of the categories
is amazing, but I must leave them, as by no means unin-
structive pastimes, to others.   My greatest regret is that
space forbids the unfolding of the latent possibilities of
Harry Bailly as an exponent of the Sins!   But the *Monk's
Tale,* the *Nun's Priest's Tale,* and the *Merchant's Tale*
(together with the perfectly sound variant interpretations
of the *Summoner's Tale,* the *Man of Law's Tale,* and the
Wife of Bath's Tale given above), are enough to show that
Mr. Tupper's theory proves too much.

X

In conclusion, I wish to point out, with the utmost
brevity, that in dissenting from Mr. Tupper's thesis we
are not relinquishing those elements of Chaucer's art of
which the theory has skilfully availed itself.   Mr. Tupper has so dexterously interwoven with the other strands
of his fabric certain of Chaucer's most familiar characteristics, that, in refusing to accept this particular pattern
as Chaucer's design, we are put in the position of seeming
to deny to *Chaucer* the qualities that have been thus combined.   The fallacy is one that has been forced upon us,
and it requires a word or two in closing.

In the first place, Chaucer makes abundant use of
the Seven Deadly Sins.   He dealt with life, and life, like
the categories, is a labyrinth of the Vices and the Virtues.
And since he lived in an age when theology had a " large
place ... in the intellectual interests of cultured lay Englishmen " [1]—not to speak of cultivated lay Frenchmen,
Italians, Spaniards, and Germans — he calls the Vices

---

[1] *Journal,* p. 553.

freely by their names, and talks of them in terms of their
conventional associations.   In this he is at one with
Dante, Boccaccio, Jean de Meun, and his contemporaries
all and some.   But that is one thing, and a formal schematizing of the Seven Deadly Sins in the *Canterbury Tales*
is quite another.   To deny the second is by no means to
gainsay the first.

In the second place, Chaucer is thoroughly mediæval
in his use of *exempla*.   The " clear-eyed scholar " whom
Mr. Tupper quotes [2] spoke the words of truth and sober-
ness when he remarked that Chaucer follows " the line of
least resistance by falling into the well-worn *exempla*
track."   But when Mr. Tupper declares—putting the
words ironically into the mouth of some one of the " Peter
Bells of scholarship "—that " being of the fourteenth
century he [Chaucer] utterly failed to recognize that, as
an artist, *he was absolutely debarred from pointing the
moral*—that is in his tales of the Sins " [3]—in saying this,
Mr. Tupper is not only erecting a man of straw, but he
is also identifying Chaucer's facts with his own interpretation of those facts, and assuming that Chaucer's
moral and his own are one.   Chaucer has used *exempla*,

[2] *Journal*, p. 554.

[3] *Publications*, p. 127. The same fallacy appears on the preceding
page: "That the 'moralities' are there, he who runs may read.
That they are 'moralities' of the Sins, no one can doubt who takes
the trouble to compare them with Chaucer's own formal description
of the Vices (*Parson's Tale*) or with the traditional traits of these
evil passions in mediæval theology." With the first sentence one
may heartily concur, and I fear that the frequent proclamation of
the "utter aimlessness and irrelevancy" of Chaucer's moralizing
which Tupper deplores is "fantom and illusioun"—a ghost of his
own raising. As for the second sentence, it was precisely the comparison which Tupper there suggests that changed the present
writer's doubt to certainty, and led to this statement of the results
of the comparison.

and has used them with consummate art—an art whose fine appositeness Mr. Tupper's theory has done much to blur. Nothing more artistically perfect than the employment of the *exemplum* by the Pardoner, the Nun's Priest, the Monk, the Summoner, the Friar, and the Prioress, could well have been devised. But Mr. Tupper has read many mediæval sermons, and turned the pages of innumerable *exemplum* books. Would he venture to suggest that the range of the *exempla* is coterminous with the Seven Deadly Sins, and their application limited by the confines of the categories? Dissent from his theory admits fullest recognition of the unique place of the *exemplum* in Chaucer's art.

Furthermore, Chaucer's unsurpassed and unsurpassable *irony* is independent of any formal schematizing of a group of Tales. This mastery of irony on Chaucer's part is no discovery of Mr. Tupper's, nor would he for a moment claim it as his own. *Vixere fortes ante Agamemnona multi.* What he has seemingly overlooked is the fact that ironical inconsistency between precept and practice has been the fruitful theme of comedy and satire from Aristophanes to Meredith, with no thought of the Seven Deadly Sins. Ungracious pastors, who show the steep and thorny way to heaven, whilst themselves the primrose path of dalliance tread, and reck not their own rede, do not thereby become the formal exponents of a Vice. One may keep the " delicious inconsistency," without the Sin. And most of the ironical inconsistencies which Mr. Tupper sees are inconsistencies of his own making—the creations of pure assumption, " plausible conjecture," hypothetical " afterthoughts," adjustments " for the nonce." *For this particular type of irony* the evidence, in the case of all the Tales but one, is either wholly wanting or ambiguous. And in that one, where Chaucer *does* oppose rule of life to dogma, *he makes his meaning unmistakable:*

> *Thus can I preche agayn that same vyce*
> *Which that I use, and that is avaryce.*[4]

Chaucer does employ this sort of irony; but when he does, he relies on no ambiguous giving out. One cannot lose what one has never had, and nothing is taken from Chaucer's irony, if the tellers of the Tales are left as Chaucer drew them.

And finally, there is Chaucer's *art*. For that too Mr. Tupper has identified with his own particular conception of it. "Obviously he [Chaucer] did not share the modern tenet [5] that, while illustrations of masculine or feminine submissiveness in the married state are entirely worthy of a poet's art, *pointed revelations of the cardinal emotions must be deemed degrading to his genius.*" [6] I had thought that pointed revelations of the cardinal emotions were among Chaucer's glories, not his shame, and had been dull enough to think that others thought so too. If, however, by " pointed revelations of the cardinal emotions " Mr. Tupper means " the architectonic use of the *motif* of the Deadly Sins," I can only quote his next five words: " Fallacious indeed is the reasoning." When Mr. Tupper or anyone else shall demonstrate that Chaucer, at the height of his powers, reverted from the glorious liberty he had attained, to the more or less schematic tendencies of his earlier period, one may unhesitatingly (even though with somewhat of a sad perplexity) readjust one's opin-

---

[4] C, 427-28. Chaucer is no less unequivocal, for instance, in his matchless juxtaposition of practice and precept in the friar's suggestions for his dinner (D, 1838-47); etc.

[5] Where this tenet (which follows) is found outside Mr. Tupper's own pages it would be interesting to know.

[6] *Publications*, p. 127.

ions in conformity with established facts.   Meantime, one may hold to the conviction, based on such knowledge as we have, that the development was the other way.   If, however, as I believe, " the presence and prominence of the Sins *motif* completely collapses under scrutiny," [7] the question of its bearing upon Chaucer's art becomes a purely academic one.   And I shall not discuss it here.

This task has been entered upon and carried through reluctantly.   But the far-reaching significance of the principle of interpretation which I am combating has left me (believing as I do) without alternative.   I have examined Professor Tupper's argument with rigorous observance of the mediæval point of view, not stepping once outside what has been laid down as " absolutely essential to the proper interpretation of [Chaucer's] poetry," to wit, " his horizon, that is, his strict confinement within the bounds of fourteenth-century thought." [8]   So far as the Seven Deadly Sins are concerned, I have refrained with scrupulous care from the point of view of " the casual reader of today," and have done my devoir " to plumb the depths and shallows of mediæval thought." [9] As a result it is necessary to say that what has " sadly puzzled " some of us in the view so ably presented in the articles under review is not " a design so different from [our] twentieth-century conception of a poet's province." It is a design so acutely at variance with the modes of fourteenth-century thought.   It is not the mediæval conception that seems strange; it is the modern metamorphosis of that conception.

JOHN LIVINGSTON LOWES.

[7] *Publications*, p. 126.   Of course in Mr. Tupper's sentence the phrase which I have quoted is preceded by the words: " The *objection* to."

[8] *Journal*, p. 553.   [9] *Ibid.*, p. 554.

XII.—BEOWULF AND THE TRAGEDY OF FINNSBURG

If there were ever an occasion when, to paraphrase the words of Sir Benjamin Backbite, a neat rivulet of text might meander through a meadow of marginal annotation, the *Finnsburg Episode* would provide it. Hardly any passage in *Beowulf* has gathered to itself such a mass of exegesis. This is not surprising when we consider the highly allusive manner in which the story is told, the unusual words and idioms, and the corruptions of the text. In the *Finnsburg Fragment* the same obscurities and corruptions abound, and if the narrative itself is less broken and allusive, these textual difficulties and the loss of lines at the beginning and the end make its interpretation difficult. Unfortunately, many problems still remain to be settled; the labors of scholars have failed to bring agreement upon many important matters.

Under these circumstances, so familiar to all those who have studied *Beowulf* with care, a review of the whole much-disputed Finnsburg material seems, and is, a somewhat formidable undertaking. But the present article has a different aim from that of most criticisms on this subject; it is mainly concerned, not with the explanation of individual words or lines, but with the interpretation of the story as a whole. The chief end of the study of details is a   the narrative itself may be better understood. We have to hold the book at arm's length occasionally in order to avoid the risk of regarding these passages merely as highly-annotated lines. The emphasis here, then, will be upon this broader view, although it will constantly be necessary to consider the minutiæ of criticism, and in some cases to investigate disputed points afresh.

372

The larger outlines of the story seem, at the present time, to require some review and explanation. The original aim of the present paper was to discuss only certain special problems of interpretation. But decision in regard to any one passage is likely to depend upon the view taken of other passages, and of the personal and ethnographical relationships of the different characters. This involves so much cross-reference and explanation that it is almost simpler to give a review of the whole story. Such a review, taking due account of the latest investigations, is not, so far as the writer is aware, to be found in print at the time of writing.[1] While critics will differ as to the solution of these problems, it may be of service to have them restated, —occasionally, as in the vexed passage describing the events after Hengest and the Danes had spent the winter in Friesland with Finn, in some detail. A number of new suggestions are offered by the present writer, but no startling or revolutionary theories are proposed; the reader will rather find a modification of what may be called the traditional interpretation. Throughout, the attempt has been made to be conservative in argument and statement.[2]

---

[1] Since this investigation was undertaken, Professor Friedrich Klaeber read, at the meeting of the Central Division of the Modern Language Association of America, in December, 1914, a review of the Finnsburg Tale. The present paper was read by title at the corresponding meeting of the Eastern section of the Association. It is much to be hoped that Professor Klaeber's monograph may soon be published.

[2] It is no part of the design of the present paper to give an exhaustive bibliography of critical comments on the Finnsburg material. The advantages of such completeness are questionable; much of this criticism is valueless today. The history of opinion in regard to any vexed passage may be gained by reading the notes and consulting the bibliography suggested in an edition of *Beowulf* with full notes, like Schücking's revision of the Heyne-Socin text.

The necessity of basing general conclusions upon the unamended text, so far as this is possible, must be emphasized. By liberal conjectural emendation one may shape the interpretation to fit one's own fancies, making

It seems useless to reprint this here. References to special comments on disputed passages will be found in the appropriate places in the succeeding pages. The reader will find the following books and articles of especial value in determining the larger outlines of the story, and in deciding questions of ethnography and saga: Simrock, Beowulf, das älteste deutsche Epos, 1859, pp. 187-191; Müllenhoff, Beowulf, Berlin, 1889, pp. 105-107; Nordalbingische Studien, I, 157 ff.; Möller, Das altenglische Volksepos, Kiel, 1883 (proposes a radically different interpretation from that generally favored by earlier scholars, a book of great learning and ingenuity, but unsound in most of its conclusions); Heinzel, Anzeiger für deutsches Altertum, Vol. X, pp. 225 ff. (dissenting review of Möller); Bugge, Paul und Braune, Beiträge, Vol. XII, pp. 20-37 (reviews Möller, rejecting his interpretation, with much new criticism, a most important article); ten Brink, Paul's Grundriss, first ed., Vol. II, pp. 543 ff. (reprinted in ten Brink's Geschichte der englischen Litteratur, second ed., Strassburg, 1899, pp. 472-478, (an excellent survey; ten Brink did not accept the hypotheses of Möller); Koegel, Geschichte der deutschen Litteratur, Strassburg, 1894, Vol. I, pp. 163-169; Binz, Paul und Braune, Beiträge, Vol. XX, pp. 179 ff. (discusses traces of Germanic saga in place-names in the British Isles); Trautmann, Finn und Hildebrand, in Bonner Beiträge No. 7, 1903, see especially pp. 58-64 (an important work, chiefly concerned with textual criticism, with great freedom in conjectural emendation); Binz, review of Trautmann in Zeitschrift für deutsche Philologie, Vol. XXXVII, pp. 529 ff.; Boer, Finnsage und Nibelungensage, Zeitschrift für deutsches Altertum, Vol. XLVII, pp. 133 ff. (a suggestive comparison of the Finnsburg material with related or similar stories); R. Imelmann, Deutsche Litteraturzeitung, Vol. XXX, p. 999 (17 April, 1909); Brandl, Paul's Grundriss (second edition), 1908, Vol. II, pp. 983-1024 (an important and highly condensed review with full bibliography). Critical comments in the various standard translations of Beowulf may be consulted to advantage. Dr. R. W. Chambers's edition of Widsith, Cambridge, 1912, gives an admirable introduction to the general background of early legend and ethnography in Germanic poetry. The text of Beowulf used in the present investigation is that of Heyne and Socin, revised by Schücking, tenth edition, Paderborn, 1913.

a very pretty poem, but not *Beowulf*. Much mischief
has already been done by unnecessary alterations. Upon
them have sometimes been built most elaborate theories,
which, if true, would be of far-reaching significance. Thus
a well-known English scholar has recently conjecturally
identified the Hengest of the present poem with the
Hengest traditionally associated with Horsa, upon the
basis of a textual emendation which was both unnecessary
and unidiomatic, but which was widely adopted in early
editions of *Beowulf*.[3] His whole argument depends upon
this emendation; it falls to the ground if the reading of
the manuscript, which gives perfect sense, be retained.
Emendation is, in the present state of the text, sometimes
inevitable, but it should in most cases be the editor's last
resort, and conclusions depending upon it should be
treated as hypothetical. It is gratifying to note that the
general trend of modern text-criticism is towards greater
conservatism, rather than greater license.

These much-discussed lines deserve all the patient care
which scholars have lavished upon them, since they present
not only the fascination of an enigma, but the enduring
charm of great poetry. The Finnsburg story is one of
the most dramatic in the whole literature of the Heroic
Age. It is far superior to the main subject-matter of
Beowulf, if human passions and human struggles are
more fitting subjects for epic than contests with demons
and dragons. The two versions which have been preserved are, as has often been noted, most striking examples
of epic and lay technic. The *Episode* is retrospective and
elegiac, at once revealing the outlines of a long story, and
emphasizing its more dramatic and pathetic moments.
The *Fragment,* on the other hand, is sharp as an etching,

rapid of movement, brisk of dialog, concerned only with the moment. The moonlight gleams upon the weapons of the advancing warriors, there is a swift alarm, taunts and defiance are exchanged, and the battle is on. The whole tale of strife and bloodshed in the halls of King Finn is called by the *Beowulf*-poet *heal-gamen,*—a thing well suited to please the champions at Hrothgar's feast. If the terrible revenge meted out to the enemies of the Danes does not give us the same savage joy today, the passion and pathos of the story have not lost their charm with the passing of years.

I

The Sorrows of Hildeburg

The *Finnsburg Episode* tells of hatred and violence, of injury and insult atoned for in sorrow and slaughter. But there is also a place for the tragedy of an innocent victim of the struggle,—the unhappy Queen Hildeburg. The emphasis upon her sufferings gives the beginning of the *Episode* an elegiac note, which recurs later on, in the passage describing her lamentations at the funeral pyre upon which lie the bodies of her brother and her son. An examination of the significance of the figure of Hildeburg in this story, and a consideration of other stories similar to this, will serve to indicate the general type to which the tale of Finnsburg belongs, and prepare the way for the subsequent investigation of other matters.

The main outlines of the situation at the opening of the narrative are fairly clear. Whatever view is taken of other circumstances, so much seems certain: Hildeburg, a princess of the Hocings, a tribe allied with or forming a component part of the Danes, is the queen of

Finn, king of the Frisians. A conflict, the result of treachery, breaks out at her husband's court between her kinsmen, led by her brother Hnæf, and her husband's men. In this conflict Hnæf and a son of Hildeburg are killed.[4] The queen is thus torn between affection for her husband and her son, and for her brother; for her adopted people on the one hand, and for her kinsmen and countrymen on the other. On whichever side she arrays herself, she will be guilty of disloyalty to those to whom she is bound by affection and by ties of family. This tragic situation was, we may be sure, not uncommon in actual fact in early days. Often a queen was given in marriage as a means of healing enmities between hostile peoples. One of the regular epithets of a queen in Anglo-Saxon poetry is *freoþuwebbe,* "weaver of peace," used by Widsith of Ealhhild, the princess who, according to his tale, married Eormanric the Goth.[5] But often the smoldering fires of ancient hatred or of newly kindled passion were too

[4] Hildeburg is the daughter of Hoc (1076); Hnæf is prince of the Hocings (*Widsith* 29). Hnæf and his men are referred to as Danes 1108 (cf. 1114), (1069 is ambiguous) 1090 (cf. 1158). Hildeburg is nowhere stated to be the wife of Finn, but there can be no doubt of this; she is called *cwēn,* a term only applied to queens in Beowulf, and Finn is the only *cyning* save Hnæf (*Fragment* 2 cannot refer to Hengest, see below). The carrying off of Hildeburg at the end of the story, with the treasures of Finn, suggests that she was his queen; compare the experiences of Ongentheow's consort. See for an outline of events in the story, Trautmann, *Finn und Hildebrand,* pp. 59 ff. That treachery was at work in causing the fight between the men of Hnæf and of Finn seems clear from the statement that Hildeburg "could not praise the good faith of the Eotenas" 1071, which of course means that she had good cause to blame their treachery (cf. Schuchardt, *Die Negation in Beowulf,* Berlin, 1910, p. 70).

[5] See discussion of this word by the present writer in *Modern Philology,* Vol. IV (1906), p. 350; also by R. W. Chambers, *Widsith,* pp. 21-28.

strong, and strife broke out between the very peoples whom the queen was to unite in bonds of love.

The frequency with which this tragic situation appears in early poetry accounts for its presence here. We cannot be absolutely certain that Hildeburg was given to Finn to cement peace between her people and his, but it should be remembered that this is antecedently very likely, as the Danes and Frisians were ancient enemies. Siebs says,[8] "During the Middle Ages, to the end of the eleventh century, the Danes were the worst foes of the Frisians, and through their depredations on their coasts were in constant conflict with them." Probably the ill-feeling between Danes and Frisians revealed in the tale of Finnsburg was of long standing. The whole story appears to belong to a type which may be reduced to its simplest form somewhat as follows: Two peoples are united by a royal marriage. But this era of peace is broken by an attack upon one of the queen's countrymen, or upon a band of her countrymen, while at her husband's court. In the midst of the conflict the figure of the queen, who is tortured by conflicting duties and emotions, stands out full of tragic pathos. The causes of the quarrel vary: an ancient feud, a real or a fancied insult, the avarice or ambition that overrides the keeping of pledges.

It will be instructive to review briefly episodes of this general character in early story, especially those in *Beowulf* itself and those which must have been familiar to the audience for which that poem was composed, to note the motivation which underlies these episodes, and to observe the moments of the action which poets have chosen to make especially prominent. One might, indeed, make a very pretty collection of such incidents in the

---

[8] Paul's *Grundriss*, (second edition), Vol. II, p. 524.

manner of Boccaccio, a kind of *De Casibus Feminarum Illustrium* of the Heroic Age. A few *exempla* must suffice here.[7]

One of these unhappy ladies is Hrothgar's own daughter Freawaru, betrothed to Ingeld, prince of the Heathobards, a people with whom the Danes had previously been at war. Upon his return to the court of Hygelac, Beowulf speaks of Freawaru as having carried the ale-flagon to the nobles of Hrothgar at the banquet, and as having dispensed treasure in the hall. She was, then, in all likelihood, one of the company who had listened to the minstrel's tale of King Finn, and she might have seen in the misfortunes of Queen Hildeburg a forecast of her own future.[8] For, says Beowulf,

2024   She is betrothed,
     Young and gold-adorned, to the gracious son of Froda.
     It hath seemed good to the friend of the Scyldings,
     Shepherd of the people, and he accounteth it policy,
     To lessen by her marriage[9] a deal of deadly feuds,
     Of contests.

The fatal danger of this " policy " is all too well realized by Beowulf; he knows that revenge for blood-spilling is stronger than oaths of peace or the gracious presence of a queen.

2029   Rarely anywhere
     After the death of a warrior[10] is for a little time
     The murderous spear lowered, though the bride be fair!

---

[7] For a review of earlier interpretations of the Finnsburg-story, see Boer, *Zeitschrift für deutsches Altertum*, Vol. XLVII, pp. 148 ff. Boer sees the closest analogy in the second part of the Nibelungen-saga.

[8] See below, p. 380, note 11.

[9] Literally, " by the woman."

[10] *Leod-hryre* may also mean " people-death," the slaying of warriors, but I prefer the rendering " death of a prince," as in 2391.

These words may well serve as the *leit-motif* not only of this story, but of the whole group of stories with which we are here dealing. Beowulf sketches, in pursuance of this thought, the train of events after Freawaru shall have gone to live at the Heathobard court. It may well be an annoyance to the Heathobards, he says, to see a thane in the retinue of Freawaru wearing spoils taken in the past from a Heathobard warrior, and trouble will follow. The *Beowulf*-poet here violates the propriety of strict logic in making his hero outline the well-known story of Ingeld and Freawaru, which must be supposed to be subsequent to Beowulf's visit to Hrothgar.[11] The poet himself often

Here it would refer to the death of Froda, Ingeld's father. According to Saxo Grammaticus, Bk. VI, Froda was killed by the father of his son's wife. Saxo, however, tells the story in so late and altered a form that we must draw conclusions from him as to the earlier form of the story with great reserve. As Olrik points out (*Danmarks Heltedigtning*, Vol. II, p. 38), this does not necessarily refer to the death of Froda, since in the form of the story represented in *Beowulf* the revenge is of a young Heathobard warrior for his father. The transference of the revenge to Ingeld belongs to a later form of the tale. The "young warrior" (2044) can hardly be Ingeld; the old hero addresses him (2047) as *mīn wine*, too familiar for a retainer to his king, and the avenger (*sē ōðer* 2061) escapes from Ingeld's court, whereupon the king feels his anger rise and his love for his wife diminish. In Saxo, however, Ingeld is the avenger.

[11] Olrik, in his very thorough and suggestive discussion of the Ingeld-story (*Danmarks Heltedigtning*, Vol. II, pp. 37 ff.), says "I must utter a warning against the very common but very meaningless assertion that what Beowulf relates in the Danish royal court at this point is not a narrative of what has already happened, but a prophecy of future events." His view of the situation is that Freawaru had already had these experiences at the court of Ingeld— the slaying of her thane, and the loss of her husband's love—and had "either been cast off or had returned home of her own accord (selv)" (p. 38).

I cannot agree with Olrik. 1) The tenses referring to Hrothgar's plans, *hafað þæs geworden* (2026), where according to O.'s view we

gives us glimpses of the future, as in regard to the burning of the hall Heorot (83-85), or the future troubles in the Danish royal house, and he utilizes the present opportunity for reference to the tragic outcome of the feuds between Danes and Heathobards. An old Heathobard warrior "eggs on" to revenge the son of the man whose armor Freawaru's thane is wearing; the thane is killed, but the murderer escapes, because he knows the land well. Then Ingeld's love for his wife grows cool, and hatred against the Danes begins to rage in his breast (*weallað wæl-niðas*). And so, says Beowulf, foreseeing such trou-

should expect the pluperfect, and *talað* (2027), where we should expect the preterit or the perfect, are contrary to this hypothesis. O. does actually translate the second of these phrases, incorrectly, as "har fundet det raadeligt," which makes the sense better accord with his view. If these sad events at Ingeld's court had already taken place, moreover, Hrothgar's notions about the excellence of his "policy" would probably be somewhat modified! 2) Against O.'s view are the tenses in Beowulf's narrative, which opens with *mæg þæs þonne ofþyncan* (2032), a clear reference to future time, and continues throughout in the present tense, frequently equivalent in Anglo-Saxon to the future, of course. Moreover, there is, I think, no other long passage in the poem in which the "historical present" is used in relating past events, as O. assumes to be the case here. 3) It would hardly be natural for Beowulf to say, even in view of Anglo-Saxon fondness for understatement, that he does not consider the good faith of the Heathobards'sincere and their friendship firm, if Ingeld had already lost his love for Freawaru and caused her to return to her father's court, if he was already feeling "slaughterous enmity," and if the oaths of peace had already been broken on both sides (2063).

Moreover, this prophetic glimpse into the future is in entire accord with the peculiarities of Anglo-Saxon epic technic. Cf. *Beowulf* 83 ff.; 1240 ff.; 3021 ff., and see Hart, *Ballad and Epic*, Boston, 1907; and Klaeber, *Archiv*, Vol. cxxvi, pp. 46-47, where many bibliographical references to this stylistic habit are noted. Klaeber calls particular attention to a similar peculiarity in the *Æneid*. There is at all events no need of viewing with suspicion Beowulf's temporary excursion into vaticination.

17

ble as this, " I do not account the good faith of the Heathobards to the Danes sincere."

In much this strain Hrothgar's poet speaks in the lay
of Finn.

1071   Surely Hildeburg could not praise
       The good faith of the Eotenas; innocent,
       Was she bereaved of her dear ones in the play of shields,
       Of her son and brother.

So far as the woman is concerned, the general situation
underlying both stories is much the same. How famous
was the story of Ingeld is shown by the references elsewhere in *Beowulf* and in *Widsith,* also by its elaborate
though distorted form in Saxo, and by the well-known
letter of Alcuin, in which he laments that men are fonder
of hearing about Ingeld than about Christ,—" Quid
Hinieldus cum Christo?"

Other striking parallels will occur immediately to the
reader, and have already been pointed out by scholars.
In the *Volsungasaga,*[12] Signy, the daughter of King Volsung and sister of Sigmund, is wedded to King Siggeir
of Gothland, who, to avenge what he considers an insult
on the part of Sigmund, invites Volsung and his sons to
visit him in his own land at the end of three months'
time after the wedding festivities. The invitation is accepted; Volsung and his men come to Siggeir's court.
The unhappy queen, realizing that treachery is afoot,
comes out to meet her father and brothers, and implores
them to return. But Volsung scorns to be thought a
coward; he will neither go back nor allow his daughter
to leave her husband, despite her tears. " Thou shalt

---

[12] Ed. Ranisch, Berlin, 1891; German translation by Edzardi,
Stuttgart, 1881; English translation by Magnússon and Morris (no
date).

certainly go home to thy husband and dwell with him, howsoever it fare with us." At daybreak the next morning Volsung and his warriors land, in armor, and are attacked and most of them slain by the forces of King Siggeir. Throughout the narrative it is Signy who engages the chief attention, down to her death with Siggeir in the flames of the burning hall,—one of the greatest scenes in Germanic poetry. With her brother Sigmund and their child Sinfjotli she takes a dreadful revenge upon Siggeir, burning him and his warriors to death.

Even more familiar is the tale of the marriage of Gudrun, the widow of Sigurd, to Atli, King of the Huns, of his treacherous invitation to her kinsmen to visit his court, of their death at his hands, and of Gudrun's revenge. The Scandinavian version, as represented in the *Poetic Edda*,[13] is to be preferred to the narrative of the *Nibelungenlied,* since it represents an earlier form of the story. The motive of Atli is desire of the great Nibelung Hoard, in the possession of Gudrun's brothers. Gudrun's consent to the marriage is gained by a drink of forgetfulness given her by Grimhild, the mother of Atli, who is wise in magic. Gudrun's kinsmen are treacherously invited to the Hunnish court, their men are cut down by Atli's warriors, Hogni's heart is cut from his living body, and Gunnar is thrown into a den of serpents. For the death of her kinsmen Gudrun takes a dreadful revenge, in putting her two sons by Atli to death, and in giving him their blood to drink and their hearts to eat. Finally she kills Atli himself, and setting fire to the hall,

---

[13] Cf. *Guþrúnarkviþa II; Atlakviþa; Atlamál.* German translations by Gering, Leipzig and Vienna (no date) ; and by Genzmer, with notes by Heusler, Diederichs, Jena, 1914. There is at present no modern English translation of this portion of the Edda which is easily accessible (1914).

perishes in the flames.[14]   Here, as in the story of Signy,
the woman is loyal to her kin rather than to her husband.
We do not learn how Hildeburg and Freawaru decided;
their helpless figures are lost in the dark deeds about
them.   In the Nibelung tale there is no antecedent feud
to explain the quarrel, as in the Freawaru-Ingeld story;
no rankling insult as in the *Volsungasaga;* it is a case of
treacherous violation of hospitality through greed for
gold.   But it is noticeable in all these stories that the
immediate injury, the initiation of hostilities, comes, not
from the kinsmen of the queen, but from her husband
or his retainers.[15]

In these tales no figure commands more interest, either
for the ancient poet or for the modern reader, than the
unhappy woman married to the foreign king.   The episode in which Beowulf tells the story of Ingeld is apparently introduced to make more effective and pathetic the
mention of the lovely Danish princess Freawaru.   In the
story of Finn, as told in the *Episode,* no character is
more individualized or prominent than Hildeburg.   Finn
is only the conventional king and leader; the poet wastes
no time in making him seem real or in describing his

[14] In other lays, of course, her fortunes are different; cf. *Guþ-
rúnarhvot.*

[15] These parallels are cited only with a view to illustrating the
type of story with which we here have to deal, and the prominence
and significance of the role played by the queen. Into the difficult
question of how the Finn-story developed and of its relationship to
the great legends of Signy and Gudrun-Kriemhild, I do not care to
enter here. Interinfluence among these stories there may have been,
but the nature and extent of this are exceedingly difficult to determine. For a discussion of these relationships, the reader is referred to Boer, Finnsage und Nibelungensage, *Zeitschrift für
deutsches Altertum,* Vol. XLVII, pp. 125 ff. Conclusive results in
these matters are very difficult to attain. I cannot agree with Boer's
theories.

emotions. Hengest receives more attention, but Hnæf is
scarcely mentioned. Hildeburg is kept prominently before the hearer; the beginning, the middle, and the end
of the *Episode* all make mention of her. First of all, her
misfortunes are told:

> Surely Hildeburg could not praise
> The good faith of the Eotenas; innocent
> Was she bereaved of her dear ones in the play of shields,
> Of her son and brother; they fell as Fate decreed,
> 1075 Wounded by the spear. A sad woman she!
> Not without reason did the daughter of Hoc
> Bemoan her fate when morning dawned
> And she beheld beneath the skies
> Her kinsmen dead by violence, where once she [16] had enjoyed
> The greatest of earth's joys.

After the carnage at Finnsburg, the dead warriors are
burnt upon a huge funeral pyre. Once more the poet·
seizes the occasion to arouse sympathy with the unfortunate queen.

> Then at the pyre of Hnæf, did Hildeburg command them
> 1115 To give unto the flames her own son,
> To burn his body and to place him on the fire.
> The wretched woman wept on his shoulder,
> Lamented him in lays.

And in the closing picture of all, the very last words of
the *Episode,* the avenging Danes are represented as bringing Hildeburg back to her old home.

> 1157   Over the sea-waves
> Did they carry the noble lady to the Danes,
> Brought her back to her people.

This elegiac treatment of the career of the unhappy
Hildeburg recalls the fondness of the Anglo-Saxons for
themes similar to this. They often drew the inspiration

[16] See note 18, page 402 below.

for their lyric poetry from heroic story, and they were particularly fond of dwelling in these lyrics upon the misfortunes of distressed ladies. It is scarcely necessary to cite instances,—*The Banished Wife's Lament,* in all probability the lyric cry of the queen of the Offa-saga; *The Lover's Message,* in which Professor Schofield has noted a similarity to an incident of the Tristram-story; *The First Riddle,* variously interpreted as the lament of Signy or as an episode connected with Odoacer or some other hero; the stanzas in *The Song of Deor,* dealing with the princess Beadohild, the beloved of Weland, and perhaps also with Hild, the betrothed of Hedin.[17] Lyric and epic technic are occasionally very close to each other. Miss Rickert has even conjectured that the Anglo-Saxon lyrics may have formed portions of lost epics, though we must be cautious about accepting this suggestion. Certain it is that both in mood and form the two are often strikingly similar.

The most distinguished lady at Hrothgar's banquet, his queen, is of foreign birth. We know little of her people, the Helmingas, or of their relations with the Danes. The name *Wealhþēow* itself is puzzling; it does not fall into line with Scandinavian traditions, and is perhaps, as Olrik has suggested, of English origin.[18] It is interesting

---

[17] For the *Banished Wife's Lament,* see article by the present writer in *Modern Philology,* Vol. v, pp. 387-405; for Schofield's suggestion, see his *English Literature from the Norman Conquest to Chaucer,* p. 202; for the so-called *First Riddle,* see *Publications of the Modern Language Association,* Vol. xvii, pp. 247 ff., and Bradley, *Athenæum,* 1902, p. 758; for the *Song of Deor,* an article by the writer in *Modern Philology,* Vol. ix, pp. 23-45; also by Tupper, *ibid.,* pp. 265-267.

[18] *Danmarks Heltedigtning,* Vol. i, p. 27; cf. R. W. Chambers, *Widsith,* pp. 81 ff. Deutschbein, *Zeitschrift für deutsches Altertum,* Vol. liv, p. 224 f., suggests that it may be an abstract name

to note that for her, as for Freawaru, tragedy is impending.
Immediately after the lay of Hildeburg is finished,
Wealhtheow, addressing her husband, pleads for the peaceful succession of her children Hrethric and Hrothmund,
and appeals to the king's <u>brother</u> Hrothulf to assure it ↑
to them.   How terribly her hopes were destined to be
disappointed we can gather from hints in various places
in the epic and elsewhere.   Apparently estrangement
came at length between Hrothgar and Hrothulf, and still
later Hrothulf forced Hrethric from the royal power, and
killed him.   Vengeance followed, however, and he was
himself slain by Heoroweard, the son of Hrothgar's elder
brother Heorogar.   " It is in contrast with this tragic background," says Dr. Chambers, " that the poet of *Beowulf*
.emphasizes the generous confidence towards each other of
Beowulf and his kinsman, king Hygelac." [19]   May it
not also be that the tragedy of Wealhtheow, which must
have been well known to the audience for which the
Beowulf-poet wrote, is designedly brought into connection
with the tale of Hildeburg?   The irony of it all is heightened by the rejoicings which fill the hall, and by the
happiness which is at present the lot of Wealhtheow.   Of
such contrasts as this Germanic poets were exceedingly
fond, as many passages in *Beowulf* illustrate.   This is no
episode of the Hildeburg type; but the telling of Hildeburg's story, in the presence of a queen who was herself
of another people than that of her husband, whose efforts
to keep the peace were destined to come to naught, and
whose daughter Freawaru [20] was to experience much the

invented by the Anglo-Saxon poet. He compares such names as
Widsith and Unferth, and suggests, although realizing that Wealhtheow is very sympathetically portrayed, that it may be " ein
scherz- oder spott-name . . . . ein ehrenname geworden."
        [19] *Loc. cit.*, p. 83.   [20] Possibly her step-daughter.

same melancholy destiny as the wife of King Finn, is
surely not without significance.[21]

[21] It has been conjectured that the tale of Hildeburg is an " abduction-story " of the type familiar in the story of Hilde and Hedin.
This view has commanded some acceptance, and is occasionally repeated today. It was originated and most fully set forth by Möller
(*Altenglisches Volksepos*, pp. 70 ff.). Möller based his proof upon
deriving both the Finn-story and the Hilde-Hedin story from the
myth of Frey and Skirnir and the wooing of the giant-maiden Gerd,
familiar in the *Poetic Edda*. He found further confirmation for his
theory in a late *märchen* from the island of Sylt.

It behooves us to be cautious in assigning " mythical " origins to
matter as modern in much of its present form as the Hilde-Gudrun
story. Even Müllenhoff's derivation of the Hildesage from the
" necklace-myth "—a far more convincing interpretation—must be
regarded with some scepticism. " Our sources are too late to draw
such far-reaching conclusions in regard to the original form of the
story " (Jiriczek, *Deutsche Heldensage*, p. 187, Leipzig, 1906).
And it is impossible to assent when Möller attempts to connect the
Finn-sage with the Gudrun portion of the Middle High German epic.
There is little real similarity save that one of the characters is
named Hildeburg. The same is the case with the *märchen* just referred to; it tells of a king named Finn, but presents little further
likeness. The name Finn or Fin is not unknown in popular literature which has nothing to do with the Finn-story in *Beowulf*, witness the " diabolic personage or warlock " of the ballad " The Fause
Knight on the Road " (Child, *English and Scottish Popular Ballads*,
Vol. I, p. 21). Moreover, Möller's arguments depend to a large extent upon his very arbitrary interpretation of the text, which has
already been criticized in detail by Heinzel, Bugge, and others, and
cannot command acceptance today. Boer (*Zeitschrift für deutsches
Altertum*, Vol. XLVII, p. 150) has some good comments on Möller's
view that this is an abduction-story of the Hilde-type, pointing out
that Möller has no support from the text in reconstructing the events
preceding the first clash between the Danes and the Frisians, and
continuing: " If the Finn-sage were a variant of the Kudrunsage,
one would expect that Hrolf's revenge for Hoc [i. e., as Möller conceived the story] would be crowned with success. . . . The idea that
Hengest is desirous of avenging his lord Hnæf is everywhere prominent; nowhere does the revenge concern Hildeburg. That she is
carried away by the victors, moreover, does not prove that she had
earlier been abducted by Finn,—what is to be done with a lady who

It is important to note that the *Finnsburg Episode* is, in the main, a story of vengeance.   This theme is partly motivated and is rendered more effective by the opening passage, and by the further description of the sorrows of Hildeburg.   The prominence of the revenge motive is not to be wondered at;—a song sung by a Danish minstrel in the hall of a Danish king on an occasion of great national rejoicing should leave no insult to Danish pride unavenged.

The treachery of the Frisians has brought great misfortune upon the Danes; their prince and leader Hnæf has been slain.   Although many Frisians have been killed, the Danes are obliged to compromise with them, and to accept Finn as their lord,—a bitter humiliation.   Oaths

belonged to the [Danish] royal family, and whose husband has been killed? She could not be left behind all alone in the devastated country." Boer is also quite right in denying (p. 160) the presence of mythical elements in the story. Möller's attempt to bring the tale of Finn into the class of *Entführungssagen* may, then, be considered sufficiently refuted. There is no need to traverse ground already fully covered by earlier critics. But the notion that Hildeburg was abducted still persists. Schücking says (*Beowulf*, ed. of 1913, p. 119) "Hildeburg ist wahrscheinlich eine von Finn im Kriege geraubte Dänin (vgl. 1159, 2930)." But what bearing do these references to the abduction of Ongentheow's queen have on the story of Finn and Hildeburg? It must first be shown that both tales have enough general similarity to warrant our identifying these two episodes as of the same character. There is nothing in the text to support the view that Hildeburg was abducted; the circumstances of her union with Finn are left quite untold. In any case, Hildeburg enjoyed a time of great happiness at Finn's court (1079-80) as his queen (*cwēn* 1153). In *Beowulf* *cwēn* always means "queen" (62 is of course defective), and the context *cyning on corðre ond sēo cwēn numen* makes this still plainer. The burden of proof is certainly on the shoulders of those who would make of the Finn-story a tale of abduction. For an elaborate attempt to connect the Finn-saga with the Hilde-saga "mythically," see Much's review of Panzer, *Archiv*, Vol. CVIII, pp. 406 f.; not a convincing piece of work.

of peace are sworn on both sides, but the Danes take the
first advantageous opportunity to break their compact,
and to revenge themselves upon Finn and his men.
Throughout the tale every effort is made by the poet
to enlist the sympathy of the hearer in the Danish cause,
and to exalt Danish valor. Although Hnæf has been
killed, nothing further is said of any Danish loss, while
Finn has been "deprived of all his thanes, save only a
few " (1080 ff.). It is he who is forced to sue for peace,
not the Danes (1085 ff.). His own promises are detailed
at length, but nothing is said of the Danish side of the
bargain, though the implication is clearly that Finn is
to become lord of all the Danes who have survived. Perhaps any special mention of the Danish pledges is avoided
because the final consummation of revenge involves a
breaking of these pledges. The death of Hnæf, then, and
the humiliation of the Danes in being forced to follow
the "slayer of their lord " [22] provides ample logical justification for Danish revenge, according to Germanic ideas,
but the sufferings of Hildeburg through Frisian faithless-
ness touch the heart, and make retaliation seem all the
more necessary and justifiable.

The revenge of the wife or of her kin for the treacherous attack by her husband's followers forms a prominent part of the stories of Signy and Siggeir, and of
Gudrun and Atli, as we have just observed. It is not so
clear in the tale of Ingeld and Freawaru. A passage in
Beowulf seems to connect the burning of the hall Heorot
with a feud between Hrothgar and his son-in-law Ingeld,
but the exact circumstances which motivate this feud are
not plain.

[22] See below, p. 406, note 21.

The hall arose
82   High and wide-gabled; it waited for the hot surges,
.   For the hostile flames. Not long was it to be
     Ere deadly hatred between son-in-law and father-in-law
.   Should wake to life through bloody feud.

And Widsith relates that

45   Hrothwulf and Hrothgar for a very long time
     Kept peace together, uncle and nephew,
     After they drove away the race of the Vikings
     And beat down the power of Ingeld,
     Cut to pieces at Heorot the hosts of the Heathobards.

Axel Olrik, in his very detailed study of the Ingeld-
Starkad story, expresses the belief that these passages
represent another conception of the " strife " after the
marriage of Ingeld and Freawaru narrated in *Beowulf*
2032-2067, with the difference that it is localized at
Heorot, instead of at the court of the Heathobards. The
testimony of Saxo upon this point is interesting, but in-
conclusive. The most natural reconstruction of the story
seems to be that proposed by Müllenhoff,[23] that the defeat
of the Heathobards at Heorot was a sequel to the earlier
outbreak of strife at Ingeld's court, that it was a punishment for the insult to Freawaru, for the death of her
thane, and for the breaking of the oaths, and that with
this decisive victory at Heorot the Danish-Heathobard
feud came to an end. But Olrik rejects this interpretation.[24] The point is in any case obscure and difficult of
decision. It may not do to rely confidently for the later
events in the Ingeld-story upon the passages just cited.
But the implication of impending trouble between Danes
and Heathobards is clear. No Dane could let the matter

[23] *Deutsche Alterthumskunde*, Vol. v, p. 316 (Berlin, 1891).
[24] *Heltedigtning*, Vol. ii, p. 39; " Müllenhoff's opfattelse . . . . . .
lader sig næppe opretholde."

rest with the killing of the bride's thane. Revenge is in the air, even if its course cannot be traced with certainty.

Before considering in more detail the nature of the vengeance in the Finn-story, the events leading up to this vengeance must be somewhat more carefully examined, with particular reference to the interpretation of the text.

II

The Treachery of the Frisians

The actors in this drama are members of two North Sea tribes, or rather groups of tribes. For purposes of convenience we may call one group Danes and the other Frisians. The original leader of the Danish group was apparently Hnæf, who on being killed in the Frisian onslaught was succeeded by Hengest. We are told in *Widsith* that Hnæf ruled the Hocingas (29). *Beowulf* seems to make it clear that he was the son of Hoc, and brother of Hildeburg. His men are called *Dene,* and he himself is " battle-warrior of the Here-Scyldings " (1108), and " hero of the Half-Danes," *hæleð Healf-Dena* (1069).[1] The exact relation of " Half-Danes " to Danes proper is not clear. Possibly they were an allied folk who had strengthened by intermarriage the ties which bound them

---

[1] Or *hæleð* may be plural, referring to his warriors. There are many interpretations of these opening lines. In the present argument in regard to the tribes it makes little difference whether *hæleð* be taken as singular or plural. For the arbitrary alteration of the MS. reading to *Healfdenes* there is no justification. Bugge rightly rejected it: " ich finde kein beispiel davon, dass ein anführer als der *hæleð* seines königs bezeichnet wird." The best modern editors print the reading of the MS.; see texts of Wyatt, Sedgefield, Holthausen, Schücking, etc.

to the Danes. The name *Healfdene* is commonly held
to indicate that the hero's mother was from another people. Probably such an epithet as " Half-Dane" need not
be taken too literally. Elsewhere in the poem " West-
Danes " and " East-Danes " are terms somewhat loosely
used, perhaps chosen for their picturesque suggestion of
the extent of the Danish territory, perhaps for metrical
reasons or for the sake of alliteration.[2]   Sigeferth, the
Secgena lēod of Frag. 24, is clearly an ally of the Danes.
It is sometimes said that his people were one of the Half-
Danish tribes, but there appears to be no conclusive evidence of this.[3]   It seems doubtful if, especially in poetry,
the nicer geographical and political distinctions between
these peoples were carefully maintained. Indeed, such
distinctions may well not have been understood either by
the Anglo-Saxon poet or by his hearers. But the broader
lines of contrast are clear. Opposed to the Danes are
the Frisians, the men of King Finn, who are also called
Eotenas (1072, 1088, etc.). Explanation of this term is
difficult, and further complicated by being involved in the
discussion over the ethnography of the Jutes. A reasonable solution seems to be that the word *Eotenas* is the
result of confusion of the tribal name *Eotas* (*Widsith,
Ȳtas* or *Ȳtan*), probably the *Iutae* of Bede, and the *Eutii*
or *Eutiones* of Theudebert's letter to Justinian, with the
appellative *eotenas* " elves," " supernatural beings." This
is the view of Siebs, perhaps the foremost authority on

[2] Cf. 828, 383, 392, etc.
[3] The reason for grouping the Hocingas and the Secgan in this
way seems to be that Hnæf the Hocing is called a Half-Dane, and
that among the forces under his command are the Secgan. But
even if the Secgan were allied folk, under the command of a leader
of the Half-Danes, and included in the general term Dene, they
may not themselves have been Half-Danes.

Frisian conditions, who conjectures that the *Eutii* or *Eutiones* were once the nearest neighbors of the Frisians, and that the occupation by the Frisians of Jutish territory after the Conquest of Britain assisted the confusion between the two names.[4] It may also be suggested that the name Finn, occasionally applied to supernatural beings in Germanic story, may have further helped in this process. Finn, King of the *Eotas,* might easily be confused with a Finn of the *eotenas.* It should be said that the Frisian king mentioned in *Beowulf* has nothing supernatural about him, nor is there any evidence of his connection with mythology. The explanation here offered for the term *Eotenas* may be regarded as conjectural, but of one thing we may be sure: that the Eotenas were not Danes; they were the group of men opposed to the Danes.[5]

[4] See Paul's *Grundriss*, Vol. II, p. 524, and Vol. I, p. 1158. For a careful review of the chief questions connected with the location of the Jutes, and the forms of the proper name applied to this people, with bibliographical references, see Chambers, *Widsith*, pp. 237 ff.

[5] Möller's unfortunate theory that the *Eotenas* are the men of Hnæf the Dane, which has done much to obscure understanding of this story, is revived in Miss M. G. Clarke's *Sidelights on Teutonic History During the Migration Period,* Cambridge (Eng.) University Press, 1911, pp. 181 ff. Her arguments are not weighty, and she does not appear to have considered the criticisms of this interpretation made by previous scholars. See especially Heinzel's review of Möller's *Altenglisches Volksepos,* Kiel, 1883, in *Anzeiger für deutsches Altertum,* Vol. X, p. 227, Trautmann, *Bonner Beiträge,* VII, p. 13; also Bugge, ten Brink and Boer (cf. p. 374 above), Sedgefield, Schücking, and Wyatt in their editions, and Gering in his translation of the poem, in which he renders Eotenas "Friesen." Others might easily be cited.

Miss Clarke says: "In the first case, l. 1072, the use of the word (*i. e. Eotenas*) is ambiguous; there is nothing to show to which party it refers. We will let Heinzel reply to this: "'fürwahr Hildeburg hatte keinen grund die treue (oder vielmehr "güte") der Eotenas zu preisen, sie wurde ohne schuld des bruders und des sohnes

The view that the name *Eotenas* really points to the
Jutes, or by confusion, to Frisians inhabiting Jutish territory, seems to be confirmed by the passage which describes the fortunes of King Heremod.   After distin-
guishing himself by savage and unkingly violence towards
his own people (cf. 1718 ff.), Heremod suffered the consequences.

901   . . . Heremōdes hild sweðrode,
               eafoð ond ellen. Hē mid Eotenum wearð
               on fēonda geweald forð forlācen,
               snūde forsended.

" Heremod's prowess in battle waned, his strength and
might.   He among the Jutes was betrayed into the hands

im kampfe beraubt.'—Dieser bruder, den sie durch die feindseligkeit
der Eotenas verloren hat, soll auch ein Eote sein, und sie selbst eine
Eotin! "
    She continues: " In the second case, *viz.*, l. 1088, Eotena seems
clearly to refer to Hnæf's men: *hie*, which is the subject of the
clause, which must denote the same persons as the *hig* in l. 1085,
which is the subject of the principal clause, and which evidently
refers to the Frisians." Miss Clarke forgets the freedom with which
the subject often shifts in Anglo-Saxon poetry; let her look at
the plural verb *gemænden* 1101, a few lines below in this same passage, the subject of which is clearly the Frisians. Does she think
the *hie* in the next line refers to the same people? (See also Heinzel,
loc. cit.)
    As to 1141, Miss Clarke says: " Commentators who wish to make
Eotena correspond to *Fresna* translate *gemunde* as ' remember,'
i. e. take vengeance on; but it is much more natural to suppose that
the feeling described by *gemunde* was one of sorrow for lost friends,
in which case *Eotena bearn* refers of course to Hengest's own men."
How is it possible to maintain that this is " more natural " after
the lines just preceding, in which Hengest's desire for vengeance is
expressly emphasized, *hē tō gyrn-wræce swiðor þōhte þonne tō sæ-
lāde?* Such special pleading as this hardly deserves refutation, but
it is perhaps well that the futility of the attempt to support this
general theory should be made as plain as possible. For the interpretation of the vexed passage 1140 ff. see below.

of his enemies, quickly sent forth." Joseph [6] proposed to render *eotenas* " Jutes," while otherwise accepting Bugge's reading " durch verrat in die gewalt der teufel gegeben, schnell zur hölle entsendet," [7] which has been accepted by many translators.[8] I see no reason for assuming that *fēonda,* which usually refers to mortal enemies in *Beowulf,* has a different meaning here.[9] Sievers and Sarrazin have done much to illuminate the passage, by citations from Saxo and from the Swedish chronicler Messenius.[10] The passage quoted by Sarrazin from Messenius is especially interesting in the present connection. " Lotherus igitur Danorum rex, ab Othino vehementer infestatus, & ope suorum propter nimiam destitutus tyrannidem superatusque *in Iutiam* profugit." The resemblance of this to the lines just quoted is obvious. Defeated in battle, and on account of his tyranny hated by his own people, Heremod' was forced to take refuge in the land of his enemies *the Jutes* (cf. *mid Eotenum,* 902). Here again, then, as in the Finnsburg story, we have an illustration of the hostilities of these two neighboring countries, reflected in saga.

Comparison of episodes of the general type to which the Finn-story belongs, or appears to belong, and the occurrence of the significant words " Surely Hildeburg

---

[6] *Zeitschrift für deutsche Philologie,* Vol. XXII, p. 388.

[7] Paul and Braune, *Beiträge,* Vol. XII, pp. 39 ff.

[8] As for example by Gering and Gummere.

[9] It was urged by Bugge that 1720 ff. mean " dass Heremod für sein böses tun und treiben in der hölle strafe leidet." I can see no necessity for so understanding the later passage, which really begins with line 1711. The " departure from the revelry of men " seems probably to refer to his exile.

[10] Sievers, " Beowulf und Saxo," *Berichte der kgl. sächs. Gesellschaft der Wiss. zu Leipzig,* 1895, pp. 175 ff.; Sarrazin, *Anglia,* Vol. XIX, p. 392.

could not praise the good faith of the Eotenas " (1071-2), make it altogether probable that Finn's invitation of Hnæf and the Danes to his court was but a ruse to get them into his power, and so satisfy some earlier injury or enmity.[11] What the nature or cause of this hostility was, we are not informed. Possibly the ancient and traditional ill-feeling between the two peoples is sufficient to explain it; possibly vengeance was sought to satisfy some particular grudge. Of direct evidence in regard to this there is, so far as I am aware, not a trace. The tale begins, appropriately enough for a Danish audience, with the treacherous attack of the Frisians upon their guests.

The opening lines of the *Episode* raise various difficulties. Perhaps it will be clearest to print the text as given by Holthausen, which seems to embody the best solution of these difficulties.[12]

	þǣr wæs sang *ond* swēg	samod ætgædere
	fore Healfdenes	hildewīsan,
1065	gomenwudu grēted,	gid oft wrecen,
	ðon*ne* healgamen	Hrōþgāres scop
	æfter medobence	mǣnan scolde,
	Finnes eafer*an*, ðā hīe sē fǣr begeat.	
	Hæleð Healf-Dena,	Hnæf Scyldinga
1070	in Frēswæle feallan scolde.	

The chief stumbling-block in this passage has been the construction of *eaferum* 1068, here read *eaferan*. The best explanation seems to be that by Klaeber, following up a suggestion of Trautmann:[13] "*healgamen* is the first,

---

[11] See p. 378 above.

[12] References to Holthausen are to the second edition, Heidelberg and New York, 1908. I have not, however, retained the marking of vowels and diphthongs peculiar to this text. The marks of quotation preceding 1068 are also omitted, the reason for which is explained below.

[13] Trautmann (*Bonner Beiträge*, VII, p. 11) proposed the reading *eaferan*, to be regarded as a corruption of *gefēran*.

18

eaferan the second object of *mǣnan*. The collocation of
such dissimilar substantives, which offends our modern
feeling for style, is not seldom to be found in Anglo-Saxon
poetry." [14] A literal translation into modern English is
therefore of necessity somewhat awkward; the following
rendering does no violence to the sense:

> There were song and music, blended together
> Before Healfdene's battle-chieftain;
> 1065 The harp was struck, a lay oft recited,
> When Hrothgar's minstrel o'er the mead-benches
> Brought to men's mind the joys of the hall,
> The swift attack falling on warriors [15] of Finn.
> The hero of the Half-Danes, Hnæf of the Scyldings,
> 1070 In Frisian slaughter was doomed to fall.

Editors have read the passage in a great variety of
ways. Wyatt follows Grein " in regarding *eaferum* as an
instrumental plural with reference to *feallan scolde.*"
Others have sought to avoid this harsh and unusual construction by reading *be Finnes eaferum* or *Finnes eaferum
fram.* Sedgefield and Holthausen in his first edition
assume a gap after *mǣnan scolde* 1067. Schücking, while
accepting Klaeber's reading, places a comma after *begeat*
1068, ending the sentence with *feallan scolde.* It is hard
to reconcile this punctuation with syntax. The passage
is in any case a difficult one, and a thorn in the flesh for
the editor.

The interpretation here followed is sustained by the
character of the episode and the circumstance of its recita-
tion. One point of some importance has, I think, been
overlooked, that the contest mentioned in 1068, *Finnes*

---

[14] *Anglia*, Vol. xxviii, p. 433, where parallels and comment are
given. See also Herrig's *Archiv*, Vol. cviii, 'p. 370.

[15] Cosijn, *Aant.*, p. 26, points out that *eaferan* means 'warriors,'
and compares 1710.

eaferan, ðā hīe sē fǣr begeat, is in all probability not that in the beginning, in consequence of which the Danes were forced to conclude a peace, and become dependents of Finn, but the last struggle of all, that in which they took vengeance upon Finn for their wrongs. This is the fight in which the Danes are the aggressors, in which " a sudden attack fell upon the men of Finn," whereas everything goes to show that in the earlier contest, related in the *Fragment,* the attack was made by the Frisians. It has already been pointed out that the whole interest of the *Episode,* after the lyric opening referring to the sorrows of Hildeburg, is focussed upon the revenge at the end. A reference to the final struggle, in which the Danes were completely victorious over their enemies, doing great injury to them, and completely wiping out a bitter old score, surely makes a better parallel for the *healgamen* at Hrothgar's banquet than the first fight at Finnsburg, which is indeed a glorification of Danish valor, but does not relate a contest in which the Frisians were attacked.

The introduction, then, as I conceive it, states that Hrothgar's scop sang of a thing pleasing to the Danish warriors in the hall, the vengeance taken upon Finn. The lay proper, or a paraphrase of it, then begins, recounting the injuries which motivated that vengeance.

There is considerable difference of opinion among editors and translators as to the point at which the lay itself begins. For it has generally been assumed that the *Beowulf*-poet, after this short introduction, quotes the words of the poet in Hrothgar's hall. Consequently the *Episode* is generally printed within marks of quotation. Holthausen, Wyatt, Sedgefield begin this quotation with 1068 *Finnes eaferum* (or *eaferan*); Schücking with 1071 *Nē hūru Hildeburg;* the old Heyne-Socin text (1903) with 1069, *Hæleð Healfdena,* so also Trautmann, *loc. cit.,* p. 30.

Gering, Child, Tinker, and Clark Hall begin with 1068; Lesslie Hall with 1069. But is the *Episode* to be regarded as a direct quotation at all? Is it not rather the *Beowulf*-poet's résumé of the scop's lay? Consider the earlier Sigemund-Episode (871-915), in which this is certainly the case. As the warriors return from the Haunted Mere, on the morning after Beowulf's victory over Grendel, they amuse themselves with horse-racing and with song. A thane of the king, skilled in story, who has the treasures of past lore at his command, entertains the company, improvising a song in honor of Beowulf, in which the hero is compared to Sigemund the dragon-slayer [16] and contrasted to Heremod, the wicked and cruel king.

>   Secg eft ongan
>   sïð Bēowulfes   snyttrum styrian,
>   ond on spēd wrecan   spel gerāde,
>   wordum wrixlan; wēl-hwylc gecwǣð,
> 875 þæt hē fram Sigemundes secgan hȳrde
>   ellen-dǣdum, uncūðes fela,
>   Wælsinges gewin, wīde sïðas,
>   þāra-þe gumena bearn   gearwe ne-wiston,
>   fǣhðe ond fyrena . . . .

The general method of introducing the episode here is much the same as in the tale of Finn, but it is impossible to treat the account of Sigemund and what follows as a direct quotation of the lay sung by the improvisator; the introductory sentence and the narrative are too closely welded for any line of division. No one of the editors just mentioned has included the Sigemund-Heremod episode within marks of punctuation. Had the original lay been directly quoted, the comparison between Beowulf and

---

[16] Almost by implication; but the point is none the less obvious. It is hardly necessary to mention the confusion between Sigemund and Sigurd or Siegfried.

Sigemund would probably have been much more clearly emphasized.

I do not believe, then, that we are justified in treating the Finn-*Episode* as reproducing the very words of Hrothgar's poet, but rather as a paraphrase of his words. This conclusion is further supported by the reminiscential and allusive tone of the *Episode,* contrasting so strongly with the vigor and concreteness of the *Fragment.* Since the *Episode* is merely a paraphrase, forming a part of the main narrative, it is probably impossible to mark off its beginning, and certainly an error to print it as a direct quotation.

The scene of the treacherous attack upon the Danes is Finn's royal residence in Friesland, the *hēa-burh* (1127), called *Finns-buruh* (*Fragment* 36). The details of this attack, as told in the *Fragment,* we shall consider presently; we may first look at the narrative in the *Episode.*[17]

---

[17] It has been held that the earlier scenes of the poem do not take place in Friesland (Trautmann, *Finn und Hildebrand,* p. 60; Boer, *Zeitschrift für deutschem Altertum,* Vol. XLVII, p. 137). Trautmann says: "Hnæf trifft mit seinen friesischen verwanten zusammen nicht im eigentlichen Friesland—in dies ziehn die Friesen und Dänen zusammen erst später (Einlage 1125-27)—, sondern in einem nicht genannten lande, in welchem Finn einen herrschersitz hat (Finnes buruh)." The contrary is asserted by Binz, *Zeitschrift für deutsche Philologie,* XXXVII, p. 532, and Klaeber, *Journal of English and Germanic Philology,* Vol. VI, p. 193. The latter remarks, "After the conclusion of the treaty between the two parties and the completion of the funeral rites, the Frisian warriors—presumably men who had been summoned by Finn in preparation for the encounter with the Danes—return to their respective homes in the country (*heaburh* is a high-sounding epic term that should not be pressed), whilst Hengest stays with Finn in *Finnesburh* (where the latter is subsequently slain: *æt his selfes ham* 1147)." It needs but little reflection to see that Binz and Klaeber are right. It is, furthermore, reasonable to suppose that the place where Hildeburg had experienced the greatest of earthly joys (1080) and where gold was lifted from Finn's hoard (1107) was not an outlying and temporary abode,

The general situation in the opening lines (1071 ff.) is clear. In the morning after the night attack by the Frisians in which Hnæf lost his life, Hildeburg looks on her slain kinsmen, in the very place [18] where she had experienced the greatest happiness that the world had to give (1079). This points to a time of peace and tranquillity preceding, during which she was living in happiness at the Frisian court. Apparently the son who is killed, and later burnt on the funeral pyre with his uncle, is her child by Finn. Otherwise we must assume that she had been married years before, and had had a child by her former husband. The poet then explains with great care the terms of the peace concluded between the rival peoples. The reasons for this peace are:

> War had swept away
> All the thanes of Finn save a few only,
> So that he could not on the place of combat
> Offer to Hengest aught of conflict,
> Nor in battle protect the woeful remainder (of his force)
> From the prince's thane.

---

but Finn's chief city. *Hēa-burh* does not seem to me too high-sounding an epic term to be in keeping as applied to that city. I do not attach any importance to Binz's argument that the fight must have taken place in Friesland because it is called *Frēs-wœl* (1070.). "Frisian slaughter" might take place wherever Frisians were to be found, at home or abroad. As for 1125 ff., the paratactic construction so characteristic of Anglo-Saxon makes it natural for the poet to say "to look upon Friesland, the homes and high city" rather than "to look upon the homes and the high city of Friesland." Cf. *þæt hē fram Sigemunde secgan hȳrde ellen-dǣdum* 875 (the emendation *Sigemundes* is to my mind an error, resting upon forgetfulness of Anglo-Saxon idiom).

[18] This is altogether the most simple and unforced reading of *þǣr* 1079. MS. *hē* is altered to *hēo* by all modern editors. There can scarcely be a doubt that this is right; to construe the pronoun as referring to Finn would be very awkward. Moreover, there is an obvious contrast between Hildeburg's witnessing the *morðor-bealo mága* and her previous enjoyment of *mǣste . . . worolde wynne*.

So the *Episode* expressly says that Finn had too few men to wage offensive or defensive warfare; it was not merely that the narrow passage which they were defending gave the Danes an advantage which the Frisians could not overcome.   Yet the poet tells us that the Danes were " forced by necessity " to make peace and " follow the slayer of their lord " (1102 f.).   But if Finn's men were too few to prevail over the Danes, why did the latter assent to a condition which, according to Germanic ideas, was in the highest degree dishonorable?

It seems probable that the present narrative does not preserve the original motivation of the story, but that in their desire to set forth the situation to the advantage of the Danes, story-tellers had altered this motivation. [The original narrative perhaps related that Finn, after inflicting severe punishment on the Danes,[19] concluded to offer the survivors terms of peace, which, in view of the superior power of the Frisians, were perforce accepted.   Finn's offer would be natural enough.   There would be no profit for him in exterminating all the Danes; such good fighters might on the other hand form a valuable addition to his own forces, if they could be induced to swear allegiance to him.   But singers forgot, as time went on, that acceptance of the terms of peace offered by Finn becomes plausible only if the Danes cannot contend against the Frisians longer.   So, in their desire to exalt the prowess of the Danes, they altered the story a little, and said that so many Frisians were killed in the hall-fight that Finn was obliged to come to terms.   It is certain, as has been pointed out in the preceding pages, that the poet is making every effort in the *Episode* to present Danish valor in the most

---

[19] Cf. 1098, in which the term *wéa-láf* is clearly applied to the *Danish* forces.

favorable light. Finn is forced to sue for peace, and his promises are detailed at great length, while nothing is said of the pledges of the Danes, excepting, by implication, that they are to become Finn's men.

How such a shift in the telling of the story took place is well shown by the *Fragment*. Here there are still further divergences from the epic, and they are all in the direction of the exaltation of Danish valor; a five days' fight, as against that in a single night in the *Episode,* and no Danish loss in the defence of the hall,—not even the death of Hnæf is mentioned, but it is said explicitly that no one of the sixty Danish warriors fell. Such alterations are all the more natural in a single incident detached from a longer epic. Perhaps the form of the story in the *Fragment* affected the motivation of the epic itself. For a discussion of these questions, as they affect the *Fragment,* the reader is referred to the appropriate place in the following chapter. In order to understand the present form of the poem, we must take due account of the history of the material in *Beowulf* before it reached the man who put it into the form in which we now have it. The Finn-story is, of course, old epic tradition, which was in circulation in oral form for many years before it was written down, and so was subject to all the shifts and inconsistencies which arise in popular narrative poetry. Such differences in motivation are conspicious in other parts of the poem; witness the varying conceptions of the nature and location of the Haunted Mere, or the different motives that impel Beowulf to do battle with the dragon.[20] The original motivation here suggested is of course purely

[20] See on this general subject an earlier article by the present writer, "The Haunted Mere in Beowulf," *Publications of the Modern Language Association of America,* Vol. xxvii, pp. 223 ff. (1912).

hypothetical, but only by some such hypothesis as this does the situation become reasonable. It must be remembered that the Danish submission to the leader of the men who had slain Hnæf was, according to the notions of that age, not at all a heroic act under any circumstances, however great the Danish straits might be, and that it was almost incomprehensible if the force opposing the Danes was so small that their leader was obliged to propose peace on highly liberal terms. The humiliation of such a submission is sufficiently shown by the fact that one of the terms of peace was that no Finnish warrior should suggest that the Danes were following the slayer of their lord, and that if any were so rash as to call this to mind, he should be punished by the sword (1099-1106).

The duty of warriors under such circumstances is well shown by a familiar passage in the *Anglo-Saxon Chronicle,* which in many ways affords a close and instructive parallel to the situation in the *Finnsburg Episode.* In the year 755, it is related that King Cynewulf was attacked by an enemy named Cyneheard, whose men surrounded the house in which the king was tarrying. Although Cynewulf fought bravely, he was killed. Then the king's thanes, hearing the commotion, ran out. " The ætheling (Cyneheard) offered each of them life and property (*i. e.,* if they would come to terms with him), but *none of them would accept this,* fighting on until they all lay dead save one British hostage, and he was sore wounded." In the morning more thanes of the dead king came to meet the ætheling, who had shut himself up in the town where the king had fallen. Cyneheard once more offered them property, as much as they would have, if they would recognize him as king, and told them that kinsmen of theirs were with him, who would not desert him. " And they replied that no kinsman was dearer to them than their

lord, and *that they would never follow his slayer."* [21]   The
king's party then offered their kinsmen with the atheling
a chance to depart in safety before the fight began, and
the kinsmen replied that the same.chance had been offered
the comrades of those outside who had been slain with the
king (and refused), and that they considered it would be
no more worthy of them to accept this offer than it was of
the king's defenders.   The attacking party then rushed
at the gates, forced an entrance, and slew all those within
save one, and he was grievously wounded.

In this vigorous old narrative, told with spirit despite
its clumsy syntax, we see the exact alternative which was
accepted by the Danes in the *Episode* proudly refused.
" They would never follow the slayer of their lord."   That
the Danes did choose to become the liegemen of Finn was
an intolerable state of affairs which could not, in the
nature of things, last long. · The next stage of the story
deals with the terrible revenge which was to wipe out the
memory of this humiliating submission.

After peace has been solemnly confirmed by oath, and
gold lifted from the hoard,[22] the dead are burnt upon a

[21] Compare the similarity of phraseology: *Chronicle: ond hie næfre
his banan folgian noldon,* and *Episode* 1102 *þēah hīe hira bēag-gyfan
banan folgedon.* We are not to understand, of course, that Hnæf
actually fell at the hands of Finn, but that Finn was responsible
for the attack resulting in his death. Cf. Heinzel, *Anzeiger*, Vol.
XV, p. 192.

[22] I take this to mean that Finn rewarded his warriors on the
conclusion of the treaty of peace with presents of gold. They might
well expect this reward after their hard fighting. By the terms of
the treaty (cf. 1089), the Danes would have their share when the
presents were distributed. This would also be appropriate to the
sealing of a compact of peace. It is to be noted that the lifting
of gold from the hoard is mentioned in direct connection with the
swearing of the solemn oath. *Āð wæs geæfned ond icge gold
āhæfen of horde* (1107). Klaeber's explanation (*Journal of English*

magnificent funeral 'pyre, raised in honor of Hnæf, as most illustrious of the heroes.   Upon it lies also the body of Hildeburg's son, the nephew of Hnæf.   As the curling smoke rises to the heavens, the lamentations of the unhappy queen break forth anew.   It is a terrible and moving picture which the poet here makes vivid in a few graphic lines; the crackling flames, the curling smoke, the blood bursting from the bodies.

Flame swallowed all,
Greediest of spirits,   whom war had claimed
of either people;   their prosperity was done!

With this picture the first phase of the tragedy with which we are acquainted, the phase which we have called the Treachery of the Frisians, comes to an end.   Before we consider in detail the vengeance taken by the Danes, we must examine briefly the hall-fight as related in the *Finnsburg Fragment.*

III

The Defence of the Hall

The relation of the *Finnsburg Fragment* to the *Episode* does not offer serious difficulties.   There can hardly be a doubt that the *Fragment* sets forth, as the majority of critics have agreed, the fight at the opening of the story. Finn's men are clearly the aggressors, and the Danes the defenders.   The *Episode* is much concerned with the Danish desire for revenge after a treacherous attack; it is natural to see in the *Fragment* a more detailed descrip-

---

and Germanic Philology, Vol. VIII, p. 256), does not seem to me so convincing,—unless *að* "oath" be emended to *ád* "pyre."   Possibly if we knew the meaning of the obscure word *icge* some light might be thrown on the matter.

tion of that attack, which is obviously one of the most
important and interesting moments in the whole story.
The defence of a hall was of course a favorite episode of
Germanic story-tellers; as Professor Ker puts it, " No
kind of adventure is so common or better told in the earlier heroic manner than the defence of a narrow place
against odds."

Like the visitors to Etzel's court in the *Nibelungenlied,*
the Danes have been quartered in a hall. While they are
asleep at night, they are set upon by the forces of their
host. The "battle-young king" Hnæf, probably with a
companion, is on the watch while his men are sleeping.[1]

---

[1] Möller maintained that the "battle-young king" is not Hnæf,
but Hengest. He admitted that this would not agree with the
Episode, which calls Hengest 1085 *þeodnes þegn,* and his men
þeodenlease, 1103, but he thought that " diese bezeichnungen im
Beowulf können vom zusammensteller der episode sein." We must
admit the possibility of discrepancies between *Episode* and *Fragment,* but the chances are against making Hengest a king, since he
nowhere gets that appellation in the *Episode.* Again, is is expressly
stated that in the ensuing fight Hnæf's warriors repaid him for
sweet mead 39, f. Bugge (Paul and Braune, *Beiträge,* XII, p. 21)
has shown that this cannot, as Möller proposed, be a tribute to the
memory of the dead leader, with no reference to the living one.
Möller thought that *sylf* 17 is most naturally taken as referring to
the *cyning* 2, but he admitted that if Hengest had already been
mentioned in the (lost) opening of the lay, this argument would
have no force. It is quite possible that Hengest is the other watcher,
possibly the man who speaks the words . . . *hornas byrnað næfre.*
There seems to be no reason why *sylf* should not be applied to a
prominent character like Hengest even if he has not been already
mentioned. The background of the story and the characters in it
were of course familiar to hearers of the *Fragment,*—these old stories
were not new to their audiences in plot. For Möller's discussion,
see his *Volksepos,* p. 65.

One would think that Möller's theories about the interpretation
of *Episode* and *Fragment* might now be regarded as obsolete. But
we continue to find them set forth in books about *Beowulf.* Indeed,
one editor, Sedgefield, goes so far as to give them the place of

A gleam of light is mistaken for a moment for a fire in
the gable of the hall, or for the breaking dawn, or the
passing of a dragon, but only for a moment; it is the
moonlight shining on the accoutrements of advancing warriors. Moonlight reflected on burnished weapons and
armor is apparently a part of the poetical " machinery "
of a secret attack by night, just as the raven and the wolf
were the common adornments of a place of combat.   In
the *Völundarkviþa,* the men of King Nithad attack the
cunning smith in his hall:

> By night fared the warriors,
> Bossed were their breastplates,
> Shining their shields
> In the waning moonlight;
> They stepped from their saddles
> Close by the gable,
> Thence stole they in
> Down through the hall.[2]

And in the *Nibelungenlied,* as Volker and Hagen together
keep watch, while their companions sleep, Volker sees in
the distance the gleam of helmets, and knows that enemies
are approaching.

> Des nahtes wol enmitten, i'ne weiz iz ê geschach,
> daz Volkêr der küene einen helm schînen sach
> Verre ûz einer vinster . . .[3]

So the " battle-young king " in the *Fragment* calls out in
a loud voice to his men, warning them of the impending

honor (second edition, p. 258, *sub* Finn). While this can still happen, there is justification for criticising Möller's position once more.
It should be said that while the textual work in Sedgefield's edition
is good, his remarks on the history of the material are not authoritative.

[2] From the edition of Hildebrand, Paderborn 1876, p. 133.

[3] Ed. Bartsch, Leipzig, 1886, strophe 1837, Aventiure XXX.

attack.[4] His stirring words find immediate response;
Sigeferth and Eaha rush to guard one of the entrances to
the hall, apparently the one where the king has been standing, while Ordlaf and Guthlaf, beyond doubt the Oslaf
and Guthlaf of the *Episode,* and Hengest, apparently the
next in authority after Hnæf, take their stand at the
opposite entrance. In the attacking party an impetuous
warrior, Garulf, the son of Guthlaf,[5] is restrained from
an immediate onslaught by Guthere, who urges that it is
better for Garulf not to risk losing his life in the very
beginning by an attack on the doorway. But Garulf,
recklessly brave, calls out in a clear voice above the tumult
and demands to know who the defender of the door
may be. Sigeferth answers proudly and provocatively.
Thereupon Garulf can restrain himself no longer, and in
the conflict of warriors about the entrance to the hall he
is the first to be struck down. Many others fall; the
fight lasts five days; the Danes defend the hall successfully,
without losing a man. Then the conflict seems to cease.
A "wounded hero" goes away from the place of conflict,
his armor shattered. He is in all probability one of the
attackers, as they would naturally be the ones to retire,
in case the defence of the hall were successful. Possibly he

---

[4] His meaning is not quite clear. Bugge (*Beiträge*, XII, p. 23)
renders *fremman* (9) "zur ausübung bringen." If *nið* is here close
to its original meaning of "activity," or "malicious activity," the
meaning may be: "now arise deeds of woe, which will put into
execution the hatred of this people" ("this hatred of the people").
If *nið* is to be rendered "tribulatio," "afflictio," and *fremman*
"facere," we may translate "which will bring tribulation to this
people." Gering (*Übersetzung*) renders it thus: "Wehgeschick
droht, da mit grimmigem Hass der Gegner uns heimsucht." Gummere (*Oldest English Epic*) : "foul deeds rise to whelm this people
with peril and death."

[5] For a discussion of the identity of this Guthlaf, see below, pp.
425-6.

is Guthere. The " shepherd of the people " who asks after the warriors, how they are recovering from their wounds, is probably Finn. It would be in accordance with the constant effort to exalt Danish valor in this tale that the Frisians should be the first to withdraw from the fight, and that their wounds should be so grave as to be a matter of solicitude to their king. The *Fragment* ends as abruptly as it begins ; but this very abruptness is not without its effect in a scene so full of rapid action.

The *Fragment* does not agree in all its details with the *Episode*. The implication in the *Episode* is clearly that the fight lasted but a single night (1077) ; while in the *Fragment* it continued for five days. Moreover the *Fragment* states that no Danish warrior fell in the defence of the hall, whereas the *Episode* makes it plain that Hnæf and other warriors (*wēa-lāfe,* 1098) had been killed. The five days' fight is probably epic exaggeration, like the whole day that it took Beowulf to reach the bottom of the Haunted Mere, or the brilliancy of Heorot, " which shone over many lands " (311). Similarly, the poet of the *Fragment* emphasizes Danish valor by asserting that no one of the warriors of this people was slain in the defence of the hall. It is very generally agreed that the *Fragment* is not a part of a longer epic, but that it is an epic lay, and " ein besonders gedrungenes Lied " at that (Brandl).[6] " It most probably confined itself to the battle in the hall,' so Ker thinks, and this seems entirely plausible.[7] The poet, then, is concerned only with this single episode or some extension of it ; he is making his effect by a single scene ; he is not endeavoring to fit his narrative without inconsistencies into the longer epic tale of which it forms

---

[6] Paul's *Grundriss,* (second edition), Vol. II, p. 985.
[7] *Loc. cit.,* p. 84.

a part. We know that in heroic story different accounts of the same event or series of events seldom if ever tally exactly. Even within a single poem, like *Beowulf* itself, the contradictions and inconsistencies are considerable. Brandl, in commenting upon the discrepancies between *Finnsburg* and *Beowulf,* warns us that such discrepancies " zwischen verschiedenen Fassungen mündlich überliefer- ter Geschichten immer und überall auftauchen." On the whole, the surprising thing is that the divergences between the *Episode* and the *Fragment* are so slight. But this detached treatment of a single incident drawn from a longer epic narrative shows how the details of that inci- dent may be slightly altered so as to make it more effective in itself, though less in agreement with the longer story.

It seems hardly necessary to review once more the details of Möller's theory of the relation of the *Fragment* to the *Episode,* or of the interpretation of the Finn-saga as a whole. The weakness of Möller's position is obvious to the careful reader; and it has already been pointed out in detailed criticisms by Bugge, Heinzel, and others. His conception of the story depends not only upon his novel interpretations of the text, but also, to a considerable de- gree, upon his now universally discredited " strophen- theorie," and his view that the *Episode* was made up of two separate lays, one dealing with Hildeburg and the burial of Hnæf, and the other with Hengest.[8] Much of his reconstruction is purely imaginative. He maintained that Finn had carried off Hildeburg, and that her father Hoc had pursued the fugitives, and was slain in the ensu- ing fight, whereupon, after the lapse of many years, Hnæf attacked Finn.[9] There is not the least warrant for this

[8] *Das altenglische Volksepos*, Kiel, 1883, p. 54.
[9] *Ibid.*, p. 70.

in the text. The event which he thinks the *Episode* relates is not referred to at all in the *Episode*. He proposed to place this event between lines 1145 and 1146,
" grade an die stelle wo das Hengestlied abbricht: das
fragment behandelt einen zweiten kampf in dem der mit
Hengest geschlossene vertrag von Finn gebrochen wird."
The *Episode* affords no ground for supposing that this
" second fight " ever took place. Similarly, his explanation of the events between this and the final contest is
spun out of thin air. " Dass Hengest im kampfe fiel steht
nirgends, wir müssen aber erraten dass er und andere
seiner mannen nach dem fünften tage des kampfes fielen,
worauf Guðlaf und Oslaf da die geschwächten Friesen es
nicht mehr hindern konnten sich durchschlugen." After
some metrical meditations he continues: " also müssen
die genannten helden sich durchgeschlagen haben und in
die heimat entwichen sein um mit neuen mannen wieder
zu kommen. Gegen diese fiel dann Finn mit allen seinen
mannen im letzten vernichtungskampfe." The danger
of such methods of reconstructing an old legend are obvious. Möller's general interpretation of the relation of
the Finnsburg story to early literature, his view that the
Eotenas were the men of Hnæf, and that Hengest is the
" battle-young king " of the *Fragment* have already been
discussed here.[10]

---

[10] Miss M. R. Clarke, following in part Kögel, assigns a different
significance to the *Fragment*. Her arguments are not of much importance, but they may be briefly reviewed. She says: " It is difficult to see in this story (*i. e.*, the *Fragment*) either of the two
fights alluded to in the Finn episode in *Beowulf*, as the circum-
stancs under which it took place do not seem to apply exactly to
either." (*Sidelights on Teutonic History during the Migration
Period*, Cambridge, 1911, p. 179.) Her reasons for not identifying
it with the second fight may be passed over, since we can agree fully
with her on that point. But she also refuses to identify it with the

19

We may now turn to the last act of the drama, in which the Danes take final vengeance upon Finn and his men. For a time the ominous and bloodstained peace is observed; but the demands of wild justice can be satisfied only by another murderous combat, not less bloody, but more decisive than the heroic defence of the hall.

IV

The Vengeance of the Danes

Leaving behind them the smoking brands of the balefire upon which the bodies of the slain warriors have been consumed, the Frisians return to their homes and their city (*hēa-burh*). There Hengest and his warriors stay the winter with Finn. But Hengest's thoughts dwell constantly upon his native land, although the storms sweeping over the wintry sea make return as yet impossible.[1] His chief desire is for the vengeance which a

---

first fight because "*Beo.* l. 1068, *thâ hie se faer begeat* [sic!] does not seem to indicate that the first attack was made by the Frisians: nor does it appear from ll. 1071-2 that any treachery practised was on the part of Finn (*i. e.* if we take *Eotena* as referring to Hnæf and his followers)." It has already been shown that *Eotena* cannot refer to Hnæf and his followers, and also that *þā hie sē fǣr begeat* may well refer, not to the first combat, but to the final struggle of all, in which the Danes took vengeance. Miss Clarke then proposes another solution for the *Fragment*. "It might very well be a description of part of the first struggle, and refer to the events immediately following on Hnæf's death, when we might suppose that the strangers took up as strong a position as possible in anticipation of a counter-attack. The *heatho-geong cyning*, Finn, l. 2, would then aptly enough denote Hengest," etc. This is much the same sort of interpretation as Möller's; there is no warrant in the text for any counter-attack.

[1] I do not at all agree with Klaeber (*Anglia*, Beiblatt, Vol. XXII, p. 373), who defends the MS. reading *þēah-þe hē meahte* 1130. This

return to his native land will make possible. It is clear that upon his shoulders rests the responsibility for this duty.[2] As soon as spring comes and sea-travel. becomes practicable, he leaves Finn's court. There is no reason to suppose that he " escapes " by stealth.[3] It is far more

is directly contradicted by the context; the description of the stormy weather of winter and the statement that Hengest left when spring came. It is easy to understand the omission of the *ne*, which directly follows two words very like it in appearance,—*þe he*.

[2] Hengest has sometimes been held to be the brother of Hnæf. The alliteration of the names favors this theory, but it must be remembered that names beginning with H are very common. The evidence of the poem is against making him Hnæf's brother; he is called only *þēodnes þegn* (1085), and his men after the death of Hnæf are *þēodenlēase* (1103).

Mr. H. M. Chadwick (*Origins of the English Nation*, Cambridge, 1910, p. 52) attempts to identify him with the Hengest of the Saxon Conquest, the associate of Horsa. His reasons are these: Hengest was the follower of Hnæf, " who appears to have been a prince in the service of the Danish king Healfdene." The date of Healfdene's reign, reckoning from *Beowulf*, would be " before the middle of the fifth century," making the two Hengests contemporaries. Bede calls the tribe to which the Hengest of the Conquest belonged Iutae (Iuti), while " the tribe to which the other Hengest belonged is called in Beowulf *Eotena* (Gen. pl.), *Eotenum* (Dat. pl.)." The Hengest of the *Historia Brittonum* is said to have been driven into exile, and the scribe who wrote the genealogy of the *Historia* appears to have been familiar with the story of Finn, the son of Folcwalda.—This identification of the two Hengests must be unhesitatingly rejected. Hnæf was not in the service of Healfdene; that notion rests on an emendation of the text which does violence to idiom (Bugge) and is today rejected by the best editors. (See above, p. 392, note 2). The tribe to which Hengest belongs is certainly not the Eotenas—a point which has already been discussed in detail. (See above, pp. 393 ff.). The minor points urged in support of the theory are not worth consideration if the main arguments fail. It should be said that Mr. Chadwick merely states he thinks his theory " more probable than not," and makes it conditional upon dating the invasion of Kent after 440.

[3] My colleague Professor H. M. Ayres called my attention to this point.

probable that he goes with Finn's consent. The Frisian king could hardly expect to keep as prisoner a chieftain whose men he had admitted to an equal standing in the state with his own (1087). We are not informed as to how many of his men, if any, accompanied him; but he can hardly have sailed back to Denmark all by himself. Had he tried to escape secretly, this would have meant to Finn hostility and rebellion, and the consequences to the Danish warriors still at his court would have been unpleasant. It would be quite natural for Hengest to ask to set forth upon a sea-voyage with the coming of spring. This was a common desire after the passing of the long, dull winter, as many sagas tell us. *The Seafarer,* too, reminds us how strong an appeal sea-voyaging in summer made to the Anglo-Saxons,—there was no worldly joy, says the poet, comparable to its strange fascination.[4] Finn, then, could hardly refuse a request of this sort from Hengest, excepting by manifesting open hostility and suspicion. And Hengest had sworn deep oaths to keep the peace. But in Hengest's mind the duty of revenge outweighs that of keeping his pledge.

The passage which narrates the events which follow is the most difficult in the whole *Episode.* The narrative becomes highly allusive and laconic, and the text contains an unusual number of obscure expressions. Possibly the poet did not care to dwell upon the circumstances under which the Danes broke their solemn pledges. He hurries on as rapidly as he can to the consummation of the Danish vengeance. It is probably impossible to determine exactly the events leading up to this vengeance; but the alternatives and probabilities must be considered.

4 For an analysis and interpretation of this lyric, see an article by the present writer, *Journal of English and Germanic Philology,* Vol. IV, p. 460 (1902).

The whole passage reads as follows:

```
                 þā wæs winter scacen,
        fæger foldan bearm;      fundode wrecca,
        gist of geardum;      hē tō gyrn-wræce
        swīðor þōhte      þonne tō sǣ-lāde,
1140    gif hē torn-gemōt þurhtēon mihte,
        þæt hē Eotena bearn      inne gemunde.
      . Swā hē ne-forwyrnde      worold-rǣdenne,
        þonne him Hūnlāfing      hilde-lēoman,
        billa sēlest,      on bearm dyde.
1145    þæs wǣron mid Eotenum      ecge cūðe.
        Swylce ferhð-frecan      Fin eft begeat
        sweord-bealo slīðen      æt his selfes hām,
        siððan grimne gripe      Gūðlāf ond Ōslāf
        æfter sǣ-sīðe      sorge mǣndon,
1150    ætwiton wēana dǣl;      ne-meahte wæfre mōd
        forhabban in hreðre.      þā wæs heal roden
        fēonda fēorum,      swilce Fin slægen,
        cyning on corðre,      ond sēo cwēn numen.
```

The first point of importance [5] to consider is the meaning of *worold-rǣdenne* 1142. The suffix *-rǣden* is regularly used to form abstracts [6]; as the Bosworth-Toller *Lexicon* states, its force is much the same as that of the suffixes *-ship, -hood, -red,* denoting a state or a condition. A fairly

[5] 1141 has given some trouble. The best reading seems to be that adopted by Grein, Nader, and Schücking: "worin er (in feindlicher Begegnung) der Kinder der Eoten gedächte (d. h. Rache an ihnen nähme) " as Schücking puts it. Sievers would alter *þæt* to *þǣr,* and render "wo, wie er wusste, die Helden sich befanden" (Paul and Braune, *Beiträge,* Vol. xII, p. 193). But emendation, even by an authority like Sievers, is to be rejected in favor of the ms. reading, if the latter can possibly be retained.

[6] Das produktive ags. *rǣden* . . . bildet feminine abstracta aus substantiven und zwar aus persönlichen substantiven, um das verhältnis der personen zu einander anzugeben: *frēondrǣden* 'freundschaft;' *fēond-, gefēr-, geþoft-, gebēod-, folc-, brōþor-rǣden.* Daneben erscheinen sonstige aus substantiven abgeleitete abstracta wie *camprǣden* 'kampf,' *gecwid-, folc-, þing-, hiw-, gēbed-, heorð-rǣden* usw. (Kluge, *Nominale Stammbildungslehre,* Halle, 1889, p. 81.)

close approximation to the literal significance of *woorold-rǣdenne* would then be " what pertains to the world." The common connotation of *worold* in Anglo-Saxon compounds, as already pointed out in this connection by Mr. Clark Hall,[7] is " secular affairs," as opposed to the religious life. The Abbess Hild advised Cædmon, as the Anglo-Saxon version of Bede tells us, *þæt hē woruldhād ānforlēte ond munuchād onfēnge.* In the *Cura Pastoralis, negotiis secularibus* is rendered by *woruldscipum.*[8] It seems probable that the general meaning of *worold-rǣdenne* is similar. So 1142 appears to mean that Hengest " did not reject what pertained to the world, worldly business." But this figurative expression obviously admits of various interpretations. To me it seems very probable that it may mean " he did his worldly duty," that is, the duty of revenge. This seems somewhat closer to the literal meaning of the phrase than most of the other suggested renderings. Heinzel[9] explained it as a paraphrase for " he met his fate," remarking that a medieval Latin writer might have expressed it " tributum naturae solvere non recusavit." Imelmann translates, " daher verweigerte er es dem Geschick nicht (sah darin seinen Wink und gehorchte ihm)."[10] Clark Hall suggests, " he did not run counter to the way of the world, *i. e.,* he fell into temptation, as most people would have done under the circumstances (*swā*) "—maintaining this to be " more likely than the too Oriental fatalism of ' he did not resist his fate.' " We must, however, be cautious about denying fatalism to a poem which proclaims *Gǣð ā Wyrd swā hīo scel!* Schücking has proposed to connect the line with

---

[7] *Modern Language Notes,* Vol. xxv, p. 113.
[8] See Bosworth-Toller, sub *woruldscipe.*
[9] *Anzeiger für deutsches Altertum,* Vol. x, p. 226.
[10] *Deutsche Litteraturzeitung,* Vol. xxx (1909), p. 998.

what precedes, and translates " ohne dass er das Weltge-
setz versagte (d. h. bräche), d. h. ohne dass er seine
Schwüre bräche." [11] So highly specialized a meaning for
this vague phrase seems unlikely; we must ask ourselves
if an Anglo-Saxon would have understood it. Moreover,
as Imelmann has pointed out,[12] this interpretation is
not very well supported by the context. Möller's emendation of *worold* to *worod,* and reading " so wehrte er dem
willen der gefolgschaft nicht " [13] should certainly be
rejected. We beg the whole question of the interpretation
of a difficult passage by altering a very common word like
worold to *worod,* which occurs in *Beowulf* only in the
forms *werod* or *weorod,* never *worod.* *Worod-rǣdenne* is
not a compound found elsewhere in Anglo-Saxon poetry.
The possibility of confusion between similar words, which
Möller urged, does not make the substituted word preferable to the original reading, if this reading is of more
frequent occurrence, and makes good sense.

The interpretation of *worold-rǣdenne* will depend to
some extent upon the meaning assigned to the lines immediately following,

1143   þonne him Hūnlāfing   hilde-lēoman,
           billa sēlest,   on bearm dyde.

Critics have hitherto been divided between two general
conceptions in explaining *on bearm dyde:* either " plunged
into the breast "; or " laid upon his bosom " or " lap," as
a present, or possibly as a military ceremony or " obscure

[11] Glossary sub *worold-rǣden.*
[12] " Darf man Hengest so gewundene Gedankenpfade und dem
Dichter so verstiegene Redeweise ernsthaft zutrauen? Hengest hat
die Friedenseide mit beschworen, plant aber Friedensbruch; und da
soll er sich einbilden, er könne um die Eide herumkommen, ohne sie
zu brechen? " (*loc. cit.*).
[13] *Altenglisches Volksepos,* p. 68.

rite of the *comitatus.*" So far as the phraseology itself
is concerned, either meaning seems defensible. The parallels, while on the whole rather favoring the second of
these alternatives, are not conclusive evidence. The meaning of *dōn* varies, of course, in accordance with the particles used in connection with it; and *on* means both " in "
and " on." *Dōn* with *on* can obviously mean " thrust in,"
as 2090, where Beowulf relates the desire of Grendel to
thrust him into his pouch. But a parallel to the expression (*sweord*) *on bearm dōn,* if we take it to mean " slay,"
is not easy to find. A passage in the *Heliand* may be
compared:

> Tha muoder uuiepun
> 745   kindiungero qualm. Kara uuas an Bethleem,
> hofno hludost: thoh man *im* iro hertun an tue
> sniði midi suerdu, thoh ni mahta im io serora dad
> uuerðan an thesaro uueroldi uuibon managon
> brudion an Bethleem: gisahun iro barn biforan,
> 750   kindiunga man qualmu sueltan
> blodaga an iru barmon.[14]

The phrase in the *Cotton Gnomes, sweord sceal on bearme*
25, is quite as obscure as the one now under consideration.

On bearm implies, in various passages, possession, as
him tō bearme cwōm māððum-fæt mǣre 2404 (cf. 1210
and 2775), and *on bearm dōn* may well mean " place in
possession of." 2194 is often cited as a parallel. Hygelac presents Beowulf with the sword of Hrethel:

> þæt hē on Bīowulfes bearm ālegde,
> 2195   on him gesealde seofan þūsendo,
> bold ond brego-stōl.

The parallel is not quite perfect, since *ālecgan* is a word
of very definite meaning, and *dōn* is very indefinite. But

¹⁴ Ed. Sievers, Halle, 1878, p. 54.

it is clear that the rendering " lay upon the bosom or lap " receives considerable support from other passages; more, on the whole, than " plunge into the breast " can command. It does not seem safe to assume that this presentation of the sword had any ceremonial significance,[15] it is sufficiently explained by the fact that for the execution of his duty of revenge Hengest might well have been presented with a supremely good weapon. The giver may have been some one with a grudge of his own against Finn; possibly a kinsman of a warrior whom Finn had slain. To this question we shall have occasion to revert later.

However much the details of the translation may vary, the general interpretation of this vexed passage will either be that Hengest carried out his scheme of revenge on being given a supremely good sword, or that he met his fate when this sword was thrust into his breast. In either case the transition of thought from the preceding lines is natural enough; perhaps it is a little more convincing with the first interpretation. Hengest, while his thoughts were fixed on vengeance, took the opportunity offered by the possession of a very excellent sword, and carried out his purposes; this sword was to kill—or had killed in the past—many of the Eotenas. " Its edges were known among the Eotenas " is the grimly ironical Germanic way of putting the matter. It is to be noted that the line can mean nothing else if we suppose that the passage just

[15] For references to discussions of this matter, and of the meaning of the passage in the *Cotton Gnomes*, see Miss B. C. Williams, *Gnomic Poetry in Anglo-Saxon*, N. Y., 1914.

[16] I think *fundode* here means " he hastened " (*i. e.*, actually went) rather than " he was eager to go." This verb obviously oscillates in meaning between desire and performance, in other instances of its use. The following *gist of geardum* seems to favor the latter alternative, which is well enough supported by parallels. See Bosworth-Toller's *Lexicon*.

preceding tells how Hengest received the sword as a gift. For the line following narrates how Finn suffered sword-bale; how he was killed in his own home, and this is introduced by *swylce*. The regular function of *swylce* is to introduce a clause of content similar to the one preceding.[17] If we do not assign the meaning " Eotenas were slain " to 1145, we must see in the lines preceding a reference to the death of Hengest. In that case, the sequence of thought introduced by *swā* 1142 will be: Hengest brooded over revenge and so he accepted his fate when it came. It is to be observed that it does not appear that Hengest slew Finn; Guthlaf and Oslaf are the ones who reproach him openly, in the midst of his men, not Hengest, who seems to have been the leader of the band. There is here a slight presumption in favor of the previous death of Hengest,— but only a slight one. The whole narrative is so allusive and broken that arguments of this sort must be accepted with great caution.

If we can definitely identify " Hunlafing " as a Dane, a choice between the two alternatives here presented will be much easier. Obviously, if Hunlafing were a Dane, he would not be likely to have been the slayer of Hengest, but it would have been natural for him to present Hengest

---

[17] Cf. Schücking, *Die Grundzüge der Satzverknüpfung im Beowulf*, Halle, 1904, p. 84: *swylce:* Es leitet einen Satz ein, der einen dem vorhergehenden ähnlichen Inhalt hat. Und zwar werden vom selben Subjekt ähnliche Handlungen ausgesagt oder von ähnlichen Subjekten gleichartige Handlungen, oder es wird die Aehnlichkeit einer Situation mit einer andern angedeutet, u. s. w. Die Handlung in beiden Sätzen ist oft gleichzeitig. Der *swylce-* Satz zeigt sich in der Regel als für den Gang der Handlung wichtig; er dient selten bloss einem erweiternden Zusatz.—This point is also referred to by Clark Hall, *loc. cit.* The implication seems to be that the sword *later on* caused the death of Frisians, since this makes a better parallel to 1146 ff.

with a good trenchant sword. Most recent writers seem
to agree [18] that this identification has been made by the
discovery of the passage in Arngrim Jonsson's version of
the *Skjoldungasaga,* in which three Danish princes are
mentioned, whose names are Hunleifus, Oddleifus, and
Gunnleifus, and who may thus be identified with the
Hunlaf(ing), Oslaf, and Guthlaf of the passage under
discussion. There seems to be no reason to doubt that
the Ordlaf and Guthlaf of *Fragment* 16 are the same
persons as those mentioned in the *Episode.* It may be of
some interest to reprint the whole passage in Arngrim's
text, as it seems to have been more ardently discussed
than examined.[19]

CAP. IIIII HERLEIFUS,

rex Daniæ quartus ordine.

Hæredem Frodo reliquit, avo cognominem, Leifum, qui cessante
pace et tranquillitate publica et bellis ac rapinis recrudescentibus a
fortitudine bellica nomen mutuatus est, Herleifus dictus. Filios is
multos reliquit, quorum duo præcipue commemorantur; quos etiam
hic cum posteris aliquot propter sequentium rerum seriem in subjecta
tabula recensuimus.

---

[18] Clark Hall, for example, says: "It is a great relief to find that
the personage of 1143 is a Dane, as it clears out of the road translations which must have been felt to be unsatisfactory." See also
Chambers, *Widsith,* p. 201, note; Imelmann, *loc. cit.;* Huchon,
Revue Germanique, Vol. III, p. 626; Sedgefield (second edition), p.
128; Schücking, p. 119.

[19] Hunlafing cannot, of course, be the name of the sword, as Chadwick and Miss M. G. Clarke suppose (Chadwick, *Origin of the
English Nation,* p. 52, note; Miss Clarke, *Sidelights on Teutonic
History,* p. 183). The impossibility of this view was pointed out
long ago by Möller, p. 68, and more recently by Huchon, *loc. cit.*
Clark Hall called attention to the fact that Hunlafing could not be
identical with the Hunleifus of Arngrim, as Chadwick thought.
Hunlafing would be the *son* of Hunlaf, and consequently, if the
equation with the list in Arngrim be accepted, the nephew of
Guthlaf and Oslaf.

Herleifus

Havardus hinn handramme	*Leifus* cogn. *hinn frekne* quod epitheton in luctatores strenuos competebat					
Frodo	Her- leifus	Hun- leifus [20]	Alei- fus	Odd- leifus	Geir- leifus	Gunn- leifus

Vermundus hinn vitre: sapiens
Olufa, filia, nupta Dan II, r. D., de quo postea.
Cap. V. [Havardus] r. D. quintus.

Successit patri Herleifo filius Havardus Handramme (sic appellantur, qui rem aliquam manu apprehensam pertinaciter. retinent), de quo nihil ulterius memoriæ proditum est. Huic [21] deinde frater Leifus, et illi filii sex ordine unus alteri: omnes in Selandia, Lethra regiam fixam habentes. De Aleifo quidem memoratur, quod nullum apparatum ab aulicis suis diversum habere voluerit. Hos patruelis Frodo et ex patruele nepos Vermundus in regno secuti sunt. Quos omnes si prædictis Daniæ regibus ordine annumeremus, jam ad XV numero regem pervenimus." [22]

The supposed identification of the personages in *Beowulf* with the princes in Arngrim's chronicle is not quite as convincing as one could wish. Obviously, the coincidence is somewhat less striking when it is seen that the names of all the seven brothers end in -*leifus* (*lāf*). There seems to be nothing else in the chronicle at this point which suggests a connection with the story of Finn, but genealogies of the Danish kings of course differ greatly, and it may be that these seven brothers were inserted into the genealogy in a place where they did not belong, having been taken from some floating story or tradition. The number seven and the ending of all their names in -*leifus* create a suspicion that they are fictitious. But this is

[20] MS. Humleifus.
[21] MS. Hinc.
[22] For the text of the *Skjoldungasaga*, and discussion, see Axel Olrik, *Aarböger for nordisk oldkyndighed og historie*, Vol. IX (Second Series), 1894, pp. 83 ff.

of no particular consequence; their presence in the chronicle makes it likely that tradition had in any case made them Danish heroes. The importance of the parallel depends almost wholly upon how great the probability is that the correspondences of the names are the result of chance. We must, I think, be exceedingly cautious about concluding that a proper name in Germanic story is necessarily, in the absence of evidence to the contrary, to be fastened upon the same hero or heroine. A large number of stories have been lost; it is perhaps to one of them that we should turn for the explanation of a proper name, rather than to one of the tales which has been preserved. Imelmann has called attention to the occurrence of the name *Hunlapus* in an early *Brut,* and his identification of this worthy with the Hunlaf(ing) of *Beowulf* seems to have been generally accepted.[23] But is not this somewhat questionable? Hunlaf, Oslaf (Ordlaf) and Guthlaf were names of common occurrence, as a glance at Searle's *Onomasticon* [24] will show. We have in the very story now under discussion an illustration of the frequency of the name Guthlaf. The Guthlaf whom we have just been considering is of course one of Hengest's companions. But the Guthlaf of *Fragment* 33, the father of Garulf, who is of the opposite party, cannot be the same person as the companion of Oslaf, unless we assume a tragic complication, kinsmen fighting on opposite sides, as in the passage from the Anglo-Saxon *Chronicle.* Möller tried to

---

[23] See *Deutsche Litteraturzeitung,* 17 April, 1909: "In diebus illis, imperante Valentiniano imperatore vel principe, regnum barbarorum et germanorum exortum est. Surgentesque populi et naciones per totam europam consederunt. Hoc testantur gesta rudolphi et hunlapi, Unwini et Widie, horsi et hengisti, Waltef et hame, quorum quidam in Gallia, alii in britannia, ceteri uero in Germania armis et rebus bellicis claruerunt." *Brut;* Cott. Vesp. D iv. fol. 130 b.

[24] Cambridge (Eng.) University Press, 1897.

avoid this confusion by emending F. 33 to Guthulf, and Trautmann by emending to Guthere. But the plain truth is that we must expect to find a common name like Guthlaf borne by more than one person; it is only the modern scholar who tries to remove such repetitions.[25] Why should it be more disturbing than to find two people named Jacques in *As You Like It,* or two named Bardolph in *Henry IV, 2?* In Germanic story we have only to consider such names as Theodoric, which occurs in the *Widsith* referring to two different kings; Gudrun, the heroine of the Nibelung legend, and Gudrun, the daughter of Hetel and Hilde; Hagen, the murderer of Siegfried, and Hagen, the father of Hilde; or such recurring names as Sieglind, Sigebant, Ute, Hildeburg. How then can we feel sure that the obscure Danish prince in Arngrim, the hero in Beowulf, and the Hunlapus of the *Brut* are one and the same person? We have already seen the failure of the attempt to identify the Hengest of the *Brut* list with the Hengest of our poem;[26] is the case more certain with Hunlapus?[27]

While the evidential value of this passage in Arngrim seems much slighter than has generally been supposed, its weight falls on the side of the interpretation which we have already seen, on other grounds, to be somewhat more

[25] Since writing the above I see that Klaeber has expressed himself in *Englische Studien,* Vol. xxxix, p. 308, to the following effect "Gūðere zu Gārulf's vater zu machen (35 nach Trautmann Gūðheres [statt Gūðlāfes] sunu), liegt kein genügender grund vor. Warum sollten denn nicht zwei personen denselben namen Gūðlaf haben? Auch in der schlacht bei Maldon treten zwei kämpfer namens Godrīc auf."

[26] See above, p. 415, note 2.

[27] These considerations apply also to Bugge's division of Hunlafing into Hun (a warrior) and Lafing (a sword), and his identification of Hun with the worthy mentioned in *Widsith* 33. Hun was a common name.

plausible,—that the " son of Hunlaf " presented Hengest with a sword, with which slaughter was done amongst the Frisians. But this part of the story remains in any case exceedingly obscure. If Hunlaf were the brother of Guthlaf and Oslaf, his son might present Hunlaf's sword to the man who was to lead an attack against the family enemy. It would perhaps be venturing too far to suggest that Hunlaf had already fallen in the struggle at Finnsburg, and that the son of Hunlaf gave the sword to Hengest in order that his father might be avenged. Apparently Hengest had brought reinforcements from Denmark for the final struggle, although this is not stated in the text. It is strange, as already noted, that Hengest is not mentioned in connection with the death of Finn, but that " after the sea-journey " it is Guthlaf and Oslaf who cast old scores in the teeth of the Frisian king. Was Hengest already dead ? These are questions which cannot be settled without further evidence; the main lines of the interpretation of 1142-1151 must still remain, after the most patient scrutiny, debatable. It is easy to construct ingenious hypotheses, and equally impossible to prove and to disprove their accuracy.

The rest of the tale is clear enough. In the bloody conflict at Finnsburg Finn is slain, and his queen carried off. The royal treasure is plundered, and everything of value which the Danes can find is loaded upon their ships. Then, with queen and treasure, their vengeance accomplished, they sail back to Denmark.

It may be well, in closing, to review briefly the main events of the story, adding as little as possible to the direct statements in the text. A certain amount of reading between the lines is necessary; it is for instance nowhere stated that Hildeburg is the queen of Finn, but there is no doubt that this is the case. Two serious omissions make a well-rounded outline of the story impossible; we are not told the cause of the Frisian hostility which leads to the attack upon the Danes in the hall, nor the exact train of events leading up to the final struggle in which Finn is killed. Otherwise the general course of the story is sufficiently plain.

Finn, king of the Frisians, has married a Danish princess, Hildeburg, the daughter of Hoc. Hildeburg's brother Hnæf, accompanied by a band of Danish warriors, is staying at Finnsburg, the residence of Finn in Friesland. The Danes are quartered by themselves in a hall. For reasons with which we are not acquainted,—probably an old feud between Frisians and Danes, temporarily healed by the marriage of Hildeburg—Finn attacks his visitors as they are sleeping in the hall at night. The Danes make a brave and successful defence.

This defence is described in the *Finnsburg Fragment*. . . . Hnæf, probably with a companion, has been on the watch. There are sixty men inside the hall, of whom Hengest, Sigeferth, Eaha, Ordlaf, and Guthlaf are particularly mentioned. The attacking party is discovered by the gleam of moonlight upon their weapons or armor. Hnæf arouses his men, who immediately rush to the doors to prevent the enemy from entering. Garulf, an impetuous warrior of the Frisian party, is restrained by Guthere from at once attacking, but Garulf demands the name of the warrior defending the door, and receives from Sigeferth a defiant reply. Restraining himself no longer, Garulf, followed by the rest, rushes to the attack, and is the first to fall. For five days the struggle continues, but not a single Dane is killed. Then a chief of the attacking party withdraws. . . .

According to the *Episode*, Hnæf is killed, and the fight takes place in a single night. Hengest, a thane of Hnæf, assumes the leadership upon the death of his lord. All of Finn's thanes save a few have been slain, so that he can no longer continue the combat. The Frisians therefore offer terms of peace, agreeing, on their part, to give the Danes a hall of their own, to allow them equal power with the Frisians, and an equal share of treasure, when this is dispensed by Finn to his warriors. It is further agreed that the Frisians are to treat the Danes with great courtesy, not recalling the feud, nor taunting them with following the leader of the men who slew their lord. The Danish part of the bargain seems to consist solely in giving allegiance to Finn. These promises are duly confirmed by oath. A great funeral pyre is erected, upon which the dead warriors, chief among them Hnæf and a son of Queen Hildeburg, are burnt. Frisians and Danes then settle down for the winter.

At the coming of spring, when travel by sea becomes possible, Hengest, who has been nursing his desire for revenge, sails away. The subsequent events are exceedingly obscure. Apparently Hengest reaches Denmark and brings back reinforcements, and perhaps he is presented by "the son of Hunlaf," probably a Dane, with a supremely good sword. It is clear, however, that Finn is slain in his own home, after bitter reproaches have been uttered by Guthlaf and Oslaf. The Danes then plunder Finn's treasures, and sail back to Denmark with this booty and with Queen Hildeburg.

Hrothgar's minstrel was truly a man of tact and discretion. At a celebration in honor of the great Geat hero who had performed a feat which the Danes themselves had been unable to accomplish, there might well have been some who, like Unferth, would not be free from jealousy. Nothing could better have appeased wounded pride than this tale of Danish heroism and Danish vengeance. It was " a thing pleasing to hear in the hall " not alone because it was a great and moving story, but because it was admirably adapted to the particular occasion upon which it was recited. And it left nothing more to be told. After the final contest at Finnsburg, Danish revenge for past injury and insult was complete. The song comes to an end, and once more the revellers in Hrothgar's hall give themselves over to the pleasures of the feast.

WILLIAM WITHERLE LAWRENCE.

Since the above article was written, the admirable revision of the Wyatt text carried out by Dr. R. W. Chambers has been issued. In this edition (Cambridge University Press, 1914, p. 168) is noted the difficulty involved in supposing the Danes to have entered the service of the Frisian king, who was responsible for the death of their lord. This problem has been fully discussed above (pp. 403 ff.), and an explanation of it offered. Dr. Chambers holds a different view, to which I cannot assent. He believes "the Eotenas to be a distinct tribe, possibly identical with the Ēote or Ȳte, whom modern historians know as Jutes." While the Frisians were a great nation, the Eotenas were, as he thinks, "a small and obscure clan," and "the Hōcingas or Healf-dene, though Danish, are not identical with the Danish nation proper." . . . "Finn, king of the Frisians, probably called a meeting of chieftains of subordinate clans, subject to or allied with him, such as we read of in the Norse sagas. At this meeting a night attack was made upon Hnæf and the Hocingas by Garulf, presumably prince of the Eotenas. It may be assumed that the supreme chief, Finn, had no share in this treachery, though he had to interfere in order to end the conflict, and to avenge his son, who had fallen in the struggle. . . . Such a succession of events would explain allusions in the poem not explicable on other hypotheses, and the action of the Danish survivors, in making peace with Finn, becomes less unintelligible if Finn had no hand in the original treachery, and interfered only to avenge a slain son." Dr. Chambers's argument should of course be read entire, but the preceding extract gives the most important points.

Serious objections to this argument immediately present themselves. There is no warrant in the text for assuming a meeting of allied clans called by Finn, nor for his vengeance for his slain son, nor for the statement that Garulf is "presumably prince of the Eotenas." Nothing is said in the *Fragment* about the nationality of the attackers. There is no reason to suppose they were not Frisians. The fact that Finn is not the first to attack the door certainly does not mean that they were not. And how is it possible to shift the blame for the attack from Finn to the Eotenas when Finn is called the *bana* of Hnæf? It does not matter whether he killed him with his own hands or not; he is clearly held responsible; the lines tell us it was regarded as disgraceful for the Danes to have to follow him, and the revenge at the end falls heavily upon him. The insult and hurt to Danish pride would be very little lessened by the assumption that some one else started the quarrel; and for this assumption, too, the lines give no warrant. Moreover, there is no evidence that the Eotenas were "a small and obscure clan." We have already seen that the name is probably, as Dr. Chambers admits may be the case, identical with that of the Jutes, and that probably the Frisians came to be called by this name in consequence of having settled in Jutish territory. (See above, p. 394). The names *Frȳsan* and *Eotenas* seem to be used interchangeably in the *Episode*. Whether the *Hōcingas* or *Healfdene* are identical with the Danes proper or not is of no particular consequence for the present argument; it may be noted, however, that they are called Dene (1000) and their prince a Scylding (1108), and that on the usual interpretation of 1069 Half-Dane and Scylding were synonymous terms. It seems likely that the Half-Danes were one of the allied clans making up the Danish people, and hence were treated as to all intents and purposes Danes by the poet. It is *tó Denum* that the avengers return (1158). The complete union of the Danish people into a state took place in the eighth century; even then the divisions of this people were marked (cf. Bremer, Paul's *Grundriss*, Vol. III, p. 837). At the time when the present poem was put into shape we surely have to assume for the Danes and Frisians, not compact and unified political units, but groups of tribes held somewhat loosely together, and sometimes known by tribal names.

Altogether, then, I feel that Dr. Chambers's hypotheses are to be decidedly rejected, as lacking evidence in the text, and indeed as being contradicted by it.—W. W. L.

PUBLICATIONS

OF THE

Modern Language Association of America

1915

VOL. XXX, 3	NEW SERIES, VOL. XXIII, 3

XIII.—STENDHAL AND FRENCH CLASSICISM

In *Rouge et Noir,* Stendhal (Henri Beyle) defines a novel as a miroir: qui se promène sur la grande route. We may apply this figure to his *Correspondance*[1] which, less open to the suspicion of pose than his other writings, reflects much of *la vie littéraire* of France during the first four decades of the nineteenth century. Stendhal was brought up on a classicist régime, he saw the passing of pseudo-classicism, he contributed to the triumph of romanticism and was himself a realist, before the term had been invented. In a letter to Mr. Stritch of London, written in 1823 ·in the midst of the romanticist ebullition, he declared: Le caractère principal de la nation française est la méfiance (II, p. 296). No one could offer more natural qualifications for recognition as the spokesman of his nation in this regard, than this man, who, French by birth, wrote under a German pseudonym and had himself buried as a citizen of Milan under the Italian inscription which he had composed for his own tombstone.

---

[1] Paris, 1908, 3 vols.

The entirely classic nature of Stendhal's early literary
training, such as it was, is revealed in his early correspondence with his sister, whose education he attempted to
direct. Si ton goût est juste, tu placeras Corneille et
Racine au premier rang des tragiques français, Voltaire et
Crébillon au deuxième . . . Je finis en te recommandant
de lire sans cesse Racine et Corneille, je suis comme
l'église, hors de là, point de salut (I, p. 33). She was to
commit to memory certain rôles from the plays of the
French classic authors in order to form her language (I,
p. 145), and he joined example to precept: Je lis chaque
soir avant de me coucher, quelque fatigué que je sois, un
acte de Racine pour apprendre à parler français. Les
jours où je n'ai pas mon maitre d'anglais, je lis, en me
levant, une pièce de Corneille (I, p. 33). Such was his
enthusiasm that: quand je lis Racine, Voltaire, Molière,
Virgile, l'Orlando Furioso, j'oublie le reste du monde (I,
p. 124).

His taste was so severely classic that he could see very
little merit in the successors and imitators of the classic
French authors. In 1801, at the age of eighteen, he assures his sister that she will see: l'immense distance qui
sépare Racine de Crébillon et la foule des imitateurs de
ce dernier (I, p. 16). If, in 1802, he is disposed to recommend La Harpe for: les premiers principes (I, p. 32),
he recognizes that his " taste is not sure," and his contempt for him finally developed even unto hatred (III,
p. 258). Le Cours Analytique of Lemercier he judged:
assez ridicule (II, p. 382), and he characterized Nisard
as: un fat qui n'a pas une idée (III, p. 125). None of
the pseudo-classic poet-celebrities find favor in his eyes.
Delille is an: amant tartuffe de la nature (I, p. 32); Ray-
nouard is a: savant qui avait de l'esprit dans sa jeunesse
(II, p. 282); Lemercier a fait douze ou quinze tragédies

barbares pour le style (*ib.*) ; Picard . . . le plus vrai de
nos poètes comiques . . . rend ce qu'il vit comme dans
un miroir (II, p. 370) ; but: rien, ou presque rien ne valait
la peine d'être dit (II, p. 281) ; Andrieux . . . est un
élève de Voltaire, ingénieux et sans force . . . ses ouvrages ne conviennent plus au siècle vigoureux au milieu
duquel nous vivons (II, p. 283) ; if he makes an exception
in favor of M. de Jouy, it is because: il a osé peindre un
grand caractère et lui faire dire des mots simples (II,
p. 262).

At the same time Stendhal was thoroughly imbued with
the eighteenth-century skepticism: Je ne saurais trop vous
répéter: n'ayez aucun préjugé. C'est-à-dire, ne croyez
rien parce qu'un autre vous l'a dit, mais parce qu'on vous
l'a prouvé, . . . en tout cherche la vérité, il n'y a qu'elle
qui dure; j'aime mieux que tu saches une vérité de plus
que d'avoir lu dix volumes d'histoire (I, p. 56). Faguet,
on the basis of such statements, characterizes him as a
déplacé, as a Frenchman of 1770, ill at ease in the midst
of nineteenth-century conditions.[2] But the campaigns
under Napoleon, various affaires du cœur, many disap-
pointments, an ardent temperament, all served to modify
the character of the author of *Rouge et Noir*. He even
came as a result of his experiences and of his temperament to be dissatisfied with his favorite eighteenth-century
philosopher, Helvetius: Helvétius a eu parfaitement
raison lorsqu'il a établi que le principe de l'utilité ou
l'intérêt, était le guide unique de toutes les actions de
l'homme. Mais comme il avait l'âme froide, il n'a connu
ni l'amour ni l'amitié, ni les autres passions vives qui
créent des intérêts nouveaux et singuliers (II, p. 217).
The romanticist note sounds frequently in these confiden-

[2] *Politiques et Moralistes du dix-neuvième siècle*, Paris, 1900.

tial letters of his. In 1804 he writes to his sister: j'étais
ce qu'on appelle tout cœur. Cette folie me donna quelques moments de la plus divine illusion (ɪ, p. 130); in
1807, une église gothique environnée d'arbres décrépits
et couverte de neige me touche (ɪ, p. 312); in 1810, ce
qui m'a touché le plus dans mon voyage d'Italie, c'est le
chant des oiseaux dans le Colisée (ɪ, p. 373); in 1813,
quand je suis seul, je ris et pleure pour un rien, mais les
pleurs sont toujours pour les arts (ɪ, p. 406); in 1832,
describing a certain man, he declares: il aime comme moi,
avec passion, folie, bêtise (ɪɪɪ, p. 66), and the character
of this man is: passionné et ombrageux (*ib.*, p. 70). But
he anticipated Flaubert in his impatience for the exces-
sive mal de siècle of his contemporaries, and no one has
characterized more picturesquely than he the romantic
sentimentality of the period. C'est un homme (speaking
of J. J. Rousseau) qui fendant une racine de noyer au
milieu de la cour, s'efforcerait de faire entrer son coin
par le gros bout, ne parviendrait qu' à casser sa masse, et
sur le midi, dégoûté de ses efforts, irait pleurer dans un
coin de la cour; bientôt il s'exalterait la tête, se mettrait
à croire qu'il y a de l'honneur à être malheureux et, de
suite, qu'il est excessivement malheureux. . . . En
général les malheureux de ce genre dans le monde, ne
sont que des sots, les trois quarts de ces mélancolies ne
sont que des folies. C'est malheureusement la maladie
des jeunes gens du siècle et des jeunes femmes (ɪ, p. 184).

Instead of seeing in Stendhal a déplacé, we should
rather go to the opposite extreme and regard him as very
much a man of his period. It was that and nothing else
that made him such an ardent champion of the romantic
movement. In 1818 he predicted: L'invasion des idées
libérales va amener une nouvelle littérature (ɪɪ, p. 86).
Two years later he wrote to a friend: Vous vous moquiez

de moi quand je vous disais que le romanticisme était la racine ou la queue du libéralisme, il fait dire: examinons et méprisons l'ancien (ii, p. 187). L'ancien synonymous with classicism, had become: une vieille platitude (ii, p. 112); romanticism offered something new: Voilà le principe du romanticisme que vous ne sentiez pas assez. Le mérite est d'administrer à un public le drogue juste qui lui fera plaisir (ii, p. 168).[3] He believed that the French nation desired to see upon its stage tragedies derived from its own national life, just as the English could see their national life portrayed in the tragedies of Henry VI. and Richard II. But: cela est impossible en employant le vers alexandrin français, qui, dit La Harpe, n'admet que le tiers de la langue (ii, p. 296).[4]

But Stendhal was not at all inclined to bow before the foreign romanticist influences which were so potent with his contemporaries. In 1816, he declared: Il faut bien séparer cette cause (romanticism) de celle de ce pauvre et triste pédant Schlegel qui sera dans la boue au premier jour (ii, p. 12.) None of the Germans pleased him, not even Schiller, whom he almost admired, but who bored him because: on voit le rhéteur (ii, p. 187). As for the English: Je ne connais pas de gens plus bavards et plus froids. Ils n'ont produit qu'un grand homme et qu'un fou. Le grand homme est Shakespeare et Milton le fou (i, p. 98). Walter Scott, whom he presents as the most

---

[3] Letter of 1820. Cf. *Racine et Shakespeare*, Paris, 1823. Le romanticisme est l'art de présenter aux peuples des œuvres littéraires qui, dans l'état actuel de leurs habitudes et de leurs croyances, sont susceptibles de leur donner le plus de plaisir possible.

[4] In this connection Stendhal suggests the subject of *La Mort de Henri III*, which, treated by Dumas (1829), was to win the first great theatre-triumph of the romanticists. See, Le Roy, *L'Aube du théâtre romantique*, Paris, 1904, pp. 72 f.

popular author in France in 1823,[5] impresses him as
being: un peu grossier et un peu brut; ses éternelles
descriptions de costumes ennuient et fatiguent (II, p.
393); he is: injuste avec l'amour; il le peint mal, sans
force, décoloré, sans énergie. On voit qu'il a étudié
l'amour dans les livres et non dans son propre cœur (II,
p. 272). He considered Byron: le plus grand poète
vivant. When he met him for the first time he confesses:
Si j'avais osé, j'aurais baisé la main de Lord Byron en
fondant en larmes (II, p. 501). But this enthusiasm
passed upon closer acquaintance: Les plaisanteries de
Lord Byron sont amères dans *Childe Harold* . . . au lieu
de gaieté et d'insouciance, la haine et le malheur sont au
fond. Lord Byron n'a jamais su peindre qu'un seul
homme: lui-même (I, p. 502).

He manifested the same sort of discontent with the
French romanticists of his day: La poétique de Madame
de Staël est plus mauvaise que celle de La Harpe ou de
l'*Edinburgh Review* (I, p. 117). He saw in René: la
plus belle peinture de ces sentiments vagues et mélan-
coliques (II, p. 373) which were the essence of romanticism. But his general attitude towards Chateaubriand is
summed up in a sentence from a letter of 1834: J'ai
horreur de la phrase à la Chateaubriand (III, p. 135).
As for Benjamin Constant: C'est de la bouillie pour les
enfants (II, p. 63); and in 1840, when Sainte-Beuve was
greeting with enthusiasm the publication of the collected
works of Xavier de Maistre, Stendhal declared point
blank: je ne puis souffrir M. de Maistre (III, p. 258).

As for the poets of the period, a letter of 1825 makes
this rather startling choice: Lamartine est le second ou
le premier poète de la France, selon qu'on voudra mettre

---

[5] *Racine et Shakespeare*, Paris, 1823, p. 6.

M. de Béranger avant ou après lui (II, p. 373). Here is the explanation of Stendhal's rather exaggerated appreciation of Béranger: On voit que M. de Béranger, le plus grand poète peut-être que la France possède, ne laisse échapper aucune grande circonstance, aucune grande émotion de l'opinion publique, sans exprimer dans ses vers, ce que le monde de Paris exprime de vive voix. Ses *Chansons* sont donc exactement des odes nationales; elles s'adressent au sens intime des Français (II, p. 358). As for Lamartine, Stendhal recognized his gift of self-revelation: Au contraire de nos autres poètes français, il a quelque chose à dire (II, p. 295); M. de Lamartine rend avec une grâce divine les sentiments qu'il a éprouvés (II, p. 373). But at the same time he was very keenly alive to Lamartine's limitations: Mais dès qu'il sort de l'expression de l'amour, il est puéril, il n'a pas une haute pensée de philosophie ou d'observation de l'homme, c'est toujours et uniquement un cœur tendre au désespoir de la mort de sa maitresse (II, p. 282). Victor Hugo was less likely than any other to appeal to Stendhal. In 1823 he wrote this appreciation, the concluding sentence of which has been the cause of so many exclamation points: Ce M. Hugo a un talent dans le genre de Young, l'auteur des *Night Thoughts;* il est toujours exagéré à froid; son parti lui procure un fort grand succès. L'on ne peut nier, au surplus, qu'il ne sache fort bien faire des vers français; malheureusement, il est somnifère (II, p. 284). He never contests Victor Hugo's ability in the art of versification (II, p. 363); as for the rest, he judged him much as posterity has judged: M. Victor Hugo n'est pas un homme ordinaire, mais il veut être extraordinaire (II, p. 518).

Most of ·the romanticist battles in the theatre were fought out during Stendhal's absence from Paris. He would hardly have been satisfied with the efforts of those whose cause he had so noisily adopted. A letter of 1829 announces the *Henri III et sa cour* of Dumas, with this characterization: Ceci est encore Henri III à la Marivaux (II, p. 493). He seems to have preferred Scribe among all the dramatists of his time, and for reasons quite similar to those which made him esteem so highly the *Chansons* of Béranger. As for the novels, they lack force, like those of Picard (II, p. 370); or, like those of Madame Cotin, they are so sentimental that: ils sont difficiles à lire pour des gens âgées plus de vingt-cinq ans (II, p. 394); or, they are absurd in their attempts at a resuscitation of the past: ce qu'il y a de plaisant, c'est que ces grossiers chevaliers du treizième siècle ne disent pas vingt paroles sans faire une allusion pleine de grâce à la mythologie grecque (II, p. 356).

There will be a strong inclination to see in these sharp criticisms of Stendhal so many more evidences of his misanthropy, of his notoriously recalcitrant disposition. But surely that is not the whole explanation. If the exaggeration and sentimentalism of the romanticists irritated his critical faculties, their abuse of the personal element offended his finer sensibilities, and he was not as deficient in sensibility as one is often tempted to think. One finds ample proof of this throughout his *Correspondance,* but nowhere so convincingly as in his admirable letter of protest written, as it were involuntarily, in 1830, to Sainte-Beuve, after reading "in a single sitting," the latter's collection of verse, entitled *Les Consolations.* Je suis choqué que vous autres qui croyez en Dieu, vous imaginez que, pour être au désespoir trois mois de ce qu'une maitresse vous a quitté, il faille croire en Dieu. . . . Vous parlez trop de la gloire. On aime à travailler. . . . Qui diable sait si la gloire viendra? Mais pourquoi parler tant de ces choses-là? La passion a sa pudeur; pourquoi révéler ces choses intimes? . . . Voilà Monsieur, ma pensée et toute ma pensée. Je crois qu'on parlera de vous en 1890. Mais vous ferez mieux que *Les Consolations,* quelque chose de plus fort et de plus pur (II, pp. 531 f.).

From this rapid review it is apparent that Stendhal was quite as much dissatisfied with the romanticism as with the classicism, or rather the pseudo-classicism of his time. What was this " something stronger and purer " demanded of Sainte-Beuve? Let us seek to piece together the answer from this *Correspondance,* just as literary historians have long since pieced together and clearly defined the literary system of Malherbe from the marginal notes on the poems of Desportes and the scattering precepts preserved for us by his disciple, Racan. We shall try to prove that Stendhal, like Malherbe, like Boileau, represents that national French trait which demands in intellectual and æsthetic products, fidelity to that which is in the thought, and logical precision in the expression of it; qualities which, in his time, were being lost sight of in the midst of the ardent discussions which divided the literary men of France into two hostile camps. And since these qualities are the essence of French classicism, we shall go a step farther in concreteness and say that what Stendhal desired and fought for, in his fashion, was a return to classicism; that is to say, an adaptation to modern subjects of the processes of Boileau, Molière, and Racine.

Much confusion has resulted from the failure to distinguish between Stendhal's literary and his personal attitude. An officer of Napoleon, considerably affected by the democratic enthusiasm of the period, he saw much in the social relations of the seventeenth century to make

him impatient. In 1804 he writes to his sister: J'ai
étudié Louis XIV ces jours-ci, nommé le grand par les
bas coquins Voltaire et compagnie, et bassement flatté par
Boileau, Molière, etc., j'ai été étonné de sa bassesse et de
sa bêtise (I, p. 125). Three years later he writes to her
from Berlin, from the entourage of Napoleon: Je méprise
sincèrement Racine; je vois d'ici toutes les platitudes
qu'il faisait à la cour de Louis XIV. L'habitude de la
cour rend incapable de sentir ce qui est véritablement
grand (I, p. 298). He always maintained this personal
attitude which is quite characteristic of him.

But this aversion for what he considered the sycophancy
of the classic writers does not seem to have affected his
literary judgment. He asks his sister if she perceives
the *sens profond* of the *Fables* of La Fontaine; he urges
her to get La Bruyère and " read him " (I, p. 68). He
instructs her to read often *L'Art Poétique* of Boileau
(I, p. 68), and many years later he refers to that: homme
de sens, un nommé Boileau (III, p. 96). Molière he
characterizes as: le poète qui a le mieux connu le cœur
humain (I, p. 131). *La Princesse de Clèves* is " divine "
(III, p. 258). In 1838 he writes to a young poet who
has sought counsel: Je vous dirai franchement, Monsieur,
que pour faire un livre qui ait la chance de trouver quatre
mille lecteurs, il faut étudier deux ans le français dans
les œuvres composées avant 1700. Je n'excepte que le
Marquis de Saint-Simon (III, p. 209). According to Faguet (*op. cit.*, p. 49) Stendhal ne pouvait souffrir Racine; but, we repeat, this is true only in the personal
sense. To be sure he speaks somewhat disdainfully of:
l'amour fade peint de Racine dans Hippolyte, dans Ba-
jazet, dans Xipharès (II, p. 296), but that conforms very
well with the judgment of modern standard literary his-

torians;[6] and he concludes the outbreak against Louis XIV, cited above: c'est le grand roi des sots comme *Iphigénie* de Racine est leur belle tragédie (i, p. 125), wherein again he conforms with modern critics.[7]   On the other hand, Stendhal uses Racine currently as a standard by which to measure his favorite modern poets.   In 1817 he thus characterizes Monti: C'est le Racine d'Italie, du génie dans l'expression (ii, p. 65).   In 1824, one year after the publication of *Racine et Shakespeare,* he declares: La *Francesca da Rimini* est ce que la langue italienne a produit de plus ressemblant à Racine. . . . Pellico a su peindre l'amour italien de la manière la plus vraie, la plus touchante, et en vers dignes de Racine (ii, p. 339).   And as for the *Corsair* of Lord Byron, "the greatest living poet": Le style est beau comme Racine (ii, p. 12).   Nor was it merely the style or the verses of Racine that enlisted Stendhal's admiration.   In 1801, he wrote to his sister: Peut-être Voltaire te plaira-t-il d'abord autant comme eux (Corneille and Racine); mais tu sentiras bientôt combien son vers coulant, mais vide, est inférieur au vers *plein de choses* du tendre Racine et du majestueux Corneille (i, p. 24).   And he remained true to that opinion, as we can see in his letter of 1840 to Balzac: Le demi-sot tient par-dessus tout aux vers de Racine. . . .   Mais tous les jours le vers devient une moindre partie du mérite de Racine.   Le public, en se faisant plus nombreux, moins mouton, veut un plus grand

---

[6] Cf. Lanson, *Histoire de la Littérature Française*, Paris, 1908, p. 541: Les hommes sont plus faibles, les amoureux aimés sont des galants agréables, et rien de plus.

[7] Cf. J. Lemaître, J. *Racine*, Paris, 1908, p. 224: *Mithridate* et surtout *Iphigénie* me semblent les deux pièces où le poète s'est le plus plié, sciemment ou non aux mœurs de son temps, et à l'idée que ce temps se faisait de la beauté.

nombre de *petits faits vrais* sur une passion, sur une situation de la vie (III, p. 260). In this last passage, of which the italics are Stendhal's, it seems clear that, in his opinion, it is the realism (les petits faits vrais) of Racine that is gradually winning a deserved though long delayed recognition.

Stendhal was an admirer of his time. Far from regretting or ridiculing the existing social and political conditions, he welcomed them as a real progress: Les enrichis donnent de l'énergie à la bonne compagnie. . . . Nous sommes bien loin de la fadeur du siècle de Louis XVI (III, p. 209). In face of the cool contempt of the classicists for the philistinism of the bourgeois, Stendhal asserted: Des gens qui ont agi mettront plus de pensées en circulation que des gens de lettres uniquement occupés pendant toute leur jeunesse, à peser un hémistiche de Racine, ou à chercher la vraie mesure d'un vers de Pindare (II, p. 271). Instead of adopting the robustious attitude of the romanticist brethren toward these same philistines, Stendhal declared: Un banquier qui a fait fortune a une partie du caractère requis pour faire des découvertes en philosophie: c'est-à-dire voir claire dans ce qui est; ce qui est un peu différent de parler éloquemment de brillantes chimères (II, p. 515). To meet these conditions it was necessary to apply once more the primary precept of Boileau:

N'offrez rien au lecteur que ce qui peut lui plaire.

To satisfy this eminently French desire of "seeing clearly in that which is": il faut faire ressemblant (III, p. 181). A letter of 1804 presents Stendhal's earliest conception of literary realism in regard to natural things: Une vérité aussi complète que possible est une description complète d'une· chose. Par exemple: la vérité complète sur tout ce qui est vivant à Grenoble (la maison, les arbres, etc.), serait celle d'après laquelle un dieu tout-puissant pourrait bâtir un nouveau Grenoble exactement semblable et égal au Grenoble où tu es (I, p. 100). The same letter suggests how characters must be painted: Envoie-moi vite trois ou quatre caractères peints par les faits: raconte-les exactement (I, p. 101). He complains that his sister's letters: manquent toujours de détails physiques, nécessaires pour bien entendre les réflexions sur les choses et les sensations qu'elles donnent (I, p. 189). But he had no patience with the exuberant descriptions undertaken by contemporary romanticists in the interest of a much bespoken local color. He ridicules the fashion, prevalent, according to him, in the novel of 1830, when: on était sûr de succès en employant deux pages à décrire la vue que l'on avait de la fenêtre où était le héros, deux autres à reproduire son habillement, et encore deux pages à représenter la forme du fauteuil sur lequel il était posé (III, p. 91). It was precisely the criticism of Boileau:

> Un auteur, quelquefois trop plein de son objet,
> Jamais sans l'épuiser n'abandonne un sujet:
> S'il rencontre un palais, il m'en dépeint la face; etc.

Boileau attributed the success of his own writings to the fact that: mon vers, bien ou mal, dit toujours quelque chose. That was precisely what was lacking in the works of the period, according to Stendhal. Faire correctement des vers est devenu un métier, he complains, le mal est qu'à peine en a-t-on lu quinze ou vingt, l'on se sent une très grande envie de bailler (II, p. 284). And as for the style of Chateaubriand and Villemain, it seems to him to say: 1. Beaucoup de petites choses agréables, mais inutiles à dire; 2. Beaucoup de petites faussetés agréables à entendre (III, p. 259). To those rare individuals who sought his advice, Stendhal insisted: En décrivant un homme, une femme, un site, songez toujours à quelqu'un, à quelque chose de réel (III, p. 114); 1. Dans un roman, dès la deuxième page, il faut dire du nouveau, ou, du moins, de l'individuel sur le site où se passe l'action; 2. Dès la sixième page, ou, tout au plus, la huitième, il faut des aventures (III, p. 209).

In his youth, when he had his first visions of " literary glory," Stendhal was convinced that: Il ne faut écrire que lorsqu'on a des choses grandes ou profondément belles à dire, mais alors il faut les dire avec le plus de simplicité possible, comme si l'on prenait à tâche de les empêcher d'être remarquées (I, p. 179). When he became a writer he remained true to this ideal, imitating the style of *Le Code Civil* and the *Causes Célèbres* (III, pp. 103, 135). Je dirai comme les enfants,[8] he writes to Balzac in 1840, je ne veux pas par des moyens factices, fasciner l'âme du lecteur. . . . Je cherche à raconter avec vérité et avec clarté ce qui se passe dans mon cœur. Je ne vois qu'une règle: être clair. Si je ne suis pas clair, tout mon monde est anéanti (III, p. 258). In this constant insistence upon the principle that the writer must first have something to say and then say it in the simplest and clearest way ·possible, Stendhal renews the traditions of Malherbe, Boileau, and their successors, who had formed the: génie de la langue française, qui, naturelle-

---

[8] Cf. Boileau, *Epître* IX, vv. 81 ff.:

> La simplicité plaît, sans étude et sans art.
> Tout charme en un enfant, dont la langue sans fard,
> A peine du filet encor débarrassée,
> Sait d'un air innocent bégayer sa pénsee, etc.

ment, est ennemie jurée des grandes phrases à la Chateaubriand (II, p. 290).[9]

The analogy between the position of Stendhal and that of Malherbe has been touched upon. Malherbe found French diction in a state of anarchy resulting from an excess of enthusiasm on the part of the Pléiade and its successors. Stendhal found a very similar state of things, a literary battlefield, on which the two opposing forces of the pseudo-classicists and the romanticists were contending: the one, to hold French literature within its old consecrated channels, the other trying to break down the barriers and let it flow wherever it listed. While Malherbe " forged the instrument which the genius of the seventeenth century was to use with success " (Brunetière), Stendhal opened the way at least for Balzac, Flaubert, and Maupassant. If he did not succeed in " reducing the Muse to the rules of duty " as fully as Malherbe succeeded, it was because, or largely because, the times no longer permitted a man like Stendhal, or Malherbe, to assume a power in the domain of letters so absolute as that wielded by the seventeenth-century critic and poet. Had the conditions been similar, it is quite possible that the *tyran des petits faits vrais* [10] would have taken the place of the *tyran des sillabes* in the talk of men of letters.

Finally Stendhal's conception of style was that of

---

[9] Cf. also his criticism of Xavier de Maistre: " l'auteur n'ose jamais être simple . . . par exemple, a-t-il à parler de Newton, il ne dit pas simplement: Newton; cela sera trop plat à Turin, il faut dire l'immortel Newton. Pour approcher de l'esprit français il faudrait commencer à être soi-même, n'imiter personne (II, p. 390). Cf. Boileau:

Ce n'est que l'air d'autrui qui peut déplaire en moi.

[10] Des faits, morbleu! · des faits (III, p. 90).

Malherbe and Boileau; it was based on "the power of
a word put in its place." In 1804, he wrote to his sister:
Coligny les suivait à pas précipités, ou, à pas précipités,
Coligny les suivait, sont deux choses différentes pour une
âme sensible (I, p. 124). Two years later he declared:
Le style est une pensée . . . je t'aime véritablement,
et véritablement je t'aime, ne sont pas la même chose
(I, p. 246). When Mérimée's *Chronique de Charles IX*
appeared (1829), Stendhal wrote: Je serai trop sévère
pour votre style que je trouve un peu portier: j'ai eu
du mal à faire etc., pour: j'ai eu de la peine à faire
(II, p. 509). In 1840 he wrote to Balzac: Souvent je
réfléchis un quart d'heure pour placer un adjectif avant
ou après son substantif (III, p. 258).

Like Boileau, Stendhal was convinced of the necessity
of taking pains; it was one of his grievances that: Les
gens de lettres ne se donnent pas le temps de travailler
(II, p. 360). La haine de détails est ce qui perd notre
littérature (II, p. 521). And Boileau's famous verses
which might serve as the epitome of the *Art poétique:*

Avant donc que d'écrire, apprenez à penser;
Selon que notre idée est plus ou moins obscure,
L'expression la suit, ou moins nette, ou plus pure,

are repeated in the prose of Stendhal's letters: Tous les
jours nous voyons dans la vie, que l'homme qui comprend
bien une chose l'explique clairement (II, p. 513).

Les pensées de tout le monde dans les paroles de
quelques-uns is a trite definition of French classic literature. That definition suggests, and rightly, the idea of
something chosen, something aristocratic. It was that ideal
that Stendhal wished to see restored; moreover, he believed
it was to be restored as a result of the convulsions and the
invasion of new ideas through which France had passed.

STENDHAL AND FRENCH CLASSICISM

Le jour immortel où M. l'abbé Sieyès publia son pamphlet: *Qu' est-ce que le tiers-état?* . . . il croyait attaquer l'aristocratie politique; il créait sans le savoir l'aristocratie littéraire. Celle-ci ose encore aimer les phrases simples et les pensées naturelles (III, p. 184). He was enough a man of his time to realize that this literary aristocracy must adapt itself to the spirit and needs of the time. Because: Nous avons infiniment plus d'idées qu'on avait du temps de Plutarque . . . La Bruyère a bien peint les mœurs de la bonne compagnie de son temps: le tableau serait bien différent aujourd'hui (I, pp. 130 f.). Les gens qui croient avoir raison ne sauraient être trop claires et trop lucides; ils cherchent à écrire avec les mots et les tours de phrases employés par La Bruyère, Pascal et Voltaire. Mais cependant, quand il se presente une idée nouvelle il faut bien un mot nouveau (II, p. 425).

The citations given above, chosen from a very large number of similar import, give a fair presentation of Stendhal's literary point of view as manifested by his *Correspondance*. Whatever boutades he may have indulged in, in writings destined for the public, we find him here quite consistent and sincere: Je désire pour mon compte la vérité toute entière et la vérité la plus âpre (II, p. 363). The conclusion that he represents to a certain and rather important extent a persistence of French classicism would probably have greatly surprised his contemporaries, while completely staggering him. And the conclusion is very likely absurd, unless one is prepared to admit that French classicism is, par excellence, the manifestation of what Lemaitre calls in his book on Racine: le génie de notre race, which he defines as the striving for: ordre, raison, sentiment mesuré et

2

force sous la grâce. It has at least appeared from the foregoing pages that Stendhal was constantly insisting on the first two of these four qualities, that the sentimental excesses of the romanticists no less than the aridity of the pseudo-classicists irritated him; that, finally, he demanded of a recognized leader of the new school: quelque chose de plus fort et de plus pur.

COLBERT SEARLES.

XIV.—"TO BE STAIED"

Possibly no entry in the Stationers' Register has given rise to more discussion than the puzzling "to be staied" entered in the margin beside the titles of four plays on one of the fly-leaves of "Register C." The item occurs on page 37 of volume iii of Arber's *Reprint:*

My lord chamberlens menns plaies Entred

27 May, 1600   A moral of ' clothe breches and velvet hose '
To Master Roberts

27 May   Allarum to London
To hym

                 4 Augusti

As you like yt / a booke
Henry the Ffift / a booke   to be staied
Every man in his humour / a booke
The commedie of ' much Adoo about nothing ' / a booke

The entry has provoked curiosity chiefly because it has been assumed that here was a definite injunction against a threatened piracy, an assumption which fits into the generally accepted theory that playwrights were indifferent about the publication of their plays, if not really averse from it, and that the acting companies to whom they sold their plays were habitually opposed to the publishing of plays still in use, on the ground that it would lessen their profits; and therefore, when we find plays published that were still popular on the stage, we should immediately suspect them of being issued surreptitiously.

The theory in its simplest form is expressed by Sir Sidney Lee in his *Life of William Shakespeare:*[1] " This was one of the many efforts of the acting company to stop

[1] Macmillan, 1898, p. 207.

451

publication of plays in the belief that the practice was injurious to their rights. The effort was only partially successful." Practically the same view appears in the preface to the new Hudson *As You Like It* (p. xvii, 1906): " There is more probability that the ' staying ' was the result of a direct attempt on the part of Shakespeare or someone acting for him, to prevent the publication of a popular new play, the circulation of which in book form would seriously interfere with its business success and the receipts at the theatre." Fleay [2] gives the theory a novel turn by his suggestion that *Every Man in his Humour* was published " without Jonson's supervision, no doubt by the company, as acted by them, after an ineffectual effort had been made to ' stay ' it on August 4, by Jonson, I suppose."

Surprisingly ineffectual, this effort to " stay " the publication, whether it originated with acting company or author! It is true that, so far as we know, *As You Like It* was not published in quarto form. But ten days after the " staying " entry, *Henry V.* was entered to Thomas Pavier. It was printed in 1600 by Thomas Creede for Thomas Millington and John Busby, and in 1602 " by Thomas Creede for Thomas Pavier," and again " for T. P., 1608 " (really for William Jaggard in 1619). The play had been acted at the Globe by the Chamberlain's men in 1599, and was later acted at Court, January 7, 1605.[3] On the same date, August 14, 1600, Master Burby and Walter Burre " entred for their copie under the bandes of Master Pasuill and the Wardens, a booke called Fuery man in his humour." [4] It was printed " as it hath been sundry times publikely acted by the right Honorable the

---

[2] *Biographical Chronicle of the Eng. Drama*, I, p. 358.
[3] Murray, *History of the English Dramatic Companies*, I, p. 173.
[4] Arber, III, p. 169.

Lord Chamberlen's servants, written by Ben. Johnson, for Walter Burre, 1601." The play had been acted in 1598, and was acted at court Feb. 2, 1605. Nine days after these entries (23 August), Andrew Wyse and William Aspley " enterd for their copies under the bandes of the wardens Two bookes, the one called Muche a Doo about nothinge. Thother the second parte of the history of kinge Henry iiijth with the humours of sir John Ffallstaff: Wrytten by Master Shakespere." [5] *Much Ado* was published " as it hath been sundrie times publikely acted by the right honorable, the Lord Chamberlaine his seruants. Written by William Shakespeare. V. S. for Andrew Wise and William Aspley, 1600." Its earlier stage history is obscure. It was acted at Court 1612-1613 under the title of *Benedicite and Bettris.*

We may place beside these cases of ineffectual " staying" yet another from the same year—that of *Patient Grissel.* Henslowe records payment to Chettle, Dekker, and Haughton, in behalf of the Admiral's Company, of a total of £10 10 s. between Oct. 16, 1599 and 28 Dec., 1599; then, " to buy a grey gowne for gryssell £1 " on 26 Jan., 1600,[6] and finally [7]

Lent unto (the c) Robarte Shawe the 18th of March 1599 (1600) to geue unto the printer to staye the printing of patient grisell the some of 40 s.

by me Rob. Shaa.

But, says Greg, " the play was entered S. R. 28 Mar., 1600 (i. e. ten days after it was stayed!) to C. Burby, and printed in 1603 for H. Rocket as acted by the Admiral's men." Mr. Pollard suggests [8] that this may have been a

---

[5] This is the first entry of Shakespeare's name on the registers.

[6] *Diary,* ed. Greg, II, p. 206.

[7] *Ibid.,* I, F68, line 19.

[8] *Shakespeare Folios and Quartos,* p. 12.

compromise payment to induce the printer to relinquish his printing right. Others seem to regard Burby as a brazen pirate entering (apparently with the approval of the Stationers) a copy to prohibit whose publication the owners had paid two pounds just ten days before. Belated justice then would seem to have overtaken the pirate; for the play was, after all, not printed till 1603, and then was printed for another man.

We have, then, in 1600 five plays clearly " to be staied " ; and, after intervals of ten days in three cases and nineteen days in one, four of these five plays are entered for publication. Two are published within the year of the entry, one the following year, and one apparently not until three years later. Shall we suppose that the owners of the plays were at first eager to prohibit publication, and then suddenly " removed the bar " ?

Various solutions have been proposed; but most of them are based upon the theory that the company objected to publication because the play was still new on the stage. It is beyond the purpose of this paper to discuss the general conditions of dramatic publication; but it may be permissible to suggest that this theory should be accepted with an interrogation point, in view of the Chamberlain's powerful patronage and his evident interest in protecting the players' rights, of the absence of any positive evidence that this particular company was at this time opposed to the publication of its plays save as such publication may have been unauthorized; in view of the many plays actually published while still good for stage use; and in view of the evident success with which Bieston's Boys protected their stage rights [9] in plays which had been long in print,

---

[9] " Cockpitt playes appropried." MS. in L. Chamberlain's Office. Murray, *Hist. of the Eng. Dramatic Companies*, I, p. 368.

and of the fact that they thought it worth while to protect old printed plays.

But, whether or not the theory is well founded, it fails to account in a satisfactory way for any play but *As You Like It*. If we regard the actors as still opposed to the publication when the other plays come to be entered after the "staying," we must suppose the Stationers to be either deliberately and openly promoting piracy or utterly helpless to enforce a prohibition which they still, however, record to their own shame. But the promptness and efficiency of the Stationers in cancelling false entries (as in the case of Bacon's *Essays,* 1597), in taking up pirated editions, as Newman's edition of Sidney's *Astrophel & Stella,* 1591, in regulating the behavior of the pirates, as in the Jeffes-White quarrel over the *Spanish Tragedy,* 1592, make it impossible to suppose the Stationers helpless, especially in a case like this, where the Chamberlain, as well as the Court of Star Chamber, would back them up. And it is to be hoped that we shall not be driven to assume that the Company of Stationers deliberately put itself in league with pirates.

In order to evade this conclusion, it has been suggested that the acting company first put up a bar to publication and then, for reasons of its own, removed the bar. Clearly not in the interest of stage receipts, if the regular entry is supposed to carry with it the right to print at the printer's convenience; for the interval between the "stay" and the regular entry is too brief to conserve the players' interests for more than a single run. And unless this were expected to be the last or only run, it is hard to see why a company originally opposed to publication of these plays should so quickly change their minds. The plays were all successful, and were all used at Court after publication. And anyone who has looked through Henslowe's

Diary or has studied successive editions of plays will understand that the custom of revising and rewriting plays, cutting here, expanding there, or even reviving them with only verbal alterations, was so nearly universal that it would be absurd to suppose that a good play by Shakespeare or Jonson could possibly have appeared to the company to have outlived its usefulness to the stage when it had finished its first few runs. If seriously opposed to publication on 4th of August, 1600, because of expected lessening of theatre receipts, doubtless the company remained opposed to publication throughout the month of August.

Of the three or four theories offered by Fleay,[10] the first, that the plays " were ordered to be stayed; they were probably suspected of being libellous and reserved for further examination," seems peculiarly unfit. It cannot be made to account for the seemingly permanent " staying " of *As You Like It;* nor does it fit the character of the other plays, in which there is nothing to suggest a reason for a special challenge.

More reasonable are the theories based on the idea that the acting company was opposed not to the publication of plays in general or these plays in particular, but to the entry of these plays to others than the publishers authorized by the company. Aside from a possible preference for good printers rather than bad ones, the company may reasonably be assumed to prefer that the plays should be entered to printers who bought their copies from the company instead of securing them through circuitous means, whether by purchase from individual actors, by snatching up strayed or stolen manuscripts, or by patching up the texts from short-hand notes taken at the theatre.

[10] *Life and Works of Shakespeare*, 1886, pp. 40, 140.

Collier was one of the first to suggest that the staying was for the sake of favoring a particular printer as against some others. In his introduction to *Much Ado,* he says that the object of the stay was probably to prevent the publication of *Henry V., Every Man in His Humour,* and *Much Ado* by any other stationers than Wise and Aspley. But he offers no reasons for this preference.

Fleay's most recent conjecture [11] is a variation of Collier's: " It seems clear that the delay, of which so many hypothetical interpretations have been offered, was simply to enable Millington and Busby, who probably had the copyrights of all four plays, to complete the sales thereof to the other publishers." This, like Collier's theory, is founded on air; but here the air is considerably thinner. For Wise and Aspley did properly enter one of the plays, produced a text good enough to form the substantial basis of the Folio version, and transferred their property by regular entry so that we can trace it to the Folio owners. All this favors the assumption of legitimacy. But Millington and Busby do not appear at all on the registers in connection with any of these plays (unless, indeed, they are mentioned in the part of the registers which Mr. Arber was not permitted to publish, folios 427-486). They merely printed without entry a very short and garbled *Henry V.,* bearing on its face the evidences of its illegitimacy; slipped it on, by some obscure means, to a new stationer, Pavier, who retained the original printer for his work, but apparently waited two years to issue an edition. The text was secured by Jaggard in 1619 and printed " for Pavier," dated " 1608," remaining to the end a version decidedly inferior to the widely differing Folio text. To suppose the delay to have been arranged to shield Milling-

[11] *Chronicle History of the English Drama,* 1891, II, p. 184.

ton and Busby is to accuse the Stationers' Company of the grossest and most obvious misuse of power in checking publication merely to permit a team of pirates to sell out a property that they had never owned.

The most ingenious and elaborate explanation is that set forth by Mr. Furness in the prefaces to the Variorum editions of *As You Like It,* 1890, and *Much Ado,* 1899. In the former volume, he declares (p. 294):

At the bottom of all this entanglement over the printing of *As You Like It,* was James Roberts. If we look back at the entries in the Stationers' Registers, we shall see that his is the last name before the *As You Like It* item set down as an applicant for an entry; and the same needlessness which deterred the clerk from repeating on this informal sheet the date of the year, deterred him from repeating in the margin opposite the titles of these new " bookes " the name of the applicant; who was (is it not probable?) this very same James Roberts. Now this same James Roberts was far from being one of the best of the Stationers, at least if we can judge from the fact that he came more than once under the ban of the wardens and was fined by them. . . . He once made an attempt on the Queen's Printer's realm of Catechisms, and was promptly repressed by the Master Wardens of the Stationers' Company. Next he seems to have turned his attention to the stage, and clasped itching palms with some of my Lord Chamberlain's men. In a mysterious way he gained possession of a copy of the *Merchant of Venice* and would have incontinently printed it, had not the Wardens " staied " it, and staied it for two years, too, at the end of which time James sold his copy to young " Thomas haies " and at once proceeded to print a second and better copy for himself. Clearly, James Roberts was what the Yankees would call " smart " . . . I believe he made some friends with the mammon of unrighteousness among my Lord Chamberlain's men, and by underhand dealings obtained possession of stage copies of sundry plays of Shakespeare's which happened to be unusually popular. His name does not appear often in the Registers in these years. After he was foiled in his attempt to print the *Merchant of Venice* in 1598, he made one other entry toward the close of that year, and succeeded in getting permission to print Marston's *Satires.* Then in March of the next year he tried to enter a translation of Stephan's *Herodotus,* but was " staied." Again, in the following October he was permitted to print a *History of Don Frederigo,* but

with the permission was coupled the very unusual condition that
he should print "only one impression and pay sixpence in the
pound to the use of the poore"; manifestly, James Roberts was in
ill repute. His next venture was in May, when he tried to enter
"A morall of Clothe breches and velvet hose, As yt is Acted by
my lord Chamberlens servantes," but there follows the proviso "that
he is not to putt it in prynte without further and better aucthority."
Two days later, on the 29th of May, he again tried to enter a book:
"the Allarum to London," and again there follows the inevitable
caveat "that yt be not printed without further Aucthoritie." These
two items, which appear in their proper order in the main body
of the Registers, the clerk, as I suppose, briefly jotted down on
the blank page at the beginning of the book, as a reminder to
keep his eye on James Roberts. When, therefore, on the 4th of
August, James Roberts brought forward four more plays that were
performed by "my lord chamberlen's men," the clerk noted them
down on his fly-leaf under the others, and did not take the trouble
to repeat James Roberts's name, which was already there in the
margin opposite the "clothe breches and velvet hose," but added
(what was almost the synonym of James Roberts) "to be staied."

This it was, the bad reputation of James Roberts, which caused
the printing of these plays when first offered to be forbidden. . . .
Where the line was among printers, blessing some and banning others,
we cannot know, only that it looks as though where all were bad
James Roberts was somehow among the worst, and that to his
unsavory reputation is due the fact that we have no quarto edition
of *As You Like It.*

In the preface to *Much Ado,* Mr. Furness presents practically the same line of argument. He calls attention
again (p. xi) to the fact that all editors have assumed the
date 1600 for the entry of August 4 because it immediately
follows the dated Roberts entry of two plays. "Now if
the clerk thought it needless to repeat the 1600, why is
it not equally likely that he thought it needless to repeat
the name, James Roberts, if to him both entries belonged?
What may be assumed of a date may surely be assumed
of a name, especially since all six plays belonged to the
Chamberlain's Company. . . . Is it straining the plain
facts before us too far to assume that all these plays were

entered by James Roberts, and that the caveat was due to his shifty character ? "

Decidedly, it is, as we shall see if we look more closely into the record of James Roberts. We should remember, the entries to Roberts are in ink of a different color from the staying entries, and a separate dating (4 Augusti) serves also to mark off the staying entry as distinct. Only the location on the page, the absence of printer's name for the staying entry, and the lack of the year 1600 in its date favor Mr. Furness's assumption. The location on the page may mean nothing more than that this was the next of the Chamberlain's plays to be entered after Roberts's entry, and that all plays of this company were being watched for some special reason that had nothing to do with Roberts's character. In answer to Mr. Furness's query why it is not equally likely that a clerk would omit the name of a claimant, in an informal note, if he omitted the year, it may be said that the omission of the name of the owner would certainly be a more serious drawback in conserving copyright than the omission of the year, when the month and day of the month were given, and there were often auxiliary means of determining the year if a dispute as to priority of entry should by chance occur. At any rate, it is rather idle to speculate as to which is more likely to be omitted; for it is only necessary to look through the registers to discover that not only here in these informal notes (some of which, in spite of their informal character, did service as real entries), but also in the body of the Register, the clerk does often omit the year when it is the same as that of the entry above, noting merely the month and day; but he is very careful, even in successive entries to one man, to repeat that man's name. The " to hym " of the second Roberts entry is in effect a repetition of the name of Roberts just above. Why not again " to hym " or some other indication of a connection with James Roberts? The very next entry to that of the staying is an example of careful repetition of the owner's names, Thorpe and Aspley, where two books in succession are entered on the same day to the same men. Two pages back in these fly-leaves Millington's name appears twice in succession in provisional entries belonging to the year 1603, but simply dated 25 April and 28 April. There are more probabilities against than for the accidental omission of Roberts's name in connection with the staying entry.

Mr. Furness has pounced upon the reputation of James Roberts with considerable enthusiasm; but he has not quite demolished it. The researches of Pollard and Greg in Shakespeare texts, strengthened by the disclosure by Mr. Neidig of the real facts as to the " Roberts 1600 " quarto of the *Merchant of Venice,* have tended to put Roberts back within the bounds of respectability. A comparative study of his record with that of other printers of his day will show that he was very far from being one of the worst, and that there is no evidence that he remained under any sort of ban among the stationers. His business in general, players' bills included, was acquired in a normal way. The entry of the *Merchant of Venice* is unique only in its explicit mention of the Lord Chamberlain as the one who must furnish the authority to print, and not at all extraordinary because of its being provisional. The entries of *Clothe Breches* and the *Allarum to London* are unusual in that they are repeated in the memorandum on the fly-leaf, not in that they are provisional. The permission to print only one impression of the *History of Don Frederigo* and pay sixpence in the pound to the use of the poor was not " a very unusual condition." A cursory examination of the registers will show that it was a common practice to allow printers in need of work to reprint old copies (some belonging to the whole Company and some simply derelicts through age and lack of claimants), with the condition that a percentage of the profits go to the Company's poor whom they were obligated to look out for. The worst that this arrangement could be supposed to imply is, that at this time James Roberts was out of work. Mr. Furness's statement that the publication of Herodotus is to be "stayed" is altogether misleading, when taken in connection with his theory. For this is only one of many entries of books to be translated, with the proviso that after translation the book is to be submitted to authorities for licensing publication. In other words, it is a mere advance claim to copyright in a work not yet produced. The most reputable of publishers did exactly the same thing.

The most extraordinary suggestions are those which Mr. Furness makes with reference to the entry of the *Merchant of Venice*. The wardens, not being so 'smart' as James Roberts, after being cautious enough to grant only a provisional entry in the first place and staying the publication for two years because the condition was not removed, still allowed him to retain and sell a copy he never owned, and meekly recorded his sale in their registers. And the buyer must stand back and see this smart stationer reprint a second and better edition for himself!

Much of this theorizing vanishes with the emergence of the facts about the 1619 quartos. We know now that William Jaggard, who succeeded Roberts in business, printed the "Roberts, 1600" quarto. And, as Roberts, though consenting to Hayes's entry of the copyright, reserved the printing to himself, it is safe to assume that is was by succeeding to Roberts's business that Jaggard acquired his text of the play. He no doubt knew that Roberts had once claimed, if not actually owned, the copyright; and, having no permission from the descendants of Thomas Hayes to reprint the play, hit upon the "Roberts, 1600" imprint as likely to give his issue a show of right. That it did not pass unchallenged may be guessed from the fact that Laurence, son of Thomas Hayes, re-entered the *Merchant of Venice* in his own name 8 July, 1619 "by consent of a full court" as one of two copies of Thomas Hayes his father. He held the copyright till 1637, when an edition was printed for him. So that it was Jaggard in 1619, not Roberts in 1600, that invaded the rights of the Hayes family.

The question now arises, did Roberts ever really own the copy of the *Merchant of Venice?* If the acting company refused permission to Roberts and granted it to Hayes, it is hard to see why the consent of Roberts should be recorded, as the entry on the registers was conditional on the company's approval. Miss Porter, in the Folio edition of the play, supposes the Roberts entry to indicate a stolen copy, and the appearance of the play two years later to be "subject to some sort of compromise between the rival publishers." But what is there to indicate rivalry, rather than ordinary business relations, between Roberts and Hayes?

Mr. Pollard's suggestion is more interesting:[12] "It is obvious that, if an applicant could obtain provisional protection merely by mentioning the name of a play and promising that he would produce subsequently sufficient authority for printing it, then here was a way in which an obstacle could be raised against piracy without any need for going to press inconveniently early." He discusses in this connection several provisional entries of Roberts as possible attempts of this sort: *Merchant of Venice, Ham-*

[12] *Shakespeare Folios and Quartos,* pp. 66 ff.

let, Troilus, and the two plays entered in May, 1600 and
noted just above the staying entry. The theory would
seem to be rather more applicable to the *Merchant of
Venice* entry than to any other, in view of its wording
and the subsequent history of the copyright and text. But
in his next discussion of the topic (p. 71), Mr. Pollard
seems to have abandoned the idea, at least so far as it
concerns this play. " This book was re-entered by Thomas
Haies by consent of Master Roberts, this course being taken
in preference to an ordinary transfer most probably because the terms of the previous entry had never been
complied with. If Roberts had produced a written authority from the Lord Chamberlain, the fact would almost
certainly have been mentioned. It was simpler, now that
a bogie was no longer needed, to enter the book afresh,
the mention of Roberts in the new entry being a sufficient
compliment to the old, while it helped to secure for him
the printing of the book." But it is not easy to see why
the Stationers should " compliment " the old entry if it
turned out to be unauthorized. Their behavior on similar
occasions was not complimentary. And why should they
record consent of a man who had never really owned the
copy ? The phrasing " by consent of " is not so unusual
a formula for an ordinary transfer of property as to call
for so ingenious an explanation as this of Mr. Pollard's.
We meet it on 6 Sept., 1602, for example, where *The Ethi-
opian History of Heliodorus* is transferred to Hayes "by
consent of Master Coldocke," the rightful owner. If anything special is indicated by it, it seems to be, that a
signed note of transfer is in the hands of the applicant for
re-entry or that the original owner retains a part interest.

That the authorizing of Roberts by the Chamberlain
would certainly have been mentioned does seem a reasonable statement, and it receives support from similar cases

where such notes are found appended. For example, a
comedy, " the fleare," entered to John Trundell and John
Busby 13 May, 1606 " provided that they are not to printe
yt tell they bringe good Aucthoritie & license for the
Doinge thereof (6d.)," is transferred by regular assignment to Busby and Johnson 21 Nov., 1606 with this note
appended: " This booke is aucthorised by Sir George
Bucke, Master Hartwell, and the Wardens." And the
provisional entry of Marston's *The Dutche Curtizan,* 26
June, 1605, to John Hodgets is followed by a similar note:
" This is alowed to be printed by Aucthoritie from Master
Hartwell." But, on the other hand, there are cases where
such notes were not entered, whether or not they should
have been. Another of Marston's plays, *The Faun,* was
entered 12 Mar., 1606, to William Cotton, " provided that
he is not to put the same at prynte before he gett alowed
lawfull aucthoritie." It was printed by Cotton in 1606
with a preface by the author which shows clearly that he
saw it through the press.[13] In two other instances near
the time we are considering we can see clearly from subsequent history that the provisional entry became a real
entry, though there was no special noting of the fact that
permission to print had been granted. On the 25th of
April (1603) *England's Mourning Garment* was entered
to Millington as not to be granted to anyone else " nor to
hym neither unles he bring my Lord Graces hand or my
Lord of Londons hand for aucthoritie." Here the only
clue to authorization is a W (probably the initial of Water-
son, a warden) placed after the 6d. fee. On 7 June of
this year Matthew Lawe was fined 20s. for printing " Eng-

---

[13] Marston, by the way, is the unhappily chosen example in Mr.
Walder's discussion of the playwright's unwillingness to see his
plays in print (*Cambridge History of English Literature,* v, ch. xi,
p. 289).

3

lands Mourning Garment beinge Thomas Millingtons copie." There is nothing whatever to indicate removal of condition in the entry of Lyly's *Sappho* to Thomas Cadman, April 6, 1584 ("if he get it lawfully allowed unto him"); but Cadman published the play twice in that year, and, in spite of an issue "by Thomas Orwin for William Broome, 1591," the copy seems to have remained Cadman's, as it was entered "in full court" to Joan Brome, widow of William Brome, 12 April, 1597 with two others, " the whiche copies were Thomas Cadman's." [14]

A possible reason for carelessness of clerks in checking up conditional entries that were authorized may have been the fact that they had a habit of checking up in several ways the ones that were definitely forbidden. Sometimes the whole entry is struck through; sometimes the note *vacat*, or *this is no entry*, with the reason for the statement, will appear in the margin, or "struck out by order of" some authority, often "cancelled by a court." *Westward Ho*, provisionally entered to Henry Rockett 2 Mar., 1605, is so struck out, and below Rockett's name is written *vacat*. Similarly *The Returne of ye Knighte of the poste from Hell, with the Devilles Answere to Pierce Pennylesse Supplicacon*, provisionally entered to Nathanael Butter, 15 Jan., 1606, is cancelled by a court, 7 Feb., 1606, and so crossed out. Lack of cancellation cannot at all be insisted on as showing that a provisional entry held good; but it is well to note that this method was used when the Sta-

---

[14] Bond, in editing Lyly's works, seems to assume that the copy passed out of Cadman's hands into William Brome's because of the 1591 edition. William Brome was dead before 4 October, 1591 (Arber, II, p. 596), and in 1591 Orwin had his presses seized for dishonest printing (Arber, v, p. li); so that the 1591 edition will bear investigation as to its legitimacy. However, the transfer to Joan Brome clearly recognizes Cadman as owner and makes no mention of a right on the part of Joan's former husband.

tioners knew an issue to be definitely forbidden, whether by the author, as in the case of Bacon's *Essays,* 1597, or by authorities, as in the cases noted above. Simple failure on a printer's part to get permission probably often went unrecorded, if the matter was amicably settled and the printer gave up his claims. Whether or not a fee was taken for the entry is not a guide as to its authoritative character; for the fee was often received in advance of complete authorization to print a work.

As there are some entries which turn out to be unconditional, though no note of removal of condition is appended, and as there is a recognition of Roberts's rights in the entry to Hayes, it seems simpler to suppose that Roberts got his permission and then sold out the copyright, retaining the printing for himself. Plenty of similar arrangements can be found. The entry to Roberts, then, would be regarded merely as an advance entry, to secure the copyright, either chiefly in his own interests or in the interests of the company.

In spite of the trouble over the invasion of a great patent in the printing of catechisms, when Roberts was obliged to submit to the order of a court,[15] his record as a whole compares pretty favorably with those of contemporary printers of good repute. From 1593 to 1605 Roberts printed works of Harvey, Marston, Nash, Breton, Daniel, Drayton, Lyly, Spenser, and Shakespeare; he seems, indeed, to have been a rather important figure in the printing world. Comparing him with men like Jeffes, the warden Edward White, Sims, Danter, Pavier, and Waldegrave, one finds it easy to listen to Mr. Pollard's suggestion that Roberts was a trusted printer of the Chamberlain's company, who was used to enter and protect their copyrights,

[15] Arber, II, p. 824.

with the understanding that the publishing was to be done
at the company's convenience.   But there is in the case
of the staying entry no sufficient evidence to connect Roberts with the matter, and, as his name does not occur in
any of the subsequent mentions of these copies, it is hardly
safe to assume connection.

It may possibly occur to someone that the company may
have entered these plays themselves, to secure the copyright, in this informal way, before they had decided upon
the printers.   The title of the group entry "My Lord
Chamberlens menns plaies entred" might suggest this; but
it precedes the note concerning the Roberts entries, and
not the "to be staied" group.   And besides, we have no
evidence to show that an acting company could take out
a copyright, formally or informally, except through the
services of a stationer who should claim, hold, and protect
that right.

In the case of *Patient Grissell,* at least, it seems likely
that the Admiral's Company, in arranging, through Henslowe, to "stay" the printing, really meant to have a chosen
printer, Burby, enter the play in his name, and reserve and
defend the copyright, refraining from printing or selling
out the right to print until the play should be released for
publication by the company.   It will be remembered that
Burby entered the play ten days after the 40s. were lent
by Henslowe to arrange the staying, but the play was not
printed till 1603, and then "for Henry Rockett."   Sir
Sidney Lee interprets the situation in this way: [16] "Many
copies of a popular play were made for the actors, and if
one of these copies chanced to fall into a publisher's hands,
it was habitually issued without any attempt to obtain
either author's or manager's sanction.   In March 1599

[16] *A Life of William Shakespeare,* 1898, p. 48.

[it is really 1600] the theatrical manager, Philip Henslowe, endeavoured to induce a publisher who had secured a playhouse copy of the comedy of *Patient Grissell* by Dekker, Chettle, and Haughton, to abandon the publication of it by offering him a bribe of £2."

That the theatrical manager had to buy off an intending pirate is an absurd notion. The whole history of piracy, as one may trace it through the registers, shows that it was the pirate that did the paying. In some cases an amicable settlement was made between printers, resulting in the authorized printer's buying up the printed sheets at cost or a low rate and using them for his own edition. Mr. Pollard seems to have something like this in mind, where he discusses the usual interpretation of the matter and offers a more reasonable solution: [17]

Patient Grissell. . . was eventually published in 1603, but according to the usual interpretation of the entry the players thought it better in 1599 to buy off a piratical printer at the earlier date with a couple of pounds, than to allow it to be printed or to be at the trouble of getting the play stayed by authority. As it is certain that some plays were pirated, there is no impossibility in this, but the entry may equally well be explained as caused by the revocation of a permission to print previously given, the forty shillings being the compensation offered to the printer, either for pages he had set up, or for surrendering his bargain.

Possibly Mr. Pollard has in mind a hypothetical third printer, preceding Burby, who was bought off in this manner; but as no entry had been made in the registers before this date, clearly this printer must have been issuing his edition surreptitiously, if there was any of it in print at the time of this entry in the *Diary;* so that we should have, after all, the buying off of a pirate, at least in the sense of an unauthorized printer. If Mr. Pollard means

[17] *Shakespeare Folios and Quartos*, p. 12, note C.

that Burby had permission to print and was then bought
off, it is hard to see why he should have entered his copyright on the registers not before, but ten days after the
arrangement to pay him two pounds to surrender his bargain.   Without some theory to account for the entry to
Burby ten days after the company determined to spend
two pounds on staying the play, we can only echo Greg's
(!).   If Burby was paid to enter the play and refrain
from publication until a time satisfactory to the company,
the tangle begins to resolve itself.

But why was the play printed " for Rockett " if Burby
was authorized by the company to enter and defend the
copyright?   Not, probably, because Rockett pirated it in
spite of Burby's claim, nor because Burby was prohibited
or bought off from publication, but most probably because
he found it worth his while to sell the whole or a part
interest to Rockett, or simply to use Rockett as book-seller,
as no transfer is recorded.   Rockett, as an apprentice, was
turned over from Andrew Wise to C. Burby 25 December,
1594, and did not become free until 31 January, 1602,
his first registered publication being 30 March, 1602.   If
anyone imagines that in March of 1600 the Admiral's
Company preferred to grant the publication of one of their
plays to Burby's apprentice rather than to Burby, he must
still admit that the apprentice was not as yet entitled to
enter copies in the registers or to print them for himself.
So, if the work were to be saved for this particular sta-
tioner-to-be, Burby or some other freeman would have to
do the entering.   But with no reason for assuming such
a preference on the part of the company, it is simpler to
suppose that whatever transfer of rights occurred was by
an amicable private business arrangement between a
printer and his apprentice.   Even if the property were
wholly turned over to Rockett, the transfer would not

necessarily be recorded in the registers. Stansby held a
note transferring to him copyrights in Jonson's plays from
10 June, 1621, until 4 July, 1635 before he thought it
worth his while to have it recorded. Where stationers
trusted each other and were not particularly afraid of
invasion of their rights, there must have been numerous
private transfers of this sort. In this case, Burby may
even have retained a silent interest in the copy; for the
assignments of part interests show clearly that they were
often not recorded until occasion arose for a division of
interests, as, for example, when a part owner died or went
out of business.

We may get a little light on Burby's habits by comparing with his failure to print *Patient Grissel* his failure to
print *Every Man in His Humour,* also to be stayed. Ten
days after the staying note, just as in the case of *Patient
Grissel, Every Man in His Humour* is entered uncondi-
tionally (14 August, 1600) to Burby and Burre. It was
printed in 1601, not for Burby, the first partner, but "for
Burre," though there is no record of assignment of Burby's
share to Burre. That in this case, at least, Burby retained
his rights is clear from the fact that among the 38 copies
assigned by Burby's widow to Welby 16 Oct., 1609, is
" her parte with Master Burre in Every man in his humor."

·'And there is another play printed " for Rockett,"
though it was entered to another stationer, the circumstances of whose printing suggest an amicable private business arrangement. *Blurt, Master Constable,* is entered
June 7, 1602 to Edward Aldee. With no recorded transfer, it was published in quarto in 1602 as "printed for
Henry Rockytt, and are to be solde at the long shop under
St. Mildreds Church in the Poultry." Turning to the

history of shops,[18] we find that in 1600 the widow Margaret
Aldee, who succeeded her husband in business, kept the
Long Shop with Rockett as her partner. The Edward
Aldee who entered *Blurt, Master Constable* was her son.
It is entirely possible that Aldee did the printing or had
it done, and that Rockett only sold the book for him. Pos-
sibly some similar arrangement existed between Rockett
the book-seller and his old master, Burby, in the case of
Patient Grissel.

And now, lest some follower of Furness cast up Burby's
record as unfitting him for the position of trusted printer
authorized by the companies to defend copyright, let us
hasten to admit that, although McKerrow sums up his
record, in his dictionary of printers, with the statement
that "nothing disreputable is known about him," he had
his little sins. He was fined along with twenty-seven
others for selling *Humors lettinge bloode,* 4 Mar., 1601,
and again in the fall of 1602 for selling a book which
Pavier had printed without entry; and again, in June
of the same year, he was fined 20s. for printing, along
with Dexter, *The Englische Scholemaster* without allowance. This had been entered to Jackson and Dexter 18
December, 1596, and was finally re-entered to Burby and
Bishop 14 March, 1605. The history of this last case is
too obscure for safe comment. It seems to be the only
case of unlicensed printing on his own account that can
be proved against him. The catalogue of his sins is
comparatively brief. The Shakespeare quartos that he
printed, the 1595 *Edward III.,* the 1598 *Love's Labor's
Lost,* and the 1599 *Romeo and Juliet* are all, as Mr. Pollard would say, " good "—*i. e.,* they bear no *prima facie*
evidences of being surreptitious. Burby handled general

[18] Arber, v, p. 207.

literature of a fairly good class, and was also interested in publishing accounts of current events. Eight of his entries are provisional, and for this reason many will persist in regarding him as crooked; but perhaps we should regard this fact only as a testimony to his enterprising business habits; for in no case is there any sign of trouble with the authorities in connection with these conditional entries.

Burre, his partner in *Every Man in his Humor,* was also in the habit of entering in advance of complete authorization. But, in spite of the fact that we find *Catiline* recorded in the registers for the first time as transferred, the facts that he published besides this and *Every Man, Cynthia's Revels* in 1601, *The Alchemist,* 1612 (licensed by the Master of the Revels), and that he acquired by assignment from the rightful owners *Sejanus, Volpone,* and *Epicœne* and finally assigned all seven of these copies by due transfer to William Stansby, publisher of the 1616 Folio, put Burre before us as unquestionably an authorized printer of Jonson's plays.

But in the case of the Chamberlain's men's plays we have not, as in the case of *Patient Grissel* for the Admiral's, any positive evidence that the company is doing the staying, though the title under which the entries are grouped on the fly-leaf does suggest that the company was in some way specially interested. We have no evidence of any attempt on the part of the company to check a proposed piracy 4 August, 1600, though it is entirely possible that in the case of *Henry* V. a piracy may have been going on at just this time. Documents of later date, however, show that it was the custom of the Chamberlain to guard the players' printing rights. On June 10, 1637 the Chamberlain, Philip Earl of Montgomery, wrote to the stationers [19] concerning the efforts of his brother William Herbert, Earl of Pembroke, to " stay further impression " of some stolen plays; complaining that in spite of the caution (which should have sufficed) some plays had recently been stolen or gotten indirectly, and were about to be printed; requesting, in conclusion, that if any of the plays of the King's men were already entered or should be entered later, notice should be given to the company, and a certificate in writing from their representative be required before the play should be put in print. A similar warrant from Essex, August 7, 1641 is printed by E. K. Chambers in his article on *Plays of the King's men in 1641*,[20] mentioning the complaints of the players that certain printers intended " to Print and publish some of their Playes which hitherto they haue beene usually restrained from by the authority of the Lord Chamberlain." The reason given by the Lord Chamberlain for issuing the warrant is not that it is against the players' interests to have the plays published at all, but simply that copyright as well as stage right belongs to the players to dispose of: " Their request seemes both just and reasonable, as onely tending to preserue them Masters of their proper Goods, which in Justice ought not to be made comon for another mannes profitt to their disadvantage. Upon this Ground therefore I am induced to require your care (as formerly my Predecessors haue done) that noe Playes belonging to them bee put in Print without their knowledge and consent." A list of unprinted plays belonging to the *répertoire* is enclosed for the convenience of the stationers. The closing request is, that when their plays appear for entry " they be made acquainted with it

---

[19] *Prolegomena*, III, pp. 160-1.

[20] *Malone Society, Collections*, parts iv and v, p. 367.

before they bee recorded in the hall and soe haue Oportunity to shew their right unto them."

It is open to question just how far back we may safely assume this " usual restraint " of the Lord Chamberlain to have occurred. Positive evidence stretches back only to 1616, the beginning of William Herbert's term of office. Whether it is safe to extend " our predecessors " to include Carr, Earl of Somerset, Howard, Earl of Suffolk, and George Carey, Lord Hunsdon, the last of whom was Chamberlain in 1600, is a matter of speculation. It seems not unreasonable to expect that so powerful a patron would do his utmost to protect the interests of the players; but whether he did it in just this way is an open question. Perhaps it was only the unusually large number of plays belonging to this company that aroused the stationers' suspicions; perhaps someone knew of trouble over *Henry V.*, or perhaps the Chamberlain himself issued warning. If the caution of the stationers were aroused, for one reason or another, shortly after Roberts entered his two plays conditionally, the memorandum would naturally begin with these. Then the next printers to appear with plays belonging to this company would meet a challenge and a refusal to enter the plays to them without complete authorization—perhaps a written permission from the company. The titles and the staying notice on the flyleaf would, then, be no entry, but a memorandum not to enter these plays to anyone till the Chamberlain's company had been heard from. The intervals of ten to nineteen days are reasonable ones for the transaction of such business, involving as it did in the case of plays, not only the company's approval, but that of official censors, in addition to the wardens'. The entry, then, would mean not an injunction against any printer or printers intending to pirate all these plays, but a memorandum that the plays had been brought for entry but held up for fuller authorization. The staying, in this case, would be as much to the advantage of the prospective printer as to that of the company; for it would be in effect, though not in form, a reservation of copyright to the applicant while his claim was being investigated.

This is not an attempt to argue that the term *to stay* never meant *to check, withhold,* or even, in some cases, *permanently to prohibit.* Real suppression seems to be meant in a letter from Fulke Greville to Sir Francis Walsingham (Nov., 1586) concerning an unauthorized reprint of Sidney's *Arcadia:* " I think fit there be made a stay of that mercenary book." [21] And it is probable that permanent prohibition was intended when the Lord Chamberlain wrote to the stationers " to take orders for the stay of any further impression " of unauthorized publication of the Chamberlain's men's plays. Bacon uses the term quite frequently. In his letter to the Marquis of Buckingham, 18 Oct., 1621, he clearly implies only a temporary prohibition when he says: " My Lord Keeper hath stayed my pardon at the seal. But it is with good respect. For he saith it shall be private, and that he would forthwith write to your Lordship and would pass it if it received your pleasure." Lincoln's letter to Bacon, of the same date, confirms our judgment that here the "stay" is temporary: " May it therefore please your Lordship to suspend the passing of this pardon until the next assembly be over and dissolved, and I will be then as ready to seal it as your Lordship to accept of it, and in the mean time undertake that the King and my Lord Admiral shall interpret this short delay as a service and respect issuing wholly from your Lordship." [22] The same idea, of tempo-

[21] *Gentlemen's Magazine,* 1850, pt. i, pp. 370 ff.
[22] *Life and Letters,* Spedding, VII, p. 308.

rary délay, attaches itself to Bacon's use of the term with reference to the holding back of his *History of Henry VII*. The manuscript had been approved by the King in the fall, had been printed and was ready for delivery, when the issue was stayed by Dr. George Mountain, Bishop of London, who was, of course, an official licenser. In a letter to Thomas Meautys (21 Mar., 1621), Bacon writes: " For my Lord of London's stay, there may be an error in my book; but I am sure there is none in me, since the King had it three months by him, and allowed it. If there be anything to be amended, it is better if it be spied now than hereafter." [23]

Continued delay becoming in effect prohibition or suppression is illustrated also by Bacon's usage. He writes concerning a patent [24]: " When it came to the great seal, I stayed it. I did not only stay it but brought it before the council-table, as not willing to pass it, except their Lordships allowed it." The lords heard the business for two days, disallowed it, and " ordered that it should continue stayed; and so it did all my time."

One cannot say quite so positively what the term means where it occurs in the *Prefatory Epistle* to Bacon's *Essays* (Jan. 30, 1597): " These fragments of my conceits were going to print: to labour the stay of them had been troublesome, and subject to interpretation: to let them pass had been to adventure the wrong they might receive by untrue copies, or by some garnishment it might please any that should set them forth to bestow upon them; therefore I held it best discretion to publish them myself, without any further disgrace than the weakness of the author." But probably what Bacon means here by " labour the stay " is only a considerable postponement of

[23] *Life and Letters*, VII, pp. 352-3.
[24] *Life and Letters*, VII, p. 514.

publication. His letters show clearly that it was never
his intention to keep the essays permanently out of print.
He was not at all averse from publication in general; and
the essays in particular he wanted translated into Latin,
that they might be a monument for posterity. But he
did feel, apparently, that the essays were at this time un-
ripe, and he would have preferred to keep them longer
out of print, to revise and polish. But the entry to Serger
might make it seem, if the essays were long withheld from
publication, that they contained matter offensive to the
authorities. At any rate, "labouring the stay " is here
very certainly not merely the suppression of a piratical
edition; for at the very time Bacon writes the preface he
is succeeding in having that edition suppressed and the
entry to Serger cancelled, and with very little delay. Serger entered the *Essays* Jan. 24, Hooper made his authorized entry February 5, and Serger's entry was cancelled
by a court on February 7. The authorized edition was
on sale already when the court cancelled the unauthorized
entry, as is indicated by the date of a note on the title-page
of a copy in the British Museum. Clearly it was in
Bacon's power to choose, after getting a court to cancel
Serger's entry, whether he would put his work in print
or not. The Stationers' Court could not compel him to
publish against his will; nor could a discovered pirate,
except indirectly, as above suggested,—by making explanations for witholding publication needful.[25] It is just

[25] One good reason for not continuing to keep the essays out of
print was, no doubt, that they were known from the manuscript
version already, and subject to quotation without acknowledgment.
The Essay *On Studies* was freely plagiarised by a member of the
suite of the Earl of Lincoln on an embassy to the Landgrave of
Hesse, in an account of that journey published within three months
of Bacon's entry of the *Essays* (S. R., Oct. 26, 1596). Bacon may
have thought it better to publish earlier than he had intended, to
avoid having more of his thunder stolen.

possible that "labouring the stay" meant continuing to conserve copyright through his chosen printer for a considerable period without publishing.

This may be a forcing of the meaning of the phrase, as Bacon's use of the term *stay* throughout his letters seems most commonly to be in the sense of *postpone*. But there are some instances where it is quite clear that "to be staied" entered in connection with a printer's claim to a copy carries with it no suggestion whatever of an attempt, in the interest of the author or owner of the manuscript, at prohibiting that printer from intended piracy, but is rather a general prohibition of anyone from printing the work, and hence in effect a temporary and conditional reserve [26] of copyright to the claimant. Such protection would be particularly useful in dramatic publications, where consent must be had from several authorities.

These examples, however, taken from the fly-leaves to Register C that we are concerned with, have to do with non-dramatic works:

18 May, 1603. Henry Gosson. A booke called *a warninge peece to bribers* is to be staied and not entred to any but hym when he hathe aucthority for it.[27]

31 March, 1603. William White. *The Erle of Essex going to Cales.* a ballad to be stayed for hym, begyns *gallantes &c.*[27a]

[26] Outside the field of copyright a clear instance of the use of "stayed" in the sense of "preserved" in the interests of the owner occurs in *Remembrancia*, VII, p. 6 (1629):

"Anciently the custom was that if any man lost any pewter he should come to the Hall and give notice to the Company's officer, with the marks, whereupon the goods were stayed & restored to the owner, & the parties punished."

[27] The subsequent history of this piece I do not know.

[27a] No fee is entered here. We find the real entry in the body of the registers (Arber, III, p. 238), just sixteen days after the note that the ballad is to be stayed for him. ("Gallantes all come mourne with me".)

A similar use of the term *stayed* is found in a provisional entry in the body of the registers (III, p. 302) where, on September 27, 1605, *The estate of Russia with the tragicall endes of the Late Emperour, Empresse & prynce* is "to be staid for John Trundel till he bringe further aucthority for yt." Here the fee is entered, and the provisional entry is made to serve as a real entry by appending a note, "he bathe Master Norton's hand for this entrance."

Clearly, then, two works to be stayed for the printers who first claimed them turned out to be authorized entries, and the other one is doubtful. The conclusion is inevitable that these printers were simply so eager to secure copyright that they entered the works in advance of complete authorization; that "staying" was a restraint which might prove to be temporary or permanent, according to the circumstances in any case; and that it was imposed by the stationers not to the disadvantage, but even, in a sense, to the advantage of the prospective printer, securing him in his claims while they were being investigated in accordance with some printing regulations.

An examination of the other entries on the fly-leaves of Register C shows that many of the eleven items preceding our staying entry are provisional, as the entry of *England's Mourning Garament* to Millington, for example: "This book is not to be entred to any but hym, nor to hym neether unles he bring my Lord graces or my Lord of Londons hand, for auctoritie." Four more provisional entries follow the staying note. The miscellaneous character of the notes may be illustrated by the last two entries, one of which (as late as 1615) concerns the indebtedness of one stationer to another, and the other, May 16, contains the caution that "if any of Master Deane of Windsor [Nicholas West's] copies come to be entred, Master Knight is to haue notice thereof." The fly-leaf entries were apparently not intended for real entries, in the first place, but for an informal memorandum; but four entries are made to do service as real entries by the addition of a fee and a warden's initial, or "per token from Master Man" or some other sign of authorization.

The entry in advance of complete authorization was apparently a recognized business transaction. For many years it had been the practice, even among the best printers, to reserve printing rights for works to be translated, with the proviso that, when the work was completed, it should be submitted for examination and license. As competition grew keener and there came to be an increasing demand for works of current interest—fresh plays, ballads, satires, and news letters—other works came to be entered in advance, to secure the copyright. Gradually works of more permanent interest were added to the list.

The advance entry was made by many of the most important publishers, Ponsonby, Burby, Trundell, Ling, Aspley, for example; and it seems to be not a symptom of rascality or poverty of the stationers, but rather a testimony to the keen competition of the rival stationers, whose eagerness to protect their newly acquired copies outstripped the delays imposed by the elaborate system of censoring and licensing.

That a sort of partial authorization was occasionally granted by an official licenser, so that the stationer might get temporary protection of his copyright, may be inferred from the defence of a licenser of William Prynne's *Histriomastix*, 1634: [28]

Mr. Buckner in his defence saith, hee lycenced but 64 pages of it; that that was not lycenced to bee published, but onely att the request

[28] *Proceedings against William Prynne, Camden Society,* 1877, p. 15.

4

of Sparckes to bee entered into the Stationers' Hall, to entitle
Sparckes to the sale of it; that hee advised the booke should not
bee published, and said to Sparckes, hee would loose his eares yf hee
published it; that when it was published, by his meanes warrant was
obtayned from the late Lord Bpp. of Canterburye for calling in of
the same.

The excuse was not held to be satisfactory, as Buckner
was fined £50 because, as the King's Attorney puts it,
" it doth appear hee eyther lycenced, or begann to lycence
it." But still the defence of the licenser leaves no doubt
that the stationers did enter books and secure copyright
without expectation of immediate permission to publish
and without complete authorization. A similar instance
of partial licensing is that of *Nosce Teipsum,* entered to
John Standish 14 April, 1599. " This is aucthorised
under the hand of the L Bysshop of London. Provyded
that yt must not be printed without his L hand to yt
agayne."

We find, then, that *staying* as applied to publication at
this time may indicate suppression or prohibition; but
that it is more generally used in the sense of postponement or delay; that there is no need of interpreting a
staying order as a sort of injunction against a threatened
piracy, inasmuch as the delay may arise in the ordinary
course of business; and that in some instances the order
for staying is given in the interests of the printer who
brings the work to be entered, for whom it serves as a
temporary protection against invasion of the rights he
claims.

In the case of our entry, the evidence is insufficient to
determine whether the order arose as a result of the ordi-
nance of 1599 stimulating the stationers to greater dili-
gence in the oversight of plays in general, whether it
arose as a result of a special request for care in regard to
the issuing of plays belonging to the Chamberlain's Com-

pany, or whether it arose in the ordinary course of business. The grouping and labelling of items, however, suggests some special watchfulness of the interests of the Chamberlain's men at this time. The circumstances surrounding the publication of *Patient Grissel* somewhat favor the theory that the Admiral's men were interested in reserving the copyright of this play through a chosen printer, Burby. A similar purpose on the part of the Chamberlain's men in the case of their four plays is not unplausible; but the evidence is insufficient to establish such a theory. In the absence of proof that the Chamberlain's Company was entering its plays, it is perhaps safer to assume that the plays were presented by individual printers; that they were delayed for fuller authorization; that two were found to be authorized, one (*As You Like It*) definitely unauthorized, and the fourth (*Henry* V.) also unauthorized, but perhaps even then in print or being printed.

If we regard staying as either an ordinary or extraordinary precaution on the Stationers' part, flexible in limits of duration, merely safeguarding property in the interest of the claimant until an investigation of his right is made, we may proceed to study the plays independently of one another. We are relieved of the necessity of choosing between the theory that the Chamberlain's men attempted to check a threatened piracy of four (possibly six?) plays at once and found the Stationers so incompetent as to fail in every case but one, though backed by Star Chamber, Privy Council, and Lord Chamberlain, and, on the other hand, the theory that the Stationers were competent but openly crooked in their business. We do not need to suppose that the acting company whimsically changed their minds. And in the case of *Patient Grissell* we have found a rational use for those forty shillings! Also, we are re-

lieved of the embarrassment of supposing that, because
one of the plays was not published in quarto, all should
not have been; and of placing on a par so good a text as
the quarto of *Much Ado* with so wretched a text as that
of the first or second quarto of *Henry* V. We may take
each of these texts upon its individual merits.

In the case of *As You Like It* there is no positive evidence as to why it was stayed in 1600 and not published,
apparently, until 1623. Current opinion is fairly represented by the attitude of the editors of the new Hudson
As You Like It, Boston, 1906 (pp. xvii-xviii):

> There is more probability that the 'staying' was the result of a
> direct attempt on the part of Shakespeare or someone acting for him
> to prevent the piratical publication of a popular new play, the cir-
> culation of which in book form would seriously interfere with its
> business success and the receipts at the theatre.

This will doubtless remain the accepted theory unless a
more thorough study of the history of dramatic publication shall sometime unsettle the popular conviction that
before the Restoration all dramatic companies feared the
publication of plays still running would spoil their business and lessen their receipts.

It is more profitable to speculate concerning the plays
that did appear in quarto. Mr. Pollard, who has made
a careful study of the text of *Much Ado about Nothing,*
says: That the manuscript was obtained from the Chamberlain's men and printed with their full authority "is
as certain as anything can make it save the discovery of a
statement to that effect in Shakespeare's autograph." His
chief reasons are: that no pirate would dare appear so
soon after the staying notice (no doubt the regularity of
the entry as compared with that of *Henry* V. was in his
mind in connection with this); and that the actors' names
and stage-directions indicate a playhouse copy as a source.

Of course, the actors' names might be jotted down by a spectator who was familiar with the names of these famous actors, if he were taking short-hand notes of the performance. But the text does not furnish ground for suspicion of having been pirated by stenography. Its close resemblance to the Folio text, taken with the fact that one of its publishers, Aspley, helped finance the Folio, unites with the other evidence in favoring the assumption that this quarto was authorized.

The really problematic case is that of *Henry V.*—not as to whether the quarto text was authorized (for on that there can hardly be two opinions), but as to why it should have been tolerated, and how it came to be entered on the Registers. Rolfe, in his *A Life of William Shakespeare,* (1904, p. 255), says: " The prohibition was soon removed, at least with regard to *Henry V.* and *Much Ado,* the former being duly licensed for publication on the 14th and the latter on the 23d of August, and editions of both were issued before the end of the year." But this smoothes the matter over too easily. *Henry V.* was not " duly " licensed, if duly means regularly; and the edition which came out that year was apparently not for Pavier at all, unless he had a silent partnership; for the 1600 quarto is printed " by Creede for Millington and Busby," and is to be sold " at the house in Carter Lane next the Powle head," which is the Millington and Busby shop; and it is not till 1602, so far as we know, that an edition was printed by Creede for Pavier, to be sold at his shop.

It is just possible that the unprinted portions of the Registers, folios 427 to 486, may contain some item that will throw light upon the Pavier entry of 14 August, 1600, but unless something of that sort appears to explain the situation, we must regard the entry as unusual and obscure in meaning.

Entred for his Copyes by Direction of Master White warden under his handwrytinge. These Copyes followinge beinge things formerly printed and sett over to the sayd Thomas Pavyer.

Among the twelve copies listed is *The historye of Henry the Vth with the battell of Agencourt.*

Whether the Millington and Busby edition was printed before or after the staying notice is not known. Pavyer's "printed and sett over," if true of *Henry V.*, suggests that Millington and Busby's edition was published or at least in print before 14 August; but of course the phrase may be in this case nothing but a subterfuge.

The text of 1600 is notoriously bad; that of 1602 is practically a reprint, in spite of over a hundred minor variations in spelling and wording, some for the better, some for the worse. The 1602 quarto is in no sense a revised version, as there are no substantial changes in the sense. The first quarto version is less than half the length of the Folio text. It lacks the first scenes of Acts I and III, the second of Act IV, and the choruses; it interchanges scenes 4 and 5 of Act V, and condenses or omits many of the best speeches. The French of the English lesson and wooing scene is exceedingly corrupt. Prose is often set up as verse. One cannot say with confidence just what is the relation of the quarto versions to the folio; but apparently it is a very bad transmission of an unskilfully cut version of the text which underlies the Folio—marred not only by bad cutting but either by failure to read copy, or, what is more likely, by a clumsy attempt to patch out a text from short-hand notes. The badness of the text is not corrected; for even in 1619, when William Jaggard had printed the quarto "for T. P., 1608," he made only a few corrections here and there, evidently with no fresh sources.

Mr. Pollard suggests[29] a reason for the failure to

---

[29] *Shakespeare Folios and Quartos*, p. 68.

improve the text: that, as pirates had put *Henry V.* on the market in spite of the company's opposition, "they could only revenge themselves by abstaining from setting right the text, a form of vengeance which seems to show that Shakespeare cared more for his business relations with the Chamberlain's men than for his literary reputation." This does not fit in very well with his theory that the 1598 (first extant) edition of *Love's Labor's Lost,* printed without entry by Burby for W. W. as "newly corrected and augmented," is an authorized re-issue replacing a former piracy, and that the 1599 edition of *Romeo and Juliet,* by Creede for Burby, is an authorized edition to supplant that of Danter in 1597. It is hard to see why the company should adopt such a form of "vengeance" in the one case and not in the others.

Mr. Pollard's explanation of the irregular character of the entry on the registers is not entirely satisfactory, owing to an accidental slip resulting from the confusion of the first names of two printers. He remarks:[30]

This entry is thoroughly characteristic of the way things were done in the Stationers' Company. Master Warden White was the printer, William White, and Pavier was contracting with him for some of his 'copyes,' *e. g.,* the *Spanish Tragedy* and Peele's *Edward Longeshankes,* both of which are named in the list. White, being Warden, could make the entry in any form he chose, and so Pavier slipped into the list *the historye of Henry the Vth with the battell of Agencourt,* thus obviating the necessity for mentioning that he was obtaining it from persons who had omitted to apply for a license for it and who could probably show no shadow of a claim to its possession.

In correcting a slip in the date (in a list of *Errata* prefixed to the volume) Mr. Pollard holds to this theory: "Thus it was ten days, not two years after the staying order, that Pavier, with the connivance of the Master of

---

[30] *S. F. & Q.,* p. 67.

the Stationers' Company, from whom he was buying copy-rights, slipped in a false entry of this play under the guise of a transfer, and the discreditable transaction is thus made a good deal worse than I thought it."

The vagueness of reference in the "things formerly printed and set over" does seem to suggest great negligence if not crookedness on someone's part. But the motive for crookedness in this case disappears when we see that the warden of the company was not William but Edward White. It was William who, up to 1600, owned the copies of Peele's *Edward Longshanks* and Kyd's *Spanish Trag-edy*. The former was printed by Abel Jeffes in 1592 and reprinted by William White in 1599. The *Spanish Trag-edy* was presumably printed twice before 1594, once with-out date by Edward Aldee for Edward White (probably before the end of 1592), and probably once before this, by Jeffes, as Aldee's quarto is advertised on the title-page as being "corrected and amended of such grosse faults as passed in the first impression." A third edition was printed in 1594 "by Abell Jeffes. sold by Edward White"; a 1599 edition was printed by William White, and sev-eral later editions for Thomas Pavier after the "setting over" to him. But Jeffes assigned the copy not to Edward, but to William White, and it passed from William White to Pavier. The relations between the quartos of the *Spanish Tragedy* were for a long time obscure. Not the rightful owner Jeffes's first edition but Edward White's somehow survived. And White's early quarto printed by Aldee offers a text freer from error than the later one printed by Jeffes and sold by White. So that, up to 1901, when Schick's revised edition of the text appeared, it was commonly supposed that the "Allde for White" quarto was the authoritative one, and that the copyright somehow passed from Jeffes to Edward White. One argument of

Schick's is sufficient to prove beyond a doubt that the undated "Allde for White" quarto was used for setting up
the "Jeffes, sold by Edward White" quarto of 1594. The
compositor of the Jeffes quarto, in setting up fol $K_2{}^a$, fell
short one line in his pagination, and retained (out of
place) both a stage-direction and the former compositor's
catch-word, She stabs
her helfe
Enter,
an error unaccountable on any
other supposition than that the second compositor had the
first text before him. Mr. Schick has also shown that, in
spite of White's having a text which lays claim to being
better than its predecessor and actually is purer than its
successor issued by the rightful owner, the better text is
the piratical one. This is an unwelcome bit of news to
such text critics as assume that a bad text is an inevitable
indication of surreptitiousness; but in this case all we can
do is to accept it, and acknowledge that it was simply a case
of E. White's having a more careful printer get up his
edition. For an entry on the Registers not reprinted by
Arber but quoted by Herbert in his edition of *Typographical Antiquities,* (II, p. 1160), taken together with a note
in Arber's reprint (II, p. 864), leaves no doubt as to the
White piracy:

Whereas Edw W & Abell Jeffes haue each of them offended, *viz.*
E W in having printed The Spanish Tragedie belonging to A J And
A J in having printed The tragedie of Arden of Kent, belonging to
E. W. Yt is agreed that all the books of each impression shalbe
confiscated & forfayted, according to thordonances, to thuse of the
poore of the company. Item, yt is agreed that either of them shall
pay for a fine 10 s a pece, presently or betweene this & our Lady day
next. And as touching their imprisonment for the said offence, yt
is referred ouer to some other conuenient tyme, at the discrec'on of
the Wardens and Assistants. Item. Abell hath promised to pay
the 6 d. in the li. to thuse of the poore which he oweth for Quintus
Curtius.

In the margin is " solut. x s. per E. White , May 1593 .."
And in May, 1593 in Arber (II, p. 864) occurs this receipt:

Edw White Receaued of him for a fine accordinge to the order
sett downe betwene him and A Jeffes 18 Decembris ultimo [1592]
x s.

Jeffes made submission before a full court 18 December,
1592, and promised to live honestly. As he was the first
offender, as the pirate had bettered the text, and the Stationers had arbitrated the difficulties by punishing both,
Jeffes and White seem to have come to an agreement per-
mitting Jeffes to set up copy from White's better text, and
White to have the selling.

There is no evidence that the warden, Edward White,
retained an interest in the copy of the *Spanish Tragedy*
after it passed by duly recorded transfer from Jeffes to
William White; nor that E. White was ever interested in
Peele's *Edward Longshanks*. Mr. Daniel,[31] while keeping
the Whites distinct, has supposed it necessary to assume a
tie of relationship or business between them. But the
name White is too common to justify such an assumption
without evidence; and there appear in the registers no
traces of relationship where we should expect them. The
only entry that could be supposed to connect them significantly is that concerning fines ordered by Court June
25, 1600. Edward Aldee and William White are fined
5s. apiece for printing the "ballad of the wife of Bathe,"
and Edward White 10s. for selling it. But we know
Aldee to have been Edward White's printer, and it is possible that the only business tie here is between Aldee and
Edward White. Even should we suppose that in this case
Edward White sold some books printed by William, the
single instance would be insufficient to prove either family

---

[31] *Academy*, 1891, II, p. 197.

ties or special business partnership. It certainly would
furnish no reason for Edward White's interest in slipping
in a false entry of *Henry V.* to Pavier; for the transfer
of the *Spanish Tragedy* to Pavier was regular and needed
no concealment, as William White really owned the copy
and continued to print for Pavier after assigning the copy
to him.

So, if Edward White deliberately misused his power as
a warden, it must have been simply as an act of favoritism
to one of the chief parties concerned: Millington and
Busby, anxious to get the questionable property disposed
of, or the new stationer, Pavier, eager to acquire copy even
at a risk. Entries in 1602 and 1603 show that at this
time Edward White had ordinary business relations with
Pavier, but no direct connections appear in 1600.[32] It is
unlikely that Pavier had in August, 1600 any strong business ties with any of the stationers, as he was only two
months old at the business. His first entry on the registers is that of two copies on the 4th of August (the date
of the staying), only ten days before the entry we are considering.

It would·be rather easier to find a reason for assuming
favoritism toward Millington. The recently discovered
1594 quarto of *Titus Andronicus* was printed by John
Danter and " to be sold by Edward White & Thomas Millington, at the little North doore of Paules at the signe of
the Gunne." That there was a temporary partnership in
a copy is perfectly clear. The shop named is E. White's,
however, and there is no evidence that Millington sold
there. During the whole time in question, 1594-1600,
Millington had his own shop to the east of St. Paul's,

[32] The E. White who assigned him twelve copies Dec. 13, 1620, is
a younger man. The warden E. White died in 1612.

under St. Peter's Church, in Cornhill. So that the tie
between E. White and Millington was not the equivalent
of a real partnership in general book-selling.

The personal record of Edward White is such as to
suggest that he would not scruple to misuse his powers as
warden, given a sufficient motive for doing so and a fair
chance of not being called to account by a Court of
Assistants. During the general house-cleaning at Stationers' Hall which succeeded the printing ordinances of
1586, White was among those who entered the long lists
of ballads, some of which were no doubt published earlier
without entry, as they are entered on condition that the
copies belong to no others. He was fined even when he
was warden, 25 June, 1600, to the extent of 10s. for
printing a "disorderly" ballad, and was fined again in
1603. The question is, though, why he should risk the
unpleasantness of possibly being called to account so soon
after the trouble in June, unless he were personally interested in the transfer. For the warden of the Company
was certainly not immune to criticism and punishment
for irregularities of behavior. Christopher Barker, elder
warden, printer to the Queen, and much more prominent
as a stationer than White, was fined 20s. in 1586 for
holding an apprentice "a certen space" unpresented.
And on March 1, 1596, a court took away a copy from
Master Dawson, Warden. That wardens now and then
broke rules is evident; that they broke them oftener than
they were caught and punished is very probable; but
that the making of false entries to serve their own interests was "thoroughly characteristic of the way things
were done in the Stationers' Company" is not, I believe,
a conclusion that can be justified by the facts. The war-
denship was a position of trust and responsibility; but if
this was not sufficient to steady a stationer of shaky prin-

ciples, he might be inspired to caution by the fact that it was also a position of publicity. Stationers subject to fines and regulations were excellently qualified to keep an eye on the behavior of a warden who was also subject to fines and regulations.

It is quite true, as Mr. Pollard says, that a work once printed without entry was sometimes " made an honest woman" by late entry on the registers. The intention is clear in the following instances:

> Veale on 2 Sept., 1578, has " lycenced unto him The Regiment of lyfe uppon condycon that if it heretofore be lycenced to any other that then this license graunted to him shalbe void.
> he fined for printynge this before he had lycence (II, p. 336)
> 2 August, 1578. he is fined for printinge the regiment of lyfe without Lycence lo s.   pd."
> 7 Feb., 1597. Thomas Myllington " is ordred that he shall pay 2s. 6d. for a fine for printing a ballad to the wrong of Thomas Creede, and shall also pay to the said Thomas Creede iiis. iiiid. for amendes for ye sayd wrong. The fine is to be paid for that the ballad was not licenced, and Myllyngton performing this order is to enjoy the ballad."

But other entries already quoted show that a pirate could not always get his work recognized after it was printed, simply by paying a fee for entry. The fact appears clearly in a note after the entry of Beza's *Psalmorum Dauidis et aliorum Prophetarum,* 26 October, 1579: " Master Vautrolier had printed this without Licence before this was entred to master bishop " (II, p. 361).

Where we have sufficient data for studying the settlements between rightful owners of copies and piratical stationers, we find that the rightful owner as a rule takes over the copyright; but sometimes, if amicable settlement is made, he buys up printed copies for his own use. In other cases the pirated editions are confiscated to the use of the Stationers' Hall, or destroyed. Newman's unauthorized edition of *Astrophel and Stella,* 1591, was taken up, and the edition suppressed. Jeffes and White, as we have seen, had their piratical issues of plays confiscated in 1592. When complaint was made in time, false entries could be cancelled, as in the case of Bacon's *Essays,* 1597, and Sidney's *Apologie for Poetry,* wrongly entered to Olney, 12 April, 1595, and crossed out because it belonged to Ponsonby by an entry about five months earlier under a slightly different title.

Apparently, the degree of satisfaction to be obtained through the Stationers for invasion of the owner's rights depended, first of all, upon promptness of discovery of the invasion, and also, to some extent, upon the amount of pressure brought to bear upon the Stationers by the rightful owner. Obviously, the Stationers wished all copies printed to be duly recorded on the registers, and were more concerned with this than with the question as to how the stationer got hold of his copy. That there was inquiry on this point, however, is perfectly clear, in the case of transfers from one stationer to another, because there is often recorded the fact that a note of hand from the original owner gave the second stationer the copyright. What inquiries were made when the stationer first brought his copy to be entered is not so clear. I think it likely that the official censors and licensers handled the matter in many cases. Surely the Master of the Revels, as licenser of plays, was best fitted to inquire into sources of copy. The Stationers' chief interest was, to keep straight their records of ownership; they were most anxious to have all works entered on the registers; and it is only natural that, after a piracy had been aired, it would seem wise to them to make the best of a bad situation by starting a record which would at least do away with the possibility of future entanglements about the printing rights. In the eyes of the lover of literature, such a practice can never, in any sense, make " right " a bad text; but to a business man it might have something to commend it. Where the bad text continued to be printed, there were doubtless reasons for this—indifference on the part of the owners, or disinclination to put themselves to the necessary trouble to prove their claims.

So far as the accessible records from Stationers' Hall can testify, the trouble over *Henry V.* was not aired in the Stationers' Court. The quietness of the entry to Pavier, too, seems to suggest that the entry was slipped in. In the "setting over" of *Henry V.,* 14 August, 1600, there are several possibilities. Millington and Busby may have tried to enter the work, met with a delay Aug. 4, and, failing to get authority for publishing their poor, ill-gotten text, decided to get rid of it as quickly as possible, in spite of the fact that they had already printed some copies in the hope of getting their entry allowed. That Millington did assign one copy before he had it properly allowed to him is clear from the entries concerning *Jack of Newbery:*

7 Mar. 1597 Millington entered " Jack of Newbery so that he haue it laufully aucthorised. 6d." (III, p. 81)

25 May, 1597 Humfrey Lownes had " assigned ouer to hym for his copie from Thomas Myllington A booke called Jacke of Newbery: with this condicon that yt be Laufully aucthorized whiche booke was entred for the said Thomas Myllington 7 Marcii 1596(7) upon the same condicon. 6d.
This is entred by Direction from Master Warden Dawson."

The same sort of setting over of a work entered provisionally (but in this case " stayed " and not entered to him by name), may have occurred in the case of *Henry V.*

Another possibility is, that some private agreement may have been reached by which Pavier should make the effort to do what Millington had failed in—get the copy recognized by the Stationers and recorded—and Millington and Busby should retain an interest and be responsible for the

sale of the work.   As Pavier had been transferred from
the Company of Drapers to the Stationers as recently as
June 3, 1600, he must have been eager for copy; his later
history shows that he was not very particular as to the way
the copy was acquired.   As yet, he could have little or no
business reputation, and even stationers of questionable
repute, such as Millington, might be better able to sell the
book.   Pavier's newness as a stationer, however, would be
a valuable asset as giving a presumption of innocence to
an obscure transaction.   Later developments show amicable business relations between Millington and Busby and
Pavier; for on 19th of April, 1602 (the year in which the
Pavier *Henry* V. came out) Pavier took over by assignment under the warden's hand *saluo Jure cuiuscunque*
three copies, among them *Titus Andronicus* and the first
and second parts of *Henry VI.*

If the entry of *Henry* V. to Pavier was a slippery transaction—and everything seems to favor the supposition that
it was—is it not possible that the warden was deceived as
to the identity of the *Henry* V. and, because the printer,
Thomas Creede, was the same, was misled into supposing
that he was only giving consent to a transfer from Creede
to Pavier of the copyright in the old Queen's play, *The
Famous Victories of Henrye the Ffyfth conteyning the
honorable battell of Agencourt,* properly entered on the
register 14 May, 1594, to Thomas Creede? As Creede
retained the printing of the new *Henry V.,* the deception
would not be impossible, if the copy were only glanced at
by a careless warden.   The entry of the *Apologie for Poesie* to Olive, when it had been entered, under a title rather
different, to Ponsonby five months before, shows that a
differently worded title did not always rouse the suspicion
of the warden at the time the work was entered.   And
there are substantial resemblances in the wording of the

title (e. g., "with the battle of Agincourt" and "con-
teyninge the honourable battell of Agincourt") which,
taken together with the fact that the same printer was involved in both cases, make it possible that the warden was
careless rather than dishonest. That the work continued
to be printed in its corrupt form, however, can be explained only by indifference on the part of the company
or peculiar difficulties in the way of settlement.

It is possible that, if the play was patched up from
stenographic notes taken at performance, it would have
put the company to some expense to defend itself against
this particular kind of piracy. There is no doubt that the
law gave better security for property in manuscripts at
this time than it gave against reproduction from oral delivery by memory and short-hand. The whole history of
stage right shows that this must have been the case. The
legality of reproducing a play from short-hand notes and
printing it was solemnly discussed in 1770,[33] and reproduction by stenography forbidden. But reporting and reproducing from memory was upheld by J. Buller in
1793.[34] Again, in Keene v. Wheatley and Clarke, decided
by the Circuit Court of the U. S., E. D. Pa. in equity,[35]
it was stated that, if the piracy had been committed
through the defendants' memorizing the play or hiring
others to memorize it, there would be no case; but, as the
defendants had got the manuscripts from actors, a breach
of confidence might be pleaded. Even as late as 1882, in
the case of Tompkins v. Thomas E. Hallock,[36] a play was
committed to memory a section at a time, by repeated
visits to the theatre, and dictated by sections after the performance. The judge who heard the case against the man

[33] Macklin v. Richardson (Ambler, *Cases in Chancery*, II, p. 694).
[34] Coleman v. Wathen (5 T. R. Durnford and East, p. 245).
[35] Phila. *Reports* 4, vol. XVII, p. 349.
[36] 133 Mass., p. 32.

5

Byron ruled that there was no violation of trust or confidence, and therefore no injunction could issue. The
question was then brought before the full court and argued.
Many precedents were cited to show that, while the manager of a theatre might, if he chose, prevent phonographic
or stenographic report, " the privileges of listening and
of retention in the memory cannot be restrained. Where
the audience is not a select one, these privileges cannot be
limited in either their immediate or ulterior consequences."

That stenography was commonly used in the late sixteenth and early seventeenth centuries is well known;
indeed, by 1630 it was probably in more common use at
public performances than it is today, if we may judge
from contemporary statements. And we have proof that
it was used as early as 1600. Frequent allusions show
that it was a common practice of the theatre-goers of this
time to memorize parts of plays. When there were fewer
things to memorize, there were doubtless stronger memories; and it is not improbable that numerous attempts
were made to reproduce plays from stenographic notes
aided by memory, or from memory aided by stenographic notes on details. The garbled texts of the first
quartos of *Henry V.* strongly favor such an origin;
and I believe, when some one shall have studied them in
detail with this in view, he will be able to make us
reasonably certain that this was the means by which the
text was actually acquired. If so, perhaps the company
refrained from taking the matter up because it was too
late to check the piracy entirely, through stationers or
Lord Chamberlain, when they discovered the trouble, and
because they shrank from the time, trouble, and expense
involved in proving that the issuing of a text so acquired
really violated their stage rights. That the reporting of

a play by stenography was regarded as reprehensible we
guess from Heywood's allusions to the practice; but this
gives us only the playwright's point of view, and it is only
natural that the legal protection should be far behind the
author's conception of his rights: it always has been far
behind. Even if there were any generally accepted legal
attitude that tended to protect plays from stenographic
piracy (which we may reasonably doubt when we see how
lately the problem has worried learned judges), the company must have been aware that there were some addle-
headed individual judges who could not be made to see the
matter straight. Going to law about violations of stage-
right in the last two centuries has been anything but a
pleasant pastime. If the Chamberlain's men were really
busy in the summer of 1600, it is not inconceivable that,
in the difficult matter of a text got up from short-hand
notes and memory, they may have preferred to shirk the
task of proving their case. The text is so extremely bad
that the reading of it would not be likely to rival the pleasure of seeing and hearing the real thing. But inquiry
into the motives of the company in not pursuing their
claims to property is, of course, highly speculative. A
really satisfactory solution of the problems surrounding
the publication of *Henry V.* has never yet been set forth.
Possibly we may hope for one after the quartos have been
thoroughly studied with reference to the possibilities of
their having been made up entirely from short-hand notes
and memory, and after the activities of the Chamberlain's
men in 1600 have been more thoroughly investigated. It
is the purpose of this paper to isolate this problem from
those connected with the other plays " to be staied " at the
same time, on the ground that it is a different kind of
problem and one that merits investigation independently
of the others.

EVELYN MAY ALBRIGHT.

XV.—GAILLARD'S CRITICISM OF CORNEILLE, ROTROU, DU RYER, MARIE DE GOURNAY, AND OTHER WRITERS

A quaint piece of dramatic writing, the *Cartel* or *Monomachie* of Antoine Gaillard, is one of the earliest of seventeenth-century French plays in which an author puts his contemporaries on the stage and makes fellow writers the butt of his jests. It clears the way for Desmarest's *Visionnaires,* Saint-Evremond's *Académistes,* a half-dozen of Molière's plays, and a number of other pieces by Molière's contemporaries, whose satire is devoted to living individuals or to groups of literary persons; but the work has so little dramatic value that it would remain merely a date, were it not for the fact that by selecting real persons as the object of his satire, Gaillard has criticized from the standpoint of a contemporary a number of writers who flourished with greater or less distinction in 1633. In discussing the work I shall therefore dwell upon its biographical qualities, rather than upon its slender merit as a drama.[1]

Antoine Gaillard sieur de la Porteneille jests about being a lackey and a " philosophe naturel," but the first claim should be regarded no more seriously than the second; for, as the *Catalogue de Soleinne* [2] points out, a lackey would not be likely to write the letters which Gaillard addresses to the princesse de Guéménée and the duchesse de

---

[1] The play has been little studied. A short analysis can be found in La Vallière, *Bibliothèque du théâtre français,* I, pp. 556, 557. The frères Parfaict, IV, pp. 472, 495, 511, mention it briefly. Goujet, *Bibliothèque,* XV, pp. 328-333, gives the most complete account of it, citing a large number of verses.

[2] No. 1024 and first supplement, No. 189.

Chevreuse. He published a pastoral called *La Carline* in 1626 and with it several poems, one of them on the exile of Théophile de Viaud. The *Monomachie*, or, as it is called here, the *Comédie qu'on peut intituler le Cartel ou le Défi entre Braquemart et Gaillard sur la bonté de leurs ouvrages,* appeared along with various poems and letters in Gaillard's *Œuvres Meslées* [3] of 1634. That it had been composed as early as 1633 is shown by the reference to Auvray given below, who must have been alive when the line was written and who died in November, 1633. It was probably republished as the *Monomachie* in 1636; for the frères Parfaict [4] mention only that name and date.

The piece is written in verse and is divided into five short acts. It should be considered a farce from the simplicity and triviality of the theme, which is destitute of intrigue; from the treatment of character, which interests us without the slightest emotional appeal; and from the tone, which lacks fineness of touch and shows a constant effort to excite laughter. Gaillard himself supports such classification by his preliminary letter to the reader, in which he disclaims any intention of hurting the victims of his satire, begs that his jokes be not taken too seriously, and that, if anything is found in his work contrary to the rules of twenty-four hours, unity of scene, and " ornement du Theatre," the reader should remember that it is extremely difficult to be satisfactory at the same time as lackey and as author.

The plot can be summarized in a few words. Gaillard and Braquemart quarrel over the relative merit of their verses, agree to submit them to some authority, discuss various dramatic poets, and finally appeal to Neuf-Germain, who refers them to Mademoiselle de Gournay and

[3] Pp. 27 f.   [4] IV, p. 472.

a certain Doctor Govino. After some interesting talk about literary questions, the judges select Gaillard as the better poet. It may be doubted whether this theme would interest a popular audience in 1633, but wé have no proof that the play was not acted. Its brevity may have made its representation possible at the Hôtel de Bourgogne; but it is more likely that, if acted at all, it found its audience at some noble or literary house. However this may be, its interest for us lies chiefly in its presentation of Neuf-Germain and Marie de Gournay, and in its lines on ten dramatic poets.

Louis de Neuf-Germain (1574-1662), the "poète hétéroclite de Monseigneur frère unique du Roy," is known to us chiefly through his *Poésies et rencontres,* published in 1630 and 1637, and various anecdotes that tell of his strange methods of verse making.[5] Gaillard represents him as a venerable old man, intensely self-centered, who has a low opinion of all literary persons except himself and Mademoiselle de Gournay and who, in the course of the play, eliminates this one rival as a result of a dispute over the nature of poetry. *Vers à contretemps,* which lack number, measure, and cæsura, are recited by Neuf-Germain as evidence of his inventive genius. They are really prose lines of unequal length, written according to a system that seems to have remained peculiar to their author until the middle of the nineteenth century. Strange to say, despite this striving for originality and lack of all attempt at regularity of rhythm, Neuf-Germain argues for labor rather than enthusiasm, and thus places himself in theory where we should least expect to find him, among the followers of Malherbe.

---

[5] Cf. especially the dictionaries of Bayle and Jal; and Goujet, *op. cit.,* XVI, pp. 156-161.

Mademoiselle de Gournay is more fully described. Her fondness for Montaigne and Ronsard, classical mythology, and the language of the sixteenth century, her great age, her learning, her poetic doctrine are brought out, but no use is made of her feminism. To Neuf-Germain she is "la sçavante Gourné," whom Montaigne judged worthy of his amours and whom Saint-Amant was wrong to call a *buse.* Evidently the seventeenth century had grown cynical about the sage's affection for his "fille d'alliance." The reference to Saint-Amant supports Tallemant's statement that Marie de Gourné is the unnamed woman attacked in the *Poète crotté,* where, to be sure, Saint-Amant does not use the word *buse,* but he substitutes for it every equivalent epithet in his command.

Neuf-Germain hails her as

> Pucelle de mille ans, vieille muse authentique,
> Scauante iusqu'aux dents,[6] sage Metaphysique.

She uses *iaçoit que, ores, pieça,* praises Ronsard, Du Bellay, Desportes, disapproves of Malherbe and a dozen poets then engaged in forming the French Academy.[7] She quizzes the rival poets on classical mythology, objects to Neuf-Germain's verses, and places herself with the sixteenth-century poets by defending enthusiasm against correctness.

This representation of Mademoiselle de Gournay recalls Saint-Evremond's treatment of her in his *Académistes* (published, ab. 1650). Both authors emphasize her age, her devotion to Montaigne and the speech of his times, her

---

[6] An illusion to her false teeth, which Saint-Evremond ridicules in *Académistes,* I, sc. 3, and which are mentioned by Tallemant, *Historiettes,* edition of Monmerqué and Paris, 1862, II, p. 154.

[7] L'Estoille, Colletet, Colombi, Racan, Godeau, Barro, Malville, Cerisé [Serisay or Cerisy], Alber [Habert?], Faret, Gombaut, Mainard.

opposition to the Academicians and their attempts at re-
forming the language; but the details of the satires are so
obviously different that Saint-Evremond can scarcely have
taken from Gaillard more than the idea of placing her
upon the boards.   Similarly these two writers may have
shown Molière the dramatic possibilities of satirizing a
woman of letters, but the fact that neither of them availed
himself of his opportunity to laugh at Marie de Gournay
as a feminist shows us that the *Femmes Savantes* is largely
free from their influence.

The most important passage in Gaillard's work is the
one in which the rival poets discuss the merits of various
dramatists with a view to choosing a judge for their verses.
The facts stated in these lines are in many cases confirmed
by other evidence.   The opinions are probably representative of those held generally in 1633, though some allowance should be made for the author's striving after comic
effect, as he suggests in his word to the reader.   The lines
run as follows: [8]

> Corneille est excellent, mais il vend ses ouvrages:
> Rotrou fait bien des vers, mais il est Poëte à gages:
> Durier est trop obscur, et trop remply d'orgueil:
> Dorval est tenebreux, il aime le cercueil:
> Raziguier est Gascon, par consequent il volle,
> Marcassus est sçavant, mais il sent trop l'escolle:
> Gomer nous seroit bon, s'il n'estoit pas si gueux.
> De coste escrit parfois, mais il est malheureux.
> Auvray ce gros camart, plaide pour les suivantes.
> Claveret est rimeur, mais c'est pour les servantes.

The charge against Corneille can scarcely be simply that
he sold his work, certainly not an uncommon thing to do,
but it is rather that he was already celebrated for avarice.
Both La Bruyère and Tallemant charge him with this vice
in passages that have been often cited: "Il ne juge de la

[8] Pp. 33, 34.

bonté de sa pièce que par l'argent qui lui en revient; " [9]
" La troupe du Marais à laquelle Corneille par politiqué,
car c'est un grand avare, donnoit ses pièces; " [10] " Il a
plus d'avarice que d'ambition, et pourveû qu'il en tire bien
de l'argent, il ne se tourmente guères du reste." [11] Gaillard's statement appeared, of course, much earlier than
these passages, and shows that, while still young, Corneille
was notorious for the canny qualities of his province.

The reference to Rotrou's productiveness is consistent
with that poet's remark that his *Cléagénor et Doristée*, published the same year as the *Cartel*, was the " cadette de
trente sœurs." Stiefel [12] cites the line to prove Chardon's
conjecture that Rotrou had succeeded Hardy as the hired
dramatist of the troop which played at the Hôtel de Bourgogne. Indeed, it furnishes the best evidence we have of
that interesting and generally accepted fact.

Pierre Du Ryer is said to have been reduced to poverty
by his marriage and to have sold in consequence his position as secretary to the king. I have argued that this sale
took place in 1633 or 1634.[13] If the word *obscur* refers
to his poverty, the passage gives new evidence in support
of this theory. The expression *remply d'orgueil* implies
in him something less pleasant than the simple self-respect
with which he bore his misfortunes at a later date. If
Gaillard's criticism was just in 1633, it probably did not
long remain so, except in regard to Du Ryer's poverty.

J. G. Durval, who is evidently intended by the name
Dorval, had composed before the end of 1633 the *Travaux*

---

[9] *Les Caractères, des Jugements.*

[10] *Historiettes,* edition of Monmerqué and Paris, 1862, v, p. 491.

[11] *Ibid.,* VI, p. 58.

[12] *Zeitschrift für französische Sprache und Litteratur,* 1894, pp.
13, 14.

[13] *Pierre Du Ryer Dramatist,* Washington, 1912, p. 13.

d'Ulysse and, perhaps, *Agarite,* published in 1636 and certainly played as early as the beginning of 1634. The description of him furnished by Gaillard was probably suggested by the first of these plays, which portrays Ulysses' visit to Hades and the loss of his companions through various ghastly episodes, also, it may be, by the wedding entertainment depicted in *Agarite,* which ends in the murder of the prospective bridegroom.

N. de Rayssiguier, author of pastoral plays, was a native of Albi, Tarne, and was imprisoned at Paris, a misfortune which, according to poems written by him and studied by the frères Parfaict, he attributed to the hatred of some influential person. Gaillard's accusation does not prove that Rayssiguier was a thief, but it makes it extremely probable that theft was the charge brought against him at the time of his incarceration.

Marcassus was professor of rhetoric " au collège de la Marche à Paris." He translated Vergil, Horace, Ovid, and other Latin authors. His place in Gaillard's list is due to his having written a pastoral, *l'Eromène,* which was published in 1633.

Gomer is probably a misprint for *Gombaud,* who was poor most of his life [14] and was at this time quite celebrated as a dramatist on account of his *Amarante* (published, 1631). The only other dramatist I can find whose name resembles *Gomer* is Chaulmer or Chomer, translator of Baronius and author of *La Mort de Pompée* (published, 1638); but as this play was probably not represented as early as 1633 and as we know nothing of its author's life, it seems likely that Gombaud rather than Chaulmer is the dramatist here indicated.

De Coste evidently refers to G. de Coste, author of

---

[14] Cf. Goujet, *op. cit.,* XVII, p. 126.

Lizimène, a pastoral whose privilege was obtained Nov. 28, 1631; for La Calprenède, whose name was Gautier de Costes, not only had a less satisfactory name, but began writing too late to be referred to here. In what way de Coste was unfortunate I have not been able to discover.

Lachèvre [15] raises the question as to whether Jean Auvray, the lyric poet, author of the *Banquet des Muses,* composed all the works commonly assigned to him. If, as he believes, he died in 1622, he could not have been the author of the plays, *Madonte* and *Dorinde,* which would then be the work of the second Auvray, who died Nov. 19, 1633. Gaillard's reference is evidently to the latter writer. That his uncomplimentary line is inspired, as Goujet [16] thinks, by the obscenity of the *Banquet des Muses,* cannot, of course, be held, if Lachèvre's theory is established.

Jean Claveret, most of whose plays had been written by the end of 1633, is known to us chiefly as the rival whom Corneille offended so deeply by using his name as a synonym for lack of literary ability: " Il n'a plus tenu à vous que du premier lieu où beaucoup d'honnêtes gens me placent, ie ne sois descendu au dessous de Claveret." [17] Gaillard's opinion of Claveret differs little from that of his eminent contemporary.

Finally, it is worth noting that the order in which the dramatic poets are named is not very different from that which would be assigned to their relative merits today; also, that the selection of these as the most prominent

---

[15] *Bibliographie des Recueils collectifs de poésies,* Paris, 1901-1905, III, p. 192. He does not give the special authority for the statement that Jean Auvray died in 1622 and, as I have not had access to all the works he mentions in his bibliography for Auvray, I have been unable to verify it.

[16] *Op. cit.,* xv, p. 322.

[17] *Lettre apologétique du Sr Corneille.*

dramatists in the year 1633 is not far wrong. Hardy, Théophile, and Pichou were dead. Scudéry, Baro, and Boisrobert were only beginning to be known. The only important name omitted is that of Mairet. The passage is especially interesting in showing the dominant position already taken by Corneille in the opinion of his contemporaries.

H. CARRINGTON LANCASTER.

XVI.—*RICHARD CŒUR DE LION* AND THE *PAS SALADIN* IN MEDIEVAL ART

I

Every student of the literature of the Middle Ages is aware that Richard I was a highly popular figure in medieval England, and that about the historical facts of his career there grew up with rapidity and luxuriance a considerable growth of romantic legend. As his fame challenged the pre-eminence of Arthur among British heroes,[1] so his exploits, like Arthur's, multiplied and grew more marvelous in the imagination of the people, though for obvious reasons the process never went so far. To Richard's prestige among his own people we have abundant testimony in the seven manuscripts of the Middle English romance of *Richard Cœur de Lion* extant and in the three printed editions of the sixteenth century. As Ellis pointed out, as early as 1805, in introducing his synopsis of the romance, it is a curious texture of narrative mainly historical concerning the Third Crusade, interwoven liberally with bits of this legendary material. It will be profitable, before dealing with illustrations of certain episodes occurring in the romance, to devote some attention to its development and structure. In a review of Dr. Karl Brunner's critical edition of *Richard Cœur de Lion,* to be published elsewhere, I hope to deal fully with the subject, and merely summarize here the results of my investigations. I owe much to Dr. Brunner's discussion, but more to that of Gaston Paris, whose conclusions in general I adopt.[2]

[1] *Romania,* 1897, p. 387, n. 5. [2] *Ibid.,* pp. 353 ff.

As I have already said, certain well marked parts of
the romance adhere roughly to the historical facts of
Richard's career, whereas other parts as clearly are utterly
fabulous. Since in three places the Middle English text
makes acknowledgment to a French authority,[3] it is clear
that the closely historical portions represent an Anglo-
Norman poem. Despite Gaston Paris's uncertainty as to
the verse form of this poem,[4] I am convinced by the comparatively large number of rhymes in French words in
these historical parts of the Middle English text that they
reproduce the rhymes of the original French octosyllabic
couplets. The parts of the Middle English text as given
in Brunner's edition which are in my judgment translations from the Anglo-Norman are the following:

1269-1341, b1057/126-130, 1430-1436, b1437/1-4,
1667-2039, b2040/1-13, 2042-2649, b2650/1-12, 2683-
3040, 3125-3128, b3129/1-10, 3151-3176, b3177/1-6,
3229-3346, b3346/1-36, 3699-3758, 4817-5188, 5931-
5950, b5950/1-28, 5951-end.

What can we learn of the translator? Koelbing had
shown the presence of many Kentish forms in the rhymes
of the Middle English text,[5] and with some exceptions
these occur in the parts translated from the Anglo-
Norman. He also pointed out a large number of parallel
passages in the Kentish romance of *Arthour and Merlin*.[6]
We are justified then in believing that the author was a
Kentishman and that he is probably identical with the
author of *Arthour and Merlin*.

With the exception of the introductory thirty-four lines,
which are certainly the Kentish poet's, all the rest of the

[3] Ll. 21, 5100, 7028.
[4] *Romania*, 1897, p. 362, n. 2.
[5] Koelbing, *Arthour and Merlin*, pp. xcvii ff.
[6] *Ibid.*, pp. lxxiii ff.

poem .is to be attributed to one or more interpolators. The bulk of it' is, I believe, to be attributed to one man, who seems to have a particular interest in extolling the deeds of two knights unknown to the chroniclers of the Third Crusade, Thomas de Multon and Fulke Doilly. H. L. D. Ward pointed out that these two knights are to be identified with two lords of the district of Holland in South Lincolnshire, who flourished from about 1190 to 1240.[7] It seems likely that our interpolator, a minstrel, having enjoyed the patronage of their descendants, determined as a stroke of policy to associate these obscure heroes in the renown of the Lion Heart. He therefore composed narratives of tournament, battle, and siege, wherein his patrons distinguished themselves by their prowess, and fitted these into the framework of the Kentish romance. This hypothesis is confirmed by the general Midland character of his rhyme words.

Gaston Paris dates the various stages in the composition of the romance as follows: Anglo-Norman poem, ca. 1230, Kentish translation, end of the thirteenth century, interpolations, fourteenth century.[8] I see no reason to disagree with these conclusions, except, perhaps, the first.

Besides the fictitious exploits of Doilly and De Multon, the South Lincolnshire minstrel is probably responsible for' the fabulous interpolations concerning Richard himself: his demon birth, his imprisonment by the King of Almayne and his revenge, his cure from fever, the banquet for the Saracen ambassadors, his overthrow of Saladin before Babylon. Much of this material is clearly based upon tradition, oral and written. It is among these interpolations that we find related two of the episodes which

---

[7] *Catalogue of the Romances in the British Museum, I, p. 946.*
[8] *Romania, 1897, pp. 362, 385 ff.*

enjoyed a great vogue, as we shall see, among medieval
artists. It will be our task in examining their illustrations to see what they indicate as to the literary and
traditional sources of these episodes.

II

Of the fabulous adventures attributed to Richard that
which seems most to have fascinated the imagination of
medieval England was his personal encounter with Saladin. Let me outline the account of the combat as given
in lines 5481-5797 of the romance. Saladin sends a challenge to Richard to meet him in single combat on the
plain, and offers him the gift of a horse: Richard accepts
both the challenge and the offer. Saladin then causes a
necromancer to conjure two fiends of the air into the
shape of a mare and her colt. The latter, which will
instinctively run at its mother's neigh and kneel beside
her for suck, he dispatches to Richard, and keeps the dam
as his mount. But an angel warns Richard by night of
the intended treachery, instructs him to procure a tree
forty feet long and truss it overthwart the colt's mane,
and gives him a spear head of steel to fasten on the end
of it. With these directions Richard complies, and in
addition stops the colt's ears with wax and conjures it in
the name of God to obey him. When the time of the combat arrives, Richard, besides other equipments, carries a
shield of steel, "With þree lupardes wrouȝt ffull weel"
(l. 5710). Saladin, expecting Richard's steed to betray
him, carries as his only weapon a falchion. But though
the mare begins to neigh, the colt cannot hear her, and
Richard comes hurtling into the Sowdan. Bridle and
poitrel, girth and stirrups give way. The mare falls to
the ground, and the Sowdan shoots

Bakward ouyr̄ hys meres croupe,
His feet toward þe ffyrmamente.
Behynde hym þe spere out wente. (ll. 5778-80)

That this account of the overthrow of Saladin as it stands is the work of the South Lincolnshire minstrel is clear owing to the part which the two South Lincolnshire knights play in lines 5812 f. But there are several reasons for seeing behind it a source which has been appropriated with only slight modifications. Frequent reference is made to an authority: twice it is called a " booke," twice a "geste." Furthermore, it is significant that in this passage of 450 lines Saladin is never mentioned by name, but is called simply the Sowdan, " the Cheff Sawdon of Hethenysse," or "the Sawdan, that cheef was told of Damas," as if the minstrel were simply copying, almost word for word, some manuscript he had before him. Finally, Gaston Paris has detached the element of the treacherous gift of the horse from the account of the actual combat, and skilfully traced its separate origin and development.[9] I believe it has not yet been pointed out that the other element, the combat itself between Richard and Saladin, exists separately in accounts of the battle of Arsour given by two early fourteenth century chroniclers, Peter de Langtoft and Walter de Hemingburgh.[10] The latter's version runs as follows: " Obviantem ei Saladinum, militem quidem strenuissimum, et congressu militari cum lancea exceptum, equum etiam cum assessore in terram prostravit." This account represents probably a much earlier tradition. Finally, there is the early mention of the single combat of King Rich-

---

[9] *Journal des Savants*, 1893, pp. 489-91.
[10] Peter de Langtoft, *Rolls Series*, II, p. 102. Walter de Hemingburgh, ed. H. C. Hamilton, p. 183.

ard as the subject of mural decoration to demonstrate that the story was an old one.

This notice is to be found among the Liberate Rolls of the reign of Henry III. This royal patron of the arts showed a peculiar fastidiousness in the decoration of his residences, and in his commissions for mural paintings he nearly always specified the subject, be it sacred or profane, which was to cover a given wall space. In an order of the year 1250 to the Sheriff of Wiltshire he directed that the history of Antioch and the single combat of King Richard be painted in the royal chamber at Clarendon Palace.[11] The paintings, which have long since perished, consisted, then, of a long series of illustrations of the romantic history of the First Crusade and one single illustration of an episode from the romantic history of the Third Crusade. The literary authority for the first was probably the well-known *Chanson d'Antioche,* that of the latter was either the " geste " mentioned by the South Lincolnshire minstrel or its source.

A second illustration of this episode is furnished by a pair of the so-called Chertsey Tiles. These tiles were found in a very fragmentary state on the site of Chertsey Abbey and form the subject of an unsatisfactory monograph by Dr. Manwaring Shurlock, to whom their discovery and preservation are due. The original tiles were circular and about nine and a half inches in diameter. They are of a dark terra-cotta color, the design being inlaid with white clay. Their date as based on the evi-

---

[11] Rot. Liberat. 35 Hen. III. De operacionibus apud Clarendon Rex vicecomiti Wiltes salutem. Precipimus tibi quod facias lambruscari cameram nostram sub capella nostra et murum ex transuerso illius camere amoueri et in eadem camera historiam Antiochie et duellum Regis Ricardi depingi et lambruscariam illam depingi viridi colore cum scintillis aureis, etc. *Vetusta Monumenta,* vol. VI, Painted Chamber at Westminster, p. 23.

FIG. 1.

dence of the armor depicted on them lies between 1270
and 1280. They are generally considered by experts to
be the finest examples of tile design and manufacture
which have come down to us from the Middle Ages.[12]
Prof. Lethaby has made the plausible suggestion that
they were commissioned by Henry III. and presented by
him to Chertsey Abbey.[13]

On examining the reproduction of the pair of tiles
(Fig. 1), we note certain features of the Middle English
romance, namely, the shield blazoned with three leopards
(l. 5710), the broad falchion (l. 5759), the broken girth
and stirrups (l. 5775), the spear athwart the colt's mane
(l. 5561), the Sowdan's body thrown backward (l. 5778),
and the falling mare (l. 5780), more or less faithfully
reproduced in the design. Before, however, we come to
any rash conclusion, we must realize that three of these
features, the falchion, the body thrown backward, the
falling steed, were part of an artistic tradition for representing the overthrow of pagan warriors by Christian
champions. There was before the French Revolution in
the Abbey of St. Denis a stained glass window containing
medallions of subjects from the First Crusade, and though
the window was destroyed, engravings of it survive in
Bernard de Montfauçon's *Monumens de la Monarchie
Française,* vol. I, and the particular medallion which concerns us occurs on Plate LIII,[14] and represents the Saracen
Corbaran overthrown by Robert Count of Normandy, as

---

[12] I have in preparation a study of these tiles, which will appear
in the Series of Philological Studies published by the University of
Illinois. I hope to improve on the out-of-date material of Dr. Shurlock's text and to furnish illustrations that more accurately reproduce the original designs.

[13] *Walpole Society* (London), *Annual Volume* II, 1913, pp. 78 f.

[14] Figured also in S. Lane-Pool, *Saladin,* p. 30.

described in the *Chanson d'Antioche,* ll. 985 ff. Both poem and stained glass window date from the first half of the twelfth century. This design shows the Saracen, armed with the falchion, struck backward in his saddle, while his horse collapses beneath him as in the tile design.

Accordingly, the only features of the tile design which are not adequately accounted ·for by this artistic tradition and the legendary tradition incorporated in Walter de Hemingburgh are the broken girth and stirrups, and the spear resting between the colt's ears. This latter feature is, however, of so marked and unusual a character, even though it does not correspond in full detail to the description of the beam trussed athwart the colt's mane, that it is inconceivable that the artist supplied it without knowing some more elaborate tradition than that related by Walter de Hemingburgh. Very likely he used the " geste," if we may take that to be an Anglo-Norman poem.

Passing to the third illustration of the combat (Fig. 2), we find that the artist has diverged from the version of the Middle English romance in providing Saladin with a spear instead of a scimeter, and in other details is not a whit closer than the Chertsey Tiles save for the introduction of the bells fringing the mare's trappings. This illustration is to be found on folio 82 of the *Louterell Psalter,* on loan at the British Museum. It was done for Geoffrey Louterell of Irnham in South Lincolnshire about the year 1340, when the East Anglian School of illumination was beginning to lose its decorative feeling and harmony of color.

To the second half of the same century belongs a fourth illustration. In Burgate church, Suffolk, there is a chest which, while originally intended for secular use, has for a long period served the purpose of a parish chest. The front, besides some painted designs of a purely ornamental

FIG. 2.

FIG. 3.

character, shows on the sinister side the much obliterated but clearly decipherable figure of a mounted knight, who was evidently opposed to a knight now vanished on the dexter side (Fig. 3). The still discernible participant in this tilting scene wears a jupon decorated with red designs, a hawberk appearing at the thighs, a camail, and vambraces,—all combining to place the date of the painting in the second half of the fourteenth century. A straight black line representing a spear strikes the knight in the midriff, and blood is flowing from the wound. The shock causes the knight to lean back, while his horse stoops its head and seems to stagger. The knight's right arm is raised over his head and grasps a sword with curving blade. The left arm droops at his side, holding an egg-shaped shield charged with a red wyvern. The scimeter is enough to distinguish the warrior as a Saracen, and the wyvern on the shield is almost the counterpart of one on the shield of Saladin carved on a handsome chest in the Musée de Cluny, of which I shall have more to say later. This wyvern also corresponds to ll. 5769 f. of the romance, which read:

> In hys blasoun, verrayment,
> Was jpaynted a serpent.

In two manuscripts we find illuminations which cannot be described as illustrations of this episode but which can be set down with some confidence as reminiscences of paintings or illuminations directly illustrating it. One manuscript is that masterpiece of medieval English craftsmanship known as *Queen Mary's Psalter,* dating from the early fourteenth century. On folio 184 there is depicted a combat between two knights, one of whom exhibits the familiar features of the upraised right arm, the scimeter, the body thrown back into an almost horizontal position,

and the collapsing steed.[15]   In the so-called *Douai* P*salter*
(No. 171 in the Public Library at Douai) the same features occur in an illumination on folio 48 verso.[16]   This
manuscript was originally given as a present by Thomas,
vicar of Gorleston in Suffolk, to a certain Abbot John,
and its date lies between 1322 and 1325.   These two illuminations, then, while lacking any conclusive details
which would show that the artists had in mind the story
of the encounter of the Lion Heart and Saladin, do show
that they were familiar with the pictorial representations
of it and testify to the popularity of the *motif*.

The evidence of these illustrations, then, tends to show:
first, that as early as 1250 an account of Richard's combat with Saladin, probably in Anglo-Norman, so stood
out from the rest of the traditions concerning Richard's
prowess as to have been alone selected for the decoration
of Clarendon palace; secondly, that about 1275 a version
existed embodying certain features, the scimeter, and the
spear resting between the horse's ears, which reappear in
the version contributed to the Middle English romance
by the South Lincolnshire minstrel and which tend to
prove that in that version the treacherous gift *motif* was
already combined with the *motif* of the unhorsing of
Saladin; finally, that by the opening of the fourteenth
century illustrations of the encounter had become so common that artists unconsciously in depicting encounters
between Christian and Saracen warriors reproduced the
familiar features of Richard's triumph over Saladin.   It
was this same popularity which induced the South Lincolnshire minstrel early in the fourteenth century to incorporate a version which he calls the " booke " or " geste "
into his redaction of the Richard romance.

---

[15] Figured in *Queen Mary's Psalter*, ed. G. Warner, Pl. 207.
[16] Figured in *New Palaeographical Society*, Part I, Pl. 16.

III

Next to his overthrow of Saladin, Richard's most renowned exploit was that of tearing the heart out of a lion.
Apparently it had occurred to some professional raconteur
to invent a story in explanation of Richard's familiar
sobriquet.   If we accept the evidence of the two thirteenth
century illustrations which I shall presently examine, that
story had already won a vogue before it was interpolated
in the Middle English romance.   It is retained in the
printed editions of the sixteenth century, is the subject
of references in the play printed in 1591 called *The
Troublesome Reign of King John,* which is the basis of
Shakespeare's play.[17]   These references are repeated in
King John, Act I, Scene I, l. 265:

> Against whose fury and unmatched force
> The aweless lion could not wage the fight,
> Nor keep his princely heart from Richard's hand.

Also in Act II, Scene I, l. 3:

> Richard that robbed the lion of his heart.

Briefly, the story, as related in ll. 738-1118, is this:
Richard, returning from Palestine as a palmer, was imprisoned by King Modard of Almayn.   He managed to
crack the skull of the king's son and to violate the king's
daughter.   Naturally Modard was in high dudgeon, but
had scruples about shedding royal blood by process of law.
One of his wisest councillors suggested that the difficulty
might be avoided by letting a starved lion into Richard's
cell, and thereby shifting the responsibility upon the
beast.   The king, much relieved, gave commands that so it
should be done.   His daughter, however, warned Richard

[17] G. H. Needler, *Richard Cœur de Lion in Literature,* p. 57.

and brought him forty silk handkerchiefs. These he wound about his arm and when the lion rushed at him, thrust it down his gaping throat, and rent out the heart. Walking in triumph to the hall where the king and his court were seated, he calmly salted the bleeding lump of flesh and devoured it before the gasping assemblage.

The feat of tearing out the heart of a lion presents a similarity to the well-known exploits of Samson and David, which are portrayed countless times in medieval art. The first illustration (Fig. 4) of it which I wish to bring forward would naturally be identified as Samson and the lion if it occurred alone. It belongs, however, among the Chertsey Tiles, none of which illustrate Biblical or religious scenes, which do, however, afford at least one other illustration of the romance of Richard, namely, the unhorsing of Saladin with which I have already dealt. I believe, therefore, we are justified in taking this to be Richard, despite the fact that it represents no distinctive details of the story and is much like the conventional portrayals of Samson bestriding the recalcitrant beast.

We can be more certain of our identification in the case of an illumination in the so-called *Peterborough Psalter,* Nos. 9961, 9962 at the Royal Library at Brussels. This manuscript was the product of the monastery at Peterborough and belongs to the end of the thirteenth century. On folio 33 (Fig. 5) there stands in the middle of the text the picture of a crowned, bearded man, with one hand grasping the mane of a lion and thrusting it back on its haunches, and with the other reaching down its throat. Father Van den Gheyn, who edited a very complete series of reproductions from this manuscript in a volume of the *Musée des Enluminures,* in one place explains this as " Samson et le lion," and in another as " David terassant le lion." The first suggestion we may discard at once,

FIG. 4.

FIG. 5.

FIG. 8.

FIG. 6.

FIG. 7.

since Samson was never a crowned king. The case for David derives plausibility from the fact that this illumination occurs in the midst of the Psalms. But David's adventure with the lion took place when he was a boy, before he could boast a beard and long before he wore a crown. In fact, we have on folio 64 of this very MS. a representation of David rescuing the sheep from the lion's mouth, so faithful to the Biblical account as to show that the illuminator could not have been guilty of the blunders which the identification of the picture with David would impute to him. King Richard, then, remains the only likely subject, and I think the arm thrust down the lion's throat a feature I do not remember seeing in any representation of Samson's struggle, conclusive.

A third illustration occurs among the bosses in the cloister of Norwich Cathedral (Fig. 6). These exceedingly interesting bosses have been the subject of a monograph by Mr. M. R. James, the Provost of King's College, Cambridge. The cathedral records show that the north walk in which our boss occurs was built between 1420 and 1428, and give us the names of several workmen employed on it.[18] Mr. James numbers the boss in question VI, 1, and on page 24 suggests that the subject is King Richard. Two peculiar features are here present: the background is composed of trees, and Richard in his upraised hand grasps a dagger. The latter is explained by the fact that according to three MSS. of the romance Richard received not only forty handkerchiefs from the King of Almayn's daughter but also an Irish knife, and while he strangled the lion with the swathed left arm, cut open its breast and took out the heart with his right.[19] The reproduction of

[18] M. R. James's monograph on bosses of Norwich Cathedral cloister, p. vii.
[19] Version b, ll. 1035-1057/44.

these features, in conjunction with the maturity of the man and the crown, justify our overlooking the incongruous background and accepting the figure as Richard.

One striking fact emerges from the consideration of these illustrations of the Lion Heart's triumph over the Saracen and the beast, namely, that save the Clarendon painting, the Chertsey Tiles, and Queen Mary's Psalter, which were probably the work of artists under royal patronage,[20] all the rest are known to have been made in East Anglia, with the exception of the Burgate chest which, since it is now to be found there, has also a claim to having been made in the district. Thus the names, Burgate and Gorleston, in Suffolk, Irnham in South Lincolnshire, Peterborough and Norwich, indicate a special local cult of Richard. Whether to any extent the minstrel who enjoyed the patronage of the two knightly families of South Lincolnshire encouraged and confirmed the cult, whether, as he sang about in ale houses and monastic halls, he infected his fellows of a sister craft with a devotion to the fame of Richard, remains mere matter of conjecture. It is not likely that he met in the flesh any of the particular artists whose illustrations of Richard's feats we know.

IV

Besides these illustrations scattered over the domain of English decorative art, there is also one accompanying the earliest text of the romance (Fig. 7). This is to be found on folio 326 of the famous *Auchinleck Manuscript* in the Advocates' Library, Edinburgh. A galley, bristling with oars and spears, flying banners, approaches a walled city, whose battlements are crowded with armed men. In the

---

[20] Sir George Warner, *Queen Mary's Psalter*, pp. vi f., suggests that the Psalter was destined for Edward I or II.

bow of the galley stands a bearded knight, on whose red surcoat white leopards are distinguishable, grasping a large ax in his hands. Above the illumination is the rubric *King Richard:.* There can be no doubt that this illustrates the following lines from the Auchinleck text as given in *Englische Studien,* VIII, p. 118:

> & king richard þat was so gode
> Wiþ his ax afor schippe stode
> & whan he com ouer þe cheyne
> He smot astrok wiþ miȝt and mayn
> þe cheyne he smot on peces þre
> & boþ endes fel down in þe se.　(ll. 45-50)

V

So far I have dealt with Richard in English literature and English art, and with the evidence there afforded that as a sort of embodiment of bravado and knock-down strength and rough humor he was very dear to the Anglo-Saxon heart. Across the Channel, however, Richard's standing was, to say the least, dubious. When a small boy calls out to another small boy across the back fence "You're a sneak, you're a sissy," the easiest retort is, "No, I'm not. You're a sneak, you're a sissy." So when the English had turned out a romance which through many folio pages called the French and their king traitors and cowards, the French replied in almost identical terms. While Richard is the hero of English accounts of the Third Crusade, Philip is the hero of the French literature ef the same Crusade. In *Jean d'Avesnes* it is Philip who is given the credit of overthrowing Saladin at a tournament at Cambrai, while Richard is exposed as a blustering, quarrelsome adventurer.[21] In other French

---

[21] P. Chabaille's résumé in *Mémoires de la Société d'Emulation d'Abbeville,* 1838-40, p. 477.

poems, however, especially in those originating in the neighborhood of Flanders, Richard is treated more leniently.   In the *Pas Saladin* he is by no means the principal figure, but together with eleven other knights of great prowess he holds a defile into the Holy Land against an invading Saracen host.   Readers of the poem will remember that twelve champions of the Christian army undertake, with the permission of their leader, Philip, to hold a pass against the paynim foe.   Saladin coming up with his army, is held at bay, and many of his chieftains are slain by the redoubtable twelve.   Wondering who can be the cause of the delay, he despatches a spy, Tornevent, who is familiar with the blazonry of the Christian knights, to an eminence overlooking the defile where the fight is raging.   Tornevent scrutinizes closely the shields of the twelve champions, and returns to Saladin to report their names.   The Saracens at last abandon the attempt to force a passage and retreat, while the victorious heroes return to their camp and celebrate in feasting their marvelous exploit.

The short poem of the *Pas Saladin,* belonging to the late thirteenth century, does not represent the first form of the story.   Evidently it had been a current tradition for some time, for the poem itself bears witness that the paintings of the subject were found in many a hall.[22]

---

[22] Gaston Paris in the *Journal des Savants,* 1893, pp. 491-96, elaborates a theory that the literary versions of the *Pas Saladin* were each inspired by pictorial representations, that artists were responsible for the spread of the story, and that writers merely developed independently suggestions afforded by the paintings. He furthermore (p. 492), says that it is probable that those paintings had a very ancient point of departure and had originally represented, perhaps at the instance of Richard himself, his marvelous relief of Jaffa and discomfiture of the Saracen host with the aid of only a few companions. Now, that the several literary versions of the *Pas*

Gaston Paris has pointed out that in the will of the Black
Prince made in 1376 he bequeathes to his son Richard
" une sale darras du pas Saladyn." [23]   We learn from the
records concerning the castle of Valenciennes that in the
same year payment was to be made to " Loys, le pointre,
pour plusieurs ouvrages de pointure qu'il a fait a le Sale,
c'est assavoir le Pas Salehadin, etc." [24]   It has furthermore been frequently pointed out that Froissart has an
elaborate account of a pageant given to celebrate the entry
of Isabel of Bavaria into Paris in 1389, in which the
story of the Pas Saladin was acted out.   Upon a scaffold
" estoit ordonne le pas du roy Salehadin, et touz faiz de
personnages, les chretiens d'une part, et les Sarrazins de
l'autre, et la estoient par personnages tous les seigneurs
de nom qui jadis au pas Salhadin furent, et armoiez de
leurs armes ainsi que pour le temps de adonc ilz s'ar-
moient." [25]   So that we may see that not only the episode

Saladin owe their origin to the exploits of Richard and his ten
knights at Jaffa, Paris has amply demonstrated. But his general
theory that the *motif* was diffused by paintings alone rests on the
slight basis of the references to paintings in the *Pas Saladin;* and
his suggestion that Richard had himself given the order for a painting of the original battle at Jaffa rests upon the incorrect assumption (p. 492, n. 3) that Henry III's commission for the painting at
Clarendon of the *duellum Regis Ricardi* referred to the same battle.
The word *duellum* itself precludes such an identification. Accordingly, while I may not deny that paintings and tapestries played
some part in the diffusion and modification of the story of the *Pas
Saladin*, yet I regard Paris's theory as stretching far beyond the
bounds of ascertained fact, and it is unfortunate that it should have
been repeated with such assurance by Dr. Lodeman in editing the
Pas Saladin. See *Mod. Lang. Notes*, XII, p. 93.

[23] *Journal des Savants*, 1893, p. 491, n. 1. J. Nichols, *Collection of
Wills of Kings and Queens of England*, p. 72.

[24] *Jahrbuch der Kunsthistorischen Sammlungen des Allerhöchsten
Kaiserhauses*, XVI, p. 223. Ch. Dehaisnes, *Documents concernant
l'Histoire de l'Art dans la Flandre*, p. 533.

[25] Froissart, Bk. IV, ch. I.

and the participants were familiar to the artists of the
fourteenth century, but also that a recognized tradition
assigned to each warrior a distinctive heraldic device.
This is confirmed by the fact that in the libraries of Lille,
Valenciennes, and Besançon, manuscripts of the sixteenth
and seventeenth century are found giving the arms of the
heroes of the Pas Saladin.[26]

Furthermore, as an additional proof of their fame, there
is preserved in the Hôtel de Cluny a magnificent carved
chest, made in Northeastern France about the year 1300.
On one end of the chest we see depicted Saladin with his
chivalry (Fig. 8), and we may note the wyvern on his
shield to which I have already alluded in connection with
the Burgate chest. On the left of the design, Tornevent
is perched on a hillock, spear in hand, reporting the names
of the Christian knights. On the front of the chest the
twelve knights themselves appear standing under an ar-
cade (Fig. 9). Unhappily I am not as familiar as Tornevent with medieval heraldry nor have I had access to the
manuscripts aforementioned, so that I cannot read all
their shields with certainty. I am doubtful in particular
as to the identity of the first, sixth, and twelfth figures,
but an identification of the twelve by their family arms
may prove useful until the manuscripts can be consulted.
I give first the numbers of the knights as they stand on
the front of the chest from left to right, then my suggested
identification, then the basis of it in a heraldic blazoning
quoted from an armorial.

I. Hues de Florine. Florins—D'azur à la croix
recercelée d'or au sautoir de gueules brochée sur le tout.
Rietstap, *Armorial Général*, i, p. 682.

II. Bernars de Horstemale. Horstmar—D'or à VII

---

[26] K. Brunner, *Richard Löwenherz*, p. 69.

fasces d'azur au lion de gueules couronné d'or brochant sur le tout. Rietstap, I, p. 991.

III. Tierris de Cleves. Cleves—De gueules à l'écusson d'argent en cœur, au rays d'escarboucle fleurdelisé et pommeté d'or brochant sur le tout. *Gelre's Wappenboek*, ed. V. Bouton, IV, Pl. 124.

IV. Guillaume Longe Espée. F. E. Lodeman in his notes on the *Pas Saladin, Mod. Lang. Notes*, XII, p. 33, is at a loss to know who this William Longsword is. There can be no question that it is the fourth Earl of Salisbury, who distinguished himself in the Seventh Crusade, and in honor of whom an Anglo-Norman romance was written. See *Histoire Littéraire*, XXIII, p. 429. Chronology was obviously nothing to the author of the *Pas Saladin*. The arms of William Longaspata, as recorded by Matthew Paris, *Chronica Majora, Rolls Series*, VI, p. 470, were, azure six lioncels or. Here the carver for lack of space has substituted three lioncels for six.

V. Simon de Monfort. Montfort l'Amaury—Gueules à un lion d'argent rampant à la queue fourchiée. M. Douet D'arcq, *Armorial de France*, p. 8, no. 16.

VI. If all the other identifications be right, this should by the process of elimination be Gofroy de Lasegnon or Lusignan.

VII. Renars de Boulogne. Daumartin—Fessié d'argent et d'asur de VI pièces à une bordeure de gueules. Douet D'arcq, p. 8, no. 19.

VIII. Valerans de Lemborc. Limburg—D'argent au lion de gueules, la queue en sautoir. *Gelre's Wappenboek*, IV, Pl. 158.

IX. Guillaume de Barre. Barres (Auvergne)— Lozengez d'or et de gueules. Douet D'arcq, p. 49, no. 661.

X. Phelippons de Flandres. Flandres—D'or à un lion noir rampant. Douet D'arcq, p. 79, no. 1163.

XI. Roi Richars d'Engleterre.

XII. Gautier de Chastillon. Chatillon—Paalé de vair et de gueules à un chief d'or à une molette d'or ou chief. Douet D'arcq, p. 48, no. 643.

Of Flemish or North French origin, doubtless, are the various tapestries of King Richard mentioned in medieval inventories. An inventory of the tapestries of Richard II made in the year of his death, 1399, mentions "two pec (pieces) de Regi Ricardo." [27] Among the tapestries of Arras work in the possession of John Duke of Berry in 1416 were two " tappis du Roy Richart." [28]

ROGER SHERMAN LOOMIS.

[27] W. G. Thomson, *History of Tapestry*, p. 100.
[28] J. Guiffrey, *Inventaires de Jean Duc de Berry*, II, pp. 209 f.

XVII.—THE MIDDLE ENGLISH *EVANGELIE*

The Middle English metrical paraphrase of the gospel narrative bearing the title *La Estorie del Euangelie* has been printed hitherto only from the fragmentary text in the Vernon MS.[1] Indeed, Horstmann was not aware that any other MS. of this poem existed. In the following pages, the *Evangelie* is printed from two additional MSS.:[2] (1) a fragment of 519 lines in Dulwich Coll. MS. XXII (*D*), which Sir George Warner dates about 1300, and (2) a complete text from Bodl. MS. Add. C 38 (*B*), which according to Mr. Madan was written between 1410 and 1420.

The Dulwich fragment—seventy years earlier than the Vernon MS. (*V*)—is particularly important, since it pushes back the composition of the poem to a date before the beginning of the fourteenth century. The Bodleian MS. also, though later than the Vernon by forty or fifty years, is indispensable for the reason that it is the only MS. in which the narrative is completed.[3] Comparison of

---

[1] Printed by Horstmann, with introduction, in *Engl. Stud.* VIII, pp. 254-259; also in *Minor Poems of the Vernon* MS., EETS. XCVIII, pp. 1-11.

[2] These MSS. were called to my attention by Professor Carleton Brown, who also kindly placed at my disposal rotographs of the text in the Dulwich MS.

[3] The title of *V* indicates the complete scope of the poem as follows (EETS. XCVIII, p. 1; cf. also the English index to the Vernon MS., *ibid.*, p. 11, note) : " I ceste liuere est escrit la estorie del Euangelie en engleis solum ceo ke ele est escrit en latin, et continue de la Anunciacion nostre seignour Ihesu crist. De la Natiuite benette. De sa Passion. De sa Resurexion. De sa Ascension e de sa Glorificacion. Et de soun Auenement a Jugement et de nostre presentement en cors en alme."

the three MSS., however, shows that B and V present **an**
abridged text; if the scale of D had been followed in B,
we should have a poem of some 3000 lines.

I.   DESCRIPTION OF THE MSS.

Dulwich Coll. MS. XXII is described in the Catalogue [4]
as follows: "Vellum.   Small·quarto. . . .   Theological
Tracts and other pieces in prose and verse, in different
hands of the thirteenth and fourteenth centuries. . . .
[Art. No. 9, ff. 81 b-84 b.]   Poem on the Life of Christ
in *English:* a fragment, containing the first 519 lines.
Written, about 1300, on part of a quire (the two outside
leaves of which are lost) originally forming part of another MS.   The first three pages remaining (ff. 80-81)
contain the end of some theological treatise, notes on the
plagues of Egypt, etc., in *Latin.*"   The pages of this inserted quire are about 14 x 18 cm., having been trimmed
along the outer margin so closely that in some cases letters
of the text are cut off.   At the bottom of fol. 84 b, a seventeenth-century hand has written the words *Carolus Carolus dei gratia Anglie R.*   On the lower part of the pages
is a blot or stain, diminishing in size and intensity from
fol. 81 to fol. 84.   The poem is written in double columns,
from 30 to 41 lines to the column.   The Latin passages
are rubricated.   The initial letter of each line is colored
and slightly separated from the rest of the line.   Space is
left at the beginning of each stanza for an illuminated
initial, and a small letter is usually written far out at the
left as a guide to the illuminator.   The same symbol,
occasionally dotted, is used for y and $\wp$.[5]   The original

---

[4] *Catalogue of the Manuscripts and Muniments of Alleyn's College
of God's Gift at Dulwich,* by George F. Warner, 1881, I, pp. 344-5.
[5] *Y* is dotted in *day* 18, *y* 34, *may* 38, *day* 49, *may* 70, *inewardly*

hand has added a number of corrections, which consist chiefly in the insertion of words or letters above the line.

Bodl. MS. Add. C 38 is thus described in the *Summary Catalogue:* [6] " in English, on parchment: written about A. D. 1410-20: 11⅜ x 7⅞ in., i + 121 leaves: with an illuminated border and capitals: stained in parts and imperfect at end. Part of an English Festial, [*i. e.,* the South English Legendary] containing Lives of Saints, &c., in English verse, in the order of the calendar from Dec. 25 to May 26 (St. Augustine): the first, on the Nativity, *beg.* ' Nou blometh the nuwe frute that late bigan to sprynge ': about forty-two Lives in all: *ends* with the 35th line of the Life of St. Augustine ' receyued hem faire ynough.' " The *Evangelie,* which stands as Art. 26 in the MS. under the title *Novum Testamentum* (ff. 71 b-82 a), is preceded by the legend of St. Benedict (March 21) and followed by verses on the Feast of the Annunciation (March 25).[7] Like the other pieces in the collection, it is written in single column, from 40 to 46 lines to the page, each line, as a rule, containing the two verses of an original couplet. The Latin is not rubricated.

The following table shows the line correspondences be- tween *DB* and V. In the following study, the line refer- ences are to *DB* unless otherwise specified.

89, *may* 125, *may* 160, *syhende* 375, *fleschly* 385, *lay* 404, *may* 407, *eye* 462, *hye* 518. þ is dotted in þi 13, þat 20, þouht 27, þat 30, þe 36, þe 39, þere 67, þar-inne 86, þouru 388.

[6] *Summary Catalogue of Western MSS. in the Bodleian Library,* F. Madan, Oxford, 1905, v, p. 764.

[7] For the relationship of such poems as the *Evangelie* to the South English Legendary, cf. *The Early South English Legendary,* ed. Horstmann, EETS. LXXXVII, Introd., pp. vii-viii.

DB	V	DB	V
1–12	1–12	345–379	177–211
15–68	13–66	380–395	213–228
145–150	67–72	398–429	229–260
189–206	73–100	431–433	261–263
221–268	101–148	466–477	293–324
283–296	149–162	482–487	325–330
300a–d	163–166	492–493	331–332
301–304	167–170	498	333
311–328	275–292	501–503	334–336
329–336	264–274	504	338
337–341	171–175	508–519	339–350
343	176	520–565	351–396

II. RELATIONSHIP OF THE TEXTS

Neither V nor B, the later texts, can derive from D, as both agree in preserving a good reading in 373-377, where D is corrupt. V and B also agree in the disarrangement of material at 311, 329, and 433,[8] and in the insertion of an extra stanza (300 a-d) to patch up the resulting chronological disarrangement. Finally, V and B agree against D in a number of less significant readings: e. g., 5, 46, 65-6, 329-32, etc.

On the other hand, B cannot derive from V, since it agrees with D against V in several readings, of which the most important are DB 318 (V 282), and DB 430-1 (V 261).[9] The character of the divergences in V seems to indicate oral transmission at some point in its descent.

---

[8] D follows the story in Luke in the following order: (a) annunciation and conception 224-82, Luke i, 26-37; (b) visit to Elizabeth 283-336, Luke i, 38-56; (c) St. John's birth and naming 337-445, Luke i, 6-25, 58-77; (d) Mary's return 446-9, Luke i, 56. V and B insert (c) in the midst of (b), after Elizabeth's greeting 283-310, and follow it by the account of Mary's stay 329a-336, and the Magnificat 311-29.

[9] $\dot{D}$ 318, þat is of mihte to leyse ant binde; B þat mightful is to lese & bynde; V 282, þat mihtful is to lame and blynde. DB 430-1, Of gret mihte scal be þi speche / To godis folc þou schalt preche; V 261, þis speche to godus folc þou schalt preche.

Finally, *D* and *V,* as might be expected, agree against
B in many readings where the later text has substituted
Romance for Scandinavian words, or more modern for
archaic forms: *e. g., DV fele* 16, 61, 255, etc., *B many;
DV al-swonge* 324, *B ydel gonge; DV pynis* 6, *B peynes;*
etc. *D* and *V* agree against *B* in numerous other cases,
notably wherever the latter transposes the lines of a couplet; *e. g.,* 24-5, 293-4, 364-5, etc.

In addition to these three texts, portions of the *Evangelie* are incorporated in a text of the *Northern Passion*
in MS. Rawlinson C 655 (*R*), a MS. described by Dr. Foster as " written in the South of England, perhaps at Wells,
about the middle of the fourteenth century. . . ." [10]   *R*
contains several interpolations, in particular an account
of the baptism, temptation, and preaching of Christ, forming an introduction to the *Passion* proper, and an account
of the thieves at the Crucifixion. Besides these, *R* contains other interpolated lines and passages which also may
have been taken from the *Evangelie,* but are not in the
extant texts. Unfortunately, the text of *R,* although older
than either *V* or *B,* is extremely corrupt.

The following table shows the line correspondence between *B* and *R.*

B	*R*
821–2	184ʹ–5ʹ
855–6	19ʹ–20ʹ
857–934	23ʹ–100ʹ
937–1020	101ʹ–184ʹ
1023–1028	5ʹ–10ʹ
1536–1547	1714c–n
1548–9	1714s–t
1556–1563	1792a–h
1584–1591	1808a–h

[10] *The Northern Passion,* ed. Miss F. A. Foster, *Introduction,*
Bryn Mawr diss., 1913, p. 10.

III. Sources

Although the main source of the poem is of course the gospel narrative of the life of Christ, it is evident from the freedom shown in the arrangement of the Latin rubrics and of the English narrative that the author did not draw directly from the Vulgate text, but used as his immediate source some compilation of the Biblical material. This compilation may have been a Gospel Harmony, like Victor of Capua's and Clement of Llanthony's, or it may have been a breviary. In the latter case the homiletical material may have been already combined with the narrative. In either case, the story shows some curious omissions. Of the events of the Ministry, only the Sermon on the Mount is related; of the events of the Passion, the Last Supper is not mentioned, nor the cutting off of Malchus's ear, nor the service rendered by Simon the Cyrenean in bearing the Cross—incidents which would naturally be included in any Harmony or compilation. I have been unable to find any compilation which presents the material in the form which we find here.

To the gospel narrative is added apocryphal and homiletical material from various sources. The apocryphal incidents are few—Herod's journey to Rome and burning of the ships at Cilicia (753-761), the downfall of the idols in Egypt at the coming of the infant Jesus (774-783), and the presence of the devil at the Crucifixion (1584-7). Since all this is found in Peter Comestor, who is specifically cited as the source for at least one other passage (*D* 461), it is probable that Comestor, and not the Apocryphal Gospels, was the immediate source.

The material on the hart (69-102), the serpent (103-130), and the eagle (131-170), with the accompanying moralizations, is of a type familiar from the Latin *Physi-*

ologus and the *Middle English Bestiary;* [11] to the latter work, which was probably contemporary with the original of the *Evangelie,* these passages show some resemblance in content, though not in phraseology. Parallels of content are also to be found in various Latin bestiaries, notably in *De Bestiis et Aliis Rebus* ascribed to Hugo de Folieto. The form in which the material appears here, however, indicates that it has been independently derived from Augustine's *Commentaries on the Psalms;* [12] and slight divergences from Augustine in the moralizations, as well as the incorrect ascription to Isidore (*D* 72), point to an intermediate source.

The homiletic passages are based ultimately on the Church Fathers, though the variety of the sources quoted [13] and occasional inaccuracies indicate that the author was using some compilation and giving references at second-hand. If this be the case, the compilation which served as the source can hardly have been composed earlier than the beginning of the 13th century, as appears from a reference at *D* 198 to " Martinus," who is evidently Martinus Legionensis (d. 1203).[14]

---

[11] For discussion of the relationships of these works to one another and to Augustine, see Lauchert, *Geschichte des Physiologus*, Strassburg, 1889, pp. 77-79.

[12] See Notes on these passages.

[13] The citations include *Ysydorus 72, philosophus libro de animalibus* 130, *Boethius libro consolationis* 142, *Martinus in sermone quodam* 198, *Augustinus* 220, *Beda in glossa* 336, *Beda predicator* 446, *cantor* 439, *magister in historiarum glossa* 462, *historiarum* 503; besides anonymous references at 14, 198, 268, 282, 469, and references in the text of B to *Seint Austyn* 1549, *Bede* 1286, *Jerome* 527, 1271, *Bernard* 943, *Anselm* 1789. The majority of these defy identification; see Notes.

[14] See note on *D* 198, *infra*, p. 611; for Martinus, cf. *Catholic Encyclopedia*, art. *Martin of Leon*.

IV. DIALECT

(I) *The Dialect of D.*—The dialect of *D* is obscured by certain orthographical peculiarities, some of which are due to the scribe and others possibly to his original. Among the former are several which occur also in *Havelok,* where Skeat [15] explains them as mistakes made by an Anglo-French scribe who was writing in an unfamiliar dialect. In the present MS., this explanation would account also for the large number of corrections and for the confusion in the dotting of *y* and *þ*.[16] That the scribe, moreover, was not only unfamiliar with the dialect of his original, but was also exceptionally illiterate, is evident from the mistakes made by him in copying the Latin rubrics.[17]

a) Initial *h* is omitted:[18] *este* 202.

b) Inorganic *h* is inserted: [19] *hold* 80, 103, *holde* 85, *ohld* 367; *herþe* 106; *heue* 152; *his* 77, 175, 485.

c) Guttural *h* before *t* is transposed or omitted: *þot* 11, *þoutis* 15, *þouthe: wroute: broute: bouhte* 171-4, *þout: wrouht: to-brouht: nouht* 265-8, *broute: þoute: rouhte: wrouhte* 410-13, *lith: nowiht* 83-4, *lithte: in-sihte* 169-70, *mihte: lithe* 271-2, *nouth: brouht: bi-souht: wrouht* 352-6, *nohut* 381, *brouth* 397, *ritte* corrected to *rihte* 43, etc. This confusion is common in East Midland texts of this period.[20]

[15] *Havelok,* ed. Skeat, Oxford, 1902, p. x.

[16] For other examples of this confusion in the dotting of *y* and *þ,* cf. Heuser's comments on MS. Bodl. 425, in *Anglia* XXIX, p. 395.

[17] *E. g.,* at *D* 198 *lumbum* is written for *limbum, infirnum* for *infernum, signum* for *sinum.* The more usual error consists in the omission of letters; all these cases are noted in the printed text.

[18] Cf. *Havelok* 2254, *is* for *his;* ed. Skeat, EETS., p. iv.

[19] Cf. *Havelok,* ed. cit., Glossary under *olde, ende, be.*

[20] For other examples, cf. Foerster, *A 13th-century Dream-book from MS. Harl. 2253,* in Herrig's *Archiv,* XIX, p. 36, note.

d) O. E. *hw,* where it is not represented by the South-ern *w,* $>$ *w* . . . *h:* [21] *wahm* 32, *waht* 411, *wihlc* 124, *woh* 64, *wehn* 69, 92, 131, 168, 174, *vehn* 103, *wihl* 185; *weher* 218, *wehr* 220, are for Northern *wher,* A. S. *hwæþer.*

e) *Z* stands for medial *r* in *i-chozin* 250 (r. w. *borin, bi-forin, lorin*)*;* for final *th* in *soz* 363, *moniz* 330; fre-quently for final *s,* as in *eggiz* 24, *bi-houiz* 32, *giuiz* 50, etc.

f) Note *foulh* 55, *fuhl* 139, *fouhl* 149, *foul* 155, for A. S. *fugel; wiht* (= *with*) 197, 227, 456, 462; *trouhe* 298; *buth* [22] 158; *cham* [23] 450. A. S. *cild* appears once as *schild* 357, once as *gildre* (pl.) [24] 154. *Il* 145 is for *ilk.* [25]

The language of *D* shows an East Midland dialect, with some Southern forms and with very distinct Northern traces, especially in the forms of the pronouns. The con-fusion in dialect and orthography is such as might result from the efforts of a foreign scribe to copy a Northern MS. into an East Midland dialect.

a) O. E. *a* $>$ *o: sore* 10, *non* 31, *olde* 41, *no* 45, *ston* 46, etc. Exc: *a* stands in *gastis* 491, *fra* 58, 240, 489, *fram* 320, 384, *mare: lare* 330, 332 (r. w. *kare* 331), *nammare: sare* 374-5 (r. w. *þare: ware*).

O. E. *a* $+$ *h* $>$ *auh* in *sauh* 335, 350, 462: elsewhere *saw* 347.

---

[21] For similar instances from Layamon and *M. E. Genesis and Exodus* of inorganic *h* due to French scribes, cf. Diehn, *Die Prono-mina im Frühmittelenglischen, Kieler Stud. zur engl. Philol.* I, Heidel-berg, 1901, p. 45.

[22] Cf. *Havelok* 752, *neth,* and Skeat's remark in ed. Oxford, 1902, Introd., p. xiii.

[23] Cf. *Havelok* 1873.

[24] This may, however, be dialectical; cf. Note on *D* 154.

[25] Cf. *Havelok* 218, 1644, and ed. Oxford 1902, Introd., p. xii.

O. E. $a + w > ou$: *soule* 101, 169, *soulis* 199, 226, *outhir* 465.

b) O. E. *æ* before $r > a$ in *ar* 335, *ware* 376, *þare* (*þar*) 28, 36, 60, 86, 171, 198, 268, 274, 306, 315, 373, 383, 408, 438, 466. Elsewhere *æ* before $r > e$: *er* 80, 270, etc., *were* 15, 51, etc., *þere* (*þer*) 56, 267, 301, 404, 413.

c) O. E. $ea > o$ in *oc* 442, a form found in the East Midland texts *Gen. and Ex., M. E. Bestiary,* and *Have-lok.*[26]

d) *C* and *g* are not palatalized: *seke* 71, *swink: drinke* 75-6, *brekis* 135, 166, *fullic* 335, 457, etc.

e) 2nd sg. pres. ind. of the verb ends in *-ist:* 3rd sg. and pl. in *-s, -z,* except *abide* (pl.) 326.

Preterites of strong verbs are without personal endings, except *comin* 401, which may be taken as a pret. part.

Note *longyt* 10, *bi-fellit* (pret.) 472, *blessit* (pret. part.) 296.

f) The 3rd sg. and pl. of pret. pres. verbs are alike: *may* (sg.) 60, 106, etc., (pl.) 38; *schal* (sg.) 87, 95, etc., (pl.) 37, 220, etc.

g) The pret. part. of strong verbs usually retains the *n: drunkin* 78, *bundin* 115, 119, 182, *ileyn* 86, *istungin* 94, etc. Exc.: *i-bunde* 1, (r. w. *grunde*), *i-write* 68, 144, 305, *i-funde* 298 (r. w. *stunde*), *vndir-fonge* 325 (r. w. *al-swonge*).

h) Note the Northern contracted forms *ta* (*inf.*) 139, *maz* 124, *mas* 306; also the noun *clos* (pl.) 79.

i) The pronouns are Northern, with occasional South-ern forms, and with *w* or *wh* for O. E. *hw* in the rel. and interr. forms. 1st sg. nom. *i* 1, 5, 12, etc.; *y* 34, 171; *ic* 293; *ich* 367. 2nd sg. nom. *þou* 11, 14, 20, etc; *þo* 493;

[26] Cf. Björkmann, *Scandinavian Loan Words in M. E.;* Morsbach's *Studien für engl. Philol.* vii, p. 72, note 1.

woldistu 209, *als tu* 264, *þat tu* 369. 2nd sg. obj. *þe* 5, 8, 9, etc.; *dred te* 353. 2nd sg. poss. *þi* 7, 13, 20, etc.; *þin* 10, 161, 166, 168; *þine* 3. 3rd sg. nom. fem. *scho* 132, 134, 135, 138, 163, 263, 404, 449, 461, 463; *sco* 291, 332, 334, 335, 393, 394, 395, 396, 450, 453; *scha* 258. 3rd sg. poss. masc. *his* 63, 79, etc.; *hise* 88, 129, 140; *is* 128, 236, 420. 1st pl. obj. *vs* 32, 143, 210, 218; *us* 173, 174; *ws* 206. 1st pl. poss. *vr* 276. 3rd pl. nom. *þei* 37, 45, etc.; *þe* 401, 402. 3rd pl. obj. *þeim* 153, 429, 432, 443, 489, 505; *þem* 43; *þeym* 46; *hem* 68, 240. 3rd. pl. poss. *þeire* 158, 240, 316, 399, 429; *þere* 44, 67, 217, 346; *þer* 201; *here* 409. Rel. and interr. *woh* 59; *wahm* 32, *wam* 337; *wat* 182, *waht* 411; *wihlc* 124.

j) *Til,* prep., stands at 225, 475, 477.

(II) *The Dialect of B.*—B is a South Midland text, from a region further south than the home of the original.

a) Pres. 3rd sg. and pl. and impv. pl. of verbs end in -(e)*th* where the original had -*es*. 3rd sg. *hath* 2, 7, 8, 256, etc. (pl. *han* 4, *haue* 488), *greueth* 6, *eggeth* 25, *herith* 59, *gyueth* 145, etc.; but note *drawes* 1309 (r. w. *lawes*). 3rd pl. *doeth* 406; but note *lede* 1210 (read *ledes,* r. w. *dedes*). Impv. pl. *goeth* 634, *takith* 1009, *wakith and beeth* 1113, etc.

The inf. ends once in *n: comen* 570.

Occasional syncopated verb forms occur: *hath* 2, 7, 8, etc.; *had* 184, 194, 222, etc.; *lost* 186; *made* 42, 46, etc.; but *maked* 608.

b) The pronouns show Midland and Southern forms. 1st sg. nom. *i* 1, 5, 12, etc. 3rd sg. nom. fem. *she* 258, 291, 300 c, etc. 3rd pl. nom. *þei* 45, 48, 51, etc. 3rd pl. obj. *hem* 43, 46, 68, etc. 3rd pl. poss. *her* 44, 51, 67, etc. Rel. nom. *who* 59, 977, etc.; obj. *wham* 32, 536, 838, etc.

c) *Oe* stands for *ō* in *wroeth* 1854, and throughout the text in *goed,* O. E. *gōd* (adj.).[27]

d) Note the Southern forms *hielde* 48, 1144, 1563, etc., beside *helde* 501; *deeth* when not in rhyme (orig. *dēd*), 7, 751, 1078, etc.

The following forms indicate the Southwest rather than the Southeast Midland.

a) *U* occasionally stands in final syllables: *hungur* 823, 1817, *custum* 1355, *drunkun* 1787, *vndrun* 1788.

b) *Gh* before *t* represents guttural *ʒ*: *thoght* 5, *noght* 6, *broght* 7, *wroght* 8, etc.

c) The form *thenke* (A. S. *þencan*) 12, 1011, 1530, etc., would be *thinke* at this date in the Southeast.[28] The unpalatalized *k* is doubtless due to Northern descent, as the other poems in the MS. have *thenche.*

d) Note *þulke* 686, *truvth* 941.

The following evidence indicates descent from a Northern or North Midland text.

a) *Thenke;* see above.

b) Pret. pres. verbs form Northern plurals, with the same root-vowel as the sg. Exc.: *gun* 652, 1705, *shul* 668, 868, 941, 1356, 1805, 1834, *witen* 1280, *wite* 1390, *mowe* 1464.[29]

---

[27] The spelling *goed* is apparently used to distinguish *gōd* from *gŏd;* it is found in the North Yorkshire text of Hampole's *Commentary on the Psalter,* preserved in MS. Univ. Coll. LXIV, of the 15th cent.; cf. Bramley's ed. of the *Psalter,* Oxford, 1884, and Skeat's note, p. 527. The spelling is also found in MS. Digby 86, where both spellings are used for both words; cf. *Middle English Humorous Tales in Verse,* ed. McKnight, Belles Lettres Series, 1913; Glossary s. *god.*

[28] Cf. Van der Gaaf, The transition from the impersonal to the personal construction in Middle English, *Anglistische Forschungen* XIV (1904), pp. 77 ff.

[29] With the exception of *shul* 1356, *mowe* 1464, and *gun* 1705,

(III) *The Dialect of V.*—The Vernon MS. is written in a Southern dialect, with traces of West Midland influence.[30]

(IV) *The Dialect of R.*—According to Miss Foster,[31] this MS. was written " in the South of England, perhaps at Wells, about the middle of the 14th century," and is descended from a lost MS., probably written in the North as early as the first half of the 14th century. The dialect is Southwestern, with West Midland peculiarities possibly due to an earlier scribe.

(V) *The Dialect of the Original.*—The rhyme forms point to an East Midland original, and this evidence is strengthened by the large number of Scandinavian loanwords found in *D,* the oldest text. Since the rhymes show

these Southern plurals stand in glossarial and homiletic passages which could have been easily inserted or omitted at the pleasure of the scribe; cf. the bestiary passages in *D.* If these passages were interpolated, however, the source cannot have been another poem, as portions of these passages are included in *R.* Moreover, *R,* although a Southern text, has the Northern pl. *schal* 105, where *B* has *shul;* these passages, therefore, must have stood in Northern dialect in the original of *R.* That the scribe of *B* had two MSS. before him appears from the error in the account of Jesus' baptism by John, 825-868, where 825-836 are repeated as 843-854, with textual changes in 828 and 834 which show that the scribe did not merely repeat from the same MS. but must have copied the same passage from two different MSS. with slightly different readings. The presence of the Southern plurals may be accounted for on the supposition that the first MS., the basis of B, was a Northern text, in a condensed form similar to *V,* without the homiletical passages, and that the second MS. was a Southern text in an expanded form, from which the scribe inserted the didatic and other passages in their proper places.

[30] For a detailed study of the dialect of the Vernon MS., cf. J. Schipper, *Englische Alexius-legenden,* in *Quellen und Forschungen,* XX, 1877.

[31] *The Northern Passion, ed. cit.,* Introd., pp. 10, 24, 38-39. For a detailed study of the dialect of *R,* see pp. 24-26.

a marked absence of such Northern characteristics as the present participle in *-and* found in Robert of Brunne, and the North Midland *o* for O. E. *æ* before *r* found in *Havelok,* it is probable that the poem was composed somewhat further south than those works.

a) O. E. *a*> *o*: *euirlkon* 193 (r. w. *jon*: *salamon*: *won*), *anon*: *gon*: *on*: *non* 257-260, *þo*: *go*: *wo*: *mo* 392-5, *non*: *jon* 408-9; etc. *A* stands in rhyme with proper names in *Iuda*: *fra* 624-5, *alane*: *Baraban* 1361-2.

b) O. E. *a* + *w* >*aw*: *lawe*: *slawe* 1526-27, *felawe*: *sawe* (noun) 1544-5.

c) O. E. *a/o* before a single nasal > *a*: *man*: *bigan* 871-2, *þam*: *man* 1265-6, *bynam*: *man* 1293-4, *man*: *þan* 1389-90, *þanne*: *man* 1592-3.

d) O. E. *a/o* before nasal + *e* > *a*: *name*: *blame*: *fame*: *scame* 341-4, *blame*: *shame* 1422-3.

e) O. E. *æ* before *r* > *e* in *were, a* in *þare*: *preiere*: *were* 1109-10, 1496-7, *were*: *eere* 1231-2, *eer*: *were* 1381-2, *were*: *bere* 688-9, 1369-70, 1636-7, *bysmer*: *were* 1783-4; *fare*: *þare* 758-9, *care*: *þare* 1709-10, 1872-3. Exc.: *þere*: *were* 690-1.

f) O. E. *i, y* remains *i*: *blisse*: *kisse*: *wisse*: *misse* 9-12, *winne*: *biginne*: *sinne*: *inne* 179-82, etc.

g) O. E. *c, g* are palatalized: *leche*: *spreche*: *wreche*: *reche* 319-22, *speche*: *spuse-breche*: *bi-teche*: *wreche* 466-9, *leche*: *eche* (v.) 885-6, etc. Note *biswiche* 1839, r. w. *riche;* the form is elsewhere found unpalatalized even in Southern texts such as the *Ancren Riwle;* neither Mätzner's *Sprachproben* nor the *N. E. D.* gives an example of the palatalized form.

h) Inflectional *n* is dropped, except in monosyllabic infinitives: *drede* (inf.): *quede*: *lede* (inf.): *dede* 23-6, *lede* (inf.): *dede* 43-4, etc. Exc.: *gon* (inf.) 416 (r. w. *a-non*: *ion*: *on*), 478 (r. w. *a-non*).

i) The pres. 3rd sg. and pl. of the verb end in -es: dedes: lede (3rd pl.; read ledes for rhyme) 1209-10, drawes (3rd sg.): lawes 1309-10.

j) The subst. pl. ends in -s or -e, except three monosyllabic plurals in -n: walles: palles 538-9; [32] ʒere (pl.): fere (sg.) 255-6, þinge (pl., r. w. metinge: kissinge: wendingge) 301, etc. Exc.: fons: home 766-7, gone: fone 812-3, stone: tone 899-900.

k) The pres. part. ends in -ende; in all cases the rhyme has been destroyed by the substitution of -ing in B: wende: tiding (read tidende) 550-1, ende: wende: thanking (read thankende): sende 582-5, comyng: went (read comende: wende) 1031-2.[33]

V. Genealogy of the Texts

A poem of the character of the Evangelie would in all likelihood enjoy great popularity and a correspondingly wide circulation; there were probably many versions, both oral and written, and consequently a considerable amount of contamination. It is, therefore, impossible to determine the genealogy of the three extant texts with any precision; the appended diagram is intended to indicate merely the most obvious relationships.

---

[32] The reading palles, however, is found only in B; V reads "Heo leyden him in Bestes stalles," which may be the original reading.

[33] Another example of this change of final de to t, destroying the syntax, is found in biwent: shent (inf.) 736-7; read biwende : shende.

z^1

B

B

EXPLANATION

x. East Midland original, of the latter half of the 13th century(?).

x^1. Northern text, immediate ancestor of D.

D. Dulwich text, written c. 1300 by a Norman scribe.

y. Text with displaced material, ancestor of V and B, and possibly R(?).

y^1. Oral version, ancestor of V.

V. Vernon text, c. 1370.

z. Text with homiletical passages, Northern ancestor of R.

R. Rawlinson interpolations, middle of 14th century.

z^1. Text with homiletical passages, Southern ancestor of B(?).

y^2. Text without homiletical passages, Northern ancestor of B(?).

B. Bodleian text, c. 1420.

VI. Texts of the Middle English *EVANGELIE*

N. B.   In printing the texts, I number the lines after *D,* as far as it goes.   The lines of *B* are restored to couplet form.   The punctuation is that of the MSS., except the hyphens.   The capitalization is that of the MSS.   Where a small letter stands in *D* as a guide for the illuminator, it is printed in parentheses; where the small letter is lacking, the initial is supplied in brackets.

DULWICH COLL. MS. XXII	BODL. MS. ADD. C 38
[S]Um wyle i was wyt sinne ibunde	Sum tyme i was with loue boundeȝ [fol. 71 b]
Ant sinne me hauid cast to grunde	& synne me hath kest to grounde/
Bot swete iħu þine fif wundis.	But suete iħu þi woundesȝ
Lesid me hauis of harde stundis.	han losed me of harde stoundes /
5 Se hu i to þe wende mi þouht.	When i to þe turne my thoghtȝ
Pynis to þole greuis me nouht.	peynes to sofir greueth me noght/
þi ded me hauis of serue al brouht.	þi deeth me hath out of sorwe broghtȝ
Ant loue to þe in me hauis wrouht.	& loue to þe in me hath wroght /
þe to loue is al mi blisse.	þe to loue is al my blisseȝ
10 Me longyt sore þin wndis kisse	me longeth sore þi woundes to kisse/
Swete iħu mi þot þou wisseȝ	Suete iħu my thought þou wisseȝ
þe to loue þat i ne¹ misse.	on þe to thenke þat i ne mysse /
Do me² iħu aftir þi name.	
þat þou me schilde from sinne ant schame.	

¹ MS., *ine* as one word.   ² MS., *Dome* as one word.
³ MS., title in margin opp. v. 1. *Nouum testamentum/ domini nostri ihasu christi./*

8

DULWICH COLL. MS. XXII   BODL. MS. ADD. C 38

Ihu ihu propter hoc
nomen / tuum Fac michi
secundum hoc nomen /
tuum. nomen dulce. nomen
delectabile. nomen / con-
fortans peccatorem ihu
saluator propter temet
ipsum/ esto/ in ihc ne
peream./

15 [F]Ole þoutis me were   ffoule thoughtes were wont to
        inwnid to tille   tiller
    Fele sithis to don ille.   many tymes to do ille/ ·
    In word. *in* dede. in wikke   Ageyn my soule & goddes willer
        wille.
    Nicht ant day al me to   night & day al me to spille/
        spille.
    [B]ot ᵣwan⁴ þat i me*   But when i me vndirstoder
        vndir-stod.
20 þat þou for me scheddist   þat þou for me shaddest þi blode/
        þi blod.
    Folye to lete me þouhte   ffolie to leef me thoght goedᵧ
        god.
    Ant to þe iħu torne mi   & to þe iħu turne al my mode/
        mod.

    i. petri. quia aduersarius
    noster diabolus / circumit
    querens quem deuoret. [I
    Peter v, 8]

    [B]Ote þat i me bi-gan to   But ȝit i me bigan to dreder
        drede.
    þat he þat man eggiz to   þat sum foule thought wolde me
        quede.   lede/
25 Wyt sum fol þot me   Thorou him þat eggeth man to
        scholde lede.   queeder
    To wicke wille. or folye   to wikked wille or to folie dede/
        dede.

⁴ MS., two letters erased after *wan; hu*(?) faintly legible.
⁵ MS., *ime* as one word.

DULWICH COLL. MS. XXII   BODL. MS. ADD. C 38

95 Ant þouru þat drink he
      schal biginne
    A new lif and leue sinne
    Dauid [14] þe king of þis
      drinkinge.
    In his sauter þan makis
      muninge
    Alse þe hert he seiz ne wil
      nouht dwel[le]
100 þat ȝerniz watir of þe
      welle.
    Aswo [15] þe soule þat is in
      me.
    Hauiz ȝerning iesu to þe.

    *Sicut   ceruus   fontes
    aquarum   ita   desiderat/
    anima   mea   ad   te   deus
    [Ps. xli, 2] & in ysaya
    xii./   Haurite   aquas   in
    gaudio de fonti/bus salu-
    atoris/ [Is. xii, 3]*

    (þ)e neddre vehn he is
      hold bi-comin.
    þat his mihte is him bi-
      -nomin.
105 Ant hard an streit . . .[16]
      is his hide.
    þat he ne may on herþe
      glideʔ
    He sekis ouiral a-non
    Til þat he finde a þirlid
      ston.
    (a)nt þoru þat he crepiz
      ofte.

[14] MS., *d* written at the left of the line for insertion.

[15] *? alswo.*

[16] The stain here in the MS. renders three letters illegible; possibly *mad.*

DULWICH COLL. MS. XXII   BODL. MS. ADD. C 38

110 Til þat his hide bicome al
    softe. [fol. 82 b, col 1]
    Ant til þat he a-wey al
    caste.
    His olde skin þat him
    bond faste.
    Ant newe bi-ginnis vp to
    rise.
    Ant ȝung bi-comiz vp-on
    þis wise.
115 [þ]E skin þat þe neddre is
    bundin inne
    Is old liking of mannis
    sinne
    þat lettis man wel for to
    spede.
    In eni god werc or eni god
    dede.
    [F]or-þi man bundin wyt
    sinne.
120 þat wile a neu lif bi-ginne.
    Wel he may forbisine take.
    Of þe neddre ant of þe
    snake.
    Ant seke þe ston til he
    finde
    Of wihlc þe apostil paul
    maz minde.
125 þat is þe ston þat we may
    se.
    þirlid on þe rode tre.

    petra autem erat x̄p̄o.
  cor. x./ [I Cor. x, 4]

    [þ]e sinful schal þoreu þo
    þirlis crepe.
    And so is olde s[i]nnis
    wepe.
    And sore for hise dedis
    rewe.
130 Ant so bi-ginne his lif al
    newe.

DULWICH COLL. MS. XXII

BODL. MS. ADD. C 38

aquila ut dicit philoso-
phus libro de animalibus
& etiam in glossa super/
psalmo dicitur senio gra-
uatur crescente rostro ut/
possit cibum capere: sed
inde languescit. Sed/ na-
turali modo colidit ros-
trum collidit rostrum/ ad
petram & excuti[t] rostri
honus quo cibus impe/-
diebatur & redit ad cibum
& omnia reperiebuntur/ ut
ut fiat/ iuue/ nis./

(þ)E erne wehn is with
    eld of gon.
þat scho ne may mete take
    non.
Hire bile oi-ginnis hard to
    clinge.
þat scho ne mai liue wit
    no likinge.
135 Agenis a ston scho brekis
    hire bile.
þoureu kinde ant þoreu
    non oþir skille.
Ant þat er was old ant of
    vn-mihte.
þan may scho ete ant take
    hire flihte.
(o)f best of fuhl. man
    schal ta ȝeme.
140 And hise dedis alle deme.
þat he in him no þing ne
    finde.
þat be wrout agenis his
    kinde.

boecius libro consola-
tionis dicit quod omni ho-
mini naturaliter in serta/
est boni/ cupiditas./ [Bk.
III, Prose ii]

DULWICH COLL. MS. XXII   BODL. MS. ADD. C 38

(a)nt a wis man vs dos
to wite.

Alse we of him finde
iwrite.

145 þat kinde giuez il man   þat kynde gyueth iche man egg-
eginge.   yng؟

Of god þing to haue ȝer-   .of iche goed thing to haue desir-
ninge.   yng/

(b)ot betir þing mai no   But bettir thing may no man
man finde.   fynde؟

þan þe louerd of alle kinde.   þan þe lord of al kynde/

þat best ant fouhl ant alle   þat beest & al thing dight؟
þinge dihte.

150 To be vndir mannis mihte. at wille to be vnder mannes
In holi writ þus we lere.   myght/

Wen adam was mad and
heue his fere.

God þeim bad waxe ant
þriue.

Ant gildre gete ant bringe
to liue.

155 Ant fisch ant foul a best
ant tre.

Ant al þat scholde on
erthe be.

On lift. on watir ant on
londe.

Al made god buth sinn to
þeire honde.

*gen. i. crescite & multi-
plicamini & domi/ namini
piscibus maris & uolatili-
bus celi/ & bestuis terre.
& cetera./* [Gen. i, 28]

(f)orbisine ob [27] bestis man
þou mai here.

160 þat þou may þe betere lere.
Ant skil in þin herte finde
þe louerd to loue of alle
kinde.

[27] ? of.

Ant do al scho þe ern þe
wile teche.

Ant kest a-wei þi fule
speche

165 Ant loue god wit al þi
skile

Ant swo þou brekist þin
olde bile.

On þe ston þat is godis
sone.

Wehn þu leuist þin old
wne.

Ant þanne þou mai þi
soule lithte. [fol. 83 a,
col. 1]

170 Of god to speke and haue
in-sihte

[þ]are-fore of him y write
þouthe.

þat kinde in alle þingis
wroute.

And us from ded to liue
broute.

Wehn he us on þe rode
bouhte.

175 [F]or ne his þinge writin
in þis liue. '

þat swo wel may ne swo
bliue.

Mannis herte of sworue
bringe

Alse haue in iħu al his
likinge.

[F]or-þi iħu þi luue to
winne.

180 þou giue me grace to bi-
-ginne.[13]

Loue to sende to for-do
sinne:

Wat al mankinde was
bundin inne.

þerfor iħu þi loue to wynne:

gyf me grace to bigynne/

Loue to þe sende & do awey
synne:

þat al mankynde was bounden
inne/

---

[13] MS., in written above the line. .

DULWICH COLL. MS. XXII

primo Io[han]*nis scitis*
quia œc apparuit ut pec-
cata/ tolleret [I John iii,
5] *& iiii. in hoc est caritas*
dei in nos quia misit/
filium suum propiciaci-
onem pro peccatis nos-
tris./ [I John iv, 10]

[E]r godis sune in þe
maydiñ lihte.

Agenis þe deuil hauide
we [19] no rihte.

185 For wihl we were vndir
his mihteᵧ

Of god to do we lesid sihte.

[þ]at time was sinne so
rif.

In old in ᵹung. in man in
wif.

þat sone so [20] þei lefte þe
lif.

190 To helle bi-houid wit-
-houutin strif.

[H]abraham. ysaac. ant
sen jon.

Dauit þe king. ant sala-
mon.

þider þei wente euirlkon.

Hauide þei þanne non oþir
won.

195 [T]il godis sone was don
on rode

þider wente wikke ant
gode

þe wikke to pine wiht
dreri mode.

þare to be þe deuilis fode.

boniᵧ iи/ lumbum. maliᵧ
in ·infirnumᵧ lucas. œvi.

BODL. MS. ADD. C 38

Er goddes sone in þe maide
alightᵧ

ageyn þe feende had we no
myght/

ffor while we were vndir his
myghtᵧ

of goed to do we lost þe sight/

þat tyme was synne so ryfᵧ

& in olde & ᵹonge man & wyf/

þat as sone as þei lete þe lyfᵧ

þei went to helle without stryf/

Abraham Isaac & seint Iohnᵧ

Dauid þe king & Salomon/

þidir þei went ichoneᵧ

had þei þan none oþir wone/

Til goddes son was done on rodeᵧ

þe wikke to pyne with drery
modeᵧ

þere to be without goed./

---

[19] MS., *we* written above the line.
[20] MS., *so* written above the line.·

DULWICH COLL. MS. XXII

BODL. MS. ADD. C 38.

laza/rus in sinum abrahe.
diues in infirnum. per
la/zarum boni per diuitem
mali designantur per
signum/ abrahe requies.
    [col. 2] *martinus in ser-*
mone quodam deus erat a
patriar/chis predictus./ &
a prophetis/ predica/tus./

(b)ote þo ilke soulis
swete.

But þo soules suete:

200 þar her on liuis sinnis
lete.

þat here in lyf her synnes did
bete/

In fre prisun þan was þer
sete.

In free prison was her sete:

To abide þe este of þe
prophete.[21]

to abyde þe bihest of þe pro-
phete/

In limbo exspectabant anime
sanctorum promissionem pro-
phete de aduentu x̄p̄i./ psalmo.
vi: Ecce veniet & saluos nos
faciet. [Ps. lxxix, 3] *zakar. ix:*
Ecce veniet etc./ [Zach. ix, 9]

(p)rophetis were i-winde [22]
to grede.

Prophetes were wont to grede:

on shal come wyt-vtin
drede.

one shal cum without drede/

205 þat flesch schal take in
maidin [23]-hede.

þat flesshe shal take in maiden-
heed:

Ant ws of pine to yoye to
lede.

& vs to ioie fro pyne lede/

ysaye.- vii. ecce virgo
concipiet [Is. vii, 14] *&*
lxiiii./ utinam dirumperes

---

[21] At the left of v. 202 in the MS. is an incomplete paragraph
sign, stroked out.

[22] ? iwnide.

[23] MS., first *i* written above the line.

DULWICH COLL. MS. XXII

BODL. MS. ADD. C 38.

celos & descenderes.[24] [Is. lxii, 1]

(þ)e prophe[te] ysaye.
Iwnid was[25] to gode þus crie.
Wi ne[26] woldis-tu þe heuene riueȝ

210 Ant do vs dun lihte bliue.
Ant þe prophetis alle hauide gret longinge
Of god to se þe to-cuminge
Ant ȝernide alle on liue to be.
Godis to-come for to se.

215 Seint austin seiz þat in þo dawis.
þe holi men of þe olde lawis.
Ofte seide in þere preiere.
Weher þat chil schal finde vs hereȝ
þat we of him in writ þan rede.

220 Wehr we schal se in dede.

Augustinus. Sciebant inquid antiqui regem esse venturum/ & dicebant. O. si hic me inueniat illa nati/uitasȝ O si quod credo in scripturis videam oculis m[eis].

(w)en god of heuene ·herde þis cri.
Of mankin hauede he merci.

When god of heuenȝ hard þis crieȝ
of man-kynde he had merci/

---

[24] MS., on the left of the paragraph sign at the beginning of the Latin quotation is a capital B, stroked out. A space of two lines is left after the Latin.

[25] MS., *was* written above the line.

[26] MS., *wine* written as one word.

DULWICH COLL. MS. XXII	BODL. MS. ADD. C. 38
Ant a maidin ches of gret ferli. In soule clene ant in bodi.	And chees a maide of greet ferly. clene in soule & in bodi/

*missus est angelus ga-
briel/ ad mariam vir-
ginem. lucas. .i./* [Luke
i, 26, 27]

	Til hire he sende a swete fere.	To hir he sent a suete fere.
225	Til hire he sende a swete fere. þat him was swiþe lef ant dere. [fol. 83 b, col 1] Gabriel wiht swete chere. þat hire gan grete on þis manere.	To hir he sent a suete fere. þat him was ful leue & dere/ Gabriel with suete chere. þat hir gan grete on þis manere. *lucas. x./*

*aue gratia plena/ domi-
nus tecum./* [Luke i, 28]

*Missus est angelus Gabriel ad
Mariam virginem &c. Que &c.
Que cum au/disset. turbata est
in sermone eius. et cogitabat
qualis &o./* [Luke i, 26-29]

	[H]el ful of grace god is wyt þe.	Heil ful of grace god is with þe.
230	Among wimman blessid þou be. þe maidin dred on him to se. Ant þouhte hu þis mihte be.	amonge alle wymmen blessed þou be/ þe maide was dradde on him to se. & thought what þis myght be/

*que cum audisset tur-
bata est in sermone/ eius
& cogitabat &c. ne timeas
maria/ invenisti gratiam
apud dominum ecce con-
cipias/ &c./* [Luke i, 29-
31]

[þ]anne þe aungil him spak fre. Marie nout ne drede þou þo.	þan spake þe aungel free. marie drede not þe/.*

* MS. B, in the margin opp. v. 234 are the words (n)e timeas
maria &c.

235 A child schal be borin of   A child shal be borne of þe/
   þe.
   Ihu schal is name be.   ihc shal his name be/
   [H]e scal þe fadir of   He shal þe fadir of heuen queme/
    heuene queme[28]
   In dauiis sete sitte an   in Dauid seete sitte & deme/
    deme.
   þe folc of israel he scul   þe folc of Israel he shal ȝeme/
    ȝeme/
240 Ant þeire[29] fos fra hem
   al fleme.

    Dabit illi dominus deus
    sedem dauid patris/ eius
    & regnabit in domo iacob./
    [Luke i, 32]

   [þ]anne answeride þat   þan ansuerde þat suete maide/
    swete maide.
   To þe angel gabriel ant   to þe aungel Gabriel & seide/
    seide
   Hu scal þis be neuir me   Hou shal þat be neuer i leide/
    leide.
   Mi þout. to lust of man   my thoght to lust of man opon
    upbraide.   braide.[30]/

    quomodo fiet istud quo-
    niam virum non cognosco/
    &c./ [Luke i, 34]

245 [þ]anne gan þe aungil   þan gan þe aungel hir hert dight/
   hire herte dihte
   Ant of his gretinge to   & of his greting had insight/
    haue insihte
   þe holy gost schal in þe   þe holi gost shal in þe light/
    lihte/

---

[28] MS., *s* written at end of line.

[29] MS., *re* written above the line.

[30] MS., in the margin opp. v. 244 are the words *Quomodo fiet istud*
quoniam/ virum non cognosco./

DULWICH COLL. MS. XXII	BODL. MS. ADD. C 38
Ant in þe wirke þourue his mihte.	& in þe wirche thorou goddes myght./ [31]
[þ]e child þat of þe schal be borin.	þat childe þat shal of þe be borne⸝
250 Godis sone s c h a l be i-chozin	goddes son shal be corne./ [32]
þat folk he schal þat was bi-forin.	He shal alle þat were biforne⸝
To blisse bringe þàt þei haue lorin.	to þe blisse bringe þat þei had *lorne/*
spiritus sanctus super veniet in te & virtus al/- tissimi obumbrabit tibi. quod. n[ascetur] ex te &c./ [Luke i, 35]	
Ant þat þou þe sothe lere. [col. 2]	And þat þou þe sothe lere⸝
þi nece elizabeth lo here.	þi neece Elizabeth loo here/
255 þat is in eld fele ꝫere.	þat is in eelde with many ꝫeere⸝
Child nou hauis takin of hire fere.	nou hath taken childe of hir fere/
Ecce elisabet cognata tua & ipsa concepit/ filium in senectute sua./ [Luke i, 36]	
(þ)e sixth monith nu is anon.	þe sixt moneth nou is agone⸝
þat scha hauis wit childe gon.	þat she hath with child gone/
For to god of heuene þat is on⸝	ffor to god of heuen þat is one⸝
260 Ne is word of vn-mihte non	ne is worde of vnmyght none/
Hic mensis sextus est illi qua uocatur sterilis./ quia non est impossibile	*Ecce Elizabeth cognata tua. et ipsa concepit filium in senec- tute sua. hic/ mensis est sextus*

[31] MS., in the margin opp. v. 248 are the words *Spiritus sanctus superueniet in te &c./*

[32] MS., in the margin opp. v. 250 are the words *Quod enim ex te nascetur &c./*

9

DULWICH COLL. MS. XXII	BODL. MS. ADD. C 38
apud deum omne uerbum./ [Luke i, 36, 37]	*ille &c. quia non erit impossibile apud deum omne verbum, &c./* [Luke i, 36-37]

Ne wolde marie no len-gire plaide.	Ne wolde marie no lengar duelle ne pleder
Bote þis wrd on hire herte leyde.	but þis on hir hert leide/
Lo here scho seide godis hand-maide.	Loo me here goddes hande-maider [fol. 72 b]
With me be don als tu saide.	¹with me to do as þou seide/

Ecce ancilla domini fiat mihi secundum uerbum tuum./ [Luke i, 38]	*Ecce ancilla domini fiat michi secundum verbum tuum/* [Luke i, 38]

265	Sone so þis was in hire þout.	As sone as þis was on hir thoghtꝝ
	In hire was mannis kinde wrouht.	in hir was mankynde wroght/
	Ant soth-fast god was þere-to brouhtꝝ	And sothfast god was þer-to broghtꝝ
	Man þare-offe ne drede þou nouht.	man þerof drede þou nought/

ut solis radius intrat innoxius fenestram/ vit-ream sic dei filius immo subtilius aulam uirgi/-neam./

	(a)ls þe sunne þirlis þe glas.
270	Ant hol bi-leues as hit ˢˢ er was.
	Wel sleyliker þure þe fadir mihte.
	þe sune in þe maidin lithe
	þe fadir his sone in þe maydin sende
	Ant þe holigost þarto wende.

ˢˢ MS., *h* written above the line.

DULWICH COLL. MS. XXII	BODL. MS. ADD. C 38

275 Ant alse þat swete [34]
    maidin þouhte.[35]
Vr kinde wit þe godhed
    wrouhte.
Ant þoreu þe holi gostis
    dede.
Was mad in on wit þe
    godhede.
þo bar þe maidin hire wit-
    inne.
280 God ant man wit-vtin
    sinne.
Maidin at þe bi-gini[n]ge.
Bi-fore ant at hire end-
    ingge.

    *Virgo ante partum . vir-
go in partu. virgo post
partum./*

þe angil marie god bi-
    kende. [fol. 84 a, col. 1]
Ant to him ȝede þat him
    sende.
285 Ant sone aftir þe maide
    wende.
To elisabet þat was hire
    frende.

    *et discessit ab ea ange-
lus. exurgens/ autem
maria abiit ad elizabet &
salutauit/ eam./ luca*s
i./ [Luke i, 38-40]

(s)one so þe maide marie
cam to þe hus of zakarie.
Elizabe in prophecie.
290 þe maidin kiste ant þus
    gan crie.

þe aungel marie god bikende.

& to him ȝeode þat him sende/

To Elizabeth þat was hir frende/

As sone as þe maide marie.
entred þe hous of zakarie/
Elizabeth in prophecie.
þe maide kissed & þus gan crie/`

[34] MS., *te* written above the line.
[35] MS., *h* written above the *o*.

DULWICH COLL. MS. XXII

BODL. MS. ADD. C 38

Unde hoc michi vt benedicta
mater domini veniat ad me &c./
[Luke i, 43]

[A] sco seide hu mai þis be

A. she seide hou may þis beʔ

þat mi louirdis modir comiz to meʔ

þat my lordes modir cometh to
. me/

Wen þat ic herde þe steuene of þe.

þe childe in my wombe makith gleeʔ

þe child in mi wombe made gle.

as sone as i harde þe steuen of þe/

vt audiuit salutacionem
beate marie. eli/zabet ex-
clamauit & dixit vnde hoc
mihi ut/ ueniat mater do-
mini mei ad meʔ ecce.
&c./ [Luke i, 41-43]

295 Among wimmen blessid þou be.

Ant blessit be þe frut of þe.

benedicta tu i[nter]
m[ulieres] & b[enedictus]
f[ructus] v[entris] tui.
amen./ [Luke i, 42]

(a)nt seli þou be þat ilke stunde.

þat in þe was trouhe[36] i-funde.

For al schal god þuru-vt his willeʔ

300 þat he hauis seid in þe ful-fille.

et beata que credidisti
quoniam perficientur/ in
te que dicta sunt tibi a
domino./ [Luke i, 45]

[36] MS., *u* written above the o.

DULWICH COLL. MS. XXII BODL. MS. ADD. C 38.

	300 *a* þere bileft þat suete may:
	b wit*h* Elizabeth many a day/
	c Ne loued she no foles play:
	d but loued god and thanked ay/
þer þan was a swete met-inge.[37]	Here was a suete metyng:
A swete cuple a swete[38] kissinge.	a suete kissing a suete clipping/
A maide bar god of alle þinge.	A maide bare þe lord of al thing:
A wif seint jon i*n* holi wendi*n*gge.	a wyf seint Iohn in holi wedding/
305 Iwrite on þis steide i finde.	
þar a wis man here-of mas minde.	
þat þe joie in þis met-i*n*gge.	
þat seint jon made was biginge.	
Bi-fore god go[39] ant p*r*eche	
310 Ant of him þe folc to teche.	
[col. 2] *glossa super illud exultauit infans. quod li[n]gua/ non poterat. animo exultante salutat &/ sue precursionis officium inchoat./*	
(þ)anne þankid marie god ful of blisse	þe while thanked god ful of blisse:[40] [fol. 73 a]
þat he se wolde hire meke-nesse.	þat she wolde se hir mekenesse/
Ant sende his sone i*n* swetenesse.	And his son sende suetnesse:
In hire to take ma*n*nis likenesse.	to take in hir ma*n*nes liknesse/

[37] MS., *metigie;* *i* deleted by dot.

[38] MS., *aswete* as one word.

[39] Infinitive.

[40] In MS. B, vv. 311-328 stand after vv. 329a-336, and the whole section stands after v. 433.

DULWICH COLL. MS. XXII	BEDL. MS. ADD. C 38

& ait maria magnificat anima mea dominum/& exultauit spiritus meus in deo salutari meo/ [Luke i, 46-47]

315 (þ)are-fore me schal al mankinde.	þer-fore shal al man-kynde꞉
Blisful telle in þeire minde.	blisful be in her mynde/
þat he wold in me swo gret þing finde	þat he wolde in me mekenesse fynde꞉
þat is of mihte to leyse ant binde.	þat mightful is to lese & hynde/

ecce enim ex hoc beatam me dicent omnes generationes. quia/ &c./ [Luke i, 48-49]

(o)f mercy þanne he was leche.	Of merci he was þe best leeche꞉
320 Fram kin to kinde. þat dredde his speche	fro kynde to kynde dred was his speche/
Of þe prude in herte he dide wreche.	Of þe pride of hert he did wreeche꞉
Ant dide þe meke on hey to reche.	& did þe meke on hye to reeche/

Et misericordia eius a progenie in pro[genies] ti-[mentibus] e[um]. fecit &c./ [Luke i, 50]

(þ)e hungery in god he made stronge.	þe hungry in goed he made stronge꞉
Ant þe riche꞉ he lette al--swonge.	& þe riche lete ydel gonge/
325 þe folc of israel hauiz vndir-fonge.	þe folc of Israel he hath vndir-fonge꞉
þe child꞉ þat þei abide longe.	þe childe þat þei abyde longe/
Alse bi-fore spak heuinis king.	Also bifore spake heuen king꞉
To abraham꞉ ant his o[f]-spring	to abraham & his ofsprynge/

DULWICH COLL. MS. XXII   BODL. MS. ADD. C 38.

esurientes imple[vit]. *&*
di[vites] *inanes. Suscepit*
&[*c*]. [Luke i, 53, 54]

þanne bi-lefte marie

329*a* As i er seide þe ´maide
        marieʸ
    b harde lyf ladde wi*th*out
       folie/
    c Wi*th* Elizabeth & zakarieʸ
    d blessed was þe companye/

330 þre moniz oþir mare

330*a* ffor with hem she was þareʸ
331   wi*th*out synne wi*th*out care/

Withoutin sinne with-out-
in kare.

331*a* Three moneths ful or moreʸ
332   she loued god þat was hir
      lore/

Sco louid god. þat was hire
lare

Alse seit þe holi man seint
bede.

As seith þe holi sein*t* Bedeʸ

Fram hire nece nouht sco
ne ʒede

fro hir neece she ne ʒeode/

335 Ar sco sauh fullic i*n* dedeʸ
Elizabet [41] seint jon fede.

Er she sawe fulliche in dedeʸ
Elizabeth seint Iohn seide/

beda in glossa/tam diu
mansit maria cum Eliza-
bet donec/ uideret precur-
soris natiuitatem propter
quam max/ime uenerat./

þis was sen jon for wam
bi-forin

þis ʀwas seint Iohn for wham bi-
forneʸ   [fol. 72 b]

His fadir hauide þe speche
for-lorin. [fol. 84 b, col.
1]

his fadir had his speche lorne/

Al to þe time þat he was
borin.

Vnto þe tyme þat he was boreʸ

340 Alse þe aungil hauid sei
bi-forin.

as þe aungel seide bifore/

[Z]acarie was his fadir
name

Zakarie was his fadir nameʸ

[41] MS., *a* written above the *z*.

DULWICH COLL. MS. XXII	BODL. MS. ADD. C 38

His lif he ledde with-vtin
blame

God man he was and of
god fame?

To do sinne him þoute
scame.\

erant autem *ambo iusti*
incedentes in omnibus/
mandatis & iusticiis domi-
ni sine querela. lucas i./
[Luke i, 6]

ne ladde his lyf without blame/

To do synne him thoght shame?

greet man he was & of goed fame/

Erant autem ambo iusti
incedentes in omnibus
mandatis et iusti deo sine/
querela. cum sacerdocio
fungeretur forte exiit vt
incensum poneret in tem-
plum domini appar/uit ei
angelus domini stans a
dextris a latere incensi &
zakarias turbatus est./
[Luke i, 6, 8, 9, 11, 12]

345 Time com of þe seruise
  þat he do scholde on þere
  wise.

  In þe temple he saw up
  rise.

  A man? ant him bi-gan to
  grise.

  cum sacerdocio fu[n]-
  geretur sorte exiit ut in/-
  censum poneret in tem-
  [*plum*] *domini & apparuit*
  ei an/gelus domini & zac-
  arias turbatus est [Luke
  i, 8, 9, 11, 12]

þe tyme come of seruice?
þat he do shulde in al wise/

In þe temple he sawe up rise?

bifor him a man & him gan
agrise/

  [H]it was an angil godis
  sonde.

350 Bi þe auter þat he sauh
  stonde.

  þat hider was sent him to
  fonde.

  Ant do his seruise bad him
  nouht wonde.

It was an aungel of goddes sonde?

þat gan at þe auters ende stonde/

DULWICH COLL. MS. XXII	BODL. MS. ADD. C 38
[Z]acarie he seide ne dred te nouth.	Zakarie ne drede þou noughtɣ
353 a	to do his seruice ne lette him noght/
Bi-fore god þi bed is brouht.[42]	Bifor god þi beed is broghtɣ
355 þat þou hauist him bi--souht.[43]	þat þou hast him bisought/
schal in elizabet be wrouht.	Shal in Elizabeth be wroght/

Ne timeas za[caria] quoniam exaudita est de/-precacio tua & elizabet uxor &c./ [Luke i, 13]

[A] schild þou schal on hire winne.	A childe þou shalt on hir wynneɣ
þat be schal joie to al his kinne	þat shal be ioie to al his kynne/
Halewid he bez hire wit--hinne.	Halwed he is hir withinneɣ
360 Jon he schal hote clene of sinne.	Iohn he shal hight clensed of synne/

et uocabis nomen eius Johannem./ [Luke i, 13]

[A]t his burthe me schal gamine ant pleye	At his birthe men shal game & pleyɣ
Ant schal greithe godis weie.	he shal make redy goddes weye/
To þe folk he schal soz seye.	And foule bileue he shal doun layɣ
Ant juil bileue dun he scal leye.	to þe folc he shal sothe sey/

et multi in natiuitate eius gaudebunt/ & spiritu sancto reple[bitur] ad huc ex utero matris sue./ [Luke i, 14, 15]

---

[42] MS. *wrouht, w* deleted by dots, *b* written above.
[43] MS. *wrouht, wr* deleted by dots, *s* written above.

DULWICH COLL. MS. XXII	BODL. MS. ADD. C 38.
365 [Z]acarie answerede with dreri chere.	Zakarie ansuerd with drery chere;
Hou may þis be on eni manere.	hou may þis be on any manere/
Bothe " is ohld ich ant mi fere. [col. 2]	Bothe ben olde i and my fere;
Ant forth gon in fele yere.	forth gone in many a ȝeere/

vnde hoc sciam. ego enim
sum senex & vxor me/a
processit in diebus suis./
[Luke i, 18]

(þ)e angil seide ȝis schal þat tu se.	þe aungel seide þis shalt þou se;
370 Ant for þat þu ne leuist me.	& for þou ne leuest me/
þou schalt be dumb. i telle hit þe.	Til þat childe borne be;
Til þat þe child borin be.	þou shalt be dombe i sey þe/

pro eo quod non credi-
disti uerbis meis eris ta-
cens/ vsque in diem quo
haec fiant. [Luke i, 20]

(þ)e angil lefte no lengire þare.	þan went þe aungel to his lord;
Ne zacarie ne spak nam-mare.	& zakarie spake no worde/
375 Bote vt he ȝede syhende sare.	But out he ȝeode & sought sight;
þe folc hauid wundir war--fore hit ware.	þe folc wondirde hou it be myght/
Bote þei seide al bi-den.	But þei seide alle in fere;
þat he hauid sum wndir sen;	þat he had som wondir here/
For þat he hauid so longe ben.	So longe he hath þerinne be;
	ne liketh him neiþir game ne glee/

" MS., h written above the t.

DULWICH COLL. MS. XXII | BODL.- MS. ADD. C·38'

egressus a*utem* n*on po-*
terat loqui & cognouer-
unt/ quod *visionem vidis-*
set i*n templo.* [Luke i,
22]

380 Zacarie þanne dide his
dede.
Nohut for his fleschly nede,
Bote child to gette ჳif he
muhte spede꙳
Of god þare þoureu to
winne mede.
(þ)at swete cuple ant þat
meti*n*ge.
385 Of fleschly lust hauide he
no likinge.
Bote holi wille ant long-
inge꙳
To gidis⁴⁵ seruise a child
for to bringe.
(a) childe þei gat þouru
godis mihte.
Of godis hest and hauid
i*n*-sihte.
390 In elizabet þe holi gost
lihte꙳
Ant þe child in hire dihte.

Zakarie þan did his dede꙳

not for his flesshely nede/
But childe to geet if he **myght**
spede꙳
& so of god to wynne mede/

þat suete couple i*n* þat metyng꙳

of flesshely lust had no likyng/

But holi wille & suete desiryng꙳

to goddes seruice childe forth to
bringe/
A childe he gate thorou goddes
myght꙳   [fol. 73 a]
of godes hest he had insight/

In Elizabeth þe holi gost alight꙳

& þat childe in hir dight/

post dies hos concepit
elizabet & dixit quia/ *sic*
fecit/ michi dominus i*n di-*
e*bus* quibus *respexit au-*
ferre/ opprobrium meum.
[Luke i, 24, 25]

(e)lizabe*t* hire felid þo.
þat sco bi-gan wyt childe
go.
Awei sco lette al hire wo.

Elizabeth hir feled þo꙳
þat she gan wi*th* child go/

Awey she lete al hir woo꙳

---

⁴⁵ ? *godis.*

395 þat sco hauide fourti " ȝer   þat she had fourty ȝere & mo/
    ant mo.

God sco seide me hauis
    ben milde.

þat me hauis nou brouth
    with childe. [fol. 85 a,
    col. 1]

[W]en þe childe scolde   When þe child shulde borne beɣ
    borin be.

þeire frendis alle of þe   his freendes aboute of þe cun-
    cuntre.   tree/

400 Wyt blisful chere. an   With blisful chere game & gleeɣ
    gamin ant " gleɣ

Alle þe comin þ child to se   alle þei come þat child to se/

Ant þe seide þe frendis   þan seide his frendes alleɣ
    alle.

Zacarie þei wolde him   zakarie þei shulde him calle/
    cal[l]e.

*Vicini & cognati eius
congratulabantur ei & uo/-
cabant eum nomine patris
sui zacariam.* [Luke i, 58,
59]

[þ]at herde þe modir þer   þat harde þe modir þere she layɣ
    scho lay.

405 And answerede ant seide   & ansuerde & seide nay/
    nay.

Mi leue frend doz alle   Mi leef frendes doeth al aweyɣ
    away.

Jon he schal bi-hote ȝif   Iohn he shal hight if i may/
    þat i may.*

Ant þei seide þat þare was   And þei seide þer was nonɣ
    non

In al here kinde þat hete   in al her kynde þat hight Iohn/
    jon.

*& respo/ndens mater
eius dixit nequaquam sed
uocabitur Johannes.*/[Luke
i, 60]

DULWICH COLL. MS. XXII	BODL. MS. ADD. C 38
410 [T]o zacarie þe word þei broute	To zakarie þis worde þei broght⸝
Ant bad him schewe waht him þoute.	& bad him sey what him thought/
Ant he a tablet sone souhte.	And he a tablet sone soght⸝
Ant þer-on þe name of ion he wrouhte.	and þer-on þe name he wroght/

et postulans zacarias pugillare scripsit dicens./
[Luke i, 63]

[I]n þat tablet he wrot[49] a-non.	In þat tablet he wrote on-one⸝
415 þ childis name þan schal be ion.	þe childes name shal be Iohn/
Bi-fore god he schal cume ant gon.	God bifore he shal gone⸝
Ant him to bringge wel mani on.[50]	& to him turne many one/

Iohannes est nomen eius preibit ante faciem domi-ni/ parare[51] *vias eius./*
[Luke i, 63, 76]

[W]ndir þan hauide al his kinde.	Wondir þan had many of his kynde⸝
Hu he muhte þat name finde.	hou he might þis name fynde/
420 Bote god is[52] tunge þan gan unbinde.[53] .	But god his tunge gan vnbynde⸝
Ant he him louede with al his minde	& he him thanked with al his mynde/

& mirati sunt vniuersi./
[Luke i, 63]

[49] MS., *t* written above the line.
[50] MS., *manion.*
[51] MS., *_parare.*
[52] MS., *godis.*
[53] MS., *imbinde.*

DULWICH COLL. MS. XXII	BODL. MS. ADD. C 38
[G]od he seide b[l]essid þou be.	God he seide blessed he beȝ
þat of þi folc woldist [54] haue pite.	þat of his folc wolde haue pitee/
Ant hauist þi merci scehwed in meȝ	And his merci had shewed in meȝ
425 þat þis child scholde borin be.	where thorou al folc shal turne to þe/
[A]nt þou child be icald [55] prophete	þat þis child shulde be cleped propheteȝ
þou scal greþe [56] godis strete	
Godis folc þou schalt gete.	goddes folc þou shalt geet/
Ant þeim teche þeire sinnis bete. [col. 2]	And hem teche her synnes beteȝ/

& prophetauit zacarias dicens. Benedictus dominus deus &c./ [Luke i, 68]

430 (o)f gret mihte scal be þi speche.	Of greet myght shal be þi specheȝ
To godis folc þou schalt preche.	to goddes folc þou shalt preche/
þou þeim schalt þe sothe teche.	þou hem shalt þe sothe techeȝ
Hu þei scal to heuene reche.	hou þei shal to heuen reeche/[56]

addandam scienciam salutis plebi eius &c./ [Luke i, 77]

(w)en þe child bi-gan to belde.

435 Wel to þriue ant waxe in elde.

Of worlddis blisse nouht him ne rouh[te]

[54] MS., *l* written above *o*.
[55] ? *i-cleped.*
[56] MS., r written above the line.

DULWICH COLL. MS. XXII   BODL. MS. ADD. C 38

Bote wildernesse sone he
souhte
In penaunce þare his lif to
lede.
þát neuire ȝet iuil dide in
dede.

antra deserti teneris sub
annis &c. sicut can[t]/*or.*

440 (v)pon þis word þan seiz
seint bede.
Penance to do was him no
nede.
Bote he þat oc[57] scholde
penance preche
þeim þat him herde swo
scholde teche.
þe world to lete ful of
serue.[58]

445 Ant wit penance him to
folewe.

beda predicator inquit
penitentie futurus asperi/-
[tatem] *solitudinis elegit*
ut ab amore[59] *mundi/*
auditores suos reuocaret.

(w)en marie hauid sen in   When marie had seyen þe dede꞉
dede.
Elizabet seint jon fede.   of þe child & al þe nede/
þe maidin hire to spede.   þe maide bigan hir to spede꞉
Ant leue tok꞉ and hom   & leeue toke & home ȝeode/
scho ȝede.

cum peperisset elizabet꞉
maria rediit in domum
suam./ [Luke i, 57, 56]

[57] MS., *t* written above the line, *oc* slightly below, with a blur
from erasure.
[58] MS., *ofserue*, as one word.
[59] MS., *amare*, *a* deleted by dot and *o* placed above.
[60] In the MS. B, vv. 329 a-336 and vv. 311-328 follow at this point.
I print them opp. the corresponding lines in the Dulwich text.

DULWICH COLL. MS. XXII	BODL. MS. ADD. C 38
450 (w)en sco hom cham josep to queme.	When she home cam ioseph to queeme᷄
þat alse hire spouse hire hauid to ȝeme/	þat as hir spouse hir had to ȝeme/
In his herte he gan hire deme.	In his hert he gan hir deme᷄
Hu sco muhte wiht childe seme	hou she myght with childe seme/
qua *reuersa inuenta est in utero habens de spiritu sancto./* [Matt. i, 18]	
(w)are-of hit were nouht he ne wiste.	Wherfore it were noght he ne wist᷄ [fol. 73 b]
455 Swo alse he neuir hire muht kiste.	
Wiht wille of sinne. ne neuir liste.	with wille of synne neuer he ne lyst/
Hire maidinhod fullic vp-briste.	hir maidenheed fully up-briste/
(a)nt for *in* him ne was falsehed.	And for in him was no falseheed᷄
In word. *in* þouht. ne in dede.	in worde *in* thought ne in dede/
460 In him of hire was no drede.	In his hert was no drede᷄
þat scho hauide lorin hir maidinhede [fol. 85 b, col. 1]	þat she had lost hir maidenheed/
ma. dicit in histor[iar]-*um glossa quod iosep pocius credidit/ mulierem concipere sine viro quam mariam posse peccare./*	
[B]ut [a] for þat he neuere sauh wiht eye.	And for he neuer sawe with eye᷄
[þ]at scho hire gan to folye beye.	þat she to foleheed hir gan beye/

[a] The page has been trimmed along the outer margin so that very few of the initials in the first column are visible.

DULWICH COLL. MS. XXII

[L]oth him were on hire to' leye.

465 Outhir of eni sinne wreye.
[F]or wel he wiste was þare no speche.
þoruu þe laue of spusebreche.
[B]ote hire þe domisman bi-teche.
[S]one of hire to take wreche.

noluit eam traducere id-est in domum suam ducere vel ad/ penam quia sicut adultera lapidaretur.

470 [A]geinis þe laue him likid ille.
[þ]at men scholde a maide[62] spille.
[F]or bi-fellit in his willeʒ
[þ]e maidin lete and leue stille.
[W]il iosep in his herte wende.

475 [H]u þis þing scholde come til ende.
[I]n slep he fel alse god him kende.
[A]nt þan til him his an-gil sende.

Hec cogitante ecce an-gelus domini apparuit/ in somp[nis] iosep. [Matt. i, 20]

[þ]e angil was redi for to gon.
[A]nt to iosep wente a-non.

BODL. MS. ADD. C 38

Lothe him was on hir to lyeʒ

or to flesshely dede wrye/
ffor wele he wist was þere no specheʒ
þorou þe lawe of spousebreche/

But hir þe domes-man bitecheʒ

sone of hir to take wreeche/

Ageyn þe lawe him liked illeʒ

þat men shulde a maiden spille/

þerfore bifel it in his willeʒ
þe maiden bileef & lete stille/

While ioseph in hert wendeʒ

hou þis shulde cum to ende/

On slepe he fel as god him kendeʒ

& to him his aungel sende/

[62] MS., *amaide.*

10

480 [A]nt to him þe sothe
    seide.
    [O]f þe child ant of þe
    maide.
    [I]osep he seide nouht   Ioseph he seide nought þou dredeʳ
    þou ne drede.
    Marie alse þi spuse lede.   marie as þi spouse lede/
    þe child in hire þou schalt   þe childe in hir þou it shalt feder
    fede.
485 Bote hit his þe holi gostis   but it* is þe holi gostis dede/
    dede.

    Noli timere accipere ma-
    riam in coniugem tuam/
    hoc quod in/ ea natum est
    de spiritu sancto. [Matt.
    i, 20]

    [þ]e holi gost hauiz hire   þe holi gost hir hath be mylderʳ
    ben milde.
    [þ]at hire hauis brout wiht   & marie hath broght with childe/
    childe.
    His folc þat er hauis ben   þe folc þat hidir-to haue be
    wilde.   wilderʳ
    He þeim schal fra sinne   he hem shal fro synne shilde/
    schilde.

    Pariet autem *filium ipse*
    *en*im saluum faciet/ popu-
    lum suum a peccatis eo-
    rum. [Matt. i, 21]

490 (g)odis sone in þe maidin
    lichte.
    þoureu þe holi gastis
    mihte.
    God in hire hauis don   God in him hath done vertuʳ
    vertue.
    þo schalt clepe þe child   his name þou shalt clepe i̅h̅u̅/
    ihesu.

    et uocabis nomen eius
    *ih*esum. [Matt. i, 21]

  * MS. *e*, deleted by dot.

DULWICH COLL. MS. XXII   BODL. MS. ADD. C 38

(h')*v* a child schulde be
borin.

495 Of a maidin*y* [64] longe bi-
forin.

Ysaye þou seide wel*y*

Ant his name schal be
emanuel.[65]

*Hic factum est. ut ad
impleretur illud ysaie.
vii./ Ecce virgo & pariet
&c.* [Matt. i, 22, 23]

(w)en josep he*r*de þis   When ioseph harde þis tidyng*y*
tiþinge.

And awok of his slepinge.

500 He þonkede þe louird of
alle þinge

And held marie in clene   marie he helde i*n* clene wed-
wedi*n*gge.   ding/

And wid þe maidin. i*n*   And þe maide in goed likyng*y*
god likinge.

Maidin bi-lefte to his end-   maide bileft to his endyng./
i*n*gge.

*exurgens iosep a somp*n*o
accepit spon/sam in u-
xorem* [Matt. i, 24] *& cum
virgine uirgo per/mansit
dicit histor*[iar]*um.*

(þ)an wiste Iosep god   When ioseph wist þat god shulde
schulde be borin   be borne*y·*

505 To sauue þeim þat were   to saue he*m* þat were forlorne*y*
for-lorin.

Ant was i*n* longinge þe
time to se.

þat þe child scholde borin
be.

---

[64] MS., *amaidin* written as one word.

[65] MS., *u* written above the line.

DULWICH COLL. MS. XXII	BODL. MS. ADD. C 38

tunc cognouit iosep de-
um nasciturum qui/ solus
peccata dimittit.

þat time was mihtful ant fer	þat tyme was myghtful & sterer
Augustus cesar ant strong ant ster	augustus cesar was stronge & fere/
510 In al þat lond was non his per.	In al þat londe was none his perer
Ouir al þe lond was his pouer.	ouer al þat londe was his powere/
He criid his ban and sende his sonde.	He cried his bane & sent his sonder
To alle þat were vndir his honde.	to alle þat were in his londe/
þat vndir him non schulde stonde.	þat vndir him ne shulde stonder
515 þat were of a-nothir londe.	þat were of a-noþir londe/

In diebus illis exiit a.
ce[sar]. *au*[gustus]. *&c.*
precepit/ tunc cesar ut
singuli irent ad propria/
sua loca. lucas. ii. [Luke
ii, 1-3]

Wen josep herde hem þus crie.	When ioseph harde þus þis crier
þe maidin he tok with him marie	with him he toke þe maide marie/
Ant of nazaret him bi-gan to hye	Out of Nazareth he him gan hier
519 Ant to bethleem weys guye.	& to Bedleem his wey guye/

END OF DULWICH COLL. MS. XXII

	520 In Bedleem he toke his wonyngr
	for marie was nye child-yng/
	And for hir kynde & hir ofspringer

were of dauid hous þe
   king/
In Bedleem hous he toke⸗
525 litel & pore as seith þe
   boke/
An olde cote al to-falle⸗
had þei þan none oþir
   halle/
Seint Ierom a maide
   kende⸗
In a writte þat he hir
   sende/
530 þat Marie wan hir breed⸗
with hir nedil & with hir
   threde/
When þe childe was forthe
   broght⸗
litil she had or right
   noght/
ffor to ly in þat berne⸗
535 but a litil hay or ferne/
Of wham þat she myght
   biȝete⸗
& leide him þer bestes
   shulde ete/
Loken bituene two olde
   walles⸗
had þei þan none oþir
   palles/
540 þan was fulfilled þe pro-
   phecie⸗
þat bifore seide Isaye/
þe oxe & þe asse had
   kennyng⸗
of oure lord in her stall-
   yng/
And abacuc had also
   seide⸗
545 bituene tuo beestes he shal
   be leide/
þan bifel þat ilke tyde⸗

þat in þe cuntree þere
   bisyde/
Heerdes waked in a faire
   meede⸗
her bestes & her shepe to
   fede/
550 Sone to hem an aungel
   gan wende⸗
& to hem broght þe suete
   tiding/
But sore gan hem doute⸗
   [fol. 74 a]
of þe light þat was so
   clere aboute/
þe aungel seide noght ȝee
   ne drede⸗
555 i ȝou telle a blisful dede⸗
a childe is borne for ȝoure
   nede⸗
þat shal his folc out of
   peyne lede/
And þat i ȝou þe sothe
   bringe⸗
þis is gyuen ȝou to token-
   yng/
560 In clothes in a cribbe
   bounde⸗
in Bedleem he is founde/
In a cribbe he is leide⸗
as i haue bifore ȝou seide/
His folc he shal out of
   synne bringe⸗
565 as crist & lord ouer al
   thing/ **
þan harde þei a companye⸗
of aungels nygh in þe sky/
þat with steuen & crie⸗
blesse god þat sitte on
   hye/
570 And pees þei seide comen
   in londe⸗

** End of the Vernon text.

þat in goed stedfast wille
wil stonde/
When   þei   harde   þis
steuen:
þe herde men thanked god
of heuen/
And amonge hem bigan to
sey:
575   to Bedleem take we þe
wey/
To wite þere þat we ne
duelle:
if it so be as we harde
telle/
To Bedleem þei gan hye:
& of þis worde þe sothe
aspye/
580   And þere þei fonde þe
maide marie:
& þe childe in a cribbe by/
Of þis thing when þei
sye þe ende:
home ageyn þe herdes gan
wende/
With greet ioie god thanking:
585   þat hem þidir wolde sende/
Nought to hem marie
selde:
but on hir hert þe wordes
leide/
When þat was comen to
þe tyde:
men shulde þat childe cir-
cumscide/
590   His flesshe þei share þe
eght day:
so bad moyses in his lay/
þe tuelft day come þe
kinges:
& in her hondes bare of-
frynges/

Where is þat childe þat is
bore:
595   þat is king of iewes core/
To him present we haue
broght:
fro 'fer londe we haue him
soght/
We be aboute kinges here
by:
of Tharsis saba & arabie/
600   His sterre in þe *[67] est hath
gone:
vs bifore hidir on-one/
Of þis worde when þe
tidyng:
broght was to herode þe
king/
Sone him toke euyl liking:
605   sorwe of hert care &
mornyng/
Sorwe had al his bareyn-
teme:
& al þe folc of Ierusalem/
With him þei maked drery
chere:
þat þei þis tidyng shulde
here/
610   Herode was with care
bounde:
where any childe þan were
founde/
Of alisaundre þe king:
þat him shulde put bi-
hynde/
ffor herode as comlyng:
615   & ageyn right was kinge/
þan did herode bifor him
calle:
preest & clerk & princes
alle/
And of hem he gan spye:

*[67] MS., h deleted by dot.

wheþir he were borne þat
is messye/

620 To herode þei ansuerde
ichone؟

& acorded alle in one/

Of Bedleem shulde cum
messye؟

as is written in prophecie/

And þou Bedleem londe of
Iuda؟

625 a' lodes man shal cum þe
fra/

þat gouerne shal in israel؟

my folc þat i loue wele/

And cleped herode þe
kinges stille؟

and bad hem go & do her
wille/

630 In Bedleem of her offryng؟

& of þe childe soth worde
him bringe/

Tyde & tyme of þe sterne؟

of þe kinges he aspyed
ȝerne/

Goeth he seide þat ȝee ne
duelle؟   [fol. 74 b]

635 of þe child þe sothe ȝe me
telle/

At ȝoure ageyn comyng
fro him to oure؟

i haue thoght him wele to
honoure/

But he him bithought of
oþir quede؟

þat childe to bringe to
deed/

640 When þe kinges him harde
þus sey؟

to Bedleem þei toke þe
wey/

And þe sterre in þe est
on-one؟

bifor hem forthe gan
gone/

fforthe it ȝeode biforne
hem ay؟

645 til it come aboue þer þe
child lay/

þus þei sawe þe sterre hem
wisse؟

to þe child þei ȝeode with
ioie & blisse/

When þe[68] sterre stode
stille on hye؟

þe hous þei wist þei were
nye/

650 And in þei ȝeode with ful
greet hye؟

& fonde þe child with his
modir marie/

When þei come in. him þei
gun grete؟

modir & maide with
wordes suete/

On knees þei fel on þe
flore؟

655 & offred þe childe golde
myrre & store/

[T]o[69] þis childe þat
suete offryng؟

shewed him þis in token-
yng/

In golde þat he was
myghtful king؟

in encense lord ouer al
thing/

---

[68] ms., h, deleted by dot.

[69] ? ms., faint paragraph sign and illegible initial.

BODL. MS. ADD. C 38

660　In myrre þat oynement is
　　　　to þe deedᵹ
　　　þat he shulde dye in his
　　　　manheed/
　　　Of þat comyng of þo
　　　　kingesᵹ
　　　of her presentz of her of-
　　　　frynges/
　　　Bifore was seide many
　　　　ᵹeereᵹ
665　of Dauid þe king in þe
　　　　sautere/
　　　Kinges he seide of Saba
　　　　þoᵹ
　　　arabie tharsis & oþir moo/
　　　Presentes of gyftes to him
　　　　shul bringeᵹ
　　　& to him ⁷⁰ make her of-
　　　　fryng/
670　Gyf shal alle kinges oureᵹ
　　　and alle princes him hon-
　　　　oure/
　　　When þei had made her
　　　　offryngᵹ
　　　& home to wende had ᵹern-
　　　　yng/
　　　To hem come þe aungel
　　　　þere þei slepeᵹ
675　& bad þei shulde hem
　　　　kepe/
　　　ffrom herode þat hem
　　　　wolde shendeᵹ
　　　& bad hem home bi a-noþir
　　　　wey wende/
　　　When þe kinges of her
　　　　slepe wokeᵹ
　　　a-noþir wey home þei
　　　　toke/
680　And left herode in greet
　　　　longyngᵹ

BODL. MS. ADD. C 38

　　　þat abode her comyng
　　　　ageyn/ ⁿ
　　　　þan come þe tyme þei
　　　　　shulde bringeᵹ
　　　þe childe to þe temple
　　　　with his offringe/
　　　with tuo turtils or with
　　　　tuo culuyrbirdesᵹ
685　as þe lawe of Moises
　　　　biddes/
　　・ So was þe wone in þulke
　　　　dawesᵹ
　　　as moyses bad in his
　　　　lawes/
　　　þat when a knaue childe
　　　　borne wereᵹ
　　　first of þe modir men
　　　　shulde him bere/
690　To þe temple & offre him
　　　　þereᵹ
　　　as he to god halwed wereᵹ
　　　In Ierusalem þan was oneᵹ
　　　þat had to name Simeon/
　　　Rightwise man & god he
　　　　draddeᵹ
695　& his lyf without synne
　　　　ladde/
　　　Olde man he was & in
　　　　greet longyngᵹ
　　　for to abyde goddes com-
　　　　yng/
　　　ffor þe holi gost had
　　　　wroghtᵹ
　　　sothfast opon his thought/
700　þat he shulde neuer dyeᵹ
　　　er he sawe goddes son
　　　　with his eye/
　　　þat tyme þis holi proph-
　　　　eteᵹ

⁷⁰ MS., hem, e deleted by dot and i written above.
ⁿ Read ageyn comyng, for the rhyme.

BODL. MS. ADD. C 38

gan in þe temple marie
mete/
And to þe child he toke
goed sete:

705 & him in his armes toke
suete/
When Simeon þis childe
toke:
he seide to him as seith
þe boke/
Nou leef lord þi seruant
stille: [72]
for he hath sene to wille/

710 Nou is tyme lord þat i
dye:
for i haue sene þe with
myn eye/
Seen i haue lord þi light:
þat þou hast to þi folc
dight/
Of þi to-come i haue in-
sight:

715 israel þat þi folc is right/
Simeon þan to þe maide:
[fol. 75 a]
þe childes peyne bifore
seide/
þat thorou sorwe of his
pinyng:
shulde hir hert thorou-
out stynge/

720 þer was in þe temple
þanne:
an holi widou hir name
was Anne/
þat in þe temple nyght &
day:
in fasting & in bedes lay/

BODL. MS. ADD. C 38

ffoure score & foure she
had in eelde:

725 of þis child many thinges
she teelde/
To alle þo þat had long-
yng:
him to se & his comyng/
Herode þe while had
greet longyng:
of þe childe to here tid-
yng/

730 And wondir had & greet
ferly:
þat þe kinges ne come him
by/
But he wened & not right:
þat þei had lost her sight/
Of þe sterre þat hem gan
lede:

735 & so myght þei not for
drede/
Or of oþir thing him bi-
went:
þat he hem myght of les-
ing shent/
So a stounde he him bi-
thoght:
þe childe to slee him ne
rought/

740 In ierusalem þis worde
gan sprede:
& in Iuda as it must nede/
ffor þe heerdes þat sawe þe
dede:
ouer al þat londe it gan
to grede/
þe prophet Simeon &
Anne:

---

[72] MS., in the margin opp. v. 708 are the words [N]unc dimittis/
[s]eruum tuum domine. The page is trimmed, and the initial letters
are cut off.

745 þat were in þe temple
þanne/
And þe childe sawe with
her eye꞉
alle thanked god þat sit-
tith on hie/
When þei to herode þis
worde broght꞉
of felonie he him bithoght/
750 Of his londe alle þe
childir spille꞉
& bringe to deeth it was
his wille/
þe while þis in his hert
wende꞉
augustus cesar aftir him
sende/
And bad him on his quikke
lyue꞉
755 þat he shulde cum to
Rome bilyue/
While he to Rome toke þe
wey꞉
in Cisile he harde say/
þat þe kinges were ouer
fare꞉
in þe shippes þat were
þare/
760 And he in felonie & greet
ire꞉
alle þe shippes sette on
fyre/
While herode to Rome
went꞉
to ioseph god his aungel
sent/
And bad him in-to Egipt
hye꞉
765 with þe childe & with
marie/
And be þere for þe childes
fons꞉

til þe aungel bid him go
home/
ffor herode is in wille꞉
al þe childir to spille/
770 Ioseph in-to Egipt fledde꞉
forthe marie & þe childe
he ledde/
And þere he was without
drede꞉
til herode þe king was
dede/
When þe childe come in-to
þe londe꞉
775 no maument ne false god
might stonde/
In iche temple þer he was
founde꞉
þei fel doun to þe grounde/
Here was fulfilled þe
prophecie꞉
þat bifore seide Isaye/
780 God shal into egipt go꞉
alle þe maumentz shal
falle þo/
In no temple shal false
goddes stonde꞉
þat is made & wroght with
honde/
When herode had done
his nede꞉
785 wherfore he to Rome
ȝeode/
Home he went to fulfille꞉
in wikke dede his wikked
wille/
ffor of his folc he sent his
route꞉
sone al þe londe aboute/
790 To Bedleem & þe cuntree꞉
toun castel & eke citee/
And bad þei shulde blyue꞉

alle þe childir bringe out
of lyue/
þat tuoo ȝeere had & lesse
in eelde͛
795 aftir þe tyme þe kinges of
teelde/
So wende herode þe childe
to queller͛
& his wikke dede fulfille/
þer-fore he had hem ouer
alle gone͛
of tuoo ȝeere olde ne spare
none/
800 þe deuyles forth gan hye͛
[fol. 75 b]
& did þat greet folie/
þei slough þe child on þe
modirs barme͛
at þe teet in þe modirs
arme/
Herode here-aftir gan to
fonde͛
805 shame to do ouer al þe
londe/
And þerfore god him
sende͛
a shendeful lyf & euyl
ende/
So þat aftir his endyng͛
archelaus his son was
kinge/
810 Sone aftir þe aungel
wende͛
to ioseph as god him
kende/
And to israel bad him
gone͛
for deed were alle þe
childirs fone͛
As ioseph him toke þe
way͛
815 to israel he harde say/

þat archelaus þe kinges
son͛
for his fadir king was bi-
come/
þidir to wende ioseph him
dredde͛
forthe marie & þe childe
he ledde/
820 To galilee þere bisyde͛
in Nazareth a stounde to
abyde/
In wildirnes seint Iohn
ȝeode͛
in hungur & thirst & pore
wede/
To þe folc in þulke dawes͛
825 preching goddes lawes/
Aboute he ȝeode þe folc to
preche͛
to baptize & to teche/
þat god of heuen shulde
not take wreeche/
One he seide shal cum
aftir me͛
830 strengar þan i shal he be/
þat shal þe folc bringe out
of synne͛
þorou his might þat þei
be inne/
I am not worþi þer-to͛
to lese þe thwonge of his
sho/
835 As he stode þe folc to
preche͛
of ihu had he knouleche/
þer stondith he seide ȝou
bituene͛
of wham ȝee nothing
wene/
þat þis worde is bounden
inne͛
840 ȝou shal saue fro synne/

BODL. MS. ADD. C 38

To þe folc he shal þe sothe
   sey·
shal he stonde of hem
   none eye/
Preching goddes lawes
   aboute he ʒeode þe folc
   to preche·
to baptize & to teche/
845 To heuen hou þei shulde
   reeche·
þat god of hem shulde not
   take wreeche/
One he seide shal cum
   aftir me·
strengar þan i he shal be/
þat shal þe folc bringe out
   of synne·
850 þorou his myght þat þei
   be inne/
I am not worþi þer-to·
to vndo þe lace of his sho/
But as he stode þe folc to
   preche·
of iħu had he knouleche/
855 Iħc seide be nou stille·
þus us bihoueth us to ful-
   fille/
al rightwisnes & þan seint
   Iohn·
baptized iħu in flum Ior-
   don/
Out of þe flum iħu ʒeode·
860 as we in þe gospel rede/
þan heuen opened thorou
   goddes myght·
& þe holi gost on iħu
   alight/
As seith seint luke in a
   culyr liknes·
& seint Marc berith witnes/
865 And þan on him was harde
   a steuen·

BODL. MS. ADD. C 38

þat com fro þe fadir of
   heuen/
þis is my son leue & dere·
in him me likith him ʒee
   shul here/
   þe holi gost þan radde·
870 & him to wildirnes ladde/
ffonded to be a sothfast
   man·
of him þat fonding bigan/
In wildirnes was his won-
   yng·
fourty daies in fasting/
875 And fourty nyghtes as
   seith þe boke·
& aftir þat hungyr him
   toke/
þan come þe feende him to
   fonde·
& broght stones ful his
   honde/
If þou be goddes son·
880 nou shewe a newe wone/
And make þise stones
   turne to breed·
þan iħu ansuerde þe quede/
And seide noght al-one in
   brede·
lyueth a man but with
   goed reed/
885 þat to mannes soule is
   leche·   [fol. 76 a]
& wil him gostly strengthe
   eche/
When he iħu with no wile·
myght with glotonye bi-
   gyle/
Him to fonde oþir pride
   he thoght·
890 & him to þe temple broght/

And on þe pynacle he him
sette⸝
and him on þis wise grette/
If þou be goddes son doun
light⸝
of þe pynacle thorou þi
myght/
895 ffor of þe it is writen in a
stede⸝
þat god to his aungels hath
bede/
þe to bere & þe to queme⸝
and fro fallyng þe to ꝣeeme/
þat þou spurne on no stone⸝
900 þi fote to hurt or þi tone/
And it is writen iħu seide⸝
þat þou shalt not þi lord
vpbreide/
Nor þi god fonde wham
þou shalt drede⸝
al þi werk in al þi dede/
905 ꝣit 'wende þe foule quede⸝
iħu to bringe to synful
dede/
And him bithoght in al
wise⸝
iħu to fonde with couetise/
þan ladde he iħu to an hie
doun⸝
910 & him shewed felde &
toun/
Wode watir meede &
grasse⸝
& al þat on þe erthe was/
Al þis he seide i wil gyf
þe⸝
if þou falle doun & honoure
me/
915 To him þan gan iħu sey⸝
þou Sathanas go þi weye/
God þi lord þou shalt hon-
oure⸝

& him al-one serue iche
houre/
þe deuyl left iħu þore⸝
920 & þer aftir spake with
him no more/
And þe aungels come to
his seruice⸝
iħu to serue on al wise/
Man be wise in al þi deede⸝
& kepe þe fro þe feendes
reed/
925 ffor if he fonded to bi-
gynne⸝
him þat neuer myght do
synne/
Wele þou maist wite he
wil not wonde⸝
þe synful man for to fonde/
ffonde he wil in synne þe
cast⸝
930 but if þou ageyn him
stonde fast/
And do þe þi sight of iħu
mysse⸝
& out þe cast of heuen
blisse/
þerfore vs techith & lere⸝
seint Petir if we wil here/
935 Ageyn him hou we may
stonde⸝
when us wil of synne
fonde/
þe feende he seith þat
is ꝣoure foo⸝
styntith not aboute to go/
As a lyon his preye to
fynde⸝
940 wham so he may of synne
bynde/
In truyth ꝣee shul ageyn
him fight⸝

þat he in ȝou haue no
myght/
Seint Bernard seide he
may þe fonde꞉
but in þe it is to falle or
to stonde/
945 He may þe to synne egge
& tille꞉
but in þe it is to graunt
him wille/
  There iħu nolde no
  lengar duelle꞉
for of seint Iohn he harde
telle/
þat herode þe king him
had founde꞉
950 and in prison ful fast
bounde/
þan bigan iħu to prechen꞉
in galilee and þe folc to
teche/
Penaunce to do & leef
synne꞉
and heuen riche blisse
wynne/
955 Bi þe see side as iħu
ȝeode꞉
with his worde þe folc
to fede/
Tuo men he sawe her
nettes slake꞉
& out of þe see þe fisshe
take/
þat one was Petir andreu
þe toþir꞉
960 þat fissher was as was his
broþir/
Iħc hem bad aftir him
gone꞉
& þere þei left her bote
on-one/
Her mete where-with þei
shulde hem fede꞉

& at o worde with Iħu
ȝeode/
965 fforþirmore when he was
gone꞉
Iame he sawe & his broþir
Iohn./
Her nettes drye bi þe see
syde꞉   [fol. 76 b]
& of fisshing þe tyme
abyde/
Iħu hem seide þei shulde
him folwe꞉
970 & þei without any sorwe/
Sone þei lete her nettes
falle꞉
& left her freendys alle/
And al þat þei had nette
& bote꞉
& ȝeode with iħu fote hote/
975 þan iħu ȝeode in þat
cuntree꞉
preching þe folc of galilee/
And who so was in sekenes
falle꞉
with his worde he heled
hem alle/
Halt croked wode & blynde꞉
980 & alle þat he þere myght
fynde/
þe folc him folwed al
aboute꞉
of þe cuntree with greet
route/
Som were wikke & som
were goed꞉
som him folwed for her
fode/
985 Som of her sekenes to
haue rightyng꞉
som of him to se tokenyng/
Som of him som thing to
here꞉

    & som of him som thing
      to lere/
    Wherethorou þei might on
      him lyeᵹ
990 & him to þe .iewes bewrie/
    When he sawe þe folc him
      nyghᵹ
    opon an hil he sate on
      high/
    And bigan þe folc to techeᵹ
    & on þis maner hem to
      preche/
995   Blessed be þe pore in
      willeᵹ ⁷³
    þat her pouert sofir stille/
    And here on erthe suffre
      nedeᵹ
    for þe kyndom of heuen is
      her mede/
    þe debonere & meke be
      selyᵹ
1000 & blessed be man of merci/
    So he þat him with right
      ledeᵹ
    & þat wepith for his mys-
      -dede/
    Also haue he þe blessyngᵹ
    þat kepith his hert fro
      foule ⁷⁴ likyng/
1005 And þei þat pees loue hem
      bitueneᵹ
    & for þe right sofir tene/
    And þat haue shame for
      þe loue of meᵹ
    & be mys-seide blessed ᵹee
      bee/
    Takith it with ioie &
      mekenesᵹ

1010 for ᵹoure shal be heuen
      blisse/
    þerfore thenk man to ful-
      filleᵹ
    with þi myght goddes
      wille/
    Be ⁷⁵ pore meke & debon-
      ereᵹ
    clene in soule and of suete
      ansuer/
1015 Loue pees & merci folweᵹ
    to hem þat fallith euer in
      sorwe/
    Prey god & wepe for þi
      mys-dedeᵹ
    & iħu wil gyf þe þi mede/
    Of ioie & blisse with goed
      likyngᵹ
1020 in heuen riche at þine
      ending/
      þerfore more i wil
      shewe þeᵹ
    þat þou might bothe here
      and se/
    Hou he sofirde for þe &
      þineᵹ
    ᵹou to bringe out of pyne/
1025 And þat þou his pyne haue
      in thoghtᵹ
    þat he hath þe so dere
      bought/
    And be aboute his loue to
      wynneᵹ
    & do goed & hate synne/
    When þat worde of iħu
      sprongeᵹ
1030 ierusalem þe folc amonge/

---

⁷³ MS., in the margin opp. v. 995 are the words *Beati pauperes
spiritu./*
⁷⁴ MS., *from euyl, m euyl* deleted by dots and *foule* written above.
⁷⁵ MS., in margin opposite this line is placed the word *Nota.*

þat he to hem was com-
yng·/
alle þei ageyn him went/
Ageyn him þei come al bi-
-dene·/
& bare al þat þei fonde
grene/
1035 ffloures & palme & grene
tree·/
& alle were glad iħu to se/
ffloures þei cast ouer al þe
strete·/
& clothes þei leide vndir
his fete/
þei þat bifore & aftir
ʒeode·/
1040 Osanna bigan to grede/
Goddes son blessed þou be·/
& blessed be þat cometh
of þe/
þe pharisens when þei
harde·/
þat þe folc þus with iħu
ferde/
1045 And þat þei him cleped
king·/
of israel & dauid of-
springe/
Sone þei hem toke to reed·/
iħu for to bringe to deed/
And to þe princes him gan
wrie·/
1050 & seide he was worþi to
dye/
ffor if he longe þus forthe
ʒeode·/   [fol. 77 a]
þe folc he wolde with him
lede/
On him to leue & him to
folwe·/
& hem alle bringe out of
sorwe/

1055 þan bad þe princes þei
shulde him holde·/
& do bi him as þei wolde/
Sone þeraftir iħu gan
calle·/
to him his apostles alle/
And to hem bigan to telle·/
1060 þat one of hem shulde him
bitraye & selle/
þan ansuerde petir & Iohn·/
& aftir euerichone/
A lord wheþir it i be·/
we be redy to dye for þe/
1065 þan seide iudas one of þe
tuelf·/
& iħc seide it was him-
-self/
And bade him go fast &
spede·/
and his thoght fulfille in
dede/
Euyl iudas ʒeode iħu to
bitraye·/
1070 & of þe iewes take his
pay/
Thirty penys of her
money·/
iħc gan to his apostles
sey/
Alle ʒee shal sclaundred
be·/
þis nyght for loue of me/
1075 þe herde man shal smyten
be·/
& þe shepe shal alle flee/
But when i ryse i shal ʒou
see·/
fro deeth to lyue in gali-
lee/
þan spake petir boldest of
alle·/
1080 þat shal me not bifalle/

BODL. MS. ADD. C 38

ffor þowe alle sclaundirde
 be꞉
þat shal neuer bifalle in
 me/
  iħc seide wiþ mylde
  chere꞉
petir er þou shalt here/
1085 þis night þe koc crowe꞉
thrys þou shalt me forsake
 to knowe/
þat may he seide in no
 wise be꞉
þowe i shulde lord dye for
 þe/
And þe apostles seide alle
 one꞉
1090 rather þei wolde wiþ him
 to deeth gone/
þan toke iħu ouer Cedron꞉
petir wiþ him Iame &
 Iohn/
And to his fadir þise
 wordes seide꞉
& him in orison he leide꞉
1095 ffadir if it þi wille be꞉
turne þis passion fro me/
Not for þan at my de-
 siryng꞉
but as þou wolt on al
 thing/
When iħc had seide his
 bede꞉
1100 Ageyn he ȝeode to þe
 stede/
þer petir was Iame &
 Iohn꞉
& fonde hem on slepe
 ichone/
ffortraueiled þei were &
 fer agone꞉
& þerfor þei slepe on-one/
1105 þe while iħu was in þis
 dede꞉

BODL. MS. ADD. C 38

man for þe to sofir deed/
þe suette on his face
 stode꞉
as it were dropes of blode/
Thrise iħc made his pre-
 iere꞉
1110 and euer þei on slepe
 were꞉
þe thirde tyme he bad hem
 wake꞉
for nygh þei were þat
 wolde him take/
Wakith & beeth in prei-
 ere꞉
he þat wil me bitraye is
 nye here/
1115 Me bitraye wil he not
 wonde꞉
in to synful mannes honde/
 While iħc þis worde
 forthe broght꞉
in þat stede iudas him
 sought/
Wiþ fel iewes him bi-
 hynde꞉
1120 for wele he wist him þere
 fynde/
þan come iudas wiþ fikil
 chere꞉
& iħu kissed on þis man-
 ere/
Heil maistir iudas him
 seide꞉
& honde on him þe iewes
 leide/
1125 Iudas hem gaf to tokyn
 þis꞉
wham i kisse he it is/
Holdith him & ledith
 stille꞉
& doeth wiþ him al ȝoure
 wille/

11

When he him kissed on þis
mañere꞉

1130 iħc him seide with mylde
chere/

Iudas wherto is þi com-
yng꞉   [fol. 77 b]

goddes son to bitraye with
kissing/

þan seide iħc to þe deuyles
lymes꞉

þat were comen him to
nym/

1135 With suerdes & staues ȝee
cum to me꞉

in to take as i a theef be/

While i was þan ȝoure
fere꞉

in þe temple þe folc to
lere/

Iche day. none i fonde꞉

1140 þat on me þan leide honde/

And to þe prince of þe
lawe him ledde꞉

& alle his disciples fro
him fledde/

But petir folwed som-
what nygh꞉

& as he durst him hielde
awey/

1145 And in amonge þe folc he
ȝeode꞉

of þe iewes to se þe dede/

þan gan þer a woman
gone꞉

& to petir seide on-one/

þou art of his companye꞉

1150 nay i am not petir gan
crie/

A-noþir him seide þat he
was sene꞉

go with iħu of Nazarene/

And of his disciples one
be꞉

for he was a man of gal-
ilee/

1155 Nay seide him petir sone꞉

i haue noght with him to
done/

Sone þeraftir come moo꞉

and to petir seide also/

Petir swore & seide ywis꞉

1160 i note what þat man is/

Nor i no thing him knowe꞉

& þan bigan þe koc to
crowe/

þan gan iħc petir bi-
holde꞉

& petirs hert bigan to
colde/

1165 ffor sore to his hert he
leide꞉

þat iħc bifore to him
seide/

And out he ȝeode wepyng
sore꞉

and in come he no more/

þan bigan þei ihu to
wrie꞉

1170 to þe prince and on him
lye/

And of him seide many
thinges꞉

but none þei myght to
sothe bringe/

And þe prince him made
his askyng꞉

of his disciples & of his
teching/

1175 Iħc bifor þe prince stode꞉

and þus ansuerde with
mylde mode/

Openly i am wont to
  teche꙼
þe folc in þe temple &
  preche/
What is þine asking to
  me꙼
1180 aske hem þat þere were
  wont to be/
Wele þei wote & can telle꙼
what i was wont to spelle/
þan cam one fote hote꙼
þat þere stode & ihū
  smote/
1185 A buffet he him gaf & to
  him seide꙼
shaltou so þe prince vp-
  breide/
ffaire ihc to him seide꙼
þat him smote & honde
  on leide/
If i spake euyl or wikked-
  nes꙼
1190 of þe euyl berith wit-
  nesse/
If i wele seide i haue no
  wite꙼
wherfore shaltou me þan
  smyte/
þan him sent þe prince
  annas꙼
to þe bisshop Caiphas/
1195 ffast bounde him to deme꙼
& so þe false iewes queme/
When þei to Caiphas him
  broght꙼
on him to lye þei hem
  bithoght/
And when þei so on him
  lye꙼
1200 þat he were worþi to dye/
Vp ros tuoo & gan him
  vpbreide꙼

he þis þat here stondith
  seide/
þis temple i destroye may꙼
& make it al newe þe
  thirde day/
1205 When Caiphas on ihū
  sawe꙼
þat was bisshop in þe lawe/
þo lesinges on him wele
  he harde꙼
& to ihū þus ansuerde/
Herestou not in hou many
  dedes꙼
1210 þise men bewrie þe þat þe
  lede/
But þan ihc stille stode꙼
& no worde spake euyl ne
  goed/
When Caiphas myght in
  no wise꙼
of ihū crist do sacrifice/
1215 Bi god he seide i coniure
  þe꙼
sey us if þou crist be/
            [fol. 78 a]
I it am ihc him tolde꙼
and fro þis tyme shal be
  holde/
Goddes son in myche
  myght꙼
1220 doun of heuen in cloudes
  light/
þan him ros þe bisshop
  blyue꙼
& his cloths bigan to
  Ryue/
And to þe folc seide what
  haue nede꙼
witnesse ageyn him to
  lede/
1225 þis same ꝫee here what
  ꝫoure reed꙼

BODL. MS. ADD. C 38

alle þei ansuerd he is worþi be deed/
þan sette þei iħu hem
amydder
& with a clothe his eyen
hidde/
And in his face þei gan
speter
1230 & his heed aboute bete/
And bad him rede as he a
fole werer
who him smote vndir þe
eere/
As sone as þe day bigan
to dawer
alle þe princes of þe lawe/
1235 Pharisen scribe & iewer
alle þei come to deme iħu/
To pilat þei ladde iħu
bounder
we haue þei seide þis man
founde/
Turnyng þe folc aftir his
deder
1240 & thorou-out þe londe for-
bede/
To Cesar gyf any thingr
& seith þat he is bore crist
& king/
Pilat him ledde to his
mote haller
and him asked biforne
hem alle/
1245 þe first tyme of þis o
thingr
if he were iewes king/
Iħc seide to Pilat on-oner
as in þe gospel seith seint
Iohn/
Wheþer seistou þat of þer
1250 or þei it seide to þe of me/
Pilat ansuerde to iħur

wheþer þou wene þat i be
a iewe/
þi folc þe haue bitake to
mer
what hastou done hem þat
toke þe/
1255 þan seide iħc my kynde
richer
to þis worlde is no thing
lyche/
If i king were in þis lyuer
my disciples wolde for me
stryue/
ffor me fight & bi me
stonder
1260 þat i were not taken into
iewes honde/
When iudas hem sawe
iħu þus leder
& þe iewes deme him to
deed/
þe penys wherfore he iħu
solder
bifor þe iewes he broght
& tolde/
1265 And seide i haue synned
in þamr
i haue bitraied þe right-
wis man/
þere wolde iudas no lengar
ber
but ȝeode & hange him-
self on a tree/
And þere his wombe he
brake a tuoor
1270 þat alle his guttys gan
out go/
More synned iudas of þis
deder
as we of seint Ierom rede/
þan he did þat ilke whiler
þat he wold iħu bigyle/

1275 Iudas what was þi wikked
   wille⁊

   in wan-hope þi-self to
   spille/

   þat þou noldest merci
   calle⁊

   him þat wil merci haue of
   alle/

   Wele we rede & fynde
   writen⁊

1280 & for soth wele we it
   witen/

   þat þer is no man in so
   greet synne⁊

   but þat he may merci of
   iħu wynne/

   If he wil his synne lete⁊

   & þat he hath mys-done
   ageyn him bete/

1285 ffor more is his merci þan
   oure mys-dede⁊

   as seith þe holi man seint
   Bede/

   Seint Petir oure lord for-
   soke⁊

   three tymes as seith þe
   boke/

   Marie Maudeleyn had hir
   withinne⁊

1290 alle þe seuen deedly
   synnes/

   Dauid þe king did greet
   folie⁊

   for he slough his knyght
   Vrye/

   ffor his wyf þat he him
   bynam⁊

   while þat he was liuyng
   man/

1295 Of oþir ynowe ȝee rede⁊

   þat did greet synne in
   worde and dede/

   And thorou penaunce þei
   had space⁊

   merci to wynne of·god ·&
   grace/

   But þine hert was so
   drie⁊   [fol. 78 b]

1300 þat þou ne mightest merci
   crie/

   Of god þi lord for þi mys-
   -dede⁊

   þerfor helle is þi mede/

   So is of þe fulfilled in
   dede⁊

   þat we in þe sauter rede/

1305 þe iewes stode iħu to
   wrie⁊

   bifor pilat on him to lye/

   And seide fro galilee⁊

   to ierusalem al þe cun-
   tree/

   Aboute he goeth & þe folc
   drawes⁊

1310 with his lore fro oure
   lawes/

   When pilat harde of gal-
   ilee⁊

   þat herode had in his
   poustee/

   To herode he sent iħu
   sone⁊

   to wite what were of him
   to done/

1315 ffor of herode þan spronge
   wide⁊

   þat he was in. ierusalem
   þat ilke tyde/

   And in·his hert had greet
   longyng⁊

   of iħu to here som token-
   ynge/

And þan bigan his hert
light⁊

1320 when he of iħu had þe
sight/
To herode þe iewes feller⁊
and thinges bigan him to
telle/
Of iħu & of his lore⁊
as þei raþer had done bi-
fore/

1325 ᵗ To Caiphas Pilat &
anne⁊
and iħc no worde ansuerde
þanne/
When þe iewes had seide
her wille⁊
& herode sawe iħu be
stille/
And to him gyf none an-
suer⁊

1330 sone he him droof by
bysmere/
And of him þan made his
game⁊
as he a fole were & did
him shame/
Vilanye & hething⁊
& did him chaunge his
cloþinge/

1335 And to iewes him bi-
kende⁊
and ageyn to pilat sende/
When iħc was pilat
bitaught⁊
herode & pilat were
saught/
And forgaf him wreeche &
tene⁊

1340 þat longé bifore was hem
bituene/

When þei to pilat iħu
broght⁊
& him to deeth bringe
thoght/
Pilat gan þe iewes caller⁊
and þus seide biforne hem
alle/

1345 þis man biforne me ȝee
wrie⁊
as he were worþi to dye/
ffor with his worde & with
his preching⁊
he wil al þe folc to him
bringe/
But i in him fynde no
thinge⁊

1350 no more did herode þe
kinge/
Of no thing þat ȝee him
wrie⁊
wherfore þat he shulde
dye/
þerfore i wil aftir my
wille⁊
him chastise & lat him go
stille/

1355 Custum it is thorou oure
lay⁊
þat ȝee shul on pasche
day/
Som prison ȝee prey of
me⁊
do vnbynde & lat free/
Wil ȝee lat þe iewes king⁊

1360 & þei cried nay. for no
thinge/
But to him þei seide al
ane⁊

ᵗ The paragraph division should be at v. 1327, instead of v. 1325,
as it is in the MS.

BODL. MS. ADD. C 38

> þat he shulde graunt hem
> Baraban/
> Theef he was as seith
> þe boke of seint Iohnꝭ
> & him delyuerde pilat on-
> -one/
> 1365 þan wolde Pilat þe iewes
> quemeꝭ
> & iħu crist bigan to deme/
> And him bitaught in his
> mennes hondeꝭ
> pyne to do þat þei ne
> wonde/
> And þe iewes redy wereꝭ
> 1370 & in stede of croun þat
> kynges bere/
> Of sharpe thornes a croun
> platteꝭ
> & iħu heed it sette/
> And þerto so fast it
> boundeꝭ
> þat iche thorne made his
> wounde/
> 1375 Shamefully with him þei
> ferdeꝭ
> & in stede of kinges ȝerde/
> A rede þei him gaf to bere
> on hondeꝭ
> as he were king of londe/
> And bifor him on knees
> hem setteꝭ
> 1380 & on þis wise þei him
> grette/
> Heil iewes king. & vndir
> þe eerꝭ
> him smote þat aboute
> were/
> To Pilat þan sent his wyfꝭ
> for iħu to saue his lyf/
> 1385 And him noght to haue in
> willeꝭ   [fol. 79 a.]
> þat rightwise man so to
> spille/

BODL. MS. ADD. C 38

> þan did Pilat, þe iewes
> calleꝭ
> & iħu broght bifor hem
> alle/
> And hem seide lo here þe
> manꝭ
> 1390 þat ȝee alle it wite bi þan/
> þat i in him no thing seeꝭ
> wherfore he ·shulde nou
> deed be/
> When þe iewes iħu syeꝭ
> alle þei bad he shulde dye/
> 1395 And to pilat alle cried oneꝭ
> him to do on rode on-one/
> And pilat bad þei shulde
> him takeꝭ
> for i fynde in him no
> sake/
> And of him doeth nou ius-
> tiseꝭ
> 1400 and doeth him on rode on
> ȝoure wise/
> þe iewes ansuerde & seide
> nayꝭ
> for þat lawe we haue in
> oure lay/
> And thorou þat lawe he
> shal deed beꝭ
> & þat bihoueth to be þorou
> þe/
> 1405 ffor he doeth ageyn oure
> woneꝭ
> and seith þat he is goddes
> sone/
> And we no man shulde do
> to deedꝭ
> þan was pilat in more
> drede/
> And þan bad pilat iħu sey
> nouꝭ
> 1410 Of what londe artou/
> To his demaunde iħc was
> stilleꝭ

BODL. MS. ADD. C 38

and þat liked pilat ille/
And seide spekèstou not
    to me⸱
wotestou not i haue pous-
    tee/
1415 þe to do on rode & lete
    free/
ihc him seide no might of
    me/
Hast þou. but if it were
    gyuen þe⸱
of man þat hath more
    poustee/
þan Cesar gode þat al shal
    dight/
1420 þerfore he þat bitaught
    me⸱
in þi bandoun & þi pous-
    tee/
Haue more synne & eke
    blame⸱
þan þou þat doest me al
    þis shame/
þerfor pilat bifel in wille⸱
1425 ihu bileef and lete stille/
And þe theuys with greet
    envie⸱
to pilat bigan to crie/
If þou lat him scape so⸱
Cesar loue þou shalt for-
    goe/
1430 When Pilat sye þat he
    might with no reed⸱
ihu delyuyr fro þe deed/
Watir he toke in a bacyne⸱
and his hondes wesshe þer-
    -inne/
And seide to alle þat
    aboute stode⸱
1435 gyltles i am of þis right-
    wise blode/
And þei ansuerde alle⸱

BODL. MS. ADD. C 38

his blode on vs & on oure
    childir falle/
þan demed pilat ihu to þe
    deeth⸱
& forthe bad hem þei
    shulde him lede/
1440 But first to a piler þei
    him bonde⸱
aftir þe maner of þe londe/
And him bette while þei
    might drye⸱
as þou man maist se nou
    with þine eye/
þere was fulfilled þe pro-
    phecie⸱
1445 þat of him seide Isaye/
Mi face no thing i ne
    wende⸱
a-weye from hem þat me
    shende/
Lord god myn help in
    nede⸱
þerfore i am not shent in
    dede/
1450 Of betyng when þei were
    sade⸱
þei did as pilat hem bade/
And lede him forthe þei
    gan hye⸱
to þe mount of Caluarie/
To wikked men þat shulde
    him lede⸱
1455 him to pyne & do to deed/
Opon his shouldir þat ran
    on blode⸱
þei made him bere his
    owne rode/
To þe deeth as ihc ȝeode⸱
as vs alle bihoueth nede/
1460 Many wymen he sye him
    folwe⸱

þat for him wepe & made
sorwe/
Hem he bad stille beꝛ
and bileef ȝoure weping for
me/
ffor ȝoure-self ȝee mowe
wepeꝛ
1465 and for ȝoure childir þat
ȝee kepe/
ffor ȝit shal come þe dayꝛ
þat men to ȝou sey may/
Blessed be wele and myldeꝛ
[fol. 79 b]
þe wombe þat neuer was
with childe/
1470 þe bodi þat nadde be-geetꝛ
and no mylke gaf hir
teete/
When þe to þe stede
him broghtꝛ
þere þei on rode him hange
thoght/
þei bigan first to bore þe
treeꝛ
1475 þere inc shulde nailed be/
Isaye seith þei toke her
sorweꝛ
& bare her pynnes vs to
borwe/
In Ieremye also we fyndeꝛ
þat þus of him makith
mynde/
1480 I am ledde opon þat wiseꝛ
as a meke lombe to sac-
rifice/
When þei had nailed þe
one hondeꝛ
to þe toþir a rope þei
bonde/
ffor þei myght not a-noþir
takeꝛ
1485 nor þei wolde none oþir
make/

But so his lymes draweꝛ
þat his bones were sene al
raweꝛ
Suete iħu þat was vnlaweꝛ
þi bodi so to be drawe/
1490 Mi soule & my thought þou
rightꝛ
here on to thenke day &
nyght/
When þe rode was sette on
hieꝛ
tuoo þeues þei hanged
him nye/
ffor Isaye þan of him toldeꝛ
1495 with wikke men men shal
him biholde/
þan made iħc his prei-
ere
for alle þat aboute him
were/
And aboute him þere stodeꝛ
him to pyne and hange on
rode/
1500 ffadir forgyf hem for wele
þou mightꝛ
for what þei do þei wote
no-wight/
Alle goddes werkes ben
oure techingeꝛ
þerfore we shal with goed
likyng/
Hem forgyf & for hem
preieꝛ
1505 þat vs mys-doeth or mys-
sey/
While iħc þus hanged on
þe rodeꝛ
þe wikke men þat aboute
stode/
Scornyng him did &
shameꝛ
& of him made al her
game/

1510 And shoke her hedes &
lough & pleied⁊

& bituene hem þe princes
seide/

Oþir to hele he hath
broght⁊

and him-self he may help
noght/

Lat him light doun þat
we may see⁊

1515 and we wil þat he king be/

Of þe theues spake þe
tone⁊

& iħu mys-seide on-one/

With foule wordes wikke
& kene⁊

& to him seide lat nou be
sene/

1520 Of israel if þou king be⁊

light doun & delyuyr us
and þe/

þe toþir liked þise wordes
ille⁊

& him gan blame & bad be
stille/

Wheþir þou he seide ne
drede⁊

1525 and for þi gylt art done
to deed/

ffor oure deed jas with
dome & lawe⁊

we haue deserued to be
slawe/

Of euyl may him no man
wrye⁊

wherfore he shulde on rode
dye/

1530 þan bad he iħu lord thenk
on me⁊

in þi kyngdom when þou
shalt be/

Iħc seide with' mylde
chere⁊

to-day þou shalt be my
fere/

In paradys i sey it þe⁊

1535 in rest þere to be with
me/

In þis theef se we may⁊

three thinges at his end-
yng day/

þat in him were on þe rode
tree⁊

feith hope and charite/

1540 ffeith " he had in þat
thing⁊

when he on rode god knewe
for kinge/

Hope ¹⁸ in him men myght
se⁊

when he preied god: lord
thenk on me/

Charite ¹⁹ when he his
felawe⁊

1545 vndirnom of· wikked sawe/

And him bad god to drede⁊

and him preie for his mys-
-dede/

þerfore i trowe he be
goddes leef⁊ [fol. 80 a]

seint austyn him clepith
þe blessed theef/

1550 þe sonne left his light⁊

& þe day hore as it were
myd-night/

Ouer al þe londe was
derknesse/

" MS., *fides* in margin.

¹⁸ MS., *spes* in margin.

¹⁹ MS., *caritas* in margin.

BODL. MS. ADD. C 38

fro mydday to none with
  greet distresse/
    Of none when þe tyme
      was nygh꞉
1555 iħc bigan to crie on high/
  To his fadir & made his
    mone꞉
  þat he him had left al-one/
  Al-one in mannes kynde꞉
  none ne myght men þan
    fynde/
1560 þat stedfastly in trouthe
    stode꞉
  but þe theef þat hange on
    rode/
  And þe maide in wham he
    toke man-heed꞉
  she hielde up þe trouthe of
    his godheed/
  þan thirst iħc as seith þe
    boke꞉
1565 and one of þe knightes a
    sponnge toke/
  And in vynegre it wette꞉
  & to iħu mouthe it sette/
  ffor som þer were þat gaf
    þe [60] rede꞉
  of þe iewes to hast his
    deed/
1570 Vinegre þei him gaf &
    galle to drinke꞉
  so shulde þei no more
    swynke⌐
  þer to stonde al nyght to
    wake꞉
  til þe deeth him wolde
    take/
  þan sawe iħc þe deeth him
    nye꞉
1575 & to his fadir cried on
    hye/

In-to þi hondes · fadir I
  bikenne꞉
my soule nou i wende
  henne/
But of þe knightes a spere
  fette꞉
and to his side fast it
  sette/
1580 And his hert thorou-out
    stonge꞉
  þat þe blode thorou-out
    wronge/
  So þat þe prophet it shulde
    be꞉
  in wham þei stonge he
    shulde se/
  When iħc deeth was
    nygh꞉
1585 þe deuyl sate on þe rode
    on high/
  And fonded if he myght
    wynne꞉
  in him any filthe of synne/
  þan shaltou þi self deme꞉
  and in þi lyf fro synne
    ȝeeme/
1590 þat no gylt at þine endyng
    day꞉
  þe deuyl in þe ne fynde
    may/
  ffor wele þou maist wite
    bi þanne꞉
  þat he wil spare no synful
    man/
    þe night when it bi-
    gan to dawe꞉
1595 þer was a goed man in þe
    lawe/
  Ioseph of Aramathie꞉
  þat him bigan to Pilat
    hye/ ·

Iħu doun to take er it
were euen⁊

þat he shulde not on rodc
bileuen/

1600 Pilat graunted ioseph his
bone⁊

& bad gyf him þat bodi
sone/

And ioseph went *with*
gladde chere⁊

& Nichodeme he toke to
fere/

When þe bodi was done to
grounde⁊

1605 in clene cloþes þei it
wounde/

With oynement þei did it
smere⁊

þat no wormes shulde it
dere/

And in þe graue it leide
on-one⁊

þat was al newe made of
stone/

1610 And sith þere-opon þei
leide a lidde⁊

ioseph & Nichodemus did/

And with a greet stone þe
dore fest⁊

& lete þat bodi stille rest/
When þe iewes sawe
þis dede⁊

1615 to pilat on-one þei ⁊eode/
And seide we us vndir-
stonde⁊

þat while þe traitour was
in oure londe/

He seide he shulde on al
wise⁊

þe thirde day fro deeth
up rise/

1620 þerfore if it be þi wille⁊

comaunde þe graue ⁊eme
stille/

þat of hem ne cum none⁊

þat with him were wont to
gone/

And stele þat bodi with-
out drede⁊

1625 & sey þat he is risen fro
deed/

And pilat hem graunted
her askinge⁊

of þe bodi to haue lokyng/
As sone as it bigan to
nyght⁊

iħu thorou his owne
myght/

1630 ffro deeth to lyue he aros⁊
[fol. 80 b]

and þe sepulcre left clos/
On Esterne day at þe
mornyng⁊

when þe day bigan to
springe/

þe maudeleyn þe suete
marie⁊

1635 and oþir in her companye/
Atte sepulcre redy were⁊
and oynementz *in* her
hondes bere⁊

þat bodi to smere as were
þe lawes⁊

with riche myrre in three
dawes/

1640 As þei stode þere al-one⁊
bituene hem þei made her
mone/

Who shal us help þis stone
were went⁊

fro þe dore of þe monu-
ment/

As þei lyft up her eye⁊

1645 þe stone lyft up þei sye/

BŎDL. MS. ADD. C 38

And þei bigan to loke and
    prye⁊
& sye þere no thing but
    cloþes ly/
Wondir hem toke and were
    in doute⁊
hou þat bodi was broght
    without/
1650 But þe maries so in ȝeode⁊
& fonde an aungel in white
    wede/
With steryn loke & sitte
    on þe stone⁊
and to him seide on-one
No thinge be ȝee in doute⁊
1655 wele i wote ȝee ben aboute/
Iħu to seke of Nazarene⁊
þat nailed hath on rode
    ben/
He is risen þat may ȝou
    lere⁊
þer þei him leide þe stede
    is here/
1660 And goeth to his disciples⁊
and tellith he shal be⁊
bifor ȝou & hem in galilee/
þe maries on hert leide⁊
þat iħc biforne had seide/
1665 þe maudelyn ȝeode on-one⁊
and seide to petir & Iohn/
Out of þe sepulcre my
    lord is nom⁊
i note whidir he is bicom/
þan ran petir þan ran
    Iohn⁊
1670 to þe sepulcre on-one/
But no thing þere þei
    founde⁊
but þe clothes þat he was
    in wounde/
þe maudeleyne ageyn she
    ȝeode⁊

BODL. MS. ADD. C 38

with petir & Iohn to take
    hede/
1675 If she might on any man-
    ere⁊
of iħu oght se or here/
She wepe with greet
    mournyng⁊
of him to se som tokenyng/
    As she wepe and
    wronge hir honde⁊
1680 she sawe iħu biside hir
    stonde/
And she hir went & ȝeode
    nere⁊
& wende it were a gar-
    dyner/
þan spake iħc with mylde
    chere⁊
& asked hir on þis manere/
1685 Woman whi wepestou so
    sore⁊
for i haue my lord lore/
þat awey is hennes bore./
If þat ȝee him bare she
    seide⁊
telle me where ȝee him
    leide/
1690 And i shal if it be þi wille⁊
him hennes take & bere
    stille/
Bi name iħc marie gan
    neuen⁊
& she him knewe bi þe
    steuen/
And to his fete she fel
    doun sone⁊
1695 as she was wont to done/
But iħc bad hir wonde⁊
for to lay on him hir
    honde/
But go to my disciples
    blyue⁊

& telle hem þat i am on
lyue/
1700 And þis he seide to me:
he wil ʒou se in galilee/
At euen þat þe disciples
alle/
Were in o hous for þe
iewes doute͛
but Thomas þan was with-
out/
1705 And amonge hem þei gun
stryue͛
if þat iħc were risen to
lyue/
Amyddes hem þei sawe him
stonde͛
& shewed hem his fete &
honde/
Wondir þei had & greet
care͛
1710 a gost þei wende had
stonde þare/
But pees he seide amonge
ʒou be͛
i it am þat ʒee nou see/
And þat ʒee see vndir-
stonde͛
gropeth my feete & myn
honde/
1715 When þei were sikir of þis
dede͛   [fol. 81 a]
awey þei lete sorwe and
drede/
And ioie þei made with al
her myght͛
of iħu þat þei had a sight/
Mo tokenynges he shewed
hem ʒit͛
1720 for as sothfast man with
hem he ete/
And might hem gaf alle to
preche͛

goddes worde þe folc to
teche/
As sone as he was agone͛
Thomas of Inde come in
on-one/
1725 And þei him asked where
hastou ben͛
for we haue oure lord
seen/
Nay but i his woundes
fonde͛
and in his syde do myn
honde/
I leeue in no wise͛
1730 þat he myght fro deeth
arise/
þe nyent day was eft
bifalle͛
þat Thomas and þe dis-
ciples alle/
Iħu þei sawe hem stonde
amydde͛
and to Thomas þus sey &
bidde/
1735 þi fyngyr Thomas put nou
here͛
and on þat wise may þou
lere/
In honde and fote where
þe nayles stode͛
when i hange opon þe
rode/
In-to my side þine honde
þou reche͛
1740 & of my wounde haue
knouleche/
þat i for þe sofirde sore͛
and in mysbileue be þou
no more/
Thomas answerde with
drery chere͛
my lord my god þou art
nou here/

1745 Iͨ him seide for þou me
      syeͬ
      Thomas with þi flesshely
      eye/
      þou it leuest wele forþiͬ
      but þei be blessed and sely/
      þat of me sawe right
      noghtͬ
1750 & wele it leeuen with
      stedfast thoght/
      With his disciples first he
      spake & eteͬ
      and sith to þe mount of
      Olyuete/
      Hem ladde & hem gaf his
      blessingeͬ
      & stey up without duell-
      yng/
1755 And alle þei stode loking
      on hyeͬ
      tuo aungels hem stode nyeͬ
      And seide ȝee men of gali-
      leeͬ
      stondyng what biholde
      ȝee/
      Iͨ þat is fro ȝou nomͬ
1760 opon þat wise he shal
      come/
        Opon a day it was
        bifalleͬ
      þat þise disciples alle/
      In-to an hous were comen
      on-oneͬ
      þere petir andreu & Iohn/
1765 Philippus Iacob Thomas &
      Matheuͬ
      Simond Iude & barthel-
      meu/
      And oþir in her companyeͬ
      in bedes were with þe
      may marie/

      Ahd þan with lot & with
      bedeͬ
1770 in iudas þe traitours stede/
      Apostle þei ches Mathi
      soneͬ
      and of þe tuelf him made
      one/
      þan out of heuen doun þei
      hardeͬ
      þat as a greet fyre com-
      yng ferde/
1775 And sere tunges þere were
      seneͬ
      as it fyre were hem bi-
      tuene/
      þat amonge hem alle
      alightͬ
      þe holi gost thorou goddes
      myght/
      Of þe holi gost þei were
      filled on-oneͬ
1780 & alle maner langage spake
      ichone/
      þe iewes seide hou may þis
      beͬ
      were not þise men of gali-
      lee/
      But som hem droue to
      bysmerͬ
      and seide þat þei dronken
      were/
1785 þan stode petir up hem
      bitueneͬ
      it is not breþir as ȝee
      wene/
      þat þise men drunkun be
      mayͬ
      for it is but vndrun of
      þe day/
        Seint anselme seith
        ᴅweilaweyͬ [81]

---

[81] MS., *nota* in margin.

1790 what shal i do þat ilke
day/
On iche syde shal be my
sorwe꞉
and is no man þat me may
borwe/
Mi synnes me shal on iche
half wrie꞉
as i be worþi for to dye/
1795 On þe toþir half shal hem
shewe꞉ [fol. 81 b]
my goed dedes none or
fewe/
Vndir me helle so [52] foule
& lothe꞉
aboue me my domes-man
so goeth꞉
Myn inwitte with-inne me
mys-likyng꞉
1800 without þe world al bren-
nyng/
þe [53] rightwise shal vn-
neeth borwed be꞉
þe synful man whidir may
he flee/
Abyde him bihoueth on al
wise꞉
til þat he here þe hie
iustise/
1805 Of þe domes-man shul þei
here꞉
to hem sey on þis manere/
Hungur i had thirst &
nede꞉
ꝫee gaf me no drynke ne
wolde fede/
Seke i was ꝫee nolde me
se꞉

1810 in prison ꝫee nolde com to
me/
Naked gyf me no cloþinge꞉
ne ꝫee me nolde to hous
bringe/
þan shal þei ansuer with
drery chere꞉
as we in þe gospel may
lere/
1815 Lord when sye we þe꞉
seke or in prison be/
Hungur haue thirst or
nede꞉
& we þe warned for to
fede/
Naked or in any sorwe꞉
1820 and we þe warned har-
borwe/
þan shal ansuer þe right
iustice꞉
& shal sey to hem on þis
wise/
þat ꝫee did not to one of
my meynee꞉
of þe leest ꝫee did not for
me/
1825 þan shal here he þat drery
speche꞉
when god of hem shal take
wreeche/
ꝫee cursed gostes hennys
ꝫee wende꞉
in-to þe fyre þat hath
none ende/
In-to þe pyne fro me &
myn꞉
1830 þere to be in sorwe and
pyne/

---

[52] MS., *so* repeated, deleted by dots.
[53] MS., *via saluabitur iustus* in margin.

BODL. MS. ADD. C 38

Of þe deuyl to take ȝoure
mede⁊
aftir þat ȝee haue wroght
in dede/
Beeth þere none þat may
flee⁊
but þe deuyles shul redy
be/
1835 Hem to bere drugge and
drawe⁊
to helle pyne with dome &
lawe/
ffor sikir þer nys king nor
erle⁊
baroun knyght squyer ne
cherle/
Olde ne ȝonge pore ne
riche⁊
1840 þat may þan god biswiche/
Nor bisshop preest ne clerk
none⁊
but þat shal dome take
aftir one/
Alle þat out of þis worlde
wende⁊
in deedly synne at her
ende/
1845 Mi suete frendes take here
goed hede⁊
hou marie þat maide
suete/
Hir brest she vndoeth hir
son to queme⁊
fro helle pyne þat man to
ȝeme/
Thenke also opon þe
stoundes⁊
1850 þat ihc for þe sofirde
woundes/
And is aboute þi pees to
wynne⁊

BODL. MS. ADD. C 38

þat þou hast forgylted
thorou synne/
To þe fadir he is oure
forespeche/
ffor þowe he be wroeth
founde⁊
1855 us to chastise & amende a
stounde/
He shal ageyn wende eft-
-sone⁊
to his seruauntz & graunt
her bone/
ffor he us to þe lyf broght⁊
when he us on þe rode
boght/
1860 With his blode he gaf us
grace⁊
in his kyndom to se his
face/
On him to loke him to see⁊
in ioie & blisse with him
to be/
Of þat blisse may no man
telle⁊
1865 hou miche it is ne no man
spelle/
Ne hert thenk nor eye see⁊
nor eere here whitche it
shal be/
þere is plentee without
nede⁊
sikirnesse without drede/
1870 Ydil ⁸⁴ to do is þere no
myght⁊
þere is day without
nyght/ ⁸⁵
Without sorwe without
care⁊
al þat is goed. men shal
haue þare/
To þat blisse ihc us bringe⁊

BODL. MS. ADD. C 38

1875 þat to þe fadir made his
      offrynge/
      Of his suete flesshe and
      blode↗
      on þe rode tree for oure
      gode/

BODL. MS. ADD. C 38

      þat o god is and euer shal
      be↗   [fol. 82 a]
      fadir & son & þe holi gost
      in trinite. Amen./

VII. NOTES

1-14. Anselm, *Meditation* II.[1]

72. The ascription to Isidore appears to be incorrect. Cf. Augustine, *Commentary on Ps. xli.*[2] "[Cervus] serpentes necat et post serpentium interemptionem majori siti inardescit, peremptis serpentibus ad fontes acrius currit. *Mor.*—Serpentes vitia tua sunt; consume serpente iniquitatis, tunc amplius desiderabis fontem veritatis." Augustine does not mention the renewal of youth, and does not quote Isaiah. The author of *De Bestiis et Aliis Rebus* (probably Hugo de Folieto) Bk. II, ch. xIV,[3] has the account of the loss of horns and hair, with a different moralization. According to the *Mid. Eng. Bestiary*[4] vv. 307-328, the hart draws out the snake from the stone, swallows it, and drinks water as a cure for the venom; he afterwards casts his horns and renews his youth. The moralization identifies the poison with original sin and the horns of the hart with pride. In this case, the *Mid. Eng. Bestiary* offers on the whole a closer parallel than Augustine.

103-126. Cf. Augustine, *Commentary on Ps. lvii*, 5, 6,[5] "Sed gravat quasi pondus corii cuiusdam et quasi senecta veteris hominis. Audi Apostolum dicentem, Exuentes vos veterem hominem, et induentes novum . . . Et quomodo exuo, inquis, veterem hominem? Imitare astutiam serpentis. Quid enim facit serpens, ut exuat se veterem tunicam? Coarctat se per foramen angustum . . . " In the moralization, the narrow hole is the strait and narrow way of eternal life; the skin is our *vetus tunica*. The moralization in the poem at 119-126, based on 1 Cor. x, 4, is used by Augustine in his moralization of the story of the eagle. *Comm. on Ps. cii.*[6] In *De*

[1] Migne, *Patr. Lat.*, 158, col. 724-5.
[2] *Ibid.*, 36, col. 465-6.
[3] *Ibid.*, 177, col. 64.
[4] *An OE. Miscellany*, EETS. xLIX, pp. 1-25.
[5] Migne, *Patr. Lat.* 36, col. 681-2.
[6] *Ibid.*, 37, col. 1324.

Bestiis, Bk. III, ch. LIII [7] the moralization resembles ·that in our poem. In the *Mid. Eng. Bestiary*, vv. 120-143, 165-215, the serpent first fasts, then creeps .through the pierced stone, which is the path of penance, and then drinks his fill from a spring and spews out his venom.

130. *Philosophus libro de animalibus, i. e.*, Aristotle in *Historia Animalium*, Bk. XI, ch. 32. Aristotle, however, has only the statement that the eagle perishes because of its ·overgrown beak. For· the whole passage, cf. Augustine, *Commentary on Ps. cii.* [8] "Dicitur aquila, cum senectute corporis pressa fuerit, immoderatione rostri crescentis cibum capere ·non posse . . . Praegravatur languore sen- ectutis· et .inopia comedendi languescit nimis . . . Itaque modo quodam ·naturali in mensura ·reparandae quasi juventutis, aquila dicitur collidere et percutere ad petram ipsum—atque ita conterendo illud ad petram excutit, et caret prioris rostri onere, quo cibus impediebatur. Accedit ad cibum,· et omnia reparantur; erit post senectutem tanquam juvenis aquila . . ." Augustine's moralization does not refer to evil speech; in this particular the *Mid. Eng. Bestiary* vv. 111-119 affords a closer parallel. Cf. also *De Bestiis et Aliis Rebus*, Bk. I, ch. LVI. [9]

154. *Gildre=childre;* 357, *schild=child.* Cf. *gildes* (=*childes*) *Gen. and Ex.* [10] 2624. The consonant change seems analogous to that in the fem. pron. *ge, ghe, sge* in *Gen. and Ex.*, *ge* in *M. E. Best.*, for Midland *sche;* it will be noted that these forms occur in early East Midland texts. See Introd.

187-220. Compare with this passage vv. 33-80 of the poem printed by Horstmann under the title of *Geburt Jesu.* [11] The similarity of the passages indicates that they are translated from a common original.

198. The source of the first rubric I have been unable to identify. —*Martinus in sermone;* cf. Martinus Legionensis, *Sermon* II, *In*

[7] *Ibid.*, 177, col. 102.

[8] *Ibid.*, 37, ·col. 1323.

[9] *Ibid.*, 177, col. 55.

[10] *The Middle English Genesis and Exodus*, ed. ·Morris, EETS. VII, p. 75.

[11] *Altenglische Legenden*, ed. Horstmann, Paderborn, 1875, pp. 67- 69. The introduction of 80 lines is ·prefixed to the *Geburt Jesu* in MSS. Ashmole 43 and Egerton 1993, both of the early 14th century, and also stands as a separate poem in Laud MS. 622, of the latter 14th century (printed by Furnivall in *Adam Davy*, EETS. LXIX, pp. 93-96.)

Adventu. Domini[13] which contains an account of the prophecies ·and symbols of. the Advent found. among the patriarchs and prophets; also Sermon III,[13] " Hos vero prophetas et patriarchas verissimos Domini·praecones," etc. The exact words of the rubric do not occur in the sermons; but the similarity of thought and phrase identifies the author. See Introd.

269–280. For instances of this favorite medieval simile, cf, Napier's note on *A M. E. Compassio Mariae*, l. 35.[14]

282. Cf. Augustine, *Sermon* CXCV; [15] also Peter Comestor, *Sermon* II, *In Adventu Domini* II.[16]

296 ff. (*V* 162 ff.) Horstmann[17] points out disarrangement in the text of *V* at vv. 162, 246, and 275. *D* appears to preserve the best sequence, according to which vv. 275 ff. should follow v. 170. and not, as Horstmann suggests, v. 162.

308. *Biginge:* probably a mistake of the scribe for *biginninge* (cf. Latin *inchoat*, and a similar error in *biginige* 281); possibly, however, from A. S. *bigenge*, worship, honor. Cf. *English Metrical Homilies*,[18] p. 11, where the form is referred by the editor, probably incorrectly, to A. S. *bycgan*, build.

324. *Al-swonge:* so *V;* B, *ydel gonge;* Latin *inanes*=very hungry; a Scandinavian loan-word from O. N. *all-svangr, admodum jejunus*.[19] This appears to be the only occurrence of the word in this sense, although *swong* is used in *Promptorium Parvulorum* to gloss *gracilis*.[20] Cf. ·Björkmann, *Scandinavian Loan Words in M. E.*,[21] p. 221. The word does not appear in the *N. E. D.*

434-439. *Antra deserti*, etc.; three hymns beginning with these words are listed by Chevalier.[22]

---

[12] Migne, *Patr. Lat.* 208, col. 9.

[13] *Ibid.*, col. 72.

[14] *History of the Holy Rood-Tree*, etc., ed. Napier, EETS. CIII, p. 81.

[15] Migne, *Patr. Lat.* 39, col. 2107.

[16] *Ibid.*, 198, col. 1726.

[17] *Minor Poems of the Vernon MS.*, ed. Horstmann, EETS. XCVIII, p. 5, note on v. 162.

[18] Ed. Small, Edinburgh 1862. The passage runs, " For it falls to a mighty king/ That messager word of him bring/ Ar he com til his biging/ Als sain Jon broht of Crist tithing."

[19] Egilsson, *Lexicon Poeticum Antiquae Linguae Septentrionalis*, 1860.

[20] *Promptorium Parvulorum*, ed. Mayhew, EETS. CII, pp. 189, 484.

[21] Morsbach's *Studien für engl. Philol.* vii.

[22] *Hymnologicum Repertorium*, Louvain, 1892, I, p. 74, nos. 1213-1215.

442. *Oc:* variant form of *eac, eke.* Cf. Introd.

454-461. *Ma. in historiarum glossa* should refer· to· a gloss·on the *Historia Scholastica* of Peter Comestor (Magister); but I have been unable to find the passage in Migne's edition of Comestor.. For the tradition, however, cf. Ludolphus de Saxonia, *De Vita Christi,*[23] Part i, ch. VIII, B, quoting Chrysostom: " Possibilius enim credebat virginem sine viro posse concipere quam mariam posse peccare."

462-469. Cf. Ludolphus de Saxonia, *op. cit.,* Part I, ch. viii, A: " Ac (nolens eam traducere) in publicum, idest diuulgare & difamare ne scilicet tanquam adultera lapidaretur. Uel (nolens eam traducere) in domum suam ad cohabitationem assiduam."

502-8. Peter Comestor, *Hist. Schol. in Evang.,* ch. III.[24] "Et accipiens sponsam in uxorem, cum Virgine virgo permansit," etc.

655. *Store:* A. S. *stor,* incense. The word is found elsewhere only in a few Southern texts.[25]

752-761. The story of Herod's journey to Rome and destruction of the ships at Cilicia (*Cisile* 757) is found in Peter Comestor, *Hist. Schol. in Evang.* xi.[26]

1271-4. For Jerome on Judas, cf. Peter Comestor, *Hist. Schol. in Evang.* clxii.[27]

1472-95. I have been unable to find a source for the statement that only one nail was used in the Crucifixion. For the account of the rope, cf. pseudo-Anselm, *Dialogus de Passione Domini,* ch. x.[28] The statement that the Jews had no nail for the second hand, and would not make one, perhaps furnishes a clue to the origin of the story, first found in the French *Passion,* of the smith who is asked by the Jews to forge three nails.[29]

1585-1593. For the story of the devil on the cross, cf. Peter Comestor, *Hist. Schol. in Evang.,* ch. CLXXII.[30]

1789-1879. Cf. Anselm, *Meditations* I, II, III.[31] Details, however, are introduced from other sources; *e. g.,* the inquisition of the souls 1805-1824, the list of the condemned 1836-1844, the intercession of Mary 1845-1848.

GERTRUDE H. CAMPBELL.

[23] Ed. Lyons, 1530.   [24] Migne, *Patr. Lat.,* 198, col. 1539.

[25] *I. e., Geburt Jesu,* v. 749 (*Alteng. Leg.,* ed. Horstmann, Paderborn, 1875, p. 96), Kentish *Sermon on the Offering of the Magi* (EETS. XLIX, pp. 26-29), *Ayenbite·* (ed. EETS. XXIII, p. 211), and Wm. of Shoreham (EETS. LXXXVI, p. 120).

[26] Migne, *Patr. Lat.,* 198, col. 1543.

[27] *L. c.,* col. 1625.   [28] *Ibid.,* 159, col. 282-3.

[29] See Miss Foster, *Northern Passion, Introd., ed. cit.,* pp. 64-5.

[30] Migne. *Patr. Lat.,* 198, col. 1630.   [31] *Ibid.,* 158, col. 721-729.

XVIII.—THE ACADEMIC STUDY OF FRENCH CIVILIZATION

If history is to giv us a tru picture of human life in the past, it cannot limit itself to political events. The chief end of man never was to frame, uphold, and overthro governments, stil les to wage war and sign treaties. These ar accidents or epiphenomena. Man's primary concern is and was from the first his daily fight for existence, the necessity of getting food and shelter, the desire of getting them with a minimum of painful exertion. Man does not merely adapt himself to his surroundings: he attempts to alter his surroundings so as to suit himself. Thus he creates new conditions from which new problems arise. Human society groes ever farther away from that brutish state of automatic adaptation which poets call the Erthly Paradise. From the erliest stone implement to the aeroplane, from the first concerted hunt to the elaborate insurance system of the German Empire, we see the progres of this warfare against nature. The result of these efforts is what we understand by civilization.

But man does not liv by bred alone. He has other needs, no les real, altho les imperius. Sharpend in his lifelong struggle for existence, his intellect, his imagination, his soul, crave for satisfactions which science, philosophy, art, religion, endevor to provide. The sum of these nobler efforts is culture.

The fruits of civilization and culture may not all be equally sweet; Rousseau may not be wholly wrong in his arrainment of what most men call progres; but no one wil dispute that man's combat against brute nature and his wrestling with the secrets of the universe ar worthier of record than his wasteful strife with his fello-man.

No revolution, no conquest, wil ever compare in importance with the discovery of fire, the invention of printing,
or the revelation of Jesus. In our own times, the battle of
Sedan was undoutedly a most dramatic event; yet its consequences—the doom of one empire, the rise of another—
wer trifling, even for France and Germany, compared with
those of the introduction of railroads. Thus political history tels at best but a small part of the truth: and even
that part which lies within its own narro field it cannot
study thoroly without including civilization and culture.
For it is a delusion to consider political events as forming
an autonomus series. Any of them may be linkt immediately and apparently to another of the same order; but
the deeper cause wil generally be found in economic or
cultural conditions. Human activities form a whole
which cannot be safely divided into artificial sections.
Tru history must be synthetic, or, to use a term of which
modern French writers are inordinately fond, it must be
"integral." It is this all-inclusiv study that the Germans
call *Kulturgeschichte* and we History of Civilization.

Unfortunately the conception of such a universal science
is self-destructiv. No scolar, even at the end of a long
career, wud be qualified to write "integral" history.
Thus the work of the specialist, incomplete and even misleading tho it may be, remains the indispensable basis of
any synthesis. · For the historian of civilization, original
reserch into every part of the field, and exhaustiv treatment of the whole, ar out of the question. Yet his rôle
is not simply that of a compiler. A mere juxtaposition
of unrelated monographs wud serv no purpose. What
we need is a synthesis of their results. The field of the
historian of civilization is not politics, art, literature, religion, science, industry, in themselvs, but the study of their
interaction. It includes only so much of each as wil facili-

tate the comprehension of the rest. It provides the common background on which scientist, artist, statesman, trader, warrior, and prophet stand boldly out.

In a sense, all special histories ar but the auxiliaries of the history of culture, which coördinates them all, and thru their combination goes beyond any of them; this is the lofty point of view of the " philosophers of history," from Vico and Herder to H. S. Chamberlain. In another sense, the history of culture and civilization is but the exchange-counter, the clearing-house of all special studies, and as such, a useful but subordinate instrument of genuin science. In this case, the laws of progres, the mysteries of ethnic and national psychology, all theories as to the destinies of mankind, if tucht upon at all, ar used with the utmost caution, as mere working hypotheses for the convenient grouping of facts. This modest point of view, in our opinion, is the more suitable for university teaching. A course on the history of French civilization may hav its philosophy: what human production has not?—but its purpose is not to establish theories: it is to giv as complete an idea of French history as its compas wil permit.

" There is a Chinese civilization, but there is no such thing as a French or a German civilization—for that reason their history cannot be written." Thus H. S. Chamberlain, in his *Foundations of the XIXth Century.*[1] We agree for once with the uncompromising apostle of racial exclusivness in general and of Teutonism in particular. For centuries, national differences hav been so trivial, and the unity of European culture so evident, that any scientific history of civilization must disregard political and linguistic frontiers almost entirely. Yet the convenient title: History of French Civilization is not unjustifiable.

[1] London, 1911, II, p. 232.

It might mean History of Civilization in France: the description of the local effects of world-wide, at least of European, causes. It might mean: Contribution of France to the common civilization of Europe—a singularly difficult, dangerus, but fascinating subject, which obviusly supposes a complete mastery of the first. For practical reasons, a middle course shud be elected. When writing for men who belong to the same cultural group as the French, there is no need of emphasizing those points of similitude which might be of interest to the Martians, or even to the Chinese. Whilst tru history of civilization shud deal only with collectiv movements, and neglect accidental and personal variations, local history must insist on the disturbing factors which explain the different rate of progres on either side of a given frontier. For instance, science and industry hav revolutionized the modern world, yet little space need be devoted to this tremendus change, which is in no way specifically French. The growth of democracy is also a world-wide phenomenon: but as its manifestations wer not simultaneus and similar in all the cuntries it affected, it is entitled to more detaild treatment. The evolution of literature from some form of classicism, thru a period of romanticism, to the realism of yesterday, is European in its sweep; so was the four-cornerd and ever-shifting fight between rationalism, science, theology, and religion. But, in these last two cases, the barrier of language, the potency of literary and ecclesiastical traditions wer such that the same movements wer variusly colord in one cuntry and in another. *Die Aufklärung,* the enlightenment and "les lumières" of the xvinth century ar subtly different. Thus the history of civilization referd to a particular nation has a system of perspectiv all its own, in which essentials may often be taken for granted, whilst minor deviations from the common type ar strongly emphasized.

A course of study such as we ar outlining is ment to be, first of all, a complement to all Histories of French Literature. Even in its most tecnical aspects, literature cannot be divorced from civilization. The formal caracter of French classical tragedy is in harmony with the tremendus wigs and majestic colonnades of the period. The Romantic reform in French versification implied a whole revolution in French society.[2] If we ar interested not merely in the instrument of literature, but in its message and the sources of its inspiration, we cannot possibly limit ourselvs to purely literary facts and documents. Authors ar first of all human beings; they ar influenced by the whole life of their community, and influence it in their turn. In every book, the culture of the public it was ment for is unconsciusly or not taken for granted, and that whether the writer share or combat the prejudices of his contemporaries. Every literary work is a dialog between author and public, which we cannot understand if we ignore the " tacit interlocutor."

It wud be sheer waste of time further to demonstrate such a truism. A few words of warning may be more appropriate. In their enthusiasm for *Kulturgeschichte* as the basis of literary history, some modern scolars wud fain revive Taine's extravagant claims for the theory of " race, environment, and time." [3] Perhaps it is not idle to reassert the old-fashiond truths that man is man all the world over and in all ages; that, in the present state of science, the individual differences we ar most interested in ar not

---

[2] This is exprest with great *verve* and some exaggeration in Victor Hugo's *Réponse à un Acte d'Accusation.*

[3] Preface to *History of English Literature; Lafontaine and his Fables.*

àccounted for. La Fontaine, born in Champagne, "bears fables as an apple-tree bears apples"; Racine, born within fifteen miles and in the same decade, wrote tragedies; and no other nativ of Champagne has rivald them yet in either field. Much of our modern dout and despair may be explaind by historical causes: but in the XIXth century, we find faith side by side with dout, and the great pessimist Leconte de Lisle is but the echo of Job and the Preacher. Social conditions under Louis XIV "explain" Pradon as wel as Racine. They fail to explain why Racine is not Pradon. When textual criticism has prepared the ground, when history has "restored the atmosphere," as the phrase goes, in which a masterpiece was composed, when reserch has done its best—then almost everything is explaind except what is really worth while, and the actual task of the student of literature begins. Historical knowledge removes artificial causes of misapprehension: it contributes next to nothing to the positiv appreciation of a work of genius. It defines the literary problem: it does not solv it. The one key to literary tresures is not erudition but sympathy.

If social history, within certain limits, lends valuable assistance to the study of literature, literature in its turn, as the most comprehensiv manifestation of culture, is not without influence on social history. It provides a welth of captivating documents. Novels and plays claim to be the mirror of contemporary life; letters and memoirs giv us acces to the inmost thoughts and feelings of brilliant men and women, traind in the arts of observation and expression. In addition to this documentary valu, literature often plays a more activ rôle. Some books and some authors hav helpt to shape the history of a nation. Chateaubriand's *Génie du Christianisme* was an event in the world of politics and religion as wel as in that of pure letters. The Napoleonic poems of Béranger and Victor Hugo fosterd the imperial legend and thus wer partly responsible for the creation of the second Empire. Such immediate response to literary stimulus is particularly tru of France, and of France in the xixth century. Many wer the writers of note who posed as prophets and as leaders of men, from Chateaubriand to Zola. Michelet's and Quinet's courses at the Collège de France wer battles in the great democratic campain against "clericalism." Lamartine said of the Revolution of 1848: "Voilà mon Histoire des Girondins qui passe!"; George Sand wrote bulletins for the provisional government; Victor Hugo considerd himself as the soul of the resistance against the *Coup d'Etat,* and European history from the 2nd of December 1851 became in his eyes a grand duel between himself and Napoleon III. Sainte-Beuve's later years wer made feverish by political and religius strife. Even Renan, retiring scolar tho he was, was brutally dragd into the very thick of the fray. Taine devoted the last twenty years of his life to an arrainment of the Revolution in eleven volumes. Zola, Jules Lemaitre, Anatole France, Paul Bourget, Maurice Barrès, came to be the spiritual and even the actual leaders of political, social, and religius factions. If "Social Forces in Literature" ar worth studying,[4] so ar literary forces in social life. The interaction of these phenomena is evident.

But here again caution is indispensable. Literature reflects the life and the opinions of the classes who ar able to expres themselvs and who care to do it. But the overwhelming majority of any generation is dum, and almost as def as it is dum. It leavs no trace in literature: no genuin, unsophisticated pesant cud giv us a record of

---

[4] Prof. Kuno Francke's *Social Forces in German Literature.*

pesant life. It is practically unaffected by literature: all essentials of its existence—the daily task, the family, religion—ar profoundly instinctiv and traditional, and hav hardly changed thruout the ages. Men educated in the artificial atmosphere of cities often fail to realize the invincible conservatism of the rural classes. It was only yesterday that it dawnd upon a village minister that German pesants had not yet been converted to Christianity.[5] The fact is tru of continental Europe as a whole and of Great Britain in part: the old gods ar stil worshipt in the guise of saints, or feard as goblins and demons. This huge immovable mas seems to play a small part in national history: yet it is the constant reservoir of forces without which the self-devouring upper classes cud not perpetuate themselvs. In national as wel as in individual psychology, the domain of the subconscius is by far the more extensiv. These conditions, we ar bound to ad, hav been changing with surprising rapidity within the last five or six decades. With "universal" suffrage (1848), conscription, cheap transportation, telegraphs, compulsory education, and popular newspapers, the masses ar waking up to cultural life—a revolution of untold consequences. In France at least, and as late as 1848, literature, even in its widest sense, was written by a handful of men and red by the chosen few.

, Furthermore, what is literature? If we cud include under that name every written word, the mas of these documents might giv us a tolerably tru picture, if not of the whole people, at least of certain classes: the upper middle class before the Revolution, an ever-groing proportion of the urban population, even the poorest, during the xixth century, and, in our own times, no inconsider-

[5] Paul Gerade, *Meine Beobachtungen und Erlebnisse als Dorfpastor,* 1896.

able portion of the urbanized pesantry. But, in every cultivated nation, several thousand books or pamphlets ar publisht every year: who cud handle these tons of literary material? What survives as "literature"—one book in a thousand, and, if we take periodicals into account, one page in a million—is likely to represent, not an average, but an exception. Histories of French literature rightly devote pages to the noble philosophical poet Alfred de Vigny. The serial stories in *Le Constitutionnel* or *La Presse* had thousands of readers to Vigny's hundreds. If literature is intellectually superior to the general level, it may also be morally inferior. Before drawing inferences from *Les Fleurs du Mal,* one shud remember that there never wer more than a handful of Frenchmen who enjoyd Baudelaire. The yello-back novels, a cosmopolitan poison put up in Parisian bottles, ar less typically French than the "feuilletons" of *Le Petit Parisien* or *Le Petit Journal,* wherein vice is punisht and virtu rewarded as in any Sabbath-School book. Indeed, even the best kind of literature may be not so much a picture of society as a protest against it. If we shud attempt to study France under Louis-Philippe thru the works of Hugo, Dumas, George Sand, and the erlier novels of Balzac, we shud get a grotesquely distorted image of reality. Béranger, Delavigne, Paul de Kock, and Scribe, because of their literary mediocrity, wud be infinitly more significant. Finally, authors ar emphatically misrepresentativ men: all ar more or les exceptional, all more or les artificial. Even as documents on their own lives, their memoirs and letters must be taken *cum grano;* for general history, they ar worse than useles except in the hands of the most careful critic. As to the personal rôle of writers in political and social life, it seldom was so great as they imagind. Poets ar echoes rather than prophets. As leaders of

:thought, they often found themselvs in the same plight as the Republican politician who ingenuusly confest: " How cud I refuse to follo my.troops, since I am their chief?" Lamartine and Hugo discoverd that all their glory did not weigh a straw against the name of Napoleon. Yet there is no dout that Victor Hugo, for instance, in clothing with eternal beauty the common aspirations of his contemporaries, in preaching great ideals to the mas of his readers with such force and freshnes as to make the most hackneyd theme seem new, was a factor in French culture. And what is preëminently tru of this the greatest and most popular of French poets is tru only in a lesser degree of many others.

We hav conscientiusly playd the part of *advocatus diaboli,* and sought to circumscribe as narroly as possible the field of reserch common to the students of literature, civilization, and culture. No cause is permanently servd by making extravagant claims for it. It is the bane of the history of culture that in too many cases there has been a great discrepancy between promis and performance. Disgusted alike by a surfeit of frivolus anecdotes or of unsupported generalizations, many serius-minded scolars hav been driven back to the most mecanical labors of textual criticism: all other work they brand as amateurish. If they wud remove the stigma, historians of civilization shud first of all imitate the modesty and conscientiusnes of their more specialized colleags. Then it may be realized that tru science is caracterized not by the nature of the material handled, but by the love of truth and a rigorusly objectiv method.

The history of national civilization is of particular interest in our times. In the world of material activities, frontiers ar fast crumbling down and wil soon cease to exist; in the world of the spirit, national differences stil

seem exceedingly strong. One of the greatest problems
of our century wil be to harmonize nations who can no
longer liv apart, and ar not yet redy to merge their separate existence. The cosmopolitan wishes to emphasize whatever is broadly human at the expense of local traditions;
the nationalist tries to save whatever can be saved of his
cuntry's historical individuality. Both, if they ar not
guided solely by abstract principles or by prejudices, shud
study in a disinterested spirit these vast entities, the nations, to which they ascribe so much of our weal and wo.

They wil find it an alluring but a difficult task. Nothing is so puzzling to the average Frenchman as the English turn of mind; if the average Englishman is not equally
nonplust by foren peculiarities, it is because he calmly
condemns or ignores whatever he fails to understand. The
ideal student of alien civilizations shud be a tru cosmopolitan, ripend by extensiv and varied experience. He
shud avoid the attitude of the travelers who, dong before
they landed at a treaty port, had always branded the Chinese as "inscrutable"; such lazy agnosticism has no
place in real science. But even more dangerus wud be the
example of the globe-trotter, who, in six weeks, after a
dozen interviews, a presentation at Court and a slumming
expedition, has inventoried the depths of a nation's soul.
Each center of culture speaks a language of its own, whose
subtle connotations ar not always found in the best dictionaries. For instance, in French political parlance,
" Progressivs " ar retrograde, " Liberals " ar conservativ, " Conservativs " ar revolutionary in aim and
methods,[6] " Radicals " ar trimmers and time-servers,
whilst one of the most reactionary administrations of
recent years was heded by three " Socialists." Hence the

* Les Camelots du Roy.

need of interpreters, whose task is not purely mecanical, but requires a certain amount of imaginativ sympathy. Each nation shud send frendly spies to investigate the intellectual and spiritual secrets of its rivals; and ambassadors, even missionaries, to spred its own message abroad. This, we are proud to say, was fully realized by the three leading democracies, England, America, and France, when they sent forth such men as Lowell, Bryce, Prévost-Paradol, and Jusserand. But the influence of these ambassadors of culture cannot be felt everywhere: in every scool, college, and university, the teacher of languages cud and shud be their modest and efficient assistant, the consular agent of ideal commerce. Whatever his nationality, he shud teach, not merely French and German, but France and Germany. The practical valu of linguistic study may hav been over-estimated, so far at least as English-speaking cuntries ar concerned. But, if we considerd it as a key to foren thought, its cultural, humanistic valu cud be immensely enhanced.

That French Civilization in particular deservs to be studied with thorones and sympathy is, fortunately, a point which I need not demonstrate. The splendid contributions of France to universal history ar universally acknowledged. French was the favorit vehicle of culture as erly as the XIIIth century, and in the middle of the XVIIIth it was spoken even by those kings who had humbled the pride of the French armies: the man whose genius framed the destinies of modern Prussia, Frederick the Great, used French almost exclusivly. From the time when a mystic dove brought down from heven the Holy Chrism for the coronation of the first French king, to the time, thirteen centuries later, when the armies of Napoleon enterd every European capital, there has been a peculiar glamor about French history. Roland, Oliver,

13

and the other knights of Charlemagne, whose glories ar recorded in French rather than in German epics; the first crusaders and the last; Saint Louis and Joan of Arc, the most ideal figures of the middle ages; Francis I, Henry of Navarre, Richelieu, Louis XIV, the Revolution, Napoleon—how familiar these names ar in every cuntry; what a welth of gorgeus or tragic memories they bring in their train! On the greatness of France in the past I need not insist. But it is the study of Modern France that I am pleading for. France is a living nation, and wishes to be judged les on her storied past than on her present achievments, efforts, and dreams. A course in French civilization shud be an introduction to the problems of xxth century France, not an inventory of tresures heapd up in a museum.

But is the France of today, wil the France of tomorro, be worth our while, in the same way as medieval or monarchical France? Has not France lost her long-unchallenged supremacy? In a sense, she has. Supremacy on the part of any one nation has invariably proved precarius, more or les illusory, and harmful in the end: let us be thankful that nations ar growing wiser, and ar gradually dropping that silly and offensiv talk about national supremacy. But if France is les aggressiv and les boastful than in the past; if she has been outdistanced in point of numbers and welth, this does not prevent her from retaining her rank as one of the mightiest cultural forces in the modern world. It might wel be the teacher's endevor to sho his audience how in science, industry, politics, art, literature, religion, France is stil a prodigius laboratory, where bold and possibly dangerus experiments ar carried on for the benefit of mankind.

Some fifteen or twenty years ago, for reasons which it is singularly interesting to analyze, a certain number of

Frenchmen raised the cry of decadence, which was soon taken up by some not over-frendly neighbors. Such fits of self-depreciation ar not rare among nations. England, Germany, even certain elements in our own United States, hav at times taken a very gloomy view of their own destiny. This tonic despair, in a political body that is sound at the core, is generally the prelude of renewd activity. No one believs at present that France is a decaying nation. Even in purely material affairs, France, with a colonial empire second only to that of Great Britain, with a total welth and a foren trade greater *per capita* than those of Germany, can hold her own against any rivals.

There is no dout that the study of the German language, of German literature, and of German life and institutions has been given more attention in America than the study of the corresponding French subjects. Fortunately, the historical feud which divides France and Germany in Europe cannot be exported into this cuntry. Every thoughtful Frenchman can honestly repeat with Michelet and Victor Hugo " Germania Mater," or with Renan: " When we first penetrate into the majesty of German philosophic literature, we ar struck with awe and as tho we wer entering a temple." But our deep gratitude for the services of Germany shud not blind us to the different and no les valuable services of France. Before the recent invasion of our New England States by French Canadians, there wer barely half a million people in this immense cuntry of ours who cud claim French descent, however remote. The roll of famus Franco-Americans can not therefore be so extensiv as that of distinguisht German-Americans. Yet I hav been assured that in the percentage of prominent citizens, the Franco-American element comes first, ahed even of the justly appreciated Scotch-Irish.

Other nations hav given America more of their flesh and blood: none has given more of her soul. For the special appeal that French civilization stil has for Americans is based on intellectual kinship, whose bonds may be stronger than the community of blood and speech. The arms of Lafayette and Rochambeau wer but the symbols of a deeper fact: it was for the principles of the French political philosophers, grafted on the constitutional traditions of old England, that America and France wer fighting in common; and trite as the expression " sister republics " has become, the common ideal of liberty, equality, fraternity, which is struggling to assert itself in both, is nothing to be jeerd at. Most of the other great nations ar stil swathed in medievalism: theoretically at least, France and America ar free. It cannot be forgotten either that French art and American art ar really two branches of the same tree. For all these reasons, America is the only foren cuntry where a Frenchman, even a Parisian, feels absolutely at home, whilst, as we all know, " good Americans, when they die, go to Paris."

It is therefore our contention that no undergraduate curriculum in French is complete without at least one course on the history of French Civilization: and that for graduate work, the three-fold division now adopted by French universities shud be recognized: linguistics, literature, civilization.

ALBERT LÉON GUÉRARD.

XIX.—THE ARRANGEMENT AND THE DATE OF SHAKESPEARE'S SONNETS

There are so many points at issue regarding Shakespeare's Sonnets,—the authenticity of the Quarto arrangement, the question of their autobiographical interest, the date, the identity of W. H., of the Dark Lady, and of the Rival Poet,—there has been so much written on all these problems, and the solution of them is so wholly a matter of conjecture, that I shall be obliged for the most part merely to record my own convictions and refer to rather than repeat the sets of arguments which have led me to one opinion instead of to the contrary view; and even in presenting what I offer as my own contribution to the subject I must omit many if not most of the minor considerations which have influenced me.

It has seemed to me from the start that the mere absence of direct evidence to the contrary has unduly influenced most writers on the Sonnets to accept as authoritative the Quarto arrangement. It is true that the first 125 sonnets and the "envoy" may be read as a continuous series addressed to the "beauteous and lovely youth." Professor Dowden has read them so; and Mr. Wyndham and others have made only very mild reservations. But Professor Alden has more recently shown [1] that the burden of proof rests not with those who would deny but with those who would assert that the order of the first series of the Sonnets is chronological, or is at all as the poet himself might have arranged it.

Professor Alden seems to me completely to have proved

---

[1] The Quarto Arrangement of Shakespeare's Sonnets, in *Anniversary Papers by Colleagues and Pupils of George Lyman Kittredge,* Boston, Ginn, 1913.

his point; and indeed, in the face of such facts as we have, it seems odd that the arrangement of the Sonnets in the Quarto of 1609 should ever have been taken as of any authority whatever. The Sonnets were presumably written at intervals during several years and given out in small groups or singly; they were copied and recopied; we know from the *Passionate Pilgrim,* as well as from a preserved manuscript of Sonnet 8, that there existed various differing copies; it is conceded by all that Shakespeare did not supervise nor authorize Thorpe's quarto (note both the errors and the dedication by the publisher); no one denies that Thorpe took *some* liberties with the arrangement, since he removed to the end those Sonnets that did not apply to the youth; we find in the first series of 125, which alone is supposed to be chronological, innocence attributed to the young man after guilt has been recorded; we find sequences interrupted by Sonnets which have nothing to do with the Sonnets about them. There can be no real possibility, therefore, that Thorpe's collection of manuscripts could have been supplied in their proper order either by the author or by the person to whom so many of them were addressed, or by any " only procurer " of them in his family, as is asserted by the indefatigable Fleay.[2]

The first conclusion to be drawn from this fact is that any Sonnets among the first 125 which seem to be addressed to a woman *may* have been.[3] The second conclu-

---

[2] It is no answer to Mr. Walsh's excellent introduction and rearrangement to say, as one critic does, that no one will accept any one else's order. We need not believe, as Mr. Walsh points out, that the folio order of the plays was chronological, even though we do not agree as to what the order was.

[3] Sir Sidney Lee notes that Sonnet 21 may be addressed to a woman. Professor Alden cites 21-24, 29-30, 46-47, 99, 115-116 as examples of those that " would be thus interpreted were it not for

sion is that it is not only our privilege to reconstruct the order of the Sonnets, but, if this will aid us in the appreciation of them, our duty to do so.

The question at once arises, however, as to how we are to account for the fact that Sonnets 1-126 can be read as relating to a certain young man if they did not all relate to him, and how it happens that there is something faintly resembling a time order in the group. The answer is obvious enough. Thomas Thorpe came into possession of 154 Shakespeare's Sonnets; he knew (apparently) that many of them were addressed to a young man who in 1609 was a person of some importance; Thorpe knew his name (O happy Thorpe!), and took it upon himself to dedicate his book of Shakespeare's Sonnets to their " only begetter " (using, of course, and wisely, merely the initials). He had obviously two conflicting desires,—to publish all the Sonnets in his possession, and to make them, so far as was by any means possible, seem to apply to Mr. W. H. Accordingly he removed and put at the end all those Sonnets which he thought could not be read as applying to the youth; he began his sequence with the longest obvious series; he put as far along as possible those Sonnets which say that the poet has been silent, that three years have passed, and that the poet's friend has once wronged him; [4]

their connection with those in which a person of the other sex is referred to " (p. 285, *n*).

[4] Sonnets 100-125 may have come to his hand in a single manuscript. See below, with reference to the italicized words. Thorpe was, of course, right in supposing 1-17 early and 100-125 later sonnets. This accounts (if it is necessary to account) for the fact noted by Dowden that the pronoun *thou* preponderates in the earlier Sonnets and *you* in the series 100-125. Nothing is to be made of the use of the pronouns from 50 to 100, where they are apparently used at haphazard. One might carry this kind of argument to almost any length. The opening sequence of 17 Sonnets might be

the rest Thorpe distributed, not very carefully, between these two series; and having brought them all together, he marked off this main division with the " envoy " and added all the sonnets that he had left over. Of course he kept the smaller groups as he found them; but he was not always careful, in inserting a sonnet or two into his little pile of manuscript, to see that he did not interrupt one of the minor sequences. Thus Sonnet 81 got right in the middle of the Rival Poet series, and Sonnets 36-39 were pushed in between the closely connected 35 and 40.[5] If Thorpe had taken more pains he would have avoided this; he might also have brought together all the " Heart and Eye " sonnets; or, worse still, he might have set in a row all the sonnets written in absence,—in which case we should have had to identify this very long absence with some extended journey of Shakespeare, or of his friend.

If Professor Alden is not mistaken in his proof that the Quarto arrangement of the Sonnets is in all probability not Shakespeare's, and if my own conjecture as to Thorpe's general purpose and method is reasonable, we may discover from certain peculiarities of his text what was the exact nature of some of his inversions.

The misprint of " their " for " thy " occurs in Sonnets 26, 27, 35 (twice), 37, 43, 45, 46 (four times), in 69 and 70, and twice in 128, fourteen times in all. It has been noted [6] that this error is most naturally to be accounted for by a peculiarity in the particular manuscript which contained these Sonnets. Sonnet 128 Thorpe, of course,

---

divided into a group of *thou* sonnets, 1-12, in which we have only a general friendliness and fondness, and a second group, 13-17, of *you* sonnets (except for Sonnet 14), where we have a deepening of tone and a manner of greater intimacy.

[5] But note my later reservation on this point.

[6] Beeching, p. lxv.

removed; as addressed to a woman, and the pair 69, 70, he
likewise removed on the same count. But later Thorpe
discovered that there was no absolute reason why 69, 70
could not be read as addressed to the youth, and he rein-
stated them in their present position. But 70 is the sonnet which speaks of the " pure unstained prime," and
ought not to have been put after 40-42. Perhaps it was
the line " Thou hast pass'd by the ambush of young days "
(in 70) which at first (coming to him in the same manuscript as 40-42) led Thorpe, as it still leads me, to believe
that this pair of sonnets could not well have been written
to that " lovely boy " whose " straying youth " is still the
excuse for his sinful conduct.[7]

The problem of the italicized words in the Quarto of
1609 is generally discussed with relation to the word (or
name) *Hews,* in Sonnet 20. The peculiarity does seem
to demand some explanation. A type-setter would not go
over to another font for a word unless the manuscript
clearly called for it. Italicized words other than proper
names occur seven times in the series 100-126, and only
six times in all the rest of the Sonnets. There are none,
for example, in the *their*-for-*thy* manuscript. "Alchemy"
is italicized in 114 and not in 33; " audit " is italicized
in 4 and 126 and not in 49; " autumn " is italicized in
104 and not in 97; " rose " is italicized only in Sonnet 1,
though elsewhere used in the same sense.[8]

---

[7] I am obliged to notice that the mistake of printing " their " for
" thy " comes twice in the sequence 33-35, 40-42 (in 35), and that it
comes once in the intervening Sonnets 36-39 (in 37); so that the
manuscript itself must have contained this faulty arrangement
(which is not at all against my theory), or the pages of this manuscript were shuffled. It is possible, however, that the " their " in
37, line 7, is not a misprint.

[8] Mr. Wyndham has made an elaborate *ex post facto* effort to
account for all the words which are italicized, and even for all the

The conclusion to be drawn from these inconsistencies and from the grouping of the italicized words, as well as from the *their* for *thy* peculiarity, if these are to be weighed at all, is that neither the author nor compositor is responsible, but that various manuscripts of sonnet groups came into Thorpe's hands, some of the manuscripts bearing characteristics not found in the others, and that Thorpe seems not to have disturbed his manuscript groups more than was necessary to remove duplicates and to put at the end sonnets which *could* not be read as concerned with Mr. W. H.   Indeed, the very fact that every sonnet which *can* be read as addressed to the youth is placed in the first series, and that no other sonnet, though dealing with the same theme, is to be found there, is evidence of just such an obvious sorting out as Thorpe could and would be responsible for.   Because, however, it is more likely than not that the majority of the sonnets came to Thorpe's hand in a few fairly large groups or collections (for he could otherwise scarcely have gathered so many), and since these collections would be apt to be of sonnets

capitals. He does not try to account for the fact that other words which by analogy should be so marked are not so, nor for the inconsistency where the same word occurs.

It seems futile to try to account for the fancy of some reader of one of the manuscript groups who may have indicated as significant, for example, the word "Autumn" in Sonnet 104, perhaps supposing that Shakespeare was using the word in its frequent metaphorical sense, or who may have thought (or known) that "every Alien pen" had special point as referring to the Rival Poet.

As I shall not recur to this matter of the italicized words, I may as well say frankly that the type of pun contained in the line

"A man in hue, all hews in his controlling,

seems to me so uncharacteristic that the italicized word gives us the only name which Shakespeare's friend could *not* have borne. If Shakespeare used this sort of cryptogram, then there is little to say against the Baconian theory.

given out at the same time (and the general character of the text as we have it indicates this), I believe that Mr. Walsh has gone too far in his rearrangement of them.[9]

With these considerations before us, we are at liberty to reconsider the problem of the date. Without going into the argument *pro* and *contra,* I may say that I am personally fully convinced that the Sonnets record Shakespeare's own experience. I cannot understand Dean Beeching's distinction that they are autobiographic in feeling but not in incident. Lyric poetry is necessarily autobiographic in feeling. If not autobiographic in incident, the Sonnets are not autobiographic at all, and we are reduced at once to the blank agnosticism of the "literary exercises" theory. There is one complete answer to this view: If Shakespeare had been writing as much of a story as these Sonnets tell, and writing it as an imaginary or a borrowed or reflected experience, this Prince of Dramatists would have done it better.[10]

With this preamble, I shall endeavor to set down in the smallest possible space first the main considerations in

[9] *Shakespeare's Complete Sonnets,* Unwin, 1908. Mr. Walsh considers each sonnet as a law unto itself, and he breaks up the obvious sequences rather needlessly. Still, one who came to the Sonnets for the first time in his edition would, I think, gain a truer impression of their meaning and their value than he would from the Quarto arrangement.

[10] The only comment I have found in favor of the "literary exercises" view which is not fully answered by other writers on this subject is that suggested by Price (in *Studies in Honor of Basil S. Gildersleeve,* 1902). Professor Price noted that Shakespeare was most successful in the sonnets containing the highest proportion of native words, and he counted, assorted, proportioned, and tabulated all the metrical features of the Sonnets to show with what expedients the young experimenter most expeditiously sped,—forgetting that it is precisely the genuineness of the emotion that most often and most surely produces the remarkable "effects" of the greatest sonnets.

favor of choosing an early date for the Sonnets, then those for selecting a later date, and finally my own reasons for taking an intermediate date which will not fit either Pembroke or Southampton. And as usual I shall give less attention to the more important arguments, because they are familiar.

First, then, as to the early date:

(1) The remarkable appropriateness of Southampton to sustain the part of the "beauteous and lovely youth" must here be reckoned with. One feels, with Acheson, that any such expressions of adoration as Shakespeare uses in the Sonnets might seem disloyal if addressed to a later patron.[11]

(2) The sonnet sequences reached their climax in 1594 with the publication of Spenser's *Amoretti*. It is presumable that Shakespeare would not have begun to write sonnets several years after the fashion had gone out.

(3) *Venus and Adonis* was published in 1593, and *Lucrece* in 1594. It would be natural to suppose that Shakespeare would at this time be more concerned with the writing of his non-dramatic poems and the establishment of himself as a man of letters than he would later.

(4) Taking the most generally accepted dates, we have the *Dream* in 1594, *Richard II.* in 1595, and *Romeo and Juliet* (revised) in 1596-7. That is, Shakespeare's most lyrical comedy, his most poetic history, and his most fanciful tragedy come in the years immediately following his narrative poems; and the lyrical mood would be both cause and result of his sonnet writing.

(5) Parallels have been found between the Sonnets and the early plays.

---

[11] Sonnets 82, 83, however, *could* not have been written to Southampton, who had twice received Shakespeare's "dedicated words."

(6) Relinquishing the lady to the friend has been noted as a similarity of idea in the Sonnets and the *Two Gentlemen of Verona*.

(7) The fantastic assumption that Shakespeare is W. S., the "old player" in *Wyllobie his Avisa* (1594) need hardly be mentioned, though Fleay regards it as "indubitable." [12] This would bring the whole Sonnets story to a still earlier period.

As to the chief arguments for a later date:

(1) A large supply of parallels point to *Henry IV., Henry V.,* and *Hamlet.*

(2) The arguments for and against the Pembroke theory need not be reviewed. The facts are that W. H. comes nearer to William Herbert than to Henry Wriothesley; that the *Will* sonnets are vastly more appropriate if Will was the young man's name; but that this young earl's father lived till 1601; and that Mary Fitton can scarcely be counted as an argument; [13] that the "Mr." is in either case a bit hard to get around, [14] and that the young earl who was beautiful and who closely resembled his mother was whichever you please,—it depends upon which you have chosen for your theory; in short, that Southampton and Pembroke can play each other to a tie, but neither can show any compelling reason for the choice of him.

---

[12] *Life and* Works *of Shakespeare*, p. 124. Mr. Acheson devotes a whole book to the elaboration of this impossible theory.

[13] Dean Beeching says that "Mistress Mary Fitton turns out when her portraits are examined to be conspicuously fair" (p. xlii). I agree with Professor Alden that the attempt to find out the name of the Dark Lady is not only impossible but impertinent. (Introduction to *The Sonnets*, p. xx, in "The Tudor Shakespeare.")

[14] In this connection one may remember the articles by Archer and Lee in the *Fortnightly Review*, December, 1897, and February, 1898, wherein each critic makes the "Mr." impossible for the opposing theory.

(3) Sonnet 107 is assigned with complete assurance to the year 1603 by various excellent critics. Tyler found that Sonnet 55 reflected Meres's *Palladis Tamia,* 1598. Beeching and Dowden agree that '71-74 echo the tone of *Hamlet* and *Measure for Measure.*

(4) Beginning about 1602, there is a sequence of plays which are concerned with women's infidelity. *Troilus and Cressida, Hamlet, All's Well, Othello, Measure for Measure, Pericles* (if Shakespeare wrote it), and even *Lear* and *Antony and Cleopatra* may all be read as due to the attitude of mind brought about by such an experience as the Sonnets record. In this case, Hero, in *Much Ado,* would represent the state of mind in which Shakespeare was when he believed the lady unjustly suspected and maligned. But all this presents peculiar difficulties. If the "three years later" sonnets were 1602, then the time of disillusionment and fury should not be that of *Hamlet* and succeeding plays, but of the years which extended from the sunny Rosalind to the saucy Viola. Indeed the disillusionment *could* not come so late; for the *Passionate Pilgrim* in 1599 already contained the "Two loves I have" (144) and the

> When my love swears that she is made of truth
> I do believe her though I know she lies (138).

And finally, the argument for an intermediate date:

In 1596 (the year usually assigned to *The Merchant of Venice,* we have the story of an older man of melancholy mood who loves his *débonnaire* and somewhat frivolous young friend so much that he would risk his life for that friend's happiness. Bassanio goes awooing and forgets all about Antonio, who would pay dearly for his generosity but for Portia's own splendid intervention in his behalf. I would not point to a factual analogy between this and the story of the Sonnets, nor suggest that the wish was father to the thought; what *is* notable is the exaltation of friendship and the isolation and self-pity of Antonio.

If the usual dating is correct, we have in the next year, 1597, the story of love in place of the story of friendship. It is, of course, a predetermined tragedy; circumstances have doomed it in advance. Romeo is ever the man who is happy in love but who is out of favor with fortune. Again, the play takes its own course and follows its sources, as the *Merchant* did, sources which were not to be found in the poet's life. But I believe, as I have elsewhere stated,[15] that *Romeo and Juliet* could not have been written by anyone but a lover, were he never so many times a Shakespeare. The "out of favor with fortune but happy in love" sonnets are closely akin, both in attitude and circumstance, to the unfortunate Romeo. No correspondence of phrase could be half so significant as this amazing similarity of idea.

` Both Antonio and Romeo are characters who have been taken, and I think justly taken, as showing much of Shakespeare's own mood and attitude.[16] I see no reason for supposing it should be otherwise. Great dramatists do write great dramas out of the deepest experience of their souls. We know it to be the case with the dramatist who stands perhaps next to Shakespeare in intensity and power; and Shakespeare was after all not necessarily more "objective," nor more remote from his characters and their experiences, than was Ibsen.[17] Why should he

[15] "Romeo, Rosalind and Juliet," in *Modern Language Notes*, November, 1914.

[16] Frank Harris, *The Man Shakespeare*, Kennerley, 1909.

[17] "Everything that I have written has the closest possible connection with what I have lived through, even if it has not been my own personal—or actual—experience." Letter of Ibsen to Passage. Goethe, objective as he is, frequently testifies to his use of his own experiences.

have been? Though I am no follower of Mr. Frank Harris, still I affirm that Shakespeare was like others in that he derived the form of his plays from his " sources " and his imagination, and the inspiration for them largely from his own experiences. We know the personal inspiration of *Le Misanthrope* and *An Enemy of the People;* why should we believe it impossible in the case of *Romeo and Juliet* and *The Merchant of Venice?* The friendship and the love which produced the Sonnets would more likely than not have found expression in just such plays as these.

But there is always a grave danger in such conjectures as we have now come into. I am well aware that in giving so subjective and personal a significance to Shakespeare's dramas that they may throw light upon the interpretation of the Sonnets, I shall encounter the prejudice not of the unlearned but of scholars. Even Shakespeare's mid-career turning from comedy to tragedy has been said by such sane and logical professors of literature to be due to a following of the fashion:

> Why with the time do I not turn aside
> To new-found methods, and to compounds strange?
>   *—Shakespeare*, Sonnet 76.

that one must appear behind the times and " unscientific " if one does not sedately acquiesce. Just as it is considered heresy for the psychologist to give himself any possible aid from the realms of philosophy, so the Sonnets-critic is forbidden to invoke the one source of enlightenment that he has, except that he may note verbal correspondences.

But to continue in my evil course: In 1597-8 Shakepeare revised *Love's Labour's Lost*,[18] and, as I have tried

---

[18] *Love's Labours Lost* was published in 1598, with the words " As it was presented before her Highness this last Christmas. Newly corrected and augmented by W. Shakespeare." If this first

to show in another paper,[19] added all those portions which refer to Rosaline as "dark." The Rosaline of 1590 or so was "a whitely wanton with a velvet brow," and an irresponsible madcap. The later added portions deepen her character, as they do that of her lover, Biron, and they give him a truly noble expression of his love for her. It is notable that the analogies so often cited [20] between this "early" play and the Sonnets occur almost wholly in the additions of 1597-8. Note for example:

> O, if in black my lady's brows be deck'd,
>   It mourns that painting and usurping hair
> Should ravish doters with a false aspect;
>   And, therefore, is she born to make black fair—
> (IV, iii, 258-261).

But Shakespeare could not in 1597 have made such a point of the "blackness" of his heroine, and have treated her with such easy grace, just after his betrayal by the Dark Lady of the Sonnets. And, as I have said, the two sonnets contained in the *Passionate Pilgrim* (1599) come after this crucial event. 1598 would accordingly be the year of the "key sonnet" (144), and from this date we should have to build out our sequence in both directions if my theory is to be tried. Only the "sugred" sonnets need come before 1598, and indeed it is more appropriate that the others should not.

Sonnet 104 states definitely that three years have passed

---

quarto was published after March 25, the reference would be to the Christmas of 1597. But a play at court does not look as if Shakespeare were wholly out of favor with fortune in this year.

[19] "The Original Version of *Love's Labour's Lost*" has not yet been sent out for publication, but an abstract of it may be found in the Proceedings of the American Philological Association for 1911 (Vol. XLVI).

[20] For example by McClumpha in *Modern Language Notes*, June, 1900.

since first the poet saw the lovely youth who had inspired
him. It cannot therefore be later than 1599, if what I
have said about *The Merchant of Venice* is to hold.[21]
Unless 104 does not go with the sequence beginning with
100, this " three years later " sonnet came after a considerable interval of silence, perhaps after an entire year in
which sonnets had been addressed only to others. In this
case, 1599 would be the date of the majority of the sonnets from 100 to 125. It is easier (as well as more natural) to get a period of silence after the betrayal than
before that time. After this silence, in the calmness of
triumphant friendship, the poet says

> That better is by evil still made better;
> And ruined love, when it is built anew,
> Grows fairer than at first, more strong, far greater.—(119).

I do not like the idea of spreading the Sonnets out over
too long a period of time; but I must admit that some of
them—such bitter ones as 152 and such closely wrought
and philosophic ones as 107,—may belong to the *Hamlet*
period. No doubt earlier sonnets are preserved in 153,
154; and others in Thorpe's collection may well have been
written in the years before 1596.

As I have said, the dates I have been giving scarcely
accord with either the Southampton or the Pembroke theory. Even if this were not so, I should not be greatly
tempted to connect the youth of the Sonnets with either
of these noblemen. In the first place, there is one matter
which I have not seen mentioned and which I believe to be

[21] One must allow some time for a friendship to ripen and for
a play to be written. I should like, if I could, to get the beginning
of the friendship, and such sonnets as 1-17, as early as 1595. Sarrazin argues for the date 1592-6, with Sonnet 104 as a point of
departure, in the *Jahrbuch*, xxxiv, p. 368.

of some significance. In Shakespeare's plays of this period no character addresses another of superior rank with the pronoun *thou* except by way of deliberate insult.[22] I admit that Shakespeare may not have held to his rule in addressing sonnets to a patron; but many of the sonnets are so conversational and immediate in their tone that I am sure he would have felt his " thou " an insult to a man of the rank of Southampton or Pembroke. It seems to me incredible that Shakespeare should have told either of these earls, even in jest, that only sex stood in the way of his grace's marriage to an actor. The tone of many of the sonnets seems to me far removed from what it would necessarily have been in addressing one of the great noblemen of the realm. I am not impressed by the similarity of phrase in Sonnet 26 and the dedication of *Lucrece,* though this sonnet (unfortunately a " thou " sonnet!) need not by any means be addressed to the " lovely boy." [23]

There is something sad about working over a vexed problem and getting in the end only negative results. One so *wishes* to say " Southampton " or " Pembroke," or even, in desperation, " William Hughes! " But as Shakespeare said, " What's in a name? " Superficially, it looks as if his elaborate attempt to " eternize " his friend had ended quite in failure, from his having neglected to mention who his friend was! And yet we know all that we need to of this pretty and wayward youth, whom the greatest man of the ages loved with genuine passion (by

---

[22] I say this under correction. I may easily have overlooked instances to the contrary. "Thou" is, of course, used in apostrophizing the dead; and Laertes, who has *thou'd* Hamlet in his rage, also *thou's* him after giving him his mortal wound.

[23] In this connection see Beeching, p. xxxi, and Butler, *passim.* The dedications of *Venus and Adonis* and of *Lucrece* of course use the appropriate " you."

no means, it seems to me, with the criminal and unnatural passion of a degenerate) ; and I am not sure that any other source of information regarding him than the Sonnets themselves, even the mere knowledge of his name, would not give a tinge of something earthly and transient to his assured immortality. · .

HENRY DAVID GRAY.

XX.—A POSSIBLE FORERUNNER OF THE NATIONAL EPIC OF FRANCE

In Richer's History of France, written in 996 for Gerbert of Rheims, there is an account of one of Odo's campaigns against the Normans, which critics have uniformly rejected as being too romantic to rest on facts.

The time of the campaign, according to Richer, would be the spring of 892, when Odo had withdrawn his troops from France proper, and was refitting them at Le Puy (now in Haute-Loire). The Normans had overrun Britanny, had reached the Loire, and were preparing to raid the country to the south of that river. When this news reached the king, he at once put himself at the head of his army and marched to meet the invaders. His way led him by Brioude, where he stopped to offer gifts at Saint Julian's shrine, through Clermont and on to the north. He found the pirates in the act of laying siege to Montpensier (near Aigueperse, in Puy-de-Dôme). A council of war gave Odo the opportunity to exhort his nobles to remember the military prowess of their ancestors, who had subdued nearly the whole world and humbled even the pride of Rome, and then battle was joined. The foe fell by thousands. Victory was within the grasp of the French, when a Norman ambush advanced on the field. But its presence was betrayed by its shining weapons, and the French had time to reform their lines, and listen to another appeal from Odo to undergo death even in the defense of their fatherland and for Christianity's sake.

However, the ranks hesitated. Leaders were lacking. The nobles to a man had been wounded in the first fight, and now pleaded their wounds as excuse. There was no

one to carry the royal standard. At this crisis Ingo
stepped forward. He was a mere squire, perhaps even
lower (the Latin word, *agaso,* seems to signify " groom "),
but his heart was high, and with the king's permission,
and should the dignity of the nobles allow, he would bear
the banner. Consent was given, the Normans were over-
whelmed, only a handful escaping under cover of the dust
raised by the onset to a thicket, from which they were
soon hunted out and put to the sword, all save their leader,
Catillus, who became Odo's prisoner.

The campaign now over, the French marched to Limoges, where the Norman chieftain was offered the choice
of baptism or death. He chose baptism. Many prelates
had gathered at Limoges for Pentecost, and in their presence, with Odo as sponsor, Catillus was plunged three
times into the font of St. Martial's. But before he could
leave it Ingo rushed at him and stained the holy water
with the pirate's blood. Then eluding the guards who
were ordered to seize and execute him, the assassin gained
the high altar of the abbey, from where he implored Odo
to hear him.

For he had done this sacrilege, he said, because of his
loyalty to his king and the king's subjects. Unusual, extraordinary as it was, it was wholly justifiable. Catillus
had feigned conversion in order to save his life. Once
free, he would have wreaked vengeance on the French for
his defeat, and sunk all Christians into one common ruin.
Such a disaster he, Ingo, had forestalled. Would that
now by his own death he might bring peace and safety
to land and people! He was in the king's power. Yet
should he die, it would be for having rescued king and
nobles, and his fate would prove a sad warning to all
others. Indeed, could it be worth the while to fight
merely to receive such a reward? Should fidelity to the

crown merit this recompense? Uttering these words Ingo bared his fresh wounds and his older scars to the crowd about him. The suffering they had caused him had worn him out, he declared. Death would be a welcome end to his ills, if the king so willed.

At this the soldiers murmured. They surrounded Odo. What profit, they demanded, would he find in the death of a loyal servant? Rather should they all rejoice at Catillus' end. For the Norman had either entered into everlasting joy through a sincere repentance, or been rightly punished for deceit. These arguments promptly secured Ingo's pardon. He was also invested with the castle of Blois and the hand of its widowed mistress. Fortune seemed to smile upon him, but it was only for a time. Malpractice had aggravated his wounds. Tumors appeared. Two years he resisted the malady. Then he succumbed to it, leaving a son, the king's ward, joint heir with his widow.[1]

This account of Odo's campaign and Ingo's exploits seems entirely plausible. It contains numerous touches of realism. Its various parts are consonant with one another. And yet all historians consider it apocryphal. Odo's biographer, Édouard Favre, calls it " de la légende," "un grand épisode fantaisiste," [2] and Philippe Lauer, won by its dramatic power, saw in it only a " récit épique," a " heroïca cantilena." [3] Why this scepticism? Is it due to the surprising incidents of Ingo's career, a commoner shaming the nobles by soliciting the post of danger, and

[1] Richer, *Historiarum Libri Quatuor*, I, c. VI-XI.

[2] *Eudes, comte de Paris et roi de France*, Paris, 1893 (" Bibliothèque de l'École des Hautes Études," no. 99), pp. 230, 232.

[3] *Les Annales de Flodoard*, Paris, 1905 (" Collection de textes pour servir à l'étude et à l'enseignement de l'histoire," no. 39), p. 12, n. 3; p. 45, n. 2.

triumphant, then incurring the sin of sacrilege to assure the safety of his countrymen? Or are these deeds suspect because they are first recorded, in quite a romantic manner, some three generations after they were supposed to have occurred?

Now Richer could rightfully protest this judgment and advance reasons for his confidence in his sources, whatever these sources may have been. In the first place, the topography of Odo's campaign is exact. The king was at Le Puy when he heard of the inroad. He advanced to Brioude, Clermont, and Montpensier. In so doing he followed a well-known highway, the Via Aegidiana of the Middle Ages.[4] The battle fought, he went from Montpensier to Limoges. Here Richer fails to aid us by mentioning intermediate stations, but a Roman road did connect Clermont—less than twenty miles south of Montpensier—with Limoges, in passing by Ahun (Creuse).[5] As for the Normans, Montpensier was easy of access. If they came by river, the Allier flows near by, if by road, a turnpike led from Bourges to Aigueperse.

The year is also correctly given. Odo had withdrawn his army from France proper, exhausted by piratical forays and civil strife, and in 892 was refitting it in Aquitania, but where we are not told outside of Richer's pages. Here again, however, Richer is entirely consistent. He makes Odo visit Saint Julian's altar at Brioude before the fight. After the sacrilege, on his return to France, the king is also seen in our chronicler paying his devotions to Saint Martin at Tours, Saint Denis, and leading saints at Paris, exhibiting to all the same generosity he had

[4] J. Bédier, *Les Légendes épiques*, vol. I, pp. 339 ss.
[5] E. Desjardins, *La Géographie de la Gaule romaine*, vol. IV, pp. 147, 148, and planche X.

shown to Saint Julian.[6] And if we are asking why the Normans should follow up their raids in the North with a dash into the Center, would not the fame of the treasures amassed at Brioude by Saint Julian's worshippers suggest a reasonable answer? And such an expedition was possible at this time, because the country in their path had been left defenseless through the withdrawal of Odo's army.

Far less probable, however, than locality and date seem Richer's conversion and baptism of Catillus, perhaps because of our remoteness from the Middle Ages. For in 897 the Norman, Huncdeus, who had sailed up the Seine in 896 and established himself in the interior, was baptized at Cluny, at Easter, under the name of Catillus, Charles the Simple being sponsor.[7] The parallelism is certainly suggestive. Are both conversions true, and both baptisms? Is one a reflection of the other, and which one? At all events, the ceremony at St. Martial's was in keeping with the times. Richer needs no apologist for it—unless in connection with the added particular of the murder.

For this incident we are reduced to pure argumentation. It is not to be presumed that the meager, laconic records of the Norman invasions, which afford only the briefest mention of matters of the greatest import or edification, would incorporate in their labored phrases the mention of an unedifying sin. Ecclesiastics were the recorders. We could trust them to pass such deeds by. Yet a murder like the one at St. Martial's font could well have been committed. Years of ravages and cruelty, the killing of

[6] Richer, *loc. cit.*, c. XIII.
[7] Favre, *op. cit.*, pp. 187, 188; *Richer's Vier Bücher Geschichte*, Leipzig, 1891 (" Die Geschichtschreiber der deutschen Vorzeit," vol. 37), p. 10, n. 1; p. 17, n. 1.

monks and the burning of convents being by no means
exceptional, had exasperated the population of the river
valleys to the highest degree. It would have hailed any
form of vengeance with unbounded joy. And because of
their own peril the mass of the clergy must have been of
one mind with the people. The suspicion of a feigned
conversion on the part of a ruthless Viking, and the fear
of his release, generally harbored, were enough to change
desire to action, with an independent spirit like Ingo's.
And had the deed not been done at St. Martial's, it is difficult to understand why it was located there. The abbey
was a center of piety. It stood on the highways of commerce. However unscrupulous an inventor of incidents
might be, he would have scarcely dared to debase a shrine
so revered and so accessible. Too many witnesses would
have come forward to controvert him.

Therefore the main features of Richer's account of
Odo and Ingo may be conceded historical plausibility, if
not historical actuality. The conditions obtaining in
Central France at the time indicated may have given
rise to any or all of them. It might also be added that
what we can glean from the annals of the day about Odo's
character and the popular opinion about the king himself
is wholly in sympathy with the tenor of Richer's narrative.[8] Consequently it must be not the contents of his
narrative, but the manner of telling it, that brought its
pages under uniform suspicion. A tinge of romance per-
vades it. A career which passed through such dramatic
crises creates doubt as to its consistent reality and unity.

[8] Odo had stood as the especial defender of the land against the
Normans. He had become so endeared through his efforts to check
them, while still Count of Paris, that his coronation called out an
especial hymn of rejoicing, handed down to us in the hymnal of the
abbey of Moissac (Favre, *op. cit.*, pp. 235-236; Dreves, *Analecta
Hymnica*, vol. II, no. 127).

Were these the experiences of one man or of several men? The story is too well rounded out. It reads like a biography, if not like a eulogy. And then there are details interwoven with it, which are of a decidedly poetical turn, or at least call up correspondences that medieval poetry has rendered famous.

Take the scene where the nobles offer their wounds as excuses for not engaging a second battle, and thereby oblige the honor of the king to depend on the voluntary act of an ambitious squire. Is the plot of *Aimeri de Narbonne* any other? Cannot we imagine Odo, another Charlemagne, making vain appeals to this vassal and that one until Ingo steps forth unannounced? We read that Catillus escaped death under the cover of the dust stirred up by the fight. So will William of Orange, concealed by dust and mist, slip through the Saracen lines to solace dying Vivien,[9] or Girard profit by thick weather to flee from the disaster of Larchamp.[10]

And if these lesser touches avail to shake our faith in the genuineness of Richer's story, what may be said of the idea on which Odo bases his repeated exhortations to his soldiery? Let them remember their race, which surpassed all others in strength, boldness, and arms![11] Let them win the glory that is the reward of him who dies for country and fellow Christians![12] Not otherwise will Charles's rear-guard be heartened to stand in the fatal pass.[13]

[9] *Aliscans*, ll. 611-613, 679, 680.

[10] *Chevalerie Vivien*, l. 1001.

[11] Aliis quoque gentibus eos esse potiores, tam viribus quam audatia et armis, memorabat (*loc. cit.*, c. VII).

[12] Decus pro patria mori, egregiumque pro Christianorum defensione corpora morti dare (*loc. cit.*, c. VIII).

[13] *Roland*, ll. 1063, 1064, 1076, 1090, 1091, 1129, 1210, etc. This idea of a militant Christianity was not at all restricted to the Loire

Further incidents could be cited from the episode, familiar to us because they constantly recur in the epic poems of the twelfth century, though none the less facts arising from observation of life. Odo's visits to shrines before the battle and on his return to France, and the disclosure of an ambush by the glint of the soldiers' weapons have undergone many repetitions in romance. Catillus may not have been the first Pagan offered the choice of baptism or death, but his progeny in medieval verse is legion.

Too much weight should not be laid on the presence of these elements, which were to penetrate so deeply into the romantic tradition of the later centuries. They all undoubtedly proceeded from direct observation. Each and every one in its origin—if we make exception of Odo's appeals—was purely objective. It is their combination here in one continued account which really gives that account the appearance of fiction. The campaign of Odo against the Normans in 892, Ingo's rise from the ranks and his sacrilege at St. Martial's at Pentecost, may well be historically exact and historically connected—as we believe them to be—and yet the form in which these events reached Richer may have been artistically composed, and embellished with ideas of patriotism and faith, and various poetical conceptions quite foreign to the campaign and the sacrilege. In other words, Richer's ultimate source might have been the literary presentation of an historical event, by an author who invoked for himself the privilege of poetic license.

Could we get at the phraseology of the original story,

basin in the last decade of the tenth century. In 897, the year of Huncdeus' baptism at Cluny, we find Archbishop Foulques of Rheims soundly rating Huncdeus' sponsor, Charles the Simple, for proposing an alliance to the heathen Normans. Favre, *op. cit.*, pp. 187, 188.

we could of course test this supposition easily. An author is not a chronicler, a recorder of facts, and the language he might use would prove a sufficient guide to the purpose he had in view. Now while this evidence is not plainly attainable, still there are passages in Richer's version which seem to differ in kind from the main body of the episode, and which accordingly may furnish a hint as to the nature of the material that had come to his hand. These passages comprise about one-sixth of the whole. Furthermore, they are all included in the scene where Ingo offers himself as standard-bearer and the scene where he defends his crime. They are put in the first person, but their difference in style does not come from this substitution, of the first person for the third, oratory for narration. Richer was fond of speeches and scattered them freely throughout his history. The difference in these passages arises rather from the form of the period itself, which, to me, frequently drops into cadence, or rhythm. Here are the words with which Ingo offers his services to the king: "Ego ex mediocribus regis agaso, si majorum honori non derogatur, signum regium per hostium acies efferam. Nec fortunam belli ambiguam expavesco, cum semel me moriturum cognosco." [14]

His apology for his crime begins as follows: "Deum voluntatis meae conscius testor, nihil mihi fuisse carius vestra salute. Vester amor ad hoc me impulit. Ob vestram salutem in has me miserias praecipitavi. Pro omnium vita tantum periculum subire non expavi." [15]

Of these phrases, "mediocribus regis agaso," "honori non derogatur," "me moriturum cognosco," from the first citation, sound rhythmical to me, and "meae conscius testor," "carius vestra salute," "Vester amor ad hoc me

---

[14] *Loc. cit.*, c. IX. [15] *Loc. cit.*, c. XI.

impulit" and "miserias praecipitavi," from the second. From the remainder of the second speech might be added, "visus est, ferrum converti," "haec me ad scelus impulit," "salutem occisus videbor," "pro hujusmodi mercede," "et an pro fide servata" and "malorum finem exspecto." The other five-sixths of the episode, however, where Ingo is not speaking, apparently yield only three such clauses: "decus pro patria mori," "sin minus mortem promittens" and "multis clamoribus petens."

Now elsewhere in Richer it is difficult to detect anything of the sort. He will occasionally lean toward rhymed phrases,[16] never, even in his many speeches, toward rhythm. And his very limited employment of rhyme is all the more noticeable when we recall the positive mania of his day for rhymed prose, a mania which reaches its culmination in the *De Gestis Normanniae Ducum,* of Richer's neighbor and contemporary, Dudo of St. Quentin († 1029). Put beside this remarkable effort, the rare instances of rhymed periods to be skimmed from Richer's work can hardly be interpreted in any other way than as marking our author's decided aversion to this species of rhetorical ornamentation.

Consequently, if these points are well taken, would it be too hazardous to conclude from them that the supposedly rhythmical clauses of Ingo's two speeches, fortified by the distinctively romantic or poetical elements of other sections of the story, indicate a rhythmical, poetical composition as Richer's original? We mean the ultimate original, of course, for the speeches of Ingo in Richer's rendering may alone retain traces of the primitive poem. Their difference in style indicates that. And if the original were a poem, would it not further follow that it was a

---

[16] As in Book II, c. 52, 71-77, etc.

poem in the vernacular? The Latin poetry of the day was extremely learned and rhetorical. But in our whole episode there is only one solitary rhetorical phrase, the "fortunam belli ambiguam" of the first citation, and one phrase only which hints at a loan from classical Latinity: "decus pro patria mori." [17]

There is no difficulty at all in assuming a vernacular composition for this time and place. *Ste. Eulalie* dates from the end of the ninth century, and St. Martial's abbey was about to take over from St. Gall the primacy of music and Christian poesy, a primacy it was to retain during the first two-thirds of the tenth century. And the whole region round about the abbey was imbued with poetical fervor. Native talent and literary training, therefore, met at Limoges, and it was no accident that within another hundred years the Limousin echoed with the first notes of Troubadour song. These considerations may serve to explain the artistic shaping of the Ingo story, its artistic completeness, and they may also furnish a reason for its lack of erudition. For if this story was addressed to the people, in a language which was familiar to all, erudition would be out of place. Direct, concise statements were needed to convey the speaker's (or singer's) ideas, brevity of phrase to awaken the desired response. And by this assumption, of an original composition in Romance, intended for the crowd of peasants and burghers, would also be explained the popular tone of the story, its setting of the humble Ingo over the highest noble in devotion to monarch, fatherland, and faith. Conjectures like these may have prompted Lauer's qualification of "heroïca cantilena," and his keen ear may have caught in some of Ingo's phrases the hesitating accents of the mother tongue.

[17] Even here the quotation is not an exact one. Horace's words are, "Dulce et decorum est pro patria mori" (*Odes*, III, c. 2).

The spirit that animates the substance of the episode may also call for comment. Patriotism and the sense of religious solidarity are its base. It is therefore evident that public opinion in Gaul did not await the growth of the political units of the eleventh century and the crusades against the Saracens of Spain to crystallize these two great conceptions of medieval France. For here they are found developed, already fully expressed. They may have been indeed survivals of the time of Charlemagne, preserved perhaps by nobler minds in church and monastery, and now widening out and deepening among the laymen under the pressure of the Norman inroads. Nor should we in our hesitation ascribe them here to Richer. They are indeed of Odo's day. A Latin poem on the siege of Paris by the Normans in 885 and 886, by Abbo of St. Germain, gives them clear and full voice. Abbo praises the saints for their aid to the city, he commends Odo for his resistance to the pirates on one occasion, he blames him for his desertion of the helpless folk during other raids. Yet neither his praise nor his blame, nor his rhetoric and his abundant quotations from standard Latin authors succeed in beclouding his fervent belief in the oneness of French blood and faith.[18]

In the concluding volume of his *Légendes épiques,* Joseph Bédier looks back from the known epic poems of the twelfth century to possible narratives of earlier days which would have expressed similar ideas and essayed similar forms of verse.[19] These ideas, with the exception

[18] *Poetae Latini Aevi Carolini,* vol. IV, pp. 77 ss.

[19] Placer au XIe siècle la naissance des chansons de geste, c'est dire que les âges antérieurs n'ont pas légué au XIe siècle des poèmes tout faits, mais seulement, par l'œuvre des clercs, quelques-unes des idées qui, l'heure venue, inspireront les chansons de geste, et quelques-uns des procédés de narration et de versification qui, l'heure venue, constitueront la technique des chansons de geste. (*Les Légendes épiques,* vol. IV, p. 462.)

of the idea of the feudal relation, of later development, are present in the Ingo episode. These forms of poetic narration are foreshadowed in its simple directness, its conciseness, its strokes of the picturesque, even if we cannot unqualifiedly grant it the further attribute of rhythmical phrasing.

F. M. WARREN.

XXI.—THEODOR FONTANE UND ENGLAND[1]

In Theodor Fontanes Roman *Effi Briest* heisst es einmal: " Auf zwanzig Deutsche, die nach Frankreich gehen,
kommt noch nicht einer, der nach England geht. Das
macht das Wasser. . . Das Wasser hat eine scheidende
Kraft." Zu dem Wasser, d. h. der geographischen Lage,
kommt die Geschichte Englands, um einen Inselgeist aus-
zubilden, den die fremden Besucher Englands während
der letzten 300 Jahre alles andere nur nicht entgegen-
kommend und liebenswürdig nennen. Man lese etwa nur
das Buch von Edward Smith: *Foreign Visitors in England.*[2] Und die Haltung der Engländer dem Ausländer
gegenüber ist nur ein Symbol für die geistige Abgeschlos-
senheit und Unzugänglichkeit ihres Landes, dem das Ge-
fällige und Mitteilsame der französischen Kultur mindestens ebenso fehlt wie Deutschland.

Natürlich finden sich nun die Deutschen mit den Engländern anders ab als z. B. die Franzosen. Aber Deutsche
und Franzosen entdecken in England bis 1900 etwa—
keine reizvolle Kultur, sondern nur Zivilisation, und zwar
finden dabei die Franzosen den Hauptmangel im Ästhe-
tischen, während die Deutschen, denen Kultur hauptsächlich Innerlichkeit bedeutet, vom englischen Materialismus
oder besser von dem, was sie englischen Materialismus
nennen, von vornherein abgestossen werden. Das lässt

[1] Dieser Aufsatz ist im wesentlichen der Vortrag, den ich am 30.
Dezember 1914 vor der M. L. A. of America in New York gehalten
habe. Die Zusätze und Erweiterungen ergeben sich zumeist aus der
neuen Form. Schliesslich sind auch Berührungen mit zwei meiner
Aufsätze in der *New Yorker Staatszeitung* vom 13. XII. 1914 und
30. v. 1915 nicht zu vermeiden gewesen.

[2] The Book-Lover's Library, London, 1889.

sich im einzelnen durchs 18. und 19. Jahrhundert nach-
weisen. Hier muss ein kurzer Hinweis genügen. .

Im 18. Jahrhundert waren den Deutschen von den
Engländern (ausser Hogarth) eigentlich nur der Schau-
spieler Garrick und der Weltumsegler James Cook näher
bekannt; der eine, weil man sich für Shakespeare und das
Theater lebhaft interessierte, der andere, weil man ein
modisches Gefallen an Reisen und Reisebeschreibungen
fand. Einen allgemeinen Sinn für England als Eigenart
haben beide nicht erweckt. Das beste Beispiel dafür ist
Georg Christoph Lichtenbergs Bericht über seine Eng-
landreisen zwischen 1770 und 1775.

Mit dem literarischen Sturm und Drang erwacht dann
in Deutschland ein regeres Interesse an England, aber
wirklich aufs Inselland treibt es nur den Ästheten Carl
Philipp Moritz 1782, und auch sein Reiseziel ist nicht
"England," sondern ein Naturwunder, die Höhle von Cas-
tleton bei Matlock; und seine Aufmerksamkeit gilt ebenso
sehr der herrlichen Beleuchtung der Londoner Strassen
wie dem Parlament.

Unsere Klassiker haben keine umfassende, lebendige
Kenntnis Englands gehabt. Was sie wussten, stammte
aus Büchern. Selbst Goethe täuschte sich, als er unterm
10. Januar 1825 zu Eckermann bemerkte: "Käme ich
nach England hinüber, ich würde kein Fremder sein."
Zuerst wär's ihm wie Moritz u. a. ergangen, er wäre mit
viel zu hohen Gedanken gekommen und entsprechend ent-
täuscht worden. Und dann hätte gerade er sich vom
englischen Materialismus abgestossen gefühlt, vielleicht
mehr noch als Lichtenberg und Moritz, und hätte auch die
Kunst Englands genau wie sein Freund Wilhelm von
Humboldt oder die Religiosität Englands wie Schleier-
macher verworfen, kurz, er hätte mit seiner deutschen
Persönlichkeit in England so allein gestanden wie z. B.

sein grosser Verehrer Carlyle mit der Schätzung Deutschlands unter den Engländern.

Von den Romantikern dann hat nur Achim von Arnim
(1803-1804) England besucht, und er ist sehr ernüchtert
zurückgekehrt. Seine Urteile sind nicht viel weniger ab-
sprechend als die Heines aus den 1820er Jahren. Heines
unbedingte Abneigung gegen England erklärt sich aber
nicht nur aus seinem Napoleonkult, sondern auch aus romantischen Zeitstrebungen und deutschen Idealen, so wenn
er ganz frei den Engländer einen "zivilisierten Barba-
ren" (mit dem Ton auf "zivilisierten"!) nennt. Fast
gleichzeitig mit Heines erscheinen 1830 Fürst Pücklers
Reisebriefe "eines Verstorbenen," die ausser Politik und
Theater hauptsächlich die Moden und Parks Englands be-
handeln. Im Jahre 1836, nach einem Abschied von
Heine in Paris, macht Grillparzer seine Englandfahrt
von ungefähr einem Monat, freilich ohne bedeutende
Ergebnisse, was hauptsächlich in seiner eigenen See-
lenverfassung begründet liegt. Und so wie Heine im
Vorwort zur ersten Auflage des vierten Bandes von seinen *Reisebildern* der Pücklerschen Briefe erwähnt, macht
uns Grillparzer seinerseits auf Raumers Werk über England aufmerksam. Gemeint ist das gründliche Buch
des Geschichtsforschers Friedrich von Raumer, nämlich *England im Jahre 1835*. In diesem, das erst von
Lothar Buchers und Gneists Forschungen überholt worden ist, wird die Lichtseite Englands viel mehr als die
Schattenseite gesehen; und wenn auch manches Lob Englands aus einer Abneigung gegen Frankreich zu erklären ist, so hat sich doch Raumer ernstlich bemüht:
"England nicht mit deutscher Schere zurechtzuschnei-
den." Doch am Ende seines mehrbändigen Werkes stehen
die Worte, die im grossen und ganzen alle deutschen Besucher Englands kennzeichnen: "So unendlich anziehend

und lehrreich auch alles war, was ich ringsum in Grossbrittannien sah und hörte, ergriff mich doch nicht selten eine Sehnsucht nach Gesprächen über die Geschichte vergangener Zeiten, über spekulative Philosophie, schöne Kunst, Musik, Schauspiel und ähnliche Gegenstände. Dem Roastbeef des Staatslebens hätte ich gern einige leichtere und mannigfaltigere Speisen jener Art beigemischt." . . . Diese blosse Aufzählung des Fehlenden verrät die innerste Stellungnahme des Deutschen zum Problem: England.

Man könnte den erwähnten Schriftstellern und Dichtern und einem Wissenschaftler wie Raumer noch Künstler anreihen wie schon Schadow und später Passavant oder Kunstforscher wie Dr. Waagen, Raumers Freund und Fontanes öfter erwähnten Gewährsmann, aber eine wesentliche Änderung des oben Gesagten ergäbe das nicht. Erst das Jahr 1850 stellt einen Wendepunkt in der seelischen Haltung der Deutschen England gegenüber dar: England als Ganzes wird jetzt den Deutschen auf einmal lebendig interessant, und zwar als geschichtliches Wesen.

England ist Deutschlands letzte Liebe. Die erste war Frankreich, aber nach der grossen Revolution von 1789 mit ihren Greueln begann das Erwachen. Doch die Julirevolution von 1830 und das tolle Jahr 1848 zogen die Deutschen immer wieder in französische Kreise, bis sich endlich um 1850 aller Augen nach England wandten. Dorthin waren die verfolgten deutschen Demokraten geflüchtet, und von dort aus ward dann durch sie und ihre Nachfolger das neue Evangelium einer Demokratie gepredigt, als deren Paradies natürlich England erschien. Was damals Bismarck von der Königin Augusta gesagt hat, gilt von den Deutschen allgemein: ein Wohlwollen für England galt als ein Zeichen für einen höheren Grad von Zivilisation und Bildung.

Die politischen Machtverhältnisse erklären nur etwas.
Im ganzen muss es eine besondere Zeit für die Deutschen
gewesen sein. Will doch Herman Grimm damals eine
neue Weltepoche angefangen wissen. Man kann an
Goethes 100. Geburtstag und an die Blütentage des echt-
deutschen " poetischen Realismus " erinnern. Und nicht
zuletzt haben wir noch tiefer Einwirkungen des Jahres
1848 zu gedenken, das besonders das Geschichtsinteresse
hoch aufschnellen liess. Kein Wunder, dass die Deutschen, die ihre zerrissene Geschichte im Herzen trugen,
vor Englands einheitlicher, ununterbrochener Geschichte
und Machtpolitik ehrfurchtsvoll staunend standen. Und
die englische Revolutionsgeschichte mit Oliver Cromwell
wird nun ständiger Gegenstand in politischen Schriften
wie im Drama. Man studiert aber nicht nur die englische
Geschichte, was Namen wie Ranke, Dahlmann, Gneist,
Gervinus und Hettner beweisen, man reist auch nach England selbst, um England zu sehen. Und diese Welle ge-
schichtlicher Neugier, sozusagen, hat neben Levin Schücking, Julius Rodenberg, Lothar Bucher, Karl Elze u. a. m.
auch Theodor Fontane hinüber geführt.

Theodor Fontane war dreimal in England: 1844 zu
einem kurzen Ausflug, 1852 auf einige Monate und 1855
auf fast vier Jahre. 1844 war es eine Vergnügungsreise
mit wenig Geld, aber viel Freude und jugendlicher Be-
geisterung unternommen. Der Apothekergehilfe Fontane
diente gerade als Freiwilliger beim Kaiser-Franz-Regi-
ment in Berlin, als ihn ein Freund zu der Englandfahrt
einlud. Die zweite Reise, die Fontane, jetzt ein 33 jähri-
ger, machte, geschah im Auftrage zweier " offiziöser " Zei-
tungen Berlins und zwar zum ausdrücklichen Studium der
politischen Verhältnisse in London. Inzwischen hatte
Fontane seinen Apothekerberuf aufgegeben und war ein
freier Schriftsteller geworden. Die letzte Reise verdankte

Fontane dem Entschluss der preussischen Regierung, zur
Unterstützung ihrer Politik eine ständige deutsch-eng-
lische Korrespondenz zu gründen. Mit dem Ministerium
Manteuffel, das diese Korrespondenz eingerichtet hatte,
fiel auch Fontanes englische Berichterstattung. Fontane
kehrte 1859 nach Berlin zurück: aber ganz sollte er seine
journalistische Vermittlungsrolle noch nicht aufzugeben
haben. Denn die nächsten zehn Jahre hatte er den " englischen Artikel " für die *Kreuzzeitung* zu schreiben.

Verschieden nun wie der Anlass zu den drei Reisen
waren auch ihre Art und ihre schliesslichen Ergebnisse.
Was bei der ersten Reise den Charakter von Anregungen
des Augenblicks besass, wurde in den beiden andern
regelrechtes Studium. Die letzten Jahre waren noch besonders anregend durch den persönlichen Verkehr mit
Max Müller, dem berühmten Oxfordprofessor, und aller-
hand Deutschen, die 1848 nach London gekommen waren,
wie Edgar Bauer, Heinrich Beta und vor allen Julius
Faucher.

Fontane kam schon bei der ersten Englandfahrt, bei
kurzen Ausflügen nach Schloss Windsor, Hampton Court,
dem Lieblingsaufenthalt Heinrichs des Achten, und bei
der Besichtigung von Londons Sehenswürdigkeiten überall
Englands Geschichte gross entgegen geschritten. Ein
Bild der Maria Stuart machte solchen Eindruck auf ihn,
dass er noch viele Jahre ein Stuart-Schwärmer blieb, was
zahlreiche seiner Gedichte beweisen. Vor dem Tower und
der Westminster Abtei bekommt er ein gewisses roman-
tisches Gruseln, oder wie er sagt: " Ganz unmittelbar
wirkt der historische Zauber, der in diesen Steinen
geheimnisvoll verkörpert ist." Wie lebhaft ihm das historische alte London vor der Seele stand, zeigt sein phan-
tastisches Gedicht *Der Towerbrand,* das er " noch voll von
Londoner Eindrücken " (im Dezember 1844) schrieb.

Als er zum zweiten Male in London eintraf, schrièb er seiner Mutter, er sei beileibe kein "Anglomane, der seit Jahr und Tag in alles englische Wesen verrannt ist." Sein Urteil über London werde diesmal anders ausfallen als vor acht Jahren (1844): "Ich war damals unerfahren, gutmütig und wenn ich so sagen darf, schwärmerisch genug, alles was ich anders fand, auch sofort besser zu finden."

Seine historische Schwärmerei für England hörte auch bei der zweiten Reise nicht auf. Dazu steckte ihm seit frühester Jugend sein allgemeines Interesse für Geschichte zu tief im Blut. Und ausserdem hatte er sich inzwischen noch eingehender mit der englischen Literatur und Geschichte befasst, was (seit 1848) zahlreiche Übersetzungen aus den Balladensammlungen von Bischof Percy und Walter Scott und der Romanzen-Zyklus *Von der schönen Rosamunde* (1850) beweisen. Auch ihn nahm damals, wie viele andere, die schimmernde Romantik der englischen und schottischen Vergangenheit gefangen.

Mit einem vertieften Interesse kommt also Fontane 1852 nach London, dessen Seele er suchen wollte.

"Der Zauber Londons ist—seine Massenhaftigkeit," so schreibt er. Architektonische Schönheit findet er ebenso wenig wie die vielen Besucher Londons vor und nach ihm, wie er ja auch von der englischen Kunst, besonders der Malerei nicht viel hielt. Grossartig erscheint ihm nur das Britische Museum und die St. Pauls Kathedrale. Samt Westminster ist ihm im Grunde die ganze Stadt "mehr interessant als schön," und zwar weil sie ihm das Symbol des ganzen "soliden Englands" ist: reich, aber ohne Geschmack und daher ohne Schönheit.

Nach den geschichtlich merkwürdigen Stätten in und um London zieht es ihn wieder sehr, aber überall ist jetzt eine Kritik zu spüren, die mit einer sittlichen Verdammung Englands schliesst. In seinem Reise-Tagebuch, das uns seit Oktober 1914 bekannt ist,[3] heisst es, aus dem Augenblick heraus gesagt: "England stirbt am Erwerb und Materialismus." England stehe auf "tönernen Füssen," und "der Anfang vom Ende" sei da.

Theodor Fontane steht mit seiner Prophezeiung nicht allein. Burke, Carlyle, Ruskin sind Propheten unter den Engländern selbst. Die sehr interessanten geschichtlichen Gründe hierfür lassen sich hier nicht erörtern.

Natürlich kann auch Fontane, gleich Lichtenberg, Moritz, Pückler, Heine und selbst Raumer, nicht über England urteilen, ohne immer an Deutschland zu denken, ohne zu vergleichen. Und so fragt er: Was steht der Kultur nach, also nach dem, was ein Volk im innersten Wesen ist, was steht höher: Deutschland oder England?

Das führte Fontane zeitweise in einen wirklichen Zwiespalt. Sein geschichtliches und sein politisches Interesse gehörte England in einem hohen Grade. Die Frage nach der Form im Deutschtum war ihm ein ernstes Problem, weil er selbst einen ausserordentlichen Sinn für die Form besass. Ja, in seinen letzten Lebensjahren hat er mehrfach gesagt, er habe mehr Sinn für Form, als die Mark Brandenburg geben könne. Und doch, wenn wie hier die Frage galt: Form oder Inhalt, war ihm alles klar. Deshalb entscheidet er sich gegen England, wenn er sagt: "Deutschland und England verhalten sich zu einander wie Form und Inhalt, wie Schein und Sein." Er wendet das ebenso auf die innerste Volkssittlichkeit an, wie auf den persönlichen Umgang von Mensch zu Mensch, auf Lebensweise wie Lebensformen. Beurteilt man beide Länder nach dem "Allgemeingut der Bildung," und hat ein Volk mit höherer Durchschnittsbildung den grösseren Kultur-

[3] *Die Neue Rundschau,* S. 1385 ff.

wert, dann steht ihm Deutschlands Gesamtkultur tatsäch-
lich höher als die Englands. Noch 1898, zwei Tage vor
seinem Tode wiederholt er das. Und mag England
Deutschland noch an äusserer Macht und " Repräsenta-
tion " überlegen sein, dem Wesen nach ist ihm das
Deutschtum weiter und tiefer, weil es innerlicher als
das Engländertum ist.

Zu diesem Endergebnis gelangte Fontane endlich auch
bei seinem letzten Studienaufenthalt in England. Er
hoffte, wie schon vor drei Jahren, auf ein gutes persön-
liches Fortkommen, aber wieder vergeblich. Er blieb
" eine Pflanze im fremden Boden," er blieb ein Deutscher.

Er hatte zunächst nicht viel Ruhe, sich " dem alten
Zauber der Londongrösse " hinzugeben; denn England
lebte im Zeichen des Krimkriegs und bald auch des grossen
Sepoy-Aufstandes (1857). Die denkbar beste Gelegenheit, allergegenwärtigste Geschichte mitzuerleben. Und da
kam er endgültig zu einer Ablehnung des, wie er sagte,
" englischen Kattunchristentums," d. h. der Verquickung
von Geschäft und Politik mit Religion und Moral. Einige seiner Gedichte enthalten das, z. B. das sehr ironische
Britannia an ihren Sohn John Bull oder *Fire, but don't
hurt the flag.* Und seine Briefe sind voll davon.[4]

Fontane haben die Londoner Tage im ganzen reichen
geistigen Gewinn gebracht. Bei seiner journalistischen
Tätigkeit mit Studieren und Schreiben arbeiteten immer
der Poet und Politiker Hand in Hand.[5]

Die wertvollsten Zeitungsaufsätze aus den Jahren 1852
bis 60 sind jetzt in zwei lesenswerten Büchern vereinigt:
Ein Sommer in London (1852) und *Jenseit des Tweed,
Bilder und Briefe aus Schottland* (1858 und 59). Ein

---

[4] *Freundesbriefe*, Bd. I, S. 179, bringt sein stärkstes Wort.
[5] *A. a. O.*, S. 189.

Aufsatz von 1860 behandelt die Londoner Theater. Dazu kommen an weiteren Zeugnissen für Fontanes Anschauungen über England zahlreiche Briefe des Dichters an die Familie und Freunde, sodann Gedichte über englische Gegenstände und schliesslich gelegentliche Äusserungen in Romanen wie *Cecile* und vor allen im *Stechlin* (1898), der als letzter und persönlichster Roman auch des Dichters letztes und klarstes Bekenntnis über sein inneres Verhältnis zu England gibt. Es habe für ihn eine Zeit gegeben, wo er bedingungslos für England schwärmte, so heisst es in diesem Roman. "Aber das ist nun eine hübsche Weile her. Sie sind drüben (in England) schrecklich runtergekommen, weil der Kult vor dem goldenen Kalb beständig wächst, lauter Jobber und die vornehme Welt obenan. Und dabei so heuchlerisch, sie sagen Christus und meinen Kattun."—

Ungefähr dieselben fünfzehn Jahre von 1844 bis 1859, die Fontane mit dem ernstlichen Studium Englands beschäftigt sehen, haben nun auch dem Übersetzer Fontane seine besten Werke eingebracht. Dass die eigentliche Übersetzertätigkeit mit seiner Rückkehr nach Deutschland aufhört, ist bedeutsam. Die anempfindende Hingabe an das fremde Schrifttum hört nun auf, und unser Dichter ist hinfort nicht nur bewusst deutsch, sondern auch selbsttätig. Seine Persönlichkeit drängt gereift nach Aussprache, nach ihrem eigensten Ausdruck und Stil. Und wie man sagen muss, dass Fontanes Lyrik um 1845 in Berlin erwacht ist, so auch, dass der Schriftsteller Fontane die entscheidenden Anregungen in England bekommen hat. Ein Blick auf die Entstehungsgeschichte der *Wanderungen durch die Mark Brandenburg* bestätigt das. Mit dem Jahr 1859 oder besser 1860—denn 1860 erscheinen seine *Balladen*—endet jene Zeit des Fontaneschen Schaffens, die wir am besten *Der junge Fontane*

überschreiben. Während dieser Zeit seines Schaffens ist
er immer ein echter und schlichttiefer Dichter ohne den
geringsten Ansatz zu der "amüsanten Selbstpersiflage"
seiner Alterslyrik, und während dieser Jahre hat er auch
sein Schönstes als Übersetzer geleistet.   Daher bleibt
denn auch beim Übersetzen seine "Absicht, nicht literar-
historisch interessante Beiträge, sondern Gedichte liefern
zu wollen."

Fontane übersetzte fast alle seine englisch-schottischen
Balladen f r e i, mit der ihm eigenen Kürze, aber zugleich
auch t r e u, d. h. nach dem innersten Geist der alten Bal-
ladenpoesie.   Fontanesch an allen Übersetzungen ist die
grössere Sensitivität und das dichterische Feingefühl des
Modernen. Ein glänzendes Beispiel hierfür ist *Lord
Athol.* Diese Ballade kennzeichnet zugleich Fontanes
Selbständigkeit gegenüber den Fassungen Walter Scotts.
Scotts epischer Balladenstil und Scotts Modernisierung
("Verschlimmbesserung" sagt Fontane) waren ihm un-
angenehm.   Bei der Ballade von *Sir Patrick Spence* z. B.
tritt er unbedingt für das "rührend-schöne Original" ein.[6]

In diesen Zusammenhang gehört Fontanes allgemeines
tiefes Verständnis der englischen Literatur, die für ihn
mit Shakespeare beginnt.   Nächst dem schon erwähnten
Aufsatz über die Londoner Theater (1860), in dem es
sich hauptsächlich um geistreiche Gegenüberstellungen
der deutschen und englischen Auffassung Shakespeares
handelt, geben die *Causerien über Theater*[7] Fontanes
Erkenntnisse über Shakespeare. Diese *Causerien* sind
sein künstlerisches Programm als Theaterrezensent, der
er zwischen 1870 und 89 für die *Vossische Zeitung* war.
Hierin stellt er sich nicht nur als moderner Mensch zu

[6] Vgl. Jahrbuch *Argo*, 1854, S. 232.
[7] 1905 aus dem Nachlass veröffentlicht.

Shakespeare, sondern vergleicht auch immer wieder die deutsche und die englische Bühnenüberlieferung, wobei er meistens der englischen Recht gibt.[8] Denn das hatte er in London erfahren, dass dort Shakespeare ein Dichter für alle Volksschichten ist, während man ihn in Deutschland hauptsächlich für die Gebildeten spielt. Dort kommt der Mensch auf der Bühne zur Geltung, während hier im ganzen die Schauspielkunst höher steht. Alles in allem wünscht sich Fontane in Deutschland mehr von dem " Naturburschentum der englischen Bühne." Wiewohl er sich nie als Kunstsachverständiger " gehabt," so wird er doch eine hervorragende Rolle in dem Buch " Shakespeare in Deutschland im 19. Jahrhundert " beanspruchen.

Und Scott kritisiert er wohl im einzelnen, nennt ihn im ganzen jedoch einzig und bewahrt ihm sein Leben lang eine persönliche Zuneigung, wie sie ganz rührend in zwei Gedichten zum Ausdruck kommt: *Walter Scotts Einzug in Abbotsford* und *Walter Scott in Westminster-Abtei.* In seinem Roman *Unwiederbringlich* überlegt der Graf bei der Abreise, welche Reiselektüre er mitnehmen solle. Schliesslich sagt er dem Diener, der den Koffer packt: " Nimm ein paar Bände Scott mit, man kann nicht wissen, und der passt immer." Genau so dachte der Dichter, wie seine Familienbriefe beweisen.[9] Scott ersetzt ihm " das Geplauder mit einem geliebten und geistreichen Menschen."

Eine andere Frage ist: wie weit Fontane in seinem poetischen Schaffen von Scott beeinflusst worden ist. Hier zeigt sich vor allem Fontanes Märkertum. So viel nämlich die Märker und Preussen im allgemeinen für das

---

[8] Vgl. u. a. *Causerien*, S. 23 f.
[9] Im I. Bd. z. B. S. 149 f.; 156; 160; 247 f.; 282 ff.

Verständnis Englands in Deutschland getan haben, weil
ihnen als Norddeutschen das englische Wesen näher kam
als den Süddeutschen, so sehr haben sie sich stets ihre
geistige Selbständigkeit zu bewahren gewusst. Man lese
hierzu Fontanes schönen Aufsatz über Wilibald Alexis.
Von dem märkischen Romantiker Achim von Armin, der
von Scott merkwürdig unberührt bleibt, laufen ge-
schichtliche Fäden zu Fontane, dessen einzige wirkliche
" Anlehnung an Scott " in seinem ersten Roman *Vor dem
Sturm* zu finden sein dürfte,[10] und über diesen Roman
fehlt noch eine gründliche Einzeluntersuchung.

Im übrigen hat Scotts künstlerisches Programm als
solches—in einem einseitigen Wort gesagt: die innige
Durchdringung von Landschaft und Begebenheit, von
geschichtlichem Hintergrund und Charakter—mächtig auf
Fontane gewirkt, und ebenso auf W. H. Riehl und Gustav
Freytag. Scott hat die Deutschen wohl nicht erst " das
einfache ruhige Erzählen gelehrt," wie Karl Lamprecht
in seiner *Deutschen Geschichte* [11] annimmt, aber der
Begriff " Land und Leute " in der deutschen Literatur
zeigt Scotts tiefe Anregung, und zwar im ausgesprochenen
Sinn für die Poesie des Kulturgeschichtlichen.

Scott hat neben mehrseitiger künstlerischer Anregung
noch ein letztes für Fontane und die Deutschen seiner
Zeit geleistet: *he did the honors for all Scotland.* Auch
für Fontane ist Schottland nicht ohne Scott denkbar, was
seine schottischen Reisebriefe auf jeder Seite verraten.
Denn er beschliesst seinen langen Ausflug nach Schottland
im Jahre 1858 wie symbolisch mit einer Pilgerfahrt nach
Abbotsford. Und wie er sich auch bemüht, mit seiner
Anteilnahme nicht in der Vergangenheit, in der " ro-

---

[10] *Freundesbriefe*, Bd. I, S. 246.
[11] Bd. x, S. 171.

mantischen Hälfte," also in Scotts eigentlichster Welt, stecken zu bleiben, sondern auch das moderne Schottland zu sehen, immer wieder lauscht er auf die "stille romantische Sprache" der althistorischen Stätten und der schönen Landschaft Schottlands. Ein Beweis mehr übrigens, wie romantisch gestimmt der junge Fontane selbst war.

Es wäre jetzt noch mehr über andere englische Dichter zu sagen, über Dickens und besonders über Thackeray, der für den " alten Fontane," den Verfasser der Berliner Romane etwa bedeutet, was Scott für den " jungen Fontane "—ein neuer Zug kommt damit nicht in Fontanes Gesamtverhältnis zu England.

Um zusammenzufassen: Fontane verdankte England viel. Wir können es vielleicht am besten so ausdrücken: Die starken und tiefen Anregungen und Erlebnisse, die er in England empfing, gaben ihm die letzte Klarheit zu seinem eigenen deutschen Schaffen. Vielleicht ist sogar, mit einem Wort von Fontanes Freund Wolfsohn zu reden, England die bedeutende " Quelle seiner poetischen Bildung." Jedenfalls erklärt die künstlerische Hinneigung zu England mit Fontanes Gesamtauffassung Englands.

FRIEDRICH SCHÖNEMANN.

PUBLICATIONS

OF THE

Modern Language Association of America

1915

VOL. XXX, 4	NEW SERIES, VOL. XXIII, 4

XXII.—THE SIEGE OF TROY IN ELIZABETHAN LITERATURE, ESPECIALLY IN SHAKESPEARE AND HEYWOOD

I

No traditional story was so popular in the Elizabethan age as that of the siege of Troy and some of its episodes; because of its antiquity and undying beauty, of the fame and greatness of the early writers who had treated it, and to some extent of the tradition that the Britons were descendants of the Trojans, a tradition which certainly often determined the point of view. After the close of the Middle Ages its popularity had increased rather than diminished, among both educated and uneducated. And nothing better than this story illustrates the true relation of the age to the nearer and the remoter past,—the continuation of mediæval tradition and taste, especially among the little-educated; and the often uncouth modification of it by an increased knowledge and a sharpened understanding of the classics. To Chaucer and the fol-

673

lowers of Guido delle Colonne were added a more intelli-
gently-read Virgil and Ovid, and a new-found Homer.
But for the most part they were subdued to what they
worked in, the romantic and rather undiscerning taste of
the not highly educated.

There is curious evidence of the popularity of the Troy-
saga in the talk of uneducated people in Shakespeare, especially in the historical plays. With Shakespeare's clear-
sighted veracity of imagination we may well suppose that
the characters and events of the saga were really familiar
to such people. They certainly did not read Homer or
Virgil in any language. Those who read at all may doubtless have read Caxton and Lydgate, and probably heard
and read ballads;[1] but easiest of all is to believe that
they knew the story through stage-plays. In fact, in some
of these passages there is clear evidence that such was
the source of information or misinformation, and we
know from the preface to Heywood's *Iron Age* (part I,
printed 1632) how long and successful had been its run
on the boards. Falstaff's harum-scarum hangers-on are
especially fond of Trojan language. Pistol says,

> Shall I Sir Pandarus of Troy become,
> And by my side wear steel?[2]

Within a few lines he parodies Marlowe's *Tamburlaine*
and talks of "Trojan Greeks" (*II. Henry IV.*, ii, iv,
178-81). To him Fluellen is a "base Troyan" (*Henry
V.*, v, i, 32). He gracefully calls Doll Tearsheet, speaking to Falstaff, "Thy Doll, and Helen of thy noble
thoughts" (*II. Henry IV.*, v, v, 35). In *Henry V.* he is

---

[1] I find no record of any early chap-books on the Troy or Troilus
stories (unless as noted on p. 676). For ballads, cf. pp. 678-9.

[2] *M. W. W.*, I, iii, 83-4; my line-references are to the *Tudor Shakespeare* (Macmillan, 1911-13).

less chivalrous to her; she is "the lazar kite of Cressid's kind" (ii, i, 80). Doll Tearsheet was doubtless no great reader, but she tells Falstaff, "Thou art as valorous as Hector of Troy, worth five of Agamemnon" (*II. Henry IV.*, ii, iv, 237). The host of the Garter calls Falstaff "bully Hector" (*M. W. W.*, i, iii, 12); and calls Caius, "Hector of Greece, my boy!" (*ib.*, ii, iii, 35). Fluellen calls the Duke of Exeter "as magnanimous as Agamemnon" (*Henry V.*, iii, vi, 6). The clown in *Twelfth Night* (ii, iii, 29) with his precious irrelevance says "the Mermidons are no bottle-ale houses," and is called by Sebastian "foolish Greek" (iv, i, 19). He "would play Lord Pandarus of Phrygia, sir, to bring a Cressida to this Troilus. . . . Cressida was a beggar" (iii, i, 58-62).[3] All this is not only of interest in itself; the fact that these signs of popular interest seem to be confined to plays dated between 1598 and 1602 is evidence, confirmed by other matters,[4] that the especial vogue of the Troy-Troilus story in the drama was around that time. Mr. Greg remarks,[5] "The popularity of Greek subjects at this date [1599] is striking." The use as common nouns (and verbs), even to the present day, of such words as Hector, Myrmidon, Trojan, may be traced in part to these plays.

It is in the drama especially that I mean to study the

---

[3] Some of these collections and remarks I owe to one of my students, Miss Marjorie L. Walker. Of course in other plays other references are made by characters of higher station. The popularity of the fighting in Elizabethan Trojan plays is shown by Davenant in 1643, who says of his auditors' ancestors at the theatre (prologue to *The Unfortunate Lovers*):

> Good easy judging souls, with what delight
> They would expect a jig, or target fight,
> A furious tale of Troy, which they ne'er thought
> Was weakly written, so 'twere strongly [f]ought.

[4] See pp. 676-8, below.   [5] *Henslowe's Diary*, ii, p. 202.

subject, partly with the hope of throwing new light on Shakespeare's *Troilus and Cressida,* and its puzzling and graceless position among his plays,[6] by showing it against a clearer and fuller background. By the way, however, I shall show some new facts about certain contemporary treatments of the subject, dramatic and non-dramatic, especially by Thomas Heywood. First I give a list of the plays on the subject, lost and extant, the names of the latter being italicized. I divide them into four groups,— those dealing, so far as we can tell, (I) with the story of the siege in general, (II) with Troilus and Cressida, wholly or in part, (III) with the episode of Ajax's jealousy of Ulysses, (IV) with the calamities of some of the Greek chiefs after the fall of Troy.[7]

I. Troy, acted at the Rose, 1596 [8] (perhaps Heywood's *Iron Age*).

The Siege of Troy, a tragi-comedy, often acted (annexed to an early chap-book called *History of the Trojan Wars,* n. d.; Hazlitt, p. 210).

The Greeks and Trojans, mentioned 1654 (Hazlitt, p. 99).[8a]

II. Troilus and Pandarus, at court, 5 Jan., 1516-7 (Hazlitt, p. 239).

---

[6] Anyone solely interested in this may turn immediately to p. 726

[7] On all these plays cf. W. C. Hazlitt, *Manual for Collectors of Old English Plays, Henslowe's Diary* (ed. by W. W. Greg), Griggs and Stokes' reprint of the *Troilus and Cressida* Quarto, Ward's and Schelling's histories of the Elizabethan drama, W. W. Greg's *English Plays Written before 1643 and Published before 1700 (Bibliogr. Soc. Publ.,* 1900), and his *List of Masques, etc.,* 1902.

[8] This may be what is referred to in the following entry in the *Stationers' Register,* 6 Apl. 1601: "The old *destruction of Troye* to print one Impression onely thereof for the Company." Or this may be still another play.

[8a] Perhaps the same as one of the others.

" Troilus ex Chaucero," by Nicholas Grimoald (*ib.*, p. 238).

Troilus and Cressida, by Chettle and Dekker (Hazlitt, p. 238)', mentioned by Henslowe in 1599.[9]

A play on Priam, Troilus and Cressida, 1617 (Collier, *Annals of the Stage,* I, p. 387).

The *Admiral Fragment* on Troilus and Cressida (about 1599).[10]

Shakespeare's *Troilus and Cressida* (printed 1609).

The Welsh Troilus and Cressida (before 1613).

Heywood's *Iron Age* (two parts, printed 1632).[11]

III.[12] Ajax Flagellifer, in Latin; at Cambridge, 1564, and Oxford, 1605.[13]

Ajax and Ulysses, at court, 1572.[14]

Contention of Ajax and Ulysses for the Armour of Achilles (a dramatic dialogue); by James

[9] This play, together with *Agamemnon* (on which see below), of the same year and by the same authors, affords a perfect parallel to the two parts of Heywood's *Iron Age.* Perhaps it is the play referred to in 1600 (Halliwell-Phillipps, *Outlines of the Life of Shakespeare,* II, p. 301). Halliwell-Phillipps and Small (*Stage-Quarrel,* p. 152) think *Troilus* and *Agamemnon* the same play, but this seems very unlikely; cf. pp. 703, 707 below.—One of the dumb-shows in *Rare Triumphs of Love and Fortune* (printed in 1589; Hazlitt-Dodsley, VI, p. 155) is on Troilus and Cressida; and so is one of the fragmentary plays acted in *Histriomastix.*

[10] Cf. p. 703 below. The preceding play also may be identical with some other.

[11] A still later work is John Banks's *Destruction of Troy,* 1678-9; in blank verse. It suggests Shakespeare's play, the scene being in the Greek camp and in Troy; Troilus is rather prominent, but Cressida does not appear. Dryden's *Troilus and Cressida* need hardly be mentioned.

[12] This group is included because its subject is that of the fifth act of Heywood's *Iron Age,* pt. I; see pp. 707, 746 below.

[13] Malone Soc., *Collections,* 1909, p. 249, and Hazlitt, p. 4; probably two plays.

[14] *Old Sh. Soc.,* VII, p. 13.

Shirley, 1640, printed 1659 (from Ovid's
  Metamorphoses).

Here also belongs Act V. of Heywood's *Iron Age,* pt.
  I (1632).

IV.[15] Seneca's *Agamemnon,* tr. by John Studley, published 1566, 1581.[16] .

Agamemnon and Ulysses, at court, 1584.

Ulysses Redux, by William Gager, played at Oxford,
  1591, published 1592 (Latin).

Troy's Revenge, by Chettle, written in 1598; the
  same (?) as

Agamemnon, by Dekker and Chettle, acted 1599.

Polyphemus or Troy's Revenge, 1599.[17]

Heywood's *Iron Age,* pt. II (1632), as to its latter
  part, belongs here.

The following are the non-dramatic works on the subject
in the period in question:

Peele's Tale of Troy (1589, 1604: written earlier).

Greene's *Euphues his Censure to Philautus* (1587).

Heywood's *Troia Britanica: Britayne's Troy* (1609).

The Life and Death of Hector (1614; anonymous).[18]

---

[15] This group consists wholly or almost wholly of plays dealing,
as II. *Iron Age,* IV and V do, with the later history of some of
the Greek besiegers of Troy; sometimes with a view to showing how
they came to grief. The popular sympathy for the Trojans is very
apparent, the supposed ancestors of the western Europeans.—I
should add that Seneca's *Troades* was translated by Jasper Heywood
(1559, 1563, 1581); there was an *Orestes,* 1599 (*Hens. Diary,* II,
p. 202).

[16] Greg, *List of English Plays,* pp. 92-3; *List of Masques,* etc.,
p. xlvii; reprinted, Spenser Soc., 1887.

[17] Greg, *Henslowe's Diary,* II, p. 201; cf. Orestes' Furies, 1599 (*ib.*
p. 202).

[18] I should further mention a ballad on Troilus and Cressida, coarse
and not serious, based entirely on Chaucer; Old Shakespeare Soc.,
1846, XXXI, pp. 101-5; *Shakespeare's Works,* Boston, 1857, V, p. 240;

II

I take up first the non-dramatic works. In the dedication to his first edition (1589; second edition 1604) Peele calls his *Tale of Troy* [1] "an old poem of mine own," whence Dyce conjectured that it was written while he was at Oxford (between 1572 and 1581), where Anthony à Wood says he was noted as a poet.[2] In nearly 500 lines, of rather rough [3] ten-syllable couplets, the poem tells of the progeny of Priam and Hecuba, the story of Paris, his judgment and his abduction of Helen, and the siege and

Halliwell's *Folio Shakespeare*, XII, p. 307. One or two other ballads are known of, one of them in dialogue form. Cf. the above references; *Irving Shakespeare*, VIII, p. 164; Jusserand, *Lit. Hist. of Engl. People*, II, p. 410; Griggs-Stokes' reprint of the *T. and C.* Quarto, p. ix. Dares Phrygius, tr. T. Paynell, was printed in 1553 (Esdaile, *Engl. Tales and Prose Rom. Printed bef. 1740*, Bibl. Soc., 1912). Among other indications of the popularity of the Troy story, cf. the following, from Tyndale's *Obedience of a Christian Man* (*Works*, London, 1831; I, p. 196; pointed out by one of the critics): "They [the Papists] permit and suffer you to read Robin Hood, Bevis of Hampton, Hercules, Hector, and Troilus, with a thousand histories and fables of love and wantonness, and of ribaldry, as filthy as heart can think," etc. (first printed apparently in 1528, earlier than Thynne's *Chaucer*).

[1] In Bullen's edition of Peele (1888), II, pp. 241-265; Dyce's (Routledge), pp. 550-558.

[2] Cf. Bullen's edition, I, p. xvii; Dyce's (1829), I, p. ii.

[3] The hermaphrodite rhyme is common: thus—Patroclus (306-7), treason—son (318-9), this—Aulis (233-4). See also 9-10, 21-2, 39-40, 75-6, 103-4, 227-30, 282-3, 444-5. It occurs occasionally in contemporary writers, and is doubtless due to the supposed example of Chaucer,—to the natural 16th-century way of reading such Chaucerian rhymes as occasioun—soun; honour—flour. But it is curious that in Irish-Gaelic poetry the same sort of rhyme is regularly used in the so-called Deibhidh metre (Douglas Hyde, *Lit. Hist. of Ireland*, p. 483), and also in Welsh poetry. It is highly melodious when we feel it is not a mere license and when the rhythm is adapted to it.

destruction of Troy. The main sources are not difficult
to make out. To Ovid's *Heroides* are probably due the
account of Hecuba's dream of a firebrand, Paris on Mount
Ida,[4] his love of Oenone, his return to Troy, his kind reception at Sparta, the departure of Menelaus, and Helen's
willing elopement.[5] Paris' letter to Helen (*Heroides*,
XVI) is referred to (ll. 173-4). To the *Metamorphoses* is
due the account of the contest of Ajax and Ulysses for
the arms of Achilles; [6] and perhaps to Hyginus the account
of the detection of Ulysses' feigned madness and Achilles'
disguise.[7] Virgil's *Æneid* contributed most of the account
of the fall of the city,—the device of the horse, Sinon,
Priam's death, the flight of Æneas.[8] There are reminiscences of Chaucer's *Troilus* in the slurs cast on "uncon-
stant Cressed" and "unworthy Diomed" (281-7). But
the main groundwork of the poem is probably due to Caxton's *Recuyell of the Historyes of Troye;* we may note the
welcome of Helen in Troy, the council of war, the warning
of Cassandra, the coming of Penthesilea (earlier than in
other versions), Achilles' love of Polyxena [9] and forgetting

[4] The golden ball is said to have been brought from hell by Ate,
not Eris; this seems to be unparalleled in ancient or modern literature, except in Peele's *Arraignment of Paris* (II, i; printed in 1584).
This is a further bit of evidence for Peele's authorship of that play,
which otherwise rests on a statement in Nashe's preface to Greene's
Menaphon.

[5] Ll. 46, 61, 123, 143, 152, 175, 192; cf. *Her.* XVI, 43 ff., 53 ff.,
89 ff., 127; v; XVII, 195 ff., 115; XVI, 298 ff.; XVII, 154; XVI, 183-4.

[6] Ll. 346-75; cf. *Met.* XIII, 1 ff. To *Met.* XIII, 430 ff., 551, rather
than *Aen.* III, 22 ff., is due the account of Polydorus (392 ff.).

[7] Ll. 213, 227; *Fabulae*, 95, 96; but cf. *Met.* XIII, 36 ff., 162 ff. and
Cicero's *De Officiis*, III, 26.

[8] Ll. 376, 400, 430, 480; cf. *Aen.* II, 13 ff. etc., 506 ff. etc.

[9] Ll. 294 ff. remind one of the festive meeting in Greene's *Euphues
his Censure* (see below), which however was not published till after
Peele's poem was written. It is not impossible that both remembered some earlier play. Peele's *Tale* has almost exactly the com-

her to kill Hector, Hecuba's plot for revenge on Achilles
and offer of Polyxena in marriage, the return of his body
to the Greeks, the sacrifice of Polyxena; [10] finally, at the
end a sort of postscript-account of Helen's elopement, more
favorable to her character, representing it as forced, is

pass of the two parts of Heywood's *Iron Age*. There is another hint
that it may have been suggested by some play. Ll. 262-7 describe
a council of Priam and his princes to deliberate on the war, at
which Cassandra makes an outcry, and urges the restoration of
Helen. This scene in Caxton, Lydgate and the *Iron Age* comes
before Paris abducts Helen, but here, as in Shakespeare's *Troilus*,
the Admiral fragment and the Welsh *Troilus*, comes after the war
has begun (cf. pp. 698-9, 740-5, 744-5 below). This scene may be
called traditional in the plays we have, and may possibly be inherited
from an earlier play on the subject. The shift in time is natural in
a drama, but not in a sketchy narrative like Peele's.

[10] Ll. 192, 264, 265, 272, 297, 313, 325, 331, 344, 470; cf. Caxton,
pp. 536, 515, 537, 644, 621, 637, 642, 670. Or the source may
possibly be Lydgate's *Troy-Book*. At the death of Hector there is a
combination of the accounts in the *Iliad* and Caxton, p. 613. A
further sign of Homer's influence may be Hecuba's twenty children
(l. 15; *Il.* xxiv, 496 says nineteen). Throughout, my references to
Caxton are to H. Oskar Sommer's edition (London, 1894), and those
to Lydgate's *Troy-Book* are to the E. E. T. S. edition. Caxton's
and Lydgate's works are generally identical in contents to the most
minute points, so it is often impossible to tell which has been used;
except for the fact that Caxton begins with the reign of Saturn,
Lydgate only with the Argonauts. The popularity of both, especially of Caxton, was due not only to their historical and modern air,
minimizing the pagan supernatural, and the like, but also to the
fact that they gave the whole story of Troy in order, while Homer,
Virgil and Ovid gave only parts. Yet, so mediæval in their ways
were some writers even as late as the 17th century, that in the
dedication of Heywood's *Troia Britanica*, mainly founded on Caxton, the only authorities mentioned are Homer and Virgil, who were
used comparatively little.—Caxton was much oftener reprinted than
Lydgate, was more easily read, and is known to have been oftener
used; the presumption in doubtful cases is that he was used rather
than the other. Caxton's book was printed in 1475(?), 1502, 1553,
1596, 1607, 1617 (Esdaile, *op. cit.*); Lydgate's in 1513 and 1555,
apparently as a rival to Caxton. The continued popularity of
Caxton is almost incredible; there were some fourteen other editions
to 1738.

fathered on "my author" (488 ff.), who is probably
Caxton (pp. 533-4). The tone of the poem also reflects
Caxton's loose style and chivalric spirit (277 ff., 290 ff.).
There are some small inconsistencies in these parallels, and
some points are unaccounted for; probably Peele wrote
carelessly and from memory. Altogether the poem has little
merit, and is a juvenile performance, put in, Dyce conjectures, to swell the bulk of the volume which contains it.[11]

Poor Robert Greene with his usual journalistic instinct
seized upon the popular subject and treated it in the popular (and very inappropriate) Euphuistic style. In *Euphues his Censure to Philautus*,[12] published in 1587, a
number of the Trojan knights and dames are entertained
at the Greek camp, and later the Greek knights and dames
in Troy; telling long-winded stories and discussing abstract
subjects, such as the ideal soldier, in the approved half-
Italianate manner. The scene is probably a reminiscence
from Ovid's *Metamorphoses* (XII, 146 ff.), where the
Greeks (alone) have a banquet and discuss valor and the
like, and perhaps also from the presence of Achilles and
other Greeks in Troy at the anniversary-service in honor
of Hector (Caxton, p. 620). The work shows a memory
of Chaucer's *Troilus;*[13] and Achilles' love of Polyxena

---

[11] The same explanation of its presence seems to have occurred
to a less kindly critic. In all probability Thomas Nashe is alluding to the *Tale of Troy* when he says, in his preface to Sidney's
Astrophel and Stella (published two years later, in 1591; *Nashe's
Works*, ed. McKerrow, III, p. 332): "Others are so hardly bested for
loading that they are faine to retaile the cinders of *Troy*, and the
shiuers of broken trunchions, to fill vp their boate that else should
goe empty," etc.

[12] See Greene's works in the Huth Library (VI, pp. 147-284).

[13] Cf. the prominence of Cressida (164, 166, 233). There are
verbal reminiscences on pp. 162 (cf. *T. and C.* V, 485) and 163
(IV, 1457-8). Cf. also the *Canon's Yeoman's Tale*, 1413-4 (also

and references to the rape of Hesione as a cause of the war doubtless reflect Caxton's *Recuyell*.[14]

The little-known *Troia Britanica*,[15] 1609, is the product of the journalistic as well as the poetic side of a more engaging personality than Greene, Thomas Heywood. The title, as well as the last two canti, was meant to gratify the fond belief of the British that their nation was founded by Trojans.[16]   The verse-form and general style were timely.   Sir John Harington's translation of Ariosto's *Orlando Furioso,* 1591, and Edward Fairfax's of Tasso's *Gerusalemme Liberata,* 1600,[17] to say nothing of other

Gower's *Confessio Amantis*, VI, 1280) with p. 164; *Reeve's T.*, 4054 and *Mill. T.*, 3457-60 with p. 250.

[14] Cf. pp. 156, 159, 160, 284, 167-8 with Cx. pp. 621 and later, and 509, etc. Or the source may be Lydgate's *Troy-Book*, IV, 596 ff., II, 2106 ff.

[15] *Troia Britanica: or Great Britaines Troy;* the dedication is to Edward, Earl of Worcester, and next comes an address " To the two-fold Readers: the Courteous, and the Criticke," which suggests Ben Jonson's addresses " To the Reader in Ordinary " and " To the Reader Extraordinary," preceding *Catiline.* Chapman's Homer has prefatory addresses " To the Reader " and " To the Understander." This cavalier manner affected toward the public contrasts oddly with the same men's servility to patrons, and is suggestive of literary conditions at the time. *Troia Britanica* was printed by W. Jaggard, in quarto. The only copy I know of came from George III's library to the British Museum. The work is briefly described by Franz Albert, *Münchener Beiträge*, XLII, 150-1.

[16] Similarly Jasper Fisher entitled his play on the valiant defence of the Britons against the first Roman invasion *Fuimus Troes* (printed in 1633; see W. W. Greg's *List of English Plays*, Bibliogr. Soc., 1900). As to the prevalence of this belief at an even later date, cf. the introduction to my edition of *Troilus and Cressida* in the *Tudor Shakespeare*, p. xvii.

[17] The former was reprinted in 1607 and 1634; the *Gerusalemme* had been partially translated also in 1594 by Richard Carew, and Boiardo's *Orlando Innamorato* by Robert Tofte in 1598. The verse and other points assimilate the *Troia* to such works rather than to Spenser's *Fairy Queen* (1590-6); though the general influence of that is also visible.

translations, had popularized the *ottava rima* and a type of narrative-poem somewhat rambling, long, varied, romantic, warlike, sentimental and pseudo-historical. Accordingly, in some 13,000 lines, mainly in the *ottava rima,* and dividing the poem " into XVII. severall Cantons," Heywood narrates with occasional digressive episodes [18] the

[18] "Intermixed with many pleasant poeticall Tales," the title-page announces. *E. g.,* cf. the beginning of canto XII, and pp. 367-377. After each canto is a prose historical and genealogical commentary, such as he proposed in the preface to *Iron Age* II. The work is so rare that it is worth while to show its contents and style by reprinting the longer of the two summaries of each canto:

   I. Tytan and Saturne differ, their great strife,
      Is by their carefull mother (Vesta) ended:
      Saturne, his Sister Sybill takes to wife,
      And the heyre-males that are from the descended
      He doomes to death: faire Sybil saves the life
      Of Iupiter, grim Saturne is offended,
         And to the Oracle at Delphos hyes,
         Whiles Titan thrugh the earth his fortune tries.

  II. Young Dardanus his brother Iasius slew,
      And leaves the Countrey where he sought to rayne
      Warre twixt th' Epirians and Pelagians grew,
      Lycaon is by Iove exilde, not slaine:
      Iupiter of Calisto taking view,
      A votresse, and one of Dians traine;
         Loves, and is loath'd, the Virgin is beguild,
         Clad like a mayd, he gets the Mayd with child.

 III. Calista knowne to be with Child, is driven
      From Dians Cloyster: Archas doth pursue
      His mother: unto him Pelage is given,
      Now termed Archady: when Tytan knew
      Saturne had sonnes alive, his hart was riven
      With anger: he his men togither drew
         To Battayle: the two brothers fight their fils,
         Iove saves his Father, and his Uncle kils.

 IV. Ihove Esculapius kils, Apollo drives
      To keepe Admetus sheepe in Thessaly,
      And next his beautious sister Iuno wives,

siege of Troy and allied mythological story and history
from the falling out of Titan and Saturn to the accession
of James I.

As to the source, two things are apparent on a single
reading.   One is that the poem is rather closely parallel

> At her returne from Creet to Parthemy,
> The father with the sonne in battell strives,
> But by his puissance is inforst to fly:
>> Acrisius keepes his daughter in a Tower,
>> Which amorous Ihove skales in a golden shower.

V. King Tantalus before the Troians flyes,
Saturne arrives in Creet and by Troas ayded
Once more intendes his Kingdome to surprise,
Creet is by Troian Ganimede invaded,
In ayde of Iupiter the Centaures rise,
Ægeons ful-fraught Gallies are disladed:
> Danae and her young sonne are turnd afloate,
> By Arges King, into a Mast-lesse boate.

VI. Perseus the Gorgon kils, then takes his way
To Ioppen, on his flying horse alone,
Destroyes the Monster, frees Andromeda,
Acrisius saves, turnes Atlas into stone:
King Pricus Wife, the beauteous Aurea
Doates on the valiant Knight Bellerephon:
> The Troians are with fearfull pests annoyde,
> By Hercules, great Troy is first destroyde.

VII. Euridia stung with a Snake and dying,
Sad Orpheus travels for her sake to Hell,
Among th' Infernals Musickes vertue trying,
Much honoured (even where fiends & devils dwel)
Ceres to Hercules for vengeance crying,
Th' undaunted Greeke, seekes Pluto to expell
> Iasons rich Fleece, & proud Troy once more racst
> By Hercules, in our next skeades are placst.

VIII. The twice sackt Troy with all abundåce flowes,
Her walls inlarg'd, hir spacious bounds augmentĕd,
Fortune on Priam all her favour strowes,
Her populous streets from all parts are frequented,

to Heywood's series of five plays, the *Golden, Silver, Brazen* and *Iron Ages* (two parts), published 1611-32 but probably written long before.[19]   The other is that it is not a mere retelling of them, but contains episodes which they lack,[20] and is mainly based on Caxton's *Recuyell*,[21]

> Proud of his sonnes, the King impatient growes,
> And with all Greece for wrongs past, discontented:
> Warlike Anthenor by Embassage seekes,
> To have the Kings faire Sister from the Greeks

IX.   Paris departs from Troy, & Greece doth enter
Whom Menelaus welcomes, having seene;
The King is cald thence by a strange adventer
And to his Troian-guest he trusts his Queene:
Paris fayre Hellen Loves, & doth present her
With a long sute, to heale his wound yet greene:
> First Paris writes, she answers; Then with ioy
> Greece they forsake, & both are shipt for Troy.

X.   Hellen re-wrytes, the Troians sute prevails,
And of the appointed Rape they both agree,
Proud of so fayre a purchase, Paris sailes
To Troy, from whence the Græcians seek to free
The ravisht Spartan: Menelaus bewailes
The absence of his Queene, longing to see
> Revenge on Troy, to which the Græcians meet,
> Castor and Pollux perish with the Fleet.

XI.   The Græcians Land, Prothesilaus fals
By Hectors sword, King Diomed is sent
With wise Ulisses to debate their brals,
And fetch the Spartan to her Husbands Tent:
Hellen denide: the Greekes begirt Troy wals,
But are by Hector raisd incontinent:
> Troylus and Diomed in Armes contend
> For Cressida, so the first battels end.

XII.   Achilles transformation: Palimed
Accusd of Treason and condemnd to die:
After long battaile, honor Hector led
The boldest Argive Champion to defie:
The Græcians storme to be so chalenged,
Hector and Aiax the fierce Combat try:

with much use of other authorities. Chief among these is Ovid's *Heroides,* of which the sixteenth and seventeenth, the epistles from Paris to Helen and from Helen to Paris, in a skillful translation in ten-syllable couplets, form a large part of the ninth and tenth canti.[22] The *Iliad* is

> A Truce, a Banquet: at this pompous feast,
> Queene Hellen is invited a chiefe guest.

XIII.   Achilles dotes on beauteous Polixaine,
And at her faire request refraines the fielde,
The Truce expierd, both Hoasts prepare againe
For battaile, with proud harts, in valour steel'd:
The Greekes are beate backe, many kild and taine,
Patroclus don's Achilles Arms and shield:
> Him Hector, for Achilles tooke and slew,
> Whose Armor gone, his Mother seeks him new.

XIV.   Troylus, Achilles wounds, and is betraid
By his fell Myrmidons, which being spread,
The bloody Greeke still loves the beautious Maid
Pollixena, and for her love is lead
To Pallas Church, whom Paris doth invade,
And with an Arrow in the heele strikes dead:
> Penthisilea with her valiant Maydes,
> Assists sad Troy, Greece lofty Pyrrhus ayds.

XV.   On th' Hellesponticke Sands Epeus reares
A brazen horse: the Græcians hoise up saile
And feigning to depart: Synon with teares
Tels to the invaded King an ominous tale,
The Fleete returnes by night: After ten yeares
Troy is surprisde, and the proud Greeks prevaile,
> The Citty's burnt, and after tragicke broyles,
> The Greekes returne, laden with Asiaes spoyles.

XVI.   The yeares from Brute to Christ   .   .   .
. . . .
From Christ to Norman William   .   .   .

XVII.   Of all great Brittans Kinges, truely descended
From the first Conqueror   .   .   .   .   .
. . . .
Till royall James claymes his Monarchall Seate;

evidently drawn on,[23] and also Ovid's *Metamorphoses*.[24]
The account of the withdrawal of the Greeks, the wooden
horse, and the capture and destruction of Troy (xv, 10 ff.)
is taken in great detail from Virgil's *Æneid*, bk. ii. There
would seem to be some knowledge, direct or indirect, of

[19] There are details not found elsewhere and common to both.
One episode in both, unknown in other accounts of the Trojan War
(but cf. Peele's *Tale*, p. 680 above), is the feast given in Troy to
the Greeks (*T. B.* xiii; *I. A.* 301-9); much of the detail is closely
parallel. That it is a reminiscence from Greene's *Euphues his
Censure* is shown by the fact that it is here, and not in a Trojan
temple at Hector's anniversary service, as in Caxton, p. 621, that
Achilles falls in love with Polyxena (*T. B.*, pp. 335-6, xiii, 17 ff.;
I. A., pp. 303, 306; cf. p. 725 below).

[20] *E. g.*, Apollo and Admetus (canto iv; Caxton, p. 84); Troilus'
taunt to Helenus (*T. B.*, p. 188; Cx. p. 524; also in Shakespeare's
Troilus and in the Welsh play). That Heywood used Caxton directly, and not merely the *Ages*, is proved by such passages as pp.
186-7 (nearer Cx. 518-9 than *I. A.* 266-7), and pp. 184-5 (cf. Cx.
511-5 and *I. A.* 268).

[21] Certainly not Lydgate's *Troy-Book*, which begins only with the
story of Jason. Such a form as *Ioppen* (c. vi) proves the use of
Cx. (214-21). Likewise the word *ortiges* is interpreted as *quails*
in the *Troia* and Caxton (p. 549); as *curlews* in Lydgate (ii, 5445).
The names of the six gates of Troy (*T. B.*, p. 180) are nearer to the
forms in Caxton than to those in Lydgate. The form *Tytanoyes*
(p. 409) is from Caxton (cf. p. 719 below). That Caxton is the
main source is the conclusion of Hofberger in an apparently unpublished Staatsexamenarbeit (1907), referred to by Franz Albert
(*Münch. Beitr.*, xlii, p. 151).

[22] On these two pieces see pp. 715-8 below. They had a curious
fortune. The thoroughly unprincipled printer of the *Troia*, William
Jaggard, had published *The Passionate Pilgrim* in 1599, and
attributed it to Shakespeare (he also printed the 1623 folio). In
its third edition, 1612, he included these two translations as by
Shakespeare, and though Heywood at the end of his *Apologie for
Actors*, 1612, immediately protested with tact and firmness, and
declared that Shakespeare was equally displeased, they remained
in the 1640 edition of Shakespeare's poems, and in such later ones
as those of 1710 (Gildon's), 1725 (Sewell's) 1775 (?) and 1804.
Cf. Farmer's *Essay on the Learning of Shakespeare* (in Reed's

Sophocles' *Ajax,* according to which (ll. 661, 817, 1029) Ajax and Hector had exchanged a sword and girdle as presents, which latter was used by Achilles to tie Hector's corpse to his chariot.[25]

As to the date, the poem was clearly published (1609) soon after it was written.[26] Guy Fawkes and his plot, 1605, are mentioned in canto xv. (st. 5 ff., pp. 386-7). Better yet, about half-way through (viii, 59, p. 182) is this allusion:

Shakespeare, 1822; I, p. 137); Furnivall in the *Leopold Shakespeare,* p. xxxv; Collier's edition, viii, p. 227; Halliwell's *Folio Shakespeare,* xvi, p. 467; Halliwell-Phillips' *Outlines of the Life of Shakespeare,* I, pp. 236-7; Heywood's *Apologie for Actors* (Sh. Soc., p. 62; he complains bitterly also of the inaccurate printing of the *Troia*). Heywood was unlucky as to his translations from Ovid; in the preface to the *Brazen Age* he taxes one Austin, a schoolmaster at Ham, with claiming as his own Heywood's youthful versions of three books of the *Ars Amatoria* and two of the *Remedium Amoris.* In *The Nation,* N. Y., 9 Apr., 1914, (vol. 98, p. 390) I pointed out that in these versions from the *Heroides* Heywood seems to have been the pioneer in the English closed couplet, the traits of which are not regularly but frequently found in them, and which therefore is directly traceable to the Latin elegiac distich, the verse of the *Heroides.*

[23] *E. g.,* for the death of Patroclus, and Thetis' seeking new arms for Achilles (c. xiii; *Il.* xvii, xviii); for some parts at least of the single-combat scene between Hector and Ajax (c. xii; *Il.* vii); and probably for the figure of Thersites (p. 171; who curiously is said to have been "well featur'd" but made "*Stigmaticke* and lame" by the angry Muses).

[24] The debate of Ajax and Ulysses for Achilles' arms, and Ajax's madness and death (p. 407; *Met.* xiii); a printed marginal gloss says "Ouid metamor· " In the pre-Trojan part of the work I have no doubt he used the *Metamorphoses* now and then (though his main source was Caxton); *e. g.,* for the story of Orpheus and "Euridia" (c. vii; *Met.* x, 1 f.).

[25] *T. B.,* p. 333. The presents are exchanged in *Il.* vii, 299, but nothing is said of their later use. Chapman in his commentary merely says they were later the cause of the heroes' deaths.

[26] It was entered S. R. 5 Dec., 1608, for W. Jaggard.

With as great state as *Troian Priam* could,
I have beheld our Soveraign, Strangers feast,
In Boules as precious, Cups, as deerly sould,
and hy-prizd Lyquors equall with the rest,
When from the *Lands-grave* and the Browns-wicke bold,
The *Arch-duke* and the *Spaniard* Legats prest:
    But chiefely when the royall Brittish *James*,
    at Greenwitch feasted the great King of *Danes.*

King Christian IV. of Denmark visited James I. on 17 July, 1606.[27] There is evidence that the poem was begun not earlier than 1602, when Heywood seems to have joined Lord Worcester's company.[28] In the dedication to him of *Troia Britanica,* Heywood says Lord Worcester's

    Favour gave my Muse first breath,
To try in th' Ayre her weake unable wing,
And soare this pitch . . . . . .
Your Noble hand, to her, supportance gave,
Even in her Pen-lesse Age about to fall,
Her Cradle then had beene her Infant grave,
Had not your power and Grace kept her from thrall:

.   .   .   .

Though smothered long, yet she findes time at length
To shew her office to her Patron-Lord.

---

[27] S. R. Gardiner, *Hist. of Engl.* (London, 1883), I, p. 300. The general drunkenness among the Danes gave great scandal; the author of *Hamlet* might have said "I told you so." An account of *The King of Denmarkes welcome*, July, 1606, is attributed to Lyly (ed. Bond, I, pp. 505-7). The other rather vaguely-mentioned festivities may have been connected with the treaty between England and Spain in 1604, in which the Archduke of Austria, the Duke of Brunswick, and the Landgrave of Hesse were involved (Gardiner, I, pp. 208-14; Rymer's *Foedera*, London, 1715, XVI, pp. 581, 591, 617, 624). In his *Apologie for Actors*, p. 40, Heywood says English actors had been especially patronized by the late King of Denmark, the Duke of Brunswick, the Landgrave of Hesse, and others.

[28] Fleay, *Chron. of the Engl. Drama*, I, p. 281; Greg, *Henslowe's Diary*, II, pp. 106-8, 284-5; J. T. Murray, *Engl. Dram. Companies* (Boston, 1910), I, pp. 52-3, II, pp. 141-3. Late in 1603 Worcester's players became the Queen's, till whose death in 1619 Heywood was one of her servants (Murray, I, pp. 185-96; Malone Soc. Collections, p. 266).

Pretty clearly the patron of his company had encouraged him to write this poem, and (the dedication naturally postdating the poem) Heywood maintained relations with him even after as a theatrical man he had passed under the Queen's patronage.   Pretty much the whole poem, then, is later than 1602, and most of it later than 1606.

The literary quality of no modern poem on the siege of Troy is likely to get full credit since the world has been brought up on Homer and Virgil, but in the absence of more fitting and long-revered accounts that of Heywood would rank high.   It shows no strong imagination or great distinction of language, yet a practised literary hand,—deft and racy phrasing, metrical skill and no more dilute-ness than the *ottava rima* inevitably tends to.   When the very desirable complete edition of Heywood's works shall appear, *Troia Britanica* will give pleasure to the literary student.

To its popularity is probably due the last non-dramatic work I have to describe, *The Life and Death of Hector,* 1614.[29]   This big, bad book, monstrous not only in the sense of running to some 30,000 lines, is worth mentioning chiefly for two reasons, that it belongs to our subject and that it also has been ascribed to Thomas Heywood.   Its sources and authorship have been studied by Dr. Franz Albert, in the *Münchener Beiträge,* vol. XLII.   The title-page anounces it as "written by Iohn Lidgate Monke of Berry," and it is hardly more than a modernizing of the decasyllabic couplets of Lydgate's *Troy-Book* in a quatrain-

---

[29] The only copy known to me is in the British Museum, inscribed "Bequeathed by Th. Tyrwhitt Esqr 1786." Notes on a back fly-leaf, in Tyrwhitt's handwriting apparently, show that he was think-ing of the poem or its source as a parallel or source for Shake-speare's *Troilus and Cressida.* The work was entered S. R., 3 Jan. 1614.

and-couplet stanza, printed in black-letter. Both works begin with the causes which led to the Argonautic expedition, and the adaptation is very close, not to say slavish, with half a dozen longish insertions, amounting to seven or eight hundred lines, and some short ones, mostly from Ovid's *Metamorphoses* and Virgil's *Æneid*.[30]

Unimportant as the work is in itself, anything possible should be done to settle the question of authorship, for Heywood's sake if for no other reason. An examination of the work entirely convinced me that the current opinion is wrong, and Dr. Albert's argument in its favor has only confirmed this view. The work is entirely anonymous, but the idea of Heywood's authorship antedates even Dr. Richard Farmer, at the end of the eighteenth century, who says it was generally attributed to him; this ascription has been steadily repeated, sometimes ignored, but seemingly never dissented from, to the present day,[31] and appears in the British Museum catalogue.[32] Dr. Albert seems to be impressed by this unanimity; which, however, loses its force when one realizes that, the work being unimportant and hardly accessible, the statement has been handed down and taken on faith, largely by mere compilers, though also by well-known scholars. As to the reviewers who accepted Dr. Albert's evidence,[33] one cannot but feel that they were so much impressed with his usually remarkable industry, care, and thoroughness as to overlook the weakness of his arguments on the question of the authorship, which appear at the end of his 185 pages.

---

[30] Albert, pp. 125-142.   [31] Albert, pp. 2-5.

[32] There is absolutely no ground for the implication there that the book attributes itself to " T. H."

[33] See G. C. Moore-Smith in *Mod. Lang. Rev.*, V, pp. 222-3; Ackermann in *Angl. Beibl.* XXII, pp. 173-4; Glöde in *Literaturblatt*, XXXII, pp. 95-6.

But now to look at his chief arguments. *The Life and Death of Hector* and Heywood's *Brazen Age* both borrow from some of the same passages in the *Metamorphoses,* bk. IX, for their accounts of Hercules, both introducing Cacus from elsewhere in Ovid or from the *Æneid;* both borrow from book VII. for Medea's soliloquy (this also in the *Troia*) ; *Hector* and *Iron Age* II. and *Troia* all borrow the account of the fall of Troy from the *Æneid,* book II. (though Dr. Albert admits the use of Virgil in *Troia* is freer and better than that in *Hector*).[34] The very few agreements in language are unimportant.[35] To say nothing of the possibility that the author of *Hector* had witnessed *Brazen Age,* he may even have read it (published 1613),[36] and it is highly probable that he had read *Troia* (1609) ; or is it unlikely that two men should in the same connection have remembered conspicuous passages from the two best-known poems in Latin literature? If these works proceed from the same author, there should be far

[34] Albert, pp. 152-165 (especially 154 and 159).

[35] *E. g.,* Crete and Iberia modernized as Candia and Spain. It is true that Crete is not mentioned here by Ovid, but the sire of the Minotaur was certainly well-known, and his connection with Crete is clear in the early part of *Met.* VIII.

[36] If it seems unlikely that *Hector* was entirely written within the year, he might have read and made insertions borrowed from a play published by the author of *Troia,* which he was more or less imitating. Such verbal agreements as exist, together with the author's general ignorance, of which Dr. Albert gives cases, favor the idea that resemblance to Heywood's undoubted works are due to imitation. Dr. Albert hardly considers this possibility, and in the absence of the texts I cannot do so fully. It is striking that the resemblances are in the parts not due to Lydgate, as if the author were consciousl supplementing by consulting Heywood's works. The idea of imitation is confirmed by the striking fact that Albert shows no parallels of the slightest consequence between *Hector* and the two parts of *Iron Age* (cf. Albert, pp. 158, 162), which (published 1632) he could not have read.

2

more striking agreements in contents and language, such
as I show later between the *Ages* and *Troia;* considering
the extent of the works, even believing *Hector* not to be by
the same author, I rather wonder that there are so few.
As to supposed general resemblances in versification and
style between *Hector* and *Troia* (Albert, pp. 170-85), it
is hard to know what to say.   So far as they exist, they
are of the most trivial and commonplace kind.   Dr. Albert
is struck (p. 167) with certain trifling agreements as to
the use of proper names, such as calling the moon
Cinthia(!); this calls for no comment.[37]   He admits (p.
172) that *Hector* is much more licentious metrically, more
disturbing and unpleasant to read, and much less exact
and careful as to rhymes.   This is partly because linguistic
changes and growth in metrical strictness since Lydgate's
day made its author's natural attempt to carry over Lydgate's lines and rhymes (Albert, p. 20) rather difficult.
Yet no one who has read all through Heywood's authentic
works will believe him so helpless as to have written (*metri
gratia*) Cassandera (p. 274), pat*a*ron (for pattern),
sac*a*red (several times, for sacred), Emperesse, childeren
(pp. 184, 194); or to have frequently written lines a whole
foot short;[38] or, writing usually Palladiowne (p. 261),
have used Palladowne a little later because he wanted one
syllable less.   What has Heywood done that he should be
suspected of such things?   Dr. Albert's explanation, that
the author was metrically skillful but careless, will not
hold; skill does not fall down before every obstacle, nor is

[37] Sometimes he is mistaken as to fact.   The name Margariton
(Albert, pp. 92, 167) does not come from Caxton or Heywood,
but is in Lydgate, III, 5204, etc. (the 1555 edition is not accessible
to me).

[38] Albert, pp. 26-35, 149.   *Troia* shows little of the laxity in
rhyme and verse common in contemporary long narrative poems
(including the *Fairy Queen*).

the elasticity of the artistic conscience as great as he thinks. Another of his arguments is this (p. 169),—that when in the preface to the *Troia* Heywood says that if that poem is well received "it may incourage me to proceed in some future labour," the reference is certainly to *Hector,* written earlier, he believes, and finally published anonymously because Heywood was ashamed of its careless style. Not to remark on the want of plausibility in this suggestion, if we need apply Heywood's aspiration to any particular work, what more natural than to apply it to his three plays of like subject, which went through the press two and four years later than the *Troia?* [39] These are all of Dr. Albert's main arguments.

Now for evidence on the other side. To start with, we may note cases where *Hector* differs from Heywood's usage as to proper names, in a manner surprising if he wrote it. Troilus' name appears as Troyelus (*passim*), Troielus (pp. 223, 355, etc.), etc., nearly always as three syllables; in the *Troia* I counted twenty-six instances with two syllables and none with three. The name of Priam's stolen sister, Exione in Lydgate, Caxton and *Hector,* the *Troia* corrects to Hesione. Again, Heywood is a free and individual and versatile writer, none more so among the second rank of dramatists. This poem is plodding and servile to the last degree; Dr. Albert (pp. 39-54) marshals no less than eighteen of Lydgate's traits of style, prejudices, etc. (including "Weiberhass" 1), all of which faithfully reappear in it. Again, Heywood was a university man, very well read and fairly accurate; this other man, in spite of some reading, was ignorant. He turns unfamiliar

---

[39] *Golden Age,* 1611, *Silver* and Br*azen Ages,* 1613. *The Iron Age* seems to have been too popular on the stage to print as yet. For much clearer evidence that he had these unprinted plays in mind when writing the *Troia,* see pp. 714-5 below.

names into familiar ones; [40] *e. g.,* Helmyus into Helenus,
Thesalus to Theseus (Albert, p. 81), and substitutes
Cinthia for Citherea (p. 89).   At the end of his prose
preface he speaks of Dares and Ditus (for Dictys).
Finally, there is this oddity; Lydgate's line

> To Petrack frauceis was giuen in Itayle [a]

appears thus,

> Given unto *Patricke Francke* in Italie (p. 183).

Are we to believe the cultivated Heywood represented
Francis Petrarch as Patrick Frank?   Above all, there is
the consideration of antecedent probability.   Heywood had
written a series of five full-sized plays, and (later doubtless) about 1607-9 a very long poem on precisely the same
subject.   This is not surprising, since the plays were unpublished, yet had prepared a sale for the poem; modern
novelists dramatize their novels.   Now Dr. Albert seems to
assume a likelihood that within a few years Heywood
might have written another prodigious poem covering
nearly as much of precisely the same ground.   But a repetition which is likely once is very unlikely twice.   The
fact that Heywood wrote *Troia Britanica* establishes a
presumption that he did not write *The Life and Death of
Hector.*   On the other hand, it is natural enough that
another publisher and another author, a poor hack, might
bring out a rival publication, founded on a rival source,

---

[40] It is true that the poem is not very accurately printed, but
there are too many other things which cannot be unloaded on the
printer to make it plausible to exonerate the author on all these
points.   Heywood himself complains bitterly of the careless printing
of the *Troia,* but it contains nothing like this.

[a] Edition of 1555 (sig. R. ii^{vo}), which was that used for *Hector*
(Albert, p. 6 ff.).   The poet is called " Franciscus Petrarcha " in
Northbrooke's *Treatise,* about 1577 (O. Sh. Soc., XIV, p. 112).

written in a more popular style and printed in black-letter, with a catch-penny title. This would explain resemblances as due to imitation. As to the author's name, nothing in his work became him like the leaving of it out.

Having discussed the contents, date, authorship, and sources of these four non-dramatic works, it remains for me to say a word about their common tone or spirit. In all, it is mediæval or early modern, superficially chivalric in the contemporary manner. They are not simple, digni- fied, unified; in other words, they are not in the least " classic," in the sense used by æstheticians. These works bring to our mind's eye no picture of white and plastic forms against a background of immortal brightness. The material is treated just as any other would be treated, with no sense that it is entitled to especial reverence or reserve; it was valued as a mine of romantic and exciting incident and of vivid human character. And the same we shall find to be true of the dramatic versions; including Shakespeare's.

III

We now come to the plays on Troilus and the Trojan war. The Admiral Fragment is found in a British Mu- seum MS., Addit. 10449, " written in two columns on paper mounted on pasteboard." [1] It contains none of the text, but for thirteen scenes gives the entrances and exits, and the names of the characters and of some of the actors; with scarcely a doubt, it is the outline of a regular play and was made for the guidance of the call-boy or whoever

---

[1] Greg, *Henslowe Papers* (Bullen, London, 1907), pp. 129, 142. Mr. Greg was the first to publish this interesting outline, though other similar ones had been published earlier by Malone and others. For lack of another convenient name, I call the play after the com- pany which performed it.

directed the performance from behind the scenes.[2]   I give each scene as given by Mr. Greg, and then my interpretation.   As an archæologist reconstructs a building from the foundation which he has unearthed, so we can form a good idea of the contents of this lost play.[3]

	]at[	
	]reoue,	
	Vlisses A[	
	dore Herrauld[	
	[pr]iam, Hecto[r	D]eiph[obus
	e[x]eunt( ) [	Di]omed, [
3. seuerall	& [D]eiphob[us] the rest &
tucketts	Her[r]aulds to [them] menalaus
	]s & Diomede, to them Hector
	D[eip]hobus, to them Cassandra exit

Scene 1 is clearly the council-scene, found in all versions, in which Priam consults with his sons and chief counsellors as to whether they are to return Helen.[4]   The presence of Priam and Cassandra proves the scene to be in Troy; the heralds and tuckets indicate an embassy; the presence of Ulysses and Diomed suggests that its purpose was to demand the return of Helen;[5] Hector is always

---

[2] This is shown by the fact that the other similar documents have holes near the top to facilitate hanging on a peg in the play-house. This one happens to be badly mutilated near the top; the two bottom lines in each column are also injured, and there are holes elsewhere. My former colleague Dr. C. H. Van Tyne kindly examined the MS. for me.

[3] The similar outline of *The Battle of Alcazar* (Greg, pp. 138 ff.) agrees very closely with Peele's extant play. Though there are some things in one which are not in the other, we could restore the play very satisfactorily from the outline, if we had as much knowledge of the material as we have in this case.

[4] As in Shakespeare's *Troilus* (II, ii), the Welsh play and Peele's poem. In Heywood's *Iron Age* (pp. 265-271), the *Troia*, Lydgate's *Troy-Book* and Caxton (515 ff.), the scene comes before Paris has eloped with Helen.

[5] *I. A.*, 292-3; Cx. 558 ff. Menelaus also seems to appear in person to demand his wife, as later in *I. A.* (p. 307).

one of the counsellors, Deiphobus is in Caxton (522-3), and other names are missing at this point; the entrance of Cassandra at the end can only be to lament their fatal decision.[6]

	Alarū		Excursions		
			Priam Mr Jones		
	excursions	Enter Hector &	(Antenor)	exeunt

Sc. 2.   In this fighting scene the presence of Hector and Priam[7] alone is hard to account for.   Priam may be warning Hector against the battle, in Sc. 4 he is not fighting, as much later in other versions; or this parallels a scene in Caxton (pp. 577-8), where Hector leaves Priam with reënforcements outside the walls, and fights gallantly.

exeunt | Enter A[   ]

Sc. 3.   ? ? ?

Alarū | [En]ter Antenor pursued by Diomede
       | to them Aiax to the[m] on the
       | walls Hector Paris [&] Deiphobus
[   ] | & mr Hunt   exeunt

Sc. 4.   Antenor is evidently captured (Cx. 600); this is important because later he would be exchanged for Cressida.[8]

En[t]er Troyl[us] & Pandarus
to them Cressida & a waight[in]g
maid with a l[i]ght, mr. Jones his boy
Pand[ar]us to him Deiphobus exit
De[i]p[ho]b[us] to him Helen & Paris
exit Pandarus, exeunt omnes

_____

[6] As in Shakespeare, II, ii, 97 ff.; *I. A.*, 269-271; Cx. 526-7.
[7] "Antenor" had been erroneously written, like "Priam" in sc. 9 (Greg, p. 150).
[8] As in Chaucer's *T. C.*, IV; Shakespeare's *T. C.*, III, iii.

Sc. 5.   In this night-scene evidently Pandarus brings
Troilus and Cressida together (cf. Shakespeare, III, ii).
The presence of Deiphobus and Helen suggests the meeting
is at Deiphobus' house, as in Chaucer (II, 1555 ff.).

> Enter Priam, Hector, Deiphobus, Paris
> Hel[len] Cassandra (to them) exit
> De[ipho]bus & Enter [   ] vlisses and

Sc. 6.   This is probably a council-scene (Hel [ ] may be
Helenus).   The entrance of Ulysses and (Diomed?) may
be in order to ask a truce (Cx. 601, immediately after the
possible original of Sc. 4), or to effect the exchange of
Cressida and Antenor (in Chaucer, bk. IV, and Shakespeare, IV, i, Diomed is the envoy).

[ ]	E[De[	
Alarū	Enter[Diomede, menalay [& beat Hector in	Antenor
	'(Priam mr Jones)	
Alarū	Enter Hector and ∧ (Antenor) exeunt	

Sc. 7, 8, 9.   Fighting (De [is doubtless Deiphobus).
As to 8, in Caxton, 607, Hector and other Trojans are
driven to the walls, and are ashamed because the women
are watching thence.[9]

> Enter Diomede to Achillis [   ]
> to them menalay, to them Vlisses
> to them Achillis in his Tent to
> them· Aiax wth patroclus on his
> back.   exeunt

Sc. 10.   Achilles stubbornly stays in his tent, and is
entreated by Diomed, Menelaus, and Ulysses.   Evidently

---

[9] "Antenor" of sc. 8 belongs in sc. 9; "Priam" is a mistake in
sc. 9 (Greg, p. 150).

the bringing in of Patroclus' body is a more effective argument. The scene reflects *Iliad*, IX, 168 ff. (Odysseus, Phœnix, and Ajax are sent to Achilles), and XVIII, 22 ff., rather than Caxton (pp. 580-1, 630, 634).

> Enter Cressida, wth Beggars, pigg
> Stephen, mr Jones his boy & mutes
> to them Troylus, & Deiphobus & proctor
> **exeunt**

Sc. 11. Cressida among the beggars and the passing of Troilus are of course due to Henryson's *Testament of Cresseid*.[10]

> Enter Priam· Hector, Paris Hellena
> Cassandra Polixina to them Antenor

Sc. 12. In Troy. Antenor is perhaps chosen to treat with the Greeks for peace, but in Caxton (p. 655) this is after the deaths of Hector and Troilus. Possibly Antenor's treason is foreshadowed here.

> Alarū | Enter D[io]med · & Troylus · to them
> | Achillis [t]o them Hector & Deiphobus
> | to them on the walls Priam Paris
> | Hellen Polixina & Cassandra to them
> | vlisses Aiax : menalay & Hea[ralds]
> | Priam & they on the wall descend to them

·' Sc. 13. The jealous Troilus and Diomed fight (as in Chaucer, Caxton, Heywood, and Shakespeare). Achilles probably kills Hector in the sight of the Trojans on the walls; Deiphobus being with Hector seems to be a reminiscence from the *Iliad*, XXII, 227 ff., where just before Hector's death Athene stands by him in the form of Deiphobus. Priam perhaps descends to beg his body back (*Iliad*,

---

[10] Printed in 16th century editions of Chaucer. This scene is unparalleled in Shakespeare, Heywood, and Caxton, but is in the Welsh *Troilus*.

xxiv). This being apparently the final scene of the play, this general interpretation must be right; Shakespeare's play ends with the death of Hector.[11]

There is probably not a very large amount lost. The other outlines have from sixteen to a couple of dozen scenes, a good average number for a play. It is clear that the present sc. 1 must have come very near the beginning, as in other versions, probably preceded by love-making between Troilus and Cressida, preparing for sc. 5; the corresponding amount lost in the middle probably related chiefly to Cressida, her departure, affair with Diomed, and abandonment by him, needed to connect sc. 5 with sc. 11. There is no sign of the single combat between Hector and Ajax, or of the peaceful meeting between the two sides, which are so prominent in Shakespeare and Heywood. According to my reconstruction the play resembled Shakespeare's in the prominence of the loves of Troilus and Cressida, and probably bore their names.[12] On the whole it seems constructed with some method and unity, centering on the guilt and punishment of Cressida and on the impending fate of Hector. The main source is clearly Caxton or Lydgate.[13] Yet an acquaintance with Homer is apparent, especially in scene 10. Chaucer's *Troilus and Criseyde* underlies the figure of Pandarus and the loves of Troilus and Cressida, and Henryson's *Testament of Cresseid* her punishment.

[11] In *I. A.* I it is followed by those of Troilus and Achilles (act v contains the contest for the latter's armor).

[12] Other striking features are the prominence of Deiphobus, Antenor, and Polyxena.

[13] Polyxena never appears in the *Iliad,* Cassandra but twice (insignificantly, with nothing on her prophecies), and Antenor is an aged sage (III, 148; similarly in Ovid, *Her.*, v, 95). The form "menalay" appears three times, and "Menelaus" but once; the latter is Caxton's and the usual form, "Menelay" generally Lydgate's. This looks as if Lydgate were the chief source.

Light on the date is to be had from the actor's names, as Mr. Greg shows. "Mr Jones" (Richard) is in a list of the Admiral's men for 1594-5 and earlier, and was with them in 1597-8 and apparently in 1599, 1600 and 1601; early in 1602 he left the company.[14]   Hunt is mentioned, probably as an actor, in 1596, and was in the Admiral's company in 1597-8 and 1598-9.[15]   Pigg or Pyk was in the company in 1597-8.[16]   Stephen Maget was a tireman in 1596, probably promoted to be the " Stephen " of the plot.[17]   " Mr. Jones his boy " is mentioned in Nov. 1599, and perhaps in 1598; he was an actor about 1598 and 1602.[18]   The date of the play is evidently before 1602, and probably after 1596; the date about 1599 fits the above items best.   Mr. Greg's conjecture is inevitable, and the probability strong, that the play is to be identified with Dekker and Chettle's " Troyeles & creasse daye," paid for in April, 1599.[19]

On the Welsh *Troilus and Cressida* (" Troelws " and "Kressyd") I shall merely summarize my results published

[14] *Henslowe's Diary*, ed. Greg, II, pp. 99, 288; Greg, *Henslowe Papers*, pp. 136, 140.   Richard Jones trained the children of the queen's revels in 1610 (Malone Soc. *Collections*, 272).   See also Fleay's list of actors in *Hist. of the Stage*, pp. 370 ff., and J. T. Murray, *Engl. Dram. Companies*, I, pp. 120, 124, 131.

[15] *Diary*, I, p. 45; II, p. 285; *Hensl. Papers*, pp. 136, 138, and cf. pp. 18, 111; also Murray, *l. c.*   He is mentioned in various connections in 1611 and 1621 (G. F. Warner, *Catalogue of MSS. at Dulwich*, 1881, pp. 188, 240, 340).

[16] *Hensl. Papers*, pp. 115, 136; cf. *Diary*, I, p. 106; II, 303; Murray, *l. c.*

[17] *Diary*, I, p. 31, 44-5.

[18] *Diary*, I, pp. 26, 106; II, pp. 286, 288.

[19] *Diary*, II, p. 202; cf. M. L. Hunt, *Thomas Dekker* (N. Y., 1911), p. 49.   In the very next month, May, 1599, Dekker and Chettle were paid for *Agamemnon* (licensed in June); in this entry "troylles & creseda" had first been written by mistake (*Hensl. Diary*, I, p. 109).   This was probably a continuation of the other, relating the return and death of Agamemnon.   So this pair of plays would parallel the two parts of the *Iron Age* (as noted earlier).

more at large elsewhere.[20]   This practically unknown
dramatic poem is extant in MS. Peniarth 106, since 1909
in the National Library of Wales at Aberystwyth.   The
MS. bears the dates 1613 and 1622, and the handwriting
is that of John Jones, a well-known copyist and lover of
the Welsh past, who flourished in the first half of the 17th
century.   The identity of the author is unknown; certainly not John Jones, he was a man of little literary or
dramatic originality or power, and no dramatic experience,
but some skill in Welsh style and verse (he was not a
bard, however), considerable classical reading, and an excellent reading knowledge of English.   As to sources, for
the most part the work is no more than a translation
and would-be dramatization of Chaucer's *Troilus,* ending with Kressyd's expulsion by Diomedes, blasphemy
of the gods, leprosy and death, borrowed from Henryson's
Testament of Cresseid, which follows the *Troilus* in 16th-
century black-letter editions of Chaucer, beginning with
Thynne's of 1532.

The first two scenes of the interlude have more originality and interest.   In the first, Kalkas with the
assistance of his acolyte-servant Sinon ceremonially consults Apollo as to whether he shall stand by the Trojans
or slip over to the Greeks.   In the second we find the
council-scene which we noticed in the Admiral fragment
and shall find in Heywood and Shakespeare.   " Priaf "
(Priam) consults his sons and chief counsellors as to
whether or not they shall return Helen to the Greeks;
after which Kressyd is threatened by the Trojans with
death for her father's treason, but is saved by Troelws and
Hector (this is developed from Chaucer's *Troilus,* I,

---

[20] See *Mod. Lang. Review*, x, 265-282 (July, 1915), where also the
more interesting scenes are fully printed in translation for the
first time.

106 ff.).   The most interesting question about the interlude is as to the source of the first part of this scene.   It
is almost surely not from Caxton or Lydgate, to whose
works there seem to be no other parallels.   The probability is that not only this scene, but the very fact that
the story of Troilus was dramatized in Welsh at all, is
due to the influence of the Elizabethan drama.   Certain
resemblances to *The Iron Age* and Shakespeare's *Troilus*
make it possible, though far from certain, that the author
had witnessed performances of these plays and been
thereby moved to emulation.   Or it may have been a
source common to them that he had seen.   Some English
play or plays we may be sure he had witnessed on the
stage, for no English play on the subject is known to have
been published before 1613 except Shakespeare's (1609),
to which this poem which translates Chaucer and Henryson
with such fidelity shows no verbal resemblances.

All this fixes the date of the interlude with fair probability.   The limits 1532 (when Henryson's poem was
first published)—1613 may be narrowed by the fact that,
while plays on Troy and Troilus are found through larger
limits, their especial vogue was within a few years of
1600.   This fact and the chance that the author knew
Heywood's and Shakespeare's plays allow the conjectural
date 1595—1610.

The plays of Thomas Heywood which we are chiefly
concerned with are the two parts of *The Iron Age,* both
published in 1632.   But the three earlier plays of the
same series are too closely connected with them to be
disregarded,—*The Golden Age* (published in 1611), *The
Silver Age* (1613),[21] and *The Brazen Age* (1613).[22]

[21] Parts of these two plays were made over into a play called
Calisto, and probably played about 1624 (Bullen, *Old Plays,* II, p.
419; IV, p. 99-101; Hazlitt, *Manual of O. E. Plays,* p. 33).
[22] The five plays form the third volume of the 1874 edition of

None of the four divisions between the five plays, except that before *Iron Age* I., marks a grand division in the material. The *Ages* contain a large number of separate episodes from mythology, and really form a cycle of a dozen or two miracle-plays, as it were, for which the material happens to be pagan and not Christian. The series which begins with Saturn's accession to the throne of Crete, and ends with the revenge executed by destiny on the chief foes of Troy, the tragedy of the house of Atreus and the suicide of Helen, has even less unity than the series which begins with the creation and ends with the last judgment. These " bright, easy-going, desultory plays," as Swinburne calls them, seem like the work of a young man full of uncritical enthusiasm for ancient myth and modern drama, too eager to pour the one into the mould of the other to care how he did it. The humanizing and modernizing runs into a riotous incongruity or extravagant quaintness even beyond the example set by Caxton. But when we look at each episode or miracle-play separately, we are amazed to see how much dramatic skill, homely humor, and rare poetry have gone into this strangely undramatic material; and chiefly at the perpetual vitality of it all.

It is of interest to determine, from internal evidence,

Heywood's dramatic works. *The Golden* and *Silver Ages* were also published by the Shakespeare Society in 1851 (vol. 46). The former was entered S. R. 14 Oct., 1611; there are no entries for the others. *The Golden Age* was acted by the Queen's company at the Bull, the title-page says: The former players of Lord Worcester were the Queen's from 1603 to 1619; the Red Bull theatre was used from 1609 to 1642 (Greg, *Henslowe's Diary*, II, pp. 97, 107; Fleay, *Hist. of the Stage*, p. 368). The Queen's men were associated with it from 1609 to 1623 (Murray, *Engl. Dr. Co's.*, I, p. 190). So *Golden Age* must have been acted between 1609 and 1611; how long before no one can say with certainty. *Silver Age* was performed at Court 12 Jan., 1612 (Murray, I, pp. 174, 201).

the order in which the plays were written.[23]   *The Golden, Silver* and *Brazen Ages* were certainly written in this order.   At the end of the first comes Danae's clandestine bearing of Perseus and her father Acrisius' severity to her; *Silver Age* begins with his consequent dethroning, and proceeds with Perseus' rescue of Andromeda.   The first plainly leads up to the second, which would hardly have begun where it does had the other not preceded. *The Silver* and *Brazen Ages* divide the labors of Hercules between them, which were certainly not too much for a single play.   Clearly then the three were written in the above order; and close together, since each necessarily implies the others.   Further it is pretty clear that *Iron Age* I. was written before *Iron Age* II., but that they were more or less planned together.   The former ends with the deaths of Hector, Troilus, and Achilles, the contest of Ajax and Ulysses for Achilles' arms, and Ajax's suicide.   The latter makes a fresh start with the arrival of Pyrrhus on the Greek side and on the Trojan the first appearance of Penthesilea, whose arrival had been announced at the end of *Iron Age I.* (p. 334); half-way through, the city falls, and the rest of the play deals with the ruin of the house of Atreus.   The strictly siege-of-Troy material being rather too much for a single play, more or less that might be called filling was inserted in each, especially at the end; it is clear that the second part implies the first, and its contents, certainly its beginning, cannot be accounted for without the first.

As to the relation of *Iron Age* to the trilogy, there is probability and evidence that when the latter was written

---

[23] Speaking generally, of course conclusions as to plays published long after they were written are imperfectly reliable because this or that part cannot be proved not to be a later addition. But a high probability is attainable.

Iron Age either was contemplated or already existed.[24] While *Brazen Age* ends with some finality in the death of Hercules, the later history of Troy is repeatedly foretold, as by Hercules just before his death (p. 254), by Hesione when carried off by Telamon (p. 225); further, the rape of Hesione and the earlier destruction of Troy (pp. 222-5, 204-8) derive their point and significance from the later history. Such a collection of miscellaneous mythology would hardly have been put into three plays, with a plain slope toward the Trojan channel, unless a play on the better-known subject were to follow. This is especially clear because the third book of Caxton's *Recuyell,* the main source of the pentalogy all through, deals with the siege and fall of Troy. Whether *The Iron Age* was actually written before or after the trilogy is not quite certain, but I am inclined to think it was written before. A gradual growth in the design, first a play or two on the popular subject, then an expansion to cover the whole ground of Caxton, seems more natural than that this strange undramatic series of dramas should have been conceived at once. Further, at the beginning of *Iron Age* the exposition of the situation (pp. 265-6), the previous destructions of Troy and the rape of Hesione, shows perhaps needless fulness and iteration, if *Brazen Age* was presupposed; is certainly fuller than the exposition at the beginning of *The Silver* and *Brazen Ages.* There are also some small contradictions of the account of things in the latter play. Troy is said to have been twice destroyed by the Greeks (265), or by Hercules (266);[25]

---

[24] This was certainly true when the preface to *The Silver Age* was written (1613).

[25] Later in *I. A.,* pt. I (p. 335), Telamon is incorrectly said to have been at "Isliums second sacke"; this is not in *Metam.* XIII, whence the context is derived.

this happens only once in *Brazen Age* (224-5), but the idea in *Iron Age* is accounted for by the rubric preceding Caxton's third book, the beginning of which Heywood was following at the beginning of *Iron Age:*—" In · these two bokes precedente. We haue by the helpe of god tretyd of the. two first destruccyons of Troye [26] with the noble faytes and dedes of the stronge and puissant Hercules," etc. Had *Brazen Age* already been written, this rubric would hardly have been followed. Moreover, in *The Iron Age,* as in Caxton, nothing is said of Hercules at the time being one of the Argonauts, as he is in *Brazen Age.* One thing more; throughout the trilogy Homer frequently appears as prologue, epilogue, and expounder, but never in *Iron Age,* where he would have been much more in place, the *Iliad* being an important source. On the whole, the above evidence establishes a probability, though hardly a certainty, that *Iron Age* was written before the trilogy.[27]

As to the date of the trilogy, the latest possible is fixed by the date, 1611, when *Golden Age* was published. The prefixed address " To the Reader " states that the play was printed without Heywood's knowledge, but that he had time to legitimize it by writing this address. Further, he calls it " the eldest brother of three Ages, that haue aduentured the Stage "; therefore the whole trilogy, anyway, had been acted at latest by 1611.[28] Probably it

---

[26] Caxton probably refers to the destruction by Hercules (296) and the inundation by Neptune (271); the latter is referred to in B. *A.* also (204), but had nothing to do with the Greeks. The passages in *I. A.* under discussion were an addition to the corresponding passages in Caxton, and were doubtless due to the rubric and a confused memory. In *Troia Britanica,* canti VI, VII, Troy is twice destroyed by Hercules, but this was written later.

[27] This is contrary to Collier's opinion (O. Sh. Soc., XLVI, p. v),

[28] On performances of *G. A.,* cf. p. 706 above. With the ambiguities of Elizabethan style, it is impossible to be sure whether this

3

had been written at least a year or two before, and perhaps
many years. We can get much nearer if we accept the
identification of the three plays first suggested, apparently, by Fleay, and since more or less adopted as a *pis
aller* by others.[29]   *The Golden Age* is supposed to be the
" Selio and Olimpo " mentioned in *Henslowe's Diary* in
1594-6; *Silver* and *Brazen Ages* to be the play *Hercules*
in two parts mentioned in 1595-6; [30] and " troye," a new
play, June and July, 1596, is accepted as either *Iron Age*
I. or an earlier shorter version of the two parts (which
latter supposition seems unlikely).[31]   Further, certain
properties for the Admiral's men mentioned in inventories
may have been used in these plays: a suit, " forcke &
garland " for " Nepton," " Nepun," (1598) would fit
Golden Age; " Hercolles lymes," " j gowlden flece," " j
lyone skin," Iris' head and rainbow, an altar, a boar's

play had three younger brothers, or was the eldest of three brothers;
that is, whether or not *Iron Age* had been already performed.
Most citics understand the former, which fits my evidence as to the
order of the plays and is certainly not ruled out by the language.
Heywood may have been thinking of his own *Ages* when he wrote
in his *Troia*, p. 105, " In Saturne ended the golden world, and in
his sonne Iupiter began the Brazen age "; this was probably written
about 1607. But he might have been thinking of *Ovid*, Met. I, 89-
124. A careful examination of the trilogy with the early part of the
Troia, which is closely parallel, I suspect might show clear evidence
that the former came first. There is a fairly clear reference to the
Silver and *Brazen Ages* in Heywood's *Apologie for Actors,* 1612
(O. Sh. Soc., 1841, p. 21).

[29] Fleay, *Chron. Engl. Drama*, I, pp. 283-5, but cf. Collier's edition
of Henslowe's diary, pp. 51, 74; Schelling's *Elizabethan Drama*, II,
p. 20.

[30] *Hercules* was bought by Henslowe in May, 1598 (*Diary*, I, p.
86).

[31] *Henslowe's Diary*, I, pp. 22, 24, 28; 25, 27, 86, 90, 151; 42.
Heywood was writing for Henslowe at least as early as October,
1596 ("hawodes bocke"; *Diary*, I, p. 45); and was writing for the
Admiral's men in 1598-9 (II, p. 284).

head, Cerberus' three heads, a caduceus, a snake, Mercury's wings, dragons and a bull's head (all 1598) are suitable for *Silver* and *Brazen Ages*.[32]   For *Iron Age* may have been " pryams hoes " (in a list of about 1590-1600, possibly 1598, written by Alleyn), "] great horse with his leages " (1598, for the Admiral's men).[33]   It seems likely enough that the bipartite *Hercules* is really *Silver* and *Brazen Ages,* and that the above properties were for them; the fact that the story of Hercules is by no means too extensive to be put into a single play makes it unlikely that there were two bipartite plays on it. The properties for Neptune seem very likely to be for *Golden Age,* but it is hard to accept " Selio and Olimpo " (for " Coelo et Olympo " ?) as a conceivable title for it, genuine or Henslowian; why Latin, and why name the play after Jupiter's dominions, which he does not receive till the last page ?[34]   Further, Priam's hose might have been for the Admiral fragment, or for Chettle and Dekker's *Troilus and Cressida* (if that is not the same). On the whole, all this evidence for dating the series must be deemed very uncertain.

There are various other, rather shaky, evidences that the *Ages* were early plays.[35]   One is their mythological,

[32] *Henslowe Papers* (ed. Greg), pp. 114-8. The suggestion is Fleay's.

[33] *Henslowe Papers*, pp. 55, 118.

[34] It is odd that these plays, written in series and doubtless originally named as now, should have these arbitrary designations from Henslowe, though he often does misname plays. Of Heywood's other plays, or properties for them, almost none are mentioned in the *Diary*.

[35] Meres's *Palladis Tamia* (1598; see Gregory Smith, *Eliz. Crit. Ess.*, II, p. 320; Haslewood, II, p. 154) mentions Heywood as among the best writers of comedy; this fits the *Ages* pretty well, and none of his other plays are known to be so early (but of course many of his plays are lost). I would suggest also that

unrealistic character, in contrast with Heywood's usual dramatic subjects. Another is the abundance of rhyme. Another is the great abundance of allusions to their subject-matter in Heywood's other works, dramatic and otherwise, from the first, before the time of *Troia;* it would not pay to record them, but at least it may be said that if these plays are early we should be surprised at a lack of such reminiscences. Finally, the preface to *Iron Age* II. (1632) tells us, " These Ages haue beene long since Writ, and suited with the Time then : I know not how they may bee receiued in this Age." [36]

As to the date of *Iron Age* there is more light. The *terminus a quo* is given, not very closely, by reminiscences from other plays. Helen just before her death (pt. II, p. 430) says, looking in a glass,

> this the beauty,
> That launch'd a thousand ships from Aulis gulfe?

obviously recollected from the exclamation of Marlowe's Faustus (sc. XIV) when he sees Helen,

> Was this the face that launched a thousand ships? [37]

---

[36] these mythological plays of Heywood are what is referred to in Kempe's well-known speech in *The Return from Parnassus,* pt. II, IV, iii: " Few of the vniuersity pen plaies well, they smell too much of that writer *Ouid,* and that writer *Metamorphosis* and talke too much of *Proserpina* and *Iuppiter.* Why heres our fellow *Shakespeare* puts them all downe, I and *Ben Ionson* too." This part was acted in 1602 and printed in 1606. The passage may even be meant to compare Shakespeare's *Troilus* with *Iron Age.*

[36] This is curiously like the " Prologue spoken at Court " written by Heywood (1633) for Marlowe's *Jew of Malta:*

> To present this; writ many yeares agone,
> And in that Age, thought second unto none.

The Jew of Malta was written about 1589-90.

[37] Also quoted in Shakespeare's *Troilus* (II, ii, 81 ff.):

The date of *Dr. Faustus* has not been ·fixed with certainty more exactly than 1587-93.   Better yet, there is
an obvious allusion to Shakespeare's *Richard III.*, 1592-6,
probably about 1593.   Richard's

> A horse! a horse! my kingdom for a horse!   (v, iv, 7.)

is parodied in connection with the wooden horse (p. 369):

> *Sinon.*   A horse, a horse.
> *Pyrrhus.*   Ten Kingdomes for a horse to enter *Troy.*"

>   Why she is a pearl,
>   Whose price hath launch'd above a thousand ships,
>   And turn'd crown'd kings to merchants,

a passage which also alludes to St. Matthew's Gospel, XIII, 45-6.
It was so natural to quote Marlowe that it may have been done
independently.   The passage was often quoted or parodied; *e. g.*,
All's Well, I, iii, the clown's song, "·Was this fair face the cause,
quoth she, Why the Grecians sacked Troy?" In *Metam.* XV, 231
the aging Helen weeps over her mirror, which may have suggested
Prior's familiar epigram, "Venus, take my Votive Glass," etc.   Cf.
Troia, Commentary, p. 384; Koeppel in Bang's *Materialen,* IX, p. 25,
compares *Rich. II.*, IV, i, 283-4 and Middleton's *Fair Quarrel,* III, ii.
   " This was often quoted and parodied, from 1598 on; cf. *Shake-
speare's Centurie of ·Prayse* (New Sh. Soc.), *Allusion Books* and
Fresh Allusions, which do not give the Heywood passage.   In the
True Tragedy the words are merely, " A horse, a horse, a fresh
horse."—It is doubtful if there is any evidence in the following
parallel, mentioned by one or two critics.   In a tavern-scene in II.
Henry IV., II, iv̲ (1597-8), one drawer sends another to "find out
Sneak's noise." In *I. A. I.* (p. 312), Thersites taunts Achilles with
abandoning arms for a lute,—

>   Wee shall have him one of sneakes noise,
>   And come peaking into the Tents of the *Greeks,*
>   With will you have any musicke Gentlemen."

It should be noted that there is the same allusion in Marston's
Dutch Courtesan (printed 1605), II, iii, 120; Mulligrub asks, " Is
there any fiddlers in the house?", and his wife answers, "Yes,
Master Creak's noise." It seems less likely that Heywood and
Marston are alluding to so obscure a passage as that in *Henry IV.*
than that the key to all three allusions is lost.

As to the other *terminus,* there are two clear pieces
of evidence that *Iron Age* antedates *Troia* (written about
1607).[39] One is a probable allusion to it in the latter.
Just after the beginning of canto XIII (p. 332) Heywood
says to the earl of Worcester, to whom he dedicates the
poem,[40]

> And you (great Lord) to whom I Dedicate
> A second worke, the yssue of my braine,
> Accept this Twin to that you saw of late,
> *Sib* to the first, and of the selfe-same straine.

He had clearly seen some other work by Heywood on
the same subject as the *Troia.* The seeming suggestion
that the work mentioned had been published and dedicated
to Lord Worcester is by no means hard to avoid; no other
of Heywood's dramatic [41] or other works (so far as known)

---

[39] In *A Funerall Elegie, upon . . . Prince, Henry* (1613) Heywood
says none ever acted better on the stage of the universe than the
Prince,—

> Nay who so well? yet as oft-times we see
> (Presented in a lofty buskind stile)
> *Achilles* fall, *Thersites* to scape free
> The eminent *Hector* on the dead-mans file
> Numbred and rankt, when men more base than he
> Survive the battell of lesse worth and stile.   (sig. B⁰)

No extant play except *Iron Age* shows Achilles' fall, and probably the
reference is to it, though it might be to Dekker and Chettle's play
(if not identified with the Admiral fragment) or some other. He
alludes transparently to his own plays in saying that to reproduce
the prince "*Ages* must backward runne" (sig. B⁰).

[40] Edward Somerset, fourth earl, 1553-1628; succeeded William,
third earl, 1589; patron of a theatrical company, to which Heywood seemingly belonged for a year or so from 1602. See *Dict. Nat.
Biogr., Henslowe's Diary, passim,* Fleay's *History of the Stage,* pp.
86-7, 113, 369, 372, Murray's *Engl. Dram. Companies,* and p. 690
above, note.

[41] One or two of the *Pleasant Dialogues and Dramas* (not published till 1637) cover a very little of the same ground. There is
a list of his works in Fleay, *Chron. of the Engl. Drama,* I, pp. 278-
281, and cf. the Brit. Mus. catalogue.

is of similar subject, few of the former and none of the latter were published before the *Troia,* and none of the former (or of the latter, so far as I find) was dedicated to Lord Worcester. The conclusion is obvious that he had seen *Iron Age,* which is certainly *Sib* to the *Troia,* and which we know from the address to the first part had been popular for long before it was published (1632) ; we need not take the phrase " of late," rhyming and hence not to be forced, to mean that the work had been originally produced only shortly before *Troia* was written.

The other evidence that *Iron Age* preceded *Troia* is certain copious borrowings in the former from part of the latter. At first sight this should prove just the opposite. But we shall see. I have said before that most of canti IX and X are a faithful translation of Ovid's *Heroides* XVI and XVII. It is perfectly clear that they were an earlier (probably youthful) work, somewhat inappositely inserted here. In the first place, the poet protests too much in justifying their presence.[42] In his youth he had done a good deal of other translating from Ovid, complaining in 1613 of the theft of his versions of three books of Ovid's *De Arte Amandi* and two of *De Remedio Amoris,* " which out of my iuniority.and want of iudgement, I committed to the view of some priuate friends." [43] These translations from the *Heroides* are in the ten-syllable couplet, and come in oddly among the *ottave rime* of the rest of the poem. Now many couplets are bor-

---

[42] " These two Epistles being so pertinent to our Historie, I thought necessarie to translate, as well for their elegancy as for their alliance, opening the whole proiect of the Love betwixt Paris and Hellen, the preparation to his iourney, his entertainment in Sparta, as also Hecubaes dreame, Paris his casting out among Shepheards, his Vision, and the whole prosecution of his intended Rape " (p. 211).

[43] Address to the *Brazen Age.*

rowed from them almost *verbatim* in the account of the visit
of Paris to Sparta and the reception of Helen in Troy.[44]
There cannot be the smallest question that *Iron Age* was
the borrower; the original Ovid is unlikely to have been
pillaged so largely, or the scattered pillagings to have been
later reassembled and sorted ·out and connected; the
common passages must have appeared first in the complete and continuous translation.   The connection is distinctly better in the *Troia* in several cases (marked * in
the last note).   Certain otherwise odd incoherences in
Iron Age can be explained by Heywood's desire to work
in bits of his old verse, but not, surely, by direct translation from Ovid.   It is plain then that these epistles, so
largely borrowed from in the play, were written before
the rest of *Troia* and before *Iron Age*.   The priority of
Iron Age to the rest of *Troia* is pretty clearly indicated
by the scarcity of other close verbal reminiscences from
one to the other.[45]   Such as exist are nearly all in the

---

[44] *I. A.*, 275-290. "How shall I doe " . . . (*I. A.*, p. 275, *T. B.*, p. 209);
"But more then " . . . (278, 201); * "Because once . . . ravish't
twice?" (278, 216); "That *Theseus* stole . . . tane this head" (278-
9, 202); * "I am not " . . . (279, 217); * "And heare . . . your
face" (279, 226); * "Say I . . . pleasure" (279, 224); * "Your
Husband . . . properer man" (279, 204); "When my . . . pro-
claime" (279, 220); "Harke how . . . heate" (290, 210); * "Alone
. . . " (290, 210); "And who would . . . contend" (290, 211);
"My father " . . . (290, 210); "Be held . . . Troy" (290, 199).
This does not exhaust the verbal borrowings. The passages borrowed from may easily be found in the reprints of the two epistles
mentioned above (p. 688, note). I may add that Heywood seems
to have made no use of Turberville's translation of the *Heroides*
(1567).

[45] I find only the following:—"She dipt him in the Sea, all save
the heele; . . . But what her dainty hand (forbore to drowne) As
loath to feele the coldnesse of the wave" (*I. A.*, 331, Thetys making
Achilles invulnerable); "Plung'd him into the Sea, all save the
heele, . . . Had she but drown'd her hand, . . . her nicenesse would

account of the fall of the city, from the *Aeneid,* which
makes it seem that when Heywood was making his second
borrowing from Virgil, he reread his first.   And they are
by no means as close as the others,—reminiscences rather
than borrowings.[45a] There are very few cases of whole lines
borrowed from the 12,000 lines of stanzas, in contrast with
the dozens already mentioned as borrowed from the couplets.   Obviously, while epistles might more easily than
narrative be drawn on for dramatic dialogue, the difference
of verse did not prevent the borrowing of lines or even
longer bits.   Further, the fact that a poet would be less
likely to quote largely from a work already published
than from one in MS. inclines one to think that the extracts
from his translations of the *Heroides* were made before
he thought of publishing them entire in the *Troia.*   To
sum up, a small part of *Troia* is often and exactly par-

not feele The coldnesse of the waves" (*T. B.,* 308). ". . . Will
spurne down these our wals" (*I. A.,* 373, of the wooden or brazen
horse) ;—"are made to spurne your mure" (*T. B.,* 389). ". . .
Witnesse you gods, that Synon cannot lye" (375, cf. 374); "Witnesse you Gods, that Synon cannot lye" (*T. B.,* canto xv, st. 31 and
cf. 22). ". . . I lept downe from the Altar, and so fled" (375);
"I leapt from of the Altar, thence I fly" (st. 27). ". . . Of this
sacred place Durst sprinke the childs blood in the fathers face"
(391); ". . . in the same place Sparkled the Sons blood in the
Fathers face" (75). ". . . And hew her peece-meale on my fathers
Tombe" (392); "He piece-meale hewes upon Achilles tombe" (92;
Polyxena does not appear in *Aeneid,* II, which is followed here-
about). ". . . *Æneas,* with twenty two ships well furnish't, (The
selfe same ships in which young *Paris* sayl'd When hee from *Sparta*
stole faire *Helena*)," (395); "Rigging to sea these two and twenty
sayle . . . The selfe-same shippes in which the Troian stale The
Spartan Queene . . ." (st. 105). Other trifling parallels are
on p. 373 of *I. A.* (*T. B.,* xv, 18, 19); 374 (29); 375 (31); 379
(45); 382 (51).

[45a] The former passages, being accessible, were not given in full, in
order to save space. There can be no question that they are much
more significant.

alleled in *Iron Age,* and the bulk of the. poem is seldom
and less exactly paralleled; the inference is unavoidable
that *Iron Age* was written after the Ovidian and before
the other part of the *Troia Britanica.*[46]

To sum up what evidence there is as to the dates of
these plays, the trilogy was written before 1611, probably
a good while before; if we accept the identification of it
with certain plays mentioned in *Henslowe's Diary,* it dates
from 1594-6. *Iron Age* was written after 1593, since it
quotes from Shakespeare's *Richard III.* An allusion and
other evidence in the *Troia* show that it antedates that
poem; this will carry it an uncertain distance back of
1607 or so, when Heywood must have been working on
the *Troia.* If we accept the identification with " troye,"
mentioned as new in June, 1596, the date 1596 is indicated for performance. The evidence that *Iron Age* was
written before the trilogy does not necessarily contradict
this. Therefore what evidence there is points to 1594-6
as the date of the five plays, which were perhaps
Heywood's earliest works. At latest they were written
in the very first years of the seventeenth century.[47] An

---

[46] With other evidence, there would be a suggestion of a date
before 1603 in the following. There is a curious parallelism between
the relations of Frankford, his wife, and Wendoll in *A Woman
Killed with Kindness,* and those of Menelaus, Helen, and Paris in
Iron Age I, though both cases might have been suggested by the *Heroides.* Frankford urges his wife to make much of their guest in his
absence (II, iii), as Menelaus does (p. 277); after her fall he asks
her, " Or in thine eye seemed he a properer man? " (IV, vi), which
recalls Paris' " You needes must say I am the properer man " (p.
279). Here the context is from Ovid's *Heroides,* this line being from
XVI, 203-4, " Nec, puto, collatis forma Menelaus et annis, Iudice te,
nobis anteferendus erit." This point was noticed by one of my
students, Miss Edith P. Rings. *A Woman Killed with Kindness*
was printed in 1607, but acted in 1603 (*Hensl. Diary,* I, p. 188).

[47] Sir A. W. Ward, writing on Heywood in the *D. N. B.,* says *The
Four Prentices of London,* written about 1599-1600, is called in its

earlier date for *Iron Age* than for Shakespeare's *Troilus* (1601-2) is favored by some of this evidence and opposed by none of it.

The main source of the trilogy is Caxton's *Recuyell,* without any doubt.[48]   It cannot be Lydgate's *Troy-Book,* which, beginning with the Argonautic expedition, has nothing to correspond with the greater part of Heywood's plays.   Heywood constantly uses for the Titans and their party (*G. A.,* 22, 40, etc.) the word " Tytanoys," a French form which indicates a source ultimately French, as the *Recuyell* is, and which is constantly used by Caxton.   Both

preface Heywood's first play. This is hardly correct. Heywood merely with mock modesty says it was an early play. But cf. J. T. Murray, *Engl. Dram. Co's.,* II, p. 141; he sees a fair probability that *Iron Age* I and II were acted by the Admiral's men in 1597 (p. 142). One more point, on the date of *Iron Age* II. No one can read the story of Orestes and Clytemnestra in acts IV and V without being strongly reminded of *Hamlet* (probably 1600-2). One detail, especially, the appearance of the father's ghost while the son is reproaching the erring mother (p. 423), seems to be common only to these two plays. But it may have been in the proto-*Hamlet.* A. C. Bradley (*Shakespearean Tragedy,* p. 419) thinks many passages in *I. A.* indicate that Heywood knew Shakespeare's *Hamlet;* I must dissent, even from the author of the best book of Shakespeare-criticism ever written, as to the convincingness of his parallels. A lecture on *Hamlet and Orestes* by Sir Gilbert Murray, just published (Clarendon Press, 1914), considers the underlying resemblances of the two stories.

[48] Yet almost everyone says Ovid's *Metamorphoses* (cf. Hazlitt's *Manual of O. E. Plays,* p. 30, Schelling's *Eliz. Drama,* I, p. 19), or else Lydgate's *Troy-Book* (cf. Fleay, *Chron. Engl. Drama,* I, p. 285, Sommer's edition of Caxton, p. xlii ff.). In Bang's *Materialen zur Kunde d. ält. engl. Dr.* IX, pp. 14-20, Koeppel remarks that we lack a thorough study of sources for these plays, but points out Caxton as a main source, and also Plautus' *Amphitruo* (p. 19). Swinburne also (*Nineteenth Century,* XXXVII, 651-2) suggested Caxton as source. There is a University of Pennsylvania thesis on *Classic Myth in the Poetic Drama of the Age of Elizabeth,* by Miss H. M. Blake (1911?).

thoroughly euhemerize the mythology. The parallelism in contents and order is most striking, especially in the earlier part of the trilogy, though from time to time Heywood may add details from other sources. Both begin with Vesta and others making Saturn king of Crete (*G. A.* 7, Cx. 11; not in the *Metamorphoses*); the dispute and bargain with Titan follow (7-10, 13-5; not in the *Metamorphoses*); and so the two proceed, *pari passu*.[49] Ovid, especially the *Metamorphoses,* is used a good deal, but not constantly. The story of Jupiter and Semele (*S. A.,* 146-55), not in Caxton, is from *Metamorphoses* III, 253 ff. Ascalaphus sees Proserpina eat a pomegranate seed, and is transformed for telling of it; this is from book V, 534 ff. The story of Achelous and Dejanira (*B. A.* 173 ff.) is probably from book IX, 1 ff., for in both Achelous goes through transformations (as not in Caxton, 370 ff., who as usual euhemerizes); that of Hercules, Nessus, Dejanira and Omphale (*B. A.* 178 ff., 239 ff.) is from book IX, 101 ff.[50] The account of the Argonauts, Absyrtus'

[49] The following may be compared: the birth and hiding of Jupiter (*G. A.,* 13-20, Cx. 18-33); Lycaon's cannibal banquet (20 ff., 38 ff.); Jupiter's seduction of Callisto (very close; 23-35, 48-57); Jupiter saves Saturn from Titan (36-52, 60-80), dethrones Saturn (53, 100-2); the story of Danae (57-71, 102-31); Ganymede is conquered and carried off (72-7, 131-64). This brings us to the end of *Golden Age*. *Silver Age* begins with the story of Bellerophon (86-96, Cx. 201 ff.); Jupiter and Alcmena (98 ff., 226 ff., but mainly from another source). All these matters are either not in Ovid, or are scattered here and there in a different and shorter form.

[50] Heywood simplifies by identifying Iole with Omphale. For the account of Hercules and his labors in *Silver* and *Brazen Ages*, he seems to have drawn on no single account, but to have used Caxton chiefly, and Ovid. With p. 126, cf. Cx. 242 (also *Heroides* IX, 21-2); with 127-8, cf. Cx. 261; 128 ff., 297 ff. (briefly in *Met.,* IX, 197); 132, 315 ff. (briefly in *Met.,* IX, 192, XII, 210 ff.; *Heroides,* IX, 87-8); 144-6 and 156 f., 328 ff. (briefly in *Met.,* IX, 185); 159-60, 334 ff.; 183-4, 305-8; 239 f., 483. It is notable that Heywood follows almost exactly the order of Caxton.

murder, etc. (*B. A.* 208 ff.), certainly not from Caxton
(348), may be from *Metamorphoses* vii, 1 ff., *Tristia* iii,
ix; or possibly from Valerius Flaccus' *Argonauticon*.
Medea's scruples before helping Jason (*B. A.* 212) are
from *Metamorphoses* vii, 11 ff. The story of Venus and
Adonis (*B. A.* 184-194) is clearly from book x, 529 ff.[51]
Of course the names *Golden, Silver, Brazen,* and *Iron Age*
are from *Metamorphoses* i, 89-126 (cf. xv, 96 ff.), though
the accounts of the ages by no means agree. From certain
other writers the borrowings are important but less frequent. The whole story of Jupiter, Alcmena and
Amphitryo is from Plautus' *Amphitruo,*[52] as is proved
instantly by the name " Socia " assumed by Ganymede.
To the story of the detection of Mars' and Venus' loves
in the *Metamorphoses* Heywood adds the capital story of
Gallus, the servant of Mars, who lets the lovers oversleep
and is changed by Mars into a cock; this is from Lucian's
Ὄνειρος ἢ Ἀλεκτρυών, §3.[53]

As to *Iron Age,* it shows a general parallelism to
Caxton, the resemblances to whose work run through both

[51] The fact that Venus tells Adonis, in *Metamorphoses* x, 560 ff.,
the story of Atalanta's race, may be what suggested to Heywood
uniquely to represent Adonis as killed by the Calydonian boar, the
story of which is in *Met.,* viii, 270 ff.

[52] This I have said was noted by Koeppel; also by A. H. Gilbert
in *Journ. Engl. Germ. Philol.,* xii, pp. 593-6,604-7. I find no evidence of a connection with *The Birthe of Hercules,* a five-act play
in a British Museum ms. of about 1610-20. It is supposed to be a
university play, written perhaps 1600-6, " a loose adaptation " of
Plautus. It was published and studied in a Chicago University
dissertation (1903) by M. W. Wallace, whose work is ignored in
the Malone Soc. reprint of the play (1911).

[53] A Hellenistic addition to the original story. Heywood may have
read Lucian in Greek; but a full translation of Lucian into Latin
by Jacob Micyllus, of Heidelberg, was published in 1538, 1543,
1546, 1549, 1615 (see the dissertation by Hautz, Heidelberg, 1842,
p. 63).

parts of the play, even through the fall of the house of Atreus (*I. A.* 414-29; Cx. 680-95). That the main source is Caxton rather than Lydgate [54] is the presumption when we find the former used in the trilogy and in the *Troia,* but it is shown by evidence as well. In *Iron Age* II, act IV (396 ff.), the two sons of King Naulus are called Cethus and Palamides; in Caxton, Cetus and Palamydes, but in Lydgate,[55] Pallamydes and Oetes. Ovid is much used. The interview of Paris and Oenone (271-3) seems to show reminiscences of *Heroides* v, *Oenone Paridi.*[56] Extracts from Heywood's own translation of *Heroides* XVI and XVII I have shown are much used in the first two acts of part I, and the whole account of the meeting and elopement of Paris and Helen is founded on the same epistles,[57] and is quite different from the version

[54] Lydgate is given as the source by Fleay and Sommer, because they think Heywood wrote *Hector;* also doubtfully by Koeppel (*Studien über S's. Wirkung auf zeitgenössische Dramatiker,* in Bang's *Materialien,* IX, 22). Even if he had written *Hector* this would prove nothing about a play written years before.

[55] v, 701, 921, 954, 987, etc. (E. E. T. S., no variant readings).

[56] "To see Ida . . . For Paris" (271-2); cf. *Her.* v, 41-2. "'Tis decreed . . . farewell (272); cf. 35-6, 52-4. "What needst . . . stranger" (272); cf. 89-92, 99-106, 125-129. "Though now . . . thy state" (272); cf. 79-82, 9-12. Probably Heywood had consulted and remembered, but not previously translated, the epistle of Oenone to Paris. (I find no traces of the answering epistle of Paris to Oenone, by Sabrinus.) An English version of Ovid's epistles was entered S. R. in March, 1600.

[57] *E. g.,* Paris feigns drunkenness (281-2), Menelaus leaves to become king of Crete (273, 282), Helen elopes willingly (286). A curious speech of Diomed's (p. 287), "Let some ride post [from Sparta] to *Creete* for *Menelaus,*" is probably due to certain lines in Heywood's versions of Ovid: Menelaus is said to have "rid unto the farthest West" to become king of Crete (P. to H., about l. 525), is "mounted on his Steed, Ready on his long journey to proceede," "Hee's on his journey to the Isle of Creete" (H. to P., about l. 270), "about great affairs is posted."

in Caxton (527-36). Most of act v of *Iron Age I,* the contention of Ajax and Ulysses for the arms of Achilles, is taken from *Metamorphoses* xiii, 1-381.[58] To Virgil's *Æneid,* bk. ii, are due acts ii and iii of part II, the account of the feigned departure of the Greeks, the wooden horse, Sinon's treachery, Laocoon's fate, and the fall of the city (371-395). Homer, no longer prologue and expounder in *Iron Age,* as in the trilogy, is of far more importance than there as source of action, character, and allusion. Diomed's wounding of Venus is referred to (*I. A.* 316; *Il.* v, 335 ff, 376);[59] so are Achilles' arms and shield, made by Vulcan and "with the whole world ingrauen" (321-2; *Il.* xviii); and Agamemnon's taking of Briseis from Achilles (402; *Il.* i, 345); Priam's fifty sons (284; *Il.* xxiv, 495, vi, 244); when the Greeks beg him to fight, Achilles plays the lute (311-2, 329; *Il.* ix, 186,—the lyre). The name "Astianax" (298, 316) is doubtless due to the *Iliad,* and so also "Thetis sonne" used of Achilles (299). The name and in part the personality of Thersites are from the *Iliad,* ii, 211-277; though he has come up in the world.[60] The chief Homeric incident in *Iron Age* is Hector's challenge of the Greeks

[58] In Cx. 671-3 and Lydgate, bk. v, the dispute is as to whether Ajax or Ulysses shall have the Palladium as a keepsake! At the end of this act there is a probable reminiscence (direct or otherwise) of Sophocles' *Ajax,* in which the hero after his disappointment goes mad, slaughters cattle thinking them the enemies who have foiled him, and when he returns to his right mind kills himself by the seashore. In *I. A.* (341-2, 344) he seems mad, persists in taking Thersites for Ulysses, threatens to slaughter a school of porpoises, and kills himself by the shore. None of this, except his death, is in Ovid.

[59] Wound but not wounder mentioned by Ovid, *Fasti,* iv, 119-20.

[60] In fact, in Heywood he cuts the most respectable figure he does anywhere,—is witty, penetrating, and judicious (274, 280-2), though still cynical, scurrilous, and misanthropic (cf. p. 747-9 below).

to a single combat; nine lots for the Greeks are cast into
a helmet, Ajax is selected, the two assail each other with
rocks and stones and trees, and in parting exchange a
sword and belt as gifts (296-300); this follows *Iliad* VII,
66-312 very closely, sometimes verbally.[61]   There is no
reason to doubt that Heywood's knowledge came directly
from the original, and it certainly was not all due to
Chapman's version of Homer, for chronological reasons.[62]
There is perceptible influence of several English works.
In Peele's *Arraignment of Paris* (printed in 1584) Ate
" trundles " the apple of discord in among the goddesses,
on which " The brief is this, *Detur pulcherrimae* " (II, i,
45; repeated 48, 51).   The Latin inscription might indicate an ancient source, but it proves to be otherwise, being
unmetrical, and not found in the classics.[63]   It is merely

---

[61] In Caxton, 588-90, Hector and Ajax have two unpremeditated
jousts together; later Hector challenges Achilles and takes his gage
(603). In Caxton and Heywood (not in Homer) they talk of their
cousinship. *Il.* III, 85 ff., the single combat of Menelaus and Paris
for Helen, may have suggested their contest of persuasion in *Iron
Age*, pp. 306-9.

[62] We have seen that *I. A.* dates from before, probably long before,
1607. In 1609 the first half of Chapman's *Iliad* appeared, the completed *Iliad* appearing in 1611 or later. Only books 1, 2, 7-11, and
" Achilles' Shield " appeared in 1598. On other translations cf.
p. 742 below. The so-called *Ilias Latina* of the so-called " Italicus "
or Pindarus Thebanus was well-known in the 16th century: it is an
epitome of the *Iliad* in 1070 lines, supposed by Lachmann to have
been written in the time of Tiberius. It was not, however, the source
of Heywood's Homeric knowledge. All the above points (except
Priam's fifty sons and Achilles' lyre) are there; but Hector's speech
of challenge, of which so many details agree in Heywood (p. 296)
and Homer (VII, 67-91, is mentioned in only two lines (577-8).

[63] The nearest parallel I find in the ancients is in Lucian's *Dialogi
Marini*, V, ἡ καλὴ λαβέτω; Hyginus (*Fab.* 92) has " quæ esset for-
mosissima attoleret." Heywood's own *Deorum Iudicium* (*Dram.
Wks.* VI, p. 248) has " Give to the Fairest this as Beauties due."
On Ate cf. p. 680 above.

translated from Caxton (521): "And ther was wreton aboute thys forsayd apple in grekysh langage be hit gyuen to the fayreste." In *Iron Age* (p. 268) Paris at Priam's council gives the inscription in the same form,—

> On which was writ, *Detur pulcherrimae,*
> Giue't to the fairest.

We can hardly avoid seeing the influence of a second Elizabethan work, already described, Greene's *Euphues his Censure to Philautus* (1587). In *Iron Age*, act III (pp. 300-9), after the duel of Ajax and Hector, Priam invites twenty-three Greek princes to his palace; each Trojan escorts a Greek prince to the city, where they all sit in pairs at a banquet, with Hecuba, Polyxena, Cressida, and other ladies in attendance. It is here (303), not at Hector's anniversary requiem, as in Caxton (621), that Achilles falls in love with Polyxena. In Greene too (p. 164) the princes and ladies go in pairs to dinner in the Greek camp, the visit afterwards being returned in Troy (234 ff). Here Achilles likes Polyxena's looks and makes love to her (159-60). In both there is talk of returning Helen (*I. A.* 306-9; Greene, p. 199). Of the influence of Chaucer's *Troilus* there is scarcely a sign, except the name Cres(s)id(a) instead of Caxton's Breseyda; Pandarus is wanting, the love-story is reduced to its lowest terms, and the woman's prominence is on a level with her character. To Henryson's *Testament of Cresseid,* accessible in the 16th century editions of Chaucer, is due a casual reference to Cressida's leprosy (p. 386).

All these facts and probabilities may be interpreted thus. The young Heywood, perhaps casting about for a safe subject with which to win his dramatic spurs, chose the ever popular Troy-story. His rough but spirited ver-

4

sion, founded for the most part on the usual sources, was
so successful that it not only ran for years and was
therefore withheld from the press till 1632, but it inspired
him to hope for and win popularity for three plays dealing with the earlier parts of the same body of tradition.
So Heywood's five plays are a striking sign of the vogue
of the story which Shakespeare was to use very little later.

IV

To an understanding of Shakespeare's *Troilus and
Cressida* nothing is more of a prerequisite than to know
whether it is to be taken merely at its face value, or
whether it contains a hidden satiric meaning.   The only
such meaning which we need regard is its supposed connection with the so-called war of the theatres, which raged
between 1598 and 1602, and involved chiefly Jonson,
Marston, and Dekker.   There is no reason for connecting
Shakespeare with it except the well-known speech of
Kempe in the second part of *The Return from Parnassus,*
IV, V, written about January, 1602,—"O, that Ben Jonson is a pestilent fellow, he brought up Horace giving the
Poets a pill [in *The Poetaster*], but our fellow Shakespeare hath given him a purge that made him beray his
credit."   If the purge exists in any of Shakespeare's extant works, all believe that it is in *Troilus and Cressida.*
We must agree with the late Dr. R. A. Small, however,
that there is no sign of personal satire on Jonson or anybody unless against Jonson in the personality of Ajax.[1]

---

[1] *The Stage-Quarrel between Ben Jonson and the So-called
Poetasters* (Breslau, 1899), pp. 167-171. Mr. John Masefield is
indignant at the idea of even so much as this; perhaps others will
agree with him. Professor Penniman (*War of the Theatres*, 146)
is doubtful if the play has any connection with the War, and thinks
Ajax is not Jonson.

Perhaps it is not impossible that he whom Jonson lamented as the gentle Shakespeare may have publicly insulted Jonson in a way in which admittedly he himself had not been insulted. Shall we agree with Dr. Small that the personality of Ajax contains a caustic portraiture of Ben Jonson? Personally I cannot, and I· believe that Dr. Small's remarkable acuteness and learning will supply evidence against his own opinion.

First we must note that Ajax as a comic figure is amply accounted for in earlier literature.[2] In the *Iliad* it is true he is altogether heroic; there is doubtless no derogation in the long simile (XI, 558 ff.) where he is compared to a lazy ass strayed into a corn-field and belabored by boys, though it may have aided in the later development.[3] In the *Odyssey* (XI, 543 ff.) he is still heroic, though angry and resentful, among the dead. In Sophocles' *Ajax* he is still dignified,—tragic though condemned, a fine example of insolent impiety, or ὕβρις, and its punishment. Angered because the Greeks adjudge Achilles' arms to Odysseus, he goes mad, whips[4] and slaughters cattle thinking them his personal enemies, and when he comes to his right mind kills himself; he is full of hatred, revengefulness, brag, and insolence toward the gods (ll. 762 ff. etc.). From this the later conception flattens out.[5] In Ovid's account

[2] Ulrici in 1874 (*Jahrbuch d. deutschen Shakespeare Gesellsch.*, IX, p. 29) thought Shakespeare made Ajax comic without any literary precedent, in order to heighten the comedy in the play. I wish to show that the comic Ajax was natural if not inevitable. But Sir Sidney Lee seems to exaggerate in saying that all the traits of Shakespeare's Ajax might have been suggested by Chapman's Homer (*Life*, p. 237 *n.*).

[3] Palmer (*Trans. Roy. Soc. of Lit.*, II. Ser., XV, p. 66) errs in thinking this the main or sole origin of Shakespeare's comic Ajax.

[4] Hence the play is sometimes called Αἴας Μαστιγοφόρος or *Ajax Flagellifer*.

[5] According to Lucian he is punished in hell and still resentful

of the contest for Achilles' arms (*Metam.* XIII.), Ulysses' victory is treated merely as one of fluency over valor, but Ajax's arrogance is such that he declares Ulysses' sufficient reward will be the repute of having contended with him. Though Ajax's speech hardly bears Ulysses out, Ulysses calls him *stolidus* (327) *rudis et sine pectore miles* (290), who could not understand the devices on ・ Achilles' shield if he should win it (291), a man of a *stolida lingua* (306), a boaster yet a trembler (340), strong without intelligence (363). In killing himself, Ajax arrogantly declares that none but Ajax can conquer Ajax (390). Everyone in Shakespeare's day knew this account; and three plays or dialogues founded on Ovid or Sophocles are known of in the 16th or earlier 17th centuries.[6] Even among the ancients, Ajax' mad exploits among the cattle could be used to point a pun or adorn a jest; in Apuleius' *Metamorphoses* or *Golden Ass* (III, xviii), Potis ends her *lepidum sermonem* to Lucius, " audacter mucrone destricto in insani modum Aiacis armatus, non ut ille, . . . sed longe fortius, . . . ut ego te . . . non homicidam nunc sed utricidam amplectarer."

The suggestion of savagery and absurdity in the classical accounts is fully realized and greatly developed by the Elizabethans. Chapman, always inclined to read too much individuality into the heroes of the *Iliad,* in his commentary takes a beautiful passage in book XVI, 119 ff. merely as a " most ingenious and spriteful imitation of

there (*Vera Historia,* II, 17; *Mort. Dial.* XXIX) ; in his *De Saltatione,* 83, Lucian describes a distressing and ludicrous overdoing of the madness of Ajax on the stage. Pindar (7th *Nemean Ode,* 24-30) champions Ajax as, next to Achilles, the most valiant of the Greeks at Troy, justly entitled to Achilles' arms.

  [6] On p. 677-8 above I gave a list of Elizabethan dramatic versions of the story of Ajax. In Spenser's *Fairy Queen,* III, ii, 25, Achilles' arms are won by Arthegall(1).

the life and ridiculous humour of Ajax"; to take it seriously "is most dull, and, as I may say, Aiantical." "A plain continuance, therefore, it is of Ajax' humour, whom in divers other places he plays upon, as in likening him.... to a mill-ass, and elsewhere to be noted hereafter." Gosson's *Schoole of Abuse* (1579, p. 21) speaks of poets as "wresting the rashness of Aiax, to valour; the cowardice of Vlisses, to Policie," etc. *The Return from Parnassus* (pt. I, act I, i, 352), speaking of an arrogant, miserly, ignorant literary patron, has the phrase " in Mounsier's Ajax vaine," meaning apparently pretentiousness.[7]   In *Iron Age* I, though the old heroic Ajax revives again, with his gallantry and magnanimity (p. 333), he is Ovidian enough to relapse, under provocation, into an arrogant braggart (299, 328-9), and out of jealous disappointment to take his own life.[8]   One thing more must be mentioned, that the Elizabethans were in the habit of making a coarse pun on Ajax's name, a pun which is at the basis of a skit by Sir John Harington, the clever translator of Ariosto.   The prologue to *The Metamorphosis of Ajax* characterizes the hero thus in the received style: " Great Captain AJAX, as is well known to the learned, and shall here be published for the unlearned, was a warrior of Greece, strong, heady, rash, boisterous, and a terrible fighting fellow; but neither wise, learned, staid, nor politic "; Harington goes on in a very facetious style to tell of Ajax's dispute with Ulysses, his madness and his

---

[7] Nashe's *Pierce Penilesse* (O. Sh. Soc., XII, p. 79) speaks of spirits of earth which make men "run mad through excessiue melancholy, like Aiax Telamonious."

[8] It may be added that the account of Ajax Telamon in Caxton, Lydgate, *Troia* (p. 235) and *Hector* (p. 101) has little resemblance to any of the others, in fact contradicts them, mentioning his modesty.   The account of Ajax Oileus is a little more like the usual account of the other.

killing beasts and finally himself; and then proceeds with
the vulgar conceit of his metamorphosis into a jakes.
Harington's immediate success is shown by the two editions of this book in 1596 (and one of unknown date), by
his *Ulysses upon Ajax* (1596), merely scurrilous *badinage*
on his earlier work, telling how the world had laughed
over it, and by *The Anatomy of the Metamorphosed
Ajax* (1596). The pun also appears in two of his epigrams (I, 51; II, 13).[9] That it got into colloquial usage
is shown by Cotgrave's French dictionary.[10]

In Shakespeare the nine references to Ajax outside our
play mostly express the contemporary view. Biron in
Love's Labor's Lost (IV, iii, 7) says, " By the Lord, this
love is as mad as Ajax. It kills sheep; it kills me, I a
sheep "; later in the same play the vulgar pun appears
(V, ii, 580). In *Titus Andronicus* (I, i, 379-81) we read,

> The Greeks upon advice did bury Ajax
> That slew himself; and wise Laertes' son
> Did graciously plead for his funerals.[11]

The Duke of York in II. *Henry VI.* (v, i, 26-7) says,

> And now, like Ajax Telamonius,
> On sheep or oxen could I spend my fury.

---

[9] All these works were reprinted by the Chiswick Press, 1814 (only
100 copies printed). Cf. *Stat. Reg.* III, p. 15. Harington's skit
seems to have been more or less imitated in the graceful and witty
mock-Ovidian *Metamorphosis of Tabacco*, published in 1602, and in
a contemporary hand on the title-page of the British Museum copy
ascribed to John Beaumont.

[10] See the definition of *Retraict* (mentioned in the *Oxford Dictionary, s. v. Ajax*).

[11] This last point, Ulysses' urging of Ajax's burial, seems to be
found only here and in Sophocles' *Ajax* (ll. 1332 ff.). This may
possibly be an argument against the Shakespearean origin of these
lines. I am glad to acknowledge on all this matter the assistance
again of Miss Edith P. Rings. On Ajax in Shakespeare, cf. R. K.
Root, *Class. Myth. in S.* (*Yale Studies in English*, XIX), pp. 35-6.

In the painting described in *Lucrece* (1394-1400),

> In Ajax and Ulysses, O, what art
> Of physiognomy might one behold!
> The face of either cipher'd either's heart;
> Their face their manners most expressly told:
> In Ajax's eyes blunt rage and rigour roll'd;
> But the mild glance that sly Ulysses lent
> Show'd deep regard and smiling government.

Not to mention two colorless references in *Taming of the Shrew* and *Antony and Cleopatra,* in two plays written after *Troilus* Ajax appears in a more dignified guise: Kent says of Oswald in *Lear* (II, ii, 131-2),

> None of these rogues and cowards
> But Ajax is their fool;

and Guiderius in *Cymbeline* (IV, ii, 252-3),

> Thersites'[12] body is as good as Ajax',
> When neither are alive.

Perhaps Shakespeare's full portrait of the unfortunate hero left him with a kindlier feeling.

It is clear, then, that the traits of Ajax which were familiar to Shakespeare's auditors were valor, heaviness physical and mental, pride, insolence, jealousy. The incidents which had most struck the imagination were his unsuccessful pleading, his madness, his lashing and slaughtering of cattle, his suicide. The slaughter of cattle under a hallucination could not have struck the Elizabethans as anything but comic, and we must not forget the probability that they often saw humor in mere madness.[13] It seems plain that the Ajax of *Troilus and Cressida* is sufficiently accounted for by what has been

---

[12] Mentioned nowhere else outside *Troilus.*

[13] See John Corbin, *The Elizabethan Hamlet,* pp. 55 ff. I do not mean that I accept all his deductions.

shown. He was recognized by Ulrici long ago as one of
the comic characters of the play. He is envious (II, i,
35-8), a glutton of flattery (II, iii.), heavy and slow (v,
v, 18), a valiant ass (II, i, 50), a braggart, proud, surly-
borne, strange and self-affected (I, iii, 188 ff., II, iii,
247 ff.), yet stupid enough to accuse Achilles of the same
faults (II, iii, 169, 218, etc.); his dulness and slowness of
speech are repeatedly mentioned (I, iii, 375, 381, II, i, 13,
III, iii, 127), though Thersites says there is wit dormant
in him (III, iii, 255 ff.). All this is simply a development
of his stock traits. It is also probable that Shakespeare
alludes to Harington's coarse pun.[14]   Ajax is the only warrior who condescends to tussle with Thersites (II, i.), and
much of the ridiculous description of him is through Thersites' mouth.[15]   The most striking description of him is
that in Alexander's speech to Cressida, which makes her
smile (I, ii, 19-32):

This man, lady, hath robb'd many beasts of their particular additions: he is as valiant as the lion, churlish as the bear, slow as the
elephant; a man into whom nature hath so crowded humours that
his valour is crush'd into folly, his folly is sauced with discretion.
There is no man hath a virtue that he hath not a glimpse of, nor
any man an attaint but he carries some stain of it. He is melancholy without cause, and merry against the hair.[16] He hath the joints
of everything, but everything so out of joint that he is a gouty
Briareus, many hands and no use, or purblind Argus, all eyes and
no sight.

---

[14] So Dr. Small, p. 169; cf. III, iii, 244, II, i, 70, 80, 120. It is possible, however, in the first passage, that Ajax is simply, like Malvolio, rehearsing imaginary conversations; cf. ll. 248-62.

[15] But Thersites talks much the same of Achilles (III, iii, 313-6).

[16] A recognized trait of the mentally deficient. Of a half-witted
country fellow, who would laugh when he was whipped, it is said,
" it was his manner euer to weepe in kindnesse, and laugh in ex-
treames." This is in Shakespeare's colleague Armin's *Nest of Nin-
nies* (O. Sh. Soc., x, p. 38); he seems to apply to Ajax later an allusion to this very same fool (see note on III, iii, 215 in the *Tudor
Shakespeare*).

The keynote of this is paradox, and in Shakespeare's Ajax paradox is inevitable, for he is a combination of the traditional Elizabethan Ajax, a mass of absurdity and egotism, and the Ajax of Homer, fighting a mighty and chivalrous duel with one of the Nine Worthies. This thoroughly comic description of him, like the description of Thersites in I, iii, 73-4, 192-4, is meant to prepare for the farcical scene (II, i) in which both at once make their first appearance.

Now it is true that some of these traits are repeatedly ascribed to Ben Jonson by his enemies, especially pride, arrogance, railing, "humours," egotism.[17] Perhaps I should not dwell on the fact that he is given none of the paradoxical combinations, and none of the stupidity, which are essential in Ajax's personality; a satirist may make his victim still more unlovely by adding new traits (if they leave him still recognizable), though it would be strange to accuse of stupidity the sour scholar whose shrewd tongue had been making everybody squirm. It was more important on the stage that the physical resemblance should be striking. Now it is clear that Ajax is a large, heavy and probably gorbellied fellow. He is "the elephant Ajax," "slow as the elephant," "a very horse," a "lubber," with "lusty arms" (II, iii, 2; I, ii, 21; III, iii, 126, 139; IV, v, 136); his wisdom confines his "spacious and dilated parts" (II, iii, 261, in Ulysses' ironical speech), he is a "thing of no bowels" (II, i, 53, with a pun and doubtless ironical), "who wears his wit in his belly and his guts in his head" (II, i, 80).[18] But Jonson

---

[17] Small, pp. 29, 89, 99, 111 f., 122. So no wonder a man writing a monograph on the stage-quarrel should be inclined at first to recognize Jonson in Ajax.

[18] This means that while his belly should be small and his head large, he has a pot-belly and a "pin-head."

was just the reverse of all this. Dr. Small says of a character in Marston's *What You Will,* "Quadratus is an
epicure and fat . . .; this alone is enough to prove that
Quadratus is not, as Penniman says, Jonson" (p. 112).
Horace in *Satiromastix,* who represents Jonson, has a
scanty beard, with a face "like a rotten russet apple, when
'tis bruised," is "a lean, hollow-cheeked scrag" (pp. 200,
260, 241). "All this," says Dr. Small (p. 125), "accords
exactly with what we know of Jonson from other
sources."[19] It is necessary to remember that at the date
of the *Troilus* Jonson (1573-1637) was under thirty, and
not at all the ponderous person he became later. All this
makes it illicit to urge that Ajax's make-up might have
imitated him. It is impossible, of course, to prove that
Ajax is not Jonson. All one can hope for is to show that
what evidence there is does not favor the idea. Ajax as a
comic figure, and most of his traits are traditional; and
in some essentials he is unrecognizable as Jonson.[20] How
much evidence is there left? The purge given Jonson by
Shakespeare may never be recognized; there is no finding
it in *Troilus and Cressida.*

As to the date of the play there is little new to say,
and little to add to my discussion of it in the introduction to the *Tudor* edition. The versification[21] is that

[19] *E. g.,* the anonymous play *Mucedorus* refers to Jonson as "a
lean and hungry meagre cannibal"; this is in the editions of 1606
(cf. Small, p. 116), and 1610 (sig. F 3ro).

[20] It would be fully as defensible to see Jonson in Achilles, to whom
Ajax is a comic counterpart. Achilles appears over and over again as
proud, insolent, scurrilous, undignified (he encourages Thersites, just
as Ajax scuffles with him). He is "lion-sick of a proud heart," full
of "humorous predominance" (II, iii, 93, 138), and his insolence to
Hector contrasts with the courtesy of the other Greeks (IV, v).

[21] Thoroughly treated by Small, pp. 143-8, who gives other references; see also Fleay, *Shakespearean Manual,* p. 136, and bibliography in S. Lee's *Shakespare,* p. 49. For evidence from vocabulary

of Shakespeare's middle period, which is as specific as one should venture to be on the basis of verse technique. The entry in the *Stationers' Register* on 7 February, 1603, is pretty surely for Shakespeare's play; [22] and a reference to an incident probably heard of through a member of his company, and two probable references to the two pro- logues of Jonson's *Poetaster*,[23] will put the date in or after 1599 and 1601 (respectively). A further sugges- tion of a date after 1599 is afforded by Professor C. W. Wallace.[24]   In II, iii, 227-230, Nestor and Ulysses are

looking in the same direction, cf. Sarrazin in the *Jahrbuch* of the German Shakespeare Society, xxxiv, pp. 148-9, 168.

[22] It seems unlikely that the Chamberlain's company had two Troilus plays within a few years (though it is true that Heywood's, and Dekker and Chettle's, were both for the Admiral's men). Furth- er, the licensee of this play in 1603 published in 1604 the second quarto of *Hamlet*, and also others of Shakespeare's plays (Lee, *Life of S.*, 1904, p. 225-6). As early as 1790 Malone assigned the above date for the above reason; he thought the play "not one of our authour's happiest effusions." I have pointed out that there is a little change in Shakespeare's way of speaking of Ajax in plays written after 1603 or so. Again, if he had already in 1599-1600 his later familiarity with the Troy-story, Rosalind would hardly have said, "Troilus had his brains dash'd out with a Grecian club; yet he did what he could to die before, and he is one of the patterns of love" (*A. Y. L. I.* IV, i, 96 ff.). The first clause contradicts Caxton, Lydgate, and others, according to whom Achilles cut off Troilus' head. Further, the Henrysonian and not the Shakespearean Cressida, "the lazar kite," the "beggar," appears in *Henry V.* and *Twelfth Night* (1599 and 1601).

[23] Envy also appears in *Histriomastix*, III, end, VI, end. In the epilogue of *Mucedorus*, 1610, Envy *does* say Amen (cf. *T. C.* II, iii, 24, but also p. 748 below, note), and there is something similar in the prologue to the 1606 edition and at the end of the 1598 edition. But Shakespeare was hardly alluding to this. See the *Tudor Fac- simile* edition of both plays (1912, 1910); *Academy*, IX, p. 402; H. P. Stokes, *Chron. Order of S.'s Plays*, p. 105. On the date see Boyle in *Engl. Stud.* XXX, p. 21, whose paper, of doubtful value, is reviewed in *Jahrbuch*, xxxviii, pp. 308-10.

[24] *Shakespeare's Money-Interest in the Globe Theatre, Century*

whetting Ajax against Achilles, and relieving their own feelings by *sotto voce* digs at Ajax:

Ajax. 'A should not bear it so, 'a should eat swords first. Shall
    pride carry it?
Nest. An 'twould, you'd carry half.
Ulyss. 'A would have ten shares.   ·

Dr. Wallace shows that from February, 1599, the stock in the Globe Theatre was divided into ten equal shares. So Ulysses seems to correct Nestor,—Ajax would carry not half but all the pride.   Far-fetched as the allusion seems, it is the almost inevitable explanation of an otherwise meaningless phrase.   The agreement of these small evidences makes the date 1601-2 fairly firm, and no sufficient ground has been shown for Fleay's view that Shakespeare's work on the play is of various periods.[25]

On the ultimate sources of *Troilus and Cressida* there is little or nothing, except on one point, to add to Dr. Small's admirable treatment of the subject.[26]   He shows

---

Magazine, LVIII, pp. 506, 509.   Wallace believes he finds many other allusions in *T. C.* to Kempe and the Globe-Rose rivalry.

[25] Cf. Small, *Stage-Quarrel*, p. 147.   There seem to be no certain contemporary allusions to the play.   *Saint Marie Magdalens Conversion* (1603-4; see *Centurie of Prayse*, New Sh. Soc. 1879, p. 57) deems itself to be on a nobler subject than that " Of *Helens* rape and *Troyes* beseiged *Town*, Of *Troylus* faith, and *Cressids* falsitie, Of *Rychards* stratagems for the english crowne, Of *Tarquins* lust and lucrece chastitie."   This is regarded by Small (p. 142) and others as a reference to Shakespeare's *Troilus, Richard III.*, and *Lucrece.*   But it may as well refer to *Iron Age, Rape of Lucrece* (acted 1603), and *II Edward IV.* (printed 1600, and containing Richard's III's usurpation), all by Heywood; the *Troilus* does not tell of Helen's rape, *Iron Age* does.   But it need not refer to dramas, to works all by the same man, or even to any works in particular. The supposed allusion to Shakespeare's play, and supposed pun on his name, in *Histriomastix* (1599 or earlier), are absolutely unreliable.

[26] Pp. 154-167.   He partially follows Hertzberg (*Jahrbuch*, VI, pp. 169-225), who in part follows Delius, Moland, and d'Hericault, etc.

clearly that Shakespeare made much use of Chaucer's *Troilus,*[27] more use than was made by any of the above-mentioned works except the Welsh *Troilus* and probably the Admiral fragment. The prologue and scene 5 of act v show knowledge of Caxton, and not of Lydgate.[28]   In the rest of the play one or the other is certainly used. But since the prologue is suspected by some, and the last few scenes are believed by many, not to be by Shakespeare, it is no more than probable that Caxton is used throughout.[29]   The suggestion[30] that certain scenes, or the gen-

See also Eitner in *Jahrbuch,* III, pp. 252-300; Koeppel in Bang's *Materialien,* IX, p. 14.

[27] I ignore for the nonce the probability that the play is founded on an earlier one. On the relations of the two poets see also E. Stache, *Verhältn. v. Sh. T. u. C. zu Ch.'s gleichnamigem Gedicht* (Programm-Abhandlung, Nordhausen, 1893). It is hardly true, however, that he " adopts the character of Pandarus from it without change " (Small). Though with the degeneration of the character of Cressida from the earlier poem to the later, his guilt toward her would naturally seem to grow less, he is a far baser person in Shakespeare. His earlier humor and unmoral loyalty to Troilus have become ribaldry and second-hand voluptuousness. He gives the impression of being a much older man than in Chaucer (v, iii, 101 ff.). though it is his pose to seem in love. Of course he had long deteriorated in popular tradition; the proper noun Pandar had become the common noun pander early in the 16th century. The procuress in Gascoigne's *Glass of Government,* 1575, is named Pandarina (cf. Wallace, *Birth of Hercules,* p. 58).

[28] " The Sagittarye," however, (*pace* Small) is mentioned by Lydgate (rubric before III, 3484, E. E. T. S.). As early as 1733 Theobald said Caxton was used even more than Chaucer.

[29] Cf. p. 681 above and pp. 755-6 below. Yet Mr. Saintsbury (*Camb. Hist. Engl. Lit.,* v, 221) says merely that the play " may have been suggested by Chaucer," and " owes much to other forms of the tale of Troy—perhaps most to Lydgate's." Stevens and Deighton also err in attributing certain things necessarily to Lydgate. As early as the *Merchant of Venice* (III, ii, 55 ff.; 1598 or so) Shakespeare knew the story of Hercules' rescue of Hesione; given at length in Caxton, 274-9 (not in Lydgate at all), and very briefly in Ovid (*Met.* XI, 211-4). On p. 681 I showed how much more popular Cax-

eral chivalric or sociable tone of the play, show the influence of Greene's *Euphues his Censure to Philautus* seems
to have little basis. We lack here the resemblance found
in *Iron Age*. Act IV, v, and v, ii, are sufficiently accounted for by Caxton (pp. 589-90, 602-3) and by the *Iliad*
book VII.).[31]

The knowledge of Homer's *Iliad* shown in the play is
always attributed to Chapman's translation; this has been
repeated constantly, at least since Dr. Johnson.[32] The
assumption (it is nothing else) is based on the belief that
Shakespeare had small Latin and less Greek, and would
be likely to use the translation made by his fellow-
dramatist, and is sometimes connected with the theory
that Chapman is the rival poet of the Sonnets, and even
that the unsympathetic spirit of the *Troilus* is traceable
to antipathy for Homer's poem because Chapman trans-

ton was than Lydgate; the latter's work seems to have come out as a
rival to the former's, just as *Hecto*r did to *Troia*.

[30] Cf. Herford's article in *Trans. New Sh. Soc.*, 1887-92, pp. 186 ff.;
Mabie, *Shakespeare*, p. 255, etc. One little parallel is probably accidental; Greene, pp. 166-7; II, ii, 175-6.

[31] It is not surprising that there seems to be no important use of
Virgil, since the play does not reach to the fall of the city; or of
Ovid, whose influence in other works appears in parts of the story
not found in this play. Cf. pp. 758, 760 below. Churton Collins
(*Studies in Sh.*, p. 64) and others compare I, iii, 85 ff. with Sopho-
cles' *Ajax*, 669 ff., but no connection seems certian.

[32] See his postscript to the play. H. R. D. Anders, *Shakespeare's
Books* (*Schriften d. deutschen Sh.-Ges.* I; 1904), p. 42, is a little
less sure than most. Even so thorough and informed a scholar as
Dr. Small (*Stage-Quarrel*, 164-7) says, "The Iliad was accessible
to Shakespeare only in Chapman's translation." His opinion is
accepted by Koeppel (Bang's *Materialien*, IX, 14). See also J. F.
Palmer in *N. & Q.* IX, vi, pp. 316-7, and in *Trans. Roy. Soc. Lit.*, II,
xv, 63 ff. On debts to Homer cf. Small, 164 ff., W. W. Lloyd's *Critical Essay* on the play (e. g., in Singer's edition, London, 1856, VII,
p. 325), etc.

lated it.[33]   Therefore the matter is of more interest than a trifling question of source.   If Shakespeare did not use Chapman, we have less excuse than ever for believing that he was consciously degrading the Troy-story.

Now, strangely enough, no one has seen that all this is impossible, simply on chronological grounds.[34]   The complete translation of the *Iliad* appeared in 1611 or later, twelve books in 1609 (when the quartos of the *Troilus* were published) or later, and only seven books (and also the description of Achilles' shield, from book XVIII) in 1598, the seven being I, II, VII-XI, though numbered continuously, I.-VII.[35]   Now the play contains many Homeric particulars from outside these seven books.[36]   The fol-

[33] Cf. Furnivall's introduction to the *Leopold Shakespeare;* Boas' *Shakespere and his Predecessors,* p. 378.

[34] Ulrici (*Jahrbuch,* IX, p. 37) in his admirable article on *Troilus* as a comedy pointed out that the dragging of Hector by Achilles' horse could not be from Chapman, but might be from Salel and Jamyn (see below).

[35] The assumption that Chapman is the source is explained by the fact that some of these editions were issued undated.   Hudson, *e. g.,* dates two of them from two to eleven years too early.   The date of the twelve books is established by a complimentary sonnet to Lord Salisbury, addressing him as Lord Treasurer, a title he received 4 May, 1609 (Bullen, in *D. N. B.*).   Of course some use may have been made of Chapman's version so far as available; a slight verbal resemblance between Ulysses' reference to Nestor (I, iii, 172) and Chapman's bk. VIII, is given by Palmer, *Trans. Roy. Soc. of Lit.,* II, XV, p. 67, but probably means nothing.

[36] In order to collect all the possible indications of Homer's influence, I put in a note those that might have come through Chapman.   The characterization, mostly original or due to Caxton or Chaucer, shows signs of Homer's influence occasionally, and strongly in case of Nestor and Thersites.   Nestor in Caxton is little distinguished; a strong fighter (571, 579, 585), he is only once spoken of as old (545), and his wise eloquence is little dwelt on (542, 630-32).   As the venerable and eloquent sage of Shakespeare he is probably due to the *Iliad.*   (In like manner he appears in other plays and poems of Shakespeare, even earlier, but cf. also *Metamorphoses,*

lowing may be mentioned. In ɪ, i, 112-3 Æneas tells
Troilus "That Paris is returned home and hurt" by
Menelaus. This probably refers to the earliest combat
described in the *Iliad*, in which Paris is wounded by
Menelaus, and snatched away homeward in a thick darkness by Aphrodite (ɪɪɪ, 355-83).[37]—Hector is struck down
by Ajax (ɪ, ii, 34-5); so in the *Iliad*, xɪv, 409 ff.—Ulysses
reminds Achilles that his

> glorious deeds, but in these fields of late,
> Made emulous missions 'mongst the gods themselves,
> And drave great Mars to faction (ɪɪɪ, iii, 188-90).

Obviously Homeric, this refers to *Iliad* xxvɪ, where Achilles has made havoc of the Trojans and fought against the

xɪɪ and xɪɪɪ.).—Thersites, more important, and entirely absent from
Cx., is developed but otherwise little changed from *Il.* ɪɪ, 212-277.
His abjectness, cowardice, and scurrility in Homer are simply extended, regularized, and accounted for in Shakespeare by his position
as the Fool of the play, much in demand among the less dignified
Greeks as a purveyor of base amusement. (He appears in *Met.* xɪɪɪ,
233, and is mentioned by Pindarus Thebanus, Juvenal, Seneca, etc.;
Small, p. 165. Erasmus, *Colloquies, Love and the Maiden*, p. 115,
speaks of him as a type of the physically loathsome fellow.).—
Small pointed out that Achilles' exaggerated pride (and insubordina-
tion) is from the *Iliad* rather than from Caxton (*Stage-Quarrel*,
165).—Achilles is twice referred to in an off-hand way as
"Thetis' son" (ɪ, iii, 212; ɪɪɪ, iii, 94). This is hardly a reminiscence from Cx., where she is barely mentioned, at the very end, long
after the fall of Troy (692, 694); and hardly from Ovid or Virgil;
but rather from the *Iliad*, where she frequently appears as Achilles'
mother.—Most important of all, Hector's challenge to single combat, the choice of Ajax by lot, and the fight (ɪ, iii, 260 ff.; ɪv, v)
follow *Iliad* vɪɪɪ, though less closely than the corresponding scene
in *Iron Age* does. (Cf. also ɪ, iii, 75 ff. with *Il.* ɪɪ, 203-6, and ɪ, iii,
171 with x, 131). The name of Cressida's servant Alexander is
probably due to the name Alexandros used often in Paris. Many of
the passages I mention are given by Small, 165-6, and Gervinus, *Sh.
Comm.*, pp. 687-8.

[37] In four lines Caxton (p. 595) mentions Menelaus' wounding
of Paris, among many other combats; possibly the source.

river Xanthus, is aided by Poseidon and Athene (284) and Hephæstus (sent by Here, 330); there is great strife (385) among the gods, and Ares, driven to faction, starts the fight, taunting and attacking Athene (391).[38]— Achilles surveys Hector (iv, v, 231-246) at their peaceful meeting to see where later he shall destroy him; so in the *Iliad* (xxii, 317-27) Achilles at the last fight examines Hector to find the best place to strike him.[38a]—It is Patroclus' death that rouses Achilles to action (v, v, 30 ff.; *Il.* xviii, 79 ff.), and not the slaughter of the Myrmidons, the only cause (besides his own danger) in Caxton (637).—Hector's body is fastened to the tail of Achilles' horse and dragged (v, viii, 21-2, x, 4, 5); this is from *Il.* xxii, 395 ff.,[39] where it is dragged from Achilles' chariot.[40]

No one will doubt after reading this that the play shows a rather extensive knowledge of the *Iliad,* all of which cannot be explained by hearsay;[41] and a knowledge of

[38] In the *Iliad* of course this comes later, after the death of Patroclus, before which Achilles does not fight at all. Ares is driven to faction also in *Il.* xv, 113 ff., in anger for the slaughter of his son, but by Deiphobus, not Achilles; in v, 461, he is driven by the exploits of Diomed to stir up the Trojans. Root (*Class. Myth. in S.,* 83) refers to v, 864-98, where also Ares is driven to faction by Diomed. Of course the dramatist's memory may have slipped.

[38a] But cf. Cx. 602.

[39] In Cx. 639 it is Troilus' body that is fastened to the tail of Achilles' horse; the dramatist combines the two accounts. Very likely the dragging of Hector was well known.

[40] Other parallels that have been or may be pointed out are i, ii, 2-4, 192-267, and *Il.* iii, 139-242 (but cf. Cx. 578); ii, iii, 272 and xx, 435; iv, i, 8-9, and v, 300-14, 430-45, xxiii, 290 ff.; iv, v, 119 ff., and vi, 119-236; v, x, 19, and xxiv, 602 ff.

[41] Nor by the so-called *Ilias Latina* of Pindarus Thebanus, said to have been used in Shakespeare's day as a school-book, and suggested as a source by von Friesen (W. *S. Dramen,* pp. 362-3). This epitome, in 1070 ll., has little about Thersites, and lacks Mars driven to faction (see Baehrens, *Poetae Latini Minores,* vol. iii). It is quoted by Chapman in his commentary on bk. i.—If Shakespeare used an earlier play (pp. 755 ff. below), we cannot tell how much of the Homeric material came from it.

passages that were not accessible in Chapman's translation till long after the date of the play. As to whether
the dramatist had read Homer in Greek it is best not to
venture a decided opinion;[42] I shall dwell a little more
on another alternative. Accessible to Shakespeare there
were the following translations of the *Iliad*. *English:*
1) Arthur Hall's, printed in London, 1581, translated
from the French of Salel, first ten books only, in four-
teeners.[43] *French:* 2) Jehan Samxon, Paris, 1530, in
prose, from the Latin. (3) Hugues Salel: bks. i.-x.,
1545, 1555; xi, xii, 1554; i-xii, 1570; complete, 1580,
1584, 1599; in verse, from the Greek, completed by
Jamyn. *Latin:* 4) Lorenzo Valla, in prose, 1474, 1502,
1522 (Cologne). 5) H. Eobanus Hessus, in verse, 1540,
1543 (first three books), 1545, 1549 (complete).
6) Greek and literal Latin, 1551, 1560-7, 1561, 1570,
1580, etc. 7) V. Obsopoeus and others, in verse, complete, 1573. 8) Spondanus, Basle, 1583. Any one of
these, except one or two incomplete versions, would have
given Shakespeare the knowledge he shows.[44]

[42] The late Churton Collins, who collected a remarkable number of
striking parallels between Shakespeare and Greek poetry, admits,
"Nothing warrants us in pronouncing with certainty that he read
the Greek classics in the original, or even that he possessed enough
Greek to follow the Latin version of those classics in the Greek
text" (*Shakespeare as a Classical Scholar*, in *Studies in Shakespeare*, p. 15); "by 1570, Greek was commonly, though not universally, taught in the schools" (p. 13). As a counterblast to
Collins, cf. Root, *Class. Myth. in S.*, pp. 4 ff.

[43] From the 1555 edition of Salel's French; the copy of it which
Hall used, containing his autograph, is in the British Museum.
Hall adds the "catalogue of the ships," omitted by Salel, from the
Latin. Thomas Drant's English translation of the *Iliad* (before
1580) is unpublished. My list of translations does not profess to
be complete.

[44] We should have some positive evidence as to the source of the
dramatist's Homeric knowledge, if we could know that he had any-

Far the most interesting and illuminating fact about the sources of Shakespeare's play is the clear evidence that it is not independent of *Iron Age*,—the existence of similarities too great to be accounted for merely by their common relation to Caxton and Homer. Some of them

thing to do with the phrasing on the title-page of one of the 1609 quartos (the second, probably): "The Famous Historie of Troylus *and* Cresseid. *Excellently expressing the beginning* of their loues, with the conceited wooing of *Pandarus* Prince of *Licia.*" (One of the editors of the quarto-reprint, Mr. Stokes, thinks this description fits so ill that it must have been borrowed from some old and lost play. This idea is not only unlikely (especially on the second printing), but unnecessary; the first two scenes of the play are full of Pandarus' clever and witty wooing of each lover, and act III, sc. ii, excellently expresses the beginning of their loves in one sense at least.) Passing over the humor in this Homeric air given to Chaucer's disillusioned worldling and Shakespeare's cynical reprobate, we must observe that the title hardly came from the Greek Homer. Pandarus appears about three times in the *Iliad*, as an expert bowman. In the list of the Trojan allies, he appears as son of Lycaon, leading the Troes of Zeleia (II, 824-7), on the Sea of Marmora in the N. W. of Asia Minor; wounding Diomed, he exults that Apollo has "sped him on his way from Lycia" (v, 105), in the S. W. of Asia Minor; Æneas tells him that none of this land rivals him, "nor any in Lycia boasts to be his better" (v, 173; on him cf. also IV, 88; v, 246, 795). How the Zeleian can have come from Lycia still' puzzles Homeric commentators, and the two vague and obscure references to Lycia hardly account for his title in the quarto; but when we look at the translations all is explained. In the first passage, the catalogue of the Trojan allies, Eobanus Hessus has "Qui vero Lyciam populi coluere Zeleam . . . Pandarus illustris duxit" (p. 67); and later "Pandarus . . . Lycio genitore Lycaone cretus" (p. 126). Spondanus, more than any other translator quoted and praised by Chapman (who mentions Salel, Valla and Hessus also), has "Pandarus, Lycaone genitus ex Lycia" (p. 46). Similarly the French: "Pandarus le Duc des Liciens" (Salel-Jamyn, 1580, f. 66vo), "Pandarus de Licie" (*ib.* 68ro) and Hall's English, "The bands of *Zele* in *Lycie* land" (p. 42), "Pandarus, the Lycian head" (p. 80), "the *Lycian* Pandarus" (82, 84 etc). These passages quoted are all cases where Lycia is not mentioned in the Greek; other translations show the same confusion, sometimes

have been noted by Koeppel,[45] who assumes that Heywood must have borrowed from Shakespeare. Before considering the points and their meaning, it is so difficult to grasp two plays in their entirety that it is worth while to summarize them in parallel columns. I indicate by symbols the scenes which correspond in each.

IRON AGE	TROILUS AND CRESSIDA
* 265-71. Council in Troy: shall Helen be seized? (Cx. 515-527)	
271-3. Paris rebuffs Oenone.	
273-87. Paris reaches Sparta, wooes Helen and carries her off, pursued by her brothers. (Cx. 540)	
† 288. Love-scene, Troilus and Cressida.	
288-91. Reception of Helen. (Cx. 536-7)	
291-3. Achilles and Calchas arrive from the oracle. (Cx. 546-52). Ulysses and Diomed arrive from Troy (Cx. 558-62).	
293-5. Defiant talk and fighting. (Cx. 589-90, 601-2).	I. i. Troilus talks with Pandarus of his love. ii. Cressida talks with

clearly caused by Pandarus' father's name. The title-page of the quarto pretty clearly reflects it, possibly derived from an original *dramatis personae* or something else in the MS., which might reflect Shakespeare's reading. We cannot be sure of this, but the point does show that the translations of Homer were well-known.—(There is nothing of all this in Pindarus Thebanus, nor in the early-published part of Chapman. There are articles on Chapman's Homer in *Engl. Stud.* v, pp. 1-55, etc., and on Shakespeare's possible use of French versions, cf. *Jahrbuch,* IX, p. 37).

[45] Bang's *Materialien,* IX, pp. 20-3 (1905). In collecting the above parallels I am glad to acknowledge the efficient help of one of my students, Mr. Albert A. Bennett. Fleay oddly does not note the resemblances (*Life and Work of S.,* pp. 222-4).

IRON AGE

‡ 296-8. Hector's challenge (*Iliad*, VII.)

‖ 299-301. Combat of Hector and Ajax. (cf. Cx., 589-90)

¶ 301-9. Festive meeting of Greeks and Trojans.

§ 309-10. Fighting between Troilus and Diomed. (cf. Cx. 608)

** 310-15. Princes vainly beg Achilles to fight. Various combats. Achilles finally roused. (Cf. Cx. 623-4, 628, 630, 634, 637, 580, 589-90)

†† 315-9. H e c t o r dissuaded against fighting. (Cx. 611-2)

‡‡ 319-20. Fighting. Margareton killed. (Cx. 672)

¶¶ 320-2. Hector fights and is killed. (Cx. 613)

§§ 322-4. Is lamented in Troy (Cx. 614, 641).

TROILUS AND CRESSIDA

Pandarus of Troilus' love.

iii. Greek princes talk of Achilles' pride; and plan to make him jealous of Ajax. ‡Hector's challenge.

II. i. Achilles, Ajax, Thersites, etc., learn of the proposed single combat; and quarrel.

* ii. Council in Troy: shall Helen be returned? (So in Admiral fragment.)

** iii. Achilles' pride; Greek princes flatter Ajax. (So partially Adm. fr.)

III. i. Pandarus and Helen.

† ii. Love-scene, Troilus and Cressida. (So Adm. fr.)

iii. Calchas asks Cressida back. Greeks slight Achilles and Ulysses exhorts him.

IV. i. Diomed comes for Cressida.

ii. Cressida is claimed.

iii. Cressida is claimed.

iv. The lovers part.

v. Cressida is received by the Greeks. ‖ The combat, ¶ followed by a friendly meeting; interview of Hector and Achilles.

V. i. Ribaldry by Thersites. Achilles' love of Polyxena.

ii. Troilus watches Cressida and Diomed love-making.

†† iii. Hector resists dissuasion against fighting. Pandarus and Troilus read a feigning letter from Cressida.

IRON AGE	TROILUS AND CRESSIDA
	iv.-vii. **Fighting.** (**So Adm.** fr.) *** Thersites in battle. ‡‡ Margarelon killed. § Troilus and Diomed fight. (So Adm. fr.)
	¶¶ viii. Hector's death. [So Adm. fr).
	ix. The Greeks learn of it.
	§§ x. The Trojans lament.
324-7. Troilus killed. Cx. 639)	
*** 327. Thersites in battle.	
327-30. Hecuba's message to Achilles. **His insolence to the Greek princes. (Cx. 641-2)	
330-3. Achilles treacherously shot by Paris. (Cx. 641-2)	
334. Coming of Penthesilea. (Cx. 644-5)	
334-45. Contention of Ajax and Ulysses for Achilles' arms. Death of Ajax. (Cx. 671-3)	

The chief peculiarities of the two plays are,—in Shakespeare's the much greater development of the Troilus and Cressida story (amounting to over a third of the play, as against a very small fraction in Heywood), and the knitting together of Achilles' pride and Hector's challenge by the elaborate scheme of the Greek princes to rouse Achilles by exciting his jealousy of Ajax; in Heywood's play, the accounts of what leads up to the war, *viz.,* Helen's seizure, and of what follows Hector's death, *viz.,* Troilus', and the contention for the arms of Achilles. That is, Shakespeare takes merely the central and essential part of the story and greatly develops and tightens it, with the result that, strongly as the reader feels its lack of unity, it has much, considering its in-tractable subject, certainly far more than the other.[46] A comparison makes one feel vividly Shakespeare's skill in structure (as well as in other things).

The above comparison is meant not to present evidence of a particular connection, but to set forth the broad outlines of the things we are comparing. Still, the general agreement in contents between *Troilus* and the middle part of *Iron Age* is clear. Now I mention the chief detailed resemblances. In the first place, it is curious how nearly identical are the *dramatis personæ* of the two plays. Of the twenty-five named characters in the *Troilus* all appear in *Iron Age* except Helenus, Pandarus, and Alexander; of the twenty-seven in *Iron Age* I all appear in *Troilus* except Polyxena, Oenone, Castor and Pollux (all inconspicuous).[47] The Homeric Thersites, unknown to Caxton and the Admiral fragment, is introduced and greatly developed by both.[48] He is often spoken of and

[46] The unity of the play (comparatively speaking) is well exhibited in Moulton's *Moral System of Shakespeare*, p. 362. Except for the fizzling out at the end (cf. p. 756 below), the structure shows skill-ful manipulation of material which was even more fixed in common knowledge than that of the English historical plays, with which it really belongs in regard to the relation of play to source. All this is hardly recognized by Professor Brander Matthews (*Shakespeare as a Playwright*, pp. 230-3), and other critics who condemn it on structural grounds. In my introduction to the *Tudor* edition (p. x) I pointed out the subtle skill shown by the unifying balance of character and situation; I might add that I, iii, and II, ii, balance each other. When Mr. Charles Fry put the play on in London, 1907, he cut and rearranged it very extensively; but modern theatri-cal demands are different from Elizabethan and far more stringent.

[47] Of seventeen persons recognizable in the Fragment all but one are in *Troilus*, which has nine not in the Fragment.

[48] *Iliad*, II, 211-77; also *Metam.* XIII, 233. In the interlude *Ther-sites* (1537) he is quite different, an absurd *miles glorious;* it was made over from a Latin play by Textor (*Engl. Stud.* XXXI, pp. 77-90). Thersites is a more dignified figure in *Iron Age* than in Shake-

speaks in much the same terms in both plays.   Achilles says to him,

> Dogged *Thersites*,
> I'le cleaue thee to thy Nauell if thou op'st
> Thy venemous Iawes (*I. A.* p. 327).[49]

Agamemnon and the other Greeks hardly expect

> When rank Thersites opes his mastic jaws,
> We shall hear music, wit, and oracle (*T. C.* I, iii, 73-4).

With the railing scenes in *Iron Age* (312, 325-7, 342-3) we may compare *Troilus* II, i, iii and v, iv.   In each play there is also a scene where Ajax in cynical desperation or Achilles in wanton humor bids Thersites describe Agamemnon, Thersites himself, etc.[50]   He tells Ajax and Patroclus at their own request what he thinks of them

speare or Homer.   At the court of Menelaus (274) he is a privileged railing counsellor, with both sense and wit, and in the last act of pt. I is busy preparing the scene for the debate of Ajax and Ulysses (334).   But at the beginning of pt. II he embraces the vile Sinon as a kindred spirit (359), and throughout falls little short of his namesake in Shakespeare in the quality, though he does in the amount, of his ribaldry.   The fact is that in Heywood his personality is not very firmly conceived.   The main difference is that in Shakespeare he is plainly the Fool of the play, for which reason he should be taken the less seriously.   On the whole, Thersites in the one play is hardly independent of Thersites in the other.   On Shakespeare's Thersites see M. L. Arnold, *Soliloquies of Shakespeare* (Columbia dissertation, 1911, pp. 120-1).

[49] Thersites answers, " Doe, doe, good Dog-killer," on which Achilles beats him.   Cf. *T. C.* II, i, 45-7: " Do, do," " Ay, do, do," says Thersites to Ajax, who is beating him.   Of course this is merely Elizabethan English for " Go ahead! "

[50] P. 343; II, iii, 46 ff.   In *I. A.* Thersites goes on in a kind of imitation of the formula of excommunication; Ajax responds four times " Amen," which reminds one of " and devil Envy say Amen " in the same scene in *T. C.* (l. 24), of Thersites' " Amen " when he has cursed Patroclus, and of Patroclus' " Amen " (36, 40).   Again, " *Both* [Aj. and Th.]. Amen.   *Ajax* . . . Our prayers now sayd, we must prepare to dye " (343).   " I have said my prayers, and devil Envy say Amen " (*T. C.* II, iii, 24).

(342; II, iii, 50). In both plays, Thersites is·full of ribald ·contempt for the war and its occasion, and full of vile imagination; in fact, he is the chief vehicle of the apparent bitterness, full of a sense of the futility of it all. In *Iron Age* he says:

> So many heauy blades to flye in peeces
> For such a peece of light flesh?
>
> .   .   .   .
>
> Now all the World's turned wenchers (301).
>
> .   .   .   .
>
> The *Troians* are all mad, so are the *Greeks*,
> To kill so many thousands for one drabbe,
> For *Hellen:* a light thing (325).
> What makest thou here at *Troy* to ayde a Cuckold?
> (to Ajax, 342).

In Shakespeare:

> All the argument is a cuckold and a whore; a good quarrel to draw emulous factions and bleed to death upon (II, iii, 78-80). Nothing but lechery! All incontinent varlets! (v, i, 106). Lechery, lechery; still wars and lechery; nothing else holds fashion. (v, ii, 195). What's become of the wenching rogues? (v, iv, 35).

There is an especial resemblance between the scenes where Thersites goes into the battle-field to ridicule the fighters and is spared by Troilus or Hector:

> *Troi.* Stand if thou bee'st a souldier, do not shrinke.
>
> .   .   .   .
>
> *Ther.* And I *Thersites*, lame and impotent,
> What honour canst thou get by killing mee?
> I cannot fight (*I. A.* 325).
>
> *Hect.* What art thou, Greek? Art thou for Hector's match?
> Art thou of blood and honour?
> *Ther.* No, no, I am a rascal; a scurvy railing knave; a very filthy rogue.
> *Hect.* I do believe thee; live. (*T. C.* v, iv.)[51]

---

[51] Shakespeare assuredly did not write this helpless dialogue. Cf. also v, vii, where Thersites is challenged and spared by Margarelon.

Further, there are many parallels in the personality and actions of Achilles and especially Ajax. In *Iron Age,* 328-9, Achilles before his tent is insolent to Agamemnon, and Ulysses excites Ajax' jealousy of Achilles. In *Troilus,* II, iii, and III, iii, Achilles is much more insolent to Agamemnon,[52] and Ulysses and others much more elaborately work up Ajax' jealousy and energy. Heywood's Ajax says,

> I'le after him and dragge him from his Tent,
> And teach the insolent, manners: Giue mee way. (328)

Shakespeare's Ajax says,

> An 'a be proud with me, I'll pheese his pride.
> Let me go to him. (II, 215-6)

The curious scene at the end of *Iron Age* I (343-4) where (simply out of time-serving) " Enter ouer the Stage all the Grecian Princes, courting and applauding Vlisses, not minding Aiax," and where Ajax speaks out bitterly, is similar to that where Achilles is neglected, out of policy (III, iii). Thersites tells Ajax he is " a horse that knowes not his owne strength " (342). Likewise Ulysses tells Achilles that Ajax is

> A very horse,
> That has he knows not what. (III, iii, 126-7; cf. 309-10)

The most striking resemblance is in the choice of a champion by lot, and in the combat between Ajax and Hector, finally stopped by the latter, which is not in Caxton, the main source of both plays, but which both borrow from Homer,[53] Heywood with less change than Shakespeare;

---

[52] Achilles' insolence here is not paralleled in Caxton and Homer; in *Il.* IX and Cx. 631 Achilles refuses Agamemnon's ambassadors, but courteously, as he does the king himself in Cx. 634.

[53] *Il.* VII. In *Il.* VI, 212 ff. Diomed and Glaucus stop fighting when the former finds they are guest-friends through his father; they agree thereafter to avoid each other in battle, and exchange arms.

if Swinburne exaggerated in seeing a following of one dramatist by the other with " almost servile fidelity," [54] the verbal resemblance is unmistakable.

And C'uz, by *Iove* thou hast a braue aspect,
It cheeres my blood to looke on such a foe:
I would there ran none of our Troian blood
In all thy veines, or that it were diuided
From that which thou receiuest from *Telamon:*
Were I assured our blood possest one side,
And that the other; by Olimpicke *Iove,*
I'd thrill my Iavelin at the *Grecian* moysture,
And spare the *Troian* blood: *Aiax* I loue it
Too deare to shed it.   .   .   .   .

.   .   .   .
         Then here's thy cousins hand,
By *Iove* thou hast a lusty pondrous arme. (*I. A.* 299-300)

Thou art, great lord, my father's sister's son,
A cousin-german to great Priam's seed.

.   .   .   .

Were thy commixtion Greek and Troyan so
That thou couldst say, " This hand is Grecian all,
And this is Troyan; the sinews of this leg
All Greek, and this all Troy; my mother's blood
Runs on the dexter cheek, and this sinister
Bounds in my father's "; by Jove multipotent,
Thou should not bear from me a Greekish member
Wherein my sword had not impressure made
Of our rank feud; but the just gods gainsay
That any drop thou borrow'dst from thy mother,
My sacred aunt, should by my mortal sword
Be drained! [55] Let me embrace thee, Ajax.
By him that thunders, thou hast lusty arms. (IV, v, 120-1, 124-136)

---

[54] *Nineteenth Century*, XXXVII, p. 655; in one of his studies on Heywood. On the whole, Swinburne thought there was little to suggest the influence of Homer or Shakespeare on Heywood. He, like Koeppel, assumed that it was Heywood who would be influenced by Shakespeare, not *vice versa*. The above parallel is dwelt on by Koeppel (Bang, *Materialien, l. c.* pp. 21-2).

[55] In Heywood's *Golden Age,* p. 17, Sibilla says Jupiter is her son as well as Saturn's, and she'll not kill her part. The conceit is not in Caxton or Homer. Heywood has it again in *I. A.* (p. 303), and also in *Troia,* p. 325.

In both plays a festive meeting and banquet follows. Among other resemblances in incident, there is a close resemblance at the death of Hector. In both he is killed unchivalrously by the Myrmidons, not by Achilles, who merely eggs them on; and who after Hector's death drags the body at his horse's fetlock or tail (321-2; v, viii). The manner of his death is unparalleled anywhere; the Myrmidons are not even mentioned at this point by Caxton or Homer.[56]

Next, as to tone or feeling. This is of particular interest, being the element in *Troilus* which has caused the critics most labor and vexation of spirit. On this subject I can only phrase cautiously what I believe the well-

---

[56] The dragging of course is borrowed from Homer; in Cx. only Troilus is dragged. *Troia*, p. 353, is much the same as *I. A.* For other resemblances, both plays have the council-scene which was traditional in these Trojan plays, being also in the Fragment and the Welsh *Troilus* (cf. pp. 698, 704-5 above, and my article in *Mod. Lang. Rev.*, x, 270-2, 278-80). The scene in *I. A.* follows Cx. 515 ff. more closely and comes earlier in the story than the corresponding scene, ii, ii, in *T. C.* While in Cx. the gist of Hector's speech is that it is imprudent to fight the Greeks, in both plays the gist is that it is unrighteous; a more or less natural change, without which Hector would have seemed cowardly. In both (269-71; ii, ii, 101 ff.), at the council Cassandra cries out against the war and Hector makes much of her prophecies, which are discounted by the fire-eaters on the ground that she is mad; this is not in Cx., who puts her outcry after the council has broken up; in Homer she is seldom mentioned, and never as a prophetess. The identical stage-direction in both plays, "Enter Cassandra with her haire about her eares" (*I. A.*, 269; *T. C.*, Folio, ii, ii, 100) probably is not significant, for the phrase is commonly used of her or other distraught persons. Cf. Ovid, *Her.* v, 114, xvi, 119; Heywood's *Edw.* iv, pt. ii, p. 165; *Dicke of Devonshire*, in Bullen's *Old Plays*, ii, 92. Both plays quote as to Helen Marlowe's line, "Was this the face that launched a thousand ships?" Both seem to represent Priam as having not fifty but fifty-one sons (*I. A.* 308, but cf. 266, 271; *T. C.* i, ii, 175-7). These last points are unimportant.

informed reader will feel when he has read the two plays through close together. The tone or spirit averages up nearly the same. In Shakespeare things are intensified, for good and for ill, which gives the play less internal harmony and unity of spirit than *Iron Age* has. Nothing in the latter rises to the stately dignity reached by Ulysses and the other Greek princes in I, iii and III, iii, and by Hector in II, ii of *Troilus;* nothing sinks quite to the loathsome venom of Shakespeare's Thersites, the silliness of his Ajax, the impotent sensuality of his Pandarus. *Iron Age* no more than *Troilus* shows any consciousness that classical heroes are entitled to the reserved and ideal treatment which belongs to a semi-canonized tradition. I believe a critical reading of Heywood's play will give most people a very different feeling about the *Troilus* from what they had before, since no one will suspect a bitter or hostile spirit in Heywood.[57]

The resemblances and the nature of the relation between the two plays are very puzzling. While most of the parallelism in larger contents is due to the fact that both follow Caxton,[58] as to the smaller points one thing seems certain; without insisting on any one, they cannot all be due to coincidence, or to any known common source, or to any sort of common fund of material generally traditional in Trojan plays. The remaining possibilities are that one borrowed from the other directly, or through an intermediary play, or that both made use of a third play.

[57] The philhellene A. C. Swinburne (*Nineteenth Century*, XXXVII, p. 655) felt "that the brutalization or degradation of the godlike figures of Ajax and Achilles is only less offensive in the lesser than in the greater poet's work." Professor Herford would have found in Heywood far more likeness to the "manner" of *Troilus* than he sees in Greene's *Euphues his Censure* (*Trans. New S. Soc.*, 1887-92, p. 187).

[58] Shakespeare possibly, but not probably, Lydgate.

The first seems unlikely. Close verbal parallels, though
they exist, are few. Chronology rules out a borrowing by
either from the printed form of the other. *Iron Age* we
know from the forewords of pt. I (1632), was long popular
on the boards, which is doubtless why it was not published
when the other *Ages* were (1611-13). Therefore its MS.
can hardly have been at Shakespeare's disposal early in the
first decade of the century.[59] So primitive a play as it
hardly reflects study of Shakespeare's MS., even if chronology favored the idea. And the resemblances seem somewhat
extensive and close to be due to one author's having witnessed the other's play, even if such large-scale cribbing
were otherwise likely.[60] If this is the explanation, the
borrower was probably Shakespeare.[61] The hypothesis
of an intermediary play is much more unlikely. Some
of the above arguments apply here, and if *Iron Age* was
a successful play for years after 1607 or so and probably
after an earlier date, and if *Troilus* was written in 1601-2,
it is unlikely that another play can have been based on
one of them and used in the other; particularly that a
play intervened after *Iron Age* and before *Troilus,* which
is the only possibility which harmonizes with the characters of the two plays.

[59] Very unluckily it is so far impossible to date *I. A.* exactly. But
we have seen it cannot be much later than *Troilus,* and is probably
earlier.

[60] Of course the points could have been got by a spectator with a
note-book, with or without shorthand. Such a proceeding would
seem of doubtful honor.

[61] His play being the less primitive, and probably the later. For
another thing, the claim in the preface to the Quarto that the play
was never acted publicly shows probably that at least it cannot
have run long and successfully; while we know *I. A.* did. It would
be superficial to exclaim against the idea of Shakespeare as the
borrower. He had not been canonized in 1602, and one could show
over and over again how the greatest poets *ont pris leur bien où
ils l'ont trouvé.*

There remains the possibility that both made use of a third play.[62] The frequency with which Shakespeare and other Elizabethan dramatists made over older plays is to well-known to be more than mentioned. This explanation is favored by internal evidence in the *Troilus*. To the general agreement of critics that Shakespeare did not write all of it, and that another hand is perceptible in v, iv-x, especially vii-x, almost any attentive reader will assent. The best statement of the case is Dr. R. A. Small's.[63] With some touches in iv-vi which sound Shakespearean, the scenes are crude in action, characterization, and poetic style, and in verse are very unlike the rest of the play. Further, though this seems

[62] Which can hardly have been the one that underlies the Admiral fragment; this seems to have lacked, *e. g.*, Thersites and the duel. Nor Dekker and Chettle's *Troilus and Cressida*, if we accept its probable identification with the former.

[63] *Stage-Quarrel*, pp. 147-9. It is often stated that the prologue is generally believed to be not by Shakespeare. Having made a pretty thorough examination of editions and criticisms of the play, I can say that by no means so many critics have taken this position, and that they seem to be guided chiefly by impression. After many readings of both prologue and play I can only state, for what it is worth, a contrary impression. There is evidence besides. The allusion to Jonson's *Poetaster* recognized in ll. 23-4 shows that it probably dates from the same time as the rest of the play, and its intimate acquaintance with the sources shows that it is probably by the author of most of the play or of the end; yet it is far superior to the wretched stuff written by the latter. The Greek princes come " from isles of Greece " (l. 1); this recalls " the island kings " (III, i, 167), and " our island " (III, iii, 210), in the Shakespearean part of the play; I find nothing in Caxton to account for this (cf. the list of the Greeks on pp. 545-6). The verse agrees as nearly with that of the Shakespearean part of the play as we need expect in so short a passage (Small, 144), though there is a marked difference as to end-stop lines. Finally, the absence of the prologue from the Quarto is not due to its being a later addition; J. Q. Adams (*Journ. Engl. and Germ. Philol.*, VII, p. 58) in an able article shows that it was probably put in the Folio to fill a blank page.

not to have been generally noticed, the end does not properly link to and round off the earlier part. I have shown that a chief point of originality in Shakespeare's play is the other princes' scheme to rouse Achilles from his proud retirement by exciting his jealousy of Ajax; this is one of the two chief motives of the play, and, as we shall see later, on its elaboration Shakespeare spent his chief interest and did his most impressive writing. Now this motive grievously flattens out and even dies away toward the end; it produces no result, for it does not eventually move Achilles to change his mind, as he is on the point of doing at the end of one of the chief scenes (III, iii, 311-2; cf. 227-8). After the fight of Ajax and Hector, it is true that Achilles surveys the latter and talks of killing him next day (IV, v, 269, v. i. 2), but he is instantly diverted from the purpose by messages from Hecuba and Polyxena,[64] and is roused to fight only by the slaughter of Patroclus (v, v, 30 ff), as in Homer, and of the Myrmidons, as in Caxton. Therefore the most interesting part of the play comes to just nothing at all. The love-motive also ends inconclusively with the faithless Cressida enjoying temporary bliss, and Troilus merely cursing her and her uncle. In the other three plays at least she is punished, and in *Iron Age* Troilus dies. It is hard to fancy any skilled dramatist dropping his main threads without tying them up; and harder to fancy Shakespeare writing the end of the play and bringing the Achilles-motive to nothing.

[64] Who are very inconspicuous in the play, so it is not a case of a lesser motive giving way in order to emphasize a greater. This part may have been (rather weakly) written by Shakespeare to connect with the ending of the old play, when he saw he should have to keep it, or may have been retained from the old play (the rest of the speech rather looks so). The passage and context do not seem like the work of a continuator; but this is anticipating.

All this has been interpreted in two ways. A few critics [65] suggest that Shakespeare left the play to an inferior hand to finish, but himself added some touches to his assistant's work in scenes IV-VI; others,[66] that an older play underlies the entire work, and that at the end he took over entire scenes almost or quite unaltered. This second explanation seems best to fit the facts. The last seven scenes, indeed others not long before, perhaps, look more like remains (at times touched up by Shakespeare) from an earlier work, than like additions by a prentice-hand to the extant play. Further, if he wrote most of it and simply left the end to another, this does not account for the resemblances elsewhere to *Iron Age;* but both problems are solved at once by the supposition that he made over an earlier play, also used by Heywood. The fact is, then, that while the greater part of the *Troilus* is unmistakably Shakespeare's, toward the end the certainty of the touch seems to fail,[67] and we finally come

[65] *E. g.*, Small, *Stage-Quarrel*, p. 149. Fleay, (*Life and Work of Shakespeare*, pp. 24, 44) thinks that while most of the play dates from 1602, the prologue, the love-story and scenes iv-x of act v are from a play of about 1593, in which Shakespeare was only a coadjutor; cf. also Fleay in New Sh. Soc. *Trans.*, 1874, pp. 304 ff. This view has found little favor. It is impossible that, as some have suggested, the play originally ended with v, iii, before Hector's death.

[66] Collier, Verplanck, Dyce, Verity, White, and others; G. P. Baker (*Devel. of S. as a Dram. Artist*, p. 260); the editor of Schlegel and Tieck's translation (Berlin, 1877), XI, p. 172. The latter suggests, as evidence that another play intervened between *Troilus* and its ultimate sources, the absence of verbal likeness between them. Note also that it contains twice as many words peculiar to itself as most of the plays, about as many as the far longer *Hamlet* (cf. lists in the *Irving* edition). The fact that some of them are favorite words with Heywood further countenances the common-source theory.

[67] There are other signs of this toward the end. No discreet critic would enter without searchings of heart on such a task as

6

to something clearly not his. A reasonable explanation
is that, beginning by rewriting entirely, he became more
and more negligent. Another sign that another man's
work underlies the play is this. We have seen that not
only are several important elements due to the *Iliad;*
numerous slight casual allusions are also unmistakable.
Now in his earlier works there is no evidence whatever
of the slightest acquaintance with the *Iliad.*[68] Nothing

dividing a work among various authors on the basis of varying
literary merit, or will expect everyone to admit all the evidence
he sees fit to adduce. Therefore I consign to a footnote certain
signs of obtuseness which are as hard as v, vii-x to attribute to
the Shakespeare of 1601-2. Consider such cases as these of psychological crudity. When Cressida is being miscellaneously kissed in the
Greek camp (IV, v, 26), the first speech of Menelaus the deserted
husband is "I had good argument for kissing once." A trifle bald!
Later in the same scene (179 ff.) Hector says to him,

> Your quondam wife swears still by Venus' glove.
> She's well, but bade me not commend her to you.

Men. Name her not now, sir; she's a deadly theme.
Hect. O, pardon; I offend.

Hector's surprise that he has offended is rather *naïf* for Shakespeare. (Paris in *I. A.*, 303, similarly reminds Menelaus of the latter's kind welcome of him in Sparta!) In *I. A.* I find no positive indication that an earlier play underlies it. Probably there is none in the
great condensation of the love-story, and its curious telescoping in
act III (303-6). Visiting Troy during a truce, Calchas urges Cressida
to abandon Troilus and take Diomed; she refuses, hesitates and con-
sents; a page later it appears that Diomed's unhorsing of Troilus and
sending the horse to Cressida has already occurred. This is carried
over almost unchanged to the *Troia Britanica* (XIII, 14, 16, pp.
334-5); but it is made more intelligible, as if Heywood had now
noticed the weakness, by an earlier passage (XI, 40-2; p. 251, page
numbers muddled). Heywood could not have omitted the celebrated
love-story from *Iron Age*, but the play is so crowded that he had
to condense.

[68] Anders, *Shakespeare's Books* (*Schriften d. deutschen Sh.-Gesell-
schaft*, I), p. 42; Root, *Class Myth. in S.* (*Yale Studies in Engl.*
XIX), pp. 5-6. *Lucrece*, 1401 ff., is from Ovid and Virgil, to whom
(especially Ovid) Shakespeare owed almost all his mythological
knowledge (Root, p. 3).

we know of his methods inclines us to believe that for one play he would have been likely to secure such intimacy with the entire *Iliad,* especially for a play which we shall find good reasons for concluding he wrote without great care and interest.   In tastes, as in reading, he had not Ben Jonson's scholarship.   He shows no such intimacy with Chaucer's *Troilus,* much more important for this play.   It is more suggestive yet that works later than the *Troilus* show no more knowledge of the *Iliad* than the earlier ones do; [69] why, unless because he never had it ? All this rather looks as if he made use of a play by a man who really knew his Homer, perhaps a university man.[70]

To sum up, the best explanation of the relation between *Iron Age* and *Troilus and Cressida,* and of some internal peculiarities of the latter, is that Heywood made use of an older play in *Iron Age* I, that Shakespeare made use of the same in *Troilus,* with less and less change toward the end.   This has not been proved, I say with all possible emphasis; but seems better than any other hypothesis to harmonize with observed facts.   At the same time, it is not quite impossible that Shakespeare borrowed directly from his recollections of a performance of Heywood's play; even that a later man wrote the end of the *Troilus.* In either case Shakespeare is not responsible for the ending; and in any case the contents and tone are so far traditional as greatly to reduce his responsibility for the entire work.

[69] Anders and Root, *l. c.*

[70] One small further point; the hypothesis of a lost play agrees well with the facts as to the Welsh *Troilus.* The resemblances which I indicated (p. 705 above; *Mod. Lang. Review,* x, 279-80) to both Shakespeare's and Heywood's plays might be explained as due to their common source.   But I feel no confidence as to this.

V

It remains to see what light the facts and possibilities set forth in this article throw on the tone and spirit of Shakespeare's play. In the first place, its subject was extremely popular, in two senses,—was widely liked, and appealed to the masses. This is attested by various allusions and by two dozen or so of other works, dramatic and otherwise, mostly covering the same ground. In contents, characters, and incidents his version is substantially like the others that are known. His sources are the same,—the enormously popular Caxton (almost certainly) at bottom, with considerable secondary use of Chaucer and Homer.[71] As with the others, it is the late mediæval versions which largely determine the tone, amorous, loosely chivalric, with no consciousness of any lofty heroic dignity to be lived up to. Of a considerable part of the play nothing need be said more unflattering than this.

As to the disagreeable impression which the play on the whole undeniably makes on most moderns, more needs to be said. With all the critics who have questioned the Sphynx about it, who [72] have even called it the chief problem in Shakespeare, it is surprising that the play and its tone have not been more thoroughly analyzed. Many critics see nothing but bitterness in it; others see mainly humor and wisdom. There is truth in both views, for there is scurrility and there is nobility; *but they are not*

---

[71] Ovid and Virgil are not used as chief sources, we have seen, as in the others, because Shakespeare does not treat, as they do, the beginning and end of the story. But the play does show incidental knowledge of Ovid and Virgil (Root, *Class Myth. in S.*, p. 18).

[72] Such as Rapp and Morton Luce.

mixed. Nothing could be more entirely weighty and stately than the personalities and talk in act I, scene iii, where the Greek princes discuss the need of authority, and Aeneas brings Hector's chivalrous challenge; [73] than those in II, ii, where the Trojan peers debate the return of Helen; in III, iii (till near the end), where Achilles' words are almost as wise as Ulysses'; in IV, v, with its chivalrous cordiality (except for the beginning and for Achilles' talk toward the end); or than the heroism and pathos of v, iii. These scenes seem to be largely Shakespeare's own addition to the story, and only a very prejudiced reader can fail to see that he wrote them with perfect seriousness and sympathy.[74] We are always liable to prejudice because we inevitably come to the play with our minds full of Homer; but Shakespeare came to it with his mind mostly full of Caxton,[75] and he has here risen far above Caxton in dignity and beauty. So far as he knew Homer,[76] he probably felt towards him quite otherwise than we do. The main point is this,—we must exchange the absolute for the relative conception of literature. The normal human reaction to Homer is not one and the same, as the history of his reputation will prove.

[73] Yet, so wrong-headed have critics been, one of them saw only scornful burlesque in the aged Nestor's gallant and touching message to Hector (298-9), " that my lady Was fairer than his grandam." To the reader, Ulysses' account of Patroclus' mimicking (151 ff.) may seem undignified. But to the spectator, the dignity of what he sees and hears would prevent any such impression.

[74] Shakespeare's preference for these scenes may have been a reaction against a certain childishness in Caxton; may be due to a feeling that the world is not conducted merely by the fighting which pleases the rabble.

[75] Of course this has long been recognized by many critics, even as early as Guizot and Schlegel.

[76] I have pointed out in the play a somewhat minute acquaintance with the *Iliad;* also that it may not have been due to Shakespeare.

A poet's renown sometimes becomes fixed only because people cease to read him. To Shakespeare the *Iliad* was one book among many; read probably, if at all, in a crude translation, it may even have seemed to him thin and unreal. On his part an attitude toward the Greeks like that of such moderns as Keats and Swinburne is unthinkable; the austere and serene background of Greek sculpture and architecture against which we see them was utterly unknown to him. The greatest charm of Homer lies in the fact that *all* his people are noble and godlike, but a drama is bound to be less heroic than an epic. Analysis shows such figures as Agamemnon, Ulysses, Achilles,[77] to be more realistic and therefore less heroic or charming, but not really more debased, than Caxton. Shakespeare had no sense that Achilles must be handled with reverence. But he was no more conscious of debasing, through the necessity of humanizing and dramatizing, than conscious of incongruity through the inevitable introduction of chivalry.[78] An openminded reading of these scenes, the most original part of the play, should make it forever impossible to regard the Shakespeare of *Troilus and Cressida* as full merely of weary disillusion and angry pain.[79]

[77] To the modern he is the δῖος Ἀχιλλεύς which Homer calls him, not the selfish skulker which the average early reader would think him in Homer and Caxton. He would seem grossly unchivalrous in Homer, to an age when the tradition of chivalry was still vivid. We have seen Shakespeare is probably not responsible for his final baseness, which is little greater than in Caxton.

[78] Other arts than the literary were in transition in his day. In these scenes there is no more incongruity than in the odd architectural combination of classic and Gothic in the more or less contemporary church of St. Eustache in Paris, the Bodleian Library in Oxford, Burleigh House near Stamford, or in the classical porticoes of St. Mary the Virgin's in Oxford or of the old St. Paul's.

[79] No character whom we should heed makes pessimistic speeches;

When we consider the parts of the play which do seem to show a harsh, unsympathetic spirit, we find the chief vehicles of it to be three. The tone embodied in Ajax, Thersites, and the love-motive does need comment. Ajax generally cuts a thoroughly comic figure; but as such he had already had a long history, as we have seen, which accounts for his paradoxical character, and his absurd appearance here is a (if not the) natural conception, especially as a dramatic foil to his opponent, the always noble Hector.[80]   Thersites too is entirely explicable. Quite definitely the Fool of the play (ii, iii) he is merely filled in from the sketch in the second book of the *Iliad*; in Shakespeare he says at large what Homer says he says; [81] we have seen that Shakespeare was doubtless not the first to introduce him to the Troilus-drama, and that he is not greatly intensified beyond what he is in Heywood. Shocking as it was to Victorian Hellenolatry, hateful as it is to us, to read the epithets he applies to Agamemnon and his peers, and to see him brawling and scuffling with that undignified trio Ajax, Patroclus, and Achilles, when the play is witnessed Thersites and his deformed spite and ugly half-truths recede into the remote littleness where

there are no such despairing generalizations as are uttered by Hamlet, Macbeth, Lear.

[80] Hector is the real hero of the play so far. as it is serious and tragic, the hinge of the main action all through, who meets his death through the defects of his qualities, through his chivalrous sparing of Achilles (v, vi, 14; cf. v, iii, 40 and iv, v, 105), and disregard of Cassandra's and Andromache's warnings (v, iii). There is dramatic irony in the fact that in ii, ii, he had appealed to the other princes to heed the warnings of Cassandra.

[81] Homer describes his deformity, and his reviling of the chiefs, especially Achilles and others; he is " the uncontrolled of speech, whose mind was full of words many and disorderly, wherewith to strive against the chiefs idly and in no good order, but even as he deemed that he should make the Argives laugh " (tr. by Lang and others).

they belong. Those who see and hear the nobler Greek princes will not take his view of them. We have been in their stately presence (I, iii) and they have even prepared us for his venom (73-4, 192 ff.), before we ever see him (II, i). Elsewhere Shakespeare gives us lovers, heroes, doubters, murderers, raised to the nth power; here he gives us likewise a railer. Thersites must have vastly pleased the groundlings and brought in many a testern. As to the love-story, no sympathy is aroused, or at any rate maintained by it,—by Troilus' callow enthusiasm, Cressida's weak voluptuousness and bold coquetry, and Pandarus' elderly prurience; yet all this is developed beyond what it is in most other versions.[82] All charm in Troilus' Romeo-like loves is destroyed by their instant publicity (IV, i-iv). The poet's attitude toward this story was the only one possible in his day; Chaucer, though he would fain have excused Criseyde, had left her without excuse, Henryson had degraded and chastised her; by Shakespeare's day her good name was gone forever, and she was merely a by-word for a light woman; [83] and in her descent she had necessarily dragged down her lover and her uncle, whose name had already long become that of his trade.[84] Troilus as a man and fighter stands high in grace; [85] only

[82] *Iron Age* has far less of the love-story; the Admiral play, when complete, may have had as much, however.

[83] He could no more have made her pure and attractive than he could have given Cleopatra what the elderly English ladies called the "home-life of our own dear Queen." Cf. John Ford, *Honor Trivmphant*, p. 24 (Old Sh. Soc. XIX); *Willobie His Avisa*, canti XVIII, LXXII, and at the end; Whetstone's *Rock of Regard* (1576); Dekker's *Wonderful Year* (1603).

[84] Cf. *pander* in *Oxf. Dict.*

[85] Ulysses, the weightiest speaker in the play, calls him "a true knight,"

Not yet mature, yet matchless, firm of word,
Speaking in deeds, and deedless in his tongue;
Not soon provok'd, nor being provok'd soon calm'd;

as a lover is he abased. The loves of Paris ánd Helen fare little better, though they are less prominent; in IV, i, Shakespeare goes out of his way to apply gross language to them. For this too he had ample precedent; [86] yet the harsh fact remains that *Troilus* is Shakespeare's only play except *Timon* with no likable female character and with love prominent but debased, and that he might have slighted but chooses to emphasize them. A study of the play in the light of its sources makes his attitude toward the Greek and Trojan heroes perfectly intelligible, his attitude toward the lovers even inevitable; if it does not wholly explain the prominence he gives a base love-affair, perhaps even the " gentle Shakespeare " found an interest in portraying this new kind of love, enough interest at least to lead him to keep what he found in an older play.[87] Why not?

> Yet gives he not till judgement guide his bounty,
> Nor dignifies an impair thought with breath;
> Manly as Hector, but more dangerous. . . .   (IV, v, 96 ff.)

What a contrast to Troilus in his dealings with Cressida, Pandarus, and Diomed! Yet even as a lover he is not quite such a fool as some critics have thought him; there is no fluctuation in his outline. Why should he be expected to see through the sly-boots Cressida as the world-worn Ulysses does?

[86] *E. g.*, some delightful verses at the end of Caxton's *Recuyell* say the cause of the war was a

> Meretrix exicialis, femina letalis, femina plena malis.

In a cryptic account by Dekker (1603) of a vulgar contemporary scandal the people are called Menelaus, Helen, Paris, Cressida (*Wonderful Year*, in *Huth Libr.*, I, pp. 134-5). On Helen and Cressida cf. also *A Gorgious Gallery of Gallant Inuentions* (1578; in Collier's reprints), pp. 7-9, 18, 20, 48, 50, 58, 74, 102. To Shakespeare's Lucrece, Helen is " the strumpet that began this stir." Anyone not wholly under Homer's spell would have moments of amazement over the origin of the war. Horace had; see p. 767 below.

[87] The prominence of the love-motive in the Admiral fragment, and Cressida's final degradation among the beggars, indicate that it was similarly treated there.

Analysis then shows the harshness of the play to be less than is often deemed, and so far as it exists to be explicable without deriving it from the poet's mood when he wrote. The undeniably unpleasant effect some critics [88] and readers are penetrating enough to see is due quite as much to its confusion and want of internal harmony as to anything else. We have chivalrous gallantry, stupid and cowardly savagery, stately dignity, voluptuousness without charm, weighty wisdom, low scurrility. This means a bad play; it does not mean an angry and embittered playwright, but rather a handicapped, careless, and indifferent one. A hastily written thing may give a totally different impression from what the writer intends or is even aware of. With so experienced a dramatist as Shakespeare we should ascribe the discord to the essential incongruity of his two conceptions. He did not wish to lower one part of the play to the level of the other. Some parts he wrote with sympathy and interest, some he took as he found them and intensified to add to their effectiveness, but without liking.[89] He poured new wine into old bottles; he sewed a piece of new cloth into an old garment, and the rent was made worse. But for the very reason that the painfulness is partly due to the confusion and internal discord, matters which especially impress the casual reader, it is hard to convince him of the truth of the present interpretation, hard to do the play justice on a mere reading.

The facts seem to favor such an explanation of *Troilus*

---

[88] Such as the editor of Bell's edition (1774), Verplanck, Hebler, Raleigh.

[89] This may account for certain internal inconsistencies (cf. Small, 149-50); which indeed are not wanting in some of his other plays, including the greatest. The chief one here, the fighting in I, ii and the long truce in I, iii, may be explained by artificial dramatic time.

and Cressida as this.   Shakespeare found it expedient to
make over an older play (to write, at least) on this highly
popular subject.   He did it with no great interest, except
in the more masculine and statesmanlike scenes.   Homer,
read, if at all, probably in a poor translation, took no particular hold on him, he admitted the light of ·common
day to the *sanctum sanctorum,*[90] and the general tone of
the play followed that of the late mediæval works which
were the chief authority for the Trojan war even in the
16th century.   To relieve the heaviness of the delibera-
tions which form so much of the play he made fun for
his popular audience by a comic Ajax and by Homer's
ribald Thersites.   Sated with, perhaps, reacting from, the
ordinary light romantic love, indeed finding it incom-
patible with the material of this play, yet not wishing to
omit the love-motive in a play with a popular appeal, perhaps feeling it desirable to develop it, he produced a
masterly study of an alluring wanton and the first passion
of a full-blooded very young man.   The most valuable
pointer for interpreting the work is the probability that
he wrote it without the deep interest which he put on the
greater plays which were to follow directly, such as probably *Hamlet.* ·So far as ·we can retrace the mental processes of an impersonal dramatist three centuries dead,
this conclusion seems reasonable ; more reasonable than to
attribute the work to a fit of misanthropy, love-disillusion,

---

[90] Even Horace could sum up the *Iliad* thus

> Fabula, qua Paridis propter narratur amorem
> Graecia barbariae lento collisa duello,
> Stultorum regum et populorum continet aestus.
>
> .   .   .   .
>
> Seditione, dolis, scelere atque libidine et ira
> Iliacos intra muros peccatur, et extra (*Epist.,* I, ii).

Horace was neither embittered .nor anti-classical, but he had no
illusions.   No more had Shakespeare.

literary jealousy. It is no longer possible to think of
Shakespeare as guided only by his own taste and temper
in choosing his material from Chaucer, Homer, and Caxton, or from an earlier play; he did not care greatly to
modify the literary tradition, as is clear from the close
resemblance of his play to *Iron Age,* from its general par-
allellism to several other works, and probably to the numerous lost versions. The call for a play on a vulgarly
popular subject, the lack of our feeling of traditional ven-
eration for some of its sources,[91] want of deep interest in
the popular part of the play, will thoroughly account for
its tone and spirit. In their desire to banish all mystery,[92] critics have created much mystery where there is
little.[93]

[91] There is evidence that even more than this, an actual spirit
of contradiction toward Homer, such as some have fancied in
Shakespeare, has gone into the material of the play; but this was
many centuries before his time. Professor N. E. Griffin (*Journ.
Engl. Germ. Philol,* VII, pp. 32-52) shows that Caxton's literary
ancestors, Dares and Dictys, take pains to slight and lower heroes
magnified by Homer, and to substitute new ones of their own (pp.
45-6). This is no more than we find in other traditional sages, as
witness the neglect or vilification of such primitive heroes as Charlemagne, Arthur, Percival, Gawain, in favor of their original
subordinates or of such understudies as Galahad and Lancelot.
The new-made hero bears, like the Turk, no brother near the throne.

[92] A vain effort, for minute criticism of a literary work can
always raise questions which none but the author could answer
(and not always he, if we can believe Browning. Anecdotes to this
effect are familiar, and I can add one which has never been printed,
I believe. Mr. Charles Fry told me that when he was putting on
The Blot on the Scutcheon at its first revival, during one of the
rehearsals he said to Browning, "I'm afraid you will think me very
stupid, but I don't understand this passage I have to speak." Browning put on his glasses, looked at it, and said, "Dear me, I don't
know what it means." In such cases there may have been a little
amiable pose, since Browning did not like to be taken too seriously
as a literary man).

[93] One question often raised is whether the play is a comedy or
a tragedy. I asked it of Mr. Fry, the only Englishman in three

A few words more, on the wider bearings of this con-clusion, a large subject on which I can barely touch. One critic after another has felt the interpretation of *Troilus and Cressida* to be the chief problem in Shakespeare-criticism. It has been the main support of the theory that in the first few years of the 17th century Shakespeare was in a thoroughly pessimistic frame of mind. For the prevalence of this idea there have been two main reasons. One is the character of the plays written about this time. But it is unnecessary to argue formally that the writing of tragedies does not imply a pessimistic frame of mind; precedent would rather point to just the contrary. Such other themes as those of *Measure for Measure* and *All's Well That Ends Well,* which *may* date from this period, may well have attracted him by reason of their difficulty, and as a practise-school before coming to the exacting themes of tragedy. The other reason is the desire to understand Shakespeare the man, at his worst as at his best. Humanity is grateful to him, and wishes to know its benefactor. There has been an almost touching desire to draw near him through a sacramental Real Presence in his plays. The pessimism theory has been especially developed by critics who have attempted to trace his full spiritual history, and to relate his plays in detail to his life. But the events in his life which have been brought forward to explain the supposed pessimism are absurdly

centuries known to have put the play on. He said, "It's neither, it's just *a play*." A better answer is that it's both, it's a historical play. Shakespeare meant to give a mingled impression, and was prevented from unifying plot or feeling by the fact that the material was too well known to be much modified. There is absolutely no essential difference between the *Troilus* and *Henry IV*. The charm of seeing on the stage personages familiar in books and tradition atoned for the undramatic character of their story; we see such things today in such a play as *Becky Sharp*.

inadequate. It is the duty of sound criticism, dealing with so impersonal, objective, and practical a writer as Shakespeare, to seek first objective explanations. If we find such, as we certainly may for the plays of this period, we must put such theories in the realm of creative imagination, not of scientifically-minded criticism. Of course Shakespeare expressed himself in his plays; but, so far as we can see, it was the whole self which had resulted from his whole experience of life, not his temporary self in an instantaneous rebound from this or that immediate experience. Criticism is moving farther and farther from the 18th century view of him as a closet theorizer, and the mid-19th century idea of a closet dramatist, to that of a practical dramatist who had professional and theatrical reasons for what he did.[94]

JOHN S. P. TATLOCK.

[94] The older critics were mostly what the late William James called " tender-minded." They would have been shocked at the idea that he ever did makeshift work, or (so to speak) did not pour out his whole soul in every line.

XXIII.— CÆSAR'S REVENGE

Though three reprints of the anonymous *Cæsar and Pompey*,[1] together with the discussion devoted to it by Parrott,[2] Mühlfeld,[3] and Boas,[4] seem to represent doubtless quite as much attention as the play really deserves, I venture to add, out of materials long on hand, another note by way of summary and, in one or two places, of addition and correction. Such a review, showing the author's literary method to be one of the closest dependence on his models, may serve to raise a presumption that in his treatment of Cæsar, who resembles Marlowe's Tamburlaine without being a literal copy, he was familiar with plays about Cæsar which are now lost to us; or conscious, at least, of a dramatic tradition which made of Cæsar a boastful conqueror.

The interest of the play, apart from this, lies of course neither in its poetry nor in its dramaturgy, but in its copious draughts from classical sources and especially in its extraordinary sensitiveness, if so amiable a description is in place, to the literature, dramatic and non-dramatic, of the early nineties. As the first known university

[1] *The Tragedy of Cæsar's Revenge, Malone Society Reprints* (prepared by F. S. Boas and W. W. Greg), Oxford, 1911. W. Mühlfeld, in *Jahrbuch der deutschen Shakespeare-Gesellschaft*, XLVII, pp. 132 ff.; XLVIII, pp. 37 ff. M. Mühlfeld, *The Tragedie of Cæsar and Pompey or Cæsar's Revenge. Ein Beitrag zur Geschichte der englischen Cæsardramen zur Zeit Shakespeares* (Münster diss.). Weimar, 1912.

[2] *Modern Language Review*, Oct., 1910, pp. 435-44.

[3] In his dissertation cited above.

[4] *University Drama in the Tudor Age*, Oxford, 1914, pp. 267-78; and the *Malone Society Collections*, ɪ, pp. 290-94, where Mr. Charles Crawford is also quoted.

tragedy in English on a classical theme [5] and " the first
university play in which we can trace deliberate imitation of dramas produced on the professional London
stage," [6] it has a kind of distinction.

It is generally assumed that the date of the play should
be carried considerably back of the date of its entry in
the *Stationers' Register,* June 5, 1606,[7] and of its publication, as one form of the title-page records, in 1607.[8] By

---

[5] Parrott, p. 444.   [6] Boas, p. 277.

[7] Arber's *Transcript,* III, p. 140.

[8] In the British Museum and Bodleian copies (A). The Dyce copy
and that of the Duke of Devonshire (B) have no date and lack
the statement on the title-page, " Priuately acted by the Studentes
of Trinity Colledge in Oxford." The undated form is " Imprinted
by G. E. for Iohn Wright, and are to bee sould at his shop at
Christ-church Gate; " the dated copy is " Imprinted for Nathaniel
Fosbrooke and Iohn Wright, and are to be sould in Paules Church-
yard at the signe of the Helmet." Since the entry in the *Stationers'
Register* is to Wright and Fosbrooke jointly, Mühlfeld concludes
that the title-page on which both names appear is the earlier form;
the Malone Society editors, on the other hand, state that the *verso*
of the A title-page, containing the *dramatis personæ,* has been reset,
showing it to be a reprint. There is no material difference in the
text of the several copies.

A possible imitation noted by Crawford, *Collections,* p. 290, of
Daniel's *Rosamond* (1592),

> Out from the horror of infernall deepes
> My poore afflicted ghost comes here to plain it;

and

> Out of the horror of those shady vaultes, ...
> My restles soule comes heere to tell his wronges (ll. 1974-7)

provides a *terminus a quo,* though this is the universal whine of
the ghost. A rather elastic *ad quem* is suggested by the apparent
fact that though the imitations of the first three books of the
Faerie Queene are numerous, there is no clear case of borrowing
from the last three, published in 1596. Presumably if the author
had known these books he would have used them too. The nearest
agreement I have noted is between Spenser's description of Ate
(F. Q., IV, I, xix-xxii) and that of Discord in our play, particularly
ll. 635-9. See further p. 776, note 11.

reason of the archaic character of the verse and the author's knowledge of Marlowe and Kyd and of anonymous plays contemporary with theirs, the dates 1592-96 (Boas) or "die mitte der 90er jahre" (Mühlfeld) seem indicated. All the affinities of the play are with the literature of this period, and I should prefer to account for this by the assumption that the play really belongs there, rather than to suppose with Parrott (p. 444) that it was written by an "elderly don."

The principal sources of the play are obviously Appian's *Civil Wars* and Lucan's *Pharsalia*. Neither was ever far from the author's elbow, and he helps himself with a lavish hand. The former he had in mind when describing the murder of Pompey (ll. 642 ff. Cf. *Bell. Civ.* ii, 84), as the name Sempronius indicates;[9] and the murder of Cæsar (ll. 1694 ff.; *Bell. Civ.*, ii, 117), as the mention of Bucolian shows. Antony's funeral oration (ll. 1791 ff.) is translated from the same source (ii, 144-6) and the accounts given by Cassius and Brutus of their campaigns in the East (ll. 2152 ff.), from iv, 62 f., 80 f.

It is quite possible that the play draws on other historical sources. Such lines as

> Now *Lucius* fals, heare *Drusus* takes his end,
> Here lies Hortensius, weltring in his goare, (ll. 2376 f.)

could not have been suggested by Appian's account of. Philippi, which mentions only Lucius Cassius, (iv, 135). The names might easily come, however, from Velleius Paterculus, ii, lxxi: tum Catonis filius cecidit; eadem

---

[9] In other sources Septimius. Does *Fortunius* in l. 798 mean that he used the English version (1578) which has Photinus? Usually the eunuch is called Ποθεινός (Appian) or Pothinus (Lucan). But the Latin quotation in ll. 1380-2 suggests a Latin translation as the source.

7

Lucullum Hortensiumque, eminentissimorum civium filios, fortuna abstulit; . . . Drusus Livius, etc.

The following lament of Pompey is clearly based on Plutarch:

> Which do remember me what earst I was,
> Who brought such troopes of soldiars to the fielde,
> And of so many thousand had command:
> My flight a heauy memory doth renew,
> Which tels me I was wont to stay and winne. (ll. 67 ff.)

Cf.

> . . . ἐν διαλογισμοῖς ὢν οἵους εἰκὸς λαμβάνειν ἄνθρωπον ἔτη τέτταρα καὶ τριάκοντα νικᾶν καὶ κρατεῖν ἁπάντων εἰθισμένον, ἥττης δὲ καὶ φυγῆς τότε πρῶτον ἐν γήρᾳ λαμβάνοντα πεῖραν, ἐννοούμενον δὲ ἐξ ὅσων ἀγώνων καὶ πολέμων ηὐξημένην ἀποβαλὼν ὥρᾳ μιᾷ δόξαν καὶ δύναμιν, [ᾗ] πρὸ μικροῦ τοσούτοις ὅπλοις καὶ ἵπποις καὶ στόλοις δορυφορούμενος ἀπέρχεται μικρὸς οὕτω γεγονὼς καὶ συνεσταλμένος, ὥστε λανθάνειν ζητοῦντας τοὺς πολεμίους. Παραμειψάμενος δὲ Λάρισσαν, ὡς ἦλθεν ἐπὶ τὰ Τέμπη . . .   (Pompey, LXXIII)

Tempe and Larissa are mentioned together in ll. 323 ff. of our play:

> The flying *Pompey* to *Larissa* hastes,
> And by *Thessalian* Temple shapes his course:
> Where faire *Peneus* tumbles vp his waues.

There is nothing of this in Appian's *Civil Wars;* for *Peneus,* cf. *Peneius amnis, Phars.,* VIII, 33.

But he does not merely translate; he combines his little pedantries, drawn from a variety of sources. Cassius describing his conquests mentions

> *Laodicia* whose high reared walles,
> Faire *Lyeas* washeth with her siluer waue:
> And that braue monument of *Perseus* fame,
> With *Tursos* vaild to vs her vanting pride.
>
>   (ll. 2154 ff.)

It is clear from the context that the author had his eye on *Bell. Civ.,* IV, 63-4; but there is no mention there of the river Lycus or of Perseus in connection with Tarsus.

The first bit of information could have reached him from
a variety of sources,[10] among them Appian's *Mithridates,*
20. The latter he probably got from Lucan's *Perseaque
Tarsos* (*Phars.* III, 225).

To Lucan his debt is pervasive. He owes him both·
long rhetorical speeches and countless bits of geography
and history. Pompey's lament after Pharsalia:

> Was I a youth with Palme and Lawrell girt,   (l. 137)

recalls Lucan's *lauriferae . . . iuventae* (*Phars.* VIII,
25), though the speech begins with a reminiscence of
Appian. Brutus comforts him in words recalling *Phars.*
VII, '717 ff.; VIII, 266 ff. In reply Pompey appropriates
one of Lucan's apostrophes to Brutus (cf. ll. 158-62 and
Phars. VII, 588-96) and comments on his own hard alternative in the words of *Phars.* VII, 710 ff.

Cæsar's description of the carnage at Pharsalia (ll.
255 f.) combines material from *Phars.* VII, 1 f. and
834 f.; his lamentation for Rome (l. 296) echoes *Phars.*
VII, 721 f. This Dolabella (ll. 307 f.) catches up with
an imitation of *Phars.* VII, 418 f., and the Lord (ll.
314 f.) turns against Pompey one of Lucan's outbursts
against Cæsar as the instigator of civil war (*Phars.* VII,
169). Cato's apostrophe to Liberty (ll. 334-53) translates with only slight rearrangements *Phars.* VII, 433-50;
but his description of the prodigies (ll. 354-58) is from
Phars. I, 529 f.; 556 f.; later (ll. 1080-4) he calls on
Cannae and Allia to give place to Pharsalia (cf. *Phars.*
VII, 407 f.); and he closes with a passage from II, 297 ff.
The parting scene between Pompey and Cornelia (ll.
369 ff.) is based on passages in the eighth book; and
Cicero's lament for Pompey (ll. 1005-11) combines the

---

[10] See Dictionaries, *s. v.*

famous *Caelo tegitur, qui non habet urnam* (VII, 819)
with the *situs est, qua terra extrema refuso Pendet in
oceano* from VIII, 797 ff.

Just as the author combines Lucan with Lucan, he
delights to mingle Lucan and Spenser.   Cleopatra, invit-
ing Cæsar to the delights of Alexandria, says

> Come now faire Prince, and feast thee in our Courts
> Where liberall *Cœres*, and *Liæus* fat,
> Shall powre their plenty forth and fruitfull store,
> The sparkling liquor shall ore-flow his bankes:
> And *Meroé* learne to bring forth pleasant wine,
> Fruitfull *Arabia*, and the furthest Ind,
> Shall spend their treasuries of *Spicery*
> VVith *Nardus* Coranets weele guird our heads.
>
> (ll. 907-914)

The opening lines are from F. *Q.* III, I, li, 3-4:

> Whiles fruitfull Ceres and Lyæus fatt
> Pourd out their plenty, without spight or spare:

but we pass on quickly to P*hars.* x, 163-4:

> Indomitum Meroe cogens spumare Falernum.
> Accipiunt sertas nardo florente coronas.

Most of the striking imitations from Spenser Mühlfeld
has noted: Cleopatra's address to Cæsar (ll. 532-6) and
Una's to the Red Cross Knight (F. *Q.* I, VIII, xxvii, 3-9),
Antony on the restless mind (ll. 1451-4) and F. *Q.* I, v,
i, 1-4; Cassius' comparison of the fallen Cæsar with the
sacrificial victim (ll. 1902-07) and F. *Q.* III, IV, xvii.[11]
I add one which he does not mention which helps to settle
a point of text.   Antony's reference to

> Siluer *Stremonia*, whose faire Christall waues,
> Once sounded great *Alcides* echoing fame:

---

[11] The figure of the storm-tossed ship in ll. 1234 ff. is almost certainly from *Amoretti*, XXXIV. If so, the play was not written before
1595.

> When as he slew that fruitefull headed snake,
> Which *Lerna* long-time fostered in her wombe:
>
> (ll. 2114-17)

becomes clearer when referred to Spenser's

> renowned snake
> Which great Alcides in Stremona slew,
> Long fostred in the filth of Lerna lake.
>
> (*F. Q.*, I, VII, xvii, 1-3)

The Malone Society editors (p. xi) suggest that we should read *Strymon,* and doubtless that river was connected in the author's mind with the " Æmathian fieldes," but he gets the form of the name and the quaint mythology from Spenser. The concluding six lines of this speech (ll. 2120-25) are lifted bodily from Vergil, *Georgics,* I, 491 ff.

Another non-dramatic source, to which attention has not been called, is Sidney's *Arcadia.* The opening lines of the play betray the acquaintance:

> The earth that's wont to be a Tombe for Men
> It's now entomb'd with Carkases of Men. (ll. 6-7)

For, though the idea of the Thracian fields covered with dead was doubtless in the first instance suggested by Lucan, *Phars.* VII, 794 f., the conceit is entirely Sidney's: " The earth it selfe (woont to be a buriall of men) was nowe (as it were) buried with men: so was the face thereof hidden with deade bodies." [12]

The same influence appears again toward the end of the play in Cassius' speech describing the defeat at Philippi:

> The horse had now put on the riders wrath,
> And with his hoofes did strike the trembling earth,
> When *Echalarian* soundes then both gin meete:

---

[12] *The Countess of Pembroke's Arcadia* (1590) ed. by H. Oscar Sommer, London, 1891, Bk. III, ch. 7, p. 268.

> Both like enraged, and now the dust gins rise,
> And Earth doth emulate the Heauens cloudes,
> Then yet beutyous was the face of cruell war:
> And goodly terror it might seeme to be,
> Faire shieldes, gay swords, and goulden creats did shine.
> Their spangled plumes did dance for Iolity,
> As nothing priuy to their Masters feare,
> But quickly rage and cruell *Mars* had staynd,
> This shining glory with a sadder hew,
> A cloud of dartes that darkened Heauens light,
> Horror insteed of beauty did succeede.
> And her bright armes with dust and blood were soyld.
>
>   (ll. 2361-75)

The following selections from the *Arcadia,* Bk. III, are in point:

The verie horses angrie in their maisters anger . . . (p. 268); a great dust arise (which the earth sent vp, as if it would striue to haue clowdes as well as the aire) . . . (p. 265 b); which the Sunne guilding with his beames, it gaue a sight delightfull to any, but to them that were to abide the terrour. (pp. 265 b-6)

For at the first, though it were terrible, yet Terror was deckt so brauelie with rich furniture, guilte swords, shining armours, pleasant pensils, that the eye with delight had scarce leasure to be afraide: But now all vniuersally defiled with dust, bloud, broken armours, mangled bodies, tooke away the maske, and sette foorth Horror in his owne horrible manner. (p. 271)

To the *Arcadia* in part is owing young Cato's dying apostrophe to virtue:

> O vertue whome *Phylosophy* extols.
> Thou art no essence but a naked name,
> Bond-slave to Fortune, weake, and of no power.
> To succor them which alwais honoured thee: (ll. 2338 f.)

O Vertue, where doost thou hide thy selfe? or what hideous thing is this which doth eclips thee? or is it true that thou weart neuer but a vaine name, and no essentiall thing, which hast thus left thy professed seruant, when she had most need of thy louely presence? (Book II, ch. i, p. 98 b.)

But the phrase 'bond-slave to Fortune' shows that he had also in mind the anonymous tragic fragment put in the mouth of Brutus in Dio Cassius's account of Philippi (XLVII, 49),

ὦ τλῆμων ἀρετή, λόγος ἄρ' ἦσθ' · ἐγὼ δὲ σε
ὡς ἔργον ἤσκουν · σὺ δ' ἄρ' ἐδούλευες τύχῃ.

It is not surprising that the author of a university play, even in the vernacular, should pilfer the classics; it is more interesting that he should borrow freely from Spenser and Sidney; still more so that he should show close acquaintance with the London stage. The Parnassus plays show much knowledge, but there it is used for critical, chiefly satirical, ends. Our author seems to transcribe and combine with fidelity and satisfaction; and his borrowings extend beyond the mere appropriation of fine tags to suggestions for whole scenes and points of structure.

Boas (pp. 271 ff.) is right in pointing out the affinities between this play and the revenge type of which the *Spanish Tragedy* is the representative, with its ghost and the dismal figure of Revenge (in our play, Discord). Further, the love-sick Antony and his hopeless passion owe much to the love-story of Balthazar; it might be added that the unhistorical scene in which Cornelia stabs herself (ll. 768-94) is perhaps suggested by Isabella's melancholy end (*Sp. Tr.* IV, 2). To Boas's excellent discussion should be added a half-dozen verbal parallels noted by Mühlfeld (pp. lvi f.).

Our author's knowledge of popular drama is not confined to this famous play. The early anonymous tragedy Locrine [13] is strikingly in the vein of our play. It shows

---

[13] Printed in 1595. C. F. Tucker Brooke, *The Shakespeare Apocrypha*, Oxford, 1898.

a similar fondness for classical decoration and geography. More specifically: Pompey, crushed at Pharsalia, cries

> Where may I fly into some desert place,
> Some vncouth, vnfrequented craggy rocke,
> Where as my name and state was neuer heard . . .
> Flie to the holow roote of some steepe rocke,
> And in that flinty habitation hide,
> Thy wofull face: from face and view of men. (ll. 61 ff.; 76 ff.)

Humber, in like situation, has more self-respect remaining but his desire for solitude is the same:

> Where may I finde some desart wildernesse,
> Where I may breath out curses as I would . . .
> Where may I finde some hollow vncoth rocke,
> Where I may damne, condemne, and ban by fill.[14]
> (*Locrine*, III, vi, 1 ff., 7 ff.)

Cæsar's love-making owes something, perhaps, to Locrine's musings: cf. particularly, though the conceit is not uncommon:

> thy goulden yellow lockes,
> Which in their curled knots, my thoughts do hold,
> Thoughtes captiud to thy beauties conquering power,
> (ll. 520 ff.)

and

> The golden tresses of her daintie haire,
> Which shine like rubies glittering with the sunne,
> Haue so entrapt poore *Locrines* louesick heart,
> That from the same no way it can be wonne.
> (*Locrine*, IV, i, 97 ff.)

The figure of the murderer, Sempronius, owes a good deal to the popular stage.   In ll. 668 ff. his avarice echoes the very words of the assassin Pedringano in the *Spanish Tragedy* (III, iii, 5 f.), and his threat

> There is thy fortune Pompey in my fist (l. 701)

recalls Hieronimo's

---

[14] Cf. *Battle of Alcazar*, V, 1, 75 f.

Bearing his latest fortune in his fist (IV, iii, 177).

His conventional hard-heartedness coupled with grim jesting finds a parallel in the Messenger in *King Leir and his Three Daughters,* to whom murder is no more than the " cracking of a Flea." [15] The conclusion of Sempronius' moralizing

> Loe you my maisters, hee that kills but one,
> Is straight a Villaine and a murtherer cald,
> But they that vse to kill men by the great,
> And thousandes slay through their ambition,
> They are braue champions, and stout warriors cald,
>
> (ll. 754 ff.)

recalls *Gorboduc* (II, i, 152 ff.): _

> Murders and violent theftes in priuate men
> Are hainous crimes and full of foule reproch,
> Yet none offence, but deckt with glorious name
> Of noble conquestes, in the handes of kinges.[16]

Achillas's exclamation

> What is he dead, then straight cut off his head (l. 749),

may be an echo of Warwick's, in the *True Tragedie of Richard Duke of York,*[17]

> I, but he is dead, off with the traitors head.

Steevens noted the parallel between l. 682, " Mens eyes must mil-stones drop, when fooles shed teares " and " Your eyes drop Mill-stones, when Fooles eyes fall Teares," in *Richard III,* I, iii, 370 (Furness, *Variorum,* pp. 115 ff.). Sempronius is, in short, the typical stage

---

[15] Hazlitt, *Shakespeare's Library,* VI, p. 342. Cf. also *Arden of Fevershame,* II, i.

[16] This is, of course, based on the well-known story of Diomedes, the pirate, and Alexander; cf. Gower, *Confessio Amantis,* III, 2363 ff., and *Gesta Romanorum,* CXLVI.

[17] Hazlitt, *Shakespeare's Library,* VI, p. 55.

murderer, in which rôle he reappears in the *False One*
(especially II, ii, and IV, iii) of Fletcher and Massinger.[18]

Here may be cited a case in which reference to old plays
helps to clear up a point of text.   In Brutus's dying exclamation,

> O tis the soule that they stand gaping for,
> And endlesse matter for to pray vpon
> Renewed still as *Titius* pricked heart, (ll. 2521 ff.)

Boas (p. 276) proposes to read *Titans* for *Titius*.   The
reference, however, is not to Prometheus, but to the giant
Tityus.   Classical writers make the vulture feed upon
his liver, as he lies bound in hell; Elizabethan writers
were quite as likely to think of the heart as the seat of the
passions,· and the change in this instance occurs not un-
commonly; as in *Selimus*, 1342 ff.

> As *Tityus* in the countrie of the dead,
> With restlesse cries doth call vpon high *Ioue*,
> The while the vulture tireth on his heart.[19]

----

[18] A parallel between

> *Caron* that vsed but an old rotten boate
> Must nowe a nauie rigg for to transport,
> The howling soules, vnto the *Stigian* stronde,
> (ll. 2538 ff.)

and Jonson's *Catiline*, Act I (Everyman's Library ed., p. 98)

> The rugged Charon fainted
> And ask'd a navy, rather than a boat,
> To ferry over the sad world that came:

is due to the fact that they both rest on some common source.   In
Lucan, the ghost of Julia announces to Pompey

> Præparat innumeras puppis Acherontis adusti
> Portitor.
> (*Phars.*, III, 16 f.)

[19] Compare also *Gorboduc*, II, 1, 18; *Tancred and Gismunda*, IV, 1;
The Cuck-Queanes and Cuckolds Errants, ed. Roxburghe Club, 1824,
p. 9.

Mühlfeld hardly does justice to the debt of our play to Marlowe (pp. lviii f.). He notes Collier's parallel between ll. 564 f.

> He on his goulden trapped *Palfreys* rides,
> That from their nostrels do the morning blow,

and Marlowe's

> The horse that guide the golden eye of Heaven,
> And blow the morning from their nosterils.
>
> (2 *Tamb.*, II, IV, p. 145) [20]

But this, it should be observed, is a commonplace since Vergil:

> solis equi lucemque elatis narihus efflant.
>
> (*Aen.* xii, 115)

When Cæsar goes a-wooing it is also in Tamberlaine's high astounding terms:

> Not onely *Ægipt* but all *Africa,*
> Will I subiect to *Cleopatra's* mame.
> Thy rule shall stretch from vnknowne *Zanziber,*
> Vnto those Sandes where high erected poastes.
> Of great *Alcides,* do vp hold his name.
>
> (ll. 510 ff.)

Cf.

> I will confute those blind geographers.
>
> (1 *Tamb.*, IV, iv, p. 65)
>
> To gratify the sweet Zenocrate,
> Egyptians, Moors, and men of Asia
> From Barbary unto the western India,
> Shall pay a yearly tribute to thy sire.
>
> (1 *Tamb.*, v, i, p. 85)
>
> I conquered all as far as Zanzibar.
>
> (2 *Tamb.*, v, iii, p. 165)
>
> Hang up your weapons on Alcides' post.
>
> (1 *Tamb.*, v, i, p. 85)

Again, though this perhaps is a common enough conceit,[21]

---

[20] *Christopher Marlowe,* ed. Havelock Ellis, Marmaid Series, vol. I.

[21] Cf. Greene's *Menaphon,* ed. Grosart, XII, 37.

My *Cynthia*, whose glory neuer waynes,
Guyding the Tide of mine affections:
That with the change of thy imperíous lookes,
Dost make my doubtfull ioyes to eb and flowe·

(ll. 569 ff.)

may be compared with

Olympia, pity him, in whom thy looks
Have greater operation and more force
Than Cynthia's in the watery wilderness,
For with thy view my joys are at the full,
And ebb again as thou departest from me.

(2 *Tamb.*, IV, iii, p. 143)

And yet again

I will regard no more these murtherous spoyles,
And bloudy triumphs that I lik'd of late:
But in loues pleasures spend my wanton dayes, . . .

(ll. 895 ff.)

And I will cast off arms to sit with thee,
Spending my life in sweet discourse of love.

(2 *Tamb.*, IV, iii, p. 143)

Cassius and Brutus, though their matter is drawn from Appian, are prompted to recite to the audience the list of their conquests (ll. 2151 ff.) by the example of Usumcasane and Techelles, who report in similar vein- to Tamburlaine (2 *Tamb.* I, iii, p. 103). And I suspect young Cato owes something of the manner of his death (ll. 2330 ff.) to that of Cosroe (1 *Tamb.* II, vii, p. 36).

The description of Cleopatra's palace (ll. 849 ff.) which owes much to Lucan (x, 112 ff.) and to Spenser (*F. Q.* III, I, xxxii),[22] closes with a reminiscence of Marlowe; compare particularly

With golden Roofes that glister like the Sunne,
Shalbe prepard to entertain my Loue: (853 f.)

with

---

[22] I am indebted to Mühlfeld for this passage from Spenser.

> That roofs of gold and sun-bright palaces
> Should have prepared to entertain his grace.
>
> > (1 *Tamb.*, IV, ii, p. 58)

These might be added:

> That in the wrinkels of thine angry browes,
> Wrapst dreadfull vengance and pale fright-full death.
>
> > (ll. 2385 f.)
>
> His lofty brows in folds do figure death.
>
> > (1 *Tamb.*, II, ii, p. 22) [23]
>
> With spangled plumes, that daunced in the ayre, (l. 711.)
>
> Their spangled plumes did dance for Iolity, (l. 2369)
>
> And in my helm a triple plume shall spring,
> Spangled with diamonds, dancing in the air.
>
> > (2 *Tamb.*, IV, iv, p. 149)

Boas does no more than justice in emphasizing the fact that "the whole conception of Cæsar is manifestly inspired by Tamburlaine." I have elsewhere quoted Marlowe in illustration of this point.[24] But it should be noted that the apparent imitations of Marlowe do not show as much verbal fidelity to the original as the others that we have examined. Cæsar's proud boast, for example,

> I come awayted with attending fame,
> Who through her shrill triump doth my name resound,
> And makes proud *Tiber* and *Lygurian Poe*,
> (Yet a sad witner of the Sunne-Gods losse,)[25]
> Beare my names glory to the *Ocean* mayne,
> Which to the worlds end shall it bound it againe, . . .[26]

imitates, does not transfer bodily, Marlowe's

> Fame hovereth sounding of her golden trump,
> That in the adverse poles of that straight line,

---

[23] Cf. also 1 *Tamb.*, III, ii, p. 43.

[24] *Pub. Mod. Lang. Assn.*, XXV, 2 (1910), pp. 223-5.

[25] He cannot suppress the allusion; a reader of Lucan would know the story of Phaëton: cf. *Phars.*, II, 409 ff.

[26] Ll. 1202 ff. In citing the first line of this speech of Cæsar's (l. 1197) Boas (p. 274) prints "likes" instead of "linkes."

> Which measureth the glorious frame of Heaven,
> The name of mighty Tamburlaine is spread.
>
> (2 *Tamb.*, III, iv, p. 128)

The same is true of other passages in which Cæsar, like Tamburlaine, dares "by profession be ambitious." Says Cæsar

> Ile triumph Monarke-like ore conquering *Rome*,   (l. 1483)

and, reciting the list of his triumphs, he concludes:

> And now am come to triumph heere in *Rome*,
> VVith greater glory then ere *Romaine* did.
>
> (ll. 1293-94)

He is

> Like to the God of battell, mad with rage,
>
> (l. 1436)

and his rule on earth will be Jove-like:

> Of *Ioue* in Heauen, shall ruled bee the skie,
> The Earth of *Cæsar*, with like Maiesty.   (ll. 1510 ff.)

This is clearly Tamburlaine or nothing.[27]   But it is not copied from Marlowe with that verbal closeness which, as the long list of parallels is designed to show, is the habitual literary method of the author.   It is not impossible that he is copying not *Tamburlaine* but some Cæsar play now lost to us in which the titular hero spoke in the "'Ercles vein;" an echo of which is still heard in Shakespeare.   At least one line,

> And *Cæsar* ruling ouer all the world,   (l. 1226)

echoes not only Marlowe's

> And we will triumph over all the world
>
> (1 *Tamb.*, I, ii, p. 17)

but likewise the

---

[27] Cf. for example, 1 *Tamb.* II, iii (p. 26), IV, ii (p. 57), V, i (p. 83); 2 *Tamb.*, IV, iv (p. 149).

787

Cæsar doth triumph over all the world

of Kyd's *Cornelia* (l. 1341), which comes to him from Garnier and the Senecan tradition of Cæsar. The presentation of all these parallel passages will justify itself if it gains for *Cæsar's Revenge* some authority as a competent witness for the popular, not merely the academic, treatment of Cæsar on the Elizabethan stage.

HARRY MORGAN AYRES.

XXIV.—STUDIES IN THE DIALECT OF
BASILICATA

Basilicata is the name of that territorial division of Southern Italy which is now known as the province of Potenza and which formed a part of the ancient Lucania. It is bounded on the north by the province of Foggia, on the northeast by the provinces of Bari and Lecce, on the east by the province of Cosenza, and on the west by the Mediterranean sea and the provinces of Salerno and Avellino. It has a population of about 512,000 inhabitants and comprises the *circondari* of Lagonegro, Matera, Melfi, and Potenza. The region is mountainous and the population is given largely to agriculture and sheep-raising. Although centrally located, the province possesses no mercantile towns of any great importance. Many objects of antiquity were discovered in this region: inscriptions, vases, fragments of statues, medallions, and two bronze tables, known as the Heraclean Tables, now in the Naples Museum.

Linguistically, the dialect of this province belongs to the Neapolitan group. When we compare it with Neapolitan, we find that the differences in accent and general modulation of the voice are striking, but phonetically the two have much in common.

A peculiar phenomenon in this dialect is the tendency for accented as well as pretonic *a* to become *ua: nuase, cuane, cuanniliere* < Italian *naso, cane, candeliere*. The tonic vowels are not so prolonged as in Neapolitan, and therefore post-tonic vowels are less liable to weaken. Open *e* when not diphthongized gives close *e: prete, pedde, freve* < Italian *pietra, pelle, febbre;* in Neapolitan it remains. Pretonic initial vowels show less tendency to disappear than in Neapolitan. Pretonic *e* not initial becomes *i: riceve, nipote* < Italian *ricevere, nipote;* in Neapolitan it remains when not in hiatus. Pretonic *ĭ* non-initial remains: *vinnette, nimique* < Italian *vendetta, nemico;* in Neapolitan it becomes *e: letecare* < Italian *leticare.* Final vowels have become much more indistinct than in Neapolitan. The confusion between *b* and *v* is less frequent than in Neapolitan; the *v* never becomes a pure bilabial. Intervocalic *d* never weakens to *r* as in Neapolitan. In the latter, initial *g* before *e* and *i* develops as in Tuscan, but in this dialect it gives *š: scienere, scelà* < Italian *genero, gelare.* We find also a *w* sound as in English instead of the Tuscan *gu: wardà, waie* < Italian *guardare, guaio.* Intervocalic *l* remains, while in Neapolitan it is sometimes confused with *r*. Intervocalic *dy* gives sometimes *š: osce* < *hodie, ausce* < *gaudium,* a development not found in Neapolitan. *Ll* generally gives *dd,* which is altogether foreign to Neapolitan: *cuavadde, capidde* < Italian *cavallo, capello.* In Neapolitan intervocalic *mby* gives *gn: cagnare* < Italian *cambiare;* in this dialect it gives *ngi: cagnià.* Unlike Neapolitan, intervocalic *by* may give at times *š: curresce* < *corigiam.* The interrogatives *chi* and *che* become in this dialect *ci* and *ce,* forms not found in Neapolitan. *Cu* before *a, o, u,* becomes *qu: quiddle, quiste* < Italian *quello, questo;* but in Neapolitan we have *chillo* and *chisto.* For Tuscan *manco, dico, nemico* we have *manquo, diquo, nimique,* a development not found in Neapolitan.

The tendency for dialects to become Italianized, as well as the variation of the same dialect in the towns of the same province, make it impossible to undertake a ,thorough study of the speech of an entire region. I have gathered my material from one town, Corleto Perticara,

8

which, being situated in a central location, may be considered to give a fair example of the speech of Basilicata.

The pronunciation is the same as that of Italian, with the exception that final vowels are very indistinct and in rapid speech are scarcely audible. This, however, is not true of monosyllables like *ie*,[1] *nu, na, cu,* etc. < Italian *io, uno, una, con.* The *dd* developed from *ll* is a very difficult sound to pronounce; the tip of the tongue must strike the upper gums, producing at the same time a slight *r* sound.

I am indebted to Prof. Domenico Francolino and Mr. Franklin Francolino of Hartford, Conn., both natives of Basilicata, for valuable help rendered and for most of the selections given as specimens.

I

Tonic Vowels

a

1. Whether in position or not, *a* generally remains: *sabbate* < *sabbatum;*   *balzame* < *balsamum;*   *mare, funtane.*

2. That *a* often remains in the speech of the majority is due to the influence exercised by the study of Italian in the public schools and very probably by neighboring dialects. However, among the more unlettered classes and among the older generation one frequently finds that the *a* becomes *ua* (the *u* before *a* and *o* being pronounced almost like English *w*): *suangue* < *sanguem;*   *puane* < *panem; cuane* < *canem;*   *nuase* < *nasum;*   *suacce* < *sapeo; suai* < *sapes; piuatte* < **plattum.*

---

[1] The *i* is pronounced like English *y* in *yes.*

3. *-arium* gives *-are* and *-iere: scinnare* < **jenuarium;*
   caudare < *caldariam; varviere* < **barbarium; cuan-*
   niliere < **candelarium.*

ĭ, ē

1. Whether in position or not, ĭ, ē give close *e* unless there
   is a *u* in the following syllable, in which case they
   become *i: verde* < *viridem; pepe* < *piper; sete* <
   setam; cere < *ceram; cannele* < *candelam; piro* <
   perum; pilo < *pilum; tise* < *tensum.*
2. Some words have *e* in the singular and *i* in the plural
   under the influence of a following *i: paese, paisi;*
   turnese, tirnisi; ermice, irmici. Also *e* instead of *i*
   in *discete, descete.*

Exceptions: *cicere* < *cicer; vinte* < *viginti; diebete* < *debi-*
   tum; iedde < *illam; tridice* < *tredecim; sidice* <
   sedecim; femmina < *feminam.*

ĕ

Ĕ· diphthongizes to *ie* when followed by *u* in the next
   syllable, otherwise it gives a close *e: liette* < *lectum;*
   piette < *pectum; fierre* < *ferrum; tiempe* < *tempus;*
   mierle < **merulum;* but *prete* < *petram; pedde* <
   pellem; freve < *febrem.*

Exceptions: *iera* < *erat; iesse* < *esse; mete* < *metere* (the
   e being open).

ī

Long *i* remains: *file* < *filum; lime* < *limam; amique* <
   amicum; but *dece* < *dicere.*

ŭ, ō

Whether in position or not, ŭ, ō become close *o* when not
   followed by *u* in the next syllable or by·*i,*·be it the

plural ending or resultant from latin *s;* in the latter
case they give *u: voce < vocem; ora < horam; sole <
solem; sopra < super; sotto < subtus; vregogne <
verecundiam;* but *surque < sulcum; munnu < mundum; curte < curtum; nuie < nos; vuie < vos; raziuni < orationem.*

Exceptions: *juorne < diurnum;* close *o* became open in
Southern dialects, whence *uo; utre < uterem* instead
of *otre; polve < pulverem,* in which the *o* is open instead of close, probably through the analogy of words
having a tonic open *o; grutta < cruptam; spuorc <
spurcum; favuogne < favonium; sciure < florem.*

ŏ

When followed by *u* in the next syllable ŏ gives *uo,* but if
followed by *a, e, o,* it gives open *o: fuoque < focum;
sciuoque < jocum; uocchie < oculum; suonne < som-
num; puorc < porcum;* but *omnine < hominem;
fore < foras; notte < noctem.*

Exceptions: *nove < novem; osce < hodie;* in which the *o* is
close.

ū

Ū remains: *suque < sucum; luce < lucem; sciume < flú-
men; chiù < plus.* But *rozze < ferruginem.*

II

PRETONIC VOWELS

a

1. Pretonic *a* generally remains: *cantà, calamare, canzone, pacienza.*
2. Occasionally it gives *ua: cuappiedde < *cappellum;*

gualantome < It. *galantuomo; cuavadde* < *caballum;*
cuanniliere < **candelarium.*

3. Often we find forms compounded with *ad,* the *ad* being
assimilated to the following consonant: *accussì* < *ad
secum sic; accumenzà* < **ad cominitiare; arri-
cuordo* < It. *ricordo; abbulà* < *ad volare.*

4. Often an *a* is found in place of other vowels: *accede* <
occidere; affenne < *offendere; canosce* < *cognoscere;
quarera* < *querelam; addore* < *odorem; cainata* <
cognatam.

ĕ

1. When not initial *ĕ* becomes *i: riceve* < *recipere; finestre* < *fenestram; cirase* < **ceresiam; scinucchie* <
genuculum; nipote < *nepotem; simmane* < *septima-
nam; stirnutà* < *sternutare; scinestra* < *genestra;
risponne* < *respondere.*

2. In a few cases it falls when initial: *limosina* < *elemo-
synam; cunomia* < *oeconomiam; pifania* < *epipha-
nia; rumite* < *eremita; statie* < *aestatem; ncignà* <
encœniare.

3. It seldom remains: *vregogne* < *verecundiam; velene* <
venenum; negozio < *negotium.*

4. In hiatus it becomes *i: lione* < *leonem; criate* < **crea-
tum.*

5. A few cases of substitution are: *luvà* < *levare; arrore* <
errorem; quarera < *querelam; survizio* < *servitium;
rumase* < *remansum.*

ĭ

1. When not initial *ĭ* generally remains: *vinnette, nimique, pifania, vidè, spitale* < *hospitalem; vilanze* <
bilancem; diaulo < *diabolum; linzule* < *linteolum.*

2. When initial it falls: *nimique, ndò* < *in de ubi;*

nnante < *in ante;* *mbarà* < **imparare;* *nginucchià* < *ingenuculare.*

3. A few cases of substitution are: *ancudine* < **incudinem;* *sangile* < *gingivam.*

ē

1. Generally *ē* becomes *i: cuanniliere, sicrete, sicure, dinare, sciluse* < **zelosum, difesa, sinsale* < *censualem, cipodde* < **cepullam, riale* < *regalum.*

2. Very seldom it remains: *vescique* < **vessicam; secce* < *sepiam.*

3. We find substitution in *rumite* < *eremita.*

ī

1. Not initial *ī* remains: *vinnegna* < *vindemiam; firnì* < *finire; figliole* < *filiolam; piccione* < *pipionem; cità* < *civitatem.*

2. Initial it falls: *mbierno* < *infernum; nfame* < *infamem.*

ŏ, ō

1. When not initial *ŏ, ō* give *u: cuvierchie, murì, cutugne, purtà, cucchiare, dulore, curresce* < *corrigiam, funtane, cunsulà, prumette* < **promittere, pruvvene* < *provenire.*

2. They fall when initial: *razione, scure, spitale, riloge.*

3. Some cases of substitution are: *accede* < *occidere; dimenica* < *dominicam; addore* < *odorem; cainate* < *cognatum; aulive* < *olivam; riloge* < *horologium; affenne* < *offendere; canosce* < *cognoscere.*

ŭ, ū

1. *Ŭ, Ū* remain: *cuniglie, vuccone, curtiedde* < *cultellum, lucrà, assugà* < *ex sucare; stirnutà, scutedde* < *scutellam.*

2. A few cases of substitution are: *migliera < mulierem;* *pricine < pullicinem; ancina < uncinum.*
3. Initial *u* falls in *nu < unum.*

III

POST-TONIC VOWELS, NOT FINAL

a

A remains: *fegate, sabbate, balzame.*

ĕ, ē

1. Generally *ĕ, ē* remain: *vipere, cicere, carcere, scienere < generum, move < movere.*
2. In a few cases they give *i*: *tridice, sidice, voria < boream.*

ĭ

1. Generally *ĭ* remains: *dimenica, irmice < imbricem, debite, femmina, miedique < medicum.*
2. Cases of substitution are: *niespole < *nespilum; cuofene < cophinum; sinnaque < syndicum.*

ŏ

1. Generally *ŏ* remains: *wescowe < episcopum; quattuordici < quattuordecim; cicorie.*
2. Some cases of syncopation are: *diaulo < diabolum; arbre < arborum.*

ŭ

1, *Ŭ* gives *o*: *wedowa < viduam; setola < situlam; pergola.*
2. Cases of syncopation are: *fibbie < fibulam; uocchie < oculum.*

Most final vowels become so weakened that we have generally indicated them by a mute *e* for both genders.

Whenever an *a* or an *o* is found, it means that the sound approaches the Italian *a* or *o*, but they are still somewhat obscured in pronunciation. The *u* found in monosyllables is pronounced as in Italian. *A* and *o* are the resultants of Latin *-am* and *-um;* only in monosyllables does the *u* remain.

IV

Consonants.—Initial

B

1. In most cases *b* gives a denti-labial *v: vasce, varwa, voria, vammace, vosco, vocca* (Italian *basso, barba, boria, bambagia, bosco, bocca*).
2. In a smaller number of words it remains: *bedde, bene-dice, balzame.*

F

Initial *f* remains: *fiche, fatique, fierre, firnì* (Italian *fico, fatica, ferro, finire*).

V

1. Generally *v* remains: *vinnette, vence, vessique, venne* (Italian *vendetta, vincere, vescica, vendere*).
2. Very rarely it gives *b: bo', bene, bota* (Italian *vuole, viene, volta);* but *vo', vene,* and *vota* are also found.

P

P remains: *puane, piro, pilo, pede* (Italian *pane, pero, pelo, piede*).

D

D remains: *dimenica, debite, duppie, duce* (Italian *domenica, debito, doppio, dolce*).

T

T remains: *tele, titte, tise, tesse, tuorte* (Italian *tela, tetto, teso, tessere, torto*).

L

1. Generally *l* remains: *lime, liette, luoque, lione* (Italian *lima, letto, luogo, leone*).
2. The articles *lu* and *la* become *ru* and *ra* after the preposition *a*.

M, N

M, N remains: *mitte, mierle, move, nide, nora, nimique*.

R

R remains: *riggine, riceve, ruzze, russe*.

S

S remains: *suangue, sicrete, surde, sive* (Italian *sangue, segreto, sordo, sevo*).

C

1. Before *a, o, u*, initial *c* gives *k*: *cuavadde, caudare, cuvierchie, cainate*.
2. Before *e, i*, it gives *č*: *cinc, ceste, cera, cedde, cicere*.
3. It becomes *qu* in: *quiste* < *eccum istum; quidde* < *eccum illum; quaglie* < *coagulum*.
4. At times we find a *g* instead of a *k*: *gatte* < *cattum; gamma* < *cambam; govite* < *cubitum*.

G

1. Initial *g* before *a, o, u*, generally remains: *gode* < *gaudere: gaddine* < *gallinam; gunnedde* < *gunna*.
2. Before *e, i*, initial *g* gives *š*: *scienere* < *generum; scinestra* < *genestam; scinucchie* < *genuculum; scelà* < *gelare*.

W

W gives a sound like the English *w: wardà* < **warda;
warnì* < *warnjan; waie* < *wai.*

Z

Initial *z* before *e* becomes *š: sciluse* < **zelosum.*

DẸ, DỊ

DẸ, DỊ becomes *j: jinte* < *de intro; juorne* < *diurnum;
diaulo* is a learned form.

·J

J becomes *š: scinnare* < **jenuarium; sciuoque* < *jocum;
sciunque* < *juncum.*

V

INITIAL GROUPS OF CONSONANTS

1

Groups ending in l

BL gives *j: jastemà* < *blasphemare; janque* < *blank.*
CL gives *chi: chiuove* < *clavum; chiamà* < *clamare; chiave*
< *clavem.*
FL gives *fi, j, š: fiore* < *florem; jate* < *flatum; jume* and
sciume < *flumen; sciocà* < **floccare.*
GL gives *j: jacce* < **glacium.*
PL becomes *chi* and seldom *pi: chiù* < *plus; chiumme* <
plumbum; chiazze < *plaetam; piwatte* < **plattum;
piace* < *placere.*
STL becomes *sk: scuppetta* < *stloppus.*
VL becomes *j: jasque* < *vlascum.*

2

Groups ending in r

Remain: *brutte, croce, crai, fronte, prigà, scrive, trave.*

3

qu, cu

1. *Qu* generally remains: *quannu* < *quando;* *quatte* < *quattuor;* *quarera* < *querelam;* *quarche* < *qualis quam.*
2. It gives *č* in *ciunque* < *qui unquam; cerza* < *querceam.*
3. *Cu* becomes *qu: quiste, quidde, qua.*

4

Groups beginning with s or x becoming initial

XB becomes *sb: sbranà* < **ex branare; sbatte* < **ex-battere.*

SC, XC become *sk* before *a, o, u: scola* < *scholam; scutedda* < *scutellam; scumminicà* < *excommunicare; scangià* < **excambiare.* Before *e, i,* they become *š: scità* < *excitare; scieglie* < *exsolvere.*

SD, XD give *sd: sdegno* < **disdignare; sdradicà* < *ex-radicare.*

SF, XF give *sf: sfacciate* < **ex-faciatum; sfoco* < *ex focum.*

SP remains: *spisse* < *spissum; spranze* < **sperantiam.*

ST, XT give *st: stà* < *stare; stedde* < *stellam; strazzà* < *extractiare.*

VI

MEDIAL CONSONANTS

B

1. In most cases intervocalic *b* becomes *v: cuavadde, trave, sive, ciriviedde.*
2. In a few learned words it remains: *subito, deḅole, diebete.*

3. It falls in *facia, dicia, diaulo* (Italian *faceva, diceva, diavolo*).

4. It becomes *p* in: *veppeta < bibitam*.

E

E remains: *tufe, cuofene, bufele.*

V

1. Generally *v* remains: *chiuove < clavum; nove, pavone.*

2. It gives *j* in: *voje < bovem.*

P

1. In most cases *p* remains: *vipere, pepe, capidde, lupe, sapone.*

2. It gives *v* or *w* in: *riceve < recipere; wescowe < episcopum; cuvierchie < cuperculum.*

D

1. Generally *d* remains: *accede, pede, ancudine, vide, radeca.*

2. It becomes *t* in: *umite < humidum; sciapite < *insapidum.*

T

T remains: *fatique, discete, strumente, veppeta.*

L

L remains: *pilo, tele, cuannela, fele, mele.*

M, N

M, N remain: *sciume, fume, nome; puane, cuane, dimenica.*

R

1. R remains: *piro, cera, sere, core, fore.*

2. Infinitives lose final *re: vence, accede, move.*

S

S remains: *mese, paise, frese, cirase.*

C

1. Before *a, o, u, c* often gives *qu: amique, fatique, miedique, pequore.*
2. It remains in: *vico, dimenica, sicure, radeca, spica, frabicà.*
3. In a few cases we find a *g: fegate* < *ficatum;* assugà < *exsucare;* prigà < *precare.*
4. Before *e, i,* it becomes *č: riceve, vacile, tridice, dece, noce.*

G

1. Before *e, i, g* becomes *ǧ* or *ǧǧ: riggine, siggille, rigistre.*
2. It falls in: *paise* < *pagensem; frie* < *frigere; quaremma* < *quadragesimam.*
3. Before *a, o, u, g* generally remains: *castigà, agoste* < *augustum; chiaga* < *plagam; augurie* < *augurium.*
4. It gives *v* in: *nivre* < *nigrum; fravole* < It. *fragola.*
5. It falls in: *riale* < *regalem.*

VII

MEDIAL GROUPS

BB remains: *sabbate, gabbà.*

BL gives *ll* in: *sullieve* < **sublevio;* and *gli* in: *neglia* < *nebulam.*

BR remains: *wuttobre* < *octobrem; frabicà* < *fabricare* and *freve* < *febrem* show methathesis.

BY becomes *ǧǧ : agge* < *habeo; ragge* < **rabiam.*

BT becomes *tt: sotte* < *subtus.*

FF remains: *affenne* < *offendere, affaccià, affittà.*

FFL gives *cchi* in: *acchià* < *afflare.*

FR, FFR remain: *soffrì* < **suffrire*.

VV gives *bb: abbilì* < It. *avvilire; ebbiva* < It. *evviva*.

VY gives *ğğ: caggiola* < *caveola*.

PP remains: *cuappiedde, stoppe, cappotte*.

PY gives *čč: acce* < *apium; piccione* < *pipionem; suacce* < *sapio*.

PL, PPL give *cchi: cocchia* < *cupulam; ristocce* < **re-stipula;* but *ppi* in *duppie* < *duplum*.

PR, PPR remain: *proprio, aprì;* it gives *bbr* in *lebbre* < *leporem;* it shows methathesis in *crapa* < *capram;* the *r* falls in *sopa* < *supra*.

PS gives *š* in *cascia* < *capsam; ss* in *stesso* < **iste-ipsum*.

PT gives *tt: sette, accattà, scritte*.

DD remains: *adduce, addormì*.

DR gives *tr* in *piddietro* < **poledrum*.

DY gives *š* in: *osce* < *hodie; ausce* < *gaudium; ğğ* in *appoggià* < **appodiare; ff* in *abbaffà* < **ad-badiare;* it remains in *odio; zz* in *ruzze* < **rudium*.

TT remains: *mitte, piwatte*.

TR remains: *patrone, utre, lettre; r* drops in *quatte* < *quattuor; drete, prete* show methathesis.

TY becomes *zz* or *zi: chiazze* < *plateam; puzze* < *puteum; prezze* < *pretium; negozio* < *negotium; cunsulazione* < *consolationem*.

TC gives *ğğ: dammagge* < *damnaticum*.

TL gives *ll: spalle* < *spatulam*.

LL generally gives *dd: cuavadde, capidde, idde, stedde, quidde;* in a few cases the *ll* remains: *sollione, allegre, ballà*.

LC becomes *rc* or *rqu: carcagne* < *calcaneum; surque* < *sulcum; cuorcà* < *collocare;* it remains in *balcone;* the *l* falls in *duce* < *dulcem*. ·

LD remains in ›*suldate, solde;* the *l* becomes *u* in *caudare, caude*.

LY gives *gli: figlie, migliere, foglie, pariglia, piglià.*

LG before *e* gives *gli: sceglie* < **ex-eligere; coglie* < *colligere.*

LM remains: *salma.*

LP remains in *vulpe* < *vulpem;* it becomes *rp* in *tarpunare* < *talpa.*

LF remains in *sulfe;* it becomes *rf* in *surfariedde.*

LS gives *uz: puzo* < *pulsum; sauzizze* < It. *salsiccia.*

LT gives *ut* in *aute* < *altum; aute* < *alter; autare* < *altarum;* the *l* falls in *vutà* < It. *voltare; vota* < **voltam.*

LV remains: *polve, salviette, salvenne* (Italian *polvere, salvietta, salvando*).

MM remains: *scumminicà, mamma.*

MB becomes *mm: gamma* < *cambam; tammurre, vammace;* it remains in *umbrelle.*

MBY gives *ngi: cangià* < **excambiare.*

MY gives *gn: scigne* < *simia; vinnegna* < *vindemiam.*

MP remains in *cumpagne* < **companio; zampogne* < *symphoniam; tiempe* < *tempus; campagne* < *campaneam.*

MPL gives *ngh: anghì* < *implere.*

MPTY gives *nz: scunzà* < **excomptiare.*

MN gives *mm* or *nn: dammagge, suonno; gn* in *ogne* < *omne.*

NN remains: *cannite, penne.*

NC before *a, o, u,* either remains or gives *nqu: ancudine, janque* < *blank; sciunque* < *juncum.*

NC before *e, i,* gives *nč* or *nz: vilanze* < *bilancem; ancina* < *uncinum; vence* < *vincere.*

NCY gives *nz: onze* < **unciam.*

NCL gives *nchi* in *carvunchie* < *carbunculum;* and *gn* in *gnostre* < **inclaustrum.*

NCT gives *nt: sante* < *sanctum.*

ND becomes *nn: quannu, stinnarde, appenne, cuanniliere.*

NDY gives *gn: vregogne < verecundiam.*

NFL gives *ff* in *gruffulà < *runflare.*

NG before *e, i* becomes *nğ chiange < plangere; nginucchià < ingenuculare.*

NG before *a, o, u* remains: *sangue, luonghe, lenga.*

NGL gives *gn: ogne < ungulam.*

NY becomes *gn: castagne < castaneam; rugna < *roneam; vigna < vineam..*

NS gives *nz* in *zanzale < censualem; nzogna <* It. *sugna;* more often the *n* falls; *scipite < insipidus; paise < pagensem; frese < forensem.*

NT remains: *vinte, gente, diente, lenticchie, fronte.*

NTR gives *nt* in *jinte < de-intro;* it remains in *cintredde, cantre.*

NTY gives *nz: canzone, linzule, accumenzà.*

RR remains: *terre, fierre, arrivà.*

RB gives *rv: varviere, cuorve, survizio.*

RC before *a, o, u* gives *rk: puorche, uorche.*

RC before *e, i* gives *rč: sorce, carcere.*

RCL becomes *rchi: cuvierchie, circhie < circulum.*

RD remains: *verde, perde, surde.*

RDY gives *rš: uorsce < hordeum;* also *z* in *veze < *viri-diatam.*

RG remains before *a, o, u: purgatorio;* it gives *rğ* before *e, i; argiente.*

RM, RN, RP remain: *verme, forma, vierne, juorne, cuorpe.*

RS remains: *vorse < *bursam; forse, vierso.*

RT remains: *sporta, uorte, fuorte, sorte.*

RTY gives *rz: scorza, terze.*

RY gives *r: ferrare, scinnare < *jenuarium.*

SS remains: *iesse, gruosse, russe, vessique;* it gives also *š: vasce < bassum; casce < cassam; abbasce <* It. *abbasso.*

SC before *e, i* gives *š*: *crésce, fasce.*

SP remains: *vespe, niespole, risponne.*

ST remains: *pastore, battistero, inneste.*

STR remains: *finestre, maestre, gnostre;* also *st: nuoste, vuoste.*

SY gives *s*: *vase* < *basium; cirase* < **ceresiam.*

CC before *a, o, u* remains: *sicche, vocca, accoglie.*

CC before *e, i* gives *čč: accede, succede.*

CL becomes *cchi: aurecchie, becchie* < **veculum; uocchie;* rarely *gli: tinaglie* < *tenaculum; cuniglie* < *cuniculum.*

CR generally gives *gr: sogra* < *soceram; agruno* < *acrem; allegre* < **alecrum;* it remains in *lucrà* < *lucrare.*

CS gives *ss: lissia* < **lixivam; tuossique, lassà, assì* < *exire.*

CT gives *tt: piette, liette, vinnette.*

CY gives *zz: azzare, trezza, sauzizze, vrazze;* in a few cases it gives *čč: crapicce, jacce* < **glaciam.*

GN loses the *g: canosce* < *cognoscere; cainate* < *cognatum; aine* < *agnellum;* but *lignum* gives *levone.*

GY gives *š* in *curresce* < *corrigiam; g* in *riloge* < *horologium.*

GR gives *vr* in *nivre* < *nigrum.*

Final consonants develop as in Italian. Final *s* gives in monosyllables *ie: nuie, vuie, craie; voje* < *bos;* but *chiù* < *plus.*

VIII

Morphological Peculiarities

1. *Cases of Methathesis: frabicà* < *fabricare; freve* < *febrem; prete* < *petram; vernedie* < *veneris dies; vregogne* < *verecundiam; crapicce* < **capricium; crape* < *capram; firnì* < *finire; priesque* < *persicum.*

9

2. *Noun.*—*Caput* gives the feminine *capa* instead of *capo* as in Italian. *Vomerem* gives *gommera* instead of the masculine; also we find *scherza* instead of *scherzo;* *la razione* becomes masculine in the plural: *li raziuni.* Likewise we find *li pequore, li descete, li scinucchie* for Italian *le pecore, le dita, le ginocchia.* Some masculine nouns which become feminine in Italian remain masculine in this dialect: *lu lebbre, lu fronte, lu carcere.*

3. *Comparison of Adjectives.*—The comparative is formed with *chiù < plus.* The comparative of inferiority with *meno* is not found. *Migliore* and *peggiore* have been replaced by the adverbs *meglie < melius* and *pesce < *pejus.* *Manquo* is used for the Italian *nemmeno.* The superlative absolute in *issimo* is expressed by *assai* before the positive.

4. *Personal Pronouns.*—Subject pronouns: *ie, tu, idde, iedde, nuie, vuie, lore.*

   Direct and indirect objects: *mi, ti, lu, la, ci* (or *nci, nge*), *vi, li, le.*

   Objects of prepositions: *me, te, idde, iedde, nuie, vuie, lore.*

5. *Possessive Adjectives.*—*Mie, mia, tuve, tua, suve, suva, nuoste, vuoste, lore;* pl. *mie, meia, tuve, toia, suve, noste, voste, lore.*

   Possessive adjectives are always placed after the noun: *tatta tua* (*tuo padre*). *Frateme, sorema, mammeta* are found for Italian *mio fratello, mia sorella, tua madre.*

   The possessive pronouns are the same as the possessive adjectives, but they take the definite article.

6. *Demonstrative Adjectives.*—*Quiste* (rarely *stu*), *chesta* (rarely *sta*); pl. *quisti, cheste; quidde, chedda;* pl. *quidde, chedde.*

Demontrative pronouns are the same as the demonstrative adjectives excluding *stu* and *sta*.

7. *Definite Article.*—*Lu, la, li, le.* After the preposition *a*, the *l* often becomes *r*.
   Indefinite article: *nu, na*.

8. *Numerals.*—*Une, duji, tre, quatte, cinc, seje, sette,
   otte, nove, dece, unnici, dudici, tridice, quattuordici, quinnici, sidice, dicissette, diciotte, dicinnove,
   vinte.*

9. The Italian relative pronoun *che* as well as the conjunction *che* become *ca* in this dialect.

10. The Italian interrogatives *chi* and *che* become *ci* and
    ce; ci iè? (Italian *chi è?*); *ce iè?* (Italian *che è?*).

11. *Verb.*—The future is seldom found; when used it
    denotes probability. Futurity is expressed by the
    present indicative of the verb *to have* and the
    infinitive of the verb in question. The present
    subjunctive is not found except in stereotyped
    phrases like *nun sia mai!* The infinitive loses its
    ending but no *ne* is added. The pluperfect sub-
    junctive often replaces the imperfect subjunctive.
    Agge < *habeo* when followed by an infinitive be-
    comes *aggia*.

(a) First conjugation in *à*: *parlà, parlanne, parlate*.
   Present Indicative: *parle, parle, parle, parlame, parlate, parlene*.
   Imperfect Indicative: *parlave, parlave, parlave, par-
   lávame, parlávate, parlavane*.
   Preterite: *parlai, parliste, parlavo, parlemme, parliste, parlarene*.
   Conditional: *parlarrie, parlarrisse, parlarrie, par-
   larriemme, parlarriste, parlarriene*.
   Imperfect Subjunctive: *parlasse, parlasse, parlasse,
   parlassime, parlassive, parlassene*.

Imperative: *parle, parlate.*

(b) Second conjugation in *è* or *'e: crede, credenne, cridute.*

Present Indicative; *crewe, crenzi, crewe, cridime, cridite, credene.*

Imperfect Indicative: *cridie, cridivi, cridie, cridieme, cridiévete, cridiene.*

Preterite: *cridietti, cridisti, cridive, cridiemme, cridieste, crederene.*

Conditional: *criderrie, cridirristi, criderrie, cridirriemme, cridierrissive, cridirrienne.*

Imperfect Subjunctive: *cridesse, cridiessi, cridesse, cridesseme, cridiessive, cridessere.*

Imperative: *cride, cridite.*

(c) Third conjugation in *i: sintì, sintenne, sintute.*

Present Indicative: *sente, siente, sente, sintime, sintite, sentene.*

Imperfect Indicative: *sintie, sintive, sintie, sintieme, sintiévite, sintiene.*

Preterite: *sintivi, sintiste, sintive, sintiemme, sintiéstere, sinterene.*

Conditional: *sintarrie, sintarrissi, sintarrie, sintarriemme, sintarrissive, sintarrienne.*

Imperfect Subjunctive: *sintesse, sintisse, sintesse, sintessime, sintissive, sintessere.*

Imperative: *siente, sintite.*

The present indicative of *firnì* is: *firnisquo, firnisci, firnisce, firnime, firnite, firniscene.* The other tenses follow *sintì.*

(d) *Stà, stanne, state.*

Present Indicative: *stawe, stai, staje, stame, state, stanne.*

Imperfect Indicative: *stave, stave, stave, stávame, stávate, stavane.*

Preterite: *stietti, stisti, stette, stemme, stiste, stezere.*

Conditional: *starrie, starrissi, starrie, starriemme, starresseve, starrienne.*

Imperfect Subjunctive: *stesse, stisse, stesse, stessime, stesteve, stessere.*

Imperative (the reflexive is used): *statti, statevi.*

(e) *Dà, danne, date.*

Present Indicative: *dave, dai, daje, dame, date, danne.*

Imperfect Indicative: *dave, dave, dave, dàvame, dávate, davane.*

Preterite: *diette, diste, dette, demme, disteve, dezere.*

Conditional: *darrie, darrissi, darrie, darriemme, · darrissive, darrienne.*

Imperfect Subjunctive: *desse, disse, desse, dassime, dasteve, dassere.*

Imperative: *dà, date.*

(f) *Scì, scenne, sciute* or *giute* (Italian *andare*).

Present Indicative: *vawe, vai, vaje, sciame, sciate, vanne.*

Imperfect Indicative: *scia, scivi, scia, sciame, scívete, scienne.*

Preterite: *scive, sciste, scette, scemme, scisteve, scerene.*

Conditional: *sciarrie, sciarrisse, scarrie, sciarriemme, sciarriste, sciarrienne.*

Imperfect Subjunctive: *scesse, scisse, scesse, scesseme, sciste, scessere.*

Imperative: *va, sciate.*

(g) *Fà, facenne, fatte.*

Present Indicative: *fazze, face, face, facime, facìte, facene.*

Imperfect Indicative: *facia, facivi, facia, facienne, faciévete, faciane.*

Preterite: *fice, faciste, fece, faciemme, facisteve, fecere.*

Conditional: *farrie, farisse, farrie, farriemme, farrisseve, farrienne.*

Imperfect Subjunctive: *facesse; facisse, facesse, facessime, facisteve, facessere.*

Imperative: *fa, facite.*

(h) *Sapè, sapenne, sapute.* :

Present Indicative: *suacce, suai, sape, sapime, sapite, sapine.*

Imperfect Indicative: *sapia, sapive, sapia, sapieme, sapiévete, sapiene.*

Preterite: *sapiette, sapiste, sapive, sapemme, sapisteve, saperene.*

Conditional: *saperrie; saperrisse, saperrie, saperriemme, saperriesseve, saperrienne.*

Imperfect Subjunctive: *sapesse, sapisse, sapesse, sapessime, sapisteve, sapessere.*

Imperative: *sai, sapite.*

(i) *Volè, volenne, vulute* or *bulute.*

Present Indicative: *voglie, vuo', vo', vulime, vulite, volene.*

Imperfect Indicative: *vulia, vulivi, vulia; vuliéveme, vuliévete, vuliene.*

Preterite: *vuzi, vuliste, voze, vulemme, vulisteve, vozere.*

Conditional: *vulerrie; vulerrisse; vulerrie, vulerriemme, vulerrisseve, vulerrienne.*

Imperfect Subjunctive: *vulesse, vulisse, vulesse, vulessime, vulisteve, vulessere.*

(k) *Potè, putenne, putute.*

Present Indicative: *pozze, puoje, pote, putime, putite, potene.*

Imperfect Indicative: *putie, putive, putie, putieme, putiévete, putiene.*

Preterite: *putiette, putiste, putette, putemme, putisteve, puterene.*

Conditional: *putrie, putrisse, putrie, putriemme, putrisseve, putrienne.*

Imperfect Subjunctive: *putesse, putisse, putesse, putessime, putissive, putessere.*

(l) *Iesse, essenne, state.*

Present indicative: *so, si, iè, sime, site, so.*

Imperfect Indicative: *iere, ire, iere, ierme, jírvete, ierene.*

Preterite: It is replaced by the preterite of *scì* (*andare*).

Conditional: *sarrie, sarrissi, sarrie, sarriemme, sarriessive, sarriene.*

Imperfect Subjunctive: *fusse, fuste, fosse, fossime, fusteve, fossere.*

Imperative: *si, site.*

(m) *Avè, avenne, avute.*

Present Indicative: *agge, aie, ave, avime, avite, anne.*

Imperfect Indicative: *avia, avive, avia, avieme, avívete, aviene.*

Preterite: *ebbe, aviste, ebbe, aviemme, aviste, ebbere.*

Conditional: *avrie, avrisse, avrie, avriemme, avriesseve, avrienne.*

Imperfect Subjunctive: *avesse, avissi, avesse, avesseme, avisteve, avessere.*

Imperative: *aie, avite.*

(n) *Vedè, videnne, vidute.*

Present Indicative: *vewe, vide, vede, vidime, vidite, vedene.*

Imperfect Indicative: *vidie, vidive, vidie, vidíeme, vidiévete, vidiene.*

Preterite: *vidde, vidiste, vedde, videmme, vidisteve, viderene.*

Conditional: *vidarrie, vidarrissi, vidarrie, vidarriemme, vidarriesteve, vidarrienne.*

Imperfect Subjunctive: *videsse, vidisse, videsse, videssime, vidisteve, videssere.*

Imperative: *vide, vidite.*

(o) *Dece, dicenne, ditte.*

Present Indicative: *diquo, dice, dice, dicime, dicite, dicene.*

Imperfect Indicative: *dicia, dicivi, dicia, dicíeme, diciévete, diciene.*

Preterite: *disse, diciste, dicive, dicemme, dicisteve, dicerene.*

Conditional: *dicirria, dicirrisse, dicirria, dicirriemme, dicirrissive, dicirriene.*

Imperfect Subjunctive: *dicesse, dicissi, dicesse, dicessime, dicisteve, dicessere.*

Imperative: *di, dicite.*

IX

Specimens
Inedited

Ierano le nuvole a pecuredde,
Lu sole annammarate ne scaffava,
La terre com'a lu fumiere modde,
La vaccaredda frasche se rumava.
    E nuie sedute a re prete toste,
    Wardanne le crapecedde noste.

Pe mienza z' curnale
E scannapuddece,
Ndo le macchie se pascienne
Pover' animale.
    Nu cagnuliedde tengo ca iè fedele,
    Se meritarrie lu zucchere e lu mele.

Ma ce putie fà ?
Se mette a abbaffà,
E come vutame l'uocchie
Eccute nu lupo mberucite
    Ca·s'è menato ndo lu ruocchie,
    Tanto lu currivo e l'appetite.

Avess' avute na scuppettedde,
Le facia subito la pedde.
Mo nge vo' lu permesso d'arma
Pe sparà lu lupo ndo la manra.
    E ie restaie com'a quidde c'a bippite,
    Senza di civiedde ca iera proibbite.

Cu l'angina mmane
Me chiame l'ate crape
Chiane chiane,
E l'a vaccaredda sape
La via e se ne vene.
    A ra pagliara tutte ne trasime,
    E lu cuane abbaffa ancora
    E iè rimaso addafora,
    Ca na crapa mancante nuie vedime.

II

Quannu lu pastore vaie a sente messa,
Vede l'acquasentera:—ce bella scutedda a mangià latte!

Vede lu battistere:—ce belle papaglione a tenè robba!
Vede li femine nginucchiate:—ce bella morra di pequore
    figliate!
Vede lu confissiunile:—ce belle pagliare pi quannu chiove!
Vede l'autare maggiore:—ce bella chianca 'a pisà sale!
Vede lu core:—ce belle mungiature a duje vadi!
Vede la sacristia:—ce belle casutaro nge vinerria!
Vede lu campanaro:—ce bell' ammagnone ca sarrie!

III

Quannu lu pastore vaje'n Puglia,
Lassa na cinc rana a ra migliera:
—Migliera mia accattati lu puane,
Lu rimanente ti cuompri la luane.
Te fai na suttana a sette panni,
Quannu venguo ie te 'trove na muntagna.
—Marito mie ti puozzi necà,
Ce puane e luane aggia accattà pe cinc rana?

IV

Tu nu buo' dece quanta si filone,
La gente ca ti sape ti canosce.
E sape pure quanta so minghione,
Ca ie nu diquo a mente-cuncta-posce.
Potesse confessà lu peccatone
Ca mi pesa a re carne meia flosce,
Forse ca pure Dio darria perdone
A ci nnanti l'uocchi ave le catosce.

Maritimi iè pastore,
Si ni vene ogne doie sere
E si mette mussu a mussu

Cu li tizzuni.

—Marite mie, vatti corche,
T'agge misi li janchi linzule!
—Migliera mia, come mi voglia corche?
Ie agge rimasi li pequore sole.
Oh Dio, quant'è mprono lu pastore!
Pensa chiù li pequore di la migliera.
Amprone pastore, manquo a lu liette ti suai cuorcà,
Manquo la cammisa suai di ti luvà.

VI

Lu pastore a ra capanne
Si face lu cunto cu la penne,
L'aine ninnu cu quidde granne,
Ca diaulo aggia venne?

VII

Nge vurrie nu catacuosto,
Nge vurrie na migliera,
Na migliera nge vurrie
Pe mangià ndo na piattedda,
Tutt'e duie 'n armonia.

Ie me sewo tuosto tuosto,
Iedde com'a na quarera,
O ca se si la pigliarrie
Lu diaulo sta wagnedda
Ie starrie 'n allegria.

VIII

Bedde figliole nu sciate chiù a leune,
Ciafarielle s'è date ncampagna:
La scoppetta caricata d'atregna,
Bedde figliole nu sciate chiù a leune.

IX

A.—Buongiorno cummara, come ti la passe?

B.—E ce bo' iesse, cummara mia, ne ncielo e manquo nterre, ce ti pozze parlà, nu pozze fa lu sfoco mie. Iè quidde dulore ca m'accede chiano chiano, e nu mi passe; mi potene adaccià a picca a picca, ie pozze murì e quidde dulore iè sempe vive e mi daie pen' amare. Pover 'a me. Meglio ca nunge fosse maie venuta a ru munno.

A.—Be, nge vo' la pacienza, bene mia; tu lu suai ca senza la pacienza a nudda si pruvvene. E Gesu Cresto e la Madonna t'anne saudì e aiutà chiano chiano e t'anne dà quedde cunsulazione c'aspiette. Le grazie nu benene tutte na vota, e certe vote venene quannu nunne lu credime.

B.—O ca ti pozza sereve l'angelo mmocca e ca l'anime de lu Purgatorio preghessene sempe pe te, cummara mia, te l'aggia deco proprio, ogne vota ca ti vewo tu mi daie nu sullievo; e come te lu pozze renne iene: te lu renne Dio, quant' aiuto mi daie a me ca stawe ndo le pene amare, ndo nu fuoque ardente; tu sola anguna vota ca trase e mi puorte mo la cestaredde de fiche e mo lu panariedde de pere, e mo n'ata cosa e mi dice quedde bedde parulecchie, tu sullieve ogne bota n'anema da lu mbierne, e Dio, ca Dio ng'è, e pe fede nun si perde maie, Dio t'ave pruvvisto de lu bene e ti pozza sempe pruvvede.

A.—Ie lu suacce ca mi vuo' bene e quannu iesquo da la casa mia nummene pozze passà a aggia trasì a vedè come te la passe e ce face. Ie t'agge sempe purtate ammore e sempe tenne porte, e se Dio vole, tu aie sta chiù cuntente e chiù meglie de me. Be, ie menne vawe e tu nun t'annammarà; statt' allegra, suai come dicie na femine: pezzient' allegre peducchie a branche.

B.—Ca proprio, we, puozze sta bona: pezzien' allegre, Dio l'aiute.

A.—Hu, e accussì ti voglie. Sapissi quanta n'agge passate ie: e tu pure aie piglià lu curagge come na briganda e ie suacce ca nun t'ave mancà. Statte bona, cummara mia, ie menne vawe fora, la vi la zapparedde. Si dece: la fatica leva l'omene da lu vizio. Ie fazze pure l'omene quannu nge vo'. Nun mi chiamà saccente.

B.—Quesse cose, la lenguzze mia, nun sia maie! Pigliame lu munnu come vene e facime la vuluntade di Dio.

A.—Nun ti fa male patì.

X

GLOSSARY

Words which differ most from modern Italian.

Abbafà <*ad-babare;* Neap. abbafare; It. bava, trafelare.

Abbaffà <*ad-badiare;* abbaiare.

Abbilà < It. *bile;* inquietare.

Abbuscà, buscare.

Accattà, Neap. accattare; comperare.

Accede, uccidere.

Acchià < *afflare,* Neap. asciare; trovare.

Acchiantate < *ad-plantare,* seduto.

Accio, sedano.

Accrianzate, Neap. accrianzato; costumato.

Accussì, così.

Accuvià < *ad-cubare,* nascondere.

Asquasentera, found also in Neapolitan, fonte battesimale.

Adaccià, Neap. adacciare; ammaccare carne o pestare lardo.

Addafora, fuori.

Addonà < *adunare,* Neap. addonare; andare a vedere.

Adersce < *ad-directiare,* drizzare, sollevare.

Agruno, Neap. agrumma (limoni, cedri, etc.); It. agrume; amaro.

Aguanne, Neap. aguanno; quest' anno.

Allifà < *allevare,* Neap. allifare; azzimare.

Alluccà < *ad-loqui,* Neap. alluccare; gridare.

Ammagnone, spauracchio.

Ammoccià, Neap. ammucciare (tacere di mala voglia); nascondere.

Amprone, balordo.

Anginaglie, anguinaia.

Anguna, alcuna.

Annammarà, It. inamarire (obsolete), intristire.

Appannà, It. appannare (offuscare); socchiudere.

Appaurà, Neap. appaurare; impaurire.

Apprettà, Neap. apprettare; querelarsi.

Appilà, Neap. appilare; tappare.

Arranchelenude, totalmente povero e ignudo.

Asche < *asclam, also in Neap., scheggia.

Ate, altro.

Atteveglie, pipistrello.

Ca, in Neap. it means perciocchè; here, perciocchè and also che, both relative pronoun and conjunction.

Cacaglie, Neap. cacaglio; scilinguato.

Cacciafumo, cammino.

Calanca, in Italian it means seno di mare; here it means frana.

Camastra, catena per il focolare.

Campescia, un tratto di terreno per pascolo.

Cancariata, Neap. cancareata; paternale.

Cannarute, Neap. cannaruto; goloso.

Capisciole, Neap. capesciola; nastro.

Carosa, il luogo dove si tosano le pecore.

Carosielle, Neap. carosiello; salvadanaio.

Casorà, Neap. carosare; tosare.

Casutaro, deposito di cacio.

Catacuoste < *cata-costam, compagno.

Catosce, lucciola.

Catuosce < *cata-ostium, pian terreno.

Ce, che (interrogative and exclamative).

Cerme, It. cerme (obsolete) means tutto il capo; here it means cornicione.

Chlanca, in Neap. it means beccheria; here it means lastra.

Chiascione < jacere, lenzuolo.

Ci, chi (interrogative).

Ciarlasane, it is said of a person who stands always erect and is unable to move freely.

Cimica < cyma, testa, cervello.

Cince, focaccia.

Cingula, in Neap. it means fronzolo; here it means ramo.

Ciuccio, ciuco, asino.

Civiedde < civis in illo; nessuno, niente.

Craie < cras, domani.

Crewe, io credo.

Criduzze criduzze, lungo la spina dorsale.

Crogne, conchiglia.

Cuccemunnedda, Neap. cocciavannella; cutrettola.

Cuffiature, vaso di legno.

Cunsuprine, cugino in secondo grado.

Cuosto, fianco.

Curnale, corniolo.

Cuttinera < cutem negram, gonna.

Dece, dire.

Devacà < de vacare, Neap. devacare; vuotare.

Diquo, io dico.

Driviglià < *de revigilare, svegliare.

Farinazze, farinata, polenta.

Fascefedde, Neap. fascetillo; fascetto di legna.

Filone, It. fellone; here, minchione.

Frese, It. forese. (contadino); here, contadino impiegato a annò.

Fricena, Neap. frecola; minuzzolo.

Fucazza, focaccia.

Fumiere, It. fumiere means l'acido del letame; here, letame.

Garamedda, It. caramella; here, midolla.

Gazale, mascella.

Ghianà ⟨ *planare; Neap. nchianare; salire.

Ghette, treccia.

Gruffulà, It. gruffolare (mangiare in modo indecente come i porci; a more archaic meaning is grugnire); here, russare.

Gualane, Neap. gualano (garzone di campagna); here, colui che guarda animali vaccini.

Igli ⟨ ilia, fianchi.

Jaccà ⟨ flaccare; Neap. sciaccare; rompere la testa.

Lammordo, di colore oscuro.

Latuorno, Neap. taluorno; fastidio, seccatura.

Lenguzza, lingua.

Lotano ⟨ lotium; It. letame; here, stagno.

Leune, legna.

Lupegna, di lupo.

Luvà, levare.

Manquo, nemmeno.

Manra, mandra.

Mara ⟨ mala hora; mara me! povero me!

Masciare ⟨ *magare, fattucchiero.

Mauro, all'ecesso.

Mbarà, imparare.

Mberucite, inferocito..

Mbierno, inferno.

Mbortà, importare.

Mbriache, ubbriaco.

Meloppe, Neap. nveloppa; busta.

Mente-cuncta-posce ⟨ mente-cunctat-poscere; perdonami.

Merque, Neap. merca; segno.

Mesaruolo, mesaiolo, che lavora a mese.

Mienza, in mezzo.

Miere, vino.

Migliera, moglie.

Modde, molle.

Morra, Neap. mmorra; folla.

Mpunteddà, puntellare.

Mungiaturo, il luogo dove si munge.

Murgia ⟨ *muricem; rupe.

Musce, moscio, lento.

Muzzico, morso.

Naca, culla.

Ncincilonne ⟨ in coelo coelorum, in alto.

Ndo, dentro, nel.

Necà ⟨ necare, annegare.

Nfonne, Neap. nfonnere; bagnare.

Nfute ⟨ infultum, folto.

Ninnu, Neap. ninno; It. nini; vezzeggiativo dei bambini; giovine.

Ntrace, It. antrace (obsolete); carboncolo.

Ommole ⟨ amphoram, brocca.

Pantaschi, fianchi.

Papaglione, ripostiglio.

Papusso, figura; perhaps connected with Neap. papuscio (pianella).

Pennelare, ciglio.

Pescera, peschiera, vivaio di pesci.

Picca or pic, poco.

Pigna, Neap., Pistojese ed altre parti della Toscana; grappolo.

Pischione, pietra grande.

Pitrosine, Neap. petrosino; various obsolete Italian forms are: petrosello, petrosellino, petrosemole; prezzemolo.

Poc, Neap. pocca; allora, poichè.

Presiente, regalo.

Quarera, querela; hence, uggioso.

Rampogna, in Italian it means rimprovero; here, metafora.

Revetale, rovo.

Rizzulo, orciuolo.

Rommole, sasso.

Rumà, It. rumare (obsolete), ruminare.

Rumate, letame.

Ruocchio, rocchio.

Sarcene, virgulto di legno.

Scannapoddice, rovo.

Scarature, pettine.

Schitte, It. schietto; here, solo.

Sciummute, gobbo.

Scunzà, Neap. sconcecare; disturbare, guastare.

Sembe, sempre.

Serra, Neap. and archaic It.; sega.

Spranzone, vagabondo.

Stare, Neap. staro (antica misura); here, cesta di legno.

Stiavucche, salvietta.

Stintine, Neap. stentino; budello.

Stizze, goccia.

Suonno, tempia.

Supala, siepe.

Tanne, Neap. tanno; allora.

Tatta, padre.

Tempe, rialto.

Terza, di ——, ier l'altro.

Tizzone, tizzo.

Tomo, lento.

Tonza, vasca.

Toste, f. pl. of tuosto, duro.

Trasì, entrare.

Uffile, Neap. uffa; anca.

Uomele, morbido.

Useme, Neap. uosemo; fiuto.

Vade, guado, entrata.

Vantera, grembiule.

Vitranedde, vaiuolo.

Wagnedda, fanciulla.

Wagnone, Neap. guaglione; fanciullo, giovanotto.

Wulisce, Neap. golio; desiderio.

Zagaredde, Neap. zagarella; nastro.

Zanche, zanna.

Zenca, Neap. zenna; poco.

Zilona, tartaruga.

Zoca, fune.

Italian *povero me!* is expressed in various ways: *travaglie mie* (Corleto); *sciglie mie* (Laurenzana); *scante mie* (Montemurro); *trimintone mia* (Guardia); *tasse nui* (Viggiano).

Un morso di pane becomes: *nu murso di puane; nu muzzico di puane; na zenca di puane; nu vuccone di puane.*

Nu rusce e nu musce, Italian *non è buono a nulla.*

Ausce di chiazza e trivole di casa, Italian *gioia di piazza e tribolo di casa.*

La catena di lu cuodde, Italian *la nuca.*

La tabacchera di lu scinucchie, Italian *la rotella del ginocchio.*

Lu pesce di la gamma, Italian *polpaccio.*

La chianta di la mano, Italian *la palma della mano.*

ALFONSO DE SALVIO.

In 1905, two important contributions were made to our knowledge of the sources of Ben Jonson's *The Staple of News*. Dr. De Winter, in a critical edition of the play, pointed out several important similarities between it and the earlier *London Prodigal,* which play he urged, further, was " mainly the work of Jonson's hand." [1] In the same year, Mr. Charles Crawford showed less important similarities between *The Staple of News* and *The Bloody Brother,* notably in speeches by the Master-Cook, a character in the former play, and insisted that here also Jonson had had a large hand in the play from which he later borrowed.[2]

Scholars had earlier shown possible borrowings from still other plays and works, and Winter added to the list of possible minor sources. His summary is interesting: " From the *Plutus* of Aristophanes and the *Timon* of Lucian, through Lady Argurian in *Cynthia's Revels,* came the idea of Princess Pecunia in her more abstract aspect, money personified." The *Wasps* of Aristophanes and the *Aulularia* of Plautus are included as having given unimportant suggestions. Chaucer's *House of Fame* " contributed slightly to the conception of the news-staple. . . . From the *London Prodigal* . . . is adapted the motif of the three Peniboys, with the father's disguise, the sham will, and a considerable number of minor details." In addition, it is suggested that certain slight hints came

---

[1] *Yale Studies in English,* vol. xxviii, p. xxxiii.
[2] *Shakespeare Jahrbuch,* vol. xli, pp. 165 f.

10

from Jonson's earlier *Cynthia's Revels,* and his masks, *News from the New World* and *Neptune's Triumph,* and from Fletcher's *The Fair Maid of the Inn.*[3]   Mr. W. W. Greg, in reviewing the contributions of both Winter and Crawford, was inclined to accept all these sources.   " Jonson's play in fine," he says,[4] "·turns out to be little more than a cento made up of borrowings from earlier works," many of which, he grants, were probably Jonson's own.

It is the purpose of this paper to call attention to still another partial source, or certain analogue, of Jonson's play, a source of some significance in throwing light on Jonson's dramatic methods.

Dr. Winter says it was from the *Plutus* and the *Timon* that Jonson " got the main idea of the allegorical part of the play, the personification of money," but he admits that " his working out of this idea in the action of our play has little or no resemblance to the plot of either of his originals." [5]   Winter lists four differences, indeed, between the personifications of money in the two plays, the most conspicuous of which is, perhaps, the difference in sex. In fact, the only real resemblance between Jonson's play and the *Plutus* is the existence of *a* personification of money, the Princess Pecunia in the one, the god Plutus in the other.   Jonson, for example, makes no use of the chief device by which Aristophanes works out his idea, namely, the restoring of Plutus' sight.

The story told in Lucian's dialogue is somewhat, though only slightly, closer to the main story of *The Staple of News.*   Here Plutus exclaims against his treatment while

---

[3] *Yale Studies in English,* vol. XXVIII, pp. xxxiii f.
[4] *Modern Language Review,* 1905-1906, p. 327.   See also a more detailed review of Winter's edition, p. 143.
[5] *L. c.,* p. xxi.

in the possession of the prodigal Timon: "He insulted me, threw me about, dismembered me . . . and practically pitch-forked me out of the house. . . . What, go there again, to be transferred to toadies and flatterers and harlots?" [6]   Pecunia undergoes a similar treatment at the hands of the young prodigal, Peniboy Junior, in *The Staple of News,* as will be pointed out more fully in a moment.   Moreover, Pecunia, as with Plutus in the *Timon,* is at the end given over to the possession of the now reformed prodigal.   But with these details, again, the similarity of story ceases.   In neither the *Plutus* nor the *Timon* is the personification of money sought after and for a time possessed by two characters who represent the extremes, avarice and prodigality; and this is the essential characteristic of Jonson's treatment of the idea.

Jonson's use of the conception of money personified illustrates a further important difference between his play and the two Greek masterpieces, a difference in purpose, or moral.   Gifford, who had earlier noted the partial similarity between *The Staple of News* and the *Plutus,* points out this difference.   Jonson, he says, insists upon "the use and the abuse of riches . . . ;" both "the prodigal and the miser (are) corrected," while Aristophanes was trying only "to expose (the) general venality of his generation." [7]   Jonson's purpose was, indeed, to show the proper use of money by portraying and punishing the two extremes of misuse.   This "moral" is insisted upon throughout the play, nowhere more clearly than in the closing lines, in Pecunia's last speech:

[6] *The Works of Lucian,* translated by H. W. and F. C. Fowler; vol. I, p. 35.

[7] Gifford's *Works of Ben Jonson,* with Introduction and Appendices, by F. Cunningham; vol. v, p. 292.

> And so Pecunia herself doth wish,
> That she may still be aid unto their use,
> Not slave unto their pleasures, or a tyrant
> Over their fair desires; but teach them all
> The golden mean; the prodigal how to live;
> The sordid and the covetous how to die;
> That, with sound mind; this, safe frugality.

It is true that a similar moral is preached in both the *Plutus* and the *Timon,* but only indirectly; the story in each is the working out of a somewhat different moral. Gifford's statement may be taken to describe that of the one: " the vanity of riches " [8] well describes that of the other. For the use to which Timon declares he will put Plutus, or wealth, upon recovering it, is as much an unwise extreme, and " vanity," as his early prodigality.[9] In fact, Timon at the beginning and then at the end of the dialogue represents the two unworthy extremes, which Jonson portrays by two characters, neither of whom, unreformed, can be trusted with wealth.

Thus in plot and underlying motive Jonson's play differs radically from both the *Plutus* and the *Timon,* though it is probable that he got suggestions from both, especially from the latter. Now, *The London Prodigal* is much closer in many respects to the story of *The Staple of News,* but here, the obviously allegorical devices are entirely lacking, as is the fundamental story and moral of the wooing of wealth by the two extremes of the misuse of wealth, the temporary possession of wealth by each of these extremes in turn, and the final realization of the " golden mean," the proper use of wealth, through the reformation of the two extremes.

---

[8] See the sub-title of the *Timon* (*Works of Lucian, ed cit.,* I, p. xvi).

[9] See the closing sections of the dialogue, especially paragraph 42, p. 46.

Much closer to *The Staple of News* in these important respects than any of the partial sources thus far suggested is a late English morality play, *The Contention between Liberality and Prodigality,* first printed in 1602.[10]   The main situation, the moral, and the rôles of several of the characters are surprisingly alike.   In the earlier play, Money, a boy or young man, fills the rôle of the later Pecunia.   He, however, is the son of Mistress Fortune. Here, possibly, is the transition from the masculine Plutus to the feminine Pecunia, or, better, to Lady Argurian of *Cynthia's Revels.*[11]   Money of the morality play is sought after and for a time possessed, as is Pecunia in Jonson's play, by Tenacity, comparable to Peniboy, the Uncle, and usurer, and later by Prodigality, an equally possible prototype of the young prodigal, Peniboy Junior in *The Staple of News.*   In each play, the prodigal's dissipation of money is symbolized by a feast, from which, in the one, Pecunia is rescued, and from which, in the other, Money

[10] Reprinted in Hazlitt's *Dodsley's Old Plays,* vol. VIII.   See in the Introduction the suggestion that this was " a revival of a more ancient piece," possibly, Collier thought, to be identified with a play called *Prodigality,* presented at Court in 1568.

[11] For both the name and the sex of his personification of money in *The Staple of News,* Jonson may have been indebted to a poem by Richard Barnfield, first published in 1598, *The Encomion of Lady Pecunia,* which is not mentioned by Winter.   Barnfield says in his address To the Gentlemen Readers, " I have given Pecunia the title of a Woman, both for the termination of the word, and because (as women are) shee is lov'd of men " (Collier's *Illustrations of Old English Literature,* vol. I, No. 7).   Moreover, he calls her " the famous Queene of rich America " (p. 1, *ibid.*), which may have suggested Pecunia's title, " Infanta of the Mines," and the following lines in the play:

Piedmantle.   I have deduced her—
Broker.   From all the Spanish mines in the West Indies,
        I hope; for she comes that way by her mother.
                                                (II, i, 86-88)

runs away. During the riotous banquet in the " Devil
Tavern," Pecunia is forced to kiss Peniboy Junior's
scheming companions,[12] and in the morality, Money is
" dandled " and " kissed " by his equally unscrupulous
seducers.[13]   Access to Pecunia has to be gained through
the Broker, " secretary and gentleman usher," to her, while
in the earlier play, Prodigality and Tenacity enlist similar
services of Vanity, " Fortune's chief servant."   There are
even closer similarities, due possibly to a common source
in either the *Plutus* or, more probably, the *Timon,* in the
treatment of the personification of wealth by the personification of avarice.   Money says of Tenacity:

> He would never let me abroad to go,
> But lock'd me up in coffers, or in bags bound me fast,
> That like a boor in a sty, he fed me at last,
> Thus Tenacity did spoil me for want of exercise.[14]

And Pecunia says Peniboy, the Uncle;

> Kept me close prisoner, under twenty bolts,
>
> .   .   .   .
>
> But once he would have smother'd me in a chest,
> And strangled me in leather.[15]

Her servant, Statute, adds that,

> .   .   .   . he cramm'd us up in a close box
> All three together, where we saw no sun
> In one six months.[16]

---

[12] Act IV, sc. i.   [14] *Ibid,* p. 377.
[13] *Dodsley's Old Plays,* VIII, p. 360.   [15] Act IV, sc. i.
[16] *Ibid.* With these compare, for example, the *Timon,* paragraph
13, p. 36: Zeus says to Plutus, " You were imprisoned by rich
men under bolts and locks and seals, and never allowed a glimpse
of sunlight; . . . you were stifled in deep darkness. . . . It was
monstrous, then, that you should be kept in a bronze or iron
chamber and brought up by these stern unscrupulous tutors, Interest,
Debit and Credit." Barnfield also makes use of some of these ideas
in his *Encomion of Lady Pecunia.* See pp. 4 and 5.

Jonson is a less stern moralist than the author of the morality, for he permits Pecunia to marry the reformed and penitent Peniboy Junior, while Money goes to Liberality, who has deserved this fortune throughout and is, it must be confessed, a more likely realization of " the golden mean " than the reformed prodigal.   Liberality, however, preaches the same moral, as when he says to Money,

> . . . bide with him that can devise
> To rid you and keep you from these extremities.[17]

i. e., Tenacity and Prodigality.   Liberality, moreover, " chief steward to Virtue," bears close resemblance to Peniboy, the Father, of Jonson's play, especially in that each " is the main spokesman of morality—from him come most of the ' sentences,' " as Winter remarks of the disguised father in both *The Staple of News* and *The London Prodigal.*[18]

Other similar rôles in the two plays are those of the prodigal's companions, Tom Toss and Dick Dicer of *The Contention between Liberality and Prodigality,* and Cymbal, Madrigal, and others in Jonson's play.   Such characters as Captain Well-Done, the Courtier, and the Lame Soldier, of the morality play, are like Shunfield, " sea captain," Fitton, " the emissary Court," and Piedmantle, " pursuivant at arms," only in being what one might call " topical " characters.

These similarities of plot, characters, purpose, and, perhaps, of lines, certainly suggest that Jonson was familiar with the belated morality play, *The Contention between Liberality and Prodigality,* and that he used the framework of it and some of its minor details, as well as suggestions from Lucian's *Timon* (possibly from the *Plutus*

[17] *Dodsley's Old Plays,* VIII, p. 378.
[18] P. xxviii of Winter's edition of *The Staple of News.*

of Aristophanes), from the earlier, partially his own,
London Prodigal and *The Bloody Brother,* and from the
other plays and works listed by Winter. In fact, the similarities between *The Staple of News* and *The Contention*
would seem to be closer and more significant than in any
of the other suggested " sources."

Of particular significance, if the suggestion of this
paper be accepted, is the probability that Jonson used an
English morality play along with the works of two great
Greek satirists. Nor is the combination incongruous, or
without significance for Jonson's purpose and method as a
dramatist. Jonson, or any writer of satiric comedy, has
much in common, of course, with classical satire, comedy
or dialogue, but no less with the morality play. The
writers of each are primarily didactic, are preachers, and,
because of that fact, are always prone to preach their
moral by the means of relatively abstract symbols. Like
the scientist's, the anatomist with his chart of nerves or
arteries or the political economist with his concept of the
" economic man," theirs is the method of " simplification,"
of abstraction, of excluding all save that which serves their
ulterior purpose. In significant contrast to Hamlet's
famous declaration, a contrast the more striking because
of the similarity of figure, is a speech by Asper, the Pre-
senter, at the beginning of Jonson's *Every Man Out of
His Humour:*

> . . . . I will scourge those apes,
> And to these courteous eyes oppose a mirror,
> As large as is the stage whereon we act;
> Where they shall see the time's deformity
> Anatomised in every nerve and sinew.

The fullness and complexity of life, of " the very age and
body of the time," is sacrificed by the satirist and the

moralist to make clearer a single aspect of life, a "humour" perhaps, or a social "deformity," or a moral law; and the symbolic abstraction, a Pecunia, a Prodigal, a nerve or sinew "anatomised," is preferred to the living image. With them there is no Shakespearean clouding of the issue by a pathetic Shylock, a worthy Malvolio, or by a "grey iniquity" who wins the tears of harlots and the affections of all men. In comparison with such as these, even a Subtle or a Brainworm seems scarcely flesh and blood, seems more akin, for example, to the shadowy, if lively, Vice of the morality plays.

It is interesting to note, especially in his so-called "dotages," Jonson's recognition of the similarity between his own plays and the morality drama. In *The Devil is an Ass,* for example, he makes such a recognition clearly.[19] And in *The Staple of News* the kinship is fairly trumpeted forth. Thus, beyond question for Jonson, speak "the ridiculous gossips that tattle between the acts";

Mirth . . . How like you the Vice in the play?
Expectation. Which is he?
Mirth. Three or four: Old Covetousness, the sordid Peniboy . . .
Tattle. But here is never a fiend to carry him away. Besides he has never a wooden dagger! I would not give a rush for a Vice that has not a wooden dagger to snap at everybody he meets.
Mirth. That was the old way, gossip, when Iniquity came in like Hokos Pokos, in a jugler's jerkin . . . but they are now all attired like men and women of the time, the vices male and female.[20]

Although it can scarcely be denied that Jonson is here admitting, and even insisting upon, the similarity between his play and older morality plays, it does not, of course, follow that he was confessing to have borrowed a moral, or a plot, or characters from a particular morality play. To

[19] See, for example, I, i, and v, iv.
[20] Intermean, after Act II, sc. i.

find such clear recognition of similarity of type is something, however. And it is hoped that this paper has pointed out, in *The Contention between Liberality and Prodigality,* the particular play of the type, from which, as well as from Lucian's *Timon* and the P*lutus* of Aristophanes and from his own earlier works, Jonson took a moral and took machinery for his allegorical satiric comedy, *The Staple of News.*

ARTHUR BIVINS STONEX.

XXVI.—THE VIRTUE OF FRIENDSHIP IN THE
FAERIE QUEENE

I

No reader of Renaissance literature need be reminded that when Spenser wrote, friendship rivalled love as a poetic theme. High friendships give life whatever good it has, says one of Castiglione's courtiers; and the Elizabethan gentleman agreed with him. If the Elizabethan gentleman was also a story-teller, the thought of friendship, it seems, usually put happy devices into his plot-making, as the thought of Helen's beauty, if he was a poet, kindled his style. Yet Spenser, who himself enjoyed friendships with the best, and who of all men should have risen to the theme of friendship, wrote of it very lamely. At least, so his critics decide. Their general verdict is that of the six books in the *Faerie Queene* the fourth, on the virtue of friendship, is, in spite of splendid episodes, the least satisfactory as a story and the least comprehensible as an allegory.

In the desire to say a word on Spenser's ideal of friendship, one would not be betrayed into arguing that the book is well told. Spenser confuses us by abandoning, in part at least, the program announced in that very useful letter to Ralegh. He had said that each book was to have for patron a special knight, " for the more variety of the story," and that each knight was to undertake an adventure. In the first three books, to which alone the letter referred, he kept his promise, as he resumed it in books v and vi, but in this fourth book Cambel and Triamond, whom he names as companion knights of friendship, have no quest, and shortly disappear from the story altogether.

831

Further, Prince Arthur has appeared in the first and second books to rescue the hero,[1] and in book III, where Britomart obviously could need no rescue, he still is associated with her [2] to remind us of that complete cluster of virtues of which she, in that book, illustrates but one. We therefore come to expect Arthur's entrance as a guide to what is important in the allegory. But in book IV he does not rescue Cambel and Triamond, nor is he associated with them; he enters only a minor part of the story,[3] and if he illustrates anything, it seems to be fair play or justice rather than friendship.

A favorite explanation of these defects of plot is that books III and IV are really one, that Spenser so conceived them, and that neither should be read apart from the other.[4] But there is reason to think Spenser constructed the allegory of the fourth book after book III was in print; for in his letter to Ralegh he said that Britomart was to rescue Amoret at the end of the third book,[5] and so indeed she did in the 1590 version of the

[1] *Faerie Queene*, bk. I, canto vii; bk. II, canto viii.

[2] *Ib.*, bk. III, canto iv.

[3] *Ib.*, bk. IV, cantos viii and ix.

[4] Cf. Kate M. Warren, in the introduction to her edition of the *Faerie Queene*, Book IV, 1899.

[5] "The third day there came in a Groome, who complained before the Faerie Queene, that a vile Enchaunter, called Busirane, had in hand a most faire Lady, called Amoretta, whom he kept in most grievous torment, because she would not yield him the pleasure of her body. Whereupon Sir Scudamour, the lover of that Lady, presently tooke on him that adventure. But being unable to performe it by reason of the hard Enchauntments, after long sorrow, in the end met with Britomartis, who succoured him, and reskewed his love.

"But by occasion hereof many other adventures are intermedled; but rather as Accidents then intendments: As the love of Britomart, the overthrow of Marinell, the misery of Florimell, the vertuousness of Belphoebe, the lasciviousness of Hellenora, and many the like."

poem. He also said that certain accidents, not " intendments," are interwoven with the main plot of the first
three books; and among these accidents he mentions the
love of Britomart, the overthrow of Marinel, and the
misery of Florimel. But these " accidents " of the
third book become " intendments," or leading motives,
of the fourth; and especially the love of Britomart, which
originally, perhaps, was to remain a hope, like the quest of
Arthur for the Faerie Queene, develops into a link between book III and book V, as though in the union of
Britomart and Artegal Spenser wished to show a continuity between Chastity, Friendship, and Justice. That
this purpose involved some reconsideration is indicated
by the passages referred to in the letter to Ralegh, and by
the fact that Spenser altered the close of book III, in
order to continue the story of Amoret.[6] He put the third
book before the public as a finished story, and reopened it
later in order to work out a different plan; the exigencies
of book IV can therefore not be urged as excuse for
book III, nor the shortcomings of book III as excuse for
the shortcomings of book IV.

So much for the difficulties of the plot. Those who
criticize the allegory bring the sweeping charge that very
little in the fourth book seems to have anything to do
with friendship. We read of the quarrel between Paridel
and Blandamour, of Agapé and her sons and of their
fight with Cambel, of Satyrane's tournament, of the
House of Care, of the happy recognition of Britomart
and Artegal, of the rescue of Amoret from the Savage
Man, of the estrangement between Arthur's squire and
Belphoebe, of the Squire of low degree, of Amyas and

---

[6] For the original ending of bk. III, see Spenser's *Works*, Grosart,
vol. VII, pp. 37, 38.

Placidas, of the Temple of Venus, of the marriage of the
Thames and the Medway, and finally of the marriage of
Marinel and Florimel. Some friendship appears in these
episodes, but for the most part they seem to deal rather
with envy, hatred, and malice. .

Recent criticism of Spenser is not disposed to explain
this tangle of allegory, much less to defend it. The fashion is to dismiss cavalierly the poet's claim to be a thinker,
along with his claim to be a story-teller; we are asked to
admire only his pictorial imagination and his verbal
music.[7] This attitude helps us to forgive Spenser for the
things in him we do not understand. Yet without denying his more than Elizabethan gift for getting swamped
in his own plots, we may examine one assumption his
critics make. They assume that by friendship he meant
the same thing as, for example, the dramatist had in mind
when he gave us Romeo and Mercutio, Hamlet and Horatio. They fail to observe that Spenser's obvious purpose
was to present friendship as a moral virtue, whereas
Shakspere, and most other writers, have portrayed friendship as a social relation, like blood kinship, involving certain virtues such as loyalty, but not itself a virtue.

Without attempting, then, to justify Spenser's defects
of plot-making, it is the purpose of this paper to suggest
that he meant what he said when he called friendship a
virtue. His philosophy or the program to which he had
committed himself forced him to support what had been
among the philosophers a minority opinion, and to rank
friendship as equal in importance and identical in kind
with holiness, temperance, chastity, justice, and courtesy.

----

[7] Cf. J. M. Robertson, *Elizabethan Literature*, 1914, p. 67: " Spenser, for his age a teacher, is for us first and last a maker of the
music of words, a creator of rhythmical and phraseological beauty."

Not even the writers from whom he drew his inspiration
cared to give friendship this equality with the other virtues, nor have later writers done so, with the exception of
a few of his enthusiastic disciples. He made a lonely
attempt to define friendship as a mystical approach to
God; if his story and his allegory fail, at least one reason
may be that the subject matter in this case, as in the third
book, was essentially fit for lyrical treatment, not at all
for narrative.

II

Spenser knew that the ancient philosophers had specu-
lated on the nature of friendship, that the Greeks before
Aristotle had questioned whether friendship could exist
between bad men, and whether the mystic attraction between friendly natures was of like to like or of opposite
to opposite. Aristotle briefly summarised this discussion
and put it aside,[8] since his interest lay in the ethical
aspects of friendship, in the motives which lead men to
form this alliance. He happened to be engaged in making
a list of virtues, according to his definition of a virtue,
and finding that friendship hardly adjusted itself to his
theory of the mean, yet unwilling, with the *Lysis* and the
Phaedrus behind him, to dispose of friendship ungrac-
iously, he concluded that, if not a virtue, it was almost
as good; and he then proceeded to discuss it as a social
relation between brothers, between husband and wife, between children and parents.[9] The undoubted virtue which
friendship most nearly resembles, he said, is justice [10]—
an opinion which perhaps has some bearing on the sequence of books IV and V in the *Faerie Queene*.

[8] *Ethics*, bk. VIII, ch. ii.   [9] *Ib.*, bk. VIII, ch. iii-xv.
[10] *Ib.*, bk. VIII, ch. iv.

Aristotle was sensible of the mystical, metaphysical aspects of friendship which Plato had stressed; he probably knew by experience the abiding of two souls as in one body. But his purpose for the moment, as he said, was to discuss moral questions, whether only the good can be friends, and whether there can be more than one kind of friendship. In later ages, when Plato was but a name, Aristotle's description of friendship became standard; whether or not men thought friendship a virtue, they wrote of it as of a social and moral relation. When Bacon, for example, expounded the advantages of friendship, he was handling the traditional theme in the traditional manner, which he derived, if not from Aristotle, then probably from Cicero's *Offices*.[11]

But the interest in friendship for its own sake, in friendship as a mystic experience, never died out. Montaigne, of all persons, followed his Aristotle with a kind of protest; real friendship, he said, is distinct from the love of parents and children or husband and wife, and they who make friends for advantage, as Cicero in the *Offices* had advised, miss the point. Perhaps Montaigne had in mind that other work of Cicero's, *On Friendship,* in which the Roman, here a Platonist, said that he often considered " this question, whether friendship seems desirable because of our weakness or want, whether by exchange each receives from the other what he himself lacks; or whether this is only a by-product of friendship, which is a higher and nobler thing, more directly derived from nature herself ? " [12] Or perhaps Montaigne was thinking of a fine sentence in Plutarch—" A musical concord consists of contrary sounds, and a due composition of sharp

---

[11] *Offices,* bk. II, ch. vii, viii.
[12] *On Friendship,* ch. viii.

and flat notes makes a delightful tune; but as for friendship, that is a sort of harmony all of a piece, and admits not the least inequality, unlikeness, or discord of parts, but here all discourses, opinions, inclinations, and designs serve one common interest, as if several bodies were acted and informed by the same soul." [13]

Had Spenser read Montaigne, or Plutarch, or Cicero's *On Friendship,* or Aristotle's *Ethics?* He may have read them all, though M. Jusserand has taught us to suspect the Aristotle. If Spenser had not read the *De Amicitia,* he had probably read Lyly's *Euphues,* which bristles with paraphrases from Cicero. That he had his Plato, or rather his Plotinus, through the Italians, we know. And if he had not read Aristotle, he could find a good paraphrase, mingled with some Platonic thought, in Giraldi's *Tre Dialoghi della Vita Civile.*

It has usually been supposed that Spenser read these dialogues in English, in his friend Ludowick Bryskett's *Discourse of Civil Life.*[14] This book was not published till 1606, but it pretends to recount what took place at Bryskett's cottage near Dublin sometime between 1584 and 1589. Spenser and some other gentlemen, we are told, called on Bryskett, who asked Spenser to read to them his unpublished work, *The Faerie Queene.* Spenser declined, but urged Bryskett to read his translation of Giraldi. This Bryskett did, or rather, he said he would paraphrase the three dialogues roughly, with running comment, and he would answer any questions his guests

[13] *Moralia,* in the translations edited by W. W. Goodwin, 1870, vol. I, p. 473.

[14] There were two issues of this book in the same year, one published by William Aspley, and the other by Edward Blount. The Harvard University copy, which I have used, was printed for Aspley. The Blount issue I have not seen. Malone and Todd describe both issues as quartos.

might put to him. He then gave them the first dialogue. The next day, he says, they called on him again, and he summarized for them the second dialogue. The following day he completed his paraphrase. On each day they asked questions, and there was a general discussion of Giraldi's doctrine.

If these three conversations took place, and if Spenser was present, he must have heard, not a paraphrase, but a very slavish translation of Giraldi, for Bryskett follows the original text as closely as he knows how. Spenser must have heard also some other Italian-Platonic ideas; for Bryskett, thinking that Giraldi did not adequately discuss the nature and number of the virtues, had recourse, as he says, to Piccolomini, " in whom having found a more plain and easy method in the description of them, I have for the more perspicuity of the translation added somewhat taken from him, and, as well as I could, interlaced it with this discourse, where mine author seemed to me too brief or too obscure." [15] M. Jusserand, in his important essay,[16] having shown that Spenser did not get his list of virtues from Aristotle, suggests that he did get them, in part at least, from the conversation here reported. He takes Bryskett at his word as to the supplementing of Giraldi with Piccolomini, and concludes therefore that the conversation reported by Bryskett is " positive testimony " that Piccolomini's *Institutione Morale* was known to Spenser.[17] It may have been, but hardly on this evidence. In the first place, Bryskett borrows only one passage [18] from Piccolomini, a description of Mansuetude,

---

[15] Bryskett, p. 214.

[16] *Spenser's " Twelve Moral Vertues as Aristotle hath Devised,"* *Modern Philology*, Jan., 1906, vol. III, pp. 373-383.

[17] *Ib.*, p. 378.

[18] Bryskett, pp. 240-247. I have used the French translation of

Desire of Honor, Verity and Affability, inserted between Giraldi's account of Magnanimity and of Justice. In the second place, it is not at all clear that the conversations Bryskett described ever took place, nor that Bryskett intended to deceive us into thinking they ever took place. Spenserian scholars, from Todd, who first saw the importance of Bryskett's little book, to M. Jusserand, have accepted the conversations as historical, although the difficulties of such a view ought to have troubled them. Todd dated the conversations as having occurred between 1584 and 1589, "as Mr. Malone ingeniously conjectures." [19] Malone had mentioned the book in his Life of Shakspere, but did not give the argument of his "conjecture," nor did Todd. Professor Child, however, in his edition of Spenser,[20] gave the best of reasons for these dates. One of the chief persons represented as calling on Bryskett and taking part in the three conversations was Dr. Long, Bishop of Armagh. Dr. Long was not made Bishop until 1584, and he died in 1589. Grosart, however, ignored Professor Child's conclusion, and dated the conversations not later than 1582-83, because another of the speakers, Captain Warham St. Leger, could not possibly have been present after that date.[21] In spite of this contradiction, it seems to have entered no one's head, until quite recently, that perhaps the conversations were a fiction. Grosart quoted the passage in which Spenser gives his own account of his poem, and the passages toward the end in which he asks certain philosophical questions about im-

Piccolomini, in the copy belonging to the Congressional Library— *L'Institution Morale du Seigneur Alexandre Piccolomini. Mise en François par Pierre de Larivey Champenois.* Paris, 1581.

[19] Spenser's *Works*, Todd, 1805, vol. I, p. lvi.

[20] Spenser's *Works*, Child, 1855, vol. I, p. xxiv.

[21] Spenser's *Works*, Grosart, 1881, vol. I, p. 149.

mortality. Spenserian scholarship has followed Grosart. The only dissenting voice I know is that of a Baconian enthusiast,[22] who in 1914 showed how improbable it is that the conversations should have taken place, and gave his own theory, based on internal evidence, that Bacon wrote them as expositions of his philosophy.

It did not occur to the Baconian enthusiast, however, nor of course to the Spenser scholars, from Todd down, to compare Giraldi's dialogues with Bryskett's conversations. The fact is that except for some dramatic trimming, such as the reference to the *Faerie Queene,* except for the change of scene and persons, and except for that one passage from Piccolomini, Bryskett's book has been taken literally from Giraldi. Bishop Long's theological remarks are in the Italian, and Spenser's philosophical questions, which Grosart quoted as interesting glimpses into his character, are translated word for word.[23] Moreover, it seems quite clear that Bryskett

[22] *Edmund Spenser and the Impersonations of Francis Bacon,* by Edward George Harman, London, 1914.

[23] M. *Spenser* then said: If it be true that you say, by Philosophie we must learne to know our selves, how happened it, that the *Brachmani,* men of so great fame, as you know, in *India,* would admit none to be their schollers in Philosophy, if they had not first learned to know themselves: as if they had concluded, that such knowledge came not from Philosophie, but appertained to some other skill or science?—Bryskett, p. 163.

Yea but (said M. *Spenser*) we have frō Aristotle, that the possible understanding suffreth in

Udito ciò, disse Torquato, come volete voi, Lelio, che la Filosofia ei faccia conoscere noi medesimi, se i Brachmani, Filosofi (come sapete) d'India, non volevano insegnare ad alcuno cosa, che fosse della Filosofia, s'egli prima nō conosceva se stesso? quasi che volessero, che ciò non dalla Filosofia, ma di altrondesi apprendesse.—Giraldi, *Tre Dialoghi,* prefixed to part II of the *Hecatommithi,* Venice, 1580, p. 40, *verso.*

Qui interponendosi Torquato, disse habbiamo da Aristotile, che il possibile intelletto intendendo

was only following a well-known literary practice [24] in substituting the Irish scene and his English friends for the Italian setting and persons; as if to absolve himself in advance, he told us plainly that he assumed this transfer of names: " I must now presuppose that ye, whom I

the act of understanding: and to suffer importeth corruption; by which reason it should be mortall as is the passible.—*Ib.*, p. 271.

Why (said Maister *Spenser*) doth it not seem, that *Aristotle* when he saith, that after death we have no memorie, that he meant that this our understanding was mortal? For if it were not so, man should not lose the remembrance of things done in this life.—*Ib.*, p. 272.

Yet (sayd Maister *Spenser*) let me aske you this question; if the understanding be immortal, and multiplied still to the number of all the men, that have bene, are, and shall be, how can it stand with that which *Aristotle* telleth us of multiplication; which (saith he) proceedeth from the matter; and things materiall are always corruptible?—*Ib.*, p. 273.

But how cometh it to passe (replied Maister *Spenser*) that the soule being immortal and impassible, yet by experience we see dayly, that she is troubled with Lethargies, Phrensies, Melancholie, drunkennesse, and such other passions, by which we see her overcome, and to be debarred from her office and function?—*Ib.*, p. 274.

patisce, & il patire importa corruttione, adunque egli è come il passible mortale.—*Ib.*, p. 68, *verso.*

A me pare, disse Torquato, che dicendoci Aristotile, che non ci raccordiamo doppo la morte, ci habbia voluto dire, che questo nostro intelletto sia mortale; se cosi non fusse, non perderebbe l'huomo la memoria della cose di questa vita.—*Ib.*, p. 68, *verso.*

Sciolto questo nodo, dise Torquato, et come puote egli esser lo intelletto immortale, & moltiplicato al numera de gli huomini, che sono stati, sono, & saranno; dicendoci Aristotile, che questa moltiplicatione procede dalla materia, & la cose, che sono tali, tutti sono corrutibili? —*Ib.*, p. 69.

Havendo ciò detto Lelio, soggiunse Fabio, come esser puote, se lo intelletto è immortale, & impassibile, che si vegga nondimeno, per isperienza, ch' egli patisce da letarghi, dalla frenesie, dalle maninconie, da gli ubriacamenti, & da altre simili passioni, per le quali veggiamo, che egli occupato, non fa l'ufficio suo?—*Ib.*, p. 70.

esteeme to be as those gentlemen introduced by this author, have likewise moved the same question as they did.—And likewise where any occasion of doubt or question, for the better understanding may happen in this discourse, that some of you desiring to be resolved therein, will demand such questions as shall be needfull."

It appears, then, that the conversations did not take place. In any event, the Baconian enthusiast who from certain resemblances in the philosophy thought that Bacon wrote Bryskett, seems to have proved that Bacon wrote Giraldi. And whatever aid Spenser had from Giraldi or Piccolomini, he seems to have got from other channels.

My own opinion is that Spenser knew Giraldi's dialogues in the original, and that he drew heavily on the long passage on Friendship in the third dialogue. Giraldi says, after Aristotle, that friendship, if not a virtue, is near to virtue, for the other virtues cannot be practised without it.[25]   Friendship is a communion of minds, he

Why (sayd M. *Spenser*) doth your author meane (as some have not sticked even in our dayes to affirme) that there are in us two severall soules, the one sensitive and mortall, and the other Intellective and Divine?—*Ib.*, p. 275.

Vorreste voi forse dire, Lelio, disse Torquato, come vogliono alcuni altri della nostra età, che siano ne gli huomini due anime separate l'una dall' altra, una sensitiva & mortale, l'altra intellettiva & divina?—*Ib.*, p. 70, *verso.*

[24] Professor George Philip Krapp kindly calls my attention to a discussion of this practice in G. L. Henrickson's *Chaucer and Petrarch, Two Notes on the "Clerk's Tale,"* in *Modern Philology,* vol. iv, p. 179 *sq.*

[25] Per questa cagione è necessaria al virtuoso l'amicitia, la quale od è virtù, o non è senza virtu, & nasce dall'amore, ond'egli ama i Figliuoi i parenti, il Padre, la Madre, i Cittadini, & le altre persone straniere. Perche, quanto alla felicità civile, non pùo nè dee l'huomo vivere solo. Et però è necessaria al Felice la conversatione, & l'amicitia, a compemento della civile felicita.—Giraldi, p. 81.

continues, following Plato.[26]   This communion is possible only when friendship grows out of virtue, for evil is the principle of discord in the world, and discord makes impossible all communion, but out of true friendship no discord can arise.[27]   Beauty, according to Plato, is the chief cause of friendship, and if the mind as well as the body be beautiful, the friendship is durable, and binds men so fast that they become as one; so that, it seems, one mind is in two bodies.[28]   If, however, the beauty is not of the soul, the friendship will break, for discord cannot dwell with friendship.[29]   Friendship, says Plato, is a habit acquired by long love, yet though love be the means to friendship, it is not friendship.[30]

[26] L'amicitia è una communion d'animi, la quale non separa ne longhezza di tempo, nè distanza di luogo, nè gran felicità, ne adversa Fortuna, nè altro fiero accidente, che accada nelle cose humane.— *Ib.*, p. 81.

[27] Se il giudicio è usato prima che altri si dia ad amare, si che giudicando questo, o quello degno di essere amato, l'ami per le virtù sue, rimangono cosi ferme tali amicitie, che non pure non si sciogliono mai, ma non nasce mai fra cosi fatti amici cagione di querela. Perche è sententia di Aristotile, nel primo della Natura, che è cosa impossibile, che fra la vera amicitia posse nascere discordia.—*Ib.*, p. 81, *verso*.

[28] Et ha nella amicitia secondo Platone principalissima parte la bellezza, cioè quella dell'animo, la qual bellezza nasce dalla virtù . . . ella lega con tal nodo, & con si fermo consentimento gli animi humani, che divengono quasi una cosa medesima, & pare che una sola anima habita in due corpi, & parimente gli regga.—*Ib.*, p. 81.

[29] Et se questa bellezza del corpo tira per disaventura l'huomo ad amare un animo sozzo & dishonesto, non si pùo quella dimandare amicitia, ma più tosto un congiungimento sozzo & abominevole.— *Ib.*, p. 81.

[30] Al qual cosa mirando Platone disse, che l'Amicitia era un 'habito acquistato con lungo amore, & altrove, che l'Amicitia era uno amore invecchiato, ciò è contratto per lungo tempo: egli è vero, che Amore è il mezo dal quale nasce l'Amicitia, ma non è egli amicitia, ma si bene l'origine di essa.—*Ib.*, p. 82 *verso* (incorrectly paged, 58).

III

If the tradition among philosophers was to combine the Aristotelian portrait of friendship as a social relation with the Platonic praise of it as a spiritual state, why did general literature, fiction and the drama, side only with Aristotle? Why did Shakspere represent friendship always, in the Sonnets, in *Romeo and Juliet,* in *Two Gentlemen of Verona,* in *Hamlet, Othello,* and *Lear,* as a relation involving virtues such as loyalty, but not as a virtue itself? Why did Sidney in the *Arcadia* so represent it? Why did Lyly, who quoted from Cicero's Platonic essay, frame the story of Philautus and Euphues merely to inculcate loyalty and honor?

The reason, I think, is that chivalry had fixed in the minds of all gentlemen the idea of friendship as an obligation between equals. In every gild, and especially in the supreme gild of knighthood, to be true to one's order was an obvious duty; and all comradeship, therefore, came naturally to be defined in terms of loyalty. Malory and Froissart record innumerable friendships so defined, and even to name *Amis and Amile* and all the other Medieval and Renaissance stories which announce this ideal of the social relation would be impossible. It should be noted, however, that in the insistence upon loyalty to one's order the Platonic communion of souls dropped somewhat below the horizon. So long as the other knight played fair, you had to be friendly with him whether you liked him or not. In time comradeship was treated as a means to friendship, not a result of it. Joinville tells us that before landing in Egypt he assigned to the same duties two young squires, in order to put an end to their inveterate quarreling. " No one could make peace between them," he says, " because they had seized each other by the hair." [31]

It was against this ideal of friendship that Spenser set up the contrast of his fourth book. He was bound by the plan of his poem and I think by his temperament also, to treat friendship as a virtue; he therefore defined the virtue as a communion of souls, an achievement, in part at least, of that harmony which is the nature of God, and which once was in the universe. In accordance with this habit of commenting, at the beginning of a canto or a book, on what had gone before, he gives in the prologue to book v, on Justice, a Platonic description of the universe before discord entered it. Since the perfect harmony there portrayed can be shared only by an innocent soul, Britomart, the knight of innocence, becomes the real illustration of friendship, and her union with Artegal or justice signifies some such idea as that the innocence of ideal nature makes friendship possible, and that friendship includes justice, as Giraldi said, following Aristotle. If Spenser had not already named Britomart the patron of chastity, perhaps he would have made her in theory, as she becomes in fact, the patron of friendship; as it is, Cambel and Triamond serve to present his definition of the virtue.

One difficulty Spenser was sure to encounter in making an allegory of his kind of friendship; he had found the same difficulty in portraying chastity. This mystical union of souls, like other dreams of perfection, implied no action; you could sing about it lyrically, but how set it

[31] Sire de Joinville, *Mémoires*, ed. by Michel, Paris, 1881, p. 48. Cornish (*Chivalry*, p. 36, note) seems to think that Joinville in order to unite them "in a chivalrous friendship," actually knighted the squires. The *Mémoires* hardly warrant this interpretation. I wish they did.

forth in a story? It was the old dilemma for literature—
stationary bliss in heaven, stirring plots in hell. But
Cicero had pointed a way out. "If it be not clearly perceived," he wrote, "how great is the power of friendship
and concord, it can be distinctly inferred from quarrels
and dissensions; for what house is there so established, or
what state so firmly settled, that may not be utterly overthrown by hatred and dissension? From which it may be
determined how much advantage there is in friendship." [32]
Spenser follows a method of this kind. Had he been writing of friendship in the ordinary chivalric sense, he could
have used many an incident of loyalty or self-sacrifice;
but writing of friendship as a spiritual state, he was forced
to discuss chiefly illustrations of the lack of it, and his
book therefore seems at first sight to treat only of jealous-
ies and quarrels.

IV

What, then, is the allegory of the fourth book? I think
it is simply a variation on a few themes; it tries to put
into narrative the ways by which the virtuous enter into
the communion of friendship, the ease with which false
friends fall out, the warfare that the devil wages against
all harmony, the temporary estrangement that discord
sometimes achieves between good men and women, and the
relation of love to friendship. All these ideas had been
stated as abstractions by Giraldi.

In the first canto we see the friendship of Britomart
and Amoret, which follows Amoret's misunderstanding of
her rescuer. Then we are introduced to Até, the enemy
of Concord,[33] and in the false friendship of Paridel and

---

[32] *On Friendship*, ch. vii.
[33] *Faerie Queene*, bk. IV, canto i, stanza 19.

Blandamour we see Giraldi's Aristotelian doctrine, that comradeship entered into for profit or for evil purposes cannot last.[34] Até and Duessa meet Scudamour, Amoret's lover, and by their falsehood temporarily arouse his anger against Britomart.[35] In the second and third cantos we read of Agapé and her sons, and of their battle with Cambel. Here Spenser tries to define in allegory the mystical communion which is his theme. Agapé (or brotherly love) had three sons, Priamond, Diamond, and Triamond, who

> with so firm affection were allied,
> As if but one soul in them all did dwell.[36]

Agapé learned from the fates that these brothers would not live long; she prayed, therefore, that the soul of him who died first should pass into the soul of the other two, and that the soul of the next who died should join itself with that of the third brother, so that in him all three souls should survive. The three brothers unanimously fell in love with Canace, and fought with her brother Cambel for her hand. When Priamond was killed, his soul added itself to Diamond's and Triamond's; when Diamond was killed, his soul added itself to Triamond's; thereupon, since by this concentration of souls Triamond was now the spiritual equal of Cambel, they immediately recognized the essential harmony between them, and became fast friends. This reconciliation is symbolized in Cambina, who brings a magic to change hate into friendship.[37] Plato had enquired in vain into the secret process by which friendship is formed.[38]

These first three cantos, then, show how bad men fall

---

[34] Ib., stanza 32.

[35] Ib., stanza 52.

[36] Ib., canto ii, stanza 43.

[37] Ib., canto iii, stanza 42.

[38] Plato, Lysis.

out, and how true men become friends.. Spenser expounds
the moral at the beginning of canto IV.

> It often falls (as here it erst befell)
> That mortal foes do turn to faithful friends,
> And friends profest are changed to foemen fell:
> The cause of both, of both their minds depends,
> And th' end of both, likewise, of both their ends;
> And friendship, which a faint affection breeds
> Without regard of good, dies like ill grounded seeds.[39]

Cantos IV and V deal with the tournament which Satyrane
made for the false Florimel. Geraldi had said that a
false beauty often leads men into a false friendship, which
cannot last. Through Britomart, Artegal, Cambel, Triamond and others in this tournament are examples of virtue, discord spreads among them, and Scudamour is driven
to the House of Care, all as a result of the untruth of the
make-believe Florimel. By way of contrast, we have in
Canto VI the encounter between Britomart and Artegal,
where the knight of justice, beholding the true beauty of
Britomart, becomes her comrade forever.[40]

The seventh and eighth cantos portray three enemies
of friendship—that is, of the pure communion of mind—
lust, in the story of the savage man who captures Amoret
and Amelia;[41] jealousy, in the story of Timias and Belphoebe;[42] and slander, in the episode of Arthur, Amelia
and Amoret.[43] In the eighth canto occurs the story of
Amyas, Amelia's lover, captured by Corflambo, and of
Placidas, who woos Corflambo's daughter in order to save
his friend Amyas.[44] This episode is the only one in the
book which seems to stress chivalric loyalty, but we hap-

---

[39] *Faerie Queene*, bk. IV, canto iv, stanza. 1.
[40] *Ib.*, canto vi, stanza 19.   [43] *Ib.*, canto viii, stanza 35.
[41] *Ib.*, canto vii, stanza 5.   [44] *Ib.*, stanza 47.
[42] *Ib.*, canto vii, stanza 36.

pen to have Spenser's own statement that he meant to illustrate rather the comradeship of souls.   Commenting on the passage, after his custom, at the beginning of the following canto, he says he was considering the three kinds of friendship allowed by Aristotle—the affection of kindred, the love between man and wife, and the communion of virtuous minds.   This third and best kind of friendship he finds in Amyas and Placidas.[45]

The ninth canto is an awkward repetition, to allow Arthur an opportunity to perform his usual rescue.   Britomart meets Blandamour and Paridel and other Knights who were at Satyrane's tournament; they are still quarreling over the false Florimel, and Britomart is drawn into the fight.   Thereupon Arthur appears and rescues her—that is, reëstablishes harmony.   It should be noted that in the third book Britomart as the patron of chastity could need no rescuer.   Here as the real knight of friendship she does need to be set free by the grace of heaven from the illusions by which Até destroys concord.

When Arthur has once performed a rescue, the remainder of a book in the *Faerie Queene* always shows life as it should be; in the remaining cantos of book IV, therefore, we have three poetical dreams of friendship.   In the description of the temple of Venus [46] the relation of love and friendship is imaged; concord controls the temple, as Plato had said that friendship contains love, though love does not necessarily contain friendship.   In the marriage of the Medway and the Thames [47]—that episode which proves so intractable if by friendship we understand a social relation,—Spenser uses a favorite nature image to express union and communion.   In the marriage

[45] *Ib.*, canto ix, stanzas 1-3.   [46] *Ib.*, canto x.
[47] *Ib.*, canto xi.

of Marinel and Florimel [48] he repeats this idea in images partly natural, partly mythological. One feels that he was running out of ideas and out of allegorical material. He had already given us his definition of friendship several times. A defect of art, perhaps, but no reason for misunderstanding him.

JOHN ERSKINE.

[48] *Ib.*, canto xii.

XXVII.—THE MIDDLE ENGLISH *EVANGELIE:* ADDITIONS AND CORRECTIONS

INTRODUCTION

P. 530. *Description of the MS.* The stain in the MS. at ff. 81-84 extends through a number of preceding folios, and therefore occurred since the fragment of the quire was bound up in the present volume. The Latin fragments on the first three pages of the quire are theological commonplaces, and the conclusion of a tract which I have not been able to identify; probably a summary of one of Augustine's sermons, copied in the same illiterate Latin as that of the rubrics.

P. 536. Add to note 20: Cf. also, on guttural *h* before *t,* Richard de Caistre, and Miss Peebles's note in Harford's edition; *Norwich Guild-reports,* EFTS. XL, pp. 38, 43, 62, etc.; Capgreaves's *Life of St. Katherine,* EETS., ed. Furnivall, *Introd.,* p. 25.

P. 540, note 27, *goed.* I have since found the spelling *goed,* used apparently without regard to the length of the vowel, in a number of MSS., and am inclined to think it merely a scribal variation. The note should be cancelled.

P. 544, diagram. The left-hand dotted line z-z^1-B should be cancelled.

TEXT

P. 549, note 12*. There are no hyphens in the MS., and *all* the compound words are separated in both *D* and *V;* the printer's device of a double hyphen is therefore unnecessary.

Corrections in rubrics. P. 546, v. 14, *nomen/ tuum Fac . . . peccatorem ihu . . . esto/ mihi ihc . . .* v. 22, *i. petri.*

P. 548, v. 52.　*Neque* enim . . . *in* quo . . . .
bona . . . *quis* . . . *lunam* . . . *putauerunt* . . .

P. 551, v. 102.　. . . *&* [*i*]*ta ysaya xii.*

P. 552, v. 126.　. . . *autem* . . .

P. 553, v. 130.　. . . *dum senio grauatur crescente* . . .
Delete first *ut* in last phrase.

P. 556, v. 182.　*prima* . . .　v. 198, (p. 557, line 3)
diuitem. & a prophetis beg. new line. v. 206, *dirumperes.*

P. 559, v. 224.　. . . *angelus* . . . *mariam* . . .

P. 559, *B,* 228, *Que cum au/disset* . . .

P. 561, v. 252.　*spiritus* . . .　v. 256, *-senectute* . . .
v. 260, *-est* . . .

P. 567, v. 336.　*Beda.*

P. 568, *B,* 344, . . . *sacerdocio* . . . *exijt.*

P. 569, v. 366.　. . . *vxor* . . .　v. 364, . . . *ad hoc*
. . . .

P. 570, v. 372, *-vsque* . . .

P. 571, v. 391, for *quia* read *quod.*

P. 572, v. 409.　. . . *mater* . . . *uocabitur* . . .

P. 576, v. 453.　*qua* . . .

P. 577, v. 469.　. . . *vel* . . .　For *quia* read *quod.*

P. 578, v. 485.　Delete *hoc*; delete bar after *in.*

P. 579, v. 497.　*Hoc* . . .

Corrections in verse.　D:—80, *for* pat, *read* þat: 103,
(þ)e, *read* (þ)E: 148, louerd, d *written above the line:*
314, likenesse, *read* liknesse: 338, for-lorin, *read* for-loriin,
second i *inserted above line:* 398, childe, *read* child: 449,
second and, *read* ant: 503, bi-lefte, *read* bi-leste. *B:*—
47, here, *read* herε: 48, dere, *read* derε: 252, *lorne, read*
lorne: 288, beg. paragraph: 509, augustus, *read* augustus:
538, two, *read* tuo: 623, written, *read* writen: 681, comyng
ageyn, comyng *marked for transposition in* MS: 724, *insert*
þere *after* four-score: 798, had, *read* bad: 832, þat, *read*

þat: 838, nothing, *read* no-thing: 863, culyr, *read* culuyr: 937, þat, *read* þat; ȝoure, *read* ȝoure: 994, hem, *read* hem: 1001, he, *read* be: 1083, ihc, *read* Ihc; *insert* him *after* Ihc: 1143, somewhat, *read*-whot: 1225, *insert* is *after* what: 1268, himself, *read* him—: 1283, synne, *read* synnes: 1330, by, *read* to: 1429, forgoe, *read* forgoo: 1472, þe, *read* þei: 1484, *insert* hole *after* a-noþir: 1572, þer, *read* þere: 1621, graue, *read* graue: 1744, here, *read* here: 1768, were, *read* were: 1771, ches, *read* chees: 1787, þat, *read* þat.

NOTES

130.   The same authority is quoted by Nicholas de Lyra, *Postilla*[1] Questio 7, in his explanation of the Immaculate Conception: " vt patet iii q. xxx: ar. v et per philosophum in libro de animalibus."

198.   Rubric on " sinus Abrahae ": based on Bernard, *In festo omnium sanctorum* iv.[2]

220.   *Augustinus.* Cf. *Epistolae* clvii, 14; clxxxvii, 34, cxc, 6.[3]

269-280.   Cf. also Zupitza's note in his ed. of Rymer's Poems,[4] and Mosher's note.[5]

310.   Cf. Bede, Hom. No. 39, 40.[6]

GERTRUDE H. CAMPBELL.

---

[1] Ed. London, 1512, fol. lxxxiiii.
[2] Migne, P. L. 183, col. 473.
[2] *Ibid.*, 33, col. 858.
[4] Herrig's *Archiv* 93, p. 325.
[5] *Exemplum in England*, p. 48, note.
[6] Ed. Giles, London, 1843; v, 293, 297.

APPENDIX

PROCEDINGS OF THE THIRTY-SECOND ANNUAL
MEETING OF THE MODERN LANGUAGE
ASSOCIATION OF AMERICA
HELD UNDER THE AUSPICES OF
COLUMBIA UNIVERSITY, NEW YORK, N. Y.,
DECEMBER 29, 30, 31, 1914
AND OF THE
TWENTIETH ANNUAL MEETING OF THE CENTRAL
DIVISION OF THE ASSOCIATION,
HELD UNDER THE AUSPICES OF THE
UNIVERSITY OF MINNESOTA, MINNEAPOLIS, MINN.,
ON THE SAME DAYS

THE MODERN LANGUAGE ASSOCIATION
OF AMERICA

MEETING OF THE ASSOCIATION

The thirty-second annual meeting of the MODERN LAN-
GUAGE ASSOCIATION OF AMERICA was held under the auspices of Columbia University at New York, N. Y., December 29, 30, 31, 1914, in accordance with the folloing
invitation:

COLUMBIA UNIVERSITY

IN THE CITY OF NEW YORK

JANUARY 7, 1914.

PROFESSOR W. G. HOWARD, *Secretary,*
  Modern Language Association,
    Harvard University,
      Cambridge, Mass.

Dear Sir:

I am directed by President Butler to transmit to you in most
emphatic form an invitation to the Modern Language Association
to hold its 1914 meetings at Columbia University. You will, of course,
have to be the judge as to whether our facilities are such as to
meet the requirements of the Association, but, should they be adequate, we hope very much that you will see fit to do us the honor
of meeting here next year.

Very truly yours,

FRANK D. FACKENTHAL,
Secretary.

All sessions of the Association wer held in Earl Hall,
except the last, which opend in Havemeyer Hall and
adjurnd to Earl Hall after the reading of paper no. 22.
The President of the Association, Professor Felix E.
Schelling, presided at all the sessions except as hereinafter
noted.

FIRST SESSION, TUESDAY, DECEMBER 29

The meeting was cald to order by Professor Schelling at 3 p. m.

The Secretary of the Association, Professor W. G. Howard, presented as his report volume XXIX of the *Publications* of the Association, including the *Procedings* of the last annual meeting; and the report was unanimusly accepted.

The Secretary reported that on May 5, 1914 he had sent to all activ members of the Association the folloing letter:

THE MODERN LANGUAGE ASSOCIATION OF AMERICA

CAMBRIDGE, MASS., May 5, 1914.

Dear Sir or Madam:

The Annual Meetings of the Association and the Central Division in December, 1906 (see *Publications*, XXII, 4, pp. xi, xxxiii) voted to adopt for official use in the publications of the Association forms of spelling then recommended by the Simplified Spelling Board. Inquiry made in the spring of 1911 shoed that in both the Editorial Committee and the Executiv Council a majority was in favor of further simplification of official spelling; and at the Union Meeting of 1911 (see *Publications*, XXVII, 1, p. xxiii) the folloing proposition, announst on the program as coming up for action, was adopted by a substantial majority, to wit:

> *Voted:* that the Association hereby adopts the rules and recommendations of the Simplified Spelling Board in its circular No. 23 of March 6, 1909 as the norm of spelling in the official publications and correspondence of the Association.

The meetings of 1913 also took action on the subject of simplified spelling (see *Publications*, XXIX, 1, pp. xvi, xlvi), that at Cambridge requesting the Secretary "to ascertain by postal card the wishes of the members as to the use of the so-cald reformd spelling by the Association," and that at Cincinnati requesting the Executiv Council "to consider the whole subject of the further reform of English orthografy and to make recommendations to the Association at the Union Meeting to be held in 1915."

Since the Executiv Council wil naturally be guided in its recommendations by the wishes of the majority of the Association, you ar now invited to make known your wishes as fully and as definitly as possible.

To prevent misunderstanding I beg leav to say a word on two points:

(1) The votes of 1906 and 1911 apply to the spelling of official documents only, that is, to official publications, to official correspondence, and to editorial matter. It is especially provided, and is a matter of course, that articles contributed to the *Publications* shal be printed in the spelling of the manuscript; and in such manuscript no editorial change of spelling has been made or wil be made, except a correction according to the author's own standard. In the programs of meetings, however, summaries of papers ar held to be editorial matter. Many of them ar very much edited in every respect, and in the future stil closer editorial attention wil probably be necessary, if programs ar to be kept within a more reasonable compas than has of late prevaild.

To be sure, official documents hav themselvs not been uniform, nor can they be under the operation of a plan for progressiv simplification of spelling. The principle of progressiv simplification has, however, been approved and adopted by the Association.

(2) The term "reformd" is misleading if it suggests the accomplishment of something that nobody professes to hav accomplisht. The official spelling does not call itself reformd; it is at most in process of reformation, or of simplification; and, as "simplified," it is not at a stage that anybody regards as final. There ar those who believ the official employment of forms which ar od, but ar undeniably simpler than the conventional forms, to be useful as an example; others ar not of this opinion; and stil others approve the principle, but disapprove this or that feature of the practis.

You ar requested to set forth your views and wishes on the opposit page. A cros placed under "yes" or "no" wil indicate an affirmativ or a negativ anser to the printed questions, and the space belo the questions may be utilized for further expression of opinion. The sheet can then be detacht and maild in the accompanying envelop. An erly reply is invited, but replies wil be receivd and considerd up to the first of December next.

Thru the curtesy of the Simplified Spelling Board you wil receiv at about the time that this letter reaches you certain publications of the Board from which exact information may be derived as to what is coverd by the votes of the Association above referd to.

Faithfully yours,

W. G. HOWARD,
Secretary.

THE MODERN LANGUAGE ASSOCIATION OF AMERICA

Question   *Anser*

Question	YES	NO
1. Do you favor the use of simplified forms of spelling in the official publications and correspondence of the Association to the extent exemplified in the foregoing letter?		
2. Do you favor the use of simplified forms of spelling in the official publications and correspondence of the Association, but to a less extent than that exemplified in the foregoing letter?		
3. Do you favor the complete abandonment of simplified spelling by the Association?		

Additional Information
    Date. . . . . .   Name. . . . .

The Secretary further reported that the vote of the Association had resulted as folloes:

```
In favor of 1:     -    -    -    -    -    -    -    -              253
In favor of 2, not opposed to 1:      -    -    -    -      37
In favor of 2, but opposed to 1:      -    -    -    -      62
                                                          ——
                                                                     99
In favor of simplification, but with varius qualifications:          10
                                                                   ———
                                                                     362
In favor of 3:     -    -    -    -    -    -    -    -     262
In favor of 3, for the present:      -    -    -    -    -    1
Opposed to 1, otherwise non-committal:    -    -    -      4
                                                          ——
                                                                    267
Indifferent, or non-committal:      -    -    -    -    -              7
                                                                   ———
    Whole number of votes:  -    -    -    -    -    -               636
```

Distribution of Votes:

In favor of	1	2	3	
New England: - - - - - -	46	21	97	= 164
Middle Atlantic States: - - - -	67	27	71	= 165
South, incl. Ark., La., Tex.: - - -	28	6	27	= 61
Middle West, east of the Mississippi: -	67	34	54	= 155
West of the Mississippi, except Ark., La., Tex.: - - - - - - -	42	10	12	= 64
Canada, Philippines, Mexico: - -	3	1	2	= 6
	253	99	263	= 615

Per cent. of Membership voting: 55.2%

[The figures wer subsequently laid before the Executiv Council.]

The Tresurer of the Association, Dr. A. F. Whittem, presented the folloing report:

A. CURRENT RECEITS AND EXPENDITURES

RECEITS

Balance on hand, December 20, 1913, - -			$1,196 60
From Members, for 1909, - -	$ 6 00		
" " " 1910, - -	3 00		
" " " 1911, - -	6 00		
" " " 1912, - -	45 00		
" " " 1913, - -	181 00		
" " " 1914, - -	2,992 54		
" " " 1915, - -	78 00		
" " " Life Member-ship, - -	50 00		
		$3,361 54	
From Libraries, for Vol. XXVIII,	21 90		
" " " " XXIX, -	220 45		
" " " " XXX, -	89 10		
		331 45	
For *Publications*, Vols. VIII-XX, -	25 40		
" " " XXI-XXIX,	95 40		
		120 80	
For Reprints, Vol. XXIX, - -	17 10		
From Advertizers, Vol. XXVIII, -	150 00		
" " " XXIX, -	22 50		
Miscellaneus, - · · · -	49 57		
		239 17	
Interest, Current Funds, Charles River Trust Co., - - - -	35 31		
Interest, Permanent Fund, - -	487 06		
		522 37	
For Reprinted Vol. I, Old Series,	84 00		
" " " II, " "	92 00		
" " " III, " "	22 00		
" " " IV, " "	26 00		
		224 00	
			$4,799 33
			$5,995 93

EXPENDITURES

To Secretary, for Salary, - -	$ 400 00	
" " " Stationery and Printing, -	14 70	
" " " Postage and Expressage, '-	29 83	
		$ 444 53
To Secretary, Central Division, for Salary, . -	100 00	
Printing Program C. D. meeting,	58 25	
Stationery, Postage, etc, - -	28 60	
		186 85
To Tresurer, for Salary, - -	200 00	
" " " Stationery and Printing, -	23 79	
" " " Postage and Expressage, -	175 12	
" " " Clerical services,	45 00	
" " " Expenses, -	17 45	
		461 36
For Printing *Publications*,		
XXVIII, 4, - - - - -	629 10	
XXIX, 1, - - - - -	972 36	
XXIX, 2, - - - - -	545 46	
XXIX, 3, - - - - -	699 01	
XXIX, 4, - - - - -	625 93	
		3,471 86
For Reprinting Old Series, III, IV,	300 00	
For Printing and Mailing Inquiry on Spelling, - - - -	79 20	
For Printing and Mailing Program, 32d Annual Meeting, - - -	122 25	
Returnd Checks (later redeemd),	12 00	
Life Memberships, transferd to Permanent Fund, - - -	50 00	
Exchange, - - - - -	6 31	
		569 76
		$5,134 36
Balance on hand, Dec. 21, 1914, - - -		861 57
		$5,995 93

B. INVESTED FUNDS

Bright Fund (Eutaw Savings Bank,
    Baltimore),
    Principal, December 22, 1913, - $1,743 38
    Interest, April 1, 1914, -   -   60 90
                     ————— $1,804 28
von Jagemann Fund (Cambridge
    Savings Bank),
    Principal, December 22, 1913, - $1,204 26
    Interest, July 23, 1914, -   -   48 64
                     ————— $1,252 90
                             ————— $3,057 18

The President of the Association appointed the folloing committees:

(1) To audit the Tresurer's report: Professors Frederick Tupper, Gustav Gruener, and James Geddes, Jr.

(2) To nominate officers: Professors F. N. Scott, F. M. Warren, and Marian P. Whitney.

Professor W. A. Hervey introduced the folloing resolutions:

Whereas, at the annual meeting of the Modern Language Association of America in 1908 it was resolvd " that it is desirable to establish' a test in pronunciation and ability to understand the foren language, as part of the college entrance examination,' and

Whereas, the expediency of establishing such a test has since been affirmd by the New England Modern Language Association, by the Committee of Twelv of the National Education Association, and by the Association of Modern Language Teachers of the Middle States and Maryland, be it therefore

Resolvd: that the Modern Language Association of America reiterates its endorsement of a college entrance test in pronunciation and ability to understand the foren language, as set forth in the resolution adopted in 1908; and be it further

Resolvd: that the Secretary be requested to transmit a copy of these resolutions and of the resolution adopted in 1908 to the proper officer of each of the folloing organizations, to wit:

1. The Association of Colleges and Preparatory Schools of the Middle States and Maryland.

2. The Association of Colleges and Preparatory Schools of the Southern States.

3. The New England Association of Colleges and Preparatory Schools.

4 The North Central Association of Colleges and Preparatory Schools.

5. The College Entrance Examination Board.

The foregoing resolutions wer unanimusly adopted.
[Copies wer subsequently sent as requested.]

On motion of Professor W. A. Braun it was unanimusly

Resolvd: that the Executiv Council be authorized, whenever it may be practicable, to respond to the exprest desire of the *Neuphilologentag* by appointing without expense to the Association a delegate or delegates of the Association to attend the *Neuphilologentag* and convey to the scolars there assembled the fraternal greetings of the Association.

The reading of papers was then begun.

1. "The *Cursus* in English Prose." By Professor George Philip Krapp, of Columbia University.

[A discussion of the supposed imitation of the rithms of final clauses in classical and medieval Latin prose stile by English prose writers of the sixteenth century.—*Twenty minutes.*]

2. "The Phonetic Uniformity of German Linguistic History." By Professor Eduard Prokosch, of the University of Texas.

[Practically all changes in purely Germanic language development ar due to intensity of articulation and contrast stress. Caracteristic instances ar: vowel gradation, sound shift, weakening of final sillables, vowel mutation, standardization of quantity in M. H. G., development of compound tenses and moods.—*Twenty-five minutes.*]

During the reading of this and the folloing paper Professor J. S. P. Tatlock occupied the chair.

3. "Why is *Hyperion* Unfinisht?" By Professor Raymond D. Havens, of the University of Rochester.

[According to the publisher's announcement, *Hyperion* was abandond because its author was discouraged by the reception given to *Endymion*. This was denied by Keats and is disproved by his letters. From what he himself says about the matter, it has been generally concluded that the poem was given up because of its Miltonic inversions and diction, and it has been claimd that in the revised form, *The Fall of Hyperion*, most of these Miltonisms ar eliminated. This reason is inadequate and is *not* borne out by the changes made in the revision. What really hamperd Keats was the fundamentally Miltonic caracter of the poem, its austerity, impersonality, and aloofness, which wer foren to him. *The Fall of Hyperion* shoes an attempt to humanize the work, and return to the natural manner of its author, who, however, had several other purposes in view in revising it.—*Fifteen minutes.*]

4. "Recent French Criticism of English Literature." By Professor Edwin Mims, of Vanderbilt University.

[Increasing interest in English literature is manifested in France on the part of scolars and the reading public. Particular influence of certain English writers: George Eliot, Shelley, the Pre-Raphaelites, Newman, Kipling. Of American writers, Emerson and Walt Whitman hav drawn attention away from Poe and his folloers in France. —*Twenty minutes.*]

During the reading of this paper and to the end of the session Professor Camillo von Klenze occupied the chair.

5. "Chaucer's Burgesses." By Dr. Ernest P. Kuhl, of Dartmouth College.

[Chaucer deliberately selected from the varius gilds the five burgesses who participate in his pilgrimage. His choice was determind by political considerations. The allusions to "guildhall" and "aldermen" refer to municipal affairs and not to the gilds.—*Fifteen minutes.*]

6. "Milton's Revision of *The Ready and Easy Way to Establish a Free Commonwealth.*" By Dr. Evert Mordecai Clark, of the University of Texas.

[An original copy of Milton's boldest pamflet has been found. Tho no publisher dared risk even his initials on the title page, the treatise got into print in 1660. The principles governing Milton's revision. Milton fired the last gun, and that a doubly charged one, in defense of the Good Old Cause.—*Ten minutes.*]

At eight o'clock on the evening of Tuesday, December 29, members and gests of the Association assembled in Earl Hall. They wer welcomd to Columbia University by President Nicholas Murray Butler. Thereupon an address was deliverd by the President of the Association, Professor Felix E. Schelling, on " The American Professor."

After this address, members and gests of the Association wer receivd at the President's House by President and Mrs. Butler.

SECOND SESSION, WEDNESDAY, DECEMBER 30

The session began at 10 a. m.

The Committee on the Reproduction of Erly Texts had no report to make. On motion of the Secretary, it was

Voted: that the Committee be continued.

The Secretary red the folloing communication from the chairman of the Joint Committee on Grammatical Nomenclature:

The Report of the Joint Committee on Grammatical Nomenclature, acceded to by the National Council of Teachers of English in April, 1913, adopted by the National Education Association in July, and by the Modern Language Association and the American Philological Association in December, was reprinted at once in 1914, and has been sent out to a very large number of people who have written to ask for it. Many letters have also been received by the Committee, asking for a clearer statement of its meaning here and there in the explanatory part (Part II) or showing that there was need of such a statement. Such letters continue to come in. Several members of the Committee, as Mr. Hubbard, Mr. Rounds, and the Chairman, have also gone through the entire pamphlet in class-room work, for the purpose of seeing where greater precision or fuller explanation was necessary.

The Nomenclature itself (Part I), being the vital part of the matter adopted by the four associations, is of course, not to be changed at any point until these same associations shall commit the entire subject again to the present or some future committee for a fresh consideration, in view of the criticism which is earnestly asked for and carefully preserved when sent. It is probably best in any case that there should be no change now for several years.

The final form of the present report, accordingly, will consist of Part I as it now stands, Part II with such improvements of explanation as the Committee can make, a brief history of the movement, and probably an index. The plan was to leave the months of January to June in 1914 for the work of criticism, etc., and to prepare the final form in the autumn months. Various causes have kept the latter part of the plan from being carried out. It is believed that this can be done in the early months of 1915. The report will then be put on public sale.

It is desirable that the Committee be continued, both for this final work, and to answer the many further inquiries or suggestions that will come, as well as communications, such as have already been received, from foreign committees upon the same problems. The Modern Language Association is therefore requested to vote to continue its representation upon the Joint Committee. Corresponding action has already been taken by the National Education Association, and will be asked of the American Philological Association.

On motion of the Secretary it was unanimusly

Voted: That the representation of the Modern Language Association upon the Joint Committee on Grammatical Nomenclature be continued.

The reading of papers was then resumed.

7. " The Temptation in *Paradise Regained.*" By Dr. Allan H. Gilbert, of Cornell University.

[To interpret *Paradise Regained*, one must grasp its structure. Milton carefully folloed the Gospel accounts of the Temptation.

Biblical commentaries make his meaning clearer. The banquet scene (II, 336-405), often misunderstood, belongs to the second, not the first, temptation. In the third temptation, also, Milton did not, as some think, alter the Gospel facts, but brought out of them the effect he desired.—*Twenty minutes.*]

8. "A Proposed Classification of the Periods in the Development of the American Drama." By Professor Arthur Hobson Quinn, of the University of Pennsylvania.

[(1) From the production of *The Prince of Parthia* in 1767 to the closing of the theaters in 1774; (2) A period of comparativ inaction from 1774 to 1787; (3) From 1787 to 1829, divided into:—(a) the period of tentativ effort, under the influence of German and French models, from the production of *The Contrast*, 1787, until the closing of Dunlap's first period of managership in 1805; (b) the period of development from 1805 to 1829, largely under foren influence, English and Continental;—(4) The first creativ period, partly under the influence of Edwin Forrest, from the production of *Metamora* in 1829 to that of *Francesca da Rimini* in 1855; (5) A transition period from 1855 to the close of the Civil War; (6) The second creativ period, begining after the war with the work of Augustin Daly and Bronson Howard, and continuing to the close of the nineteenth century; (7) The contemporary drama, including the revival of the literary drama and the growth of the drama of individualism. —*Twenty minutes.*]

This paper was discust by Professor Brander Matthews.

9. "*Hamlet* without Hamlet." By Professor Brander Matthews, of Columbia University.

[A consideration of the plays in which the chief caracter never appears.—*Twenty minutes.*]

10. "The Spirit of Shakespeare's *Troilus and Cressida.*" By Professor John S. P. Tatlock, of the University of Michigan.

[An examination of other Elizabethan versions of the Troy story modifies the impression of bitterness which Shakespeare's *Troilus* makes on a modern, and shoes that the play was probably less original than it has been considerd.—*Twenty-five minutes.*]

11. "The Dream of the Golden Age: A Study of the Influence of the Mystery on the Theory and the Art of Romanticism." By Dr. Louise Mallinckrodt Kueffner, of Vassar College.

[Friedrich Schlegel's recognition of the differences between ancient and modern art, and his later realization of their identity at their starting point in the mistery. The naturalistic origins of the mistery; the themes of the mistery and the Dream of the Golden Age; medieval, romantic, and neo-romantic misticism. Fr. Schlegel's definition of romantic poetry as *eine progressive Universalpoesie.—Twenty-five minutes.*]

At one o'clock on Wednesday, December 30, members and gests of the Association wer entertaind at luncheon at the University Commons.

At two o'clock in the afternoon of Wednesday, December 30, there was a meeting of the CONCORDANCE SOCIETY.

THIRD SESSION, WEDNESDAY, DECEMBER 30

The session began at 2.50 p. m.

The reading of papers was continued.

12. "Early Influence of La Fontaine on English Fable Writers." By Professor M. Ellwood Smith, of Syracuse University.

[Causes for this revival: La Fontaine late. Addison's statement of La Fontaine's popularity in England substantiated; erly translations from La Fontaine into English verse (John Dennis, 1693, Mandeville, Swift, and the Miscellany Writers). Relation of La Fontaine to English versifiers thru Ramsay and Gay.—*Twenty minutes.*]

13. "Dante's 'Second Love.'" By Professor Jefferson B. Fletcher, of Columbia University.

[In the *Vita Nuova*, Dante condemns as wicked his desire of the *donna pietosa*, substitute on erth for Beatrice in heven. In the

Convivio he justifies this second love as realization of Christian Fi-losofy in the activ life, *l'amoroso uso della sapienza,* by which ac-quiring needful merit he may win first the perfection of human nature, *gentilezza,* and then by grace be exalted above that to the perfection of the angelical nature, and so possess *la viva Beatrice beata,* the beatific vision—here by anticipation in rapture, hereafter in eternal fruition. Thus rightly and needfully orderd to God, his second love is shown to be *nobilissima; non passione, ma virtù sì è stata la movente cagione.* Otherwise, as inordinate desire, pride, it wud be the sin of sins. The simbolic *donna gentile* of the *Convivio* foreshadoes then not Vergil, human perfection, *gentilezza,* outside the faith, but Matilda, *gentilezza* within the faith, yet subordinate as of the activ life to Beatrice, *somma beatitudine* or angelical per-fection of the contemplativ life. As *apologia pro vita sua,* Dante's argument wud at once justify his worldly activities as right and needful, and yet deplore an inordinate absorption in them that for a time blinded him to Beatrice, *la somma beatitudine.* From the enticement of the *donna gentile* so in effect like St. Paul's *angelus Satanae,* Dante was providentially saved by the chastening sorroes of exile. Beatrice's rebuke was to him what God's was to St. Paul: *Sufficit tibi gratia mea; nam virtus in infirmitate perficitur.—Thirty minutes.*]

14. "Le renouvellement de la pensée française." By Professor Albert Schinz, of Smith College.

[Le tourment religieux dans la littérature des dernières années: attitude anti-rationaliste, spiritualiste, et catholique-orthodoxe: dans le roman (Juliette Adam, Barès, Frères Tharaud, Binet-Valmer, etc.), dans le lyrisme (Ch. Péguy, Francis Jammes, etc.), au théâtre (Curel, Brieux, Claudel, etc.), et jusque dans la critique.—*Twenty-five minutes.*]

15. "Theodor Fontane und England." By Dr. Fried-rich Schoenemann, of Harvard University.

[Deutsche Ansichten über England im 18. und 19. Jahrhundert. Theodor Fontane als Persönlichkeit. Fontanes persönliche Erleb-nisse und Studien in England. Schriften darüber. Beschäftigung mit englischer Literatur: Shakespeare, Scott, Dickens. Uebersetz-zungen. Fontanes Gesamtauffassung Englands.—*Twenty minutes.*]

16. "The *Dunciad* of 1729." By Professor Reginald Harvey Griffith, of the University of Texas.

[Contemporary periodicals and pamflets illumin several dark points in the history of the second year of the *Dunciad.* Of varieties (frequently miscald " editions ") the present paper noted sixteen, as opposed to the nine described or alluded to in W. J. Thomas's bibliografy. Dates of issue for many of them wer here first establisht. The " Dob " edition was not the second, as has long been argued. The nominal publisher " Dod " was the widow Dodd. " Dob " was pretty surely the pirate publisher Curll. Professor Lounsbury's equation " Dob " = Gilliver is highly improbable. The " mithical " lawsuit was not so certainly mithical.—*Twenty-eight minutes.*]

At the close of this session there was a meeting of the AMERICAN DIALECT SOCIETY.

From four to seven o'clock in the afternoon of Wednesday, December 30, ladies and gentlemen who wer members of the Association wer admitted to the Grolier Club.

At half after eight o'clock on the evening of Wednesday, December 30, the ladies in attendance wer receivd by Dean Virginia C. Gildersleeve, of Barnard College, at Brooks Hall.

At nine o'clock on the evening of Wednesday, December 30, the gentlemen in attendance wer entertaind at a smoker in the University Commons. An address was made by Professor Calvin Thomas.

FOURTH SESSION, THURSDAY, DECEMBER 31

The session began at 10.13 a. m.

On behalf of the Committee on the Collegiate Training of Teachers of Modern Foren Languages, the Secretary reported that untoward circumstances had prevented the committee from completing its work, and moved that the committee be continued. This motion was unanimusly carried.

Professor John L. Lowes bespoke interest on the part of the Association in the *Modern Language Review* and other European scientific periodicals, and his appeal was warmly receivd.

On motion of Mrs. Camillo von Klenze, it was unanimusly

Resolvd: That arrangements be made by the Entertainment Committee of the Modern Language Association at all future meetings for an informal meeting of the women members of the Association, to take place simultaneusly with the men's smoker, the time and place of this meeting to be announst in the official program. The women of the Association appreciate the curtesy with which they hav been entertaind heretofore, but they feel the need of an opportunity for meeting their fellow-workers and for discussing questions of professional interest.

The Auditing Committee reporting thru Professor Frederick Tupper that the Tresurer's accounts wer found correct, it was unanimusly

Voted: That the Tresurer's report be accepted.

On behalf of the Nominating Committee Professor F. N. Scott presented the folloing nominations:

President: Jefferson B. Fletcher, Columbia University.
First Vice-President: Oliver F. Emerson, Western Reserve University.
Second Vice-President: Bert J. Vos, Indiana University.
Third Vice-President: Mary V. Young, Mount Holyoke College.

On motion, the Secretary was instructed to cast one ballot for the persons nominated, and they wer declared unanimusly elected to their several offices for the year 1915.

For Honorary Membership in the Association the Executiv Council nominated:

Willy Bang, University of Louvain.
Ferdinand Brunot, University of Paris.
Alfred Jeanroy, University of Paris.

On motion of Professor L. F. Mott, the nominees wer unanimusly elected Honorary Members.

On motion of Professor H. E. Greene, the folloing resolution was adopted by a rising vote:

> *Resolvd:* That the members of the Modern Language Association of America at the close of their thirty-second Annual Meeting express their harty thanks to the President and Trustees of Columbia University for their hospitable entertainment within the walls of the university bildings; to President and Mrs. Butler, to Dean Gildersleeve, to the Faculty Club, and to the President and members of the Grolier Club, for their gracius hospitality; to Professor Calvin Thomas for his wise and witty " Smoke Talk," and to Professor Arthur Remy for his memorable illustrations of medieval legend and literature; and last, but by no means least, to the Local Committee for their thoughtful provision for the comfort of their gests, and for the many curtesies, both general and personal, that hav made this meeting one of great enjoyment and profit to all who hav had the good fortune to be present.

[The thanks of the Association wer subsequently exprest to all of the persons and organizations mentiond.]

The reading of papers was then resumed.

17. " The Psychological Basis of the Variant Treatment of Germanic -iji- in Gothic suffixes." By Professor Robert James Kellogg, of James Millikin University.

> [Germanic -(i)ji- goes back to Indo-European -(e)ie-. The Gothic gradation -ji- : -ei- shoes a Germanic double leveling of the secondary suffixal accent (-ijí- or -íjī-) according to fonetic forms of the preceding root. This in turn presupposes acute accentuation of light or singly long root sillables, and a circumflexing of hevy root sillables

which groups them accentually with polysillabic roots. Hence the grouping of roots and stems into two classes and the variant secondary accent of suffixes. Application of this explanation to problems of Germanic accent and its shifting, of West Germanic gemination, of Germanic and West Germanic shifting of consonants, and 'to the interpretation of purely fonetic analogy.—*Twenty-five minutes*.]

18. "Saint Brandan and the Sea-God Bran." By Professor Arthur C. L. Brown, of Northwestern University.

[Saint Brandan inherited marine adventures from the old Celtic god. Transfer of incident, which was fosterd by a similarity of name, continued til the saint became a mere Christianization of Bran. Associated with Bran wer *Brigit* and *Manannán* (Welsh, *Mana-wyδan*).—*Twenty-five minutes*.]

19. "The Vogue of Literary Theories in the German Renaissance." By Dr. Joseph E. Gillet, of the University of Wisconsin.

[This paper reviewd the opinions exprest for or against the "Classical Rules" by German authors, mostly dramatists, from 1500 to 1730. Gottsched's *Critische Dichtkunst* was estimated in relation to the data thus obtaind. Incidentally the fortunes of Aristotle, Scaliger, and Opitz in Germany wer described and used as illustrations in point.—*Twenty minutes*.]

During the reading of this paper, and to the end of the session, Professor B. P. Bourland occupied the chair.

20. "The Influence of the Popular Ballad on Sir Walter Scott." By Professor Charles Wharton Stork, of the University of Pennsylvania.

[With two or three notable exceptions, Scott faild in his attempts to imitate the old ballad, for two reasons: (1) the influence of the modern German ballad led him in the direction of artificiality, and (2) however "romantic" we may think him, he was, at least as to stile, a son of the eighteenth century. The real influence of the ballad on Scott was, partly as with Coleridge, in poetic atmosfere. Lerning ballads by hart as a boy, collecting them and living in their midst as a man, he never lost the interest in them that descended to him from his moss-trooping ancestors.—*Twenty-five minutes.*]

This paper was discust by Professors O. F. Emerson and E. E. Hale.

21. "Some of Longfellow's Sources for the Second Part of *Evangeline*." By Dr. Murray Gardner Hill, of Western Reserve University.

[In writing the second part of *Evangeline*, Longfellow used Seals-field's *Life in the New World*, Fremont's *Expedition to the Rocky Mountains*, and Kip's *Early Jesuit Missions* as sources for his descriptions of the lower Mississippi, the prairies, and the Black Robe Missions.—*Twenty minutes.*]

This paper was discust by Professor B. J. Rees.

At one o'clock on Thursday, December 31, the members and gests of the Association wer entertaind at luncheon at the University Commons.

FIFTH SESSION, THURSDAY, DECEMBER 31

The session began at 2.30 p. m., Professor B. P. Bourland in the chair. The reading of papers was continued.

22. "Alexander the Great's Celestial Journey." By Mr. Roger S. Loomis, of the University of Illinois.

[I. The episode in Middle English. II. The episode in Erly Forms of the Alexander Legend. III. The origin of the similar exploits attributed to Oriental heroes. IV. Illustrations of the episode in medieval art. V. Tipological interpretation of the episode. —*Twenty minutes.*]

23. "Graf von Loeben and the Legend of *Lorelei*." By Dr. Allen Wilson Porterfield, of Barnard College, Columbia University.

[Since the publication of Brentano's *Godwi* (1801-02), about sixty-five *Loreleidichtungen* hav been written in German. Many investi-

10

gators hav given the prolific but now little known Loeben much credit
for his part in the development of the legend, contending that he
influenst Heine. There is no proof that Heine knew Loehen's ballad
in 1823, while there is positiv evidence that he derived his initial
inspiration from A. W. Schreiber's *Handbuch* (1818).—*Twenty minutes.*]

During the reading of this paper, and to the end of the
session, Professor F. E. Schelling occupied the chair.

24. "Tricks of Elizabethan Showmen." By Professor Thornton Shirley Graves, of Trinity College, North
Carolina.

[Impositions practist upon the public by Elizabethan rogues mas-
querading as licenst players, methods of advertizing employd by
regular actors, tricks of sharpers to attract the curius to theatrical
swindles of one sort or another.—*Twenty minutes.*]

25. "The Sources of Jonson's *The Staple of News.*"
By Professor Arthur B. Stonex, of Trinity College, Connecticut.

[Besides the *Plutus* of Aristophanes, the *Timon* of Lucian, and
certain other works, classical and English, which hav been pointed
out, Jonson seems to hav used a late English morality play, *The
Contention between Liberality and Prodigality.* The simultaneus use
of classical satire and nativ morality drama is not improbable, because the two ar similar in both motiv and method.—*Fifteen minutes.*]

26. "The Virtue of Friendship in the *Faerie Queene.*"
By Professor John Erskine, of Columbia University.

[Frendship not one of Aristotle's virtues, nor usually considerd
a virtue by ancient and medieval filosofers. The difference between
frendship as a moral virtue and frendship as a social relation involving other virtues, such as loyalty. Frendship as a social relation the classical ideal, reinforst by the institution of chivalry.
The difficulty of defining frendship as a moral virtue, and of so
representing it in an allegory. The discussions of frendship accessible to Spenser. Possible sources of his theory of frendship.—
Twenty-five minutes.]

At 4.48 p. m. the Association adjurnd.

PAPERS RED BY TITLE

The folloing papers, presented to the Association, wer red by title only:

27. "Notes on the *Speculum Vitae*." By Miss Hope Emily Allen.

[An investigation of the MSS. of the *Speculum Vitae* has not confirmd the authorship of Nassington and Waldby or the connection with the *Prick of Conscience* discust in my article on the *Authorship of the 'Prick of Conscience.'* An English prose version has been discoverd and a Latin source. A list of MSS. is appended.]

28. "The 'Character' in Restoration Comedy." By Professor Edward C. Baldwin, of the University of Illinois.

[The Restoration comedy of manners contains many "caracters." These differ, however, from the "caracter" as exemplified in the work of Overbury and the writers of the older English comedy, being more akin to the French *portrait* as written by La Bruyère and later imitated by Addison. The model for this exotic form of the "caracter" was furnisht by Molière. His art was, in turn, influenst by that of the *précieuses*, who, after serving an apprenticeship in the *salons*, had introduced the *portrait* into fiction.]

29. "The American Indian in German Poetry." By Dr. Preston A. Barba, of Indiana University.

[Chateaubriand's *Atala* and *René* in Germany. The Indian as the embodiment of the Rousseauian doctrin in poems of Schiller, Halem, Schubart, and Seume. Upon the advent of Cooper the tragic fate of the redman is a frequent theme, as in certain poems of Chamisso and Lenau. The poets among the *Achtundvierziger* and subsequent German-American poets hav often exploited Indian lore. In spite of the realistic portrayals of the Indian in the novels of Gerstäcker, Strubberg, and Möllhausen, he has in poetry remaind an essentially romantic figure.]

30. "Christian Felix Weisse's Place Among German Educators of the Eighteenth Century." By Professor Wilhelm Braun, of Barnard College.

[Tho not even mentiond by name in Rein's *Handbuch der Pädagogik* or in Munroe's *Encyclopedia of Education*, Weisse was deemd worthy to hav his portrait hung in the Education Bilding of the recent Leipzig International Exhibition of Books and Grafic Arts beside that of Basedow, Salzmann, and Pestalozzi. But practically nothing has been written about Weisse's contribution to the new pedagogy of the 18th century, altho he publisht a Primer which was widely used for fifty years, and supplied Germany with a great bulk of educational literature for children which made his name a household word thruout the land. The present paper aims to give a succinct account of Weisse's pedagogical work, without attempting at this time any final valuation of it.]

31. "Conversations as a French Literay *Genre* during the Seventeenth Century." By Professor Isabelle Bronk, of Swarthmore College.

[A list and a consideration of the extremely numerus *Conversations*, *Entretiens*, and *Dialogues* publisht in France, from the time of the *Entretiens de M. Du Mas aveo M. de Balzac* (1656) until the end of the century—*Conversations sur l'excellence du beau sexe* (1699).]

32. "Two New Texts of the *Evangelie*." By Miss Gertrude H. Campbell, of Bryn Mawr College.

[A stanzaic story of the gospels in English is printed under the title *Evangelie* in the EETS edition of *Minor poems from the Vernon MS*. Two new texts ar here produced; one the complete poem, found in a MS. fifty years younger than the Vernon MS., the other a fragment of great linguistic interest, in the East Midland dialect, dated about 1310. Notes on the text, remarks on the MSS. and their relations, and studies in the sources of the material accompany the texts.]

33. "Sources of the *Comedia Tibalda* of Perálvarez de Ayllón." By Professor J. P. Wickersham Crawford, of the University of Pennsylvania.

[The *Comedia Tibalda* (1553) of Perálvarez de Ayllón is chiefly devoted to the discussion of two themes frequently treated in sixteenth-century Spanish literature, the remedies against love and the relativ virtues and imperfections of women. For the first of these, he folloes closely Ovid's *Remedia Amoris;* for the second, he translates almost literally from Rodriguez de la Cámara's *Triunfo de las doñas*. A study of the sources servs to correct a number of mistakes in the text recently publisht in the *Bibliotheca Hispanica*.]

34. "The Uses of the Particles of Comparison in German." By Professor Edward Elias, of Hope College.

[After brief consideration of the uses of the particles of compari-

son in O. H. G. and M. H. G., the paper traces the uses from Erly
N. H. G. to the present day. Special attention is given to Lessing,
Goethe, Schiller, Jakob Grimm, Heine, and Nietzsche.]

35. "*The Merchant Prince of Cornville* by Samuel Gross and
Rostand's *Cyrano de Bergerac*." By Dr. Walther Fischer, of the
University of Pennsylvania.

[The purpose of the paper is to sho that in spite of the wel-known
court decision it is impossible, from a literary point of view, to
charge Rostand with plagiarism from Gross.]

36. "The British Isles in Norse Saga." By Professor Christabel
F. Fiske, of Vassar College.

[The Norse sagas reflect historical conditions and events in the
British Iles, and with more or less romantic modification of actualities present the Iles as an object of conquest, a place of refuge, a
rich opportunity for pillage or for trade, the home of future brides,
possible allies, and servisable recruits, and the source of Christian
influences.]

37. "The *Dunciad* of 1728." By Professor R. H. Griffith, of the
University of Texas.

[No other English poem, it is thought, presents so elaborate a bibliografical puzzle as Pope's *Dunciad*. This paper is limited to events
of 1728, and the history of this first year as previously told is corrected and amplified. The account concerns chiefly: the preparation
of the satire for the public, and of the public to receiv it; the
number and dates of editions; the advertizing campain for and
against it; and the publishers and printers.]

38. "Civilization and Literature." By Professor A. L. Guérard,
of the Rice Institute.

[French universities now recognize a three-fold division in the
study of modern languages: linguistics, literature, civilization. In
Germany, Dr. Ernst Sieper, a. o. Professor der englischen Philologie
an der Universität München, is editing a series of monografs, *Die
Kultur des modernen England*. In this cuntry, several universities
hav professorships of the history of German culture. The present
paper, which was intended as a preface to the author's *French Civilization in the Nineteenth Century*, is a plea for a similar development of the study of French culture.]

39. "Eustorg de Beaulieu and the Protestant Song-Books of the
Sixteenth Century." By Dr. Helen Josephine Harvitt.

[I. A short biografical sketch of Eustorg de Beaulieu. II. Reformation propaganda thru the medium of songs. General aspect of the movement. III. Beaulieu's method of adapting religius songs to popular tunes and words. IV. A catalog of the songs by Eustorg de Beaulieu, with their popular prototipes (opening lines only) and references to the song-books in which the original and the prototipe may be found. V. A bibliografical list of the collections of songs mentiond in the paper.]

40. "Henry Fielding's Word-Usage and Signatures in his *Covent-Garden Journal*." By Dr. Gerard E. Jensen, of Cornell University.

[This essay endevors to determin what signatures in this *Journal* ar Fielding's, and how far they may be taken as evidence of his authorship. It examins also Keightley's word-test for the author's stile and tries to sho that it is in general reliable. The writer finds that internal evidence usually supports his other tests. After having explaind the rejection of several papers, he suggests the names of their writers.]

41. "Nature and Authorship of the Anonymous *King Leir*." By Professor Robert Adger Law, of the University of Texas.

[J. J. Munro has recently suggested a common authorship for *The Troublesome Reign* and *King Leir*. Analisis of the two plays shoes that while *The Troublesome Reign* is a tipical cronicle history, the *Leir* is really a melodrama, possessing structural unity, a few mildly poetic lines, and certain distinct peculiarities of stile. All these point in one direction for the authorship.]

42. "The *Finnsburg Fragment* and the Finn-Episode in *Beowulf*." By Professor William W. Lawrence, of Columbia University.

[A study of the interpretation of the text and of the significance of the tale as a whole in its relation to *Beowulf* and to Germanic heroic story.]

43. "Leonid Andreev." By Professor Clarence L. Meader, of the University of Michigan.

[The place of Andreev among contemporary Russian writers, and his attitude toward Russian social and political questions. The development of his ideas of individualism and self-realization; his relation to Nietzsche, to Tolstoi, and to the simbolic drama of western Europe.]

44. "The Original of *The Nonjuror*." By Dr. Dudley H. Miles, of the Evander Childs High School, New York City.

[In spite of the unanimus opinion that Cibber based his play, *The Nonjuror*, directly on Molière's *Tartuffe* (1669), a critical comparison with Molière and with Medbourne's *Tartuffe* (1670), in management of the action, handling of caracter, and in frasing of ideas common to the three pieces, shoes that Cibber workt from the erlier English translation and adaptation.]

45. "The Development of Goethe's Theory of the *Novelle*." By Professor McBurney Mitchell, of Brown University.

[The first attempt at a theory of the *Novelle* in Germany is usually dated from the pioneer work of the brothers Schlegel (1798-1804). This was folloed by a slight contribution from Wieland (1805), and after a considerable interval by Goethe's famus epigrammatic definition of 1827; "Was ist die Novelle anders als eine sich ereignete, unerhörte Begebenheit?" As a matter of fact, this definition is only the quintessential result of a long investigation which can be traced definitly as far back as the *Unterhaltungen deutscher Ausgewanderten* (1795), where the later epigram is already stated in substance, thus antedating even the first attempts of the Schlegels at a definition. Only by tracing the growth of this conception in Goethe's mind between 1795 and 1827, can one arrive at a satisfactory elucidation of the definition in its final form. Incidentally, A. W. Schlegel and Wieland appear to have borroed from Goethe.]

46. "The Position of Group C in the *Canterbury Tales*." By Professor Samuel Moore, of the University of Wisconsin.

[The position which Furnivall assignd to Group C of the *Canterbury Tales*—between B and D—is an entirely arbitrary one; no internal evidence lends it probabilty, and no MS. is known to exist in which C either folloes B² or precedes D. In fact, the MS. evidence makes it quite clear that C ought to precede B². The MSS. also sho that there ar only three possible positions for CB²: (1) between B¹ and D; (2) between F and G; (3) between G and H. The internal evidence shoes that of these three positions the best is certainly between B¹ and D. The arrangement which best expresses Chaucer's intentions is A B¹ C B² D E F G H I.]

47. "The Significance of Poetry." By Dr. Harvey W. Peck, of the University of Texas.

[A view of the function of poetry as a representativ of the fine arts, especially in its relation to science and to practical activity. The subject matter of poetry may be complex or of varied nature. The test of poetry is poetic form. This is reducible ultimately to rithm. Rithm is generally regarded as the natural mode of expressing coherent emotion. Emotion is considerd the source of values, the basis of judgments of worth. The function of poetry, then, is, abstractedly stated, the preservation or creation of values. Conclusion emphasizing the social significance of poetry, and the necessity of poetry or a kindred art as a supplement to science and to industrial activity.]

48. "Poetic Thinking." By Professor Richard Rice, Jr., of Indiana University.

[The paper attempts to define and illustrate the folloing questions: (1) In relation to filosofic and scientific thought what is poetic thought?—Illustrated by the treatment of a single topic in three tipical courses of the college curriculum. (2) What kind of truth does the poetic mind choose to believ in?—Illustrated by our memory of the past and our discovery of the future. (3) How does poetry combine with the other modes of thought to help one solv the important problems of life?—Illustrated by the most important of all problems.]

49. "The Rationale of Punctuation." By Miss Constance Mayfield Rourke, of Vassar College.

[The rules for punctuation do not accord with the practis of careful writers; they offer a code rather than a comprehensiv logic, the retorics fail to agree. The function of punctuation can only be defined in terms of effect. By offering simbols different in kind from those of the printed or written word, punctuation arrests attention: its primary effect is that of emfasis. Each point not only produces stress, but by its form colors language with purpose. The effect of each point may be simply defined. This functional logic interprets both the tendencies exprest by the rules and the variations of literature. Upon the basis of this logic the amateur may be taught to punctuate according to the relativ values of his expression. His punctution will become organic, a direct and natural outgrowth from his expression.]

50. "The Theophilus Legend in Dramatic Form: A Suggested Antecedent of the Bond Story in *The Merchant of Venice*." By Miss Helen Sandison, of Vassar College.

[Dramatic and semi-dramatic versions present: (1) the "bond story" of a Christian trapt by the devil, with whom a Jew is allied and almost merged; (2) the trial scene in essentials, Mercy (i. e. Mary) overcoming Justis; (3) certain minor parallels. If not this particular miracle, one similar, similarly developing into rationalized drama, conceivably contributed to the final evolution of Shakespeare's story.]

51. "Allusions in Sixteenth-Century Dramatists (including Shakespeare) to the Puritans' 'Pensive Care for the Well Bestowal of Time.'" By Professor Morris P. Tilley, of the University of Michigan.

[The paper seeks to sho two things; the Puritans' opinion of the value of time, and the dramatists' ridicule of that opinion. Not all Puritans wer equally severe in their denunciation of recreation. But severe Puritanical denunciations cald forth violent protests from the dramatists, who for satirical purposes introduced into their plays the extreme Puritans' views with regard both to the value of time and to the restrictions of time, place, and persons placed upon amusements. Shakespeare joind in the ridicule of views of this sort.]

52. "Some Phases of the Elizabethan Epigram." By Professor Samuel Marion Tucker, of the Brooklyn Polytechnic Institute.

[However difficult to classify, the Elizabethan Epigram was the resultant of two distinct influences: the English epigrams of John Heywood, which wer general, didactic, and impersonal, and the Latin epigrams of Martial, which wer particular and personal, sometimes satirical, sometimes eulogistic, but almost always occasional. These two influences appear chiefly in the epigrams of Sir John Harrington, but they ar also to be found in the work of Davies, Bastard, Weaver, and a score of other epigrammatists of the Elizabethan and the Jacobean age.]

53. "Chaucer and the Woman Question." By Professor Frederick Tupper, of the University of Vermont.

[This article considers the large det of *The Canterbury Tales* to a contemporary tradition dominant in satires, sermons, "gospels," *exempla*, fabliaux, goliardic poems, love-disputes, etc. Chaucer's deliberate treatment of the woman question includes not only varied discussion of wives' counsels and obedience in the so-cald "Marriage Group" (which must be enlarged) and of "gentilesse" in tales of courtly love, but also ample illustrations of celibacy, jelusy, and the conventional contrast between good and bad women. The Wife of Bath is the storm-center of all fases of this *querelle des femmes*, to which class satire furnishes a background and popular theology a relief.]

54. "Shakspere's Present Indicative Singular Predicates with Plural Subjects." By Professor Frederick Tupper, of the University of Vermont. •

[A careful scrutiny of the many passages in the Shakspere Quartos and Folios containing a plural subject of one member folloed by a singular predicate seems to sho that, in the poet's use, such a subject is always impersonal. The few seeming exceptions are demonstrably printer's errors. Noteworthy is the close resemblance between Shakspere's construction (misinterpreted by all grammarians) and the Greek idiom of the subject in the neuter-form of the plural with the verb in the singular.]

55. "The Heroine of the *Dunciad.*" By Mr. George F. Whicher, of the University of Illinois.

[The public-spirited reason profest by Pope for his coarse attack on Mrs. Eliza Haywood was as usual the stalking-horse for his personal animus. He owed the author of *The Court of Carimania* a grudge for her slander of his frend, Henrietta Howard, and for a scandalus reference to himself in *The Court of Lilliput*, which he chose to attribute to her. Tho the inclusion of a novel by Mrs. Haywood in Curll's *Female Dunciad* was in no way retaliatory, Savage again took occasion to abuse the novelist in *An Author to be Let.* The effect of these attacks was not unfelt by Mrs. Haywood. The popularity of her writings declined, she produced almost nothing for a decade, and her name did not appear in connection with her later successful work.]

56. "The Influence of the Minnesong on the Early Italian *Canzone.*" By Professor Ernest Hatch Wilkins, of the University of Chicago.

[The Provençal lyric is the main, but not the only, general source of the erly Italian lyric. The poets of the court of Frederick II had ample opportunity to become acquainted with the work of the Minnesingers. The *canzone* resembles the *Minnelied* rather than the *canso* in several important respects of metrical technique: 1) in its unvarying tripartition; 2) in its preference for the *piede* of three lines; 3) in its rejection of the favorit Provençal initial rime-scheme ARBA; 4) in its preference for the initial rime-scheme ABCABC; 5) in its use of the initial rime-scheme ABCDABCD; 6) in its preference for the metabolic rather than the isometric stanza; 7) in its insistence on originality in stanza structure; 8) in its rejection of the *tornada.*]

57. "Thomson's *Seasons* in France." By Dr. Ernest Hunter Wright, of Columbia University.

[A chapter in the history of the re-awakening of nature poetry in the last half of the eighteenth century, treating especially the more direct imitators of Thomson—Bernis, Saint-Lambert, Léonard, Roucher, Lemierre, Delille, and others.]

MEETING OF THE CENTRAL DIVISION

The twentieth annual meeting of the CENTRAL DIVISION of the MODERN LANGUAGE ASSOCIATION OF AMERICA was held at Minneapolis, Minnesota, under the auspices of the University of Minnesota, December 29, 30, and 31, 1914. All the sessions except that of the first evening were held at the Minnesota Union on the University Campus. Professor Julius Goebel, Chairman of the Central Division, presided.

FIRST SESSION, TUESDAY AFTERNOON, DECEMBER 29

The Central Division met at 2.40 p. m.

The Chairman stated that he would announce the committees on Wednesday morning.

On motion of Professor T. A. Jenkins it was

Voted: That sometime during the meeting the question of support of the modern language journals be discust.

It was later arranged to have this question discust Wednesday forenoon.

The reading of papers was then begun.

1. "New Light on Some· of Cowper's Friendships." By Professor Madison C. Bates, of the South Dakota State College of Agriculture and Mechanic Arts.

[An interpretation of an unpublisht manuscript by Hayley. The manuscript is valuable chiefly for the new light it throws on Cowper's friendship with his first two biographers Hayley and Greatheed, with his cousins Theodora and Harriet, and with Mrs. Unwin. Certain of the points discust have long been matters of controversy.— *Fifteen minutes.*]

2. " A Note on the Relation of Chateaubriand to Rousseau." By Professor Barry Cerf, of the University of Wisconsin.

[The aim was to show that *Atala* and *René* were written at a time when Chateaubriand was a Rousseauist in his attitude toward religion, nature, and man, and that it is not necessary to suppose they were alterd at the time of their incorporation in the *Génie du Christianisme.—Ten minutes.*]

This paper was discust by Professor Colbert Searles.

3. " St. Anne's Day ' Sights ' at Lincoln." By Professor Hardin Craig, of the University of Minnesota.

[An attempt to ascertain the nature of the St. Anne's Day procession at Lincoln and its relationship to the mystery plays acted in the city, based upon a newly discoverd account-book of the Cordwainers' Company, the accounts of the Cathedral Chapter (now for the first time red), and upon other Lincoln documents more or less well-known. The paper began with a summary of the general question of the relationship between processions and plays.—*Fifteen minutes.*]

4. " The Mortimer Action in Schiller's *Maria Stuart.*" By Professor Carl Schlenker, of the University of Minnesota.

[Schiller has not clearly indicated how Maria Stuart is made to accept her fate with free moral conviction of its justness. Can the Mortimer episode be one device to bring this about?—*Fifteen minutes.*]

This paper was discust ·by Professors J. T. Hatfield and E. C. Roedder.

5. " British and American Pronunciation: Retrospect and Prospect." By Professor Louise Pound, of the University of Nebraska.

[Increast present-day interest in living oral speech. Attempts to record "standard" pronunciation and regional variations. The ideal of conscious supervision in speech. Present status of American pronunciation in relation to British. Duality of standard. Sketch of existing divergencies and salient tendencies. Relation to the movement for spelling reform. Is further deviation inevitable?— *Fifteen minutes.*]

This paper was discust by Professors T. A. Jenkins, M. Callaway, Jr., and Julius Goebel.

6. "Flaubert's *Education sentimentale* (version of 1845)." By Dr. A. Coleman, of the University of Chicago.

[This first novel of Flaubert, romantic in essence, sets forth his doctrin of impassibility. It reflects the literary theories of Balzac and Hugo and presents the formula on which his greatest works were constructed.—*Ten minutes.*]

7. "Some Considerations Bearing on the Fundamental Basis in Human Nature of the Doctrines of Good Use." By Professor Raphael Dorman O'Leary, of the University of Kansas.

[There are two main attitudes which men take, and perhaps have always taken, with reference to linguistic usage. These attitudes we may distinguish as that of the legalist and that of the liberal. The relation of these two attitudes to each other affords a striking illustration of the working in social phenomena of what we may call the principle of contrariness.—*Fifteen minutes.*]

This paper was discust by Professor Julius Goebel.

SECOND SESSION, TUESDAY EVENING, DECEMBER 29

This evening session was held at the home of President George E. Vincent, of the University of Minnesota, No. 1005 Fifth Street, S. E. At half-past eight o'clock President Vincent deliverd a very cordial address of welcome, which was followed by the address of the Chairman of the Central Division of the Modern Language Association of America, Professor Julius Goebel, of the University of Illinois, on " The New Problems of American Scholarship."

These addresses were folloed by a reception given by President and Mrs. Vincent to members and guests of the Central Division.

THIRD SESSION, WEDNESDAY FORENOON, DECEMBER 30

The session began at 9.50 a. m., when the Chairman announced the folloing committees:

(1)   To nominate a chairman and executiv committee: Professors T. A. Jenkins, D. Ford, E. C. Roedder, J. F. Royster, and F. E. Held.

(2)   On place of meeting: Professors C. B. Wilson, G. D. Morris, and M. Callaway, Jr.

(3)   On resolutions: Professors A. R. Hohlfeld, J. M. Manly, and A. de Salvio.

Reading and discussion of papers:

8.   " The Finnsburg Tale."   By Professor Frederick Klaeber, of the University of Minnesota.

[Synopsis of the story.   The contending parties (Frisians, Danes). Possible parallels and genesis of the legend.   Relation between the two Anglo-Saxon versions.   The Fight at Finnsburg.—*Twelv minutes.*]

9.   " The Attitude of Leopardi toward Romanticism." By Dr. John Van Horne, of the State University of Iowa.

[An examination of the effect of Leopardi's classical studies upon his esthetic theories shows him to have been a determind enemy of the ideals of the Romanticists.   The material is found in the *Zibaldone*, and in an essay on Romantic poetry, written by Leopardi and publisht only recently.—*Twelv minutes.*]

Pursuant to a resolution adopted at the first session, Professor John M. Manly presented the matter of practical support of our modern language journals. A discussion folloed, in which the folloing members participated: Professors Julius Goebel, E. C. Roedder, T. A. Jenkins, A. R. Hohlfeld, J. M. Manly, H. Craig, B. Cerf, and others.

On motion of Professor T. A. Jenkins it was voted to have the substance of the discussion recorded. It was pointed out that the greatly increast pressure for publication, in itself a welcome sign of growth and progress, should be met by an increase in the subscriptions on the part of the members of this Association. A substantial increase in income would enable the journals to enlarge their annual output. The situation is acute and calls for action. Contributors seem to be under special obligation to come to the financial support of the journals in which they publish. Groups of instructors may organize to take a series of journals which, while fresh from the press, may be past from hand to hand, each journal remaining finally the property of the member most interested. College and municipal libraries may be advised to subscribe. Advice of this kind is often welcomd.

The reading and discussion of papers were then resumed.

10. " The Comentaryes of Cæsar. . . . as much as concernyth thys Realm of England." By Professor Henry Burrowes Lathrop, of the University of Wisconsin.

[The first translation into English of a connected portion of Cæsar's *Gallic War*, printed 1530, but attributed to John Tiptoft, Earl of Worcester, (d. 1470), and cited as evidence for the language of his time, was based on Gaguin's French translation, is by an unknown hand, and cannot be earlier than about 1500.—*Fifteen minutes.*]

This paper was discust by Professor B. Cerf and the author.

11. "French Criticism of Poe." By Professor George D. Morris, of the Indiana University.

[The wide-spread belief that Poe has been almost unreservedly admired in France not justified. A study of the French criticism of his tales shows that a considerable number of well-known French men of letters have been far from according him unstinted praise, and that they have not given him a higher rank than he has been given by conservativ critics in America.—*Fifteen minutes.*]

This paper was discust by Professor S. H. Bush.

12. "Literary Relations of the *rimur* of Harald Hringsbane." By Dr. Gertrude Schoepperle, of the University of Illinois.

[Into the story of Randver and Swanhild, as told in the *Volsunga* saga, the poet has introduced from the similar Tristan tradition the *motifs* of the substituted bride and the healing at the hands of the enemy. His hero and heroin, moreover, escape the tragic fate of Randver and Swanhild.—*Ten minutes.*]

This paper was discust by Professor J. W. Beach and the author.

13. "The Auxiliary *Do*—1400 to 1450." By Professor James Finch Royster, of the University of Texas.

[Investigation of the date of the rise of the auxiliary *do* and its dialectical distribution in the fifteenth century shows that Lydgate has left the first recorded frequent use of the construction. It is sparingly found in Chaucer, in Gower, and in the later London language of Hoccleve; and in Northern English as late as *Ratis Raving*. A dialectical inconsistency is presented between the presence in Fragment B of the *Romaunt of the Rose* of (supposedly) Northern forms and of numerous cases of the auxiliary *do.*—*Ten minutes.*]

This paper was discust by Professor J. W. Beach and the author.

14. " Corneille and the Italian Doctrinaires." By
Professor Colbert Searles, of the University of Minnesota.

[The paper discust what may be termd the four or five working
principles of Corneille. Are they the result of his experience, as he
would have his readers believe, or did he derive them from the Italian doctrinaires whom he cited, and who had alredy, as a matter of
fact, stated these principles in terms very similar to those used by
him? Finally, what was the effect of these working principles upon
his work as a dramatist?—*Fifteen minutes.*]

At half-past twelv o'clock on Wednesday the members
and their friends were entertaind at luncheon by the University at the Minnesota Union.

Immediately after the luncheon the ladies were entertaind by an automobile ride.

FOURTH SESSION, WEDNESDAY AFTERNOON, DECEMBER 30

In accordance with the custom of the Central Division
this session was devoted to three departmental meetings,
representing the English, Germanic, and Romance languages and literatures. Subjects of importance to the
advancement of instruction constituted the programs of
the respectiv sections. All three sections met in the rooms
of the Minnesota Union.

ENGLISH

Chairman—Professor Hardin Craig, of the University
of Minnesota.

Secretary—Professor William Savage Johnson, of the
University of Kansas.

Professor Will David Howe, of Indiana University, had
arranged the program of the English Section, but being
detaind at home by illness in his family, he invited Professor Craig to serv as chairman.

11

Professor James F. A. Pyre, of the University of Wisconsin, red a paper entitled " The Teaching of Literature in the College."

The main purpose of the paper was to combat the tendency to deal with recent and contemporary materials in undergraduate courses in English literature. This was shown to be a phase of the movement by which so much of literary culture has alredy been obliterated from the program of modern education. In view of the tendency of our civilization to glorify the actual, it was pointed out, the teacher of literature has a special responsibility. It is for him, at least, to preserv from violation that world of imagination to which literature is our most universal means of introduction. That one object of literary interpretation is to establish in the mind of the pupil the substantiality of books, their essential liveness, their appositness to life, was allowd; but it was urged that when this is done at the expense of the virtue by which literature and literary history exist as things for the mind, something apart from mere actuality, then literary study is robd of its peculiar grace as an element of the intellectual life. How a mind nourisht upon actualities may lack the capacity to free itself from its immediate experiences and may ludicrously flounder in its efforts to enter the kingdom of the imagination was illustrated by student comments upon literary personages. To persuade the student's attention by sinking to the level of his interest in what is easy, familiar, and contemporaneous is to forfeit the chief end of literary study at the outset. A plea for the " really great classics " was formulated on this basis.

This paper was folloed by an interesting discussion by Professors W. F. Bryan, H. Craig, E. N. S. Thompson, J. F. Royster, J. W. Beach, J. M. Manly, Dr. Gertrude Schoepperle, and others. Not all speakers agreed with the main thesis of the paper, but many supported Professor Pyre in his attitude toward contemporary literature.

Professor Frederic Newton Raymond, of the University of Kansas, then red a paper on " The Teaching of Rhetoric." It was pointed out that the department of rhetoric has two sides, (1) machinery for casting a production in such a form that it will reach other men, (2) means of a general education. Among other things the paper made a plea for a closer coöperation between the department of rhetoric and other departments.

The paper was discust by Professor H. B. Lathrop and others. Professor Lathrop stated that the department of English in the University of Wisconsin felt that the work of initiating the new student into real education rests with the course in freshman English. At that institution the course is fundamentally based upon exposition, with a minimum in narrativ and description.

GERMANIC LANGUAGES

Chairman—Professor A. R. Hohlfeld, of the University of Wisconsin.

Secretary—Professor Charles Bundy Wilson, of the State University of Iowa.

Professor Ernst Voss, of the University of Wisconsin, had arranged the program of the Germanic Section, but on account of illness in his family he was unable to be present and Professor Hohlfeld was invited to serv as chairman.

Professor Hohlfeld exprest the hope that fuller reports of the departmental sections might appear in the publisht *Proceedings*. This idea receivd general approval.

Professor Charles M. Purin, of the University of Wisconsin, then red a paper entitled, "The Teachers' Course in German with Special Reference to Phonetics." Professor Purin said in part:

The chief responsibility for the poor results in our modern foren language work rests upon the institutions which are concernd with the training of secondary teachers, namely, upon our colleges and universities, the normal schools, at least for the present, being a very insignificant factor in this respect. Approximately only in 10% of our colleges and universities, however, are the requirements for a teacher's certificate in modern foren languages of such scope and nature as to warrant a fair degree of proficiency on the part of the graduates.

In order to be acceptably prepared to teach German in a secondary school, the student, in addition to a two-year course in the high school, should devote at least 33 semester hours to the study of German in college. These 33 hours might be distributed as folloes:

8 hours of advanced reading in modern and classical German authors, with grammar work by topics, some composition exercises, and a careful training in translation of especially selected passages in the text treated: *i. e.*, the work in translation ought to be *intensiv*, not *extensiv*. A goodly portion of the time should be made available for oral drill and reproduction in German.

12 hours in special literary courses, preferably 3 in novel, 3 in drama, and 6 in general outline of German literature.

6 hours in Composition, oral and written, with sufficient emphasis on " freie Aufsätze."

2 hours in Conversation on topics dealing with every-day life and German " Realien."

2 hours in History of the German language.

3 hours in the course on methods. One-half of the time in this course should deal with the organization of high school courses, selection of texts, and discussion of methods of presentation; the other half ought to be devoted to a practical training in phonetics.

In addition to this we should require of all students intending to teach German a course in the History of Europe, with special stress on the History of Germany, including its geographical features.

Further, no candidate ought to be granted a license to teach unless he has demonstrated his ability to handle both subject and classes in a satisfatory manner. Provision for observation and practis work is, therefore, an indispensable prerequisit with every institution which attempts to train teachers for secondary schools.

As to phonetics, the knowledge of this subject is of great importance to every teacher of modern foren languages. Ill-pronounced French or German creates in the mind of the pupil incorrect sound associations which hinder his progress in the oral and written reproduction. Without a thoro drill in pronunciation, the sound perceptions of the pupils are blurd insted of being clarified, and the appreciation of clear and distinct enunciation is lost forever.

In order to be of real servis to the teachers, the course in phonetics in the college ought to be more in the nature of applied phonetics. A few simple and inexpensiv pieces of apparatus, such as the laryngeal signal, the endoscope, sets of diapositivs and tuning forks, an auditory tube, Wilson's artificial palate, a hand mirror for each student, etc., should be used to illustrate a number of the most important phonetic phenomena. Particular attention would be paid to those phases in German pronunciation and intonation which are apt to cause especial difficulties to high school pupils.

Such a college course in phonetics will be an effectiv aid in solving one of the chief problems in modern language teaching, namely, that of pronunciation,—by establishing at the very beginning of the instruction a correctiv means more reliable than mere description or imitation.

Professor Purin's paper was discust by Professors M. Batt, E. C. Roedder, E. Feise, J. A. Campbell, C. M. Lotspeich, J. T. Hatfield, G. P. Jackson, J. Davies, A. R. Hohlfeld, C. B. Wilson, and others.

On motion of Professor C. M. Lotspeich it was

Resolvd: That it is the sense of this section that all teachers of German should have an elementary course in phonetics, either as an independent course or in connection with the general teacher's course.

Professor Edward Henry Lauer, of the State University of Iowa, then red a paper on " The Organization of Work in Second-Year College German."

Professor Lauer pointed out that a great diversity exists in the second-year German work in the various institutions. The main cause of this diversity is the fact that there is no general idea, commonly accepted, of the province and scope of this course. It is the critical course in the curriculum, and the demands made on it are numerous and varied. To do all that the course should do, demands careful organization and conservation of time. It is advisable that first-year students be segregated from college sophomores, and that the absolute conversational method be abandond. The course should prepare the student for real advanced work, and should, above all things, equip him with a reading knowledge of the language. To accomplish this it is advisable to eliminate the classics from second-year work.

This paper likewise cald out a very animated and interesting discussion by Professors J. T. Hatfield, A. R. Hohlfeld, M. Batt, F. E. Held, F. Briggs, C. M. Purin, C. B. Wilson, and others. Professor Batt argued in favor of having the classics in the second year and would devote one-half of the time of that year to reading and the other half to composition. Professor Hatfield divides the second year into four stages and would represent the work of the various stages as folloes: (1) Simple but not artistic prose; (2) some artistic prose; (3) classical drama; (4) lyric poetry. Professor Purin agreed with Professor Lauer and considerd his opinions the soundest that he had ever herd in a modern language meeting.

ROMANCE LANGUAGES

Chairman—Professor Everett Ward Olmsted, of the University of Minnesota.

Secretary—Mr. Edward Hinman Sirich, of the University of Minnesota.

Professor Thomas Edward Oliver, of the University of Illinois, who had arranged the program of the Romance Section, was unable to be present and had invited Professor Olmsted to take his place as chairman.

A paper entitled " The Problems and Difficulties of the First Year's Instruction in College French," which had been prepared by Professor Bert Edward Young, of Vanderbilt University, was red by Professor Casimir D. Zdanowicz, of the University of Wisconsin.

The paper spoke of the conditions particularly in Vanderbilt University where there is still a homogeneous body of students, coming chiefly from old-line preparatory schools or from schools whose curriculum is modeld largely after them. These students, for the most part, are well traind in the ancient classics. The paper treated at

some length the importance of pronunciation and urged emphasizing the teaching of the right intonation. A plea was made for a
grammar in which the verbs are treated erly so that reading may
be begun within the first few weeks. Most grammars feed out words
to the student faster than he can incorporate them into his vocabulary. As supplementary to the French club, it was urged that students be organized in smaller groups, as in the case of the English
clubs in vogue in the *lycées* in France.

Representing Professor Hugh Allison Smith, of the
University of Wisconsin, Professor Barry Cerf of that
institution spoke on some of the difficulties in first-year
instruction. Most of his remarks were based on facts as
they are in Wisconsin. The real problem there is how to
preserv uniformity in a number of sections in beginning
French without interfering with the individuality of the
various instructors. Another problem was how to make
a one-year course complete in itself for those who take no
more French as well as to make it a preparatory course
for those who plan to continue the study.

Both these papers were discust by Professors T. A.
Jenkins, D. H. Carnahan, G. D. Morris, S. H. Bush, Dr.
A. Coleman, and others. Professor Jenkins made a special plea for some periodical in which papers on modern
language pedagogy could be publisht. He spoke also of
the advantage which would accrue if there could be establisht a chair to have as its object the presentation scien-
tifically of all such problems in the pedagogy of the modern languages. Professors Carnahan and Morris and Dr.
Coleman spoke of the advantage of having special " honor
classes " for students of unusual ability.

Professor Olmsted red a paper by Professor Oliver on
" Some Suggestions Regarding the Future Work of the
Romance Section." The paper sketcht the history of the
sectional meetings, urged a more definit sequence of work

and discussion that might lead to results of greater value, and exprest the hope that these results might prove of sufficient worth to merit publication. It was also suggested that a committee be appointed to consider subjects for the program of the Romance Section and that the committee be askt to prepare a plan of campain for the triennium succeeding the union meeting of 1915. This suggestion was approved and the folloing committee was appointed: Professors T. E. Oliver, Colbert Searles, and Dr. A. Coleman.

On Wednesday evening the ladies were entertaind at dinner at her home by Miss Margaret Sweeney, Dean of Women in the University of Minnesota.

The gentlemen were entertaind at the Athletic Club. One of the interesting features of the entertainment was a chalk talk by Mr. Charles L. Bartholomew, of the *Minneapolis Journal,* otherwise known as " Bart."

FIFTH SESSION, THURSDAY FORENOON, DECEMBER 31

Reports of committees were the first order.

On behalf of the committee appointed to nominate a chairman and an executiv committee, Professor T. A. Jenkins presented the folloing nominations and suggested that in view of the fact that there would be a union meeting in 1915 these persons be elected for two years:

For Chairman:.
> Professor William H. Hulme, of Western Reserve University.

For Executiv Committee:
> Professor Colbert Searles, of the University of Minnesota.

Professor George O. Curme, of Northwestern
University.
Professor John L. Lowes, of Washington Uni-
versity.

These persons were thereupon elected to serv for the
years 1915 and 1916.

On behalf of the committee on place of meeting, the
Secretary, Professor Charles Bundy Wilson, reported that
the committee recommended that the choice of a place for
the union meeting in 1915 be referd to the Executiv
Council, as that body is representativ of the whole Association.

This report was adopted and the matter was so referd.

For the committee on resolutions, Professor A. R. Hohlfeld presented the folloing resolution:

We, the members of the Central Division of the Modern Language
Association of America in attendance at the twentieth annual meeting in the city of Minneapolis, hereby voice our appreciation of the
kind and generous hospitality with which we have been receivd, and
express our cordial thanks to the University of Minnesota, to its
Board of Regents, to President and Mrs. Vincent, to Miss Margaret
Sweeney, to the Minnesota Union, to the Minneapolis Athletic Club,
to the members and associates of the Local Committee, and to the
many others who have contributed to the plesurableness of our
gathering.

This resolution was adopted, and copies were sent to
the persons directly concernd.

On behalf of Professor W. G. Howard, Secretary of
the Association, the Secretary of the Central Division
presented, for information, a table of the results of the
recent balloting on the subject of simplified spelling. (See
Publications, xxix, 1; pp. xvi, xlvi). The figures were
found very interesting.

The chairman of the committee on the "Question of the Training of Teachers of Modern Foren Languages," Professor A. R. Hohlfeld, presented a report of progress.

For honorary membership in the Association the Executiv Council nominated Willy Bang, Professor at Louvain, Ferdinand Brunot and Alfred Jeanroy, Professors at Paris.

These nominations were approved.

The reading and discussion of the folloing paper were then taken up:

15. "The Evolution of the Phonetic Alphabet in English." By Professor Frank Gaylord Hubbard, of the University of Wisconsin.

[An examination of the chief systems of phonetic spelling in English from the middle of the sixteenth century to the present, for the purpose of ascertaining what the general tendencies have been, what signs have been most commonly used, what signs appear to have been tried and rejected, what signs, in the course of time, have become establisht in use.—*Fifteen minutes.*]

This paper was discust by Professors H. B. Lathrop, J. M. Manly, the author, Dr. G. N. Northrop, and ex-President W. W. Folwell, of the University of Minnesota.

COLLOQUIUM

In accordance with a resolution adopted at the meeting of 1913 (see *Procedings,* p. xlviii), the rest of this session was devoted to a colloquium. Professor John M. Manly, of the University of Chicago, presented the subject "The Significance of Medieval Latin Studies to Students of the Modern Languages." He set forth in a clear way the vital importance of this neglected subject. Professor Manly's address aroused much enthusiasm, and a profitable discussion folloed which was led by Professor Lucy M. Gay, of the University of Wisconsin. Others who took part in the discussion were Professors E. W. Olmsted, T. A. Jenkins, H. B. Lathrop, A. R. Benham, H. Craig, and Julius Goebel. It was shown how the influence of the Latin culture of the middle ages had been underestimated and that recognition is sure to come. It was also pointed out that in certain institutions the departments of Latin are unsympathetic toward medieval Latin. On request, Professor J. B. Pike, of the Latin department in the University of Minnesota, told of the position of medieval Latin in that institution. He stated that they maintain four courses in late Latin, but that the classes were usually very small, and he believd that the modern language teacher should be better qualified than the Latin teacher to give courses in medieval Latin.

In conclusion an expression of thanks was extended to Professor Manly for his part in the colloquium.

The members and their friends were entertaind at luncheon by the University at half-past twelv o'clock on Thursday at the Minnesota Union.

SIXTH SESSION, THURSDAY AFTERNOON, DECEMBER 31

The meeting was cald to order at 2 p. m.

Professor F. G. Hubbard red a report of progress from Professor W. G. Hale, chairman of the Joint Committee on Grammatical Nomenclature, suggesting that the committee be continued both for the final work on its report and to answer the many further inquiries that will come in. It was thereupon moved and carried that our representation upon this committee be continued.

Reading and discussion of papers:

16. "Studies in the Syntax of the *Lindisfarne Gospels.*" By Professor Morgan Callaway, Jr., of the University of Texas.

[An instalment of the author's *Studies in the Syntax of the Lindisfarne Gospels* which was restricted to an investigation of the participle and of the infinitiv, with the object of determining whether the syntax of these verbals in the Northumbrian dialects differs essentially from that in the West-Saxon dialect as set forth in his three monographs dealing with these parts in the latter dialect.— *Fifteen minutes.*]

This paper was discust by Professors F. Klaeber and Julius Goebel.

17. "Goethe's Early Conceptions of Women." By Professor Ernst Feise, of the University of Wisconsin.

[During his Leipsic and Frankfort periods Goethe's interest in women centers around the young girl. While he displays the conventional prejudices of rationalism and materialism, *Die Laune des Verliebten* marks an approach toward the ideas of the "storm and stress." The influence of his sickness and convalescence, deepening his character, prepares him for the more unprejudiced attitude and the later incisiv experiences.—*Ten-minute summary.*]

This paper was discust by Professor A. R. Hohlfeld.

18. "Thomas Warton and Eighteenth Century Interest in Medieval Romances." By Dr. Ronald Salmon Crane, of the Northwestern University.

[A study of Warton's rôle in the revival of interest in medieval fiction which took place in England during the second half of the eighteenth century, with some account of the influences which acted upon him and of the results of his work.—*Fifteen minutes.*]

19. "The Physiological Principles Underlying Sound-Changes in German." By Professor Claude M. Lotspeich, of the University of Cincinnati.

[The physiological processes underlying the more important sound-changes in German were analyzed with a view to pointing out their value in the historical study of language.—*Ten minutes.*]

This paper was discust by Professors F. Klaeber and E. Feise.

20. "*Samson Agonistes* as a Classical Drama." By Professor James Walter Rankin, of the University of Missouri.

[*Samson Agonistes* approaches the Greek drama chiefly in restraint and lucidity of style. In spirit it is no more Greek than *Paradise Lost* is Greek. As for structure, the theme, which is the omnipotence of God and the inevitableness of his decrees, is not sufficiently in evidence to entitle the drama to be cald classic from the point of view of the unities.—*Fifteen minutes.*]

21. "The *Poema Biblicum* of Onulphus." By Professor Karl Young, of the University of Wisconsin. Red by Professor Henry Burrowes Lathrop.

[A Vienna manuscript of the fourteenth century contains a cycle of eight short dramatic pieces writen by a certain Onulphus. Only one of these dialogues has been publisht. The paper discust the content and authorship of the cycle.—*Ten-minute summary.*]

This paper was discust by Professor H. Craig.

22. "The Puys." By Professor Charles Berry Newcomer, of Chicago, Ill.

[The *puys* were pious literary societies in northern France from the thirteenth to. the.eighteenth century. They gave prizes for certain poetical compositions, especially ballads. Hence their interest. The best known *puy* was that of the Immaculate Conception at Rouen, which lived three centuries.—*Ten-minute summary.*]

The Central Division adjurnd at 4.15 p. m.

PAPERS PRESENTED BY TITLE ONLY BEFORE THE CENTRAL DIVISION

23. "Dramatic Technique in Lessing's Comedies." By Professor James Andrew Campbell, of Knox College.

[In *Der junge Gelehrte* and in *Minna von Barnhelm* are a number of characters and situations which bear striking resemblances. An analysis of how Lessing develops these characters and situations throws light on the changes in his dramatic tastes and technique between 1748 and 1767. A study of the dialogue also shows that certain devices were developt which help to knit the thought and the speeches more closely together.]

24. "Some London Booksellers of the Early Eighteenth Century." By Professor John Mantel Clapp, of the Lake Forest College.]

[There is no good list extant of English publishers or booksellers of the eighteenth century. In this paper are offerd notes for such a list gatherd in the preparation of English eighteenth-century fiction, viz: names of London book-dealers of 1700-1725, lists of books issued by them, and suggestions as to their trade relations, in syndicates, etc.]

25. "The Influence of the Bible on Wordsworth and Coleridge." By Professor Solomon Francis Gingerich, of the University of Michigan.

[Wordsworth and Coleridge attempted to restore to English literature the freedom and the largeness that characterized it before Dryden, and in particular to bring back to it its Puritan religious spirit. To this end the Bible itself was an extremely important influence. The purpose of this paper is to indicate their indetedness to the Bible.]

26. "Some Spanish-American Poets." By Professor Elijah Clarence Hills, of Colorado College.

[Six poets have been chosen as representativ of the best that Spanish America has given to literature: Sor Juana Inés de la Cruz, of Mexico; Don Andrés Bello, of Venezuela and Chile; Don José Joaquin de Olmedo, of Ecuador; Don José María Heredia, of Cuba; Don Olegario Victor Andrade, of Argentina; and Don Rubén Darío, of Nicaragua.]

27. "The Development of Ideas in the *Poésies* and *Journal* of Alfred de Vigny." By Mr. Merton Jerome Hubert, of the University of Cincinnati.

[An attempt to trace the development of Vigny's political, philosophical, and religious ideas from youth to maturity, shoing the change from Byronic melancholy to logical pessimism, and finally to an idealistic optimism.]

28. "The Prophets of Christ in the Drama of Western Europe." By Miss Adeline Miriam Jenney, of the University of Wisconsin.

[A study of the Greek and Latin sermon sources, the matin *lectio*, the Latin *Processus Prophetarum*, and the subsequent development of the form in the religious drama of England, France, the Lowlands, Germany, Italy, and Spain.]

29. "Wolfram von Eschenbách as a Religious Reformer." By Professor Francis Waldemar Kracher, of the State University of Iowa.

[*Parzival* the greatest evangelical sermon of the pre-reformation period. Theological teachings of Luther anticipated: Opposition to pope and church on Bible principles; attempt to purify the church from within; the church of the time no harbor for a striving soul; no middle ground between eternal punishment and salvation; fall and redemption of man; cause and effect of sin; power of God's grace; man's seeking and finding peace; world-brotherhood of all men; justification by faith.]

30. "Place Names in the *Canterbury Tales*." By Dr. Ernest Peter Kuhl, of Dartmouth College.

[An investigation of the place names in the *Canterbury Tales* reveals some interesting facts. Two stand out prominently, allusions to the political affairs of the time, and aid in establishing the chronology of some of the tales.]

31. "Chaucer and Aldgate." By Dr. Ernest Peter Kuhl, of Dartmouth College.

[Chaucer's loss of the "mansion" over Aldgate in 1386 was probably due to the political conditions of the time. Other city gates were likewise witnessing new occupants, those who were partisans of the King. Significant in shoing Chaucer's relation to the King.]

32. "Emerson as a Romantic." By Professor Louise Pound, of the University of Nebraska.

[Emerson's idea of the poet and the poetic gift. Emerson the chief American professor of the typical romantic conception of the poet and his inspiration; his aloofness and solitude, his devotion to his own ideals, his superiority to others. Emerson's belief in self-contemplation; the note of self-sufficiency and of the anti-social qualifying his democracy. Relation of other of his teachings to those of the romanticists folloing Rousseau.]

[Publisht in *The Mid-West Quarterly* for January 1915.]

33. "Observations on the Evolution of Rime Suggested by Bede's *De Arte Metrica*." By Professor James Walter Rankin, of the University of Missouri.

[It is not sufficient to say that rime was introduced into English verse as a result of the influence of Latin hymns and French lyrics. Before the hymns could exert any influence, there was rime in ancient popular vernacular verse in charms, gnomes, and proverbs. In Latin there is much rime antedating Christianity, and the rimed French forms probably go back thru the *vulgares cantilenae* to *barbara et antiquissima carmina.*]

34. "The Rear Stage of Shakespeare's Theater." By Professor George Fullmer Reynolds, of the University of Montana.

[The paper discusses the uses of the rear stage which can be establisht from the plays, and especially the principle of recurring properties which seems to have determind the staging of many of the plays. This principle is illustrated, and the apparant exceptions to it are discust.]

35. "The Materials Considered Suitable for Literature by English Critics of the Sixteenth and Seventeenth Centuries." By Professor James Routh, of Tulane University.

[Chapter in the history of criticism. Study of what themes, and what detaild materials were consider'd by critics admissible in literature. Most notable were views on conventional, novel and learned matter in art; the function of the ugly or repulsiv, including deth on or off the stage; the supernatural; truth in art; probability; popular prejudices; satirical themes.]

36. "Schiller's *Anthologie auf das Jahr 1782*." By Professor Bert John Vos, of the Indiana University.

[The paper is an attempt to determin, more particularly thru an examination of the style, the authorship of some of the groups of poems of the *Anthologie*. The poems signd " P." (Nos. 16, 29, 35, 82) are, contrary to the conclusions of Leitzmann, *Euphorion* xv, p. 219, claimed for Schiller.]

PROCEDINGS FOR 1914   liii

37. "The Evolution of the French Novel Prior to the *Astrée*." By Professor Jacob Warshaw, of the University of Missouri.

[A few scholars have recognized that the boundaries of the French novel must be moved far back of the *Astrée* (cf. Wilmette and Wurzbach). This study seeks to sho the evolution of the novel out of the *chansons de gestes*, its separation into definit species, its mutations, its assimilation of new view-points, and the stedy addition of new principles of technique.]

38. "Clipped-Words; a Study of Back-Formations and Curtailments in Present-Day English." By Miss Elisabeth Wittmann, of the University of Nebraska.

[Linguistic importance of clipt words. Contributions to the standard language. Definition of terms and delimitations of treatment. Causes underlying word-curtailment. Classes of clipt words and their relativ popularity. Survey and analysis of contemporary clipt forms; present-day vogue of word-mutilation.]

[Publisht in *Dialect Notes*, Vol. IV, part II.]

39. "The *Mise en Scène* of the French Theatre at the Beginning of the Classic Period." By Professor Casimir Zdanowicz, of the University of Wisconsin.

[The stage-setting of this period is not as fully understood as is sometimes assumed. Some questions to be considerd. Influence of the *mise en scène* upon the dramatists with especial reference to the unity of place.]

THE PRESIDENT'S ADDRESS

DELIVERD ON TUESDAY, DECEMBER 29, 1914, AT NEW
YORK, N. Y., AT THE THIRTY-SECOND ANNUAL
MEETING OF THE MODERN LANGUAGE
ASSOCIATION OF AMERICA

BY FELIX E. SCHELLING

THE AMERICAN PROFESSOR

In the quiet of lovely Venice, some eight months ago,
in the calm of a sabbatical year, with the task that I had
come to Europe to complete, now fulfilled, and a world
within and without at peace, I thought of the future and
especially of this evening when I should have my turn to
speak to you, my friends and colleagues in the teaching
of our modern tongues, my turn to greet you and extend to
you all the hand of cordial welcome. I had been in England for months; England, dear to me on many accounts,
as the home of the language that we of America speak, the
source out of which has come a great world literature, still
potent, still vital, the abiding place—when all has been
said in detraction and misunderstanding—of justice, of
freedom, of ideals, and of hope for the future. I had
been, too, in Germany, staunch, proud, orderly and competent Germany, as the guest of an honorable association
of scholars, in their celebration of the fiftieth anniversary
of the founding of the German Shakespeare Society. And
there I had the honor to convey to that society the greetings and congratulations of our Modern Language Asso-

ciation of America. At Weimar were gathered on that occasion the very flower of German culture and learning, the more especially in these our modern languages, men whose names we all know, whose scholarship we all admire, kindly, gentle, hospitable men, intent to honor the memory of the one world poet who stands pre-eminent above national prejudice and parochial disparagement. And it seemed to me that there was an obvious theme before me, the solidarity of our modern scholarship, the union, harmony, the essential agreement as to the larger issues and purposes of learning which had come to pervade the scholarly world; its unity in the gradual advance towards a better comprehension, not only of the multitudinous subjects of scholarly investigation, but in a clearer understanding of the various methods by which that approach was being conducted, a closer bond, begotten of mutual sympathy, respect, and support. From these dreams, bred of Italian sunshine, respite from labor, and personal content, I have had, like the rest of the world, my rude awakening. Shattered in thin air are my castles, like those of many another dreamer, and we awake to a desolated world, a prey to primitive passions, in brute struggle for the right to live, with civilization a mockery and a delusion, and culture and the fine arts buffeted back a hundred years. There come to me times when I wonder with Mr. Shaw, whether a misinvoked and blasphemed God may not repent him of the misused reason with which he has endowed the human race and, revoking that precious gift, bestow it on some humbler and kindlier animal of his creation.

But despairing themes such as these are not for us, for that way lies madness. There need be here no charges, no defiances nor recriminations. Our books need be neither white books nor grey books nor yellow books. And

God forbid that we shall ever exchange our scholars' gowns for invisible grey or earth-colored khaki. By our own hearth, so to say, brothers all, let us forget, for the nonce, the tempest that is raging without, and chat contentedly of that most pleasant of topics, ourselves, teachers, scholars, investigators, be we what we may, each after his kind and each in his individual function. If I shall seem in any wise admonitory to the young among you and compact of wise saws and modern instances, remember, I beg of you, how long it is since I was of your years. If, on the contrary, I shall seem newfangled and unorthodox to my elders and betters, nothing could more flatter me than the ascription of such opinions to the long continuance of my youth.

A patronizing foreigner once acknowledged to me that American scholarship was far from discreditable. This was after dinner, and my foreign friend was in a benignant mood. Appreciating the sublimity of his condescension, I trust that I seemed, even to him, becomingly grateful. As a matter of fact, American scholarship is really amazingly creditable, when we recognize the conditions under which it flourishes. The American professor is practically the American man of science, as he is still, to a large degree, the American man of letters. He is paid primarily to teach and he is expected to teach more hours for his pay than his colleagues either in England, France, or Germany. If he continues to keep up with his subject and add his quota to its progress, so much the more credit to him; for even yet, in some of our less enlightened colleges, such activities are looked upon askance, as consuming time better spent in the class-room, as impairing the indefinable thing called " efficiency," and as productive of a spirit of discontent. I once inquired of a professor at Cambridge, England, the claim of the university on his

time, and he told me " about twenty lectures a year." Few
American professors of equal standing give less than three
times that number a month; and what shall we say of the
many that labor in the class-room four or five hours a day,
taking home the burden of preparation and incessant paper
work, not to mention the claims of faculty attendance,
committee work, student advice, and what not. We may
grant that the very drive of our American professor's
life makes for intellectual activity and acts as a spur and
exhilaration. Yet can we look for anything but disparity
in the quality of scholarly work, carried on under conditions so diverse? Impetus, project, ideals, expectation,
all are abundantly ours; elaboration, completeness in detail and thoroughness of treatment,—these things we may
confess here among ourselves, that we reach in our scholarly work less habitually than might be desired. It can
not but be a matter of regret that almost the last thing
that scholarship in America possesses is that quality of
leisure that inheres in the original significance of the word.
Scholarly leisure permits not only toiling upon a subject,
but that quiet preliminary pondering in which are embed-
ded the roots of thoroughness. Leisure allows a natural
period of incubation, without artificial heat or the pressure
of haste. It is that which gives to work the quality that
distinguishes, in scholarship as elsewhere, growth from
manufacture, that marks the difference which divides the
disinterestedness of the seeker after knowledge from the
opportunism of the writer of many books for much immediate recognition.

The effort, haste, and strenuous endeavor of American
scholarship is doubtless no more than the logical manifestation of a new temperament, begotten of new climatic
and social conditions, and one which time may modify
and readjust. A similar contrast with English condi-

tions is notorious in our manner of transacting business (of which it is unnecessary here to speak) and in our mode of education. The young English student is submitted for a period of years to the leisurely influences of culture at Oxford, often deferring his actual study to the long vacations, when the social and athletic activities of college life fall off sufficiently to permit a steady grind with a tutor. We insist on educating our boys all the time; and, even in the seasons of football and of baseball, we cruelly demand attendance on recitations, manning our courses so as to keep all busy (or seemingly busy) and visiting derelictions from the straight and narrow path with academic pains and penalties. We do everything in our American universities for the intellectual feeding of our young men and women save allowing them time for digestion. No wonder it takes some people until middle life to recover from the effects of a college education, and that some never recover at all.

Returning to the American professor, which of you does not know that overworked man? Busy with his lectures, his students, his committees, his preparations for experiment, and his workshop, whatever it may be, all and every day; stealing hours from the night, from recreation, from vacation, when his driven mind demands some relaxation, from holidays, to carry on his search for some philosopher's stone. He has passed the time in life when the acclamation of success can mean much to him, for his best hours have ever been given to others, but his search is always on, for the love of learning is strong within him, and he knows, as few men know, that the true reward of all human endeavor is in the activity, not in the achievement. Such a man is the true investigator, and all honor to him whether he attain discovery or not; for he is in the path of rectitude, as Carlyle might have put it, be out of it

who may. Very different is the type, unhappily not unknown among us, whose food is adulation and the loud
applause of men. Take the case of John Payne Collier,
the notable English Shakespeare scholar, and forger, alas.
Starting in an honorable career and enjoying good fortune
in his earlier researches, Collier developed an avidity for
praise disproportionate to the possibilities of his subject.
The time was one in which many fields still stood un-
reaped; these Collier industriously gathered in. Where
others had left him only sweepings, he discredited their
efforts, to demand for his gleanings the credit of a full
harvest. Such a man must make at least one startling
discovery a year, and each " discovery " must rise in splendid climax over what has gone before. When he has once
broached a theory, he must prove victorious over all whose
temerity has dared to impeach it; and if stubborn records
deny, they must be wrought to conformity and support.
If such a man is really a genius, as Collier was (almost),
he may amaze the ignorant again and again, though he
make the judicious grieve. If he is less than a genius, it
becomes difficult for him to preserve his integrity, and he
sacrifices before long his honor as a scholar to his vanity
as a man.

Here, in America, despite some approximation to an
understanding, it may not be too great an exaggeration to
affirm that we are only beginning to know the investigator
in pure science or in historical research. We recognize the
value of industrial experimentation, and large salaries
properly reward the chemist, the engineer, or bacteriologist
who labors in the interests of trade. We understand, too,
the need of experimentation in peace to maintain effectiveness in war, and we grudge very little—nor dare we now
begrudge at all—the continuance of experiments with pro-
jectiles that cost the nation the yearly maintenance of five

universities. Experiment in science looking towards the amelioration of health is a nobler species of research, justly recognized among us and highly and generously subsidized; whilst occasionally, as in more than one splendid foundation, known to us all, other subjects—even at times, though not too frequently, literary ones—claim a place, not a little begrudged. None the less, to mention only two examples among those who have gone before, the admirable researches into the history of the Middle Ages by the eminent historian, Henry C. Lea, were provided for out of his own purse, happily a heavy one, and the monumental *New Variorum Edition of Shakespeare* was undertaken by the late Dr. Horace Howard Furness, canny booksellers refusing, at the pecuniary risk of the editor. The man among our contemporary American scholars in English who will be remembered when the rest of us are forgotten—remembered for his additions to the materials concerning the life of Shakespeare and his contemporaries in their traffic with the stage—is expending his own slender capital in a devoted search, now protracted over a period of many years, and not an Association, an Institute, nor a University (save his own in far away Nebraska), will raise a finger to help him. In contrast to all this, it is never very difficult to find the money to fit out an expedition to ascend a new mountain or recover a lost river, to gather loot for the illustration of the *Kultur* of some barbarous race, or to dig up something or other, provided it be sufficiently outlandish and remote.

Indeed, when all has been said in praise and recognition of the fostering hand which some of our captains of industry are extending to the subalterns of science, it can scarcely be denied that American encouragement of scientific investigation remains even now to a large degree erratic and based more on the virtuoso's love of the curious and the far-fetched than on any genuine apprehension of the needs and true significance of scientific inquiry. Moreover, as always in a plutocracy such as ours, we have as yet somewhat rudimentary conceptions of the relations of the investigator to those who encourage him. The fostering of science by the condescensions of fashion is a thing not unknown in the purlieus of our intellectual life. It was prevalent in England about the time of the Restoration of King Charles; and in France it died out before the Revolution. To see a man, whom two hemispheres have united to honor, explaining the rudiments of paleontology to a bevy of Chicago fair matrons, no one of whom has ever possessed, much less forgotten, knowledge enough to have entered the humblest college, is a sight for the genius of comedy. But the eminent scholar received his subsidy and the ladies were amused at his queer manners and his foreign tongue. Seriously, the mere man of money who supports genuine scientific inquiry or fosters the arts, no matter what his benefactions, embraces a really priceless opportunity. From one of the horde who " add to golden numbers golden numbers,"—if I dare so misapply the lyrist's words—he becomes the abettor of one of the noblest activities of the race and comes to share, by reflection at least, in its intellectual victories. Among the rich men of ancient Rome, Atticus is less remembered than Maecenas. Yet Atticus was by far the richer man. It was Maecenas, not Atticus, that befriended poetry in the person of Horace, and Maecenas lives in the memory of those who revere genius. In this day of imperious money-getting—if that is our end-all and strive-all—it is well to admonish the young: " Be, if you must, a millionaire; but don't be an indistinguishable millionaire."

But let not my words be misunderstood. With the many noble foundations and magnificent charities, educational and other, for which our country is justly famous, in mind, it would ill become any lover of learning to cast a stone at those whose munificence renders these activities possible. The man of wealth and position who makes these the fulcrum with which to wield the active lever of administration, thus giving himself as well as his wealth, has achieved all that the true patron of learning can achieve; and more besides. In his disinterested love of his fellow-man, his labors and his sacrifices, he stands alike above the man who has merely given, and beyond him whose humbler mission it is to garner wisps in the fully mown fields of knowledge.

The true honors of the investigator are not such as wealth or fashion can bestow. Often his work can be justly appraised only by his peers, and his tardy reward consists in a recognition that he has brought some one stubborn block of knowledge, hewn and fashioned by his cunning hand, to its place in the structure of the temple of wisdom. This may not seem encouraging to some among us who are beginning their careers as scholars, full of ambition for immediate returns, and eager to discount the face value of promise into a cash payment for achievement. But if the true spirit of the investigator be in a man, neither time nor the praises of men will concern him in his quest, and he will find in his work itself a sufficient joy and recompense.

The true investigator in science (like the genuine artist) is the most valuable asset in a civilized nation, to be cherished and encouraged in the highest degree. For not only do such men add to the sum total of the world's knowledge, but they bring renown to the country in which they live, and make, according to the degree of their genius and success, for the uplifting of mankind. To let such a man waste valuable hours over the petty means of subsistence is wasteful beyond description. Something might be said, in these days of the cry for conservation of our physical resources, for the conservation to nobler purposes of the brains and talents of the nation. A forest will grow somehow, haphazard, if you let it sufficiently alone and do not burn it. So, too, human ambition, the exigencies of the moment, sheer accident, contrive in the struggle of life to keep our intellectual slopes, so to speak, fairly well wooded. But there is much inferior second growth flaunting its insufficiency saucily in the sun, and when some old giant of the forest falls under the axe of time we cannot but deplore our want of thought for the future.

And now as to the professor as teacher. Most people believe that any body can teach. Teaching is an excellent makeshift for youths who are working forward to medicine, law, or the pulpit, or to a fortunate business opening. Teaching is a becoming and altogether proper vocation for young women awaiting the delightful possibilities of matrimony. It has been cited as a reproach to our American education that it is, to a large degree, feminized. (I refuse parenthetically to say whether I regard this as a reproach or not.) And a man of middle life who continues to teach is looked on—often with justice—as one who in all likelihood could scarcely earn a subsistence in any other way.

I remember, some years ago, meeting a keen and clever lawyer at dinner. We had crossed swords on several subjects and, somewhat exhilarated in the process, he said to me: "You seem to me, Sir, to be a man of perhaps as much as average common sense." I naturally thanked him for his blunt compliment, and he continued: "Why don't you leave that dusty University of yours over the river and come down into the city, back to the profession of the law to which you were bred, and live like a man? I note that you do not disdain the good things of life nor yet the sparkle of its champagne. These are to be had by a man of intelligence in the world; you'll never get them in the cloister." Nor could I convince him that my fine notions about the things of the mind, about service to others, about the inward satisfaction of scholarly activity were not, all of them, perilously near cant.

There are many reasons for this disrepute of the teacher. The life of a mere teacher is narrow and confining. He is apt to magnify his office and, with it, his importance, from his daily habit of converse with those who are younger than himself and less specifically trained. Moreover, there is little to attract the able or ambitious in mere teaching, either in the position and social recognition which this profession is accorded or in the money return which in our country remains, despite some betterment in some quarters, still generally inadequate. In an article of a few years since, the average American male college teacher is rated as a wage-earner with puddlers and Pullman car conductors. How impalpably we may have risen above that standard since that time, I do not know; although we are informed that as late as 1908, " one-third of our degree-giving institutions were paying their full professors an average salary of less than a thousand dollars per annum." And the professor's plight is really worse than this might seem to indicate; for there are demands on his purse which these excellent people of iron and motion do not know; for the professor's very education and status in life demand a higher, and hence a costlier, mode of living. An acquaintance of mine, professor in one of our larger Eastern colleges, kept a list of the " legitimate demands " upon his purse that grew directly out of his position. To say not one word of books, scientific periodicals, and like tools of the trade, there were clubs, national and international, collegiate and intercollegiate,

their meetings, and attendance on them, with traveling
expenses and maintenance. To be out of these things was
to argue yourself unknown. There were student activities, athletic, dramatic, musical, class organizations, fra-
ternities and what not. To be out of them all was to make
yourself unpopular to the degree of impairing your usefulness. There were charities, the hospital, the museum, the
college settlement, the students' religious gatherings, an
occasional student to help, an occasional colleague or old
friend to " accommodate." What had such a man for his
own church, or his club, or his political party? For a
charity undirected, or for the frank and indiscreet gift of
a dollar on the street? My friend calculated that the
" legitimate demands " upon his slender purse by reason
of his position in the University of Weissnichtwo constituted nearly forty per cent. of his salary. To honor
them all was to beggar his family. How he solved the
matter, if he solved it at all, nearly anyone of you present
can tell.

I do not deny that much has been done to ameliorate
former conditions, especially in the retiring pensions
which the munificence of Mr. Carnegie has made possible;
but there still remains something to be done by the colleges
themselves in the restraint not only of superfluous buildings and dictated endowments but in what is often worse,
the restraint of supernumerary courses, too often added to
the curriculum and to the budget as well, as a stock of new
ribbons is added, because the competing tradesman keeps
the new kind. I should like to see the American college
professor so placed that he might not be compelled, as so
frequently now, to dissipate the singleness of his aim in
life by the necessity of common outside drudgery to relieve common inward wants; just as I should like to have
the dignity and the importance of his position recognized

in other ways, for his sake not alone but for the sake of
our colleges and universities, their dignity and usefulness.
Whether Professor X or Professor Y receive a larger or a
smaller salary is a matter wholly unimportant to anyone
save the gentlemen in question and their families. That
a large body of competent and intellectual men should be
compelled to practice sordid petty economies for their
families' sake and take a secondary place in the commu-
nities which they are trained to lead, is a public misfortune. On the other hand, I am not insensible of the fact
that there could be no greater misfortune to the profession
of teaching than to endow it with the glittering pecuniary
rewards that attend success in medicine or law. For woe
to our profession when it shall attract only because it is
well paid. That teacher who does not accept his profession as a trust, in the spirit of unaffected sacrifice, who
does not count his real success in his power to influence
those about him to an honest pursuit and a genuine love
of learning, should seek some employment more congenial
to his sordid soul. The great thing about teaching is the
humanity of it. The man's the thing and the contact
man to man. How often do we who concoct our big and
little books and our portentously learned notes and note-
lets, forget that where the written word may reach its tens
the spoken word, if it be sincere, may reach its hundreds,
and, radiating through them, its thousands. The fertile
thought of the true teacher may germinate a thousand fold,
and it is not alone the information imparted, important
as that may be, but the spirit, the outlook, the uplift that
the true teacher may give the student in whose spirit he
may establish a sympathy with his own.

The ideal teacher is as difficult to find as the ideal investigator. The ideal teacher must be competently, never
ostentatiously, learned, and he must be as alive as the in-

vestigator to the progress of his subject. He must be hospitable to new ideas, tenacious of the best that have been, and courteous to differences of opinion, though they tread on his most cherished preconceptions. In a word, liberality is the first essential of the ideal teacher, and he will gain for himself the confidence of his students (prime essential to the teaching of anything) by an openness of spirit that entertains the possibility of the discovery of truth even in the most unexpected places. Again, the ideal teacher must be disinterested and forgetful of self. Many a strong personality has been wrecked as a teacher on the rocks of self-esteem. It is a precious piece of impertinence for any man to stand between a class and a great subject; and obscuration and disfigurement in proportion to the bulk of the man's " selfness " (to employ a good Elizabethan word) are sure to follow. On the other hand, nothing interests the student so much as the personal note, if it be unconscious and free from real or affected vanity. The true teacher can dare anything, and with that dangerous two-edged Delphian blade, paradox, confound inattention, lack of interest, and the thousand other lets and hindrances to successful teaching.

But there are other, scarcely lesser virtues that we have a right to demand even of those who we know must fall far short of the ideal. I have never been able to rid myself of an old-fashioned conviction that the instruction of the young should be entrusted to people of gentle manners and an innate disposition to play fair in the game of life. That we have men in the profession of teaching who are examples neither in their lives, their conduct towards their students, nor their grammar is in part referable to the small returns for petty ambition which the office of the teacher holds forth, but more to our habitual failure to distinguish the processes of filling a young mind with information, from education in a truer sense. Perhaps this contrast is best expressed in the much abused antithesis between mere education and that cultivation of the whole man which alone really makes for civilization. One may educate a dog, a horse, or a pig; that is, superimpose on the nature of each of these animals a process of action regulated by habit which may produce pretty results. Cultivation is another matter, and some men, like most animals, are impervious to it. Not long ago I met for the first time a man of considerable repute in his own subject. He discussed with grasp and certainty in his own *Fach,* but in the voice of a huckster, passing even grammatical pitfalls at times precariously; and his manners were those of a yokel. That, alas, was an educated man; and his three or four degrees from as many universities, his repute, too, be it acknowledged, as a scholar, attested his education. I am not prepared to say that that man should have been blocked in his Freshman year for his notorious offenses against his own English tongue, but I do deny that his four universities exerted any appreciable influence in the nature of culture upon him. Most happily for the young, this man confines his talents to research.

I have spoken of the investigator and the teacher apart. In truth, there should be no repugnance between them, however the qualifications of one man may lead him to emphasize one of these functions of the scholar above the other. I should like to see every teacher interested in some investigation of his own, thereby keeping his work in the class-room fresh and vitalized by a larger outlook than mere pedagogy can give him; and I should like to feel that there was no investigator in science whose field had become so specialized and remote that he could not on occasion bring it down to the understandings of those in need of his instruction. It is still a moot question as to whether the teacher gains as much as some have been fain to believe by directions and organized training in how to teach. I note that those who have failed specifically often aspire to lead others to success by means of this fine art of teaching how to teach. In very truth, I confess to a frank mistrust of all the newer parasitic courses, courses which, be their titles whatsoever they may, commonly draw the bulk of their content from history, philosophy, and literature, derived too often superficially at second hand. The best specific for the teacher is a thorough knowledge of his subject, and (almost as important) a clear apprehension of its relations to other subjects. Narrow specialized training may make a man expert; it sometimes unsettles him in his bearings. It is conceivable that for the training of the teacher we might sacrifice somewhat the severity of specialization. It seems unquestionable that gain would come to our graduate schools, if we were frankly to give up the pretence of making every student a specialist and an investigator, and devote the time thus saved, not so much to teaching him how to teach as to preserving in him a greater catholicity of spirit and a larger outlook on things as they are. And yet it is a great deal for any man to know one thing measurably well. To have, so to speak, a background to his subject, to speak out of the fulness of his knowledge and, when he seems to have given all, to have an abundance yet in store.

But the teacher is responsible for more than the character of the knowledge that he imparts. Is it altogether fanciful that the typical Harvard man—may I say it?—is superior (as he has the right to be), blasé, critical, and aristocratic; the Yale man hearty, clannish, and (shall I whisper it?) at times, while an undergraduate, just a bit noisy; the Princeton man—but Princeton is too near a

13

friend for Pennsylvania to characterize her, and Columbia?—Columbia is our ever gracious host. These distinctions may arise partly from the dominion of brain or the dominion of brawn, occasionally, as in this year, remarkably united; but they can often be found in their ultimate origins in the manners of some favorite teacher or coterie of teachers who through dozens and dozens of unconscious imitations have impressed their personalities on those about them, and created in time an unmistakable air. Even fashions in scholarship seem referable at times to a powerful example. Not to be personal or to mention individual instances known to us all, the researches into Chaucer and the " old English balladry " of the late revered Professor Child of Harvard, if I dare so flippantly designate his masterly scholarship in that interesting field, have now been propagated to many a good purpose—as our present program declares—even unto the third and fourth generation.

It is only out of a university that cherishes the ideals of research that the true scholar can come, for there alone can he find the stimulus that vitalizes the slow process of the accumulation of facts into the exciting pursuit of truth. Example is always more powerful than precept, and the teacher who is known outside the walls of his own college, as a recognized authority in his subject, has a potency within, which his humbler fellows can never hope to win. The time will come when we shall recognize wherein true academic celebrity consists. It is not in the size and diversity of the thing which a certain type of trustees loves to designate largely by that hideous factory-made word, the " plant "; it is not in the beauty of buildings and the charm of a lovely campus, desirable as are all these things. Still less is it in a startling number, novelty, and variety of courses, in swarms of students, easily entered, rarely dismissed, or in the cheap advertisement of athletic prowess, even in sensational discovery or pronouncement in laboratory or lecture room. Academic celebrity, I repeat, lies in the quality of the student as a man and a scholar, and no less essentially in the scholarship that a university begets and fosters. A university whose faculty receives no recognition elsewhere is moribund and out of the race. A university, whose men remain because its atmosphere is favorable to research, gains in every scholar a tongue to tell abroad its fame. In a word, the academic atmosphere can be kept fresh alone in a nice adjustment of the claims of the teacher and the investigator, and no institution can afford to sacrifice either the drawing power of the one or the lifting potency of the other.

The life of an American professor need not be narrow, unless he himself make it so. His mind is constantly in communion with the best that has been gathered from the past, and its treasure-houses are open to him as they are not always open to other men. Nor need he answer to the reproach that the present lies, a closed book, before him; for there are few subjects that American scientific inquiry has not been busy with; precisely as there are few topics—of the streets, of the family as it should and should not be, of criminals and their converse, of the councils of princes in their spread of empire—to which American professorial activity has not confidently extended itself of late. Is it not the American professor who expounds the Nietzschean philosophy and the metaphysics of Bergson, the romantic sentiment of Maeterlinck, and the flamboyant socialism of Shaw? And is it not the American professor—or at least the professor in American occupation—who is even now expounding treaties, explaining racial antipathies, directing diplomacy, and apologising for the Kaiser? Assuredly the American professor is not, at this moment, shrinking in becoming reticence into the shadow of his class-room; and we are in danger of being heard in some things not too little, but too much.

And now will those of you who are newer comers than I into this exhilarating state of being, forgive me if I have seemed to remind you of too many things that you must long since have found out for yourselves. To return to seriousness, the actual value of any subject lies far less in its contents than in the spirit in which it is approached. He is a rhetorician not a teacher, a sophist not a true lover of wisdom, who seeks popularity in the class-room by the brilliancy of his wit, the startling novelty of his notions, and the cleverness of his delivery. In your own studies, whether you are climbing by circuitous paths the giddy highlands of research or are content modestly " only to teach," pursue your work disinterestedly, loving it for itself and for the wholesome labor which it costs you, not as an asset to be realized on to the enhancement of your next year's salary. If your goal is research, know that there is only one thing really worth while, and that is the truth. And remember that you may happen to " discover " with amazed delight many an object which has long lain along the beaten path of knowledge, " discovered " and delighted in by many who have gone before you. There was wisdom in the world before we were born and some will survive us. And to you who more modestly are satisfied " merely to teach " (if indeed there be any such truly contented man or woman present) know that there is nowhere a more dignified and more sacred trust than that of the teacher. You are needed almost above all other men. If you are a good teacher, you will never receive a salary adequate to your worth. If you are a poor teacher, you will be overpaid at any price. Your rewards will come, not in money, perhaps not in repute, or even in much recognition; but every man's recompense lies in the satisfaction of his own heart, and to have led honestly, bravely, and competently, to have left some the better for our living in the world, none deprived or misled, surely this is better than a brief day in the sunshine of repute.

The American professor, as I have known him now for many years, is kindly, hard-working, uncomplaining, and unselfish. He is commonly underpaid, though not quite so frequently overrated. He is more liberal than his immediate predecessor of clerical cut, though not nearly so courageous in expressing his convictions; but he fears God, and the President (of his college), and is too magnanimous, for the most part, to take this latter fear out in the discipline of innocent Freshmen. Once in a while he writes—or at least publishes—too many books; more commonly he writes too few. Sometimes he employs his Sabbatical year, if he gets it, to excellent scholarly purpose; he is often too genuinely wearied to do so, or too harassed with cares, not of his own making. He is a self-respecting man, even spirited at times in the defence of his convictions, his right of free speech, and his right of free teaching. But he is protected as yet by no trades union (although I hear that he is at this moment perilously near to it), and therefore at times is silent when he wishes to God that he might speak. He has less confidence in his abilities to run the world than some, not possessed of his special training, have confidence that they can run his department. To the popular impression that he is an impractical man, he gives the lie, by his general competence even in every-day affairs. In short, the American professor is of stuff good enough to make an excellent President of the United States, and even such an Atlas disdains not to become, on the lifting of his heavy load, an American professor.

THE CHAIRMAN'S ADDRESS

DELIVERD ON TUESDAY, DECEMBER 29, 1914, AT MINNE-
APOLIS, MINNESOTA, AT THE TWENTIETH ANNUAL
MEETING OF THE CENTRAL DIVISION OF
THE MODERN LANGUAGE ASSOCIATION
OF AMERICA

BY JULIUS GOEBEL

THE NEW PROBLEMS OF AMERICAN SCHOLARSHIP

The question whether there are any problems whose
solution constitutes the particular task of American scholarship has no doubt at one time or another occupied the
attention of all of us who hope to contribute our mite
to the development and possible extension of our special
field of research. It is not a narrow conception of nationality which prompts this question that I have in mind.
At the present time it seems to me more than ever necessary to emphasize the international character of the search
for truth; for here, in my opinion, lies the only guarantee
we have for the permanency of our modern civilization.
The decay of the civilization of the ancients and the petrification which finally befell the culture of the Middle Ages
were due in no small degree to national exclusiveness and
to the lack of that free interchange of the results of thought
and investigation which characterizes modern times. It
seems to me one of the greatest achievements of the Renaissance that it did away with this national exclusiveness, despite the fact that its early beginnings in Italy

were national in character. The humanistic ideal soon found its champions among the various nationalities, and there developed among these champions a sort of brotherhood which was held together by the tie of one common aim: the revival of ancient art, literature, and life. For centuries the study and the appreciation of classical antiquity thus constituted the intellectual atmosphere in which the educated of the various nations lived and moved and had their being. Yet, at the same time, we notice that in Italy, later in France and England, and finally in Germany the vernacular is gradually receiving attention. During the seventeenth century we even find the modest beginnings of a history of the various national literatures. It is significant that the first attempts in this direction should have been made in Germany, for I doubt whether a book such as Morhoff's " Polyhistor " or his " Unterricht von der Teutschen Sprache und Poesie " could have been written in any other country, showing as they do the author's study of English, French, and Italian literature. To be sure, among single individuals the knowledge of foreign languages is found at that time also outside of Germany, but it is here that for the first time this knowledge is pursued for its own sake in accordance with the spirit of universality which men such as Johann Val. Andreae and Leibniz instilled into all scientific efforts during this period. At least ten years before the publication of Bacon's " Novum Organon," Johann Val. Andreae had written a little book advocating a general reform of science based upon observation. One of the principal ideas of this book was that this new science was to be of an international character, that the society of scholars which was to bring about the new era should have its members among various nations, and that the new message was to be sent out in five different languages.

There is no question in my mind that the new scientific spirit foreshadowed in this book exerted its influence also on the study of language and literature. For the first time we notice the revolutionary effect which a great intellectual movement such as the rise of empirical science had upon the methods and aims of research in almost every field of knowledge.

The idea that henceforth the duty of science is to seek for the true nature of man, identical among all the nations of the earth, appears for the first time in Andreae's book, the famous and much misunderstood " Confessio Fraternitatis Rosaecrucis." That this idea, as far as investigation in the various languages and literatures is concerned, was not realized until the latter half of the eighteenth century was due above all to the powerful hold which the conception of the singular greatness of classical antiquity had upon the intellectual life of this period. If it was a fact that only once in the course of history had the ideal of humanity revealed itself in its perfection, and found its completest expression in the art, philosophy, and literature of the Greeks and Romans, what other nations had achieved must inevitably appear as trifling. According to such a view, the poetical heritage of modern nations, which manifests itself in their national legends, their lyric, epic, and drama, is doomed to disregard or oblivion, and literary productions in the vernacular will receive recognition only in so far as they conform to the classical tradition.

In the latter half of the eighteenth century there arose an entirely new conception of history and the historical process. It is the discovery of the naïve in contrast to the artificial, the sudden realization of the value and importance of the national as opposed to the abstract classical type of humanity, which causes the rise of the new conception of history. The products of classical antiquity are no longer regarded as the highest and the only expression of the truly human. On the contrary, humanity has developed in its diversity and beauty in every clime and under every sky. For the beautiful is no mere abstraction, but variously reveals itself in life. It is the historical point of view from which we comprehend historical variety, through which we perceive and enjoy the beautiful in all its manifestations, through which, in short, we discover a glowing life in the infinitely varying processes of history.

Herder is the man to whom we owe this new and revolutionary idea. It is through him that the study of modern languages and literatures in a large and comprehensive sense, first became possible. Although he was an ardent admirer of classical antiquity and especially of the Greeks, the application of the standards of Graeco-mania to historical phenomena was repugnant to his sense of truth. Thus it was possible for him to gain a true understanding for the so-called Dark Ages, so greatly despised by the Age of Enlightenment. In his eyes the fall of the Roman Empire and its culture was not a catastrophe eternally to be lamented, but rather the dawn of a new youth for mankind, in which much that was great and fresh had been developed.

The effect of these new and fruitful ideas upon the German Romantic School is well known. What distinguishes this school from the romantic movement in England is primarily the spirit of universality. This, as we have observed, appears first in the seventeenth century in the work of Andreae and Leibniz, but it found its completest expression in Herder.

Inspired by the spirit of universality and in accordance with Herder's ideas, the Romanticists began their search for a national spirit among all peoples. They comprehend the spirit of the Middle Ages as common to both the Germanic and Latin peoples, and at the same time seek to penetrate into the true nature of every national individuality. It is from this point of view that we can understand how Jakob Grimm, the real founder of modern philology, incorporates all Germanic dialects in his Grammar and thereby creates the foundation for the scientific study of single dialects. In the same manner that Jakob Grimm embraces the languages, the mythology, and the law of the Germanic peoples, Wilhelm Grimm and Uhland especially seek to comprehend as a unit the literature and the folklore of the Germanic and Latin nations.

We may say that it was primarily the discovery of the conception of nationality, its worth and its importance for modern culture, that made possible the study of the modern languages as we understand it today. Almost simultaneously with this discovery came the political recognition of the various nations in contrast to the abstract cosmopolitanism of the eighteenth century. But while this new political principle leads to great struggles between the individual nationalities, modern philology works toward a mutual understanding and encourages a peaceful competition in the search for truth.

No other great intellectual movement of subsequent years has had so powerful an influence upon the development of our studies as has Romanticism. It is through Romanticism primarily that the historical method gained its sway, and neither Nietzsche's attacks nor the rise of the natural sciences in the latter half of the nineteenth century was able to undermine its dominance. There was a time, of course, when it was thought that the so-called method of natural science was the magic key which would unlock the innermost secrets of the languages and

literatures. This was the time when was introduced into
our science the unfortunate separation between philology
and literature, a division which, much to its advantage,
classical philology never recognized. I am the last person
to deny that the so-called scientific method has contributed
much that is new to the purely physiological aspect of
language, but it has utterly failed in the field of literature,
and it is for this reason that at the present time scholars
are trying to revive the great and fruitful ideas of the
Romanticists.

During recent decades the conviction has gradually
arisen that the language and especially the literature of a
people is a partial expression of the entirety of national
life which we designate by the word culture. This spiritual life of a nation finds its expression also in art, in
music, in philosophy, and in science, but nowhere is the
inner and outer life which lies at the bottom of its political
activity, nowhere is the true genius of a nation and its
enduring life more faithfully and purely mirrored than
in its language and literature, where this life is embodied
in wonderful imagery.

The study of the language and literature of a people
consists in no small measure in deciphering, in reading
and interpreting this imagery. Such a study has as its
object the revelation of the entire cultural life of the nation. But since the civilization of the individual modern
nations is not exclusive nor nationally limited, and since
cultural influences pass in countless ways from one nation
to another, the study of a single modern language and
literature tends to create an understanding for the entire
modern civilization. Who can have an historical appreciation of the German language without a knowledge of
the various Germanic dialects, indeed without a knowledge of the Romance languages, and who can comprehend

the true spirit of German literature without due regard for the English, Scandinavian, French, Spanish, and Italian literatures? Today, more than ever before, the spirit which inspires the study of modern languages and literatures is the idea of universality, the idea which inspired Leibniz, Herder, and the Romanticists.

It is here, in my opinion, that we may find the new problems for American scholarship; for it is in this country that the civilizations of the various European nations meet, and it is here that they are developing into a new and individual civilization. Never before in the course of history has so great and rich a field been offered to both the philologian and the historian of literature. The point might be raised that these problems which I have in mind touch the historian more closely, but our American historiography, prejudiced by a one-sided conception of history, has up to the present time paid little or no attention to them, and I doubt whether they can ever be solved without the help of the philologian.

If we proceed from the fact that our national culture is neither complete nor shaped by a single ethnic force, but that it is of a composite nature and still in the making, one of the most immediate and important problems seems to me to be concerned with penetrating into this process of formation. First of all an inventory must be made of the cultural possessions which the various ethnic elements have brought to this country. Since the immigrants who have poured into this country during the past three centuries have come from various social classes, we may distinguish between popular tradition and higher culture. While the task which I have in mind appears relatively simple as far as the English element is concerned, it is much more complex in regard to the other ethnic groups. These groups, however, have also clung to their customs and their folklore and transmitted it to their environment, and they, too, have shown poetic and artistic activity. To-day when speaking of American poetry, we mean only that written in English. We forget that there is also an American poetry in other languages. As a German philo-logian I am thinking of course, in the first place, of Ameri-can poetry written in German. This is almost unknown to the majority of us; yet, were it collected in its entirety, it would fill many volumes.

Hand in hand with the establishment of the cultural possessions introduced during the various historical periods, and hand in hand with the careful collection of the documents of continued cultural productivity, should go the determination of the geographic distribution of the various ethnic elements in this country. Upon this basis might be achieved the solution of other important prob-lems allied to the psychological relation of the immigrants to the fatherland as well as to the new environment. Of greater importance is the weighing of conservative and progressive tendencies which we may observe in the soul of the immigrants, and which throw a most interesting light upon the character of all colonial intellectual life in general. It will be found that the culture of colonial peoples compared with that in the mother country shows a retrogression, indeed a sort of petrification; great intel-lectual movements in the fatherland are scarcely felt by the emigrants. Thus, the English revolution of the seven-teenth century as well as the intellectual renaissance in Germany during the time of the Storm and Stress and the Romantic period left scarcely a trace in America.

A national literature develops but slowly in colonial countries. The question is, what are the conditions which finally lead to its attainment, and how long does it still remain under the influence of the mother country in regard to form and content? Most closely allied to this is the important problem of how a new civilization, and concomitantly a new nationality, may develop from the various cultural elements. Does the development of a new nationality mean the destruction of the original national characteristics of the various ethnic groups? When this problem first appeared in America in practical form its solution was attempted in the light of the unhistorical and rationalistic cosmopolitanism of the eighteenth century. Even today there are those who dream of the Utopia of national uniformity as the aim of this process, and the melting pot is praised as the national fetich, the magic cauldron out of which this phantom will arise.

Grave doubts as to this miracle arise, however, in the mind of the historian and philologian. Uniformity is the goal of tyranny, be it in the garb of a monarchy or of a democracy. The highest ideal of true culture is freedom, which cannot be conceived as uniform. The native soil for all that is truly characteristic, creative, and of ethnical value in a people is the national individuality. To seek its destruction means to undermine this soil and to hasten decline. How can we students of modern philology sanction such a fatal policy, we who have made the study of nationality our life work?

All the new problems and studies which I have sought to indicate presuppose a comparative method and at the same time sharpen our vision for the countless relations between the various civilized nations which lie hidden in the several languages and literatures. In this country we recognize more clearly than anywhere else the interchange of cultural possessions between the various nationalities. The richness of modern life in its growth and in its diversity opens up before us like a land of wonder. While up to the present time the study of comparative literature has only too often consisted in mechanical juxtaposition or in superficial generalities, the comparative method as described above has a true scientific basis. By calling to our aid history, philosophy, psychology, and aesthetics it becomes possible for us philologians to penetrate into the great intellectual movements which stream back and forth between the various civilized nations of Europe, and which find their expression in the language and literatures of these people. Permit me to illustrate what I have in mind by an example.

It is a fact which has but recently been brought to light in all its bearings that from the close of the sixteenth century until far into the seventeenth a stream of mystical ideas flows from Germany to England. There it takes hold of the religious and poetical life of the nation and exercises a deep-rooted influence upon the poetry and awakening literary criticism of the latter seventeenth century; it helps to determine the fundamental conceptions of the English romantic movement, and finally returns home in the influence which English philosophy and English poetry had in Germany in the eighteenth century. A detailed and exact account of this great cultural movement which I have just tried to summarize in a single sentence would fill volumes. The discovery and presentation of similar far-reaching cultural relations between the various European nations, and ultimately between Europe and America, will open entirely new fields in linguistics and in the history of literature.

It would not be fair were I to leave unmentioned the fact that attempts have been made in this direction. If the history of comparative literature is not content to stand still satisfied with purely mechanical comparisons or with worthless and discreditable aesthetic talk, it must henceforth regard its work from the higher point of view of cultural history which I have indicated.

The objection may be raised that such a method infringes upon other scientific fields, and the guardians of the boundaries of specialization in science will try to drive us back into our own province. If such attacks are made, let us console ourselves with the experience of the great philosopher and jurist Christian Thomasius, whom the theological mediocrities of his time denounced because he had the audacity to poach upon the preserves of theology. He had actually taken the liberty of uttering sarcastic doubts concerning the orthodox teaching that Adam, our great-great-grandfather, had after his fall willed to Cain his estates, lands, and meadows, but to Abel his ready cash and furniture.

We do not deny any one the privilege of pursuing the well-known paths in his research, but in exchange we demand the privilege of seeking new and individual fields, not because of a false desire for originality but, in the final analysis, in order to serve the nation. For a science which has lost its connection with the great life of the people is in danger of petrification or of serving the ends of an unworthy utilitarianism, which after all is synonymous with petrification. The creation of a higher national culture in a composite nation, such as ours, is, as I have said on another occasion, to a large extent a conscious process, which in a certain way is dirigible and, therefore, dependent for its success on the quality of our intellectual leaders and their ideals. I cannot conceive of a greater and more inspiring mission for the American student of modern languages than to have a share in the direction of this process, the greatest which history has seen.

OFFICERS OF THE ASSOCIATION FOR 1915

President,
JEFFERSON B. FLETCHER,
Columbia University, New York, N. Y.

Vice-Presidents,

OLIVER F. EMERSON,   BERT J. VOS,
Western Reserve University, Cleveland, O.   *Indiana University, Bloomington, Ind.*

MARY V. YOUNG,
Mt. Holyoke College, S. Hadley, Mass.

Secretary,   *Tresurer,*
WILLIAM GUILD HOWARD,   ARTHUR F. WHITTEM,
Harvard University, Cambridge, Mass.   *Harvard University, Cambridge, Mass.*

CENTRAL DIVISION

Chairman,   *Secretary,*
WILLIAM H. HULME,   CHARLES BUNDY WILSON,
Western Reserve University, Cleveland, O.   *State University of Iowa, Iowa City, Ia.*

EXECUTIV COUNCIL

THE OFFICERS NAMED ABOVE AND

J. DOUGLAS BRUCE,
University of Tennessee, Knoxville, Tenn.

ARTHUR G. CANFIELD,   ALBERT B. FAUST,
University of Michigan, Ann Arbor, Mich.   *Cornell University, Ithaca, N. Y.*

CHARLES MILLS GAYLEY,   MARION D. LEARNED,
University of California, Berkeley, Cal.   *University of Pennsylvania, Philadelphia, Pa.*

JOHN L. LOWES,   RAYMOND WEEKS,
Washington University, St. Louis, Mo.   *Columbia University, New York, N. Y.*

EDITORIAL COMMITTEE

W. G. HOWARD,   CHARLES BUNDY WILSON,
Harvard University, Cambridge, Mass.   *State University of Iowa, Iowa City, Ia.*

JAMES W. BRIGHT,   F. M. WARREN,
Johns Hopkins University, Baltimore, Md.   *Yale University, New Haven, Conn.*

14

CONSTITUTION OF THE MODERN LANGUAGE ASSOCIATION OF AMERICA

ADOPTED ON THE TWENTY-NINTH OF DECEMBER, 1903

The name of this Society shal be *The Modern Language Association of America.*

II

1.   The object of this Association shal be the advance-ment of the study of the Modern Languages and their Literatures thru the promotion of frendly relations among scolars, thru the publication of the results of investigation by members, and thru the presentation and discussion of papers at an annual meeting.

2.   The meeting of the Association shal be held at such place and time as the Executiv Council shal from year to year determin. But at least as often as once in four years there shal be held a Union Meeting, for which some central point in the interior of the cuntry shal be chosen.

III

Any person whose candidacy has been approved by the Secretary and Tresurer may become a member on the payment of three dollars, and may continue a member by the payment of the same amount each year.   Persons who for twenty years or more hav been activ members in good and regular standing may, on retiring from activ servis as teachers, be continued as activ members without further payment of dues. Any member, or any person eligible to membership, may become a life member by a single payment of forty dollars or by the payment of fifteen dollars a year for three successiv years. Persons who for fifteen years or more hav been activ members in good and regular standing may become life members upon the single payment of twenty-five dollars. Distinguisht foren scolars may be elected to honorary membership by the Association on nomination by the Executiv Council. But the number of honorary members shal not at any time excede forty.

IV

1. The officers and governing boards of the Association shal be: a President, three Vice-Presidents, a Secretary, a Tresurer; an Executiv Council consisting of these six officers, the Chairmen and Secretaries of the several Divisions, and seven other members; and an Editorial Committee consisting of the Secretary of the Association (who shal be Chairman *ex officio*), the Secretaries of the several Divisions, and two other members.

2. The President and the Vice-Presidents shal be elected by the Association, to hold offis for one year.

3. The Chairmen and Secretaries of Divisions shal be chosen by the respectiv Divisions.

4. The other officers shal be elected by the Association at a Union Meeting, to hold offis until the next Union Meeting. Vacancies occurring between two Union Meetings shal be fild by the Executiv Council.

1. The President, Vice-Presidents, Secretary, and Tresurer shal perform the usual duties of such officers.

The Secretary shal, furthermore, hav charge of the Publications of the Association and the preparation of the program of the annual meeting.

2. The Executiv Council shal perform the duties assignd to it in Articles II, III, IV, VII, and VIII; it shal, moreover, determin such questions of policy as may be referd to it by the Association and such as may arise in the course of the year and call for immediate decision.

3. The Editorial Committee shal render such assistance as the Secretary may need in editing the Publications of the Association and preparing the annual program.

VI

1. The Association may, to further investigation in any special branch of Modern Language study, create a Section devoted to that end.

2. The officers of a Section shal be a Chairman and a Secretary, elected annually by the Association. They shal form a standing committee of the Association, and may ad to their number any other members interested in the same subject.

VII

1. When, for geografical reasons, the members from any group of States shal find it expedient to hold a separate annual meeting, the Executiv Council may arrange with these members to form a Division, with power to call a meeting at such place and time as the members of the Division shal select; but no Division meeting shal be held during the year in which the Association holds a Union Meeting. The expense of Division meetings shal be borne by the Association. The total number of Divisions shal not at any time excede three. The present Division is hereby continued.

2.   The members of a Division shal pay their dues to the Tresurer of the Association, and shal enjoy the same rights and privileges and be subject to the same conditions as other members of the Association.

3.   The officers of a Division shal be a Chairman and a Secretary.   The Division shal, moreover, hav power to create such committees as may be needed for its own business.   The program of the Division meeting shal be prepared by the Secretary of the Division in consultation with the Secretary of the Association.

VIII

This Constitution may be amended by a two-thirds vote at any Union Meeting, provided the proposed amendment has receivd the approval of two-thirds of the members of the Executiv Council.

ACTS OF THE EXECUTIV COUNCIL

I.   In accordance with a proposition of date January 7, 1915, *Voted:*

That the invitation of Western Reserve University and the Case School of Applied Science to hold the next annual meeting, a Union Meeting, under their auspices be accepted.

II.   In accordance with propositions of date February 1, 1915, *Voted:*

   1. That to members of the American Philological Association resident on the Pacific Coast our *Publications* be sent at the rate of $1.50 per annum for each member, said sum to be paid to us in advance by the Tresurer of the American Philological Association.

   2. That the Council approve an amendment to the Constitution combining the offises of Secretary and Tresurer.

III.   In accordance with a proposition of date February 3, 1915, *Voted:*

That Professor C. Alphonso Smith be appointed a delegate to represent the Association at the inauguration of President Graham of the University of North Carolina on April 21, 1915.

IV.   In accordance with a proposition of date February 8, 1915, *Voted:*

That the Council approve amendments to the Constitution increasing the Editorial Committee by one and making all members of said Committee members of the Executiv Council.

V. In accordance with propositions of date September 11, 1915, *Voted:*

That the Council recommend the election of Professors Charles Harold Herford, Kristoffer Nyrop, George Saintsbury, and Sir Sidney Lee to Honorary Membership in the Association.

VI. In accordance with a proposition of date October 29, 1915, *Voted:*

That Professor George N. Henning be appointed Delegate, and Mr. A. Werner Spanhoofd be appointed Alternate Delegate of the Association to the Second Pan-American Scientific Congress at Washington, D. C., December 27, 1915, to January 8, 1916.

W. G. HOWARD,
Secretary.

MEMBERS OF THE MODERN LANGUAGE ASSOCIATION OF AMERICA

INCLUDING MEMBERS OF THE CENTRAL DIVISION OF THE ASSOCIATION

Names of Life Members ar printed in small capitals

Abbott, Allan, Assistant Professor of English, Teachers' College, Columbia University, New York, N. Y.

Adams, Arthur, Professor of English, Trinity College, Hartford, Conn.

ADAMS, EDWARD LARRABEE, Assistant Professor of French and Spanish, University of Michigan, Ann Arbor, Mich. [1333 Washtenaw Ave.]

Adams, John Chester, Assistant Professor of English and Faculty Adviser in Undergraduate Literary Activities, Yale University, New Haven, Conn.

Adams, Joseph Quincy, Jr., Assistant Professor of English, Cornell University, Ithaca, N. Y. [169 Goldwin Smith Hall]

Adams, Warren Austin, Professor of German, Dartmouth College, Hanover, N. H.

Alberti, Christine, Head of the French Department, Allegheny High School, North Side, Pittsburgh, Pa. [318 W. North Ave.]

Albright, Evelyn May, Associate in English, University of Chicago, Chicago, Ill. [1227 E. 57th St.]

Alden, Raymond Macdonald, Professor of English, Leland Stanford Jr. University, Stanford University, Cal.

Alderman, William E., Instructor in English, University of Wisconsin, Madison, Wis. [1216 W. Washington Ave.]

Alexander, Luther Herbert, Instructor in Romance Languages, Columbia University, New York, N. Y. [660 Riverside Drive]

Alexis, Joseph Emanuel Alexander, Assistant Professor of Swedish and Germanic Languages, University of Nebraska, Lincoln, Neb. [1420 Elm St.]

Allen, Clifford Gilmore, Associate Professor of Romanic Languages, Leland Stanford Jr. University, Stanford University, Cal.

ALLEN, EDWARD ARCHIBALD, Professor Emeritus of the English Language and Literature, University of Missouri, Columbia, Mo.

Allen, F. Sturges, Springfield, Mass. [83 St. James Ave.]

Allen, Hope Emily, Kenwood, Oneida, N. Y.

Allen, Philip Schuyler, Assistant Professor of German Literature, University of Chicago, Chicago, Ill. [1508 E. 61st St., Jackson Park Sta.]

Allen, William H., Jr., Oxford University Press, 35 W. 32nd St., New York, N. Y.

Almstedt, Hermann, Professor of Germanic Languages, University of Missouri, Columbia, Mo.

Altrocchi, Rudolph, Assistant Professor of Romance Languages, University of Chicago, Chicago, Ill.

Anderson, Frederick, Instructor in French and Spanish, Sheffield Scientific School, Yale University, New Haven, Conn. [1007 Yale Station]

Andrews, Albert LeRoy, Instructor in German and Scandinavian, Cornell University, Ithaca, N. Y.

Andrews, Clarence Edward, Assistant Professor of English, Ohio State University, Columbus, O. [1874 N. High St.]

Ansley, C. F., Professor of English and Dean of the College of Fine Arts, State University of Iowa, Iowa City, Ia.

Appelmann, Anton, Professor of German, University of Vermont, Burlington, Vt.

Arbib-Costa, Alfonso, Instructor in Romance Languages, College of the City of New York, New York, N. Y. [500 W. 144th St.]

Armstrong, Edward C., Professor of the French Language, Johns Hopkins University, Baltimore, Md.

Arnold, Frank Russell, Professor of Modern Languages, State Agricultural College, Logan, Utah.

Arnold, Morris LeRoy, Professor of English Literature, Hamline University, St. Paul, Minn. [2628 Park Ave., Minneapolis, Minn.]

Arrowsmith, Robert, Orange, N. J. [253 Highland Ave.]

Ashley, Edgar Louis, Associate Professor of German, Massachusetts Agricultural College, Amherst, Mass.

Atkinson, Geoffroy, Instructor in Modern Languages, Union College, Schenectady, N. Y.

Austin, Herbert Douglas, Instructor in French and Italian, University of Michigan, Ann Arbor, Mich.

Aydelotte, Frank, Associate Professor of English, Indiana University, Bloomington, Ind.

Ayer, Charles Carlton, Professor of Romance Languages, University of Colorado, Boulder, Col.

Ayres, Edward, Professor of Rhetoric, Purdue University, West Lafayette, Ind. [1003 State St.]

Ayres, Harry Morgan, Assistant Professor of English, Columbia University, New York, N. Y.

Babbitt, Irving, Professor of French Literature, Harvard University, Cambridge, Mass. [6 Kirkland Road]

Babcock, Charlotte Farrington, Instructor in English, Simmons College, Boston, Mass. [11 Downer Ave., Dorchester, Mass.]

Babcock, Earle Brownell, Professor of Romance Languages and Literatures, New York University, University Heights, New York, N. Y.

Babson, Herman, Professor of German and Head of the Department of Modern Languages, Purdue University, West Lafayette, Ind.

Bach, Matthew G., Instructor in German, Teachers' College, Columbia University, New York, N. Y. [Furnald Hall]

Bachelor, Joseph Morris, Assistant Professor of English Literature, Cornell College, Mt. Vernon, Ia.

Bacon, George William, Wyncote, Pa.

Bagster-Collins, Elijah William, Associate Professor of German, Teachers' College, Columbia University, New York, N. Y.

Baker, Asa George, G. & C. Merriam Co., Publishers of Webster's Dictionaries, Springfield, Mass.

Baker, Fannie Anna, Head of the Department of Modern Languages, Fort Smith High School, Fort Smith, Ark. [515 N. 15th St.]

Baker, Franklin Thomas, Professor of English, Teachers' College, Columbia University, New York, N. Y. [525 W. 120th St.]

Baker, George Pierce, Professor of Dramatic Literature, Department of English, Harvard University, Cambridge, Mass. [195 Brattle St.]

Baker, Louis Charles, Professor of German, Lawrence College, Appleton, Wis. [490 College Ave.]

Baker, Thomas Stockham, Head Master, Tome School for Boys, Jacob Tome Institute, Port Deposit, Md.

Baldwin, Charles Sears, Professor of Rhetoric, Columbia University, New York, N. Y.

Baldwin, Edward Chauncey, Assistant Professor of English Literature, University of Illinois, Urbana, Ill. [1002 S. Lincoln Ave.]

Barba, Preston Albert, Assistant Professor of German, Indiana University, Bloomington, Ind. [412 E. 4th St.]

Bargy, Henry, Professor of French, Hunter College of the City of New York, New York, N. Y.

Barlow, William M., Assistant in German, Commercial High School, Brooklyn, N. Y.

Barney, Winfield Supply, Professor of Romance Languages, Hobart College, Geneva, N. Y. [408 Pultney St.]

Barrows, Sarah T., Assistant Professor of German, Ohio State University, Columbus, O.

Barry, Phillips, Cambridge, Mass. [83 Brattle St.]

BARTLETT, Mrs. DAVID LEWIS, Baltimore, Md. [16 W. Monument St.]

Barto, Philip Stephen, Instructor in German, University of Illinois, Urbana, Ill. [312 W. Springfield Ave., Champaign, Ill.]

Barton, Francis Brown, Instructor in Romance Languages, Williams College, Williamstown, Mass.

Baskervill, Charles Read, Assistant Professor of English, University of Chicago, Chicago, Ill.

Bates, Madison Clair, Professor of English, South Dakota State College of Agriculture and Mechanic Arts, Brookings, S. D.

Batt, Max, Professor of Modern Languages, North Dakota Agricultural College, Fargo, N. D.

BATTIN, BENJAMIN F., Professor of German, Swarthmore College, Swarthmore, Pa.

Baugh, Albert C., Instructor in English, University of Pennsylvania, Philadelphia, Pa. [638 S. 54th St.]

Baum, Paull Franklin, Instructor in English, Harvard University, Cambridge, Mass. [64 Sparks St.]

Baumgartner, Milton D., Professor of Germanic Languages, Butler College, Indianapolis, Ind.

Baur, William F., Assistant Professor of Germanic Languages, University of Colorado, Boulder, Col. [1035 15th St.]

Baxter, Arthur H., Associate Professor of Romance Languages, Amherst College, Amherst, Mass.

Beach, Joseph Warren, Assistant Professor of English, University of Minnesota, Minneapolis, Minn. [1801 University Ave., S. E.]

Beall, Mrs. Emilie, Teacher of French, German, and Spanish, High School of Commerce, Columbus, O. [420 14th Ave.]

Beam, Jacob N., Princeton, N. J.

Bean, Helen, Fairfield, Ia. [202 N. Main St.]

Bear, Maud Cecelia, Instructor in German and Latin, Bellefonte High School, Bellefonte, Pa. [Bush House]

Beardsley, Wilfred Attwood, Waterbury, Conn. [78 Clowes Ter.]

Beatty, Arthur, Assistant Professor of English, University of Wisconsin, Madison, Wis. [1824 Vilas St.]

de Beaumont, Victor, Associate Professor of the French Language and Literature, University of Toronto, Toronto, Canada. [73 Queen's Park]

Beck, Jean Baptiste, Associate Professor of Mediæval French Literature, Bryn Mawr College, Bryn Mawr, Pa. [1041 County Line Road]

Becker, Ernest Julius, Principal, Eastern High School, Baltimore, Md.

Bek, William G., Professor of German, University of North Dakota, Grand Forks, N. D. [Box 1233, University, N. D.]

Belden, Henry Marvin, Professor of English, University of Missouri, Columbia, Mo. [811 Virginia Ave.]

Belknap, Arthur Train, Professor of English, Franklin College of Indiana, Franklin, Ind.

Bell, Robert Mowry, Minneapolis, Minn. [229 Fifth Ave., S. E.]

Bender, Harold H., Assistant Professor, Preceptor in Modern Languages, Princeton University, Princeton, N. J.

Benham, Allen Rogers, Associate Professor of English, University of Washington, Seattle, Wash.

Benson, Adolph Burnett, Instructor in German, Sheffield Scientific School, Yale University, New Haven, Conn. [130 Howe St.]

Berdan, John Milton, Assistant Professor of English, Yale University, New Haven, Conn.

Bergeron, Maxime L., Instructor in French, College of the City of New York, 138th St. and Amsterdam Ave., New York, N. Y.

Bernbaum, Ernest, Instructor in English, Harvard University, Cambridge, Mass. [86 Sparks St.]

Bernkopf, Margarete, Head of the German Department, Yonkers High School, Yonkers, N. Y. [503 W. 121st St., New York, N. Y.]

DE BÉTHUNE, Baron FRANÇOIS, Louvain, Belgium. [34 rue de Bériot]

Betz, Gottlieb Augustus, Instructor in Germanic Languages and Literatures, Barnard College, Columbia University, New York, N. Y.

Béziat de Bordes, André, Professor of French, Newcomb College, Tulane University, New Orleans, La.

Bigelow, Eleanor, Radcliffe College, Cambridge, Mass. [6 Wellington Terrace, Brookline, Mass.]

Billetdoux, Edmond Wood, Associate Professor of Romance Languages, Rutgers College, New Brunswick, N. J. [324 Lincoln Ave.]

Bishop, David Horace, Professor of the English Language and Literature, University of Mississippi, Oxford, Miss. [University, Miss.]

Blackburn, Bonnie Rebecca, Associate Professor of Modern Languages, James Millikin University, Decatur, Ill. [911 W. Main St.]

Blackwell, Robert Emory, President and Professor of English, Randolph-Macon College, Ashland, Va.

Blake, Harriet Manning, Instructor in English Literature, Mount Holyoke College, So. Hadley, Mass. [The Gables]

Blanchard, Frederic Thomas, Instructor in English, University of California, Berkeley, Cal. [2610 Russell St.]

BLAU, MAX FRIEDRICH, Professor of Germanic Languages and Literatures, Princeton University, Princeton, N. J.

Blayney, Thomas Lindsey, Professor of the German Language, Rice Institute, Houston, Texas. [Yoakum Boulevard]

Blondheim, David Simon, Assistant Professor of Romance Languages, University of Illinois, Urbana, Ill. [University Club]

Blood, Edna Banks, Teacher of German, Lower Merion High School, Ardmore, Pa. [119 Coulter Ave.]

Bloomfield, Leonard, Assistant Professor of Comparative Philology and German, University of Illinois, Urbana, Ill.

Blount, Alma, Assistant Professor of English, Michigan State Normal College, Ypsilanti, Mich. [712 Ellis St.]

Blume, Carlos August, Instructor in French and Spanish, Dartmouth College, Hanover, N. H.

Bockstahler, Oscar Leo, Instructor in German and History, High School, Arcola, Ill.

Boesche, Albert Wilhelm, Assistant Professor of German, Cornell University, Ithaca, N. Y. [Forest Home Drive]

Bohn, William Edward, Teacher of English, School of Ethical Culture, New York, N. Y. [206 N. Maple Ave., East Orange, N. J.]

Boll, Helene Hubertine, Mistress in German, Rosemary Hall, Greenwich, Conn.

Bond, Otto Ferdinand, Instructor in Romance Languages, University of Texas, Austin, Tex. [3202 West Ave.]

Bonilla, Rodrigo Huguet, Instructor in Romance Languages, University of Michigan, Ann Arbor, Mich. [508 Benjamin St.]

Bonnell, John Kester, Instructor in English, University of Wisconsin, Madison, Wis. [625 Mendota Court]

Booker, John Manning, Associate Professor of English, University of North Carolina, Chapel Hill, N. C.

Borgerhoff, J. L., Professor of Romance Languages, Western Reserve University, Cleveland, O.

Borgman, Albert Stephens, Detroit, Mich. [295 Seminole Ave.]

Bothne, Gisle C. J., Head Professor of Scandinavian Languages and Literatures, University of Minnesota, Minneapolis, Minn.

Boucke, Ewald A., Professor of German, University of Michigan, Ann Arbor, Mich.

Bourland, Benjamin Parsons, Professor of Romance Languages, Adelbert College of Western Reserve University, Cleveland, O.

Bouton, Archibald Lewis, Professor of English, Dean of the College of Arts and Pure Science, New York University, University Heights, New York, N. Y.

Bowen, Abba Willard, Professor of German, Peru State Normal School, Peru, Neb.

Bowen, Benjamin Lester, Professor of Romance Languages, Ohio State University, Columbus, O. [775 E. Broad St.]

Bowen, Edwin Winfield, Professor of Latin, Randolph-Macon College, Ashland, Va.

Bowen, James Vance, Professor of Modern Languages, Mississippi Agricultural and Mechanical College, Agricultural College, Miss.

Bowman, James Cloyd, Associate Professor of English, Iowa State College, Ames, Ia. [109 Hyland Ave.]

Boyer, Clarence Valentine, Instructor in English, University of Illinois, Urbana, Ill.

Boynton, Percy Holmes, Assistant Professor of English, University of Chicago, Chicago, Ill. [5748 Kimbark Ave.]

Boysen, Johannes Lassen, Instructor in German, University of Texas, Austin, Tex.

Bradshaw, S. Ernest, Professor of Modern Languages, Furman University, Greenville, S. C.

Bradsher, Earl Lockridge, Instructor in English, University of Texas, Austin, Tex.

Brandon, Edgar Ewing, Vice-President and Dean, Miami University, Oxford, O.

Brandt, Hermann Carl Georg, Professor of the German Language and Literature, Hamilton College, Clinton, N. Y.

Braun, Wilhelm Alfred, Associate Professor of Germanic Languages and Literatures, Barnard College, Director of the Deutsches Haus, Columbia University, New York, N. Y.

Brede, Charles F., Professor of German, Northeast Manual Training High School, Philadelphia, Pa. [1937 N. 13th St.]

Brewer, Theodore Hampton, Professor of English Literature, University of Oklahoma, Norman, Okla. [111 Hammond St., Cambridge, Mass.]

Brewster, William Tenney, Professor of English, Columbia University, New York, N. Y.

Briggs, Fletcher, Professor of Modern Languages, Iowa State College, Ames, Ia. [Station A]

Briggs, William Dinsmore, Assistant Professor of English, Leland Stanford Jr. University, Stanford University, Cal.

BRIGHT, JAMES WILSON, Professor of English Philology, Johns Hopkins University, Baltimore, Md.

Bristol, Edward N., Henry Holt & Co., 34 W. 33d St., New York, N. Y.

Bronk, Isabelle, Professor of the French Language and Literature, Swarthmore College, Swarthmore, Pa.

Bronson, Thomas Bertrand, Head of the Modern Language Department, Lawrenceville School, Lawrenceville, N. J.

Bronson, Walter C., Professor of English Literature, Brown University, Providence, R. I.

Brooke, C. F. Tucker, Assistant Professor of English, Yale University, New Haven, Conn. [725 Yale Station]

Brooks, Neil C., Assistant Professor of German, University of Illinois, Urbana, Ill.

Broughton, Leslie Nathan, Instructor in English, Cornell University, Ithaca, N. Y. [110 E. Marshall St.]

Brown, Arthur C. L., Professor of English, Northwestern University, Evanston, Ill. [625 Colfax St.]

Brown, Calvin S., Professor of Modern Languages, University of Mississippi, University, Miss.

Brown, Carleton F., Professor of English Philology, Bryn Mawr College, Bryn Mawr, Pa.

Brown, Frank Clyde, Professor of English, Trinity College, Durham, N. C. [410 Guess St.]

Brown, Frederic Willis, Professor of Modern Languages, Bowdoin College, Brunswick, Me.

Brown, George Henry, Instructor in Romance Languages, Cornell University, Ithaca, N. Y. [120 Oak Ave.]

Brown, Harold Gibson, Instructor in English, University of Wisconsin, Madison, Wis. [University Club]

Brown, Kent James, Associate Professor of German, University of North Carolina, Chapel Hill, N. C.

Brown, Rollo Walter, Professor of Rhetoric and Composition, Wabash College, Crawfordsville, Ind. [607 S. Water St.]

Bruce, Charles A., Professor of Romance Languages, Ohio State University, Columbus, O.

Bruce, James Douglas, Professor of the English Language and Literature, University of Tennessee, Knoxville, Tenn. [712 W. Main Ave.]

Bruner, James Dowden, President, Daughters College, Harrodsburg, Ky.

Bruns, Friedrich, Assistant Professor of German, University of Wisconsin, Madison, Wis. [2330 Rowley Ave.]

Brush, Henry Raymond, Professor of Romance Languages, University of North Dakota, Grand Forks, N. D. [607 Walnut St.]

Brush, Murray Peabody, Collegiate Professor of French, Johns Hopkins University, Baltimore, Md.

Brusie, Charles Frederick, Principal, Mt. Pleasant Military Academy, Ossining, N. Y.

Bryan, Eva May, Associate in French, State Normal and Industrial College, Greensboro, N. C.

Bryan, Walter Speight, Assistant Instructor in German, Yale College, New Haven, Conn. [173 Park St.]

Bryan, William Frank, Assistant Professor of English, Northwestern University, Evanston, Ill.

Buchanan, Milton Alexander, Associate Professor of Italian and Spanish, University of Toronto, Toronto, Canada. [88 Wells Hill Ave.]

Buck, Arthur Ela, Associate Professor of the German Language and Literature, Grinnell College, Grinnell, Ia. [1008 Park St.]

Buck, Gertrude, Professor of English, Vassar College, Poughkeepsie, N. Y. [112 Market St.]

Buck, Philo Melvin, Jr., Professor of Rhetoric, University of Nebraska, Lincoln, Neb. [1825 Pepper Ave.]

Buck, Robert W., University Scholar in German, Columbia University, New York, N. Y. [Furnald Hall]

BUCKINGHAM, MARY H., Boston, Mass. [96 Chestnut St.]

Buffum, Douglas Labaree, Professor of Romance Languages, Princeton University, Princeton, N. J. [60 Hodge Road]

Burchinal, Mary Cacy, Head of the Department of Foreign Languages, West Philadelphia High School for Girls, 47th and Walnut Sts., Philadelphia, Pa.

Burkhard, Oscar Carl, Assistant Professor of German, University of Minnesota, Minneapolis, Minn.

Burnet, Percy Bentley, Director of Modern Languages, Manual Training High School, Kansas City, Mo. [3751 Flora Ave.]

Burnett, Arthur W., Henry Holt & Co., 34 W. 33d St., New York, N. Y.

Burnham, Josephine May, Associate Professor of English, Wellesley College, Wellesley, Mass.

Burrage, Leslie M., Instructor in Romance Languages, Pennsylvania State College, State College, Pa. [243 S. Pugh St.]

Bursley, Philip E., Instructor in French and Spanish, University of Michigan, Ann Arbor, Mich. [917 Olivia Ave.]

Burton, John Marvin, Professor of Modern Languages, Millsaps College, Jackson, Miss.

Busey, Robert Oscar, Assistant Professor of German, Ohio State University, Columbus, O. [2050 Inka Ave.]

Bush, Stephen Hayes, Professor of Romance Languages, University of Iowa, Iowa City, Ia.

Bushee, Alice H., Instructor in Spanish, Wellesley College, Wellesley, Mass.

Busse, Paul Gustav Adolf, Associate Professor of German, Hunter College of the City of New York, New York, N. Y.

Butler, Pierce, Professor of English, Newcomb College, New Orleans, La.

13

Cabot, Stephen Perkins, Head of the Department of French and German, St. George's School, Newport, R. I.

Cady, Frank William, Assistant Professor of English, Middlebury College, Middlebury, Vt.

Cairns, William B., Assistant Professor of American Literature, University of Wisconsin, Madison, Wis. [2010 Madison St.]

Callaway, Morgan, Jr., Professor of English, University of Texas, Austin, Tex. [1104 Guadalupe St.]

Camera, Amerigo Ulysses N., Instructor in Romance Languages, College of the City of New York, New York, N. Y. [575 West Ave., Kensington, Brooklyn, N. Y.]

Cameron, Ward Griswold, Professor of Modern Languages, St Stephen's College, Annandale, N. Y.

Campbell, Gertrude H., London, England. [9 Endsleigh Gardens, N. W.]

Campbell, James Andrew, Professor of German, Knox College, Galesburg, Ill.

Campbell, Killis, Associate Professor of English, University of Texas, Austin, Tex. [2301 Rio Grande St.]

Campbell, Lily B., Instructor in English, University of Wisconsin, Madison, Wis. [419 Stirling Place]

Campbell, Oscar James, Jr., Assistant Professor of English, University of Wisconsin, Madison, Wis. [15 E. Gilman St.]

Campbell, Thomas Moody, Professor of German, Randolph-Macon Woman's College, Lynchburg, Va. [College Park, Va.]

Canby, Henry Seidel, Assistant Professor of English, Sheffield Scientific School, Yale University, New Haven, Conn. [105 East Rock Road]

Canfield, Arthur Graves, Professor of Romance Languages, University of Michigan, Ann Arbor, Mich. [909 E. University Ave.]

Cannon, Lee Edwin, Professor of Modern Languages, Eureka College, Eureka, Ill.

Carhart, Paul Worthington, Assistant Editor, G. and C. Merriam Co., Myrick Building, Springfield, Mass.

Carnahan, David Hobart, Associate Professor of Romance Languages, University of Illinois, Urbana, Ill.

CARNEGIE, ANDREW, New York, N. Y. [2 E. 91st St.]

Carpenter, Fred Donald, Instructor in German, Sheffield Scientific School, Yale University, New Haven, Conn. [385 Norton St.]

CARPENTER, FREDERIC IVES, Barrington, Ill.

Carpenter, Jennette, Professor of the English Language and Literature, Iowa State Teachers' College, Cedar Falls, Ia. [412 W. 8th St.]

Carr, Muriel Bothwell, Instructor in English, University of Wisconsin, Madison, Wis. [149 Sterling Court]

Carruth, William Herbert, Professor of Comparative Literature, Leland Stanford Jr. University, Stanford University, Cal.

Carson, Lucy Hamilton, Professor of English, Montana State Normal College, Dillon, Mont.

Carteaux, Gustave A., Professor of the French Language, Polytechnic Institute, Brooklyn, N. Y.

Casés, Lilia Mary, Associate Professor of Spanish, University of Texas, Austin, Tex.

Cave, Charles Elmer, Instructor in German, Oakland Technical High School, Oakland, Cal. [2623 Parker St., Berkeley, Cal.]

Cchrs, Carrie M., Assistant Professor of German, Montana State College of Agriculture and Mechanic Arts, Bozeman, Mont.

Cerf, Barry, Associate Professor of Romance Languages, University of Wisconsin, Madison, Wis. [1911 Monroe St.]

Chamberlain, May, Professor of Germanic Languages and Literatures, University of Nebraska, Lincoln, Neb. [Station A]

Chamberlin, Willis Arden, Professor of the German Language and Literature, Denison University, Granville, O.

Chandler, Edith Beatrice, Professor of Modern Languages, Highland Park College, Des Moines, Ia.

Chandler, Frank Wadleigh, Professor of English and Comparative Literature, Dean of the College of Liberal Arts, University of Cincinnati, Cincinnati, O. [222 Hosea Ave., Clifton, Cincinnati]

Chapin, George Scott, Assistant Professor of Romance Languages, Ohio State University, Columbus, O.

Charles, Arthur M., Professor of German and French, Earlham College, Richmond, Ind.

Chase, Lewis Nathaniel, London W., England. [54 Digby Mansions, Hammersmith Bridge]

Chase, Stanley P., Assistant Professor of English, Union College, Schenectady, N. Y. [9 Glenwood Boulevard]

Chatfield-Taylor, Hobart C., Lake Forest, Ill.

Cheever, Louisa Sewall, Associate Professor of the English Language and Literature, Smith College, Northampton, Mass. [Chapin House]

Chenery, Winthrop Holt, Librarian and Associate Professor of Romanic Languages, Washington University, St. Louis, Mo.

Cherington, Frank Barnes, University of Chicago, Chicago, Ill. [111 Middle Hall]

Child, Clarence Griffin, Professor of English, University of Pennsylvania, Philadelphia, Pa. [4237 Sansom St.]

MODERN LANGUAGE ASSOCIATION

Childs, Francis Lane, Assistant Professor of English, Dartmouth College, Hanover, N. H. [Box 142]

Chinard, Gilbert, Associate Professor of French, University of California, Berkeley, Cal.

Church, Henry Ward, Professor of Modern Languages, Monmouth College, Monmouth, Ill. [1011 E. Boston Ave.]

Church, Howard Wadsworth, Instructor in German, Yale College, New Haven, Conn.

Churchill, George Bosworth, Professor of English Literature, Amherst College, Amherst, Mass.

Churchman, Philip Hudson, Professor of Romance Languages, Clark College, Worcester, Mass. [20 Institute Road]

Claassen, Peter Alden, Professor of Modern Languages, Florida State College for Women, Tallahassee, Fla. [P. O. Box 298]

Clapp, John Mantell, Professor of English, Lake Forest College, Lake Forest, Ill.

Clark, Eugene Francis, Assistant Professor of German, Dartmouth College, Hanover, N. H.

Clark, Evert Mordecai, Instructor in English, University of Texas, Austin, Tex.

Clark, Thatcher, Head of the Department of French, School of Ethical Culture, 63d St. and Central Park West, New York, N. Y.

Clark, Thomas Arkle, Professor of Rhetoric and Dean of Men, University of Illinois, Urbana, Ill. [928 W. Green St.]

Clarke, Charles Cameron, Professor of French, Sheffield Scientific School, Yale University, New Haven, Conn. [254 Bradley St.]

Clary, S. Willard, D. C. Heath & Co., 50 Beacon St., Boston, Mass.

Clementine, Sister M., Teacher of English, Saint Clara College, Sinsinawa, Wis.

Cobb, Charles W., Assistant Professor of Mathematics, Amherst College, Amherst, Mass. [Mt. Doma]

Coffman, George Raleigh, Professor of English, University of Montana, Missoula, Mont.

Cohen, Helen Louise, First Assistant in English, Washington Irving High School, New York, N. Y. [38 W. 93d St.]

Cohn, Adolphe, Professor of the Romance Languages and Literatures, Columbia University, New York, N. Y.

Cohn-McMaster, Albert Marian, Professor of Modern Languages, Sweet Briar College, Sweet Briar, Va.

Cole, George Franklin, Professor of Romance Languages, Dickinson College, Carlisle, Pa.

Coleman, Algernon, Instructor in French, University of Chicago, Chicago, Ill.

Collings, Harry T., Professor of German, Pennsylvania State College, State College, Pa. [308 S. Burrows St.]

Collins, George Stuart, Professor of German and Spanish, Polytechnic Institute, Brooklyn, N. Y.

Collins, Varnum Lansing, Professor of the French Language and Literature, Princeton University, Princeton, N. J.

COLLITZ, HERMANN, Professor of Germanic Philology, Johns Hopkins University, Baltimore, Md.

Colton, Molton Avery, Instructor in Modern Languages, U. S. Naval Academy, Annapolis, Md.

Colville, William T., Carbondale, Pa.

Colwell, William Arnold, Professor of the German Language and Literature, Adelphi College, Brooklyn, N. Y.

Comfort, William Wistar, Professor of the Romance Languages and Literatures, Cornell University, Ithaca, N. Y.

Compton, Alfred D., Tutor in English, College of the City of New York, New York, N. Y.

Conant, Martha Pike, Associate Professor of English Literature, Wellesley College, Wellesley, Mass. [25 Weston Road]

Condit, Lola M., Professor of Modern Languages, State College, Brookings, S. Dak.

Conklin, Clara, Professor of Romance Languages and Literatures, University of Nebraska, Lincoln, Neb.

Conrow, Georgianna, Assistant Professor of French, Vassar College, Poughkeepsie, N. Y.

Cons, Louis, Associate in Romance Languages, Bryn Mawr College, Bryn Mawr, Pa.

Cook, Albert S., Professor of the English Language and Literature, Yale University, New Haven, Conn. [219 Bishop St.]

Cool, Charles Dean, Assistant Professor of Romance Languages, University of Wisconsin, Madison, Wis. [1607 Adams St.]

Cooper, Lane, Assistant Professor of the English Language and Literature, Cornell University, Ithaca, N. Y. [Cornell Heights]

Cooper, William Alpha, Associate Professor of German, Leland Stanford Jr. University, Stanford University, Cal.

Corbin, Alberta Linton, Associate Professor of German, University of Kansas, Lawrence, Kas.

Corbin, William Lee, Associate Professor of English, Wells College, Aurora, N. Y.

Corley, Ames Haven, Instructor in Spanish, Yale University, New Haven, Conn. [131 Canner St.]

Cornwell, Irene Marie, Instructor in French, Newcomb College, New Orleans, La.

Corwin, Robert Nelson, Professor of German, Sheffield Scientific School, Yale University, New Haven, Conn. [247 St. Ronan St.]

Cory, Herbert Ellsworth, Assistant Professor of English, University of California, Berkeley, Cal. [2558 Buena Vista Way]

Cosulich, Gilbert, Chicago, Ill. [La Salle Extension]

Coues, Robert Wheaton, Assistant in English, Harvard University, Cambridge, Mass. [10 Mason St.]

Cowper, Frederick Augustus Grant, Assistant Professor of Romance Languages, University of Kansas, Lawrence, Kas. [1540 New Hampshire St.]

Cox, Edward Godfrey, Assistant Professor of English, University of Washington, Seattle, Wash.

Cox, John Harrington, Professor of English Philology, West Virginia University, Morgantown, W. Va. [188 Spruce St.]

Craig, Hardin, Professor of English, University of Minnesota, Minneapolis, Minn.

Crane, Ronald Salmon, Assistant Professor of English, Northwestern University, Evanston, Ill. [725 Foster St.]

Crawford, Douglas, Instructor in English, Phillips Academy, Andover, Mass. [Bishop Hall]

Crawford, James Pyle Wickersham, Professor of Romanic Languages and Literatures, University of Pennsylvania, Philadephia, Pa.

Crawshaw, William Henry, Dean and Professor of English Literature, Colgate University, Hamilton, N. Y.

Creek, Herbert Le Sourd, Associate in English, University of Illinois, Urbana, Ill.

Croissant, De Witt C., Associate Professor of English, University of Kansas, Lawrence, Kas. [1611 Tennessee St.]

Croll, Morris William, Assistant Professor of English, Princeton University, Princeton, N. J. [53 Patton Hall]

Crook, Mrs. Martha Loescher, Professor of German, Denver University, Denver, Col. [P. O. Box 913]

Cross, Tom Peete, Associate Professor of English and Celtic, University of Chicago, Chicago, Ill.

Cross, Wilbur Lucius, Professor of English, Sheffield Scientific School, Yale University, New Haven, Conn. [24 Edgehill Road]

Crowell, Asa Clinton, Associate Professor of Germanic Languages and Literatures, Brown University, Providence, R. I. [66 Oriole Av., East Side Sta.]

Crowne, Joseph Vincent, Instructor in English, College of the City of New York, New York, N. Y.

Cru, Robert Loyalty, Assistant Professor of French, Hunter College of the City of New York, New York, N. Y.

Cuenca, Tomás Leal, Director General de la Escuela Nacional de Idiomas de la Rep. de Colombia, Bogota, Colombia. [Calle 17, No. 49]

CUNLIFFE, JOHN WILLIAM, Professor of English and Associate Director of the School of Journalism, Columbia University, New York, N. Y.

Curdy, Albert Eugene, Associate Professor of French, Yale University, New Haven, Conn. [743 Yale Station]

Curme, George Oliver, Professor of Germanic Philology, Northwestern University, Evanston, Ill. [629 Colfax St.]

Curry, Walter Clyde, Instructor in English, Vanderbilt University, Nashville, Tenn.

Curts, Paul, Associate Professor of German, Wesleyan University, Middletown, Conn.

Cushwa, Frank William, Professor of English, Phillips Exeter Academy, Exeter, N. H.

Cutting, Starr Willard, Professor and Head of the Department of Germanic Languages and Literatures, University of Chicago, Chicago, Ill.

Daland, Rev. William Clifton, President and Professor of English and Biblical Literature, Milton College, Milton, Wis.

Damon, Lindsay Todd, Professor of Rhetoric, Brown University, Providence, R. I.

Dana, Henry Wadsworth Longfellow, Instructor in English and Comparative Literature, Columbia University, New York, N. Y.

Daniels, Francis Potter, Professor of Romance Languages, Wabash College, Crawfordsville, Ind. [107 Marshall St.]

Danton, George Henry, Professor of German, Reed College, Portland, Ore.

Dargan, Edwin Preston, Assistant Professor of French Literature, University of Chicago, Chicago, Ill.

Dargan, Henry M., Instructor in English, University of North Carolina, Chapel Hill, N. C.

Darnall, Frank Mauzy, Professor of English, Southwestern Presbyterian University, Clarksville, Tenn. [120 4th St.]

Darnall, Henry Johnston, Professor of Germanic Languages, University of Tennessee, Knoxville, Tenn.

David, Henri Charles-Edouard, Assistant Professor of French Literature, University of Chicago, Chicago, Ill.

Davidsen, Hermann Christian, Assistant Professor of German, Cornell University, Ithaca, N. Y. [Highland Ave.]

Davies, James, Instructor in German, University of Minnesota, Minneapolis, Minn.

Davies, William Walter, Professor of the German Language, Ohio Wesleyan University, Delaware, O.

Davis, Edward Ziegler, Assistant Professor of German, University of Pennsylvania, Philadelphia, Pa. [424 N. 34th St.]

Davis, Edwin Bell, Professor of Romance Languages, Rutgers College, New Brunswick, N. J. [145 College Ave.]

Davis, Henry Campbell, Professor of the English Language and Rhetoric, University of South Carolina, Columbia, S. C. [2532 Divine St.]

Davis, William Hawley, Professor of English and Public Speaking, Bowdoin College, Brunswick, Me. [4 Page St.]

Davis, William Rees, Professor of English, Whitman College, Walla Walla, Wash.

Daw, Elizabeth Beatrice, Fellow in English, Bryn Mawr College, Bryn Mawr, Pa. [Denbigh Hall]

Daw, M. Emily, Instructor in English, New Jersey State Normal School, Trenton, N. J. [142 N. Clinton Ave.]

Dearborn, Ambrose Collyer, Henry Holt & Co., 34 W. 33d St., New York, N. Y.

De Beck, B. O. M., American Book Co., 300 Pike St., Cincinnati, O.

Deering, Robert Waller, Professor of Germanic Languages and Literatures, Western Reserve University, Cleveland, O. [2931 Somerton Road, Mayfield Heights, Cleveland]

De Forest, John Bellows, Instructor in French, Sheffield Scientific School, Yale University, New Haven, Conn. [1019 Yale Station]

De Haan, Fonger, Professor of Spanish, Bryn Mawr College, Bryn Mawr, Pa.

Delamarre, Louis, Associate Professor of French, College of the City of New York, New York, N. Y. [237 Tecumseh Ave., Mt. Vernon, N. Y.]

Denney, Joseph Villiers, Professor of English and Dean of the College of Arts, Philosophy, and Science, Ohio State University, Columbus, O.

Dey, William Morton, Professor of Romance Languages, University of North Carolina, Chapel Hill, N. C.

Diekhoff, Tobias J. C., Junior Professor of German, University of Michigan, Ann Arbor, Mich.

Dingus, Leonidas Reuben, Professor of German, Richmond College, Richmond, Va. [108 N. West St.]

Doby, Madeleine H., Instructor in French, Wellesley College, Wellesley, Mass. [Stone Hall]

Dodge, Daniel Kilham, Professor of the English Language and Literature, University of Illinois, Urbana, Ill.

Dodge, Robert Elkin Neil, Assistant Professor of English, University of Wisconsin, Madison, Wis. [15 W. Gorham St.]

Doernenburg, Emil, Professor of German, Ohio University, Athens, O.

Doniat, Josephine C., Instructor in French and German, Carl Schurz High School, Chicago, Ill.

Donnelly, Lucy Martin, Professor of English, Bryn Mawr College, Bryn Mawr, Pa.

Douay, Gaston, Professor of French, Washington University, St. Louis, Mo.

Douglass, Philip Earle, Instructor in French, University of Pennsylvania, Philadelphia, Pa. [14 Graduate House, U. of P.]

Dow, Louis Henry, Professor of French, Dartmouth College, Hanover, N. H.

Downer, Charles Alfred, Professor of Romance Languages, College of the City of New York, 138th St. and Amsterdam Ave., New York, N. Y.

Doyle, Henry Grattan, Instructor in Romance Languages, Harvard University, Cambridge, Mass. [29 Berkeley St., Somerville, Mass.]

Drummond, Robert Rutherford, Assistant Professor of German, University of Maine, Orono, Me.

Dudley, Louise, Professor of English, Lawrence College, Appleton, Wis.

Dunlap, Charles Graham, Professor of English Literature, University of Kansas, Lawrence, Kas.

Dunn, Joseph, Professor of Celtic Languages and Lecturer in Romance Languages, Catholic University, Washington, D. C.

Dunster, Annie, Head of the Department of Foreign Languages, William Penn High School for Girls, 15th and Wallace Sts., Philadelphia, Pa.

Durham, Willard Higley, Instructor in English, Sheffield Scientific School, Yale University, New Haven, Conn. [1819 Yale Station]

Dutton, George B., Assistant Professor of English, Williams College, Williamstown, Mass.

Dye, Alexander Vincent, Secretary, Phelps, Dodge & Co., Bisbee, Ariz.

van Dyke, Henry, Professor of English Literature, Princeton University, Princeton, N. J.

Easley, Owen Randolph, Teacher of French and German, High School, Lynchburg, Va.

Eastburn, Iola Kay, Professor of German, Wheaton College, Norton, Mass.

Easter, De la Warr B., Professor of Romance Languages, Washington and Lee University, Lexington, Va.

Eastman, Clarence Willis, Professor of the German Language and Literature, Amherst College, Amherst, Mass.

Eberhardt, Edward Albert, Jefferson City, Mo.

Eckelmann, Ernst Otto, Assistant Professor of German, University of Washington, Seattle, Wash. [3442 Cascade View Drive]

Effinger, John Robert, Professor of French and Acting Dean of the College of Literature, Science, and the Arts, University of Michigan, Ann Arbor, Mich.

Eggert, Carl Edgar, Assistant Professor of German, University of Michigan, Ann Arbor, Mich. [924 Baldwin Ave.]

Eisenlohr, Berthold A., Professor of German, Ohio State University, Columbus, O.

Eiserhardt, Ewald, Assistant Professor of German, University of Rochester, Rochester, N. Y. [145 Harvard St.]

Elias, Edward, Professor and Head of the Department of Modern Languages, Hope College, Holland, Mich.

Elliott, George Roy, Professor of English Literature, Bowdoin College, Brunswick, Me.

Elson, Charles, Instructor in German, Adelphi College, Brooklyn, N. Y. [118 Oak St., Kane, Pa.]

Emerson, Oliver Farrar, Professor of English, Western Reserve University, Cleveland, O. [98 Wadena St.]

Emery, Fred Parker, Professor of English, Dartmouth College, Hanover, N. H.

Eno, Arthur Llewellyn, Assistant Professor of English, Pennsylvania State College, State College, Pa.

Erskine, John, Associate Professor of English, Columbia University, New York, N. Y.

Esborn, Charles Linus, Professor of Modern Languages, Augustana College, Rock Island, Ill.

Evans, Marshall Blakemore, Professor of German, Ohio State University, Columbus, O.

Evers, Helene M., Mary Institute, St. Louis, Mo.

Ewart, Frank Carman, Professor of Romanic Languages, Colgate University, Hamilton, N. Y.

Eyster, John B., Instructor in German, Horace Mann Boys' School, New York, N. Y. [417 W. 121st St.]

Fahnestock, Edith, Assistant Professor of Spanish and Italian, Vassar College, Poughkeepsie, N. Y.

Fairchild, Arthur Henry Rolph, Professor of English, University of Missouri, Columbia, Mo. [708 Maryland Place]

Fairchild, J. R., American Book Co., 100 Washington Sq., New York, N. Y.

Fairley, Barker, Professor of German, University of Alberta, Edmonton South, Alberta, Canada.

Fansler, Dean Spruill, Lecturer in English, Columbia University, New York, N. Y.

Farley, Frank Edgar, Professor of English, Simmons College, Boston, Mass.

Farnham, Willard Edward, Harvard University, Cambridge, Mass. [18 Conant Hall]

Farnsworth, William Oliver, Professor of Romance Languages, University of Pittsburgh, Pittsburgh, Pa. [103 Orchard St., W. Somerville, Mass.]

Farr, Hollon A., Assistant Professor of German, Yale University, New Haven, Conn. [351 White Hall]

Farrand, Wilson, Head Master, Newark Academy, Newark, N. J.

Farrar, Thomas James, Professor of Germanic Languages, Washington and Lee University, Lexington, Va.

Faulkner, William Harrison, Professor of Germanic Languages, University of Virginia, Charlottesville, Va. [Box 228]

FAUST, ALBERT BERNHARDT, Professor of German, Cornell University, Ithaca, N. Y. [Cornell Heights]

Fay, Charles Ernest, Professor of Modern Languages, Tufts College, Tufts College, Mass.

Fay, Percival Bradshaw, Assistant Professor of Romanic Philology, University of California, Berkeley, Cal. [Faculty Club]

Feise, Richard Ernst, Associate Professor of German, University of Wisconsin, Madison, Wis. [1011 Edgewood Ave.]

Ferguson, John De Lancey, Instructor in English, Heidelberg University, Tiffin, O. [216 Jefferson St.]

Ferren, Harry M., Professor of German, Allegheny High School, North Side, Pittsburgh, Pa.

Ferrin, Dana Holman, The Century Co., 623 S. Wabash Ave., Chicago, Ill.

Ficken, Hilbert Theodore, Professor of German, Baldwin-Wallace College, Berea, O.

Fife, Robert Herndon, Jr., Professor of German, Wesleyan University, Middletown, Conn. [347 High St.]

Files, George Taylor, Professor of Germanic Languages, Bowdoin College, Brunswick, Me.

Fisher, John Roberts, Professor of Modern Languages, Randolph-Macon College, Ashland, Va.

Fiske, Christabel Forsyth, Associate Professor of English, Vassar College, Poughkeepsie, N. Y.

Fitz-Gerald, John Driscoll, Professor of Spanish, University of Illinois, Urbana, Ill.

FITZ-HUGH, THOMAS, Professor of Latin, University of Virginia, University, Va.

Fletcher, Jefferson Butler, Professor of Comparative Literature, Columbia University, New York, N. Y. [112 E. 22d St.]

Fletcher, Robert Huntington, Professor of English Literature, Grinnell College, Grinnell, Ia.   .

Flom, George Tobias, Assistant Professor of Scandinavian Languages, University of Illinois, Urbana, Ill.

Florer, Warren Washburn, Assistant Professor of German, University of Michigan, Ann Arbor, Mich. [910 Olivia Ave.]

Flowers, Olive, Teacher of French and English, West High School, Columbus, O. [763 Franklin Ave.]

Foerster, Norman, Associate Professor of English, University of North Carolina, Chapel Hill, N. C.

Fogel, Edwin Miller, Assistant Professor of German, University of Pennsylvania, Philadelphia, Pa.

Fogg, Miller Moore, Professor of Rhetoric, University of Nebraska, Lincoln, Neb.

Fogle, David Edgar, Professor of German, Georgetown College, Georgetown, Ky.

Fontaine, Camille, Assistant Professor of Romance Languages, Columbia University, New York, N. Y.

Ford, Daniel, Assistant Professor of Rhetoric, University of Minnesota, Minneapolis, Minn. [315 4th St., S. E.]

Ford, J. D. M., Professor of the French and Spanish Languages, Harvard University, Cambridge, Mass. [9 Riedesel Ave.]

Ford, R. Clyde, Professor of Modern Languages, State Normal College, Ypsilanti, Mich.

Forsythe, Robert Stanley, Instructor in English, Adelbert College, Western Reserve University, Cleveland, O. [18 Adelbert Hall]

Fortier, Edward J., Instructor in Romance Languages and Literatures, Columbia University, New York, N. Y. [Hamilton Hall]

Fossler, Laurence, Head Professor of the Germanic Languages and Literatures, University of Nebraska, Lincoln, Neb.

Foster, Finley Melville, Instructor in English, New York University, New York, N. Y. [112 Moore Ave., Rutherford, N. J.]

Foster, Irving Lysander, Professor of Romance Languages, Pennsylvania State College, State College, Pa.

Fowler, Earle Broadus, Chicago, Ill. [6029 Ellis Ave.]

Fowler, Thomas Howard, Professor of German, Wells College, Aurora, N. Y.

Fox, Charles Shattuck, Professor of Romance Languages, Lehigh University, South Bethlehem, Pa. [330 Wall St., Bethlehem]

Francke, Kuno, Professor of the History of German Culture and Curator of the Germanic Museum, Harvard University, Cambridge, Mass. [3 Berkeley Place]

Frank, Colman Dudley, Head of the Department of Romance Languages, De Witt Clinton High School, 59th St. and Tenth Ave., New York, N. Y.

Franklin, George Bruce, Assistant Professor of English, Simmons College, Boston, Mass. [22 Trowbridge St., Cambridge, Mass.]

Frantz, Frank Flavius, Acting Professor of Romance Languages, Vanderbilt University, Nashville, Tenn. [Vanderbilt Campus]

Fraser, William Henry, Professor of Italian and Spanish, University of Toronto, Toronto, Canada.

Freeman, Clarence Campbell, Professor of English Literature, Transylvania College, Lexington, Ky. [515 W. 3d St.]

Frelin, Jules, Assistant Professor of French, University of Minnesota, Minneapolis, Minn.

French, George Franklin, Instructor in Modern Languages, Phillips Academy, Andover, Mass. [12 School St.]

French, John Calvin, Associate Professor of English, Johns Hopkins University, Baltimore, Md.

French, Mrs. W. F. (M. Katherine Jackson), London, Ky.

Friedland, Louis Sigmund, Instructor in the English Language and Literature, College of the City of New York, 138th St. and Amsterdam Ave., New York, N. Y.

Froelicher, Hans, Professor of German, Goucher College, Baltimore, Md.

Fuentes, Ventura P., Assistant Professor of Spanish, College of the City of New York, 138th St. and Amsterdam Ave., New York, N. Y.

Fuess, Claude Moore, Instructor in English, Phillips Academy, Andover, Mass. [183 Main St.]

Fulton, Edward, Associate Professor of English, University of Illinois, Urbana, Ill.

Galloo, Eugénie, Professor of Romance Languages and Literatures, University of Kansas, Lawrence, Kas.

Galpin, Stanley Leman, Professor of Romance Languages, Trinity College, Hartford, Conn.

Galt, Mary Meares, Teacher of French, Williams Memorial Institute, New London, Conn.

Gambrill, Louise, Instructor in French, Wellesley College, Wellesley, Mass.

Gardner, Edward Hall, Assistant Professor of English, University of Wisconsin, Madison, Wis. [1924 Kendall Ave.]

Gardner, May, Instructor in Romance Languages, University of Kansas, Lawrence, Kas.

Garver, Milton Stahl, Instructor in French, Sheffield Scientific School, Yale University, New Haven, Conn. [811 Yale Station]

Gaston, Charles Robert, First Assistant in English, Richmond Hill High School, New York, N. Y. [215 Abingdon Road, Richmond Hill, N. Y.]

Gauss, Christian, Professor of Modern Languages, Princeton University, Princeton, N. J.

GAW, MRS. RALPH H., Topeka, Kas. [1321 Filmore St.]

Gay, Lucy Maria, Assistant Professor of Romance Languages, University of Wisconsin, Madison, Wis. [216 N. Pinckney St.]

Gayley, Charles Mills, Professor of the English Language and Literature, University of California, Berkeley, Cal.

GEDDES, JAMES, Professor of Romance Languages, Boston University, Boston, Mass. [20 Fairmount St., Brookline, Mass.]

Geissendoerfer, John Theodore, Instructor in German, University of Minnesota, Minneapolis, Minn. [216 Folwell Hall]

Gerig, John Lawrence, Associate Professor of Celtic, Columbia University, New York, N. Y.

Gerould, Gordon Hall, Assistant Professor, Preceptor in English, Princeton University, Princeton, N. J.

Getz, Igerna Miriam, Instructor in German and English, Marshalltown High School, Marshalltown, Ia. [5 S. 4th St.]

Gideon, Abram, Professor of German and French, University of Wyoming, Laramie, Wyo.

Gilbert, Allan H., Instructor in English, Cornell University, Ithaca, N. Y. [202 Miller St.]

Gilbert, Donald Monroe, Morgantown, W. Va. [749 N. Front St.]

Gildersleeve, Virginia Crocheron, Dean and Professor of English, Barnard College, Columbia University, New York, N. Y.

Gillet, Joseph Eugene, Associate in Comparative Literature and German, University of Illinois, Urbana, Ill. [806 S. 3d St., Champaign, Ill.]

Gingerich, Solomon Francis, Assistant Professor of English, University of Michigan, Ann Arbor, Mich. [517 Elm St.]

Gingrich, Gertrude, Professor of the German Language and Literature, University of Wooster, Wooster, O. [575 University St.]

Glascock, Clyde Chew, Assistant Professor of Modern Languages, The Rice Institute, Houston, Tex.

Goddard, Eunice Rathbone, The Knox School, Tarrytown, N. Y.

Goddard, Harold Clarke, Professor of English, Swarthmore College, Swarthmore, Pa.

Goebel, Julius, Professor of Germanic Languages, University of Illinois, Urbana, Ill.

Goettsch, Charles, Assistant Professor of Germanic Philology, University of Chicago, Chicago, Ill.

Good, John Walter, Assistant Professor of English Literature, Kansas State Agricultural College, Manhattan, Kas. [807 Osage St.]

Goodale, Ralph Hinsdale, Professor of English, Hiram College, Hiram, O.

Goodnight, Scott Holland, Associate Professor of German, Director of the Summer Session, University of Wisconsin, Madison, Wis. [2130 W. Lawn Ave.]

Goodsell, Marguerite, Teacher of French and German. Gilbert School, Winsted, Conn.

Gordon, Robert Kay, Lecturer in English, University of Alberta, Edmondton South, Alberta, Canada.

Gorham, Maud Bassett, Instructor in English, Swarthmore College, Swarthmore, Pa.

Gould, Chester Nathan, Assistant Professor of German and Scandinavian Literature, University of Chicago, Chicago, Ill.

GRANDGENT, CHARLES HALL, Professor of Romance Languages, Harvard University, Cambridge, Mass. [107 Walker St.]

Graves, Isabel, Associate Professor of English, The Temple University, Philadelphia, Pa.

Graves, Thornton Shirley, Assistant Professor of English, Trinity College, Durham, N. C.

Gray, Charles Henry, Professor of English, Tufts College, Tufts College, Mass. [57 Dartmouth St., Winter Hill, Somerville, Mass.]

Gray, Henry David, Assistant Professor of English, Leland Stanford Jr. University, Stanford University, Cal.

Gray, Jesse Martin, Instructor in German, Columbia University, New York, N. Y. [410 Hamilton Hall]

Gray, Roland Palmer, Professor and Head of the Department of English, University of Maine, Orono, Me.

Green, Alexander, Instructor in German, University of Illinois, Urbana, Ill. [1001 S. 5th St., Champaign, Ill.]

Greene, Ernest Roy, Assistant Professor of Romance Languages, Dartmouth College, Hanover, N. H. [19 Maple St.]

Greene, Herbert Eveleth, Collegiate Professor of English, Johns Hopkins University, Baltimore, Md. [1019 St. Paul St.]

Greenfield, Eric Viele, Assistant Professor of German, Purdue University, West Lafayette, Ind.

Greenlaw, Edwin Almiron, Professor of English, University of North Carolina, Chapel Hill, N. C.

Greenough, Chester Noyes, Professor of English, Harvard University, Cambridge, Mass. [26 Quincy St.]

Greever, Gustavus Garland, Associate Professor of English, Washington and Lee University, Lexington, Va.

Griebsch, Max, Director, National German-American Teachers' Seminary, 558-568 Broadway, Milwaukee, Wis.

Griffin, James O., Professor of German, Leland Stanford Jr. University, Stanford University, Cal.

Griffin, Nathaniel Edward, Assistant Professor, Preceptor in English, Princeton University, Princeton, N. J. [14 N. Dod Hall]

Griffith, Dudley David, Professor of English, Simpson College, Indianola, Ia.

Griffith, Reginald Harvey, Associate Professor of English, University of Texas, Austin, Tex. [University Station]

Grimm, Karl Josef, Professor of the German Language and Literature, Pennsylvania College, Gettysburg, Pa.

Gronow, Hans Ernst, Assistant Professor of German, University of Chicago, Chicago, Ill.

Grünbaum, Gustav, Instructor in Romance Languages, Johns Hopkins University, Baltimore, Md.

GRUENER, GUSTAV, Professor of German, Yale University, New Haven, Conn. [146 Lawrance Hall]

Grumbine, Harvey Carson, Professor of the English Language and Literature, The College of Wooster, Wooster, O.

Grummann, Paul H., Professor of Modern German Literature, University of Nebraska, Lincoln, Neb. [1967 South St.]

Gubelmann, Albert Edward, Assistant Professor of German, Yale College, New Haven, Conn. [806 Yale Station]

Guérard, Albert Léon, Professor of the History of French Culture, The Rice Institute, Houston, Tex.

Guerlac, Othon G., Assistant Professor of French, Cornell University, Ithaca, N. Y. [3 Fountain Place]

Guitner, Alma, Professor of German, Otterbein University, Westerville, O. [75 W. College Ave.]

Gummere, Francis B., Professor of English, Haverford College, Haverford, Pa.

Gutknecht, Louise L., Instructor in Modern Languages, J. Bowen High School, Chicago, Ill. [7700 Bond Ave., Windsor Park]

Guyer, Foster Erwin, Assistant Professor of French, Dartmouth College, Hanover, N. H.

Gwyn, Virginia Percival (Mrs. H. B.), Chicago, Ill. [5612 Madison Ave.]

Haertel, Martin H., Assistant Professor of German, University of Wisconsin, Madison, Wis.

Hale, Edward E., Professor of English, Union College, Schenectady, N. Y.

Hale, Wm. Gardner, Professor of Latin, University of Chicago, Chicago, Ill.

Hall, Edgar A., Professor of English, Adelphi College, Brooklyn, N. Y. [420 Park Place]

Hall, John Lesslie, Professor of the English Language and Literature, College of William and Mary, Williamsburg, Va.

Hall, Margaret Woodburn, Acting Chairman of the French Department, Evander Childs High School, St. Lawrence and Westchester Avenues, Bronx, New York, N. Y.

Haller, William, Instructor in English, Barnard College, Columbia University, New York, N. Y.

Halley, Albert Roberts, Head of the Department of Modern Languages, Chatham Academy, Savannah, Ga. [1230 E. 31st St.]

Hamilton, George Livingstone, Assistant Professor of Romance Languages, Cornell University, Ithaca, N. Y.

Hamilton, Theodore Ely, Assistant Professor of Romance Languages, Ohio State University, Columbus, O.

Hammond, Eleanor Prescott, Chicago, Ill. [1357 E. 57th St.]

Handschin, Charles Hart, Professor of German, Miami University, Oxford, O.

Haney, John Louis, Professor of English Philology, Central High School, Philadelphia, Pa.

Hanford, James Holly, Associate Professor of English, University of North Carolina, Chapel Hill, N. C.

Hardy, Ashley Kingley, Assistant Professor of German and Instructor in Old English, Dartmouth College, Hanover, N. H.

Harper, Carrie Anna, Associate Professor of English Literature, Mount Holyoke College, So. Hadley, Mass.

Harper, George McLean, Professor of English, Princeton University, Princeton, N. J.

HARRIS, CHARLES, Professor of German, Western Reserve University, Cleveland, O

Harris, Lancelot Minor, Professor of English, College of Charleston, Charleston, S. C.

Harrison, Frederick Browne, Instructor in English, Jacob Tome Institute, Port Deposit, Md.

Harrison, John Smith, Assistant Professor of English, Kenyon College, Gambier, O.

14

Harry, Philip Warner, Associate Professor of Romance Languages and Literatures, Colby College, Waterville, Me.

HART, CHARLES EDWARD, Professor Emeritus of Ethics and Evidences of Christianity, Rutgers College, New Brunswick, N. J. [33 Livingston Ave.]

HART, JAMES MORGAN, Professor Emeritus of the English Language and Literature, Cornell University, Ithaca, N. Y. [English Seminary, Cornell University Library]

Hart, Walter Morris, Associate Professor of English Philology, University of California, Berkeley, Cal. [2255 Piedmont Ave.]

Hartmann, Jacob Wittmer, Assistant Professor of the German Language and Literature, College of the City of New York, New York, N. Y. [468 W. 153d St.]

Harvitt, Helen J., Assistant in French, Teachers' College, Columbia University, New York, N. Y. [192 Hooper St., Brooklyn, N. Y.]

Hastings, Harry Worthington, Assistant Professor of English, New York State College for Teachers, Albany, N. Y.

Hastings, William Thomson, Assistant Professor of English, Brown University, Providence, R. I. [13 John St.]

Hatcher, Orie Latham, Associate Professor of Comparative and Elizabethan Literature, Bryn Mawr College, Bryn Mawr, Pa.

HATFIELD, JAMES TAFT, Professor of the German Language and Literature, Northwestern University, Evanston, Ill.

Hauhart, William F., Assistant Professor of German, University of Michigan, Ann Arbor, Mich.

Haussmann, John Fred, Instructor in German, University of Wisconsin, Madison, Wis. [531 State St.]

Havens, Raymond Dexter, Assistant Professor of English, University of Rochester, Rochester, N. Y.

Hayden, Philip Meserve, New York, N. Y. [1120 Amsterdam Ave.]

Heaton, H. C., Instructor in Romance Languages, New York University, New York, N. Y. [University Heights]

Heck, Jean Olive, Instructor in English, Hartwell High School, Cincinnati, O. [3757 Darwin Ave.]

Heiss, John, Associate Professor of German, Purdue University, West Lafayette, Ind. [403 University St.]

Held, Felix Emil, Associate Professor of German, Miami University, Oxford, O. [110 University Ave.]

Heller, Anna Marie, Teacher of German and French, William Penn High School, Philadelphia, Pa.

Heller, Otto, Professor and Head of the Department of German, Washington University, St. Louis, Mo.

Helmholtz-Phelan, Mrs. Anna Augusta, Assistant Professor of Rhetoric, University of Minnesota, Minneapolis, Minn.

Helmrich, Elsie W., New Rochelle, N. Y. [8 Franklin Ave.]

Hemingway, Samuel Burdett, Assistant Professor of English, Yale College, New Haven, Conn.

Hempl, George, Professor of Germanic Philology, Leland Stanford Jr. University, Stanford University, Cal.

Hénin, Benjamin Louis, Professor of French, High School of Commerce, 157 W. 65th St., New York, N. Y.

Henning, George Neely, Professor of Romance Languages, George Washington University, Washington, D. C.

Henry, Laura Alice, Teacher of German, West High School, Minneapolis, Minn. [217 8th Ave., S. E.]

Herford, Charles Harold, Professor of English Literature, University of Manchester, Manchester, England.

Hermannsson, Halldór, Curator of the Icelandic Collection and Lecturer in Scandinavian, Cornell University, Ithaca, N. Y.

Herrick, Asbury Haven, Instructor in German, Harvard University, Cambridge, Mass. [34 Maple Ave.]

Hersey, Frank Wilson Cheney, Instructor in English, Harvard University, Cambridge, Mass. [61 Oxford St.]

HERVEY, WILLIAM ADDISON, Associate Professor of the Germanic Languages and Literatures, Columbia University, New York, N. Y.

Heuser, Frederick W. J., Assistant Professor of the Germanic Languages and Literatures, Columbia University, New York, N. Y.

Heusinkveld, Arthur Helenus, Instructor in English, Hope College, Holland, Mich.

HEWETT, WATERMAN THOMAS, Professor Emeritus of the German Language and Literature, Cornell University, Ithaca, N. Y.

Hewitt, Theodore Brown, Instructor in German, Williams College, Williamstown, Mass.

Heyd, Jacob Wilhelm, Professor of German, State Normal School, Kirksville, Mo.

Hicks, Fred Cole, Professor of Modern Languages, Dakota Wesleyan University, Mitchell, S. Dak.

Hicks, Rivers Keith, Associate Professor of French, Queen's University, Kingston, Ont.

Hildreth, Walter A., Instructor in German, Williams College, Williamstown, Mass.

Hill, Herbert Wynford Professor of the English Language and Literature, University of Nevada, Reno, Nev.

Hill, Hinda Teague, Professor of Romance Languages, State Normal College, Greensboro, N. C.

Hill, John, Dresden, Tenn.

Hill, Murray Gardner, Instructor in English, Adelbert College, Western Reserve University, Cleveland, O.

Hill, Raymond Thompson, Instructor in French, Yale University, New Haven, Conn.

Hills, Elijah Clarence, Professor of Romance Languages and Literatures, Colorado College, Colorado Springs, Col. [12 College Place]

Hinckley, Henry Barrett, New Haven, Conn. [83 Grove St.]

Hinsdale, Ellen C., Professor of the German Language and Literature, Mount Holyoke College, So. Hadley, Mass.

Hochdörfer, K. F. Richard, Professor of Modern Languages, Wittenberg College, Springfield, O. [The Elbridge]

HODDER, Mrs. ALFRED, Baltimore, Md. [33 Mt. Vernon Place, East]

Hohlfeld, Alexander R., Professor of German, University of Wisconsin, Madison, Wis.

Holbrook, Richard Thayer, Associate Professor of Old French and Italian, Bryn Mawr College, Bryn Mawr, Pa.

Hollander, Lee M., Instructor in German and Scandinavian, University of Wisconsin, Madison, Wis. [202 Forest St.]

Holt, Josephine White, Head of the Department of Romance Languages, John Marshall High School, Richmond, Va. [113 N. 3d St.]

Holzwarth, Franklin James, Professor of the Germanic Languages and Literatures, Syracuse University, Syracuse, N. Y. [911 Walnut Ave.]

Hopkins, Annette Brown, Associate Professor of English, Goucher College, Baltimore, Md.

Hopkins, Edwin Mortimer, Professor of Rhetoric and the English Language, University of Kansas, Lawrence, Kas.

Horning, Lewis Emerson, Professor of Teutonic Philology, Victoria College, Toronto, Canada.

Hosic, James Fleming, Professor of English, Chicago Normal College, Chicago, Ill. [10423 Seeley Ave.]

Hoskins, John Preston, Professor of the Germanic Languages and Literatures, Princeton University, Princeton, N. J. [22 Bank St.]

Hospes, Mrs. Cecilia Lizzette, Teacher of German, McKinley High School, St. Louis, Mo. [6429 Berlin Ave.]

House, Ralph Emerson, Instructor in Romance Languages, University of Chicago, Chicago, Ill.

House, Roy Temple, Professor of German, State University of Oklahoma, Norman, Okla. [321 W. Symmes St.]

HOWARD, WILLIAM GUILD, Assistant Professor of German, Harvard University, Cambridge, Mass. [39 Kirkland St.]

Howe, Thomas Carr, President, Butler College, Indianapolis, Ind. [30 N. Audubon Place]

Howe, Will David, Professor of English, Indiana University, Bloomington, Ind.

Hoyt, Prentiss Cheney, Professor of English, Clark College, Worcester, Mass. [940 Main St.]

Hrbkova, Šárka B., Assistant Professor, Head of the Department of Slavonic Languages and Literatures, University of Nebraska, Lincoln, Neb. [105 M. Arts Hall]

Hubbard, Frank Gaylord, Professor of English, University of Wisconsin, Madison, Wis. [409 N. Murray St.]

Hubert, Merton Jerome, Instructor in French and Italian, University of Cincinnati, Cincinnati, O.

Hughes, Mrs. Charlotte Condé, Tutor in Romance Languages and Literatures, Grand Rapids, Mich. [20 North College Ave.]

Hulbert, James Root, Assistant Professor of English, University of Chicago, Chicago, Ill.

Hulme, William Henry, Professor of English, College for Women, Western Reserve University, Cleveland, O.

Humphreys, Wilber R., Assistant Professor of English, University of Michigan, Ann Arbor, Mich. [1435 Cambridge Road]

Hunkins, Charles H., Assistant Professor of Romance Languages, Brown University, Providence, R. I.

Hunt, Theodore Whitefield, Professor of English, Princeton University, Princeton, N. J.

Hurlburt, Albert Francis, Instructor in Romance Languages, University of Michigan, Ann Arbor, Mich. [513 Elm St.]

Hutchins, Henry Clinton, Instructor in English, Lafayette College, Easton, Pa.

HYDE, JAMES HAZEN, New York, N. Y. [23 W. 50th St.]

Ilgen, Ernest, Associate Professor of German, College of the City of New York, New York, N. Y.

Imbert, Louis, Instructor in Romance Languages, Columbia University, New York, N. Y. [Hamilton Hall, Columbia University]

Ingraham, Edgar Shugert, Professor of Romance Languages, Ohio State University, Columbus, O.

Jackson, George Pullen, Assistant Professor of German, University of North Dakota, University, N. D. [813 Belmont Ave., Grand Forks, N. D.]

von Jagemann, H. C. G., Professor of Germanic Philology, Harvard University, Cambridge, Mass. [113 Walker St.]

von Janinski, E. R., Instructor in German, Municipal University, Akron, O.

JENKINS, T. ATKINSON, Professor of French Philology, University of
Chicago, Chicago, Ill. [5411 Greenwood Ave.]

Jenney, Adeline Miriam, Huron, S. D.

Jensen, Gerard Edward, Instructor in English, University of Pennsylvania, Philadelphia, Pa.

JESSEN, KARL DETLEV, Professor of German Literature, Bryn Mawr
College, Bryn Mawr, Pa.

Johnson, Amandus, Instructor in Scandinavian and German, University of Pennsylvania, Philadelphia, Pa. [Box 39, College Hall]

Johnson, Carl Wilhelm, Assistant Professor of German, Williams
College, Williamstown, Mass.

Johnson, Henry, Professor of Modern Languages, Bowdoin College,
Brunswick, Me.

Johnson, Herman Patrick, Adjunct Professor of English Literature,
University of Virginia, University, Va.

Johnson, Ida Petrine, Instructor in German, University of Minnesota, Minneapolis, Minn. [214 Folwell Hall]

Johnson, William Savage, Associate Professor of English Literature,
University of Kansas, Lawrence, Kas. [1135 Ohio St.]

Johnston, Oliver Martin, Associate Professor of Romanic Languages,
Leland Stanford Jr. University, Stanford University, Cal.

Jonas, Johannes Benoni Eduard, Teacher of German, DeWitt Clinton
High School, New York, N. Y. [50 Turner Ave., Riverside,
R. I.]

Jones, Clara V., Teacher of German, Princeton Township High
School, Princeton, Ill.

Jones, Harry Stuart Vedder, Assistant Professor of English, University of Illinois, Urbana, Ill.

Jones, Jessie Louise, Assistant Professor of German, Lewis Institute, Chicago, Ill.

Jones, Raymond Watson, Instructor in German, Dartmouth College,
Hanover, N. H.

Jones, Richard, Professor of English, Tufts College, Tufts College,
Mass. [9 Concord Ave., Cambridge, Mass.]

Jones, Richard Foster, Instructor in English, Western Reserve University, Cleveland, O.

Jones, Virgil Laurens, Professor of English, University of Arkansas,
Fayetteville, Ark.

Jordan, Daniel, Assistant Professor of the Romance Languages and
Literatures, Columbia University, New York, N. Y.

Jordan, Mary Augusta, Professor of English, Smith College, Northampton, Mass. [Hatfield House]

JOYNES, EDWARD S., Professor Emeritus of Modern Languages, University of South Carolina, Columbia, S. C.

Judson, Alexander-Corbin, Instructor in English, University of Texas, Austin, Tex.

Kammaín, William F., Assistant in German, University of Pennsylvania, Philadelphia, Pa. [3439 Chestnut St.]

Kaufman, J. Paul, Harvard University, Cambridge, Mass. [56 Brentford Hall]

Kayser, Carl F., Professor of the German Language and Literature, Hunter College of the City of New York, New York, N. Y. [71 E. 87th St.]

Keep, Robert Porter, Instructor in German, Phillips Academy, Andover, Mass.

Keidel, George Charles, Library of Congress, Washington, D. C.

Keidel, Heinrich C., Instructor in German, Ohio State University, Columbus, O.

Keith, Oscar L., Professor of Modern Languages, University of South Carolina, Columbia, S. C. [1518 University Place]

Keller, May L., Professor of English, Dean of Women, Westhampton College, Richmond, Va.

Kellogg, Robert James, Professor of Modern Languages, James Millikin University, Decatur, Ill. [912 W. Main St.]

Kelly, Edythe Grace, Teacher of French, High School, Stamford, Conn. [135 Hamilton Place, New York, N. Y.]

Kent, Charles W., Professor of English Literature, University of Virginia, University, Va.

Kenyon, John Samuel, Professor and Head of the Department of English, Butler College, Indianapolis, Ind. [5339 University Ave.]

Keppler, Emil A. C., Tutor in Germanic Languages and Literatures, College of the City of New York, New York, N. Y. [353 W. 85th St.]

Kerlin, Robert Thomas, Professor of English, Virginia Military Institute, Lexington, Va.

Kern, Alfred Allan, Professor of English, Millsaps College, Jackson, Miss.

Kerr, William Alexander Robb, Professor of Modern Languages, and Dean of the Faculty of Arts and Sciences, University of Alberta, Edmonton South, Alberta, Canada.

Kind, John Louis, Assistant Professor of German, University of Wisconsin, Madison, Wis. [425 Sterling Court]

King, James Percival, Professor of German, University of Rochester, Rochester, N. Y.

King, Robert Augustus, Professor of German, Wabash College, Crawfordsville, Ind.

Kip, Herbert Z., Professor of German, Connecticut College for Women, New London, Conn.

KITTREDGE, GEORGE LYMAN, Professor of English, Harvard University, Cambridge, Mass. [8 Hilliard St.]

Kittredge, Rupert Earle Loring, Professor of French, Trinity College, University of Toronto, Toronto, Canada.

Klaeber, Frederick, Professor of Comparative and English Philology, University of Minnesota, Minneapolis, Minn.

KLEIN, DAVID, Instructor in English, College of the City of New York, New York, N. Y.

von Klenze, Camillo, Professor of the German Language and Literature, Brown University, Providence, R. I.

von Klenze, Henrietta Becker, (Mrs. Camillo), Teacher of German, Miss Wheeler's School, Providence, R. I.

Knoepfler, John Baptist, Professor and Head of the Department of German and French, Iowa State Teachers' College, Cedar Falls, Ia.

Knowlton, Edgar Colby, Instructor in English, Lafayette College, Easton, Pa. [226 Porter St.]

Kolbe, Parke Rexford, President, Municipal University of Akron, Akron, O.

Koller, Armin Hajman, Instructor in German, University of Illinois, Urbana, Ill. [1110 S. 3d St., Champaign, Ill.]

Kotz, Theodore Franklin, Instructor in German, Ohio State University, Columbus, O. [2178 Summit St.]

Kracher, Francis Waldemar, Assistant Professor of the German Language and Literature, State University of Iowa, Iowa City, Ia. [405 N. Linn St.]

Krapp, George Philip, Professor of English, Columbia University, New York, N. Y.

Krause, Carl Albert, Head of the Modern Language Department, Jamaica High School, Jamaica, New York, N. Y. [1087A Prospect Place, Brooklyn, N. Y.]

Kroeh, Charles F., Professor of Modern Languages, Stevens Institute of Technology, Hoboken, N. J.

Krowl, Harry C., Associate Professor of English, College of the City of New York, New York, N. Y.

Kruse, Henry Otto, Associate Professor of German, University of Kansas, Lawrence, Kas.

Kueffner, Louise Mallinckrodt, Instructor in German, Vassar College, Poughkeepsie, N. Y.

Kuersteiner, Albert Frederick, Professor of Romance Languages, Indiana University, Bloomington, Ind.

Kuhl, Ernest P., Instructor in English, Dartmouth College, Hanover, N. H. [6 College St.]

Kuhne, Julius W., Associate Professor of Romance Languages, Miami University, Oxford, O.

Kuhns, Oscar, Professor of Romance Languages, Wesleyan University, Middletown, Conn.

Kullmer, Charles Julius, Professor of German, Syracuse University, Syracuse, N. Y. [505 University Place]

Kurrelmeyer, William, Associate Professor of German, Johns Hopkins University, Baltimore, Md. [Ellicott City, Md.]

Lambert, Marcus Bachman, Teacher of German, Allentown, Pa. [1816 Fairmount St.]

Lambuth, David, Instructor in English, Dartmouth College, Hanover, N. H.

Lancaster, Henry Carrington, Professor of Romance Languages, Amherst College, Amherst, Mass.

Lang, Henry R., Professor of Romance Philology, Yale University, New Haven, Conn. [176 Yale Station]

Lange, Carl Frederick Augustus, Professor of German, Smith College, Northampton, Mass.

Langley, Ernest F., Professor of French, Massachusetts Institute of Technology, Boston, Mass.

de La Rochelle, Philippe, Head of the French Department, Franklin School, New York, N. Y. [153 Manhattan Ave.]

Lathrop, Henry Burrowes, Associate Professor of English, University of Wisconsin, Madison, Wis.

Laubscher, Gustav George, Professor of Romance Languages, Randolph-Macon Woman's College, Lynchburg, Va. [54 Garden St., Cambridge, Mass.]

Lauer, Edward Henry, Assistant Professor of German, State University of Iowa, Iowa City, Ia. [306 N. State St., Ann Arbor, Mich.]

Lavertu, Francis Louis, Head of the Modern Language Department, Hill School, Pottstown, Pa.

Law, Robert A., Associate Professor of English, University of Texas, Austin, Texas. [2108 San Gabriel St.]

Lawrence, William Witherle, Associate Professor of English, Columbia University, New York, N. Y.

Layton, Katherine A. W., Instructor in German, Smith College, Northampton, Mass. [11 Arnold Ave.]

Leach, Henry Goddard, Secretary, The American-Scandinavian Foundation, 25 W. 45th St., New York, N. Y.

Learned, Henry Dexter, Instructor in German, University of Pennsylvania, Philadelphia, Pa.

Learned, Marion Dexter, Professor of the Germanic Languages and Literatures, University of Pennsylvania, Philadelphia, Pa.

Lecompte, Irville Charles, Assistant Professor of French, Yale University, New Haven, Conn. [764 Yale Station]

Le Duc, Alma de L., Instructor in French, Smith College, Northampton, Mass.

Lemmi, Charles W., Instructor in English, Simmons College, Boston, Mass.

Leonard, Arthur Newton, Professor of German, Bates College, Lewiston, Me. [24 Riverside St.]

Leonard, William Ellery, Assistant Professor of English, University of Wisconsin, Madison, Wis.

Lessing, Otto Eduard, Professor of German, University of Illinois, Urbana, Ill. [905 S. Lincoln Ave.]

Levi, Moritz, Professor of French, University of Michigan, Ann Arbor, Mich.

Lewis, Charlton Miner, Professor of English Literature, Yale University, New Haven, Conn.

Lewis, Edwin Herbert, Professor of English, and Dean of the Faculty, Lewis Institute, Chicago, Ill.

Lewisohn, Ludwig, Assistant Professor of German, Ohio State University, Columbus, O. [23 Sixteenth Ave.]

Licklider, Albert Harp, Assistant Professor of English, Williams College, Williamstown, Mass.

Liddell, Mark Harvey, Assistant Professor of English, Purdue University, West Lafayette, Ind. [523 Waldron St.]

Lieder, Frederick William Charles, Instructor in German, Harvard University, Cambridge, Mass. [6 Holyoke House]

Lincoln, George Luther, Instructor in Romance Languages, Harvard University, Cambridge, Mass. [2000 Commonwealth Ave., Boston, Mass.]

Lindsay, Julian Ira, Instructor in English, University of Vermont, Burlington, Vt.

Lipari, Angelo, Lecturer in French, Trinity College, University of Toronto, Toronto, Canada.

Livingston, Albert Arthur, Assistant Professor of Romance Languages, Columbia University, New York, N. Y.

Lockwood, Francis Cummins, Professor of the English Language and Literature, Allegheny College, Meadville, Pa.

Lockwood, Laura E., Professor of English, Wellesley College, Wellesley, Mass. [8 Norfolk Terrace]

Logeman, Henry, Professor of English Philology, University of Ghent, Ghent, Belgium. [343 boulevard des Hospices]

Loiseaux, Louis Auguste, Associate Professor of the Romance Languages and Literatures, Columbia University, New York, N. Y.

Lomax, John Avery, Secretary of the Faculties, University of Texas, Austin, Tex.

Long, Orie William, Professor of Modern Languages, Worcester Polytechnic Institute, Worcester, Mass.

Long, Percy Waldron, Instructor in English, Harvard University, Cambridge, Mass. [18 Willard St.]

Longden, Henry Boyer, Professor of the German Language and Literature, De Pauw University, Greencastle, Ind.

Loomis, Roger Sherman, Tutor in English, University of Illinois, Urbana, Ill. [907 Oregon St.]

Lorenz, Charlotte Marie, Assistant Professor of German, Iowa State Teachers' College, Cedar Falls, Ia.

Lotspeich, Claude Meek, Associate Professor of German, University of Cincinnati, Cincinnati, O.

Lowes, John Livingston, Professor of English, Washington University, St. Louis, Mo.

Luebke, William Ferdinand, Assistant Professor of German, State University of Iowa, Iowa City, Ia.

Luker, Benjamin Franklin, Instructor in French, Vanderbilt Unisity, Nashville, Tenn.

Luquiens, Frederick Bliss, Professor of Spanish, Sheffield Scientific School, Yale University, New Haven, Conn. [97 Canner St.]

Lustrat, Joseph, Professor of Romance Languages, University of Georgia, Athens, Ga.

Lutz, Frederick, Professor of Modern Languages and Acting Professor of Latin, Albion College, Albion, Mich.

Lynch, Samuel Adams, Head of the Department of English, Iowa State Teachers' College, Cedar Falls, Ia.

Lyon, Charles Edward, Assistant Professor of German, Clark College, Worcester, Mass. [21 King St.]

Lyons, Jessie M., Instructor in English, Vassar College, Poughkeepsie, N. Y.

McBryde, John McLaren, Jr., Professor of English and Editor of the *Sewanee Review*, University of the South, Sewanee, Tenn.

McClelland, George William, Instructor in English, University of Pennsylvania, Philadelphia, Pa. [3706 Locust St.]

MacClintock, William D., Professor of English, University of Chicago, Chicago, Ill. [5629 Lexington Ave.]

McCobb, Arthur Lewis, Instructor in German, Clark College, Worcester, Mass.

MACCRACKEN, HENRY NOBLE, President, Vassar College, Poughkeepsie, N. Y.

MacDonald, Wilbert L., Professor of English, University of New Brunswick, Fredericton, N. B.

Mackall, Leonard Leopold, Hon. Member, Georgia Historical Society, Foreign Member, Bibliographical Society of London. [Jena, Germany, Forstweg 14]

Mackenzie, Alastair St. Clair, Professor of English, and Dean of the Graduate School, State University of Kentucky, Lexington, Ky. [Box 208]

McKenzie, Kenneth, Professor of Romance Languages, University of Illinois, Urbana, Ill.

Mackenzie, William Roy, Associate Professor of English, Washington University, St. Louis, Mo.

McKibben, George Fitch, Professor of Romance Languages, Denison University, Granville, O.

MacKimmie, Anderson, Assistant Professor of French, Massachusetts Agricultural College, No. Amherst, Mass.

McKnight, George Harley, Professor of English, Ohio State University, Columbus, O.

McLaughlin, William Aloysius, Assistant Professor of French, University of Michigan, Ann Arbor, Mich. [644 S. Ingalls St.]

McLean, Charlotte Frelinghuysen, Professor of English, Philosophy, and Greek, College of Montana, Deer Lodge, Montana.

Macmillan, Beulah A., Instructor in English, Wilson College for Women, Chambersburg, Pa.

Mahr, August Carl, Instructor in German, Sheffield Scientific School, Yale University, New Haven, Conn. [116 Vanderbilt Hall (Sheff.)]

Maloubier, Eugène F., Instructor in Romance Languages, Adelphi College, Brooklyn, N. Y.

Manchester, Frederick A., Instructor in English, University of Wisconsin, Madison, Wis.

Manley, Edward, Englewood High School, Chicago, Ill. [6100 Lexington Ave.]

Manly, John Matthews, Professor of English, University of Chicago, Chicago, Ill.

Manthey-Zorn, Otto, Associate Professor of German, Amherst College, Amherst, Mass.

Marcou, Philippe Belknap, Paris, France. [28 quai d'Orléans]

Marden, Charles Carroll, Professor of Spanish, Johns Hopkins University, Baltimore, Md.

Marquardt, Carl Eugene, Assistant Professor of German, Pennsylvania State College, State College, Pa. [113 Heister St.]

Marsh, George Linnæus, Extension Associate Professor of English, University of Chicago, Chicago, Ill.

Marvin, Robert B., Head Teacher, Department of German, Commercial High School, Brooklyn, N. Y. [826 Marcy Ave.]

Mason, James Frederick, Professor of Romance Languages and Literatures, Cornell University, Ithaca, N. Y.

Mason, John Edward, Jr., Fellow in English, University of Pennsylvania, Philadelphia, Pa. [251 S. 44th St.]

Mason, Lawrence, Instructor in English, Yale College, New Haven, Conn. [18 Elm St.]

Mathews, Charles Eugley, Assistant Professor, Preceptor in Modern Languages, Princeton University, Princeton, N. J.

MATTHEWS, BRANDER, Professor of Dramatic Literature (English), Columbia University, New York, N. Y. [337 W. 87th St.]

Maxfield, Ezra Kempton, Assistant Professor of English, Colby College, Waterville, Me. [17 West St.]

Mayfield, G. R., Assistant Professor of German, Vanderbilt University, Nashville, Tenn.

Maynadier, Gustavus H., Instructor in English, Harvard University, Cambridge, Mass. [24 Fairfax Hall]

Mead, William Edward, Professor of the English Language, Wesleyan University, Middletown, Conn.

Meader, Clarence Linton, Professor of General Linguistics, University of Michigan, Ann Arbor, Mich. [1941 Geddes Ave.]

Medici de Solenni, Gino V., Assistant Professor of French and Spanish, Oklahoma Agricultural and Mechanical College, Stillwater, Okla.

Meisnest, Frederick William, Professor of German, University of Washington, Seattle, Wash.˙ [4705 Sixteenth Ave., N. E.]

Mensel, Ernst Heinrich, Professor of Germanic Languages and Literatures, Smith College, Northampton, Mass.

Mercier, Louis Joseph Alexander, Instructor in French, Harvard University, Cambridge, Mass.

Metcalf, John Calvin, Dean, and Professor of English, Richmond College, Richmond, Va.

Meyer, Edward Stockton, Associate Professor of German, Western Reserve University, Cleveland, O.

Michaud, Régis, Assistant Professor, Preceptor in Modern Languages, Princeton University, Princeton, N. J.

Miles, Dudley Howe, Chairman of the English Department, Evander Childs High School, Bronx, New York, N. Y. [509 W. 122d St.]

Miles, Louis Wardlaw, Assistant Professor of English, Princeton University, Princeton, N. J.

Miller, George Morey, Professor of the English Language and Literature, Wabash College, Crawfordsville, Ind. [502 W Wabash Ave.]

Miller, Raymond Durbin, Associate Professor of English, University of Missouri, Columbia, Mo. [305 Hicks Ave.]

Mims, Edwin, Professor of English, Vanderbilt University, Nashville, Tenn.

Mitchell, Robert McBurney, Assistant Professor of Germanic Languages and Literatures, Brown University, Providence, R. I. [144 Congdon St.]

Monroe, Robert Emmett, Professor of Modern Languages, Transylvania University, Lexington, Ky.

Mookerjee, H. C., Assistant Professor of English, Calcutta University, Calcutta, India. [1 and 2 Dehi Serampore Road]

Moore, Cecil Albert, Assistant Professor of English, Trinity College, Durham, N. C. [9 Lamont Ave.]

Moore, Clarence King, Professor of Romance Languages, University of Rochester, Rochester, N. Y.

Moore, Olin Harris, Instructor in Romance Languages, University of Illinois, Urbana, Ill. [University Club]

Moore, Robert Webber, Professor of German, Colgate University, Hamilton, N. Y.

Moore, Samuel, Associate Professor of English, University of Michigan, Ann Arbor, Mich. [1044 Ferdon Road]

Morgan, Bayard Quincy, Assistant Professor of German, University of Wisconsin, Madison, Wis. [1710 Adams St.]

Morgan, Charlotte E., Instructor in English, Mrs. Randall-McIver's Classes (Miss Davidge's Classes), New York, N. Y. [1173 Bushwick Ave., Brooklyn, N. Y.]

Moriarty, William Daniel, Assistant Professor of English, University of Michigan, Ann Arbor, Mich. [309 Thompson St.]

Morley, Sylvanus Griswold, Assistant Professor of Spanish, University of California, Berkeley, Cal.

Morris, Amos Reno, Professor of English, Parsons College, Fairfield, Ia.

Morris, George Davis, Associate Professor of French, Indiana University, Bloomington, Ind.

Morris, John, Professor of Germanic Languages, University of Georgia, Athens, Ga.

Moseley, Thomas Addis Emmet, Instructor in Romance Languages, Princeton University, Princeton, N. J.

Mosher, William Eugene, Professor of the German Language and Literature, Oberlin College, Oberlin, O.

Mott, Lewis F., Professor of the English Language and Literature, College of the City of New York, 139th St. and Convent Ave., New York, N. Y.

Moyse, Charles Ebenezer, Vice-Principal, Professor of English, McGill University, Montreal, Canada.

Mueller, Eugene, Teacher of German, Shortridge High School, Indianapolis, Ind.

Mulfinger, George Abraham, Professor of the German Language and Literature, Allegheny College, Meadville, Pa.

Murch, Herbert Spencer, Assistant Professor of English, Princeton University, Princeton, N. J. [A-1 Campbell Hall]

Murray, William Henry, Assistant Professor of Modern Languages, Tuck School, Dartmouth College, Hanover, N. H.

Mutterer, Frederick Gilbert, Professor of German, Indiana State Normal School, Terre Haute, Ind. [667 Oak St.]

Myers, Clara Louise, Associate Professor of English, College for Women, Western Reserve University, Cleveland, O.

Myers, Walter R., Assistant Professor of German, University of Minnesota, Minneapolis, Minn.

Myrick, Arthur B., Professor of Romance Languages, University of Vermont, Burlington, Vt. [86 Williams St.]

Nadal, Thomas William, Dean and Professor of English, Olivet College, Olivet, Mich.

Nason, Arthur Huntington, Assistant Professor of English, New York University, Instructor in English, Union Theological Seminary, New York, N. Y. [P. O. Box 84, University Heights]

Neef, Francis J. A., Instructor in German, Dartmouth College, Hanover, N. H.

Neff, Theodore Lee, Assistant Professor of French, University of Chicago, Chicago, Ill.

Neidig, William J., Chicago, Ill. [1156 N. Dearborn St.]

NEILSON, WILLIAM ALLAN, Professor of English, Harvard University, Cambridge, Mass. [34 Kirkland St.]

Nelson, Clara Albertine, Professor of French, Ohio Wesleyan University, Delaware, O.

Nettleton, George Henry, Assistant Professor of English, Sheffield Scientific School, Yale University, New Haven, Conn. [570 Prospect St.]

NEWCOMER, CHARLES BERRY, State College, N. M.

Newport, Mrs. Clara Price, Assistant Professor of German, Swarthmore College, Swarthmore, Pa.

Nichols, Charles Washburn, Assistant Professor of Rhetoric, University of Minnesota, Minneapolis, Minn.

Nichols, Edwin Bryant, Professor of Romance Languages, DePauw University, Greencastle, Ind. [529 Anderson St.]

Nicolay, Clara Leonora, Teacher of Latin, Romance, and German, Ruth Hargrove Institute, Key West, Fla.

Nitze, William Albert, Professor and Head of the Department of Romance Languages, University of Chicago, Chicago, Ill. [1220 E. 56th St.]

Noble, Charles, Professor of the English Language and Rhetoric, Grinnell College, Grinnell, Ia. [1110 West St.]

von Noé, Adolf Carl, Assistant Professor of German Literature, University of Chicago, Chicago, Ill.

Noé, Rachel, Teacher of French, Bayonne High School, Bayonne, N. J. [105 W. 8th St.]

Nolle, Alfred Henry, Instructor in German, University of Missouri, Columbia, Mo.

Nollen, John S., President, Lake Forest College, Lake Forest, Ill.

Nordmeyer, Heinrich Waldemar, Instructor in German, Ohio State University, Columbus, O. [70 Twelfth Ave.]

Northrop, George Norton, Assistant Professor of English, University of Minnesota, Minneapolis, Minn. [2213 Grand Ave.]

NORTHUP, CLARK SUTHERLAND, Assistant Professor of English, Cornell University, Ithaca, N. Y. [407 Elmwood Ave.]

Northup, George Tyler, Assistant Professor of Italian and Spanish, University of Toronto, Toronto, Ont. [10 Cornish Road]

Nykerk, John Bernard, Professor of the English Language and Literature, Hope College, Holland, Mich.

O'Connor, Horace W., Instructor in English, Indiana University, Bloomington, Ind.

Odebrecht, August, Assistant Professor of Modern Languages, Denison University, Granville, O. [Box 365]

Ogden, Phillip, Professor of Romance Languages, University of Cincinnati, Cincinnati, O.

O'Leary, Raphael Dorman, Associate Professor of Rhetoric, University of Kansas, Lawrence, Kas.

Oliver, Thomas Edward, Professor of Romance Languages, University of Illinois, Urbana, Ill. [912 W. California Ave.]

Olmsted, Everett Ward, Professor and Head of the Department of Romance Languages, University of Minnesota, Minneapolis, Minn. [901 Fifth St., S. E.]

Osgood, Charles Grosvenor, Assistant Professor, Preceptor in English, Princeton University, Princeton, N. J.

Osthaus, Carl Wilhelm Ferdinand, Professor of German, Indiana University, Bloomington, Ind. [417 S. Fess Ave.]

Osuna, Andrés, Instructor in Spanish, Vanderbilt University, Nashville, Tenn. [3021 Beech Ave.]

Owen, Arthur Leslie, Associate Professor of Romance Languages, University of Kansas, Lawrence, Kas. [536 Ohio St.]

Owen, Edward Thomas, Professor of French and Linguistics, University of Wisconsin, Madison, Wis. [614 State St.]

Owen, Ralph Woodland, Instructor in English, University of Wisconsin, Madison, Wis. [520 N. Pinckney St.]

Pace, Roy Bennett, Assistant Professor of English, Swarthmore College, Swarthmore, Pa.

Padelford, Frederick Morgan, Professor of English, University of Washington, Seattle, Wash. [University Station]

PAGE, CURTIS HIDDEN, Professor of the English Language and Literature, Dartmouth College, Hanover, N. H.

Paine Henry Gallup, Offis Manager, Simplified Spelling Board, 1 Madison Ave., New York, N. Y.

Palmblad, Harry V. E., Instructor in Germanic Languages and Literatures, University of Kansas, Lawrence, Kas. [1845 Illinois St.]

Palmer, Arthur Hubbell, Professor of the German Language and Literature, Yale University, New Haven, Conn. [221 Everit St.]

Palmer, Earle Fenton, Assistant Professor of English, College of the City of New York, New York, N. Y.

Palmer, Philip Mason, Professor of German, Lehigh University, So. Bethlehem, Pa. [University Park]

Panaroni, Alfred G., Instructor in Romance Languages, College of the City of New York, New York, N. Y.

PANCOAST, HENRY SPACKMAN, Chestnut Hill, Philadelphia, Pa. [Spring Lane]

Park, Clyde William, Assistant Professor of English, University of Cincinnati, Cincinnati, O.

Parker, Eugene Fred, Instructor in Romance Languages, University of North Carolina, Chapel Hill, N. C.

Paton, Lucy Allen, Cambridge, Mass. [Strathcona Hall, Charles River Road]

Patterson, Arthur Sayles, Professor of French, Syracuse University, Syracuse, N. Y. [415 University Place]

Patterson, Frank Allen, Assistant Professor of English, Columbia University, New York, N. Y.

Patterson, William Morrison, Columbia University, New York, N. Y. [704 Furnald Hall]

Patton, Julia, New York, N. Y. [417 W. 120th St.]

Paul, Harry G., Assistant Professor of the English Language and Literature, University of Illinois, Urbana, Ill.

15

Payne, Leonidas Warren, Jr., Associate Professor of English, University of Texas, Austin, Tex. [2104 Pearl St.]

PEARSON, CALVIN WASSON, Professor Emeritus of the German Language and Literature, Beloit College, Beloit, Wis. [Wallingford, Pa.]

Peck, Harvey Whitefield, Instructor in English, University of Texas. Austin, Tex. [506 W. 33d St.]

Peck, Mary Gray, Geneva, N. Y. [R. F. D. 2]

Peebles, Rose Jeffries, Assistant Professor of English, Vassar College, Poughkeepsie, N. Y.

Peirce, Walter Thompson, Assistant Professor of Romance Languages, Ohio State University, Columbus, O.

Pellissier, Adeline, Assistant Professor of French, Smith College, Northampton, Mass.

PENNIMAN, JOSIAH HARMAR, Vice-Provost, Professor of English Literature, University of Pennsylvania, Philadelphia, Pa. [4326 Sansom St.]

Perrin, Ernest Noël, Long Lake, Hamilton Co., N. Y.

PERRIN, MARSHALL LIVINGSTON, Professor of Germanic Languages, Boston University, 688 Boylston St., Boston, Mass.

Perring, Roy Henderson, Professor of German, Grinnell College, Grinnell, Ia. [916 Sixth Ave.]

Perrow, Eber Carl, Professor of English, University of Louisville, Louisville, Ky.

Perry, Bliss, Professor of English Literature, Harvard University, Cambridge, Mass. [5 Clement Circle]

Petri. Edoardo, Director of the Chorus School of the Metropolitan Opera Company, in charge of the Italian Department of the Institute of Musical Art, New York, N. Y. [540 W. 122d St.]

Pettengill, Ray Waldron, Instructor in German, Harvard University, Cambridge, Mass. [12 Rutland St.]

Phelps, Ruth Shepard, Instructor in Italian, University of Minnesota, Minneapolis, Minn.

Phelps, William Lyon, Professor of English Literature, Yale University, New Haven, Conn.

Pierce, Frederick Erastus, Assistant Professor of English, Sheffield Scientific School, Yale University, New Haven, Conn. [188 Canner St.]

Plimpton, George A., Ginn & Co., 70 Fifth Ave., New York, N. Y.

Poll, Max, Professor of German, University of Cincinnati, Cincinnati, O.

Pope, Paul Russel, Assistant Professor of German, Cornell University, Ithaca, N. Y. [Cayuga Heights]

Porterfield, Allen Wilson, Instructor in Germanic Languages and Literatures, Barnard College, Columbia University, New York, N. Y.

Potter, Albert K., Associate Professor of the English Language, Brown University, Providence, R. I. [220 Waterman St.]

Pound, Louise, Professor of the English Language, University of Nebraska, Lincoln, Neb. [1632 L St.]

Preston, Herbert French, St. George's School, Newport, R. I.

Prettyman, Cornelius William, Professor of German, Dickinson College, Carlisle, Pa.

Price, Lawrence Marsden, Instructor in German, University of California, Berkeley, Cal. [1531 Milvia St.]

Price, William R., State Inspector of Modern Languages, Albany, N. Y.

Priest, George Madison, Professor of Germanic Languages and Literatures, Princeton University, Princeton, N. J.

Prokosch, Eduard, Professor of Germanic Languages, University of Texas, Austin, Tex.

Puckett, Hugh Wiley, Instructor in German, University of Illinois, Urbana, Ill.

Pumpelly, Laurence, Assistant Professor of Romance Languages and Literatures, Cornell University, Ithaca, N. Y.

Purin, Charles M., Assistant Professor of German, University of Wisconsin, Madison, Wis.

PUTZKER, ALBIN, Professor Emeritus of German Literature, University of California, Berkeley, Cal.

Pyre, James Francis Augustine, Associate Professor of English, University of Wisconsin, Madison, Wis.

Quinn, Arthur Hobson, Dean of the College, and Professor of English, University of Pennsylvania, Philadelphia, Pa.

Raggio, Andrew Paul, Professor and Head of the Department of Spanish and Italian, University of Maine, Orono, Me. [102 Main St.]

Ramsay, Robert Lee, Associate Professor of English, University of Missouri, Columbia, Mo. [25 Allen Place]

Rand, Albert Edward, Instructor in German, Brown University, Providence, R. I. [134 Lloyd Ave.]

Rand, Edwin Watson, Master in Classics, Montclair Academy, Montclair, N. J., and Head Master, Rand Summer School, Allenhurst, N. J. [Hodge Road, Princeton, N. J.]

Rankin, James Walter, Assistant Professor of English, University of Missouri, Columbia, Mo.

Ransmeier, John Christian, Professor of German, Tulane University of Louisiana, New Orleans, La. [St. Charles Ave.]

Rau, Charlotte, Teacher of German, Laurel School, 1956 E. 101st St., Cleveland, O.

Raymond, Frederic Newton, Associate Professor of English, University of Kansas, Lawrence, Kas. [812 Illinois St.]

Rea, John Dougan, Professor of English, Earlham College, Richmond, Ind.

Read, William A., Professor of the English Language and Literature, Louisiana State University, Baton Rouge, La. [338 Lafayette St.]

Réau, Anie Cécile, Instructor in French, Vassar College, Poughkeepsie, N. Y.

Reed, Albert Granberry, Professor of English Literature, Louisiana State University, Baton Rouge, La. [746 Boyd Ave.]

Reed, Edward Bliss, Assistant Professor of English Literature, Yale University, New Haven, Conn. [Yale Station]

Reed, Frank Otis, Assistant Professor of Romance Languages, University of Wisconsin, Madison, Wis. [401 Wisconsin Ave.]

Reed, William Howell, Assistant Professor of Modern Languages, Tufts College, Tufts College, Mass.

Rees, Byron Johnson, Assistant Professor of English, Williams College, Williamstown, Mass.

Reeves, William Peters, Professor of the English Language and Literature, Kenyon College, Gambier, O.

Reichard, Harry Hess, Instructor in German, Atlantic City High School, Atlantic City, N. J. [16 N. Sovereign Ave.]

Reid, Elizabeth, Professor of German, Huron College, Huron, S. D. [718 Illinois St.]

Reining, Charles, Instructor in German, Leland Stanford Jr. University, Stanford University, Cal.

Remy, Arthur Frank Joseph, Assistant Professor of Germanic Philology, Columbia University, New York, N. Y.

Rendtorff, Karl G., Associate Professor of German, Leland Stanford Jr. University, Stanford University, Cal. [1130 Bryant St., Palo Alto]

Reynolds, George Fullmer, Associate Professor of English, Indiana University, Bloomington, Ind. [718 University St.]

Rice, John Pierrepont, Assistant Professor of Romance Languages, Williams College, Williamstown, Mass.

Rice, Richard Ashley, Associate Professor of English, Indiana University, Bloomington, Ind.

Richards, Alfred Ernest, Professor of English Literature, New Hampshire State College, Durham, N. H.

Richardson, Henry Brush, Master in French, Lake Forest Academy, Lake Forest, Ill.

Riddle, Lawrence Melville, Professor of the French Language and Literature, University of Southern California, Los Angeles, Cal.

Ridenour, Harry Lee, Instructor in English, University of Wisconsin, Madison, Wis. [424 S. Mills St.]

Riemer, Guido Carl Leo, Professor of Modern Languages, Bucknell University, Lewisburg, Pa.

Riethmüller, Richard Henri, Philadelphia, Pa. [P. O. Lock Box 1615]

Rinaker, Clarissa, Instructor in English, University of Illinois, Urbana, Ill. [321 University Hall]

Ristine, Frank Humphrey, Professor of the English Language and Literature, Hamilton College, Clinton, N. Y.

ROBINSON, FRED NORRIS, Professor of English, Harvard University, Cambridge, Mass. [Longfellow Park]

Rockwell, Leo Lawrence, Instructor in German, Bucknell University, Lewisburg, Pa.

Rockwood, Robert Everett, Instructor in French, Harvard University, Cambridge, Mass. [32 Conant Hall]

Roe, Frederick William, Assistant Dean, and Assistant Professor of English, University of Wisconsin, Madison, Wis. [2015 Van Hise Ave.]

Roedder, Edwin Carl, Associate Professor of German Philology, University of Wisconsin, Madison, Wis. [1614 Hoyt St.]

Roessler, John Edward, Professor of German, Valparaiso University, Valparaiso, Ind.

Root, Robert Kilburn, Assistant Professor, Preceptor in English, Princeton University, Princeton, N. J.

Rosenberg, S. L. Millard, Professor of French and Spanish, Girard College, Philadelphia, Pa.

Roulston, Robert Bruce, Associate in German, Johns Hopkins University, Baltimore, Md.

Rourke, Constance Mayfield, Instructor in English, Vassar College, Poughkeepsie, N. Y.

Routh, James, Associate Professor of English, Tulane University of Louisiana, New Orleans, La.

Royster, James Finch, Professor of English, University of Texas, Austin, Tex.

Rudd, Robert Barnes, Instructor in English, Dartmouth College, Hanover, N. H.

Rudwin, Maximilian Josef, Instructor in German, Purdue University, West Lafayette, Ind. [120 Andrew Place]

Ruthrauff, Mary Josephine, Teacher of German, Owosso High School, Owosso, Mich.

Ruutz-Rees, Caroline, Head Mistress, Rosemary Hall, Greenwich, Conn.

de Salvio, Alfonso, Assistant Professor of Romance Languages, Northwestern University, Evanston, Ill. [1115 Davis St.]

Sampson, Martin Wright, Professor of English, Cornell University, Ithaca, N. Y.

Samra, Emile Sam, Professor of Modern Languages, Mt. St. Mary's College, Emmitsburg, Md.

Sanderson, Robert Louis, Assistant Professor of French, Yale University, New Haven, Conn.

Sandison, Helen Estabrook, Instructor in English, Vassar College, Poughkeepsie, N. Y.

de Santo, Vincenzo, Instructor in Romance Languages, University of Pennsylvania, Philadelphia, Pa.

Sbedico, Attilio Filippo, Instructor in Romance Languages, University of Washington, Seattle, Wash.

Schappelle, Benjamin Franklin, Acting Professor of Romance Languages, Pennsylvania College, Gettysburg, Pa.

Schelling, Felix E., Professor and Head of the Department of English, University of Pennsylvania, Philadelphia, Pa. [College Hall, University of Pennsylvania]

Schenck, Eunice Morgan, Associate in French, Bryn Mawr College. Bryn Mawr, Pa. [Low Buildings]

Scherer, Peter J., Director of German, Public Schools, Indianapolis, Ind.

Schevill, Rudolph, Professor of Spanish, Head of the Department of Romanic Languages, University of California, Berkeley, Cal.

Schilling, Hugo Karl, Professor of the German Language and Literature, University of California, Berkeley, Cal. [2316 Le Conte Ave.]

Schinz, Albert, Professor of the French Language and Literature, Smith College, Northampton, Mass.

Schlatter, Edward Bunker, Assistant Professor of Romance Languages, University of Wisconsin, Madison, Wis. [2259 Regent St.]

Schlenker, Carl, Professor of German, University of Minnesota, Minneapolis, Minn. [514 Eleventh Ave., S. E.]

Schmidt, Friedrich Georg Gottlob, Professor of the German Language and Literature, State University of Oregon, Eugene, Ore. [609 E. 14th Ave.]

Schmidt, Gertrud Charlotte, Head of the German Department, Miss Wright's School, Bryn Mawr, Pa. [631 Montgomery Ave.]

Schmitt, Bertram Clarence, Instructor in English, University of Pennsylvania, Philadelphia, Pa.

Schoenemann, Friedrich, Instructor in German, Harvard University, Cambridge, Mass. [3 Avon St.]

Schoepperle, Gertrude, Associate in English, University of Illinois, Urbana, Ill.

SCHOFIELD, WILLIAM HENRY, Professor of Comparative Literature, Harvard University, Cambridge, Mass. [21 Commonwealth Ave., Boston, Mass.]

Scholl, John William, Assistant Professor of German, University of Michigan, Ann Arbor, Mich. [917 Forest Ave.]

Scholz, Karl W. H., Instructor in German, University of Pennsylvania, Philadelphia, Pa. [24 Morgan House, U. of P.]

Schreiber, Carl F., Instructor in German, Sheffield Scientific School, Yale University, New Haven, Conn. [368 Norton St.]

Schultz, John Richie, Instructor in English, Yale College, New Haven, Conn. [16 York Sq.]

Schwabe, Henry Otto, Instructor in German, University of Michigan, Ann Arbor, Mich. [720 S. 12th St.]

SCOTT, CHARLES PAYSON GURLEY, Editor, Yonkers, N. Y. [49 Arthur St.]

Scott, Franklin William, Assistant Professor of English, University of Illinois, Urbana, Ill.

Scott, Fred Newton, Professor of Rhetoric, University of Michigan, Ann Arbor, Mich. [1351 Washtenaw Ave.]

Scott, Mary Augusta, Professor of the English Language and Literature, Smith College, Northampton, Mass.

Searles, Colbert, Professor of Romance Languages, University of Minnesota, Minneapolis, Minn.

Segal, Myer, Columbia University, New York, N. Y. [301 St. Nicholas Ave.]

Segall, Jacob Bernard, Professor of Romance Languages, University of Maine, Orono, Me.

Sehrt, Edward H., Fellow in German, Johns Hopkins University, Baltimore, Md. [3425 Eastern Ave.]

Seiberth, Philipp, Assistant Professor of German, Washington University, St. Louis, Mo.

Semple, Lewis B., Teacher of English, Bushwick High School, Brooklyn, N. Y. [229 Jefferson Ave.]

Seronde, Joseph, Instructor in French, Sheffield Scientific School, Yale University, New Haven, Conn. [1009 Yale Station]

Severy, Ernest Elisha, Instructor in French, Agusta Military Academy, Fort Defiance, Va.

Seymour, Arthur Romeyn, Associate in Romance Languages, University of Illinois, Urbana, Ill. [909 Nevada St.]

Seymour, Clara Gertrude, Editorial Department, *The Survey*, 105 E. 22d St., New York, N. Y.

Shackford, Martha Hale, Associate Professor of English Literature, Wellesley College, Wellesley, Mass. [7 Midland Ave.]

Shafer, Robert, Fellow in English, Princeton University, Princeton, N. J. [The Graduate College]

Shanks, Lewis Piaget, Assistant Professor of Romance Languages, University of Pennsylvania, Philadelphia, Pa.

Shannon, Edgar Finley, Professor of English, Washington and Lee University, Lexington, Va.

Sharp, Robert, Professor of English, Acting President, Tulane University of Louisiana, New Orleans, La.

Shaw, Esther Elizabeth, University of Michigan, Ann Arbor, Mich. [520 E. Jefferson St.]

Shaw, James Eustace, Associate Professor of Italian, Johns Hopkins University, Baltimore, Md.

Shearin, Hubert Gibson, Professor of English, Occidental College, Los Angeles, Cal.

Sheffield, Alfred Dwight, Instructor in Rhetoric and Composition, Wellesley College, Wellesley, Mass.

SHELDON, EDWARD STEVENS, Professor of Romance Philology, Harvard University, Cambridge, Mass. [11 Francis Ave.]

Shelly, Percy Van Dyke, Assistant Professor of English, University of Pennsylvania, Philadelphia, Pa.

Shepard, Grace Florence, Assistant Professor of English, Wheaton College, Norton, Mass.

Shepard, William Pierce, Professor of Romance Languages, Hamilton College, Clinton, N. Y.

Sherman, Lucius A., Professor of the English Language and Literature, University of Nebraska, Lincoln, Neb.

Sherman, Stuart Pratt, Professor of English, University of Illinois, Urbana, Ill. [1016 W. Nevada St.]

Sherzer, Jane, President and Professor of English, The Oxford College for Women, Oxford, O.

Shulters, John Raymnod, Assistant in Romance Languages, University of Illinois, Urbana, Ill. [309 University Hall]

Shumway, Daniel Bussier, Professor of German Philology, University of Pennsylvania, Philadelphia, Pa.

Shute, Henry Martin, Instructor in German, Phillips Exeter Academy, Exeter, N. H.

Sibley, Robert Pelton, Associate Professor of English, Lake Forest College, Lake Forest, Ill.

Siebens, Thekla Maria, Head of the Modern Language Department, Riverside-Brookfield High School, Riverside, Ill.

Sievers, John Frederick, Professor of German, Acadia University, Wolfville, N. S.

Sills, Kenneth Charles Morton, Dean and Professor of Latin, Bowdoin College, Brunswick, Me.

Simonds, William Edward, Professor of English Literature, Knox College, Galesburg, Ill.

SIMONTON, JAMES SNODGRASS, Professor Emeritus of the French Language and Literature, Washington and Jefferson College, Washington, Pa.

Sisson, Louis Eugene, Associate Professor of English, University of Kansas, Lawrence, Kas. [1236 Louisiana St.]

Skidmore, Mark, Assistant Professor of Romance Languages, University of Kansas, Lawrence, Kas. [1725 Indiana St.]

Skillings, Everett, Professor of German, Middlebury College, Middlebury, Vt. [133 Main St.]

Skinner, Prescott Orde, Professor of the Romance Languages, Dartmouth College, Hanover, N. H.

Skipp, Henry John, Teacher of German, High School of Commerce, New York, N. Y. [155 W. 65th St.]

Smart, Walter Kay, Professor of English, Armour Institute of Technology, Chicago, Ill. [1122 E. 54th Place]

Smith, Charles Alphonso, Professor, Head of the Edgar Allen Poe School of English, University of Virginia, University, Va.

Smith, Edward Laurence, Professor of Modern Languages, Delaware College, Newark, Del.

SMITH, FRANK CLIFTON, Gurleyville, Conn.

Smith, Horatio Elwin, Instructor in French, Yale College, New Haven, Conn. [837 Orange St.]

Smith, Hugh Allison, Professor of Romance Languages, University of Wisconsin, Madison, Wis. [15 Prospect Ave.]

Smith, Mahlon Ellwood, Assistant Professor of English, Syracuse University, Syracuse, N. Y. [202 Waverley Ave.]

Smith, Pinckney Freeman, Brownington, Mo.

Smith, Reed, Professor of English, University of South Carolina, Columbia, S. C. [1628 Pendleton St.]

Smith, Richard R., Manager, College Department, The Macmillan Company, 66 Fifth Ave., New York, N. Y.

Smith, Stanley Astredo, Assistant Professor of Romanic Languages, Leland Stanford Jr. University, Stanford University, Cal.

Smith, Winifred, Instructor in English, Vassar College, Poughkeepsie, N. Y.

Smyser, William Emory, Professor of English, Ohio Wesleyan University, Delaware, O.

Snavely, Guy Everett, Professor of Romance Languages, Allegheny College, Meadville, Pa. [588 Baldwin St.]

Snow, William Brackett, Head Master, English High School, Boston, Mass.

Snyder, Alice Dorothea, Instructor in English, Vassar College, Poughkeepsie, N. Y.

Snyder, Edward Douglas, Assistant Professor of English, Haverford College, Haverford, Pa.

Snyder, Henry Nelson, President and Professor of English, Wofford College, Spartanburg, S. C.

Spaeth, J. Duncan, Professor of English, Princeton University, Princeton, N. J.

Spalding, Mary Caroline, Professor of English, Wilson College, Chambersburg, Pa.

Spangler, Glen Harwood, Fellow in Romance Languages, Harvard University, Cambridge, Mass.

Spanhoofd, Arnold Werner, Head of the Modern Language Department in the High and Manual Training Schools, Washington, D. C. [2015 Hillyer Place, N. W.]

Spanhoofd, Edward, Head of the Department of German, St. Paul's School, Concord, N. H.

Speare, Morris Edmund, Instructor in English, University of Wisconsin, Madison, Wis. [803 State St.]

Spencer, Matthew Lyle, Professor of Rhetoric, Lawrence College, Appleton, Wis. [8 Alton Place]

Spiers, Alexander Guy Holborn, Assistant Professor of Romance Languages, Haverford College, Haverford, Pa.

SPINGARN, JOEL ELIAS, New York, N. Y. [9 W. 73d St.]

Spooner, Edwin Victor, Instructor in French, Phillips Exeter Academy, Exeter, N. H.

Sprung, Annette Mabel, Instructor in German, Lincoln High School, Lincoln, Neb. [1500 S St.]

Squire, William Lord, Instructor in English, Trinity College, Hartford, Conn. [Wethersfield, Conn.]

Stair, Bird Williams, Instructor in English, College of the City of New York, New York, N. Y.

Starck, Adolf Ludwig Taylor, Instructor in German, Smith College, Northampton, Mass. [32 Paradise Road]

Stathers, Madison, Professor of Romance Languages, West Virginia University, Morgantown, W. Va.

van Steenderen, Frederic C. L., Professor of Romance Languages, Lake Forest College, Lake Forest, Ill.

Steeves, Harrison Ross, Assistant Professor of English, Columbia University, New York, N. Y.

Stempel, Guido Hermann, Associate Professor of Comparative Philology, Indiana University, Bloomington, Ind. [400 E. 2d St.]

Sterling, Susan Adelaide, Assistant Professor of German, University of Wisconsin, Madison, Wis. [109 W. Washington Ave.]

Stevens, Alice Porter, Associate Professor of German, Mount Holyoke College, So. Hadley, Mass.

Stevens, Clarence Dimick, Assistant Professor of English, University of Cincinnati, Cincinnati, O.

Stewart, Morton Collins, Assistant Professor of German, Union College, Schenectady, N. Y. [725 Van Vranken Ave.]

Stewart, William Kilborne, Professor of German and Instructor in Comparative Literature, Dartmouth College, Hanover, N. H.

Stewart, Robert Armistead, Professor of Romance Languages, Richmond College, Richmond, Va. [Commonwealth Club]

STODDARD, FRANCIS HOVEY, Professor Emeritus of the English Language and Literature, New York University, University Heights, New York, N. Y. [22 W. 68th St.]

Stoll, Elmer Edgar, Professor of English, University of Minnseota, Minneapolis, Minn. [504 Fifth St., S. E.]

Stone, Herbert King, Instructor in Romance Languages, University of Minnesota, Minneapolis, Minn.

Stonex, Arthur Bivins, Assistant Professor of English, Trinity College, Hartford, Conn. [76 Vernon St.]

Stork, Charles Wharton, Assistant Professor of English, University of Pennsylvania, Philadelphia, Pa. [Logan P. O., Philadelphia]

Stowell, William Averill, Associate Professor of Romance Languages, Amherst College, Amherst, Mass.

Strauss, Louis A., Professor of English, University of Michigan, Ann Arbor, Mich. [1601 Cambridge Road]

Streubel, Ernest J., Assistant Professor of German, Brooklyn Polytechnic Institute, Brooklyn, N. Y. [85 Livingston St.]

Stroebe, Lilian L., Associate Professor of German, Vassar College, Poughkeepsie, N. Y.

Struck, Henriette, Assistant Professor of German, Vassar College, Poughkeepsie, N. Y.

Strunk, William, Jr., Professor of the English Language and Literature, Cornell University, Ithaca, N. Y. [107 Lake St.]

Stuart, Donald Clive, Assistant Professor, Preceptor in Modern Languages, Princeton University, Princeton, N. J. [Western Way]

Sturtevant, Albert Morey, Assistant Professor of German and Scandinavian, University of Kansas, Lawrence, Kas. [924 Louisiana St.]

Supple, Edward Watson, Instructor in French and Spanish, Sheffield Scientific School, Yale University, New Haven, Conn.

van Sweringen, Grace Fleming, Professor of the Germanic Languages, University of Colorado, Boulder, Col. [Hotel Boulderado]

Swiggett, Glen Levin, Professor of Romance Languages, University of Tennessee, Knoxville, Tenn.

Sykes, Frederick Henry, President, Connecticut College for Women, New London, Conn.

Sypherd, Wilbur Owen, Professor of English and Political Sciences, Delaware College, Newark, Del.

Taft, Arthur Irving, Instructor in English, Yale College, New Haven, Conn.

Talamon, René, Instructor in French, University of Michigan, Ann Arbor, Mich.

Tatlock, John Strong Perry, Professor of English Philology, Leland Stanford Jr. University, Stanford University, Cal.

Taylor, Archer, Instructor in German, Washington University, St. Louis, Mo.

Taylor, George Bingham, Instructor in French and Spanish, The Tome School, Port Deposit, Md.

Taylor, Marion Lee, Assistant Teacher of German, Bushwick High School, Brooklyn, N. Y. [1152 Pacific St.]

Taylor, Robert Longley, Professor of Romance Languages, Williams College, Williamstown, Mass.

Telleen, John Martin, Assistant Professor of English, Case School of Applied Science, Cleveland, O.

Temple, Maud Elizabeth, Hartford, Conn. [28 Highland St.]

Thaler, Alwin, Instructor in English, Northwestern University, Evanston, Ill.

Thayer, Harvey Waterman, Assistant Professor, Preceptor in Modern Languages, Princeton University, Princeton, N. J.

Thayer, Mary Rebecca, Instructor in English, Vassar College, Poughkeepsie, N. Y.

Thieme, Hugo Paul, Junior Professor of French, University of Michigan, Ann Arbor, Mich. [3 Geddes Heights]

Thomas, Calvin, Professor of the Germanic Languages and Literatures, Columbia University, New York, N. Y.

Thomas, Daniel Lindsey, Professor of English, Central University, Danville, Ky.

Thomas, May, Assistant Professor of German, Ohio State University, Columbus, O. [233 W. Eleventh Ave.]

Thompson, Elbert N. S., Assistant Professor of English Literature, State University of Iowa, Iowa City, Ia. [714 Iowa Ave.]

Thompson, Everett Edward, Editor, American Book Co., 100 Washington Sq., New York, N. Y.

Thompson, Garrett William, Professor and Head of the Department of German, University of Maine, Orono, Me.

Thompson, Guy Andrew, Professor of English Literature, University of Maine, Orono, Me.

Thormeyer, Bertha, Instructor in German, Manual Training High School, Indianapolis, Ind. [93 Butler Ave.]

Thorndike, Ashley Horace, Professor of English, Columbia University, New York, N. Y.

Thornton, Donna Marie, Instructor in French, Lake Erie College, Painesville, O.

Thurber, Charles H., Ginn & Co., 29 Beacon St., Boston, Mass.

Thurber, Edward Allen, Professor of Rhetoric and American Literature, University of Oregon, Eugene, Ore. [751 Eleventh Ave., E.]

Tieje, Arthur Jerrold, Instructor in Rhetoric, University of Minnesota, Minneapolis, Minn. [1314 6th St., S. E.]

Tilley, Morris Palmer, Junior Professor of English, University of Michigan, Ann Arbor, Mich.

Tinker, Chauncey B., Professor of English Literature, Yale University, New Haven, Conn. [38 Vanderbilt Hall]

Tisdel, Frederick Monroe, Associate Professor of English, University of Missouri, Columbia, Mo.

Titsworth, Paul E., Professor of Modern Languages, Alfred University, Alfred, N. Y.

TODD, HENRY ALFRED, Professor of Romance Philology, Columbia University, New York, N. Y.

Todd, T. W., Professor of German, Washburn College, Topeka, Kas.

Tolman, Albert Harris, Professor of English Literature, University of Chicago, Chicago, Ill.

Towles, Oliver, Associate Professor of Romance Languages, University of North Carolina, Chapel Hill, N. C.

Toy, Walter Dallam, Professor of Germanic Languages and Literatures, University of North Carolina, Chapel Hill, N. C.

Traver, Hope, Professor of English, Mills College, Oakland, Cal.

Trebein, Bertha E., Professor of German, Agnes Scott College, Decatur, Ga.

Trent, William Peterfield, Professor of English Literature, Columbia University, New York, N. Y. [139 W. 78th St.]

Tressmann, Conrad A., Instructor in German, University of Washington, Seattle, Wash.

Truscott, Frederick W., Professor of Germanic Languages, West Virginia University, Morgantown, W. Va.

Tucker, Samuel Marion, Professor of English, Polytechnic Institute of Brooklyn, 85 Livingston St., Brooklyn, N. Y.

Tufts, James Arthur, Professor of English, Phillips Exeter Academy, Exeter, N. H.

Tupper, Frederick, Professor of the English Language and Literature, University of Vermont, Burlington, Vt.

Tupper, James Waddell, Professor of English Literature, Lafayette College, Easton, Pa.

Turk, Milton Haight, Professor of the English Language and Literature, Hobart College, Dean of William Smith College, Geneva, N. Y. [678 Main St.]

Turner, Leslie M., Assistant Professor of Romance Languages, University of California, Berkeley, Cal.

Turrell, Charles Alfred, Professor of Romance Languages, University of Arizona, Tucson, Arizona.

Tweedie, William Morley, Professor of the English Language and Literature, Mount Allison College, Sackville, N. B.

Tynan, Joseph Lawrence, Instructor in English, College of the City of New York, New York, N. Y. [911 Ogden Ave.]

Umphrey, George Wallace, Assistant Professor of Spanish, University of Washington, Seattle, Wash.

Underwood, Charles Marshall, Jr., Assistant Professor of Romance Languages, Simmons College, Boston, Mass. [15 Upland Road, Cambridge, Mass.]

Underwood, George Arthur, Instructor in French, Smith College, Northampton, Mass. [123 Elm St.]

Upham, Alfred Horatio, Professor of English, Miami University, Oxford, O. [315 E. Church St.]

Uterhart, Henry Ayres, New York, N. Y. [27 Cedar St.]

Utter, Robert Palfrey, Associate Professor of English, Amherst College, Amherst, Mass.

Van Doren, Carl, Assistant Professor of English, Columbia University, New York, N. Y.

Van Horne, John, Instructor in Romance Languages, State University of Iowa, Iowa City, Ia. [809 Iowa Ave.]

Vaughan, Herbert H., Instructor in Romance Languages, University of Pennsylvania, Philadelphia, Pa.

Vestling, Axel E., Professor of German, Carleton College, Northfield. Minn.

Vogel, Frank, Professor of German and Head of the Department of Modern Languages, Massachusetts Institute of Technology, Boston, Mass. [95 Robinwood Ave., Jamaica Plain, Mass.]

Vollmer, Clement, Instructor in German, Cornell University, Ithaca, N. Y.

Vos, Bert John, Professor of German, Indiana University, Bloomington, Ind.

Voss, Ernst Karl Johann Heinrich, Professor of German Philology, , University of Wisconsin, Madison, Wis. [175 Nelson Ave.]

Voss, John Henry, Associate Professor of German, University of Oklahoma, Norman, Okla.

Wagner, Charles Philip, Associate Professor of Romance Languages, University of Michigan, Ann Arbor, Mich. [900 Lincoln Ave.]

Wahl, George Moritz, Professor of the German Language and Literature, Williams College, Williamstown, Mass.

Wait, William Henry, Professor of Modern Languages, University of Michigan, Ann Arbor, Mich.

Waldron, Albert Ladd, Instructor in German, St. Paul's School, Concord, N. H.

Wales, Julia Grace, Instructor in English, University of Wisconsin, Madison, Wis. [411 Lake St.]

Walter, Hermann, Professor of Modern Languages, McGill University, Montreal, Canada.

WALZ, JOHN ALBRECHT, Professor of the German Language and Literature, Harvard University, Cambridge, Mass. [42 Garden St.]

Ware, John Nottingham, Professor of Romance Languages, University of the South, Sewanee, Tenn.

WARREN, FREDERICK MORRIS, Professor of Modern Languages, Yale University, New Haven, Conn.

Warshaw, Jacob, Assistant Professor of Romance Languages, University of Missouri, Columbia, Mo. [721 Missouri Ave.]

Waterhouse, Francis Asbury, Waltham, Mass. [Greenwood Lane]

Watson, Isabella. Professor of French, Carleton College, Northfield, Minn.

Watt, Homer Andrew, Instructor in English, University of Wisconsin, Madison, Wis.

Wauchope, George Armstrong, Professor of English, University of South Carolina, Columbia, S. C. [6 Campus]

Waxman, Samuel Montefiore, Assistant Professor of Romance Languages, Boston University, Boston, Mass.

Weber, Hermann Julius, Associate Professor of German, University of California, Berkeley, Cal. [1811 La Lama Ave.]

WEBSTER, KENNETH G. T., Instructor in English, Harvard University, Cambridge, Mass. [Gerry's Landing]

Weeks, Raymond, Professor of Romance Languages and Literatures, Columbia University, New York, N. Y.

WELLS, EDGAR HUIDEKOPER, Boston, Mass. [16 Hereford St.]

Wells, John Edwin, Professor of English Literature and Head of the Department of English, Beloit College, Beloit, Wis. [911 Park Ave.]

Wells, Leslie C., Professor of French and Spanish, Clark College, Worcester, Mass.

Wernaer, Robert Maximilian, Cambridge, Mass. [8 Prescott St.]

Werner, Adolph, Professor of the German Language and Literature, College of the City of New York, New York, N. Y. [401 West End Ave.]

Wesenberg, J. Griffith, Assistant in Romance Languages, University of Illinois, Urbana, Ill.

Wesselhoeft, Edward Karl, Professor of German, University of Pennsylvania, Philadelphia, Pa.

West, Henry Titus, Professor of German, Kenyon College, Gambier, O.

Weston, George Benson, Instructor in Romance Languages, Harvard University, Cambridge, Mass. [21 Craigie St.]

Weygandt, Cornelius, Assistant Professor of English, University of Pennsylvania, Philadelphia, Pa.

Wharey, James Blanton, Adjunct Professor of English, University of Texas, Austin, Tex.

Whicher, George Frisbie, Associate Professor of English, Amherst College, Amherst, Mass.

Whitcomb, Selden Lincoln, Associate Professor of English Literature, University of Kansas, Lawrence, Kas.

White, Florence Donnell, Assistant Professor of French, Vassar College, Poughkeepsie, N. Y.

White, Horatio Stevens, Professor of German, Harvard University, Cambridge, Mass. [29 Reservoir St.]

Whiteford, Robert N., Head Professor of English, University of Toledo, Toledo, O. [2415 Warren St.]

Whitelock, George, Counsellor at Law, Baltimore, Md. [1407 Continental Trust Building]

Whiteside, Donald Grant, Instructor in English, College of the City of New York, New York, N. Y.

Whitman, Charles Huntingdon, Professor of English, Rutgers College, New Brunswick, N. J. [116 Lincoln Ave., Highland Park, N. J.]

Whitman, Frederick Wyman, Assistant Professor of Modern Languages and Latin, New Hampshire State College, Durham, N. H.

Whitmore, Charles Edward, Instructor in English, Harvard University, Cambridge, Mass. [10 Remington St.]

Whitney, Marian P., Professor of German, Vassar College, Pough-keepsie, N. Y.

Whittem, Arthur Fisher, Assistant Professor of Romance Languages, Harvard University, Cambridge, Mass. [9 Vincent St.]

Whoriskey, Richard, Professor of Modern Languages, New Hampshire State College, Durham, N. H.

Whyte, John, Instructor in German, New York University, New York, N. Y. [2336 Loring Place, Bronx, N. Y.]

Widtsoe, Osborne J. P., Professor of English, University of Utah, Salt Lake City, Utah. [382 Wall St.]

Wiehr, Josef, Associate Professor of German, Smith College, North-ampton, Mass.

Wightman, John Roaf, Professor of Romance Languages, Oberlin College, Oberlin, O.

Wilkens, Frederick H., Associate Professor of German, New York University, University Heights, New York, N. Y.

Wilkins, Ernest Hatch, Associate Professor of Romance Languages, University of Chicago, Chicago, Ill.

Williams, Cecil Heyward, Instructor in German, Sheffield Scientific School, Yale University, New Haven, Conn. [122 Canner St.]

Williams, Charles Allyn, Instructor in German, University of Illinois, Urbana, Ill. [907 W. Oregon St.]

Williams, Grace S., Associate Professor of Romance Languages, Goucher College, Baltimore, Md.

Williamson de Visme, Hiram Parker, Directeur de l'Ecole du Château de Soisy, Soisy-sous-Etoilles, Seine et Oise, France.

Wilson, Charles Bundy, Professor and Head of the Department of the German Language and Literature, State University of Iowa, Iowa City, Ia. [323 N. Capitol St.]

Winchester, Caleb Thomas, Professor of English Literature, Wesleyan University, Middletown, Conn.

Winkler, Max, Professor of the German Language and Literature, University of Michigan, Ann Arbor, Mich.

Winter, Irvah Lester, Associate Professor of Public Speaking, Department of English, Harvard University, Cambridge, Mass. [Hubbard Park]

Winton, George Beverly, Instructor in Spanish, Vanderbilt University, Nashville, Tenn. [401 24th Ave.]

Wischkaemper, Richard, Instructor in German, University of Minnesota, Minneapolis, Minn.

Withington, Robert, Instructor in English, Indiana University, Bloomington, Ind.

Wittman, Elisabeth, Lander, Wyo. [P. O. Box 164]

Wolfe, Howard Webster, Professor and Head of the Department of Modern Languages, Trinity University, Waxahachie, Tex.

16

Wolff, Samuel Lee, Instructor in English, Extension Teaching, Columbia University, New York, N. Y. [90 Morningside Drive]

WOOD, FRANCIS ASBURY, Professor of Germanic Philology, University of Chicago, Chicago, Ill.

Wood, Henry, Professor of German, Johns Hopkins University, Baltimore, Md. [109 North Ave., W.]

Woodbridge, Benjamin Mather, Adjunct Professor of Romance Languages, University of Texas, Austin, Tex.

Woods, George Benjamin, Professor of English, Carleton College, Northfield, Minn.

Woolley, Edwin Campbell, New York, N. Y. [53 Washington Sq.]

Worthington, Hugh S., Instructor in Romance Languages, Johns Hopkins University, Baltimore, Md.

Wright, Arthur Silas, Professor of Modern Languages, Case School of Applied Science, Cleveland, O.

Wright, Charles Baker, Professor of English Literature and Rhetoric, Middlebury College, Middlebury, Vt.

WRIGHT, CHARLES HENRY CONRAD, Professor of the French Language and Literature, Harvard University, Cambridge, Mass. [5 Buckingham Place]

Wright, Ernest Hunter, Assistant Professor of English and Comparative Literature, Columbia University, New York, N. Y.

Wright, Rowe, Instructor in English, University of Wisconsin, Madison, Wis.

Wylie, Laura J., Professor of English, Vassar College, Poughkeepsie, N. Y. [112 Market St.]

Yost, Clemens Andrew, Instructor in French and German, Trinity College, Durham, N. C.

Yost, Mary, Assistant Professor of English, Vassar College, Poughkeepsie, N. Y.

Young, Bert Edward, Professor of Romance Languages, Vanderbilt University, Nashville, Tenn. [Acting Professor at Columbia University, New York, N. Y.]

Young, Bertha Kedzie, Assistant Professor of English, University of Cincinnati, Cincinnati, O. [The Maplewood, Clifton]

Young, Charles Edmund, Professor of Romance Languages, Beloit College, Beloit, Wis.

YOUNG, KARL, Professor of English, University of Wisconsin, Madison, Wis.

Young, Mary Vance, Professor of Romance Languages, Mount Holyoke College, So. Hadley, Mass.

Zdanowicz, Casimir Douglass, Assistant Professor of Romance Languages, University of Wisconsin, Madison, Wis. [1818 Madison St.]

Zeek, Charles Franklyn, Jr., Adjunct Professor of French, Southern Methodist University, Dallas, Tex.

Zeitlin, Jacob, Associate in English, University of Illinois, Urbana, Ill.

Zembrod, Alfred Charles, Professor of Modern Languages, University of Kentucky, Lexington, Ky. [456 W. 4th St.]

Zeppenfeld, Jeannette, Professor of Modern Languages, Franklin College, Franklin, Ind.

Zeydel, Edwin Hermann, Fellow in German, Cornell University, Ithaca, N. Y.

Zinnecker, Wesley Daniel, Instructor in German, Cornell University, Ithaca, N. Y. [707 E. State St.]

Zwierzina, Konrad, Ord. Professor für deutsche Sprache und Literatur an der Universität, Graz, Austria. [Zinzendorfgasse 19]

LIBRARIES

Subscribing to the Publications of the Association

Akron, O.: Library of the Municipal University of Akron
Albany, N. Y.: New York State Library
Amherst, Mass.: Amherst College Library
Ann Arbor, Mich.: General Library of the University of Michigan
Austin, Texas: Library of the University of Texas
Baltimore, Md.: Enoch Pratt Free Library
Baltimore, Md.: Goucher College Library
Baltimore, Md.: Johns Hopkins University Library
Baltimore, Md.: Library of the Peabody Institute
Baton Rouge, La.: Hill Memorial Library, Louisiana State University
Beloit, Wis.: Beloit College Library
Berkeley, Cal.: Library of the University of California
Berlin, Germany: Englisches Seminar der Universität [Dorotheenstrasse 5]
Bloomington, Ind.: Indiana University Library
Bonn, Germany: Englisches Seminar der Universität
Boston, Mass.: Public Library of the City of Boston
Boulder, Col.: Library of the University of Colorado
Brooklyn, N. Y.: Adelphi College Library
Bryn Mawr, Pa.: Bryn Mawr College Library
Buffalo, N. Y.: Buffalo Public Library
Burlington, Vt.: Library of the University of Vermont
Cambridge, Eng.: University Library
Cambridge, Mass.: Child Memorial Library
Cambridge, Mass.: Harvard University Library
Cambridge, Mass.: Radcliffe College Library
Cedar Rapids, Ia.: Coe College Library
Chambersburg, Pa.: Wilson College Library
Chapel Hill, N. C.: Library of the University of North Carolina
Charlottesville, Va.: Library of the University of Virginia
Chicago, Ill.: General Library of the University of Chicago
Chicago, Ill.: Newberry Library
Cincinnati, O.: Library of the University of Cincinnati [Burnet Woods Park]
Cleveland, O.: Adelbert College Library
Columbia, Mo.: Library of the University of Missouri
Concord, N. H.: New Hampshire State Library

Crawfordsville, Ind.: Wabash College Library
Decorah, Iowa: Luther College Library
Detroit, Mich.: The Public Library
Earlham, Ind.: Earlham College Library
Easton, Pa.: Van Wickle Memorial Library, Lafayette College
Edmonton South, Alberta, Canada: Library of the University of Alberta
Emporia, Kan.: Library of the State Normal School
Eugene, Ore.: University of Oregon Library
Evanston, Ill.: Northwestern University Library
Gainesville, Fla.: Library of the University of Florida
Galesburg, Ill.: Lombard College Library
Giessen, Germany: Grossherzogliche Universitäts-Bibliothek
Granville, O.: Denison University Library
Graz, Austria: K. K. Universitäts-Bibliothek
Halifax, Nova Scotia: Dalhousie College Library
Hartford, Conn.: Watkinson Library
Houston, Tex.: The Wm. Rice Institute Library [P. O. Box 17]
Iowa City, Ia.: Library of the State University of Iowa
Irvington, Ind.: Bona Thompson Memorial Library
Ithaca, N. Y.: Cornell University Library
Knoxville, Tenn.: University of Tennessee Library
Laramie, Wyo.: University of Wyoming Library
Leipzig, Germany: Englisches Seminar der Universität
Lincoln, Neb.: University of Nebraska Library
London, England: London Library [St. James Square, S. W.]
Louisville, Ky.: Library of the University of Louisville
Lynchburg, Va.: Library of the Randolph-Macon Woman's College
Lyons, France: Bibliothèque de l'Université [18 quai Claude Bernard]
Madison, Wis.: Library of the University of Wisconsin
Manchester, England: The John Rylands Library
Manchester, England: Library of the Victoria University
Middletown, Conn.: Wesleyan University Library
Minneapolis, Minn.: Minneapolis Athenæum
Minneapolis, Minn.: University of Minnesota Library
Missoula, Mont.: University of Montana Library
Munich, Germany: Königliche Hof- und Staats-Bibliothek
Nashville, Tenn.: Library of the Peabody College for Teachers
Nashville, Tenn.: Vanderbilt University Library
New Haven, Conn.: Yale University Library
New Orleans, La.: H. Sophie Newcomb Memorial Library [1220 Washington St.]
New York, N. Y.: Columbia University Library

New York, N. Y.: Library of New York University [University Heights]
New York, N. Y.: New York Public Library [476 Fifth Ave.]
New York, N. Y.: University Club Library [Fifth Ave. and 54th St.]
Northampton, Mass.: Smith College Library
Northfield, Minn.: Scoville Memorial Library, Carleton College
Northfield, Minn.: St. Olaf's College Library
Oberlin, O.: Oberlin College Library
Olivet, Mich.: Olivet College Library
Orono, Me.: University of Maine Library
Oxford, O.: Library of Miami University
Peoria, Ill.: Peoria Public Library
Painesville, O.: Murray Library of Lake Erie College
Philadelphia, Pa.: Free Library [13th and Locust Sts.]
Philadelphia, Pa.: University of Pennsylvania Library
Pittsburgh, Pa.: Carnegie Library
Poughkeepsie, N. Y.: Library of Vassar College
Princeton, N. J.: Princeton University Library
Providence, R. I.: Library of Brown University
Providence, R. I.: Providence Public Library [Washington St.]
Pullman, Wash.: Library of the State College of Washington
Rennes, France: Bibliothèque de l'Université
Reno, Nev.: University of Nevada Library
Rochester, N. Y.: Library of the University of Rochester [Prince St.]
Rock Hill, S. C.: Winthrop Normal and Industrial College Library
Sacramento, Cal.: State Library of California
St. Louis, Mo.: Library of Washington University
St. Paul, Minn.: Hamline University Library
St. Paul, Minn.: St. Paul Public Library
Sofia, Bulgaria: Bibliothèque de l'Université
Seattle, Wash.: University of Washington Library
Sioux City, Ia.: Library of Morningside College
South Bethlehem, Pa.: Lehigh University Library
Stanford University, Cal.: Leland Stanford Jr. University Library
Swarthmore, Pa.: Swarthmore College Reading Room
Syracuse, N. Y.: Library of Syracuse University
Tallahassee, Fla.: Library of the Florida State College for Women
University, Miss.: Library of the University of Mississippi
Urbana, Ill.: Library of the University of Illinois [University Station]
Washington, D. C.: Library of the Catholic University of America
Wellesley, Mass.: Wellesley College Library
Williamstown, Mass.: Library of Williams College
Worcester, Mass.: Free Public Library

HONORARY MEMBERS

K. VON BAHDER, University of Leipzig
WILLY BANG, University of Louvain
JOSEPH BÉDIER, Collège de France, Paris
HENRY BRADLEY, Oxford, England
ALOIS L. BRANDL, University of Berlin
W. BRAUNE, University of Heidelberg
FERDINAND BRUNOT, University of Paris
KONRAD BURDACH, Akademie der Wissenschaften, Berlin
BENEDETTO CROCE, Naples, Italy
FRANCESCO FLAMINI, University of Pisa
ALFRED JEANROY, University of Paris
OTTO JESPERSEN, University of Copenhagen
J. J. JUSSERAND, French Ambassador, Washington, D. C.
FR. KLUGE, University of Freiburg
EUGEN KÜHNEMANN, University of Breslau
GUSTAVE LANSON, University of Paris
ABEL LEFRANC, Collège de France
RAMÓN MENÉNDEZ PIDAL, University of Madrid
PAUL MEYER, Ecole des Chartes, Paris
W. MEYER-LÜBKE, University of Vienna
ERNESTO MONACI, University of Rome
ARTHUR NAPIER, University of Oxford
FRITZ NEUMANN, University of Heidelberg
ADOLF NOREEN, University of Upsala
FRANCESCO NOVATI, University of Milan
FRANCESCO D'OVIDIO, University of Naples
H. PAUL, University of Munich
PIO RAJNA, R. Istituto di Studi Superiori, Florence
GUSTAV ROETHE, University of Berlin
AUGUST SAUER, University of Prague
EDWARD SCHROEDER, University of Göttingen
H. SCHUCHARDT, University of Graz
EDUARD SIEVERS, University of Leipzig
JOHAN STORM, University of Christiania
ANTOINE THOMAS, University of Paris
FRANCESCO TORRACA, University of Naples

ROLL OF MEMBERS DECEAST

J. T. AKERS, Central College, Richmond, Ky. [1909]

GRAZIADO I. ASCOLI, Milan, Italy [1907]

ELYSÉE AVIRAGNET, Bucknell University, Lewisburg, Pa. [1908]

T. WHITING BANCROFT, Brown University, Providence, R. I. [1890]

DAVID LEWIS BARTLETT, Baltimore, Md. [1899]

GEORGE ALONZO BARTLETT, Harvard University, Cambridge, Mass. [1908]

W. M. BASKERVILL, Vanderbilt University, Nashville, Tenn. [1899]

ALEXANDER MELVILLE BELL, Washington, D. C. [1905]

A. A. BLOOMBERGH, Lafayette College, Easton, Pa. [1906]

FREDERICK AUGUSTUS BRAUN, Princeton University, Princeton, N. J. [1915]

DANIEL G. BRINTON, Media, Pa. [1899]

FRANK EGBERT BRYANT, University of Kansas, Lawrence, Kas. [1910]

SOPHUS BUGGE, University of Christiania [1907]

FRANK ROSCOE BUTLER, Hathorne, Mass. [1905]

GEORGE RICE CARPENTER, Columbia University, New York, N. Y. [1909]

JOSEPH W. CARR, University of Maine, Orono, Me. [1909]

HENRY LELAND CHAPMAN, Bowdoin College, Brunswick, Me. [1913]

CHARLES CHOLLET, West Virginia University, Morgantown, W. Va. [1903]

J. SCOTT CLARK, Northwestern University, Evanston, Ill. [1911]

PALMER COBB, University of North Carolina, Chapel Hill, N. C. [1911]

HENRY COHEN, Northwestern University, Evanston, Ill. [1900]

WILLIAM COOK, Harvard University, Cambridge, Mass. [1888]

ADELAIDE CRAPSEY, Rochester, N. Y. [1914]

SUSAN R. CUTLER, Chicago, Ill. [1899]

A. N. VAN DAELL, Massachusetts Institute of Technology, Boston, Mass. [1899]

ALESSANDRO D'ANCONA, University of Pisa [1914]

EDWARD GRAHAM DAVES, Baltimore, Md. [1894]

W. DEUTSCH, St. Louis, Mo. [1898]

ERNEST AUGUST EGGERS, Ohio State University, Columbus, O. [1903]

A. MARSHALL ELLIOTT, Johns Hopkins University, Baltimore, Md.
[1910]
FRANCIS R. FAVA, Columbian University, Washington, D. C. [1896]
WENDELIN FOERSTER, University of Bonn [1915]
ALCÉE FORTIER, Tulane University of Louisiana, New Orleans, La.
[1914]
FREDERICK JAMES FURNIVALL, London, England [1910]
WILLIAM KENDALL GILLETT, New York University, New York, N. Y.
[1914]
LEIGH R. GREGOR, McGill University, Montreal, Canada [1912]
GUSTAV GRÖBER, University of Strassburg [1911]
THACHER HOWLAND GUILD, University of Illinois, Urbana, Ill. [1914]
L. HADEL, Norwich University, Northfield, Vt. [1886]
JAMES ALBERT HARRISON, University of Virginia, Charlottesville, Va.
[1911]
B. P. HASDEU, University of Bucharest, Bucharest, Roumania [1908]
RUDOLF HAYM, University of Halle [1901]
RICHARD HEINZEL, University of Vienna [1905]
GEORGE A. HENCH, University of Michigan, Ann Arbor, Mich. [1899]
JOHN BELL HENNEMAN, University of the South, Sewanee, Tenn.
[1908]
RUDOLF HILDEBRAND, University of Leipzig [1894]
JULES ADOLPHE HOBIGAND, Boston, Mass. [1906]
JULIAN HUGUENIN, University of Louisiana, Baton Rouge, La.
[1901]
THOMAS HUME, University of North Carolina, Chapel Hill, N. C.
[1912]
ANDREW INGRAHAM, Cambridge, Mass. [1905]
J. KARGÉ, Princeton College, Princeton, N. J. [1892]
GUSTAF E. KARSTEN, University of Illinois, Urbana, Ill. [1908]
F. L. KENDALL, Williams College, Williamstown, Mass. [1893]
PAUL OSCAR KERN, University of Chicago, Chicago, Ill. [1908]
EUGEN KÖLBING, University of Breslau, Germany [1899]
CHRISTIAN LARSEN, Utah Agricultural College, Logan, Utah [1913]
EUGENE LESER, Indiana University, Bloomington, Ind. [1915]
J. LÉVY, Lexington, Mass. [1891]
AUGUST LODEMAN, Michigan State Normal School, Ypsilanti, Mich.
[1902]
JULES LOISEAU, New York. [1890]
JAMES RUSSELL LOWELL, Cambridge, Mass. [1891]
J. LUQUIENS, Yale University, New Haven, Conn. [1899]
ALBERT BENEDICT LYMAN, Baltimore, Md. [1907]
THOMAS MCCABE, Bryn Mawr College, Bryn Mawr, Pa. [1891]
J. G. R. MCELROY, University of Pennsylvania, Philadelphia, Pa.
[1899]

EDWARD T. McLAUGHLIN, Yale University, New Haven, Conn. [1893]
JAMES MACNIE, University of North Dakota, Grand Forks, N. D.
   [1909]
EDWARD H. MAGILL, Swarthmore College, Swarthmore, Pa. [1907]
FRANCIS ANDREW MARCH, Lafayette College, Easton, Pa. [1911]
JOHN E. MATZKE, Leland Stanford Jr. University, Stanford Univer-
   sity, Cal. [1910]
MARCELINO MENÉNDEZ Y PELAYO, University of Madrid [1912]
LOUIS EMIL MENGER, Bryn Mawr College, Bryn Mawr, Pa. [1903]
CHARLES WALTER MESLOH, Ohio State University, Columbus, O.
   [1904]
GEORGE HENRY MEYER, University of Illinois, Urbana, Ill. [1915]
JACOB MINOR, University of Vienna [1912]
SAMUEL P. MOLENAER, University of Pennsylvania, Philadelphia,
   Pa. [1900]
EDWARD PAYSON MORTON, Chicago, Ill. [1914]
JAMES AUGUSTUS HENRY MURRAY, Oxford, England [1915]
JAMES O. MURRAY, Princeton University, Princeton, N. J. [1901]
ADOLF MUSSAFIA, University of Vienna [1905]
BENNETT HUBBARD NASH, Boston, Mass. [1906]
C. K. NELSON, Brookville, Md. [1890]
W. N. NEVIN, Lancaster, Pa. [1892]
WILLIAM WELLS NEWELL, Cambridge, Mass. [1907]
AMALIE IDA FRANCES NIX, St. Paul, Minn. [1913]
CONRAD H. NORDBY, College of the City of New York, New York,
   N. Y. [1900]
FREDERICK CURRY OSTRANDER, University of Texas, Austin, Tex.
   [1913]
C. P. OTIS, Massachusetts Institute of Technology, Boston, Mass.
   [1888]
GASTON PARIS, Collège de France, Paris, France [1903]
W. H. PERKINSON, University of Virginia, Charlottesville, Va.
   [1898]
HERBERT T. POLAND, Harvard University, Cambridge, Mass. [1906]
SAMUEL PORTER, Gallaudet College, Kendall Green, Washington,
   D. C. [1901]
FRANCES BOARDMAN SQUIRE POTTER, University of Minnesota, Min-
   neapolis, Minn. [1914]
MURRAY ANTHONY POTTER, Harvard University, Cambridge, Mass.
   [1915]
F. YORK POWELL, University of Oxford, Oxford, England [1904]
RENÉ DE POYEN-BELLISLE, University of Chicago, Chicago, Ill.
   [1900]
THOMAS R. PRICE, Columbia University, New York, N. Y. [1903]
SYLVESTER PRIMER, University of Texas, Austin, Tex. [1912]

EUGEN REINHARD, University of Wisconsin, Madison, Wis. [1914]
LEWIS A. RHOADES, Ohio State University, Columbus, O. [1910]
HENRY B. RICHARDSON, Amherst College, Amherst, Mass. [1906]
CHARLES H. ROSS, Agricultural and Mechanical College, Auburn, Ala. [1900]
OLIVE RUMSEY, Westfield, N. Y. [1912]
MARY J. T. SAUNDERS, Randolph-Macon Woman's College, College Park, Va. [1914]
M. SCHÈLE DE VERE, University of Virginia, Charlottesville, Va. [1898]
JAKOB SCHIPPER, University of Vienna [1915]
ERICH SCHMIDT, University of Berlin [1913]
O. SEIDENSTICKER, University of Pennsylvania, Philadelphia, Pa. [1894]
JAMES W. SHERIDAN, College of the City of New York, New York, N. Y. [1902]
WALTER WILLIAM SKEAT, University of Cambridge, England [1912]
MAX SOHRAUER, New York, N. Y. [1890]
CARLO LEONARDO SPERANZA, Columbia University, New York, N. Y. [1911]
F. R. STENGEL, Columbia University, New York, N. Y. [1890]
CARLTON BEECHER STETSON, University of Vermont, Burlington, Vt. [1912]
CAROLINE STRONG, Portland, Ore. [1908]
HERMANN SUCHIER, University of Halle-Wittenberg [1914]
HENRY SWEET, Oxford, England [1912]
H. TALLICHET, Austin, Tex. [1894]
ADOLF TOBLER, University of Berlin [1910]
RUDOLF TOMBO, JR., Columbia University, New York, N. Y. [1914]
HIRAM ALBERT VANCE, University of Nashville, Nashville, Tenn. [1906]
E. L. WALTER, University of Michigan, Ann Arbor, Mich. [1898]
KARL WEINHOLD, University of Berlin [1901]
CARLA WENCKEBACH, Wellesley College, Wellesley, Mass. [1902]
HÉLÈNE WENCKEBACH, Wellesley College, Wellesley, Mass. [1888]
MARGARET M. WICKHAM, Adelphi College, Brooklyn, N. Y. [1898]
R. H. WILLIS, Chatham, Va. [1900]
CHARLES F. WOODS, Lehigh University, Bethlehem, Pa. [1912]
RICHARD PAUL WÜLKER, University of Leipzig [1910]
CASIMIR ZDANOWICZ, Vanderbilt University, Nashville, Tenn. [1889]
JULIUS ZUPITZA, University of Berlin [1895]

INDEX

clxi

Lightning Source UK Ltd.
Milton Keynes UK
UKHW052250230119
335699UK00019B/997/P